2495
1875

Physiological Psychology

Physiological Psychology

Mark R. Rosenzweig
University of California, Berkeley

Arnold L. Leiman
University of California, Berkeley

D. C. Heath and Company
Lexington, Massachusetts • Toronto

We dedicate this book affectionately to our wives and children.
We appreciate their support and patience over the years of this project.

	Janine			*Lannon*	
Anne	*Suzanne*	*Philip*	*Jessica*	*Timothy*	

Cover photograph: Cross-sectional positron emission computed tomography images of glucose metabolism in the brain of a normal human subject while listening to a mystery story with background music. Lighter and warmer colors correspond to higher metabolic rates. Note the high metabolic rate in the left and right auditory cortices and frontal cortex. Since the eyes are open, there is also activation of visual cortex in the occipital lobe. (Courtesy of Michael E. Phelps and John Mazziota, UCLA School of Medicine, Los Angeles, California.)

Illustrations: Nelson W. Hee and Carmela Ciampa.

Published simultaneously in Canada.

Printed in the United States of America.

International Standard Book Number: 0-669-02901-7

Library of Congress Catalog Card Number: 82-80606

Acknowledgments

Figure 3-10 (p. 91): Adapted by permission from *Nature*, vol. 203, p. 592. Copyright © 1964 Macmillan Journals Limited.

Figure 3-28 (p. 125): Figure adapted by permission of *La Recherche*.

Figure 4-14 (p. 151): Adapted, with permission, from the *Annual Review of Neuroscience*, volume 2. © 1979 by Annual Reviews, Inc.

Figure 4-21 (p. 161) and Figure 4-22 (p. 162): Figures adapted by permission of *Acta Physiologica Scandinavica*. Karolinska Institutet, Box 60400. S-104 01 Stockholm-Sweden.

Figure 4-25 (p. 171): Reproduced, by permission, from E. Callaway, *Brain electrical potentials and individual psychological differences* (New York: Grune & Stratton, Inc. 1975), p. 13, Figure 1-3.

Box Figure 5-1 (p. 191): Adapted from J. A. Brasel and R. M. Blizzard in R. H. Williams (Ed.), *Textbook of endocrinology, fifth edition* (Philadelphia: W. B. Saunders, 1974), p. 1049.

Figure 6-15 (p. 242): From *Acta Physiologica Scandinavica*. Karolinska Institutet, Box 60400. S-104 01 Stockholm-Sweden.

Figure 6-22 (p. 253): Reproduced, by permission, from E. Callaway, *Brain electrical potentials and individual psychological differences* (New York: Grune & Stratton, Inc., 1975), p. 18, Figure 2-1.

Figure 7-13 (p. 275): Reprinted with permission from *Vision Research, 14*, R. L. De Valois and H. Morgan, "Psychophysical studies of monkey vision—III. Spatial luminance contrast sensitivity tests of macaque and human observers," copyright 1974, Pergamon Press, Ltd.

Figure 9-2 (p. 362): Adapted from F. A. Beach, "Cross-species comparisons and the human heritage," in F. A. Beach (Ed.), *Human sexuality in four perspectives* (Baltimore: Johns Hopkins University Press, 1977), p. 300, Figure 11.1.

Quotation (p. 363): From F. A. Beach, "Human sexuality in four perspectives," in F. A. Beach (Ed.), *Human sexuality in four perspectives* (Baltimore: Johns Hopkins University Press, 1977), p. 18.

Figure 9-18 (p. 387): Based on col. 1 of Table 27 in E. Bourguignon and L. S. Greenbaum, *Diversity and homogeneity in world societies*. New Haven, HRAF Press, 1973, p. 51.

Figure 9-22 (p. 397): Adapted from *Physiology and Behavior, 3*, J. M. Davidson, E. R. Smith, C. H. Rodgers, and G. J. Bloch, "Relative thresholds of behavioral and somatic responses to estrogen," copyright 1968, Pergamon Press Ltd.

Figure 9-23 (p. 398) and Figure 9-24 (p. 399): From "Neuro-hormonal integration of sexual behavior in female primates" by J. Herbert, in J. B. Hutchison (Ed.), *Biological determinants of sexual behavior,* copyright 1978 by John Wiley & Sons, Ltd. Reprinted by permission of John Wiley & Sons, Ltd.

Figure 10-9 (p. 420): From E. Satinoff, "Neural organization and evolution of thermal regulation in mammals," *Science, 201,* (1978):16–22. Copyright 1978 by the American Association for the Advancement of Science.

Figure 10-11 (p. 421): Adapted with permission from *Neurology, 4,* J. Bligh, "The Central neurology of mammalian thermoregulation," Copyright 1979, Pergamon Press, Ltd.

Box Figure 11-1 (p. 446): Adapted from A. G. Reeves and F. Plum, "Hyperphagia, rape, and dementia accompanying a ventromedial hypothalamic neoplasm," *Archives of Neurology, 20*(1969):621, Figure 3. Copyright 1969, American Medical Association.

Figure 12-2 (p. 471): From A. Kales and J. Kales, "Evaluation, diagnosis, and treatment of clinical conditions related to sleep," *Journal of the American Medical Association, 213*(1970):2230, Figure 1.

Figure 12-18 (p. 507): From A. Kales and J. Kales, "Evaluation, diagnosis, and treatment of clinical conditions related to sleep," *Journal of the American Medical Association, 213*(1970):2231, Figure 2.

Box Figure 12-4 (p. 501): Graph based on Tables 1 and 2 in Fisher-Perroudon, "Sur un cas d'agrypnie," *Electroencephalography and Clinical Neurophysiology, 36*(1974):1–18.

Table 12-4 (p. 481): From G. Gulevich, W. Dement, and L. Johnson, "Psychiatric and EEG observations on a case of prolonged (264 hours) wakefulness," *Archives of General Psychiatry, 15*(1966):29–35. Copyright 1966, American Medical Association.

Figure 13-14 (p. 534): From G. C. Wagner, L. J. Beuving, and R. R. Hutchinson, "The effects of gonadal hormone manipulations on aggressive target-biting in mice," *Aggressive Behavior, 6, no. 1* (1980):4, Figure 1.

Figure 14-2 (p. 560) and Figure 14.3 (p. 561): Adapted from K. E. Hagbarth and K. Kugelberg, "Plasticity of the human skin reflex," *Brain, 81*(1958):305–318, Figures 1, 3, and 5, by permission of Oxford University Press.

Figure 14-8 (p. 570): Adapted from B. Milner, "Memory disturbance after bilateral hippocampal lesions," in P. M. Milner and S. E. Glickman (Eds.), *Cognitive processes and the brain* (Princeton, N.J.: Van Nostrand, 1965), Figure 6, p. 108, by permission of Brooks/Cole Publishing Company.

Figure 16-1 (p. 641): Reprinted by permission of the Smithsonian Institution Press from *Birdsong: Acoustics and physiology,* C. H. Greenwalt; figs. 33, 35, and 39, © Smithsonian Institution, Washington, D.C. 1968.

Figure 16-8 (p. 650): Adapted from G. Ojemann and O. Mateer, "Human language cortex: Localization of memory, syntax, and sequential motor-phoneme identification system," *Science, 205* (September 1979):1401–1403, Figure 1. Copyright 1979 by the American Association for the Advancement of Science.

Complete sources for the following figures can be found in the References (beginning on p. xvii): 3-1, 3-7, 3-8, 3-16, 3-19, 3-27, 4-26, Box Figure 5-1, 6-20, 6-21, Box Figure 6-4, 7-4, 7-5, 7-22, 8-18, 8-25, 9-4, 9-5, 9-9, 9-11, 9-15, 9-20, 9-25, 10-9, 12-4, 12-5, 12-8, 12-11, Box Figure 12-2, Box Figure 12-3, 13-4, 13-6, 13-9, 13-14, 13-18, 14-4, 14-10, 14-17, 14-18, 15-10, 15-16, 15-17, 15-18, 15-20, quotation p. 655, 16-2, and 16-15.

Preface

In recent years frequent press coverage of topics in physiological psychology has reflected the growth of popular interest in this field. Scholarly articles illustrate the rapid pace of research and indicate the relevance of brain research to pressing human problems. Newspapers and magazines herald new findings that improve our understanding of why we do what we do and why we are what we are. Research in physiological psychology and related fields is illuminating many aspects of normal behavior, including sex, learning and memory, language and communication, sleep and daily rhythms, and the sensitivity and selectivity of our perceptual processes.

Behavioral problems and deficiencies are also being illuminated by brain research. Certainly some of the accomplishments of research on brain-behavior relationships would have been hailed as miracles only a generation ago. These findings have led to curing psychoses, abolishing pain, restoring sight to blind people, and stimulating the growth of the brain, thereby improving the capacity to learn. As science writer Arthur Clarke has stated, "The science of one generation was the magic of the preceding one."

In *Physiological Psychology* we explore the ways in which bodily states and processes produce and control behavior and the ways in which behavior influences bodily systems. This theme has great scope and breadth; it spans many scientific disciplines. Thus we draw on the research of psychologists, anatomists, chemists, endocrinologists, engineers, geneticists, neurologists, physiologists, and zoologists. In order to gain a panoramic view of the rapidly developing field of physiological psychology, we try to rise above the limits of any single specialty.

We have attempted to accommodate students from a variety of interests and backgrounds. Thus, both the behavioral and biological foundations are provided for each main topic. Well-prepared students can skip or skim some of this material, but those who need it should study it carefully before proceeding.

We present *Physiological Psychology* in a logical, progressive order of four main parts:

1. Since the interrelated functions of the nervous system and the endocrine system are fundamental to all behavior, in Part One we first examine the basic properties and functions of these two systems and then apply our knowledge to problems of behavior and its biological mechanisms.

2. Sensory inputs to the brain do not merely provide "pictures in the head"; they often incite the individual to act. The movements elicited range in complexity from slight eye motions to elaborate sequences of movements. These classes of movements are not directly driven or triggered by sensory events but reflect intrinsic programs of action that may involve sensory inputs only as modulators. How this information processing occurs in both perceptual and motor systems is the theme in Part Two.

3. An organism, in selecting among many options from its behavioral repertoire, requires some motor acts that are incompatible with others—an animal can't flee danger and feed at the same time. Responding to one motive often precludes satisfying another at the same time, and different motives may have to be satisfied in succession. How bodily systems function so that all the basic needs are satisfied is the overall question of motivation that we take up in Part Three.

4. Hardly a living creature cannot change its behavior as a result of experience. The capacity to learn and remember makes it possible to deal with a complex and changing world and thus increases adaptive success. Storing the lessons of experience implies that the properties of the nervous system can be enduringly changed. How this feat is accomplished is the major mystery of the biological sciences. In Part Four we consider many aspects of research in the biology of learning. We also discuss the most elaborate products of brain function, the biology of language and cognitive states that are distinctively human.

We believe this order of presentation to be a practical and effective one. We realize, however, that some instructors may prefer a different ordering of topics or may want to omit some areas of study, so we have written each chapter as a relatively self-contained unit. Recognizing that courses also vary in length from a single quarter or semester to two semesters, we should point out that most of this text can be covered in a single quarter; in that case the instructor may decide to omit a few chapters depending upon his or her emphasis. On the other hand, the text provides most of the basic material for a two-semester course; in this case the instructor can assign some supplementary reading to fill out particular areas.

Many features of the text are designed to enhance students' mastery of the material:

- We have put together what we feel is one of the finest two-color illustration programs in a physiological psychology text available today. A medical illustrator collaborated with us to produce hundreds of meaningful illustrations specifically designed to clarify important concepts. Graphs and data from many sources have been reorganized and redrawn for student comprehension.
- To aid student understanding, each chapter (1) is preceded by an outline that functions as an organizational framework for the chapter, (2) contains an "orientation" that lays the groundwork for the discussion, (3) concludes with summary/main points to highlight and review important concepts, and (4) lists recommended readings.
- Concepts and data have been carefully chosen and presented at a level appropriate for students with widely varying backgrounds.
- Key terms are written in boldface and defined at their first main use; they are also included in the glossary.
- Brief boxed articles feature contemporary applications and historical information, providing relevant examples from real life and a broad perspective on specific topics.
- A study guide offers a complete chapter outline, a review of general concepts, a list of study objectives, illustrations from the text with study questions, chapter tests, self-evaluation exercises, concept applications, and answers to all questions and exercises.

It is a pleasure to acknowledge the help and assistance we have received in the preparation of this book. First we want to thank our colleagues in physiological psychology who have made this field so stimulating and on whose work we have drawn so liberally. Next we want to thank our thousands of students whose questions and comments impelled us to write a text that would serve students as well as can be done. We are happy to thank the friends and colleagues who have offered their comments and suggestions on parts of the text: Frank A. Beach, Edward L. Bennett, K. L. Chow, Verne Cox, Karen K. De Valois, Russell L. De Valois, Leonard Flynn, Walter Isaac, Sheri Mizumori, Lawrence I. O'Kelly, Michael Renner, Edward Roy, Frederic J. Seil, Larry R. Squire, Suzanne Washburn, and Irving Zucker.

In the preparation of our manuscripts, we benefited from discussions with developmental editor Betty Smith. We are grateful to John Harney, who induced us to undertake this project and who set up a favorable financial program to realize the book, and to the staff of D. C. Heath and Company: Harvey Pantzis, College Science Acquisitions Editor; Cathy Cantin, Senior Production Editor; and Mark Fowler, Senior Designer.

We are pleased to acknowledge the skilled assistance of Heather Allen in the preparation of the manuscript, glossary, and index. Jessica Langford also helped ably with the manuscript and correspondence.

As we write this preface, we are in the final stages of preparation of the book—reading page proof and compiling the index. We are looking forward to receiving the comments of students and colleagues soon. We would be happy to hear from you.

Mark R. Rosenzweig
Arnold L. Leiman

Contents

3 | *Development of the Nervous System over the Life Span and through Millions of Years*

4 | Communication and Information Processing in the Nervous System

5 | Hormones: A Chemical Communication System

Box 5-1 Stress and growth:
   Psychosocial dwarfism   191

Part Two

INFORMATION PROCESSING IN PERCEPTUAL AND MOTOR SYSTEMS

6

Principles of Sensory Processing and Experience

Box 6-1 Black light and inaudible
   sound   218

Box 6-2 Unusual receptors in
   unusual animals   222

Box 6-3 Evolution of hairs that
   hear distant objects   232

7 | *Information Processing in Perception: Seeing, Hearing, Feeling*

8 | *Movements and Actions*

Box 8-1 How muscles contract 314

Part Three

CONTROL OF BEHAVIORAL STATES: MOTIVATION

9 *Sex*

10 | Homeostatic Mechanisms I: Heating/Cooling, Drinking

11 | Homeostatic Mechanisms II: Eating

Box 11-1 Effects of a hypothalamic tumor on human
behavior 446

12 | *Sleeping and Waking*

Box 12-1 Circadian rhythms 478

13 | *Emotions and Mental Disorders*

Part Four

LEARNING, MEMORY, AND COGNITION

16 | *Language and Cognition*

Box 16-2 The heart and cognition 665

Box 16-3 Childhood loss of one hemisphere 672

DON JUAN: . . . Will you not agree with me . . . that it is inconceivable that Life, having once produced [birds], should, if love and beauty were her object, start off on another line and labor at the clumsy elephant and hideous ape, whose grandchildren we are?

THE DEVIL: You conclude then, that Life was driving at clumsiness and ugliness?

DON JUAN: No, perverse devil that you are, a thousand times no. Life was driving at brains—at its darling object: an organ by which it can attain not only self-consciousness but self-understanding.

George Bernard Shaw
Man and Superman, Act III

What Is Physiological Psychology?

A neurochemical revolution in psychiatry

The body can kill pain

Two brains in one head?

Ways of Looking at Behavior

Describing behavior

Studying the evolution of behavior

Observing development of behavior over the life span

Determining the biological mechanisms of behavior

Levels of Analysis in Studying Brain and Behavior

Comparing Species and Individuals

Finding Relationships between Brain and Behavior

Nonexperimental ways

Experimental approaches to brain-behavior relations

1

Physiological Psychology

What is physiological psychology?

A legend from India (retold by Thomas Mann in his book *The Transposed Heads*) illustrates how both head and body contribute to identity and personality. In this story, the beautiful Sita marries a slender, intellectual young merchant. She is also attracted to his strong, brawny best friend, a blacksmith. One day each young man beheads himself in a temple of the goddess Kali. Sita enters the temple, looking for them, and finds them lying in pools of blood in front of the statue of Kali. Horrified, Sita prays to Kali, begging her to restore the men to life. Kali grants the wish and instructs Sita to place the heads carefully on the bodies. Sita undertakes the task with feverish energy and soon sees the men come back to life. Only then does she realize that she has placed each head on the wrong body! Now the three young people are faced with a baffling problem: Which young man is Sita's spouse? The one with the merchant's head and the smith's body? Or the smith's head on the merchant's body? While the legend explores the complexities of this puzzle, it also considers how each head affects the body which it now controls and also how the body exerts reciprocal influences on the head.

Fortunately we need not solve Sita's dilemma. We can accord priority to the brain in its integration and control of most aspects of behavior, without neglecting the influences on the brain of other bodily systems, such as glands.

This book explores the ways in which bodily states and processes produce and control behavior and the ways in which behavior influences bodily systems. This

3

TABLE 1-1 Disorders of Communicative Processes and the Nervous System

CONDITION	NUMBER OF PEOPLE AFFLICTED*
Alcoholism and drug dependency	10,000,000
Deafness	2,000,000
Seriously impaired hearing	11,000,000
Blindness	500,000
Seriously impaired vision	1,400,000
Convulsive disorders (e.g., epilepsy)	2,500,000
Stroke	2,500,000
Mental retardation due to congenital defects or birth injuries	2,500,000
Psychosis (e.g., schizophrenia)	2,500,000
Dementia (deterioration of mental ability)	2,000,000
Speech impairment (number of children in special school programs)	1,400,000
Aphasia (loss of language ability due to brain injury)	1,000,000
Head injury with resultant impairment	600,000
Parkinson's disease	500,000
Multiple sclerosis	200,000
Brain tumors	200,000

*Approximate numbers of people with these conditions in the United States, out of a total population of 220,000,000.

theme has great scope and breadth; it spans many scientific disciplines. Thus we will draw on the research of psychologists, anatomists, chemists, endocrinologists, engineers, geneticists, neurologists, physiologists, and zoologists. In order to gain a panoramic view of the rapidly developing field of physiological psychology, we will try to rise above the limits of any single specialty.

The frequent coverage in the press of topics in physiological psychology reflects growing popular interest in this field. Articles illustrate the rapid pace of research and indicate the relevance of brain research to pressing human problems. Newspapers and magazines herald new findings that improve our understanding of why we do what we do and why we are what we are. Research in physiological psychology and related fields is throwing light on many aspects of normal behavior, including sex, learning and memory, language and communication, the behavioral roles of sleep and daily rhythms, and the sensitivity and selectivity of our perceptual processes.

Behavioral problems and deficiencies are also being illuminated by brain research. By a conservative estimate, at least one person in five around the world suffers from one or another of these disabilities. (Table 1-1 shows estimates of numbers of people in the United States who suffer from sensory or neural-behavioral disabilities.) Estimates of the number afflicted vary widely from source to source, and there is some overlap among categories. Nevertheless, the figures in Table 1-1 do indicate the magnitude of these human problems.

Fortunately, many impairments and disorders may now be alleviated. For example:

1. Electronic and computer devices can now replace (although admittedly to a limited extent) the functions of the eyes and ears. In some cases, visual or auditory information can be delivered to another sensory channel such as the skin.

2. It is now believed that by the year 2000 the incidence of mental retardation can be reduced by half through the application of principles learned in research. Factors contributing to this reduction will be genetic counseling, early diagnosis of certain metabolic disorders, better nutrition, and adequately stimulating environments.

3. Before the introduction of effective antipsychotic drugs in the 1950s, half the hospital beds in the United States were occupied by mental patients. Now the number of people who require hospitalization is dramatically lower. New drugs engender hopes of returning more psychiatric patients to full roles in the community.

4. Discoveries that reveal the mode of action of habit-forming drugs and their effect on the nervous system give hope that there will be effective cures of people addicted to drugs and prevention of damage to infants born to mothers who take drugs.

Some of the examples that we will consider may seem almost as fantastic as the legend of the transposed heads. Certainly some of the accomplishments of research on brain-behavior relationships would have been hailed as miracles only a generation ago. These findings have led to curing psychoses, abolishing pain, restoring sight to some blind people, and stimulating the growth of the brain and thereby improving the capacity to learn. These and other achievements that are now becoming familiar to us would have seemed unbelievable a few decades ago. As science writer Arthur Clarke has stated, "The science of one generation was the magic of the preceding one."

Let us consider three examples of such advances. We will see others in succeeding chapters.

A neurochemical revolution in psychiatry

Throughout the world—whether in rural societies in remote areas or in industrial centers—some people spend each day in deep anxiety, plagued by hallucinations, delusions of persecution, and irrational thoughts and sentiments. Psychotic disorders have played a tragic part in world history.

For many years there was little hope of relief for this suffering. All sorts of nostrums derived from plants and animals were tried in an effort to reverse the course of these disorders. But for centuries the main method of treatment of severely disturbed people was prolonged confinement, often in the squalor of overcrowded mental hospitals. A turning point came in the 1940s, as a result of research on drugs. By now this research has led to a revolutionary new perspective in the treatment of psychiatric patients.

While searching in the 1940s for a chemical to relax muscles during surgery, Henri Laborit and other French investigators came across a substance that did that and more. This substance—**chlorpromazine**—seemed to produce a tranquilizing effect without putting people to sleep. The tranquilizing effect seen in surgical patients inspired psychiatrists in the 1950s to test this drug as a treatment for psychosis. Early research with compounds of this type was hampered by their rather weak effects and undesirable side effects. Therefore an important advance was the introduction of tests with experimental animals to screen compounds for their sedative effects (Swazey, 1974). Many studies indicated that these chemicals have remarkable antipsychotic properties. Because of the use of these substances, the number of hospitalized mentally ill persons has been halved since the middle 1950s. Today so many people can lead useful, rewarding lives while controlling psychosis with these drugs that some psychiatrists even believe that the main role of psychotherapy is to encourage patients to accept medication.

As is true of many areas of research, the successes have not been without costs. The drugs that alleviate many psychoses have come into such widespread use that they pose social problems. Drug taking has become for many people an accepted way of dealing with daily problems. It can rule the lives of some people. Have the advances of psychiatry that have aided the few led to impairment of the lives of the many? Knowledge of the responses of the brain to chemical treatments is essential in this continuing assessment.

The body can kill pain   Humans have always sought remedies to relieve pain. In China, for more than 3000 years, **acupuncture,** the insertion and rotation of needles in various parts of the body, has been used for blunting pain. Seeking freedom from pain through the use of opiates has almost as long a history. In fact, trying to understand how opiates control our perception of pain has brought us close to an understanding of normal body mechanisms for suppressing it.

Studies of heroin addiction during the 1970s resulted in the discovery that opiates accumulate in particular sites in the brain and that these regions are especially important in controlling pain. Opiates accumulate in these areas because they attach to particular cells that seem to "recognize" them. This attraction suggested that perhaps the brain manufactures and uses opiatelike substances, since it did not seem likely that evolution could have anticipated the availability of addictive drugs. Rather, it seemed that opiates mimic a natural process: the body's ability to produce opiatelike substances that control pain.

In just a few years a great deal has been learned about this built-in mechanism for inhibiting pain. Various regions of the brain do indeed contain naturally produced chemicals that are now called **endorphins,** short for "endogenous morphines." Such compounds can relieve pain, and in some cases they are more effective than morphine. Stimulation by electrodes implanted in regions of the brain containing endorphins produces dramatic relief of pain, relief that outlasts the period of stimulation.

The discovery of the endorphins has also increased our understanding of other pain remedies. For example, people who suffer from pain frequently get relief from inert pills, such as sugar tablets. This result, called the **placebo effect,** usually takes place when the pills are given in a medical environment, accompanied by the confident reassurances of a physician. The psychological factors that underlie the placebo effect have long been a mystery. Now some researchers suggest that the placebo gives relief because the clinical setting promotes the release of endorphins. Acupuncture too may work by causing the release of endorphins, since chemicals that block the action of endorphins also inhibit the pain relief produced by acupuncture. Perhaps some of the magic that banished suffering in ages past was simply the workings of natural brain chemicals that evolved to enable us to cope with pain.

Two brains in one head?

Suppose that each time a right-handed person buttoned a shirt, the person's left hand sought to unbutton it! Two separate controllers would seem to be in charge. Most of us are saved from such frustration because information from the right and left sides of the body is integrated by pathways that connect the two sides of the brain. But what happens when these connections are severed? Can we then observe two different types of consciousness? To consider this prospect, we should know that the structures of the two sides of the brain are very much alike, although some anatomical differences are present.

Functional differences between the cerebral hemispheres of human brains become especially evident after brain damage such as that resulting from a stroke. For instance, injury to certain parts of the left cerebral hemisphere can produce striking changes in speech and language, whereas injury to the right hemisphere rarely affects speech. Damage to these parts of the left hemisphere causes speech impairment in virtually all right-handed individuals and in about 50% of left-handers. This situation used to be described as "cerebral dominance," implying that a talkative left cerebral hemisphere dominated a mute right hemisphere.

New information about hemispheric specialization of function has come from studies of patients in whom the connections between the right and left cerebral hemispheres have been severed surgically: **split-brain** individuals. Tests of these patients by Roger Sperry (1975) and his collaborators have shown remarkable functional differences between the cerebral hemispheres. This has prompted Sperry to speak of separate forms of consciousness in the two hemispheres of the brain. Indeed, one of his patients *was* seen to button a shirt with one hand and try to unbutton it with the other.

Tests have indicated differences in cognitive style between the two hemispheres. The left is said to be analytic and verbal, whereas the right has been characterized as spatial and holistic. The differences in the ways the cerebral hemispheres process information have prompted some researchers to suggest that the educational needs and capabilities of the cerebral hemispheres differ. Those who urge attention to the creative potential of the right hemisphere have alleged that the educational system has "left-sided" prejudices. This is surely an exaggeration. We suggest that you hold off before you choose favorite cerebral sides. Chapter 16 offers some moderating ideas.

Ways of looking at behavior

Most subjects can be understood best if they are studied from several different perspectives. For example, when you eat a dish of pasta made from a new recipe, you may concentrate on the flavor and try to guess the ingredients of the sauce. You may also be interested in their nutritional value. Knowing the history and origin of the dish can also add to your appreciation. And if you are planning a menu, you'll consider what other foods would go well with it.

To study and understand behavior—be it the behavior of a single nerve cell or of an active person—we can adopt any of several different perspectives. Each one brings out further information. The approaches that we will adopt here are these: (a) describing behavior, (b) studying the evolution of behavior, (c) observing development of behavior over the life span, and (d) determining the biological mechanisms of behavior.

Describing behavior

Until we describe what it is we want to study, we can't get very far. Depending on the goals of our investigation, we may describe behavior in terms of detailed acts and processes or in terms of results or functions. Thus an *analytical* description of limb movements might record the successive positions of the limb and its parts (Figure 1-1) or the contraction of the different muscles. A *functional* behavioral description would state whether the limb was being used in walking, running, hopping, swimming, or shooting dice.

To be useful for scientific study, a description must be precise and analytical. That is, it must help reveal the essential features of the behavior. It must employ accurately defined terms and units. The methods and operations used by researchers must be specified so that other investigators can repeat and verify them.

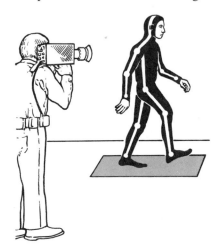

Figure 1-1 Describing behavior accurately is an indispensable step in studying it. Thus in studying locomotion, some investigators obtain a graphic display by photographing a person wearing a black suit with white lines that accentuate the axes of the body. This research will be mentioned in Chapter 8.

Studying the evolution of behavior

Darwin's theory of **evolution through natural selection,** as updated and elaborated, is central to all modern biology and psychology (Figure 1-2). This perspective provides rich insights into many kinds of behavior and behavioral mechanisms, so we will use it in most of the chapters to come. From this perspective emerge two rather different emphases: (a) the *continuity* of behavior and biological processes among species and (b) the *species-specific adaptations* in behavior and biology that have evolved in different environmental niches. At some points in this book we will concentrate on continuity, that is, on features of behavior and its biological mechanisms that are common to many species. At other points we will look at species-specific behaviors.

Figure 1-2 Studying the evolution of behavior provides rich insights concerning its functions and mechanisms.

● **Continuity**   Nature is conservative. Bodily or behavioral inventions once arrived at may be maintained over millions of years and may be seen in animals that otherwise appear to be very different. The nerve impulse, for example, is essentially the same in a jellyfish, a cockroach, and a human being. Some of the chemical compounds that transmit messages through the bloodstream (hormones) are also the same in diverse animals (although the same hormone may affect different metabolic processes in different species). Similar—but not identical—sex hormones occur in all mammalian species. Male and female mammals produce the same sex hormones, although in different relative amounts and during different time cycles.

But similarity of a feature between species does not guarantee that the feature can be traced back to a common ancestor. Similar but not identical solutions to a problem may have evolved independently in different classes of animals. For example, color vision has emerged independently in insects, fish, reptiles, birds, and mammals. Much current research on neural mechanisms of learning and memory is being done with relatively simple invertebrates. The assumption here is that there is an evolutionary continuity of mechanisms among a very wide range of species. Some findings suggest, however, that more complex animals may have evolved additional mechanisms of learning beyond those that they share with simpler organisms.

● **Species-specific behaviors**   Different species have evolved specific ways of dealing with their environments. An earthworm's sensory endowments, for example, are quite different from those of a robin. Certain species of bats rely almost exclusively on hearing to navigate and to find their prey. The vision of these species has degenerated until it has become unusable. But other species of bats are visually oriented and depend on their eyes to find their way around and to secure their food. Human beings use both vision and audition. However, we are not sensitive to electrical fields in the environment, whereas certain kinds of fish are highly sensitive to them. These fish emit electrical pulses and use the resulting electrical fields to guide their locomotion.

Communicative behavior differs greatly among species. Some species rely chiefly on visual signals, some on auditory signals, and some on olfactory signals. In many species the production of signals does not require learning but simply follows an inherited species-specific pattern. In other species (including some songbirds), the young bird must learn the song. And although there are many varieties of song, they all conform rather closely to the pattern of the species.

Human beings can produce a wide variety of vocal sounds, but any language uses only a fraction of them. Moreover, the functional significance of sounds is rather arbitrary in human languages, since the same sequence of sounds may have different meanings in different languages.

Observing development of the behavior over the life span

Observing the way a particular behavior changes during the life span of an individual may give us clues to its functions and mechanisms (Figure 1-3). For example, we know from observation that learning ability in monkeys increases over several years of development. Therefore we can speculate that prolonged maturation of neural circuits is required for complex learning tasks. In rodents the ability to form long-term memories lags somewhat behind the maturation of learning ability. Young

Figure 1-3 Observing behavior over the lifespan yields valuable clues about its functions and mechanisms.

rodents learn well but forget more quickly than older ones. This difference provides one of several kinds of evidence that learning and memory involve different processes. We can study the development of reproductive capacity and of differences in behavior between the sexes along with changes in bodily structures and processes. This enables us to throw light on bodily mechanisms of sex behaviors.

Determining the biological mechanisms of behavior

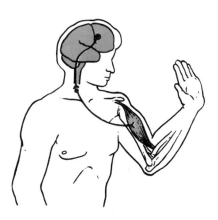

Figure 1-4 Physiological psychology is especially concerned with the bodily mechanisms that make particular behavior possible.

The history of a species tells us the evolutionary determinants of its behavior, and the history of an individual tells us the developmental determinants. To learn about the actual mechanisms of an individual's behavior, we study his or her present bodily endowments and states (Figure 1-4). Our major aim in physiological psychology is to examine those bodily mechanisms that make particular behaviors possible. For example, in the case of learning and memory, we would like to know the sequence of electrophysiological and biochemical processes that must occur between the initial capture of an item of information and its eventual retrieval from memory. We would also like to know what parts of the nervous system are particularly involved in learning and memory. In the case of reproductive behavior, we would like to know the developmental processes in the body that produce the capacity for reproductive behavior. We also want to understand the neuronal and hormonal processes that underlie reproductive behavior.

We have defined four ways of looking at behavior, and Table 1-2 shows how each of them can be applied to three kinds of behavior. We will take up each of the entries in the table in a later chapter. In fact we will use these four perspectives to examine all the categories of behavior that we consider in the later parts of this book: sensation, perception, and motor coordination (Part Two); motivation (Part Three); and learning, memory, and cognition (Part Four).

Levels of analysis in studying brain and behavior

The body's systems are organized hierarchically. Therefore finding explanations for behavior often involves dealing with several levels of biological organization. Each level of analysis deals with units that are simpler in structure and organization than the level above. Table 1-3 shows how we can analyze the brain into successively less complex units, until we get down to single nerve cells and their still simpler constituents.

Scientific explanations usually involve analyzing something on a simpler or more basic level of organization than that of the structure or function to be explained. In principle it is possible to reduce each explanatory series down to the molecular or atomic level, though for practical reasons this is rarely done. For example, the organic chemist or the neurochemist usually deals with large complex molecules and the laws that govern them and seldom seeks explanations in terms of atoms.

Naturally in all fields different problems are carried to different levels of analysis,

TABLE 1-2   Four Research Perspectives Applied to Three Kinds of Behavior

RESEARCH PERSPECTIVES	KINDS OF BEHAVIOR		
	Sex and Behavior	*Learning and Memory*	*Language and Communication*
1. Describing behavior (a) Structural description	What are the main patterns of reproductive behavior and sex differences in behavior?	In what main ways does behavior change as a consequence of experience; for example, conditioning?	How are the sounds of speech patterned?
(b) Functional description	How do specialized patterns of behavior contribute to mating and to care of young?	How do certain behaviors lead to rewards or avoidance of punishment?	What behavior is involved in making statements or asking questions?
2. Studying evolution of behavior	How does mating depend on hormones in different species? How did seasonality of reproduction evolve?	How do different species compare in kinds and speed of learning?	How did the human speech apparatus evolve?
3. Observing development of behavior	How do reproductive and secondary sex characteristics develop over the life span?	How do learning and memory change over the life span?	How do language and communication develop over the life span?
4. Finding biological mechanisms of behavior	What neural circuits and what hormones are involved in reproductive behavior?	What anatomical and chemical changes in the brain hold memories? How are different brain regions involved in different functions, such as formation of memories and storage of memories?	What brain regions are particularly involved in language? How are particular impairments of language related to local damage in the brain?

TABLE 1-3   Levels of Organization of Nervous System

LEVEL	EXAMPLES
Organ	Brain, spinal cord
Major region	Cerebral cortex, cerebellum
Subregion	Motor cortex, visual cortex
Basic processing unit	Circuits of nerve cells
Nerve cell	Two hundred or more varieties of nerve cells (e.g., pyramidal cell, Purkinje cell)
Functional contacts between nerve cells	Chemical synapse
Functional regions of nerve cell membranes	Synaptic receptor region

and fruitful work is often being done simultaneously by different workers at several levels. Thus in their research on visual perception, behavioral psychologists advance analytical descriptions of behavior. They try to determine how the eyes move while looking at a visual pattern, or how the contrast among parts of the pattern determines its visibility. Meanwhile, other psychologists and biologists are studying the differences in visual endowments among species and trying to determine the adaptive significance of these differences. For example, how is the presence (or absence) of color vision related to the life of a species? At the same time other investigators are tracing out the brain's structures and networks that are involved in different kinds of visual discrimination. Still other neuroscientists are trying to ascertain the electrical and chemical events that occur at synapses in the brain during visual learning.

Useful applications can be found at many levels of analysis of a system. For a given problem one level of analysis is often more appropriate than another. For example, common problems of visual acuity are caused by variations in the shape of the eyeball. These problems can be solved by prescribing corrective lenses without having to analyze the brain processes involved in pattern vision. On the other hand, a partial loss of sight in certain parts of the visual field suggests pressure on the two optic nerves where they run together. This may be an early sign of a tumor whose removal restores full vision.

Other restrictions of the visual field are caused by localized damage to the visual area of the cerebral cortex. Recent research shows that training can help to enlarge the field in some of these cases. If epileptic attacks of a person are regularly preceded by a peculiar visual image, this suggests the possibility that the person may have a scar or an injury to the visual cortex. Understanding how color vision works has been advanced by studying how information from different kinds of retinal cells converges on nerve cells and how the nerve cells process this information. Investigators are also studying the way visual patterns are analyzed by the brain at the level of nerve cells and their connections.

As we consider explanations of many kinds of behavior in terms of bodily events, we will point out the main levels of analysis that are currently being used to study each problem. We will also indicate some of the applications of each level of research.

Comparing species and individuals

How do similarities and differences among people and animals fit into physiological psychology? The anthropologist Clyde Kluckhohn once observed that each person is in some ways like all other people, in some ways like some other people, and in

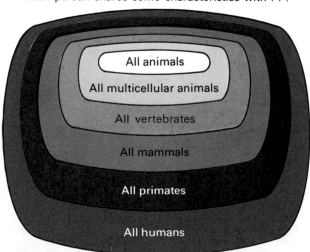

Each person shares some characteristics with . . .

All animals
All multicellular animals
All vertebrates
All mammals
All primates
All humans

Figure 1-5 Similarities and differences among species.

some ways like no other person (Kluckhohn, 1949). As indicated in Figure 1-5, we can extend this observation to the much broader range of animal life. In some ways each person is like all animals (for example, in needing to ingest complex organic nutrients). In some ways each person is like all multicellular animals, in some ways like all vertebrates (for example, in having a spinal column). In some ways each person is like all mammals (for example, in suckling the young), and in some ways like all other primates (for example, in having a hand with an opposable thumb and a relatively large and complex brain).

Areas of similarity define regions within which findings about one kind of animal can be properly applied to other kinds. Thus much of the fundamental research on the mechanisms of inheritance has been done with the bacterium *E. coli*. The findings proved to be so widely applicable that some molecular biologists proclaimed, "What is true of *E. coli* is true of the elephant". More recently it has been found that—although more complex animals do share many basic processes and chemistry of genetics with *E. coli*—there are also some important differences in their genetic mechanisms. With respect to each biological property researchers must find which animals are identical and where differences arise. When we seek model animal systems with which to study human behavior or biological processes, we must ask this question: Does the proposed model really share the same sphere of identity with human beings with respect to the aspect to be studied?

Findings made with animal subjects have been successfully applied to biological mechanisms of many kinds of behavior in people. You will see examples in every chapter of this book. For example, in all animals that have nervous systems there are both excitatory and inhibitory influences of one nerve cell on another. Study of these processes in one species can be successfully applied to other species. Again, in the case of hormones some mechanisms of hormone action are the same in invertebrates, birds, and mammals. Some hormones are very similar among widely different orders of animals. Research with animals has helped to illumine relations between body and behavior in people in many areas, among them (a) perception of color and form, (b) mechanisms of pain and relief from pain, (c) drug addiction, (d) muscular coordination, (e) roles of hormones in sex behavior, (f) control of hunger and thirst, and (g) methods of aiding people with impaired memory.

But even within the same species, individuals differ from one another: cat from cat, bluejay from bluejay, and person from person (Figure 1-6). Physiological psychology seeks to understand individual differences as well as similarities. This interest in the individual is one of the most important differences between psychology and other approaches to behavior. The lottery of heredity ensures that each individual draws a unique genetic makeup (the only exception being identical twins). The way the individual's unique genetic composition is translated into bodily form and behavioral capacities is part of our story. Furthermore, each individual has a unique set of personal experiences. Therefore the way each person is able to process information and store the memories of these experiences is another part of our story. Our focus on physiological approaches to behavior will not ignore the individuality of people but will help to show how this individuality comes about.

We will be drawing on animal research throughout this book. Therefore we should comment on some of the ethical issues of experimentation on animals. Human beings' involvement and concern with other species goes back into prehistory. Early humans had to study animal behavior and physiology in order to escape some species

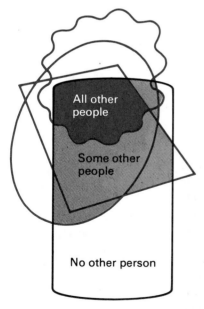

Each person shares some characteristics with . . .

All other people

Some other people

No other person

Figure 1-6 Similarities and differences within a species. The different forms represent different individuals with partially overlapping traits.

and to hunt others. When humans domesticated some species about ten thousand years ago, closer observation and interaction became possible. Formal studies of animal physiology and behavior began only in the nineteenth century.

Without experimentation on animal subjects in the last hundred years, there would not have been the enormous progress we have seen in medicine, physiology, and psychology. Today animals—or animal tissues—are used in a wide variety of medical tests and in the development of new medical treatments. The fact that these tests work testifies to the basic resemblance of our physiology to that of other species.

In view of these resemblances people have also become increasingly concerned about humane use of animal subjects. Many scientific associations have prescribed ethical standards for experiments on animals, codes derived from scientists' own concerns with their subjects. Governments also set standards for the care and housing of animal subjects. In many cases experimenters today are trying to use simpler and more abundant species rather than complex, rare ones. These precautions are important, because learning about human behavior and its biological bases inevitably requires research on animals of other species as well as on human beings.

Finding relationships between brain and behavior

The quest to understand the workings of the body takes many forms, from intuition to sophisticated experimental research to mathematical modeling of bodily processes. Each approach offers a different glimpse of the intricate ways in which the brain generates behavior and experience.

Nonexperimental ways

Although most of the advances that we discuss here have come from experimental research, nonexperimental observations have also contributed importantly to physiological psychology. Clinical observations have provided valuable data as well as incentives to learn more.

● **Looking at ourselves**   We humans are driven by curiosity about ourselves and our surroundings. Our thoughts about how we function as human beings and our informal observations about how other animals manage their lives are often the source of astute hunches about how our brains must work. All too often, however, many of us are intimidated by contemporary science and its complicated gadgetry. We forget that our own brains are quite complex, capable of searching for information and finding answers to questions about our existence. It is well to keep this in mind. The vitality of inquiry in physiological psychology depends on students asking questions about how they themselves work.

Of course, opinions are mixed as to how far we can go in understanding the physiological mechanisms of our behavior. The pessimistic view was expressed by the writer Ambrose Bierce in his definition of *mind* [*Devil's Dictionary* (1911)]:

> A mysterious form of matter secreted by the brain. Its chief activity consists in the endeavor to ascertain its own nature, the futility of the attempt being due to the fact that it has nothing but itself to know itself with.

Most scientists, as they see the accelerating pace of advances in biology and psychology, are more optimistic than Bierce. They have formed groups and societies and have established specialized publications to inform each other and to keep abreast of the tremendous amount of information that is being produced. Clearly human brains *are* making progress in understanding the biology of their own behavior as well as that of other animals.

● **The mind-brain problem**   For centuries philosophers and religious thinkers have debated about the relationship between body and "mind." This distinction is deeply rooted in many cultures. Although opinions about what is called the "mind-body problem" have little influence on day-to-day research, many people still want to understand how mental life can be explained in terms of bodily events.

Different schools of philosophy have taken opposed views about relations between mind and body. Some hold that the world of the mind and the world of the body are separate systems, with varying aspects of relatedness. Others feel that mind and matter are fundamentally just two aspects of the same system. For some philosophers brains are part of a physical world, a system separate from the world of mental phenomena. But for modern scientists they are not separate.

The notion that mind and matter are fundamentally the same usually amounts to an assumption that mental processes are at the same time brain processes. One version, known as monism, holds that mind is an "emergent" property of the organization of nerve cells. To draw an analogy: The properties of water appear when hydrogen and oxygen are combined, although neither element has the properties of water.

One can relate the concept of emergence to the evolution of brain and behavior. Thus the monist doctrine accords well with the research that we will be discussing here. We will see the ways that different organizations of neural circuits are related to different behaviors. We will see that intervention in brain processes (such as electrical stimulation of localized sites in the brain) can alter behavior and mental experiences. And intervening in mental activity (such as telling a person to imagine a certain scene or an action) can change the electrical activity of brain cells. It can even alter the distribution of blood in the brain.

● **Views from the clinic**   Viruses, wars, and accidents provide clinics with many examples of brain abnormalities and present urgent problems that must be solved. A major focus of contemporary psychology—the interest in localization of functions in the brain (which we will discuss in Chapter 2)—comes from the study of the impact of localized brain injuries on behavior. Behavioral dysfunctions in humans frequently arise from localized brain damage. In the late nineteenth century clinical neurologists, seeing the variety of behavioral changes that came about as a result of different brain injuries, concluded that different mental states had different "seats" in the brain.

The study of brain-injured people can reveal some of the plans of behavioral and motor organization in the brain. Chemical treatments of neurological and psychiatric disorders have also helped us to better understand the neurochemistry of the brain. The successes and failures of such treatments throw light on the roles of various substances found in the brain and the impact that changes in their concentration have on behavior. As the biological sciences have developed, clinical neurology and psychiatry have benefited from experimental investigations using animal subjects as models for human conditions.

Experimental approaches to brain-behavior relations

Experiments and theories in many disciplines have contributed to our understanding of the working of the body in relation to behavior. Since the focuses of different disciplines vary, they provide insights that complement each other. The anatomist portrays the structure of nervous systems, the components and the pathways of the brain. The physiologist examines how these components work, often studying the electrical signals of the nervous system. The chemist identifies the chemicals found in the brain and charts the metabolic pathways that generate different substances. The engineer seeks to determine whether quantitative concepts derived from inanimate systems can be applied to brain functions. Physiological psychologists are a bit more eclectic, but generally start with an interest in the mechanisms of behavior. Their investigations include both (a) observing and measuring behavior and (b) observing and measuring bodily structures and processes.

Figure 1-7 illustrates three approaches to relating bodily and behavioral variables. At the top, part (a), is the most commonly employed approach: **somatic intervention,** which involves altering some structure or function of the brain or body and seeing how this alters behavior. Here somatic intervention is the independent variable and the behavioral effect is the dependent variable. We will describe many kinds of somatic interventions with both humans and other animals in different chapters of this text. A few examples are these:

1. A hormone is administered to some animals but not to others. The two groups are later compared on various behavioral measures.
2. A part of the brain is stimulated electrically, and behavioral effects are observed.
3. A connection between two parts of the nervous system is cut, and changes in behavior are measured.

The opposite approach, part (b) of Figure 1-7, is **behavioral intervention,** which involves intervening in the behavior of an organism and looking for resultant changes in bodily structure or function. Here behavior is the independent variable and bodily measures are the dependent variables. Among the examples that we will consider in later chapters are the following:

1. Putting two adults of opposite sex in the presence of each other may lead to increased secretion of certain hormones.
2. Exposing a person or animal to a visual stimulus provokes changes in both electrical activity and blood flow in parts of the brain.
3. Giving animals training is accompanied by electrophysiological, biochemical, and anatomical changes in parts of their brains.

The **correlational approach** to brain-behavior relations, part (c) of Figure 1-7, consists of finding the extent to which a given bodily measure covaries with a given behavioral measure. Some questions examined in later chapters will be these:

1. Is there a significant correlation between brain size and intelligence?
2. Are individual differences in reproductive activity correlated with levels of certain hormones in the individuals?

Finding such correlations should not be taken as proof of causal relationship, however. For one thing, even if a causal relation does exist, the correlation does not

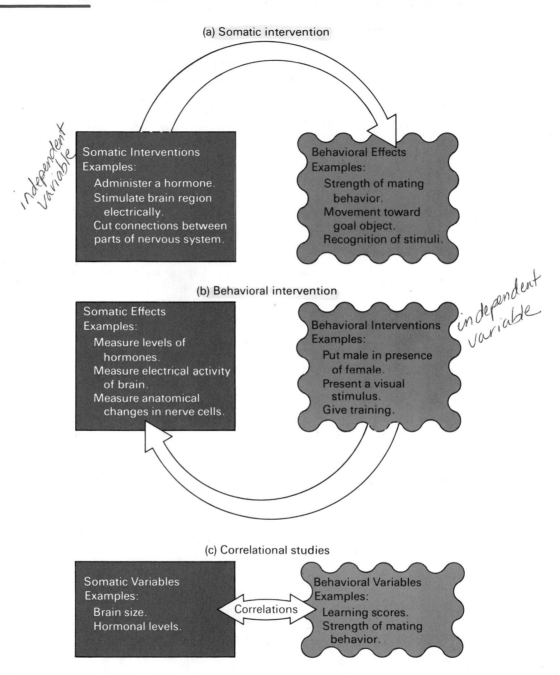

Figure 1-7 (a) Somatic intervention. When some aspect of bodily structure or function is altered, how does this affect behavior? (b) Behavioral intervention. When some aspect of behavior is altered, how does this affect bodily structure and/or function? (c) Correlational approach. To what extent does a particular bodily measure covary with a particular behavioral measure?

reveal its direction, that is, which variable is independent and which is dependent. For another, two terms might be correlated only because a third factor determines the values of the two factors measured. The existence of a correlation does indicate, however, that there is some link—direct or indirect—between the two variables. This often stimulates investigators to formulate hypotheses and to test them by interventive techniques.

Some interventive experiments are purely exploratory ("What would happen if we did this?"). Some attempt to confirm or to disprove casual observations or impressions ("Is it really true that doing A leads to B?"). Exploratory studies and careful descriptive work are first steps in research. But to obtain more penetrating knowledge, researchers must formulate hypotheses that might account for a phenomenon and devise experiments to test them. Any hypothesis that is disproved is rejected, and the remaining hypotheses are subjected to further tests. As researchers make new observations, they formulate (and test) more powerful and far-reaching hypotheses. By these stepwise procedures investigators can arrive at fuller understandings of any scientific domain, including behavioral and bodily phenomena, and the relationships between them.

Putting these three approaches together yields the circle diagram of Figure 1-8. This diagram incorporates the basic approaches to studying relationships between bodily processes and behavior. It can also serve to emphasize the theme (brought out in the legend of the transposed heads) that the relations between brain and body are reciprocal; each affects the other in an ongoing cycle of bodily and behavioral interactions. We will see such reciprocal relationships in each of the main sections of the book: Part One, "Bodily Systems Basic to Behavior"; Part Two, "Information Processing in Perceptual and Motor Systems"; Part Three, "Control of Behavioral States: Motivation"; and Part Four, "Learning, Memory, and Cognition."

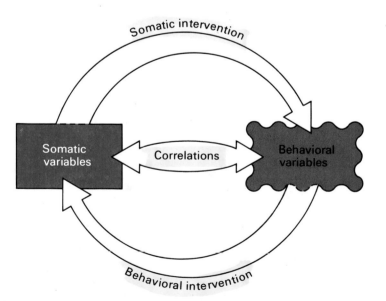

Figure 1-8 The three main approaches to studying relations between bodily processes and behavior.

Our goal in writing this book has been to provide an interesting and coherent account of the main ideas and research in physiological psychology. Because there are so many pieces to tie together, we have introduced a given piece of information when it makes a difference to the understanding of a subject rather than withholding it until we arrive at the precise pigeonhole in which it belongs. We have sought to communicate our own sense of interest and excitement about the mysteries of mind and body. We hope you will join us in seeking knowledge of this fascinating field.

RECOMMENDED READING

Bindra, D. (Ed.) *The brain's mind: A neuroscience perspective on the mind-body problem.* New York: Gardner Press, 1980.

Hebb, D. O. *Essay on mind.* Hillsdale, N.J.: Lawrence Erlbaum Associates, 1980.

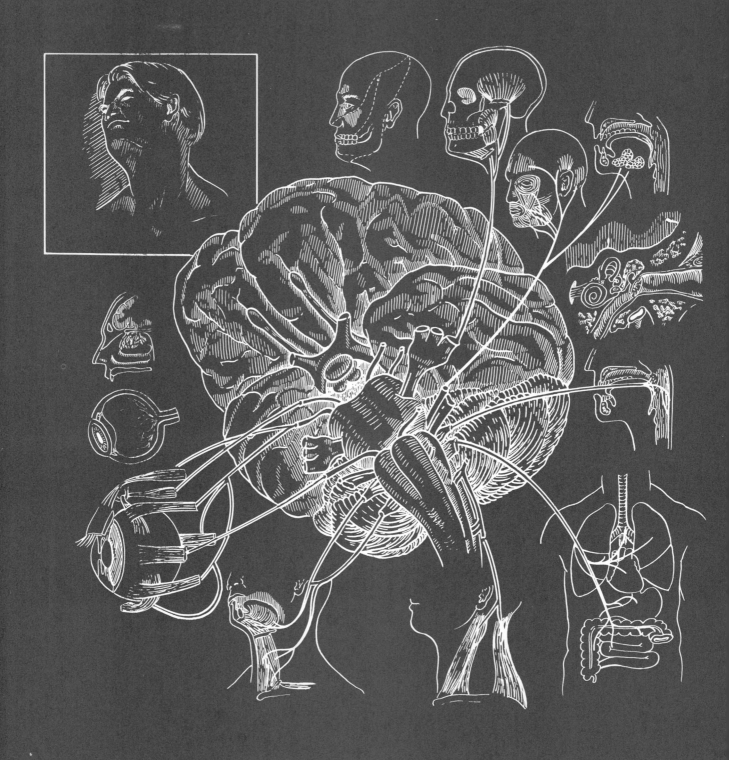

Part One

BODILY SYSTEMS
BASIC TO BEHAVIOR

Within your head is an information-processing system that contains at least 150 billion nerve cells. The workings of this vast assembly make possible our perceptions, movements, thoughts, motives, and feelings. Modulating the organization and activation of the nervous system are hormones, the secretions of endocrine cells located in your head and trunk.

Since the interrelated functions of the nervous system and endocrine system are fundamental to all behavior, we begin this book by examining the basic properties and functions of these two systems, starting with the architecture of the nervous system. Once we know how the nervous system is structured, we will analyze how it conveys and processes information. Then we will examine the structures and functions of the endocrine system and show how it works in collaboration with the nervous system. At the same time that we survey these basic mechanisms, we will begin applying our knowledge to problems of behavior and its biological mechanisms.

Orientation

Historical Views of the Brain

The central importance of the brain

Renaissance studies of the anatomy of the brain

Nineteenth-century concepts of brain localization

Contemporary Large-Scale Views of the Human Nervous System

The central nervous system

The ventricular system of the brain

Circulation of blood in the brain

Peripheral nervous system

Looking into the living human brain

Microscopic Views of the Human Nervous System

Hierarchy of brain structures

Nerve cells and their connections

Glial cells

The evolution of nerve cells

Regions of the Brain and Their Circuitry

The cerebellum

The cerebral cortex

Comparing Brains Among Species

Why compare?

Similarities and differences among nervous systems

Summary/Main Points

2

Neuroanatomical Bases of Behavior

Orientation

Thoughts, feelings, perceptions, and acts—all are products of the workings of the brain. Psychologists analyze complex psychological events like these in terms of simpler behavior processes. In a like manner, neuroscientists seek to understand the brain by examining its composition and the workings of its parts. Physiological psychologists try to combine these two approaches by studying behavior in terms of brain structures and processes. Early on in the effort to achieve this synthesis, two major questions arose: First, how are types of experience and behavior related to specific brain parts and the ways they function? Second, are particular psychological processes controlled by particular places in the brain? These questions form the core of an issue called the **localization of function.**

Investigators have been concerned with this issue for centuries; to address it, they first had to master the brain's anatomy. Within the last hundred years researchers have begun to show that the brain is not a homogeneous mass of similar components but is composed of different structures. Most importantly, we now know that differences in structures are related to variations in behavior. Structures in different places in the brain may correspond to behavioral differences. From another point of view we can hypothesize that behavioral specializations or categories of experience may correspond to different parts of the brain.

Studies of the changes in behavior that arise from head injuries supply examples of the localization of brain mechanisms of behavior. For example, in a landmark case of 1848 a workman named Phineas Gage suffered major brain damage when a crowbar was blasted into his skull in an accident. The principal site of his injury was in the frontal lobe of the brain. After the accident his physician noted dramatic changes in Gage's personal habits and a curious lack of concern for matters he had formerly cared about. This syndrome has since been seen most often as a consequence of psychosurgical treatment for mental disease. (This is discussed in greater detail in Chapter 13.)

Brain damage much less extensive than that suffered by Phineas Gage can also produce marked changes in motivation. Certain small localized lesions deep in the brain, for example, can cause both humans and rats to overeat and rapidly become obese. Other lesions, just millimeters away, can produce the opposite effect: refusal to eat and starvation. (Such striking changes in behavior are discussed in Chapter 11.)

Other psychological processes also show distinctive localization within the brain. Each sense—vision, hearing, touch, smell, and taste—has its own areas of representation in the brain. Limited injury in the back of the brain can produce regions of blindness—literally, blind spots. The size of the blind region is determined by the size of the injury, and the position is determined by the position of the injury. (We will see more about maps of sensory areas in the brain in Chapters 6 and 7.)

Observations like these have impelled investigators to search for the relations between particular brain structures and the regulation of specific behaviors. Such pursuits start from one of two general perspectives: (1) the "top-down" perspective and (2) the "bottom-up" perspective.

Scientists who use the top-down perspective examine general properties of structure of the nervous system and relate them to general properties of behavior. They emphasize examining large-scale properties of behavior and anatomy first and then scrutinizing finer details. Those who use the bottom-up perspective claim that the best scientific payoffs come from working at the finest levels of the structure of the nervous system. These researchers emphasize explanations of simple behaviors at the most elementary levels of nervous system structure. They stress the study of animals that are relatively simple in both behavior and nervous system, as witness the title of a symposium at a recent meeting of the Society for Neuroscience: "The proper study of mankind is crayfish."

Chapter 1 discussed the way explanations can involve different levels of analysis. In this chapter, we will first look at some historical ideas about the brain and then analyze—from the top down—the principal levels of the structure of the nervous system.

Historical views of the brain

It is only recently that the central role of the brain has been recognized. We will consider briefly how this recognition came about and then take up the development of anatomical knowledge of the brain, a discovery process that began during the Renaissance.

The central importance of the brain

The knowledge that the brain mediates and controls behavior is rather recent in human history. When Tutankhamun was mummified (around thirty-three hundred years ago), four important organs were preserved in alabaster jars in his tomb: the liver, the lungs, the stomach, and the intestines. The heart was preserved in its place within the body. All these organs were considered necessary to ensure the pharoah's continued existence in the afterlife. The brain, however, was removed from the skull and discarded. Obviously it was not considered important for the afterlife.

Neither the Old Testament (written from the twelfth to the second century B.C.) nor the New Testament mentions the brain. However, the Old Testament mentions the heart hundreds of times and makes several references each to the liver, the stomach, and the bowels as the seats of passion, courage, and pity. "Get thee a heart of wisdom," said the prophet.

The heart is where Aristotle, the most prominent scientist of ancient Greece, located mental capacities. He considered the brain to be only a cooling unit to lower the temperature of the hot blood from the heart. Other Greek thinkers, however, did consider the brain to be the seat of intellect and the organ that controls behavior. Thus Hippocrates, the great physician of Greek antiquity, wrote as follows:

> Not only our pleasure, our joy and our laughter but also our sorrow, pain, grief and tears rise from the brain, and the brain alone. With it we think and understand, see and hear, and we discriminate between the ugly and the beautiful, between what is pleasant and what is unpleasant and between good and evil.

The dispute between those who located intellect in the heart and those who located it in the brain still raged two thousand years later, in Shakespeare's time: "Tell me, where is fancy bred, in the heart or in the head?" (*Merchant of Venice,* Act III, Scene 2). We still reflect this ancient notion when we call people "kindhearted," "open-hearted," "hardhearted," "fainthearted," or "heartless." Only in the nineteenth and twentieth centuries, with gradually increasing knowledge of the nervous system, did educated people in the Western world finally accept the brain as the mechanism that coordinates and controls behavior.

Renaissance studies of brain anatomy

Although Renaissance anatomists did not necessarily share our views of the brain's importance, they did accurately describe the gross appearance of the human nervous system. Protected within the skull is the brain, with its elaborately furrowed or convoluted surface. Descriptions of the brain by Renaissance anatomists emphasized the shape and appearance of the external surfaces of the brain, since these were the parts that were easiest to see when the skull was removed. It was immediately apparent to anyone who looked that the brain has an extraordinarily strange shape. The complexity of its gross form led to the use of an elaborate, precise vocabulary to label different regions. Many of these labels are still in use. Most of them are Latin or Greek names of common shapes, forms, objects, and animals. We will introduce a number of these terms here, but only the ones that will be needed again in this book.

When the skull is opened, the surface of the brain is seen to be convoluted, or ridged and furrowed (Figure 2-1). Thus the early anatomists described it as showing

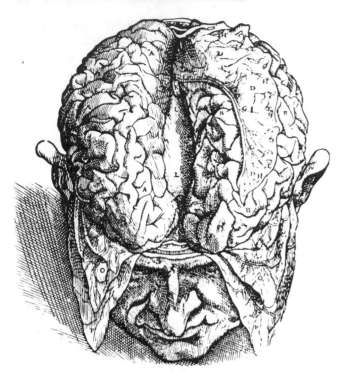

Figure 2-1 The surface of the brain, as depicted by a Renaissance anatomist of the sixteenth century.

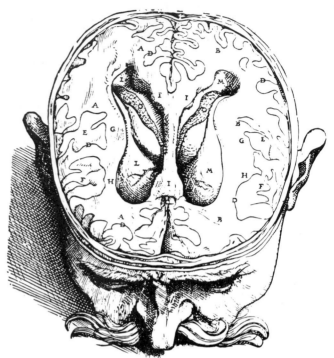

Figure 2-2 The interior of the brain, including the cerebral ventricles, as depicted by a Renaissance artist.

gyri (from the Latin "gyrus," meaning "a ridge or rounded form") separated by **sulci** (from the Latin "sulcus," "a furrow"). We still use the terms gyri and sulci today to describe the same features. The brain is divided into two halves, the right and left **cerebral hemispheres.** The hemispheres, which are soft to the touch, are connected to each other by a tough band of tissue. Renaissance anatomists gave this band the name **corpus callosum** (Latin for "hard body").

When the anatomists cut away the top part of the brain to see what lay inside, they saw that the outer bark or cortex of the cerebral hemispheres was pinkish gray in color, in contrast to the underlying **white matter.** Cutting deeper into the hemispheres, they found hollow chambers filled with fluid, which they called the **ventricles** (from the Latin for "stomach") (Figure 2-2). The Renaissance anatomists believed that the fluid (which they called "animal spirits") not only filled these cavities, but also filled the nerves and carried messages from one part of the body to another. The tissue surrounding the ventricle in the center of the brain they called the **thalamus** (from the Greek for "room" or "bridal chamber"). They gave other brain structures such names as **amygdala** ("an almond"), **pons** ("a bridge"), **colliculus** ("a little hill"), **hippocampus** ("a seahorse"), **mammillary bodies** ("breasts"), **fornix** ("an arch"), and **cingulum** ("a belt"). (See Figure 2-3.)

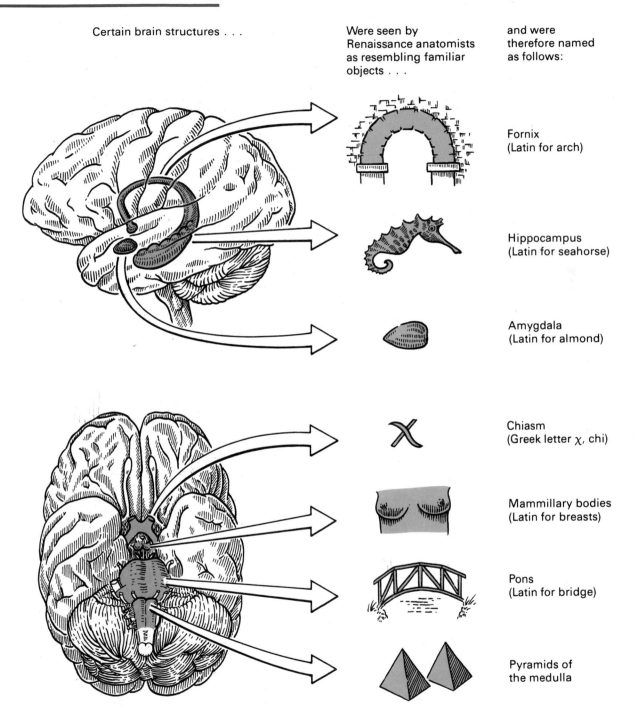

Certain brain structures . . .

Were seen by Renaissance anatomists as resembling familiar objects . . .

and were therefore named as follows:

Fornix
(Latin for arch)

Hippocampus
(Latin for seahorse)

Amygdala
(Latin for almond)

Chiasm
(Greek letter χ, chi)

Mammillary bodies
(Latin for breasts)

Pons
(Latin for bridge)

Pyramids of
the medulla

Figure 2-3 How some brain structures got their names.

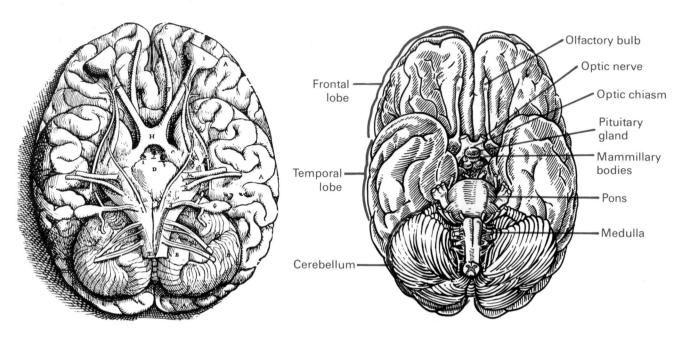

Figure 2-4 The base of the brain. On the left is a drawing by a Renaissance anatomist; on the right, an illustration by a modern artist. The sixteenth-century drawing is rather imprecise and inaccurate compared to the modern illustration.

Deep within the cerebral hemispheres the Renaissance anatomists found darker structures, looking much like the cerebral cortex. They named them the **basal ganglia** (from the Greek "ganglion," "swelling" or "enlargement"). A collection of nerve cell bodies may be called either a **ganglion** or a **nucleus** (from the Latin "nucis," "a nut"). One of the basal ganglia is called the **caudate nucleus** (Latin "caudus," "a tail") because it has a long extension.

From the base of the brain the Renaissance anatomists saw a number of nerves exit (Figure 2-4). One pair went to the inner part of the nose, one pair to the eyes, and others to the tongue and other parts of the head. Still other nerves branched off from both sides of the stalk of the brain. The spinal cord was found to give off pairs of nerves, one on each side between each of the vertebrae.

Although they lacked knowledge of the cellular structure of the nervous system and of the principles of its activity, the Renaissance anatomists patiently traced, described, and named the main nerves and brain structures that were visible to the naked eye. Modern gross anatomy grew from their diligent work.

Nineteenth-century concepts of brain localization

A popular notion of the nineteenth century was that of **phrenology.** This view stated that the shape of a person's skull reflects greater or smaller development of parts of the brain, and each brain region is responsible for a behavioral faculty such as "love of family," "ambition," "intellect," or "curiosity" (Figure 2-5). The assignment of functions to brain regions was rather arbitrary in phrenology, but soon a more

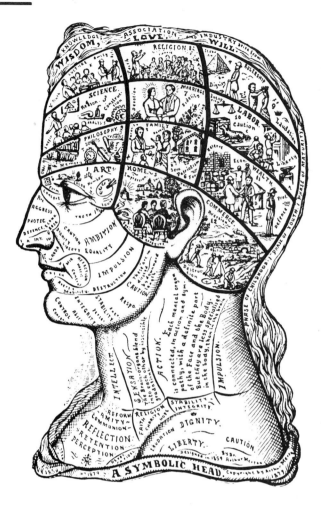

Figure 2-5 A phrenological head, illustrating concepts of brain localization that were popular in the early nineteenth century.

rational system of localization was discovered. The clues came from observations of effects of damage to the brain.

Injuries to the head have long provided evidence about the brain's functions and about location of function. In the 1860s French neurologist Paul Broca examined the brains of two patients who had lost the ability to speak after strokes. On a small amount of evidence Broca located the "speech center" in the frontal lobe of the left hemisphere (see Figure 2-6). Later research confirmed this location for most people. (We will learn more about the cerebral representation of speech in Chapter 16.) In 1870 a war injury exposed the brain of a soldier, and physicians tried stimulating the brain tissue with a weak electrical current; this was found to produce muscular movements on the opposite side of the body. Soon other investigators followed this clue to map the motor regions of the brains of experimental animals with electrical stimulation. Locations were also tested by removing small regions of animal brains and studying the effects on behavior. Not only muscular representation but also sensory abilities could be related to specific positions in the brain. The modern era of functional study of the brain had begun!

Figure 2-6 The location of Broca's speech area in the left hemisphere of the human brain.

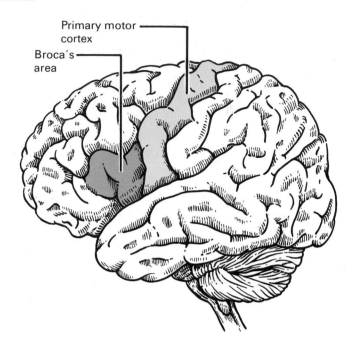

Primary motor cortex

Broca's area

Contemporary large-scale views of the human nervous system

The complex form of the adult human brain makes it hard to understand why anatomists use such terms as forebrain and hindbrain the way they do. For example, the part of your brain closest to the *back* of your head is labeled as part of the forebrain. How can we make sense of this?

The clue to subdividing the brain according to its structure lies in the way the brain develops early in life. In Chapter 3 we will consider brain development as a subject in its own right. But for now we will use brain development simply to help us describe the structures of the brain.

The central nervous system

In a very young embryo of any vertebrate, the central nervous system looks like a tube (Figure 2-7). The walls of this tube are made of nerve cells and the interior is filled with fluid. A few weeks after conception, the human neural tube begins to show three divisions at the head end (Figure 2-7a): the **forebrain** (or **prosencephalon**), the **midbrain** (or **mesencephalon**), and the **hindbrain** (or **rhombencephalon**). (The term encephalon, meaning brain, comes from the Greek roots "en" meaning "in," and "kephalon" meaning "head.")

Six weeks after conception the forebrain and hindbrain have already developed clear subdivisions (Figure 2-7b). At the fore end of the developing brain is the **telencephalon,** which will become the cerebral hemispheres. The other part of the forebrain is the **diencephalon** (or "between brain"), which will include the thalamus and the **hypothalamus.** The mesencephalon ("midbrain") comes next. Behind it the hindbrain has two divisions: the **metencephalon,** which will develop into the cerebellum and the pons, and the **myelencephalon** or **medulla.** Figure 2-7c shows the positions of these main structures and their relative sizes in the human brain; the shading is the same as in part (b). The telencephalon has expanded so greatly that

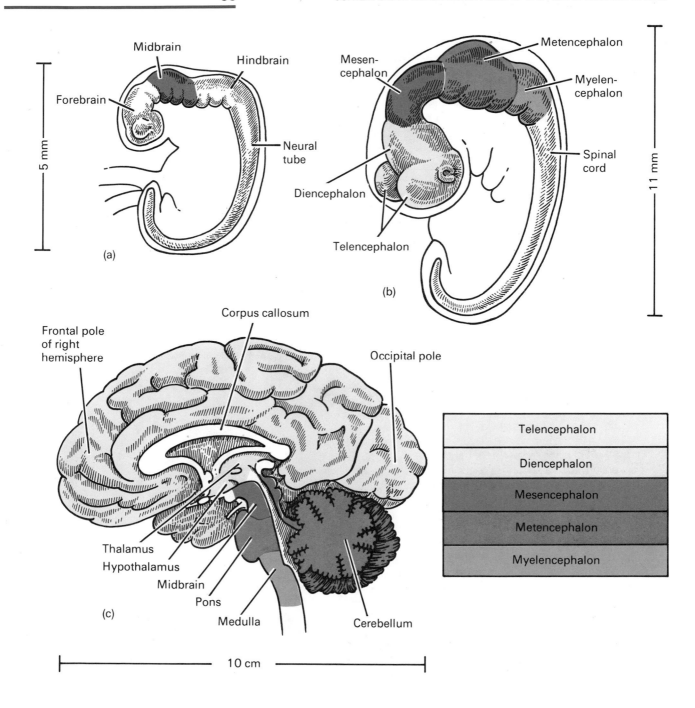

Figure 2-7 The embryological development of the human brain. (a) A few weeks after conception the head end of the neural tube shows three main divisions. (b) Six weeks after conception the five main divisions of the brain are visible. (c) The positions of these divisions are shown in the adult brain.

BOX 2-1   Orientation in the Nervous System

Note: If you don't know the terms used to designate directions in the nervous system, study this box. If you are familiar with such terms as sagittal, coronal, and rostral, as applied to the nervous system, you can skip this box.

Because the nervous system is a three-dimensional structure, two-dimensional illustrations and diagrams cannot represent it completely. Three-dimensional representations of the brain do exist, however, in several forms: (a) models of the brain (some can be taken apart to show main structures), (b) stereoscopic slides of the brain and of brain dissections, and (c) simplified models that show sections of the three main planes of the brain. If you have access to any of these, you'll find them an excellent study aid.

There are three main planes in which the brain is usually cut in order to get a two-dimensional section from the three-directional object. The brain sections that appear at many places throughout this book are for the most part made in one of these planes. Thus you will find it useful to know the terminology and conventions that apply to them. See Box Figures 2-1 and 2-2.

The plane that bisects the body into right and left halves is called the **sagittal plane** (from the Latin for "arrow"). The plane that divides the body into a front (anterior) and back (posterior) part is called by several names: **coronal** (from the Latin for "crown") or frontal or transverse. By convention, such a section is usually viewed from behind, so that the right side of the figure represents the right side of the brain. The third main plane is the one that divides the brain into upper and lower parts. This is called the **horizontal plane** and is usually viewed from above.

The same main planes are used to describe the whole body. In addition, several directional terms are used, as also shown in Box Figure 2-1. **Medial** means "toward the middle" and is contrasted with **lateral,** "toward the side." The head end is referred to by any of several terms: anterior, **cephalic** (from the Greek for "head"), or **rostral** (from the Latin for "prow of a ship"). The tail end is called posterior or **caudal** (from the Latin for "tail"). **Proximal** (from the Latin for "nearest") means near the trunk or center, and **distal** means "toward the periphery" or "toward the end of a limb" (distant from the origin or point of attachment).

One pair of terms must be used carefully because their meanings are somewhat different depending on whether

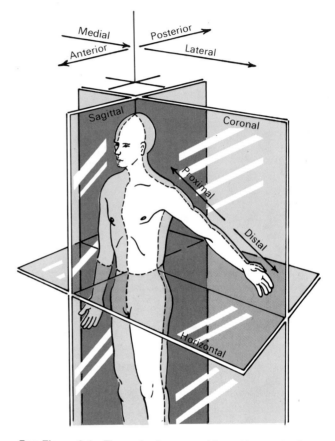

Box Figure 2-1   The main planes used in making anatomical sections, shown here in relation to the human body.

you're discussing four-legged or two-legged animals. These are **dorsal,** meaning "toward or at the back," and **ventral,** meaning "toward or at the belly or front." In four-legged animals, such as the cat or the rat, dorsal refers to both the back of the body and the top of the head. For consistency in comparing brains among species, dorsal is also used to refer to the top of the brain of a human or of a chimpanzee, even though in primates the top of the brain is not at the back of the body. Similarly ventral is used to designate the bottom of the brain of a primate as well as that of a quadruped.

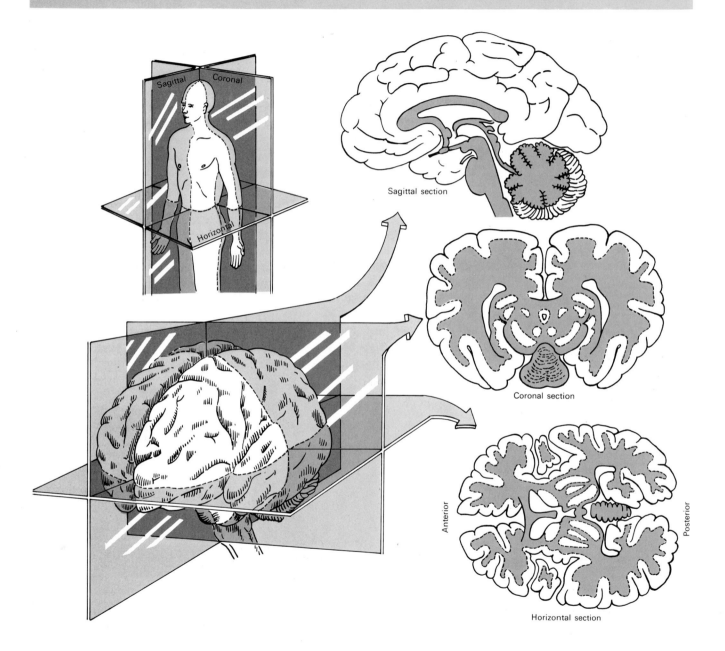

Box Figure 2-2 The main planes used in making anatomical sections of the brain.

in a side view it would hide most of the other parts. That is why we present a medial view in part (c). Even when the brain achieves its adult form, it still remains a fluid-filled tube but one of very complicated shape. All the cerebral cortex, from front to back, is part of the telencephalon, a division of the forebrain.

Using the top-down approach, let us go over major subdivisions of the brain. Looking at Figure 2-8, we will work our way from the largest, most general divisions at the left of the figure to more specific ones at the right. The variety of terms may be confusing at the beginning. But all these structures will appear again and again in later chapters, and you will have the chance to grow familiar with them.

The nervous system is made up of central and peripheral parts. The **central nervous system (CNS)** consists of the brain and the spinal cord. The **peripheral nervous system** includes both the nerves that run to and from the skeletal muscles and the skin and also the **autonomic nervous system**, which supplies connections to glands and to the smooth muscles of internal organs.

Each of the five main sections of the brain can be subdivided in turn. This is shown in Figure 2-8. When cross sections of the cerebral hemispheres are made, the outer bark or **cerebral cortex** is seen to be pinkish gray in color. This layer, about 3 or 4 millimeters thick in an adult human brain, consists largely of nerve cell bodies and their branches. Underneath the cortex is the shiny **white matter,** consisting largely of neural fibers **(axons)** with white fatty coatings. Most of the cortex is called the **neocortex** ("new cortex") because it is relatively recent in an evolutionary sense. A region of old cortex, the **hippocampus,** is found curled into the basal medial part of the temporal lobe. The basal ganglia, like the cortex, are darker in color than the associated fiber tracts because they include many cell bodies and relatively little of the white fatty insulating material that characterizes the white matter.

Figure 2-8 The major subdivisions of the central nervous system.

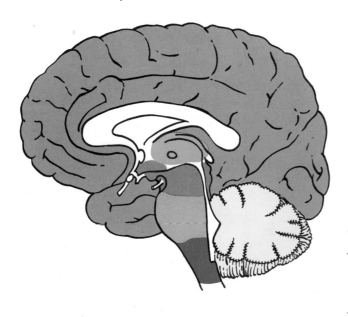

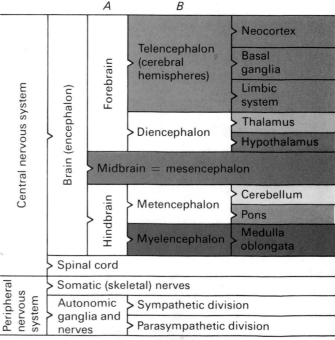

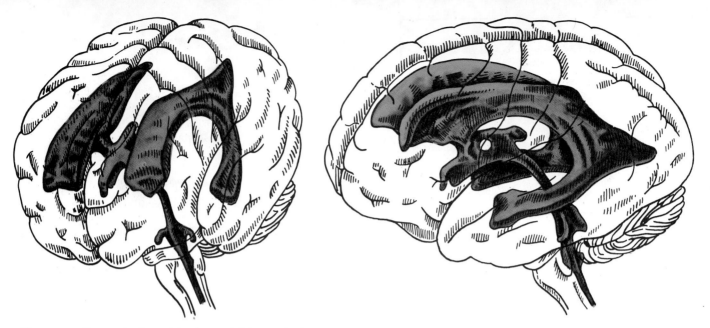

Figure 2-9 The cerebral ventricles in an adult human brain.

At the back of the human brain is a large structure, the **cerebellum,** made up of many folds of tissue. The outer surface of each fold, the **cerebellar cortex,** is made up of cell bodies. Below it is white matter, made up of fibers that run to nuclei in the base of the cerebellum.

The ventricular system of the brain

Inside the brain are cavities filled with a clear, colorless fluid (Figure 2-9). This fluid (formerly known as "animal spirits") is now called **cerebrospinal fluid.** It has two main functions:

1. The fluid that fills the space between the brain and the inside of the skull acts mechanically as a shock absorber for the brain. The brain floats in cerebrospinal fluid as the head moves.
2. Cerebrospinal fluid also mediates between blood vessels and brain tissue in exchange of materials.

Each hemisphere of the brain contains a complexly shaped lateral ventricle. The third ventricle lies on the midline, surrounded by the two halves of the thalamus. The cerebrospinal fluid is formed in the lateral ventricles. It flows through the third ventricle and down a narrow passage to the fourth ventricle, which lies anterior to the cerebellum. A little below the cerebellum is a small aperture, through which cerebrospinal fluid leaves the ventricular system to circulate over the outer surface of the brain and spinal cord.

Circulation of blood in the brain

Because the brain works intensely, it has a strong metabolic demand for its fuels, oxygen and glucose. Since the brain has very little reserve of either, it therefore depends critically on its blood supply to bring these fuels. Blood is delivered to the brain via two main channels, the carotid and the vertebral arteries (Figure 2-10).

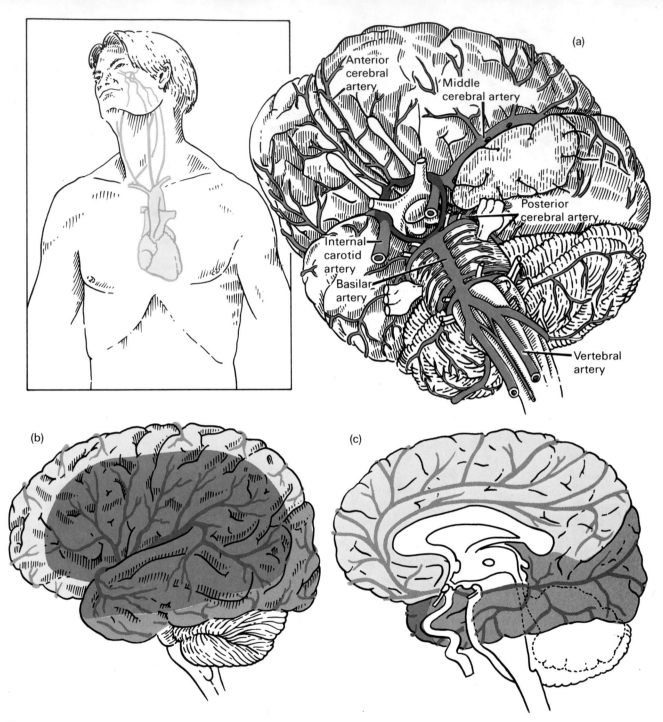

Figure 2-10 The blood supply of the human brain. The orientation of the brain in (a) is shown by the figure at the upper left. Part (a) shows the principal arteries. The basilar and internal carotid arteries form a circle at the base of the brain known as the Circle of Willis (shown in dark blue). Different regions of the cerebral cortex are supplied by the anterior, middle, and posterior cerebral arteries. This is shown in (b) for the lateral surface of the brain and in (c) for the medial surface. The field of the branches of the anterior artery is shown in light blue; the field of the branches of the middle cerebral artery is shown in dark blue, and the field of branches of the posterior cerebral arteries is shown in an intermediate shade of blue.

The **common carotid arteries** ascend the left and right sides of the neck. The **internal carotid artery** enters the skull and branches into anterior and middle cerebral arteries (Figure 2-10), which supply blood to large regions of the cerebral hemispheres. The **vertebral arteries** ascend along the bony vertebrae and enter the base of the skull. They join together to form the **basilar artery,** which runs along the ventral surface of the brainstem. Branches of the basilar artery supply blood to the brainstem and to posterior portions of the cerebral hemispheres. At the base of the brain the carotid and basilar arteries join to form a structure called the **circle of Willis.** This joining of vascular paths may provide some needed "backup" if any of the main arteries to the brain should be damaged or blocked by disease.

The actual delivery of nutrients and other substances to brain cells and the removal of waste products take place at very fine capillaries that branch off from small arteries (see Figure 2-11). This exchange in the brain is quite different from exchanges between blood vessels and cells in other body organs. We speak of the **blood-brain barrier** because many substances move from the capillaries into the brain cells with greater difficulty than they move from capillaries into the cells of other organs. The brain is thus protected from exposure to some substances found in the blood. This barrier to passage occurs because the cells that make up the walls

Figure 2-11 Exchange between capillaries and brain cells. The special structure of the walls of brain capillaries accounts for the blood-brain barrier.

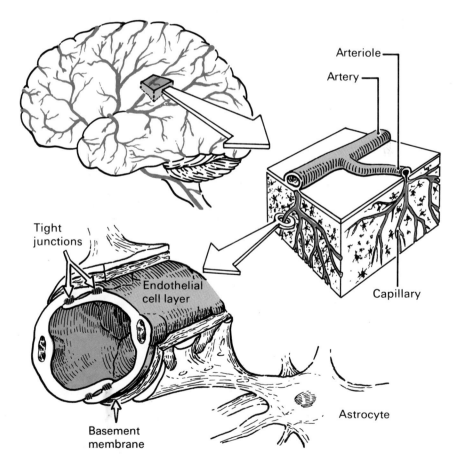

BOX 2-2   Measuring How Cortical Blood Flow Changes with Mental Activity

The great neurophysiologist Charles Sherrington once imagined a fanciful way of visualizing the complex electrical activity of the brain: If the body were transparent and each nerve impulse were a moving point of light, we would see shifting, shimmering patterns of illumination as one brain region after another became active. Some of the current techniques of measuring the ongoing activity of the brain are approaching Sherrington's dream. One of these is the measurement of local variations in blood flow in the human cerebral cortex—from outside the head! The result is a map of the surface of the brain, with activity

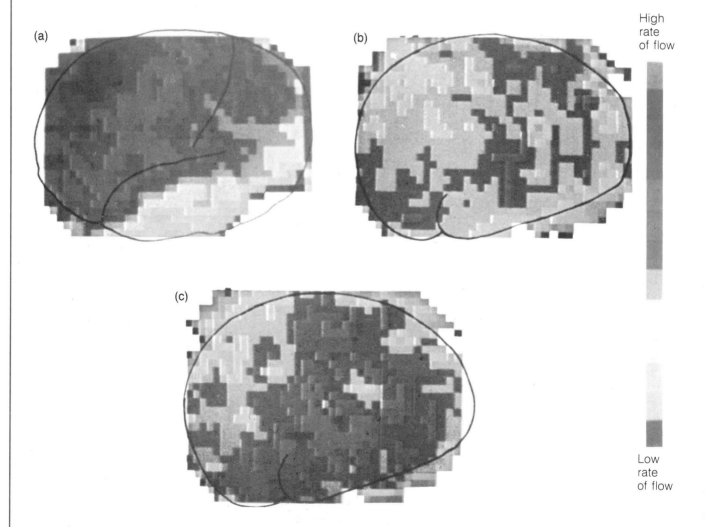

High
rate
of flow

Low
rate
of flow

Box Figure 2-3   Cortical blood flow and mental activity. (a) Average of awake normal subjects. (b) Awake severely demented person. (c) The same demented person while speaking. Although motor and sensory areas now show increased activity, the frontal cortex still shows abnormally low blood flow. In the original displays, levels of activity were coded in color, giving a vivid appearance. (Adapted from Ingvar and Lassen, 1979)

represented either in shades of gray or by a color scale, as in Box Figure 2-3. This technique makes it possible to observe localized changes of cortical blood flow that take place not only as a result of brief sensory stimulation or motor activation but also as a result of thinking, such as when a person does mental arithmetic or thinks of performing a given movement.

The technique, elaborated by David Ingvar and his colleagues in Sweden, works this way: Many counters of radioactivity are aligned along the subject's scalp. Just before the start of the test, a small amount of radioactive xenon gas is inhaled (Prohovnik and Risberg, 1982) or injected into the bloodstream. This gas does not react chemically in the body, and the level of radioactivity is very low. The rate at which the radioactivity declines at a given counter is proportional to the rate of blood flow through the underlying cortex. During the several minutes that it takes to complete a test, the subject may be asked to speak or inspect a visual display or open and close the right hand repeatedly. The pattern of blood flow clearly reflects the regions of the brain activated by the particular behavior.

Increased activity of brain cells calls for greater local blood flow. This is caused both by the release of substances that cause nearby blood vessels to dilate and by neural innervation of blood vessels.

This technique has some clinical applications in assessing brain disorders that may involve changes in blood flow, such as senile dementia and some metabolic disorders. Drugs that might be helpful in treating these disorders can be evaluated with this procedure. Records of patients, as well as of normal subjects, can also help to show how different regions of the brain cooperate in mediating many kinds of complex behavior.

of capillaries in the brain (**endothelial cells**) fit together very tightly, so they do not readily let large molecules through. In the hypothalamus, however, the blood-brain barrier is relatively weak. This feature may be what enables the hypothalamus to sense and react to circulating substances.

Peripheral nervous system

The central nervous system is linked to sensory organs, muscles, and glands via the pathways that compose the **peripheral nervous system.** There are three main sets of pathways in this system: **cranial nerves** (connected directly to the brain), **spinal nerves** (connected at regular intervals to the spinal cord), and **autonomic ganglia** (including the two chains of sympathetic ganglia and the more peripheral parasympathetic ganglia). Let us look in more detail at each of these three.

● Cranial nerves   The 12 pairs of cranial nerves in the human brain are mainly concerned with sensory and motor systems associated with the head (Figure 2-12). Some cranial nerves are exclusively sensory pathways to the brain, for example, the olfactory, optic, and auditory nerves. Others are exclusively motor pathways from the brain, for example, oculomotor nerves (to eye muscles) and facial nerves (to face muscles). The remaining cranial nerves have mixed sensory and motor functions. The trigeminal, for example, serves facial sensation and controls chewing movements. All these nerves pass through small openings in the skull to enter or leave the brain. The vagus nerve is one cranial nerve that extends far from the head. It runs to the heart and intestines. Its long and involved route is the reason for its name, which in Latin means "wandering."

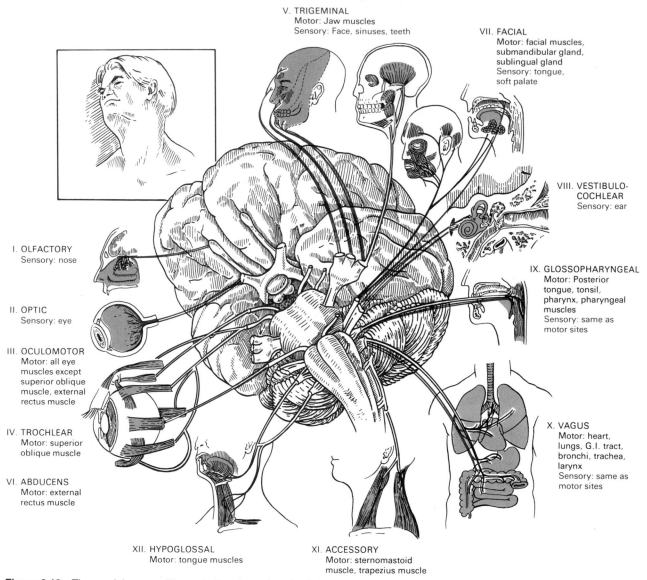

V. TRIGEMINAL
Motor: Jaw muscles
Sensory: Face, sinuses, teeth

VII. FACIAL
Motor: facial muscles,
submandibular gland,
sublingual gland
Sensory: tongue,
soft palate

**VIII. VESTIBULO-
COCHLEAR**
Sensory: ear

I. OLFACTORY
Sensory: nose

IX. GLOSSOPHARYNGEAL
Motor: Posterior
tongue, tonsil,
pharynx, pharyngeal
muscles
Sensory: same as
motor sites

II. OPTIC
Sensory: eye

III. OCULOMOTOR
Motor: all eye
muscles except
superior oblique
muscle, external
rectus muscle

X. VAGUS
Motor: heart,
lungs, G.I. tract,
bronchi, trachea,
larynx
Sensory: same as
motor sites

IV. TROCHLEAR
Motor: superior
oblique muscle

VI. ABDUCENS
Motor: external
rectus muscle

XII. HYPOGLOSSAL
Motor: tongue muscles

XI. ACCESSORY
Motor: sternomastoid
muscle, trapezius muscle

Figure 2-12 The cranial nerves. The main functions of each of the 12 pairs of cranial nerves are shown.

● Spinal nerves   Along the length of the spinal cord there are 31 pairs of spinal nerves, with one member of each pair for each side of the body (Figure 2-13). These nerves join the spinal cord at regularly spaced intervals through openings in the bony structures of the spinal column. Each spinal nerve consists of the fusion of two distinct branches called **roots.** These are functionally different. The **dorsal** ("back") **root** of each spinal nerve consists of sensory pathways to the spinal cord. The **ventral** ("front") **root** consists of motor pathways from the spinal cord to the muscles.

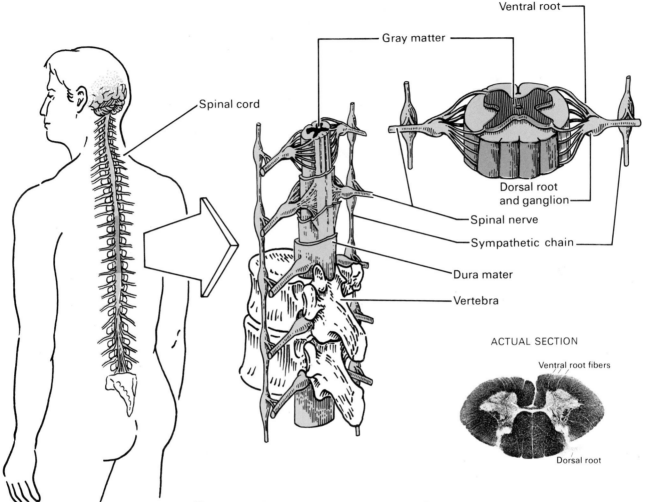

Figure 2-13 The spinal cord and spinal nerves. The diagram to the left shows a general view of the spinal column with a pair of nerves emerging from each level. The diagram in the center shows how the spinal cord is surrounded by bony vertebrae and enclosed in a membrane, the dura mater. Each vertebra has an opening on each side through which the spinal nerves pass. The diagram at the upper right shows the location of spinal cord grey matter and the white matter that surrounds it. In the grey matter are interneurons and the motoneurons that send axons to the muscles. The white matter consists of axons that run up and down the spinal column. The photograph at the lower right shows an actual cross section of the cord, magnified 6 times; it comes from the cervical (neck) region. The stain used on this section turns the fatty sheaths of the axons dark, as the white matter looks dark in this presentation. (Photograph from *Structure of the Human Brain: A Photographic Atlas, Second Edition,* by Stephen DeArmond, Madeleine Fusco, and Maynard Dewey. Copyright © 1976 by Oxford University Press, Inc. Reprinted by permission.)

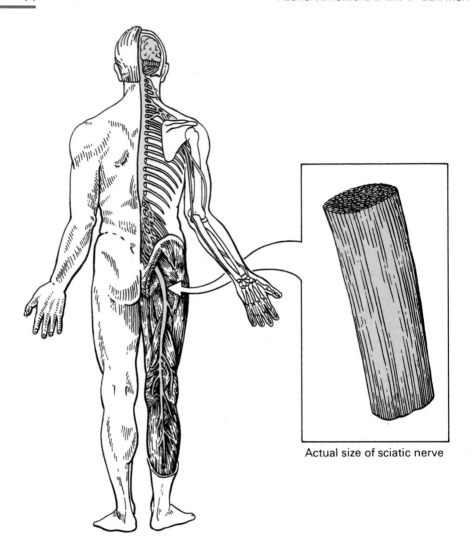

Actual size of sciatic nerve

Figure 2-14 The sciatic nerve contains nerve fibers from all the lumbar spinal nerve roots.

The name of a spinal nerve is the same as the segment of spinal cord to which it is connected: **cervical** ("neck"), **thoracic** ("trunk"), **lumbar** ("small of the back"), or **sacral** ("bottom of the spinal column"). Thus the "T12" spinal nerve is the spinal nerve that is connected to the twelfth segment of the thoracic portion of the spinal cord. Fibers from different spinal nerves join to form peripheral nerve segments, usually at some distance from the spinal cord. For example, the big sciatic nerve that runs down the leg contains fibers from all the lumbar spinal roots (Figure 2-14).

● Autonomic ganglia   The **sympathetic chains** form part of the **autonomic nervous system** (Figure 2-15). This system controls smooth muscles in organs and in the walls of blood vessels. Therefore one of its vital functions is shifting blood from one part of the body to another to adjust for different activities.

Besides the sympathetic chains, the other main part of the autonomic system is the **parasympathetic division.** This gets its name ("para," "around") because its outflow from the spinal cord occurs both above and below the sympathetic connections. As Figure 2-15 shows, the parasympathetic division arises from both the cranial and the sacral parts of the spinal cord. For many bodily functions the sympathetic and parasympathetic divisions act in opposite directions, and the result is very accurate control. For example, the rate of heartbeat is quickened by the activity of sympathetic nerves during exercise. The heartbeat is slowed by the vagus nerve (part of the parasympathetic system) during rest. In the case of the pupil of

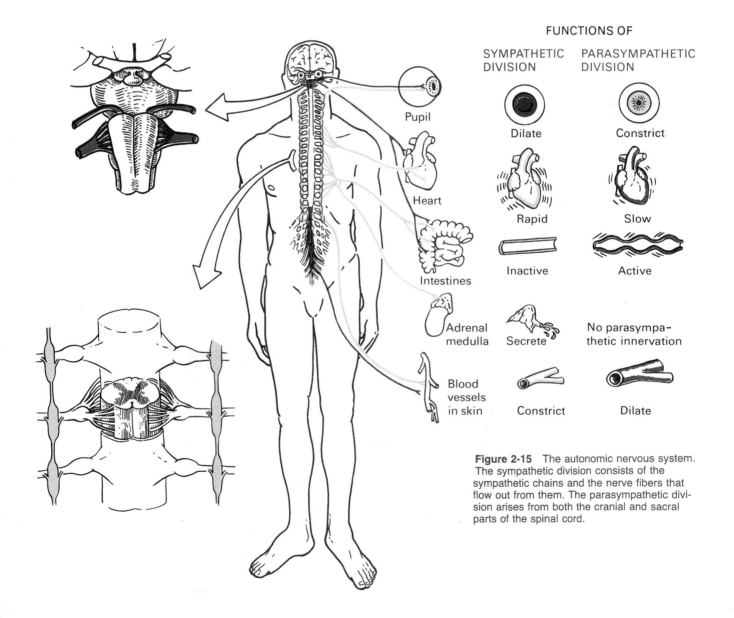

FUNCTIONS OF

SYMPATHETIC DIVISION	PARASYMPATHETIC DIVISION
Pupil	
Dilate	Constrict
Heart	
Rapid	Slow
Intestines	
Inactive	Active
Adrenal medulla	
Secrete	No parasympathetic innervation
Blood vessels in skin	
Constrict	Dilate

Figure 2-15 The autonomic nervous system. The sympathetic division consists of the sympathetic chains and the nerve fibers that flow out from them. The parasympathetic division arises from both the cranial and sacral parts of the spinal cord.

the eye, sympathetic nerves cause the muscles of the iris to contract in dim light so that the pupil enlarges, whereas in bright sunlight parasympathetic nerves relax the muscles and narrow the pupil.

Most of the time both divisions of the autonomic system are active, with a carefully modulated balance between the two. We can generalize by saying that the sympathetic division predominates during muscular activity and aids the expenditure of energy. On the other hand, the parasympathetic division predominates during building up of bodily resources and helps the body to conserve energy. The autonomic nervous system got its name during the last century, when people supposed that it acted rather independently of the rest of the nervous system. Now the autonomic system is known to be under the control of brain centers. Its activities have been found to be carefully monitored and closely integrated with ongoing bodily events.

Looking into the living human brain

The accurate assessment of possible brain disorders in humans often requires detailed views of the living brain. To be useful, these views should provide precise localization of diseased tissue, such as a tumor. Furthermore, under the best conditions one should be able to obtain pictures of brain structures without causing distress or potential harm to the patient. But is it possible to see the brain of intact humans without opening the skull? Intense research during the 1970s has led to remarkable developments in the ability to do just that. A review of some of the procedures used in clinical neurological settings will give us a glimpse of the progress in this area.

Figure 2-16 The living human brain visualized by different techniques. (a) Angiogram, lateral view, anterior to left. Dye was injected into the carotid artery. The numbers refer to branches of the arteries. (From *Structure of the Human Brain: A Photographic Atlas, Second Edition,* by Stephen DeArmond, Madeleine Fusco, and Maynard Dewey. Copyright © 1976 by Oxford University Press, Inc. Reprinted by permission.)

(a)

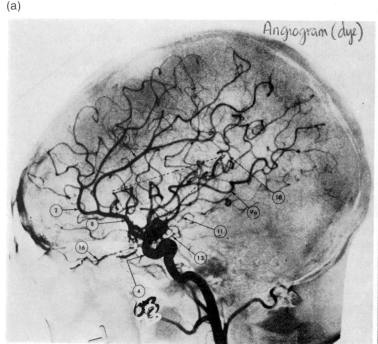

(b)

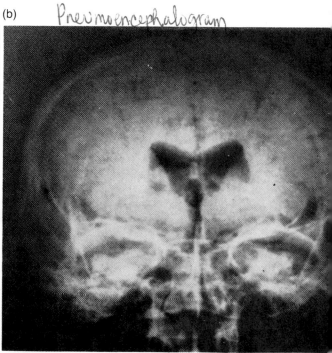

An ordinary X ray of the head, a technique that has been used since early in the twentieth century, reveals an outline of the skull with little or no definition of brain tissue. Since the X-ray density of virtually all parts of the brain is the same, there is very little contrast between regions of the brain. To provide contrast between brain tissue and blood vessels, investigators inject substances into blood vessels. The resultant X-ray pictures are called **angiograms.** To visualize the ventricles, they inject gases into the ventricles of the brain, giving pictures that are called **pneumoencephalograms.** A recent development makes use of computerized enhancement of contrast among brain tissues. We will discuss each of these techniques briefly.

Angiograms are X rays taken after special dyes are injected into blood vessels in the head (Figure 2-16a). Such pictures provide possible evidence of vascular disease. They also form the basis for inferences about adjacent tissue. It is possible to make these inferences because the outline of the principal blood vessels is rather constant from one human being to another. Therefore deformations in the shape of blood vessels provide a basis for concluding that adjacent neural tissue is abnormal. For example, an expanding brain tumor may be revealed by an angiogram.

Pneumoencephalograms are X rays made after air or other gases are injected into the ventricular system (Figure 2-16b). This produces a striking outline of the ventricles. However, this procedure is quite hazardous and is declining in use because of developments in brain scan techniques. But in its day it could be used to show changes in the shape or size of the ventricles. Such changes may have resulted from a malfunction in the circulation of cerebrospinal fluid (for example, enlarged ventricles) and changes in surrounding brain tissue.

Figure 2-16 (continued) (b) Pneumoencephalogram, frontal view. (From Netter, 1957) (c) Computerized axial tomogram, horizontal section. (Courtesy of Dr. Robert Friedland) (d) and (e) Positron emission tomographs, horizontal section. While (d) was being made, the subject listened to speech, and the auditory cortex of the left hemisphere was especially active. In (e), the subject listened to music, and the auditory cortex of the right hemisphere was especially active. Compare these with the figure on the cover of the book when the same person listened to both speech and music. [(d) and (e) Courtesy of M. E. Phelps and J. Mazziotta, Division of Biophysics, UCLA School of Medicine]

(c)

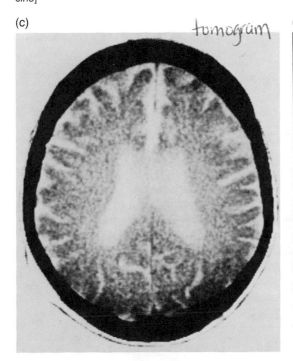

(d)

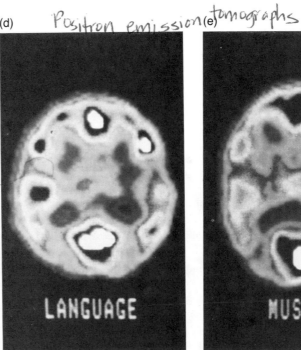

(e)

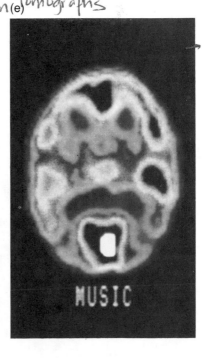

Thanks to recent developments in computers we can now generate portraits of the brain that resemble cross sections (Figure 2-16c). This technique achieves a virtually direct view of the brain rather than the inferential view afforded by angiograms or pneumoencephalograms. Making a **tomogram** (from "tomus," "a crosscut or section," and "gram," "a record or picture") involves moving the X-ray source in an arc around the head. A record of X-ray absorption at all positions around the head is analyzed by a computer program that constructs an image with optimal contrast. Side-by-side comparison of a tomogram with an actual brain section demonstrates remarkable similarity and shows why tomography has become so important in neurological diagnosis. The one deficiency of X-ray tomography is that it furnishes a static portrait of brain anatomy. It cannot distinguish between a live brain and a dead one.

A powerful new development is **positron emission tomography** (Figure 2-16d and 2-16e). This technique reflects regional differences in ongoing metabolism in the brain. It requires the injection into the bloodstream of radioactive forms of substances used by the brain, such as a radioactive form of glucose. It is possible to analyze from outside the skull exactly where in the brain the metabolism of these substances is occurring. The result is a dynamic picture of the functioning brain. The investigators use color coding to bring out the gradients of brain activity, as shown on the cover of this book.

Microscopic views of the human nervous system

In this chapter, and in many other places in this book, we will be considering structures that vary greatly in size—from the intact human brain [which measures about 15 centimeters (cm) from front to back] to the walls or membranes of neurons [which are about 7 nanometers (nm) thick, that is, seven-billionths of a meter]. If we compare these two measures—the size of the brain [15 cm, or 15×10^{-2} meter (m)] and the thickness of a cell wall (7 nm, or 7×10^{-9} m)—the first is 20 million

TABLE 2-1 Sizes of Brain Structures, Levels of Magnification, and Units of Measure

MAGNIFICATION	STRUCTURES SEEN AT THIS MAGNIFICATION	SIZES OF STRUCTURES	UNITS OF MEASUREMENT
× 1 (life size)	Whole brain	Adult human brain measures about 15 cm from front to back	1 centimeter (cm) = 10^{-2} meter (m)*
× 10	Cerebral cortex; large tracts of fibers	Cortex of human brain is about 3 mm thick	1 millimeter (mm) = 10^{-3} m
× 100 (10^2)	Layers of cortical cells	Large neuron cell bodies are about 100 μ in diameter (0.1 mm)	0.1 mm = 10^{-4} m = 100 micrometers (or microns) (μ)
× 1000 (10^3)	Parts of individual neurons	Large axons and dendrites are about 10 μ in diameter (0.01 mm)	0.01 mm = 10^{-5} m = 10 μ
× 10,000 (10^4)	Synapse (end bouton and dendritic spine)	An end bouton is about 1 μ in diameter	1 micrometer (micron) (μ) = 10^{-6} m
× 100,000 (10^5)	Detailed structure of synapse	The gap or cleft between neurons at a synapse is about 20 nm across	0.1 μ = 100 nanometers (nm) = 10^{-7} m

*The meter, the unit of length in the metric system, equals 39.37 inches. A centimeter is one-hundredth of a meter (10^{-2} m); a millimeter is one-thousandth of a meter (10^{-3} m); a micron (micrometer) is one-millionth of a meter (10^{-6} m); and a nanometer is one-billionth of a meter (10^{-9} m).

times as large as the second. Table 2-1 lists aspects of the brain that can be studied at different degrees of magnification. It also lists some of the main organizational levels of the brain, from large to small. (See also Box 2-3, "Techniques of Visualizing the Fine Structure of the Brain.")

Hierarchy of brain structures

The organization of the brain can be thought of as hierarchical. It is made up of interrelated subsystems, and each subsystem is in turn composed of smaller subsystems down to some lowest level. Figure 2-17 illustrates the main successive levels of organization. These go from the whole brain down to the tiny connections between nerve cells called **synapses** (from the Greek for "clasp together").

The brain is composed of several large functional systems. The visual system, for instance, brings visual information from the eyes up through various relay stations to the cerebral cortex. The brain can also be divided into large regions, such as the cerebral cortex, the basal ganglia, and the cerebellum. A region like the cerebral cortex can in turn be divided into functional subregions, for example, the primary motor cortex, the primary auditory cortex, and the primary visual cortex. Such subregions can be shown to be different from each other not only in function but also in the architecture of the layers and cells of the cortex. There are still some disagreements over the exact boundaries of some subregions and the number of such regions, but it seems safe to say that the human cerebral cortex contains 50–100 such specialized areas (Hubel and Wiesel, 1979).

Some regions have distinctive geometrical arrangements of cells that can function as information-processing units. In the cortex one can see columns of nerve cells, which run the entire thickness of the cortex from the white matter to the surface (Figure 2-18). In humans they are about 3 mm deep and about 400–1000 microns (μ) in diameter. Within such a column the functional connections among cells (synaptic connections) are mainly in the vertical direction, but there are also some horizontal connections. Mountcastle (1979) calls these units "macrocolumns" and estimates their number in the human cerebral cortex to be about one million. Macrocolumns are thought to be the functional modules of cortical operations.

The macrocolumns are composed, in turn, of what Mountcastle has called "minicolumns." These are vertical columns of neurons. On the average, such columns are about 30 μ in diameter in the human cortex, and there are an estimated half billion of them. The number of cells per minicolumn has been counted in five species, from mouse to human, and in several cortical regions (Rockel et al., 1974). Regardless of species and of cortical region, a minicolumn contains about 110 neurons (with a standard deviation of about 10%).

An even smaller unit is the **local circuit.** These are a small number of cells with intimate functional contacts that make up the smallest circuit typical of a particular region.

Researchers often use the concept of a **circuit** of neurons to mean an arrangement of neurons and their interconnections. Often it is implied that such an assemblage performs a particular limited function, so one speaks of a neural circuit that enhances visual contrast, or a circuit for rhythmic locomotor behavior, or a circuit for the copulatory response. This usage of the term circuit is an analogy to electrical or electronic circuits, in which an arrangement of components (such as resistors, capacitors, transistors, and connecting wires) accomplishes some function such as

Figure 2-17 The main levels of organization of the brain, ranging from the whole brain at the upper left to synaptic contacts at the lower right.

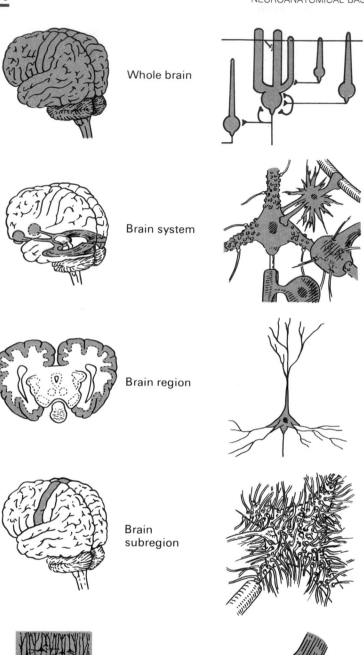

Whole brain

Local circuit

Brain system

Basic neuroglial compartment

Brain region

Nerve cell

Brain subregion

Synaptic assembly

Basic processing unit

Synapse

BOX 2-3 Techniques of Visualizing the Fine Structure of the Brain

If you cut a thin slice of brain tissue and look at it under a microscope, it is hard to see any brain cells. They are barely visible because contrast with surrounding areas like extracelluar space is quite poor. In order to see the details of cells using the light microscope, you have to use chemical agents to make cells or parts of cells stand out. In the middle of the nineteenth century dyes used to color fabrics provided the breakthrough. Dead, preserved nerve cells treated with these stains suddenly become vivid, and hidden parts become evident. Dyes produce this effect because different dyes have special affinities for parts of the cell, such as membranes, the nucleus, or the myelin sheath. Optical filters attached to the microscope can increase the clarity.

Some staining methods outline the full cell, including details like dendritic spines. The Golgi method, which is the most common (Box Figure 2-4a), is often used to characterize the variety of cell types in any region. For reasons that remain a mystery, this technique stains only a small number of cells. As a result, they stand out in dramatic contrast to adjacent unstained cells.

Dyes can also be injected directly into living cells. Another method uses stains to outline the cell body. This Nissl method can be used in such measurements as size of cell body and density of cells in particular regions (Box Figure 2-4b). Stains of myelin sheaths outline axons. Recent innovations also include techniques that cause certain nerve cells to light up when exposed to ultraviolet light (Box Figure 2-4c). This happens because nerve cells have particular ingredients that become fluorescent when treated in certain ways. Some antibodies, when attached to membranes of nerve cells, provide a fluorescent surface. Such techniques from immunology are increasingly being applied to studies of the brain's structure.

Some histological techniques can reveal aspects of the dynamic neurochemistry of nerve cells, particularly the cell's metabolic processes. One of these procedures, **au-**

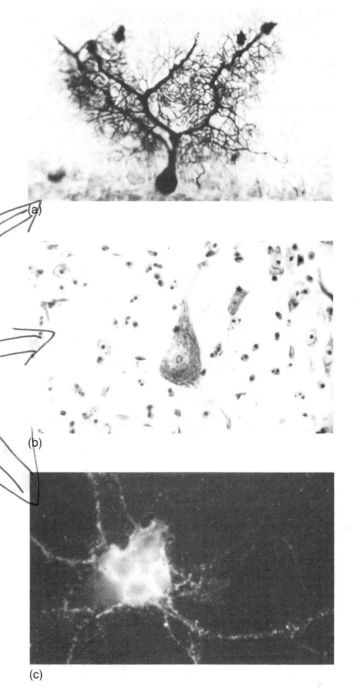

(a)

(b)

(c)

Box Figure 2-4 Various methods of visualizing nerve cells. (a) Golgi stain of Purkinje cell (Leiman). (b) Nissl stain of hippocampal neurons (Leiman). (c) Fluorescence picture of sympathetic neurons. [From Marchisio et al., *Journal of Neurocytology*, vol. 10, no. 1: 49 (Figure 3). Reprinted by permission of Chapman & Hall.] (d) Scanning electron micrograph of neuromuscular junction. [From Desaki and Uehara, *Journal of Neurocytology,* vol. 10, no. 1: 103 (Figure 7.)]

BOX 2-3 (continued)

toradiography, involves administering a radioactive substance that nerve cells use, such as glucose or amino acids. Experimenters give such a substance to a living animal, then present the animal with a stimulus condition that results in neural activity. This activity produces a need for the radioactive nutrient, which the animal's active brain cells take up. The experimenters then sacrifice the animal, cut thin sections of brain tissue, and place them on slides, which they then cover with photographic emulsion. Radioactivity emitted by the compounds in the cell causes deposition of silver, just like the effect of light on film. This produces fine dark grains in cell bodies that have taken up the radioactive substance.

Improved methods of viewing tissue have also broadened our understanding of the fine structure of cells. For years light microscopy was all that was available. Observations with light microscopes provide good detailed resolution down to about 2 μ. The advent of electron microscopy, however, extended the range of resolvable structures a hundredfold. It became possible to see some of the smallest details within cells. Scanning electron microscopy adds a dimension of depth. The synaptic endings and other structures take on a startlingly intimate appearance (Box Figure 2-4d).

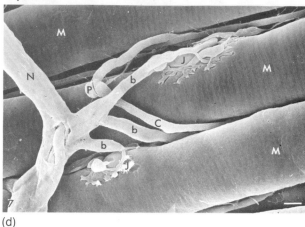

autoradiography

(d)

All these forms of microscopic study are now being coupled with computers, providing rapid, automatic, quantitative assessment of aspects of nerve cells, such as dendrite length. In the years ahead these techniques will increasingly supplement the heretofore intuitive judgments of anatomists.

amplification or oscillation or filtering. None of the components by itself could perform the function of the circuit.

A great deal of current research is devoted to trying to determine neural circuits for well-defined units of behavior. This activity may take either of two forms: (a) tracing neural connections by anatomical or electrophysiological techniques or (b) making inferences about possible neural circuits from results of varied behavioral tests. In later chapters we will see attempts to discover neural circuits that may be responsible for aspects of perception, control of movement, regulation of motivated behaviors, learning and memory, and cognitive behaviors.

Although usage is not precise, usually a **system** is considered to be a larger and higher level of organization than a circuit. Thus the visual system is composed of many specialized circuits that account for part functions of the visual system.

Subdividing still further, we come to a single nerve cell with all its synaptic endings, associated glial cells, surrounding extracellular space, and vascular elements. This is called a **basic neuroglial compartment.** At a simpler level we come to individual cells—nerve cells or **glial cells.** Current estimates hold that there are about 50 billion neurons in the cerebral cortex of the average person (Powell, 1978). This is a staggering number—it is more than ten times as great as all the people on earth. An even less imaginable number is the total number of synaptic connections: The number of synapses for each individual cell range from several hundred to many thousands. In fact, some cells in the human cerebellum may have as many as a hundred thousand connections. There must be over 50 trillion synapses in the cortex of the average person!

The term **synaptic assembly** refers to the total collection of all the synapses on a single nerve cell. The lowest level of organization that we will consider in this chapter is the single synapse, that is, the basic functional connection between two nerve cells. Now that we have briefly surveyed the scale of brain anatomy, let us follow the "bottom-up" approach and consider some of the smaller anatomical features of the brain that have relevance for behavior.

Nerve cells and their connections

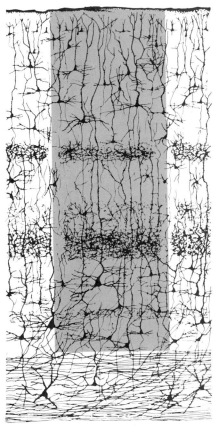

Figure 2-18 Columns of nerve cells in the cerebral cortex. One column is shaded in color, and one half column is shown on each side. (From Rakic, 1979. Reprinted by permission of MIT Press from *The Neurosciences: Fourth Study Program,* edited by Francis O. Schmitt and Frederic G. Worden, copyright © 1979 by The Massachusetts Institute of Technology.)

In the late nineteenth century anatomists sought to understand the bases of differences among brains by making microscopic studies of the finer elements. Their studies showed that brains were composed of a large assembly of oddly shaped cells. Seeing this variety, some anatomists thought that these cells were continuous with one another, a kind of nearly endless series of interconnected tubes. In this view information in the nervous system was carried through continuous channels. However, a brilliant Spanish anatomist, Ramon y Cajal, offered a forceful rejoinder. His elegant anatomical observations, begun at the end of the nineteenth century, are cited to this day. From his studies, Cajal offered a perspective that is called the **neuron doctrine.** This says that the brain is composed of separate cells that are distinct units; that is, the cells are separate structurally, metabolically, and functionally. These nerve cells (also called **neurons**) are the basic units of the nervous system. According to this doctrine information is transmitted from cell to cell across a space at specialized junctions called **synapses.** The advent of electron microscopic studies of the nervous system in the early 1950s reinforced the neuron doctrine.

A look through a light microscope at a section of a brain reveals an incredible range of cell sizes and shapes woven together in very elaborate networks whose designs vary in different brain regions. Our focus in this section is on the structural properties of these elements, particularly those properties most directly related to the fundamental tasks of a nervous system: to transmit, integrate, and discriminate information. The main constituents of brains related to these functions are these:

1. Individual nerve cells linked at specialized regions called synapses.
2. A second class of cells called glial cells (or glia or neuroglia).
3. The space between these cells called the **extracellular space.** This space constitutes 10–15% of the volume of the brain. It contains many ions and large molecules in the extracellular fluid.
4. Fluid compartments, including blood vessels and compartments containing cerebrospinal fluid.

Types of nerve cells The variety of cell types in the brain is far greater than in any other organ. Roughly two hundred geometrically distinguishable types of nerve cells are found in the brains of mammals (for examples, see Figure 2-19). Distinctions among these cells are made in terms of size and shape. These differences in size and shape reflect the ways neurons process information. It must be kept in mind that nerve cells are not simple relays that transmit the information they receive. Rather, the typical neuron collects signals from several sources, integrates

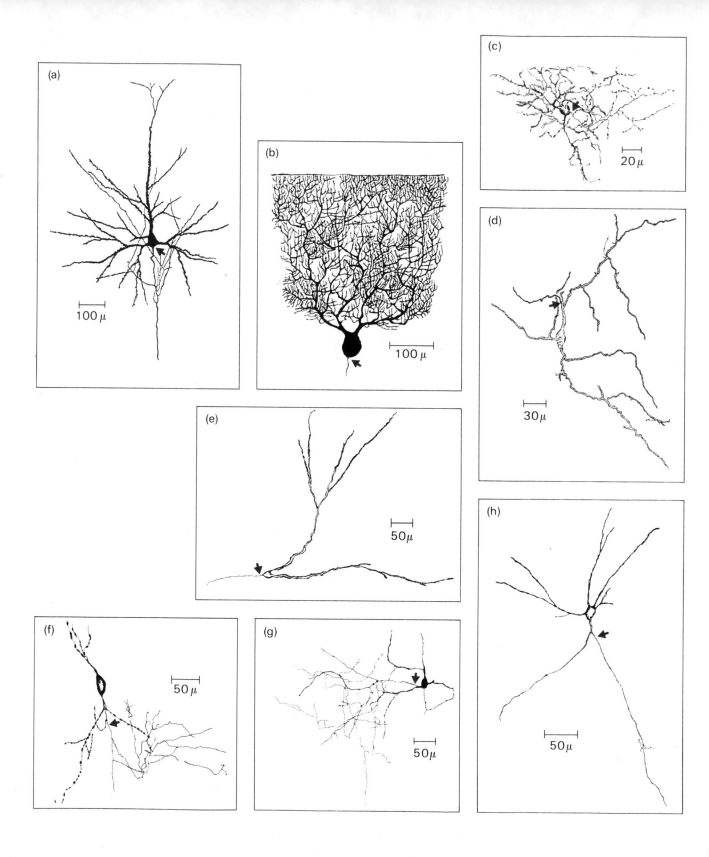

(a)

100 μ

(b)

100 μ

(c)

20 μ

(d)

30 μ

(e)

50 μ

(f)

50 μ

(g)

50 μ

(h)

50 μ

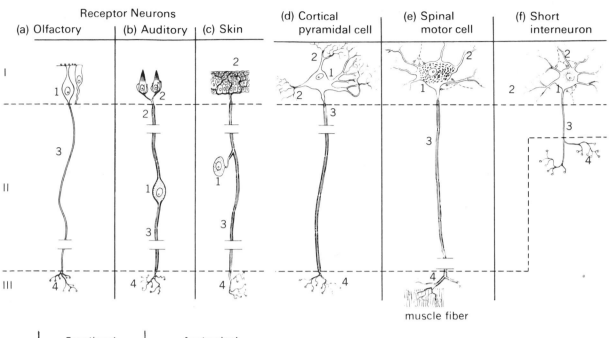

	Functional	Anatomical
I	Input zone	Dendrites, and sometimes also cell body
II	Conducting zone	Axon, and sometimes also dendrites
III	Output zone	Axon terminals

1	cell body
2	dendrites
3	axon
4	axon terminals

Figure 2-20 Structural and functional parts of neurons.

this information, transforms it, encodes it into complex output signals, and distributes these signals to a large number of other cells. The ways in which information is represented and processed in the nervous system are determined by the transactions of nerve cells. (We will discuss these processes in detail in Chapter 4.)

Although this structural diversity vastly complicates our task, there are some simplifications we can use to understand the fundamental structural properties of nerve cells. Many kinds of neurons have three distinct structural zones or parts that are directly related to the functional properties of the cell (Figure 2-20). These are (a) a **cell body** region, which is defined by the presence of the nucleus, (b) exten-

Figure 2-19 Some kinds of nerve cells. (a) Pyramidal cell from cerebral cortex. (From Sholl, 1956) (b) Purkinje cell, cerebellar cortex. (From Zecevic and Rakic, 1976) (c) Basket cell, cerebellar cortex. (From Palay and Chan-Palay, 1974) (d) Multipolar cell from pons. (From Mihailoff, McArdle, and Adams, 1981) (e)–(f) Four of the 21 identified kinds of cells in the hilar region of the hippocampus. (From Amaral, 1978) The beginning of the axon of each cell is indicated by an arrow. Other types of neurons are seen in Figure 2-20.

sions or processes of the cell body called **dendrites** (from the Greek "dendron," "tree"), which increase the receptive surface of the neuron, and (c) a single extension, the **axon.** In many neurons the axon is only millimeters in length, but in spinal sensory and motor neurons it can reach a meter or more. When you wiggle your toes, long axons carry the instructions from the spinal cord to muscles in your foot. Long fibers of sensory neurons then carry messages back to the spinal cord.

Anatomists use the shapes of cell bodies, dendrites, and axons to classify the many varieties of nerve cells into three principal types: multipolar, bipolar, and monopolar neurons. **Multipolar neurons** are nerve cells with many dendrites and a single axon. Most of the neurons of the vertebrate brain are multipolar (for example, the cells at d, e, and f in Figure 2-20). **Bipolar neurons** are nerve cells with a single dendrite at one end of the nerve cell and a single axon at the other end (a and b in Figure 2-20). This type of nerve cell is found in some vertebrate sensory systems, including the retina and olfactory system. **Monopolar neurons** are nerve cells with a single branch leaving a cell body, which then extends in two directions. One end is the receptive pole, the other the output zone (c in Figure 2-20). This is the dominant type of neuron in invertebrate nervous systems. It is also found in the mammalian nervous system.

Another common way of classifying nerve cells is by size. Examples of small nerve cells are the types called **granule** ("grains"), **spindle,** and **stellate** ("star-shaped"). Large cells include the types called **pyramidal, Golgi type I,** and **Purkinje.** Each region in the brain is a collection of both large and small neurons. Mammalian nerve cell bodies range from as small as 10 μ to as large as 50 μ.

Related to classification by size is the division of neurons into two classes: **projection neurons** and **local-circuit neurons.** We have been discussing mainly neurons that carry messages to widely separated parts of the brain or body; these are called projection neurons, and they tend to be large. Most neurons, however, make all their contacts only with other neurons that are located close by and are within the same function unit; these are local-circuit neurons, and they tend to be small. Within the human retina, for example, there are hundreds of millions of tiny neurons that form local circuits, but only one million retinal ganglion cells carry messages to the brain. Local-circuit neurons are relatively more abundant in more complex animals. For example, in the frog, whose movements are relatively simple and stereotyped, the ratio of local-circuit neurons to projection neurons in the cerebellum is about 20 to 1. In the mouse, which has more complex and elaborate motor patterns, the corresponding ratio is 140 local-circuit neurons for each cerebellar projection cell. In human beings this ratio is 1600 to 1!

The cell body The nerve cell body contains the nucleus, which includes the genetic instructions and also the plans for all the metabolic activities of the cell. We can get some idea of the complexity of the chemical processes within a nerve cell by knowing that a typical nerve cell contains, among other constituents: millions of protein molecules, billions of lipid molecules, hundreds of billions of RNA molecules, and trillions of potassium ions! Moreover, many of the molecules are metabolized and broken down at a rapid rate, so new molecules must be produced at a rapid rate. The membrane of the cell body has many tiny specialized subregions. Some of these are receptors for hormones; others pass food or waste materials into or out of the cell.

Dendrites

Axon

0 10 20
microns

Myelin
sheath

Nodes of
Ranvier

From a functional viewpoint, the cell body and the dendrites are specialized for receiving and integrating information. The axon is specialized for the conduction of information toward other cells.

The axon   All the illustrations to this point have shown the axon as a rather uniform tubular extension of the cell body. But a typical axon has several regions that are structurally and functionally distinguishable (Figure 2-21). In multipolar neurons the axon originates out of the cell body from a cone-shaped region called the **axon hillock.** (Chapter 4 will describe the functional features that distinguish the axon hillock from the main portion of the axon.) The axon beyond this region is tubular in form, with a diameter ranging from 0.5 μ to 20 μ in mammals and as large as 500 μ in the "giant" axons of some invertebrates. The length of an axon also varies appreciably, ranging from a few microns to a meter or more. With very few exceptions, nerve cells have only one axon. But axons often divide into many branches called collaterals. Because of this extensive branching, a single nerve cell can exert influence over a wide array of other cells. Toward its ending, an axon or collateral typically divides into numerous branches of fine diameter. At the end of the branches there are some specialized structures forming the synapse, the connection to the next nerve cell. We will discuss the structural properties of the synapse shortly.

Most axons are embedded in a sheath formed by nonneural accessory cells that lie close to the axon. For many axons, mainly larger-diameter ones, these accessory

Figure 2-21   A typical myelinated axon. At the upper left, the axon starts at the axon hillock of a cell body. Note that the diameter of the axon is much smaller than the diameter of the dendrites. A short distance after it emerges from the hillock, the axon acquires a myelin sheath. The segments of myelin, shown at the left, are about 1 mm long, and they are interrupted by nodes of Ranvier where the axon is uncovered. Near its termination, the axon loses its sheath and divides into many fine branches.

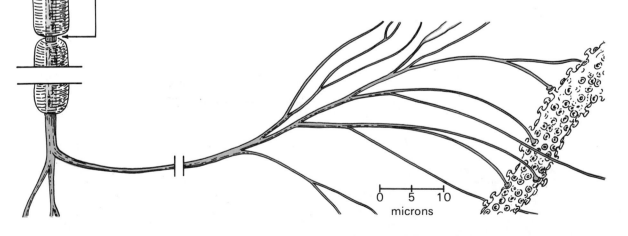

0   5   10
microns

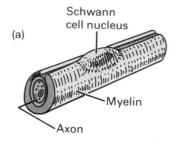

(a)

Schwann
cell nucleus

Myelin

Axon

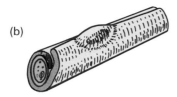

(b)

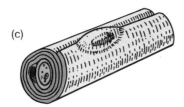

(c)

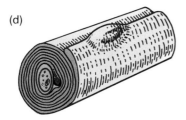

(d)

Figure 2-22 Sequence of formation of myelin sheath in the peripheral nervous system by a Schwann cell. The flat Schwann cell surrounds a length of the axon in (a) and then wraps itself several times around the axon (b)–(d). An electron microscopic picture of the final stage is shown in Figure 2-23.

Figure 2-23 Electron micrograph of myelinated and unmyelinated axons. In the upper part of the figure is a cross section of a myelinated axon with highly regular concentric layers of myelin. At lower right are four unmyelinated axons embedded in troughs in a Schwann cell. (From Peters, Palay, and Webster, 1976)

cells come close to the axon and form a regular wrapping around it. This coating around the axon is called **myelin,** and the process of the formation of this wrapping is called **myelinization** (Figure 2-22). This sheathing improves the speed of conduction of neural impulses. Anything that interferes with the myelin sheath can have catastrophic consequences for the individual. This is seen in various demyelinating diseases, such as multiple sclerosis.

Within the brain and spinal cord the myelin sheath is formed by a kind of glial cell (of which we'll be seeing more soon). For axons outside the brain and spinal cord (that is, in peripheral nerves), the accessory cell that forms myelin is called the **Schwann cell.** A single Schwann cell produces the myelin coat for a very limited length of the axon, seldom extending for more than 200 μ. Hence numerous Schwann cells are needed to myelinate the length of a single axon. There are small gaps in the coating provided by successive Schwann cells. Such a gap, where the axon membrane is exposed, is called a **node of Ranvier.** The regularity of the wrapping process is nicely illustrated in cross sections of the axon (cuts across the width) as shown in Figure 2-23. A subsequent section will describe the development of myelin in the brain. Its importance is demonstrated by the fact that myelinization increases over very extended periods of time in human beings, in some brain regions up to 10–15 years.

Many axons do not have a close wrapping of myelin. These axons generally have very fine diameter; they are commonly referred to as **unmyelinated** fibers or axons.

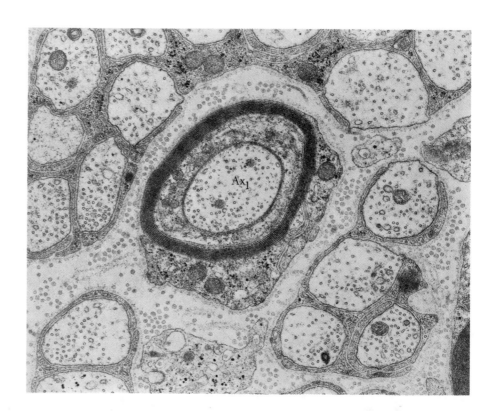

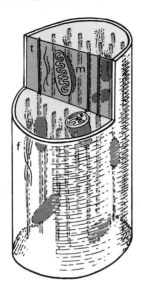

|— 10 microns —|

Figure 2-24 Diagram of an axon to illustrate tubule systems that may be involved in axonal transport: microtubules (t) and neurofilaments (f). A mitochondrion (m) is also shown.

Although these fibers do not have an elaborate coating, they do have a relationship with an accessory cell. What happens is that several axons become embedded in troughs of the Schwann cell and no regular wrapping is elaborated.

Many of the materials synthesized in the cell body are transported to distant regions in the dendrites and axons. This transportation of materials within the axon is referred to as **axoplasmic streaming** or protoplasmic streaming. Measurements of the rate of flow of substances in axons range from a "slow" system (1–3 mm/day) to a "fast" system (400 mm/day). Many constituents of the cell have been shown to flow within axons and dendrites. How does anything move in these structures? This has been studied mainly in axons whose length and uniformity (in some types of neurons) facilitates such investigation. Some investigators have observed structures in axons referred to as **microtubules** (20–26 nm in diameter) that look like hollow cylinders (Figure 2-24). There are also systems of smaller diameter (10 nm) called **neurofilaments;** these look like rods.

Experiments using drugs that selectively interfere with the structure of the microtubules give a hint as to how substances flow down an axon. One such substance, colchicine, seems to have the effect of blocking the flow of some materials in the axon while not interfering with its electrical excitability. This kind of evidence suggests that the microtubule system is important for the phenomenon of axoplasmic streaming. Some of the most exciting aspects of contemporary neurobiological research have been concerned with deciphering the molecular machinery of this phenomenon and many other aspects of the molecular properties of individual nerve cells.

● **Dendrites and synapses**   The diversity of shape of nerve cells arises primarily from the variation in the shape of **dendrites,** the extensions of nerve cells that arise from the cell body and branch out in highly complex ways. The shape of the **dendritic tree**—the full arrangement of a single cell's dendrites—provides clues about a particular cell's information processing. All along the surface of the dendrite there are many contacts, the synapses. In cortical pyramidal cells dendrites have been found to account for 95% of the cell volume.

A synapse, or **synaptic region,** has three principal components (Figure 2-25): (a) the presynaptic specialization, in many instances a swelling of the axon terminal called the **synaptic bouton** (button), (b) a specialized postsynaptic membrane in the surface of the dendrite or cell body, and (c) a **synaptic cleft,** that is, a space between the presynaptic and postsynaptic elements. This gap measures about 20–40 nm.

Detailed electron microscopic examination of the presynaptic terminal reveals the presence of many small spherical components called **synaptic vesicles.** They range in size from 30 to 140 nm. There is strong evidence that these vesicles contain a chemical substance that can be released into the synaptic cleft. This release is triggered by electrical activity in the axon. The released substance flows across the cleft and produces changes in the postsynaptic membrane. Such a chemical is called a **synaptic transmitter.** Many different transmitters have been identified in the brain, and other substances are being tested to determine whether they too are synaptic transmitters. The changes in the postsynaptic membrane are the basis of the transmission of excitation or inhibition from one cell to another. The synaptic cleft

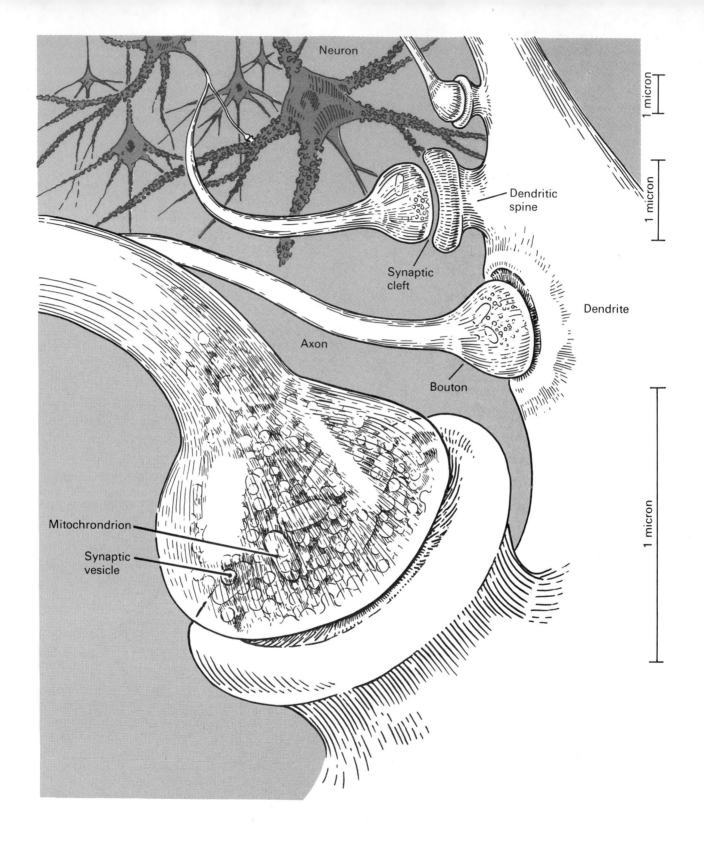

Neuron

1 micron

Dendritic
spine

1 micron

Synaptic
cleft

Dendrite

Axon

Bouton

1 micron

Mitochrondrion

Synaptic
vesicle

Figure 2-26 This shows how densely synaptic endings cover the surface of a nerve cell body and the dendrites. A few endings even occur on the initial segment of the axon. (From Poritsky, 1969)

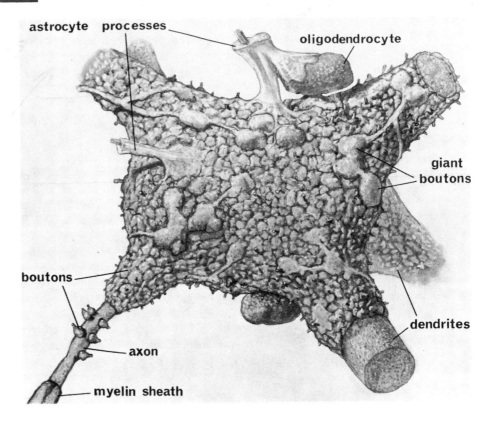

is filled with a dense material that is different from nonsynaptic extracellular regions. Similarly, the surface of the postsynaptic membrane is different from adjacent regions of the membrane. It contains special receptors that capture and react to molecules of the transmitter agent.

Numerous synapses cover the surfaces of dendrites and of the cell body. Some individual cells of the brain have as many as a hundred thousand synapses, although the more common number for larger cells is around 5,000 to 10,000. Figure 2-26 illustrates the density of the synaptic contacts on the surface of a nerve cell in the spinal cord whose axon goes to muscles. (Such a cell is called a **motoneuron,** a contraction of motor neuron.) Synaptic contacts are particularly numerous in nerve cells with elaborate dendrites.

Along the dendrites on many nerve cells of the brain there are outgrowths called **dendritic spines** or thorns (Figure 2-25). These spines give some dendrites a rough or corrugated surface. They have become the focus of considerable attention, since they seem to be quite variable elements, which may be modified by experience (Chapter 15). Chapter 3 will discuss developmental studies of the growth of dendritic spines.

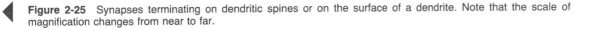

Figure 2-25 Synapses terminating on dendritic spines or on the surface of a dendrite. Note that the scale of magnification changes from near to far.

Glial cells   In some regions of the primate brain the cells that are most abundant are not neurons but **glia** or **neuroglia.** Their name is derived from the original conception of their function—that these cells serve as something like glue (in Greek, "glia" means "glue"). They provide the structural support for an extensive matrix of nerve cells. Unlike nerve cells, neuroglia can increase in number throughout the life of an animal. Although many aspects of the functional roles of neuroglia remain a puzzle, there are some facts—and many interesting ideas—about their function.

Microscopic observation of glial cells enables us to distinguish several different types (Figure 2-27). One type, called an **astrocyte** (Latin "astra," "star"), is a star-shaped cell with numerous processes or extensions that run in all directions. Some astrocytes form end feet on the blood vessels of the brain. These end feet look as though they are attached to the vessels by suckerlike processes.

Another type of glial cell is the **oligodendrocyte.** This cell is much smaller than an astrocyte and has fewer processes (Greek "oligo," "few"). Oligodendrocytes are commonly associated with nerve cell bodies, especially the bodies of larger neurons. Because of this association, they are frequently regarded as satellite cells of neurons (hence their designation as perineuronal satellite cells).

There is a third type of glial cell: the **microglia.** As their name suggests, they are extremely small. Microglia migrate in large numbers to sites of injury in the nervous system. They are apparently activated by disease states to remove cellular debris from injured or dead cells.

The functions of glial cells differ with their appearances (Figure 2-27). Initially glia were presumed to provide structural support for the neural elements within the central nervous system. It was suggested that they occupied spaces among the neurons and their extensions. Clearly structural support—or some aspects of it—is one biological role of glial cells. Extensions of astrocytes form the tough sheets that wrap around the outer surface of the brain, the dura mater we saw in Figure 2-1. It also appears that bundles of extensions of astrocytes interweave among nerve fibers, as though acting as a structural support. Glial cells may also serve a nutritive role, providing a pathway from the vascular system to the nerve cells, delivering raw materials that nerve cells use to synthesize complex compounds.

The manner in which glial cells surround neurons, especially the synaptic surfaces of neurons, also suggests that one of their roles is to isolate receptive surfaces to prevent interactions among axons in the vicinity of synapses. This indicates that part of the action of glial machinery may be directed toward segregating inputs to nerve cells.

Oligodendroglia produce myelinization of axons in the CNS. This process differs from myelinization involving Schwann cells in the periphery as follows: A single oligodendroglial cell may myelinate several segments of the same axon or several different axons, whereas a single Schwann cell myelinates only a single segment of one cell.

Figure 2-27   Some types of glial cells and some of their functions.   ▶

(a) Extensions of oligodendrocytes form myelin sheaths.

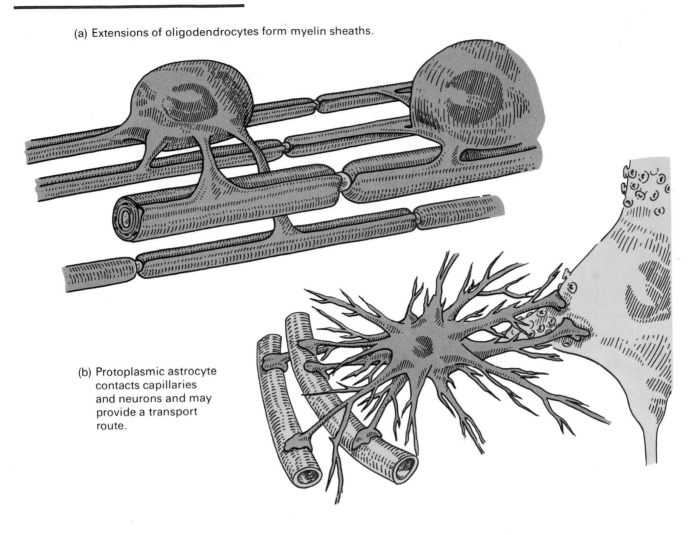

(b) Protoplasmic astrocyte
contacts capillaries
and neurons and may
provide a transport
route.

(c) Perineuronal oligodendrocyte
isolates synaptic
junctions.

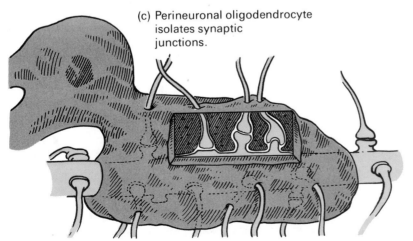

(d) Ependymal cells
line ventricular walls.

Glial cells are of clinical interest because they are the cells that form the principal tumors of the brain and spinal cord. Furthermore, some classes of glia, especially astrocytes, respond to brain injury by changing in size, that is, by swelling. This process is referred to as **edema.** The swelling interferes with the function of neurons and is responsible for many symptoms of brain injuries.

The evolution of nerve cells

Nerve cells share many attributes with other cells in the body but are distinctly different in at least one regard: *Only nerve cells have the ability to generate and transmit electrical signals over a distance.* In the evolution of cells it is the emergence of this property that is of primary significance in understanding the biological origins of the nervous system.

One view of the evolutionary development of this attribute suggests that there is a relationship between the appearance of the electrical capabilities of nerve cells and increases in body size of primitive creatures. Originally, cells that made up external, skinlike surfaces of these creatures were quite close to the muscles that moved them. In such primordial creatures, composed of only a few compact groups of cells, communication was readily achieved by the passage of substances across closely abutted membranes. When body size gradually increased over the eons, in response to various evolutionary pressures, nerve cells became an interesting solution to the problem of communication between sensory surfaces and muscles. The emergence of the electrical responsiveness of nerve cells made possible the communication of messages over longer distances. Some support for this picture of the evolution of nerve cells is offered by the fact that skin surfaces and neurons develop from the same layer of embryonic tissue. This view of evolution implies that the shape of a nerve cell is a critical feature, which predicts the functional attributes of a given nerve cell. This is a theme we will return to in several sections of this book.

Regions of the brain and their circuitry

The different regions of the brain are defined by the kinds of neurons they contain, by the way the neurons are spaced or grouped, and by the way axons are distributed. The larger fiber tracts or bands inside the brain can be seen in brain sections with the naked eye (Figure 2-28). Microscopic inspection of brain sections discloses finer features. When the field of view seen through a microscope consists of hundreds of nerve cells, different brain regions can be identified or characterized by their distinctive patterns or groupings of neurons. For example, in some brain regions cells are arranged in a kind of horizontal layering. This is referred to as a **laminar** form of organization (Figure 2-30). In this arrangement the different layers may consist of cell bodies of different size; that is, smaller cells are found at one level and larger cells at another. In other regions, the cells may be arranged in vertical columns as well as in horizontal layers. In still other regions, the orientation of nerve cell bodies and their processes may appear quite random, with dendrites and axons coursing in all directions.

These structurally different regions of the brain also differ in function. In fact, the different kinds and connections of cells in each brain region are believed to reflect the organization of circuits that process and control information. Each circuit uses

BOX 2-4   Viruses in the Brain: Discoveries in a Stone Age Tribe

A few years ago newspapers in the United States reported an unusual case of a neurological disease involving a slow course of brain degeneration and a progressive profound impairment in cognitive abilities. What made this report unusual was the fact that this brain disorder was induced by a corneal transplant! How could a corneal transplant cause a brain disorder? Research done halfway round the world provided the clue.

The particular disorder is one of several brain diseases with a slow course of degeneration paralleled by a continuous decline in behavior capacities. The beginnings of answers to the question of what causes these disorders may have come from the joining of anthropological, behavioral, and neurological approaches in studies of a Stone Age people in New Guinea.

This story starts during the 1950s, in the New Guinea highlands. Carleton Gajdusek and his collaborators came across an unusual progressive degenerative disorder of the brain that was the principal cause of death in some New Guinea groups. About 2% of the population died each year with this disorder which mainly affected women and children. The tribes called this disorder kuru, which means to shake with fear or to tremble. Persons with this disorder showed an initial clumsiness of walking that progressed to trembling of legs, which became severe enough to prevent standing. In time virtually all arm and leg movements become impossible, and in about 20% of the patients mental deterioration was also evident.

Gajdusek found clues to the nature of this pathological process in certain unusual cultural practices. In many of these communities ritual cannibalism was practiced. In the rites of mourning, women and children especially participated in eating the dead. The tribes believed that eating the flesh of their dead friends would protect them from bad spirits. Since these people did not recognize kuru as an infectious disease, there were no constraints on this form of cannibalistic behavior.

With these observations Gajdusek began a series of studies to see whether this disease was transmissible to experimental animals by inoculating the animals with brain tissue from kuru victims. He noted that kuru developed in chimpanzees after a latent period of one to four years after inoculation. Manifestation of the disease in these animals closely resembled that seen in humans. The transmissible agent has now been characterized as an unusual virus, a "slow" virus that reaches high levels in the brain. It now appears that many kuru victims may have initially been exposed to the virus 10–15 years before to the onset of symptoms. In 1976 Carleton Gajdusek received the Nobel Prize in medicine for this work, which has led to a new perspective on chronic, degenerative brain disorders.

Scientists currently believe that, among humans, several severe degenerative disorders that involve the nervous system may be caused by similar slow viruses. This has been clearly established in several disorders, including one called Creutzfeldt-Jacob's disease. This was the disorder, mentioned at the beginning of this box, that was transmitted by the donor of the corneal transplant to the recipient.

a specialized set of electrical and chemical signals. (The forms of these signals will be discussed in Chapter 4.) To understand fully the role of any region in producing a particular behavior, we must understand the circuit arrangements that are characteristic of it. Here we will briefly discuss the basic circuitry of two major regions of the brain: the cerebellum and the cerebral cortex.

The cerebellum   The general position of the **cerebellum** in the human brain was shown in Figures 2-4 and 2-7. In gross appearance the cerebellum has numerous folds or convolutions (called **folia**). If a single fold were rolled out into a flat sheet, it would have a surface area approximately 2 cm (anterior to posterior) by 10 cm (medial to lateral).

The cellular arrangements in a single folium of the cerebellar cortex are shown in

Figure 2-28 Tracts shown in a dissection of a human brain. The right hemisphere is seen from the medial aspect. Part of this hemisphere has been dissected to reveal three kinds of tracts: (1) Long projection fibers running to and from the cerebral cortex. Some of these go through the corpus callosum. (2) Short tracts that arch between nearby parts of the cortex; these are called arcuate fibers. (3) Long tracts that run in an anterior-posterior direction. The long tract shown here is the cingulum (Latin for "belt") which lies just over the corpus callosum near the medial wall of each hemisphere. It has been cut in order to show the full length of the projection fibers.

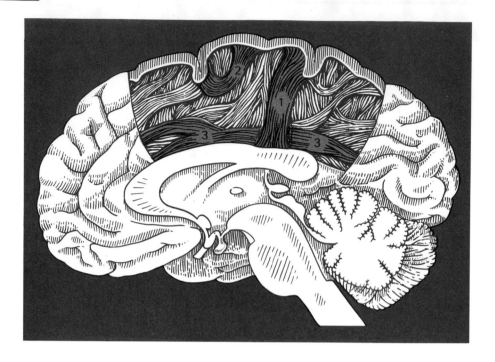

Figure 2-29. There are three quite distinct layers: a molecular layer, a layer of Purkinje cells, and a layer of granule cells.

1. At the surface of the cerebellum is the molecular layer. In its outermost part are parallel fibers; these are axons of the granule cells whose bodies lie down in the third layer. The cell bodies of the molecular layer— **stellate** (star-shaped) **cells** —are in the deeper part of the molecular layer.

2. The middle layer is a sheet composed of a single row of cells with extraordinarily elaborate dendritic trees. These are called **Purkinje cells,** after a nineteenth century Czech physiologist. The dendritic tree of the Purkinje cell extends up into the molecular layer. The tree of each cell is like a Japanese fan. When viewed from the side (toward the right of Figure 2-29), it branches extensively. When viewed head-on (just to left of center at the top of Figure 2-29), it is very narrow.

3. The deepest layer is made up of very densely packed small neurons, called **granule cells.**

These three layers comprise the cerebellar cortex; below them is white matter. This basic pattern can be noted throughout the cerebellum.

The only output from the cerebellar cortex to other brain regions goes via the axons of Purkinje cells. The intimate circuitry of the cerebellar cortex (Figure 2-29) is designed to regulate the activity of this cell type. (Chapter 8 will discuss the functional properties of the cerebellum.)

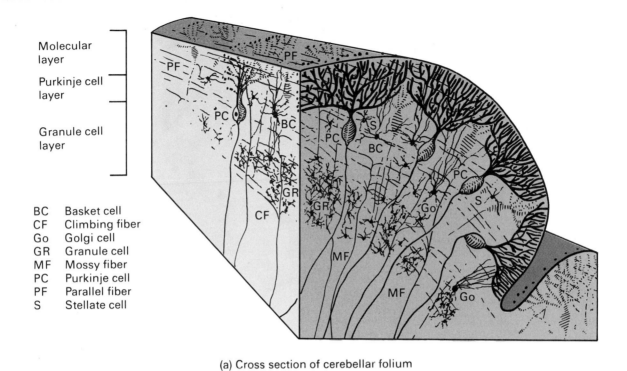

Molecular layer

Purkinje cell layer

Granule cell layer

BC Basket cell
CF Climbing fiber
Go Golgi cell
GR Granule cell
MF Mossy fiber
PC Purkinje cell
PF Parallel fiber
S   Stellate cell

(a) Cross section of cerebellar folium

(b) Intrinsic cerebellar circuit

(c) Cerebellar circuit including input connections

Figure 2-29 A folium of the cerebellum and the basic neural circuits of the cerebellum.

The cerebral cortex The cellular arrangements of the cerebral cortex are considerably more elaborate and varied than those of the cerebellar cortex. Unlike the cerebellum with its repeated pattern, the cerebral cortex has distinct regions that differ from each other in cell arrangements. The common feature of all cerebral cortical areas is that they are composed of six different layers, as shown in Figure 2-30.

The most prominent kind of neuron in the cerebral cortex—the **pyramidal cell** —usually has its cell bodies in layers 3–5. At the right of Figure 2-30 is an enlargement of a single pyramidal cell. One dendrite of each pyramidal cell (called the apical dendrite) usually extends to the outermost surface of the cortex. The pyramidal cell also has several dendrites (called basal dendrites) that spread out horizontally from the cell body. Frequently nerve cells of the cortex appear to be arranged in columns, as we have seen (Figure 2-18). Nerve cells in a single column tend to have similar functional properties, as we have learned from studies of cortical functions in the analysis of sensory inputs.

The variation in thickness of the different layers of cerebral cortex is related to differences in their functions. Incoming fibers from the thalamus terminate especially in layer 4, so this layer is particularly prominent in regions that represent sensory functions. In fact, in part of the visual cortex in the occipital lobe, layer 4 is so prominent that it appears to the naked eye as a stripe in sections cut through this area. This is why this part of the visual cortex is known as **striate** (striped) **cortex.** Fibers that leave the cerebral cortex arise especially from layer 3, which is particularly prominent in the main motor regions of the cortex. Layer 3 is also characterized by rather large pyramidal cells.

Figure 2-30 The layers of the cerebral cortex, (a) and (b), and a cortical pyramidal cell (c). Part (a) is stained (Nissl stain) to show cell bodies. Part (b) shows shapes and positions of typical cells, using the Golgi stain. Parts (a) and (b) are enlarged about 60 times. Part (c) shows a pyramidal cell enlarged about 200 times. All of the cell is seen, except the axon continues off the bottom of the figure. [Parts (a) and (b) from Rakic, 1979; part (c) from Sholl, 1956. Parts (a) and (b) reprinted by permission of MIT Press from *The Neurosciences: Fourth Study Program,* edited by Francis O. Schmitt and Frederic G. Worden, copyright © 1979 by The Massachusetts Institute of Technology.]

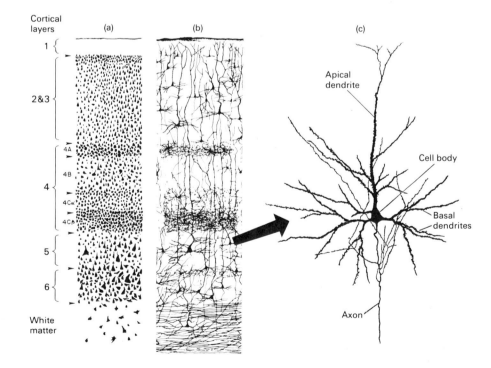

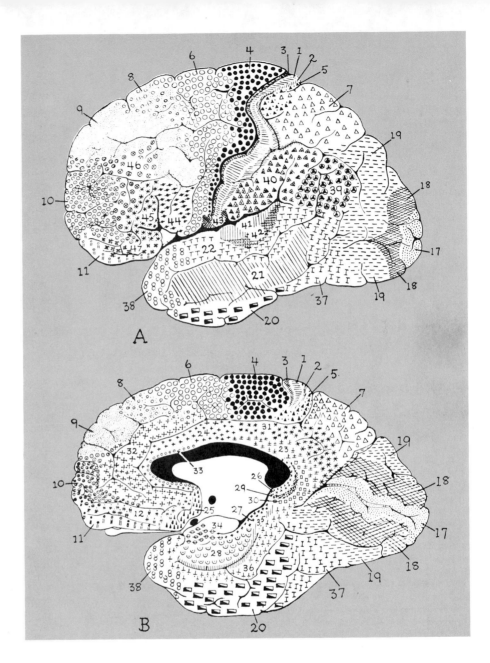

Figure 2-31 Regions of the cortex as delineated in a classical cytoarchitectonic map by Brodmann (1909).

On the basis of kinds and spacing of cells and distribution of axons, anatomists have divided up the cortex into many subregions. The study of this "cellular architecture" is called **cytoarchitectonics.** These anatomical divisions have been found to correspond to functional zones. Different criteria lead to slightly different maps. Figure 2-31, which illustrates a commonly used one, also shows the sharpness of cytoarchitectonic boundaries between some adjacent cortical areas. In other cases boundaries are not sharp and clear. The unraveling of the internal circuitry of the cerebral cortex is a very complex task.

These two examples—from the cerebral and cerebellar cortices—show that nerve cells form orderly patterns that are probably related to the functional capabilities of these regions. In other chapters we will see the special anatomical arrangements of some other regions of the brain. One of the principal tasks of physiological psychology is to ascertain the functional properties of such arrangements.

As we review this section on organization of the brain, it becomes apparent that the brain is an enormously complex structure, with a vast, nearly incredible number of cells connected in myriad ways. Efforts to understand the workings of the brain depend on knowledge of its structure, its form, and its interconnections. As we have seen, the way the brain is organized can be described at several levels, ranging from quite fine (for example, a single synapse) to very broad (the shape and size of the whole brain).

Comparing brains among species

The brains of different vertebrates vary greatly in size and shape, as Figure 2-32 shows. Between the small, relatively simple brain of the frog and the large, elaborate brain of the human, there are important differences. But there are also basic similarities. What can we learn by studying this variety, without being overwhelmed by it?

Why compare?

It would be a tall order to describe the nervous systems of all the different creatures in this world. By some estimates the insects alone—buzzing, crawling, and flying about us—account for over one million species. Even mammals number more than ten thousand species. Obviously the task of describing, cataloging, and understanding the relationships between nervous system and behavior in even a small fraction of these creatures would be awesome (and dull) unless we had some rationale beyond mere completeness in accounting for the worlds about us.

One reason for interest in comparative studies is human-centered, based on the question: "Why does the human being alone end up on top of the animal order?" Believers in the human-centered perspective consider other animals to be potentially "little humans," which is not a valid basis for comparison. Some observers poke fun at this self-centered view of evolutionary supremacy. As the humorist Don Marquis noted, "To a mosquito, man is just something good to eat."

Most comparative biological research today is concerned with quite a different theme: differences in the animal world, which reflect the long evolutionary struggles for adaptation. Different animals with varying biological histories show different solutions to the dilemmas of adaptation. Instead of worrying about the alleged evolutionary supremacy of our species, those who are studying comparative anatomy and behavior are trying to figure out how behavioral differences or specializations are related to bodily differences. Figure 2-33 provides examples. It shows that adaptations to particular ecological niches are related to differences in brain structure. As a general rule, the relative size of a region is a good guide to the importance of the function of that region for the adaptations of the species. In this sense "more is better." Our understanding of how these differences in size and structure of the brain promote behavioral specializations should help us understand the neural basis of human behavior. For example, the size of some regions in the human temporal lobe seem to be related to language function, as Chapter 16 will show.

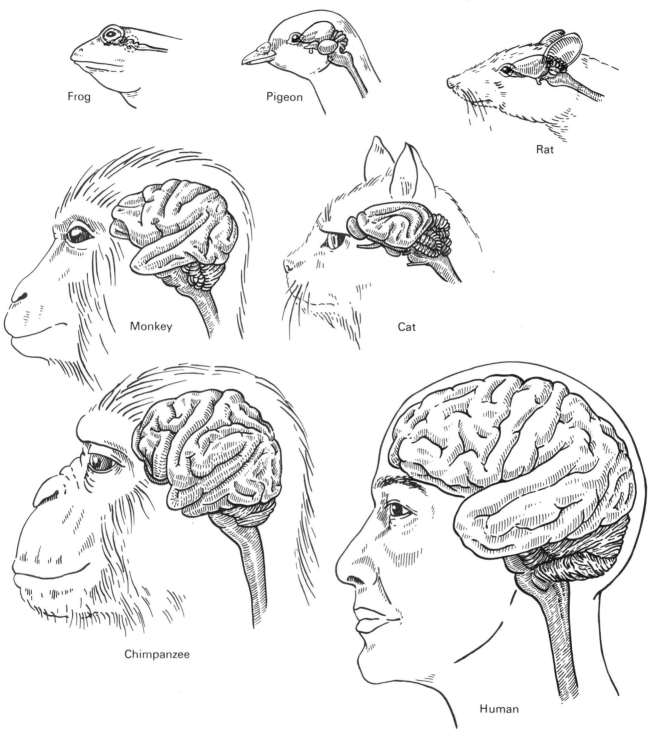

Figure 2-32 Comparison of the sizes and shapes of the brains of several representative vertebrates, all drawn approximately four-tenths life size.

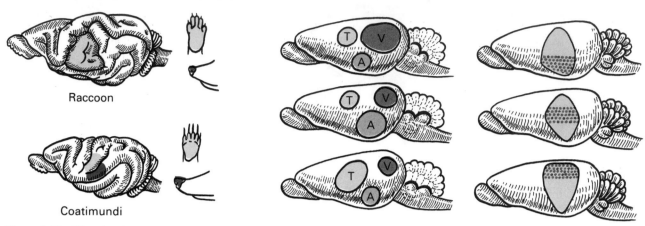

Figure 2-33 Diversity of organization of cerebral cortex in relation to differences in behavioral functions. The left column shows the brains of the North American raccoon and its Central American relative, the coatimundi. The coatimundi uses olfaction as much as touch. The raccoon cortex contains a large area representing the forepaw but a tiny olfactory area, whereas in the coatimundi cortex, olfaction has as large a representation as does the forepaw. The middle column shows schematically the differential sizes of cortical representations in animals that emphasize vision (top), audition (middle), and touch (bottom). Note also that in the midbrain the superior colliculus (midbrain visual center) is large in the visual animal, while the inferior colliculus (midbrain audition center) is large in the animal that relies on hearing; such a difference is observed in bats that use mainly vision versus bats that use mainly audition. The right column illustrates the different expansion of the tactile area according to whether an animal feels chiefly with its mouth and snout (top), its hands (middle), or its tail (bottom).

Similarities and differences
among nervous systems

Study of many species has shown that the main divisions of the brain are the same among all mammals, and the overall organization is basically similar in all vertebrates. Figure 2-34 shows medial views of the brains of the human being and of the rat. You can see that each of the labeled structures in the human brain has its counterpart in the rat brain. This comparison could be extended to much greater detail, down to nuclei and fiber tracts. Even small structures in the brains of one species are found to have their exact correspondences in the brains of other species. The types of neurons are also similar throughout the mammals. So is the organization of the cerebellar cortex and the cerebral cortex.

The differences between the brains of humans and of other mammals are mainly quantitative. That is, they concern both actual and relative sizes of the whole brain, brain regions, and brain cells. The brain of an adult human being weighs about 1400 grams (g), whereas that of an adult rat weighs a little less than 2 g. In each case the brain represents about 2% of total body weight. The cerebral hemispheres occupy a much greater proportion of the brain in the human than in the rat. Because the human cerebral cortex is so large, it develops gyri and fissures so that a great deal of cortical surface can surround the rest of the brain. The rat cerebral cortex, on the other hand, is smooth and unfissured. The rat has, relatively, much larger olfactory bulbs than the human. This difference is probably related to the rat's much greater use of the sense of smell. The size of neurons also differs significantly between human and rat. In the case of large neurons in the motor cortex, the difference in

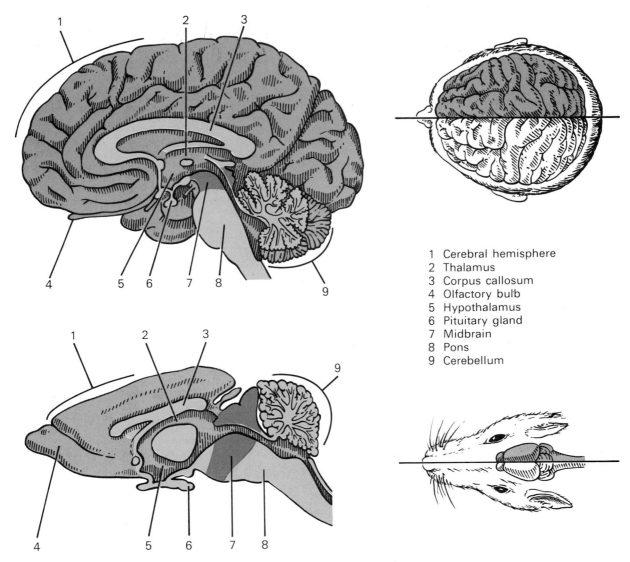

1 Cerebral hemisphere
2 Thalamus
3 Corpus callosum
4 Olfactory bulb
5 Hypothalamus
6 Pituitary gland
7 Midbrain
8 Pons
9 Cerebellum

Figure 2-34 Comparisons of human and rat brain structures in mid-sagittal views of the right hemisphere. The rat brain has been enlarged about six times in linear dimensions in relation to the human brain. Note that the cerebral hemispheres are relatively much larger in the human brain, whereas the rat has the relatively larger midbrain and olfactory bulbs.

volume between human and rat is about 30 to 1. With respect to the large Purkinje cells in the cerebellar cortex, the difference is about 4 to 1. In addition, there are great differences in the extents of dendritic trees in humans and in rats.

Behavioral adaptations of species have been related in some cases to differences in relative sizes of brain structures. To give one example, some species of bats find their way and locate prey by audition; other species of bats rely almost entirely on vision. In the midbrain the auditory center (the inferior colliculus) is much larger in bats that depend on hearing, whereas bats that depend on sight have a larger visual center (the superior colliculus).

Findings from comparative research provide important perspectives for understanding the relationships between brain and behavior in humans. We will discuss these findings at several points in later chapters; for example, in connection with sensory processes and perception, with motivation, and with learning and memory. Comparative research also furnishes important suggestions about evolution of the brain. Chapter 3 will give a fuller treatment of this topic.

SUMMARY / MAIN POINTS

1. Study of the anatomy of the nervous system is necessary in order to investigate the question of localization of function. How do different parts of the nervous system determine different kinds of behavior?

2. The main divisions of the brain can be seen most clearly in the embryo. These divisions are the forebrain, composed of the telencephalon and diencephalon; the midbrain or mesencephalon; and the hindbrain, composed of the metencephalon and myelencephalon.

3. Each main division of the brain is made up of several subdivisions. For example, the cerebral hemispheres include the cerebral cortex, white matter composed of nerve fibers, and the basal ganglia, such as the caudate nucleus.

4. The brain contains the ventricles, which are cavities filled with cerebrospinal fluid. This fluid mediates between blood vessels and brain tissue in exchange of materials. It also fills the space between the brain and the inside of the skull and acts as a shock absorber for the brain.

5. Large cerebral arteries bring blood to the brain. The exchange of nutrients and other materials between capillaries and the brain is controlled by the blood-brain barrier.

6. Sensory and motor links between the central nervous system and the body are made through 12 pairs of cranial nerves and 31 pairs of spinal nerves.

7. The autonomic nervous system is composed of the sympathetic chains and the parasympathetic (cranial and sacral) division. The two divisions work together. The sympathetic predominates during muscular activity and the parasympathetic during rest and repair.

8. The structure of the brain can be studied at many anatomical levels, from the whole organ to parts of cells. The hierarchy of levels, from broadest to finest, includes the brain, brain systems, brain regions, brain subregions, basic processing units, local circuits, basic neuroglial compartments, single neurons, synaptic assemblies, and synapses.

9. A typical neuron of most vertebrate species has three main parts: (a) the cell body, which contains the nucleus, (b) dendrites, which extend the receptive surface of the cell body, and (c) an axon, which carries impulses from the neuron.

10. Neurons make functional contacts with other neurons, or with muscles or glands, at specialized junctions called synapses. At most synapses a chemical transmitter liberated by the presynaptic terminal diffuses across the synaptic cleft and is taken up by special receptor molecules in the postsynaptic membrane.

11. The brain is made up of glial cells as well as neurons. There is a variety of glial cells, which serve many functions: They produce myelin sheaths around neurons, exchange nutrients and other materials with neurons, and remove cellular debris.

12. Regions of the brain differ from each other in the types of neurons that compose them and in their circuitry.

13. The main divisions of the brain are the same in all vertebrates. Differences among species are mainly quantitative. That is, species differ in the actual and relative sizes of the whole brain, brain regions, and brain cells. The major thrust of studies of comparative evolution is to find how differences or specializations in behavior among species are related to differences in the nervous system.

RECOMMENDED READING

Gluhbegovic, N., and Williams, T. H. *The human brain*. New York: Harper & Row, 1980.

Netter, F. *Nervous system*. Vol. 1 in the Ciba Collection of Medical Illustrations, 1957.

Noback, C. R. *The human nervous system*. New York: McGraw-Hill, 1981.

Peters, A., Palay, S. L., and Webster, H. de F. *The fine structure of the nervous system*. Philadelphia: Saunders, 1976.

Orientation

In the Beginning

Brain weight from birth to old age

The emergence of brain form

Cellular aspects of the development of the nervous system

Developmental processes after birth

Examples of the formation of neural regions

Why Neural Connections Go Where They Go

Layout of the amphibian visual system

Specificity of retinal-tectal connections

Limits to neurospecificity

Determinants of the Growth and Development of the Brain

Genetic determinants

Biochemical influences

Experience and brain development

Aging of the Brain

Normal aging

Senile dementia: A pathological exaggeration of aging

Maldevelopment of the Brain and Behavior Impairments

Genetically determined states

Prenatal maternal conditions

Birth processes and disorders of the nervous system

Evolution of the Brain

Changes in vertebrate brains through evolution

Evolution of brain size

Two Calendars for Brain Development

Summary/Main Points

3

Development of the Nervous System over the Life Span and Through Millions of Years

Orientation

The human brain has been sculptured over time. Two calendars provide the necessary time frames in which we can see its development. With one we observe its development over the life span of the individual. With the other we trace its development over the millions of years of its evolution. By following first one calendar and then the other, we will see how the brain and behavior have developed in relation to each other.

Age puts its stamp on our behavior and that of all animals. The pace, progression, and orderliness of changes are especially prominent early in life. However, the life sciences now emphasize change as a feature of the entire span of life. Change is a relentless property of biological states. Shakespeare put it well, in *As You Like It,* when he said:

> . . . from hour to hour, we ripe and ripe,
> And then, from hour to hour, we rot and rot.

In the first part of this chapter the focus is on the structural flux of the brain during the course of life. Later chapters will give examples of behavioral and physiological changes in the brain that accompany development.

Features of adult brains, described in Chapter 2, will now be seen as they progress during life from the womb to the tomb. For example, the fertilization of an egg leads to a body with a brain that contains billions of neurons, with an incredible number of connections. The pace of this process is extraordinary. During the height of prenatal growth of the human brain, neurons are added at the rate of 500,000 per minute!

We will examine several major questions here, including the way nerve cells form and what controls the formation of connections among various regions of the brain. Does the brain develop by an intrinsically guided process that obligingly follows blueprints "written in genes"? How does experience help to guide the emerging brain?

The growth and development of a nervous system is an intriguing process, especially in its relation to the ontogeny of behavior. Many psychological theories emphasize development and try to assign relative weights to the roles of nature and nurture. How important is early life to later cognitive and emotional behavior? Studies of the structural and functional developments of the brain can provide insights into these issues.

Using comparative and evolutionary approaches, as we will do in the last sections of this chapter, helps us to understand how, over the vast stretches of geological history, the human brain attained its relatively large size. We will see how brain size is related to both body size and behavioral capacity. Special attention will be given to the evolution of brain size among some families of mammals, particularly the hominids.

In the beginning

The journey from fertilized egg to mature organism is exceedingly complicated. Picture, if you can, the number of neurons in the mature human brain. Recent estimates have suggested a figure of around 200 billion (Kandel, 1976). Yet these billions of cells show highly ordered species-characteristic patterns of organization—an awesome achievement of developmental and evolutionary processes! Many aspects of the brain are being investigated, ranging from chemical influences to the ways in which experience affects the "wiring" of the brain.

Brain weight from birth to old age

One index to brain development is afforded by measurements of the weights of the brain at different stages of life. Weight can be considered as a kind of summary of many developmental processes. A study by Dekaban and Sadowsky (1978) gives a definitive portrait of the weight of the human brain over the life span. This study was based on measurements of the brains of 5826 persons, selected from more than 25,000 cases from several cities. Researchers weighed the brains of individuals who died from causes that do not exert major influences on the brain. Figure 3-1 shows the changes with age in the weights of brains in males and females. Note the rapid increase over the first five years. Brain weight is at its peak from about age 18 to about age 30, after which there is a gradual decline. Now let us see how the brain starts its developmental journey.

The emergence of brain form

A new human being begins when a sperm about 60 microns (μ) long penetrates the wall of an egg cell 100–150 μ in diameter. This event occurs in a region of the Fallopian tube, the duct leading from the ovary (Figure 3-2). From this union results

Figure 3-1 Human brain weights as a function of age. Note that the age scale has been expanded for the first five years in order to show data more clearly during this period of rapid growth. (Adapted from Dekaban and Sadowsky, 1978)

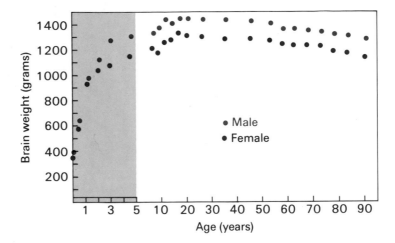

a cell with 46 chromosomes, the normal number for humans. These chromosomes contain the complete genetic blueprint for the new individual. (Box 3-1 discusses the way that genetic information is encoded in the chromosomes.) Within 12 hours this single cell has divided into two cells, and after three days these have become a small cluster of homogeneous cells, like a cluster of grapes, about 200 μ in diameter.

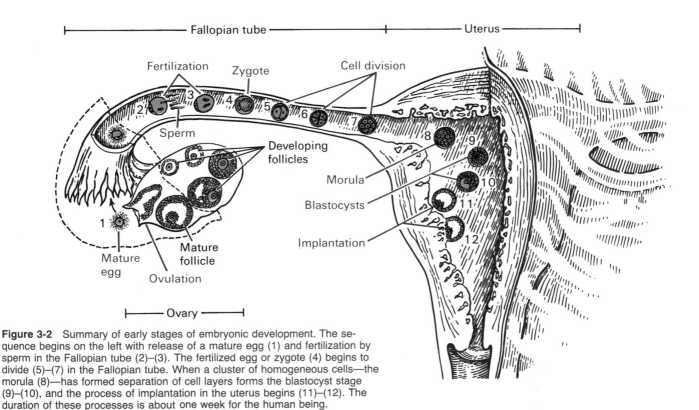

Figure 3-2 Summary of early stages of embryonic development. The sequence begins on the left with release of a mature egg (1) and fertilization by sperm in the Fallopian tube (2)–(3). The fertilized egg or zygote (4) begins to divide (5)–(7) in the Fallopian tube. When a cluster of homogeneous cells—the morula (8)—has formed separation of cell layers forms the blastocyst stage (9)–(10), and the process of implantation in the uterus begins (11)–(12). The duration of these processes is about one week for the human being.

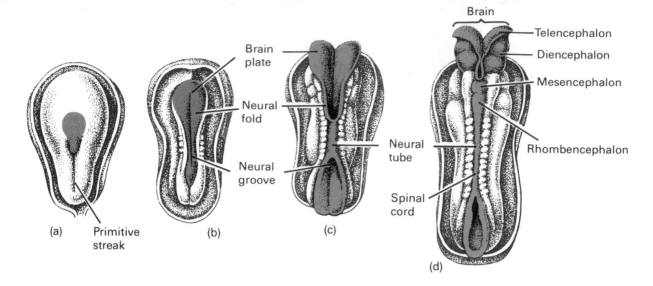

Figure 3-3 Human embryonic development during weeks 2 through 4. (a) The embryo has begun to implant in the uterine wall and consists of two cell layers. (b) Formation of three layers of cells and thickening of one of these layers—the ectoderm—leads to the development of the neural plate. (c) Beginning of neural groove. (d) Neural groove has closed along the length of the embryo; the closing of the groove at the anterior end of the anterior neuropore results in the rudimentary beginning of the brain.

During this period the ball of cells has been moving toward the uterus. After several days it arrives there. Fluid from the uterine cavity then enters this ball of cells and separates them into two groups: (1) an outer cell group that later becomes the placenta and (2) an inner cell mass that becomes the embryo itself. A cavity forms within the ball of cells. At this stage our organism is called a blastocyst (this term comes from the Greek "blastos," "sprout or bud," and from the Greek word for bladder, to denote a budding hollow organism). At the end of the first week the blastocyst is implanted in the uterine wall, as the placental cells extend into this wall.

During the second week three distinct cell layers form. These layers are the beginnings of all the tissues of the embryo (Figure 3-3). The nervous system will develop from the outer layer, called the **ectoderm** (from the Greek words for "outer" and "skin"). As the cell layers thicken, they grow into a flat oval plate. In the ectodermal level of this plate a middle or median position is marked by a groove—the primitive groove. At the head end of the groove there is a thickened collection of cells. This stage occurs two weeks after fertilization. Ridges of ectoderm then form on both sides of the middle position. These are the neural folds. The groove between them is then known as the neural groove.

The pace of events now becomes faster. The neural folds come together and convert the groove into the **neural tube.** At the anterior part of the neural tube three subdivisions become apparent. These subdivisions correspond to the future forebrain **(prosencephalon),** midbrain **(mesencephalon),** and hindbrain **(rhombencephalon).** (Recall these regions from Chapter 2, Figure 2-7.) The cavity of the neural tube ends up as the cerebral ventricles and the passages that connect them. (The morphology of the ventricular system was depicted in Figure 2-9.)

By the end of the eighth week the human embryo shows the rudimentary beginnings of most body organs. The rapid pace of development of the brain during this period is reflected in the fact that at the end of eight weeks the head is one-half the total size of the embryo. (Note that the developing human is called an embryo during the first ten weeks after fertilization; thereafter it is called a fetus.) Figure 3-4 (see p. 84) presents a sequence of views of the prenatal development of the human brain from weeks 10 through 41.

BOX 3-1 Molecular Genetics and Protein Synthesis

For the discussion of cell division and cell growth in this chapter, you need some basic knowledge of molecular genetics. You also need this knowledge to understand the mechanisms of hormonal action (Chapter 5) and of memory formation (Chapter 15). If you are familiar with molecular genetics—involving such topics as deoxyribonucleic acid (DNA), ribonucleic acid (RNA), the genetic code, messenger RNA (mRNA), protein synthesis, and ribosomes—then you can skip this box.

● **The encoding of genetic information** In 1953 James D. Watson and Francis H. C. Crick announced one of the major discoveries of this century: the structure of the genetic code of the cell. People already knew that the genetic information of the cell was somehow encoded in long complex molecules of DNA. But the precise structure of these molecules and the way in which they hold genetic information were still a mystery. Nor did scientists know how this information is used to govern the synthesis of the thousands of different proteins that the cell manufactures. Watson and Crick's discovery led to research that clarified many aspects of cellular function and that yielded many applications in the control of disease. Even today the scientific community still cannot foresee all the ultimate consequences of this discovery.

A molecule of **deoxyribonucleic acid (DNA)** is built somewhat like a tall ladder, with long sides connected by rungs. The sides are twisted in spiral fashion so that the long molecule is a double helix (Box Figure 3-1). The sides are composed of repeating units, each consisting of a sugar (deoxyribose) and a phosphate group. There are four different kinds of rungs, as the figure shows. Each rung is composed of two groups called bases. The four bases in DNA are adenine (A), thymine (T), cytosine (C), and guanine (G). Adenine always links with thymine and cytosine always links with guanine. So if one half of a rung is A, the other is T. If one half is G, the other is C. A single base and the adjoining sugar-phosphate unit of the strand is called a **nucleotide.** The order in which the bases occur along a strand was found to encode the genetic information, as we will see next.

● Direction of protein synthesis by DNA and RNA
DNA carries instructions for the synthesis of molecules of protein, which are chains made up of hundreds (or even

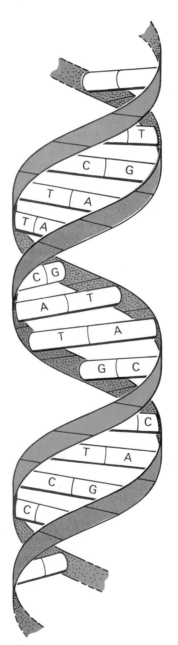

Box Figure 3-1 Diagram of a portion of a molecule of DNA. The rungs are made up of the four bases: adenine (A), thymine (T), cytosine (C), and guanine (G).

BOX 3-1   (continued)

thousands) of amino acids linked together. There are only 20 common amino acids that are incorporated into the proteins of all cells, but different sequences of them make it possible for there to be complex proteins with elaborate three-dimensional conformations. Three successive bases specify a particular amino acid. This is called a **triplet code.** A sequence of three bases is called a **codon.** There are also codons that signal the end of a chain.

The messages in a molecule of DNA must be conveyed accurately from the nucleus of the cell, where the DNA remains, out to the cytoplasm, where proteins are synthesized. This is done by means of a related compound, **ribonucleic acid (RNA).** RNA is a single strand with four kinds of bases. Three of the bases are the same as those in DNA. But in place of thymine, RNA has uracil (U). Also, the strands of RNA contain the sugar ribose instead of the deoxyribose found in DNA. (Ribose differs from deoxyribose in that it has one more atom of oxygen.)

RNA is said to "transcribe" a portion of the DNA molecule. In **transcription** the RNA forms a series of bases that are complementary to one of the two strands of DNA. Apparently the same strand of DNA is always the one that

is transcribed. Thus along a stretch of DNA with the sequence of bases TTCACG, the RNA transcribes the sequence AAGUGC. (AAG codes the amino acid lysine, and UGC codes cysteine.) The kind of RNA that carries the information out to the cytoplasm is called **messenger RNA (mRNA).** It goes to assembly points called **ribosomes,** where amino acids are linked together in the sequence specified by the mRNA molecule (Box Figure 3-2). This is called **translation** of the mRNA message into protein molecules.

Amino acids are conveyed to the ribosome by small molecules of RNA called **transfer RNA (tRNA).** Groups of ribosomes are called polyribosomes or polysomes. Some of these aggregate on the endoplasmic reticulum, which forms a network in the cytoplasm around the nucleus. The endoplasmic reticulum is what is colored by Nissl stains (recall Box Figure 2-4). Each strand of mRNA is translated by many ribosomes in succession and can direct the synthesis of thousands of molecules of protein. The formation of protein chains can be inhibited by various drugs. Some of these drugs have been used to test the hypothesis that synthesis of proteins is necessary for for-

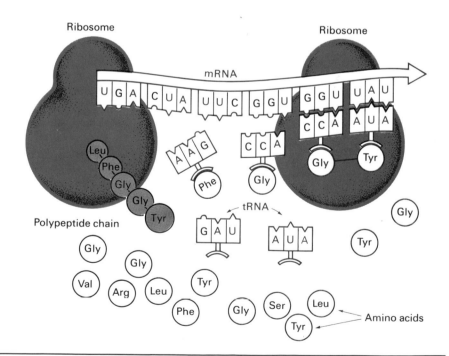

Box Figure 3-2 Translation of messenger RNA sequence into protein molecules.

mation of long-term memories. We will look at some of this research in Chapter 15.

At any given time mRNA molecules transcribe only particular portions of the long DNA molecule. The set of DNA molecules is the same in every cell of an individual's body. It contains the genetic instructions for heart, liver, kidney, skin, and so forth, as well as for different kinds of neurons. Therefore much of the information in DNA is never used by any individual cell. Most parts of the DNA molecule are kept from transcription and only small sections are made available to mRNA. Most of the length of DNA is covered by special proteins that are said to repress DNA. However, chemical reactions, some of them triggered by the arrival of hormones or neural messages, can unblock particular regions of DNA and thus cause **derepression** of a genetic message. Other reactions can activate regions of DNA and cause them to be transcribed. Thus chemical or neural signals can call for changes in the metabolic and structural activities of the cell.

● Duplication of DNA   As we have said, every cell in the body contains a full set of genetic information in the form of DNA. Therefore each time a cell divides, it must duplicate its DNA. Box Figure 3-3 illustrates the process of **duplication of DNA.**

1. The double strand of DNA separates into single strands when an enzyme breaks the bonds that have held the two bases of each rung together.

2. Then under the influence of other enzymes, each separated base attracts its complementary nucleotide (that is, a base attached to deoxyribose and a phosphate group).

3. When this process has proceeded along the entire length of the DNA strands, then the duplication (also called replication) is complete, and the new DNA is an exact copy of the original. Thus in division of somatic cells (the process called **mitosis**), the two cells receive identical genetic instructions.

Since differentiated neurons do not divide, their molecules of DNA must last a lifetime. There is evidence that there are mechanisms to repair DNA molecules over the life span of long-lived animals. Furthermore, species and

Box Figure 3-3 Duplication of DNA. (a) Part of a double-stranded molecule of DNA. (b) The two strands separate under the action of a special enzyme. (c) New complementary nucleotides attach to each base. (d) Two new molecules of DNA have been synthesized; both are identical to the original molecule.

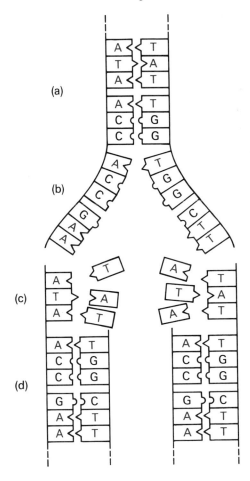

individuals differ in the rates at which they can repair errors in duplication of DNA. One hypothesis to account for aging is that it is the result of the gradual accumulation of uncorrected errors in an individual's molecules of DNA.

BOX 3-1 (continued)

The nucleus of each cell in the body (except sex cells) contains pairs of **chromosomes.** In human beings the 46 chromosomes consists of 22 different pairs (called **autosomes**) in which the two chromosomes are identical and one pair of **sex chromosomes.** In normal females the two sex chromosomes are identical (XX). But in normal males they are different (XY). Each chromosome consists of a molecule of DNA along with associated protein molecules. The sex cells or **gametes** differ from other cells in that they contain only 23 unpaired chromosomes. Since the gametes contain only half the usual number of chromosomes, they are called haploid cells. When gametes are formed, in the process called **meiosis** (or meiotic division), each gamete receives one chromosome of each pair. Therefore duplication of DNA is not required at this point.

Figure 3-4 Lateral views of the human brain during fetal development. Note the gradual process of development of gyri and sulci. The numbers show gestational ages in weeks. Brains are shown at one-third actual size. [From J.-C. Larroche, Chapter 11, Part II, "The development of the central nervous system during intrauterine life," Figure 1 (p. 258) and Figure 2 (p. 259). In F. Falkner (Ed.), *Human development* (Philadelphia, Pa.: W. B. Saunders, 1966).]

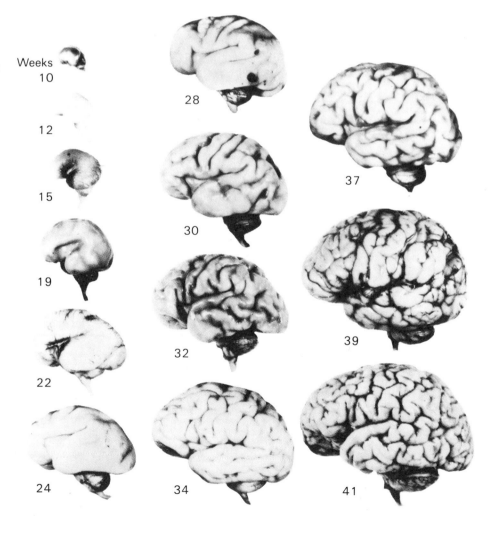

Cellular aspects of nervous system development

Four delicately controlled cellular processes underlie the gross anatomical changes in the nervous system during embryonic and fetal life: (1) cell proliferation, (2) cell migration, (3) cell differentiation, and (4) cell death. These events occur at different rates and times in different parts of the neural tube. (Our focus here is on the nervous system; however, similar events are, of course, involved in the formation of other organs.)

● Cell proliferation   The production of nerve cells is called **cell proliferation.** Nerve cells have their beginnings along the inner surface of the neural tube. Initially the walls of the neural tube are composed of a population of like cells. These cells gradually then form a closely packed layer, the **ventricular layer** of cells (ventricular cells) which keep on dividing (Figure 3-5). (The ventricular layer is also called the ependymal layer.) All neurons and glia are derived from a common kind of cell that originates in the ventricular layer. In most mammals the process of forming neural cells in the ventricular layer continues until birth, but very few are added after birth. In primates most cortical nerve cells have formed by the end of the sixth fetal month (Rakic, 1974). Postnatal additions of cells do occur in some instances, however, and we will see some examples of this later in this chapter.

● Cell migration   At some stage the nerve cells that form in the ventricular layer through mitotic division begin to move away. This process is known as **cell mi-**

Figure 3-5 Proliferation of cellular precursors of neurons and glia. Part (a) shows a small section of the wall of the neural tube at an early stage of embryonic development when only ventricular (V) and marginal (M) layers are seen. Later, as shown in (b), an intermediate (I) layer develops as the wall thickens. Part (c) shows the migration of nuclei of neurons from the ventricular layer to the outer layers. Some cells, however, return to the ventricular layer and undergo division, and then the daughter cells migrate to the outer layers.

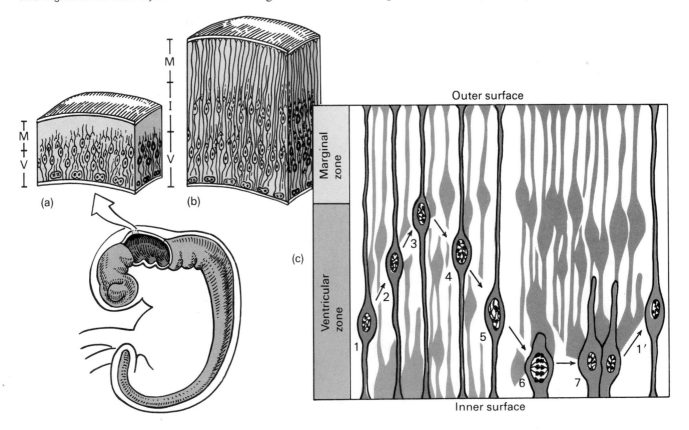

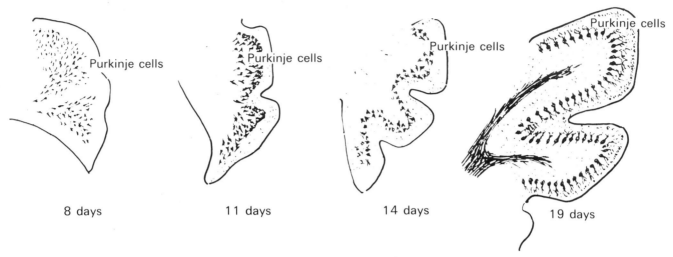

Figure 3.6 Migration of the precursors of the Purkinje cells of the chick cerebellum. At 8 days, these cells appear as a large group of "ants" streaming away from the region of the initial formation. At 11 days, these cells have begun to form a distinct layer. This layer becomes more spread out by 14 days, and at 19 days it is a single cell layer over an extended surface of tissue that has begun to form folds. (From Levi-Montalcini, 1963)

gration. Nerve cells at this stage are known as **neuroblasts.** They acquire short extensions at the "head" and "tail" ends. Some descriptions of the migrating cells compare them to a trail of active ants (Figure 3-6)! In primates the migration of nerve cells is virtually complete by birth. But in rat brains, nerve cells continue to migrate in some regions for several weeks following birth.

● Cell differentiation   At first, new nerve cells bear no more resemblance to mature nerve cells than they do to the cells of other organs. Once cells reach their destinations, however, they begin to acquire the distinctive appearance of neurons characteristic of their particular region. This process is **cell differentiation.** Figure 3-7 shows the progressive unfolding of Purkinje cells of the cerebellar cortex. Any given region in the mature nervous system contains a collection of nerve cells which may include two or more types. For example, in the cerebellar cortex there are Purkinje cells and granule cells. However, all the cells that migrate to a region are neuroblasts that at first look just alike. Thus a given neuroblast has the potentiality of being transformed into one of several different types of nerve cells.

The multiple potentialities of the growing neuroblast in any region seem to be programmed in an orderly fashion. One general rule that reflects this order is this: In a region that becomes organized into layers (for example, the cerebral cortex or cerebellar cortex) large cells are produced first, followed by small cells. Thus in the cerebellum the large Purkinje cells form first. When they are aligned in a row, the neuroblasts that will become the smaller granule cells begin to migrate.

Figure 3-7 Development of Purkinje cells in the human cerebellum at various fetal and postnatal ages, showing differentiation of form. (From Zecevic and Rakic, 1976)

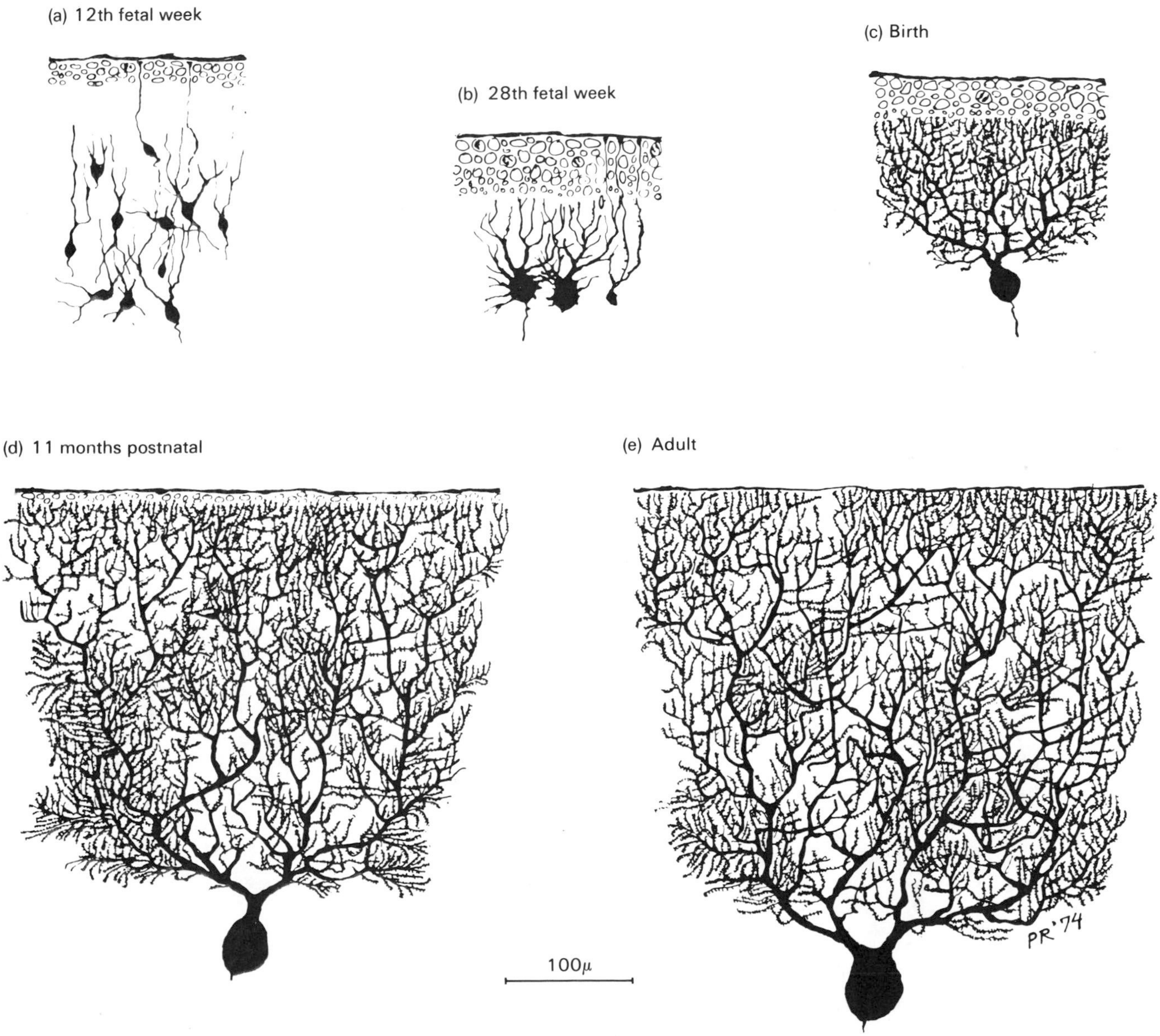

(a) 12th fetal week

(b) 28th fetal week

(c) Birth

(d) 11 months postnatal

(e) Adult

100μ

The formation of the typical shape of a neuron depends in part on determinants within the individual cell and in part on influences from neighboring cells. Some parts of a given cell grow in a typical manner no matter what the environment. Other components seem to respond to features of the environment in the brain, such as the presence of other cells.

● Cell death   The final process in the shaping of the neural system is, paradoxically, **cell death.** In some regions of the brain as much as 50% of the population of cells may die early in life! Several factors control this process. Among these is the size of the field on the body surface that will ultimately be connected to a region of the brain. For example, in tadpoles, if an investigator removes a leg before the connections from the spinal cord have formed, many more developing spinal motoneurons die than if the leg had remained in position. Grafting on an extra leg—which is possible in amphibians—appreciably reduces the usual loss of cells, so that the mature spinal cord has *more* than the usual number of neurons.

Another determinant of the pace and extent of cell death is the level of certain chemicals in the periphery of the body. (We will discuss one of these substances, nerve growth factor, later in this chapter.)

Developmental processes after birth

Between birth and maturity the human brain increases fourfold in weight and size. Similar changes from infancy to adulthood are also evident in cats, rabbits, rats, and other animals (Table 3-1). What kinds of postnatal changes in structure account for such growth in weight and size of the brain? Let us consider four types of structural changes at a cellular level that characterize brain development during early postnatal periods.

● Myelinization   The development of the sheath around axons—a process called **myelinization**— greatly changes the rate at which axons conduct messages. This should have a strong impact on behavior, since it greatly affects the temporal order of events in the nervous system. Unfortunately, there are few studies using both modern biological and behavioral techniques to relate biological attributes of the nervous system to changes in behavior. So the job of relating changes in behavior to myelinization is still open and in need of recruits.

In humans the most intense phase of myelinization occurs shortly after birth. (However, some investigators believe that myelin can be added to axons over the

TABLE 3-1   Increments in Brain Weight from Birth to Maturity in Some Mammalian Species

SPECIES	NEWBORN	ADULT	INCREMENT
Guinea pig	2.5 g	4 g	60%
Human	335 g	1300 g	290%
Cat	5 g	25 g	400%
Rabbit	2 g	10.5 g	425%
Rat	0.3 g	1.9 g	530%

SOURCE: From Altman (1967).

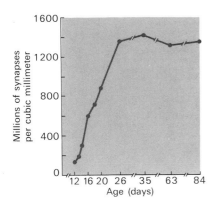

Figure 3-8 Increase in numbers of synapses per unit of volume of cortex as a function of age. This graph is based on synapses in layer I of the cortex of the rat. Although the number of synapses per unit of volume levels off at about 26 days after birth, the volume of the cortex continues to increase, so the total number of synapses also continues to rise. (Adapted from Aghajanian and Bloom, 1967)

entire course of life.) The first nerve tracts in the human nervous system to become myelinated are found in the spinal cord. Myelinization then spreads successively into the hindbrain, midbrain, and forebrain. The earliest myelinization in the peripheral nervous system is evident in cranial and spinal nerves about 24 weeks after conception. Within the cerebral cortex, sensory zones myelinate before motor zones; correspondingly, sensory functions mature before motor ones.

● Formation of synapses and dendrites   The biggest changes in brain cells from birth to maturity take place in the branches and connections among neurons. Figure 3-7 has already shown the huge increase in the length of dendrites, which seems to involve processes akin to those involved in the growth of axons. At the tips of dendrites there are growth cones, which are swollen ends from which extensions emerge. Some investigators have even found dendrite growth cones in adult animals. This can be related to the exciting finding that elongation of dendrites may continue throughout life in response to functional demands.

Synapses increase at a rapid rate, particularly on dendrites (Figure 3-8). In many nerve cells, synapses are formed at dendritic spines. The spines themselves proliferate rapidly after birth. These connections can be affected by postnatal experience, as we will see in Chapter 15. In order to support the metabolic needs of the expanded dendritic tree, the nerve cell body greatly increases in volume.

● Production of neurons after birth   Traditionally many investigators of nervous system ontogeny have believed that most mammals at birth have all the nerve cells they will ever have. They have explained the postnatal growth in the brain entirely in terms of growth in the size of neurons and the addition of nonneural (**glial**) cells. Within recent years, however, they have modified this belief, primarily because it now appears that small neurons are added for some period following birth. Some investigators have even argued that birth may trigger an acceleration in the rate of production of these small cells. This view has not gained wide support, however. Other investigators have argued that it is the maturity of the brain that determines the time of birth.

The most widely accepted current view is that all the larger neurons the brain will ever contain are there at birth. However, there are a few regions around the brain ventricles, called the subventricular zones, in which mitotic division of the precursors of nerve cells remains evident after birth. Several regions of the brain of rats, including the olfactory bulb and the hippocampus, appear to add small neurons derived from this region. In fact, it has been claimed (Graziadei and Monti-Graziadei, 1978) that nerve cells of the olfactory end organ are replaced throughout life.

● Formation of glial cells   Glial cells develop from the same populations of immature cells as neurons. The influences that determine whether the cell develops into a neuron or a glial cell remain a mystery. Unlike neurons, glial cells continue to be added throughout life. At times that process can become aberrant, resulting in glial tumors (gliomas) of the brain. The production of glia continues longer than the production of neurons and shows its greatest change later. In fact, the most intense phase of glial proliferation in many animals occurs after birth. After birth, glial cells are added from immature cells located in the subventricular zones.

Examples of the formation of neural regions

As we saw in Chapter 2, different regions of the brain have characteristic types of nerve cells arranged in distinctive patterns, such as layers. To show how a particular region acquires its characteristic orderly form, let us take the cerebellar cortex and the cerebral cortex as examples.

● **Formation of the cerebellar cortex**   As we saw earlier, the adult cerebellar cortex consists of a structure with numerous folds (called folia) and a laminar (layered) arrangement, as follows:

1. An outer molecular layer with small cells and a band of fibers (axons)

2. A middle layer of large cells (the Purkinje cell layer)

3. A deep, thick layer of very small cells—the granule cell layer

We saw this laminar arrangement of the adult cerebellum in Figure 2-29. The initial migration of cells that form the cerebellum involves the Purkinje cells, which initially are small and scattered but which later become a single, uniform row of large cells (Figure 3-9).

In human beings, Purkinje cells grow most rapidly between late pregnancy and about a year after birth. In the rat, they grow most rapidly after birth, from day 2 to day 30. After the Purkinje cells arrive on the scene, the smaller cells of the cerebellum form. Initially their migratory pattern takes them to the external granular

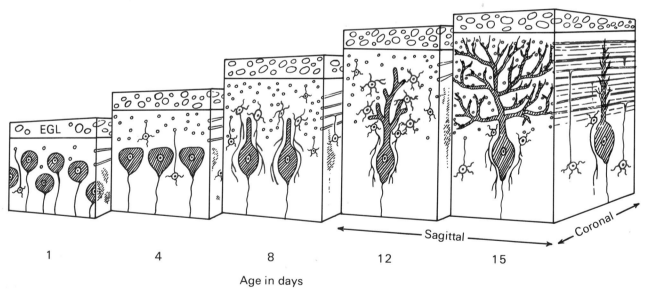

Age in days

Figure 3-9 Schematic drawings of the development of cells in the cerebellum of the rat, emphasizing the maturation of Purkinje cells. EGL stands for the external granule layer to which cells migrate during early cerebellar development. By postnatal day 4, the Purkinje cells are arranged in a single layer. From day 4 through day 7, basket cells develop (shown in blue at day 8), and the main dendrite of the Purkinje cell grows toward the surface of the cerebellum. From day 8 through day 11, stellate cells form (shown in blue at day 12), and the main branches of the Purkinje cell dendrites grow. From day 12 on, a large number of granule cells form (shown in blue in the day 15 block); the granule bodies migrate down below the Purkinje cells but their axons form the parallel fibers that synapse with the small spiny branches of the Purkinje dendritic tree. (Adapted from Altman, 1976)

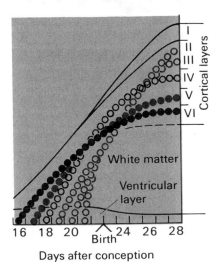

Figure 3-10 Migration of cells into cerebral cortex in the rat. Cortical cells of the rat originate and start their migration before birth. The earliest cells to originate migrate to the lowest layers of the cortex; the cells produced in the few days before birth form the upper cell layers (II and III). Migration of cells to the upper layers continues for several days after birth. (Adapted from Berry, Rogers, and Eayrs, 1964)

surface. They then descend around and past the Purkinje cells to form the deeper cell populations. The fact that in the rat most of the development of the cerebellum occurs after birth has made these developmental processes relatively easy to study. Any of a number of treatments, including mild exposure to X rays, interferes with newly developing neuroblasts but does not harm cells that are already differentiated or that are relatively mature.

Three different populations of small cells develop in sequence: basket cells, stellate cells, and granule cells. Altman (1976) exposed young rats to X rays over the course of a few days, which prevented the development of one or more kinds of these small cells in the rats' brains. This had disastrous consequences for the development of the large dendritic fan of the Purkinje cells.

Giving a burst of irradiation on each of days 4 through 7 prevents the formation of basket cells. This in turn prevents the regular upward growth of the main dendrite of the Purkinje cells; the main dendrites may grow in any direction and become twisted. Irradiation on days 8 through 11 prevents formation of the stellate cells and thereby interferes with growth of the main branches of the Purkinje cell dendrites. Finally, irradiation on days 12 through 15 reduces the number of granule cells and diminishes the complex branching of the dendritic tree of the Purkinje cells (Altman, 1976). The irradiation also produces behavioral effects; it interferes with posture, and impairment of maze learning has also been reported (Pellegrino and Altman, 1977).

● Formation of the cerebral cortex   The 50 billion neurons of the human cerebral cortex are arranged in layers, the cells of each layer differing in form and size. This arrangement of layers shows variations in different parts of the brain. These variations have been used to define the borders of different cortical regions. Here we will look at the way the cerebral neocortex grows and achieves this distinctive layered organization.

Examining the closed neural tube of a human embryo at the end of the third week after fertilization reveals a zone of cells all around the inner surfaces. This early proliferation of cells at the rostral end results in the formation of the cortical plate, the beginnings of the cerebral cortex. Intense cell division at this end continues to produce cells that will in time become the neurons of the cerebral cortex. This rapid proliferation continues until the sixth month of fetal life, by which time the cerebral cortex has its full complement of neurons. They are now aligned in layers, although they scarcely resemble the cortical layers that you see in the adult brain.

The formation of cell layers in the cerebral cortex follows a regular process, although the guiding mechanisms remain controversial. Cells that are formed along the ventricular (ependymal) surface migrate away from it. Each new cell migrates beyond those born earlier (Figure 3-10). Thus new cells move closer to the cortical surface. The oldest cells are found at the deepest layer. The generation time—the mitotic cycle for the production of a cortical cell—is about 11 hours and remains constant throughout the development of the cortex. However, migration time—the interval between cell birth and arrival at its final position—becomes progressively longer. This time is about five days for the last group of new cortical cells. The most intense phase of dendritic growth and synapse formation in the cerebral cortex occurs after birth.

Why neural connections go where they go

All members of a species generate similar types of nerve cells. Furthermore, these cells have a characteristic arrangement. This order is evident in the ways in which the cells are grouped together in different brain regions. The structural feature that is of particular interest for behavior is the orderliness and specificity of connections among individual cells and among regions. Clearly the adaptive behavior of any animal depends on how the brain is "wired"—that is, on the ways in which connections are formed. Is the process of the formation of connections an unvarying one, specified by mechanisms controlled by the genetic machinery? Three current answers to this question can be summarized as follows:

1. The main connections that form during development are closely specified by innate mechanisms.

2. Detailed aspects of central connections can be modified by training or experience.

3. There is intense competition among individual neurons and among groups of neurons to form connections, so that if some units are inhibited or removed, their connections are taken over by adjacent neurons.

Let us examine some of the research that has given rise to these conclusions.

Billions of nerve cells, all growing at once, somehow manage to make appropriate connections with each other and to form the intricate circuits that mediate complex behavior. One neuron sends out an axon that is less than a millimeter long. Another neuron sends its axon along a particular tract for more than a meter. At the end of its path each axon forms connections at specific sites within a specific brain region. Indeed, some axons terminate on particular *portions* of the dendrites of specific nerve cells. When you think about this formation of pathways and connections in the nervous system, it seems as though each nerve cell has instructions about a particular address, a site at which it must establish connections. How can we account for the highly ordered connections that are formed during the development of the brain?

Pioneering research on this complex problem was done by Roger Sperry, an American neuropsychologist and neuroembryologist who was awarded a Nobel Prize in 1981. In the 1940s he started a series of experimental observations of the visual systems of amphibia and fish. These studies capitalized on the remarkable abilities of these animals to regenerate tissue, including neural tissue. As we will see, many studies of neural development concern the visual system, partly because vision plays such an important role in behavior, and partly because of the orderly spatial projection of the visual field, from the retina up through the visual centers of the brain (Figure 3-11). Later we will see that development of the visual system in mammals is clearly influenced by early experience with visual stimuli.

Layout of the amphibian visual system

To understand some of Sperry's main experimental observations, let us briefly consider the layout of the visual system in amphibia and fish. The **retina** is a population of photosensitive elements that provides a map of the visual world (Figure 3-11). The axons of the output nerve cells in the retina form the **optic nerve.** In amphibia these fibers cross to the opposite side of the brain and terminate in an orderly way in a structure called the **optic tectum.** This is the chief neural center for vision in these animals. The surface of the tectum provides, in a sense, a map of the

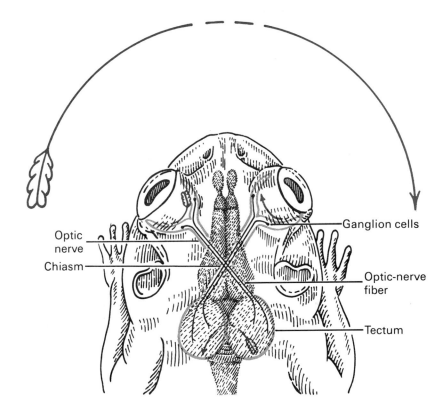

Figure 3-11 An outline of the frog's visual system. The visual field is represented by the large arrow in front of the frog's head. The lateral parts of the field stimulate the nasal parts of the retinas; the central part of the field stimulates the temporal parts of the retinas. The output of the retina (the axons of ganglion cells) is directed to the tectum on the opposite side of the head. Temporal parts of the retina project to rostral parts of the tectum and nasal parts of the retina go to more caudal regions. Upper parts of the retina (not shown in this illustration), also called dorsal, are directed to lateral portions of the tectum, and lower parts of the retina (ventral) go to medial portions of the tectum.

retina. Thus an object at a given place in the outside world excites a particular place in the retina, which in turn activates a specific locus in the optic tectum. It almost seems as if each point in the retina "knows," or becomes aware in the course of development, which place to connect to in the optic tectum. One could imagine that there is some sort of a label in each growing axon that tells the axon where to go.

The initial studies of Sperry (and others) did not require any fancy anatomical or physiological tools. Instead, experimenters let the visual behavior of amphibia tell the experimenter about connections in the brain that are related to perceptions of visual space. Many amphibians show highly stereotyped responses to visual stimuli. They correctly orient toward and attack small moving objects with the flick of a tongue, especially when the objects resemble small insects like flies. Therefore their responses can be used to reveal the representation of the visual field in the brain.

Specificity of retinal-tectal connections

In initial experiments Sperry cut the optic nerve and watched the way visually guided behavior reappeared. After the nerve fibers grew back to the optic tectum (a period of months), the animals were able to perform just as accurately as before! What does the restoration of this behavioral response imply about the reestablishment of connections between the retina and the optic tectum? Two alternative possibilities must be considered:

1. The regrowing axons enter the tectum in a tangle of random connections, and

BOX 3-2 Degeneration and Regeneration of Nervous Tissue

When a nerve cell is injured, several forms of regrowth of mature nerve cells can occur. However, complete replacement of injured nerve cells is rare in mammalian nervous systems. Box Figure 3-4 illustrates several characteristic forms of degeneration and regeneration in the peripheral and central nervous system. Injury close to the

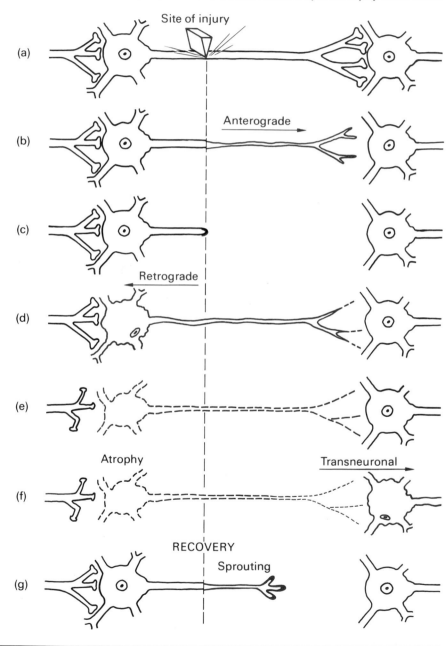

Box Figure 3-4 Types of degeneration of nerve cells. (a) Prior to injury. (b) and (c) Anterograde degeneration; injury causes loss of the distal section of the axon. (d) and (e) Retrograde degeneration. Injury also causes degeneration of the cell body, resulting in some cases in complete atrophy. (f) Transneuronal degeneration. Loss of input may produce changes in other cells in the pathway. (g) Recovery Injured axons may sprout new endings.

cell body of the neuron produces a series of changes that result in the eventual destruction of the cell. This process is called **retrograde degeneration**.

Transecting the axon at some distance from the cell body produces loss of the distal part of the axon (the part separated from continuity with the cell body). This process is called Wallerian or **anterograde degeneration**. The part of the axon that remains connected to the cell body may regrow. Severed axons in the peripheral nervous system regrow readily. Sprouts emerge from the part of the axon that is still connected to the nerve cell body and advance slowly toward the periphery. Some animals

have an enviable advantage. After an injury to the brain, several fish and amphibians appear to be able to regenerate large parts of the brain itself.

From an experimental point of view, our interest in regeneration of the nervous system lies principally in the fact that regeneration involves processes that seem similar to original development. Studying regeneration may thus increase our understanding of the original processes of growth of the nervous system. From a therapeutic viewpoint, these studies may help scientists learn how to induce repair and regrowth of damaged neural tissue in humans.

experience (success or failure in locating food) determines the survival of connections for reporting locations in space. That is, the networks are reeducated about location of objects.

2. Fibers in the nerve grow back to their original positions on the optic tectum and simply reestablish the original map of the visual world

Several now classic experiments enabled Sperry to choose between these alternatives. What he did was to rotate the eyes of a newt 180 degrees. This inverted the newt's visual field completely (Figure 3-12). Both up and down and right and left were reversed. After the visual connections regenerated, the animal's behavior was found to be reversed: When a small lure was presented in the upper half of the visual field, the tongue flicked down. When the lure was presented near the nasal portion of the horizontal axis, the animal aimed to the side. These reversals of behavior persisted for years! Despite the fact that these responses were markedly maladaptive, there was no apparent "reeducation" of location behavior.

These observations led Sperry to conclude that the regenerating optic axons reconnect to their original positions in the tectum. They recreate a pattern of orderly connections. Sperry's explanation has come to be known as the doctrine of **neurospecificity.** He argued that during the differentiation of the cells of the retina, each cell acquires a unique identity. It becomes specified, as though it had a label relating it to a certain position in the animal's visual field (Figure 3-13a). Axons emerging from such cells, according to Sperry, are unique biochemically. When they reach the tectum, they seek cells that have a similar chemical identity. There is thus a matching of cells according to a chemical label.

Limits to neurospecificity

Suppose that we were to extend the concept of neurospecificity to cover the genesis of all nervous system connections. That is, suppose that we maintained that there was virtually total, rigid, genetic specification of neural connections. We would run

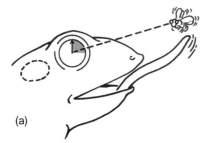

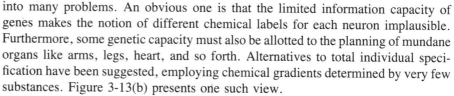

Figure 3-12 Vision with normal and rotated eyes. (a) Normal. (b) Eyes rotated 180°, reversing both the vertical and horizontal directions. (c) Exchange of right and left eyes, reversing vision right for left but preserving the vertical direction. (d) Left eye inverted and placed in right eye socket, inverting up for down but preserving the horizontal direction. In each case, the place where the animal strikes with its tongue shows where it perceives the target.

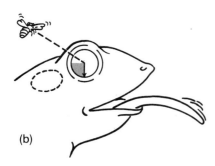

(a)

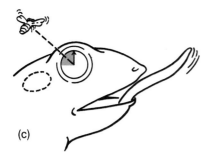

(b)

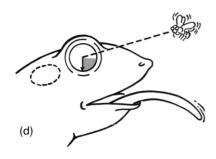

(c)

(d)

into many problems. An obvious one is that the limited information capacity of genes makes the notion of different chemical labels for each neuron implausible. Furthermore, some genetic capacity must also be allotted to the planning of mundane organs like arms, legs, heart, and so forth. Alternatives to total individual specification have been suggested, employing chemical gradients determined by very few substances. Figure 3-13(b) presents one such view.

Several experiments have also cast doubt on the likelihood that there is complete predetermined specification of all neural connections. These experiments have shown that there is some plasticity in retino-tectal connections. Such plasticity or adaptability suggests that, at the very least, it is possible that tectal neurons might be able to respecify their properties during the regrowth period. Good examples are the so-called size disparity experiments. To cite one such experiment, Yoon (1979) showed that when half of the tectum is removed, the entire retina will then map onto the remaining half tectum. This suggests that connections within the tectum are capable of modification.

Experiments on retino-tectal specificity also reveal that there is a kind of recognition process that may involve specific chemical agents. Attempts to ascertain the details of this process have directed attention to the molecular features of chemical recognition.

Rigid genetically predetermined invariance of neural connections may characterize only one class of neuron. Jacobson (1974) argued that control of neurons' development may vary between two classes of neurons: Class I neurons are large neurons, "born" early, with long axons. Jacobson suggests that these develop in ways that indicate rigid genetic specification. In contrast, Class II neurons are small neurons, born later, with more variable axon length. Jacobson believes that Class II neurons may be less completely specified genetically and thus more amenable to the impact of experience. This theory may account for some of the varying data, but it does not yet have a significant body of research to support it.

Determinants of brain growth and development

Many states, both internal and external, influence the emergence of the form, arrangements, and connections of the developing brain. In the case of development, as in the cases of some other topics that we will consider in later chapters, it is useful to think of both direct determinants and modulatory influences. A direct determinant (or intrinsic factor) is one that is involved in the basic processes that produce or control a phenomenon. In the development of the nervous system, certain genes and the processes they control are direct determinants. For example, some kinds of

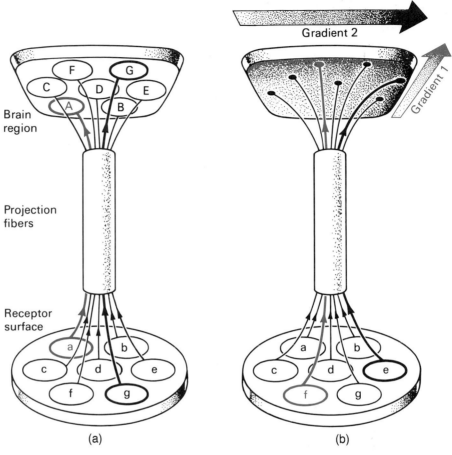

Figure 3-13 (a) Neurospecificity hypothesis of determinations of neural connections. Specific sites on the receptor surface are represented by different letters. Connections to the brain are made only to like sites (a to A, b to B, and so forth). Each position is coded by some unique state or chemical. (b) Chemical gradients as determinants of neural connections. Here connections are not defined by a specific unique chemical but by gradients of two dimensions (shown here by black and blue gradients). Every locus can be identified by a position on the two gradients.

neurons receive genetic instructions to form dendritic spines, whereas other kinds of neurons in the same organism never form spines. A modulatory influence (or extrinsic factor) is one that can either facilitate or inhibit basic processes but that does not directly control them. In the development of the nervous system, modulators such as nutrition and experience can influence the rate or extent of development. For example, in neurons that form dendritic spines, modulating factors determine how many spines are formed.

The effectiveness of modulating influences is often critically dependent on the stage of development at which they are present. A particular biochemical state present in the early life of an embryo may exert vastly different influences than the same state present during fetal development or early postnatal stages. In this section we will discuss some examples of intrinsic and extrinsic factors that can exert significant influence in the development of brain structure. We will not give an exhaustive list but only describe a few well-investigated phenomena.

Genetic determinants

Geneticists are embarked on an ambitious program designed to find genetic determinants not only of bodily structure but also of behavior. The geneticist Seymour Benzer (1973) describes this program as follows. Geneticists analyze four levels and processes that control transitions from one level to the next:

1. Genetic information is coded in a unidimensional sequence in each gene. (See Box 3-1.)

2. This genetic information determines the development of the two-dimensional array of cells in the blastocyst.

3. This hollow ball of cells develops into the three-dimensional organism with its nervous system, muscles, glands, sensory receptors, and other organs.

4. These complex structures give the organism its capacities to interact with the environment—to behave in a multidimensional way.

Not much of this vast scientific program has yet been realized. But in this section we will see some promising attempts to find genetic determinants for development of the nervous system and of behavior.

Genes are not, of course, the only influences that shape bodily structure and behavior. Experience and environment do so too. It is hard to differentiate the roles of genes and experience in the structural and functional development of the nervous system. However, intensive experimentation in this field, which some researchers call neurogenetics, has begun to reveal examples of genetic control of brain structure and function.

Selective breeding procedures have been used for years by scientists and farmers to produce distinctive animals. These techniques have also been used by researchers in behavioral genetics, who have charted changes of behavior through generations. Use of these techniques with simpler animals has begun to connect genetic effects on the nervous system with effects on behavior. Bentley (1976) has shown that the calling songs of crickets have intricate patterns that can be manipulated by selective breeding. These song patterns change in distinctive ways as genes of a particular type are introduced by controlled mating through several generations. Recordings made from neurons in the crickets' nervous system reveal that the genetically controlled variability in songs is directly related to the impact of genes in changing the arrangements of neural networks.

An unusual breeding technique is one that produces genetically identical animals called **clones,** which used to be known mainly in science fiction and horror films. But life imitates fiction! Studies of the genetics of the development of the nervous system are using carbon copy creatures. Researchers develop these animals by means of asexual reproduction, and all offspring have the same genes. Using clones of grasshoppers, Goodman (1979) compared the uniformity and variability in the growth and development of different neurons. Although the basic shape of larger cells showed considerable uniformity, many neurons of cloned grasshoppers showed variability in the fine branching patterns. Occasionally extra cells also appeared. Differences in cell structure among clones also contributed to physiological differences in cell responsiveness. Thus even animals with identical heredity do not possess identical fine structure of neurons.

Sometimes nature, with the help of researchers, produces unusual animals which show a sudden change in genetic structure, a mutation that is related to marked anatomical or physiological change. These effects may appear in the course of selective breeding, especially in highly inbred strains, or may result from exposure to toxic substances that produce genetic changes.

Mutants—animals that display these changes—are interesting to study because their suddenly changed genetic characteristics may be quite specific and striking. This gives evidence of genetic controls in their development that are more subtle in other animals. For example, Dudai and Quinn (1980) described mutants of the fruit fly *Drosophila* that had memory problems. These mutants—affectionately labeled "Dunce," "Amnesiac," and "Turnip"—either failed to learn or *could* learn but forgot rapidly. New evidence points to a biochemical deficit in one of these mutants that might account for failures of memory.

Many mutants of *Drosophila* have highly specialized defects in some part of the nervous system (Hall and Greenspan, 1979). The strength of research on *Drosophila* mutants derives from the wealth of specific mutations, each one involving a distinct impaired development process. For example, a lethal *Drosophila* mutant, "Notch," has an enlarged nervous system because too many precursor cells are produced. Studies of this mutant may enable researchers to attain a better understanding of processes that control the number of cells produced during early embryological development.

Over 150 mutations in mice involve the nervous system (Sidman, Green, and Appel, 1965). In these animals special defects appear during the development of the nervous system. Some mice fail to grow in particular brain regions. Others show specific anatomical derangements, such as a failure to myelinate or to arrange cells in their characteristic alignments. One group of mutants, especially intriguing to researchers, all have impairments due to single genes that affect the postnatal development of the cerebellum. The names of these animals—"Reeler," "Staggerer," and "Weaver"—reflect the locomotor impairment that characterizes these animals. The impact of these genes on the size and arrangement of the cerebellum is illustrated in Figure 3-14. The cerebellum of Reeler shows an abnormal positioning of cells. There are no characteristic layers in the cerebellum, hippocampus, and cerebral cortex. Strangely, although cells of these regions are in abnormal positions, many connections to these cells are appropriate (Caviness, 1980). The cerebellum of Weaver has far fewer granule cells than a normal cerebellum, which might arise from a failure of these cells to migrate or form appropriate connections. Atrophy of the cerebellum is also evident in Staggerer, according to Sotelo (1980), who has shown that this animal fails to form synaptic connections between granule cells and Purkinje cells. The axon of the granule cell—the parallel fiber—comes close to the dendritic surface of the Purkinje cell, but postsynaptic specializations simply do not develop. Each of these mouse mutants shows impairment due to a single gene, related to the development of a specific kind of cell. Studies of these animals are bringing deeper understanding of the processes of neural development and their behavioral consequences.

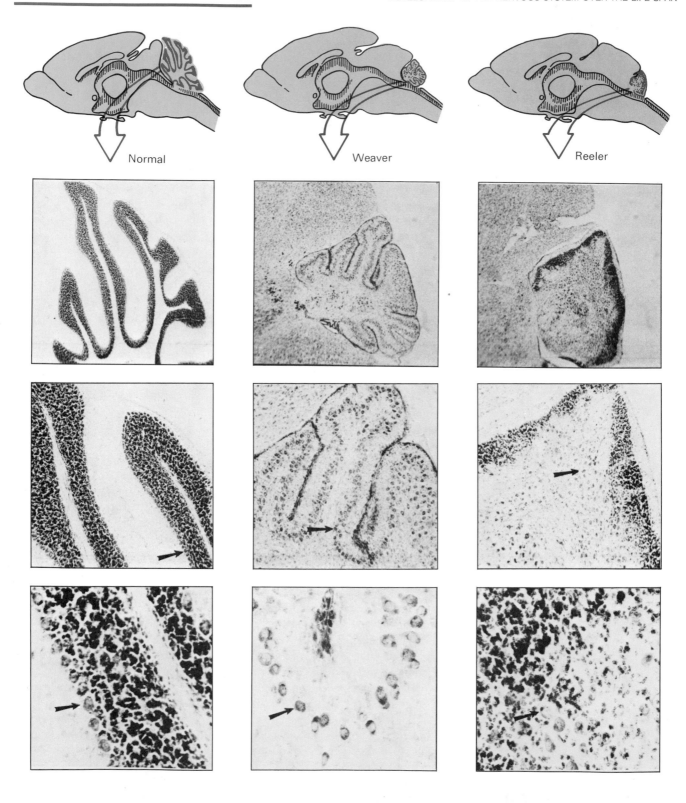

Biochemical influences

The brain consists of many different cell groups that develop at different times. The rules that orchestrate the emergence of this complex structure are undoubtedly elaborate. But one notion that all investigators share is that various bodily substances regulate this process.

This section gives examples of two kinds of biochemical conditions that regulate neural growth. An example of intrinsic control is **nerve growth factor (NGF),** a substance that seems to control development of a particular class of nerve cells. An example of extrinsic biochemical influence is the role of nutrition in brain growth.

● Nerve growth factor   More than twenty years ago investigators discovered a substance that markedly affects the growth of neurons of spinal ganglia and of the ganglia of the sympathetic nervous system (Levi-Montalcini, 1982). This substance is nerve growth factor. Originally, it was found in a variety of unusual places, including the salivary glands of mice, certain skin tumors, and the venom of a snake. More recently precise biochemical techniques have revealed its presence in the nervous system. Researchers found that if they administered NGF to an animal fetus, it resulted in the formation of sympathetic ganglia with many more cells than usual. These cells were also larger and had many extensive processes (Figure 3-15). If they administered it postnatally, NGF produced enlarged sympathetic nervous system cells. More recently it has been shown that nerve growth factor can reverse the degenerative effects of a drug that selectively destroys brain cells containing particular synaptic transmitters.

Part of the interest in NGF arises from the possibility that it is an example of control mechanisms in the development of the nervous system. There may be many such substances, each one controlling a particular cell type at a specific developmental period.

● Nutrition and brain growth and development   The good fortune of having adequate nutrition is not uniformly shared by people throughout the world. Periodic starvation confronts many, and this problem grows more urgent as population growth threatens to overwhelm the food resources of many nations. For many years people believed that the brain was less susceptible to the effects of diet than other parts of the body. It is certainly true that the adult brain is much less affected by dieting or overeating than are most other organs. But there is now evidence that malnutrition is detrimental to the brain, especially during early development. In fact, various forms of malnutrition that occur during critical growth periods of the brain in humans and other animals can produce irreversible changes in brain structure (Winick, 1976). Relating these cerebral changes to behavior is a complicated issue. It is hard to disentangle the effects of social disadvantage from the effects of dietary deficiencies, since most of these studies involve mothers and infants living in impoverished circumstances (Balderston et al., 1981).

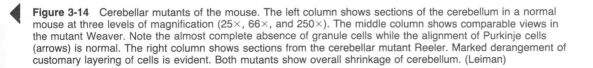

Figure 3-14   Cerebellar mutants of the mouse. The left column shows sections of the cerebellum in a normal mouse at three levels of magnification (25×, 66×, and 250×). The middle column shows comparable views in the mutant Weaver. Note the almost complete absence of granule cells while the alignment of Purkinje cells (arrows) is normal. The right column shows sections from the cerebellar mutant Reeler. Marked derangement of customary layering of cells is evident. Both mutants show overall shrinkage of cerebellum. (Leiman)

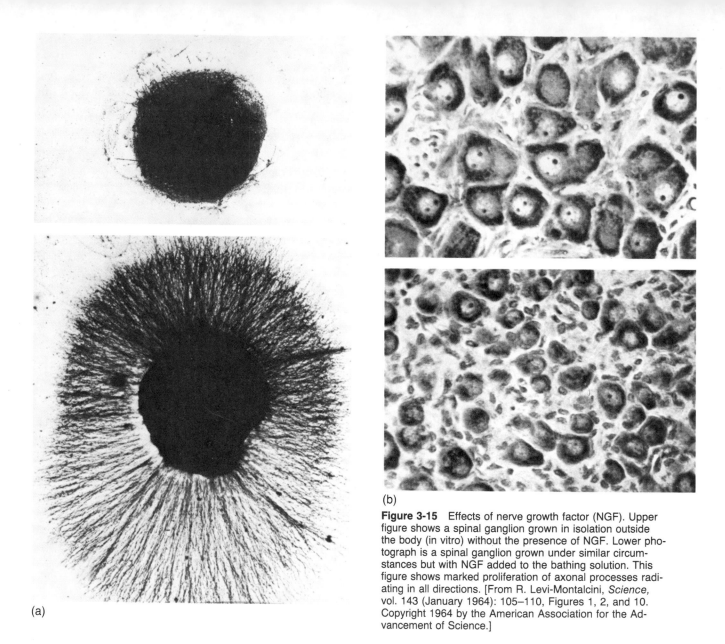

(a)

(b)

Figure 3-15 Effects of nerve growth factor (NGF). Upper figure shows a spinal ganglion grown in isolation outside the body (in vitro) without the presence of NGF. Lower photograph is a spinal ganglion grown under similar circumstances but with NGF added to the bathing solution. This figure shows marked proliferation of axonal processes radiating in all directions. [From R. Levi-Montalcini, *Science*, vol. 143 (January 1964): 105–110, Figures 1, 2, and 10. Copyright 1964 by the American Association for the Advancement of Science.]

We have learned something about the effects of early malnutrition from studies that compared undernourished children with matched controls who had no early nutritional deficiency. Studies in Mexico, Chile, Yugoslavia, and South Africa have shown that early malnourishment reduces later performance on many kinds of tests of mental capacity (Tizard, 1974). Malnourishment occurs more commonly in families that live in the kind of poverty that also poses other potent barriers to children's development. However, many of these studies show that later behavioral impairment depends on the time of life at which the child underwent a period of malnutrition. Children have a greater chance of behavioral recovery if the malnutrition occurred later rather than earlier in life.

The effects of severe early malnutrition can be counteracted to a large extent by nutritional and behavioral rehabilitation, especially if it begins by the age of 2 and is maintained into adolescence (Winick, Meyer, and Harris, 1975; Nguyen, Meyer, and Winick, 1977). This research was done with Korean orphans who were adopted by middle-class American families. All the children came from orphanages and were less than 5 years old when they were adopted. The study was done retrospectively; that is, it was based on records available when the children were adolescent. The children were divided into three groups according to their height at the time of admission to the agency:

1. Severely malnourished, below the 3rd percentile (according to Korean norms)

2. Moderately malnourished, from the 3rd through the 24th percentiles

3. Well-nourished, at or above the 25th percentile

The malnourished groups developed well in their adoptive families, and they all came to exceed Korean norms of height and weight, although not reaching American norms. In IQ and school achievement tests the means for all three groups adopted by the age of 2 later exceeded American means (Figure 3-16). Among those adopted after the age of 2, the children in group 1 (who suffered from severe early malnutrition) did not quite reach American norms, but children in the other two groups did. Although some differences related to their early malnutrition persisted, these differences were rather small. This is an important study because it demonstrates that the effects of severe early malnutrition can largely be overcome, if rehabilitation starts early and is kept up.

The critical importance of early malnutrition with respect to later impairment of mental capacities has been emphasized in neuroanatomical and neurochemical studies. Dobbing (1974) stresses the fact that the brain is most vulnerable to malnutrition during the period of rapid brain growth. These periods vary for different animals

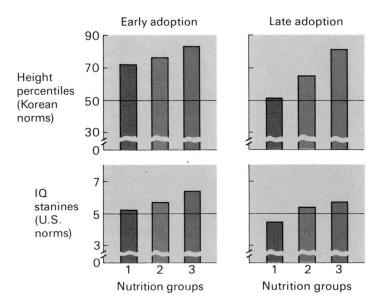

Figure 3-16 Effects of early and late adoption of malnourished infants on growth, intelligence, and achievement. Nutrition groups: 1, severely malnourished upon admission to adoption agency; 2, moderately malnourished; and 3, well-nourished. (Early adoption results from Winick, Meyer, and Harris, 1975; late adoption results from Nguyen, Meyer, and Winick, 1977)

Figure 3-17 Rate of development of the brain in relation to birth. The time scale is different for various animals, ranging from days to months. This figure shows that the peak periods for brain development are quite different for various animals. The rat, for example, shows mainly postnatal increments of brain weight. In contrast, the main development of the guinea pig brain occurs before birth. (Adapted from Dobbing, 1972)

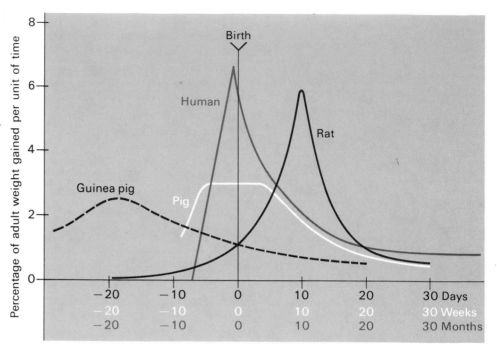

(Figure 3-17). In humans the period of fastest brain growth and, according to Dobbing, maximum vulnerability to malnutrition occurs in late pregnancy and the first months of postnatal life. Similar malnutrition in the adult produces negligible effects.

Some permanent effects of malnutrition during early periods of rapid brain growth have been shown in experiments with animals. Body size and weight as well as brain structure and behavior are affected (Dobbing, 1974). For example, the size of the cerebellum in rats is especially sensitive to postnatal malnutrition, since this structure forms mainly just after birth in the rat.

Experience and brain development

The young of many species are born in a highly immature state, both anatomically and behaviorally. For example, in humans the weight of the brain at birth is only one-fourth of its adult weight. Behaviorally, the infants of many species are totally dependent on the parents. In these species developments in brain and in behavior seem to vary together. According to recent studies, the successes and failures of early experience can affect the growth and development of brain circuits.

Varying experience during an individual's early development has been found to alter many aspects of behavior, brain anatomy, and brain chemistry (Gottlieb, 1976; Rosenzweig and Bennett, 1977, 1978). Interpretation of these findings suggests that experience can play three different roles in development and that it is important to distinguish among them: It can *induce* development, it can *modulate* development, and it can *maintain* ongoing development or results (Figure 3-18).

Induction of development is the most impressive possible role of experience. Some experimental treatments, such as administration of sex hormones early on, can channel development into the male or the female body type (as we will see in Chapter 9). But can experience have an equally striking role? Evidence is scant, but **imprinting** may be an example of experiential induction of a behavior pattern. For example, male mallard ducklings were raised for their first 8–10 weeks with other duck species. As mature drakes, they were given the choice of mating with mallard ducks or with ducks of the species with which they had been raised. Whereas normally reared mallards all choose mallards, about two-thirds of the experimental animals chose the other species (Schutz, 1965).

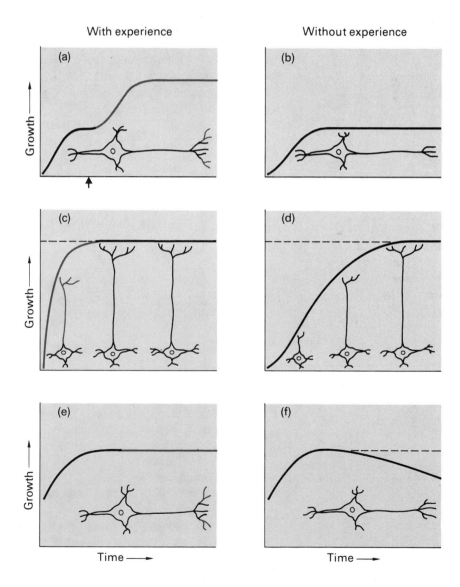

Figure 3-18 Schematic illustration of different kinds of effects of experience on brain development. (a) versus (b) Experience can *induce* changes—here the growth of a set of axon terminals. (c) versus (d) Experience can *modulate* development—here causing growth to reach a plateau earlier. (e) versus (f) Experience can maintain growth —here the endings decline unless experience occurs.

When it comes to experience modulating development, we have more evidence. There can be negative as well as positive effects. For instance, "Exposure to certain sounds can either accelerate or decelerate hatching time in quail embryos. . . . Prior exposure to light facilitates the young chick's behavioral approach to a flickering light, whereas prior exposure to sound delays the approach to a source of visual flicker . . ." (Gottlieb, 1976, p. 32).

The role of experience in maintaining development has been shown in experiments with the visual system, as we will see below. Sensory deprivation that begins shortly after birth and continues for several weeks can cause some of the developing cells to atrophy. "If you don't use it, you'll lose it."

● Visual deprivation and disuse   Some people do not see forms clearly with one eye, even though it is intact and a sharp image is focused on the retina. Such impairments of vision are known as **amblyopia** (from Greek words for "dull" or "blunt" and for "vision"). An example of this disorder is seen in persons with a "lazy eye": one that is turned inward (cross-eyed) or outward. Some children are born with this kind of misalignment of eyes. They "see double" rather than seeing a single fused image. If the deviated eye is not surgically realigned by the time the person reaches late childhood, vision becomes dimmed. By the time the person reaches adulthood, there is virtually total suppression of pattern vision in the deviated eye. Realignment of the eyes in adulthood does not restore acute vision to the turned eye. This is quite striking, since throughout the person's development light enters this eye in a normal manner and the nerve cells of the eye continue to be excited. Similar misalignment of the eyes, when it appears for the first time in adulthood, produces double vision; the eye sees two quite separate images. This condition shows no change with further aging. These clinical observations of humans suggest that unusual positioning of the eyes during early development might change connections or circuits in the brain.

Other forms of amblyopia can be more subtle. Partial deprivation of form vision for long periods during childhood can result in deficits that persist even when the optical problems are corrected by eyeglasses in adulthood. This is especially likely to occur when defects are partial or subtle and not easily assessed in young children. Astigmatism is a visual disorder in which lines at some orientations do not appear as clear as lines at other orientations. This happens when the shape of the eyeball is not exactly spherical. Children with such a disability are partially deprived of visual input, since they do not receive clear stimuli in certain directions. Later in life, when their astigmatism is discovered, eyeglasses cannot provide completely adequate correction. Since this abnormal visual input started early in life, brain circuits were apparently changed in a lasting way.

Understanding the cause of amblyopia in people has been greatly advanced by visual-deprivation experiments with animals. These experiments have revealed some startling changes that are related to disuse of the visual system during early critical periods. Depriving animals of light to both eyes (binocular deprivation) produces structural changes in visual cortical neurons. Animals reared without visual input show a loss of dendritic spines and a reduction in synaptic density. Cragg (1975) emphasized that these effects occur most extensively during the early period of synaptic development in the visual cortex (Figure 3-19).

Figure 3-19 Brain development in the visual cortex of the cat. Synaptic development occurs most intensely 8–37 days after birth, a period during which use can have profound influence. Note also that brain weight and cell volume rise in a parallel fashion and precede synaptic development. (Adapted from Cragg, 1975)

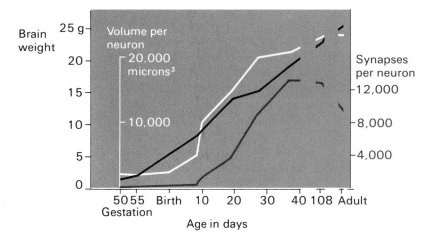

Pioneering work by Hubel and Wiesel, who shared a Nobel Prize in 1981, showed that restricting the deprivation of light to one eye (monocular deprivation) produces much more profound structural and functional changes in the visual cortex. Depriving an infant cat or monkey of vision in one eye leads to an absence of response by the deprived eye when the animal reaches adulthood. This is illustrated by a graph, usually called an **ocular-dominance histogram,** that portrays the strength of a neuron's response to stimuli presented to either the left or the right eye. Most cortical neurons are excited equally by input to either eye (Figure 3-20). Fewer neurons are activated solely by inputs to one eye. When there has been monocular deprivation during an animal's early development, there is a striking shift in this graph. Most cortical nerve cells respond only to input to the nondeprived eye. In cats the susceptible period for this effect occurs during the initial 4 months of life. In nonhuman primates the sensitive period is extended to age 6 months. The mechanisms proposed for this effect bring us to a possible understanding of the forms of amblyopia described at the beginning of this section. It has been suggested that during a person's early development, axons representing input from each eye "compete" for synaptic places. Active, used synapses become effective connections and predominate over inactive, disused synapses.

Researchers also offer an explanation like this to account for amblyopia produced by misalignment of the eyes. An animal replica of this human condition was produced by cutting muscles on one side of the eye in young cats (Hubel and Wiesel, 1965). The ocular-dominance histogram of these animals reveals that cells of the visual cortex show binocular sensitivity that is greatly reduced. A much larger proportion are excited by stimulation of either right or left eye than can be seen in control animals. This effect occurs because after surgery the cells of the visual cortex do not receive synchronous input from both eyes.

● Early exposure to visual patterns   At birth the visual cortex is quite immature, and most synapses have yet to form. This raises the question of whether early experience affects the development of the visual cortex. Evidence cited in the previous section shows that profound disuse results in changes in both structure and

Figure 3-20   (a) Ocular dominance histogram of cells recorded from visual cortex of normal adult cats. (b) Ocular dominance histogram after early eye misalignment, that is, squint. (c) Ocular dominance histogram following monocular visual deprivation through the early critical period. (d) Ocular dominance histogram following binocular deprivation. (Adapted from Hubel and Wiesel, 1965; Wiesel and Hubel, 1965)

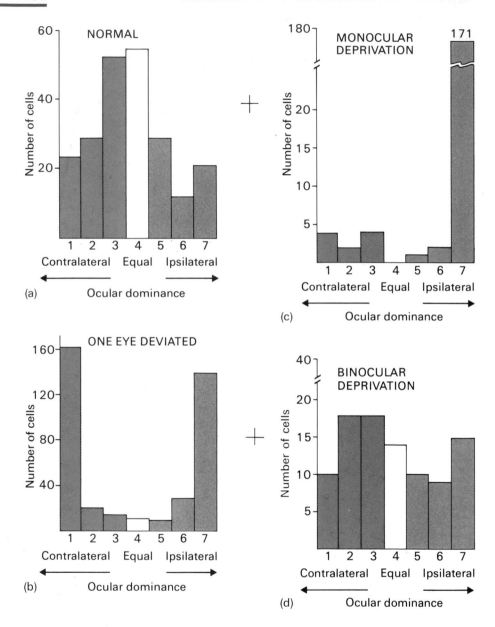

response of visual pathways. The modifiability of the developing brain is also evidenced when animals are exposed to certain visual patterns during early development.

Experiments in which visual patterns are manipulated early in an animal's life have used patterns such as horizontal or vertical lines (Blakemore, 1976; Figure 3-21b), a field of such stripes seen through goggles (Hirsch and Spinelli, 1971; Figure 3-21a), or small spots of light (Pettigrew and Freeman, 1973). This is a very controversial field. Some research groups report results that differ from those reported

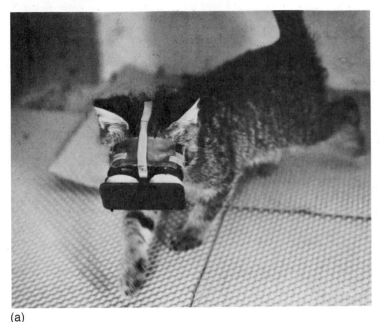

(a)

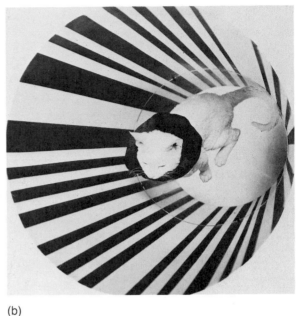

(b)

Figure 3-21 Methods used to restrict visual experience during development. (a) Kitten wearing a mask used to provide selective visual stimulation. The stimulus patterns are mounted on the inside surface of the black, rectangular sheet of plastic at the ends of the two white cylinders. (b) Kitten exposed to vertical stripes in a drum. [(a) From Hirsch and Spinelli, 1971. (b) From Blakemore, 1974.]

by others. Nevertheless, the weight of current results suggests that these various visual experiences during the critical early periods of life modify the responses of nerve cells in the visual cortex. The sensitive period for these effects is the same as that for producing the effects of monocular deprivation.

According to a detailed survey (Movshon and van Sluyters, 1981), the variety of experiments and results in this area fail to provide any simple or uniform conclusions. Various results support the hypotheses that sensory stimulation is required to induce development of the visual system, to modulate ongoing development, or to maintain development that is programmed genetically. It appears therefore that experience *can* play each of the three hypothesized roles in neural development.

● **Nonvisual experiences**   Effects of early experiences on the brain can also be produced by manipulating nonvisual sensory inputs—a rat's whiskers, for example. Thomas Woolsey and collaborators (1976, 1981) found a unique clustering of nerve cells in a region of the cerebral cortex of the rat that receives input from the vibrissae ("whiskers"). The arrangement of these hairs on the skin is distinctive. The hairs are aligned similarly for all animals of the same species (see Figure 3-22). In the region of the cortex in which the vibrissae are represented, Woolsey noted clusters of cells that he called barrels, because the way they were packed made them look like the walls of a barrel. Figure 3-22 also shows that the layout of these cortical barrels corresponds to the map of the vibrissae. If some vibrissae are cut one to four days after birth, their cortical barrels do not develop. However, the barrels that represent adjacent intact vibrissae tend to be enlarged.

Manipulating an animal's capacity to smell also affects its brain during developmental stages. Studies by Meisami (1978) showed that the two nostrils of rats are relatively independent, with cross connections evident only at the pharynx. When

Figure 3-22 Locations of whiskers and cortical barrels in young mice. Arrangements of barrels in the somatosensory cortex is shown on the right. (a) Each barrel receives its input from a single whisker on the opposite side of the mouse's snout. (b), (c) If one row of whiskers is destroyed shortly after birth (as indicated by the color dots), the corresponding row of barrels in the cerebral cortex later will be found to be missing and the adjoining barrels to be enlarged. (d) If all whiskers are destroyed, the entire group of barrels will have disappeared. The illustration is based on work of Thomas A. Woolsey of Washington University School of Medicine. (From W. M. Cowan, "The Development of the Brain." Copyright © 1979 by Scientific American, Inc. All rights reserved.)

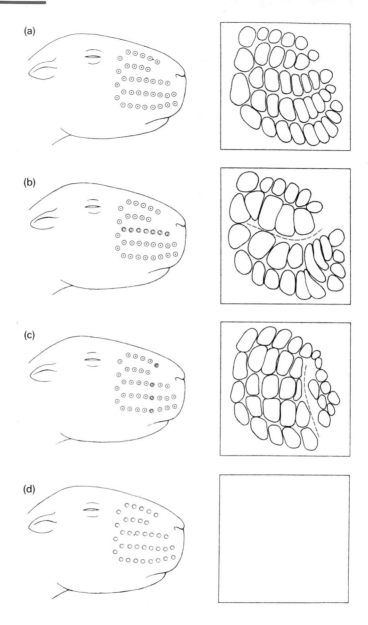

one nostril is occluded early in life, the rat can breathe, but the olfactory mucosa—the sensory surface in the nose—is not stimulated on the occluded side. After causing rats to experience this occulusion for some weeks, Meisami compared the growth of the rats' olfactory bulbs—the region of the brain that receives inputs from sensory receptors in the nose. There was a marked difference in size between the bulbs receiving inputs from the occluded and the normal nostrils. The olfactory bulb connected to the blocked nostril exhibited atrophy.

We have given only a few examples of the many experiments showing that sensory stimuli influence the development of the brain with respect to both structure and function. The effects differ depending on variables such as age of the subject, duration of the experience, and the stimulation given.

Aging of the brain

The passage of time brings us an accumulation of joys and sorrows—perhaps riches and fame—and a progressive decline in many of our abilities. Changes with age seem to be inevitable in biological systems. Let us first survey some of the characteristics of normal aging. Then we will look on some of the pathological exaggerations of the aging process, notably senile dementia.

Normal aging

Many aspects of structure and function change through the span of a human life. Though responding more slowly seems inevitable with aging, many of our cognitive abilities show little change throughout the adult years until we reach an advanced age. What happens to brain structure from adolescence to that day when we all get a little forgetful and walk more hesitantly? Does the structure of the brain change continuously throughout the life span of any animal? Data from autopsies on humans give us a few clues about how the brain changes progressively during adulthood.

Changes in the structure of the brain that accompany aging can be viewed at different levels, from subcellular structures to overall brain morphology. Differences in brain weight have often been examined in relation to aging. For years people have questioned the relevance of aging to these weight changes, since it was hard to distinguish changes due to aging from changes that arise from disease states that shortly lead to death. An excellent recent study eliminated such confounding factors (recall Figure 3-1). Changes are very small up to the age of 45, after which time the weight of the brain begins to decline markedly. The course of these changes is the same for men and women, even though women generally live seven to ten years longer than men. Data also emphasize that aging is a variable state. Declines are evident in all people, but the declines are exaggerated in some. To some investigators this serves to emphasize the genetic contribution to aging and reinforces the idea that if you want to live long, choose parents and grandparents who have lived long.

In the brains of aged persons one frequently finds that the folds of cerebral cortex have atrophied and that the lateral ventricles have enlarged. These changes are marked, however, only in cases of severe senile dementia, which we will discuss shortly.

A common measurement of structure used in studies of brain aging is the number of neural and glial cells in particular volumes of tissue. Investigators map specific regions and count the number of cells in various areas, using tissue taken from persons who have died at different ages. These studies suggest that cell changes begin as early as the third decade and are specific to particular regions. Even more noticeable than the decrease in the number of cells is the loss of synaptic connections, which is especially prominent in the frontal regions.

Two regions of the motor system can be used to show how different aging functions can be. In the motor cortex a type of large neuron—the Betz cell—starts to change by about age 50, and by the time the person reaches about age 80, many of these cells have virtually shriveled away (Scheibel, Tomiyasu, and Scheibel, 1977). In contrast, other cells involved in motor circuitry—those in an area of the brain stem called the inferior olive—remain about the same in number over at least eight decades of life.

In young nervous systems, lesions in many parts of the brain and spinal cord induce the regrowth of axons and the formation of new connections (Chapter 16). But in adults, though axonal sprouting is also seen, it is much less vigorous. Furthermore, several investigators (for example, Scheff, Bernardo, and Cotman, 1978) have shown that the brains of aged rats are much less able to grow axon collaterals after lesions of a brain tract. Thus it appears that the brains of aged animals are less able than the brains of young ones to compensate anatomically for progressive reduction in cells and synapses.

Senile dementia:
A pathological exaggeration
of aging

Because the average age of people in advanced countries has been rising during this century, we are seeing both the advantages and the costs of old age. Along with those who lead happy and productive elderly years, there are other people for whom old age brings not only aches and pains but severe mental deterioration. **Senile dementia** is the diagnostic label used to refer to a generalized condition of progressive behavioral deterioration. This condition encompasses both personality changes and profound intellectual decline, including confusion and loss of memory. This is an increasingly serious problem that may affect as many as 10–15% of people over the age of 65.

Many of the changes in the brains of people with senile dementia appear to be exaggerations of the aging process that everyone else undergoes. The brains of senile people show a greater number of cytological changes. Tomlinson and Henderson (1976) have shown that behavioral ratings on a dementia score correlate highly with two major neuroanatomical changes: (1) neurofibrillary tangles, and (2) senile plaques.

Neurofibrillary tangles are abnormal whorls of neurofilaments within nerve cells (Figure 3-23a). They first attracted interest as a marker for senile dementia many years ago when the neurologist Alzheimer described a form of dementia that occurs in middle age (45–60) and is characterized by the formation of these tangles. He thought that this was a discrete disease (now called **Alzheimer's disease**), a unique presenile dementia. Neurofibrillary tangles are now viewed as a marker of aging in all brains. But they are especially apparent in demented individuals, both old and young. They are found to a much lesser extent in nondemented older persons.

Senile plaques (Figure 3-23b) are small areas of the brain that contain degenerated nerve cells, an excess of glial cells, and a substance called amyloid that is composed of chains of unusual protein related to the immune system. Actually, amyloid probably leaks from blood vessels and destroys axon terminals. The plaques invade all areas of the brain, especially the cerebral cortex. Once again, more plaques are found in demented persons than in normal aged persons.

Striking neurochemical changes have been found in the brains of patients with

Figure 3-23 (a) Neurofibrillary tangles seen in a cross section of the cerebral cortex of an aged person. One example is pointed out by the colored area. (b) Senile plaques in the cerebral cortex of an aged patient. Examples are shown within blue circles. (Photographs courtesy of F. J. Seil)

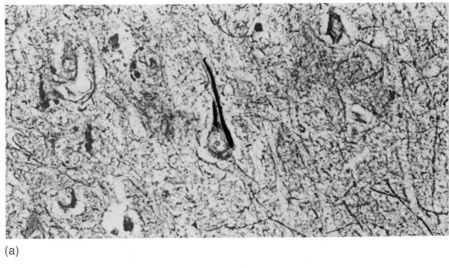

(a)

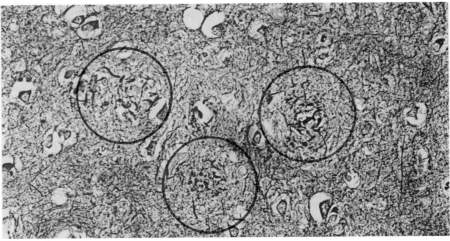

(b)

Alzheimer's disease. In fact, at least six independent researchers have shown a significant decline in a chemical needed for communication among nerve cells (Kolata, 1981). This inspires hopes for a scientifically based drug therapy for senility.

Maldevelopment of the brain and behavior impairments

The fact that the processes that guide development of the human brain are so multiple, intricate, and complex also means, unfortunately, that there are many ways in which they can go wrong. The many factors that control brain development—those that govern cellular proliferation, migration, differentiation, and formation of synapses—are subject to failures that can have catastrophic consequences for adaptive behavior. The magnitude of this problem is reflected in the incidence of disorders that produce marked cognitive impairment. In the United States approximately 3.6 children per 1000 between the ages of 5 and 17 have IQ levels below 50.

BOX 3-3   Brain Transplants or Grafts: Help for the Future?

Research on surgery of the nervous system sometimes makes the present look like the future. We have grown accustomed to heart transplants, kidney exchanges, corneal gifts, and so forth. But what about brain transplants? Journalists once asked Christiaan Barnard, the first surgeon to transplant a human heart (in 1967), what he thought about a brain transplant. He noted all the awesome technical difficulties: connecting axons, blood vessels, nerves, and all else. Then he seemed to recoil from the very idea by noting that such surgery should really be called a *body* transplant. (Shades of the transposed heads in Chapter 1!)

A short while ago brain or body transplants were unreal, the stuff of science fiction. The boundaries of the real have been extended a bit further, however, with demonstrations of the successful isolation of the entire brain of a chimpanzee by White (1976). He was able to maintain an isolated brain for at least one to two days by connecting it to machines that supplied oxygen and nutrients in the circulation.

More immediate, less quixotic hopes for humans come from work on a less grand scale, transplanting small portions of the brain as grafts. Can a piece of the brain be removed from one animal and donated to a second? This prospect is particularly important for possible compensation in brain disorders that involve deficiencies of specific chemicals generated in certain brain regions.

Fetal tissue can be removed from the brain of one animal and be maintained in various body cavities (eyeball, chest) of another animal. Lund and Hauschka (1976) removed fragments of the superior colliculus of a fetal rat and donated these to a host animal. Interconnections formed between the donated fragment and the host's superior colliculus.

More exciting prospects for applications to humans are apparent in the recent work of Perlow and colleagues (1979). These investigators first injected a drug that killed cells that produce a chemical transmitter needed in some motor centers in rats. As a result, the animals showed motor impairment. Then the investigators were able to achieve a reduction in the motor abnormalities by giving a graft of neurons containing chemicals that were missing in the recipient animals. Specifically, they implanted fetal neurons containing the missing substance (dopamine; see Chapter 4) into the caudate nucleus of the adult rat, where they survived and grew axons. The rat's recovery of functional abilities after the experimenters had induced motor disorder was clearly related to the maintenance of the transplant. This research poses the possibilities of similar replacements for humans in some deficiency states, especially Parkinson's disease (see Chapter 8).

In this section we will review developmental disorders of the brain that can cause major cognitive impairment. Three common sources of such disorders are genetically controlled states, prenatal maternal conditions, and processes related to birth.

Genetically controlled states   Genetically controlled states that cause developmental disorders include both the actions of mutant genes and chromosomal anomalies.

● Actions of mutant genes   Many metabolic disorders profoundly affect the developing brain. Some, which are associated with **autosomal** recessive inheritance (recall Box 3-1), generally appear very early in life. In this category are about a hundred different disorders involving disturbances in the metabolism of proteins or carbohydrates or lipids. Characteristically the genetic defect is the absence of a particular enzyme that controls some critical biochemical step in the synthesis or breakdown of a vital body product. Two main results that can affect metabolic and structural states of the brain are: (1) certain compounds build up to toxic levels; (2) compounds needed for either function or structure fail to be synthesized.

An example of the first kind is **phenylketonuria (PKU),** a disorder of protein metabolism that at one time commonly resulted in mental retardation. It is a recessive hereditary disorder. One out of 50 persons is a **heterozygous** carrier; one in 10,000 births is an affected **homozygous** victim. The basic defect is the absence of an enzyme necessary to metabolize phenylalanine, an amino acid present in many foods.

The brain damage caused by phenylketonuria probably comes about because phenylalanine metabolism generates a toxic product, thought by some to be phenyl-pyruvic acid. This condition was the first inborn error of metabolism to be associated with mental retardation. Nowadays there are screening methods, required by law throughout the United States and in many other countries, that assess the level of phenylalanine in children a few days after birth. A simple method is to place a piece of treated paper in the diaper of the newborn infant; a change of color indicates possible PKU. Very effective prevention of brain impairment can be provided by giving diets that are low in phenylalanine. Recent evidence suggests that dietary control of phenylketonuria is critical during early years, especially before age 2, and that the diet can be relaxed during adulthood. Since there has been considerable success in treating phenylketonuria, we may hope eventually to control other genetic disorders of metabolism.

● **Chromosomal anomalies**   One in every 200 live births exhibits some kind of chromosomal anomaly: either an abnormal number of chromosomes (usually 45 or 47 instead of 46) or modifications in the structure of the chromosome. Generally, disorders involving nonsex chromosomes have a more profound impact on behavior than those involving sex chromosomes.

The commonest form of cognitive disorder due to a chromosomal anomaly is **Down's syndrome.** The disorder associated with 95% of these cases is an extra chromosome, number 21 (hence the designation trisomy 21). This disorder is strikingly related to the age of the mother at the time of conception (Table 3-2). The behavioral dysfunctions are quite varied. Most cases of Down's syndrome have very low IQs, but some rare individuals attain an IQ of 80. Brain anomalies in Down's syndrome are also varied. Recent biopsies of the cerebral cortex of Down's sufferers show abnormal formation of dendritic spines (Figure 3-24).

TABLE 3-2   Risk of Babies with Down's Syndrome Related to Maternal Age

MOTHER'S AGE AT BIRTH OF CHILD	RISK OF DOWN'S SYNDROME
Under 30	1:1500
30–34	1:1000
35–39	1:300
40–44	1:100
45 and over	1:40

SOURCE: Karp (1976).

Figure 3-24 Dendrites of motor cortex neurons from normal and Down's syndrome infants. (a) Segments of dendrite from a normal 6-month-old infant; 1 and 2, dendrite with stubby spines close to cell body; 3, distal dendritic segment; and 4, basilar dendrite with thin spines. (b) Segments of dendrite from a 10-month-old Down's child; 1–3, dendrites showing some long thin spines close to cell body. (From Purpura, 1978)

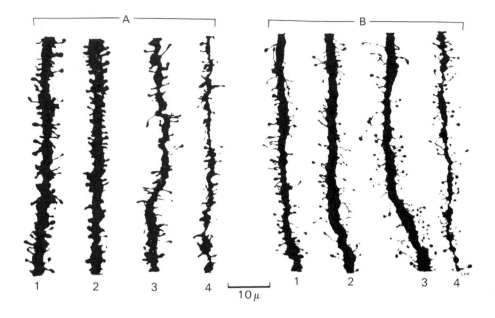

Prenatal maternal conditions

Even in its protected environment of the womb, the embryo and fetus are not immune to what is taking place in the bodily state of the mother. Maternal conditions such as virus infection, exposure to drugs, and malnutrition are especially likely to result in developmental disorders in the unborn child. Let us consider examples of disorders resulting from two of these conditions.

● Virus infection   Any infections in the mother's body during the fetal period can have potent effects on the organization of the fetus's central nervous system. Some severe neurological handicaps, including mental retardation and sensory impairments like deafness, have their origin in virus diseases of the mother during pregnancy. In recent years these causal relationships have become more apparent, particularly those involving maternal rubella infections. These data have often been cited during arguments over abortion laws. In a large-scale study in 1964, 10% of the children born to women with obvious manifestations of rubella during the first three months of pregnancy showed neurological dysfunctions at birth (Hardy, 1973). This compares with an incidence of 0.6% defects of babies born to mothers exposed to the virus at this time but who did not show the common signs of infection, such as rash.

● Exposure to drugs during pregnancy   Concern with the maternal environment as a determinant of brain development has recently spawned a new field: **behavioral teratology.** (Teratology is the study of malformations, from the Greek "teras," "monster.") Those who work in this field are especially concerned with the pathological behavioral effects of drugs ingested during pregnancy. The heavy use of behaviorally active drugs in recent years has focused attention on their connection with several developmental disorders.

Children born to mothers who habitually use certain drugs show a high frequency of behavioral and structural impairments. In fact, this is even evident with the habitual use of drugs that might at one time have been prescribed to help women during pregnancy! Such is the case with alcohol. Children born to alcoholic mothers show a portrait of impairments now referred to as the "fetal alcohol syndrome." Such children have a high mortality rate at birth. Many show behavioral symptoms such as hyperactivity, irritability, and tremors. Some investigators believe that mental retardation can result from prolonged exposure of an embryo or fetus to alcohol. These observations of humans inspired an experimental study with an animal model. This report by West, Hodges, and Stack (1981) showed that the offspring of rat mothers who were fed alcohol during gestation showed defects in hippocampal circuitry. The distribution of nerve fibers was quite aberrant. However, there were not any gross bodily malformations, such as are often found when the mother has ingested toxic drugs during pregnancy.

Birth processes and disorders of the nervous system

Complications of the birth process itself can produce an oxygen deficit in the fetus that can result in brain damage. Examples include interference with the umbilical cord or separation of the cord from the placenta. In some instances the infant may undergo brief periods of reduced oxygen before birth.

Studying the reactivity of newborns has shown that such anoxic episodes either before or during birth can affect their immediate behavioral responsiveness. The Apgar scale (1954), developed to evaluate newborns' behavioral reactivity, is based on such measures as the presence or absence of crying and the intensity of crying. Infants who suffered anoxic episodes have much poorer Apgar scores than children born after an uncomplicated pregnancy. Experimental studies of monkeys who underwent severe asphyxia at birth show marked structural changes in the brain, including loss of cells and degeneration of fibers (Windle, 1969).

Evolution of the brain

Now that we have traced the development of the brain over a single life span, let us adopt a perspective of millions of years and consider the evolution of the brain. We will see that over the last hundred million years there has been a general tendency for the size of the brain of vertebrates to increase, and that the brains of our human ancestors have shown a particularly striking increase in size over the last 2 million years. How, then, has the evolution of the brain been related to changes in behavioral capacity?

It would help us learn about the evolution of the brain if we could study the brains of fossil animals. But brains themselves do not fossilize, unfortunately. Two methods of analysis have proved helpful. One is to use the cranial cavity of a fossil skull to make a cast of the brain that once occupied that space. These casts (called **endocasts**) give a good indication of the size and shape of the brain.

The other method is to study present-day animals, choosing species that show various degrees of similarity to (or difference from) ancestral forms. Although no modern animal is an ancestor of any other living form, it is clear that some present species resemble ancestral forms more closely than others do. For example, present-day frogs are much more similar to vertebrates of 300 million years ago than any

Figure 3-25 Broad outlines of the historical record of the vertebrates. For each vertebrate class, the width of the pathway is proportional to the known number of species in each of the geological periods. [Adapted from G. G. Simpson, *The meaning of evolution, second edition* (New Haven: Yale University Press, 1967).]

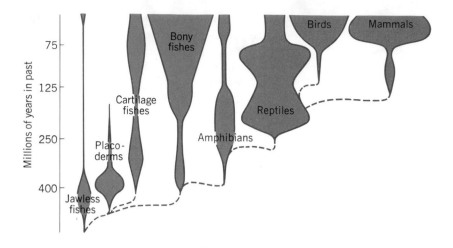

mammals are (see the historical record of the vertebrates in Figure 3-25). Among the mammals some species, such as the opossum, resemble fossil mammals of 50 million years ago more than do other species, such as the dog. Anatomists who study the brains of living species can obtain far more detailed information from them than from endocasts, because they can investigate the internal structure of the brain: its nuclei, fiber tracts, and the circuitry formed by connections of its neurons.

But care must be taken not to interpret the evolutionary record as if it were a linear sequence. Note that the main classes of vertebrates in Figure 3-25 represent different lines or radiations of evolution that have been proceeding separately for at least a hundred million years. Thus a particular evolutionary development may not have been available to mammals even if it occurred before the first mammals appeared. For example, some advanced forms of sharks long ago evolved much larger brains than primitive sharks. But this cannot account for the large brains of mammals. The line of descent that eventually led to mammals had separated from that of the sharks before the large shark brain evolved.

Different evolutionary lines have independently discovered many tricks for survival. To establish the fact that a characteristic was probably inherited from a common ancestor, one must show that it is held in common by most members of the classes that derived from that ancestor. Few species of each class have yet been studied in detail, so conclusions must still be regarded as tentative (Northcutt, 1981). However, we can present some that appear solid.

Changes in vertebrate brains through evolution

Recent research shows that even the most primitive living vertebrate, the lamprey (a kind of jawless fish), has a more complex brain than it used to be given credit for. The lamprey not only has the basic neural chassis of spinal cord, hindbrain, and midbrain, but it also has a diencephalon and telencephalon (Figure 3-26). Its telencephalon has cerebral hemispheres and other subdivisions that are also found in the mammalian brain. All these brain regions mentioned here occur in the brains of all vertebrates.

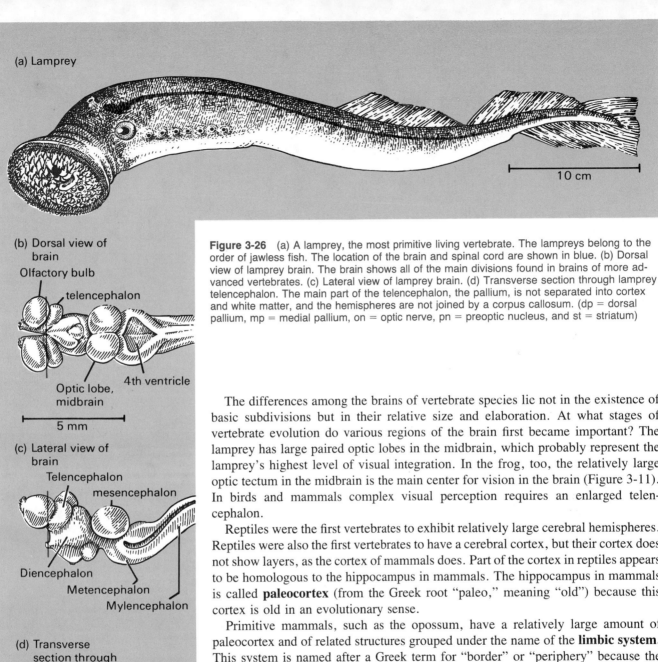

(a) Lamprey

10 cm

(b) Dorsal view of brain

Olfactory bulb

telencephalon

Optic lobe, midbrain

4th ventricle

5 mm

(c) Lateral view of brain

Telencephalon

mesencephalon

Diencephalon

Metencephalon

Mylencephalon

(d) Transverse section through telencephalon

dp

mp

st

pn

on

Figure 3-26 (a) A lamprey, the most primitive living vertebrate. The lampreys belong to the order of jawless fish. The location of the brain and spinal cord are shown in blue. (b) Dorsal view of lamprey brain. The brain shows all of the main divisions found in brains of more advanced vertebrates. (c) Lateral view of lamprey brain. (d) Transverse section through lamprey telencephalon. The main part of the telencephalon, the pallium, is not separated into cortex and white matter, and the hemispheres are not joined by a corpus callosum. (dp = dorsal pallium, mp = medial pallium, on = optic nerve, pn = preoptic nucleus, and st = striatum)

The differences among the brains of vertebrate species lie not in the existence of basic subdivisions but in their relative size and elaboration. At what stages of vertebrate evolution do various regions of the brain first became important? The lamprey has large paired optic lobes in the midbrain, which probably represent the lamprey's highest level of visual integration. In the frog, too, the relatively large optic tectum in the midbrain is the main center for vision in the brain (Figure 3-11). In birds and mammals complex visual perception requires an enlarged telencephalon.

Reptiles were the first vertebrates to exhibit relatively large cerebral hemispheres. Reptiles were also the first vertebrates to have a cerebral cortex, but their cortex does not show layers, as the cortex of mammals does. Part of the cortex in reptiles appears to be homologous to the hippocampus in mammals. The hippocampus in mammals is called **paleocortex** (from the Greek root "paleo," meaning "old") because this cortex is old in an evolutionary sense.

Primitive mammals, such as the opossum, have a relatively large amount of paleocortex and of related structures grouped under the name of the **limbic system.** This system is named after a Greek term for "border" or "periphery" because the limbic system forms a border around the underlying brain structures. (We will take up the limbic system in Chapter 13 in connection with emotion and motivation, and in Chapters 14 and 15 in connection with learning and memory.)

All mammals have a six-layered **neocortex.** In more advanced mammals the neocortex accounts for more than half the volume of the brain. (This increase in size of the neocortex was illustrated in Figure 2-32.) In many primates, such as the great apes and humans, the neocortex is deeply fissured, so that a large cortical surface covers the brain. The cortex is what is mainly responsible for many complex functions, such as perception of objects. Regions of the brain that were responsible for perceptual functions in less highly evolved animals—such as the midbrain optic lobes (in the lamprey) or the midbrain optic center (in the frog)—have in the modern mammal become visual reflex centers or way stations in the projection pathway to the cortex. (We will take up the neocortex in several chapters in connection with not only perception but also complex cognitive functions.)

Evolution of brain size   It is often said that the brain increased in size with the appearance of each succeeding vertebrate class shown in Figure 3-25. But this is a questionable generalization. For one thing, there are exceptions among the present-day representatives of the various classes—birds appeared later than mammals but don't have larger brains. For another thing, the generalization arose from the old way of viewing vertebrate evolution as being one linear series of increasing complexity rather than as a series of successive radiations.

Actually there is considerable variation in brain size within each line of evolution if we compare animals of similar body size. For example, within the ancient class of jawless fish, the hagfish, considered to be the advanced members of that class, possess forebrains four times as large as those of lampreys of comparable body size. The increase of brain size in relation to behavioral capacity has been studied most thoroughly in the mammalian line.

Study of brain size is complicated, however, by the wide range of body sizes. You wouldn't expect animals that differed in body size to have the same brain size. But exactly what relation holds between the size of the body and that of the brain? A general relationship was found first for present-day species and then applied successfully to fossil species as well. This function turns out to be useful in finding relationships between brain and behavioral capacities, as we will see.

● **Relating brain size to body size**   We humans long believed our own brains to be the largest of all brains, but this belief was upset in the seventeenth century when it was found that the elephant brain weighs three times as much as our own! Later whale brains were found to be even larger. (Table 3-3 shows brain weights and body weights of certain adult mammals.) These findings puzzled thinkers who took it for granted that human beings are the most intelligent of animals and therefore must have the largest brains. As a way of overcoming this difficulty, they proposed that brain weight should be expressed as a fraction of body weight (see column 3 of Table 3-3). On this basis humans outrank elephants, whales, and all other animals of large or moderate body size. But a mouse has about the same ratio of brain weight to body weight as a man, and the tiny shrew outranks a human on this measure. So we are left to wonder how much brain is needed to control and serve a body of a given size. Let's examine this question.

Look at the brain and body weights in Table 3-3. Do you see any pattern? When we consider a larger sample of animals and the values plotted in Figure 3-27, then some generality appears. All the brain weight–body weight points fall within one of two diagonal areas (one for higher and one for lower vertebrates). Since both scales are logarithmic, the graph encompasses a great variety of animal sizes and departures from the general rule tend to be minimized. Each diagonal area in Figure 3-27 has a slope of two-thirds. This slope reflects the fact that the weight of the brain

TABLE 3-3   Brain Weights and Body Weights of Certain Adult Mammals

LIVING MAMMALS	APPROXIMATE BRAIN WEIGHT (g)	APPROXIMATE BODY WEIGHT (g)	BRAIN WEIGHT AS PERCENT OF BODY WEIGHT	k (ENCEPHALIZATION FACTOR)
Shrew	0.25	7.5	3.33	0.06
Mouse	0.5	24	2.08	0.06
Sheep	100	40,000	0.25	0.08
Leopard	135	48,000	0.28	0.10
Malay bear	400	45,000	0.89	0.32
Chimpanzee	400	42,000	0.95	0.30
Human	1,400	60,000	2.33	0.95
Indian Elephant	5,000	2,550,000	0.20	0.27
Fossil hominids (estimates):				
Australopithecus (about 4–6 million years ago)	450	50,000	0.90	0.33
Homo habilis (about 1.75 million years ago)	550	50,000	1.10	0.41
Homo erectus (about 0.7 million years ago)	950	50,000	1.90	0.70

SOURCE: Most animal data from Crile and Quiring (1940); data on fossil hominids from Jerison (1973).

is roughly proportional to the two-thirds power of body weight. More formally stated, $E = kP^{2/3}$ where E = brain weight, P = body weight, and k is a constant for a species but varies among classes and species of animals. The constant k is greater for animals that are highly evolved or more complex than it is for the less evolved, simpler animals. Note that the upper diagonal for higher vertebrates (such as the rat, crow, baboon, and whale), taken as a group, has the equation $E = 0.07 P^{2/3}$; that is, $k = 0.07$. But on the lower diagonal, for lower vertebrates (such as the alligator, eel, and goldfish) taken as a group, $k = 0.007$. In other words, higher vertebrates

Figure 3-27 Brain size plotted against body size for some two hundred species of living vertebrates. Data for mammals and birds fall within the upper blue area, and data for reptiles and fish fall within the lower gray area. (Adapted from Jerison, 1973; based largely on data of Crile and Quiring, 1940)

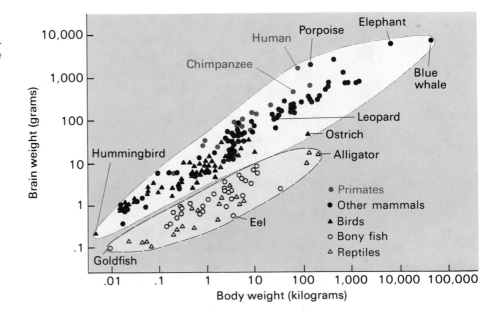

typically have a brain size that is about ten times larger for a given size of body than the brain size of lower vertebrates.

Note that the brain weight–body weight points for higher vertebrates do not fall exactly on a diagonal line running through the middle of the oval. Some are located above the diagonal (such as those for human, porpoise, and crow). Others are below it (such as ostrich and opossum). The value of the constant k for a given species is related to the vertical distance of its position from the diagonal on the graph. So, although 0.07 is the mean value of k for higher vertebrates, we can find the particular value of k for each species.

Many investigators have used k or related statistics to try to quantify the relative "brain power" of different species. In these terms human beings rate higher than any other species. You can see that on the graph the point for humans is located farther above the diagonal than the point for any other species. From the values for brain weight and body weight, we can calculate k for humans to be about 1.0. Values of k for the species in Table 3-3 are given in column 4. The primates as a group rate relatively high on this statistic; k for the great apes is around 0.3. The Indian elephant also has a k of about 0.3. On the other hand, for the shrew and the mouse k is only 0.06, and for the opossum it is only 0.02.

Brain size has been studied in many species of mammals, both living and fossil. These studies have yielded clues about the selection pressures that have led to larger brains. We will first see how brain size has evolved with regard to ecological niche, and especially the methods of obtaining food. Then we will take up the brain size among the relatively direct ancestors of modern humans.

● **Brain size and diet**   Within several families of mammals, species that eat leaves or grass have brains that are relatively smaller than those of species that feed on food sources such as fruit or insects that are distributed less densely and less uniformly. This relationship has been found among families of rodents, insectivores (such as shrews and moles), and lagomorphs (such as rabbits and pica) (Clutton-Brock and Harvey, 1980). It is also true of primates (Mace, Harvey, and Clutton-Brock, 1981). Within the order of bats, which includes several hundred species, relatively large brains have evolved several times. When body size is held constant, species of bats that eat mainly fruit or nectar or live mainly on blood have brain weights that are about 70% greater than those of species that live mainly on insects captured in flight. Finding fruit and assessing its quality requires integrating information from several senses, whereas the species that capture insects in flight rely entirely on hearing. Eisenberg and Wilson (1978, p. 750) argue that larger brains are found among those bat species whose foraging strategies are "based on locating relatively large packets of energy-rich food that are unpredictable in temporal and spatial distribution."

Study of the fossil record suggests that interaction between predator and prey has been part of the selection pressure that led to increased brain size in both kinds of animals. Harry Jerison (1973) has studied the endocasts of fossil ungulates (hoofed animals, such as horses, camels, deer, and rhinoceros) and carnivores (flesh-eating animals, such as dogs, cats, otters, and bears) in the Western hemisphere. Using large samples to reveal major trends, he classified the animals into four main time periods, as shown in Table 3-4. For each time period and each family (ungulates or

TABLE 3-4 Encephalization Quotients for Western Hemisphere Ungulates and Carnivores

MILLIONS OF YEARS AGO	MEAN ($\bar{X}$), STANDARD DEVIATION, AND NUMBER	NORTH AMERICAN		SOUTH AMERICAN UNGULATES
		Ungulates	*Carnivores*	
>63				
	$\bar{X}$	0.18	0.44	—
	S.D.	0.05	0.09	—
	n	13	4	—
36 to 63				
	$\bar{X}$	0.38	0.61	0.44
	S.D.	0.12	0.19	0.14
	n	26	11	9
2 to 35				
	$\bar{X}$	0.63	0.76	0.47
	S.D.	0.24	0.23	0.13
	n	13	6	11
<2				
	$\bar{X}$	0.95	1.10	—
	S.D.	0.33	0.31	—
	n	25	15	—

SOURCE: Jerison (1973) Tables 13.2 and 14.2.

carnivores) he calculated relative sizes of brains from measures of the endocasts and of body size. Expressed as encephalization quotients (EQs), these are simply the k values multiplied by 14.3 so that the mean EQ for higher vertebrates is 1.00.

Note in Table 3-4 that animals of both families showed a progressive increase in relative brain size across these long time periods. At each period the ungulates had smaller EQs than the carnivores. This agrees with the findings about small EQs in modern grass or leaf eaters. No modern mammal has as small an EQ as the mean of the earliest ungulates. The difference between the EQs of carnivores and ungulates was relatively large in the earliest period (the carnivore mean was about two and a half times the ungulate mean). However, in the last of the four periods, the difference was small—only 16% as compared with 240% in the earliest period. Note also that the standard deviations have increased over time, indicating increased diversity. That is, even as mean brain values grew, there remained ecological niches for small-brained species.

It is tempting to believe that the predator-prey relationship led to increases in the EQs of both families. That is, those ungulates with somewhat larger brains were more likely to evade or to ward off predators and thus to reproduce, so there was selection pressure that gradually drove up their brain size. Meanwhile, as their prey became more wily and capable, those carnivores with larger brains were better able to prey on them successfully.

Jerison suggests that South American ungulates can provide a test of this hypothesis. Until the recent geological period, when a land bridge formed between North and South America, there were many species of ungulates in South America but no species of placental carnivores. As shown in Table 3-4, the earliest South American ungulates were equivalent in EQ to their contemporary North American ungulates. But thereafter South American ungulates showed practically no increase in EQ, while the North American ungulates showed a substantial increase. The lack of change in South American ungulates in the absence of advanced predators appears to support Jerison's hypothesis that the increase in relative brain size of North American ungulates was a result of the interaction between predator and prey.

● Hominid brains   Another approach to evolutionary relationships between brain and behavior comes from the study of **hominids,** that is, primates of the family Hominidae, of which humans *(Homo sapiens)* are the only living species. This approach is intriguing for the light it sheds on our distant ancestors, and it helps us understand how the body adapts to the environment through natural selection.

The structural and behavioral features that we consider characteristic of humans did not develop simultaneously. Our large brain is a relatively late development. According to one estimate the trunk and arms of hominids reached their present form about 10 million years ago. (Note that the time span of human evolution and the dates of various fossils have been altered by recent methods of dating. All authorities do not agree on these dates; they should be considered only approximate.) Hominids began walking on two feet at least 3 million years ago. The oldest stone tools date back at least 2.5 million years. The tool users were bipedal ape-men called Australopithecines, creatures with a brain volume of about 450 cubic centimeters (cc), about the size of the modern chimpanzee brain. They made crude stone tools, which chimpanzees do not, and used them in hunting and in breaking animal bones to eat. With use of tools their jaws and teeth became smaller than the ape's and more like those of modern human beings. But the brain did not grow. A brain volume of about 450 cc sufficed for the life of Australopithecine. Moreover, this was a successful animal, lasting relatively unchanged for about 2 million years.

Campsites suggest that these early hominids lived in small nomadic groups of 20 to 50 individuals. The males hunted, and the females gathered plant foods. This life of hunting and gathering was a new life style that was continued by later hominids. In Chapter 9 we will see some implications of this life style combined with the increase in brain size for human sexuality.

About three-quarters of a million years ago the Australopithecines were replaced by *Homo erectus*. This creature, which had a much larger brain—almost 1000 cc—made elaborate stone tools, used fire, and killed large animals. *Homo erectus* had not only a larger brain than his predecessor but also a smaller face. These trends continued in the development of the modern human, *Homo sapiens*. Fossils and tools of *Homo erectus* are found throughout three continents, whereas those of the Australopithecines were found only in Africa. It may be that *H. erectus* represented a level of capacity and of cultural adaptation that allowed the hominids to expand into new environmental niches and to overcome barriers that kept earlier hominids in a narrower range.

Evolution of the brain and increased behavioral capacity advanced rapidly from the Australopithecines to modern humans (Figure 3-28). By the time *Homo sapiens* appeared, about two hundred thousand years ago, brain volume had reached the

Figure 3-28 Aspects of hominid evolution. (Adapted from Tobias, 1980)

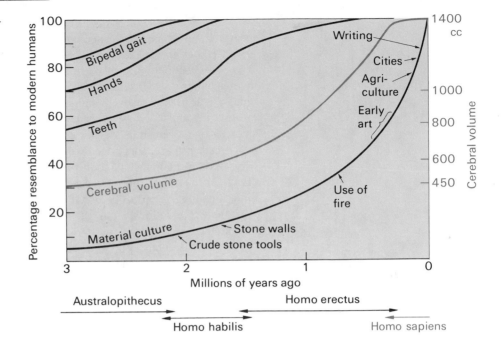

modern level, about 1400 cc. Thus after remaining virtually unchanged in size during about 2 million years of tool use by the Australopithecines, the brain almost tripled in volume during the next million and a half years.

The human brain now appears to be at a plateau of size. The recent changes in human life style—such as the appearance of language (perhaps only about forty thousand years ago), the introduction of agriculture and animal husbandry (about ten thousand years ago), and urban living (the last few thousand years)—have all been accomplished and assimilated by a brain that does not seem to have altered in size since *Homo sapiens* appeared.

A change in any organ during evolution indicates that there was pressure from the environment for modification and that the change conferred advantages with respect to the survival of the species. A rapid change, as in the size of the hominid brain, suggests that it brought strong advantages for survival. Can we then tell in what ways the evolution of the human brain accompanied and made possible certain changes in human behavior?

As we mentioned before, in size and general shape the Australopithecine brain resembled that of a modern chimpanzee. It is clear, however, that the chimpanzee is a more distant relative of humans than the Australopithecine is. Some investigators (Kohne et al., 1972) have compared DNA sequences and interpreted them as showing that our ancestors diverged from those of the chimpanzee about 30 million years ago. Another investigator (Sarich, 1971) interprets the data on DNA and also on albumin and hemoglobin as indicating that the human and chimpanzee lines diverged only 4 to 5 million years ago. Even if we take the more recent estimate as valid, the chimpanzees have still had 4 to 5 million years to evolve in their direction while we humans evolved in ours. All species that have survived to the present have been busy over the eons leading their own lives and adapting to their own environmental circumstances. We cannot think of them as sitting around to provide a picture gallery of our ancestors!

The fact that hominids made stone tools at least 2.5 million years ago and used them in hunting also distinguishes the Australopithecine from the chimpanzee, even though their brain sizes were similar. Field observations have shown chimpanzees to use some tools—twigs, branches, leaves—but they have never been seen to fashion a stone, even crudely. They catch small game occasionally, but not in the frequent manner that is suggested by the collections of bones of prey found in association with Australopithecine tools and fossils. So the Australopithecine was clearly our closer relative, further advanced toward human culture than the chimpanzee. Its brain organization probably also differed somewhat from that of the chimpanzee. With these reservations, let us see how the modern human brain differs from that of the chimpanzee.

Prominent differences between the organization of the brain of *Homo sapiens* and of chimpanzee include the following:

1. The human brain shows a larger expansion of the motor and sensory cortical areas devoted to the hands.

2. The human brain is like the chimpanzee brain in having a limbic system that is involved in vocalization. However, the human brain shows, in addition, large cortical regions devoted to the production and perception of speech.

3. When it comes to speech, manual dexterity, and other functions, the human brain shows striking hemispheric specialization of functions. In the chimpanzee the two hemispheres are more equivalent in function.

4. The primary sensory regions of the cortex are somewhat greater in the human than in the chimpanzee. But the main expansion in the human cortex lies outside these sensory regions. That is, in the human a larger proportion of the brain is devoted to more varied and more elaborate processing of information.

Thus the expansion of cortical areas and hemispheric specialization appear to have made possible human beings' social cooperation in gathering plants and in hunting and their ability to make increasingly complex tools and weapons. These behaviors, which increased humans' chances for survival, could be developed further only as the brain increased further in size and complexity. So selection for advantageous behavior also entailed selection for more powerful brains. Charles Darwin realized this when he wrote:

> In many cases, the continued development of a part, for instance the beak of a bird or the teeth of a mammal, would not aid the species in gaining its food, or for any other object; but with man we can see no definite limit to the continual development of the brain and mental faculties, as far as advantage is concerned.

The survival advantage that accrues to those with larger brains does not hold only for human beings, or primates, or mammalian predators and prey. It would even be too limited to maintain, as George Bernard Shaw did in the dialogue cited at the beginning of this book, that large brains are the specialty of the mammalian line.

Within each of the lines of vertebrate evolution there is variation in relative brain size, with the more recently evolved species usually having the larger encephalization quotients. Furthermore, in each vertebrate line it is the dorsal part of the telencephalon that has expanded and differentiated in the more advanced species. As we find more such common responses to selection pressures, they may reveal the "rules" of how the nervous system adapts and evolves (Northcutt, 1981).

Two calendars for brain development

Let us now try to bring together research on brain development along the two vastly different time scales: the weeks and months of growth of an individual and the millions of years of evolution. We might use the analogy of the different but equally essential contributions of an architect and a carpenter in building a house. The architect, in preparing the plans, calls on a long history of human knowledge about structures that meet the basic human needs: rest, work, recreation, eating, child care, and so on. The structure must be comfortable, safe, affordable, and conform to the tastes of the community. The carpenter has to use these plans to construct the house, translating the two-dimensional information given on the blueprints into a three-dimensional structure. At a number of points during the building process, the carpenter's judgment and interpretation are called for. So two houses built by different carpenters from the same blueprints will not be identical. Another reason for differences in houses is that the materials available for their construction may not be exactly the same. The architect tries to foresee some of the problems of construction and to build safety factors into the plans, so that small deviations or errors will not seriously impair the safety or utility of the completed building.

We are not the first to use such an analogy. An anonymous wit pointed out that a baby is the most complicated object to be made by unskilled labor. And psychologist-information scientist J. C. R. Licklider characterized God as a great architect but a sloppy workman.

The plans for construction of the brain have certain characteristics that we should note and comment on:

1. New plans are never started from scratch. Instead, older plans are reused and modified to adjust to specific situations.

2. Not every detail is specified. Part of the program is implicit in the list of materials and methods of construction. The plans would be hopelessly complex and voluminous if every detail had to be specified.

3. Allowances are made for interaction between the materials and the environment. An architect knows how certain shingles will weather in a given climate to produce a desired appearance and how landscape planting will stabilize the soil and beautify the home's setting. So, too, the genetic plans for the brain take advantage of information provided by the environment. These plans allow for interaction between the developing organism and its environment.

The reuse and successive modification of genetic plans mean that the early embryological stages of development of all vertebrates are similar. The early neural tubes look very much the same in the embryos of a frog, a rat, or a person.

Furthermore, the basic divisions of the brain are the same in all these forms. However, the whole structure has been scaled up in the mammals, and especially in the primates, and some parts have been enlarged relative to others.

The genetic code does not seem to have room for all the information necessary to specify the complete wiring diagram for each part of the nervous system. It achieves some economy by using the same information to apply to many different parts of the structure. Thus the same gene may specify aspects of neural circuitry in different areas of the brain. Any mutation of the gene may therefore cause an abnormal arrangement of neurons in both the cerebellar and cerebral cortex. Also, certain hormones stimulate the growth of neural connections throughout the nervous system, as we will see in Chapter 5. And some fine details of the wiring do not seem to be specified but are simply worked out locally.

Both economy of genetic instructions and adaptation to individual circumstances are achieved by counting on the environment to furnish certain information necessary for development. Each species has evolved in relation to a particular ecological niche, and its program of development utilizes the environment as a source of information and stimulation. Thus, for example, most vertebrates are exposed to patterned visual stimulation soon after birth. By the time of exposure the basic plan of the visual system has been laid down. But formation of detailed connections and maintenance of the visual circuitry require input from the environment. Precise coordination of input from both eyes requires fine tuning of the system. There are so many variables in the structure of the eyes that it would be extraordinarily costly for genetic specification to bring about perfect alignment of the two retinal images. The program of the genes has come down to us after millions of years of trial-and-error improvements, but it has its limits. So certain adjustments are required after the individual goes into operation, so to speak. Small misalignments of the two retinal images can be compensated for by minor "rewiring" of the central visual connections. But if the misalignment between the two eyes is too great, as when the eyes are crossed, then the input of one eye is usually suppressed. Double vision is thereby avoided. The ability to learn from our environment and experience enables us to adjust to particular environments and life styles. (Chapters 14 and 15 will consider the biological mechanisms of learning and memory.)

You can now see that the short-range and long-range calendars provide complementary perspectives on the development of the nervous system and behavior. We will call on both perspectives to illuminate brain-behavior relations in many areas of physiological psychology.

SUMMARY / MAIN POINTS

1. Early embryological events in the formation of the nervous system include an intrinsically programmed sequence of cellular processes: (a) the production of nerve cells (cell proliferation), (b) the movement of cells away from regions of mitotic division (cell migration), (c) the acquisition, by nerve cells, of distinctive forms (cell differentiation), and (d) the loss of some cells (cell death).

2. Fetal and postnatal changes in the brain include myelinization of the axons and development of dendrites and synapses. Although most neurons are present at birth, most synapse development in humans occurs after birth.

3. Neurospecificity is the doctrine that the formation of neural pathways and synapses follows an innate plan that specifies the precise relations between growing axons and

particular target cells. The extent to which specific connections are determined genetically is a matter of current controversy.

4. Among many determinants of brain development are (a) genetic information, (b) growth factors, such as nerve growth factors, and (c) nutrition.

5. Experience affects the growth and development of the nervous system. This is shown by experiments in which animals undergo sensory deprivation during critical early periods of their development. Results indicate that experience may induce and modulate formation of synapses and may also maintain them.

6. The brain continues to change throughout life. Old age brings a loss of neurons and synaptic connections. In some people the changes are more severe than in others and may result in the condition known as senile dementia.

7. Various kinds of maldevelopment of the brain can occur as a result of genetically controlled metabolic disorders. Each usually involves the body's inability to manufacture a particular enzyme. Each defect is probably governed by a single recessive gene.

8. Some forms of mental retardation, such as Down's syndrome, are related to disorders of chromosomes, particularly an excess number of chromosomes.

9. The brains of different vertebrates are similar in their basic subdivisions, although there are many differences in the relative sizes of different structures.

10. Evolutionary changes in brain size are apparent when one compares fossils and contemporary animals. The brain size of a species must be interpreted in terms of body size. The overall rule for vertebrates is that brain weight is proportional to the two-thirds power of body weight.

10. Some animals have larger brains than predicted by the general relation between brain and body weights. Humans, in particular, have larger brains than would be predicted from their body size.

12. Within each of the lines of vertebrate evolution there is variation in relative brain size, with the more recently evolved species usually having the larger encephalization quotients.

RECOMMENDED READING

Jacobson, M. *Developmental neurobiology*. New York: Plenum, 1978.

Lund, R. D. *Development and plasticity of the brain*. New York: Oxford University Press, 1978.

Olson, E. C. *Vertebrate paleozoology*. New York: Wiley, 1971.

Sarnat, H. B., and Netsky, M. G. *Evolution of the nervous system 2nd ed*. New York: Oxford University Press, 1981.

Orientation

Electrical Signals in the Nervous System

Resting membrane potential

Nerve impulses

Propagation of nerve impulses

Postsynaptic potentials

Electrical synapses

Information Processing by Small Neural Circuits

A model for information processing in nerve cells

Examples of processing in local circuits

Ionic Mechanisms of Excitation and Conduction

Mechanisms of the resting potential

The action potential

Gating ion channels

Chemical Properties of Synapses

Storage and release of transmitters

The role of receptor proteins

The second messenger: boosting the effect of
transmitters

Cessation of action of synaptic transmitters

Synaptic events: a recapitulation

Chemical transmitters: confirmed and candidates

Distribution and localization of transmitters

Effects of Drugs on Synapses

Gross Electrical Potentials of the Brain

Why study gross brain potentials?

Characteristics of brain potentials

Epilepsy

Summary/Main Points

4

Communication and Information Processing in the Nervous System

Orientation

Underlying all behavior—seeing, mating, eating, learning—is the processing of information. The sources of information include sensory receptors, ongoing neural activity, and endocrine events. The integrated behavior of an individual depends on the signals that communicate information within the nervous system and from one part of the body to another. In this chapter and the next we will take up basic questions about the nature of information processing in the body, the ways scientists have investigated the underlying activities, and some applications of their research. We will discuss neural communication and information processing in Chapter 4, and we will take up hormonal communication in Chapter 5. The neural and endocrine systems work together in many kinds of behavior, and some investigators believe that endocrine cells evolved from neural cells.

For ease of discussion, we can separate the signals that control and integrate behavior into two categories: neural and hormonal. Neural signals are electrochemical events produced by nerve cells and transmitted among them. The usual way of investigating these signals is to put electrodes into (or close to) nerve cells and record their electrical activity. Hormonal signals are biochemical compounds secreted into the blood by endocrine organs (such as the pituitary gland or the thyroid gland). Unlike neural messages, which are confined to nerve cells, hormonal mes-

BOX 4-1   The Discovery of Animal Electricity

The electrical aspects of neural signals were understood considerably earlier than the chemical aspects. Since at least the early eighteenth century, scientists had been speculating that neural messages might be electrical in nature (Brazier, 1959). Whether that was true became a matter of intense controversy between the pioneer investigators of electricity, Alessandro Volta (1745–1827) and Luigi Galvani (1737–1798). [Volta's name is commemorated by the volt, and Galvani's name gave rise to such words as "galvanic," "galvanize," and "galvanometer" (a device for measuring electric current).]

Galvani, a physician and professor of anatomy in Bologna, discovered what he believed to be "animal electricity." Performing experiments on frog's legs, he saw that the leg muscles would twitch if he touched the end of the cut nerve with a rod of one metal and the foot with another metal, the other ends of the two rods being joined together. Volta countered this by showing that although animal tissue in contact with two dissimilar metals does form what we now call an electric battery, the animal tissue is not an essential component. All that is needed is two dissimilar metals and an electrolyte separating them. Galvani replied with an experiment showing that metals are not required. Merely touching the muscle to the exposed nerve sufficed to cause a twitch. Many other scientists joined this field of investigation, and it became clear that both nerves and muscles do produce electrical charges. Galvani was right! Furthermore, it was demonstrated that the electrical charges change when nerves and muscles are active.

By the 1840s techniques had advanced to the point at which it was possible to measure the "action current" of a nerve, that is, the change of a few millivolts that marks a nerve impulse. The first person to accomplish this was a Swiss-German physiologist, Emil du Bois-Reymond (1818–1896). He trumpeted his claim: "If I do not greatly deceive myself, I have succeeded in realizing in full actuality (albeit under a slightly different aspect) the hundred years' dream of physicists and physiologists, to wit, the identity of the nervous principle with electricity" (1849).

sages spread throughout the body, but they are taken up only by cells or organs that are prepared to receive them. We can think of endocrine organs as broadcasting their messages to be picked up by any receivers that are tuned in.

Electrical signals in the nervous system

One of the most powerful "inventions" in animal evolution was the electrical signalling of neurons. This invention appears in animals as diverse as human beings, insects, and jellyfish—in fact, in all multicellular animals. These neural signals underlie the whole range of thought and action, from composing a symphony or solving a mathematical problem to feeling an irritation on the skin and swatting a mosquito. (A look at the discovery of "animal electricity" is given in Box 4-1.)

To understand how the nervous system works, investigators measure three different kinds of electrical events in studying the activity of single neurons:

1. The **resting potential,** or **membrane potential,** that neurons show when they are inactive. This small difference in potential between the inner and outer surfaces of the membrane results from the separation of electrically charged particles: ions. Many other kinds of cells, such as muscle cells and blood corpuscles, also have membrane potentials. The uniqueness of nerve cells is that they use changes in the resting potential as signals that can be transmitted to other cells.

2. **Nerve impulses,** or **action potentials,** brief propagated changes that travel rapidly along the axon in some kinds of neurons. These changes are conducted in chain-reaction fashion, maintaining a uniform size as they advance, and they enable axons to serve as channels for rapid communication.

3. **Local potential changes** that are initiated at postsynaptic sites. These local or **graded potentials** vary in size and duration. They are not propagated, but spread passively, so that the amplitude of such a potential decreases progressively with distance from its site of origin. These are also called **postsynaptic potentials.** Interaction among graded postsynaptic potentials is the basic mechanism by which the nervous system processes information.

Let us consider each of these three kinds of potentials in order to see the characteristic states of the neuron at rest and during activity. These potentials can be thought of as the basic vocabulary of the nervous system. Knowing this vocabulary, we can understand much about how information is communicated and processed in the nervous system. Some neurophysiologists have pushed the analysis of these potentials to another level and have investigated the ionic mechanisms of neural activity. We will review these ionic mechanisms later in the chapter.

Resting membrane potential A few simple experiments will display the characteristics of electrical potentials in nerve cells. Our initial experimental setup is shown in Figure 4-1. It includes an axon placed in a bathing fluid that resembles extracellular fluids, a pair of electrodes—the one with a very fine tip is called a microelectrode—and devices to amplify, record,

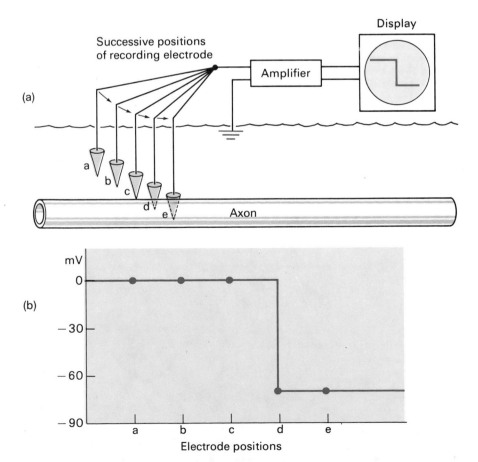

Figure 4-1 Recording the resting potential of the neural membrane. When the tip of the recording electrode is in the extracellular fluid or even touching the surface of the neuron, no potential is recorded between it and the reference electrode in the fluid. But as soon as the electrode penetrates the axon, a resting potential of approximately −70 mV is recorded.

and display electrical potentials. As we advance the microelectrode toward the axon, we see that as long as the microelectrode remains outside the axon, there is zero potential difference between the microelectrode tip and a large electrode placed at some distance from the axon in the bath. There are no potential differences between any two electrodes placed in the extracellular medium, since the distribution of ions in the extracellular fluid is uniform or homogeneous.

When the electrode suddenly penetrates the membrane of the axon (point d in Figure 4-1), we note an abrupt drop in potential to a level of −70 to −80 millivolts (mV). That is, the inside of the axon is electrically negative with respect to the outside. This difference, called the membrane potential, demonstrates that the axonal membrane separates charges. It shows that the fluid environment of the intracellular compartment is different in composition from that of the extracellular fluid. We will discuss the manner in which that difference is created in the section on ionic mechanisms.

Our hypothetical experiment would be hard to perform with just any axon. Most axons of mammals are less than 20 microns in diameter and quite difficult to pierce in this manner. Nature provided neurophysiologists with an extraordinary solution to this problem: **giant axons,** especially those of the squid. Squid axons can attain a diameter of 1 mm, so fat and apparent to the unaided eye that observers originally thought that the axons must be part of the circulatory or urinary system (Figure 4-2). The zoologist J. Z. Young discovered the squid giant axon for neurophysiology in 1938. Electrodes in the form of capillary tubes 0.2 mm in diameter can be inserted into a giant axon without altering its properties or activity. The membrane seems to seal around the inserted electrode tip. Experiments with giant axons soon led to fundamental advances in the understanding of neural membrane structure and function. We owe a nod of gratitude to the squid!

Figure 4-2 Drawing of a squid with the mantle nerve emerging from its ganglion. The giant fiber is embedded in the mantle nerve. Contraction of the mantle is produced by activity in these nerves. This results in ejection of water and powerful reverse movement. The giant axon (b) is about 400 μ in diameter. (From J. C. Eccles, 1973)

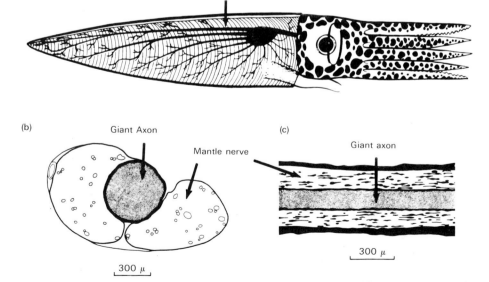

Figure 4-3 Effects of hyperpolarizing and depolarizing stimuli on the axon. The upper section of the figure shows a setup for stimulation (to the left) and for recording (to the right). When a series of hyperpolarizing stimuli of increasing amplitude are delivered, the axon shows hyperpolarized responses that are graded in amplitude. With depolarizing stimuli, graded responses occur to weak stimuli, but when depolarization of 10–15 mV occurs, the axon gives a large response called an action potential or nerve impulse.

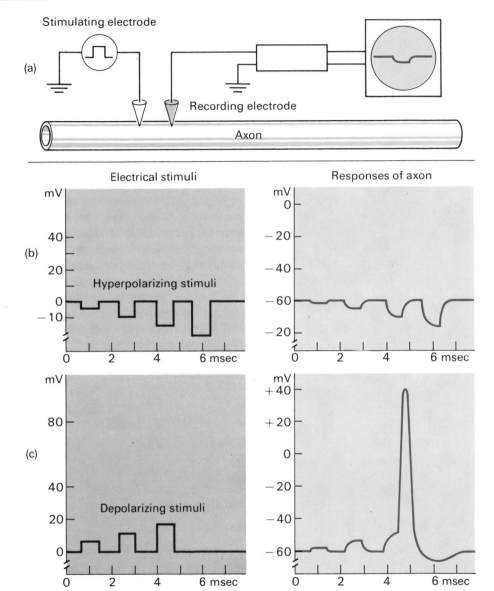

Nerve impulses The next experiments require a source of electrical stimulation. We must also add two terms to our vocabulary: **hyperpolarization** refers to increases in membrane potential (a greater negativity inside the membrane), and **depolarization** refers to reductions of the membrane potential (decreased negativity). The stimulator will provide hyperpolarizing or depolarizing electrical pulses, and our objective is to describe the effects such stimuli have on the membrane potential.

Figure 4-3 displays the changes in membrane potential that occur in response to successively stronger stimulus pulses. The application of hyperpolarizing stimuli to the axonal membrane results in responses that are almost mirrors of the "shape" of the stimulus pulse. These responses are passive reflections of the stimulus, with distortions at the leading and trailing edges due to an electrical property of the membrane: its capacitance, the ability to store electrical charges.

If we placed several fine electrodes at successive positions along the axon, but all within 1 mm of the site of stimulation, we would see another important attribute of biological potentials in a conducting medium. If we applied a hyperpolarizing pulse, we would note progressively smaller responses at greater and greater distances from the stimulus site. In fact, there is a simple law that describes this relationship: In a conducting medium, the size of a potential decays as a function of the square of the distance. Since the amplitudes of these responses decline with distance, they are examples of local or graded potentials.

Now let us present a series of depolarizing pulses (Figure 4-3). The membrane response to the initial few stimuli is a series of depolarizing changes, with some distortions. These again are local, graded responses. However, things change suddenly when the depolarizing stimulus reaches a level of 10–15 mV. At this level, a rapid, brief (0.5–2.0 msec) response is provoked: the action potential or nerve impulse. This is a brief transmembrane change in potential that momentarily makes the inside of the membrane positive with respect to the outside. Our experiment has now illustrated the notion of the **threshold** of the nerve impulse, that is, the stimulus intensity just sufficient to elicit a nerve impulse.

What happens when we increase the level of depolarizing stimuli in successive pulses until they get well above threshold? This experiment displays a significant property of axonal membranes: With further increases in depolarizing stimulation, the amplitude of the nerve impulse does not change (Figure 4-4). Thus the size of the nerve impulse is independent of stimulus magnitude. This is referred to as the **all-or-none** property of the nerve impulse. Increases in stimulus strength are represented in the axon by changes in the frequency of nerve impulses. With stronger stimuli, the interval between successive nerve impulses gets shorter.

If we continue our experiment on this axon and now employ either very strong stimuli or stimulating pulses that are closely spaced in time, we observe another important property of axonal membranes. As we offer our beleaguered axon more

Figure 4-4 When one presents depolarizing stimuli (a) that are stronger than threshold (suprathreshold stimuli), the amplitude of the nerve impulses (b) remains fixed and is not influenced by the strength of the stimulus. This fixity of amplitude is referred to as the all-or-none property of action potentials.

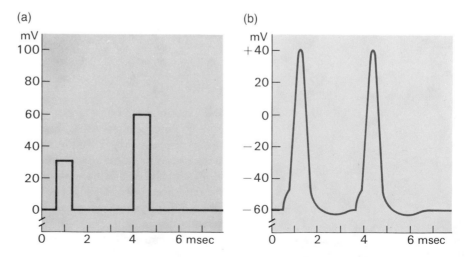

Figure 4-5 Refractory phases following a nerve impulse. The fiber is inexcitable during the absolute refractory period. This means that no matter how intense the depolarization, a nerve impulse cannot be generated. The relative refractory period is characterized by an elevated threshold. The decrease of the threshold during the relative refractory period is shown in blue. At (a) a small depolarization reaches the threshold and elicits an impulse. At (b) even a very large depolarization is unable to elicit an impulse during the absolute refractory period. At (c)–(f) successively smaller depolarizations could elicit an impulse as the threshold declines to the resting level.

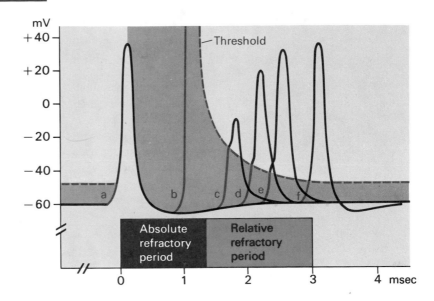

and more intense stimuli, we note that there seems to be an upper limit to the frequency of nerve impulse activity. That upper limit is about 1200 impulses per second. The same underlying property is also shown in experiments in which we compare the effects of varying the interval between two successive stimuli. That is, we space our stimuli closer and closer together until, at some brief interval, only the initial pulse will elicit a nerve impulse. In this case the axon membrane is said to be **refractory** to the second stimulus. There is a period following the initiation of a nerve impulse in which the membrane is totally insensitive to applied stimuli. This is called the **absolute refractory phase.** This is followed by a period of reduced sensitivity, the **relative refractory phase.** The excitability cycle of an axon is shown in Figure 4-5.

A closer look at the form of the nerve impulse shows that the return to baseline is not simple. Rather, many axons show oscillations of potential following the nerve impulse. These changes are called **afterpotentials,** and they are related to changes in excitability following an impulse.

Propagation of nerve impulses

The axon is specialized to communicate nerve impulses over its entire length. How is the nerve impulse conducted along the axon? To explore this process we will add to our experimental setup by placing recording electrodes at several points along the axon (Figure 4-6). The nerve impulse is initiated at one end of the axon, and records are obtained from electrodes along the length of the axon.

These records show that the nerve impulse appears with increasing delays at the successive positions along the length of the axon. The nerve impulse initiated at one location on the axon spreads in a sort of chain reaction along the length, traveling at speeds that range from less than 1 meter/sec in some fibers to more than 100 meters/sec in others.

How does the nerve impulse travel? Basically, the nerve impulse is a change in membrane potential that is regenerated at successive axon locations. It spreads from one region to another because the flow of current associated with this small and rapid potential change stimulates adjacent axon segments. The segment of axon that is just beyond the activated area is supplied with depolarizing current because an electrical circuit is formed along the length of the axon, linking successive regions. The nerve impulse established at one place on the axon is then regenerated at successive points along it.

If we record the conduction speed of impulses in axons that differ in diameter, we see that the rate of conduction varies with the diameter of the axon. Relatively large, heavily myelinated fibers are found in mammalian sensory and motor nerves. In these neurons conduction speed ranges from about 5 m/sec in axons 2 microns (μ)

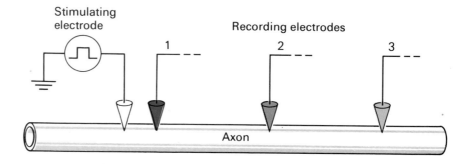

Figure 4-6 Propagation of the nerve impulse along an axon. When a stimulus is delivered at 1 msec on the trace, an action potential appears promptly at recording electrode #1, as shown in recording 1. Electrodes #2 and #3 record potential changes of exactly the same form and amplitude but delayed successively in time (as shown in records 2 and 3) as the impulse propagates along the axon.

BOX 4-2   Do Nerve Impulses Travel at the Speed of Light?

How rapid is neural activity? This problem concerned physiologists even before they knew the nature of the nerve impulse. Late in the eighteenth century the pioneer physiologist Albrecht von Haller estimated 50 m/sec for neural activity in the human being. His estimate was based on the rapidity of reading aloud, although the method by which he reached his estimate was not described very clearly. Early in the nineteenth century the great teacher of physiology, Johannes Müller, said that neural messages must travel exceedingly rapidly—because thought is so fast! He supposed that neural impulses might travel at the speed of light, or at least too rapidly ever to be measured in the short stretches of nerve available.

Hermann von Helmholtz, the outstanding physiologist and physicist and student of Müller, proved his professor wrong. In a famous experiment in 1848, Helmholtz made a frog muscle contract by shocking its nerve at two different distances from the muscle. He measured the time interval between nerve shock and onset of muscle contraction in each case. When Helmholtz applied the shock 5 cm from the muscle, the contraction started 0.0013 sec later than when he shocked the nerve 1 cm from the muscle. From these data he calculated that the speed of the nerve impulse is about 30 m/sec (about 65 mi/hr). The result amazed Helmholtz' contemporaries. It demonstrated that the nerve impulse—a concept that up to then had seemed insubstantial—could be measured quantitatively.

The discovery that nerve impulses travel at moderate speeds encouraged further investigations in both physiology and behavior. Helmholtz' colleague, du Bois-Reymond, measured the electrical action potential of the nerve. And du Bois-Reymond's student, Julius Bernstein, measured the rate of conduction of the electrical action current. He showed that it was the same as that of the functional signal measured by Helmholtz. This series of physical measurements accomplished a major advance: It related behavior to bodily processes. The discovery of the moderate speed of the nerve impulse also encouraged the study of reaction times, and this research helped found the science of psychology. More sophisticated research into reaction time continues today.

---

in diameter to 120 m/sec in axons 20 μ in diameter. The highest speed of neural conduction is only about one-third the speed of sound in air, whereas it was once thought to be as great as the speed of light! (See Box 4-2.) These relatively high rates of conduction aid the speed of sensory and motor processes. Small unmyelinated mammalian nerves have diameters of 1 μ or less, and their conduction speeds range downward from 2 m/sec.

The myelin sheathing on the larger mammalian nerve fibers speeds conduction. The myelin is interrupted by small gaps, called **nodes of Ranvier,** that are spaced about every 1 mm along the axon (recall Figure 2-21). Since the myelin insulation offers considerable resistance to the flow of ionic currents, the impulse jumps from node to node. This is called **saltatory conduction,** from the Latin "saltus" meaning a "leap" or "jump." (The more familiar word somersault comes from the Latin "supra" meaning "over" and "saltus"). The evolution of rapid saltatory conduction in vertebrates has given them a major behavioral advantage over nonvertebrates.

Invertebrate axons are unmyelinated, and most are small in diameter and slow in conduction. An exception to this rule is that many invertebrates have a few giant axons that mediate critical motor responses, such as escape movements. In the invertebrate as in the vertebrate, the speed of conduction increases with axon diameter. The giant axon of the squid has an unusually high rate of conduction for an invertebrate, but the rate still is only about 20 m/sec, considerably slower than that of many mammalian fibers.

The importance of myelin sheathing in promoting rapid conduction of neural impulses helps explain why myelinization is an important index of maturation of the nervous system, as described in Chapter 3. It also helps to explain the gravity of diseases that attack myelin.

Postsynaptic potentials

Postsynaptic potentials are electrical events elicited at postsynaptic sites by the activity of presynaptic axons. They vary in amplitude and can be either positive or negative potential changes. Interaction between these potentials, in the form of summation and subtraction, is the basis of information processing in the neuron, as we will see. Although observations of these electrochemical changes are commonplace today, this is a relatively recent scientific breakthrough. Before the early 1950s, the nature of communication across synapses was a topic of vigorous argument (Eccles, 1982).

The problem of how messages get from one neuron to another has a curious history of changes and controversies. At first it was a nonproblem. Communication among parts of the nervous system seemed to be so swift and complete that scientists in the last century concluded that nerve cells merged into each other, so that impulses flowed with no interruption. But other evidence suggested that nerve cells are separate, even though they make intimate functional contacts. One indication of independence was that when a nerve cell body is destroyed, either in an experiment or by disease, all the branches of the neuron die, but the other neurons with which it is in contact usually remain functional. In 1892 the "neuron doctrine" proclaimed that nerve cells are independent units (as noted in Chapter 2). This doctrine was based largely on extensive anatomical evidence gathered and formulated by the great Spanish neuroanatomist Santiago Ramón y Cajal. One person who remained unconvinced was the eminent Italian neuroanatomist Camillo Golgi. (In Box Figure 2-4, we saw the use of a staining technique developed by Golgi.) These two anatomists were jointly awarded the Nobel Prize in 1906, and in their lectures of acceptance, they continued to take opposite stands on the neuron doctrine. Since the 1950s, definitive evidence has come from electron microscopy. Electron micrographs have shown that even where neurons make their closest functional contacts with each other, each cell is surrounded by its own complete membrane.

Once you realize that neurons are separate entities, you have to account for their ability to communicate with each other. As early as the mid-nineteenth century, du Bois-Reymond [who provided strong evidence for the electrical nature of the nerve impulse (see Box 4-1)] proposed two possible mechanisms by which one neuron could excite another, or could excite a muscle fiber: Either the electrical nerve impulse stimulates the adjacent cell, or the neuron secretes a substance that excites the adjacent cell. Attempts to prove variants of the electrical or the chemical hypotheses provoked lively controversies for a century. Eventually it was found that the nervous system employs both mechanisms—but at different kinds of junctions.

Experimentation on postsynaptic potentials was done with a setup like that shown schematically in Figure 4-7. When a microelectrode is inserted delicately into the cell body of a neuron, the membrane seals around the electrode and the neuron

Figure 4-7 Synaptic potentials recorded when a neuron is stimulated by an inhibitory presynaptic neuron (b) or by an excitatory presynaptic neuron (c). Note that the presynaptic recordings are similar in the two cases, but the postsynaptic response to the inhibitory neuron is hyperpolarizing, whereas the postsynaptic response to the excitatory neuron is depolarizing.

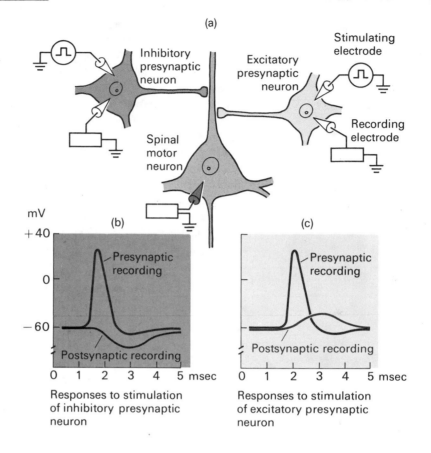

continues to function normally. During the 1950s and 1960s, experiments on synaptic transmission in mammals involved spinal motor neurons because they are large and many characteristics of their inputs were known. The receptive surface of each spinal motor neuron has many synaptic connections, some of which were known on the basis of their behavioral effects to be excitatory and some to be inhibitory. By selecting the presynaptic cell to stimulate, investigators can see how the motor neuron responds to signals from either excitatory or inhibitory connections. The responses of the presynaptic and postsynaptic cells are shown on the same records so that their time relations can be compared readily.

Stimulation of an excitatory presynaptic neuron leads to an all-or-none action potential in the presynaptic cell. In the postsynaptic cell, a small local depolarization is seen. Generally it takes the combined effect of several excitatory synapses to elicit an all-or-none potential from a postsynaptic neuron. If **excitatory postsynaptic potentials (EPSPs)** are elicited almost simultaneously by several neurons that converge on the motor cell, these potentials can summate and produce a depolarization that reaches the threshold and triggers an action potential. Note that there is a delay: The postsynaptic depolarization begins about half a millisecond after the presynaptic impulse. This delay was important evidence that the postsynaptic effect was not just an attenuated reflection of the presynaptic action current.

Further evidence that the synapse makes a special contribution came from analysis of the results of presynaptic inhibitory stimulation. This is shown in the bottom records of Figure 4-7. The action potential of an inhibitory presynaptic neuron looks exactly like that of the excitatory presynaptic fiber. Neurons have only one kind of propagated signal. But the postsynaptic local potentials show opposite polarities. When the inhibitory neuron is stimulated, the postsynaptic signal is an *increase* of the resting potential. This hyperpolarization is inhibitory for the motor neuron—it decreases the probability that the neuron will fire an impulse—so it is called an **inhibitory postsynaptic potential (IPSP).**

If a chemical step is required in synaptic transmission, this could help to explain a number of phenomena. It could explain the delay of about 0.5 msec in synaptic transmission. Time is required for the transmitter agent to be released, diffuse across the synaptic gap, and react with receptor molecules in the postsynaptic membrane. The chemical hypothesis also explains why the synapse acts as a sort of one-way valve; that is, transmission proceeds from presynaptic terminals to postsynaptic cells but not in the reverse direction. When we stimulate the axon of the postsynaptic cell, we do not see any changes in the presynaptic terminals. The reason is that the presynaptic terminal can liberate a chemical transmitter, but the synaptic membrane of the postsynaptic cell cannot. The axon also normally conducts impulses in only one direction. This is because the action potential starts at the **axon hillock,** the place where the axon emerges from the cell body. As the action potential progresses along the axon, it leaves in its wake a stretch of refractory membrane. Propagated activity does not spread from the hillock back over the cell body and dendrites because the membrane of the cell body and dendrites, although chemically sensitive, is not electrically excitable and will not produce a regenerated impulse. By the early 1950s a combination of chemical transmission and ionic mechanisms appeared to offer a complete account of transmission at synapses.

Shortly after the chemical hypothesis seemed to have won out for good, an excitatory synapse in the crayfish central nervous system was found to operate by purely electrical means (Furshpan and Potter, 1957). Then an inhibitory electrical synapse was found in the goldfish (Furukawa and Furshpan, 1963). Even more surprisingly, Martin and Pilar (1963) found synapses in the chick that employ both chemical and electrical transmission. Subsequent research has revealed electrical as well as chemical synapses in many mammals—in fact, in all species that have been investigated in this regard. However, chemical transmission occurs much more frequently (see reviews by M.V.L. Bennett, 1973, 1976).

Electrical synapses At **electrical synapses** the presynaptic membrane comes even closer to the post-synaptic membrane than it does at chemical synapses; the cleft measures only 2–4 nm, as shown in Figure 4-8. This is in contrast to the separation of 20–30 nm at chemical synapses. The narrowness of the gap at electrical junctions means a very low electrical resistance between the presynaptic and postsynaptic surfaces. As a consequence, current flow associated with nerve impulses in the presynaptic axon terminal can travel across the narrow cleft to the postsynaptic membrane. Transmission at these synapses is then quite similar to conduction along the axon. The principal contrast with axonal transmission is that most of these connections are direc-

Figure 4-8 Electrical synapse in crayfish. A_1 indicates the presynaptic axon and A_2 is the postsynaptic axon. A few vesicles are seen on both sides, but their function is not known. (magnification × 130,000) [From G. D. Pappas and D. P. Purpura, *Structure and function of synapses* (New York: Raven Press, 1972), p. 26.]

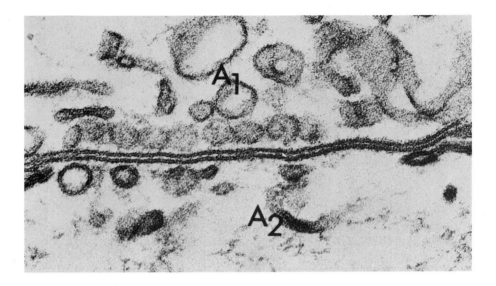

tional or polarized, which means that the connection works in only one direction. This is demonstrated by experiments that involve electrical stimulation of the postsynaptic cell with the intention of seeing whether it is possible to produce a nerve impulse that goes back across the gap to the presynaptic terminal. Depolarization of the presynaptic axon terminal cannot be produced in this manner. The mechanism of one-way transmission at electrical synapses is not as well understood as that at chemical synapses. Electrical synapses work with little time delay. They are frequently found as part of neural circuits that mediate escape behaviors in simpler invertebrates. They are also found where many fibers must be activated synchronously, as in the vertebrate oculomotor system for control of rapid eye movements.

Information processing by small neural circuits

Synaptic transmission and impulse conduction not only achieve the communication of signals but also transform messages in ways that make complex behavior possible. A few examples will show some of the capabilities of neurons for processing information.

The nerve cell, with its synaptic inputs, is able to perform both summation and subtraction of input signals. These operations are possible because of the characteristics of synaptic inputs, the way in which the neuron integrates the postsynaptic potentials, and the trigger mechanism that determines whether a neuron will fire off an impulse. As we have seen, the postsynaptic potentials that are caused by the action of transmitter chemicals can be either depolarizing (excitatory) or hyperpolarizing (inhibitory). These potentials spread passively over the neuron from their points of origin on dendrites and on the cell body. The trigger mechanism for mammalian neurons is located at the initial segment of the axon which, in mammalian multipolar neurons, is the axon hillock. Thus what determines whether the neuron will fire off an action potential is whether depolarization reaches the critical threshold at the axon hillock.

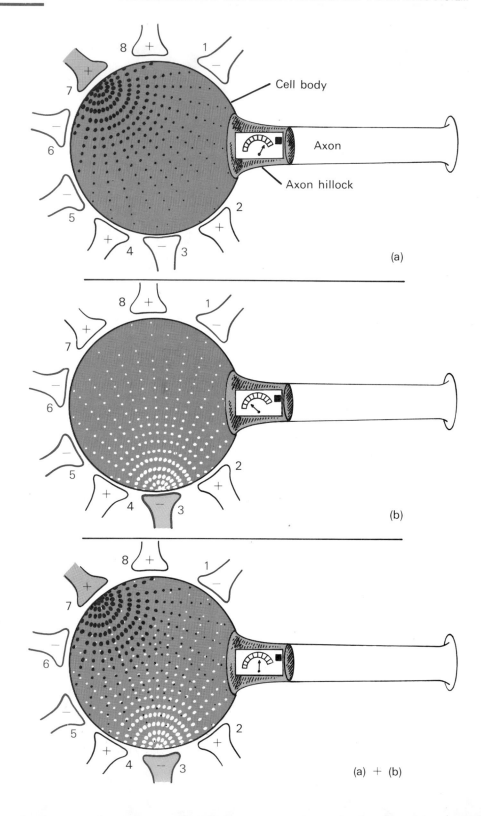

*A model for nerve cell
information processing*

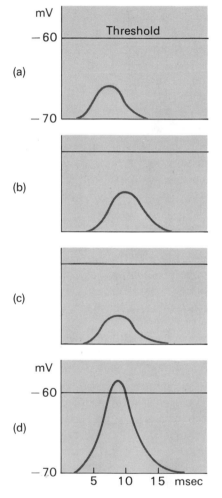

For an analogy to nerve cell information processing, look at the physical model shown in Figure 4-9. Here the cell body is represented by a metal disc. For simplicity, no dendrites are shown, and all input endings are on the cell body. The presynaptic terminals are represented by tubes through which blasts of hot or cold air can be delivered; hot air represents excitatory synaptic action and cold air, inhibitory synaptic action. The axon hillock contains a thermostat. If the temperature rises above the resting level of 30 degrees to a critical level of 45 degrees (the threshold), the thermostat closes a circuit and triggers a propagated impulse.

Suppose an impulse arrives at ending number 7, as shown at (a) in Figure 4-9. A pulse of hot air is delivered, causing local heating of the cell body. This heat spreads out over the disc, dissipating as it spreads so that only a small proportion of the heat reaches the axon hillock. Part (b) of Figure 4-9 shows what happens when a blast of cold air is delivered at ending 3. The resultant local cooling spreads passively, so that the change of temperature diminishes as it travels. Since 3 is relatively close to the axon hillock, a greater proportion of the change reaches the hillock than was true of the change that originated at 7. If 3 and 7 are activated simultaneously, since one cools and the other warms, these effects partially cancel each other. Thus the net effect is the difference between the two: The neuron *subtracts* the inhibitory postsynaptic potential from the excitatory postsynaptic potential. If two excitatory terminals are activated simultaneously, their effects sum at the hillock: The neuron *adds* postsynaptic potentials that have the same sign. The summation of potentials across the cell body is called **spatial summation.** Only if the overall resultant of all the potentials is sufficient to raise the hillock temperature to the threshold level is an impulse triggered off. Usually it requires the convergence of excitatory messages from several presynaptic fibers to fire off a neuron. Figure 4-10 illustrates how potentials add algebraically.

Summation can also take place between postsynaptic effects that are not absolutely simultaneous, since the effects last for a few milliseconds. The closer they are in time, the greater the overlap and the more complete the summation. This is called

Figure 4-10 Summation of excitatory synaptic potentials. Graphs (a), (b), and (c) represent inputs that differ in amplitude and time. Graph (d) represents their algebraic summation.

Figure 4-9 Physical model of summation of synaptic influences on activity of postsynaptic neuron. Tubes representing presynaptic endings (1–8) can each deliver a blast of hot (+) or cold (−) air to the metal disc that represents the cell body. Each arrival of an impulse at a presynaptic ending leads to a blast of air. In (a) a pulse of hot air at 7 causes local heating of the cell body. This heat spreads over the disc, dissipating as it goes; only a small proportion of the heat reaches the axon hillock. In (b) a pulse of cool air at 3 leads to local cooling of the cell body, and this effect also spreads passively, the temperature change diminishing as it travels. Since 3 is relatively close to the axon hillock, a greater proportion of the change at 3 reaches the hillock than was true of the change at 7. In (c) since 3 cools and 7 warms, these effects partially cancel each other. The hillock contains a thermostatic device that triggers activity in the axon only where the temperature reaches a certain level. The disc integrates all the temperature changes, and the axon hillock senses the algebraic sum.

temporal summation. But even successive impulses arriving at the same terminal can produce postsynaptic effects that summate. Thus, although the impulses are all-or-none, the postsynaptic effect can be graded in size: A rapid barrage of impulses produces a larger postsynaptic potential than a single impulse does.

Dendrites were omitted from Figure 4-9 for simplicity, but let us see how they add to the story. Dendrites augment the receptive surface of the neuron and increase the amount of input information the neuron can handle. The farther out on a dendrite a potential is produced, the less effect it will have on the axon hillock. When the potential arises at a dendritic spine, its effect is further reduced because it has to spread down the shaft of the spine. Thus information arriving at various parts of the neuron is weighted in terms of the distance and path resistance to the axon hillock.

Examples of processing in local circuits

Circuits of just a few neurons can accomplish quite powerful feats, because of the ability of the neuron to add and subtract and to show temporal and spatial summation of postsynaptic potentials. Thus local circuits can select one type of stimulus out of a welter of stimuli; they can enhance the difference between two stimuli; they can classify stimuli into groups; they can generate motor patterns; and they can correlate inputs, provide an internal clock, and synchronize activities with it. Let us briefly consider two examples from visual perception.

The first example shows a simple retinal circuit that detects direction of movement (Figure 4-11). Some neurons in the retina respond to a stimulus that moves to the right, but not to one that moves to the left. Others respond only to movement to the left, or to upward movement. Since the receptors in the retina are excited by any stimulus that enters their field of vision, how is such discrimination accomplished? The retinal receptor cells in Figure 4-11 stimulate **bipolar cells.** These in turn stimulate **ganglion cells,** whose axons form the optic nerve. In addition, there are **horizontal cells** that form inhibitory synapses on bipolar cells. In the case of a stimulus moving to the right (the black arrows), each bipolar cell is excited before the corresponding horizontal cell is activated, so stimulation is relayed to the ganglion cell. But when a stimulus moves to the left (the gray arrows), it stimulates each horizontal cell before stimulating the bipolar cell with which the horizontal cell forms a synapse. Thus with leftward movement the bipolar cell is inhibited when the excitatory message arrives from the receptor. Because of temporal summation, the inhibitory postsynaptic potential cancels (or at least reduces) the excitatory potential, so the bipolar cells fail to excite the ganglion cell. Therefore this ganglion cell does not respond to stimulus movement to the left, whereas it had responded to stimulus movement to the right. This example also illustrates the **convergence** of information from different sources, which occurs at many places in the nervous system.

Another example of information processing in local circuits is seen in a circuit that produces contrast effects at boundaries between two kinds or levels of stimulation. Thus red appears more saturated when it borders green, and white appears brighter next to black. Most animals with vision show such contrast effects, which are based on neural circuitry. The neurons that are connected to adjacent visual receptors make inhibitory connections with each other. Here there is **divergence** of messages from each neuron to many adjacent ones. When one patch of neurons is strongly stimulated by light and a neighboring patch is only weakly stimulated by it (Figure 4-12),

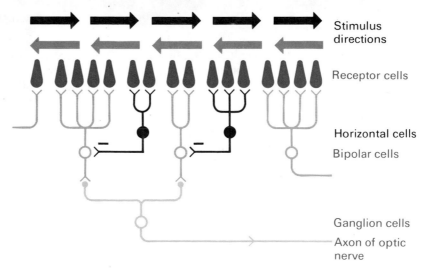

Figure 4-11 A simple circuit of retinal neurons that respond to stimuli that move to the right but does not respond to those that move to the left.

Stimulus directions

Receptor cells

Horizontal cells
Bipolar cells

Ganglion cells
Axon of optic nerve

Figure 4-12 A retinal neural circuit that sharpens contours by lateral inhibition. Lateral inhibitory connections depress neural activity, especially among cells receiving a high level of illumination. A contrast effect occurs at the boundary between cells receiving high and low levels of illumination.

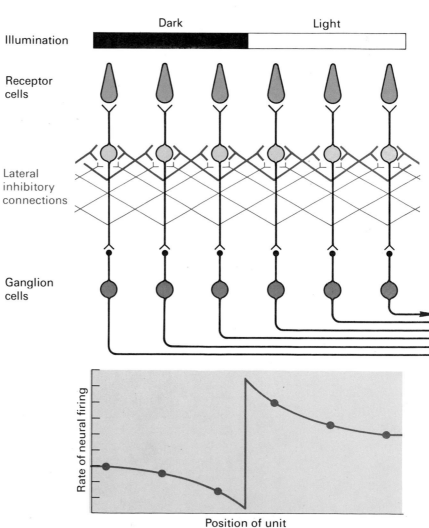

Illumination

Dark   Light

Receptor cells

Lateral inhibitory connections

Ganglion cells

Rate of neural firing

Position of unit

the inhibitory signals cause a contrast effect at the boundary. Within the strongly stimulated group of neurons, there is mutual inhibition, which reduces the level of excitation. But the units just inside the boundary of the strongly light-stimulated patch are only slightly inhibited by their neighbors on the dark side, so the greatest level of excitation occurs on the light side of the boundary. These units strongly inhibit their neighbors on the dark side, so the lowest level of excitation is found just on the dark side of the boundary. Thus the inhibitory interconnections within the spatial array of units produce contrast, or sharpening of the perception of various patterns of light.

Ionic mechanisms of excitation and conduction

Now that we have seen some of the main characteristics and functions of electrical signals in neurons, let us examine the mechanisms that produce these potentials. This section will provide a nontechnical explanation; more complete accounts can be found in many sources (for example, Kuffler and Nichols, 1976; Kandel and Schwartz, 1981).

Mechanisms of the resting potential

Consider the distribution of ions across the simplified and idealized neural membrane in Figure 4-13. Inside the cell there is a high concentration of potassium ions, each of which has a positive electrical charge (K^+). There is also a high internal concentration of large protein ions, each with a negative charge. Finally, the axon has

Figure 4-13 Distribution of ions inside a neuron and outside the neuron in the extracellular space. Note that most K^+ ions are found in the intracellular space, whereas most Na^+ and Cl^- ions are in the extracellular space. Some exchange between the intracellular and extracellular spaces occurs through channels in the cell membrane.

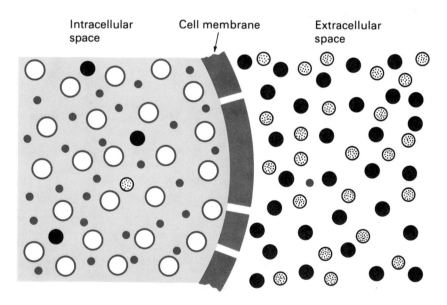

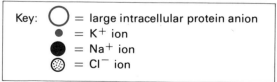

Key: ⃝ = large intracellular protein anion
      • = K^+ ion
      ● = Na^+ ion
      ⊛ = Cl^- ion

TABLE 4-1   Concentrations of Ions Inside and Outside Squid Axons (millimoles)

ION	INSIDE NEURON	IN BLOOD	IN SEA WATER
Potassium (K^+)	400	20	10
Sodium (Na^+)	50	440	460
Chloride (Cl^-)	40–150	560	540

low internal concentrations of sodium (Na^+) and chloride (Cl^-) ions. Because of their negative charges, the protein and chloride ions are called **anions.** Positively charged ions such as K^+ and Na^+ are called **cations.** The cell membrane contains many small pores through which the potassium ions can flow in or out relatively easily but which are not permeable to the other ions.

What happens when the neuron is placed in a solution that contains the same concentrations of ions as exist inside the cell? Some potassium ions may flow in or out, but there will be no net change and no charge will develop across the membrane. What happens when the neuron is placed in a solution, such as blood plasma or sea water, that has a low concentration of potassium and high concentrations of sodium and chloride? (The concentrations inside and outside the squid axon are shown in Table 4-1.) Certain laws of physical chemistry govern the movements of ions in solutions. For example, substances in solution move from regions of high concentration to regions of low concentration, unless there is some impeding force like a membrane. In the absence of other forces, potassium ions tend to move out of the cell, since their concentration is 20 times greater inside than outside. This creates a potential difference across the membrane, since positive charges (potassium ions) leave the inside and accumulate outside. If the membrane were permeable to anions, one anion would accompany each positive ion out and no potential difference would occur, but the membrane of the axon is impermeable to anions. When the potential difference across the membrane becomes large enough, it stops the net outflow of positive ions. This occurs because the positive ions outside repel each other, but are attracted to the negative ions inside.

At this point in the process, the tendency of the ions to flow from the regions of high concentration is exactly balanced by the opposing potential difference across the membrane. This potential is called the **potassium equilibrium potential.** This phenomenon is so predictable according to the laws of physical chemistry that it is possible to calculate the equilibrium potential by an equation, called the **Nernst equation.** The Nernst equation represents the voltage that develops when a semipermeable membrane separates different concentrations of ions. It predicts that the potential across the squid axon membrane will be about -75 mV, inside to outside. The actual value is about -70 mV.

The discrepancy between the predicted and observed values occurs because the membrane is not absolutely impermeable to sodium ions. Small numbers leak in gradually, and this tends to reduce the membrane potential. This in turn causes more potassium ions to move out. Eventually this leakage would cause the concentrations inside and outside the cell to become the same, and the membrane potential would disappear. The neuron prevents this by pumping sodium out of the cell, and potassium into the cell, just rapidly enough to counter the leakage. So, maintaining the membrane potential demands metabolic work by the cell. In fact, most of the energy expended by the brain—whether waking or sleeping—is thought to be used to maintain the ionic gradients across neuronal membranes so that neurons will be ready to conduct impulses.

The action potential   It used to be thought that the action potential resulted from a momentary increase in membrane permeability to all ions, so that the membrane potential dropped to zero. But research with the squid axon revealed a more interesting story. The action potential is actually larger than the resting potential. There is an "overshoot" that briefly makes the inside of the neuron positive with respect to the outside (Curtis and Cole, 1939). The change of potential was shown in Figure 4-3. The amplitude of this overshoot is determined by the concentration of sodium ions (Hodgkin and Katz, 1949), even though sodium does not affect the resting potential. At the peak of the nerve impulse, the potential across the membrane approaches that predicted by the Nernst equation with respect to the concentration of sodium ions: about +40 mV.

Thus, in its resting stage, the neural membrane can be thought of as essentially a "potassium membrane," since it is permeable only to K^+ and the potential is about that of the potassium equilibrium potential. But the active membrane is a "sodium membrane," since it is mainly permeable to Na^+ and the membrane potential tends toward the **sodium equilibrium potential.** Thus the action current occurs during a sudden shift in membrane properties, and these revert quickly to the resting state.

What causes the changes from K^+ permeability to Na^+ permeability and back again? A reduction in the resting potential of the membrane (depolarization) increases Na^+ permeability. This can be thought of as "opening gates" at the ends of some pores, or **ion channels,** in the membrane. These gates admit Na^+, but not other ions. As some sodium ions enter the neuron, the resting potential is further reduced, opening still more Na^+ channels. Thus the process accelerates until all barriers to the entry of Na^+ are removed, and sodium ions rush in. This increased permeability to Na^+ lasts less than a millisecond; then a process of inactivation blocks the Na^+ channels. By this time the membrane potential has reached the sodium equilibrium potential of around +40 mV. Now positive charges inside the nerve cell tend to push potassium ions out, and the permeability to K^+ also increases somewhat, so that the resting potential is soon regained.

Earlier in this chapter we stated that the sequence of electrical events observed during conduction of a nerve impulse could be explained in terms of ionic mechanisms. Now we see that they can be accounted for in detail by the sequence of Na^+ and K^+ currents (Hodgkin and Huxley, 1952).

The absolute and relative refractory phases also can be related to these changes in permeability. When the Na^+ channels have opened completely during the rise of the nerve impulse, further stimulation does not affect the course of events. Also, during inactivation of the Na^+ channels, when stimulation cannot reopen them, the action current falls off. So, during the rising and falling phases of an action potential, the neuron is absolutely refractory to elicitation of a second impulse. While K^+ ions are flowing out and the resting potential is being restored, the neuron is relatively refractory.

Gating ion channels   Because changes in the permeability of the nerve membrane to Na⁺ and K⁺ ions during the course of the nerve impulse are so important, many investigators are studying the mechanisms that control these events (Hille, 1976; Ritchie, 1979). In particular they are trying to find the molecular bases of the voltage sensors that indicate when the changes are initiated and also the "gates" in the ionic channels. Gating is thought to involve rearrangements in the shape or positions of charged molecules that line the channel. Making such changes requires the expenditure of energy. During the 1970s several research groups reported the measurement of tiny electrical currents that seem to be related to molecular rearrangements that open or shut gates in ion channels; these have been called gating currents.

Since the ion channels in axon membranes are too tiny to be seen even with the electron microscope, how can investigators determine their structures and modes of operation? The solution has been to test pharmacological substances that affect one or another aspect of the functioning of the channels. Important clues emerge from knowing the sizes and shapes of such molecules and knowing whether they are effective at only one or the other side of the membrane. The sodium channel has been an object of special study, and detailed understanding of its structure and mechanisms is beginning to emerge (Ritchie, 1979).

Figure 4-14 is a schematic picture of a sodium channel in the membrane at a node

Figure 4-14 The sodium channel in the neural membrane. (Adapted from Ritchie, 1979)

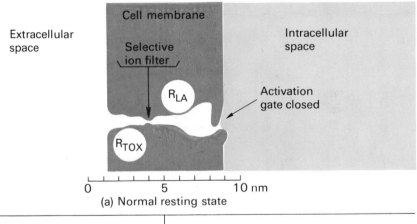

(a) Normal resting state

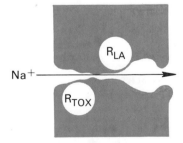

(b) Sodium channel open during rising phase of action potential

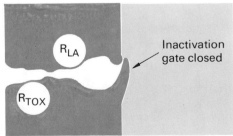

(c) Sodium channel closed by inactivation gate during falling phase of action potential

of Ranvier in a myelinated axon. Let us look at some of the features of this model and some of the main evidence on which they are based. Certain toxins of animal origin, when applied to the outer surface of the membrane, block the sodium channel (but no others). These are tetrodotoxin (TTX) and saxitoxin (STX). The size and structures of TTX and STX together with those of other molecules that do or do not alter Na^+ permeability suggest the following dimensions of the sodium channel. The outer part is an antechamber that measures 0.9 nm by 1.0 nm. Deeper in the membrane the channel narrows to a pore 0.3 nm by 0.5 nm. In this narrow ionic selectivity filter there is a binding site to which metal cations bind, as well as TTX and STX. This receptor for toxins is labeled R_{TOX} in Figure 4-14. A narrow part of the structure of the TTX and STX molecules enters the pore and sticks there because the rest of the molecule is too wide to pass. Thus the channel is blocked to Na^+ ions.

Tetrodotoxin is found in the ovaries of the pufferfish, which is esteemed as a delicacy in Japan. Fish markets in Japan display dried pufferfish, blown up like globes. If the pufferfish ovaries are not removed properly and if the the fish is not cleaned with great care, people who eat it may be poisoned, because their neurons cannot function. People die from this cause each year, and now neuroscientists know why.

In contrast to toxins that act at a site near the outer surface of the membrane, certain local anesthetics act at a different site that is accessible only from inside the membrane. This receptor for local anesthetics is labeled R_{LA} in Figure 4-14.

Whereas the action of local anesthetics is temporary and wears off, a permanent change is caused if the enzyme pronase is introduced within the axon. Pronase destroys the inactivation gate that normally shuts the Na^+ channel. Two kinds of scorpions have evolved venoms that block processes basic to neural conduction. The venom of the *Leiurus* scorpion impairs the inactivation gate, but the venom of the *Centruroides* scorpion specifically impairs the activation gate. Thus it is clear that different molecular processes control the two kinds of gating of the sodium channel. A snake that we will mention below has evolved a toxin that blocks chemical transmission at synapses that use acetylcholine. Blocking either conduction of impulses or synaptic transmission is an effective way for an animal to kill its prey.

Chemical properties of synapses

The activity of a chemical agent is essential to transmission at chemical synapses. Consequently the structures and processes involved in producing, storing, releasing, and receiving chemical transmitters are critical. Figure 4-15 shows the main structures related to chemical synaptic transmission: synaptic vesicles, the synaptic cleft, and receptor sites. We will mention them briefly and then discuss them in more detail.

Synaptic vesicles are located within the axon terminal of the presynaptic neuron. These vesicles are small globules that, in a given synapse, are all the same size and show the same staining properties but vary in size and appearance among different synapses. The size ranges from 40 nm to 200 nm. From the time that they were discovered in electron micrographs in the 1950s, synaptic vesicles were linked with chemical transmission, and they have since been demonstrated to store packets of the chemical transmitter used at the particular synapse. The size and shape of the vesicles may provide clues to the identity of the transmitter.

Figure 4-15 Electron micrograph of two synapses in the cerebral cortex of a rat. S_1 and S_2 show the synaptic junctions with prominent postsynaptic thickenings on the membrane of the dendrite (Den). The axon terminals (At_1 and At_2) are filled with synaptic vesicles. (magnification $\times$ 100,000) (From Peters, Palay, and Webster, 1976)

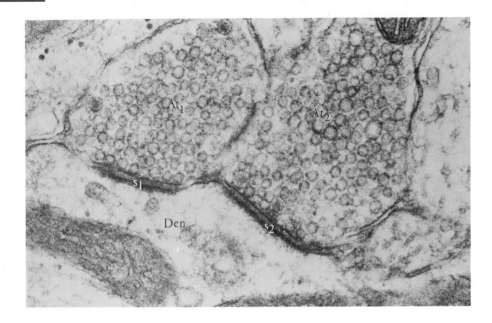

Chemical transmitters are substances liberated at presynaptic terminals that produce potential changes in the postsynaptic membrane. There are many different transmitter substances. A given neuron produces only one transmitter substance at all its terminals, but some terminals of the same cell may be excitatory and others inhibitory, depending on the receptor molecules. The transmitter is manufactured at the terminal and stored in vesicles for release into the synaptic cleft. Several substances—such as acetylcholine (ACh) and norepinephrine (NE)—have been demonstrated to be synaptic transmitters, and many more substances are presumed to be.

The **synaptic cleft** is the space between the presynaptic and postsynaptic neurons. Only about 20–30 nm separates the facing membranes of the two neurons.

Receptor sites, located on the postsynaptic side of the cleft, are regions of specialized membrane that receive and react with the chemical transmitter. These sites contain specialized **receptor proteins,** which have an affinity for certain transmitters. The transmitter–receptor reaction causes a change in membrane potential in the direction of depolarization (at an excitatory synapse) or hyperpolarization (at an inhibitory synapse). The receptor membrane has different staining properties from the rest of the membrane.

Storage and release of transmitters

When a nerve impulse reaches a presynaptic terminal, vesicles in contact with the presynaptic membrane discharge their contents into the synaptic cleft, where the molecules quickly diffuse to the receptor on the other side (Figure 4-16). Actually, there is a delay of at least 0.5 msec between the arrival of the impulse at the presynaptic ending and the first sign of a potential change at the postsynaptic membrane because chemical steps are required to release the synaptic transmitter. The arrival of the nerve impulse at the presynaptic terminal causes calcium ions (Ca^{2+}) to enter

Figure 4-16 Discharge of transmitter molecules from synaptic vesicles into the synaptic cleft. At (b) a synaptic vesicle fuses with a discharge site in the presynaptic membrane, and at (c) it ruptures, liberating transmitter molecules into the cleft. The molecules diffuse across the cleft and are taken up by special receptors in the postsynaptic membrane. Meanwhile, the emptied vesicle is recycled (d) and supplied again with molecules of transmitter.

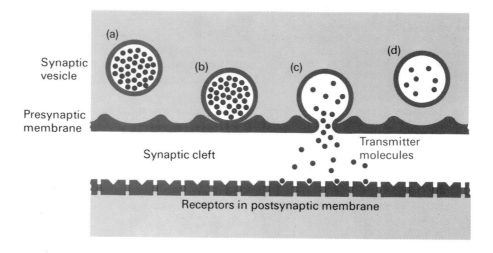

the terminal. Recent work has shown that the entry of Ca^{2+} is controlled by a substance called calmodulin (Roufagalis, 1980). The greater the influx of Ca^{2+}, the greater the number of vesicles released by the impulse. If the concentration of Ca^{2+} in the extracellular fluid is reduced, fewer vesicles are released. (Calcium is also important in the liberation of hormones from endocrine glands.) Most synaptic delay is caused by the processes related to the entrance of calcium ions (Ca^{2+}) into the terminal. Small delays are caused by diffusion of the transmitter across the cleft and reaction of the transmitter with the receptor.

The vesicles in a given synapse all appear to contain the same number of molecules of transmitter chemical. The release of each vesicle causes the same change in potential in the postsynaptic membrane. Normally a nerve impulse causes release of the contents of several hundred vesicles at a time. But if the concentration of calcium is lowered at a synapse, only a few vesicles are released per impulse, and the size of unit depolarizations can then be measured. The number of molecules of transmitter per vesicle is not yet known accurately, but it is probably in the tens of thousands. The accurate measurement of detailed synaptic events, including unit depolarizations, won the Nobel Prize for Sir Bernard Katz in 1970. The end bouton normally produces and stores enough transmitter substance to ensure that the neuron is ready for activity. Intense stimulation of the neuron reduces the number of vesicles, but after a time, more vesicles are produced to replace those that were discharged. Neurons differ in their ability to keep pace with a rapid rate of incoming signals. The production of the transmitter chemical is governed by enzymes that are manufactured in the neuron cell body close to the nucleus. These enzymes are transported actively down the axons to the terminals. If they weren't, synaptic function could not continue.

The role of receptor proteins

How does the joining of the chemical transmitter with the receptor protein in the postsynaptic membrane cause changes in the polarity of that membrane? How can the same chemical transmitter cause depolarization at some synapses but hyperpolarization at others? **Acetylcholine (ACh),** for example, is an excitatory transmitter at synapses between motor nerves and skeletal muscles, but an inhibitory one between the vagus nerve and heart muscle. It is a positively charged ion, but far too little of it is released to account directly for the positive synaptic potentials at excitatory junctions, and direct transfer of charges could not produce the negative effect at inhibitory junctions.

The action of a key in a lock is analogous to the action of a transmitter on the receptor protein (Figure 4-17). Just as a particular key can open different doors, a particular chemical transmitter can lead to the opening of different channels in the neural membrane. At excitatory synapses where it is the transmitter, ACh opens channels for both sodium and potassium ions, as Jenkinson and Nicholls (1961) demonstrated by following the movement of radioactive Na^+ and K^+ ions. Increasing the permeability to both cations drives the membrane voltage down toward zero. At inhibitory synapses, ACh opens a different door. It increases the permeability of the membrane to chloride ions (Cl^-), which increases the potential across the membrane (hyperpolarizes it). Thus the receptor protein itself must be different at different kinds of synapses. Not only must ACh react with proteins that provide different channels for Na^+, K^+, and Cl^- but other transmitter chemicals (such as norepinephrine, gamma aminobutyric acid [GABA], and probably a host of others) must fit like keys into their specific locks.

The key-and-lock analogy is strengthened by the observation that various chemicals can fit onto receptor proteins and block the entrance of the key. In the case of ACh, two blocking agents that have been studied extensively are curare and bungarotoxin. Curare is famous as the arrowhead poison used by South American Indians. Extracted from a plant, it greatly increased the efficiency of hunting: If the hunter managed to hit any part of his prey, the poison soon paralyzed the animal. Bungarotoxin is a lethal poison produced by the bungarus snake of Taiwan. This toxin has proved very useful in studying acetylcholine receptors because a radioactive label can be attached to it without altering its action. With such labeling it is possible to investigate the number and distribution of receptor molecules at various kinds of synapses, as well as details of transmitter–receptor binding.

Just as there are master keys that fit many different locks, submasters that fit a certain group, and keys that fit only a single lock, so there are chemical transmitters that fit several different receptor molecules, and others that fit only one. Acetylcholine acts on at least four kinds of receptors. Two main kinds of cholinergic receptors are called **nicotinic** and **muscarinic,** named after the compounds nicotine and muscarine. Nicotine mimics chiefly the excitatory activities of ACh, and muscarine mim-

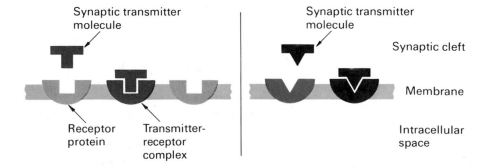

Figure 4-17 Lock-and-key model of transmitter-receptor function. Each synaptic transmitter has a particular shape that fits only one kind of receptor molecule. Two kinds of transmitters and their receptors are diagrammed here.

Synaptic transmitter molecule

Synaptic transmitter molecule

Synaptic cleft

Membrane

Intracellular space

Receptor protein

Transmitter-receptor complex

BOX 4-3 A Living, Shocking Torpedo

Mammalian nerves and muscles operate with electrical potentials of only about one-tenth of a volt, but several families of fish have evolved organs that can produce a shock of several hundred volts—enough to stun or kill their prey. The genus of fish called *Torpedo,* long known in the Mediterranean Sea, was so named because their shock rendered their prey torpid (numb and motionless). The underwater explosive devices known as torpedoes were named after the fish. Another family of fish that evolved a powerful electric shock organ is the so-called electric eel (genus *Electrophorus*). (See Box Figure 4-1.) Although long and slender in form, these fish are not eels, but relatives of carp.

In the genus *Torpedo,* the electric organs evolved from the neuromuscle endplates. As the incipient muscle cell develops, it flattens and loses its power to contract. The electroplaque units stack up in series, which provides high voltage. Stacks are also arranged in parallel, which provides considerable current. The build-up of voltage and discharge of shocks are controlled by nerves. The synaptic chemical acetylcholine (ACh) develops the voltage in the electric organs of both torpedoes and electric eels. The electric organs of these fish have been used as a rich source of the enzyme acetylcholinesterase (AChE) for research. So the same chemical transmitter (ACh) that functions at human neuromuscular junctions and elsewhere in the human nervous system builds up impressive —even shocking—voltages in other vertebrates.

Box Figure 4-1 Electric eel. (© New York Zoological Society Photo)

ics chiefly the inhibitory actions. Cholinergic receptors (those responding to ACh) at neuromuscular synapses on skeletal muscles and in autonomic ganglia are nicotinic. Cholinergic receptors on organs innervated by the parasympathetic division of the autonomic system are muscarinic; this is true of such effectors as heart muscle, the intestines, and the salivary gland. Most ACh receptors in the brain are muscarinic. They were thought to be exclusively so, but now small numbers of nicotinic receptors have been found in the brain, and some brain cells show the curious property of responding to both nicotine and muscarine. Nicotinic receptors are inhibited by the compound hexamethonium, but not by atropine, whereas muscarinic receptors are blocked by atropine, but not by hexamethonium. Some cholinergic receptors—both nicotinic and muscarinic—are excitatory and others are inhibitory. Most

Figure 4-18 Arrival of a synaptic transmitter (or a hormone) at a receptor in a neural membrane can lead to formation of a second messenger inside the cell. The transmitter activates the receptor and the associated enzyme; the enzyme then converts some of the precursor within the cell into the second messenger.

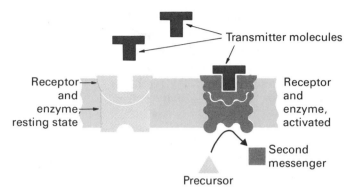

nicotinic sites are excitatory, but there are also inhibitory nicotinic synapses, and there are both excitatory and inhibitory muscarinic synapses.

Typically, receptors for synaptic transmitters are located in the postsynaptic membrane, but recently receptors for serotonin and dopamine have been found on the presynaptic side (Usdin and Bunney, 1975). It is thought that these so-called **autoreceptors** provide a negative feedback mechanism. Through them the transmitter can inform the axon terminal, "I am doing my job, no more release is needed."

The second messenger: Boosting the effect of transmitters

At many synapses, chemical transmission involves a further step. The action of the transmitter on the receptor alters the concentration of another substance in the postsynaptic cell (Figure 4-18). If we think of the transmitter as the first messenger at the synapse, then the substance within the cell is a **second messenger.** The second messenger amplifies the effect of the first and can initiate processes that lead to changes in electrical potential at the membrane. In many cases, second messengers also lead to biochemical changes within the neuron. As we will see in Chapter 5, many hormones also act by causing the release of a second messenger within their target cells. In 1971, Earl W. Sutherland was awarded the Nobel Prize for research on second messengers that he began in the 1950s. He showed that in many cases the second messenger is the small molecule **cyclic adenosine monophosphate (cyclic AMP** or **cAMP).**

The second messenger system works relatively slowly, so it seems to be involved in longer-lasting actions, such as motivational states or formation of long-term memories, rather than in relaying sensory information or motor commands. Cyclic AMP has been implicated in synaptic activities of the transmitters dopamine, norepinephrine, and serotonin. ACh acts directly, without intervention of a second messenger, at neuromuscular synapses. But many cholinergic synapses in the brain appear to use another second messenger, cyclic guanosine monophosphate (cyclic GMP). After the second messenger has carried out its activity, it is inactivated by an enzyme, phosphodiesterase. Drugs such as caffeine that inhibit this enzyme allow the second messenger to act more strongly and for a longer period. Thus they intensify the effects of the transmitter.

Cessation of action of synaptic transmitters

When a chemical transmitter is released, its postsynaptic action is not only prompt, but usually very brief as well. This brevity ensures that, in many places in the nervous system, postsynaptic neural signals closely resemble presynaptic signals in their timing; that is, the message is repeated faithfully. Such accuracy of timing is necessary to ensure rapid changes of contraction and relaxation of muscles in coordinated behavior. The prompt cessation of transmitter effects is achieved in one of two ways. In the case of some transmitters, the synapse is soon cleared of the transmitter by **re-uptake** by the presynaptic terminal. This not only cuts off the synaptic activity promptly, but also spares the terminal the necessity of manufacturing some of the needed transmitter.

No re-uptake mechanism has yet been found for ACh. ACh, as well as some other transmitters, has a special enzyme that acts with amazing speed to split up and thus inactivate the transmitter. The enzyme that inactivates ACh is called **acetylcholinesterase (AChE).** It hydrolyzes ACh into choline and acetic acid, and then these products are recycled (at least in part) to make more ACh in the end bouton. AChE is found especially at synapses, but it is also found elsewhere in the nervous system. Thus if any ACh escapes from a synapse where it is released, it is unlikely to survive and get to other synapses where it could start false messages.

Synaptic events: A recapitulation

Now we recommend that you use Figure 4-19 to review the stages in the transmission of nerve impulses at chemical synapses. This will also emphasize sources of variability in synaptic activity, since each step is subject to variation in the

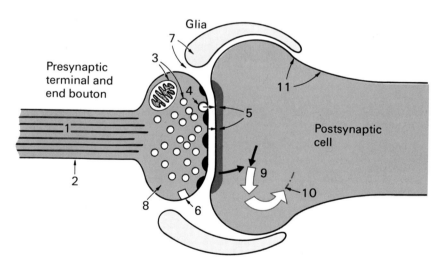

Figure 4-19 Summary of events and steps related to transmission at chemical synapses. 1. Axonal transport of enzymes and precursors needed for synthesis of transmitter agents, vesicle wall, and so forth. 2. Propagation of action potential over presynaptic membrane. 3. Synthesis of transmitter and its storage in vesicles. 4. Depolarization of presynaptic terminal causes influx of Ca^{2+} which leads vesicles to fuse with release sites and to liberate transmitter into synaptic cleft. 5. Binding of transmitter to receptor molecules in postsynaptic membrane, initiating postsynaptic potential. 6. Binding of transmitter to an autoreceptor in the bouton membrane. 7. Enzyme present in extracellular space and in glia splits excess transmitter and prevents it from passing beyond the synaptic cleft. 8. Re-uptake of transmitter stops synaptic action and provides transmitter for subsequent transmission. 9. Second messenger is released into postsynaptic neuron by certain transmitter-receptor combinations. 10. Inactivation of second messenger by enzyme. 11. Postsynaptic potentials spread passively over dendrites and cell body to the axon hillock.

TABLE 4-2   Some Synaptic Transmitters and Transmitter Candidates

TRANSMITTERS AND TRANSMITTER CANDIDATES	LOCATIONS IN NERVOUS SYSTEM	BEHAVIORAL FUNCTIONS OR RELEVANCE (E = EXCITATORY; I = INHIBITORY)
Acetylcholine (ACh)	Neuromuscular synapses; also CNS	E at neuromuscular synapses and most central synapses; I at heart and some other autonomic junctions
Serotonin (5 hydroxytryptamine, 5HT)	See Fig. 4-23	E and I; in circuits involved in mechanisms of sleep, emotional arousal
Catecholamines		
Dopamine (DA)	See Fig. 4-22	I; in circuits involved in control of voluntary movement, emotional arousal, learning and memory
Norepinephrine (NE)	See Fig. 4-21	E and I; involved in arousal and wakefulness, control of eating, learning, and memory
Epinephrine	Similar to NE but less extensively distributed in CNS	Similar to NE but less thoroughly studied in CNS
Amino acids		
Gamma-aminobutyric acid (GABA)	Widely distributed in brain	I; the main inhibitory transmitter
Glutamic acid	Widely distributed in brain	E; perhaps the main excitatory transmitter
Neuropeptides		
Enkephalins		
Met-enkephalin	See p. 163	Mostly I, for example in circuits involving pain, but E in hippocampus
Leu-enkephalin		
Beta endorphin		Mostly I, but E in hippocampus
Oxytocin		I; may inhibit neurons that project to posterior pituitary

amounts of necessary substances and the rates of reactions. The review will also set the stage for the next section, in which we consider the vulnerability of synaptic events to chemical agents and drugs that can either facilitate or impair synaptic transmission. If you are uncertain about any point, the section headings and index will tell you where to find the original discussion.

Chemical transmitters: Confirmed and candidates

No one knows how many different chemical transmitters there are. A few substances have been definitely proved to be synaptic transmitters; these include acetylcholine (ACh), norepinephrine (NE), epinephrine (or adrenalin), and gamma aminobutyric acid (GABA) (see Table 4-2). There is considerable positive evidence for many other substances, but most investigators are not yet convinced. And even if a compound is known to be a transmitter at one location, we may not be able to prove that it acts as a transmitter at another location where it is found. The same substance can serve different functions in different places. Some neurochemists suppose that there are many different synaptic transmitters, some of them having a very restricted distribution.

What does it take to place a substance on the select list of proved transmitters? The criteria come from the anatomical and functional characteristics that we have discussed. To prove that a particular substance is the chemical transmitter at a particular synapse, we must demonstrate the following facts:

1. the chemical exists in the presynaptic terminals,
2. the enzymes for synthesizing the transmitter exist in the presynaptic terminals,

3. the transmitter is released when nerve impulses reach the terminals,

4. it is released in sufficient quantities to produce normal changes in postsynaptic potentials,

5. experimental application of appropriate amounts of the chemical at the synapse produces changes in postsynaptic potentials, and

6. blocking the release of the substance prevents presynaptic nerve impulses from altering the activity of the postsynaptic cell.

Distribution and localization of transmitters

Some synaptic transmitters are widely distributed through the mammalian nervous system and others are not. It is estimated that the two major inhibitory transmitters, GABA and glycine, account for about half of all the synapses in the brain (Iversen and Bloom, 1972). Some well-known transmitters—acetylcholine, norepinephrine, serotonin, and dopamine—account for a small proportion of the excitatory synapses in the brain, but the major excitatory transmitters have not yet been identified. Among the best candidates are the amino acids glutamate and aspartate (Snyder and Bennett, 1976).

Finding whether and where a particular transmitter system is used in the brain is often difficult; several methods have been tried. For instance, specific stains may make a transmitter visible in histological sections, thus permitting detailed localization. With certain staining techniques, neurons containing a given transmitter fluoresce in ultraviolet light. Figure 4-20 illustrates the use of this technique to reveal neurons that contain norepinephrine and that enter the cerebellum from the brainstem. A method of identifying the specific receptor molecules for a particular transmitter is to bind to them radioactively tagged forms of the neurotransmitter itself, or of compounds that are agonists or antagonists of the transmitter (Snyder and Bennett, 1976). This not only shows where the transmitter is used but it also permits quantification of receptor molecules, and it has revealed new facts about synaptic mechanisms.

Figures 4-21 through 4-23 show the brain locations of a few transmitter systems that we will consider later with respect to behavior. To abbreviate long-winded phrases like "those synapses at which acetylcholine is the transmitter," investigators have devised shorter labels, using the Greek root "ergon," meaning "work"; for instance, "cholinergic synapses." When we write about the transmitters norepinephrine (or noradrenalin), dopamine, and GABA, we will use the terms "noradrenergic,", "dopaminergic," and "GABAnergic."

Norepinephrine (NE) is produced mainly in neurons whose bodies lie in brainstem nuclei although their axons project to wide regions of the brain (Figure 4-21). NE is also a hormone (see Chapter 5). We will take up the activity of noradrenergic synapses in relation to psychotic behavior in Chapter 13. Norepinephrine cells are

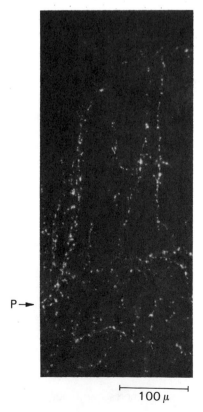

P →

100 μ

Figure 4-20 Section of the cerebellar cortex of the rat showing fluorescence of noradrenergic fibers from locus coeruleus. The P at the left margin indicates the layer of Purkinje cell bodies around which the fibers ascend to terminate in the outer molecular layer. (Micrograph courtesy of F. E. Bloom)

Figure 4-21 Diagrammatic representations of noradrenergic pathways and cell bodies in the brain of the rat. (a) Dorsal view of brain. In (b) these pathways and cell clusters are projected onto a sagittal view of the brain. The cell clusters are designated A1, A2, and so forth. (DB = dorsal bundle, VB = ventral bundle of noradrenergic fibers) (Adapted from Ungerstedt, 1971)

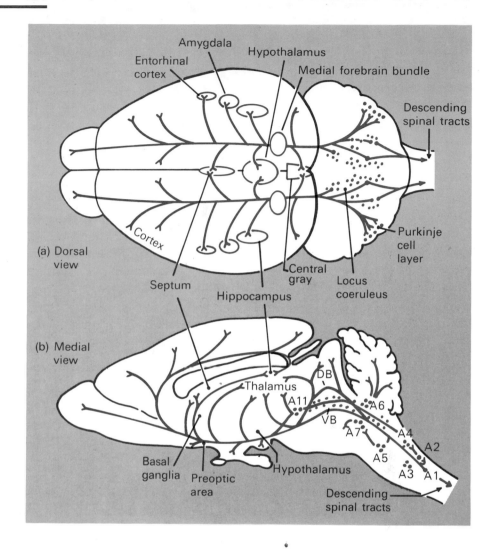

implicated in wakefulness and arousal behavior (Chapter 12), intracranial self-stimulation (Chapter 13), and learning and memory (Chapter 15). For a review of the anatomy and physiology of the norepinephrine system, see Moore and Bloom (1979).

Dopamine (DA) is produced mainly by neurons whose bodies lie in the basal forebrain and brainstem; the axons project to the basal ganglia, the olfactory system, and a limited part of the cerebral cortex (Figure 4-22). In Chapter 13 we will consider dopaminergic transmission in relation to schizophrenia and to psychotic-like behavior caused by LSD. We will also take up dopamine neurons with respect to control of voluntary movements (Chapter 8) and emotional arousal (Chapter 13). For a review of the anatomy and physiology of the dopamine system, see Moore and Bloom (1978).

Serotonin (5HT) is produced in the central nervous system, mainly by cells in the midline of the brainstem (Figure 4-23). Like some other neurotransmitters, sero-

Figure 4-22 Representation of dopaminergic pathways and cell bodies in rat brain. As in Figure 4-21, these pathways lie on either side of the sagittal plane, but for simplicity they are projected onto this diagram of the sagittal plane. (Adapted from Ungerstedt, 1971)

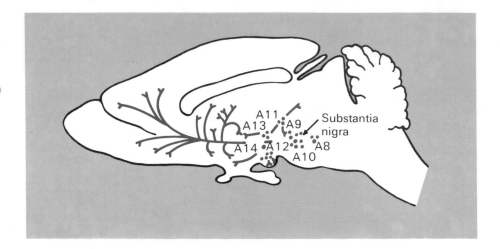

Figure 4-23 Representation of serotonergic pathways and cell bodies projected onto a sagittal diagram of the rat brain.

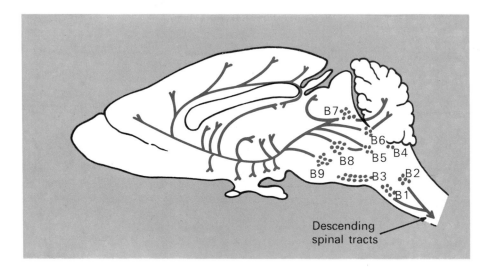

tonin was first discovered outside the nervous system. It was identified in the blood and was found to constrict blood vessels—hence its name, a serum factor that affects tonus, or muscle tone of blood vessels. The neurons that produce serotonin form the **raphe nuclei** which lie along the midline in the brainstem. (The Greek word "raphe," meaning "seam or suture," is used in anatomy to refer to a seamlike union between two parts of an organ.) These neurons send long axons to structures throughout the cerebral hemispheres. We will refer to serotonergic activity in connection with research on the mechanisms of sleep (Chapter 12). It is estimated that serotonin is the transmitter at fewer than 0.1% of brain synapses, so a transmitter can play important although highly circumscribed roles.

The **endorphins,** discovered in 1975, are called the body's own narcotics (Bloom, 1981). In fact, the term "endorphin" is a contraction of "endogenous morphine" (that is, morphine formed within the body). The discovery of these transmitters occurred in a way very different from the way the other transmitters were discovered. For

BOX 4-4   Food for Thought?

"Your brain depends very much on what you ate for breakfast." Of course, this comment should be taken figuratively, but the work of Richard J. Wurtman, who made it, has generated some interesting ideas about diet and synaptic transmitters.

For many years, it was believed that the metabolic activities of the brain were largely insensitive to the body's intake of nutrients. Recent emphasis on the special needs of the developing organism and the structural cost of protein malnutrition have led to a second look at this assumption.

Research has shown that the level of the transmitter serotonin (which controls sleep, among other behaviors) can be influenced by diet. Like every other synaptic transmitter, serotonin is synthesized within nerve cells, using precursors delivered to the brain by the vascular system. Tryptophan is a precursor of serotonin that is found widely in foods that are part of customary diets, for example, bread, milk, and corn. Wurtman and his colleagues have shown that feeding tryptophan to rats increases the brain's concentration of serotonin.

More recently, these investigators have shown that the concentration of the transmitter acetylcholine has a similar dietary influence. These data have led to a clinical contribution: Administering choline—a precursor of acetylcholine—significantly lessens the symptoms of a motion disorder that arises from the use of some tranquilizing agents. (This disorder, tardive dyskinesia, is discussed in Chapter 13.)

Wurtman has emphasized that not all transmitters are subject to dietary influences. To establish whether a transmitter is subject to such control, researchers must show that: (1) a necessary precursor for the synthesis of the transmitter is available from blood to nerve cells, (2) the level of such a substance in the blood changes after a meal that contains it, and (3) the internal regulatory devices of the nerve cell allow for variability of transmitter levels.

Wurtman entitled one of his articles (1978) "Food for thought." Perhaps future research will enable us to give a literal interpretation to his remark.

those we have already discussed, the transmitter chemical was known before its receptors were found, but the reverse was true of the endorphins.

Investigators had long suspected that narcotics might act on postsynaptic receptors in the brain. Some narcotics are effective in such small doses that they could not be acting chemically in a widespread way, but they could be affecting neural messages at specific sites. Animal studies showed that localized application of narcotics to some sites caused relief from pain, whereas application to other regions had no effect. One way to see whether a narcotic acts on certain receptors is to label the narcotic or a narcotic antagonist with a radioactive marker and see whether it binds to sites in neural tissue. This was first done with **naloxone,** a potent antagonist of several narcotics that is often administered to people who have taken drug overdoses. In 1973 researchers in the United States and Sweden found that naloxone binds to synaptic regions of cells taken from rat brains. Further work showed that the narcotic receptors are concentrated in specific regions of the brain. They are especially dense in the medial thalamus, in the periaqueductal gray of the brainstem, and in specific layers of the spinal cord. These are regions that process the perception of pain, and this receptor location seems to be related to the ability of narcotics to relieve pain. Narcotic receptors are abundant in the amygdaloid nuclei of the forebrain, and stimulation of the amygdala may be related to the euphoria that narcotics produce. The pretectal nuclei in the brainstem are also rich in narcotic receptors. One function of these nuclei is to regulate the diameter of the pupils of the eyes, so this may be why drugs such as heroin cause the pupils to constrict.

There was no reason why the body should have evolved receptors that bind external narcotics unless it also produced some substance of its own that acts on these receptors. In 1975 experimenters began to look for the key or keys that would fit the receptor locks. Success was announced by the pharmacologists John Hughes and Hans Kosterlitz (1975), who isolated from pig brain two peptides that bind to the narcotic receptors. Each of these peptides is made up of a chain of five amino acids, and the two are the same except for one amino acid at the end of the chain. Since these substances occur in brain, they were named **enkephalins** (from the Greek roots "en" meaning "within" and "kephalon" meaning "head"). Soon afterward, Simantov and Snyder (1976) isolated narcotic-like substances from calf brain and found that their chemical structures were the same as the pig enkephalins. Other enkephalins have been identified since, and undoubtedly more will be discovered in the near future. Research with animal subjects showed that the enkephalins relieve pain. It also showed that they are addictive. We will consider these substances later in regard to pain perception (Chapter 7).

Some investigators have associated certain transmitters with particular behaviors, as if a given transmitter served in only one brain circuit. For example, Substance P (a transmitter in the dorsal horn of the spinal cord) was linked with transmission of pain messages, both in the cord and centrally. But research has shown Substance P to exist in at least 18 different locations in the brain, most of which do not appear to have any connection with pain. Another example is the endorphins which, like morphine, were thought of largely in regard to inhibition of pain. But the endorphins have been found to influence a variety of behavioral and physiological processes in addition to pain: temperature regulation, respiration, cardiovascular responses, even epileptic seizures. (Morphine also affects many of these processes; respiratory depression is one of the dangerous effects of overdoses of morphine.) The endorphins have also been implicated in reinforcement or reward, memory consolidation, attention, and male copulatory performance (Bolles and Faneslow, 1982).

The fact that a transmitter may play a role in many different brain circuits means that a variety of different effects will occur if the activity of that transmitter is increased or diminished throughout the brain. Normally, however, different brain circuits act relatively independently, and transmitters play only a local role.

Effects of drugs on synapses

From time immemorial, people have sipped, swallowed, or chewed liquids, plants, and animals. They have also learned to shun toxic liquids, plants, and animals. Social customs and dietary codes evolved to protect people from harm from such sources. This long history of seeking, testing, and using different substances came not only from the need for nourishment but also from the need for relief of pain and the control of anxiety, and from the desire for pleasure. In many cases, the basis of an effect lies in the nervous system, especially in its synapses, which are particularly sensitive to drugs and poisons. The blood–brain barrier shelters the central nervous system from some of the drugs that enter the body, but many other drugs can penetrate the brain.

Practically every stage in transmission at chemical synapses (reviewed in Figure 4-19) can be influenced by particular drugs or toxins, and many drugs exert their

TABLE 4-3 Synaptic Events and Drugs (Numbers of Events Are Keyed to Figure 4-19.)

SYNAPTIC EVENTS	DRUGS
Presynaptic events	
1. Block axonal transport	Colchicine.
2. Block propagated nerve impulse	TTX and STX prevent increased permeability to Na^+.
3. Interfere with synthesis or storage of transmitter	Hemicholinium blocks uptake of choline. Reserpine inhibits vesicular storage of catecholamines.
4a. Interfere with mobilization of vesicles by Ca^{2+} influx	Low concentrations of Ca^{2+}. Calcium ion binding agents (for example, EDTA or EGTA). High concentrations of Mg^{2+} which competes with Ca^{2+} for sites.
4b. Block release of transmitter	Botulinum toxin blocks release of ACh. Tetanus toxin blocks release of GABA.
Postsynaptic events	
5. Block receptor molecules	Curare, bungarotoxin block nicotinic ACh receptors. Atropine, scopolamine block muscarinic ACh receptors. Phenothiazines (for example, chlorpromazine) block dopamine receptors. Bicuculine blocks GABA receptors.
6. Mimic transmitter at autoreceptor molecules	LSD mimics serotonin at autoreceptors and thus slows transmission at serotonergic synapses.
7. Inhibit enzyme that inactivates transmitter	Eserine, DFP inhibit AChE.
8. Prevent re-uptake of transmitter, depleting stores available for subsequent transmission	Cocaine, imipramine inhibit re-uptake of NE.
9. Inhibit release of second messenger or inhibit its activity	Nicotinate and certain heavy metals (for example, lead and lanthanum) block activation by NE of the synthesis of cAMP.
10. Inhibit inactivation of second messenger and so enhance its activity	This is done by the methyl xanthines: caffeine (in coffee and tea) and theophylline (in tea).

main effects at synapses. Table 4-3 lists some effects of such drugs, keyed to the points listed in Figure 4-19. Let us comment on some of these agents and their effects.

If axonal transport is inhibited by drugs such as colchicine, then enzymes, which are manufactured in the cell body, are not replaced in the presynaptic terminals. Since enzymes are needed to direct the manufacture of transmitter chemicals and vesicle walls, colchicine prevents the replenishment of the transmitter agent as it is used up. Thus, synaptic transmission fails. The tranquilizing drug reserpine does not interfere with synthesis of transmitters but it inhibits storage of catecholamine transmitters (dopamine, epinephrine, and norepinephrine) in vesicles.

Even if a terminal has an adequate supply of transmitter stored in vesicles, various agents or conditions can prevent the release of transmitter when a nerve impulse reaches the terminal. Low concentration of calcium in the extracellular fluid is such a condition: the impulse leads to release of transmitter by causing an influx of Ca^{2+} which guides vesicles to release sites. Also, specific toxins prevent the release of specific kinds of transmitter. (Table 4-3 gives examples.) For instance, botulinum toxin, which is formed by microorganisms that multiply in improperly canned food, poisons many people each year by blocking release of ACh.

The postsynaptic receptor molecules can be blocked by various drugs. For example, curare blocks nicotinic ACh receptors. Since the synapses between nerves and skeletal muscles are nicotinic, curare results in paralysis of all skeletal muscles, including those used in breathing. Behavior can be disrupted not only by blocking transmitter–receptor action, but also by prolonging it. Agents that inhibit the enzyme AChE allow ACh to remain active at the synapse and alter the timing of synaptic transmission. Effects can range from mild to severe, depending on the anti-AChE agent and its dosage. The drug eserine has temporary and reversible anti-AChE effects. Mild doses of it are used in certain medical conditions when ACh action at neuromuscular junctions is weak and inadequate. (See Box 4-5.) On the other hand, some organic phosphorous compounds like DFP are potent and persistent inhibitors of AChE. DFP is the active ingredient in certain insecticides which must be used with caution because they are also highly toxic to human beings.

Gross electrical potentials of the brain

In 1929 the German psychiatrist Hans Berger published a paper that illustrated the electrical activity of his son's brain. This was more than family pride. Berger had used his son as a subject in studies in which he recorded the electrical activity of the brain by using electrodes (discs about size of a dime) placed on the scalp. He had placed one such electrode at the front of the skull and the other at the back. Potential differences between these two electrodes measured a mere 5 microvolts. The record revealed regular oscillations with a frequency of about 10 Hz, which Berger called the **alpha rhythm** (Figure 4-24). At that time, electronics was in its infancy and the recording of such low-voltage biological signals was difficult and not readily accepted. Berger's accomplishment of scalp recordings of brain electrical activity was

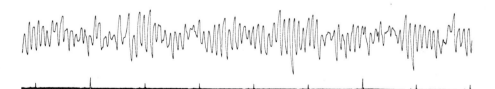

Figure 4-24 Alpha rhythm recorded from scalp in the occipital region of awake relaxed human subject with eyes closed. Time markers show 1-second periods. (Leiman)

BOX 4-5 Myasthenia Gravis: A New Look at a Disorder of Synaptic Transmission

Fundamental neurobiological research is leading to a sense of cautious optimism about our understanding of several debilitating neurological diseases. Myasthenia gravis is one such disease. This disorder is characterized by easy fatiguability and weakness of muscles. The word myasthenia comes from Greek roots "myo" meaning "muscle" and "asthenia" meaning "weakness." This condition may progress until there is paralysis, especially of the muscles involved in respiration and swallowing, and become life-threatening. The data we now have on this disease are like pieces of a jigsaw puzzle, and some already interlock. But we do not yet have a picture of the whole assembled puzzle.

For a number of years, neurologists thought that myasthenia gravis was a disorder of the presynaptic compartment of neuromuscular junctions. Data relevant to this view included observations of synaptic potentials of neuromuscular junctions called miniature endplate potentials. (The postsynaptic membrane of the neuromuscular junction is called an endplate zone or region.) Spontaneous synaptic potentials at neuromuscular junctions tend to have a standard unit amplitude, which has contributed to the view that the potentials arise from the release of the transmitter contents of single synaptic vesicles. Miniature endplate potentials of muscles of myasthenic patients have a reduced amplitude, suggesting a smaller amount of released transmitter. Other data contributing to this "presynaptic view" were pharmacological observations of the therapeutic value of drugs that inhibit acetylcholinesterase, the enzyme that destroys the transmitter at the neuromuscular junction, acetylcholine. Drugs of this type —like physostigmine—have a therapeutic effect in this disease, relieving muscle weakness, presumably by prolonging the action of released acetylcholine.

A new explanation integrates clinical and basic research findings to emphasize postsynaptic membrane changes (Drachman, 1981). Both data on endplate potentials in myasthenic muscle and the ameliorative effects of anticholinesterase drugs are compatible with such an explanation. Many observations indicate that myasthenic muscle shows a marked drop in the number of acetylcholine receptors. Evidence shows that this occurs because the patient's body produces antibodies that specifically destroy acetylcholine receptors. This conclusion was promoted by the demonstration of the induction of myasthenia gravis in rats by the use of immunological procedures. Antibodies derived from acetylcholine receptor protein of the electric eel injected into these rats produced behavior impairments like those seen in patients with myasthenia gravis. Furthermore, antibodies from myasthenic patients interfere with the binding of bungarotoxin to acetylcholine receptor protein. Converging evidence thus suggests that immune mechanisms play a vital role in the generation of this disease of synaptic transmission.

greeted with skepticism until other researchers confirmed his observations and established that the potentials really do originate in the brain. This psychiatrist in search of a physical record of the mental activity of the brain had begun the field of **electroencephalography (EEG)**: the study of the electrical activity of the brain, observed with large electrodes. This is referred to as measuring gross potentials, in contrast to measuring potentials recorded from single cells, because the EEG represents the activity of many cells and is recorded at some distance from them.

Why study gross brain potentials? Why are investigators interested in the gross electrical activity of the brain? The question is especially relevant in view of our continued insistence in this chapter that the basic electrical signals for communication and information processing are nerve impulses and synaptic potentials. We will explore several reasons presented by researchers involved in brain potential studies. One answer stresses expediency.

Techniques for studying the intact human nervous system are few, and scalp recording of human brain activity, via electrodes, offers a way of examining the functioning of the human brain.

Another rationale for the electrophysiological approach stresses clinical aspects. Brain potentials provide significant diagnostic data, for example, in distinguishing forms of seizure disorders. They also provide prognostic data, for example, predictions of the functional effects of brain injury. Indeed, in most states of the United States brain potential data are used in the legal definition of death. In the control of seizures, brain potentials may even form part of a treatment program using **biofeedback** of brain potentials. New developments in computer technology designed to offer detailed quantitative analysis of brain potentials have buoyed hopes for an even greater clinical contribution, especially in psychiatric areas. The word "neurometrics," coined by E. R. John (1977), defines a world of clinical applications that relies on sophisticated computer analysis and representation of electrical activity of the brain.

A rationale for basic research into the gross potentials of the brain has been offered by several investigators (Freeman, 1978; John, 1977). Let's consider an analogy. At college footabll games, a section of students often entertains the crowd with card stunts, spelling out messages and forming pictures. Each participant holds a single piece of cardboard, one side of which is white and the other colored. By lifting one or the other side according to a plan paced by a leader, these rooters present a coherent message: "Go Bears." No single individual can convey that message with a card, no matter how well intended or feverish the pace of moving the card. The message is a product of the entire ensemble of card-carrying fans. Furthermore, the display arises only from a plan that spells out the joint activity. A random presentation of cards would give spectators across the stadium no message—simple confusion.

Now let us return to the electroencephalography laboratory. Both John (1977) and Freeman (1978) emphasize that the functional outputs of the mammalian brain, especially behavior, depend on the spatial and temporal activation of many neurons, a vast ensemble of them. The most trivial interaction with the world involves thousands of neurons. For example, Phillips (1978) estimated the number of cortical cells that must be active in order to produce the barest observable movement of one digit of a monkey's hand. His figure was 50,000 cells. The most discrete sensory input probably activates just as many. Pointing to these estimates, John argues that single-cell data are of limited use in understanding complex behavior such as perception and learning. Instead, he argues that we need a way to portray the coherent activity of a whole population of neurons. For some investigators, gross potential descriptions fill that need.

Developments in science usually emerge from productive argument and debate, and this issue is no exception. Researchers with a more cellular focus who hope to generate significant relations between the behavior of single nerve cells and behavior offer many criticisms of this global view. Especially prominent in this criticism is the retort that there is no solid evidence that brain potentials offer a useful representation of the spatial and temporal activation of nerve cells. They also say that it is not clear how the dispersed activity of many thousands of neurons is "read out" and channeled to control behavioral events. At this stage in our knowledge about the brain, single nerve cell analyses significantly further our understanding of the neural substrates of behavior. It is understood, of course, that the single neurons are studied as units in much larger populations. In later chapters, we will consider some cases in which behavior is correlated with the activity of ensembles of neurons and even more cases in which it is correlated with the activity of single neurons or small neural circuits.

Characteristics of brain potentials   Investigators divide brain potentials into two principal classes: those that appear spontaneously without specific stimulation and those that are evoked by particular stimuli. We will consider the two classes in succession.

● Spontaneous rhythms   Electrical activity of the brain recorded from the scalp reveals several distinctive properties. The most prominent property is that, even in the absence of stimulation, there are oscillations of brain potentials. Trains of rhythmical variations of electrical activity are the hallmark of gross potentials, such as those in Figure 4-24. These potentials can be categorized according to their principal frequency components. Broad psychological categories, such as arousal or attention, are related to the principal frequency components of the gross potentials of the brain.

Scientists over the years have tried to discover the functional properties of the alpha rhythm. Ranging from 8 Hz to 12 Hz, alpha rhythm is especially noticeable in recordings from posterior regions of the skull. Many individuals readily show alpha activity when they close their eyes and relax. Easing tension is so much a part of the alpha state that in recent years we have seen the application of alpha recording to the pursuit of pleasure. Commercially available gadgets can provide a person with a record of alpha activity, usually in the form of a tone that comes on either when alpha occurs or when it reaches some desired amplitude. This is used by some people as a clue to their state of relaxation. It can also be used in a form of biofeedback training. The connection between relaxation and prominent alpha activity evident in biofeedback experiments has reinforced the view that alpha rhythms represent an "idling" state of the brain.

Clinical neurologists use alterations in spontaneous brain activity in the diagnosis of many disorders. Disordered biochemical, anatomical, and neurophysiological states of the brain can markedly change certain properties of spontaneous brain potentials. That is what happens in cases of epilepsy and other seizures.

Table 4-4 shows that the frequency of spontaneous or ongoing brain potentials varies directly with level of arousal. More rapid oscillations—beta waves of 18–30 Hz—are common in vigilant states, while quite slow oscillations—delta waves of 0.5–5 Hz in normal humans—occur in a state of deep sleep (see Chapter 12).

● Event-related potentials   Gross potential changes provoked by discrete stimuli —usually sensory stimuli, such as light flashes or clicks—are called **event-related**

TABLE 4-4 Characteristics of Human EEG Waves

TYPE OF WAVE OR RHYTHM	FREQUENCY RANGE (Hz)	AMPLITUDE OR VOLTAGE (μV)	REGION OF PROMINENCE OR MAXIMUM	CONDITION WHEN PRESENT
Alpha	8–12	5–10	Occipital and parietal	Awake, relaxed, eyes closed
Beta	18–30	2–20	Precentral and frontal	Awake, no movement
Gamma	30–50	2–10	Precentral and frontal	Awake, excited
Delta	0.5–5	20–200	Variable	Deeply asleep
Theta	5–7	5–100	Frontal and temporal	Awake, reduced vigilance

potentials (Figure 4-25). In the usual experiment, a series of evoked potentials are averaged to obtain a reliable estimate of stimulus-elicited brain activity. Sensory-evoked potentials have distinctive characteristics of waveshape and latency that reflect the type of stimulus, the state of the subject, and the site of recording. More subtle psychological processes, such as expectancy, appear to influence some characteristics of evoked potentials.

Some evoked potentials are slow potential shifts lasting for several seconds. They appear in a context of more complex psychological states than mere passive exposure to a stimulus. Foremost among such events is the **contingent negative variation (CNV)** which arises especially in the interval between a "warning" signal and a signal that directs action (for example, pressing a button). Some researchers feel that this brain potential change reflects a state of expectancy or anticipation. Manipulations of many instructional variables seem to affect the prominence of this response, but its relation to psychological processes remains hard to pin down.

Computer techniques enable us to record brain potentials at some distance from the sites at which they are generated. This started in the late 1940s when it was shown that an electrode on the cerebral cortex could pick up the electrical activity of the cochlea and all the auditory stations between the cochlea and the cortex (Figure 4-26). In the study of brain potentials, a specialty has developed that is called "far-field response recording." This phenomenon is displayed in Figure 4-27, which shows that a single electrode can record the activities of successive stations along a sensory pathway, here the human auditory system. Modern recording equipment allows the amplification of signals in tissue quite far from their source. Figure 4-27 shows the recording of click-evoked activity orginating in the cochlea; the recording electrode was about 10 cm away on the top of the skull. There is a substantial fall-off in the size of the signals over this distance, but computer averaging techniques enable their resolution. There are important clinical applications of this technique, for example, assessing hearing abilities of newborns and assessing brain integrity after a stroke.

How are EEG potentials generated? Are they another form of signalling in addition to nerve impulses and synaptic potentials? The quest for an understanding of the

Figure 4-25 Forms of averaged event-related potentials recorded from the scalp. The tracings show characteristic negative (N) and positive (P) deflections with their latencies in milliseconds. (From Calloway, 1975)

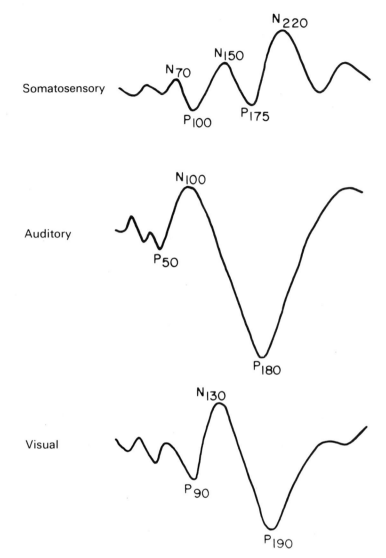

Figure 4-26 Electrophysiological response recorded at the auditory cortex of the cat when a click was delivered to one ear. The time of delivery of the stimulus is shown by the arrow labeled s. The small deflections at a represent activity at subcortical stations of the auditory system. The large deflection at b is the response of the auditory cortex. (From Rosenzweig, 1949) By means of such recording, "the activity of subcortical centers can be studied without surgical invasion of the nervous system" (Rosenzweig, 1951, p. 148).

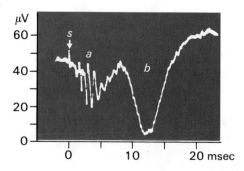

Figure 4-27 Auditory far-field evoked responses. Successive deflections reflect the travel of activity through the auditory pathway from receptor to cortex. These potentials were recorded with a scalp electrode and show that sensitive recording can pick up activity far from the field of principal excited cells. (From Starr, 1978)

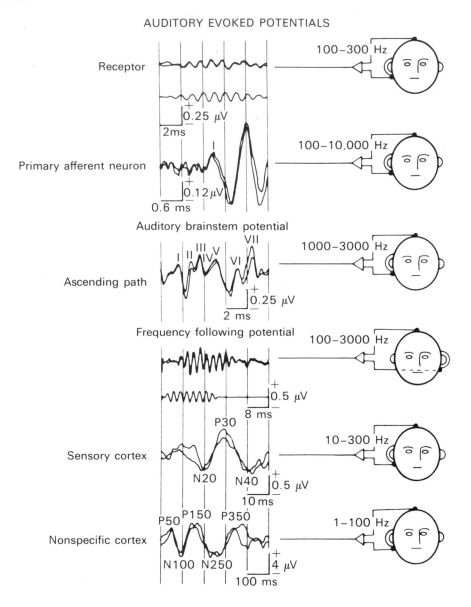

AUDITORY EVOKED POTENTIALS

cellular origin of brain waves has occupied the attention of many investigators. Some speculations have been rather whimsical, like the idea that brain potentials were a kind of movement artifact arising from small oscillatory movements of the brain within the skull. More serious understanding has developed from experiments involving recordings from single nerve cells at the same time gross potentials are measured. Experiments of this sort seek to determine the cellular basis of the gross potentials of the brain. Recent studies indicate that EEG potentials represent the summation of synaptic potentials, including both excitatory and inhibitory postsynaptic potentials.

Epilepsy

Epilepsy has provoked wonder and worry since the dawn of civilization. (The name comes from a Greek word meaning "to seize or attack.") To some ancient Greeks, epilepsy was a sacred disease—possession by a god. In the Middle Ages, afflicted humans were regarded as being possessed instead by a devil, and they were subject to many forms of cruelty. In the history of medicine, proposed cures include bloodletting, trephining (producing a hole in the skull), application to the head of high voltage electric fish, and ingestion of various plants, particularly peony and mistletoe. Views about the origin and cure of epilepsy have varied over the years. This is not surprising, since many people display seizures at some point in their life. A world total of 30,000,000 humans who suffer from epilepsy was estimated recently (O'Leary and Goldring, 1976).

● **Types of seizure disorder**   What is epilepsy? Most investigators now agree that it is a disorder marked by major sudden changes in the electrophysiological state of the brain. These changes and their behavioral accompaniments are referred to as seizures. Metaphors such as "electrical storms" have frequently been used to characterize the electrical state of the brain during seizures, and the term is apt.

There are several types of seizure disorders distinguished both behaviorally and neurophysiologically. **Generalized seizures** involve loss of consciousness and symmetrical involvement of body musculature. Grand mal and petit mal seizures are two common types of generalized seizure and account for the largest number of patients.

Grand mal seizures involve an EEG pattern evident at many places in the brain (Figure 4-28) with individual nerve cells firing in high frequency bursts. The behavior connected with this state is dramatic. The person loses consciousness, and the muscles of the entire body suddenly contract, producing stiff limbs and body. This "tonic" phase of the seizure is followed 1–2 minutes later by a "clonic" phase that consists of sudden alternating jerks and relaxation of the body. An interval of con-

Figure 4-28 Electrical activity of the brain (EEG) characteristic of a grand mal convulsion. High-voltage activity is especially evident in frontal cortex leads in this case. Arrows indicate the onset of seizure activity. (From *Neurological pathophysiology* by Sven G. Eliasson, Arthur L. Prensky, and William B. Hardin, Jr. Copyright © 1974, 1978 by Oxford University Press, Inc. Reprinted by permission.)

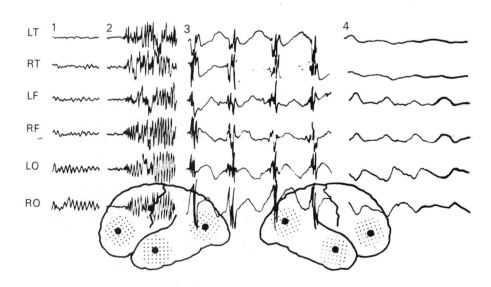

fusion and sleep follows this phase. When most nonprofessionals refer to epilepsy, they generally mean grand mal seizures.

Petit mal epilepsy is a more subtle variant of generalized seizures. It is revealed by a distinctive electrical pattern in EEG recordings called the spike-and-wave pattern (Figure 4-29). Periods of such unusual electrical activity can occur many times a day. During these periods the person is unaware of the environment and later cannot recall events that occurred during these periods. Behaviorally, the person does not show unusual muscle activity, except for a cessation of ongoing activity and sustained "staring." That is, the person's eyes do not move from a particular position for a long period. The term "absences" has been used to describe this state.

Both grand mal and petit mal are generalized seizures because they arise from pathology at brain sites that project to widespread regions of the brain. In contrast, there are **partial seizures** that arise from pathological foci that have less extensive anatomical distribution. Some partial seizures involve no impairment of consciousness. For example, focal motor seizures involve repetitive motor spasms that frequently start in the periphery of a limb and move to adjacent muscles; such a spasm may start in the fingers and move to the forearm. Partial seizures that originate in the temporal lobe may involve strange sensory impressions, sudden feelings of anxiety, and elaborate acts performed automatically such as complicated gestures.

Seizures arise from pathological electrical activity of brain cells that can be caused in many different ways. Frequent causes are mechanical events, such as head injury; various chemicals, including some environmental toxins; and metabolic faults, some of which are genetically determined. The basic cellular event is the abnormal synchronous discharge of large groups of neurons. Seizure potentials can reach 5 to 20 times the amplitude of normal EEG waves. The determination of the complete sequence of events leading to this state remains an unsolved problem.

Figure 4-29 EEG from a patient with petit mal epilepsy. The illustration shows the abrupt onset and termination of a 3-Hz high-amplitude discharge with a pattern called "spike and wave." (From *Neurological pathophysiology* by Sven G. Eliasson, Arthur L. Prensky, and William B. Hardin, Jr. Copyright © 1974, 1978 by Oxford University Press, Inc. Reprinted by permission.)

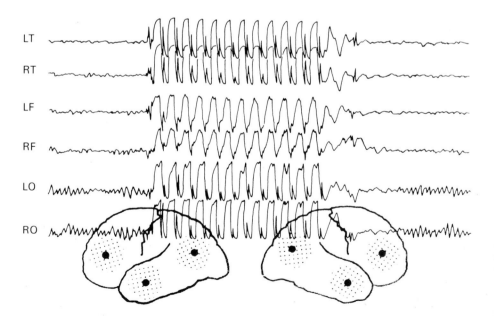

● **New approaches to controlling seizures**   Current therapeutic practice in the control of seizures usually takes one of three approaches: (a) the use of drugs, including the introduction of a new substance that is related to inhibitory synaptic transmitters, (b) surgical attempts to remove the foci of hyperexcitability, and (c) the use of learning techniques that aim to produce conditioned inhibition or suppression of seizures.

For centuries plants have been the source of a host of drugs that have been used for many different ailments, including epilepsy. Then, early in the twentieth century, pharmacological research led to phenobarbital, a synthetic barbiturate that continues to be one of the major drugs used in seizure control. Other drugs were synthesized with the intention of achieving seizure control without the sleepiness that is another effect of phenobarbital. The search for such a substance led to diphenylhydantoin (also known as Dilantin), whose chemical structure resembles that of phenobarbital, with enough difference to reduce sleepiness. Diphenylhydantoin has become the major drug tool in this therapeutic effort.

Since a small proportion of epileptics are not helped by drug treatments, neurologists have investigated surgical treatment for these individuals. Surgical efforts to relieve seizure disorders originated in the many years of neurosurgical research by Wilder Penfield at McGill University. Electrical recordings from the brains of epileptic patients during surgery led Penfield to propose that surgical removal of centers, or foci, of abnormal electrical activity might produce relief of partial seizures involving the temporal lobe. Many of these patients had suffered 60–70 seizures per day. Such a high rate of seizures is not only exhausting but actually endangers life, so it seemed worth the risk of brain surgery to attempt to remove the damaged tissue where the seizure originated—and the risk paid off! Results show that for focal or partial seizures with a temporal lobe origin, neurosurgery is a remarkable cure. Some of these brain operations have had major influences on psychological research. (In Chapter 14 we will discuss the effects of deep bilateral temporal lobe surgery on memory. In Chapter 16 we will discuss the effects of severing connections between the cerebral hemispheres on language and cognition.)

Drugs and surgery have their limitations, so some psychologists are exploring the use of learning techniques for seizure relief. Learning and memory must certainly involve modifications of circuits in the brain. It is a short step from there to suggest that circuit changes induced by learning might be used to control aberrant excitability of a population of neurons.

More than 100 years ago the neurologist John Hughlings Jackson observed that some patients were able to control the progression of motor seizures by forcibly constraining abnormal movements. Repetition of this regimen led to greater ease of control. Years later Foster (1978) reported that extinction procedures could control seizures. His program of trained control developed from the knowledge that certain external stimuli precipitate seizures. Foremost among these stimuli is flickering light around 8–12 Hz. However, Foster noted that for many patients binocular flicker provokes seizures more readily than monocular flicker. He then exposed patients to prolonged monocular flicker, having them use one eye and then the other. After patients had such prolonged exposure to monocular flicker, they no longer suffered seizures in the presence of binocular flicker.

Other attempts to control seizures by behavioral means involve biofeedback training. This training is intended to increase the prominence of an electrical event associated with reducing the frequency of seizures. The event is a burst of a 4–14 Hz rhythm of the sensorimotor cortex associated with motor inhibition. In such a biofeedback experiment, a light comes on when the frequency of the patient's EEG activity falls into the 4–14 Hz range. The patient's task is to keep the light on as long as possible by somehow keeping the EEG in this frequency range. A schedule of contingency training reduces the frequency of seizures. However, if there are only random relations between the cue (that is, the light) and the EEG frequency, no improvement occurs. This has now been observed in several studies, although the clinical characteristics of patients who succeed in this training have yet to be distinguished from those who fail. Developments in computer technology may make possible more elaborate studies of feedback control in epilepsy.

SUMMARY / MAIN POINTS

1. Nerve cells are specialized for receiving, processing, and transmitting signals.

2. Neural signals are changes in the resting potential, which is the normal small difference in voltage between the inside and outside of the cell membrane.

3. A propagated impulse (also called an action potential) travels down the length of the axon without diminishing in amplitude; the impulse is regenerated by successive segments of the axon.

4. Postsynaptic potentials are not propagated. They diminish in amplitude as they spread passively along dendrites and the cell body. Excitatory postsynaptic potentials are depolarizing (they decrease the resting potential). Inhibitory postsynaptic potentials are hyperpolarizing (they increase the resting potential).

5. Cell bodies process information by integrating (adding algebraically) postsynaptic potentials across their surfaces.

6. A propagated impulse is initiated at the initial segment of the axon when excitatory postsynaptic potentials summate to reach the threshold.

7. The potentials of a neuron can be explained by differences in the concentration and ease of movement of ions. The resting potential occurs because the neuron contains a relatively high concentration of potassium ions and the extracellular fluid contains a relatively high concentration of sodium ions. When the membrane is depolarized, sodium channels open, Na^+ rushes in, and the membrane potential reverses. Within a millisecond, the sodium channels are inactivated and the resting potential is restored.

8. During the action potential, the neuron cannot be excited by a second stimulus; it is absolutely refractory.

9. At most synapses the transmission of signals from one neuron to another requires a chemical that diffuses across the synaptic cleft and binds to receptor molecules in the postsynaptic membrane.

10. At many synapses, chemical transmission involves the release of a "second messenger," which amplifies and prolongs the transmitter's effect.

11. Many drugs exert their principal effects on chemical synapses.

12. Some synapses use electrical transmission and do not require a chemical transmitter. At these electrical synapses, the cleft between presynaptic and postsynaptic cells is extremely narrow.

13. The electrical activity of the brain can be recorded outside the skull. Such a recording is called an electroencephalogram (EEG).

14. Epileptic seizures are correlated with abnormally large EEG waves. Most cases of epilepsy can be controlled by the use of drugs. Others can be controlled by brain surgery or by training patients to control the pattern of their brain potentials.

RECOMMENDED READING

Bullock, T.H., Orkand, R. and Grinell, A. *Introduction to nervous systems*. San Francisco: W.H. Freeman, 1977.

Cooper, J.R., Bloom, F.E. and Roth, R.H. *The biochemical basis of neuropharmacology*. New York: Oxford University Press, 1978.

Kandel, E.R. and Schwartz, J. H. (Eds) *Principles of neural science*. New York: Elsevier/North-Holland, 1981.

Kuffler, S.W. and Nicholls, J.G. *From neuron to brain*. Sunderland, MA: Sinauer Associates, 1976.

O'Leary, J.L. and Goldring, S. *Science and epilepsy*. New York: Raven, 1976.

Orientation

Mechanisms of Hormone Action

How do hormones affect the body?

How do hormones act?

What regulates secretion of hormones?

Main Endocrine Glands and Their Hormones

Pituitary hormones

Hypothalamic hormones

Adrenal hormones

Pancreatic hormones

Thyroid hormones

Gonadal hormones

Hormonal Effects

Hormones and growth

Hormones and homeostatic mechanisms

Effects of hormones on learning and memory

Comparisons of Neural and Hormonal Communication

Integrated Activities of Hormonal and Neural Systems

Summary/Main Points

5

Hormones: A Chemical Communication System

Orientation

Without regular supplies of some hormones our capacity to behave would be seriously impaired; without others we would soon die. Tiny amounts of some hormones can modify our moods and our actions, our inclination to eat or drink, our aggressiveness or submissiveness, and our reproductive and parental behavior. And hormones do more than influence adult behavior; early in life they help to determine the development of bodily form and may even determine an individual's behavioral capacities. Later in life the changing outputs of some endocrine glands and the body's changing sensitivity to some hormones are essential aspects of the phenomena of aging. Endocrine glands come in a variety of sizes and shapes, and they are located in many parts of the body. Figure 5-1 gives the names and locations of the main endocrine glands.

Communication within the body and the consequent integration of behavior were considered the exclusive province of the nervous system up to the beginning of the present century. Only then did some investigators become aware that the endocrine system participates importantly in these functions.

Of course, the importance of certain glands for behavior had long been known. For instance, Aristotle accurately described the effects of castration in birds, and he compared the behavioral and bodily effects with those seen in castrated men. Although he did not know what mechanism was involved, it was clear that the testes were important for the reproductive capacity and sexual characteristics of the male. This question was approached experimentally in 1849 by A. A. Berthold, a professor at Göttingen. He castrated young roosters and observed declines in both reproductive behavior and secondary sexual characteristics such as the rooster's comb. Then in some birds he replaced one testicle, devoid of its neural connections, into the body cavity. This restored both the normal behavior of these roosters and their combs. Berthold concluded that the testes release some substance into the blood that is necessary for both male behavior and male structures. Berthold's observation did not seem very important to his contemporaries because it could not be related to the concepts of that time. Only in retrospect is it considered important—as the first experiment in endocrinology.

The creative French physiologist Claude Bernard also helped to set the stage in the nineteenth century for the emergence of endocrinology. Bernard stressed the importance of the "internal environment" in which cells exist and the fact that this environment must be regulated. As he put it, a constant internal bodily environment is a necessary condition for independent activity in the external environment. Then late in the nineteenth century clinical and experimental observations showed the importance of several glands—including the thyroids, the adrenal cortex, and the pituitary—for maintaining a constant internal environment and thus for normal health and behavior.

The emergence of endocrinology as a separate discipline can probably be traced to the experiments of Bayliss and Starling, around 1905, on the hormone **secretin.** This substance is secreted from cells in the intestinal walls when food enters the stomach; it travels through the bloodstream and stimulates the pancreas to liberate pancreatic juice, which aids in digestion. By showing that special cells secrete chemical agents that are conveyed by the bloodstream and regulate distant target organs or tissues, Bayliss and Starling demonstrated that chemical integration can occur without participation of the nervous system.

The term **hormone** was first used with reference to secretin. Starling (1905) derived the term from the Greek "hormon," meaning "to excite or set in motion." The term **endocrine** (from the Greek roots "endo," meaning "within," and "krinein," meaning "to secrete") was introduced shortly thereafter. "Endocrine" is used to refer to glands that secrete products into the bloodstream. The term endocrine contrasts with **exocrine,** which is applied to glands that secrete their products through ducts to the site of action. Examples of exocrine glands are the tear glands, the sweat glands, and the pancreas, which secretes pancreatic juice through a duct into the intestine. Exocrine glands are also called duct glands, while endocrine glands are called ductless.

We should note here a possible source of confusion: Some glands may have separate functions that lead to different classifications. Thus the pancreas is a duct gland insofar as the secretion of pancreatic juice is concerned. But other cells in the pancreas—the islets of Langerhans—do not make contact with the pancreatic ducts; instead they secrete the hormones insulin and glucagon into the bloodstream.

In the following sections of this chapter we will consider the mechanisms by which homones accomplish their functions, the main endocrine glands and their hormones, and examples of hormonal influences on physiology and on behavior. Then we will compare the endocrine and nervous systems as mechanisms of commu-

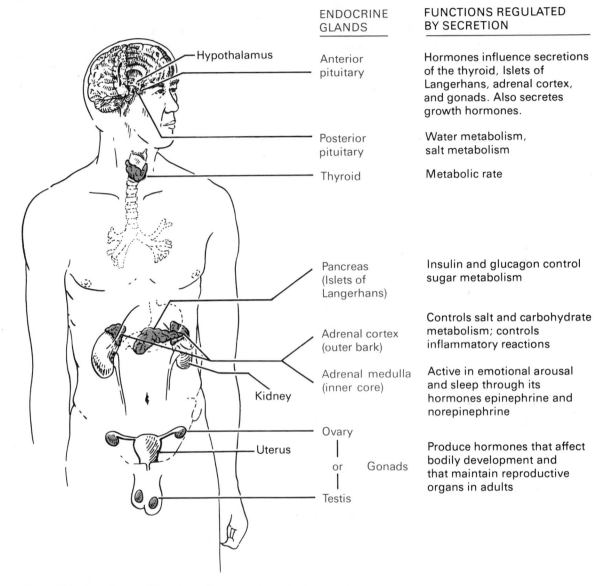

	ENDOCRINE GLANDS	FUNCTIONS REGULATED BY SECRETION
Hypothalamus	Anterior pituitary	Hormones influence secretions of the thyroid, Islets of Langerhans, adrenal cortex, and gonads. Also secretes growth hormones.
	Posterior pituitary	Water metabolism, salt metabolism
	Thyroid	Metabolic rate
	Pancreas (Islets of Langerhans)	Insulin and glucagon control sugar metabolism
	Adrenal cortex (outer bark)	Controls salt and carbohydrate metabolism; controls inflammatory reactions
	Adrenal medulla (inner core)	Active in emotional arousal and sleep through its hormones epinephrine and norepinephrine
Kidney		
Uterus	Ovary|or Gonads|Testis	Produce hormones that affect bodily development and that maintain reproductive organs in adults

Figure 5-1　Locations and functions of some major endocrine glands.

nication and coordination, and we will show how the activities of the two systems are integrated in the control of behavior.

Mechanisms of hormone action

We will soon be considering the effects of specific hormones on behavior. In preparation for this material let us look briefly at three aspects of hormonal activity: the effects of hormones, the mechanisms by which they exercise these effects, and the ways in which their secretions are regulated.

How do hormones affect the body?

Hormones affect many everyday behaviors in people and other animals, and they do so by influencing organs. Hormones exert these far-reaching effects by (a) promoting the proliferation, growth, and differentiation of cells and (b) modulating cell activity. We discussed proliferation and differentiation of brain cells in Chapter 3. The hormone of the thyroid gland, thyroxine, is important in promoting these early activities. Without it mental development is stunted. (We will discuss the effects of thyroxine further when we consider the functions of the thyroid gland in detail.) Although neural proliferation and differentiation occur mainly during early development, cells in some organs divide and grow at later stages of life, too. For example, male and female hormones cause secondary sexual characteristics to appear during adolescence—breasts and broadening of the hips in women and facial hair and enlargement of the Adam's apple in men, for instance.

In cells that are already differentiated, hormones can modulate the rate of function. For example, thyroxine and insulin promote the metabolic activity of most of the cells in the body. Other hormones modulate activity primarily in certain types of cells. For example, a hormone from the anterior pituitary gland—called luteinizing hormone (LH)—promotes the secretion of sex hormones by the testes and ovaries.

How do hormones act?

Hormones exert their varied influences on target organs in two main ways:

1. The peptides and amine hormones (see Table 5-1) usually bind to specific receptors on the surface of target cell membranes and cause the release of a **second messenger** in the cell. (As we saw in Chapter 4, the release of a second messenger can also be caused by some synaptic transmitters.)

2. The steroid hormones pass through the membrane and bind to specific receptor proteins in the cytoplasm. The steroid-protein complex then enters the nucleus. There it interacts with the genome and initiates the transcription of specific genes, leading to the production of specific proteins.

We will now consider these two main modes of action in a little more detail, and we will examine some other ways in which hormones affect cellular function.

The same second-messenger compound transmits the messages of most, if not all, of the peptide and amine hormones. This compound is **cyclic adenosine monophosphate (cAMP).** It may seem surprising that the same second messenger can mediate the effects of many different hormones, but recall from Chapter 4 that the same kind of neural impulses can convey all sorts of neural messages. The situation here is similar.

The specificity of hormonal effects is determined by the selectivity of receptors in cell membranes and in the specific genes that are affected in the cell. For example, adrenocorticotropic hormone (ACTH) is taken up selectively by receptors on the membranes of cells in the adrenal cortex, and in these cells cAMP leads to the synthesis and release of adrenal cortex hormones.

The peptide hormones usually act relatively rapidly, within seconds to minutes. While this is rapid for hormonal action, it is, of course, much slower than neural activity. There can also be prolonged effects. For example, ACTH also promotes the proliferation and growth of adrenal cortical cells and thereby increases the long-term

TABLE 5-1 Some Hormones Classified by Type of Chemical Compound

AMINES	POLYPEPTIDES	STEROIDS
Epinephrine	Adrenocorticotropic hormone (ACTH)	Estrogen
Norepinephrine	Follicle-stimulating hormone (FSH)	Progesterone
Thyroxine	Luteinizing hormone (LH)	Testosterone
	Thyroid-stimulating hormone (TSH)	Glucocorticoids
	Insulin	
	Glucagon	
	Oxytocin	
	Antidiuretic hormone (vasopressin)	

Polypeptides that are releasing hormones

Growth-hormone–releasing hormone (GrHRH)
Thyrotropin-releasing hormone (TRH)
Luteinizing hormone–releasing hormone (LHRH)

capacity to sustain production of their hormones. The surfaces of many kinds of cells are studded with receptors for peptide and amine hormones, just as the membranes of neurons are riddled with special channels for different kinds of ions.

The steroid hormones typically act more slowly, requiring hours for their effects to occur. The specificity of action of steroid hormones is determined by the intracellular receptors. The steroid hormones pass in and out of many cells in which they have no effect. However, if there are appropriate receptor molecules in the cytoplasm, these receptors bind the hormone so that it becomes concentrated in its target cells. Thus one can study where a hormone is active by observing where radioactively tagged molecules of the hormone are concentrated. For example, when tagged estrogen is administered systemically, it accumulates in several specific tissues, including the reproductive tract, and in some groups of cells in the hypothalamus.

As mentioned earlier, there are also other ways that hormones can affect cells. For example, insulin is effective even if its second-messenger activity is blocked. So it appears that insulin alters membrane properties by some other route. Some insulin enters the cells, and its action inside the cell may account for its long-term effects. Among these long-term effects are an increase in the transport of glucose across cell membranes and an alteration of ionic permeabilities of membranes. Other polypeptide hormones pass through cellular membranes, too, and intracellular activity of these hormones is now a subject of intense study.

What regulates secretion of hormones?

Some endocrine glands secrete hormones at a fairly stable rate over long periods of time, whereas others vary with stimulation. In either case, secretion is usually monitored and regulated so that the rate is appropriate to ongoing bodily activities and needs. The basic control used is a **negative-feedback system.** We will begin our study with simple negative-feedback systems; then we will move on to systems with larger numbers of links.

Figure 5-2 Negative feedback control of hormonal secretion. A black arrowhead indicates inhibition in this figure and in Figures 5-3 and 5-4.

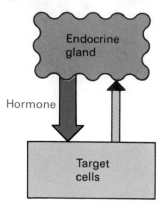

The simplest kind of system that regulates hormones is diagramed in Figure 5-2. The hormone acts on target cells, changing the amount of a substance in the extracellular fluid; this, in turn, regulates the output of the endocrine gland. Thus, for example, the hormone insulin helps to control the level of glucose circulating in the blood in the following way: Ingesting glucose leads to release of insulin. The insulin causes extracellular glucose to enter muscle and fat and stimulates increased use of glucose. As the level of glucose in the blood falls, the pancreas responds by secreting less insulin, so a balance tends to be maintained. The negative-feedback action of a hormone is like that of a thermostat: In a heating system when the temperature falls below a set level, the thermostat switches the furnace on. When the temperature rises a few degrees, the thermostat turns the furnace off, so the temperature is held rather constant. And just as the thermostat can be set to different temperatures at different times, the set points of endocrine feedback systems can also be changed to meet varying circumstances.

The next order of complexity in endocrine systems is illustrated in Figure 5-3. Here the hypothalamus controls the endocrine gland. This control may occur through a neural link, as in control of the adrenal medulla, or through a hormonal link, as in control of release of growth hormone by the anterior pituitary. The secretion of the endocrine gland affects target cells, and the negative feedback goes to the hypothalamus, bypassing the endocrine gland.

One further degree of complexity, illustrated in Figure 5-4, is exemplified by control of thyroid secretion. This secretion is regulated by the anterior pituitary hormone called thyroid-stimulating hormone (TSH). This hormone is one of several anterior pituitary hormones that affect the secretion of another endocrine gland, and these are all called **tropic hormones.** (Tropic, pronounced with a long "o" as in toe, means "directed toward.") Release of TSH is controlled in turn by the hypothalamic hormone called thyrotropin-releasing factor (TRF). Feedback in this case is from the endocrine gland hormone to the hypothalamus and to the anterior pituitary. Thus the regulation of these chemical messages can be analyzed in terms of concepts borrowed from systems analysis or servomechanisms. In Chapter 8 we will see similar concepts employed in the analysis of control of motor functions.

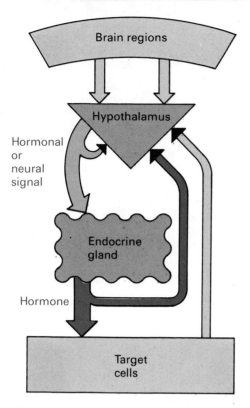

Figure 5-3 A more complex endocrine control circuit that includes the hypothalamus and other brain regions.

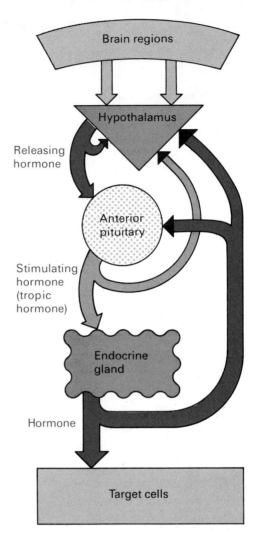

Figure 5-4 Complex control of endocrine secretion, involving the hypothalamus and the anterior pituitary gland.

Main endocrine glands and their hormones

The main endocrine glands, their secretions, and some of their principal effects are listed in Table 5-2. Our account of hormones will be simplified, and you should realize that each hormone has multiple effects and that several hormones often act together. We will discuss only a few of the main effects of each hormone we examine, and we will not even mention some of the hormones in the body. For more details, see Turner and Bagnara (1976) and Williams (1974).

TABLE 5-2 Main Endocrine Glands, Their Hormones, and Principal Effects

GLANDS	HORMONES	PRINCIPAL EFFECTS
Anterior pituitary	Growth hormone	Stimulates growth
	Thyrotropic hormone	Stimulates the thyroid
	Adrenocorticotropic hormone	Stimulates the adrenal cortex
	Follicle-stimulating hormone	Stimulates growth of ovarian follicles and of seminiferous tubules of the testes
	Luteinizing hormone	Stimulates conversion of follicles into corpora lutea; stimulates secretion of sex hormones by ovaries and testes
	Prolactin	Stimulates milk secretion by mammary glands
	Melanocyte-stimulating hormone	Controls cutaneous pigmentation in lower vertebrates
Posterior pituitary (storage organ for certain hormones produced by hypothalamus)	Oxytocin	Stimulates contraction of uterine muscles; stimulates release of milk by mammary glands
	Vasopressin (antidiuretic hormone)	Stimulates increased water reabsorption by kidneys; stimulates constriction of blood vessels (and other smooth muscle)
Hypothalamus	Releasing hormones	Regulate hormone secretion by anterior pituitary
	Oxytocin, vasopressin	*See under* Posterior pituitary
Adrenal cortex	Glucocorticoids (corticosterone, cortisone, hydrocortisone, etc.)	Inhibit incorporation of amino acids into protein in muscle; stimulate formation (largely from noncarbohydrate sources) and storage of glycogen; help maintain normal blood sugar level
	Mineralocorticoids (aldosterone, deoxycorticosterone, etc.)	Regulate sodium-potassium metabolism
Testes	Testosterone	Stimulates development and maintenance of male secondary sexual characteristics and behavior
Ovaries	Estrogen	Stimulates development and maintenance of female secondary sexual characteristics and behavior
	Progesterone	Stimulates female secondary sexual characteristics and behavior, and maintains pregnancy
Thyroid	Thyroxine, triiodothyronine	Stimulate oxidative metabolism
	Calcitonin	Prevents excessive rise in blood calcium
Pancreas	Insulin	Stimulates glycogen formation and storage; stimulates carbohydrate oxidation; inhibits formation of new glucose
	Glucagon	Stimulates conversion of glycogen into glucose
Mucosa of duodenum	Secretin	Stimulates secretion of pancreatic juice
	Cholecystokinin	Stimulates release of bile by gallbladder; may be signal of satiety for food
	Enterogastrone	Inhibits secretion of gastric juice

TABLE 5-2 (Continued)

GLANDS	HORMONES	PRINCIPAL EFFECTS
Pyloric mucosa of stomach	Gastrin	Stimulates secretion of gastric juice
Parathyroids	Parathormone	Regulates calcium phosphate metabolism
Pineal	Melatonin	May help regulate pituitary, perhaps by regulating hypothalamic releasing centers
Thymus	Thymosin	Stimulates immunologic competence in lymphoid tissues
Adrenal medulla	Epinephrine (adrenalin)	Stimulates syndrome of reactions commonly termed "fight or flight"
	Norepinephrine (noradrenalin)	Stimulates reactions similar to those produced by adrenalin but causes more vasoconstriction and is less effective in converting glycogen into glucose

Pituitary hormones   Resting in a depression in the base of the skull is the **pituitary gland,** about 1 cc in volume and weighing about 1 g. The term pituitary comes from a Latin word meaning "mucus"; it received this name from an outmoded belief that it removed waste products from the brain and secreted them into the nose! A true "mighty mite," the pituitary used to be referred to as the master gland, a reference to its regulatory role in regard to several other endocrine glands. As Figure 5-5 shows, the pituitary gland consists of two main parts. These are completely separate in function and are derived from different embryological sources. The two parts are the **anterior pituitary,** or **adenohypophysis,** and the **posterior pituitary,** or **neurohypophysis.** The term hypophysis comes from Greek roots meaning an outgrowth from the underside of the brain. The root adeno- comes from a Greek word meaning gland, because the anterior pituitary originates from glandular tissue. The neurohypophysis derives from neural tissue.

The stalk of the pituitary, called the **infundibulum** in the belief that it was a funnel into the gland, is also shown in Figure 5-5. It consists of axons and is richly supplied with blood vessels. All these axons go to the posterior pituitary; the anterior pituitary does not receive any neural input.

● Anterior pituitary hormones   The cells of the anterior lobe of the pituitary secrete a variety of substances. Most of these secretions are called tropic hormones, because their principal role is the control of endocrine glands situated elsewhere in the body. Figure 5-6 shows activities of several tropic hormones.

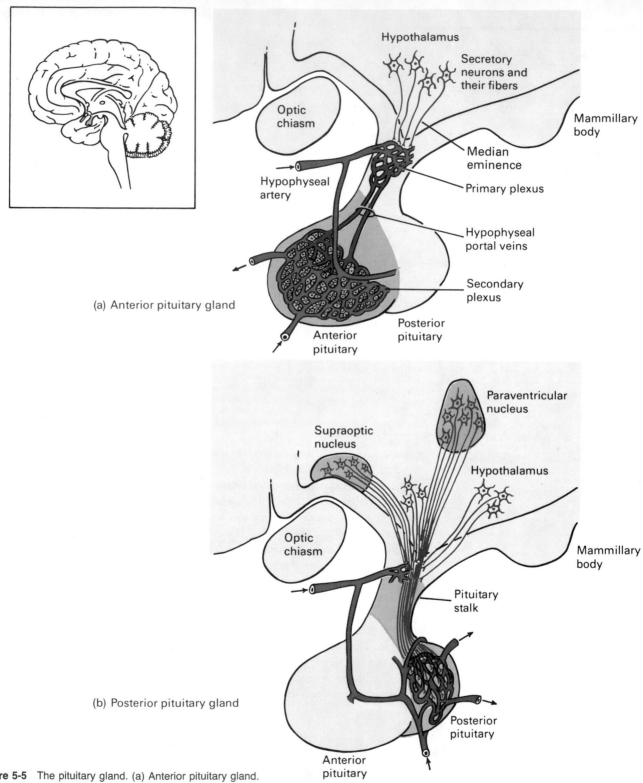

Figure 5-5 The pituitary gland. (a) Anterior pituitary gland.
(b) Posterior pituitary gland.

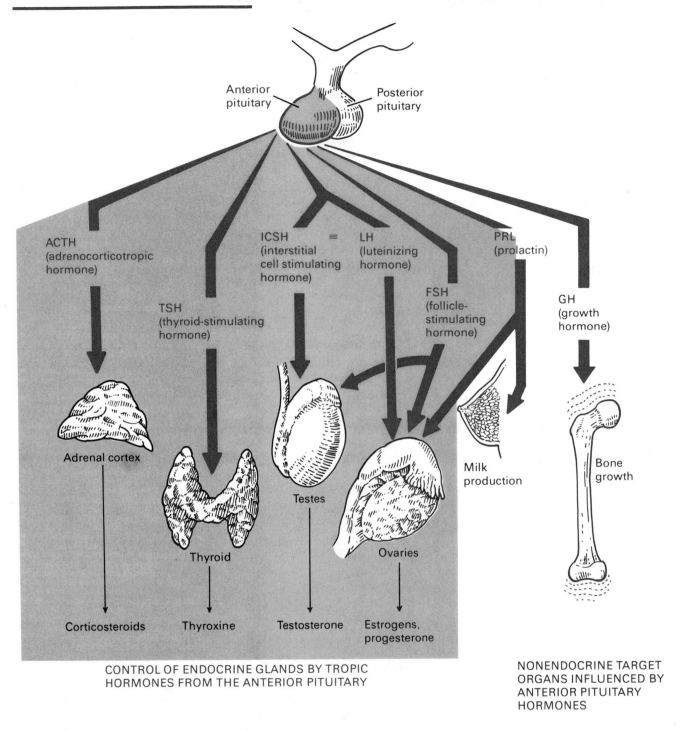

CONTROL OF ENDOCRINE GLANDS BY TROPIC
HORMONES FROM THE ANTERIOR PITUITARY

NONENDOCRINE TARGET
ORGANS INFLUENCED BY
ANTERIOR PITUITARY
HORMONES

Figure 5-6 Secretions of the anterior pituitary gland include both tropic secretions (shown in the blue area to the left) and hormones that affect nonendocrine target organs.

Growth hormone (also known as somatotropin or somatotropic hormone, STH) acts on many tissues of the body to influence the growth of cells and tissues. It exerts this action by an impact on protein metabolism. The daily production and release of growth hormone is especially prominent during the early stages of sleep. In fact, some sleep stages are needed for growth hormone release. Several other factors influence growth hormone release, such as a fall in blood sugar, starvation, exercise, and stress. (See Box 5-1.)

Many other hormones of the anterior pituitary control the production and release of the products of other endocrine glands. Let us note briefly four of these tropic hormones.

Adrenocorticotropic hormone (ACTH) controls the production and release of hormones of the adrenal cortex. Measurements of the level of this hormone in blood show a marked circadian rhythm. **Thyroid-stimulating hormone (TSH)** increases the release of thyroxine from the thyroid gland and markedly affects thyroid gland size by increasing iodide uptake.

Two tropic hormones of the anterior pituitary influence the hormone activities of the gonads. One of these is known as **luteinizing hormone (LH)** in females and as **interstitial-cell–stimulating hormone (ICSH)** in males. LH stimulates the release of the developed eggs in the ovary and affects the uterine lining by producing changes that prepare for the implantation of a fertilized egg. In males this hormone stimulates production of testosterone by the testes. The other tropic hormone that influences gonadal hormone activities is the **follicle-stimulating hormone (FSH).** This hormone stimulates the secretion of estrogen in females and of testosterone in males; it also influences both egg and sperm production.

Secretion of the tropic hormones is partly determined by "releasing hormones" that are produced in the hypothalamus and are transported to the anterior pituitary by blood vessels that run along the infundibulum. The releasing hormones will be taken up soon when we turn to the hypothalamus.

● The posterior pituitary   The posterior pituitary gland contains two principal hormones, the **antidiuretic hormone** (also called **vasopressin**) and **oxytocin.** At one time it was thought that these substances were produced and stored in cells of the posterior pituitary, to be released upon arrival of appropriate neural signals from hypothalamic centers. Justification for this viewpoint came from the clear presence of an extensive system of nerve fiber endings in this region of the pituitary. Recently, though, the view of the neural role in posterior regions of the pituitary gland has undergone a major change.

Contemporary data clearly show that cells in various hypothalamic nuclei, especially the **supraoptic nucleus** and the **paraventricular nucleus,** synthesize hormones that are transported along their axons (where they appear as dense granules) to the axon terminals. Nerve impulses in these cells result in release of this neurosecretory material into the rich vascular capillary bed of the neurohypophysis. Actually the axon terminals of these nerve cells abut capillaries; Figure 5-5(b) shows the relations of these secretory nerve cells and capillaries.

Signals that activate the nerve cells of the supraoptic and paraventricular nuclei appear to be related to osmotic pressure of blood. (Aspects of this problem are related to thirst and water regulation, which will be discussed in Chapter 10.) Secretion of antidiuretic hormone (ADH) leads to conservation of water, because ADH

BOX 5-1   Stress and Growth: Psychosocial Dwarfism

Genie had an extremely deprived childhood. From the age of 20 months until the age of 13 years, she was isolated in a small closed room, and much of the time she was tied to a chair. Her disturbed parents provided food, but nobody held Genie or spoke to her. When released from her confinement and observed by researchers at the age of 13 years 9 months, she looked as if she were only 6 to 7 years old (Curtis, 1977).

Other less horrendous forms of family deprivation have also been shown to result in failure of growth. This syndrome has been referred to as psychosocial dwarfism to emphasize that the growth failure arises from pituitary insufficiency, which in turn reflects psychological and social factors. When these children are removed from stressful environmental circumstances, many begin to grow rapidly. The growth rates of several such "psychosocial dwarfs," both before and after periods of emotional deprivation, are shown in Box Figure 5-1. These children seem to recover much of the growth deficit that occurred during prolonged stress periods.

How do stress and emotional deprivation produce impairments of growth? The effects are mediated by a reduced output of pituitary growth hormone. Assays in some of these children show virtually no release of growth hormone. Perhaps this reduced output of growth hormone develops from an absence of relevant hypothalamic releasing factors (Brasel and Blizzard, 1974). Disturbed sleep has been connected to this syndrome by Gardner (1972). He notes that these children have stress-induced changes in typical sleep patterns of growing children. This factor is significant since large amounts of

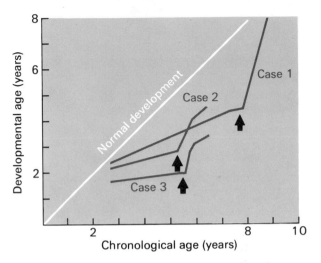

Box Figure 5-1   Growth rates of three cases of psychosocial dwarfism. Removal from environment causing psychological stress is indicated by an arrow for each case. (Adapted from Brasel and Blizzard, 1974)

circulating growth hormone are evident during some stages of sleep (stages 3–4 of slow-wave sleep; see Chapter 13). In fact, these stages of sleep are invariably connected with growth hormone release no matter what time of day they occur. The stresses of an emotionally deprived environment lead to decreased amounts of these stages of sleep, which, in turn, result in reduced growth hormone in the body. Over a prolonged period reduced growth becomes evident.

inhibits the formation of urine—hence the designation antidiuretic. The two quite different names for this hormone reflect the sequence of research on it. The first effect to be identified was its increase of vascular pressure—hence its designation as vasopressin. But later it became clear that the major physiological role of this hormone is its potent antidiuretic activity; it exerts this effect with less than one-thousandth of the dose needed to alter blood pressure. Therefore antidiuretic hormone is clearly a more suitable term, although many investigators still use the older term.

Oxytocin, another hormone stored in axon terminals of the posterior pituitary, is involved in milk "let-down," the contraction of cells of mammary glands. The mechanism mediating this phenomenon provides a good example of the interaction of behavior and hormone release. When an infant or young animal begins to suckle, there is a delay of 30–60 seconds before milk is obtained. This delay results from a sequence of events that consists of several steps. The stimulation of the nipple activates receptors of the skin, which transmit this information through a chain of several neurons and synapses to hypothalamic cells that contain oxytocin. This

Figure 5-7 The milk "let-down" response involving the hormone oxytocin.

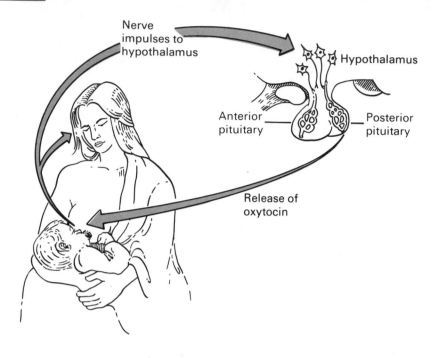

hormone is released from the posterior pituitary and travels via the vascular system to the mammary glands, where it produces contraction of cells surrounding storage sites for milk and thus results in the availability of milk at the nipple (see Figure 5-7). For human mothers this reflex response to suckling frequently becomes conditioned to baby cries, so milk appears promptly at the start of nursing.

Oxytocin also produces powerful internal contractions of the uterus and may facilitate delivery once labor has begun. Injections of oxytocin are frequently used to accelerate delivery in instances of prolonged labor that can threaten the viability of the fetus.

Hypothalamic hormones

The secretions of the anterior pituitary are controlled by releasing hormones produced in neurons of the hypothalamus. These neurons are found in various parts of the hypothalamus, including the median eminence (see Figure 5-5). The median eminence is surrounded by an elaborate profusion of capillaries (the hypophysial-portal capillaries and veins). Endings of neurons of the median eminence lie close to these capillaries. These axons convey large granules that contain hormones. The contents of the granules are released into the surrounding capillaries, through which blood flows into the anterior pituitary. The blood supply of the anterior pituitary thus contains many hormones that have been transported via the portal circulation from the median eminence. The list of these hormones now includes growth hormone–releasing hormone, thyrotropic-releasing hormone, and luteinizing hormone–releasing hormone.

The hypothalamic hormones are a further control element in the regulation of endocrine secretions. The neurons that synthesize these regulatory hormones are subject to two kinds of influences:

1. They receive neural influences from other brain regions via the synaptic contacts of these cells. In this manner the endocrine system is influenced by a wide range of neural signals originating from both internal and external events. Thus the outputs of endocrine glands can be regulated in accordance with ongoing events. Also, endocrine secretion can be subjected to learned controls.

2. The cells that synthesize the releasing hormones are directly affected by circulating messages, such as hormones and blood sugar, because they are not shielded by a blood-brain barrier.

Adrenal hormones

Adjacent to each kidney is an **adrenal gland** that secretes a large variety of hormones. There are two major portions of the adrenal structure in mammals. The outer bark of the gland is the **adrenal cortex,** which is composed of three distinct layers of cells, each producing different hormones. The core of the gland is the **adrenal medulla,** really a portion of the autonomic nervous system, which is richly supplied with nerves from autonomic ganglia. In many nonmammalian vertebrates these are two separate glands.

The adrenal cortex produces and secretes a variety of steroid hormones. One group is called **glucocorticoids** because of their effects on carbohydrate metabolism. Hormones of this type, such as **cortisol,** produce marked changes in glucose metabolism, increasing the level of blood glucose. They also accelerate the breakdown of proteins. In high concentrations they have a marked anti-inflammatory effect, which results in the decrease of bodily responses to tissue injury. More extensive biological actions of these substances are evident in their effects on appetite and muscular activity.

A second group of adrenal cortical hormones is called **mineralocorticoids** because of their effects on ion concentrations in some body tissues, especially the kidney. **Aldosterone** is one such hormone, and its secretion results in conservation of sodium and release of potassium into urine. As a consequence a homeostatic equilibrium in the distribution of ions in blood and extracellular fluids is maintained.

Regulation of the level of circulating adrenal cortical hormones involves several steps, as shown in Figure 5-8. The importance of the pituitary hormone adrenocorticotropic hormone (ACTH) can be demonstrated simply: Removal of the pituitary results in shrinkage of the adrenal cortex. ACTH promotes steroid synthesis in the adrenal; indeed, cortisol is secreted by the adrenal cortex only when ACTH is present.

A negative-feedback effect on ACTH release is produced by adrenal steroids, especially cortisol. As the level of adrenal cortex hormones increases, ACTH secretion is suppressed, so the output of hormones from the adrenal cortex then diminishes. When the levels of adrenal steroids fall, the pituitary ACTH-secreting cells are released from suppression, and the concentration of ACTH in the blood rises. This occurrence, in turn, leads to increased output of adrenal cortex hormones. ACTH secretion is also controlled by hypothalamic mechanisms and the appropriate releasing hormone, **corticotropin-releasing hormone (CRH)** or **factor (CRF).** CRH provides the signal that produces the daily rhythm of ACTH release. A prominent influence on ACTH secretion is also exerted by stress, both physiological and psychological. (Further discussion of stress and ACTH is given in Chapter 13.)

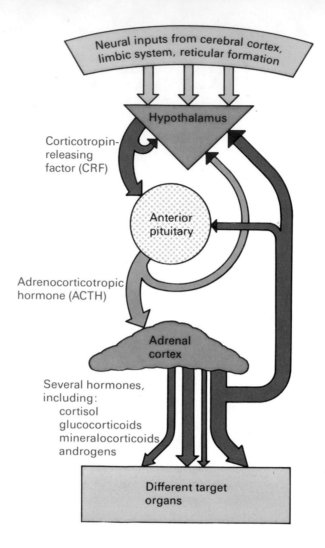

Figure 5-8 Regulation of endocrine secretions of the adrenal cortex.

Neural inputs from cerebral cortex, limbic system, reticular formation

Hypothalamus

Corticotropin-releasing factor (CRF)

Anterior pituitary

Adrenocorticotropic hormone (ACTH)

Adrenal cortex

Several hormones, including:
cortisol
glucocorticoids
mineralocorticoids
androgens

Different target organs

The hormones of the adrenal medulla are two amine compounds, **epinephrine** and **norepinephrine.** We have already discussed these compounds in Chapter 4, where we saw that they are also synaptic transmitters at certain sites in the nervous system.

Pancreatic hormones

Throughout the **pancreas** (located near the posterior wall of the abdominal cavity) are clusters of cells called **islets of Langerhans** that secrete hormones directly into the bloodstream. These collections of cells are intermingled among other cells that perform an exocrine function, secreting digestive enzymes into ducts leading to the gastrointestinal tract.

Hormones secreted by the islets of Langerhans include **insulin** and **glucagon,** both of which have potent and frequently reciprocal actions dealing with glucose utilization. Insulin is produced in one type of cell within the islets (beta cells) and glucagon is secreted by another type (alpha cells).

Both nonneural and neural factors regulate the release of insulin. The level of glucose in the bloodstream, which is monitored by cells of the islets of Langerhans, is a critical determinant of insulin release. As the level of blood sugar rises above a norm of concentration, insulin is released. Among the actions of insulin are increased glucose uptake in some tissues like muscle and reduced liver output of glucose. These effects produce a lowering of blood glucose. Note that this reaction is a direct-feedback effect that does not involve a tropic hormone.

The effects of insulin are directly antagonized by glucagon, the other hormone of the islets of Langerhans. In contrast with the actions of insulin, the actions of glucagon increase blood glucose levels. The nonneural regulation of secretion of both insulin and glucagon is summarized in Figure 5-9. The reciprocal action of insulin and glucagon help to keep blood glucose within the range that is necessary for proper functioning of the brain and of other organs.

The release of insulin is also controlled by neural impulses that arrive at the pancreas via the vagus nerve. When a person eats, insulin is released even before any glucose reaches the bloodstream. This early release occurs in response to taste stimulation in the mouth. Cutting the vagus nerve in experimental animals prevents

Figure 5-9 Regulation of blood glucose levels by (a) glucagon, (b) insulin, and (c) both glucagon and insulin.

Regulation of blood sugar (glucose) levels by

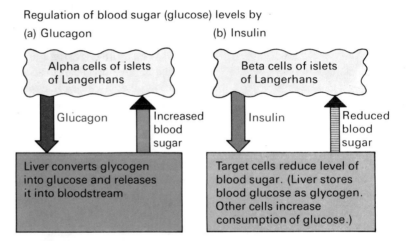

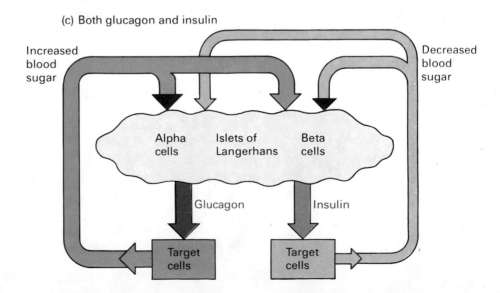

the rapid release of insulin in response to eating, but it does not interfere with the response to glucose in the bloodstream. Furthermore, even stimuli that are normally associated with eating can cause the release of insulin. This response is a conditioned one, and it also operates via the nervous system, since it is eliminated by cutting the vagus nerve.

Thyroid hormones

Situated just below the vocal apparatus in the throat is the **thyroid gland;** this gland produces and secretes several hormones, including **thyroxine** and **calcitonin.** Certain cells of the thyroid produce the hormones, and a saclike collection of cells called the thyroid colloid stores them. The thyroid is unique among endocrine glands because it stores large amounts of hormone and releases it slowly; normally the thyroid has at least 100 days' supply of hormones.

The control network for regulating thyroxine levels in blood is shown in Figure 5-10. The major control is exerted by **thyroid-stimulating hormone (TSH)** from the anterior pituitary gland. The secretion of TSH is controlled by two factors. The dominant one is a negative feedback relation with the level of thyroid hormone circulating in the blood; the second and less important factor is a hypothalamic neurohumor, **thyrotropin-releasing hormone (TRH).** When the level of circulating thyroid hormone falls, this leads to secretion of both TRH and TSH; when TSH reaches the thyroid gland, it causes release of thyroid hormone.

Knowledge of the feedback controls of thyroid output is often used in diagnosing undersecretion (hypothyroidism) or oversecretion (hyperthyroidism) of the thyroid gland. Both are relatively common disorders. The TSH level in the blood is almost invariably raised in people with hypothyroidism. As hypothyroidism develops, the TSH level rises before the person shows low circulating levels of thyroid hormone, because increased TSH keeps up the level of thyroid hormone as long as possible.

Thyroid hormone is the only substance produced by the body that contains iodine, and the manufacture of thyroxine is critically dependent on the supply of iodine. In parts of the world where iodine is in short supply in foods, many people may suffer from hypothyroidism. In such cases the thyroid gland may enlarge in the attempt to produce more hormone, a condition known as goiter. Iodized salt is now widely used to prevent this condition.

The major role of the thyroid is the regulation of metabolic processes, especially carbohydrate utilization. It also has an influence on growth, which is especially evident when profound thyroid deficiency starts early in life. Besides stunted bodily growth and characteristic facial malformation, thyroid deficiency produces a marked reduction in brain size and cellular structure. This state is called **cretinism** and is accompanied by mental retardation; we will discuss it further when we talk about the effects of hormones on learning and memory.

Gonadal hormones

Virtually all aspects of reproductive behavior, including mating and parental behavior, depend on hormones. Since Chapter 9 is devoted to reproductive behavior and physiology, at this point we will only briefly note relevant hormones and some pertinent aspects of anatomy and physiology.

The gonads of male and female vertebrates produce hormones and also gametes (sperm and eggs). Hormone production is critical both for reproductive behavior and for the production of sperm or eggs. Within the testes are several cell types. Inter-

Figure 5-10   Regulation of secretion of thyroxine.

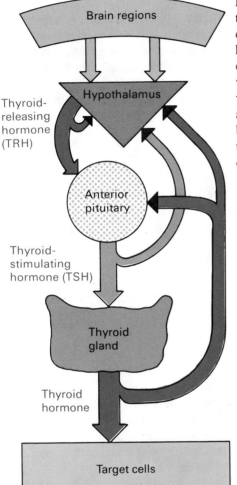

spersed among the sperm-producing cells are the Leydig cells, which produce and secrete the hormone **testosterone.** Production and release of testosterone is regulated by a hormone of the anterior pituitary; this anterior pituitary hormone is sometimes called **interstitial-cell–stimulating hormone (ICSH),** and sometimes it is called **luteinizing hormone (LH).** The pituitary hormone in turn is controlled by a hypothalamic releasing factor, **gonadotropin-releasing hormone (GnRH),** also called **luteinizing hormone–releasing hormone (LHRH).** Testosterone controls a wide range of bodily changes that become visible at puberty, including changes in voice, hair growth, and genital size. Levels of testosterone vary during the day in adult males, although the connection between daily rhythms in this hormone and behavior remains a mystery. In species that breed only in certain seasons of the year, testosterone has especially marked effects on behavior and appearance. Regulation of secretion of testosterone is summarized in Figure 5-11.

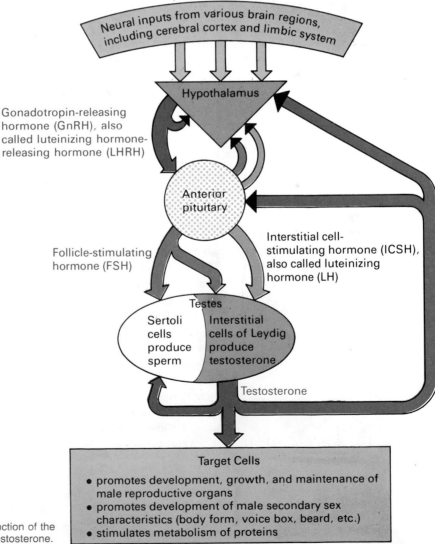

Figure 5-11   Regulation of function of the testes, including secretion of testosterone.

The paired female gonads, the ovaries, also produce the mature gametes (ova) and hormones. However, hormonal activities of the ovary are more complicated than those of the testes. Production of ovarian hormones occurs in cycles whose duration varies with species—in human beings they last about four weeks, whereas in the rat the cycles last only four days. The ovary produces two major classes of hormones: the **estrogens** and the **progestogens.** Ovarian production of these hormones is under the control of two anterior pituitary hormones, **follicle-stimulating hormone (FSH),** and **luteinizing hormone (LH).** (LH is identical to ICSH found in males.) The release of the anterior pituitary hormones is controlled by a hormone from the hypothalamus, **gonadotropin-releasing hormone (GnRH),** also called **luteinizing hormone–releasing hormone (LHRH).** Figure 5-12 presents a model of the regulation of ovarian hormones.

Hormonal effects

As we mentioned earlier, endocrine influences on structural or functional states frequently involve the interaction of several different hormones. In this section we will consider three classes of typical hormonal effects that have multiple endocrine determinants: growth, homeostasis, and learning.

Hormones and growth

Individuals of different species grow and develop at rates characteristic of their species. In addition, there is much evidence pointing to long-term trends toward increased human stature in many countries (Figure 5-13). This trend may reflect better nutrition and health care, since it is not seen in parts of the world where standards of living are low. Many factors influence body growth, and growth processes like those reflected in Figure 5-13 are especially affected by hormones and also by health, nutrition, and genetic influences.

The role of hormones becomes especially apparent in cases of deficiency. Table 5-3 summarizes hormonal disorders associated with small stature; as shown in the table, disorders at several levels in the endocrine system can cause growth failure. The rate of body growth and development is controlled by at least five hormones: pituitary growth hormone, thyroxine, insulin, androgens, and estrogens. One effect all these hormones have is to increase protein synthesis and in this way to produce the building blocks of tissue. The separate impact of each hormone can be seen in the type of growth change; some have greater impact on bone fusion, others on muscle development, and still others on fat deposits. Further, the time of life when the particular hormone exerts its greatest impact varies among hormones. For example, adolescent growth spurts appear to be especially related to androgenic hormones. Hormone deficiencies have their greatest effect early in life. Thyroid deficiency, for example, retards all skeletal growth and causes marked decline in muscle tension, "tone," and strength.

Several classes of growth failure involve pituitary growth hormone regulation. Primary pituitary failure involves either destruction of the pituitary (for example, by a tumor) or inherited tendencies toward deficiency of pituitary growth hormone. Secondary pituitary failure—the most prevalent growth hormone deficiency—develops from deficiencies in the neural regulation of the pituitary, particularly in hypothalamic regulation. In these cases there is no apparent destructive process directly

Figure 5-12 Regulation of function of the ovaries, including secretion of ovarian hormones.

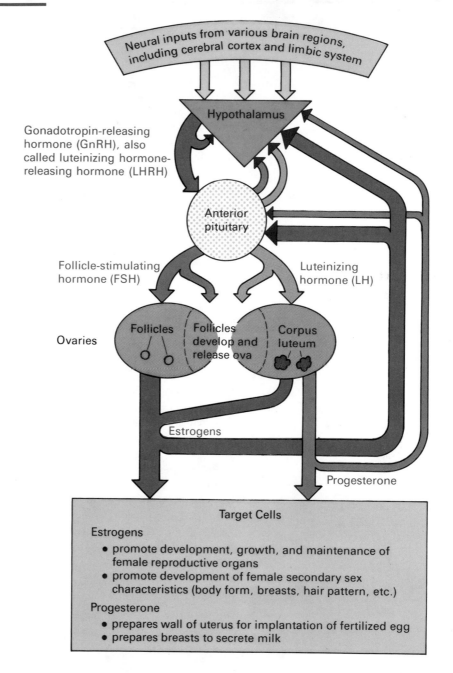

Neural inputs from various brain regions, including cerebral cortex and limbic system

Hypothalamus

Gonadotropin-releasing hormone (GnRH), also called luteinizing hormone-releasing hormone (LHRH)

Anterior pituitary

Follicle-stimulating hormone (FSH)

Luteinizing hormone (LH)

Ovaries

Follicles

Follicles develop and release ova

Corpus luteum

Estrogens

Progesterone

Target Cells

Estrogens
- promote development, growth, and maintenance of female reproductive organs
- promote development of female secondary sex characteristics (body form, breasts, hair pattern, etc.)

Progesterone
- prepares wall of uterus for implantation of fertilized egg
- prepares breasts to secrete milk

involving the pituitary. Dwarfism is a common endpoint of both classes, although there are some distinctions between them. For example, primary pituitary failure is more often accompanied by failure of sexual maturity, whereas secondary pituitary failure is not.

One class of human hormonal disorders is not characterized by failures of production or release. Rather these disorders result from the insensitivity of the target or-

Figure 5-13 Stature in the United States, 1900 and 1965.

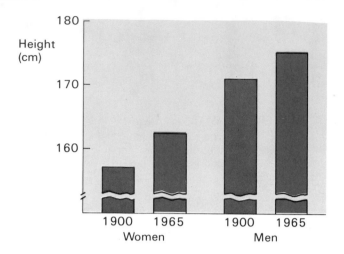

gan to the growth hormones. For instance, some children with normal levels of the growth hormone fail to show usual growth and also fail to show customary metabolic responses to elevated levels of growth hormone in the blood. It is assumed that their problems involve insensitive target tissues.

TABLE 5-3   Some Endocrine Disorders That Cause Small Stature

1. Primary disorders of the anterior pituitary gland
   (a) Tumors or trauma of pituitary
   (b) Hereditary deficiency of pituitary

2. Pituitary deficiency caused by hypothalamic dysfunction
   (a) Defect in hypothalamic control of anterior pituitary
   (b) Psychosocial dwarfism
       Stress-induced reduction of secretion of growth hormone

3. Unresponsiveness of tissues to growth hormone
   Normal secretion of growth hormone but tissues are unresponsive to this hormone. African pygmies show hereditary unresponsiveness to growth hormone. In other cases, reduced responsiveness can be induced by severe malnutrition.

4. Early hypothyroidism
   Cases are characterized by retarded growth and development; they occur frequently in regions where the diet is low in iodine.

5. Early excessive secretion of androgen or estrogen
   Growth processes end early with precocious sexual development.

Hormones and homeostatic mechanisms

Many bodily mechanisms have evolved to ensure the relative constancy of the internal environment. American physiologist Walter Cannon called these mechanisms **homeostatic** (from the Latin roots "homeo," meaning "same," and "stasis," meaning "standing or remaining"). Hormones play major roles in regulating many basic processes that are significant for homeostasis, such as those that govern the distribution of ions and fluids and those that control the concentration of glucose in blood and brain. We will consider the regulation of glucose in the blood as an example of the hormonal role in glucose homeostasis.

Glucose in blood is usually found in a concentration that varies between 80 and 130 mg/100 milliliters. Some hormones lead to an increase in glucose concentration in the blood; these include glucagon, growth hormone, and cortisol. Decrease in glucose concentration in blood is produced by insulin. The balance among these hormones maintains the glucose concentration of blood within a range that provides for maximal production of energy in a variety of circumstances. The level of blood sugar itself also inhibits the secretion of some hormones.

Failure in these controls has major consequences for bodily organs. High blood levels of glucose (hyperglycemia) can produce pathological changes in body tissues, such as diabetic blindness. Such destruction of tissue may arise from the use of metabolic pathways that produce unusual metabolites. This is evident in diabetes mellitus, a disorder characterized by insulin deficiency.

Homeostatic mechanisms dealing with glucose regulation are particularly prominent during periods of stress or strong exercise. Hormonal changes accompanying these states enhance the release of glucose from the liver. But if insufficient glucose is released, the central nervous system is unable to produce its full response. A normal rate of release is part of the alarm reaction, the prompt "fight or flight" response of the body to any stressor. If the stressful situation continues, then long-term reactions occur that involve several other hormones.

Effects of hormones on learning and memory

Hormones affect both the early development of capacities to learn and remember and the efficient utilization of these capacities after they have been formed. Thyroid hormone, as already indicated, is important in the early development of the nervous system. Insufficient thyroid secretion results in fewer synaptic connections than usual, and this condition is linked to cretinism. Experimental studies have given us more information about this condition: If a drug that inhibits thyroid function is administered to infant rats, the results are a demonstrable decrease in the formation of cortical synapses and significantly impaired learning ability. Giving such "experimental cretin" rats enriched experience as they grow has been reported to ameliorate their behavioral deficiencies to a large extent (Davenport, 1976). (The effects of enriched experience on the brain will be discussed in Chapter 15.)

After the developmental period the ability of juvenile or adult animals to learn and remember has been shown to be affected by the hormones ACTH and vasopressin (antidiuretic hormone, ADH) and also by particular fractions or analogs of these hormones (Dunn, 1980). Here, in brief, is some of the main evidence: Removal of the pituitary in rats results in the impairment of some kinds of learning, and this impairment can be overcome by administering ACTH. In fact, the impairment can be overcome by giving only a particular part of the ACTH molecule. This part includes the fourth through tenth amino acids in the chain that makes up ACTH, so it is referred to as $ACTH_{4-10}$. ACTH or $ACTH_{4-10}$ can improve acquisition even in normal, intact animals, and ACTH has been found to facilitate unlearning one habit and acquiring the reverse habit (for example, learning that a right turn will no longer avoid shock in a T maze but that a left turn now does). Conditioned avoidance behavior usually extinguishes after a number of nonreinforced trials, but the extinction can be retarded by giving the animal ACTH (or ACTH$_{4-10}$) or ADH. It should be noted that ACTH$_{4-10}$ has little or no detectable endocrine effect, although it has significant effects on learning. Such small molecules may be used as neurotransmitters in parts of the nervous system.

One plausible interpretation of these effects is that the hormones are important in reinforcing learning. That is, they may provide a chemical signal that a behavioral pattern that an individual has just performed should be retained for future use.

Comparisons of neural and hormonal communication

Now that we have surveyed hormonal communication in this chapter and neural communication in Chapter 4, we can compare the two systems and note their differences and similarities.

Neural communication works somewhat like a telephone system: Messages travel over fixed channels to precise destinations. In contrast, hormonal communication works somewhat like a broadcasting system: Many endocrine messages spread throughout the body and can be picked up by any cells that have receptors for them. (Some hormonal messages, however, have a less broad distribution; for instance, the hypothalamus sends releasing factors only a few millimeters through the portal vessels to the anterior pituitary gland.) Neural messages are rapid and are measured in milliseconds. Hormonal messages are slower and are measured in seconds and minutes. Most neural messages are "digitized," all-or-none impulses, whereas hormonal messages are "analog," that is, graded in strength.

Another difference between neural and hormonal communication involves voluntary control. You cannot, at a command, increase or decrease the output of a hormone or a response mediated by the endocrine system, whereas you can voluntarily lift your arm or blink your eyelids or perform many other acts under neuromuscular control. This distinction between neural and hormonal systems, however, is not absolute. Many muscular responses cannot be performed at will, even though they are under neural control. An example is heart rate, which is regulated by the vagus nerve to meet changing demands during exercise or stress but which very few people can change promptly and directly. Sometimes it is said that we do not have voluntary control over responses mediated by the autonomic nervous system; these involve smooth muscles and glands rather than skeletal muscles. But that conclusion is too sweeping: Children are toilet-trained to achieve voluntary control of the smooth sphincter muscles used to hold back urination and defecation. Biofeedback techniques may enable people to overcome health problems by altering their heart rate and blood pressure (Miller, 1978). Training can also produce control over hormonally mediated behavior. For example, rats whose skeletal musculature is paralyzed can be trained to alter the rate of secretion of urine into the bladder (Miller and Dworkin, 1978); this response presumably involves antidiuretic hormone. We have seen earlier examples of the conditioning of other responses that involve hormones—the milk let-down response mediated by oxytocin and the prompt release of insulin during eating. So there is a general distinction between the involuntary endocrine system and the skeletal muscular system that is accessible to voluntary control, but it should not be taken as an absolute distinction.

Figure 5-14 Comparison of (a) hormonal communication and (b) neural communication at a synapse.

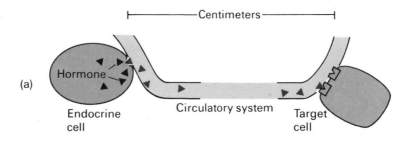

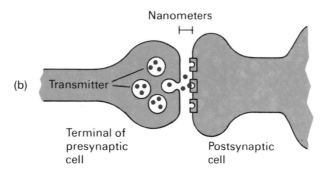

(a)

(b)

In spite of differences, the neural and hormonal systems show important similarities. The nervous system uses specialized biochemical substances to communicate across synaptic junctions in much the same way that the endocrine system uses hormones (see Figure 5-14). Of course, the distance traveled by the chemical messengers differs enormously in the two cases—the synaptic cleft is only about 30 nm wide (30×10^{-9} m), whereas hormones may travel a meter or so from the site of secretion to the target organ. Nevertheless, the analogy between chemical transmission at synapses and hormonal communication holds up in several specific respects:

1. The presynaptic ending of a neuron produces its particular transmitter chemical and stores it for later release, just as an endocrine gland stores its hormone for secretion.

2. When an electrical nerve impulse reaches the presynaptic terminal, it releases the transmitter agent into the synaptic cleft between neurons. Similarly, endocrine glands are stimulated to secrete hormones into the bloodstream, some glands responding to neural messages and others to chemical messages.

3. There are many different synaptic transmitter chemicals, and there are many different hormones, and more and more biochemical compounds are being found to serve as both. Examples are norepinephrine and epinephrine, which act as transmitters at many brain synapses and which are also secreted as hormones by the adrenal medulla. Other substances that serve as a hormone at some locations and as a synaptic transmitter at other locations include ACTH, vasopressin, and melanin-stimulating hormone.

4. The synaptic transmitter reacts with specific receptor molecules at the surface of the postsynaptic membrane. Similarly, many hormones react with specific receptor molecules at the membrane of their target cells; most organs do not have receptors for a given hormone and therefore do not respond to it.

5. In many cases when hormones act on receptor molecules, a second messenger is released within the target cells to bring about changes within the cell. This process has been studied extensively in the endocrine system, and more recently it has been discovered that some neural effects also involve the release of second messengers in the postsynaptic neuron. Moreover, the same compound—cyclic AMP—acts as a second messenger in many places in both the nervous and the endocrine systems.

Some neurons in the hypothalamus actually synthesize hormones, as we saw earlier. These so-called neurosecretions make it hard to draw a firm line between neurons and endocrine cells. In fact, it has been suggested that the endocrine glands may have evolved from **neurosecretory cells** (Turner and Bagnara, 1976). Recent evidence indicates that cells in several parts of the brain produce peptides that are identical with pituitary hormones (Krieger and Liotta, 1979). Much current research is devoted to determining the functions of these compounds in the brain. It is possible that they are used as neurotransmitters. On the other hand, the peptides typically have a slower onset of effect and a longer duration of action than do transmitters, so it has been suggested that they act as **neuromodulators,** substances that alter reactivity of cells to the specific transmitters (Barchas, 1977).

Integrated activities of hormonal and neural systems

Although we have focused on the endocrine system in this chapter, the endocrine system is part of the body, and it participates in interactions with many other organs, including, of course, the nervous system. Figure 5-15 incorporates the endocrine system into a larger schema of reciprocal relations between body and behavior. Let us examine some of the relations indicated by the figure. Incoming sensory stimuli elicit nerve impulses that go to several brain regions, including the cerebral cortex, cerebellum, and hypothalamus. Behavioral responses bring further changes in stimulation. For example, the person may approach or go away from the original source of stimulation, and this action will alter the size of the visual image, the loudness of sound, and so forth. Meanwhile the endocrine system is altering the response characteristics of the person. If the evaluation of the stimulus situation calls for action, energy is mobilized through hormonal routes. The state of some sensory receptor organs may also be altered, thus modifying further processing of stimuli.

Many behaviors require neural and hormonal coordination. For example, when a stressful situation is perceived through neural sensory channels, hormonal secretions prepare the individual to make energetic responses. The muscular responses for "fight or flight" are controlled neurally, but energy is mobilized for them through hormonal routes. Another example of neural and hormonal coordination is the milk let-down response.

Four kinds of signals from one cell to another are possible in a system with both nerve cells and endocrine cells: neural to neural, neural to endocrine, endocrine to

Figure 5-15 The endocrine system incorporated into the overall schema of reciprocal relations between body and behavior.

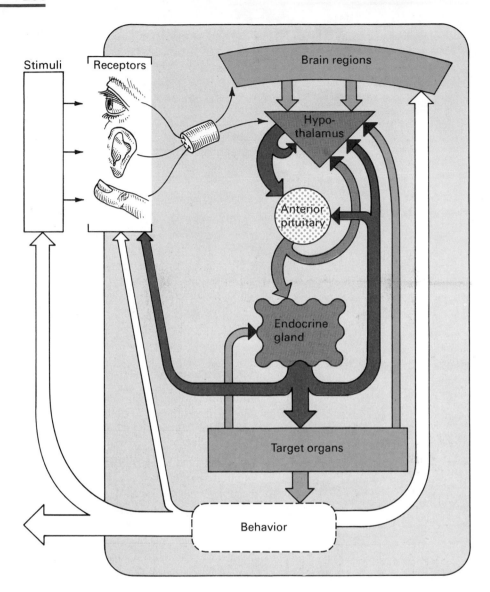

endocrine, and endocrine to neural. All four kinds can be found in the courtship behavior of the ring dove. Friedman (1977) observed this by placing a male dove in a position where he could see a female through a window. The visual stimulation and perception involve neural-neural transmission. The particular visual stimulus activates a neural-endocrine link, which causes some neurosecretory cells in the hypothalamus to secrete interstitial-cell–stimulating hormone. Then there is a series of endocrine-endocrine signals that causes increased production and release of the hormone testosterone. Testosterone, in turn, alters the excitability of some neurons through an endocrine-neural link and thus causes the display of courtship behavior. The female dove responds to this display, thus providing new visual stimulation and

Figure 5-16 Circle schema represen-tation of reciprocal relations between endocrine activity and behavior.

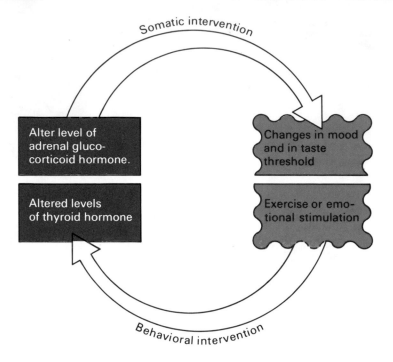

further neural-neural signals. (We will discuss the complex interactions of male and female doves further in Chapter 9, where we will see other examples of coordination of neural and endocrine activities.)

Our circle schema in Figure 5-16 can be used to consider how relations are being found between endocrine activity and behavior. Here are a few examples: The level of circulating hormones can be altered by chemical intervention, and this can affect behavior. For example, there is an uncommon disease (Cushing's syndrome) in which the level of adrenal glucocorticoid hormone is elevated, causing obesity, hypertension, and mental disorders. Since cortisone was introduced as a drug in 1949, cases of Cushing's syndrome have shown up in occasional patients who have been treated with cortisone in doses that caused an oversupply of the hormone. In experimental animals removal of the adrenals causes excretion of salts, which greatly increases the animals' preference for salty water. In fact, adrenalectomized rats show an amazing sensitivity for very weak salt solutions.

Experiential interventions also cause rapid changes in the output of many endocrine glands. For example, the output of thyroid hormone responds to many environmental influences. Starting to exercise increases the level of thyroxine in the circulation. Putting animals in a cold temperature also increases thyroid activity, and keeping them there increases the size of the thyroid gland. On the other hand, physical stresses, pain, and unpleasant emotional situations decrease thyroid output, probably as a consequence of diminished release of thyroid-stimulating hormone from the anterior pituitary gland. Sensory stimulation and emotional experience influence the thyroid system by modulating the secretion of thyrotropin-releasing hormone from the hypothalamus.

SUMMARY / MAIN POINTS

1. Hormones are chemical compounds that act as signals in the body. They are secreted by endocrine glands into the bloodstream and are taken up by receptor molecules in target cells.

2. Some hormones, such as insulin and thyroxine, have receptors in a wide variety of cells and can therefore influence the activity of most cells in the body. Others, like gonadal hormones, find receptors in only certain special cells or organs.

3. Hormones act by promoting the proliferation and differentiation of cells and by modulating the activity of cells that have already differentiated.

4. Peptide and amine hormones bind to specific receptor molecules at the surface of the target cell membrane and cause the release of molecules of a "second messenger" inside the cell. Steroid hormones pass through the membrane and bind to receptor molecules in the cell.

5. A negative-feedback system monitors and controls the rate of secretion of each hormone. In the simplest case the hormone acts upon target cells, leading them to change the amount of a substance in the extracellular fluid; this in turn regulates the output of the endocrine gland.

6. Several hormones are controlled by a more complex feedback system; a tropic hormone from the hypothalamus regulates the release of an anterior pituitary hormone, which in turn controls secretion by an endocrine gland. In this case feedback of the endocrine hormone acts mainly at the hypothalamus and anterior pituitary.

7. Endocrine influences on various structures and functions often involve more than one hormone, as in the cases of growth, metabolism, and learning and memory.

8. Neural communication differs from hormonal communication in that neural signals travel rapidly over fixed pathways, whereas hormonal signals spread more slowly and throughout the body.

9. The neural and hormonal communication systems have several characteristics in common: Both utilize chemical messages; the same substance that acts as a hormone in some locations is a synaptic transmitter in others. Both manufacture, store, and release chemical messengers. Both use specific receptors and may employ second messengers.

10. Many behaviors involve the coordination of neural and hormonal components. The transmission of messages in the body may involve neural-neural, neural-endocrine, endocrine-endocrine, or endocrine-neural links.

RECOMMENDED READING

Beach, F. A. Behavioral endocrinology: An emerging discipline. *American Scientist,* 1975, 63, 178–187.

Leshner, A. *An introduction to behavioral endocrinology.* New York: Oxford University Press, 1978.

Turner, C. D. and Bagnara, J. T. *General endocrinology* 6th ed. Philadelphia: Saunders, 1976.

Williams, R. H. (Ed.). *Textbook of endocrinology.* Philadelphia: Saunders, 1974.

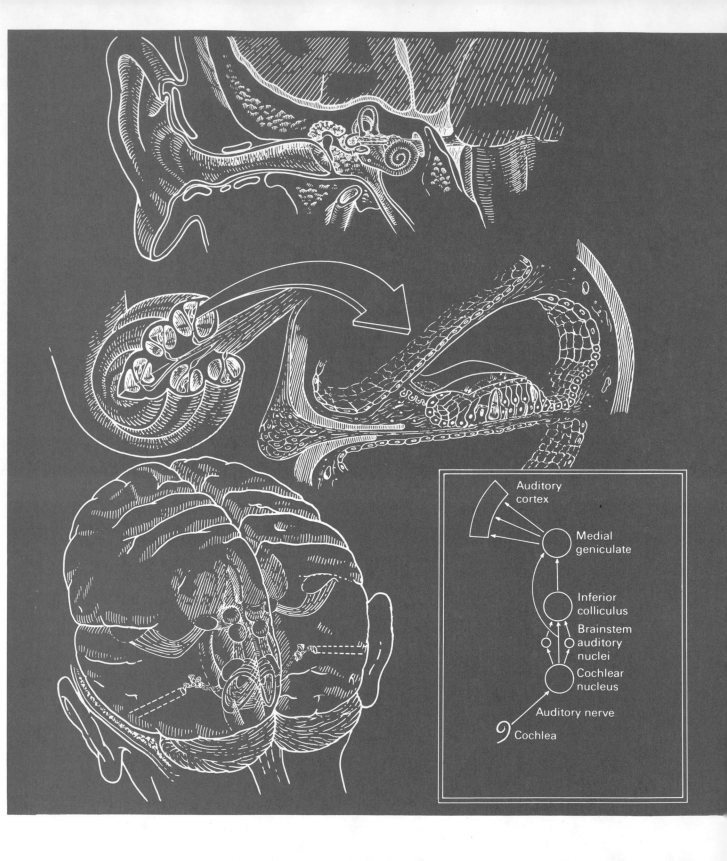

Auditory
cortex

Medial
geniculate

Inferior
colliculus

Brainstem
auditory
nuclei

Cochlear
nucleus

Auditory nerve

Cochlea

Part Two

INFORMATION PROCESSING IN PERCEPTUAL AND MOTOR SYSTEMS

LIGHT FROM THE SUN WARMS OUR SKIN and stimulates our eyes. A chorus of sounds, ranging from the songs of insects to the hearty performances of opera singers, stimulates our ears. Winds bend the hairs on the skin and carry substances that lead to a sense of pleasant or unpleasant odors. The food we eat affects receptors in the mouth, the stomach, and the brain. All about us there is a wide range of energies and substances that excite our senses and supply our brains with a vast array of information about many external and internal happenings. The success of any animal—including humans—in dealing with the tasks of survival depends on its ability to construct reliable representations of some of the physical characteristics of its environment—both internal and external. In most cases, however, sensory systems are not slavish, passive copiers and reflectors of impinging stimuli—quite the contrary. Evolutionary success calls for far more selective action. For any species sensory systems construct only partial and selective portraits of the world.

Sensory inputs to the brain do not merely provide "pictures in the head"; they often incite the individual to act. Different inputs lead to distinct adjustments of the body. Picture the simple case when a sound occurs suddenly: Our eyes almost automatically turn toward the source of the sound. Movements elicited by sensory events range in complexity from slight eye motions to elaborate sequences of movements, such as species-characteristic escape behavior. Of course, many acts are coupled to sensory information in a different way. These classes of movements are not directly driven or triggered by sensory events but reflect intrinsic programs of action, which may involve sensory inputs only as modulators. How information processing occurs in both perceptual and motor systems is our theme in Part Two.

Orientation

Design of Sensory Systems

Discriminating among forms of energy

Responding to different intensities

Responding reliably

Responding rapidly

Suppressing extraneous information

Diversity of Sensory Worlds

Stimulus responsiveness

Kinds of receptors

Events at Sensory Surfaces

Visual excitation

Auditory excitation

Vestibular excitation

Somatosensory excitation

Olfactory excitation

Gustatory excitation

Principles of Sensory Information Processing

Coding

Sensory adaptation

Lateral inhibition

Information suppression

Receptive fields

Sensory pathways in the brain

Attention

Summary / Main Points

6

Principles of Sensory Processing and Experience

Orientation

Sensory systems enable animals to recognize, appreciate, and assess aspects of the world that are necessary for survival. For each species certain features of its surroundings have become especially significant for adaptive success. Although each species in some ways has distinctive windows for viewing the world, the basic processes mediating perceptual accomplishments are much alike in many species. We will consider some of these basic principles of sensory processing and then examine how particular sensory systems work.

All animals have specialized parts of the body that are particularly sensitive to some forms of energy. These body parts—collections of receptors—act as filters in that they respond to some stimuli and exclude others. Furthermore, they convert energy into the language of the nervous system—electrical signals. In any animal, information processing related to these inputs involves codes, that is, rules that relate attributes of stimulus energy, such as intensity, to activity of nerve cells. Knowing these rules, the experimenter should be able to look at a pattern of nerve impulses and distinguish between a beautiful sunset and a tasty bit of food. Of course, we are only slowly gaining understanding of these rules, and up to now our knowledge of coding is mainly restricted to rather simple stimulus dimensions like color and spatial location. Part of the complexity of the problem comes from the fact that processing of sensory neural activity involves many different brain regions, and each may use different transformations of signals. Moreover, the way an event is represented in the nervous system can be different at various brain regions, because each region doesn't merely passively reflect the barrage of neural inputs. Rather, active processing takes place. These processes can be described as filtering, abstracting, and integrating.

All this information processing requires extensive neural circuitry, and the evolution of specialized sensory receptors has led to the development of related regions of the brain. In fact, by examining the relative sizes of sensory regions of the nervous system in a given species, one can tell the degree to which different senses contribute to the adaptation of that species to its environment. This is just one of the many ways in which the theme of localization of function comes into the study of sensory and perceptual processes.

Advances in our understanding of sensory processing are not uniform across all areas of sensory experience. In this chapter we will discuss mainly the neural processes that have offered significant advances in understanding how the brain produces an appreciation of sensory worlds.

Design of sensory systems

Before we consider the actual properties of sensory mechanisms, it is helpful to consider some ideal properties from both biological and engineering perspectives. Suppose that you had the opportunity to take part in the original design of a sensory system. (Emperor Charles V of Spain once remarked, "If I had been present at the Creation, I could have offered some useful advice.") As a participant in the planning sessions, you can suggest criteria for ideal features. You can ask for the best! Remember, however, that the best probably costs more in terms of number and precision of components. Some compromises may therefore become necessary. Also, different design criteria may come into conflict, and this may require further compromises.

What attributes would you suggest for our model? As it turns out, evolution has provided close-to-optimal sensory systems, taking into account the needs of animals in particular environmental niches and the costs and benefits of various sensory mechanisms. Let us consider some of the ideal features and also some realistic compromises.

Discriminating among forms of energy

The kinds of energies and the range of substances in the world are quite broad. Different kinds of energy, such as light and sound, need different receptors to convert them into neural activity, just as you need a camera and not a tape recorder to take a picture. The different sensory systems (or modalities) must be separate in the brain, too, rather than converging on a common system, as ancient hypotheses held.

We gain information by distinguishing among forms or kinds of stimulus energy. The poet may write, "The dawn came up like thunder," but most of the time we want to know whether a sudden dramatic sensory event was auditory or visual, tactile or olfactory. Furthermore, different senses furnish us with quite different information: We see a car hurtling toward us, hear the thin whine of a mosquito circling us, or smell gas escaping; but we might not hear the car until it was too late, and we probably wouldn't smell the mosquito or see the gas. So our model sensory system should provide for detecting and distinguishing among different forms of energy.

This requirement was considered by the pioneer physiologist Johannes Müller early in the nineteenth century. He proposed the doctrine of "specific nerve energies"; that is, the idea that the receptors and neural channels for the different senses are independent and operate in their own special ways. For example, no matter how the eye is stimulated—by light or mechanical pressure or electrical shock—the sensation that occurs is always visual. Müller formulated his hypothesis before the nature of nervous transmission was known, so he could suppose that the different sensory systems of the brain used different kinds of energy to carry their messages. Now we know that the messages for the different senses—such as seeing, hearing, touch, pain, and temperature—are kept separate and distinct not by the way systems carry their messages but by keeping their neural tracts separate.

It would be quite costly, however, for each animal species to be sensitive to all the kinds of energy in its environment. Each species therefore evolved the sensory detectors needed to respond to certain forms of stimulation, but for other forms of stimulation it is only poorly equipped or not equipped at all.

Responding to different intensities

Many forms of energy occur over a broad range of intensities. For example, a sonic boom brings to the ear millions of times more energy than the tick of a watch; from the wan light of the first quarter moon to sunlight at noon there is a difference of 1 to 10 million in energy. Our ideal system should be able to represent stimulus values over these broad ranges so that the viewer can discriminate accurately, neither groping in the dark nor being dazzled by too much light. Of course, sensitivity to very feeble stimuli may require highly specialized, and therefore costly, sensory detectors, so we will have to settle for some realistic lower limit.

If the system is to respond to a wide range of intensities, it should be sensitive to differences in intensity; that is, it should be able to provide large responses for small changes in the strength of a stimulus. Actually there are few circumstances in which the absolute value of a stimulus is of major adaptive significance. In most instances sensitivity to change in the stimulus is the important signal for adaptive success. Thus we respond mainly to changes, whether these are changes in intensity or quality or location of the stimulus.

Responding reliably

Reliability in a sensory system means that there should be a consistent relation between any signal in the external or internal environment and the sensory system's response. Imagine your confusion if a cold stimulus randomly elicited the responses cold, warm, painful, and slippery. To establish useful representations of the world, our ideal system must work reliably.

Responding rapidly

Optimal adjustment to the world requires that sensory information be processed rapidly. As a driver, you have to perceive the motion of other cars swiftly and correctly if you are going to avoid collisions. Similarly, it doesn't do a predator much good to recognize prey unless it can do so both rapidly and accurately. Alas, we have come up against a conflict between optimal properties.

A customary way to provide reliability is to increase the number of components. Using several different circuits to process the same stimulus (**parallel processing**) is a conventional way to ensure reliability. Indeed, the "backup" plans ensuring reliability in engineering designs generally provide such "fail-safe" options. However, increasing the number of components in our biological systems poses two difficulties:

1. The greater the number of components, the greater the metabolic expense.
2. Increasing the number of components generally compromises speed.

In many sensory systems there is a delicate balance between speed and reliability for optimal function.

Suppressing extraneous information

Did you ever try to hold a conversation on a disco floor? Is so, could you hear anything besides the overwhelming input of the music? This example illustrates a paradox. Previously we called for the design of a sensory analyzer with exquisite sensitivity and reliability. But now we are arguing that this extraordinary device should include a provision for ignoring some of the world! This ideal feature once again underscores the fact that the stimulus property of primary biological significance is change. Maintained stimuli provide little information to an organism.

A dramatic example of this effect comes from experiments with stabilized visual images. In these studies images are stabilized on the retina, either by affixing a microprojector to a contact lens (Figure 6-1) or by using a set of mirrors, including one on a contact lens. Both techniques ensure that whenever the eye moves, the image moves precisely with the eye. Thus, the image continues to fall on the same retinal elements no matter how the eye moves. Under these circumstances perception of the projected pattern disappears within 15 seconds to 2 minutes, depending on the

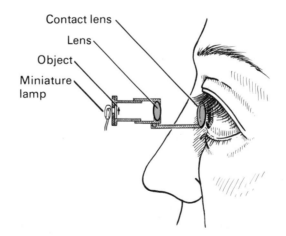

Figure 6-1 Stabilized image experiment. An image is projected on the retina using a tiny projector connected to a contact lens that is placed firmly on the surface of the eye. With every eye movement there is an exactly corresponding movement of the projector so the image stays fixed on the retina. Such stabilized images fade quickly, illustrating the importance of change in perception.

TABLE 6-1   Sensory Systems and Adequate Stimuli

TYPE OF SENSORY SYSTEM	MODALITY	ADEQUATE STIMULI
Chemical	Smell	Odorous substances dissolved in air or water in the nasal cavity
	Taste	Taste stimuli; in mammals the categories of taste experience are sweet, sour, salty, bitter
	Common chemical	Changes in CO_2, pH, osmotic pressure
Mechanical	Touch	Contact with or deformation of body surface
	Hearing	Sound vibrations in air or water
	Vestibular	Head movement and orientation
	Joint	Position and movement
	Muscle	Tension
Photic	Seeing	Visible radiant energy
Thermal	Cold	Decrement of skin temperature
	Warm	Increase of skin temperature
Electrical	[No common name because humans do not have this sense]	Differences in density of electrical currents

complexity of the figure. This experiment demonstrates the role of changing stimulus values in perception. As we will see, sensory devices of different sorts accomplish suppression in a variety of ways. These include varying thresholds, adaptation, and different forms of direct and indirect controls.

How are the ideal properties we have just discussed realized in the actual sensory systems of human beings and of other species? This chapter and Chapter 7 explore the answers to this question.

Diversity of sensory worlds   Different species detect different aspects of the world. From the physicist's point of view, the stimuli that animals detect are forms of physical energy or chemical substances that can be defined and described by using the scales or measures of physics and chemistry. But as we have said, not all the forms of physical energy that the physicist or chemist can describe are necessarily potential stimuli for any animal. Indeed, some forms of energy cannot be detected by the sensory systems of *any* existing animal. Table 6-1 classifies sensory systems and the kinds of stimuli related to each system. The term **adequate stimulus** refers to the type of stimulus for which a given sensory organ is particularly adapted. Thus the adequate stimulus for the eye is photic energy; although mechanical pressure on the eye or an electrical shock can stimulate the retina and produce sensations of light, these are not adequate stimuli for the eye.

Box 6-1 briefly describes the characteristics of two types of stimuli—visual and acoustic—as background for discussing differences among species and among sensory receptors.

BOX 6-1   Black Light and Inaudible Sound

Among the wavelengths of radiant energy only a small range is visible to us, but some wavelengths that are invisible to us are readily perceived by certain other species. Similarly, there are frequencies of vibration in the air that we can't hear but that bats can. To consider species differences in sensitivity to stimuli, we need to know some basic facts about the physical stimuli.

● **The visual stimulus**   The physical energy to which our visual system responds is a band of electromagnetic radiation. This radiation comes in very small packets of energy called **quanta.** Each quantum can be described by a single number, its wavelength (the distance between two adjacent crests of vibratory activity). The human visual system responds only to quanta whose wavelengths lie within a very narrow range, from about 400 to

700 nanometers (nm) (see Box Figure 6-1). Such quanta of light energy are called **photons** (from the Greek word meaning "light"). The band of radiant energy in which animals can see may be narrow, but it is well suited for accurate reflection from the surface of objects in the size range that we deal with in most of our behavior. Radio waves are good for imaging objects of astronomical size, while X rays penetrate below the surfaces of objects.

Each photon is a very small amount of energy; the exact amount depends on its wavelength. A single photon of wavelength 560 nm contains only 3.55×10^{-19} joules of energy. A 100-watt (W) light bulb gives off only about 3 W of visible light—the rest is heat. But even the 3 W of light amounts to 8 quintillion (8×10^{18}) photons per second! When quanta enter the eye, they can evoke visual sensations. The exact nature of such sensations

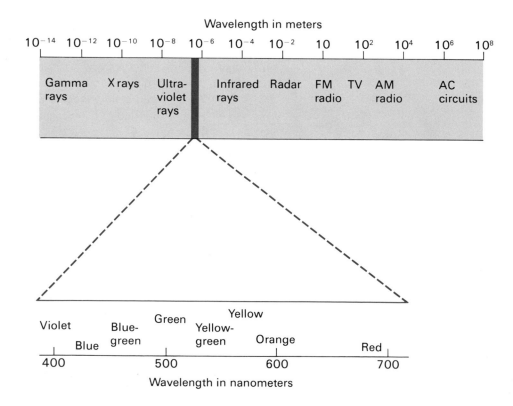

Box Figure 6-1   The electromagnetic spectrum of which visible light, enlarged below, is only a small fraction.

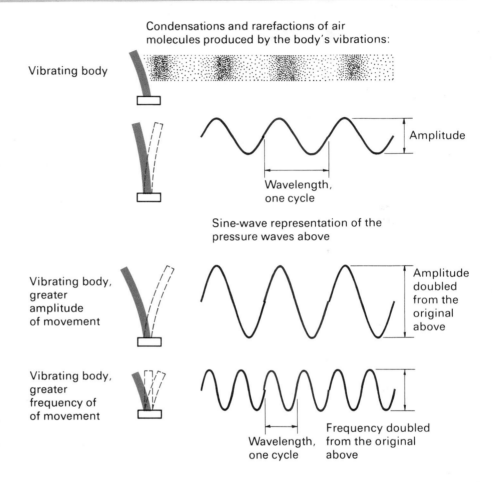

Condensations and rarefactions of air molecules produced by the body's vibrations:

Vibrating body

Amplitude

Wavelength, one cycle

Sine-wave representation of the pressure waves above

Vibrating body, greater amplitude of movement

Amplitude doubled from the original above

Vibrating body, greater frequency of of movement

Wavelength, one cycle

Frequency doubled from the original above

Box Figure 6-2 The auditory stimulus. A pure tone or sine wave vibration can vary in both amplitude and frequency.

depends both on the wavelengths of the quanta and on the number of quanta per second.

● **The acoustic stimulus** Although few animals produce light, most animals produce sound. Hearing lets us detect energies that we and other animals produce, either for communication or incidentally to other activities. Sound is a repetitive change in the pressure of some medium, commonly air or water. In air this change arises because air particles are moved by a vibrating mechanical system, such as the glottis of the larynx in speech, a tuning fork, or the cone of a loudspeaker. As the tuning

fork moves away from a resting position, it compresses air particles, which increases air pressure above atmospheric pressure. As the tuning fork swings to the other side of its rest position, air particle density is briefly reduced with respect to atmospheric pressure. An alternation of condensation and rarefaction of air is called one cycle. Box Figure 6-2 presents an illustration of the changes in the spacing of air particles produced by a vibrating tuning fork. The sound produced by a tuning fork has only one frequency of vibration, so it is called a pure tone and can be represented by a sine wave.

(continued)

BOX 6-1 (continued)

A pure tone is described physically in terms of two measures:

1. Frequency, or the number of cycles per second, measured in hertz (Hz) (for example, middle A has a frequency of 440 Hz).
2. Amplitude or intensity, the distance of particle movement in some period of time, usually measured as pressure, or force per unit area, measured in dynes per square centimeter (dyn/cm²).

Most sounds are more complicated than a pure tone. For example, a sound made by a musical instrument contains a "fundamental" frequency and "harmonics." The fundamental is the basic frequency and the harmonics are multiples of the fundamental. For example, if the fundamental is 440 Hz, then the harmonics are 880, 1320, 1760, . . . When different instruments play the same note, they differ in the relative intensities of the various harmonics, and this difference is what gives each instrument its characteristic quality, or timbre. Any complex pattern can be analyzed into a sum of sine waves, a process called **Fourier analysis** after the French mathematician who discovered it. (We will see later that Fourier analysis can also be applied to visual patterns.) Box Figure 6-3 shows how a complex waveform can be analyzed into sine waves of different frequencies.

Since the ear is sensitive to a huge range of pressures, sound intensity is generally expressed in **decibels (dB),** a logarithmic scale. The definition of a decibel is as follows:

$$N \text{ (dB)} = 20 \log P_1/P_2$$

where N is the number of decibels and P_1 and P_2 are the two pressures to be compared.

The common reference level in hearing studies (P_2 in the above notation) is 0.0002 dyn/cm²; this is the least pressure necessary for an average human observer to hear a 1000-Hz tone. In this scale a whisper is about 10 times as intense as 0.0002 dyn/cm² and a jet airliner 500 ft overhead is about a million times as intense as the reference level; in decibel notation the whisper is about 20 dB above threshold and the jetliner is about 120 dB above threshold.

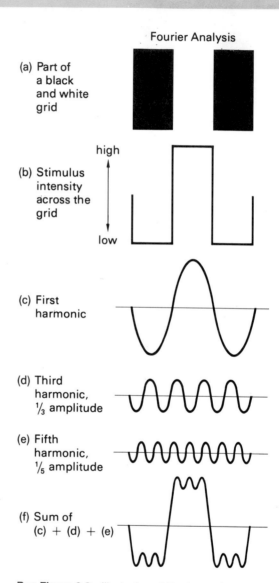

Fourier Analysis

(a) Part of a black and white grid

(b) Stimulus intensity across the grid

(c) First harmonic

(d) Third harmonic, ⅓ amplitude

(e) Fifth harmonic, ⅕ amplitude

(f) Sum of (c) + (d) + (e)

Box Figure 6-3 Illustration of Fourier analysis. A complex repeating pattern such as this square wave can be analyzed into component sine waves.

TABLE 6-2   Frequency Ranges of Hearing of a Few Species

SPECIES	APPROXIMATE FREQUENCY RANGE (Hz)	APPROXIMATE OPTIMUM FREQUENCY (Hz)
Human	20–20,000	2,000
Cat	60–65,000	10,000
Canary	250–21,000	3,000
Porpoise	150–150,000	60,000
Bat	1000–120,000	
Moth	3000–150,000	

Range of responsiveness

For any single form of physical energy the sensory systems of a particular animal are quite selective. For example, humans do not hear sounds in the frequency range above 20,000 hertz (Hz), a range we call "ultrasonic." But to a bat, air vibrations of 50,000 Hz would be sound waves, just as would vibrations of 10,000 Hz. Primates in general are deficient in the ability to hear sounds between 20,000 and 80,000 Hz, although many small mammals have good sensory abilities in this range. Table 6-2 compares the frequency ranges of hearing of several species of animal.

In the visual realm, too, other animals can detect stimuli that we cannot. Bees see in the ultraviolet range (wavelengths shorter than 400 nm; see Box Figure 6-1). Some snakes perceive the wavelengths beyond the other end of our visual spectrum, wavelengths that we can only feel as heat. Box 6-2 gives further examples of species differences in sensory abilities. These abilities are related to characteristics of sensory receptors, our next topic.

Kinds of receptors

Detection of energy starts with the properties of **receptors.** Receptors are the biological devices that initiate the body's responses to particular energies or substances in the environment. They do so either by converting energies into biological signals or by converting contact with substances into signals. Devices that convert energy from one form to another are known as **transducers,** and the process is called **transduction.** Receptors are therefore the starting points for the neural activity that leads to sensory-perceptual experiences.

The receptor itself may consist of the termination of a nerve fiber such as free nerve endings in the skin (Figure 6-2). But in most kinds of receptors the nerve fiber ending is associated with a nonneural cell, which is the actual site of energy conversion. For example, various kinds of corpuscles are associated with nerve endings in the skin. The eye has specialized receptor cells that convert photic energy into electrical charges that stimulate the fibers of the optic nerve. The inner ear has specialized hair cells that transduce mechanical energy into electrical signals that stimulate the fibers of the auditory nerve. And deep in the nasal cavity are patches of specialized cells—the olfactory mucosa—that react chemically with odorous substances and produce electrical charges that stimulate the olfactory nerve.

Across the animal kingdom, receptors offer enormous diversity. A wide array of sizes, shapes, and forms reflects the varying survival needs of different animals.

BOX 6-2   Unusual Receptors in Unusual Animals

Animals have evolved some unusual sensory receptors in the course of adapting to specialized ecological niches. Some of these receptors seem strange to us because they sense aspects of the world that we cannot appreciate without the aid of specialized gadgets. We humans are so visually oriented that "seeing" seems to be synonymous with "understanding." We say, "I see what you mean. It's clear to me now." But for some species, the most useful and accurate information about the environment comes not from seeing but from heat radiation, electrical fields, or odors.

The pit organs of some snakes are extraordinarily sensitive to heat. These organs are located on each side of the head between the eye and the nostril of the snake. They have such sensitivity to heat (referred to as infrared sensitivity) that they can detect a temperature change of just a few thousandths of a degree. Consequently snakes that have these organs can easily locate heat-emitting sources—such as their prey—and follow their movements. With the aid of its infrared "eyes" the snake can accurately locate a rodent in the immediate environment, even at night and in dark caves. Integration of information obtained through the pit organs and through the eyes occurs in the snake's tectum. Some neurons there respond to both infrared and visual stimulation (Newman and Hartline, 1981).

Some fish that live in murky waters "see" with electricity. Fish that generate large-amplitude electrical pulses to kill prey were mentioned in Chapter 4 (Box 4-3). Other fish that generate electricity are more peaceful; they generate long trains of low-voltage electrical pulses as aids to their navigation. The type of pulse emitted is characteristic of the species (Box Figure 6-4). Along the surface of the body of these animals are receptors that are sensitive to changes in the electrical field set up by their own electrical signals. Rocks, weeds, and other fish, whose electrical conductance differs from that of water, change the shape of the fish's electrical field. This change in electrical field enables the fish to locate these objects. Since the signals are species-characteristic, they may also serve a social function of communication (Hopkins, 1974).

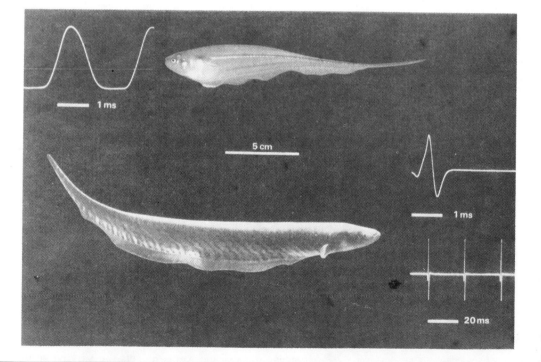

Box Figure 6-4 Examples of two types of electric fish, each emitting a species-characteristic electrical discharge. Electrical receptors are located in the skin. [From G. W. B. Westby, "Communication and jamming avoidance in electric fish," *Trends in Neurosciences* (August 1981): 205.]

Other animals find their way by smell. Salmon, which leave the streams in which they are spawned and begin a long period of ocean migration, return several years later to the exact stream in which they grew up. This amazing feat involves thousands of miles of travel and many opportunities to go wrong. Evidently, salmon recognize their parent stream because of olfactory imprinting. Researchers made this discovery by recording electrical activity from the olfactory bulb while water from different streams was washed across the gills. Water from the parent stream evoked considerable electrical activity, while that from other nearby streams did not.

These examples show that animals of other species not only find their way but accurately recognize objects by using senses that we either do not possess or have in much more rudimentary form.

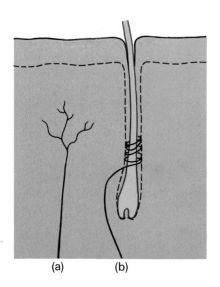

Figure 6-2 Nerve endings in the skin. (a) Free nerve endings. (b) Nerve ending around an accessory cell, a hair follicle which is shown in blue.

(a)   (b)

(See Box 6-2.) For some animals, such as some snakes, detectors of infrared radiation are essential, while several species of fish employ receptors of electrical energy. Evolutionary processes have led to the emergence of quite specialized sensors attuned to the inputs or signals characteristic of particular environmental niches. So we can look at receptors as embodying strategies for success in particular worlds. Indeed, quite often there is a close fit between optimal receptor characteristics from an evolutionary viewpoint and criteria for optimal performance derived from engineering.

Events at sensory surfaces

We have just noted that sensory receptors are transducers—devices that convert different forms of energy into neural activity. The structure of a receptor determines the forms of energy to which it will respond. In all cases the steps between the impact of energy at some receptor and the initiation of nerve impulses in a nerve fiber leading away from the receptor involve local changes of membrane potential, which are referred to as **generator potentials.** (In most of its properties the generator potential resembles the excitatory postsynaptic potentials discussed in Chapter 4.) These electrical charges are the necessary and sufficient conditions for generating nerve impulses. They are part of the causal link between stimulus and nerve impulse.

The details of the generator potential process have been explored by Loewenstein (1971) in elegant studies on a receptor called the **Pacinian corpuscle.** It is found throughout the body—in skin and muscle—but is especially prominent in tissue overlying the abdominal cavity. It consists of a neural fiber that enters a structure, somewhat like a tiny onion, that consists of concentric layers of tissue separated by fluid (Figure 6-3).

Mechanical stimuli delivered to the corpuscle produce a graded electrical potential whose amplitude is directly proportional to the strength of the stimulus. When this electrical event is of sufficient amplitude, the nerve impulse is generated (Figure 6-3). Careful dissection of the corpuscle, leaving the bared axon terminal intact, shows that this graded potential—the generator potential—is initiated in the nerve

Figure 6-3 Excitation of the Pacinian corpuscle. (a) Nerve ending within the corpuscle. Mechanical stimulation with progressively stronger stimuli produces correspondingly stronger generator potentials that reach threshold for axon firing (levels). (b) Nerve ending after the corpuscle has been dissected away. A series of stimuli delivered to the terminal also produce generator potentials and axon firing to threshold stimuli. This shows that the transducer mechanism is located in the axon terminal. (From W. R. Loewenstein, "Biological Transducers." Copyright © 1960 by Scientific American, Inc. All rights reserved.)

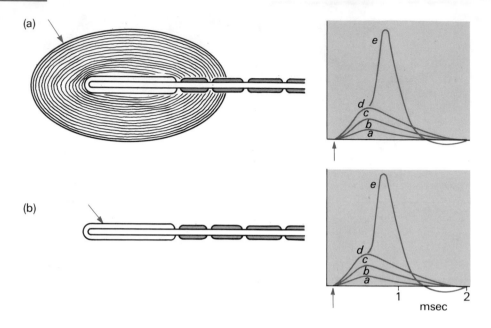

terminal. Pressing the corpuscle bends this terminal, which leads to the generator event. The sequence of excitatory events is as follows:

1. Mechanical stimulation deforms the corpuscle.

2. This deformation leads to mechanical excitation of the tip of the axon.

3. This leads to the generator potential, which, when it reaches threshold amplitude, can elicit nerve impulses.

In some receptor systems the generator events are more complicated. This is true, for example, of hair cells in the inner ear. Some researchers have suggested the following sequence of events:

1. Mechanical stimulation bends hairs.

2. Receptor potential is elicited in the hair cell by membrane deformation.

3. A chemical is released at the base of the hair cell.

4. A transmitter flows across the cleft and stimulates the nerve terminal.

5. The generator potential is produced in the nerve cell.

Let us now examine the sensory events that stimuli elicit at sensory receptors.

Visual excitation   Light passes through several parts of the eye and is affected by them on its way to the primary visual receptors. The rays of light are bent, first at the surface of the eye (the cornea) and then by the lens. The amount of light entering the eye and the depth of focus are determined by the size of the pupil. The lens and the fluid of the eyeball absorb specific wavelengths. Thus before light energy hits the retina, the visual stimulus has already been filtered, and some of its properties have been substantially modified.

The first stage of visual information processing occurs in the **retina,** the receptive surface inside the eye (Figure 6-4). Several types of cells form distinct layers within the retina (Figure 6-4b). The receptive elements proper—the **rods** and **cones** — synapse with **bipolar cells,** which in turn connect with **ganglion cells;** the axons of the ganglion cells form the **optic nerve.** From the receptive elements to the ganglion cells there is an enormous compression of input; there are about 125 million rods and cones but only one million ganglion cells. **Horizontal cells** and **amacrine cells** in the retina (Figure 6-5) complete the nerve cell population; these cells are especially significant in inhibitory interactions within the retina. The large number of retinal cells permits a great deal of information processing to occur at this level of the visual system. The resultant signals converge on the ganglion cells.

Studies of human sensitivity to light reveal the existence of two different functional systems corresponding to two different populations of receptors in the retina. One system works at low levels of light intensity and involves the rods; this system is called the **scotopic system** (from the Greek word for "darkness"). The other system operates at higher levels of light and shows sensitivity to color; this system involves the cones and is called the **photopic system** (from the Greek word for "light"). The workings of these two systems, with their somewhat different sensitivities, enable our eyes to operate over a wide range of intensities.

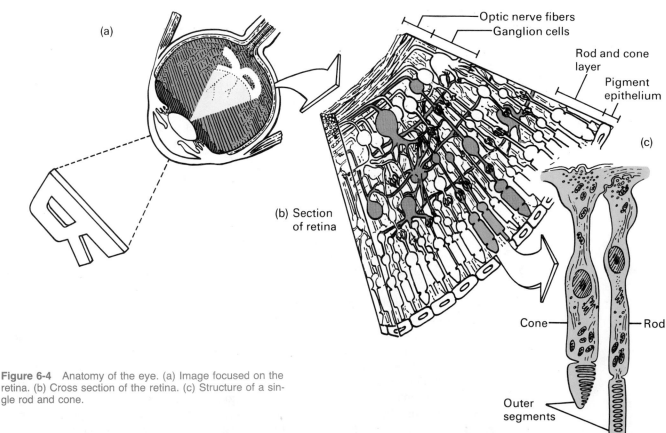

Figure 6-4 Anatomy of the eye. (a) Image focused on the retina. (b) Cross section of the retina. (c) Structure of a single rod and cone.

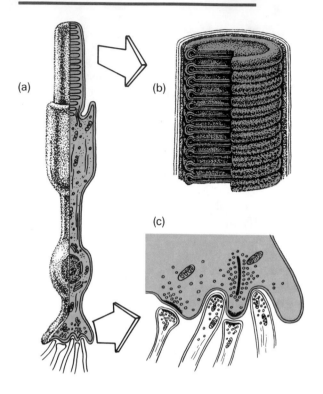

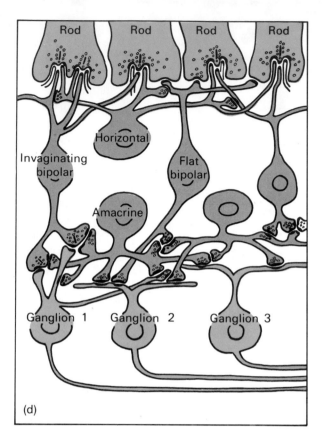

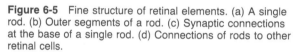

Figure 6-5 Fine structure of retinal elements. (a) A single rod. (b) Outer segments of a rod. (c) Synaptic connections at the base of a single rod. (d) Connections of rods to other retinal cells.

The extraordinary sensitivity of both kinds of visual receptors is determined by their unusual structure and biochemistry. A portion of the structure of both rods and cones, when magnified, looks like a large stack of pancakes (Figure 6-5b). Each layer within the pile is called a disc. The stacking of discs increases the probability of capturing quanta of light. This feature is especially important since light is reflected in many directions by the surface of the eyeball, the lens, and the fluid media of the eye. Because of the dispersion of light, only small amounts actually reach the retinal surface.

The quanta of light that strike the discs are captured by special photopigments. The pigment in the rods is called **rhodopsin.** The pioneering studies of George Wald (1964) established the chemical structure of this and other visual pigments. He showed that this protein molecule changes shape when exposed to light. Since the protein molecule is located in the membrane of discs, the change in molecule configuration alters the conductance of the rod membrane to ions. The flow of ions causes receptor potentials; these potentials represent the initial electrical signal of activation of the visual pathway. The size of the receptor potential is related to stimulus intensity. Sensitivity of the rod is partly determined by prior exposure to light; thus a given intensity of stimulation will cause a larger receptor potential if preceded by smaller rather than by larger stimuli. There are three different cone pigments, as will be discussed in relation to color vision in Chapter 7.

Auditory excitation   The receptor system for sound consists of the external ear, the middle ear cavity, and the mechanisms of the inner ear (see Figure 6-6). Sound enters the external ear, which acts as a kind of funnel. (Some animals can move the external ear freely, but humans are less well endowed with this talent.) At the inner end of the external ear canal, airborne vibrations strike the **tympanic membrane** (eardrum), which forms the partition between the external and **middle ear** systems. The shape of the external ear and the length and shape of the external ear canal reduce the amplitude of some frequencies of sound, while its resonance enhances other frequencies.

In the middle ear cavity a chain of small delicate bones called the **ossicles** is connected at one end to the tympanic membrane and at the other end to an opening to the inner ear, the **oval window.** Small displacements of the tympanic membrane move the ossicular chain. What is the role of these small bones in transmitting sound? They are necessary because it is extremely difficult for the minute mechanical forces of air particles to compress fluid. The mechanical linkages of the middle ear focus the pressures on the large tympanic membrane onto the small oval window; this arrangement produces a vast amplification of sound pressure that is capable of stimulating the fluid-filled inner ear.

The effects of intense sound are attenuated in transmission through the middle ear bones by muscles associated with two of these bones, the malleus, connected to the tympanic membrane, and the stapes, connected to the oval window. These muscles, when activated, prevent easy movement of the middle ear bones and limit the effectiveness of sounds. Very intense sounds activate these muscles, preventing injury to cochlea hair cells from prolonged, intense stimulation. These muscles also become active during body movement and swallowing; they are the reason we hear few of the sounds produced by the workings of our own bodies.

A detailed look at the inner ear is necessary for an understanding of sound transduction. In mammals the auditory portion of the inner ear is a coiled structure called the **cochlea** (from the Greek "kochlos," meaning "snail"; see Figure 6-6). This structure is located within the temporal bone. The region nearest the oval window membrane is the base of the spiral, and the end or top is the apex. Along the length of the cochlea are three principal canals: (1) the **tympanic canal,** (2) the **vestibular canal,** and (3) the **cochlear duct.** A cross section of the cochlea illustrating this division is shown in Figure 6-7(a). The entire structure is filled with non-compressible fluid. Hence if anything is to occur within this structure when the oval window is pushed, there must be a movable outlet membrane. This membrane is the **round window,** which separates the cochlear duct from the middle ear cavity.

The principal elements for auditory transduction are found on the **basilar membrane.** The basilar membrane of the cochlea is about five times wider at the apex than at the base, although the cochlea itself narrows toward the apex. Within the cochlear duct and riding on the basilar membrane is the **organ of Corti.** The organ of Corti sits on top of the basilar membrane and contains the sensory cells **(hair cells),** an elaborate framework of supporting cells, and the terminations of the auditory nerve fibers. There are two sets of sensory cells, a single row of **inner hair cells** and three rows of **outer hair cells** (see Figure 6-7b). The hair cells are cylindrically shaped with a diameter of approximately 5 microns (μ) and a length of 20 to 50 μ. From the upper end of the hair cell protrude hairs, or cilia (Figure 6-7c). Each cell may have as many as 100–200 of the hairs. The length of the cilia is about

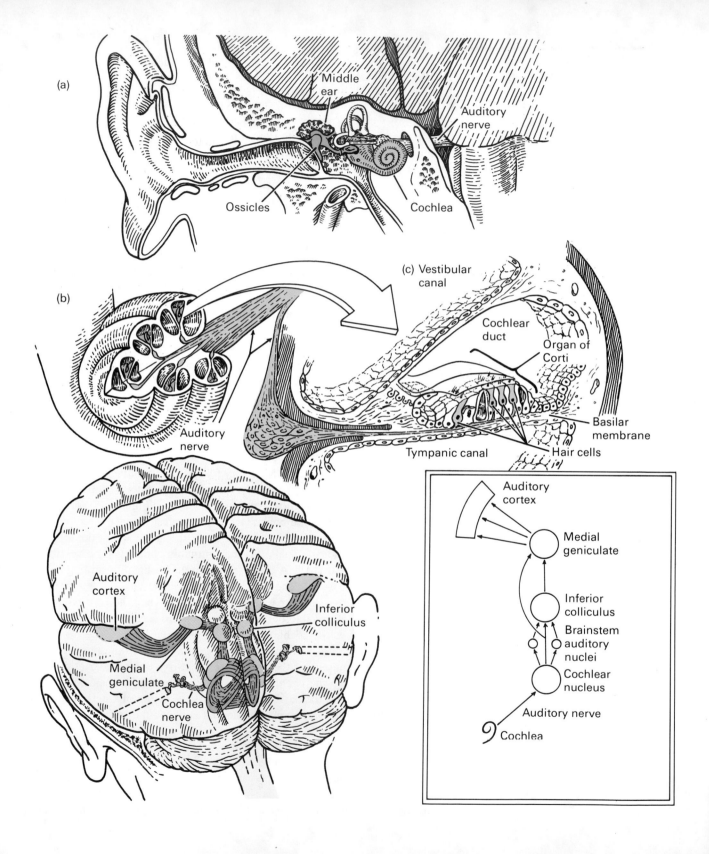

(a)

Middle ear

Auditory nerve

Ossicles

Cochlea

(b)

(c) Vestibular canal

Cochlear duct

Organ of Corti

Auditory nerve

Basilar membrane

Tympanic canal

Hair cells

Auditory cortex

Inferior colliculus

Medial geniculate

Cochlea nerve

Auditory cortex

Medial geniculate

Inferior colliculus

Brainstem auditory nuclei

Cochlear nucleus

Auditory nerve

Cochlea

2–6 μ, and the cilia of the outer hair cells extend into indentations in the bottom of the **tectorial membrane.** (Inner hair cells do not seem to make direct contact with the tectorial membrane.) Evolution of the hair cells is described in Box 6-3.

Auditory nerve fibers synapse at the base of the hair cells. Whereas each inner hair cell receives its own auditory nerve fiber, several outer hair cells share a single fiber. On each side of the human head about 50,000 auditory fibers from the cochlea enter the brainstem and synapse in a complex of cells called the dorsal and ventral **cochlear nuclei.** In addition, both the afferent fibers (running from sense organs to the central nervous system) and the efferent fibers (carrying impulses outward from the brain) make contact in the vicinity of the hair cells. The activity in the efferent fibers may modulate the excitability of the terminals of the nerve fibers and hair cells.

The processes that link mechanical events in the cochlea with auditory fiber excitation remain something of a puzzle even after many years of intense investigation. However, it is clear, at least, that the mechanical stimulation of sound causes vibration of the basilar membrane and bending of the hair cells. This bending produces at least two kinds of electrical events: (1) **cochlear microphonic potentials** and (2) **summating potentials.** The waveshape of the cochlear microphonic potential is a virtual mirror of the acoustic waveform (that is, almost as though it were the output of a microphone), while the summating potential is the envelope of the cochlear microphonic potential. [When hair cells are destroyed by drugs (for instance, some antibiotics) or by acoustic trauma, these potentials disappear. However, it is not clear whether the eliminated potentials are the generator potentials that directly excite auditory nerve fibers.]

One schema of the sequence of events leading to auditory nerve excitation is shown in Figure 6-8. Alternatives for this model consider the cochlear microphonic potential as a generator potential that directly stimulates auditory nerve terminals. The processes of auditory nerve excitation remain a matter of speculation.

Vestibular excitation

When you go up in an elevator, you feel the acceleration clearly. When you turn your head or when you ride in a car going around a tight curve, you feel the change of direction. If you are not used to these kinds of stimulation, sensitivity to motion can make you "seasick." It is the receptors of the **vestibular system** that inform the brain about mechanical forces, such as gravity and acceleration, that act on the body.

The receptors of the vestibular system lie in portions of the inner ear that are continuous with the cochlea. (The term vestibular comes from the Latin word for "entrance hall"; the term is used because the system lies in hollow spaces in the temporal bone.) In mammals one portion of the vestibular system consists of three **semicircular canals,** fluid-filled tubes, each oriented in a different plane (Figure

Figure 6-6 General structures of the ear. (a) Overall picture of peripheral components of the auditory system. (b) Cross section of the cochlea. (c) Cross section of a single cochlear duct showing main auditory components of the inner ear.

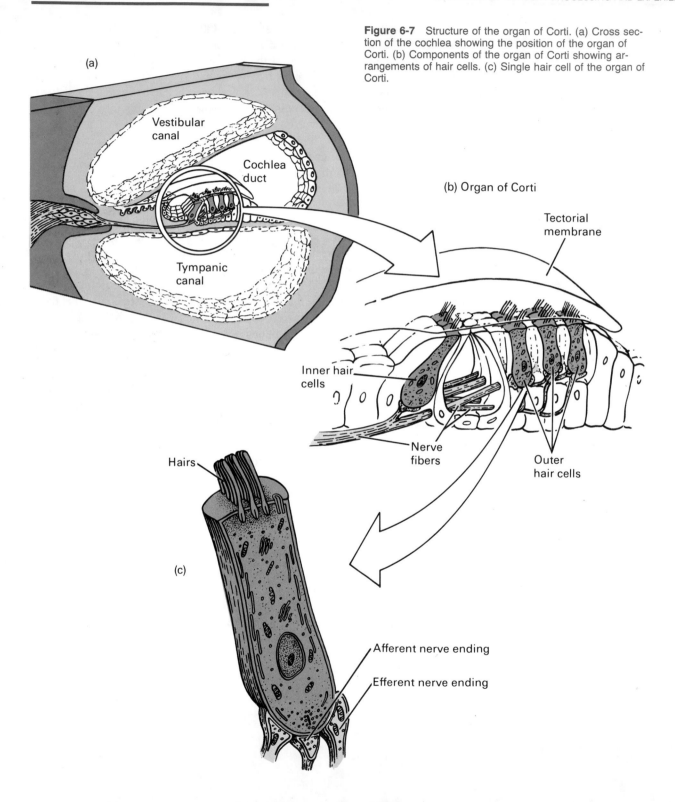

Figure 6-7 Structure of the organ of Corti. (a) Cross section of the cochlea showing the position of the organ of Corti. (b) Components of the organ of Corti showing arrangements of hair cells. (c) Single hair cell of the organ of Corti.

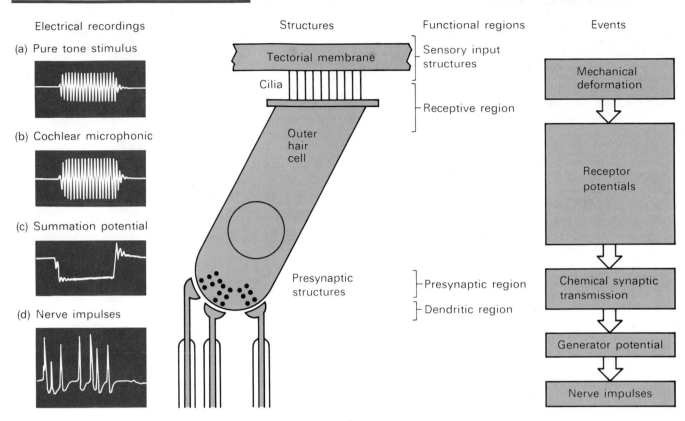

Figure 6-8 Sequences of events in excitation of the auditory nerve. (Adapted from Dallos, 1973)

6-9a and b). Connected to the end of each canal is a saclike structure called the **utricle** (a little uterus). Lying below this is another small fluid-filled sac, the **saccule** (a little sac).

The receptors within these structures, like those of the auditory system, are groups of hair cells whose bending leads to excitation of nerve fibers. In each semicircular canal the hair cells are found at an enlarged region, the **ampulla.** Here the cilia of the hair cells are embedded in a gelatinous mass. The orientation of the hairs is quite precise and determines the kind of mechanical force to which they are especially sensitive. The three semicircular canals are at right angles to each other; thus one or another detects angular acceleration in any direction. The receptors in the saccule and utricle respond to static positions of the head. At the base of these hair cells are nerve fibers whose connections to the hair cells are much like the connections in the auditory portions of the inner ear.

Somatosensory excitation

Stimulation of the body surface can yield a variety of sensory experiences. They have been classified into several groups of related sensations. A contact group includes touch, pressure, vibration, tickle, and the tingling feeling of pins and needles. A pain group includes superficial pricking, deep ache, itch, and burning. Further skin sensation groups include a thermal group (warm and cold) and sensory blends or combinations like cold pain.

BOX 6-3 Evolution of Hairs That Hear Distant Objects

The evolutionary history of the auditory-vestibular system is better known than that of other sensory systems because the receptors are encased in bone, which leaves fossil remains. Combined studies of fossils and of many living animals have yielded a detailed story of the origins of hearing (van Bergeijk, 1967; Wever, 1974). We will summarize some of the most important points here.

It is generally accepted that the auditory end organ evolved from the vestibular system, which detects movement and position. In turn, the vestibular system evolved from the **lateral-line system,** a sensory system found in many kinds of fish and some amphibians. The lateral-line system is an array of receptors along the side of the body; tiny hairs emerge from sensory cells in the skin. These hairs are embedded in small gelatinlike columns called **cupulae.** Movements of water in relation to the body surface stimulate these receptors so that the animal can detect currents of water and movements of other animals, prey or predators. Information from the lateral line also helps schools of fish stay in formation, since each fish feels the currents made by the others. A specialized form of lateral-line organ is the lateral-line canal, a groove that partially encloses the cupulae. It is speculated that the first semicircular canals developed from a stretch of lateral-line canal that migrated into the body. Having a stretch of canal away from the surface of the body gave the animal a sensor for turns to the right or left, and this receptor was free of effects of stimulation of the skin. Sensitivity to change of direction was optimized when the canal developed into a roughly circular form.

The lamprey has lateral-line receptors; some of them are shown in Figure 3-26 as the row of circles extending back from the eye. Different species of lamprey have one or two semicircular canals on each side, and these detect turning movements of the head. The lamprey also have larger chambers in the vestibular apparatus, the saccule and the utricle, which detect position and linear movements of the head. The saccule and utricle are also specialized developments from the lateral-line system. The sensitivity of these organs to position and to movements is increased by tiny bits of bone that weight the cupulae. These crystals are called otoliths (from the Latin roots for "ear" and "stone"). The sea lamprey has otoliths, as do mammals, including humans (see Figure 6-9d). The lam-

prey does not, however, possess an end-organ for hearing. That first emerged in fish with jaws.

The development of the inner ear came about in fish through the evolution of an organ, the swim bladder, that served an entirely different function, aiding balance. Many species of fish have this gas-filled cavity in the abdomen. Vibrations in water cause the air bladder to contract and expand, which increases sensitivity to such vibrations. In some families of fish the sac extended and made contact with the vestibular labyrinth; in others a series of bones connected the swim bladder with the labyrinth. In both cases, the animals acquired increased sensitivity to vibrations in the environment, and a new part of the labyrinth evolved in conjunction with this vibratory sense. This duct, the lagena (from the Latin for "flask"), is found in bony fishes, amphibians, reptiles, and birds. It corresponds to the cochlea found in mammals.

So the auditory system evolved out of the vestibular system, which in turn arose from the lateral-line system. More recently evolved animals show longer auditory ducts with greater numbers of hair cells and auditory nerve fibers (Box Figure 6-5). Presumably this larger system is the basis for the excellent discrimination of frequencies and auditory patterns in the higher animals.

Evidence of the common origin of the lateral-line system, the vestibular system, and the auditory system is of several kinds:

1. The hair cells of these three systems are similar, but so are some ciliated cells derived from ectoderm in other parts of the body.

2. The nerve fibers that innervate them come from the same brainstem nuclei.

3. The hair cells are embedded in gelatinous cupulae, and these endings are contained in fluid-filled chambers.

Although we can look at these evolutionary developments as steps toward our own vestibular and auditory organs, there is no need to think of them as having occurred for that purpose. Each adaptation was retained in natural selection because it served a function. Variability of sensitivity among animals allowed evolution of increased sensitivity and of new modes of sensation.

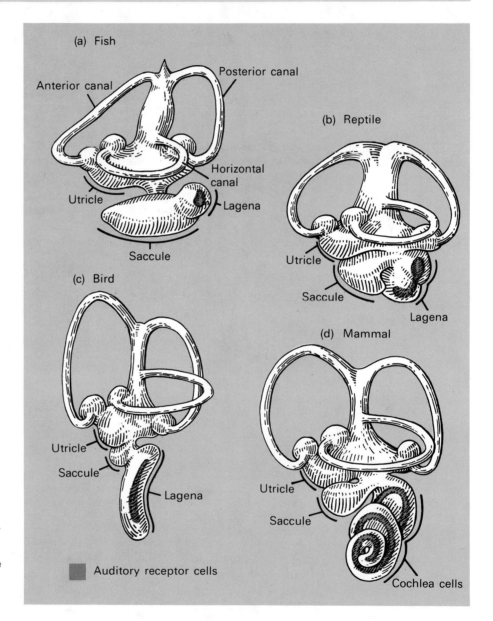

Box Figure 6-5 Evolution of the inner ear and the vestibular apparatus. During evolution the auditory end organ (shown in blue) has become progressively larger and more complex, allowing finer discrimination. (Adapted from Retzius, 1881, 1884)

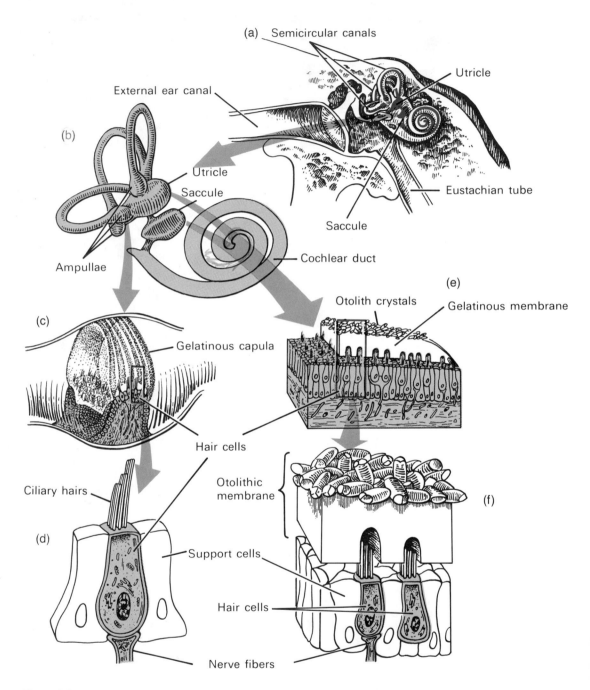

Figure 6-9 Peripheral structure of the vestibular system. (a) Position of vestibular apparatus in temporal bone. (b) Orientation of semicircular canals, utricle, and saccule. (c) An ampulla, or end, of semicircular canal and hair cells, enlarged in (d). (e) Receptor surface of saccule and utricle showing otolith crystals, enlarged in (f).

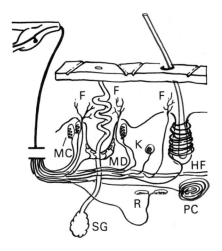

F	Free nerve ending
HF	Hair follicle
K	Krause's end bulb
MC	Meissner's corpuscle
MD	Merkel's disc
PC	Pacinian corpuscle
R	Ruffini's ending
SG	Sweat gland

Figure 6-10 Cross section of the skin showing various kinds of receptors.

Within the skin are several different kinds of receptors (Figure 6-10). One class consists of fine branches of neurons; these are called free nerve endings. A second class consists of accessory cells associated with an afferent terminal. Much has been written or argued about the relations between these receptor cells and specific sensory responses. Is there a distinct class of receptor type for each skin sensation? This is an area of continuing controversy and we will note two contrasting views.

In a review of skin senses Darian-Smith (1982) assembled a collection of research data that indicated marked functional specialization of specific types of skin receptors. For example, Pacinian corpuscles respond accurately to vibration of the skin over a wide range of stimulus frequencies. But they show little evidence of discrimination of spatial stimuli. On the other hand another type of skin receptor, Meissner's corpuscles, show a poor response to vibratory stimuli but respond to spatial features with high fidelity.

Other investigators (for example, Melzack and Wall, 1962) have cautioned us about too readily equating sensory categories and distinct structural classes of receptors. For example, one type of sensory receptor, the free nerve ending, is related to several classes of sensory response. This is the only kind of receptor found in the cornea of the eye, yet stimulation of the cornea can yield several responses, including touch and pain (Wedell, 1962). Coding of the types of sensations in the cornea must therefore be in the form of patterning of impulses rather than activation of specific receptor classes. The psychological categories of skin sensations mentioned above have been developed quite independently of structural categories of receptor types, and it is not yet clear whether these two can be related to each other in a simple way.

Olfactory excitation

Among animals the shapes of noses and other olfactory receptors provide clues to differences in the significance of odor perception in adaptive behavior. The human olfactory system is shown in Figure 6-11.

Within the noses of all mammals is a yellowish brown region that contrasts with the surrounding pinkish areas. This region is the **olfactory epithelium,** and it contains the bipolar receptor cells that are the central sites for transduction of odors. Airflow over this surface is controlled by the shape of the complex bones within the nose. Sniffing causes air to move into the parts of the nose that contain the receptors. Many animals (but not adult primates) have a second olfactory system in the nose called the **vomeronasal system** (it is found in human fetuses but disappears before birth). This system includes a separate collection of olfactory receptor cells that lies on the floor of the nose, and in some animals it is near a passage that leads into the mouth.

The nerve cells of the olfactory epithelium (Figure 6-11) are bipolar neurons from one end of which emerge cilia that can reach 200 μ in length in some animals. These cilia, which are attached to a dendritic knob, move constantly, perhaps stirring the chemical contents of the mucosal surface. The ways in which electrical activity is generated at the dendritic surface remain unknown, although there are several theories, some suggesting specific receptor sites for particular chemicals. Although the size and the shape of molecules are believed to be important in determining the

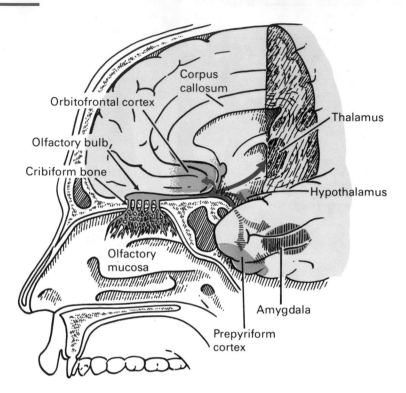

Figure 6-11 Organization of the olfactory system. This illustration shows the positions of the receptor sheet, the olfactory epithelium or mucosa, and brain structures concerned with olfaction.

identity of olfactory experience—for example, what kind of food or what perfume is present—it is not known whether there are specialized cells or different sites on all cells that are especially responsive to particular classes of olfactory stimuli. The axons of the olfactory receptor cells form the olfactory nerves. These axons are very thin and numerous. In some animals, such as the rabbit, the olfactory nerve contains 50–100 million axons.

Recently Graziadei and colleagues (1979) have shown that olfactory nerve cells are replaced every few weeks during the course of life. This result implies that there are undifferentiated cells adjacent to fully differentiated neurons that apparently take the place of dead olfactory receptors. Although we have seen that most neurons are not replaced in adult animals, here is a class of neurons that are replaced frequently. The same thing is true of taste receptors. Apparently, exposed chemoreceptors are more vulnerable than other neurons, so a process for replacing them is required.

Output of the neurons goes to the **olfactory bulb.** An adjacent structure, the accessory olfactory bulb, receives axons from the vomeronasal system. From the olfactory bulbs, olfactory information is related to further stations in the brain.

Gustatory excitation   Since the last century researchers have concluded that human beings have only four taste categories: sweet, sour, salty, and bitter. Other tastes, if they exist, are as-

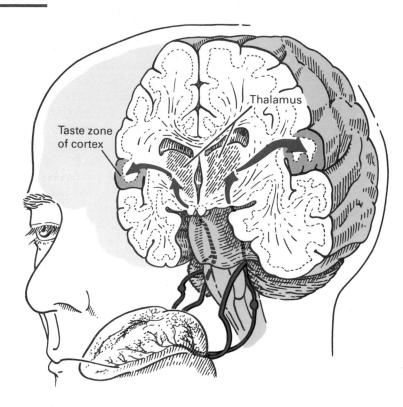

Taste zone
of cortex

Thalamus

Figure 6-12 The taste system, showing receptors in the tongue and paths
to related taste regions of the brain.

sumed to be derived qualities that represent mixtures of these fundamental categories. This view of limited chemical stimuli for taste is akin to the notion of primary
colors in vision. It is important to distinguish between taste and flavor, the latter
involving a much richer set of labels. Flavor seems to develop mostly from the smell
of substances in the mouth and partially from their textures. Deprived of these
inputs, substances lose those sensory characteristics that provide distinctive flavor
differences.

It is often assumed that for each primary taste there is a distinctive class of receptors in the tongue. Neurophysiologists have searched for such specialized receptors
by examining the sensory responses of nerves leading from the tongue. There is little
support for such specialized responsiveness—no fibers respond exclusively to a
single class of taste stimuli.

The human taste system is diagramed in Figure 6-12. Along the sides of the little
bumps on the surface of the tongue are tiny canals lined with openings to groups of
cells called **taste buds.** Nerve fibers end at these receptors. Unlike many other
receptors, but somewhat similar to the case in olfaction, each taste cell lasts only
several days, to be replaced with a newly formed unit.

Most nerve fibers associated with taste buds reach the brain via one of two cranial
nerves: (1) the geniculate ganglion of the facial nerve or (2) the inferior ganglion of
the glossopharyngeal nerve. Synaptic connections are made in the brainstem, and
postsynaptic axons run to the thalamus.

Principles of sensory information processing

Thinkers in ancient Greece believed that the nerves were tubes through which tiny bits of stimulus objects traveled to the brain, there to be analyzed and recognized. And even when accurate knowledge of neural conduction was gained in this century, many investigators still thought that the sensory nerves simply transmitted accurate information about stimulation to the neural centers. Now, however, it is clear that the sense organs and peripheral sensory pathways convey only limited—even distorted—information to the centers. The brain is an active processor of information, not a copier. In fact, a good deal of selection and analysis takes place in the peripheral sensory pathways. Here we will examine some basic aspects of the processing of sensory information—coding, sensory adaptation, lateral inhibition, suppression, receptive fields, and attention. In Chapter 7 we will apply these processes to specific sensory modalities.

Coding

Information about the world is represented in the circuits of the nervous system by electrical potentials in single nerve cells or groups of cells. One part of this process—the transformation of energy at receptors (that is, transduction)—has just been considered. Now we must ask: How are these events represented in the neural pathways? In some manner electrical events in nerve cells "stand for" or represent stimuli impinging on an organism. This process is often referred to as "coding." (A code is a set of rules for translating information from one form to another. Thus a message in English can be put into a code for transmission, such as the dot-dash Morse code of telegraphy.) Sensory information can be encoded into all-or-none action potentials in several ways: the frequency with which the impulses occur, the rhythm at which they occur (for instance, one impulse every second), the clustering of impulses, and so forth. We will examine possible neural representations of the intensity, quality, position, and pattern of stimuli.

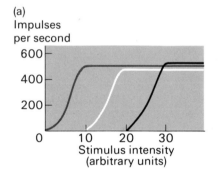

(a)
Impulses per second

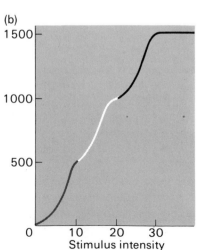

(b)

● **How intense is the stimulus?** We respond to sensory stimuli over a wide range of intensities. Furthermore, within this range we can detect small differences of intensity. How are different intensities of the same stimulus represented in the nervous system?

Within a single nerve cell the frequency of nerve impulses can represent stimulus intensity, as the graph in Figure 6-13(a) shows. However, only a limited range of different sensory intensities can be represented in this manner. The maximal rate of firing for a single nerve cell, obtained under highly artificial conditions, is about 1200/sec. Most sensory fibers do not fire more than a few hundred impulses per second. The number of differences in intensity that can be detected in vision and audition is much greater than this code could offer. Therefore variations in the firing rate of a single cell simply cannot account for the full range of intensity perception.

Figure 6-13 Range fractionation in sensory coding. (a) Rate of firing in three nerve cells, each with different thresholds. Each varies its response over a fraction of the range of stimulus intensities. (b) Combination of firing rates of the three cells. Although none of the nerve cells shown in (a) can respond more frequently than 500/sec, the sum of all three can vary in response rate from 0 to 1500/sec.

Multiple nerve cells acting in parallel provide a broader opportunity for the coding of the intensity of a stimulus. As the strength of a stimulus increases, new nerve cells are "recruited," and thus intensity can be represented by the number of active cells. A variant of this idea is the principle of intensity coding called **range fractionation** (Figure 6-13). According to this hypothesis a wide range of intensity values can be accurately noted in the nervous system by cells that are "specialists" in particular segments or fractions of an intensity scale. This mode of stimulus coding requires an array of receptors and nerve cells with a wide distribution of thresholds, some with very high sensitivity (a low-threshold group) and others with much less sensitivity (and higher thresholds).

● What type of stimulus is it?   Within any sensory modality we can readily discriminate qualitative differences among stimuli. For example, we can discriminate among wavelengths of light, frequencies of sound, and a variety of skin sensations such as touch, warmth, cold, and pain. What kind of coding underlies these qualitative differences?

An important part of the answer is the concept of **labeled lines.** This view states that particular nerve cells are intrinsically labeled for distinctive sensory experiences (Figure 6-14). Neural activity in the "line" provides the basis for our detection of the experience. Its qualities are predetermined. Clearly major separation of sensory experiences into modalities involves labeled lines; stimulation of the optic nerve, for instance, always yields vision and never gives us sounds or touches. But there is controversy surrounding coding for submodalities. Limitations to the idea are particularly evident in vision. For example, there does not seem to be a separate labeled line for each discriminable color, although there do appear to be separate lines for a few main colors. The wealth of different colors appears to result from spatial and temporal activities of only a few different kinds of cells, as we will see in Chapter 7.

Figure 6-14 The concept of labeled lines. Each receptor (C, P, T, and W) has a distinct pathway linking the receptor surface to the brain. Thus in this example, different qualities of skin stimulation are represented by distinct places in the nervous system from the periphery to the brain.

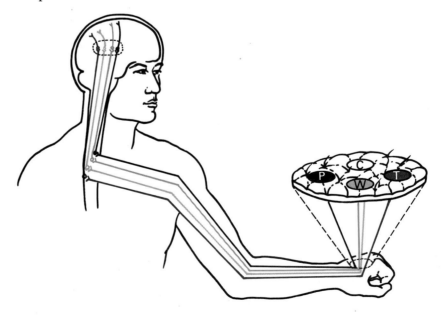

● **Where is the stimulus?**   The position of an object or event, either outside or inside the body, is an important feature of the information that a person or animal gains by sensory analysis. Some sensory systems reveal this information by the position of excited receptors on the sensory surface. This feature is most evident in the visual and somatosensory system. Seeing the position of an event or object and feeling the site of a stimulus on the skin both depend on which receptors are excited. Each receptor in either system activates pathways that convey unique position information. In these systems the spatial properties of a stimulus are represented by labeled lines that uniquely convey spatial information. In both the visual and the tactile system, cells at all levels of the nervous system—from the surface sheet of receptors to the cortex—are arranged in an orderly, maplike manner. The map at each level is not exact but reflects both position and receptor density. Thus more cells are allocated to the spatial representation of sensitive, densely innervated sites like the fovea of the eye or skin surfaces like the lips than to less sensitive sites like the periphery of the eye or the skin of the back.

Information about location is not restricted to sensory systems laid out like a map. We all know that we can detect quite accurately the source of a sound or an odor. In neither system are the peripheral receptors excited in a manner that corresponds directly to the position or location of the relevant stimulus. Locating a stimulus in these systems can involve unilateral or bilateral receptors—that is, one ear or nostril or both ears or nostrils. The mechanism for detecting position differs markedly, depending on whether bilateral or unilateral activation has occurred.

Can you tell the direction from which a sound comes if you use only one ear? Research shows that sound position can be determined with considerable accuracy with one ear if the sound lasts for several seconds but not if it is sudden and brief. Monaural (one-ear) detection of sound location depends on head movements; it is a sampling, in successive instants, of sound intensity—like radar scanning. Some animals with movable external ears (like the cat) can replace head movements with movements of the external ear. Monaural detection of stimulus location also depends on short-term memory, since successive stimuli are compared for intensity.

Bilateral receptor systems—the two ears or the two nostrils—provide a different solution to determining the location of sounds or odors. In both cases the relative time of arrival of the stimulus at the two receptors, or the relative intensity, is directly related to the location of the stimulus. For example, the only condition in which both ears are excited identically is when the sound source is equidistant from the ears, in the median plane of the body. As the stimulus moves to the left or right, asymmetrical excitation of receptors of the left and right sides occurs. Our auditory localization circuits allow us to judge accurately whether a sound source is slightly to the right or left of center when the difference in time of arrival at the two ears is only a few millionths of a second. Specialized nerve cells that receive inputs from both left and right ears and measure stimulus disparities between left and right are discussed in Chapter 7.

● **What is the identity of the stimulus?**   The main goal of sensory-perceptual analysis is the recognition of objects. It wouldn't help you much to see a moderately bright visual stimulus directly ahead if you couldn't tell whether it was your grandmother or a tiger. Being able to recognize objects requires the ability both to perceive patterns of stimulation and to recall patterns that have been learned previously. Usually these abilities go together, but in some cases of brain damage they can become divorced. (We will consider in Chapter 16 some rare cases of people who can see and describe faces but who can no longer recognize familiar faces.) For the present let us consider some questions about how patterns are perceived.

It is traditional to suppose that in perceiving a pattern, you first become aware of the main elements or features and then you reassemble them into the complete form. That is, you analyze and then you synthesize. But there is considerable controversy at present about what the elements or basic features are. In the case of vision, for example, most investigators since the 1960s have held the following hypotheses:

1. There is a hierarchy of cells in the visual cortex.
2. Simple cells respond best to a line in a given position in the visual field.
3. More complex cells require a combination of simple inputs in order to fire.
4. With enough successive levels of analysis, a unit would be able to recognize your grandmother and respond only to her.

As we will see in Chapter 7, there are challenges both to the idea of hierarchical (rather than parallel) processing and to the hypothesis that lines and angles are the basic elements of visual perception.

Perceiving patterns requires information about different parts or aspects of the stimulus display, and often this information is obtained by movements of the receptor organ. For example, we scan a scene with our eyes. We turn our heads while listening; other animals turn their ears. To identify an object by touch, we move our fingers to obtain information not only about its shape but also about its firmness, elasticity, and so on. Both skin receptors and receptors in the joints are involved in this exploration. When we taste food, we move it over our tongue, since receptors for different taste qualities are located on different parts of the tongue. Even in the case of odors, we sniff to bring new whiffs of odorous air to the receptors in our nose. So different bits of information are captured during our inspection of the stimulus pattern. How these are integrated neurally into a unified perception is a question for which we have only partial answers so far.

Sensory adaptation

Many receptors show a progressive loss of sensitivity as stimulation is maintained; a change known as **adaptation.** Adaptation can be demonstrated by recording nerve impulses in a fiber leading from a receptor (Figure 6-15); observations of the time course of nerve impulses show a progressive decline in the rate of discharges as the stimulus is continued.

Receptors can be classified into two broad categories with respect to adaptation:

1. **Tonic receptors** are those in which the frequency of nerve impulse discharge declines slowly or not at all as stimulation is maintained. In other words, these receptors show relatively little adaptation.

2. **Phasic receptors** are those that show quite a rapid fall in the frequency of nerve impulses.

Adaptation means that there is a progressive shift in perception and neural activity away from accurate portrayal of the physical event. Thus the nervous system may fail to register neural activity even though the stimulus continues. Such a striking discrepancy does not imply a weakness in the integrity of receptors; rather it emphasizes the significance of changes of state, or stimulus transients, as the effective properties of stimuli.

The eminent sensory researcher Georg von Békésy, who received the Nobel Prize in 1961, emphasized that adaptation is a form of information suppression that prevents the nervous system from becoming overwhelmed by stimuli that offer very little "news" about the world. For example, the pressing of a hair on the leg by pants may be continuous, and we are saved from a constant neural barrage repeating this fact by several suppression mechanisms, including adaptation.

The bases of adaptation include both neural and nonneural events. For example, in the visual system, adaptation emerges from depletion of photochemicals in the rod and cone cells of the retina. In some mechanical receptors, adaptation develops from the elasticity of the receptor cell itself. This situation is especially evident in the Pacinian corpuscle, which detects mechanical pressure. Maintained pressure on a corpuscle results in an initial burst of neural activity and a rapid fall to a virtual zero level. The size of this receptor enables experimenters to remove the corpuscle (the accessory cell) and apply the same constant stimulus to the terminal region of the sensory nerve fiber, that is, to bend the tip of the neuron. In this instance maintained mechanical stimulation produces a continuing discharge of nerve impulses. This result suggests that for this receptor adaptation is a property of the nonneural component, the corpuscle. In some receptors adaptation reflects a change in the generator potential of the cell. Changes in this electrical property of a receptor are probably produced by ionic changes that result in hyperpolarization.

Figure 6-15 Adaptation in receptor pathways. This illustration shows adaptation of a receptor whose receptive field is located on the fifth finger. Three different levels of stimulus intensity are shown. The decrease in rate of firing is more rapid with the least intense stimulus (A). (From Knibestöl and Valbo, 1970)

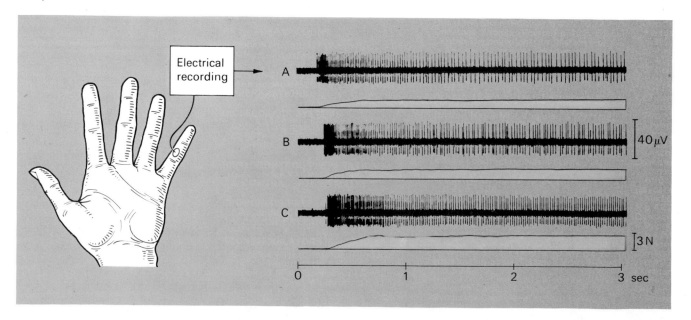

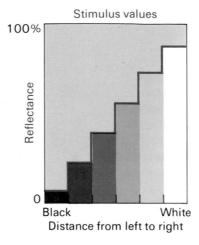
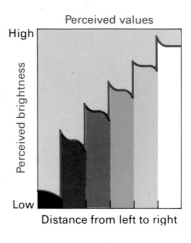

Stimulus values

Perceived values

Figure 6-16 Perceptual consequences of lateral inhibition. The series of bars at the left goes from black to white. The values of stimulus intensity are plotted in the center graph; each bar is uniform across its width. The right-hand graph plots perceived brightness; each bar appears brightest at its left edge and darkest at its right.

Lateral inhibition

In many cases when a stimulus impinges uniformly on an area of receptors, we perceive the stimulation as being strongest at the edges. For example, Figure 6-16 shows a series of bars, each one a uniform gray. But each bar *appears* to be lighter at its left side, where it touches a darker strip. Contrast also occurs in tactile sensation: If you press the end of a ruler against the skin of your forearm, you will probably feel the pressure of the corners of the ruler more strongly than the pressure all along the line of contact.

In other cases in which the stimulation is strongest in one part of its field, we may perceive the stimulus at that location only. For example, when a tone with a single frequency of vibration enters the ear, a traveling wave of motion sweeps along the inner ear. But the neural response is largely confined to receptors at the location where the amplitude of the traveling wave is the greatest, and we hear a single tone. Georg von Békésy showed that a similar phenomenon occurs on the skin. He constructed an enlarged model of the inner ear in the form of a fluid-filled tube on which the forearm could be placed (Figure 6-17). When a burst of mechanical vibration traveled through the fluid in the tube, the observer felt a thump at one or another position on his arm. The perceived location varied with the frequency of the vibration. Although in each case the vibration traveled along the whole length of the tube and stimulated the whole forearm, the pulse was perceived only at the location of strongest stimulation.

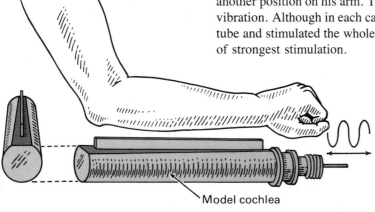

Model cochlea

Figure 6-17 An enlarged model of the cochlea used to stimulate the skin and illustrate lateral inhibition.

This sharpening of perception is based on a neural process called **lateral inhibition.** That is, the neurons in a region are interconnected, either through their own axons or by means of intermediary neurons (interneurons), and each neuron tends to inhibit its neighbors. We saw an example of this in Chapter 4 when we discussed information processing by simple neural circuits (refer to Figure 4-12). Many of these lateral inhibitory connections occur at the periphery or at lower levels of sensory systems, but they can also occur at the cerebral cortex. For example, if you use a device that allows you to view a vertical line with one eye and a horizontal line with the other eye, one line or the other will tend to be suppressed at the point where they appear to cross; this phenomenon is termed "retinal rivalry." Since the afferent messages from the two eyes are brought together only at the cortex and not at lower levels of the visual system, this so-called retinal rivalry is actually a cortical phenomenon.

Information suppression

We have noted that successful adaptation and survival does not depend on copying external and internal stimuli. Rather, our success as a species demands that our sensory systems accentuate, from among the many things happening about us, the important changes of stimuli. Without selectivity we would suffer from an overload of information and would end up with a confusing picture of the world. Suppression of some sensory inputs may also reduce the metabolic expense of nervous system activities. So it appears that, at the least, it would be extravagent to stand unsheltered from excessive sensory inputs (even if we could) and that, at worst, unselected representation of the world would be overwhelmingly confusing.

Information in sensory systems is constrained or suppressed in at least two ways. In many sensory systems accessory structures can reduce the level of input in the sensory pathway. For example, the closure of the eyelid reduces the level of illumination that reaches the retina. The constriction of the pupil of the eye accomplishes a similar result. In the auditory system contraction of the middle ear muscles reduces the intensity of sounds that reach the cochlea. Note that in this form of sensory control the relevant mechanisms change the intensity of the stimulus before it reaches the actual receptors.

A second form of information control involves descending neural connections from the brain to the receptor surface. For example, in the auditory system a small group of cells located in the brainstem have axons that exit from the brain along the pathway of the auditory nerve and connect with the base of the receptor cells. Electrical stimulation of this pathway can attenuate the effects of sounds, although in a more selective manner than the action of middle ear muscles. For years auditory physiologists have sought a connection between the activities of this efferent pathway to hair cells and selective attention. Might receptors for specific frequencies be inhibited by impulses from neural centers? Establishing this connection has proved elusive, but it continues to be a possible functional role for these fibers.

Similar efferent paths—those leading from the brain to afferent pathways or receptor surfaces—are evident in the sensory system that monitors muscles (as you will see in Chapter 8). Efferent influences have also been found in the retina and the olfactory bulb, but these have not been examined in any detail. Furthermore, during muscular movements the sensitivity of some sensory systems is reduced in the brain, as will be discussed in Chapter 8.

Receptive fields   Much current neurophysiological research on sensory processing is based on recordings made from single neurons at various levels of the sensory pathway while
sensory stimuli are presented. Investigators attempt to determine for a given type of
cell the kind of stimulation that causes the optimal rate of response. To put it another
way, they map the stimulus region and features that cause the fullest response of the
cell; this region is called the **receptive field** of the cell. For example, suppose we
are recording from a single ganglion cell in the retina (or from a neuron in the
thalamus that receives the ganglion cell's output). We first note the cell's spontaneous activity, and then we see whether this activity increases or decreases when light
or dark stimuli are presented in various parts of the visual field. Figure 6-18

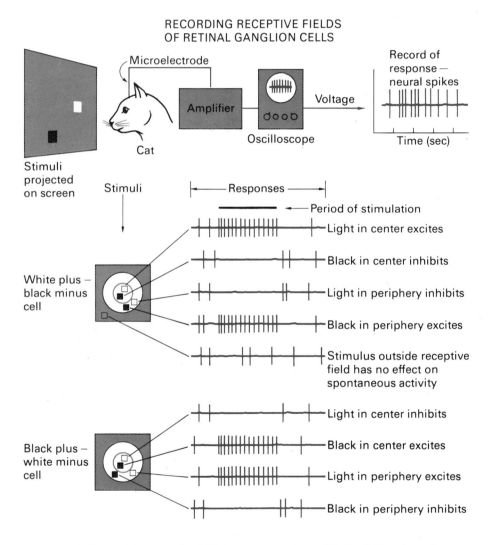

Figure 6-18 Determining receptive fields in sensory systems. This illustration shows the
procedures used to determine the receptive field characteristics of retinal ganglion cells.
Changes in the position of the stimulus are related to the record of response of neural spikes.

illustrates this process. If stimuli at one location do not alter the cell's response, then we are probably working outside the cell's receptive field; so we move the stimulus and try again. Receptive fields of retinal ganglion cells are roughly circular, and they have two concentric zones. That is, the center of the field may be excitatory and the outer ring inhibitory—or the center is inhibitory and the ring is excitatory. At the visual cortex the receptive fields tend to be more complicated; some cortical cells respond well to lines in certain orientations, some require a moving stimulus to elicit a strong response, and some cells make even more complex demands. Recent research suggests that grids or spatial arrays may be even more effective than lines in stimulating many cortical units; we will take up this idea in Chapter 7.

Cells in other sensory systems also have receptive fields. For example, cells in the somatosensory system respond only to stimuli at certain parts of the body surface. Some cells in the auditory system respond only when a sound comes from a certain direction in space in relation to the animal's head. We can therefore speak of the **trigger features** of the stimulus that evoke responses from a particular cell; these are the particular stimulus characteristics that are most effective in evoking responses from a particular cell. How to bridge the gap from receptive fields to perception of objects is a major issue in current research.

Sensory pathways in the brain

A sequence of neurons connects receptors to regions of the brain, especially to the cerebral cortex. Along these afferent pathways are multiple connections of cells— sensory relay nuclei located at various subcortical regions.

This succession of nuclei is generally thought to allow more and more elaborate information processing. Simpler analysis at lower or earlier levels in the pathways prepares inputs for more elaborate and complex information processing at cortical levels. Another view of the many steps in sensory pathways holds that different parts of the pathway may be specialized for different aspects of behavior. For example, some circuits at lower levels of the auditory pathway in the brainstem mediate acoustic control of head and eye movements toward the source of a sound. These systems seem partially separated from auditory pathways that enable us to perceive complex acoustic patterns. There appears to be a similar dual organization of visual pathways. One pathway, leading from the retina to the cerebral cortex, is involved in stimulus identification, while another pathway, extending from the retina to the superior colliculus, mediates stimulus localization (Schneider, 1969). Thus the information in a sensory nerve diverges to reach many higher cells. A major goal of contemporary studies of sensory processing is to understand the transformation of signals at each level in the chain of cells in afferent pathways within the brain.

Ideas about how the cortex processes sensory information have changed sharply in recent years (Masterton and Berkley, 1974; I. T. Diamond, 1979; Merzenich and Kaas, 1980). Early in this century a picture was formulated about perceptual mechanisms, and it remained the basis of thought until the 1970s, when a new paradigm began to emerge. The new model is not yet complete, but it contrasts in essential ways with the earlier concepts still found in many accounts of perceptual mechanisms. The classical model now being questioned can be briefly characterized as follows: Sensory input for a particular modality was supposed to be relayed to the "primary sensory cortex" that was responsible for relatively elementary sensory functions (Figure 6-19). The criteria for the "primary sensory cortex" were that it

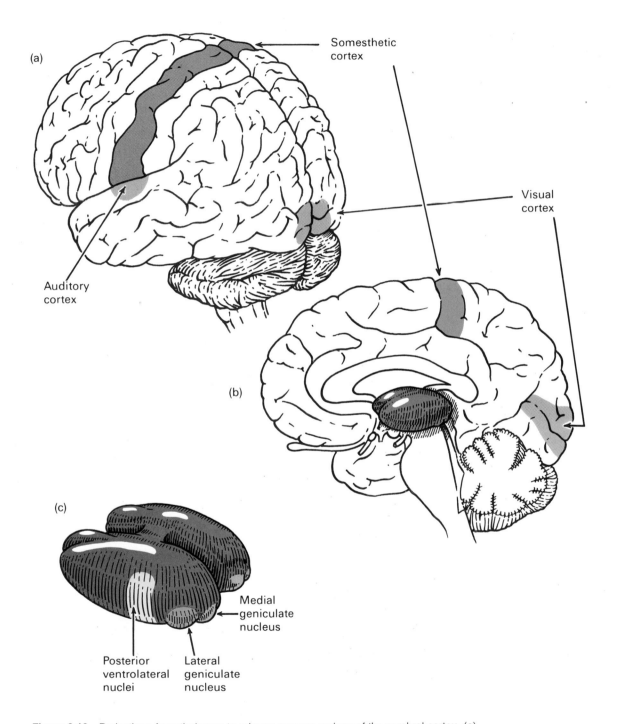

Figure 6-19 Projections from thalamus to primary sensory regions of the cerebral cortex. (a) and (b) Primary somesthetic, auditory, and visual cortices. (c) Major sensory projection nuclei of the thalamus.

received direct input from the thalamus and that it was laid out in an orderly map of the receptor surface. The "primary area" sent the transformed information to an adjacent band of a "secondary sensory" or "perceptual" cortex with more complex functions. This region in turn sent its output to the multimodal or intersensory "association" cortex for still higher-order processing that integrated information from several senses. In this strictly hierarchical scheme the "association areas" performed the highest level of perceptual processing, and their outputs could direct the activation of the motor cortex to initiate appropriate behavioral responses. Now let us see some of the features of the new model and how it contrasts with the classical one.

● **Multiple cortical representations for each sensory system**   Recent studies have revealed several cortical areas for each sensory modality, and most of these areas are laid out in an orderly topographic map of the receptor surface (C. N. Woolsey, 1981a,b,c). (By "topographic" we mean a systematic representation but one that does not necessarily preserve size relations; this is like a rubber-sheet map that preserves order but not size.) For example, recent examination of the cortex of the owl monkey (a New World monkey) reveals at least six visual areas, each of which is a topographic representation of the retina (Figure 6-20). No other species has yet been mapped as completely, but in the macaque (an Old World monkey) it also appears that most of the cortical visual regions consist of orderly maps of the retina.

In the case of somatosensory cortical fields, the owl monkey has at least seven areas, also shown in Figure 6-20. Mapping of these areas is not yet complete, but most have already been shown to be full, orderly representations of either the body surface or deep body tissues. Recent mapping of auditory areas in the cortex shows several orderly representations of the auditory receptors (the hair cells on the basilar

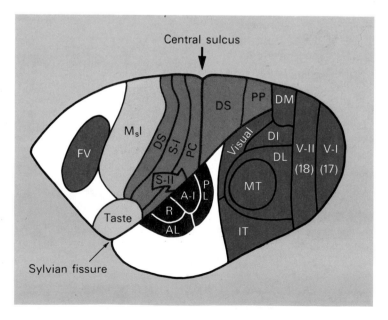

Figure 6-20 Subdivisions of neocortex with sensory functions in a New World monkey. Most of the occipital and parietal cortex shows systematic representations of sensory surfaces, as do parts of the temporal and frontal regions. *Visual subsivisions*: V-I, primary visual area (corresponding to Brodmann's Area 17); V-II, second visual area (or Area 18); DI, dorsointermediate; DL, dorsolateral; DM, dorsomedial; IT, inferotemporal; MT, middle temporal; and FV, frontal visual. There may also be visual functions in PP, posterior parietal. *Auditory subdivisions*: AI, primary auditory area; AL, anterior lateral; PL, posterior lateral; and R, rostral auditory field. *Somatosensory subdivisions*: S-I, primary somatosensory area; S-II, second somatosensory area (hidden in the Sylvian fissure); DS, deep sensory representation (muscles and joints); PC, posterior cutaneous area; PP, posterior parietal; and MSI, motor sensory area I. (Adapted from Merzenich and Kaas, 1980)

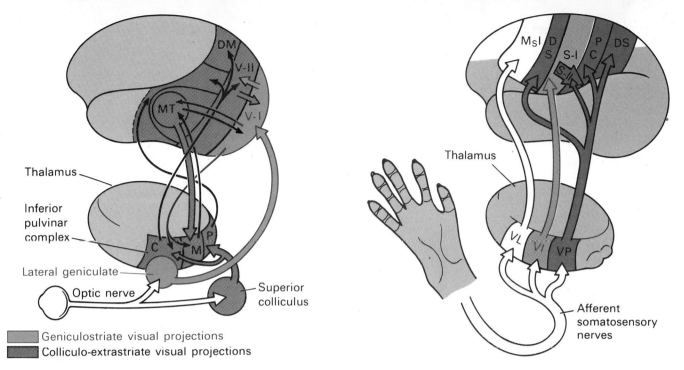

Figure 6-21 (a) Some of the thalamocortical connections of the visual system in monkeys. The optic nerve sends axons to both the lateral geniculate nucleus and the superior colliculus. The lateral geniculate projects to the striate cortex (V-I). The superior colliculus projects to the inferior pulvinar complex of the thalamus. The central (C) and posterior (P) divisions of the inferior pulvinar project to the visual cortical regions outside of V-I, and the middle (M) inferior pulvinar receives a large projection from the extrastriate cortex. Some corticocortical connections are also shown. (Adapted from Merzenich and Kaas, 1980) (b) Some of the thalamocortical connections of the somatosensory systems in monkeys. Different divisions of the ventrolateral thalamus (ventrolateral, VL; ventralis intermedius, VI; and ventroposterior, VP) send axons to different somatosensory regions of the cerebral cortex. (Adapted from Merzenich and Kaas, 1980)

membrane). These auditory "maps" represent the receptors in order from the base (high frequencies) to the apex (low frequencies) of the basilar membrane. There are at least six such maps in the cortex of the macaque and at least four auditory maps in the owl monkey.

These recent findings are in marked contrast to the earlier conclusion that each sense had one or more primary topographic representations in the cortex and that other cortical areas did not need to reflect the sensory surface accurately because they were responsible for more abstract "higher" functions.

● **Functionally distinct parallel pathways from thalamus to cortex**   Each sensory region of the cortex receives input from one or more regions of the thalamus. Some divisions of the thalamus project to a single cortical region, and some project to more than one. There is further divergence of sensory information. The sensory regions of the cortex send axons back to the thalamus, usually to their own sources of input but sometimes to other thalamic divisions as well. Some of the thalamocortical projections of the visual system of the monkey are shown in Figure 6-21a. In the somatosensory system, too, there are several pathways to the cortex from several divisions of the thalamus (Figure 6-21b). And the auditory system also has several parallel projection channels to different cortical auditory areas.

● **Exclusive sensory representation in posterior cortex**   The posterior cortex (that is, the parietal, occipital, and temporal lobes) consists almost entirely of topographically organized maps of the visual, auditory, and somatosensory systems. This feature is depicted in the recent map of a monkey brain shown in Figure 6-20. There are some exceptions to this generalization, and there are also some sensory areas in the precentral cortex. Posterior areas that are not devoted to sensory maps include the anterior and middle regions of the temporal lobe. There are also a few sensory areas that are not topographically organized; for example, there are some fields where cells respond to auditory stimuli but do not show low-to-high frequency mapping of sounds. But both of these exceptions do not account for much of the cortical surface, and most of what had been regarded as the "secondary" or "association" cortex has now been found to receive direct thalamic input and to show topographic organization.

Not so long ago it appeared that the more highly evolved the species, the greater was the area of association cortex in proportion to sensory cortex (Hebb, 1949). Now this formulation is challenged on several counts. First, topographically organized cortex with direct thalamic input is found to cover most of the posterior area in primates. Furthermore, it appears that as the area of the cerebral cortex has expanded in the evolution of the mammals, there has been an increase in the number of different cortical maps for each sensory modality. Second, the term "association cortex" has been considerably restricted in its use or even abandoned by some investigators. It is true that there are important areas of cortex that have multisensory inputs, but these usually come from the thalamus rather than from "primary" sensory areas of the cortex. Finally, the concept of "higher" and "lower" species has been replaced by the concept of species that have shown more or fewer evolutionary changes from a common starting point.

● **Different cortical fields and different aspects of perception**   Several lines of evidence indicate that the different cortical areas that represent the same receptor surface actually receive somewhat different inputs, process the information differently, and make different contributions to perceptual experiences and behavioral responses. Different inputs are shown not only by the fact that they receive fibers from different divisions of the thalamus but also by the fact that the maps, although topographic, are arranged differently from each other. Some geographic maps exaggerate a particular aspect; for example, the "New Yorker's map of the United States" magnifies New York and its environs while shrinking the rest of the country. Similarly, most cortical representations of the retina are mainly devoted to the central 10° of the visual field, but the medial area in a monkey devotes only about 5% to the central 10° (Allman and Kaas, 1976).

Differences in information processing are indicated by the fact that neurons in different cortical regions respond best to different aspects of the visual stimulus. Presumably these cells belong to circuits that extract different kinds of information from the varied visual inputs. Thus a high proportion of cells in the middle temporal visual area of the monkey respond best to stimuli that move in a particular direction, the specific direction differing from one cell to another (Newsome et al., 1978). A high proportion of cells that respond best to colored stimuli are located in a part of the superior temporal cortex of monkeys, according to Zeki (1977). Cells in other cortical areas also respond to colored stimuli, but not better than to achromatic ones. Regions also differ in their proportions of cells with relatively simple or relatively complex receptive fields.

It seems likely that different cortical regions are simultaneously processing different aspects of perceptual experience, but the details of this processing are not yet known. In spite of this specialization, it would certainly be incorrect to suppose that a given cortical sensory region receives a packet of information and processes it completely without further communication with other brain regions. For one thing, there are back-and-forth exchanges between cortical and thalamic regions. For another, the different cortical regions for a given modality are interrelated by fibers that make subcortical loops.

Even though each modality is represented by several topographically organized fields that all have direct thalamic input, there are still reasons for referring to one field as "primary" for each sense: The primary area is the main source of input to the other fields for the same modality, even though they also have direct thalamic inputs. Developmentally the primary area is the first to myelinate. The cytoarchitectural structure of the primary area has the clearest sensory characteristics; these are the small size of neurons and a thick fourth layer. But being first in these ways does not mean that the primary sensory cortex is necessarily simpler or more basic in perceptual functions than the other cortical fields for the same modality.

Discovering the separate and joint contributions of different sensory regions to perception remains a challenge. It appears that recent findings cannot be encompassed by a strict hierarchical model with its schema of primary, secondary, and association areas.

● Qualifications about cortical maps   Our description of cortical representation of sensory fields may make them seem to be too separate from each other, too fixed and static, so let us qualify this description in some major ways.

There is considerable overlap among representation of different sensory modalities. For example, some cells in a "visual" area respond also to auditory stimuli, and others respond to tactile or vestibular stimuli. Thus there is intersensory convergence at such **polymodal** cells.

There are significant individual differences in cortical maps. Lashley and Clark (1946) plotted the location and extent of striate cortex by anatomical techniques in several spider monkeys and called attention to large individual differences. Van Essen (1981) has used electrophysiological recording to map several visual cortical regions in macaques and has noted individual differences as large as two to one in the size of striate cortex. So when we describe general features of cortical representation, it should not be forgotten that there are individual differences in anatomy that may well determine differences in behavior.

Sensory maps in the brain appear to change with the current state of the individual, including both the motivational state (such as hunger, as we will see in Chapter 11) and the degree of arousal.

The maps may not be fixed permanently but may change somewhat over time, even in adults. In cases of increased or decreased use of a part of the body, such as certain fingers, the cortical representation has been reported to expand or contract and may show reorganization (Schoppman et al., 1981). Whether the cortical representations are dynamic or fixed currently is a matter of controversy, and we do not want to anticipate the final resolution of this question. But since the use of the term *map* may have suggested a fixed representation, we want to mention the real possibility that the representation may actually change over time.

Attention The concept of attention is laden with many meanings that are not easy to disentangle. One view emphasizes the state of alertness or vigilance that enables animals to detect signals. In this view attention is a generalized activation that attunes us to inputs. Another view is that attention is the process that allows selection of some sensory inputs from among many competing ones. Some investigators view attention in a more introspective manner, arguing that attention is a state of mental concentration or effort that makes it possible to focus on a particular task. As you see, a notion that may seem self-evident has considerable complexity. The treatment of this state in physiological studies has included measurements ranging from assessments of cerebral blood flow during states of alertness to firing rates of single cells during selective responding to particular stimuli. The role of the brainstem reticular formation in attention has also been the subject of intensive research. Studies of impairment of attention have helped to illuminate the mechanisms of attention.

● **Cerebral correlates of attention** Several kinds of brain measures show correlations with attention and changes in awareness. Measures of cerebral blood flow, which we discussed in Box 2-2, show shifts to the cortical region involved in attention. Thus there is increased blood flow in the upper parts of the temporal lobe when a subject listens to spoken words. The EEG shows an activation pattern of rapid, small-amplitude waves over the whole skull during attention. When a subject is alertly waiting for a signal to perform an action, a particular scalp potential appears—the contingent negative variation (Figure 6-22). Evoked potentials—those elicited in the EEG by stimuli—are significantly larger when the subject attends to the stimuli than when he or she ignores them.

Recordings from individual brain cells are also being used to find details of attentional mechanisms. In this work monkeys are trained to fixate a spot of light and then to release a lever for reward as soon as the spot dims. Responses are recorded from cortical cells whose receptive fields include the fixation spot; some cells are in the frontal cortex and some in the posterior parietal cortex. Then the situation is complicated by presenting a second spot of light, which falls within the receptive field of the cell whose activity is being recorded. In some cases monkeys are trained to shift their gaze promptly to the second light as soon as the fixation light goes off. About half the visually responsive cells in both the frontal and parietal regions show vigorous responses while the animal is preparing to shift its gaze. In other cases monkeys are trained to keep fixating on the first spot but to release the lever for reward as soon as the second light turns off. Now many of the parietal cells show enhanced responses while the monkey attends to the off-center spot, but the responses of the frontal cells are not enhanced. The investigators concluded that enhance-

Figure 6-22 Contingent negative variation, an electrical response recorded from scalp of humans. This potential appears after the warning stimulus alerts the subject to expect a stimulus requiring action (the imperative stimulus). (From Callaway, 1975)

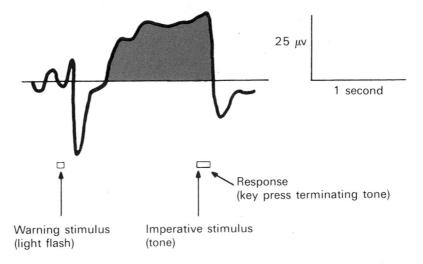

25 μv

1 second

Warning stimulus
(light flash)

Imperative stimulus
(tone)

Response
(key press terminating tone)

ment of the frontal response may reflect transfer of visual information to the oculomotor system, whereas enhancement in the parietal area "seems to function as a general attention system when the stimulus is important to the animal regardless of the motor strategy the animal uses to handle the stimulus" (Bushnell, Robinson, and Goldberg, 1978).

● **Brainstem reticular formation and attention**   As sensory neurons run toward the midbrain and diencephalon, they also send side branches to a special part of the brainstem. This region is the **brainstem reticular formation,** and it plays a major role in attention. (The word "reticular" comes from a Latin term meaning "network," and the name was chosen because this region contains small, densely branching neurons.) The diffuse pathways of the reticular formation allow messages in one sensory channel to arouse wide regions of the brain (Figure 6-23). Electrical stimulation of the reticular formation results in prompt and widespread activation of the EEG. Conversely, damage to the reticular formation or inhibition of its activity by drugs results in a depressed or even comatose individual. The many synaptic interruptions in reticular pathways make this region especially susceptible to influence by neuromodulators and by drugs.

● **Cortical regions and attention**   Certain regions of the cerebral cortex have been particularly implicated in attention. The evidence for this comes both from impairment of attention in people and animals with localized cortical damage and from recording electrical activity of cells in different cortical regions while animals attend to stimuli or await stimuli in order to obtain rewards. One cortical region that appears to play a special role in attention is the inferoparietal lobule in the posterior parietal lobe (Figure 6-24). Many cells here are polymodal. Some of them are especially

BOX 6-4　Attention and Perceptual Development

It is widely accepted that active locomotor exploration is required for development of visual discrimination of space. This conclusion comes from a classical study by Held and Hein (1963). These investigators raised kittens in the dark for 8 weeks and then allowed them daily 3-hr periods of light exposure under one of two conditions. One group actively locomoted in the stimulus field while the other kittens were moved passively in carts that prevented them from seeing their legs. Only the first group developed depth discrimination, and the investigators concluded that "self-produced movement with its concurrent visual feedback is necessary for the development of visually guided behavior."

Another possible interpretation of these findings is that attention to stimuli at different distances can promote the

development of depth perception. To test this hypothesis, Walk, Sheperd, and Miller (1978) gave some kittens their only visual experience in the set-up shown in Box Figure 6-6. The kittens seemed to watch intently as the mouse-sized cars sped down the track repeatedly. These kittens could not locomote with regard to the stimuli and could not see their legs, yet they developed good discrimination of visual space. In fact, their perceptual performance was as good as that of other kittens who were exposed at the same time to light under the active-locomotion condition of Held and Hein. Walk and colleagues also confirmed that the passive-exposure condition of Held and Hein did not lead to depth perception. They concluded, however, that attention rather than self-induced motion is the requirement for perceptual development.

Box Figure 6-6　Attention promotes perceptual development. (From Walk, Sheperd, and Miller, 1978)

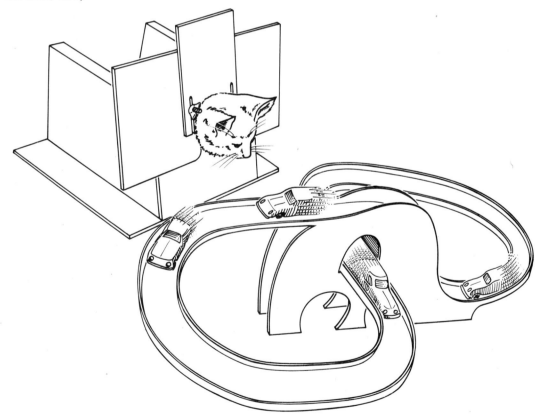

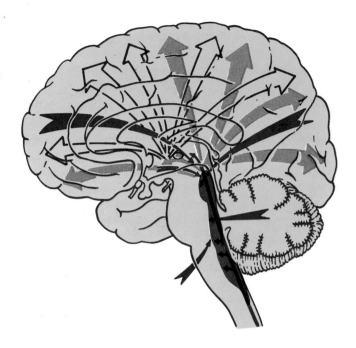

Figure 6-23 Brainstem reticular arousal system. This system, shown in blue, receives input from sensory fibers and from the cerebral cortex (black arrows). It projects widely to the cortex as shown by the open arrows.

Figure 6-24 Regions of the cortex that are implicated in attention, shown on lateral (a) and medial (b) views of the monkey brain. The inferior parietal lobule (blue) in the posterior parietal lobe seems to play a special role. It has strong connections with the three cortical regions that are shown by stippling. (Adapted from Mesulam et al., 1977)

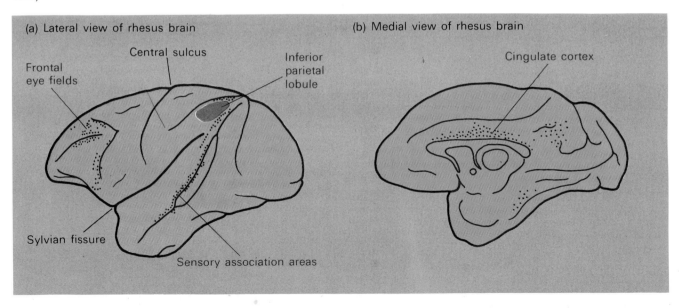

(a) Lateral view of rhesus brain

Frontal eye fields

Central sulcus

Inferior parietal lobule

Sylvian fissure

Sensory association areas

(b) Medial view of rhesus brain

Cingulate cortex

responsive when a trained monkey is expecting the appearance of a stimulus (Mount-castle et al., 1981). Lesions of this area in monkeys result in inattention or neglect of stimuli on the contralateral side. (In Chapter 16 we will see that this symptom is especially severe in people with lesions of the right parietal lobe.) The frontal eye fields (see Figure 6-24) seem to be involved in attentive visual exploration of space. The posterior part of the cingulate cortex (around the posterior part of the corpus callosum) has been implicated in motivational aspects of attention. These three cortical areas have especially prominent anatomical connections with each other, and each receives strong input from the reticular formation as well as from sensory fibers (Mesulam, 1981).

● **Understanding impairments of attention**   Several mechanisms have been proposed to explain impairments of attention, and each may be correct for certain cases. The hypotheses include (1) departures from an optimal level of cortical activation, (2) interruption of sensory transmission to the cortex, and (3) interference with central processing.

Either too much or too little arousal may impair attention and information processing. Rats with electrodes implanted in the reticular formation became hyperaroused during electrical stimulation, and this arousal state impaired their performance on tasks requiring attention. Tranquilizing drugs, such as chlorpromazine, counteracted the effects of the electrical stimulation and restored normal attention (Kornetsky and Eliasson, 1969). This study may offer an animal model for some schizophrenic cases who have been characterized as overaroused and who are aided by chlorpromazine. Barbiturate drugs, which lead to hypoarousal, interfere with synaptic transmission, especially in the reticular formation, and this effect may explain why they impair attention.

Interruption of sensory and other transmission is suggested as a cause for inattention to stimuli that come from one side after a unilateral lesion of frontal cortex. It has been observed that after removal of a region of frontal cortex on one side, monkeys neglected the contralateral visual field. These symptoms subsided in about four weeks. The investigators therefore measured metabolism in the thalamus and basal ganglia at two weeks after the cortical lesion in some monkeys and at four weeks in others. At two weeks regional metabolism was down by about 30% on the affected side versus the other hemisphere. At four weeks the deficit was less than 10%. It appears that during the first few weeks nerve impulses cannot get to and from intact cortex on the operated side as fully as usually, so the cortex is partially cut off from normal communication (Deuel et al., 1979).

The foregoing study suggests an alternative interpretation for another recent experiment. Nakamura and Mishkin (1979) have shown that monkeys are rendered functionally blind after removal of all nonvisual cerebral cortex. That is, preservation of all the known visual areas of cortex does not suffice to preserve visual function. Nakamura and Mishkin hypothesize that the intact visual system suffers from hypoarousal because it lacks activation from other cortical regions. Perhaps, however, the thalamic relays suffer from depressed metabolism, as in the study of Deuel and co-workers, so that the flow of impulses to the cortex is reduced. Electrical recordings could be used to test these alternative interpretations.

SUMMARY/ MAIN POINTS

1. A sensory system furnishes selected information to the brain about internal and external events and conditions. It captures and processes only information that is significant for the particular organism.

2. Ideal sensory systems discriminate among some of the available forms of energy, respond over a wide range of intensities, are highly sensitive to a change of stimuli, respond reliably and rapidly, and suppress unwanted information.

3. Stimuli that some species detect readily are completely unavailable to other species that lack the necessary receptors.

4. Some receptors are simple free nerve endings, but most include cells that are specialized to transduce particular kinds of energy.

5. Transduction of energy at sensory receptors involves production of a generator potential that stimulates the sensory neurons.

6. Coding is the translation of receptor information into patterns of neural activity.

7. Adaptation refers to the progressive decrease in the rate of impulses as the same stimulation is maintained. This decline is slow in the case of tonic receptors but rapid for phasic receptors. Adaptation protects the nervous system from redundant stimulation.

8. Mechanisms of information suppression include accessory structures, descending pathways from neural centers to the receptor, and central circuits.

9. The receptive field of a cell is the stimulus region that changes the response of the cell.

10. The succession of nuclei in a sensory pathway is thought to allow for different and perhaps successively more elaborate kinds of processing.

11. Each sensory system includes multiple cortical fields that all receive thalamic input; most of them are laid out topographically.

12. Attention refers to the temporary enhancement of certain sensory messages during particular states of the individual. Attention is thought to involve the reticular activating system in the brainstem reticular formation.

RECOMMENDED READING

Autrum, H., Jung, R., Loewenstein, W. R., MacKay, D. M., and Teuber, H. L. (Eds.). *Handbook of sensory physiology* (9 vols.). Berlin and New York: Springer-Verlag, 1971-1981.

Masterton, R. B. (Ed.). *Handbook of behavioral neurobiology*. Vol. 1 *Sensory integration*. New York: Plenum, 1978.

Uttal, W. R. *The psychobiology of sensory coding*. New York: Harper & Row, 1973.

Orientation

Visual Information Processing

Visual pathways of the brain

Color

Position

Pattern and form

Visual deficits and rehabilitation

Auditory Information Processing

Auditory pathways of the brain

Pitch

Localization of sound

Deafness and its rehabilitation

Vestibular Information Processing

Somatosensory Information Processing

Somatosensory pathways of the brain

Tactile intensity

Pain

Localization on the body surface

Somatosensory perception of form

Olfactory Information Processing

Gustatory Information Processing

Summary / Main Points

7

Information Processing in Perception: Seeing, Hearing, Feeling

Orientation

At every moment a barrage of neural activity originating from sensory receptors enters your brain. The pattern of nerve potentials in the array of sensory neurons is the way information is represented. In Chapter 6 we examined this process in the periphery—at receptors and the nerve fibers leading to the brain. Now we will explore the processing of these sensory inputs in various brain centers.

A useful way of viewing the brain's processing of sensory signals is to regard these various centers as arranged in a sequence, with information flowing successively from one level to another for successive kinds of processing. This is known as **serial processing**. For example, activity in the auditory nerve initially activates neurons at lower levels in the brainstem (cochlear nuclei). During successive processing stages, cells in the midbrain (inferior colliculus), the thalamus (medial geniculate), and finally the cortex alter their activity. The original pattern of neural activity in the nerve fibers entering the brain changes at each level. Complex processing at each level leads to particular emphasis on special aspects of sensory inputs. In addition to the serial organization of sensory systems, there are also many parallel pathways, which can carry out different kinds of analyses of the same sensory information. This is known as **parallel processing**.

One of the goals of physiological psychology is to understand how our representations of stimuli are related to the characteristics of information transformation at each level in a sensory pathway. A distribution of light on the retina becomes, a fraction of a second later, a face we readily recognize. To understand this cognitive process, we must examine the sensory pathways of the brain and the ways these brain centers deal with simple and complex patterns of stimulation.

In this chapter we will explore brain mechanisms of perception, looking at examples of the ways the brain deals with four sensory dimensions: intensity, quality, locus, and pattern. This subject occupies complete courses and books, so we will confine ourselves to some salient examples, most of them dealing with seeing, hearing, and pain.

Visual information processing

The brain receives from the eye basic information about the spatial distribution of various wavelengths of light, and through a variety of processes it produces recognizable perceptions. Different kinds of processing of the same input information allow us to make decisions about the color, position, depth, and form of visual stimuli. The intensity of present-day research on visual information processing is related to the preeminent role of vision in the adaptation of many animals, including ourselves. Even animals that inhabit relatively dark ecological niches, such as owls and bats and deep-sea fish, need information from light receptors. Some nocturnal animals have huge eyeballs in comparison to their body size, presumably to help them capture the small amounts of light available at night. Some invertebrates are so greedy for light that they have multiple light receptors scattered about the body, and some amphibia have photoreceptors directly in their brain! In this section we will describe the current state of experimentation in visual information processing. We begin with a brief look at the brain regions and pathways concerned with visual information processing.

Visual pathways of the brain

In any vertebrate animal some or all of the axons of the **optic nerve** cross to the opposite cerebral hemisphere (Figure 7-1). A larger proportion of axons cross over in those animals with laterally placed eyes who have little binocular overlap. In humans axons of the optic nerve are segregated into two groups at the **optic chiasm.** At this point axons from the half of the retina toward the nose (nasal retina) cross over to the opposite side of the brain. The half of the retina toward the side of the head, the temporal retina, projects its axons to its own side of the head. The degree of optic tract crossing varies greatly among species; it amounts to 90% crossing for the rat and about 50% for primates.

The **optic tract** is the term applied to the axons of the retinal ganglion cells after they cross the optic chiasm. Most optic tract axons terminate in the **lateral geniculate nucleus,** which is part of the thalamus. Some axons leave the optic tract to end in the **superior colliculus** in the midbrain. Synaptic interactions in the lateral geniculate may involve influences derived from other brain regions (for instance, the reticular formation). The axons of postsynaptic cells in the lateral geniculate form the **optic radiations,** which terminate in the primary visual areas in the **occipital cortex.** In addition to the **primary visual cortex** shown in Figure 7-1, surrounding regions of the cortex are also largely visual in function. It is at the cortical level that inputs from the two eyes converge, making possible binocular effects.

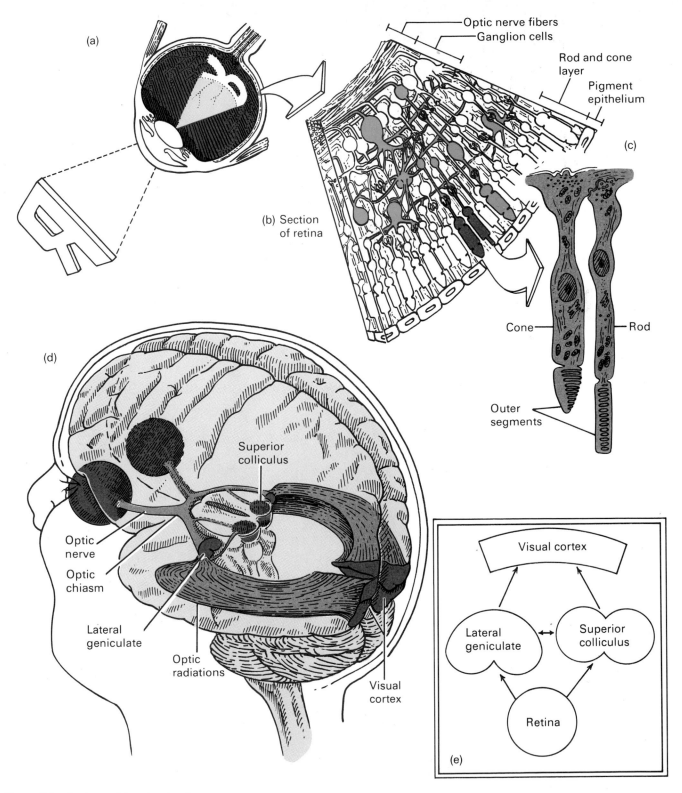

(a)

(b) Section of retina

Optic nerve fibers
Ganglion cells
Rod and cone layer
Pigment epithelium

(c)

Cone
Rod

Outer segments

(d)

Superior colliculus

Optic nerve
Optic chiasm
Lateral geniculate
Optic radiations
Visual cortex

(e)

Visual cortex

Lateral geniculate
Superior colliculus

Retina

Figure 7-1 Anatomy of the visual pathways.

Figure 7-2 The color solid illustrating three basic dimensions of perception of light.

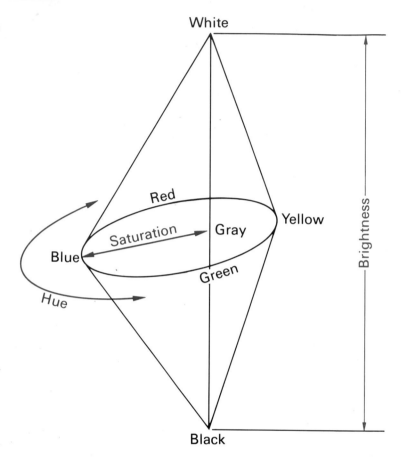

Color For most of us the visible world has several distinguishable hues, blue, green, yellow, red, and their intermediates. For about 8% of human males and about 0.5% of females, some of these color distinctions are either absent or at least less striking. Although the term color blindness is commonly used to describe impairments in color perception, even people with impaired color vision do distinguish some hues; complete color blindness in humans is extremely rare.

The appearance of a patch of light has other aspects besides its hue. The color solid (Figure 7-2) is used to illustrate three basic dimensions of our perception of light:

1. **Brightness,** which varies from dark to light and is the vertical dimension in the figure.

2. **Hue,** which varies around the color circle through blue, green, yellow, orange, and red.

3. **Saturation,** which varies from rich full colors at the periphery of the circle to gray at the center. For example, starting with red at the periphery, the colors become paler toward the center, going through pink to gray.

Color perception in mammals depends both on the existence of receptor cells that are specialized for bands of certain wavelengths of light and on the processing of this information by neurons in the local circuits of the retina.

● Receptor cells   **Cones** are the receptors for color vision. Animals that have all-rod retinas, such as the rat, are color blind. Early in the nineteenth century it was hypothesized that three separate kinds of cones provide the basis for color vision. This **trichromatic hypothesis** was endorsed in 1852 by the great physiologist-physicist Hermann von Helmholtz and became the dominant position. Helmholtz believed that blue-sensitive, green-sensitive, and red-sensitive cones would be found and that each type would have a separate path to the brain. The color of an object would be recognized, then, on the basis of which color receptor was activated. This would be like discriminating among touch, cold, and warmth on the basis of which skin receptors are activated. A different explanation was proposed by the physiologist Ewald Hering. He argued on the basis of visual experience that there are three opposed pairs of colors—blue-yellow, green-red, and black-white—and that three physiological processes with opposed positive and negative values must therefore be the basis of color vision. As we will see, both this **opponent-process hypothesis** and the trichromatic hypothesis are encompassed in current color theory, but neither of the old hypotheses is sufficient by itself.

Are there three classes of cones with different color properties? Measurements of cone photopigments in the last few years have borne out the trichromatic hypothesis in part. Each cone of the human retina does have one of three pigments. These pigments do not, however, have the rather narrow spectral distributions that Helmholtz had predicted. The color system that Helmholtz postulated would have given rather poor color vision and poor visual acuity. Color vision would be poor because only a few different hues could be discriminated; within the long-wavelength region of the spectrum there would be only red and not all the range of hues that we see. Acuity would be poor because the grain of the retinal mosaic would be coarse; a red stimulus could affect only one-third of the receptors. Actually, acuity is as good in red light as in white light.

In fact, the human visual system does not have color receptors, each sensitive only to a restricted part of the visible spectrum. Two of the three retinal cone pigments respond to lights of almost any wavelength. The pigments do have somewhat different peaks of sensitivity, but these are not as far apart as Helmholtz predicted. As Figure 7-3 shows, one peak occurs at about 419 nanometers (in the blue part of the spectrum), another at about 531 nm (green), and the third at about 559 nm (yellow green). Note that none of the curves peaks in the red part of the spectrum.

Under ordinary conditions almost any visual object stimulates cones of at least two kinds, thus providing for high visual acuity and good perception of form. The spectral sensitivities of the three cone types are somewhat different from each other, and neural processing detects and magnifies these differences to extract the color information. Certain ganglion cells and certain cells at higher stations in the visual system are color-specific, but the receptor cells are not. Similarly, the receptors are not form-specific, but form is detected later in the visual centers by comparing the outputs of different receptors. Since the cones are not color detectors, the most appropriate brief names for them can be taken from their peak areas of wavelength

Figure 7-3 Spectral sensitivity of human photopigments. The most up-to-date information on the spectral absorbance of human retinal photopigments comes from microdensitometer analyses of the outer segments of individual cones and rods. The data in this figure are based on receptors from seven eyes (3 female, 4 male). The blue curve with a maximum at 419 nm is based on 5 short-wave sensitive cones; the blue curve that peaks at 531 nm, on 45 medium-wave sensitive cones; and the blue curve with a maximum at 559 nm, on 53 long-wave sensitive cones. The black curve is the mean for 39 rods. (Data provided by H.J.A. Dartnall, J. K. Bowmaker, and J. Mollon from unpublished studies)

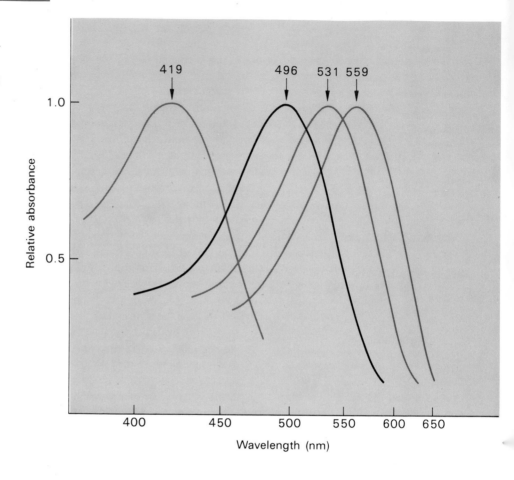

sensitivity: short (S) for the receptor with peak sensitivity at 419 nm, middle (M) at 531, and long (L) at 559.

● Retinal color circuits   The neural circuits that extract color information and that contrast the brightness of adjacent parts of the visual field are located in the retina. So a great deal of neural processing takes place in the retina, where there are hundreds of millions of nerve cells. The results of this processing are carried to the higher centers by the one million axons of each optic nerve. The complexities of retinal anatomy are indicated in Figures 6-5 and 7-1. The retinal ganglion cells are thus projection neurons and the other retinal cells are local-circuit neurons. (The distinction between projection and local-circuit neurons was made in Chapter 2.)

Recordings have been made from ganglion cells in Old World monkeys, which show color discrimination just like that of human beings with normal color vision. It was found that most ganglion cells and cells in the lateral geniculate nucleus are spectrally sensitive; they fire to some wavelengths and are inhibited by other wavelengths. Lateral geniculate cells show the same response characteristics as retinal ganglion cells but are more convenient to record from, so most of the work has been done with them. A leader in this research is Russell L. De Valois, and much of the

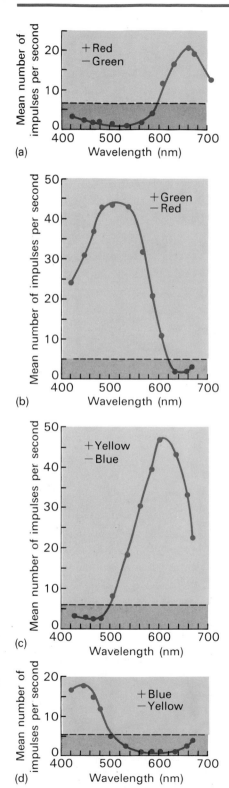

(a)

(b)

(c)

(d)

Figure 7-4 Responses of four main types of spectrally opponent lateral genic-ulate cells in macaque monkeys. These cells are called spectrally opponent be-cause each is inhibited by light in one part of the spectrum and is excited by light in another part. (From De Valois and De Valois, 1975)

information in this section comes from his reports. Figure 7-4(a) shows the response of such a cell as a spot of light in the center of the cell's receptive field is changed from one wavelength to another. The firing is inhibited from about 420 to 600 nm, then it is stimulated from about 600 nm on. Such a cell is called "plus red, minus green" $(+R - G)$. Since two regions of the spectrum have opposite effects on the cell's rate of firing, it is an example of what is called a **spectrally opponent cell.** Figure 7-4 shows examples of responses of the four main kinds of spectrally op-ponent cells.

Each spectrally opponent ganglion cell presumably receives input from two differ-ent kinds of cones through bipolar cells. The connections from one kind of cone are excitatory, and those from the other kind are inhibitory. The patterns of connections are shown in Figure 7-5. The ganglion cells thus record the difference in stimulation of different populations of cones. For example, a $+G - R$ cell responds to the difference in excitation of M minus L cones; a $+R - G$ cell responds to L minus M. (We noted in Chapter 4 that a neuron can process information by subtracting one input from another; this is an example of such information processing.) Although the peaks of the sensitivity curves of the M and L cones are not very different, the M minus L difference curve shows a clear peak around 500 nm (in the green or blue green part of the spectrum). The L minus M difference function shows a peak around 650 nm (in the orange part of the spectrum). So subtracting one cone function from the other yields two distinctly different neural response curves. The spectrally sensitive neurons can properly be called color cells, whereas the cones are best considered as light receptors that feed into many circuits—for detection of form, depth, and movement as well as of hue.

In the monkey lateral geniculate nucleus 70% to 80% of the cells are spectrally opponent, whereas in the cat very few spectrally opponent cells are found, about 1%. This difference corresponds to the ease with which monkeys can discriminate wavelengths and the extreme difficulty of training cats to discriminate even large differences of wavelength.

● **Cells of the visual cortex**   In the cortex, color information appears to be used for different kinds of information processing. Some cortical cells are spectrally opponent and may even sharpen or enhance differences of hue. These cells may contribute to perception of color. It has been reported that some cortical visual regions are particularly rich in color-sensitive cells (Zeki, 1978). Perception of color appears to require the cortex in humans, because cortical lesions destroy perception of color as well as pattern. Many cortical cells utilize color and brightness to bring out forms or movement but are not sensitive to which colors are involved. Such a cell may detect a line whether it is green on red or black on white. Thus differences in hue, as well as brightness, can contribute to perception of form and motion.

The color vision that we enjoy is rather rare among mammals. It is very poorly

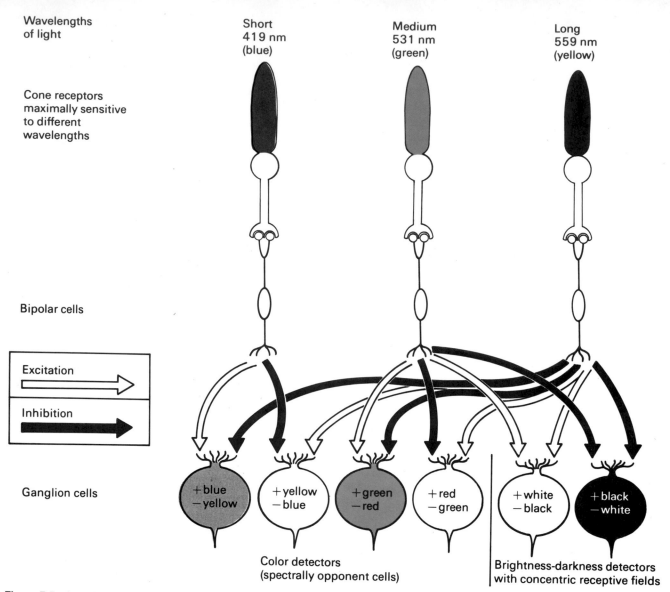

Figure 7-5 A model of the connections of the color vision systems in the retina. (Adapted from De Valois, 1969)

developed in rodents (such as rats) and in carnivores (such as dogs and cats). It is moderately well developed in prosimians (such as tupaia) and is highly developed in monkeys and apes. Perhaps human color vision goes back to our tree-living, fruit-eating ancestors. Color vision is not confined to certain mammalian species, though. Apparently it has evolved independently in several lines, including some molluscs, some insects, some fish, and some reptiles.

Position   The ability to locate visual stimuli in space depends on our ability to answer two questions: In what direction does the stimulus object lie? (This is a question about the visual field.) And how far away is it? (This is a question of depth perception.)

● **Visual field**   Each successive level of the visual system is a detailed map of the visible world. First the retina receives an accurate image, projected on it by the optics of the eye, especially the cornea and lens. Next the retina sends signals along axons to the visual areas of the diencephalon and midbrain, and these preserve the spatial array. Finally other axons then convey the visual information to several visual areas in the cerebral cortex, and again these show detailed maps of the visible world.

Although the neural maps preserve the order of the visual field, each emphasizes some regions at the expense of others; that is, each map is topographic and does not provide exact copies of spatial relations in the external world. One reason that the maps are topographic is that some portions of the retinal surface have a denser concentration of receptors than others. The region called the **fovea** (from the Latin word for a "small depression" or "pit") has a dense concentration of cones and provides a central region of maximal acuity (Figure 7-6). The rods show a different

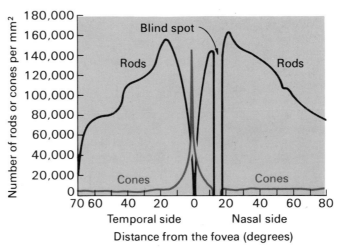

(a) Frequencies of rods and cones across the retina

Figure 7-6 Visual acuity and retinal position. Cones are concentrated in the fovea and their concentration falls off rapidly on either side. Rods are lacking in the fovea and show their greatest concentration about 20° from the fovea. About 16° to the nasal side of the retina is a disc where the ganglion cell axons leave the retina and through which the retinal arteries and veins pass. There are no receptors in this region, and small objects whose images fall on it cannot be seen, so it is called the blind spot. (From data of Østerberg, 1935) Acuity is maximum at the fovea, as shown in the lower graph. It declines with distance from the fovea rather similarly to the reduction in concentration of cones in the upper graph.

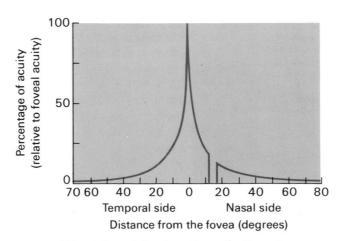

(b) Variation of visual acuity across the retina

distribution; they are absent in the fovea but are more numerous than cones in the periphery of the retina. A gap in the retinal surface, which is not noticeable under ordinary viewing conditions, is produced by the entrance of blood vessels to the retina. There are no receptors at this small region of the retina and light that strikes it cannot be seen, so this region is called the **blind spot.**

The fact that projection of visual space onto brain regions is topographic does not mean that our spatial perception is distorted. Rather it reflects the acuity of spatial discrimination, which is greatest in the central part of the field. It is for this reason that reading is done with the fovea and that the eye jumps from spot to spot along a line of printing or along any scene that is inspected.

The extreme orderliness of the mapping of the visual field is demonstrated by the study of regions of blindness brought about by injuries. The location of such a perceptual gap, or **scotoma,** in the visual field is accurately predicted by the locus of injury in the visual pathway. Although the word scotoma comes from the Latin word for "darkness," a scotoma is not a dark patch in the visual field; rather it is a spot where nothing can be perceived.

Until recently it was confidently believed that human beings needed the occipital cortex for spatial vision—or for any vision at all. Even if the lower levels of the visual system were operating normally, damage to the cortex could result in blindness. Then it was found that a monkey with its occipital cortex removed could be trained to point accurately at spots of light in order to earn rewards. The apparent discrepancy in visual capacity of humans and monkeys after damage to the visual cortex could be taken in different ways. It could be interpreted as revealing a fundamental difference in brain-behavior relations in human beings and nonhuman primates. Or it could serve as a challenge to investigate the visual capacities of brain-injured patients by employing behavioral techniques similar to those used with nonverbal animals. A few investigators have taken up this challenge.

Patients who have had only the visual cortex destroyed are rather rare, but a few of them have been studied in some detail. A patient studied by Weiskrantz and his colleagues in England is a good example (Sanders et al., 1974; Weiskrantz et al., 1974; Weiskrantz, 1977). This patient had a small tumor removed from the visual cortex of his right hemisphere, and on subsequent routine testing he appeared to be completely blind in the left-half fields of both eyes, even to intense lights. In the first experimental tests the subject was asked to reach out and touch the position on a screen at which a visual stimulus was projected briefly in the blind field. (This is the same sort of task that monkeys were trained to perform in order to obtain rewards.) It seems like an odd task to ask of a person who says he can't see, but the subject was asked to "guess" where the stimulus might be on each trial, and he cooperated. It soon became apparent that he could locate stimuli quite accurately. When the results of these trials were shown to the subject after several hours of testing, he was astonished. Later he described "feelings" that something might be present, but he consistently refused to call this the "seeing" that he had in his right-half fields. Later this subject was asked to guess if the stimulus was a horizontal or a vertical line, or X versus O. He showed about 75% accuracy with stimuli 12° in size and even greater accuracy with larger stimuli. His acuity threshold in the "blind" half field was less than 2 min of arc. The investigators termed this capacity "blindsight." The patient does not perceive, yet he performs visual discriminations. This distinction raises important questions for both application and theory.

Could patients develop both the acuity and the confidence in blindsight so that they could use it in daily life? In monkeys with lesions in part of the striate cortex, the ability to detect a spot of light in the "blind" area increased with training. Moreover, the training was specific, since the areas of the visual field that received practice recovered more rapidly than those that did not receive practice (Mohler and Wurtz, 1977). Humphrey (1970) has reported that a monkey with a completely destroyed striate cortex not only learned to discriminate targets but also used vision to avoid obstacles. Active training, rather than imposing stimuli on a passive animal, appears to be necessary for improving visual discrimination after lesions of the striate cortex (Cowey, 1967). At the outset of such training the animal seems to discover that it possesses a viable visual space; after this discovery is made, performance can improve rather rapidly. There are many kinds of performance that people carry out on the basis of barely detectable or even subliminal stimuli. But further research is needed to determine whether training of blindsight can be used in practical situations by blind people.

The spatial discrimination that occurs after removal of the visual cortex depends on circuits in the superior colliculus. After destruction of both the striate cortex and the superior colliculus, the monkey could not recover any visual discrimination in the affected part of the field (Mohler and Wurtz, 1977). It appears, then, that the circuit involving the superior colliculus has information-processing capacity for localization and has adequate connections to motor controls. However, the colliculus is only weakly connected to the parts of the brain required for identification of objects and conscious awareness. Such clues should help us elucidate brain circuits required for consciousness as distinct from those required for behavioral discrimination.

● **Depth perception**   Many people believe that the basis of depth perception was discovered by Renaissance artists who accurately analyzed scenes into lines and angles. But recent research has shown that depth can be perceived in the absence of lines and angles and that depth perception in certain targets can precede the perception of form. Also, the way in which the visual system accomplishes the perception of depth has continued to afford controversy and novel observations, even during the last decade.

New knowledge about depth perception came from work on random-dot patterns (Julesz, 1971; Julesz and Spivack, 1967); see Figure 7-7. In such stimuli the left and right random-dot targets are identical except that a central region (a square or some other form) in one of the targets is shifted horizontally by a small distance. Each of the targets appears to have the same random texture, and no form is seen in either of them. When the targets are viewed stereoscopically (the left eye viewing the left target and the right eye, the right target), the horizontally shifted region is perceived as being displaced in depth. Depending on the direction of the shift, it is seen either in front of or behind the surrounding area. Only when the depth is perceived stereoscopically does the form of the shifted region appear.

The slightly different views that the two eyes have of a scene provide the stimulus basis for perceiving depth (see Figure 7-8). This phenomenon is also called **stereopsis** (from Greek roots for "depth" and "vision"). The difference between the views of the two eyes is called **binocular disparity.** In the late 1960s a physiological correlate of binocular disparity was reported and offered as an explanation for

Figure 7-7 Demonstration of depth perception from random dot patterns. You can fuse the two figures, either by putting them in a stereoscope or by staring "through" the page until the images coincide. As soon as the images fuse, you will see a form that stands out in front of the rest of the figure. What shape is this form? (From Julesz, 1964. © B. Julesz and Bell Laboratories.)

Figure 7-8 The visual scene as viewed by each eye. The difference between the two views is called binocular disparity.

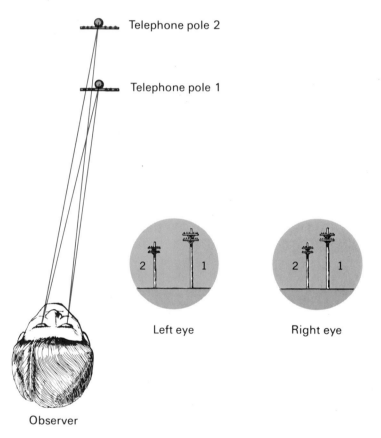

stereopsis (Barlow, Blakemore, and Pettigrew, 1967; Pettigrew, Nikara, and Bishop, 1968). Researchers found that many cells in the striate cortex are selective for binocular disparity; the particular depth with respect to the fixation plane to which the cell responded was reported to vary widely from one cell to the next. Binocular disparity could not be analyzed at lower levels in the visual system, though, because it is at the cortex that inputs from the two eyes first converge.

Work by other investigators has now produced a more accurate account of stereopsis (Poggio and Fischer, 1977; von der Heydt et al., 1978). Many cortical cells have narrowly tuned receptive fields with little or no retinal disparity; that is, they are tuned to the fixation plane, or very close to it. Other cells do show retinal disparity, but different cells are not tuned to a wide range of different depths. Rather there are only two types of cells with rather broad retinal disparities: One set is excited by stimuli in front of the fixation plane and inhibited by stimuli behind the fixation plane, and the other set has the opposite responses. The cells in both the striate and the peristriate areas thus fall into three categories: those tuned to the fixation plane, those tuned to the region beyond the fixation plane, and those tuned to the region in front of the fixation plane.

At about the same time that this research was being conducted, psychophysical results with human observers gave independent evidence of the existence of only a few pathways or channels for depth. Investigators found that some "normal" viewers are actually partially stereo-blind. That is, some subjects are specifically unable to localize, by means of stereoscopic clues alone, the depth of an object beyond the fixation plane; other subjects are unable to use such clues to locate the depth of an object in front of the fixation plane (Richards, 1970, 1977). These results point to the existence of two broadly tuned depth channels. One channel is for objects anywhere beyond the fixation plane and another is for those in front. Either channel may be missing or may function poorly in occasional individuals.

Pattern and form   We recognize individuals and classify stimuli according to their sizes, shapes, and locations in the visual field. How these aspects of spatial vision are accomplished by neural circuits has been and continues to be the object of intensive research. Much of this work involves the study of the electrical activity of neurons at various levels of the visual system and attempts to relate it to visual perception. Most investigators assume that recognition of visual scenes first requires the analysis of complex patterns into some kind of subunits, with each individual cell in the visual pathway responding only to certain aspects of the part of the pattern that occurs within the receptive field of the cell. Then these subunits must be synthesized into a complex pattern. But so far the problem of determining the initial analysis has not been solved.

The two main current models of pattern analysis are the **feature detector model** and the **spatial frequency filter model.** Let us examine each of these in turn and consider their strengths and weaknesses in accounting for the facts of form perception.

● Feature detector model   The receptive fields of cells in the visual system differ from one level of the system to another. Recall that the receptive fields of retinal ganglion cells are concentric and of two basic types: either with an "on" center and an "off" surround, or the opposite organization with an "off" center and an "on" surround (see Figure 6-18). The center and its surround are always antagonistic and tend to cancel each other's activity. This feature explains the finding that uniform illumination of the visual field is less effective in arousing a ganglion cell than is a well-placed small spot or a line or an edge passing through the center of the cell's receptive field. Ganglion cells also differ in the temporal characteristics of their receptive fields. Some show sustained activity as long as the stimulation is maintained; these tonic receptors have been called **X cells.** For other cells the activity is transient, starting strongly but then waning rapidly; these phasic receptors are called **Y cells.** We will see later that the X and Y cells project separately from the retina to the higher visual centers. Cells in the lateral geniculate body have concentric receptive fields with properties much like those shown at the retina.

The next station, the visual cortex, provided a puzzle, however. The spots of light that were effective stimuli for ganglion or lateral geniculate cells did not prove to be very effective at the cortical level. Success in stimulating cortical visual cells was announced in 1959 when Hubel and Wiesel reported that visual cortical cells require more specific stimuli—elongated stimuli, lines or bars in a particular position and at a particular orientation in the visual field (Figure 7-9). Some cortical cells also

Figure 7-9 Responses of brain cells to specific stimuli. Microelectrode recording reveals that cells in the brain vary greatly in their receptive fields. Visual cells in the thalamus have concentric receptive fields like those of retinal ganglion cells (see Figure 6-18). But cortical cells may show orientation specificity (b) or respond only to motion in a particular direction (c) or even be sensitive to only a particular shape.

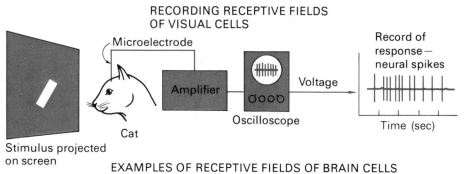

RECORDING RECEPTIVE FIELDS
OF VISUAL CELLS

Microelectrode

Amplifier

Oscilloscope

Voltage

Cat

Stimulus projected
on screen

Record of
response—
neural spikes

Time (sec)

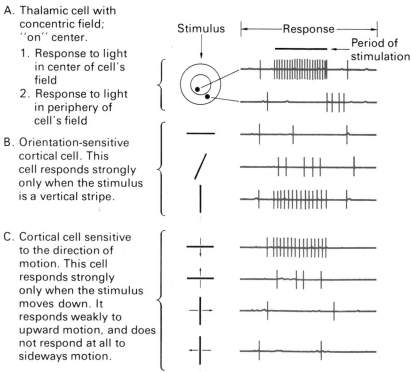

EXAMPLES OF RECEPTIVE FIELDS OF BRAIN CELLS

A. Thalamic cell with concentric field; "on" center.
  1. Response to light in center of cell's field
  2. Response to light in periphery of cell's field

Stimulus   Response

Period of stimulation

B. Orientation-sensitive cortical cell. This cell responds strongly only when the stimulus is a vertical stripe.

C. Cortical cell sensitive to the direction of motion. This cell responds strongly only when the stimulus moves down. It responds weakly to upward motion, and does not respond at all to sideways motion.

required movement of the stimulus before they would respond actively. For some of these cells just the fact of movement was sufficient, while others were even more demanding, requiring motion in a specific direction.

The ability of special stimuli to produce vigorous responses in visual cortical cells was soon verified by others, and it led to a great amount of productive research. The success of this research also led to general acceptance of the theoretical model proposed by Hubel and Wiesel, but challenges to this model have emerged in recent years. Let us first note a few more findings of Hubel and Wiesel and then take up their theoretical model.

Cortical cells were categorized into four classes according to the types of stimuli required to produce maximum responses. So-called **simple cortical cells** responded best to an edge or a bar of a particular width and with a particular direction and location in the visual field. These cells were therefore sometimes called bar detectors or edge detectors. **Complex cortical cells** had receptive fields like the simple cells, but they also showed some latitude for location. That is, they would respond to a bar of a particular size and orientation anywhere within a particular area of the visual field. Cells called **hypercomplex 1** had clear inhibitory areas at the two ends; that is, the best response was shown if the bar was of limited length, and extending the length beyond this limit reduced the response. Later work showed that even simple and complex cortical cells possess this property, at least to some extent. Finally some cells were called **hypercomplex 2;** these cells responded best to two line segments meeting at a particular angle. Hubel and Wiesel mentioned this type only briefly, but it gave rise to a great amount of theorizing.

The theoretical model of Hubel and Wiesel can be described as a hierarchical one; that is, more complex events are built up from inputs of simpler ones. For example, a simple cortical cell could be conceived as receiving input from a row of lateral geniculate cells. A complex cortical cell could be thought of as receiving its input from a row of simple cortical cells. Other theorists extrapolated from this model of Hubel and Wiesel, cascading circuits of cells to detect any possible form. Thus it was suggested that with enough successive levels of analysis, a unit could be constructed that would enable a person to recognize his or her grandmother, and there was frequent mention in the literature of such hypothetical **"grandmother cells."**

A hierarchical model of this sort might work, but critics pointed out various problems with it, some of a theoretical nature and others arising from empirical observations. For one thing, a "grandmother-recognizing" circuit would require vast numbers of cells, probably even more than the number available in the cerebral cortex. Each successive stage in the hierarchy is obviously built on the preceding one, but Hoffman and Stone (1971) found practically no difference in latency of response between simple and complex cortical cells. If anything, the complex cells had slightly faster responses, although the hierarchical theory requires the simple cells to respond earlier. Further work showed that the projection from retina to cortex was by parallel systems rather than by successive hierarchical systems. The X ganglion cells project mainly to simple cortical cells, while the Y ganglion cells project mainly to complex cortical cells (Wilson and Sherman, 1976). Also, cortical projections of the X cells are almost entirely to the primary visual cortex (also called striate cortex), whereas Y cell projections are found outside the striate area as well

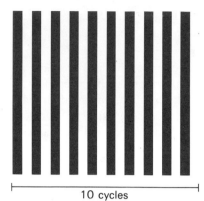

10 cycles

5 cycles

Figure 7-10 Spatial frequencies. The upper grating has twice the spatial frequency of the lower grating, since twice as many bars occur in the same space.

Figure 7-11 Visual grids with sinusoidal modulation of light intensity. If the light intensity is strongly modulated as in the black sine wave in (a), the grid has high contrast (b). If the intensity is less strongly modulated as in the blue curve, the grid has lower contrast (c). The light bands in (b) and (c) appear broader than the dark bands because of nonlinearity of the visual receptors.

(a) Spatial distribution of stimulus intensity

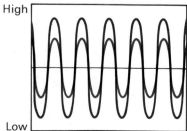

as within it. At the same time that difficulties with this model were being recognized, an alternative model was emerging.

● Spatial frequency filter model   To discuss this model, we must become familiar with a way of regarding spatial vision that is quite different from the traditional viewpoint. The idea of visual-spatial frequencies was first used to measure the precision of optical systems such as lenses. Then beginning in the 1950s it was found useful in describing the spatial vision of people and animals, and in the 1970s it was employed to describe the receptive fields of visual neurons. By the spatial frequency of a visual stimulus we mean the number of light-dark cycles it shows per degree of visual space. For example, the parts of Figure 7-10 differ in the spacing of the bars and therefore in their spatial frequencies.

The spatial frequency technique applies Fourier analysis or linear systems theory rather than an analysis of visual patterns into bars and angles. In discussing the auditory stimulus in Box 6-2, we saw that any complex, repeating auditory stimulus can be analyzed into the sum of sine waves. The same principle of Fourier analysis can be applied to visual patterns. If the dimension from dark to light is made to vary according to a sine wave pattern, we get a visual pattern like the one shown in Figure 7-11. A series of black and white stripes, like that shown in Figure 7-10, can be analyzed into the sum of a visual sine wave and its odd harmonics; that is, the sum of the first, third, fifth, . . . harmonics. A complex visual pattern or scene can also be analyzed by the Fourier technique; in this case frequency components at different angles of orientation are also used.

The spatial frequency concept allows more powerful measures of visual acuity than were available in the past. Traditionally, visual acuity has been measured in terms of the finest or smallest patterns that can be seen accurately. Much more information can be obtained, however, if we determine how the observer responds to patterns of gratings that vary both in spacing and in contrast (Figure 7-12). A pattern of gratings is hard to perceive if the spacing is too fine, but it is also hard to perceive a pattern that is too coarse. Some intermediate spatial frequency is easiest to perceive. The spatial threshold can be determined in terms of the contrast between the dark and light bars that is necessary to detect them; that is, for each frequency of spacing, one can determine the contrast necessary to perceive the pattern. The resultant psychophysical function is called a **contrast sensitivity function** or a modulation sensitivity function. An example for human observers is shown in Figure 7-13(a). The point where the curve crosses the horizontal axis (about 50 cycles per degree) corresponds to the clinical visual acuity threshold, about 1 minute of visual arc. The peak of the curve, where the eye is most sensitive, is at about 6 cycles per degree.

(b) High-contrast spatial grid

(c) Low-contrast spatial grid

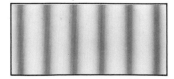

Figure 7-12 Contrast sensitivity stimulus. This photograph, taken from an oscilloscope, shows a senusoidal pattern of light intensity in which the spacing between bars decreases regularly from left to right and the contrast decreases from bottom to top. The frequency scale is correct when the figure is viewed from 50 cm (about arm's length). How high up can you detect the bars at different spacings? (Photograph courtesy of F. W. Campbell)

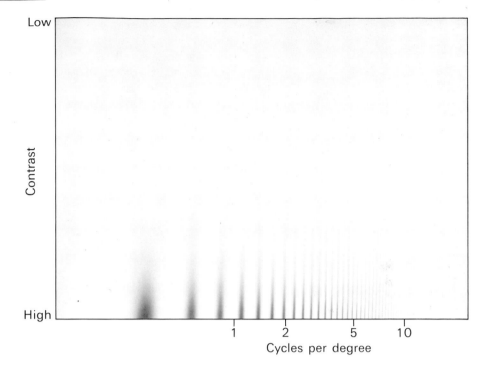

The contrast sensitivity function is useful in some clinical cases because it measures not only how well we see very small objects but also how well we see objects of all sizes. Some patients who have suffered brain damage complain that "things don't look normal," but when tested with a conventional acuity chart, they are not found to have much impairment. When the contrast sensitivity function was taken, however, some of these patients showed a selective loss of sensitivity in the middle range of sizes, which interfered with their vision of common objects (Bodis-Wollner, 1972).

Figure 7-13 Contrast sensitivity thresholds of five human and three macaque observers. Humans and monkeys were tested individually with the same stimulus display, and the contrast sensitivity functions are seen to be rather similar. (From De Valois, Morgan, and Snodderly, 1974)

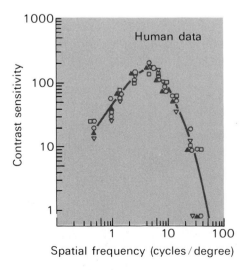 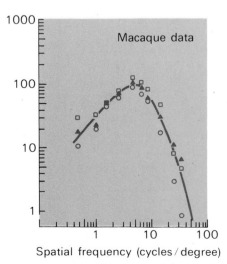

A productive suggestion was that the contrast sensitivity function (CSF) is actually the "envelope" or sum of many sensitivities of the individual, more narrowly tuned channels (Campbell and Robson, 1968). This suggestion was soon supported by results of an experiment on selective adaptation to frequency (Blakemore and Campbell, 1969). In this experiment a person spent a minute or more inspecting a visual grating with a given spacing, and then the CSF was determined. The results showed that the CSF is depressed at the frequency to which the subject adapted. The suggestion of multiple spatial frequency channels

" . . . had revolutionary impact because it led to entirely different conceptions of the way in which the visual system might function in dealing with spatial stimuli. It suggests that rather than specifically detecting such seminaturalistic features as bars and edges, the system is breaking down complex stimuli into their individual spatial frequency components in a kind of crude Fourier analysis . . . . Irrespective of the eventual judgment of the correctness of this particular model, Campbell and Robson's conjecture will remain pivotal in having opened the eyes of vision researchers to the many ways in which the visual system could analyze the world using elements not akin to our verbal descriptions of scenes" (De Valois and De Valois, 1980, p. 320).

The responses of cortical cells to spatial frequency stimuli were then measured (Maffei and Fiorentini, 1973; De Valois, Albrecht, and Thorell, 1977; Albrecht, 1978). Cortical cells were found to be tuned more accurately to the dimensions of spatial frequency grids than to the width of bars. Also, most cortical cells were more sensitive to sinusoidal gratings than to bars of the same contrast. Furthermore, when the CSF of a cell was determined, this function could be used to predict the response of the cell to black or white bars of different widths. Thus the spatial frequency model allowed quantitative prediction of responses to different stimuli, whereas such predictions could not be derived from the feature detector model.

The contrast sensitivity function also shows a sharp difference between the X and Y projection systems from the retina to higher brain centers. The Y cells perform much better than the X cells at lower spatial frequencies, whereas the X cells are somewhat better than Y cells at the higher frequencies. For this reason Sherman (1979) has suggested that the Y cell pathways are used to analyze basic spatial forms, while the X cell pathways add the detail needed for fine acuity. This difference can be related to effects of stimulus deprivation during the critical period of development. Keeping one eye of a kitten closed during its first few months causes failure of development, especially of the Y cells. The impairment in spatial discrimination of these kittens is probably due chiefly to the lack of development of their Y cell pathways.

● **Evaluating of the spatial frequency models**   Further indication that the spatial frequency approach can be applied to object perception comes from its use in analyzing optical illusions (Ginsburg, 1971 and 1975; Ginsburg and Campbell, 1977). Thus the Müller-Lyer arrowhead illusion (Figure 7-14) can be interpreted in terms of spatial filtering. The arrow with the outward arms is actually longer than the inward-arm arrow if only the low-frequency information is considered. The visual system has multiple spatial channels available simultaneously. So while

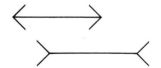

Figure 7-14 The Müller-Lyer arrowhead illusion.

higher-frequency channels give accurate information about the positions and lengths of the lines in this figure, the low-frequency channels also contribute information about size. Various patterns used as examples by Gestalt psychologists can also be interpreted from this approach. Thus Wertheimer's collection of dots that can be seen either as individual dots or as larger objects (rows or columns) in fact do have these separate characteristics depending on whether high frequency or low spatial frequency is used; when a low-pass filter is used, this classic figure consists of solid rows (Ginsburg, 1971).

No one has suggested that the visual system functions as a perfect Fourier analyzer. A perfect analyzer would have an infinite number of filters, each with infinitely narrow tuning, and the filters would be completely independent of each other. Experimental evidence indicates, however, that the visual channels interact and that the width of tuning varies with location over the retina. Nevertheless, it appears that Fourier analysis may play a useful role in visual processing, just as it does in audition.

Visual deficits and rehabilitation

In the United States half a million people are blind. The probability of blindness increases with age; in children less than 4 years of age the incidence of blindness is 9 out of 100,000, whereas for people over the age of 65 the rate is 1,500 out of 100,000. Medical advances during the past 25 years have reduced some causes of blindness but have actually increased blindness from other causes. For example, increased survival of diabetics does not overcome all effects of this disease, and many diabetics become blind.

Innovative ways of dealing with the dilemmas of blindness are coming from research on the neurobiology of vision. Early efforts to remedy some forms of blindness due to lens changes (for example, congenital cataract) provided the background for recent efforts to provide substitute vision by direct electrical stimulation of the brain. Electrical stimulation of the eyeball or sites around the eye can produce "flashes" of light called **phosphenes.** These are lightninglike sensations that illuminate the visual field. Sharp blows on the head can lead to a similar effect. In the 1940s and 1950s Wilder Penfield, an eminent neurosurgeon, was engaged in a program of surgical relief of seizures that proved quite successful. Stimulation of the visual cortex for necessary mapping in these patients yielded sensations of flashing light. This work showed that electrical stimulation of the visual system could have sensory consequences.

From this start several projects have developed in recent years that seek to replace sight with direct electrical stimulation of the visual cortex. The most ambitious of these schemes has offered startling projects still in the fledgling stage. For instance, in an individual blinded by a war injury many electrodes were placed on the visual cortex; stimulation of some of these electrodes elicited reports of visual images, such as a distant star (Dobelle and Mladejovsky, 1974). Stimulation of groups of these electrodes provoked more complicated percepts. It is hoped that a miniature TV camera replacing one eye can, with the aid of microcomputers, supply electrical stimulation that might bypass visual processing in the retina (Figure 7-15). Only rather gross images can be expected from this method, since each electrode on the cortex stimulates millions of neurons at once, and this response can hardly replace

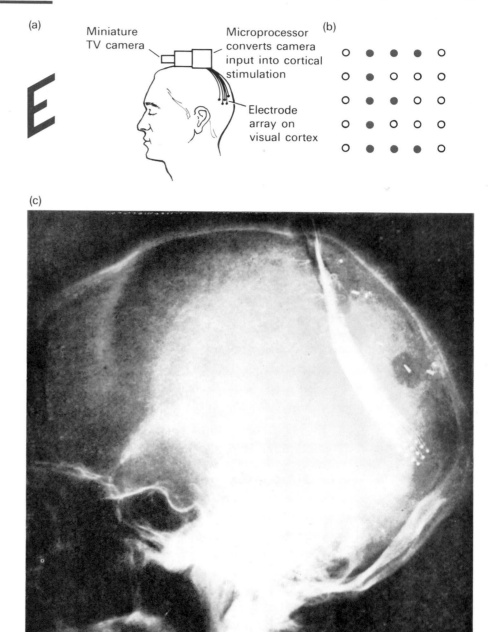

(a)

Miniature TV camera

Microprocessor converts camera input into cortical stimulation

Electrode array on visual cortex

(b)

(c)

Figure 7-15   An arrangement for a visual prosthesis. (a) Television monitoring of a pattern is translated into a spatial pattern of electrical stimulation of visual cortex. Computer circuitry of the microprocessor controls the parameters of the electrical stimuli. (b) Electrode array on the cortex, with stimulated points shown in blue. (c) An X ray showing a group of electrodes on the visual cortex of a patient. [(c) From Dobelle and Mladejovsky, *The Journal of Physiology,* vol. 243, no. 2(1974): 576.]

the detailed processing of the refined local cortical circuits. Nevertheless it may permit the person to read and to gain useful clues for locomotion. "Brave new worlds" may come to the aid of those whose hope for "sight" or a sense of light seemed, until recently, to be beyond reach.

Less drastic losses of sight are being treated by promising new techniques of training. When a patient with brain injury has an area of the visual field that is blind, it does not necessarily follow that all the cells in the cortical projection area corresponding to the deficit are destroyed. Training can sometimes produce restitution of function even though the blindness has persisted for months or even years (Zihl and von Cramon, 1979). Furthermore, training to discriminate intensity differences around the borders of the scotoma can lead to its shrinkage, especially when there is a gradual transition between the scotoma and normal parts of the visual field. Although training in these experiments was restricted to contrast sensitivity, improvement was also found in visual acuity and in perception of color. The improvement did not occur spontaneously but only during training periods. In some cases the training resulted in remarkable improvement. One patient had only a very small part of his visual field intact and was functionally blind for more than four years; he found his way around with acoustic and tactile cues. During a few months of training he regained the ability to perceive in the upper left quadrant, so that he now walks by using visual cues, and he can read a newspaper.

Auditory information processing

Sounds are an important part of the adaptive behavior of many animals. For humans sounds produced by speech organs form the basic elements of the thousands of human languages. The melodic song of a male bird attracts a female; the grunts, screeches, and burbly sounds of primates signal danger or the need for comfort or satisfaction. Whales, owls, and bats exploit the directional property of sound to locate prey and avoid obstacles. The use of sounds by all these different animals emphasizes a distinctive feature of auditory information processing—the fact that temporal features of acoustic signals can be discriminated with great accuracy. Your auditory system can detect rapid changes of sound intensity and frequency. In fact, the speed of auditory information processing is so good that the frequency analysis of the ear rivals that of modern electronic gadgets. Animals of many species have been trained to respond to small differences in auditory stimuli (Figure 7-16), and their responses have given us detailed information about their auditory capacities.

Auditory pathways of the brain

Each auditory nerve fiber divides into two main branches as it enters the brainstem. Each branch goes to a separate segment of a group of cells called the **cochlear nuclei,** consisting of a dorsal and ventral segment (Figure 7-17). The output of the cochlear nuclei is somewhat complicated and involves multiple paths. One set of paths goes to the **superior olivary complex,** which receives inputs from both right and left cochlear nuclei. The bilateral input to this set of cells is the first level for binaural interaction in the auditory system and is therefore of primary importance for mechanisms of auditory localization. Several other parallel paths all converge on the **inferior colliculus,** which is the auditory center of the midbrain. Outputs of the inferior colliculus go to the **medial geniculate nucleus** of the thalamus. Axons of postsynaptic cells of the medial geniculate in turn extend to the **auditory cortex** of

Figure 7-16 Setup for a typical auditory psychophysical study in the rat. When the animal is ready to make an observation, it presses the left disk; its head is then in the correct position under the loudspeaker. The stimulus or stimuli are then presented. If the response is correct, a food-pellet reward is delivered.

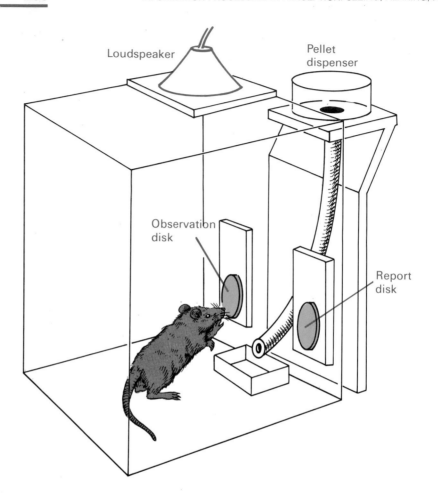

the temporal lobe. The auditory cortex consists of several adjacent regions, most of which represent the positions on the basilar membrane in an orderly map.

Many sensory systems include both ascending and descending pathways. Thus in addition to afferent pathways reaching to higher levels of the brain, there are efferent pathways that lead back to the periphery. The auditory system provides a striking example. At lower levels of the brainstem there is a group of cells whose axons form a bundle and travel out the auditory nerve to the cochlea. These efferent fibers branch profusely in the cochlea and synapse at the base of virtually every hair cell. Many studies have sought to determine the functional role of this group of fibers. Their action is predominantly inhibitory, as shown by the fact that electrical excitation of this bundle reduces the frequency of sound-provoked nerve impulses in the afferents of the auditory nerve. Some investigators have suggested that this efferent pathway can be used to suppress noise and to enhance auditory signals (Dewson, 1968).

Our auditory system makes a useful although incomplete Fourier analysis, so that we respond to the presence of different frequencies in a complex sound. For example, we discriminate vowels because each vowel sound has its own characteristic

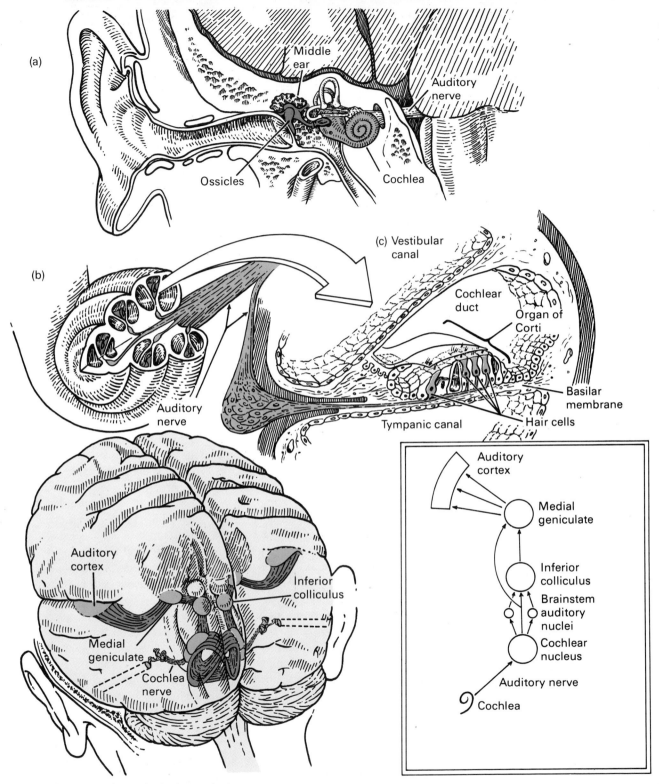

Figure 7-17 Auditory pathways in the human brain.

frequency bands, and we identify musical instruments by the relative intensities of different harmonic frequencies.

Pitch   Most of us can discriminate very small differences in frequency of sound over the entire audible range from 20 Hz up to 15,000–20,000 Hz. The ability to detect a change in frequency is usually expressed as the minimal discriminable frequency difference between two tones. The detectable difference is about 2 Hz up to 2000 Hz, at which point it grows larger. Note that pitch and frequency are not synonymous terms. **Pitch** relates solely to sensory experience, that is, to the responses of subjects to sounds, whereas **frequency** describes a physical property of sounds. The reasons for emphasizing this distinction are many, including the fact that frequency is not the sole determinant of pitch experience and changes in pitch do not precisely parallel changes in frequency.

How do we account for the ability to discriminate frequencies? Two theories have most commonly been offered. One, described as **place theory,** argues that pitch perception depends on the place of maximal displacement of the basilar membrane. "Place," according to this view, also includes which neurons are stimulated in the central auditory pathways—that is, particular nerve cells respond to particular stimulus frequencies. The alternative theory, now most commonly known as **volley theory,** emphasizes the relations between stimulus frequency of sounds and the pattern or timing of neural discharges. According to this perspective the firing pattern of a single nerve cell reveals the stimulus frequency of the input, because each time the stimulus changes frequency, the pattern of discharge is altered. The crudest representation of this idea would suggest, for example, that a 500-Hz tone is represented by 500 nerve impulses per second, whereas this same neuron represents a 1000-Hz tone by a frequency of 1000 nerve impulses per second. In both cases the firing of the nerve impulse is "phase locked" to the stimulus; that is, it occurs at a particular portion of the cycle. Such a phase lock representation can be accomplished more accurately by several fibers than by a single fiber—hence the term volley, which denotes simultaneous flight of several missiles.

These views—place and volley theory—are not necessarily antagonistic; indeed, the best contemporary view of pitch perception incorporates both perspectives. This combined view is referred to as **duplex theory.** The volley principle appears to operate for sounds from about 20 to 1000–1500 Hz, whereas the place principle holds especially for sounds above about 1000 Hz. Let us examine some physiological results that support the place theory and some data that support the volley theory.

As we noted above, the region of maximal vibration along the basilar membrane is related to stimulus frequency. With a change of frequency there is a change in the region of maximal disturbance (Figure 7-18). Von Békésy devised an ingenious way to observe directly the location of the maximal amplitude of traveling waves in animal cochleas, and he reported fairly sharp frequency tuning. He also demonstrated the representation of frequency in terms of place with an enlarged model of the cochlea (which we have seen in Figure 6-17). More recent studies employing

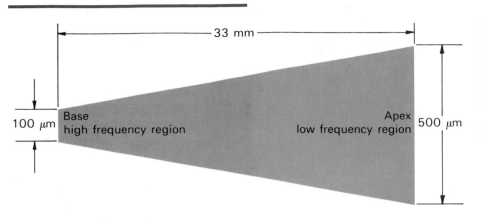

Figure 7-18 The basilar membrane and stimulus frequency. In this diagram, the basilar membrane is represented as being uncoiled. The top diagram shows the dimensions of the basilar membrane. Note that different scales are used for length and width. In the marginal column, note that as the frequency stimulation increases, the position of the peak of movement of the membrane is displaced progressively toward the base.

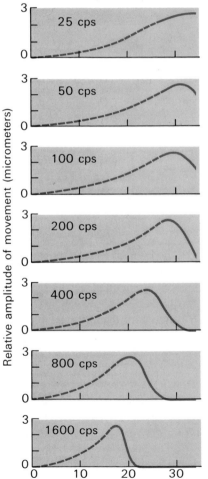

vastly different techniques for the observation of basilar membrane movement show that the relations between basilar membrane locus and stimulus frequency are even sharper than Békésy had observed (Khanna and Leonard, 1981). For complex sounds with several frequency components, the cochlea accomplishes a sort of Fourier analysis; the different frequencies are represented by peaks of vibration at different places along the basilar membrane. The accuracy of place representation of auditory frequency has improved over the course of evolution with the lengthening of the basilar membrane and an increase in the number of hair cells and auditory nerve fibers.

Place along the basilar membrane is preserved in brain representations of stimulus frequency. This arrangement was found by examining the responses of single nerve cells when an animal is presented with stimuli of varying frequency and intensity. Data obtained in these experiments are plotted as tuning curves, which describe the frequency sensitivity of nerve cells at different intensity levels. Figure 7-19 shows tuning curves obtained from single neurons in the auditory nerve. Sharply tuned neurons are evident at all levels of the auditory system, ranging from the auditory nerve to the cortex. These findings suggest that cells at successive levels are not in a hierarchical relationship with respect to frequency assessment.

In recent years an abundance of neurophysiological data has suggested that pitch sensation may also involve coding that uses the temporal patterns of discharge in nerve cells as the information signifying the sound frequency. In this way single neurons may be able to convey frequency information over a broad range. In these experiments the measurement of temporal pattern is usually the distribution of the intervals between the nerve impulses elicited by a stimulus. A neuron can be said to code the frequency of the sound if this distribution is either the same as the interval between successive cycles of the sound or some integral multiple of it. The sequence of possible discharge is displayed in Figure 7-20. This kind of coding is quite prominent at frequencies below about 1500 Hz, although it has also been noted up to 4000 Hz. It would seem, then, that the frequency properties of a sound can be coded in the auditory pathway in terms of both (1) the distribution of excitation

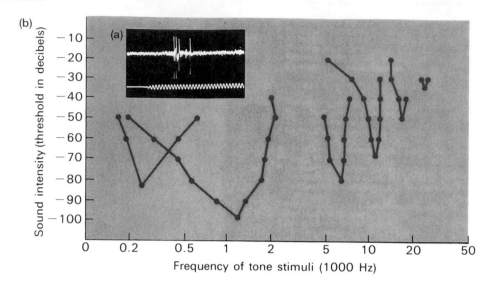

Figure 7-19 Example of tuning curves of auditory system nerve cells and how they are obtained. The curves are obtained by measuring neural responses (shown in inset, Leiman) to sounds of different intensities and frequencies. These curves are threshold measurements. The graph illustrates six neural units recorded from the auditory nerve. (From Kiang, 1965)

among cells—that is, place coding—and (2) the temporal pattern of discharge in cells extending from the auditory nerve to the auditory cortex.

Localization of sound

Under the best of conditions a person can locate the position of a sound source with an accuracy of about one degree. This ability depends on the interaction between the two ears, although under some circumstances monaural detection of acoustic sources is almost as good as binaural. (Monaural localization is possible when sounds are of long duration and the head is free to move.) What stimulus features are important for binaural analysis of auditory localization?

The cues for auditory localization used by a binaural processing system are the differences between the two ears in (1) sound intensity and (2) time of arrival. More complex differences also count, such as the frequency spectrum. Which of these interaural cues is most important in any circumstance depends on the properties of the sound and the acoustic environment (for example, sound reflection). Interaural intensity differences arise for some sounds when they are not in the median plane of the body, since the head casts a sound shadow. The sound frequencies that are effectively blocked depend on the size of the head, since long waves of low-frequency sounds get around the head. These effects are illustrated in Figure 7-21. At low frequencies, no matter where sounds are presented in the horizontal plane, there are virtually no intensity differences between the ears. For these frequencies time differences are the principal cues for sound position. At higher frequencies the

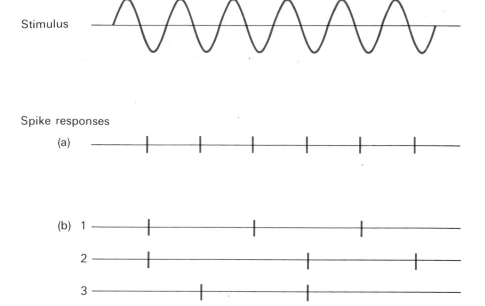

Stimulus

Spike responses

(a)

(b) 1

2

3

1 + 2 + 3

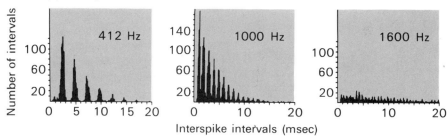

Figure 7-20 Temporal coding in the auditory system. Frequency coding in auditory neurons. (a) Some neural units can follow the stimulus frequency precisely, firing an impulse at each cycle of a stimulus, particularly if the frequency is rather low. (b) Some units are not able to fire on each cycle, but an ensemble of these cells gives one or more impulses for each cycle. (c)-(e) When the activity of a cell is recorded during prolonged stimulation, the interval between successive responses shows the cell's ability to follow the stimulus. (c) At a relatively low stimulus frequency, the most probable interresponse interval equals the period of the stimulus (e.g., for a 400-Hz tone, 2.5 msec). Longer intervals (e.g., 5.0, 7.5, and 10.0 msec) occur occasionally but the longer the interresponse interval, the less often it occurs. (d) For a higher frequency, the neuron is about equally apt to respond every second, third, or fourth cycle, as shown by the distributions of rather similar histograms over a wide range of periods. (c-e from Lavine, 1971).

Figure 7-21 Cues for binaural hearing. The two ears receive somewhat different information from sound sources located to one side or the other of the observer's midline. The head blocks some frequencies (greater than 1000 Hz), producing binaural differences in sound intensity. Also, sounds take longer to reach the more distant ear, resulting in binaural differences in time of arrival.

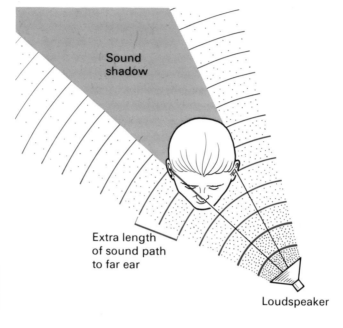

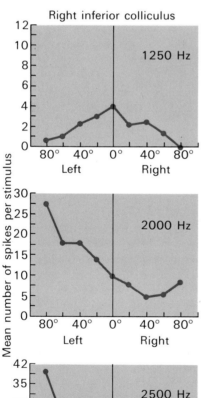

sound shadow cast by the cat's head produces significant interaural intensity differences. Human listeners cannot tell by monitoring their own performance that they are using one cue to localize high-frequency sounds and another cue to localize low-frequency sounds. In general we are aware of the results of neural processing but not of the processing itself.

How are the binaural features of an acoustic environment analyzed by the nervous system? There are many opportunities for binaural interaction at various levels of the brainstem. Thus single nerve cells can receive inputs derived from both ears. The lowest level at which interaural effects occur is the superior olivary complex; below this level of the auditory system interaural effects cannot occur. Several investigators have shown that cells within the superior olivary region are particularly sensitive to interaural differences of time or intensity. The inferior colliculus receives inputs from several brainstem nuclei with binaural inputs, so investigators have closely examined the binaural properties of neurons in this region. Are there neurons at the inferior colliculus that respond to some sound positions but not others? Different answers have been obtained for different species.

In a search for indications of feature detectors particularly sensitive to acoustic space, data were obtained from single-cell recordings in the inferior colliculus of the cat (Figure 7-22). The animal was placed at the exact center of a group of speakers arranged in a semicircle. The graphs plot the number of action potentials elicited as

Figure 7-22 Mean number of nerve impulses of inferior colliculus neurons when sound was presented at various positions in horizontal plane. Speakers were positioned at angles ranging from left 80° to right 80° in 20° steps. The frequency of the sound is indicated within each graph. Each stimulus lasted for 200 msec. (From Leiman and Hafter, 1972)

a function of sound position. These plots show that the strongest effects are exerted by contralateral sounds. However, there is little evidence for quite precise feature detectors abstracting little pieces of acoustic space. One might conclude either that the detection of acoustic position is the product of the summation of many cells active in particular spatial and temporal patterns or that feature detection relevant to auditory localization is a process at some higher level (Leiman and Hafter, 1972). Recent analysis of cortical neurons in the cat has also failed to reveal feature detectors for auditory space (Middlebrook and Pettigrew, 1981).

On the other hand, for the owl—whose livelihood depends on accurate auditory localization—detailed and elaborate neural representations of auditory space have been found. In the avian equivalent to the inferior colliculus, some of the cells are arranged rather like a spherical representation of space. That is, each space-specific cell has a receptive field that includes sounds coming from a small cone of space centering on the owl's head. Successive cells in the nucleus represent neighboring regions of auditory space (Knudsen and Konishi, 1979).

In the optic tectum of the owl, auditory and visual space are both represented, and the maps for the two senses correspond closely (Knudsen, 1981). Most cells in this region respond to both auditory and visual stimuli, and all of the auditory cells respond specifically to spatial direction. In most cases the visual receptive field of a cell is enclosed within the auditory receptive field of the same cell. Perhaps this close alignment of auditory and visual maps of space provides signals for motor responses with regard to the position of the stimulus. A further stage of this research will be to stimulate points in the optic tectum and observe effects on motor responses.

Deafness and its rehabilitation

Health surveys have indicated that at least 5 to 10 million people in the United States have some form of disabling hearing impairment. These disabilities range in severity from occasional difficulties in speech perception (41–55-dB drop in sensitivity between 500 and 2000 Hz) to a complete inability to hear anything (91-dB drop between 500 and 2000 Hz). Many of these hearing impairments arise quite early in life, and current estimates indicate that there are about 100,000 children in the United States with a major hearing handicap.

● **Types of hearing disorder**   Hearing disorders are generally classified on the basis of the site of pathological changes. The principal classes are these:

1. **Conductive deafness,** which refers to hearing impairments associated with pathology of the external or middle ear cavities.
2. **Sensorineural deafness,** which refers to hearing impairments originating from cochlear or auditory nerve lesions.
3. **Central deafness,** which refers to hearing impairments related to lesions in auditory pathways or centers including sites in the brainstem, thalamus, or cortex.

Conductive deafness involves an interference with the mechanical linkages leading to the excitation of the cochlea. This kind of deafness can result from as simple a cause as ear wax to more complex conditions like infections and changes in the

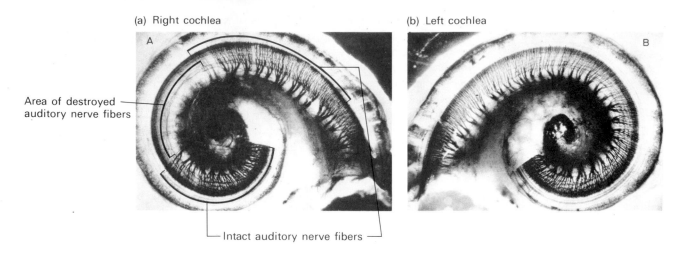

(a) Right cochlea   (b) Left cochlea

Area of destroyed auditory nerve fibers

Intact auditory nerve fibers

Figure 7-23 Right (a) and left (b) cochleas of a person who died at age 71 after long-term exposure to intense noise. The right cochlea shows marked degeneration of auditory nerve fibers. This view is obtained after removal of overlying temporal bone. (From Bredberg, 1968)

middle ear bones that prevent their easy movement. In all instances of disturbed middle ear function, the loss of sensitivity extends across all frequencies, although there is a tendency for slightly greater involvement of higher frequencies.

Sensorineural deafness involves a wide range of causal conditions, including intense noise, drugs, infection, diseases, temporal bone trauma, vascular disorders, aging, and an extensive group of hereditary hearing disorders. In all these conditions hearing impairment is observed with both air and bone conduction.

Drug-induced deafness comes particularly from the toxic properties of a group of antibiotics that includes Streptomycin, Kanomycin, and Gentamicin. The ototoxic (ear-damaging) properties of these substances were first discovered in the treatment of tuberculosis by using Streptomycin. Although this antibiotic was remarkably effective in the treatment of the disease, it became evident soon after its introduction that there was a tremendous price to pay for this cure—many patients showed severe cochlear and/or vestibular damage. In some patients Streptomycin produced total, irreversible loss of hearing. This antibiotic and several related ones produced dramatic hearing impairment by the virtually complete destruction of hair cells in the cochlea. Generally the highest frequencies are first affected. This result conforms to the histological observations of the progression of destruction; that is, the first signs of change are noted in the basal cochlear region. The endings of the auditory nerve near the hair cells remain viable.

Noise-induced hearing impairments primarily involve inner ear mechanisms. Interest in environmental issues of noise pollution and the advent of rock music have made this problem prominent and have also furnished much business to audiologists and otologists. Acoustic damage to the cochlea can be produced by exposure to either intense sudden sounds or chronic high-level sounds. The initial histological changes seen in the inner ear primarily involve hair cells, the outer hair cells being more susceptible to sound trauma than are inner hair cells (Figure 7-23). The progression of changes with continued sound exposure can in some individuals lead to a total absence of the organ of Corti. In time the initial locus of involvement in the cochlea spreads, even without additional acoustic trauma. It should be emphasized that such pathology is primarily a consequence of intense acoustic trauma—for instance, sound greater than 120 dB, such as occurs close to a jet engine.

Central deafness can occur as a result of strokes or other trauma to the brain. This is a rare cause of deafness, because the auditory tracts are bilateral and it is unusual for both sides of the brain to be impaired.

Cross-cultural comparisons of changes in hearing acuity with age have raised some interesting possibilities for the role of diet in hearing impairment. Rosen and colleagues (1970) have compared audiograms from people in different parts of the world and suggest that the evidence implicates cholesterol in the common impairment of hearing with aging noted in many industrialized nations. Minimal hearing changes occur with aging in the Mabams who live in the Sudan and have a diet virtually free of saturated fats. This result is markedly different from the aging effects observed for United States populations.

● **New treatments for some forms of deafness**   An unusual form of therapy for hearing loss has been demonstrated in a few people whose deafness is related to marked hair cell loss, usually as a consequence of substances that are toxic to the inner ear (Michelson, 1978; Bilger and Hopkinson, 1977). Since many such people have intact auditory nerves, several researchers have suggested that electrical stimulation of the auditory nerve might substitute for sound-induced excitation of these fibers. In the optimal case the stimulator would be controlled by a microphone, and the sound sensations provoked by the electrical stimulation might enable speech recognition. (This situation is analogous to the use of electrical stimulation of visual centers to replace the eyes, mentioned earlier in this chapter.)

Several different types of cochlear implants have been employed by various research groups. A comprehensive assessment of prospects for this heroic technique has been presented by Bilger and Hopkinson (1977). They noted that multiple-electrode implants in humans have had minimal success thus far. Sound sensations can be elicited by these devices, but they are limited both in frequency capabilities and in a narrow dynamic range for intensity, at least in comparison with normal hearing. After all, putting a few channels into the cochlea could hardly be expected to replace the complex mechanism of the organ of Corti. Although speech recognition has not been achieved with these devices, there is evidence that this input, coupled with lip reading, enhances speech recognition. In addition, for many patients it provides the detection of surrounding sound, which is sorely missed by those who become deaf after childhood. For these individuals it reopens a world that hearing humans take for granted but is so critical for orientation to one's surroundings.

Vestibular information processing   When your head moves as you read this page, your eyes remain fixed on the words and you don't experience blur. This would not be the case if the page moved instead of your head. Information processing in the vestibular system allows you to make compensatory movements of eyes, head, and body to counteract a variety of mechanical forces. These adjustments are usually so automatic that we are not aware of this kind of sensory stimulation.

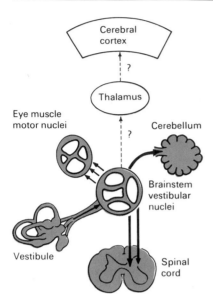

Figure 7-24 Main pathways of the vestibular system.

The structural arrangements of brain pathways dealing with vestibular excitation reflect this close connection to various muscle adjustments in the body. Nerve fibers from the vestibular receptors of the the inner ear enter lower levels of the brainstem and synapse in a group of nuclei, the vestibular nuclei (Figure 7-24). Some of the fibers bypass this structure and go directly to the cerebellum, a center for motor control. The outputs of the vestibular nuclei are quite complex, as is appropriate to their influences on the motor system.

There is one aspect of vestibular activation that many of us would prefer didn't exist. Certain types of body acceleration—such as those we experience as a passenger in an oceangoing boat, an airplane, a car, or an amusement park ride—can produce distress known as motion sickness. This same effect can be produced by "caloric stimulation," which consists of pouring warm water in one ear canal; this sets up movements of inner ear fluids, simulating mechanical stimulation. Motion sickness is produced especially by low-frequency movements that an individual cannot control. For example, passengers in a car suffer from motion sickness, but the driver does not. The biological significance of vestibular elicitation of motion sickness remains a mystery—an apparent flaw in an otherwise elegantly engineered system. People whose vestibular system has been destroyed by toxic drugs, or by side effects of some antibiotics, do not experience motion sickness.

Somatosensory information processing

From a delicate touch to unbearable pain, the skin provides a variety of sensory experiences. Embryologically, the ectoderm is the origin not only of the skin but also of most sensory receptors. Some of these have evolved into specialized receptor organs, such as the ear and the olfactory epithelium, but the skin is studded with a variety of receptors for touch, temperature, and pain. In this section we will see where information from the skin is sent and how it is processed. Special emphasis will be devoted to pain, on which much recent research has been focused.

Somatosensory pathways of the brain

Inputs from most skin surfaces are directed to the spinal cord. Within the cord, as shown in Figure 7-25(b), somesthetic fibers ascend to the brain in at least two major pathways: (1) the dorsal column system shown to the right in Figure 7-25(b), and (2) the anterolateral system (also referred to as spinothalamic). Inputs to the dorsal column system enter the spinal cord and ascend to the medulla, where they synapse at the gracile and cuneate nuclei. The axons of postsynaptic cells form a fiber bundle that crosses in the brainstem to the contralateral side and ascends to a group of nuclei of the thalamus. Outputs of the thalamus are directed to postcentral cortical regions referred to as the somatosensory cortex. The anterolateral or spinothalamic system has a different arrangement. Inputs to this system from the skin synapse on cells in

Figure 7-25 The somesthetic system. (a) General view of the system including ascending spinal tracts, thalamic relay, and primary cortical representation. The spinal tracts are seen in greater detail in (b), including crossed and uncrossed spinal pathways. All afferent messages cross before reaching the thalamus. The varieties of skin receptors are shown in (c). Bands of skin, or dermatomes, are served by different spinal nerves, as seen in (d). The main pathways are diagrammed in (e).

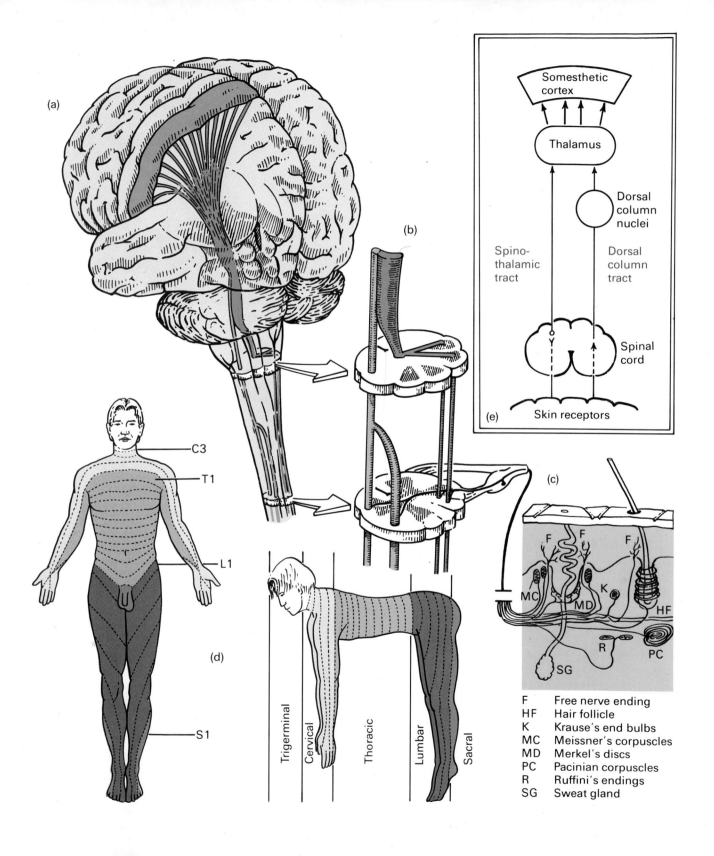

(a)

(b)

(e)

Somesthetic cortex

Thalamus

Dorsal column nuclei

Spino-thalamic tract

Dorsal column tract

Spinal cord

Skin receptors

(c)

C3

T1

L1

(d)

S1

Trigerminal

Cervical

Thoracic

Lumbar

Sacral

F   Free nerve ending
HF   Hair follicle
K   Krause's end bulbs
MC   Meissner's corpuscles
MD   Merkel's discs
PC   Pacinian corpuscles
R   Ruffini's endings
SG   Sweat gland

the spinal cord, whose axons cross to the contralateral side of the spinal cord and ascend in the anterolateral columns of the spinal cord. At least some of the input to this system is related to pain and temperature sensations.

The skin surface can be divided into bands, or **dermatomes**, according to which spinal nerve carries most axons from each region (Figure 7-25d). The pattern of dermatomes is hard to understand when seen for a standing person, but the pattern becomes comprehensible when depicted on a person in a quadrupedal posture, as shown at the bottom of Figure 7-25.

All brain regions concerned with somatic sensation have their cells arranged according to the plan of the body surface. Thus each region is a map of the body in which the relative areas devoted to bodily regions reflect the density of body innervations. Since many fibers are involved with the sensory surface of the head, especially the lips, there is a disproportionate number of cells concerned with the head; in contrast, far fewer fibers innervate the trunk, and the number of cells involved with the representation of the trunk are far fewer. The relative sizes of the cortical representations are shown in the grotesque sensory homunculus in Figure 7-26.

Tactile intensity   At what level in the system is the function determined that sets the relation between stimulus intensity and sensory intensity? In the case of touch the form of the function appears to be determined right at the level of the receptors in the skin. Mountcastle (1974) concluded this from comparing results of two sorts of experiments: (1) experiments with monkeys, where he recorded the rate of nerve impulses as a function of the strength of stimulation of the skin, and (2) experiments with human subjects who rated sensory intensity when the same stimuli were applied to their skin. When stimuli were applied to the smooth, hairless skin of the fingertips or palm, the rate of nerve impulses rose linearly with the depth of indentation of the stimulus into the skin. The same relation was found when the recording was done from neurons in the basolateral thalamus or from cortical cells in the postcentral gyrus (somatosensory cortex). The central recordings were made with indwelling electrodes in awake monkeys. When human observers rated the strength of the same stimuli, their judgments also showed a linear function.

The touch receptors in hairy regions of skin show a different relation. For peripheral nerve fibers the response was found to be related to stimulus intensity by a power function with an exponent of about 0.5. At the thalamus, too, the response to stimulation of a single tactile organ in the hairy skin gave a power function with an exponent of about 0.5. Human judgments for pressure on hairy skin followed a similar power function. (The linear function noted above for hairless skin is equivalent to a power function with an exponent of 1.0.) Thus it appears that the two sets of responses (exponent 1.0 for smooth skin and exponent 0.5 for hairy skin) are determined by the receptors; the rest of the system simply repeats what the receptor set in motion.

Pain   Most people would agree that pain is an experience characterized by unpleasantness, suffering, and even debility. It then seems hard to imagine the "biological role" of pain. Is it some perverse revenge of evolutionary gnomes?

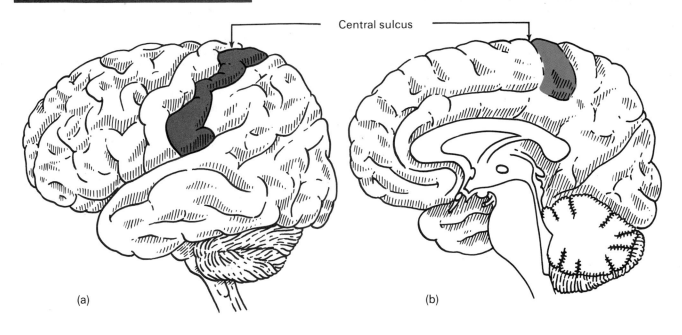

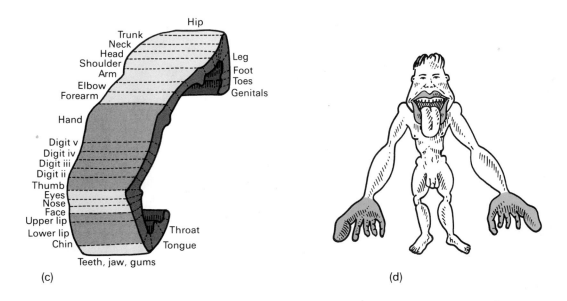

Figure 7-26 Representation of the body surface in the primary somatosensory cortex. Location of the primary somatosensory cortex on the lateral surface (a) and on the medial surface (b) of the human brain. The order and size of representations of different regions of skin are shown in (c). The homunculus (d) depicts the body surface with each area drawn in proportion to the size of its representation in the primary somatosensory cortex.

Clues to the adaptive significance of pain can be gleaned from the study of rare individuals who do not experience pain. These persons have a congenital insensitivity or indifference to pain, a condition frequently evident in several members of the same family. Case descriptions of these individuals note that their bodies show extensive scarring from numerous injuries (e.g., Manfredi et al., 1981). Deformation of fingers, hands, and legs is common. Most of these people die young, frequently from extreme trauma to body tissues. These cases suggest that pain guides adaptive behavior by providing indications of harm. Such experiences may be so commonplace that we easily forget the guiding role of pain: The experience of pain leads to behavior that removes the body from a source of injury.

● **What is pain?**   Pain is the response to noxious stimuli, those that produce tissue damage or pose the threat of damage. Receptors that respond to these stimuli are called **nociceptors,** and activation of these receptors is necessary for pain perception. This activity is not sufficient for pain experience, since pain is something more than a sensory event. Especially important to pain experience is the context; pain is strongly dependent on emotional arousal. Some models of pain experience emphasize that the integration of sensory events with emotional arousal yields pain experience (Melzack and Casey, 1968; Melzack, 1980).

● **Peripheral mechanisms of pain**   Investigators have differed about whether pain involves specialized receptors and distinct pathways. Free nerve endings are the usual form of receptor; of course, this kind of receptor provides information about other tactile events, so it cannot be regarded as a pain specialist. Pain signals travel in two groups of nerve fibers distinguished by size: (1) small unmyelinated fibers and (2) a faster-conducting, finely myelinated group of fibers. Close scrutiny shows that some forms of pain experience seem to be related to this separation into two classes of peripheral fibers carrying pain signals.

Many studies show that the pain experience has two distinct qualities. One is pain that can be described as "bright" or "pricking," like that evoked by a needle jab. This pain experience (called "first pain") is accurately localized and usually subsides quickly. The other is pain that can be described as "burning." This experience has a slower onset, is less well localized, and lasts longer than "first pain."

In humans, peripheral nerve destruction is evident in chronic alcoholism (perhaps related to thiamine deficiency) and nicotine poisoning. These neuropathies (peripheral nerve destruction) affect mainly myelinated fibers. Burning pain is the principal form of pain that can be evoked in such patients. This observation suggests that pricking pain is absent in these patients because of the destruction of the relevant set of peripheral nerve fibers.

Experiments add support for these clinical observations. Direct electrical stimulation of human skin nerves is easily accomplished by metal electrodes attached to the skin. Careful regulation of current delivered to these electrodes enables separate stimulation of fibers according to size. More specifically, the largest-diameter fibers have the lowest thresholds to electrical stimulation. At the lowest levels of stimulation humans consistently report a sense of "touch" at some discrete spot. As the current level is raised, subjects say they experience sharp pricking pain. At higher current levels this experience becomes one of intense burning pain. Other experiments using techniques that reversibly block nerve fibers by pressure on blood vessels show similar results. Blockage of larger-diameter fibers stops report of the dual quality of pain, leaving only burning pain as the experience.

Some clinical observations remind us, however, that pain is more elaborate than selective activation of two classes of fibers. By far the most enigmatic data emerge from the study of **phantom limb** phenomena. In some cases amputees report extreme pain in a limb that no longer exists, and this legacy of pain may persist for years. About 5 to 10% of amputees report pain in phantom limbs. Obviously in this case pain is not related to excitation of specialized receptors or pathways. This result poses a difficult problem for the explanatory powers of the specificity theory.

● **Central modulation of pain**   Some rare human beings with intact sensory systems can expose themselves to horrendous forms of threatening stimuli without the slightest evidence of pain. Imagine sleeping on a bed of nails or walking with a broken limb! There are many examples like these that suggest that the direct or intrinsic mechanisms of pain are subject to powerful modulatory or extrinsic influences in the brain and spinal cord. According to Melzack (1973), within the spinal cord there are "gates" that control the transmission of pain information from the spinal cord to the brain. One form of such pain modulation involves influences descending from the brain in pathways that use endorphins. Various forms of modulation of pain pathways have had significant impact on the development of pain relief therapy (Fields, 1981).

● **Relief from pain**   A major focus of current pain research deals with strategies for relieving pain. Of course, people have always sought pain relief with an extraordinary array of substances. Most recently, the helter-skelter strategy of drug firms seeking the definitive potion has been replaced by a systematic pharmacological effort based on the discovery of natural opiatelike brain substances. As mentioned in Chapter 4, studies on the neural actions of morphine showed that there are select places in the brain where morphine accumulates, especially in brainstem areas. Electrical stimulation of these areas produces insensitivity to experimentally induced pain in rats (Liebskind and Mayer, 1976). Dramatic studies in humans have recently shown potential applications of this work. Hosubuchi and collaborators (1977) implanted electrodes in brainstem regions—the periaqueductal gray area—where research using rodents had shown stimulation-induced pain blockades. Six patients suffering severe pain were stimulated, and they reported dramatic pain relief, often outlasting the stimulation for several hours. Frequent use of the stimulator to produce pain relief (self-administered by patients) resulted in tolerance—that is, it raised the threshold. After several days of rest electrical stimulation was once again effective in relieving pain. Naloxone, which blocks opiates, also blocks analgesia induced by electrical stimulation of brainstem sites in rats and humans.

Are endorphins normally released to suppress pain? (The discovery of the endorphins—"the body's own morphine"—was described in Chapter 4.) Several lines of evidence suggest that the endorphins play a part in suppression of pain, but there is also contradictory evidence. Let us review some recent findings in this rapidly advancing area.

It has been reported that the concentration of endorphins in human cerebrospinal fluid is lower than normal in people who suffer from chronic pain (Akil et al., 1978). Various kinds of analgesic treatments have been reported to raise the level of endorphins; these include stimulation of the periaqueductal gray matter with implanted electrodes (Hosobuchi et al., 1979) and peripheral stimulation with acupuncture needles. Naloxone not only blocks such stimulation-induced analgesia but it also appears to block **placebo** analgesia (Levine et al., 1979). Placebos are substances with no pharmacological properties; they either are used as control treatments in experiments or are prescribed by physicians to patients who insist on receiving some kind of medication. (The word "placebo" comes from the Latin for "I please.") In about one-third of the people placebos give relief from pain, and in these people the analgesia is terminated by administering naloxone. So it appears that simply receiving a neutral substance labeled as medication leads to release of endorphins and to analgesia in many people.

In another recent study foot shock was found to cause profound analgesia in rats, but either an endorphin mechanism or a nonendorphin mechanism was involved, depending on the temporal characteristics of the shocks (Lewis, Cannon, and Liebeskind, 1980). Pain thresholds were measured by the "tail-flick" technique that is often used in pain research: A hot light is focused on the rat's tail, and the number of seconds until the rat flicks its tail aside is recorded. Strong analgesia was produced by either prolonged, intermittent foot shock (1-sec pulses delivered every 5 sec for 30 min) or continuous foot shock administered for 3 min. Naloxone countered the effects of the prolonged, intermittent foot shock but not those of the brief, continuous shock. Apparently, then, the former kind of stimulation caused release of endorphins, whereas the latter did not. The mechanism of the nonendorphin analgesia is not known, but the results indicate that not all suppression of pain can be attributed to endorphin transmitter circuits. It should also be remembered that the endorphins act as transmitters in other neural circuits besides those involved in pain. Research in this area is flooding in, so new results will be changing the picture rapidly.

Localization on the body surface

The surface of the body is represented at each level of the somatosensory nervous system by an organization of nerve cells that provides a spatial map of the body surface. The first stage of this map of body position is seen in the organization of individual **dermatomes** at a spinal level. (A dermatome is a strip of skin innervated by a particular spinal root; see Figure 7-25.) Although individual dermatomes overlap to some extent, there is an orderly arrangement along the length of the spinal cord. At various levels of the brain the surface of the body is again represented by an orderly map of nerve cells. Thus the sensory topography of relevant thalamic cells and cortical areas preserves body topography.

As in other sensory systems, the brain maps of the body surface show much fuller representation of some parts than of others (Figure 7-26). The largest representations are given to parts such as the fingertips and the lips, where spatial discrimination of touch is especially fine and precise.

The extreme detail of somatosensory system mapping of certain body surfaces is shown in work on "cortical barrels" in rodents (Woolsey et al., 1976, 1981).

Sections of rat somatosensory cortex obtained by slicing the cortex in a plane tangential to the surface reveal some unusual groupings of cells in circular patterns. Successive sections of tissue in this plane suggested an analogy to the sides of a barrel, so these groupings were named cortical barrels. The wall of the barrel consists of tightly packed cell bodies surrounding a less dense area.

Electrical recordings of cells in a barrel revealed the startling fact that each barrel is activated by one whisker on the opposite side of the head. Further, the layout of whiskers on the face of the animal (Figure 3-22) corresponds to the layout of barrels in the cortex. (Whiskers are important to rodents in finding their way through narrow passages in the dark. In Chapter 3 we noted the importance of intact facial whiskers on the development or maintenance of cortical barrels. Rats whose whiskers were removed early in life did not form cortical barrels.)

Somatosensory perception of form

The functions of the somatosensory cortex in discriminating forms have been studied in monkeys both by observing effects of lesions in this region and by recording from individual neurons while the monkeys' hands were stimulated. Lesions impaired the ability of the animal to discriminate the form, size, and roughness/smoothness of tactile objects (Orbach and Chow, 1959). Separate lesions were later made in three anatomically distinct parts of somatosensory region I. Lesions in area 1 affected mainly the discrimination of texture; lesions in area 2 impaired mainly the discrimination of angles; and lesions in area 3 affected all forms of tactile discrimination (Randolf and Semmes, 1974).

Spatial gratings have been used to investigate mechanisms of touch (Darian-Smith et al., 1980), somewhat as gratings have been used to study vision. In this research, metal strips of varied widths and spacing were moved at different rates of speed under the fingertips of monkeys while recordings were made from sensory nerves. No single fiber could give an accurate record of each ridge and depression in the stimulus. But the ensemble of fibers provided an accurate representation, especially at optimal spacings and speed of presentation of the stimulus. Spatial discrimination of more complex stimuli is being studied in a similar way, using stimuli such as braille dots or other small forms.

Cells in the somatosensory cortex can be classified into several categories according to the characteristics of their receptive fields (Iwamura and Tanaka, 1978). About one-quarter of the cells responded to simple pressure stimulation of points on the skin. Another quarter responded best to specialized stimulation of the skin (for example, by a moving probe or by a narrow band or rod). Another quarter of the cells could be activated either by stimulation of the skin or by movement of one or more finger joints. About one-eighth of the cells responded specifically to manipulation of joints. The remainder of the cells could not be activated when the experimenter stimulated either skin or joints, but some of these cells responded strongly when the animal grasped an object and manipulated it.

Some of these "active touch" cells had highly specific response characteristics. For example, one unit responded actively when the monkey felt a straight-edged ruler or a small rectangular block, but it did not respond when the monkey grasped a ball or bottle; the presence of two parallel edges appeared to be crucial for effective activation of this cell. In the same electrode penetration another cell was found that responded best when the monkey grasped a ball, responded well to a bottle, but did not respond at all when the monkey manipulated a rectangular block. Grasping objects causes complex patterns of stimulation of skin receptors and joint receptors. This information about cutaneous and joint stimulation must reach many cortical units. Apparently different cells require particular combinations of input if they are to respond. These units with complex receptive fields in the somatosensory cortex are somewhat like units with complex visual or auditory receptive fields. These complex somatosensory units may be involved in discrimination and recognition of objects by touch, but more research will be required to learn how they function in somatosensory perception.

In human observers, the posterior part of the parietal cortex is activated during exploration of objects by touch (Roland and Larsen, 1976). This was found by recording blood flow in the cortex under three conditions:

1. The experimenter moved the passive hand of the observer over the stimulus object.

2. The person moved his hand energetically but did not touch an object.

3. The person explored an object by touch.

Only in the last of these conditions was there specific activation of the posterior parietal cortex, so this region may be particularly involved in active touch.

Olfactory information processing

The outputs of the olfactory bulb enter in the olfactory tract and are delivered to many subcortical regions, especially those that comprise portions of the limbic system (see Chapter 2). The cortical regions with synaptic inputs from the olfactory tract are mainly on the basolateral surface of the cortex (Figure 7-27). This region is phylogenetically older cortex, in contrast to the newer cortical surfaces of the dorsal and most lateral regions of the cerebral neocortex.

Recent anatomical and physiological studies of the peripheral portions of the olfactory system—the olfactory mucosa of the nose and the olfactory bulb—show a sort of topography in responses to particular odors (Moulton, 1976). Particular odorants might be absorbed at particular cells at the earliest stage of processing in the nose. This localized process could result in a map of odors, and perhaps throughout the olfactory pathways distinct places might be related to particular odors. Part of the difficulty in pursuing such ideas is that chemical senses like olfaction involve problems in classifying stimuli. In vision we know that wavelength is related to perceived color; in audition sound frequency is related to pitch. But for the chemical senses we have yet to develop an appropriate scale of the physical stimuli that is relevant to functional distinctions like quality of perceived odor. Simple features of chemical structure like variations in molecular size and shape, while providing convenient chemical grouping, may have little connection to the ways in which coding and information processing occur in this system. So information-processing studies in olfaction are hampered; we do not have the stimulus yardstick that offers a biologically significant classification.

Despite this limitation, there are some studies using various vaporized chemicals that reveal cells at all levels of the olfactory system that are "specialists," responding to only one or a few odors. However, the vast number of cells studied at various sites

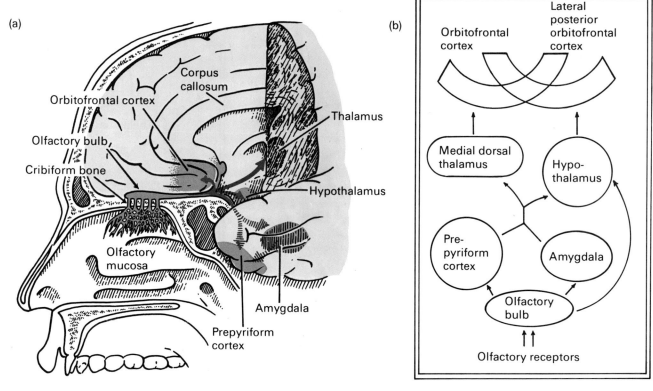

Figure 7-27 (a) Anatomy of the olfactory system, and (b) a diagram of the main olfactory pathways in the brain.

in the brain that receive connections from the olfactory bulb are "generalists," responding to many different chemicals. Even simpler animals like insects show a similar distinction between specific and general cells. Exploring the olfactory lobe of the cockroach, Yamada (1971) found that few cells responded solely to a single biologically important olfactory stimulus. Most responded slightly differently to a large class of stimuli. He notes that these slight differences in a large number of cells can produce "odor code patterns" that would allow discrimination of many odors. This process, of course, requires integration by a further stage of neural processing.

Gustatory information processing

Information about taste enters the brain through three separate cranial nerves. A portion of the **facial nerve** called the **chorda tympani** serves taste receptors in the anterior two-thirds of the tongue, while the rest of the tongue receptors connect to fibers of the **glossopharyngeal nerve.** The soft palate at the roof of the mouth and the throat includes receptors that connect with fibers in the **vagus nerve** (Figure 7-28).

Many of these diverse gustatory pathways come together in a region of the medulla called the solitary nucleus. Other parts of the central gustatory pathways include taste centers in the pons and thalamus and a cortical taste region near the somatosensory representation of the tongue.

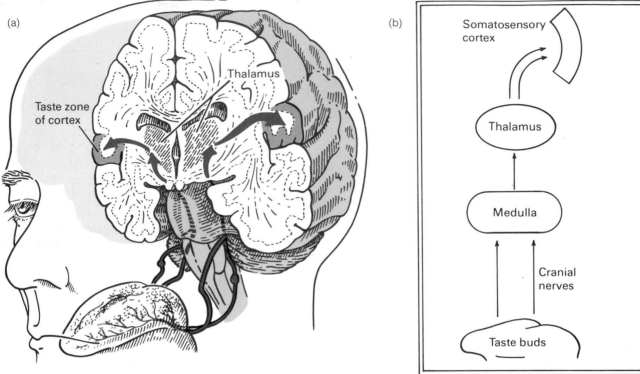

Figure 7-28 (a) Anatomy of the gustatory system, and (b) a diagram of the main gustatory pathways in the brain.

Investigation of taste processing has lagged behind that of other sensory systems partly because of the relative simplicity of taste and also because taste information does not seem vital to human survival. Neurophysiological recordings of cells in taste pathways have mainly concerned coding of the taste qualities of salty, sour, sweet, and bitter stimuli. At each level in the gustatory pathway, are particular cells responsive only to one of these discrete categories? Views on this question fall into two camps. One group of investigators emphasizes a labeled line perspective arguing that each unit serves a single category of taste. A different view emphasizes that taste processing involves patterns of activity in several cells, and the identity of a particular substance is established by the pattern of the major types. This view is called cross-fiber patterning theory (Bartoshuk, 1978).

SUMMARY / MAIN POINTS

1. Sensory systems have a sequence of information processing stages at the successive levels of the brain. There are also parallel pathways that carry out different kinds of analyses of the same sensory information.

2. Color perception depends both upon three kinds of cone cells with different spectral sensitivities and four kinds of color-opponent neurons.

3. Accurate perception of visual direction depends on the detailed maps of visual space at each level of the visual system. These maps have larger representations of the central regions of the visual field, where acuity is greatest.

4. Loss of the visual cortex in a person causes a failure to perceive stimuli; the person can nevertheless detect where a visual stimulus is located, a phenomenon called

"blindsight." This ability appears to depend on the superior colliculus, which can mediate motor performance but not object identification or consciousness.

5. Perception of visual depth depends on the tuning of cortical cells in three categories, one at the fixation plane, one for depths beyond the fixation plane, and one for positions in front of this plane. Recordings from cortical cells in animals show this threefold division. Occasionally humans lack either the far or the near channel.

6. Perception of visual form probably requires first an analysis into basic subunits. Two competing models for this analysis are the feature detector model and the spatial frequency filter model. The spatial frequency approach offers a fuller way of characterizing normal vision, and it provides a quantitative analysis of receptive fields; it also can explain some illusions and perceptual effects.

7. New methods of treating partial or total blindness include training to improve vision around the borders of a blind region, direct electrical stimulation of the visual cortex, and "sensory substitution"—stimulation of an area of skin with an array of tactile stimulators.

8. The frequency of an auditory stimulus is represented neurally by a duplex mechanism; for low frequencies neural impulses are phase-locked to the stimulus (volley theory), whereas higher frequencies are represented by the place of maximal stimulation along the basilar membrane (place theory).

9. Auditory localization depends mainly on differences at the two ears in time of arrival (for low-frequency sounds) and intensity (for high-frequency sounds). Some neurons from the brainstem to the cortex represent these binaural differences accurately.

10. Deafness can be caused by pathological changes at any level of the nervous system. Conductive deafness refers to impairments of the external or middle ear; sensorineural deafness refers to impairments of the cochlea or auditory nerve; and central deafness refers to lesions of brain pathways or centers.

11. Some cases of sensorineural hearing loss have been partially aided by devices that provide direct electrical stimulation of the auditory nerve.

12. The psychophysical functions that relate intensity of stimulation at the skin to intensity of pressure experience differ for hairless and hairy areas of the skin. These differences are determined by the skin receptors, and the higher levels of the tactile system simply repeat this information.

13. Burning pain is conducted by small unmyelinated nerve fibers, whereas pricking pain is conducted by somewhat larger myelinated fibers.

14. Pain can be modulated by central mechanisms; it can exist independently of peripheral stimulation, as in the case of phantom limb pain. Normal relief from pain often involves release of endorphins within the body.

15. Localization on the body surface is represented by maps at different levels of the nervous system. Larger regions of these maps are devoted to parts of the surface where spatial discrimination is especially fine.

16. Recognition of shape in the somatosensory system probably depends on the responses of different cells in the somatosensory cortex to different aspects of stimulation. Some respond to simple pressure on the skin, some to specific tactile stimulation, and some to movement of joints. A small percentage respond only to active touch of specific shapes.

RECOMMENDED READING

Bonica, J. J. (Ed.). *Pain*. Vol. 58 in *Research publications: Association for research in nervous and mental disease*. New York: Raven Press, 1980.

Ludel, J. *Introduction to sensory processes*. San Francisco: W.H. Freeman, 1978.

Schmidt, R. F. *Fundamentals of sensory physiology*. New York: Springer-Verlag, 1978.

Orientation

Behavioral View

Classifying movements and action patterns

Techniques of analyzing movements and acts

Acquiring motor skills

Control Systems View

Neurobiological View

Sensory and motor features of muscles and joints

Monitoring movements: External feedback

Monitoring movements: Internal feedback

Neural control of movements: Spinal mechanisms

Neural control of movements: Brain mechanisms

Brain mechanisms of movement: A conceptual model

Neurobehavioral Analyses of Certain Acts

Eye movements

Speech

Development of Motor Functions

Fetal development and activity

Child motor development

Motor changes with aging

Comparative Views of Movements and Acts

Locomotion

Vocalization

Movement Disorders

Muscle disorders

Neuromuscular disorders

Spinal injuries

Brain mechanisms and movement disorders

New Developments in Treatment of Movement Disorders

An artificial arm controlled by thought

Neural prosthesis

Biofeedback and movement disorders

Summary/Main Points

8

Movements and Actions

Orientation

Our behavior and that of other animals includes a wide range of acts that extend in complexity from finger movements to elaborate athletic feats. Elegance, grace, and complexity describe the leaps of ballet dancers and the flight pattern of an insect (Figure 8-1). But even ordinary everyday movements involve an intricate sequence of muscle activity. Think, for example, of all the muscles involved when you say a single word. The tongue, larynx, throat, lips, chest, and diaphragm must work in a highly coordinated manner to produce even the simplest speech sound. And there is little room for error if what you say is to be understood. The difference between saying "time" and "dime," for example, depends mainly on whether your vocal cords are relaxed or tensed during the start of the word. The initial consonant lasts less than 100 milliseconds (msec), and the vocal cords must be in the correct position during most of that time, so the timing must be accurate to about 10 msec (one-hundredth of a second).

Any coordinated movement implies that there are underlying neural mechanisms that can select appropriate muscles, precisely determine appropriate amounts of excitation and/or inhibition at relevant synapses, and, most importantly, activate motoneurons in the proper order. How are these tasks accomplished? The answers to this question extend from a consideration of specific muscles to a consideration of the complex control systems of the brain. As we will see, research into these control systems is yielding new methods of neurochemical treatment and physical therapy for people who suffer from faulty motor behavior.

(a)

(b)

Figure 8-1 Complex acts: (a) Graceful leap of ballet dancers. (Martha Swope) (b) An insect in flight. (Stephen Dalton FIIP FRPS)

In the next three sections we will consider movements and their coordination from different points of view—the behavioral view, the control systems view, and especially the neurobiological view. Later we will see how the capacity for movement has developed over time, in individuals and in species. We will also consider common impairments in motor behavior in relation to the underlying neural mechanisms.

Behavioral view

Crawling, walking, flying, and swimming are some of the many ways to move from one place to another. Close analysis of the movements and acts of different animals offers some notions about the underlying mechanisms. Observation of the vigorous beating of insect wings suggests that the nervous system of this animal contains a rhythm generator, an oscillator. The varied gaits of four-legged animals suggests that different oscillators are coupled in precise but flexible ways. The great versatility of learned movements in people shows the range of complex adjustments possible in the motor system. To start our discussion, we need ways of classifying movements and action patterns.

Classifying movements and action patterns

Efforts to classify movements began quite early in the study of the biology of movements when a distinction was drawn between the "machinelike" actions of nonhuman animals and the "voluntary" behavior of humans. In the seventeenth century the philosopher Descartes particularly emphasized this distinction, and in the eighteenth and nineteenth centuries it was advanced by discoveries of the basic organizational features of the spinal cord. During this time scientists noted that the dorsal roots of the spinal cord serve sensory functions and that the ventral roots contain motor fibers; sensorimotor connections seemed to provide the basis for simple movements. In the same period experiments with so-called **spinal animals** (animals whose spinal cord has been disconnected from the brain) demonstrated that stimulating the skin could elicit simple, stereotyped limb movements such as withdrawal from painful stimulation.

In the late nineteenth and early twentieth centuries the British physiologist Charles Sherrington reported an extensive series of studies on the behavioral capabilities of spinal animals. From them he argued that the basic units of movement are **reflexes.** He defined a reflex as a simple, highly stereotyped, and unlearned response to a particular stimulus. Sherrington regarded reflexes as "involuntary" acts set off by external stimuli such as pinching the skin or stretching a muscle. The size or magnitude of a reflex was, he showed, directly related to the intensity of the stimulus. His work ushered in an era of intensive attempts to identify the varieties of reflexes and to chart their pathways in the nervous system, particularly in the spinal cord. Some reflexes involve only pathways in the spinal cord linking dorsal and ventral roots, while others involve longer loops connecting spinal cord segments or even brain regions.

Many highly stereotyped responses can be elicited by stimulating skin surfaces, muscles, or joints. We owe many of our basic survival capabilities to the rapid and automatic nature of these responses. Unfortunately, a successful explanation of any concept often breeds presumption. And so it has been in this area. The reflex perspective has appropriately invited criticism when it has tried in a rather simple fashion to explain complex behaviors. For instance, Sherrington thought that the reflex was the basic unit of movement and that all complex acts were simply combinations of simpler reflexes strung out in some temporal order. The strongest criticism of this perspective has been directed toward attempts to analyze complex sequences of behavior, such as speech, in reflex terms. Portraying behaviors like speech in reflex terms has relied heavily on the control exerted by the stimuli that the movement itself produces, that is, by sensory feedback. For example, reflex explanations of speech emphasize that the movements and sounds associated with each element of speech provide the stimuli that instigate the next element. If this were true, speech would be a series of stimulus-response units chained together, each response triggering off the next unit.

But, on the contrary, it appears that the speaker has a plan in which several units (speech sounds) are placed in a larger pattern. Sometimes the units get misplaced, although the pattern is preserved: "Our queer old dean," said English clergyman William Spooner, when he meant, "Our dear old Queen." In fact, Spooner was so prone to mix up the order of words or sounds in his sentences that this type of error is called a spoonerism.

Recent investigators have shown that many complex sequences of behavior are determined by an internal plan without guidance from sensory feedback. Many acts occur so rapidly that sensory consequences cannot be fed back quickly enough to control the ongoing movements. One frequently cited example is the playing of a rapid sequence of notes on a piano; the whole sequence runs off without immediate feedback control. If the sequence is not correct, it cannot be altered in progress but must be repeated. Other examples include certain eye movements (to be discussed below) and rapid, alternating movements of the arm or leg. Furthermore, many rapid movements of invertebrates are preplanned; these include a wide repertoire of escape behaviors and insect flight mechanisms. These behaviors are distinguishable from

TABLE 8-1   A Classification of Movements

I. **Simple reflex**

Stretch	Startle
Sneezing	Pupillary contraction
Eye blink	Flexion
Knee jerk	Coughing

II. **Posture and postural changes**

Standing	Rearing
Lying	Balancing
Sitting	Urination posture

III. **Locomotion**

Walking	Creeping
Running	Crawling
Swimming	Stalking
Flying	Hopping

IV. **Sensory orientation**

Head turning	Touching
Eye fixation	Sniffing
Ear movement	Tasting

V. **Species-typical action patterns**

Ingestion: Tasting, chewing, biting, sipping, drinking
Elimination: Urination, defecation
Courtship: Display, sniffing, chasing, retreating
Copulation: Mounting, intromission, ejaculation, orgasm
Maternal: Nursing, holding, retrieving
Attack: Stalking, chasing, scratching, biting, grasping
Escape and defense: Hissing, spitting, submission posture, cowering
Grooming: Washing, preening, licking
Nest construction: Burrowing, carrying materials, arranging, weaving
Gestures: Grimacing, tail erection, squinting, tooth baring, smiling
Play behavior: Chasing, teasing, wrestling

VI. **Acquired skills**

Speech	Dressing	Sculpturing	Sports
Tool using	Painting	Auto driving	Dancing

reflexes in that input simply triggers a preexisting pattern whose magnitude is unrelated to stimulus intensity. In contrast, reflex amplitude is highly related to stimulus intensity. The existence of behaviors that are triggered and preformed offers a major challenge to the view that the reflex is the invariant basic unit of behavior and that more elaborate action patterns of any organism are simply structures built from elemental reflexes.

Ethologists have called the complex species-specific responses **fixed-action patterns.** Actually there is considerable variation in the timing and form of these response sequences, both between two individuals and within the same individual at different times. For this reason Barlow (1977) has suggested that the term **modal-action pattern** is preferable; this term implies that a typical pattern of behavior is being described, but it allows for individual variation.

An example of a movement classification scheme generated from an ethological perspective is shown in Table 8-1. This scheme focuses on the functional properties of acts rather than on their exact muscle relations. A major characteristic of many movements is that they are rhythmic—there is an orderly repetition of movements and of muscle contractions. This feature is true in locomotion, breathing, chewing, scratching, the beating of the heart, and the peristaltic movements of the intestines. How patterns of rhythmic movements are programmed and modulated will be taken up in a later section.

Table 8-1 can also be used to make a distinction between movements and acts. The upper part of the table, simple reflexes, includes brief, unitary activities of muscle that we commonly call movements. These events are discrete, in many cases limited to a single part of the body, such as a limb. The lower parts of the table list complex, sequential behaviors, frequently oriented toward a goal. Different movements of several bodily parts might be included in such behavior. This more complex event we distinguish as an act or action pattern.

Techniques of analyzing movements and acts

Bewildering variety and complexity confront the researcher who seeks to define, describe, and quantify movements and acts. Global descriptions are readily available with motion pictures, though, and high-speed photography provides an intimate portrait of even the most rapid events.

Excessive data are furnished by high-speed photography, so methods of simplification or numerical analysis have been devised. Photographic techniques that reduce the total amount of data—such as long-duration exposure or multiple exposures—have offered startling portraits of human movement. In a study of human movements using a multiple-exposure technique, subjects wore a black suit with white stripes painted along the axes of the limbs (Bernstein, 1967). Pictures taken during walking revealed an elegant portrait of coordination (Figure 8-2). The

Figure 8-2 Multiple exposures of subject walking while wearing a black suit with white tape along the arm and leg. White dots mark the head and main joints of the limbs. Shutter is opened 20 times per second. (From Bernstein, 1967)

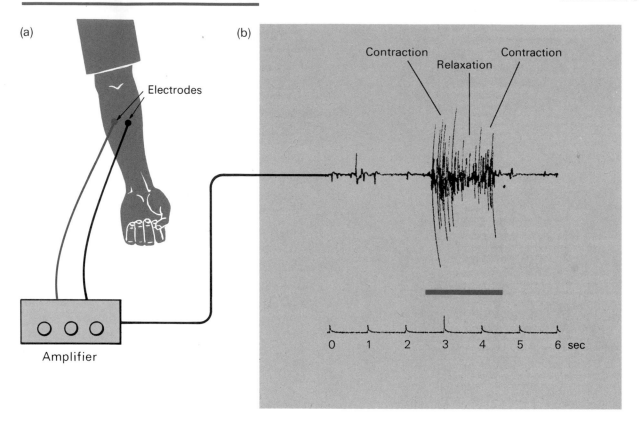

Figure 8-3 Electrical recordings from muscle called electromyograms. (a) Positions on muscles of the arm. (b) Activity with contraction and relaxation.

power of representing locomotion in this manner is shown in studies of recognition of these displays. With such simple representation of walking, viewers can recognize themselves or friends and can distinguish male from female walkers (Cutting, 1978). Recently computer graphic simulation techniques have been introduced in this area and they may offer even more simplified views of human actions.

More detailed descriptions of the activity of muscles that generate these actions can be obtained with electrical recordings. Since the contraction of muscles involves electrical potentials generated by the constituent muscle fibers, needle electrodes placed in a muscle or electrodes placed on the skin over a muscle yield electrical indications of muscle activity. This technique, called **electromyography,** is illustrated in Figure 8-3. If we put electrodes in many different muscles, we can get an electrical portrait of the contraction of the different muscles involved in a distinct act.

Acquiring motor skills   We do not have to learn how to withdraw a hand from a hot stove, or how to breath, or how to swallow. These and many other acts are highly stereotyped reflexes; no aspect of a person's attention changes their essential character. "Involuntary" is the word commonly used to characterize these responses. In contrast, we need explicit training to know how to generate speech and handwriting, to play tennis, to dial a phone, and to perform numerous other acts, ranging from trivial to extraordinary,

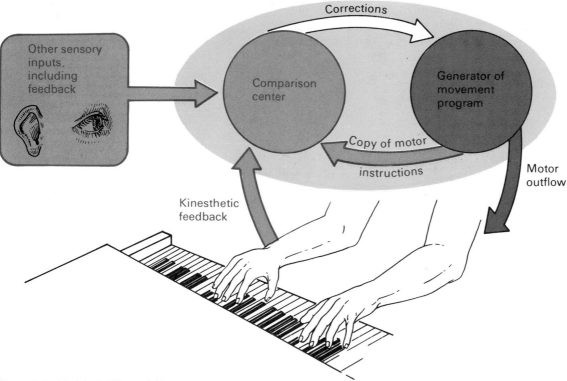

Figure 8-4 Model of skill acquisition.

that are in the general experience of humans. The characteristics of these acts are highly variable, frequently idiosyncratic, and show considerable variability among individuals. These acts are commonly referred to as "voluntary" motor skills. How are these skills acquired?

The performance of any skilled movement generates several types of information essential to acquiring a motor skill. A model of skill learning is shown in Figure 8-4 (Keele and Summers, 1976). This model posits that input to muscles is provided by a hypothetical movement program. Feedback from receptors in joints and other modes of information about movements—visual or auditory—are matched to a model of skilled performance. Feedback information thus provides input about errors, which are gradually reduced; in some cases the need for monitoring the movement may be eliminated. Welford (1974) notes that at this stage of skilled movement learning there is a loss of conscious awareness of the act—there is a feeling of automatic execution. He believes that faster performance becomes possible because feedback control loops exert less impact.

Control systems view   Engineering descriptions of the regulation and control of machines have provided a useful way of looking at the mechanisms that regulate and control the movements of animals. In designing and building machines, engineers commonly encounter two problems: (1) how to prevent or minimize error and (2) how to accomplish a task

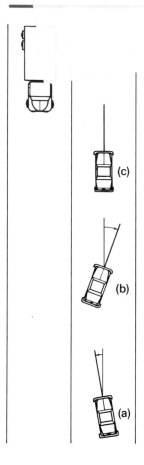

Figure 8-5 Example of feedback control in auto driving. (a) Auto veers to the left. (b) Overcorrection turns the car to the right. (c) Target is achieved.

quickly and efficiently. These are the considerations of accuracy and speed. Two forms of control mechanisms are commonly employed to optimize performance according to these criteria; they are referred to as **closed-loop** and **open-loop control mechanisms.**

The essence of closed-loop control mechanisms is that they provide for the flow of information from whatever is being controlled to the device that controls it. We have already considered closed-loop mechanisms when we discussed control of endocrine secretion in Chapter 5 (Figures 5-2 through 5-4). We used the example of a thermostat controlling room temperature to point out some of the characteristics of a negative-feedback system. Now we can consider a more complex example in which a human being—an automobile driver, for example—plays a major role. In this case the variable being controlled is the position of an automobile on the road (see Figure 8-5). Continuous information in this instance is provided by the driver's visual system, which can demand correcting movement.

Let's consider this example in terms of the formal sort of diagram customarily used for studying feedback control mechanisms (Figure 8-6). This diagram is a formal description of closed-loop (that is, feedback) systems. In terms of our analogy the controlled system is the automobile. The input is the position of the steering wheel, and the output is the position on the road. The transducer is an element that measures output, and the error detector measures differences between actual output and desired output (control signal). In this example the transducer, error detector, and controller all refer to properties of the person driving the car. Specifically, the transducer refers to the driver's visual system, the error detector to some properties of the perceptual system, and the controller to the muscle apparatus used in steering. The actual position of the car is compared with its desired position on the road, and corrections are supplied to the controlled system to minimize the discrepancy (assuming the desire to stay on the road). The only way the car could stay on the road without feedback control (as, for example, driving with your eyes closed) would be with the aid of accurate memory of all the turns and bends in the road. (In terms of our next discussion such a memory system could be considered a form of open-loop control.)

Some nonliving systems employ closed-loop controls; others employ open-loop mechanisms. Open-loop controls are those that do not involve external forms of feedback; output is measured by a sensor but the activity is preprogrammed. Open-

Figure 8-6 Diagram of feedback control mechanism.

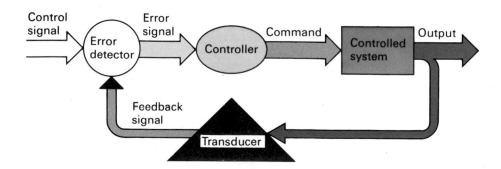

loop controls are needed in mechanical systems that must respond so rapidly that no time is available for the delay of a feedback pathway. The way elevators work furnishes a familiar example of open-loop control: Their rates of acceleration and deceleration are preset. Pressing the button for a given floor sets off the whole predetermined program.

In addition to offering speed of response, open-loop systems have the benefit of freedom from error and variability. To achieve this freedom, they employ devices that supply a control signal known to be effective or to *anticipate* potential error. In living systems such accurate anticipation may arise from prior learning. For instance, in all the acts involved in learning to play a piano, some neural elements may acquire the properties of open-loop control because some features of the brain motor system may provide anticipatory controls based on the errors initially involving closed-loop or feedback instructions. This form of open-loop control is also known as "input feed forward." Obviously it must involve a mechanism that can make educated guesses about the kind of correction that might be needed.

Neurobiological view

Posture and movements are the products of integrative mechanisms located at all levels of motor systems. Some properties of acts arise from characteristics of the skeleton and the muscle itself; others come from progressively more complicated levels of neural organization, from motor neurons to cerebral cortex. We will start by considering properties of the skeletal system, the muscles, and the muscle receptors, and then we will proceed to the spinal cord and the brain, where the main processing takes place.

Sensory and motor features of muscles and joints

Any act owes its character both to the mechanical properties of the body and to neural signals to muscles. Let us consider briefly the ways in which these mechanical properties determine and limit movements.

● Mechanics of the skeletal system   The skeletal system of any vertebrate consists of many separate bones of different shape, weight, and length. Through painful experience we know that bones themselves do not bend. The primary sites for bending occur at the joints, where bones meet. The exact appearance of different joints varies, and these differences determine how a particular body part can be used. Figure 8-7, which illustrates the human skeleton, shows examples of some joints and their movement possibilities. Note that some, like the hip, are virtually "universal" joints, permitting movement in many planes. Others, like the elbow or knee, are more limited and tolerate little deviation from the principal axis of rotation.

Both the weight and shape of any bone are also significant in the operation of a joint, since they are important properties of the leverlike actions at joints. Many features of movement differences between species can be directly predicted from comparisons of the size and shape of relevant bones. For example, a comparison of the hands of humans with those of other primates shows why humans alone are capable of the precision grip of objects between the thumb and forefinger.

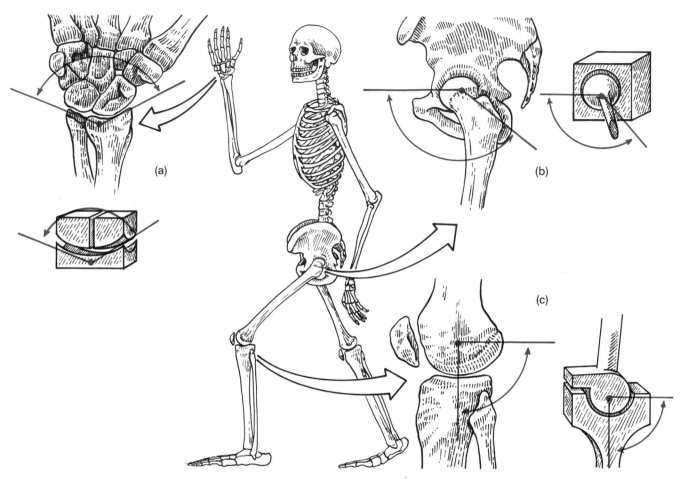

Figure 8-7 The human skeleton showing examples of joints and movements. Next to each enlarged joint is a mechanical model that shows the kinds of movements the joint can perform. (a) Wrist joint that moves in two principal planes, lateral and vertical. (b) Hip joint, a "universal joint." (c) Knee joint that has a single plane of motion.

● **Mechanics of the muscular system**   Our bare skeleton must now be clothed with muscles. The distribution of muscles on the body—their size and attachment to bones—provides direct indications of the forms of movement that they mediate. By contracting, some muscles produce forces that sustain body weight and others produce actual movement around a joint. In contrast, other muscles do not act on the skeleton at all—for example, the muscles that move the eyes, lips, and tongue and those that contract the abdomen. The molecular mechanisms of contraction of **muscle fibers** have been revealed in recent research (see Box 8-1).

The contraction of muscle fibers leads to movements or to maintenance of posture according to the ways in which any muscle is mechanically attached to a bone or bones. The arrangement around a typical joint is illustrated in Figure 8-8. Muscles are connected to bone by tendons. Around a joint different muscles are arranged in a reciprocal fashion. Thus when one muscle group contracts (shortens), the other is extended; that is, the relation of the muscles is antagonistic. Coordinated action

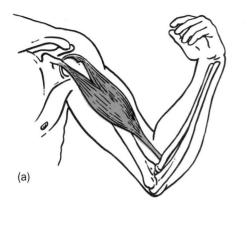

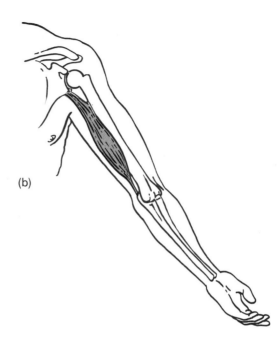

(a)   (b)

Figure 8-8 Arrangement of muscles around the elbow.

around a joint may then require that one set of motoneurons be excited while the antagonistic set is inhibited. It is also possible to lock the limb in position by graded contraction of the opposed muscles.

Speed, precision, strength, and endurance are all desirable qualities in muscular movements, but behavioral acts differ in their requirements for these qualities. Matched to these requirements are at least two main types of muscle fibers, "fast" and "slow." Eye movements, for example, must be quick and accurate so that we can follow moving objects and shift our gaze from one target to another. But fibers in the extraocular muscles do not have to maintain tension for long periods of time because the neural program uses them in rotation; that is, it allows some fibers to relax while others contract. The extraocular muscles are therefore made up of "fast" muscle fibers. In contrast, in the leg muscle "fast" fibers react promptly and strongly but fatigue rapidly; they are used mainly for activities in which muscle tension changes frequently, as in walking or running. Mixed in with them are "slow" fibers that are not as strong but have greater resistance to fatigue; they are used chiefly to maintain posture.

Because of their differential needs for rapid energy, fast and slow muscle fibers use different enzymes for metabolism. Consequently investigators have been able to stain the two types of fibers differently and to count the proportion of each type in various muscles. The proportions of fast and slow fibers are found to vary among muscles, and this variation provides a way of classifying muscles.

Differences in precision of control of various movements are also achieved by differences in the density of motor axons to muscle groups. Fine neural control is achieved when a single axon connects to only a few muscle fibers. An understanding of this concept is aided by the definition of a **motor unit;** this is a single motor axon

BOX 8-1 How Muscles Contract

The basis of most of our movements is the contraction of muscle fibers. How muscles contract has been the object of intensive investigation; in these studies the components of the fibers have been identified and their physiology analyzed (Hoyle, 1970; Murray and Weber, 1974).

Each muscle fiber is made up of many filaments of two kinds arranged in a very regular manner (Box Figure 8-1). There are bands of relatively thick filaments and bands of thinner filaments, giving the fibers a striped appearance. The two kinds of filaments always overlap somewhat, as Box Figure 8-1 shows. Contraction of the muscle increases the overlap—the filaments slide past each other, shortening the overall length of the muscle fiber.

What causes the fibers to move past each other? Under higher magnification the thick filaments are seen to have

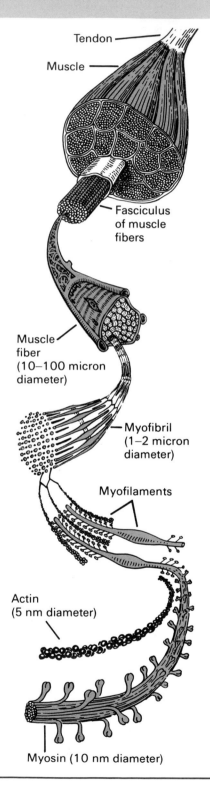

Tendon

Muscle

Fasciculus
of muscle
fibers

Muscle
fiber
(10–100 micron
diameter)

Myofibril
(1–2 micron
diameter)

Myofilaments

Actin
(5 nm diameter)

Myosin (10 nm diameter)

Box Figure 8-1 The composition of muscles. Note that successive parts of the diagram show progressively greater magnification, from lifesize at the top to 2 million times at the bottom.

paddle-shaped extensions or cross bridges that make contact with the thin filaments (Box Figure 8-2). During contraction, these cross bridges rotate, pushing the thin filaments. Actually a cross bridge moves through a certain distance and then breaks contact; it moves back, makes a new contact and pushes again. Note this action of the cross bridge shown in dark blue as it moves through a cycle in diagrams (a)–(e) of Box Figure 8-2. A single muscular contraction involves several cycles of such paddling actions. The movements of the cross bridges are initiated when calcium ions come into contact with parts of the muscle filament proteins. And the release of calcium ions is controlled by muscle action potentials that are triggered by nerve impulses. Thus the motor nerves control a series of electrophysiological, chemical, and mechanical events that accomplish mechanical contraction of the muscle fibers.

(a)

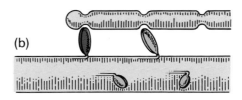

(b)

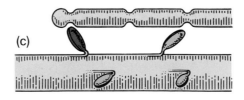

(c)

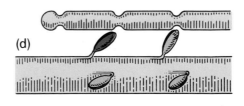

(d)

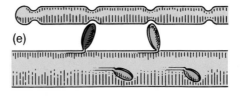

(e)

Box Figure 8-2 The movement mechanism of muscle fibers.

and all the muscle fibers it innervates. The term **innervation ratio** refers to the ratio of motor axon to the number of fibers. Low innervation ratios characterize muscles involved in fine movements, like those of the eye (1:3 ratio). In contrast, muscles of the leg have innervation ratios of one to several hundred; thus the same call for contraction goes to hundreds of leg fibers at the same time.

Monitoring movements: External feedback

To produce rapid coordinated movements of the body, the integrative mechanisms of the brain and spinal cord must have information about the state of the muscles, the positions of the limbs, and the instructions being issued by the motor centers.

The sequence and intensity of muscle activation are monitored by sensory receptors, which provide information about the state of muscles and joints, and this information is used by the circuits that initiate and guide movements. There are several kinds of sensory receptors that can provide information about the state of muscle length or contraction. Two major kinds of receptors are shown in Figure 8-9: **muscle spindles,** which lie in parallel with the muscle fibers, and **Golgi tendon organs,** which lie in series with muscles, one end attached to tendon, the other to muscle. The mechanical sensitivities of the spindles and tendon organs differ. Stretching a muscle, which occurs in many kinds of movements, activates especially

Figure 8-9 Muscle receptors. (a) Location of muscle spindles in body of muscle and Golgi organs in tendons. (b) Typical structure of muscle spindle. Two types of receptor endings are shown: primary and secondary. Gamma motor fibers control a contractile portion of the spindle. (c) Typical sensory ending of Golgi tendon organ.

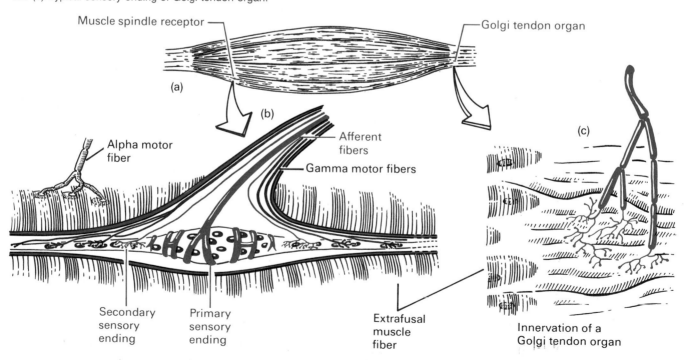

Muscle spindle receptor — — Golgi tendon organ

(a)

(b)

Alpha motor fiber

Afferent fibers

Gamma motor fibers

(c)

Secondary sensory ending

Primary sensory ending

Extrafusal muscle fiber

Innervation of a Golgi tendon organ

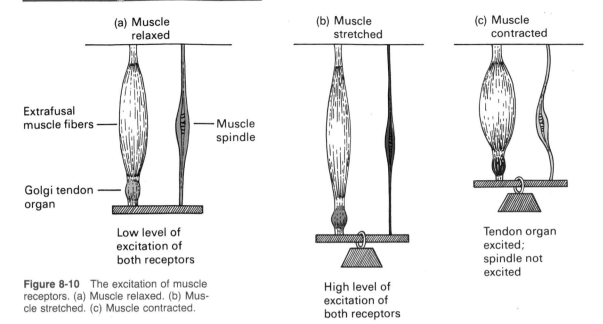

Figure 8-10 The excitation of muscle receptors. (a) Muscle relaxed. (b) Muscle stretched. (c) Muscle contracted.

the spindles and transiently the tendon organs. Shortening a muscle during contraction activates the tendon organs because they lie in series with the muscle. So together these two kinds of receptors transmit to the CNS a range of information about muscle activities (Figure 8-10).

Classical studies in physiology, especially those of Sherrington, emphasized the importance of these receptors for movement. Sherrington showed that cutting the afferent fibers from muscle results in paralysis, even if the efferent connections from motor neurons to muscles are preserved. The deafferented limb is not really paralyzed, since it can be activated, but lack of information from the muscle leads to relative disuse. Recent studies have qualified this picture. Teodoru and Berman (1980) have shown that a monkey can flex a deafferented limb in a purposive manner in response to a visual signal that is used as a conditioned stimulus for shock avoidance. Simple forearm flexion to avoid shock occurred in these animals, although during free behavior the arm looked paralyzed.

Although deafferenting one forearm leads to apparent paralysis of that limb, the result is quite different if both forearms are deafferented. In the latter case the monkey recovers coordinated use of its forearms over a few months (Taub and Berman, 1968). When one limb is deafferented, the monkey makes do with the other. But when both are deafferented, then the monkey has to learn to use them and is able to do so. The results show that the monkey becomes capable of fairly well coordinated movements even though it lacks feedback from its arms.

Even if only one arm is deafferented, forced use of it can lead to return of coordinated use of the two arms. This result was shown in experiments in which the hand of the intact limb was placed inside a ball, which prevented the monkey from grasping objects with it but allowed finger movements and thus prevented atrophy. Slowly the deafferented limb gained dexterity, and over the course of several weeks fine movements like those needed for feeding were achieved. After several months the ball on the intact hand was removed, and the monkey made coordinated movements of both limbs. However, if the forced usage lasted for less than four months, movements of the deafferented limb regressed rapidly.

● The muscle spindle   The muscle spindle of vertebrates is a complicated structure consisting of both afferent and efferent elements. Figure 8-9 illustrates the principal components of the spindle. The spindle gets its name from its shape—a sort of cylinder that is thicker in the middle and tapers at its two ends. The Latin term for spindle, "fusus," is used to form adjectives referring to the muscle spindle; thus the small muscle fibers that are found within each spindle are called "intrafusal" fibers, and the ordinary muscle fibers that lie outside the spindles are referred to as "extrafusal" fibers.

There are two kinds of receptors in the muscle spindle: (1) the primary or central sensory ending (also called annulo-spiral endings) and (2) the secondary or distal sensory ending (also called flower spray endings). As shown in Figure 8-9, these endings are related to different parts of the spindle. The primary ending wraps in a spiral fashion around a region called the nuclear bag (the central region of the intrafusal fiber). The secondary fibers terminate toward the thin end of the spindle.

How does excitation of these elements occur? Suppose a muscle is stretched, as occurs when a load is placed on it. For example, if you were trying to hold your arm straight out in front of you, palm up, and someone put an object in your hand, that would put an additional load on your biceps. The muscle spindle is also stretched, and the resulting deformation of the endings on the spindle sets up nerve impulses in the afferent fibers. When a muscle is stretched, there are two factors to consider. One is the rate of change of muscle length. In our example the rate of change is jointly a function of the weight of the load and the rate at which it is applied. The second factor is the force that must be continually exerted by the muscle to prevent dropping of the load. In our example this force is a function only of the weight of the load.

The different receptor elements of the muscle spindle are differentially sensitive to these two features of muscle length changes. The primary (central) endings show a maximum discharge early in stretch and then adapt to a lower discharge rate. In contrast, the secondary (distal) endings are maximally sensitive to maintained length and are slow to change their rate during the early phase of stretch. Because of this differential sensitivity, primary endings are called dynamic and secondary endings are called static indicators of muscle length. This distinction probably arises from the difference in the way in which these receptors are embedded in the spindle rather than from a difference in the nerve fibers themselves.

● Efferent control of the muscle spindle   Muscle spindles serve not only to help maintain postures but also to coordinate movements. Spindles are informed of planned and ongoing actions through innervation by special motor neurons that alter the tension within the spindle and thus control the sensitivity of its receptors. These motor neurons are called **gamma efferents** (to distinguish them from the faster-conducting **alpha motoneurons,** which go to skeletal muscle fibers, as shown in Figure 8-9). The gamma efferents are connected to a contractile region of the spindle (called the myotube region). The cell bodies of these fibers are found in the ventral horns of the spinal cord. The activity in the gamma fibers causes a change in the length and tension of the spindle, which modifies its sensitivity to changes in the length of adjacent extrafusal muscle fibers. Hence the number of impulses elicited in the primary and secondary afferents is a function of two factors: (1) muscle stretch and (2) the resting tension in the muscle spindle.

Corresponding to the dual nature of the afferent parts of the spindle, there are two classes of gamma efferent control. The dynamic gamma efferent fiber makes the primary sensory endings in the spindle more responsive to changes in muscle length. The static gamma efferents modulate the sensitivity of both primary and secondary fibers, resulting in an increased response to maintained stretch, while attenuating the response to varying stretch. One reflection of the importance of the gamma efferent system is the fact that about 30% of all efferent fibers are gamma efferents.

Now let us see how the gamma efferents are involved in coordinating movements. Suppose that instead of continuing to hold your arm out straight ahead, you move your forearm up and down. If the muscle spindle had only one fixed degree of internal tension, it couldn't help to monitor and coordinate this movement. As the forearm moves up, the extrafusal and intrafusal fibers both shorten. Shortening the spindle, as we have noted, removes the tension, so the sensory endings should no longer respond. But the real situation is more complicated and more effective. As the muscle shortens, the gamma efferents correspondingly increase the tension on the intrafusal fibers. We have pointed out that feedback devices can have their set points changed; for example, you can alter the desired temperature on a thermostat. In this case the muscle spindles are informed of the desired changes in muscle length, so they help to monitor any departure from the program being carried out.

Ragnar Granit, a Swedish neurophysiologist, has referred to the **coactivation** of the alpha and gamma motoneurons (1977). That is, the control program that activates or inhibits the skeletal motoneurons at the same time alters the sensitivity of the muscle spindles. Another Swedish neurophysiologist (Valbo, 1973) made recordings from single, muscle spindle afferent fibers in the median nerve of conscious human subjects while they carried out finger movements. When a subject slowly flexed a finger, using the muscle that contained the spindle whose activity was being recorded, the spindle responses increased at the start of flexion. Furthermore, any brief hesitation in the movement caused an increase in firing. Thus the spindle and the skeletal fibers were coactivated during contraction of the muscle, and the spindle probably contributed to the smooth progress of the contraction.

While the muscle spindles are primarily responsive to stretch, the Golgi tendon organs are especially sensitive to muscle contraction or shortening. They are rather insensitive to passive muscle stretch because they are connected in series with an elastic component. They function to detect overload that could threaten damage to muscles and tendons. Stimulation of these receptors inhibits the muscles that pull on the tendon and thus, by relaxing the tension, prevents mechanical damage.

Monitoring movements:
Internal feedback

At many moments during each waking hour our eyes are functionally blind, although we are not aware of the fact. These are the moments when, if we did see, muscular movements would impair the perceived continuity of vision. One type of functional blindness occurs when the eyes shift quickly from one target to another (for example, during reading); these movements are called **saccades** (from the French word meaning to jerk or move abruptly). As the eyes make saccadic movements, the retinal receptors are exposed to stimulation that moves rapidly across the retina, yet we are not aware of the scene jumping or blurring. However, if we hold our eyes steady and the target jerks at the same rate in relation to the eyes, then we notice the movements. Of if you push quickly on the edge of your eyeball with your finger, you see the world jump, although the shifting of the image across the retina is no greater than when you move your eyes during reading.

It appears that vision is suppressed just when the eyes move rapidly, and this effect is called **saccadic suppression.** This suppression has been determined by measuring the thresholds of brief flashes of light presented before, during, or after saccades. As Figure 8-11 shows, visibility begins to decline about 50 msec before the saccade begins, and it is back to normal about 100 msec later, when the movement is completed (Latour, 1962; Volkmann et al., 1969). Many investigators have concluded that information about the neural program that calls for saccadic eye movement is channeled to the visual centers and causes a central suppression of the visual input during movement. Several names have been given to this information derived from the motor program—corollary discharge (Teuber, 1966), efference copy (von Holst, 1954), and internal feedback (Evarts, 1971).

Some investigators have suggested that the physical movement of the eye, rather than the intention to move, might suppress vision. One piece of evidence against the movement explanation is that the suppression begins even before the eye starts to move, as we saw in Figure 8-11.

Complementary evidence for internal feedback comes from the fact that visual suppression also occurs during an eye blink, when the eyes remain still although the lids move. If visual stimulation of the retina is interrupted by lowering room illumination for 100 msec, this diminution is readily perceived, but people do not

Figure 8-11 Saccadic suppression. Changes in sensitivity to light before and after a saccadic movement of the eye. [Black curve from data of Latour (1962) and blue curve from study of Volkmann (1969)]

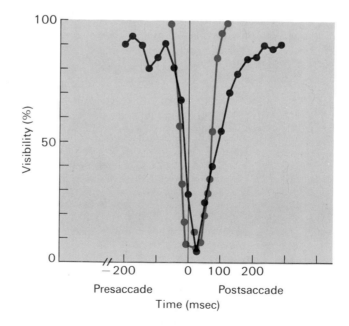

Figure 8-12 Visual suppression during eye blink. The two curves are for two different subjects. (From Volkmann et al., 1980)

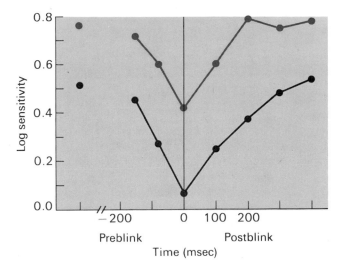

notice any reduction in brightness of a visual scene during an eye blink, which lasts even longer, about 200 msec. Recently investigators have measured sensitivity to light directed at the back of the eyeball before, during, and after eye blinks (Volkmann, Riggs, and Moore, 1980). The light was presented through a fiber optic bundle pressed against the roof of the mouth under one eye, so that the lid was bypassed; the subject wore dark goggles to eliminate all other sources of light. The results (Figure 8-12) showed that sensitivity decreased before the onset of the blinks and reached a maximum before the lid covered the pupil. Here, as in saccadic suppression, the decrease in sensitivity started before the muscular movements, so the findings again support the interpretation of internal feedback from the motor program. Such internal-feedback suppression is not confined to the visual system: For example, auditory sensitivity is suppressed during chewing movements. This suppression also occurs prior to the initiation of movement.

Although saccadic suppression prevents our perceiving motion during rapid eye movements, the input information is not completely lost. This result has been found in several different situations, of which we will mention two. In the first situation a person is placed in the dark and asked to view a small illuminated point (A) and then to shift his gaze to a second point (B) as soon as it appears. This response can be done very accurately. On some trials, however, the second point moves during the saccades to a further position (B') and then disappears before the saccade ends. What happens then is that the saccade goes to B, and then a further saccade accurately moves the gaze to B' (Hallett and Lightstone, 1976). Therefore accurate spatial information is obtained during the saccade, even though the subject is not aware of it. In the second situation subjects were instructed to strike, with a hammer, at luminous targets presented in the dark only during saccades (Skavenski and Hansen, 1978). The subjects protested that they could not really see the targets, and they believed that their performance was wildly inaccurate. Actually it was almost as good as when the target was continuously present and the eyes were stationary! Thus the suppression of conscious awareness of the stimulus during eye movement does not mean that information is not being acquired and that it cannot be used in performance. (This phenomenon is reminiscent of blindsight discussed in Chapter 7.) It appears, therefore, that internal-feedback suppression can be directed to certain brain regions and certain responses while other brain regions and responses are exempted from this suppression and benefit from the information.

Neural control of movements: Spinal mechanisms

The nerve cells directly responsible for excitation of muscle are those found in the ventral region of the spinal cord—spinal motoneurons—and those found in the brainstem nuclei of several cranial nerves. Firing patterns of these cells determine the timing of onset, coordination, and termination of muscle activity. Understanding the physiology of movement means acquiring knowledge of the source of the inputs to motoneurons, their origins, and their workings. This is a difficult task since a variety of influences converge on the motoneurons. Some arise solely at a spinal level from muscle afferents and the intrinsic circuitry of the spinal cord. Other influences are directed to motor cells from several brain pathways.

Up to this point we have described some of the basic properties of muscles and the afferent systems that monitor muscle states. We will now consider some properties of spinal and brain pathways that can control and integrate the activities of motoneurons. There are many gaps in this tale, although intensive experimental work in the last decade is filling in some of these.

Motoneurons innervating the muscles of the head region are found in motor nuclei of the cranial nerves (for example, the facial nerve nucleus and the trigeminal motor nucleus); those innervating the musculature of the rest of the body are found in the spinal cord. The motoneurons differ from each other in certain important properties. These differences contribute to graded muscle activity—coordinated contraction over time as opposed to sudden intense twitches. The principal difference among motor cells is in size which leads to important physiological differences. In general small motoneurons innervate slow muscles and are more easily excited by synaptic currents; therefore they are activated before large motoneurons are. Large motoneurons innervate fast muscles and tend to respond after small cells because they are also less readily excited by synaptic currents. Their discharge characteristics are more phasic or abrupt. Many spinal levels contain both large and small motoneurons.

● **Stretch reflex**   The motoneurons are the final common pathway to muscles. Integration of many diverse synaptic inputs is characteristic of these cells, which act as the nodal points through which the brain and other spinal cord regions address muscles. Some simple transactions fundamental to stereotyped movements have been examined by neurophysiologists. The best example is the stretch reflex.

Stretch of a muscle results in its contraction, a reaction known as the **stretch reflex.** The physiological condition for muscle stretch can be readily understood under conditions of an imposed weight or load. For example, in Figure 8-13 a weight (disturbance) is added to the hand, which imposes sudden stretch on muscle 1 (M_1). A similar condition can be imposed on many joints simply by gravitational forces (that is, the weight of the body). The circuit that precludes dropping the load, or

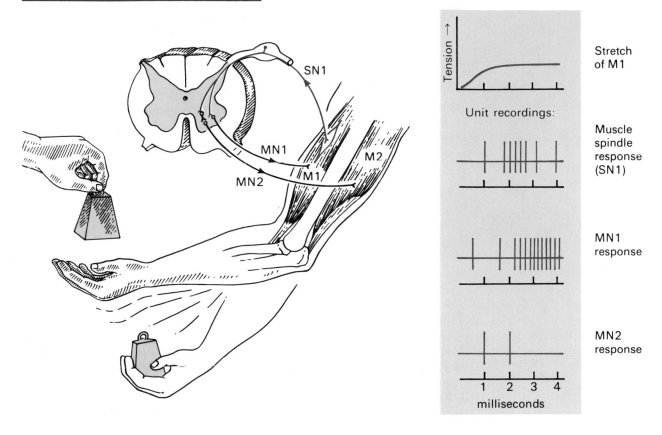

Figure 8-13 The stretch reflex circuit. MN1 is the motor nerve to muscle 1 (M1) and MN2 is the motor nerve to muscle 2 (M2). Characteristic responses at different stages in the circuit are shown on the right.

simply falling from the weight of our body, is one that links muscle spindles and the relevant muscles. The simplest depiction of the events portrayed in Figure 8-13 is the following sequence:

1. Disturbance imposed.

2. Muscle stretched.

3. Muscle spindle afferent elements excited.

4. Excitatory synaptic potentials produced by muscle spindle afferents at the synaptic junctions. (These afferents connect directly—that is, monosynaptically—to the motoneurons, whose fibers go to the stretched muscle.)

5. Motoneuron output received by muscle, producing contraction and thereby opposing muscle stretch.

This sequence describes a simple negative-feedback system that tends to restore the limb in our illustration to its "desired" position. Additional influences exerted by the activation of the muscle spindle system include the inhibition of the motoneurons supplying the antagonistic muscle (M2). These effects are exerted disynaptically ("two synapses"). Thus in the illustration of Figure 8-13 spindle information terminates on the interneuron whose output goes to the motoneuron supplying M2. At this junction inhibitory postsynaptic activity is produced. This combined action then involves spindle-produced excitation of the stretched muscle (and its synergists—that is, muscles working the same way) and inhibition of the antagonistic muscle system.

● Spinal reflexes   One way to study spinal mechanisms is to transect the connections between the brain and spinal cord (producing what is termed a spinal animal) and then observe the forms of behavior that can be elicited below the level of the section. (All voluntary movements that depend on brain mechanisms are lost, of course, as is sensation from the regions below the section.) Immediately after the cord is transected, a condition referred to as **spinal shock** occurs. This condition is an interval of decreased synaptic excitability in the neuron population of the spinal cord after it is isolated from brain communication. The period may last for months in humans, although for nonprimates like cats and dogs it may last only a few hours. During this period no reflexes mediated by the spinal cord can be elicited by either skin stimulation or excitation of muscle afferents.

Following this interval various kinds of reflexes can be elicited, and the properties of these movements in spinal animals have enabled us to gain some understanding of the basic organization of spinal nerve cells with respect to movement control. These include various stretch reflexes that may function well enough to support the weight of a standing animal for rather brief periods. Stimulation of the skin of a spinal animal can also elicit reflex effects, which can be readily demonstrated in a spinal cat or dog with intense stimulation of the toe pad. This stimulation results in abrupt withdrawal of the stimulated limb, a response called the **flexion reflex.** Unlike the stretch reflex, which involves a monosynaptic pathway, the flexion reflex involves a multisynaptic pathway within the spinal cord. Other behaviors evident in the spinal animal include bladder emptying and penile erection. Thus some very basic properties of movement are "wired in" to the organization of the spinal cord itself and do not require the brain. These responses are illustrated in Figure 8-14.

Of course these spinal reflexes do not usually function in isolation. They are integrated and modulated by the activity of brain circuits to which we now turn.

Neural control of movements: Brain mechanisms

Pathways from the brain to cranial and spinal motoneurons are many and exceedingly complex, especially from a functional viewpoint. A block diagram of the relations of major brain regions associated with movement control is presented in Figure 8-15. Complex movements clearly involve programs of the brain, and uncovering these programs is a major focus of work in this area. Some of the pathways deliver quite discrete information, which can be established by looking at the characteristic conditions that produce activity in a path. For example, the vestibulospinal pathway provides important information about head position, and this information produces an impact on postural muscles to effect body adjustments.

The variety of pathways from the brain to the spinal motoneurons is illustrated in Figure 8-15. Ideas about the differential role(s) of each of these systems in the integration and control of movement have relied heavily on observations of changes in posture and locomotion produced by natural or experimental interferences in these

STIMULATION   RESPONSE

(a) Stretch reflex

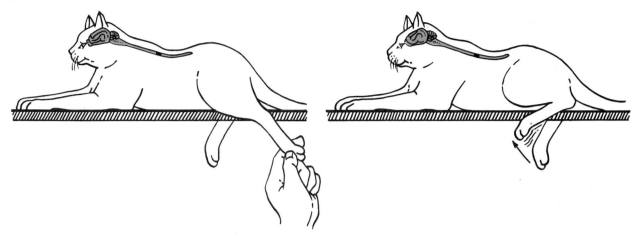

(b) Flexion reflex and crossed extension

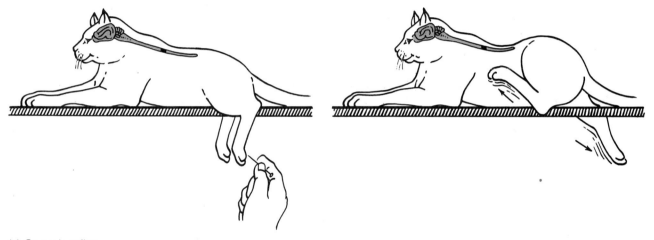

(c) Scratch reflex

Figure 8-14   Spinal reflexes in the spinal cat. The site of transection of the spinal cord is shown in blue.
(a) Stretching the hind limb evokes muscle contraction opposing stretch. (b) Painful stimulation of the pad elicits
hind limb flexion on the same side of the stimulation and extension of the contralateral hind limb. (c) Scratching
the flank below the level of section elicits accurate, rhythmic scratching movements.

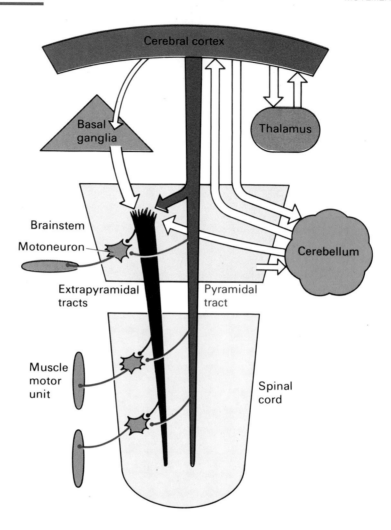

Figure 8-15 Block diagram of major brain regions and pathways associated with control of movement.

regions. Clinical data derived from people with brain damage have generated useful anatomical and functional distinctions between two motor systems, called the pyramidal and extrapyramidal motor systems.

The **pyramidal system** refers to neuron cell bodies within the cerebral cortex and their axons, which pass through the brainstem, forming the pyramidal tract (Figure 8-16). The pyramidal tract is most clearly distinguished from other motor tracts where it passes through the anterior aspect of the medulla. In a cross section of the medulla the tract is seen as a somewhat wedge-shaped anterior protuberance (pyramid) on each side of the midline. For many animals the motor cortical sector partially overlaps the somatosensory cortex.

The anatomical definition of the **extrapyramidal system** is somewhat broader and encompasses the basal ganglia of the forebrain (for example, the caudate nucleus) and various thalamic and brainstem regions. A third component not included under either category is the cerebellum.

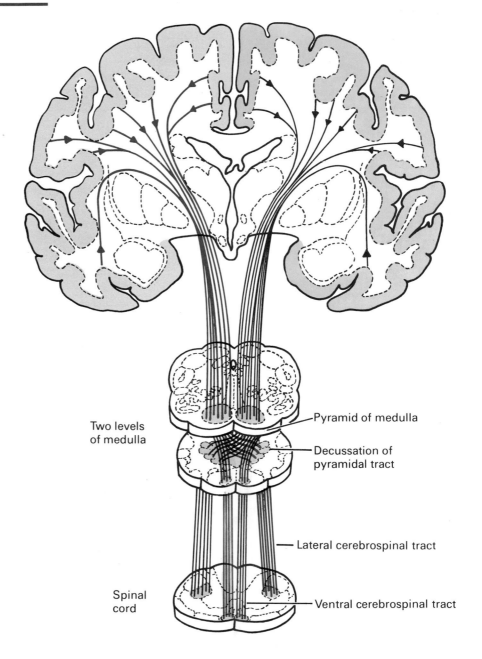

Figure 8-16 The pyramidal motor system. Most of the pyramidal fibers cross to the opposite side in the medulla (decussation of pyramidal tract).

Two levels of medulla

Pyramid of medulla

Decussation of pyramidal tract

Lateral cerebrospinal tract

Spinal cord

Ventral cerebrospinal tract

Our discussion of brain mechanisms of movement will follow this anatomical division, which we use primarily as a teaching device rather than to imply a fundamental functional differentiation, although such differentiations have been suggested by some investigators.

● **Pyramidal control: Motor cortex**   In humans brain lesions involving the pyramidal pathway commonly produce a partial paralysis of movements on the side of the body opposite the brain lesion. This disturbance is greatest in distal muscles like those of the hand, and it particularly involves flexor muscles. Humans with these lesions are generally described as "disinclined" to use the affected limb.

Because human lesions arise from accidental injury or disease, they are usually not limited to a single neural system. The symptoms of pyramidal system injury and some of the complexity of the observed changes may arise in part from involvement of extrapyramidal system injuries. In other primates experimental lesions restricted to the pyramidal tracts appear to produce some similar changes, although the overall picture is less severe. Six weeks following the bilateral interruption of the pyramidal tracts, monkeys can run, climb, and reach accurately for food. The persistent deficits they display are the limited ability in individual finger movements and the overall tendency of slower-than-normal movements, which rapidly "fatigue." Although they have difficulty in releasing food from the hand, they can readily release their grip while climbing. In mammals other than primates the impairments following pyramidal lesions are less severe.

What do these deficits mean in terms of the overall functional role of the pyramidal system? This problem has plagued many investigators, and definitive answers have not yet been found. Attempts to provide answers have involved recording from pyramidal cells during various movements and closer examination of the anatomical relations between the motor cortex and other levels of movement control systems. We will consider briefly some of the ideas emerging from these studies.

In the late nineteenth century several experimenters showed that electrical stimulation of some regions of the cerebral cortex could elicit body movements, particularly flexion of the limbs. These early findings—and many similar experiments continuing to the present—have led to maps of movements elicited by cortical stimulation, particularly those elicited by a region of the cortex just anterior to the somatosensory cortex, which has come to be known as the **motor cortex.** A map of the human motor cortex is shown in Figure 8-17. The largest motor regions in these maps are devoted to the most elaborate and complex movements in any species. For example, humans and other primates have extremely large cortical fields concerned with hand movements. More recent studies have shown that "colonies" of cells are related to particular muscle groups, and their cortical structural representation may be in vertical columns, an organizational principle similar to that noted in cortical sensory systems. Although a large fraction of the pyramidal tract fibers originate in the so-called motor area of the cortex, this fraction accounts for only about one-third of the total number of pyramidal fibers. Another large component comes from the postcentral gyrus (somatosensory cortex)—about one-fifth. Still other pyramidal fibers arise from many other cortical regions. Thus motor function is dispersed among cortical areas.

Data like those derived from clinical observation and studies involving motor cortex stimulation have suggested to many that the motor cortex–pyramidal tract system provides the executive mechanism for voluntary movements. According to this view, the motor cortex represents particular kinds of movement, and the activation of these cells is the command for the excitation of relevant spinal and cranial motoneurons. Anatomical studies that define the relations between the motor cortex and the spinal motoneurons provide only ambiguous support for this view, however. In primates the pyramidal tract has some monosynaptic connections with spinal

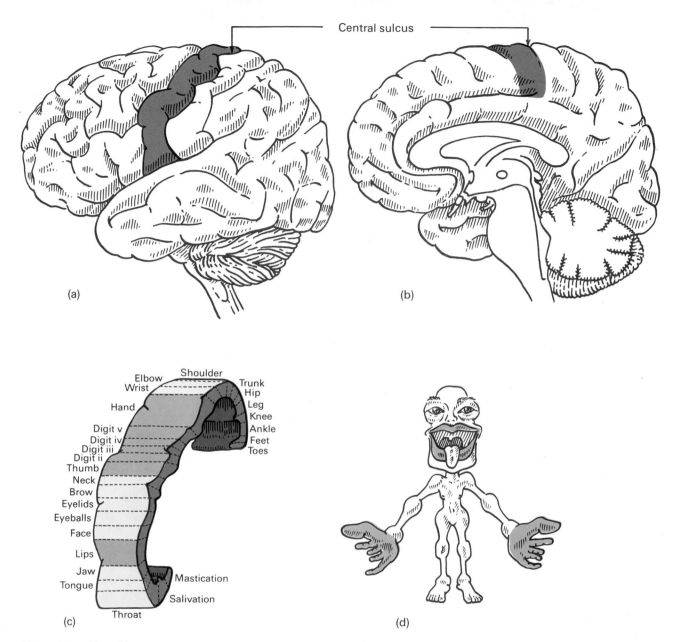

Central sulcus

(a)

(b)

Shoulder
Elbow
Wrist
Hand
Digit v
Digit iv
Digit iii
Digit ii
Thumb
Neck
Brow
Eyelids
Eyeballs
Face
Lips
Jaw
Tongue
Throat

Trunk
Hip
Leg
Knee
Ankle
Feet
Toes

Mastication
Salivation

(c)

(d)

Figure 8-17 Map of human motor cortex. The location of primary motor cortex is shown on the lateral (a) and medial (b) surfaces of the brain. (c) The sequence and sizes of motor representations of different parts of the body. (d) The proportions of the homunculus show the relative sizes of motor representations of parts of the body.

motoneurons, particularly those relevant to the control of distal segments of the upper limbs (that is, hands, wrist, and fingers). However, most pyramidal tract neurons influence spinal motoneurons through polysynaptic routes and share control of these motor cells with other descending influences. Table 8-2 lists the number of pyramidal tract fibers in a variety of mammals. Apparently the size of the pyramidal tract is principally related both to body size and to the complexity of species-typical motor behavior. It seems doubtful that the pyramidal tract is required for initiation and execution of motion, since many active mammals have very small pyramidal tracts.

TABLE 8-2   Numbers of Pyramidal Tract Fibers in
Certain Mammals

SPECIES	APPROXIMATE NUMBER OF PYRAMIDAL TRACT fiBERS
Human	1,000,000
Chimpanzee	800,000
Cow	540,000
Spider monkey	505,000
Mule	412,000
Rhesus macaque	400,000
Dog	260,000
Sheep	240,000
Hog	210,000
Cat	190,000
Rabbit	100,000
Rat	75,000
Opossum	50,000
Mouse	30,000

SOURCE: Towe, 1973.

A more direct examination of pyramidal tract function has involved recording from these cells during movements. This experiment seeks to determine the relations between measures of neural firing (for instance, velocity or force) and degree of limb displacement. Evarts (1968, 1972) recorded from brain cells in monkeys trained to make particular limb movements (Figure 8-18). He found that pyramidal tract neurons discharged prior to a movement, and the firing rate of some cells was related to the force generated by the movement. The final position of a limb—its displacement—was less obviously related to individual motor cortex cell-firing patterns.

Although most views about the motor cortex–pyramidal tract function emphasize voluntary movement and executive control as the principal functional features of this system, some investigators have posed alternatives. The neurophysiologist Arnold Towe (1971) has emphasized that this system is a rather late evolutionary development. For example, among existing vertebrates only mammals have a pyramidal system. Many nonmammalian vertebrates without a pyramidal tract, such as birds and fish, display a vast range of quite elaborate movement patterns. Towe further notes, as we described earlier, that transection of this tract does not preclude movements of the limb. He believes that this system is not the executive mechanism of voluntary movement per se but rather a mechanism for controlling the excitability of networks organized elsewhere (for example, in the brainstem). The pyramidal system is more directly involved in the monitoring of many external environmental inputs and in guiding but not initiating movement on the basis of sensory assessments. This novel perspective may provide a valuable insight for future research.

● **Extrapyramidal controls**   The first task in discussing extrapyramidal motor mechanisms is to describe this anatomical-functional category more precisely. In its

Figure 8-18 Graph of latencies of motor cortex cells in response to visually triggered movements. (a) Experimental setup. (b) Type of hand movement. (c) Graph that shows that most motor units in the precentral cortex fire before the start of a response (R), whereas most units in the postcentral cortex fire after the response starts.

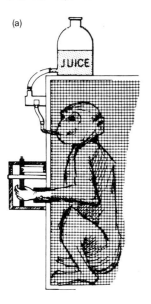

(a)

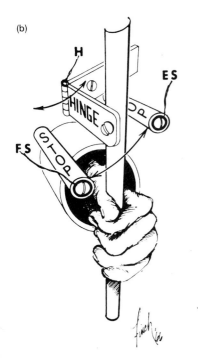

(b)

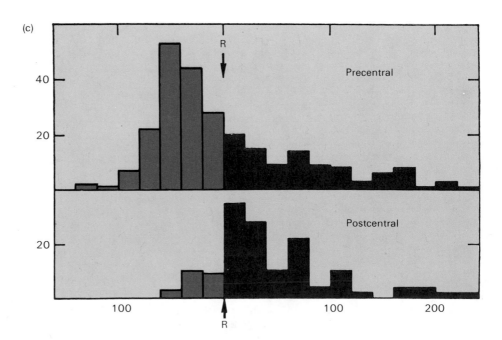

(c)

original usage the term "extrapyramidal motor system" referred to virtually any brain motor mechanism outside the pyramidal tract. Such a definition became excessively broad. Since the term had its origin in the description of some human movement disorders, its anatomical scope became narrowed as the structural basis for some of these dysfunctions was discovered. In its current use "extrapyramidal system" is generally considered to include primarily a group of forebrain nuclei—the **basal ganglia** (including the caudate, putamen, globus pallidus, and claustrum) and some closely related major brainstem connections (substantia nigra and red nucleus). The major connections of these structures are shown in Figure 8-19. Lesions of these regions in humans produce movement impairments that seem quite different from those following interruption of the pyramidal system. These impairments involve the generation of abnormal movements, especially tremors and excessive rigidity of limbs.

Single-unit studies of basal ganglia in primates during the execution of movements show a special relation to the slow phases of movements. DeLong (1974) has studied the discharge patterns of basal ganglia neurons of monkeys; these recordings are made while the animal is in an awake state sitting in a monkey chair. Animals are trained to make a variety of limb movements of varying speed and extent. Basal ganglia neurons show discharges at the onset of many movements, suggesting that they participate in initiation of movement. This effect can be seen with both slow and fast limb movements. Neural activity of one of the basal ganglia regions—the putamen—shows little discharge during the course of rapid to-and-fro limb movements. However, cells within this region display vigorous neural response through the course of slow limb activities. This observation is taken to indicate that the putamen is particularly involved in the programming and control of slower movements.

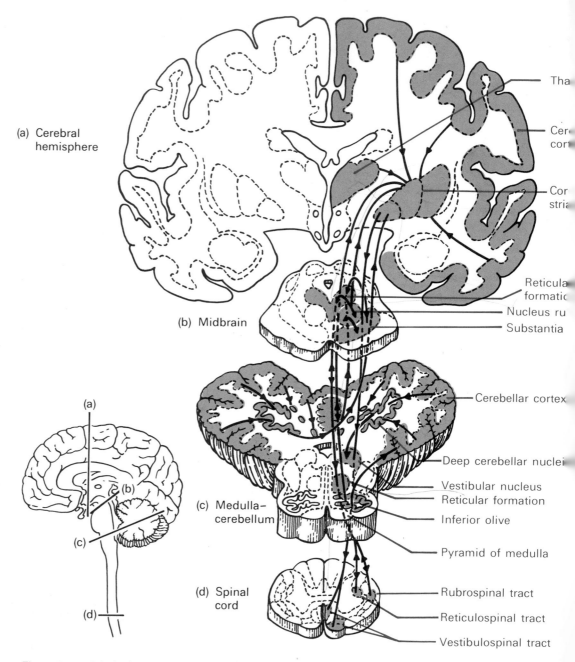

(a) Cerebral
    hemisphere

(b) Midbrain

(c) Medulla–
    cerebellum

(d) Spinal
    cord

Tha

Cer
cor

Cor
stri

Reticula
formatic
Nucleus ru
Substantia

Cerebellar cortex

Deep cerebellar nuclei

Vestibular nucleus
Reticular formation

Inferior olive

Pyramid of medulla

Rubrospinal tract

Reticulospinal tract

Vestibulospinal tract

Figure 8-19   Principal parts and relations in the extrapyramidal system.

● Cerebellar control   The cerebellum is a very important component in the central
regulation of movement. Evidence of this fact comes from the elaborate disorders
of movement that follow cerebellar injury. The manifestations of cerebellar pathology derived from disease or injury are many and seem in general to be characterized

by an interference with the accomplishment of smooth, even movement and difficulty in starting and stopping movements. The list of impairments includes these symptoms:

1. **Ataxia,** which refers to irregularity in the direction, extent, and rate of movement. Some forms of this change following cerebellar damage are difficulty in walking and in maintaining balance, with a tendency to sway and fall. Another form occurs in aiming for a target with the arm: The movement either overshoots or undershoots the target.

2. An inability to perform rapidly alternating movements.

3. **Tremors,** which may occur during some action or during postural maintenance and which may particularly involve quite irregular jerks toward the end of a movement.

4. To-and-fro movement of the eyes (called **nystagmus**), which usually occurs on attempts to fixate some position. Other eye movement changes include modification in the accuracy of saccades.

5. Disordered speech, either slurred or broken up into explosive bursts.

6. Weakness and ready susceptibility to fatigue of limb, as is evident in the inability to maintain a grip.

Various features of this syndrome are more or less accentuated depending on the specific site of disease within the cerebellum. If the pathology is extensive, virtually all features of disordered movement may be evident.

The conditions that give rise to such disorders in humans are numerous and include various types of tumors, infections, and toxins, including alcohol, lead, DDT, and the anticonvulsant Dilantin. (Patients taking this drug to prevent seizures may show a cerebellar syndrome, particularly if they display other signs of sensitivity to the drug.) In people there are also several hereditary syndromes of cerebellar degeneration. Other species also show degenerative disorders of the cerebellum. Mutant mice with cerebellar degeneration were previously discussed in Chapter 3 in the section on growth and development of the brain. The names these strains have been given reflect the varied constellations of cerebellar symptoms—"reeler," "weaver," "leaner," and "staggerer."

Deciphering this array of symptoms in terms of the functional role(s) of the cerebellum has thus far proved somewhat elusive. There are many guesses and plausible theories. The differences among various theoretical views are frequently in terms of which features of cerebellar anatomy or neurophysiology a particular investigator wishes to investigate. To explore some of these views, we will briefly consider some structural features of the cerebellum.

The cerebellum in higher vertebrates consists of a many-folded sheet (illustrated in Figure 2-29). This structure is found in virtually all vertebrates, and its size in some vertebrate groups varies according to the range and complexity of movements. For example, the cerebellum is much larger in fish with extensive locomotor behavior than it is in less active fish, and it is also large in flying birds, as compared with species that do not fly.

All the output of the cerebellar cortex travels via the axons of Purkinje cells, all of which synapse with the deep cerebellar nuclei. At this synapse they produce only postsynaptic inhibitory potentials. Hence all the circuitry of the extensive cortical portion of this system, which includes 10 to 20 billion granule cells in humans, acts to produce patterns of inhibition on motor cells.

Inputs to the cerebellar cortex are derived from both sensory sources and other brain motor systems. Sensory inputs include the vestibular system, muscle and joint receptors and somatosensory, visual, and auditory sources. Both pyramidal and extrapyramidal pathways contribute inputs to the cerebellum and in turn receive outputs from the deep nuclei of the cerebellum. Thus the cerebellum could be characterized as receiving elaborate information both from systems that monitor movements and from systems that execute movements. For this reason the cerebellum has long been considered to play a role in the feedback control of movements. More recently it has also been suggested that the cerebellum elaborates neural "programs" for the control of skilled movements, particularly when these are repeated and become automatic.

Brain mechanisms of movement: A conceptual model

Excitation of many diverse brain areas affects movements. This abundance of direct and indirect influences on motoneurons is bewildering without some scheme that can provide an outline diagram of control mechanisms of movement. A theoretical model from Hans Kornhuber (1974) has attracted wide attention in research on the neurophysiology of movement. This model will organize many of the separate discussions on previous pages that focused on the roles of particular brain regions.

At the outset, consider alternative ways that nervous systems might work to produce movements. One way would be to provide complete instructions to spinal motoneurons from the outset of movement—so complete that the precise excitation of each and every muscle is calculated in advance of actual action. Motoneurons would then simply follow, with slavish accuracy, a bombardment of descending instructions. This technique would call for very precise organization and planning prior to the execution of any movement and would allow little role for correction during the course of action.

A contrasting model of motor organization involves less detailed advance planning and proposes a functional division among various brain regions. Suppose that some brain region specifies a motor command to move a part of the body in a particular direction—for example, moving the arm and fingers in playing a series of notes on a piano. The act commanded involves the concerted activity of many muscles activated in particular arrangements. Some components of the overall act involve slower movements, like those characteristic of postural stability or maintenance of limb position. Other components of the act involve extremely rapid movements of the fingers. The time pattern of neural activity needed to effect these two dissimilar classes of muscle activation are very different. Rapid movements call for a burst of high-frequency nerve impulses that will provide enough force to produce maximum acceleration of movement, like the sudden depression of the accelerator in a car that provides power for rapid passing. Such high-frequency neural firing is maintained for short periods, in contrast with the more prolonged lower-frequency activity necessary to sustain slower movements. Investigators of movement use the term **ballistic** to define classes of rapid movements and the terms smooth or **ramp**

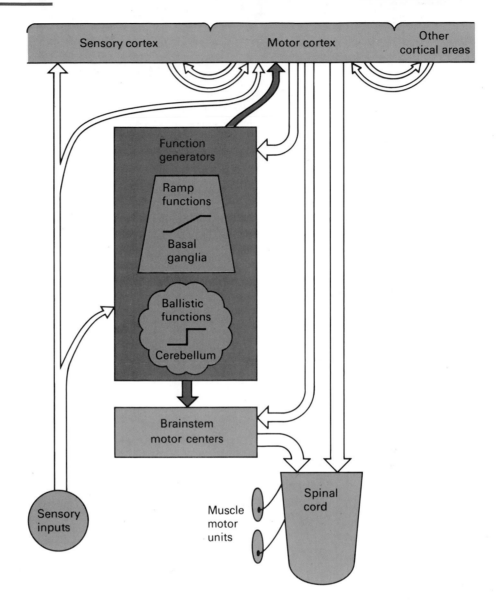

Figure 8-20 A model of the neural organization of voluntary movements proposed by Kornhuber (1974).

to define classes of slower movements. The basic feature of the Kornhuber model is the suggestion that there are separate brain regions dealing with each of these classes of movement.

The Kornhuber model, illustrated in Figure 8-20, originated from observations of human movement disorders and the recording of an unusual EEG change. Kornhuber reported that prior to the actual onset of a voluntary movement there is an electrical potential called the **readiness potential** that can be recorded over widespread posterior regions of the scalp. It starts about 700 msec before the actual movement and occurs earlier than an electrical potential that can be found over the motor cortex contralateral to the moving limb. Both events are shown in Figure 8-21. Because of the widespread distribution of the readiness potential, Kornhuber suggests that the commands that initiate movements arise in association areas of the parietal, temporal, and occipital cortex. Some clinical support for this suggestion comes from examinations of the movement impairment that is caused by injury to these areas. Many such patients show **apraxia,** an impairment in the ability to begin and execute skilled voluntary movements although there is no muscle paralysis. These patients appear stuck!

Motor commands initiated at the association cortex will involve the need to excite motoneurons by neural impulses arranged in particular temporal packets, Kornhuber argues. Such packaging involves time patterns or functions generated in two separate systems: the cerebellum and the basal ganglia. According to the model, ballistic movements are organized or programmed by the cerebellum. These movements are too fast to be directly controlled by muscle feedback systems. Cerebellar impairment from injury or disease does not completely prevent initiation of ballistic movements, but the movements are small in size and inaccurate in execution.

According to this model slow or ramp movement functions are generated in the structures of the basal ganglia. Defects of this system are seen especially in Parkinson's disease, particularly in the control of ramp movements of different speeds. Also, speech becomes very slow and difficult to understand in people with advanced cases of Parkinson's disease. These patients also show difficulty in arising from sitting or lying postures, activities that are ramp movements.

The role of the motor cortex in this model is to evaluate movement continuously in terms of consequences registered by sensory information from muscle, joint, and skin receptors. This role allows "updating" the movement instructions by providing the brain with information about consequences of movement.

Figure 8-21 Electrical potentials recorded from human scalp in anticipation of movements called the readiness potential. (From Kornhuber, 1974)

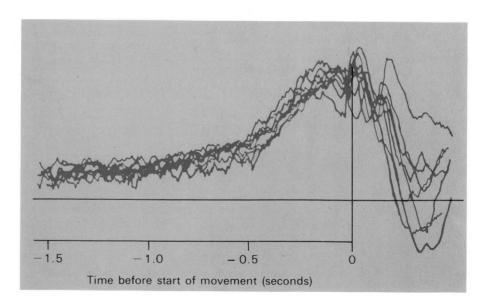

Time before start of movement (seconds)

The Kornhuber model is a current favorite in movement studies. It has provided an emphasis that is quite different from the long-standing view that suggested the primacy of the motor cortex in initiation of movement. But more research is needed to assess the adequacy of the model.

Neurobehavioral analyses of certain acts

Examining the way we perform particular acts, such as moving the eyes and speaking, may help you consolidate the concepts of motor control that have just been discussed. It will also show you how complex "simple" actions are. Just reading a page requires several kinds of eye movements, each with different control mechanisms. The physical production of speech (quite apart from the learning of a language) is also complicated, because it depends on many different groups of muscles that must be coordinated. This section includes consideration of the neural mechanisms of both eye movements and speech.

Eye movements

When we wish to examine a small object such as a letter on a page, we fix our gaze on it. Since the position of the eyes is controlled by muscles attached to the eyeball (the **extraocular muscles**) (Figure 8-22), the unavoidable fine tremor in these muscles causes the direction of our gaze to move by small irregular amounts (miniature eye movements, Table 8-3). Constant corrections must be made to counteract these errors and keep the gaze on target. Here the visual system acts as a closed-loop system; errors are detected and corrected as rapidly as possible.

Now consider what happens when you continue to look at an object while turning your head. For example, you may look at your friend while shaking your head from side to side. When you move your head 5° to the right, your eyes turn 5° to the left in their sockets and stay right on target; when your head moves 10° to the right, your eyes move 10° to the left, exactly compensating for the head movement. Isn't this just another example of the closed-loop system described in the last paragraph? No, because the closed-loop system is rather slow in operation, primarily because the whole visual pathway is slow. If the closed-loop system were the only means of stabilizing the visual world, then we would experience considerable visual slippage whenever we turned our head rapidly. Instead we benefit from the fast-acting **vestibulo-ocular reflex,** which is an open-loop system. In this reflex, head movement is transduced by the semicircular canals, and brainstem pathways convey impulses to the extraocular muscles to produce compensatory eye movement. This open-loop system is rapid and accurate; that is, there is an exact calibration of eye movement to match the angle of head movement. If human or animal subjects are given special eyeglasses that alter the relation between head movement and compensatory eye movement, the gain of the system changes slowly over several days to adjust to the new circumstances, so this open-loop reflex is plastic.

But we do not always keep the whole visual scene fixed. We may pursue an object

Figure 8-22 Muscles of the eye and the kinds of movements produced by different muscles.

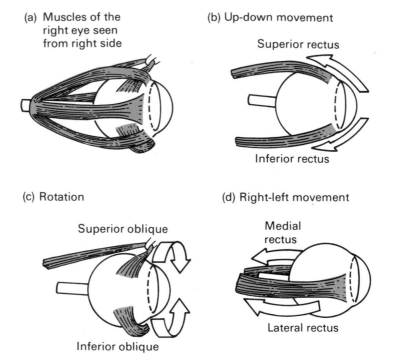

(a) Muscles of the right eye seen from right side

(b) Up-down movement

Superior rectus

Inferior rectus

(c) Rotation

Superior oblique

Inferior oblique

(d) Right-left movement

Medial rectus

Lateral rectus

that moves in relation to us and to the rest of the world. For example, we may follow a swiftly moving tennis ball, or a bird flying, or a pencil point jiggling along the paper during writing. To do this, we have to overcome the reflex that acts to oppose movement of the visual field. That is, the small target must be selected and attended to. The pursuit system is closed-loop. Its latency is over 100 msec, so that when the target starts to move, its image at first traverses the retina with the same angular velocity as the target itself. Negative feedback is used to decrease the discrepancy between the position of the target and the direction of the gaze.

Of course, we don't always keep looking at the same object. A new object may attract our attention, or we may search for a different visual target. In reading, our eyes make rapid saccadic movements from one position to another along a line of type. These movements are under open-loop control; once the target is fixated, then closed-loop optokinetic adjustments are made.

Table 8-3 summarizes the main types of eye movements and their functions; it also notes their characteristic speed, latency, and extent.

Speech   Table 8-4 and Figure 8-23 illustrate the motor mechanisms involved in speech. As you can see, the structures involved in speech are many. Since most speech sounds are made during expiration of air, let us start with respiratory movements.

TABLE 8-3   Main Types of Eye Movements

TYPE	DESCRIPTION AND FUNCTION	SIZE (DEGREES OF ARC)	LATENCY (MSEC)	SPEED (DEGREES/SEC)
Saccadic movements	Fast conjugate movements (i.e., identical in both eyes); they move the eyes from one fixation point to another to place object of interest on fovea	0.5–50	100–500	100–500
Smooth pursuit movements	Conjugate slow eye movements to follow slowly moving target so it remains on fovea	1–60	200	1–30
Convergent movements	Inward movements of the eyes to maintain foveal fixation in both eyes; necessary for binocular vision with objects close to person	1–15	—	6–15
Compensatory movements	Smooth, conjugate, involuntary movements used to compensate for passive or active movements of the head	1–30	10–100	1–30
Miniature eye movements	Tiny involuntary movements that occur during periods of fixation; some may allow for stimulation of changing population of receptors	Less than 1	—	—

TABLE 8-4   Movement Systems Involved in Speech Production

STRUCTURES	FUNCTIONS
Respiratory mechanism Chest cavity Lungs Neuromuscular systems controlling the volume of the chest cavity	Generates expiration air pressures and flows required for sound production
Vocal Folds Vocal folds (larynx) Neuromuscular systems for controlling changes in vocal folds	Vocal fold vibrations provide periodic sound source during voice production Laryngeal adjustments control vocal frequency and intensity
Vocal Cavity System Throat, mouth, and nasal cavities, including tongue, jaw, lips, and hard and soft palate Neuromuscular systems controlling movements of the tongue, jaw, lips, soft palate, and throat walls	Articulation of vowels by shaping mouth and throat to regulate resonance properties of this cavity and controlling coupling to nasal cavity Articulation of consonants by stopping and sudden release of airflow at various oral cavity locations, like lips

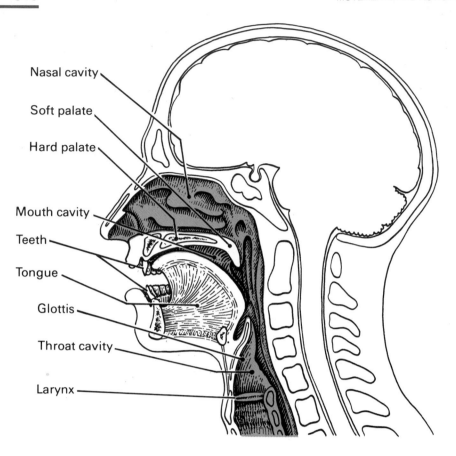

Nasal cavity

Soft palate

Hard palate

Mouth cavity

Teeth

Tongue

Glottis

Throat cavity

Larynx

Figure 8-23 Organs of speech production in the head and neck.

Muscles involved in expiration of air include those of the diaphragm and chest. These control both absolute levels of air pressure and the changes of air pressure that mark the pauses of speech. Some of the fibers of the human pyramidal tract end in the thoracic region of the spinal cord. We have noted that this tract is especially involved in control of skilled movements such as those of the fingers. In this case the thoracic connections are probably not for the control of respiration but rather for the complex use of the respiratory muscles in speech.

The detailed shaping of sounds involves muscles controlling the vocal folds (vocal cords) and the shape of the vocal cavities in the mouth and throat. Many of the relevant muscles like those of the lips involve a low innervation ratio, since delicate control is a major requirement for sounds to become intelligible signals. For example, note the very small differences in tongue position in the production of the consonants "d" and "t" or effects of equally subtle lip and tongue positions in production of "b" and "p."

Feedback control in speech is particularly interesting because it is multimodal—that is, it involves muscle receptors, tactile receptors, and sounds. The neural organization of speech—the representation in the brain of programs of movements—is presented in Chapter 16.

Development of motor functions

Understanding of motor functions is aided by seeing how they initiate early in the lifespan, how they develop during childhood and maturity, and how they decline in the latter part of the lifespan.

Fetal development and activity

Developmental views of movements must start with the womb, since the life of the fetus is not passive and quiet. Indeed, some pregnant mothers have been almost thrown out of bed by a surprising and vigorous kick of a fetal child.

The development of human fetal movements has been studied in fetuses removed by cesarean section—usually because of imperative health problems of the mother— and in other studies while the fetus remains in the womb. In isolated fetuses stimulation-induced withdrawal of the head and upper extremities can be elicited at 8–9 weeks of gestation. At this stage the fetus is about 30 mm in length, measured from the top of the head to the rump. Stimulation around the mouth can produce head turning and mouth opening. In many studies during the 1930s and 1940s Humphrey (1964) showed that localized reflexes begin to develop around 11–12 weeks after conception. These reflexes refer to selective motor changes that do not involve the entire body. An example is the squintlike contraction of the eyelid produced by tapping a nearby skin surface. Mouth opening and swallowing, which Humphrey refers to as feeding reflexes, are also evident at this stage. Tongue movements appear at 14 weeks.

The functional role of the vast range of fetal reflexes has been debated for many years. Do these movements during gestation influence fetal and postnatal motor developments? In Chapter 3 we concluded that decisive evidence is lacking for influence of fetal rehearsal on later motor performance.

Child motor development

Motor abilities of human infants have been the focus of many studies in child psychology. A common way of describing the development of motor skills early in life is to specify the ages at which infants and children reach typical motor accomplishments, such as standing, running, and object handling. The lengthening of bones and the acquisition of muscle mass along with other biomechanical changes account for many early skills. For example, the neural program for walking is available at birth, as you can see by holding a newborn infant erect (supporting its weight) and bringing its feet in contact with a solid surface. Under this condition the infant will make stepping movements of the feet. However, walking does not appear until 12–18 months, because neither the skeletal system nor muscle organization are sufficiently developed until this time—bones harden slowly.

The timetable for the emergence of various reflexes has been determined for several animals. Reflex development in the cat and the dog has been studied by Fox (1970), who examined these animals every day from birth to 2–4 months by using a set of reflex behaviors. Responses he employed included these: reflex withdrawal from painful stimuli, usually elicited by pinching a toe pad; the righting reflex, a response elicited by placing an animal on its back, which is followed by the animal attempting to turn over and position itself on its feet; the forelimb-placing reflex, which consists of extension of the forelimb when contact is made with a hard surface like a tabletop; and the auditory startle reflex. The time of onset of adultlike reflex responses is typical for each species and is related to the sequence in which different behaviors are required by the species.

Motor changes with aging

As we get older, we grow weaker and slower. This common observation may dismay us, but it is amply supported by experimental observations. Debate occurs only about estimates of the magnitude of these changes. Although speed and strength decline, is it possible that there is a bonus of aging in accuracy of skilled motor performance?

Strength in humans reaches its peak in the age range 20–29 and shows accelerating decline for each subsequent decade. Changes in strength occur in virtually all motor outputs, and this decline seems to arise from changes in properties of muscles and joints. Human performance studies in work settings indicate that this decline is less evident in people who engage in strenuous work.

Speed clearly falls prey to the ravages of the years. Both simple and complex motor tasks take longer after the peak period of 20–29. Over the life span and across many tasks this decline is from 20% to 40%. It arises from changes both in the muscle system and in information-processing networks that command movements. Some relatively simple tasks seem to show major changes. Speed of writing decreases between the age groups 20–29 and 60–69. The slowdown in this task and many similar tasks that involve small muscle movements does not arise from muscular limitations but rather from changes in central processing involving decisions that provide movement guidance. This result is demonstrated in studies showing that effects of aging are reduced when special warning signals are given that prepare the subject for the intended movement. Some benefit from slowing is evident in the form of increased accuracy of movement, provided tasks do not involve complex perceptual information.

The physiological substrates of these motor declines are evident at many levels of the neuromotor system. In the brain both neurochemical and neuroanatomical changes have been shown. McGeer and McGeer (1976) have emphasized declines in the level of transmitters within some brain regions involved in motor control. Examining the caudate nucleus of humans of different ages at autopsy, they found that a major drop in transmitter level occurs at age 40. These data are quite striking, although they have not yet been confirmed in other laboratories.

In Chapter 3 we explored some of the neuroanatomical changes that occur with aging. Scheibel et al. (1977) have drawn particular attention to the loss of Betz cells, a class of large nerve cells in the human motor cortex. Progressive loss in this cell population, Scheibel believes, reduces the number of fibers in a fast-conducting pathway from the brain to motoneurons in the spinal cord involved in locomotion.

Aged rats show movement disorders that are particularly evident during swimming. A similar impairment can be seen in young rats after injury to dopamine cells. Movement disorders of aged rats can be markedly reduced by administration of L-dopa, a precursor of dopamine and a drug that stimulates dopamine receptors, apomorphine (Marshall and Berrios, 1979). These findings are consistent with the McGeer and McGeer findings in postmortem studies of human brains. Thus it appears that movement impairments of the aged may arise from declining activities of dopamine-containing cells and their postsynaptic receptors.

Comparative views of movements and acts

Comparisons of the similarities and differences in various animals in the accomplishment of particular acts can provide a useful perspective for understanding the anatomy and physiology of movement. Some differences depend on anatomical specializations in bones, like long hind-limb bones that aid in jumping. Other differences emphasize neural specializations like the fineness of forelimb innervation that allows the dexterous use of forelimbs in primates and raccoons. In this section we will consider comparative perspectives on locomotion and vocalization.

Locomotion

In the animal world the task of moving about is fulfilled in many different ways. For some animals locomotion is accomplished by changes in body shape. Picture the sweeping curves of the body of a snake moving through the grass or the oscillations of the tail of a fish in water. More dramatic examples of changes in body shape as the basis for locomotion are the sudden jet propulsion of squid and the backward, darting escape movement of crayfish produced by sudden tail flexion. Locomotion in many other animals, like humans, is accomplished by specialized limb structures that provide the force for movements. A cross-species comparison of maximal speed of locomotion is provided in Figure 8-24. Some animals, like the cheetah, maintain their maximum speeds for only very short distances.

However locomotion is accomplished, there is a common basic characteristic—rhythm. For all animals, moving about consists of repetitive cycles of the same act, be it the endless beating of wings or the repetition of particular sequences of leg movements. In contemporary research in the neurosciences considerable attention has been given to the possible neural basis of the repetitive cycles of locomotion. Do these repetitive cycles develop from the sensory impact of movement itself, or do they reflect endogenous oscillators that provide the basic locomotor programs that motoneurons obligingly obey? In addition to the repetitive, cyclical character of locomotion, there are other features that demand a neural understanding. For example, any single cycle of a locomotor act involves the coordinative sequential activation of many muscles whose excitation is carefully graded. Comparisons in many animals, from insects to humans, indicate that the repetitive cycles of locomotor acts are generated by intrinsic oscillators.

Rhythmic movements appear to be generated by mechanisms within the spinal cord. These rhythms can be independent of brain influences and afferent inflow. Such central generation of locomotor rhythms has recently been shown by Grillner and Zangger (1979). In their study electromyographic records of hind-limb muscles of cats with spinal cord section and dorsal root cuts reveal a "walking" pattern that lasts for seconds when a single dorsal root is briefly stimulated with electrical pulses (Figure 8-25). Outputs from spinal motoneurons or muscles also show different

mph	0	10	20	30	40	50
kph	0	16	32	48	64	80

Figure 8-24 Comparisons of maximal speed of locomotion of several common vertebrate species. The fastest flier shows about twice the speed of the most rapid runner, which is twice as fast as the fastest swimmer.

types of coordination that are variants of typical locomotor patterns, like galloping. The activity of the relevant muscles shows phase relations quite similar to characteristic muscle time differences found in the observation of actual movements in intact animals. Three intact adjacent spinal segments provide the minimal amount of spinal processing necessary for generation of part of the locomotor rhythm. Spinal networks in this and other studies generate neural patterns that provide the substrate of various locomotor acts. Thus pathways to the spinal cord from the brain do not generate the essential rhythm but may control onset and provide corrections arising from other influences registered by the brain. Generation of locomotor rhythms has been demonstrated especially clearly in invertebrate preparations (e.g., Stent et al., 1978; Wilson, 1964).

344

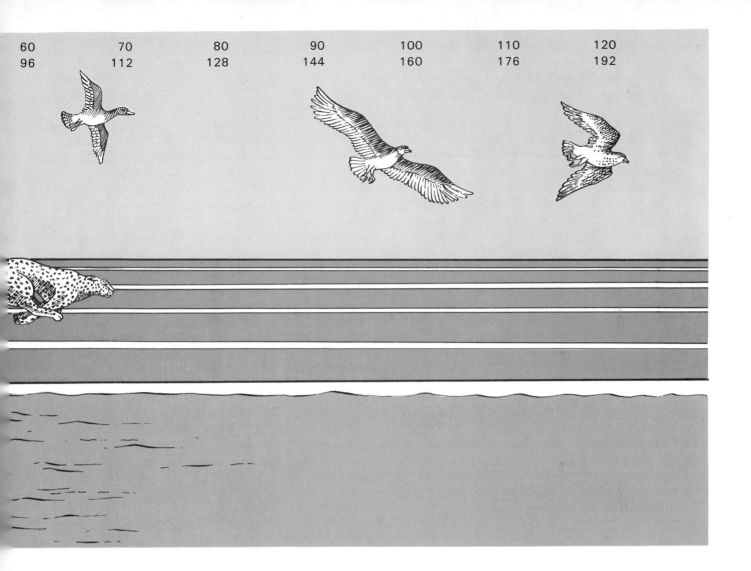

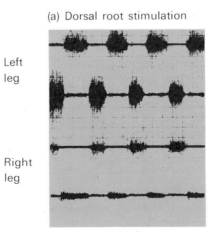

Figure 8-25 Pattern of walking shown in electromyograms of hindlimb muscles in an acute spinal and deafferented cat. (Grillner and Zangger, 1979)

(a) Dorsal root stimulation

(b) Dorsal column stimulation

Left leg

Right leg

1 second

Vocalization   In many animals, including humans, structures used for breathing are also used to produce species-typical sounds. In most cases these sounds are produced by forcing air out of either lungs or a pouch so that it flows across a structure that can vibrate when stretched in particular ways. Coordination of muscle activity is essential at several steps. Human speech production was discussed above. In other mammals, too, these steps include control of expiration from the lung, which determines airflow across the vocal folds, pressure on the vocal folds, and changes in the shape of the vocal cavities, such as the throat and mouth. Many of the vocalizations of animals are quite complicated and demand highly precise movement control lest they become acoustic gibberish.

Vocal behavior in nonhuman primates involves some startling and elaborate facial movements. Many investigators have recorded the sound repertoire of primates, and some have mapped the locus of brain regions involved in sound production. For instance, Detlev Ploog (1981) has examined the vocal behavior of the squirrel monkey, a small South American primate that lives in a dense jungle habitat. Auditory signals are particularly valuable for communication in this environment. Types of vocalizations and the social value or setting of these sounds were charted and studies were then performed to see whether characteristic vocalizations could be elicited by localized brain stimulation. Maps of the distribution of brain sites that yield vocal responses that mimic naturally produced sounds show a concentration of subcortical regions especially dense in areas that relate to control of emotional responses. Stimulation of motor pathways did not produce a characteristic sound, thus suggesting that the program for vocal behavior is not directly accessible in the motor system itself. In this case it seems to be organized in other subcortical areas. Lesions of a restricted brainstem region cause loss of vocal behavior in the monkey. (In contrast to the emphasis on subcortical control of vocalization in nonhuman primates, human speech is largely organized at the cerebral cortex.)

Intensive study of some frog vocalizations has led to a description of how frogs produce sounds. Male frogs produce several stereotyped calls. At night during the mating season males emit mating calls that draw females to ponds. A release call is produced by males when another male clasps them; this call causes the release of clasping. Robert Schmidt (1974a) has mapped the brain of frogs to determine the centers that control their acoustic behavior. Lesions in the brainstem of this animal revealed a center for the production of species-typical calls. Cutting afferent nerves in the frog does not alter the pattern of its vocalizations, showing that peripheral feedback is not required to guide this behavior (Schmidt, 1974b). In other words, the system is an open loop—which contrasts with the closed-loop control of human speech (discussed in Chapter 16).

Movement disorders   Much of the machinery of the body is involved in movement, so the behavioral characteristics of impaired movements and acts provide clues about the locus and characteristics of pathology in the motor system. In this section we will present examples of impaired movement and the bodily conditions that underlie them.

Muscle disorders   Many metabolic conditions can affect the chemistry and structure of muscle. In Chapter 5 we noted that several hormones—especially thyroid—affect muscle chemistry and function. Chronically low levels of thyroid hormone produce muscle weakness and slowness of muscle contraction. Several muscle diseases are more mysterious in origin, seemingly involving biochemical abnormalities that lead to structural changes in muscle, disorders referred to as muscular dystrophy. Many of these disorders, especially in children, appear to be hereditary metabolic abnormalities.

Neuromuscular disorders   Pathological changes in motor neurons produce movement paralysis or weakness. Virus-induced destruction of motor neurons, in the form of polio, was once a frightening prospect, especially in the United States and Western Europe. This disease involved viral destruction of motor neurons of the spinal cord and, in more severe types, of cranial motor neurons of the brainstem.

Movement disorders involving the neuromuscular synaptic junction include a variety of reversible poison states. For example, in tropical areas of the world snake bites cause neuromuscular blocks by releasing toxic substances. Venom of some highly poisonous snakes contains a substance that blocks postsynaptic receptor sites for acetylcholine. Some aspects of this form of synaptic interference were discussed in Chapter 4, where we discussed myasthenia gravis, another motor impairment involving cholinergic synapses.

Spinal injuries   War, sports, and accidents cause many forms of human spinal injuries that result in motor impairment. Injuries to the human spinal cord commonly develop from forces to the neck or back that break bone and cause compression of nervous tissue of the spinal cord. Sudden acceleration of the head with respect to the back, such as occurs in car accidents, can also produce spinal injury. Hemorrhage and circulation block produce a wide range of spinal symptoms following injury.

Complete transection of the spinal cord produces immediate paralysis with a loss of reflexes below the level of injury; a condition known as flaccid paralysis. It occurs chiefly when a considerable stretch of the spinal cord has been destroyed. In contrast, some forms of spinal cord injury produce a transection without widespread destruction of tissue. In this case reflexes below the level of injury are frequently excessive, since the intact tissue lacks the dampening influence of brain inhibitory pathways. Considerable research is currently being directed to the study of promoting the regrowth of spinal cord fibers across a region of spinal injury. Regrowth of fibers in the rodent spinal cord following injury can be readily demonstrated. To date, promoting similar regrowth in higher mammals has proved more difficult.

Brain mechanisms and movement disorders   Injury of brain motor control centers produces either diminished movement, like paralysis, or various types of increased or excessive movements. Strokes affecting cerebral-cortical motor regions typically produce partial paralysis on the contralateral side of the body. Injury and disease involving other brain motor control regions result in excessive, poorly controlled movements, including several kinds of tremor—that is, rhythmic, repetitive movements. This rhythm frequently derives from the alternation in the contraction of opposed muscle groups. Three forms of tremor can be distinguished:

1. **Tremor-at-rest,** which is movement that occurs when the affected region, such as a limb, is fully supported; it is even seen when no movement is being attempted.

2. **Postural tremor,** which is manifested when the person attempts to maintain a posture such as holding an arm or leg extended.

3. **Intention tremor,** which is provoked only during voluntary movement—for example, when the person reaches out to grasp an object.

Tremor-at-rest (usually with a frequency of 5–6 cycles/sec) is particularly characteristic of **Parkinson's disease,** which is the most common human disease involving the basal ganglia. Tremor-at-rest in this disease (which is also characterized by other movement dysfunctions) involves the extremities and can also affect the eyelids and tongue. It is a degenerative disease arising primarily between the ages of 40 and 60. Initially it involves a loss of cells in the brain region called the substantia nigra. Great advances have been made in recent years in the treatment of this disorder because of fundamental advances in knowledge of the anatomical relations between the substantia nigra and the caudate nucleus and because of the discovery of the synaptic transmitter in this pathway. Output from the substantia nigra goes to the caudate nucleus and involves dopamine as a synaptic transmitter. Parkinson's disease patients show a deficit of dopamine in the caudate nucleus; when they are given replacement therapy with a precursor of dopamine (L-dopa), there is a decrease in tremor, in addition to a relief of additional symptoms. A Parkinson's-like syndrome may also follow the use of certain tranquilizers, particularly a class called phenothiazines, the best known of which is the drug chlorpromazine. This syndrome occurs because these drugs either interfere with the storage of dopamine or block the postsynaptic receptor membrane at sites where dopamine is a transmitter.

Postural tremor can be caused by disease processes in the basal ganglia or cerebellum. There are also some forms of congenital postural tremor.

Intention tremor appears most commonly at the end of a movement and can result from any of a large number of pathological conditions that involve either the basal ganglia or the cerebellum.

The most extreme examples of increased movements involving basal ganglia dysfunctions are choreic movements and ballism. **Choreic movements** are uncontrollable, brief, and forceful; they look like strange exaggerations of normal movements. They may include a jerking movement of fingers, a facial grimace, or a dancelike movement of the feet. **Huntington's chorea** is a genetic disorder characterized by these unusual movements in addition to profound changes in mental functioning. In some of these patients a marked loss of cells in the caudate nucleus has been found. ("Chorea" comes from a Greek term for "dancing." Chorus comes from the same root, since originally a chorus danced as well as sang.)

Ballism refers to an uncontrollable, violent tossing of the limbs. The movement is sudden and may involve one side of the body. Lesions in a region called the subthalamic nucleus can produce this syndrome in humans and monkeys.

The above examples of increased movements involving extrapyramidal system diseases are hyperkinetic disorders ("hyper" means "above normal"; "kinetic" refers to movement). They demonstrate the major role that inhibition plays in normal motor control; without adequate inhibition a person is compelled to perform a variety of unwanted movements. There is also a major class of hyperkinetic effects involving motor stiffness (akinesia) and rigidity (increase of muscle tone). These deficits are also part of Parkinson's syndrome.

New developments in treatment of movement disorders

From ancient times people have sought to replace parts of the body lost by accident or disease. Artificial limbs and artificial teeth are two familiar examples of what are called **prosthetic devices** or "prostheses" (from the Greek term for "an addition"). With advances in knowledge of the mechanisms of movement and its neural controls, prosthetic devices are constantly being improved and are able to replace the missing member more completely than ever before. The use of the term "prosthesis" has been expanded to include an artificial addition that does not replace a part of the body but that aids functioning. An example is the electronic pacemaker, which ensures regularity of functioning of the heart when its own electrical pacing has become irregular. Another example is electrical stimulation to aid the cerebellum in inhibiting hyperactive reflexes, to be discussed below.

An artificial arm controlled by thought

Although artificial arms and hands have an ancient history, their usefulness was rather limited until recently. In some cases mechanical hands have had movable parts to which tendons of forearm muscles could be attached so that the amputee could have a certain amount of movement. Some people have learned to grasp and manipulate to a certain extent with these devices, but prolonged training is required. More recently, improved artificial hands and arms have been devised that an amputee can use readily with very little training (Figure 8-26). The artificial arm seems to do whatever the user intends. Small motors are installed in the arm to power the movements; the operation of the motors is controlled by a minicomputer in the arm. The computer receives information about the activity of intact muscles in the person's shoulder, chest, and neck. Whenever a person moves an arm, simultaneously there are coordinated and compensatory contractions of muscles in the nearby parts of the body, and the pattern of these contractions varies according to the particular movement of the arm. The computer can thus tell what arm movement is intended by analyzing the pattern of activation in the associated parts of the body. The different motors in the artificial arm are then operated with more or less force, depending on the pattern of activation. Feedback occurs through the pull of the arm on the rest of the body.

Researchers are now attempting to provide more complete feedback of the movements and stresses within the artificial arm. To do this, they are placing various

Figure 8-26 An artificial arm controlled by the electrical activity of intact muscles of shoulder, chest and neck. (Courtesy Liberty Mutual Insurance Company)

detectors within the arm that produce stimulation in the form of touches or vibrations on adjacent patches of skin. This technique gives more adequate feedback, but the amputee has to learn how to interpret and use it.

Neural prosthesis Muscle rigidity in cerebral palsy patients prevents or limits many movements. Routine accomplishments like reaching for objects, writing, and speech become labored and, for many patients, well-nigh impossible. Approaches to treatment over the years have involved a variety of efforts, including brain surgery, limb surgery, drugs, and physical therapy. Recently some dramatic prospects have opened up through the use of direct stimulation of the brain, particularly regions of the cerebellum.

The story starts with the recognition that all the outputs of the cerebellar cortex are inhibitory. Wherever the axons of Purkinje cells terminate, their activity produces inhibitory synaptic potentials. Experiments with cats, rats, and nonhuman primates have shown that electrical stimulation of various sectors of the cerebellar cortex can suppress some forms of muscle rigidity.

These observations led Irving Cooper, a research neurosurgeon, to suggest that cerebellar electrical stimulation might relieve symptoms of cerebral palsy and seizure disorders. Cooper and his collaborators (1976) have described remarkable relief afforded by a program of cerebellar stimulation. The patients in this study were impaired in walking, and most were restricted to wheelchairs; hyperactive reflexes impaired activity of the arms. After a group of electrodes were placed on the cerebellum, the patients received various programs of stimulation, in some cases continuing for 24 hours a day over a period of months. Following these treatments some patients who had been unable to walk could eventually move about without assistance. Improvements were also noted in speech and in relief from spasticity.

These efforts remain in the realm of clinical research. Indeed, some researchers have become critical of these data and argue that behavioral observations are too subjective for a suitable assessment of therapeutic effectiveness. Searching criticism may lead to improvements in these techniques, but even now they appear to provide a major aid to some patients whose lives have been severely circumscribed by motion disorders.

Biofeedback and movement disorders

The acquisition of complex motor skills necessary for athletic feats or playing a musical instrument shows that learning can change brain control of movement. Learned control of movement initiation, organization, and termination is evident in many of the skills we acquire during our lives, as we saw earlier. Is it possible that we can, through training, reduce or eliminate abnormal movements? Many studies have now shown that operant conditioning techniques can be employed for therapeutic purposes in a range of movement disorders that arise from brain impairments. This therapeutic technique is also known as **biofeedback**, because the signals used for operant modification are derived from the actual movements of an individual. Let us consider the procedures used in these clinical studies.

All biofeedback procedures are similar even though the applications are diverse. Some movement or postural deviation or level of muscle tension is detected by a special recording device. In some cases these motor states are observed by electromyography, which can provide accurate information about the activity of very small motor units. Information about these motor events or states is conveyed to the patient in the form of light or sound displays. More specifically, the motor events detected by the recording device are made to control the turning on and off of light or sound. The patient is thus informed about the movement, posture, or tension of some body part by exteroceptive information in addition to the usual array of muscle and joint receptor information. The subjects are instructed to try to keep the signal off (or on) for as long a period as possible, using any means, including thought, imagery, or just plain relaxation.

Major successes in using this procedure in motor disorder treatment have been reported, especially in reducing muscle tension and the strength of abnormal movements. Reduction in tension headaches produced by excessive tension of forehead muscles can result when biofeedback signals from these muscles are provided to patients. A remarkably effective use of biofeedback has been described by Brudny (1976) in the treatment of torticollis, a neuromuscular disorder characterized by extreme contraction of neck muscles producing a deviation of the head. This reaction is frequently spasmodic, producing an intermittent, marked neck muscle contraction on one side. Brudny (1976) has shown that biofeedback techniques can be used to inhibit spastic activity of neck muscles and to increase the tension of neck muscles on the opposite side of the neck in order to oppose the force that produces neck deviation. The success of biofeedback treatment in muscle disorder is also seen in cases of partial paralysis following stroke and cerebral palsy—both states of insufficient muscle activity. Poor control of the foot is evident in many cerebral palsy patients, and among those patients who can walk, foot dragging impedes success. Spearing and Poppen (1974) have shown that sounding a loud horn every time foot dragging is evident markedly reduces the instances of this impediment to walking. The effect is specific to the trained leg and is not evident in the untrained leg. This mode of treatment is very effective in providing control for many other inadequate movements of the limbs of cerebral palsy patients and seems to provide an alternative to surgery.

Exteroceptive displays that are controlled by signals provided by muscle activity enable subjects to become more aware of their muscle activity and to produce learned, corrective actions. In Chapter 12 we will discuss applications of these procedures in disorders of autonomically innervated structures, especially the heart.

SUMMARY / MAIN POINTS

1. All behavior that we see consists of either the secretion of glands or muscle contractions. Muscle contractions are regulated by neural impulses that arrive at the muscles over motor nerve fibers.

2. Reflexes are patterns of relatively simple and stereotyped movements that are elicited by stimulation of sensory receptors; their amplitude is proportional to the intensity of the stimulation.

3. The control of many reflexes occurs through closed-loop, negative-feedback circuits. Some behaviors are so rapid, however, that they are open-loop; that is, the pattern is preset and determined intrinsically without feedback control.

4. In the complex sequences of species-specific behavior that are called fixed-action or modal-action patterns, the stimulus input triggers a preexisting pattern whose magnitude is *not* related to the intensity of stimulation.

5. Many learned, skilled acts also have open-loop control and are not influenced by stimulus intensity, so long as the intensity exceeds the threshold.

6. When a muscle is stretched, a reflex circuit causes contraction, which works to restore the muscle to its original length; this response is the stretch reflex. The stretch of the muscle is detected by special receptors, called muscle spindles, that are built into the muscle.

7. The sensitivity of the muscle spindle can be adjusted by efferent impulses that call for different degrees of contraction of the muscle. This adjustment allows flexible control of posture and movement.

8. The final common pathway for impulses to skeletal muscles consists of motoneurons, whose cell bodies in vertebrates are located in the ventral horn of the spinal cord.

The motoneurons receive impulses from a variety of sources, including sensory input from the dorsal spinal roots, other spinal cord neurons, and descending fibers of the pyramidal and extrapyramidal systems.

9. Circuits within the spinal cord underlie the spinal reflexes, which can occur even when the cord is transected, severing connections to the brain.

10. The pyramidal tract is especially well developed in primates and is mainly involved in controlling fine movements of the extremities. Its fibers originate in the cerebral cortex, and they run directly to spinal motoneurons or to internuncial cells in the spinal cord.

11. The extrapyramidal system includes the basal ganglia (caudate, putamen, globus pallidus, and claustrum) and some major brainstem nuclei (substantia nigra and red nucleus). The basal ganglia have been especially implicated in generation of slow or ramp movement of functions.

12. The cerebellum receives input about pyramidal and extrapyramidal activities; it also receives input from receptors within the body, the eyes, and the ears. The cerebellum is involved in the feedback control of movements and in generation of ballistic movement functions.

13. Movement disorders can arise because of impairment at any of several levels of the motor system: the muscles, the motor neurons and neuromuscular junctions, or the spinal cord.

14. Some movement disorders can be alleviated by the use of prosthetic devices; others can be alleviated by directly stimulating a particular region of the brain. Biofeedback has proved effective in overcoming several kinds of movement disorders.

RECOMMENDED READING

Desmedt, J. E. (Ed.). *Progress in clinical neurophysiology* (Vol. 4): *Cerebral motor control in man: Long loop mechanisms*. Basel: Karger, 1978.

Stelmach, G. E. (Ed.). *Information processing in motor control and learning*. New York: Academic, 1978.

Talbot, R. E., and Humphrey, D. R. (Eds). *Posture and movement*. New York: Raven, 1979.

Towe, A. and Luschei, E. (Eds.). *Handbook of behavioral neurobiology* (Vol. 5): *Motor coordination*. New York: Plenum, 1981.

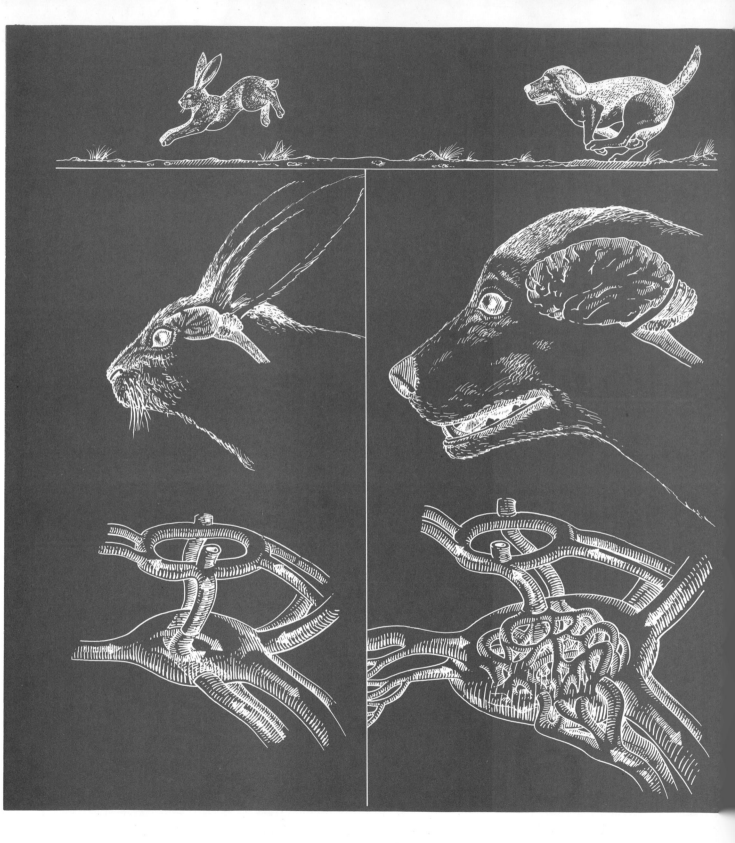

Part Three

CONTROL OF
BEHAVIORAL STATES:
MOTIVATION

So far we have considered the basic equipment and capacities of an organism: the integrative functions of the nervous and endocrine systems, the capabilities of sensory and perceptual systems, and the ways in which motor responses are formed and coordinated. But we have not yet paid much attention to how the organism selects among the many options that these systems provide. The behavioral repertoire of most mammals includes obtaining food and eating, finding water and drinking, experiencing vivid dreams, grooming, engaging in sexual behavior, communicating with others, shifting position to a somewhat warmer or cooler spot, withdrawing from painful or threatening situations, and experiencing more and less pleasant feelings. Most of these behaviors are clearly necessary to maintain the health of the individual or to perpetuate the species. But these different kinds of activities cannot all be accomplished at the same time. Some require motor acts that are incompatible with others—an animal can't flee danger and feed at the same time. Some require different times of day or places—a time and a place suitable for sleeping aren't likely to afford water to drink. So responding to one motive often precludes satisfying another at the same time, and different motives may have to be satisfied in succession. How bodily systems function so that all the basic needs are satisfied is the overall question of motivation that we will take up in Part Three.

Orientation

Descriptive Studies of Reproductive Behavior

Phases and reciprocal relations in mating

Reproductive behavior of the ring dove

Reproductive behavior of rodents

Reproductive behavior of the fruit fly

Human reproductive behavior

Development: Becoming a Man or a Woman

"It's a girl!" Prenatal differentiation of reproductive structures

Social influences on gender identity

Do sex hormones organize brain circuits?

Does prenatal sexual development influence personality?

Evolution of Sex

Adaptations for sexual reproduction

Evolutionary implications for human sexuality

Neural and Hormonal Mechanisms of Reproductive Behavior

Sexual reflexes

Brain regions and reproductive behavior

Hormonal influences on reproductive behavior

Summary/Main Points

9

Sex

Orientation

A tourist at a restaurant in France noticed a fly in his soup. Calling over the waiter, the tourist summoned up his best French and said, "Garçon, observez le mouche dans ma soupe." The waiter corrected, "LA mouche." To which the tourist replied, "What sharp eyes you have!"

In some species males and females do look a great deal alike. Species differ greatly, however, in how similar or different the two sexes appear to be. Those in which the two sexes are clearly different are said to be "sexually dimorphic" (dimorphic means different in form); see Figure 9-1. In some familiar dimorphic species the adult male is usually larger than the female (for example, humans, dogs, or turkeys), and in some the male is more highly visible either because of coloration (for example, robin or mandrill baboon) or because of some appendage (for example, antlers of a male moose or the mane of a male lion). But in other species the female is larger (for example, hyena, hamster, or marsh hawk) or more brightly colored (for example, kingfisher or phalarope).

Sex brings variety to life—in more ways than are usually realized. There are, of course, the differences in appearance and behavior between women and men and the specific behaviors involved in mating, childbirth, and parental care. There are also the marked differences that occur during development and that are related to changes in reproductive status and assumption of gender identity. The great variety among people—the differences even within a family—also is due to sexual reproduction. Sexual reproduction provides genetic permutations that are not available in non-sexual reproduction, such as occurs in many plants and some animals. In sexual

Which is the female in each pair?

(a) Mandrill baboons

(b) Peacock and peahen

(c) Ring doves

(d) Praying mantises

(e) Jacanas

reproduction each parent provides half the genetic heritage of the new individual; the precise contribution of the parent to a particular new individual is a random assortment of alternative genes. There are so many possibilities that—except for identical twins—no two human beings have exactly the same heredity.

The genetic variability due to sexual reproduction has resulted in a relatively rapid evolution. With many varied individuals alive at a given time, those better suited to current environmental challenges have a reproductive advantage. Thus life has penetrated new ecological niches, and new species have evolved.

Sexual reproduction requires a division of labor, but this can be accomplished in rather different ways, as some examples will illustrate. In many species members of the two sexes live apart for much of their lives. Reproduction requires that this separation be overcome sufficiently to permit egg and sperm to unite. When and how the two sexes unite vary enormously among species. In some species of mammals, for example, a female copulates only one day each year; in others the female copulates during a mating season that lasts a few months; and in still others the female can mate all during the year. In some species of animals, courtship is initiated by the female, in some by the male, and in some species both sexes engage in reciprocal activity from the start. Further differences are seen in care of the young. The young of some species are on their own from the moment of birth or hatching, while the young of other species need parental care for days, months, or even years. The female parent is the main care giver in most species, the male in others, and in some species both share parental responsibilities.

In the face of all the variety of sexual behavior and anatomy, are there some general conclusions that we can draw about reproductive and parental behaviors and their bodily mechanisms? Can we understand the variety of behavior and appearance in terms of some general principles? You will see that certain classes of hormones and certain neural circuits have similar functions throughout the vertebrates and that certain evolutionary principles have much explanatory value. We will start our investigation by describing some main aspects of reproductive and other sex-linked behaviors. We will then take up the evolution of these behaviors and their development during the lifetime of the individual. Finally we will survey what is known and what is hypothesized about the neural and hormonal mechanisms that mediate sex behaviors.

Descriptive studies of reproductive behavior

We will start our examination by noting the successive stages of reproductive behavior and the types of interactions that occur between the partners. Then we will see what descriptive studies have shown about the reproductive behavior of three kinds of animals that are used for many experiments in this field—the ring dove, the rat and other rodents, and the fruit fly. Descriptive studies of human sex behavior

Figure 9-1 Which is the female in each pair? In mandrill baboons (a), the male is larger and has bright blue areas on the face. In peafowl (b), the cock is larger and more brightly colored than the hen. In ring doves (c), the external appearance of the two sexes is identical, but they behave differently during courtship. Among praying mantises (d) and jacanas (e), the female is larger than the male.

will also be mentioned. In later sections we will relate many aspects of these behaviors to hormonal and neural processes and events.

Phases and reciprocal relations in mating

The mating behavior of many animals shows four successive stages (Figure 9-2), and each stage demands interaction between two individuals. Successful completion of the pattern requires exchange of stimulation between the partners. Many descriptions of mating behavior have focused on the male as initiating and showing greater variety in copulatory behavior; the female's contribution has often been described

Figure 9-2 Stages in reproductive behavior, showing interaction between male and female partners. The postcopulatory phase includes a temporary decrease in the sexual attractiveness of the partner and inhibition of appetitive (proceptive) behavior. Inhibition is represented by arrows with black arrowheads. (Adapted from Beach, 1977)

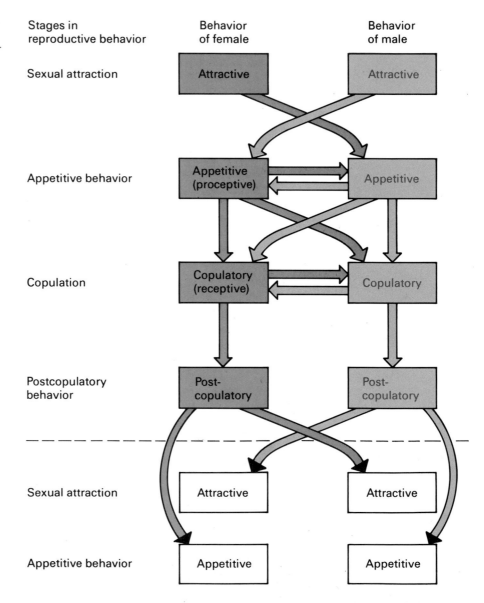

chiefly in terms of her receptivity and cooperation. But some recent treatments have emphasized a more balanced approach (Beach, 1976, p.105):

> At each stage both sexes are equally involved; which is to say that sexual attraction is mutual, sexual initiative is assumed and appetitive behavior is engaged in by both sexes, and mating involves consummatory and post-consummatory phases in females as well as males.

The first stage, **sexual attraction,** is needed to bring the male and female together, and in many species this meeting occurs only when both are in a reproductive state. Attractiveness of female animals can be scored by measuring the males' responses to them under standardized conditions; typical measures include strength or rapidity of approach and occurrence of seminal ejaculation during mating. For example, male monkeys and apes are stimulated by the sight of the "sex skin" of the female when this swells under the influence of estrogen. But attraction is not a one-way process in which females attract males. When female monkeys are in **estrus** (sexually receptive), they are likely to approach males; and they prefer to approach normal males rather than castrated ones. In the case of dogs, males are strongly attracted to the odor of vaginal secretions of a bitch in heat (estrus). The attractiveness can be reduced either by bringing the female out of heat or by castrating the male. Female dogs in heat prefer the odor of normal male dogs to castrates, but when the female goes out of heat this preference disappears.

In females, attractiveness has been found to be related to the level of estrogen; this result has been found in several species—rat, dog, monkey, baboon, and chimpanzee. Females of these species have regular cycles in which high concentrations of estrogen occur around the time of ovulation. Thus attractivity maximizes the probability of copulation when the female is fertile and susceptible to impregnation. But levels of estrogen are not the only determinants of attractivity; as has been shown in two ways:

1. In some experiments the ovaries were removed from female dogs and later they were administered equal amounts of estrogen. In spite of their having the same level of hormone, some females evoked more responses from males than did others.

2. Among dogs and monkeys not all males prefer the same females; thus attractivity resides in part in the eye (or the nose) of the beholder.

Animals do not just emit stimuli that attract members of the opposite sex. They often engage in a second stage, **appetitive behavior,** which helps to establish or maintain sexual interaction. For example, the male may pursue the female and attempt to copulate. The female may approach the male and adopt the copulatory posture. Beach (1977) has proposed the term **proceptive behavior** for female appetitive behavior to distinguish it from "receptive behavior." Types of proceptive behavior include approaching males and remaining close to them, making specific responses that invite or solicit copulation, and showing alternating approach and retreat behavior. Moving away appears to orient the male to the mounting posture necessary for copulation of quadrupeds. Female rats usually run away from the male with a special kind of hopping and darting movement that excites the male and increases the probability of copulation (Hlinak and Madlafousek, 1971). Proceptivity,

Figure 9-3 Reproductive behavior of ring doves. The cycle begins soon after a male and a female are placed in a cage containing nesting material and an empty glass bowl (1). Courtship activity is characterized initially by the "bowing coo" of the male (2). The male and then the female utter a distinctive "nest call" to indicate their selection of a nesting site (3). There follows a week or more of cooperative nest building (4), culminating in the laying of two eggs (5). The adults take turns incubating the eggs (6), which hatch after about 14 days (7). The squabs are fed "crop milk" (8). As the young birds learn to peck grain, the parents continue to feed them, but with increasing reluctance (9). When the squabs are between 2 and 3 weeks old, the adults ignore them and may start a new cycle of reproductive behavior (10). (From D. S. Lehrman, "The reproductive behavior of ring doves." Copyright © 1964 by Scientific American, Inc. All rights reserved.)

like attractivity, is greatest during that part of the estrous cycle when the concentration of estrogen is highest. If the ovaries are removed, eliminating the main source of estrogen, proceptivity wanes, but it can be restored by administering estrogens. Administration of androgens has also been reported to increase proceptivity of both monkeys and rats.

The third stage, **copulatory behavior,** comprises a species-specific pattern that is highly stereotyped in most species. The principal acts of the male mammal are mounting the female, thrusting with the hindquarters, inserting the erect penis **(intromission),** and expelling semen forcefully **(ejaculation).** The essential female acts are assuming the posture that facilitates intromission and maintaining it until ejaculation within the vagina has occurred. Readiness to show these female responses that are necessary and sufficient for the male to achieve intravaginal ejaculation is often referred to as **receptivity.** In some species (for example, the cat), estrogen is the only hormone necessary for receptivity, whereas in others (for example, the dog) receptivity occurs when estrogen is high and progesterone is

beginning to rise. In the latter case progesterone acts synergistically with estrogen. The neural mechanisms appear to be simpler for receptivity than for proceptivity, and receptivity shows fewer individual differences than does proceptivity. For instance, removing the cerebral cortex of a female rat does not impair receptivity, but it disorganizes proceptive responses. In a female rat whose cerebral cortex has been removed, her hopping, darting, and crouching responses are not oriented toward the male nor synchronized with his responses. Consequently the attractivity of such females is reduced; males consistently choose to mate with intact females even though decorticated females are equally receptive.

Some species show a fourth stage, specific **postcopulatory behavior.** This behavior may involve responses such as the after-reaction of rolling (in the cat) and grooming (in the rat). There are also changes in willingness to engage in further mating. After completion of a copulatory sequence, many animals do not mate again for a period of time, even if a receptive partner is available. The refractory period may last for minutes, hours, or days, depending on the species and the circumstances. In many species an animal will show a shorter refractory period to mate with a new partner than with the partner with which it has mated most recently.

Reproductive behavior of the ring dove

The ring dove is a small relative of the domestic pigeon; it is named for the black semicircle around the back of its neck (see Figure 9-3). The male and female are identical in appearance and can be distinguished only by examining the internal reproductive organs through a surgical procedure. In the laboratory the ring dove breeds for most of the year if the length of day and the temperature are suitable. The birds mature sexually at about 5 months of age. When a female and a male ring dove with previous breeding experience are placed in a cage containing an empty glass bowl and a supply of nesting material, the birds enter their normal behavioral cycle, which psychologists have described in detail (Lehrman, 1965; Cheng, 1979).

The male is the first to show sexual attraction; he promptly begins courtship: strutting around, bowing and cooing at the female, and chasing her. Only the male exhibits the bow-coo behavior. A day or two after the male begins to court the female, she may start to show characteristic responses, flipping her wings in a special way and approaching the male. The sight of the male's courtship behavior and the sound of his cooing are clearly attractive to the female. Even if the birds are separated by a glass partition, these stimuli evoke clear neuroendocrine responses (Friedman, 1977). After a few days together the birds usually show that they have selected a nest site by crouching on it and uttering a distinctive nest-coo. In the laboratory cage the nest site is the glass bowl; in nature it would be a concave place on the ground. If the male is paired with a female that is not easily aroused, he will continue to bow-coo and nest-coo at an undiminished frequency for weeks if the female fails to nest-coo. As soon as the female begins to nest-coo, the male's nest-coo behavior tapers off. Her behavior signals when the male should stop cooing and move on to the next behavior in the sequence, nest building. The two sexes show different and complementary activities in this phase, with the male gathering and carrying nest material to the female, who does most of the nest construction. Nest building normally occupies a week or more. Having a complete nest is an essential signal that ends nest-building activities.

When the nest is finished, or nearly complete, the birds begin the stage of copulation. For copulation the female squats low; the male mounts on her back, flapping his wings to keep his balance, and his **cloaca** contacts that of the female. (Doves, like many birds, do not have a penis or a vagina. Sperm are discharged and eggs are laid through the cloaca, which is the same passage through which wastes are eliminated.)

Once the female becomes noticeably more attached to the nest, indicating that she is about to lay her eggs, copulation ceases. About a week after the beginning of nest building she produces the first egg; the second egg appears two days later. Thereafter the male and female birds alternate in sitting on the eggs, the male for about 6 hours in the middle of each day and the female for the rest of the time.

The eggs hatch after about 14 days, and the parents feed the young "crop-milk," a thick liquid secreted at this stage of the cycle from the adult's crop (a pouch in its gullet). The squabs (young doves) leave the nest when they are about 10–12 days old, but they continue to beg for food and to receive it from their parents. Over the next few days the parents feed the young birds less and less, and the squabs develop the ability to peck for grain on the floor of the cage. The male parent often continues supplying crop-milk to the young for several days after the female has stopped. When the young are about 15–25 days old, the adult male may start courtship again. The entire cycle lasts about 6 or 7 weeks. In nature only a single cycle usually occurs each year, unless the first eggs were infertile; in that case the birds may go through the reproductive cycle again (Cheng, 1977).

Each phase of the reproductive cycle is influenced by particular hormonal states, as we will see later. The level(s) of one or more hormones affects the behavior, and in turn the behavior stimulates neuroendocrine links that alter the secretion of hormones.

Reproductive behavior of rodents

Rodents are diverse and notoriously successful at reproduction—virtually regardless of habitat. The main steps in the copulatory sequence of rodents and some main respects in which rodent species differ in copulatory behavior are classified in Table 9-1.

Unlike birds, rodents do not engage in lengthy courtship, nor do the partners tend to remain together for prolonged periods. Attraction occurs largely through odor. Appetitive behavior of the female rat was described above—darting, hopping, and withdrawing. Females of some other rodent species show similar behavior, while those of other species do not. In copulation the male mounts the female from the rear and grasps her flanks with his forelegs. If the female is receptive, she stands still and assumes a posture that aids intromission; in this female posture (called **lordosis**) the hindquarters are raised and the tail is turned to one side (Figure 9-4). When the penis has been inserted into the vagina, some species, such as the house mouse, show repetitive intravaginal thrusts, whereas other species, such as the Norway rat, have but a single pelvic thrust per intromission. (Whether or not multiple thrusts occur is shown in column 1 of Table 9-1.)

Some species can ejaculate the first time the penis is inserted into the vagina. In other species the male dismounts and then mounts again, requiring several intromissions before ejaculation (see column 2 of the table). Most rodents ejaculate more than once during a single episode of mating; the Northern pygmy mouse is an exception (column 3). After ejaculation the male in most rodent species withdraws the penis and dismounts, but in some species the penis remains swollen in the vagina for many minutes, a response called a "lock" (column 4). Locking was thought to be characteristic of carnivores, but it has also been found in several species of rodents.

The conclusion of a sequence is demonstrated when the animal does not engage in further copulatory behavior even if a receptive partner is available. The duration of the postejaculatory refractory period may last from a few minutes to 24 hours or more, depending on the species.

In the rat only the mother cares for the young. Toward the end of the 21-day period of pregnancy, the female builds a nest. Rats are born in a rather undeveloped state

TABLE 9-1　Patterns of Copulatory Behavior in Some Species of Muroid Rodents

SPECIES	MULTIPLE THRUSTS PER INTROMISSION	MULTIPLE INTROMISSIONS PER EJACULATION	MULTIPLE EJACULATIONS PER EPISODE	LOCK
Norway rat	No	Yes	Yes	No
House mouse	Yes	Yes	Yes	No
Peter's climbing rat	Yes	No	Yes	Yes
Southern grasshopper mouse	No	No	Yes	Yes
Northern pygmy mouse	No	No	No	Yes

SOURCE: Dewsbury, 1975.

Figure 9-4 Copulation of rats. The raised rump of the female (the "lordosis posture") and her deflected tail make intromission possible. (From Barnett, 1975)

(and are therefore said to be **precocial**) —they have no hair and cannot regulate their body temperature, and their eyes and ears do not open until about 13 days after birth. The mother keeps the rat pups warm, nurses them, and retrieves them if they wiggle out of the nest. Some other rodents, such as the guinea pig, are born in a much more fully developed state (they are **altricial**). Altricial young do not stay long with their mother, and if necessary they can get along without maternal care.

Reproductive behavior of the fruit fly

Study of the fruit fly, genus *Drosophila,* has been extremely important to the advancement of genetics; the inheritance of both anatomical features and behavioral characteristics has been studied extensively, and we know a great deal about the courtship and copulatory behavior of several subgenera and species of *Drosophila*. Besides providing us with genetic information about mating patterns, descriptions of this behavior in *Drosophila* provide us with an example of complex stereotyped behavior in a "simple" animal and show mating behavior mediated in part by chemoreceptors.

In brief, here are the main steps: The male taps the female with a foreleg. Receptors on the foreleg pick up chemical and tactile information necessary to species identification. If the female is of his species, the male then stands close to her side and follows her if she moves [see (a) in Figure 9-5]. He extends the wing closest to her head and vibrates it. This response may aid stimulation of chemical receptors on her antennae by emphasizing his odor, but it is also an auditory stimulus; different species vibrate their wings at different rates, and this action seems to provide distinctive auditory stimuli. (Visual stimulation is probably not involved since courtship proceeds as rapidly in the dark as in the light.) The duration of the wing-vibrating phase differs among species. If the male is successful, the female does not attempt to move away and shows receptivity. The male circles behind the female, extends his proboscis, and licks her genital region. The male then attempts to copulate, and the cooperating female spreads her wings and opens her genital plates to permit intromission.

Figure 9-5 Reproductive behavior of *Drosophila.* The male (a) orients to the female, (b) vibrates the near wing and lowers the other wing, (c) licks the genital region of the female, and (d) assumes the copulation posture. If the female is receptive, the pair then copulates (e). (From Manning, 1965)

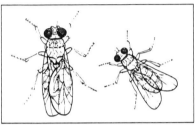

(a)

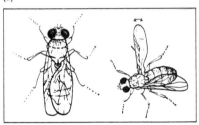

(b)

(c)

(d)

(e)

The elaborate courtship behavior of *Drosophila* probably serves more than one function. For one thing, it probably helps to keep different species of *Drosophila* reproductively separate. Different species show characteristic differences in frequency of wing beat in courtship, and a female responds only to the frequency of her own species. The courtship behavior may also play a part in sexual selection. The female is unreceptive at first and responds to a male that courts vigorously and that is more likely to be more fertile than a less active suitor.

Various kinds of mutant *Drosophila* are unable to perform one or another part of the mating sequence. Such mutants would be unable to reproduce in nature, but they can be studied in the laboratory. By use of genetic techniques investigators have been able to learn about some of the neural controls of mating in *Drosophila,* as we will see later.

Neither *Drosophila* parent cares for the young, and this is true of most insects and even of many species of vertebrates. The female *Drosophila* does, however, tend to lay her eggs where they are likely to survive and where the young are likely to find food when they hatch.

Human reproductive behavior

There wasn't much objective information about human sexual behavior in the 1940s, as biology professor Alfred Kinsey found when he started to look into the subject. To fill the gap, Kinsey began to ask friends and colleagues for detailed information about their sexual histories. Kinsey then constructed a standardized set of questions and procedures. He attempted to obtain information for representative samples of the U.S. population categorized by sex, age, religion, and education. Eventually he and collaborators obtained detailed information from tens of thousands of men, and they published an extensive survey of sexual behavior of the American male (1948). An equally detailed survey of the sexual behavior of the American female followed a few years later (1953).

A further step was to make behavioral and physiological observations of people while they engaged in sexual intercourse or masturbation. Perhaps the first person to undertake such studies was John B. Watson, the founder of behaviorism. But his research on intercourse in the early 1920s led to a scandal and the loss of his professorship. The largest and best-known project of this kind began in the middle 1950s and is headed by physician William Masters and psychologist Virginia Johnson (1965, 1966, 1970). These studies have provided greatly increased knowledge about the different physiological responses that occur in various parts of the body during intercourse, their time courses, and their relations to what the individuals experience.

Among most species of mammals, including nonhuman primates, the male mounts the female from the rear, but among humans face-to-face postures are most common. A great variety of coital postures has been described, particularly from the Orient. Many couples vary their postures from session to session or even within a session. The variety of reproductive behavior, both within and among individuals, is a characteristic that differentiates humans from other species.

Figure 9-6 Sexual response cycles of (a) men and (b) women. These are schematic diagrams and do not represent any particular physiological measure, although heart rate varies in this manner. (a) The typical male pattern with an absolute refractory phase after orgasm. (b) Three patterns often observed in women. (Adapted from Masters and Johnson, 1965)

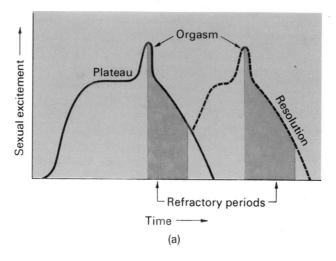

(a)

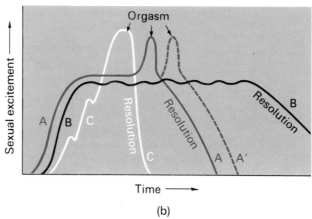

(b)

Typical response patterns of men and women have been summarized by Masters and Johnson (1965); see Figures 9-6a and b. Both sexes show four phases: increasing excitement, plateau, **orgasm** (the climax of sexual experience marked by extremely pleasurable sensations), and resolution. In spite of this basic similarity of male and female responses, there are also some typical differences. One important difference is the greater variety of commonly observed sequences in women. Whereas men have only one basic male pattern, women have three typical patterns, as shown in Figure 9-6b. The second main difference between the sexes is that men, but not women, have an absolute refractory phase following an orgasm. The male cannot achieve full erection and another orgasm until some time has elapsed; the length of time may vary from minutes to hours, depending on individual differences and on other factors. Women can have multiple orgasms in rapid succession.

In the male pattern excitement mounts in response to stimulation, which may be mental or physical or both. The rate of rise of excitement varies with many factors. If stimulation continues, the level of excitement reaches a high plateau. At some point during this stage the reflexive orgasmic responses are triggered. Then there is a gradual dissipation of excitement during the resolution phase. Usually the rising phase and the resolution phase are the longest parts of the cycle. The plateau phase typically lasts only a few minutes, and orgasm usually lasts a minute or less.

The most common pattern in women (A in Figure 9-6b) is similar in form to the male pattern. The first two phases in both sexes are marked by congestion of the blood vessels of the genitalia. This response produces penile erection in the man and vaginal lubrication and swelling in the woman. Orgasm is marked by rhythmic muscular contractions in both sexes; in the woman these occur in the muscles around the vagina. There are also typical sex differences in the temporal patterns of response. Women are usually somewhat slower than men to reach orgasm during intercourse and, as noted above, they have no refractory phase.

Two other patterns are also observed frequently in women. In pattern B the high level of excitement in the plateau phase does not quite trigger orgasmic release; after a prolonged plateau period sexual excitement dissipates gradually. Pattern C, on the other hand, is rapid and explosive. The orgasmic response is reached without a plateau, and resolution is also rapid. Orgasm in this pattern tends to be both longer and more intense than the other forms.

The similarities and differences in sexual responses exemplify the generalization of Chapter 1 that in some ways each person is like all other people, in some ways like some other people, and in some ways like no other person. The existence of differences among groups and individuals does not contradict or lessen the value of research into biological determinants of behavior. Some of the behavioral differences are related to differences in genetic makeup; some are related to differences in levels of hormones. And some of the behavioral differences can be explained by experience and learning; these, too, have biological bases, and we will consider biological mechanisms of learning in Chapters 14 and 15.

The fact that the orgasmic response is reflexive and cannot be withheld once a certain level of excitement has been reached does not mean that it is not subject to learning and other psychological influences. It is now known that many autonomic responses can be altered in their thresholds and time courses through appropriate training. Current forms of sex therapy based on studies of physiological responses are claimed to help many individuals experience sexual stimulation more fully and to help many couples coordinate their behavior more adequately (Kaplan, 1974; Masters and Johnson, 1970).

Development: Becoming a man or a woman

The developmental perspective is especially useful in the study of sex and behavior. It helps to answer the question: "How does a person assume the **gender identity** of a man or a woman?" That is, how does one identify one's self, and become identified by others, as a male or a female? The striking changes in sexual anatomy and in reproductive status over the life span are obviously important. So too are the several stages of sexual development that occur prenatally in humans and that lead to progressive divergence between the sexes. But achieving one's gender identity involves major social and cultural influences that can be even more important than the development of the anatomical-physiological endowment.

The role that hormones play in the development and differentiation of body structures is called their **organizational role.** Later in life some hormones also play an **activational role** in that they evoke or modulate reproductive behavior. In some cases activation cannot take place unless specific organization has already occurred, but in other cases activation does not require prior hormonal organization. In this section we will examine the roles that hormones and other factors play in the development of a man or a woman.

"It's a girl!" Prenatal differentiation of reproductive structures

The sequence of events that leads to development of a baby girl or baby boy can be likened to a relay race with different runners who cover different parts of the course (Money, 1977). First in line is the X or Y chromosome contributed by the male parent to pair with the X chromosome from the female parent. The XX or XY chromosomal pattern determines whether the undifferentiated embryological gonad will develop as ovary or testis. The chromosomal pattern also determines the responsiveness of the tissues to sex hormones.

Differentiation of the gonad into testes begins at about the seventh week after conception in humans; if the gonad is to differentiate into an ovary, it begins to do so later, at about the twelfth week. The testes must develop early because the androgens they produce are required for the next stages of development of males. At this stage (7 to 12 weeks after conception) two systems of primitive ducts exist in each embryo. One is the **Müllerian duct system,** which can develop into female reproductive structures—the oviducts, uterus, and upper vagina. The other is the **Wolffian duct system,** which can develop into male structures—the epididymides, the vas deferens, and the seminal vesicles. (See Figure 9-7.) The presence or absence of the testes determines which of these duct systems develops.

The testes secrete a substance that acts as the next runner in the race; it induces development of the Wolffian system and inhibits development of the Müllerian system. The biochemical nature of this testicular substance has not yet been identified. It used to be thought that the ovaries secreted a substance that promoted development of the female duct system, but it has been found that the absence of testes ensures female development, which occurs even if *no* gonads are present.

Next the testes, if they are present, promote the differentiation of the external genitalia into the masculine form by secretion of androgens such as testosterone. Until the end of the twelfth week after conception, the external genitalia remain undifferentiated. If androgens do not act upon these tissues, they then differentiate as female genitalia. Thus the glans of the predifferentiated genitalia becomes the glans penis under the influence of androgens; in the absence of androgens it develops into the glans clitoris (Figure 9-7). The fetal labioscrotal swelling develops, under the influence of androgens, into the scrotum, and the testes descend into the scrotum from their original position near the kidneys. In the absence of androgens the fetal labioscrotal swelling develops into the labia majora of the vulva. The typical male or female form of the genitalia is recognizable by the twelfth week after conception.

Figure 9-7 Fetal differentiation of human male and female reproductive structures from a common undifferentiated state in the 6-week-old embryo.

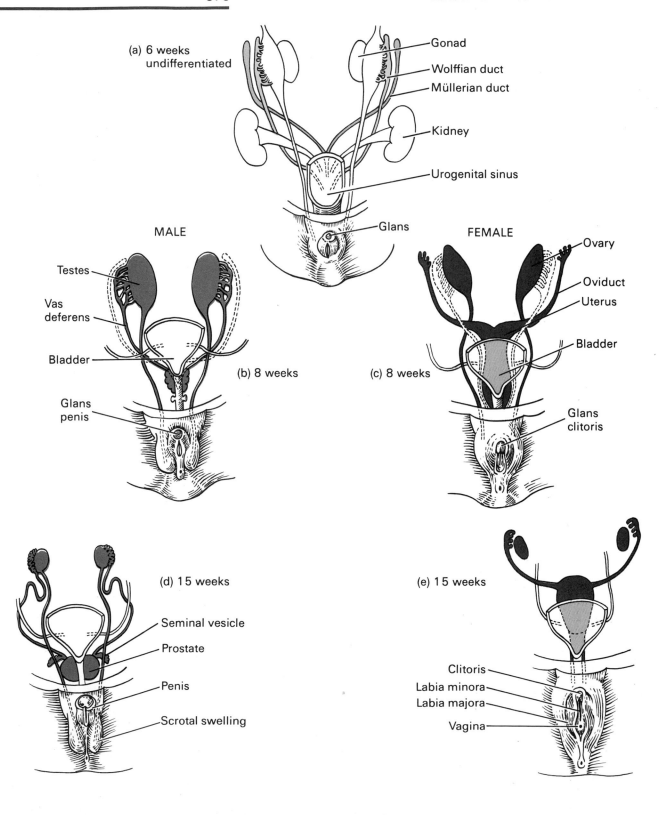

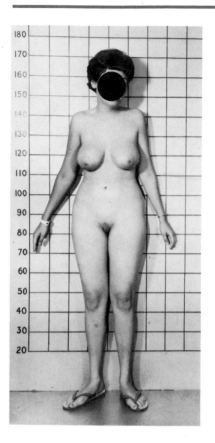

Figure 9-8 An androgen-insensitive genetic male. Although this person's chromosomes have the male XY pattern, insensitivity to male hormones caused body development to follow the female pattern. (From J. Money and A. A. Ehrhardt, *Man and Woman, Boy and Girl,* copyright 1973 by the Johns Hopkins University Press, Baltimore MD. By permission.)

Even if the fetus is female and therefore does not possess testes, its genitalia may nevertheless assume masculine form under the influence of androgens in certain clinical conditions. The adrenal cortex normally produces small amounts of androgens, but an overactive fetal or maternal adrenal gland may produce enough androgens at the critical period of fetal development to cause the genitals to assume masculine forms. Another cause of masculine appearance of the infant genitalia is the administration of androgenic drugs to pregnant women.

Despite what we have just said, the presence of circulating androgens does not, by itself, guarantee masculinization of the genitalia. The tissues must receive the hormonal message and respond to it. Tissues with the male XY chromosome pattern normally are more responsive to androgens than are tissues with the female XX pattern; but there are rare individuals with XY chromosomes whose tissues do not respond to androgens, so the person develops the external appearance of a female (Figure 9-8). (Since the differentiation of the testes does not depend on androgens, these individuals have testes, but the testes remain within the body cavity.) Thus a person with XY chromosomes can have a female appearance, and a person with the XX pattern can, if stimulated by androgens at the critical stage of development, have an external masculine appearance. The form of the external genitals usually determines how a child is classified and brought up.

Social influences on gender identity

The last runner in the relay race that determines gender identity is social experience. The relative importance of experience and of biological factors (such as sex hormones) in determining gender identity is a question of considerable current interest and investigation. Naturally it is easiest to study in people whose upbringing and biology (that is, chromosomal pattern) don't reinforce each other. In some cases the appearance of the genitals at birth is neither completely masculine nor completely feminine, and the parents or physician may err in identifying the baby's sex. For example, when an overactive adrenal cortex during the fetal period causes a girl's genitals to develop a masculine appearance, at birth this genetic female may be recognized as a girl or may be classified as a boy. In the latter case, the child raised as a boy usually acts like a boy and wants to develop into a man. At the age of puberty masculinization of the body can be induced by means of androgen therapy; this biological treatment is necessary to provide a body form that corresponds to the learned gender identity. Such a person is a man in gender identity and gender role, although his chromosomal pattern is XX.

In some cases a later, more accurate identification of sex causes a reversal of sex assignment; that is, the parents decide to shift and rear the child as a girl rather than a boy, or vice versa. When such a change is made before age 3 or 4, it proceeds easily (Hampson, 1965). Beyond this age personality problems may arise, because the child's gender identity seems to be established by about age 3. Sometimes, however, adults have apparently been able to switch successfully from one sex role to the opposite one. Hampson (1965) claims that in all such cases of successful sex reversal he has studied, the persons had had long-standing reservations about their "true sex" and had viewed themselves as a kind of role "imposter" prior to the change. Although it is widely held that sociocultural experience can predominate over biological factors in determining gender identity (for example, see Money and Ehrhardt, 1972), some recently studied cases indicate the need to reevaluate this conclusion. These cases, to be taken up shortly, suggest that exposure to normal levels of male hormones from fetal development through puberty may be able to override the effects of being reared as a girl to the age of puberty.

Do sex hormones organize brain circuits?

Much research and controversy have been stimulated by the finding that the presence or absence of androgens around the time of birth appears to determine the nature of adult sexual behavior in rats and other rodents. Since behavior is mediated by neural circuits, one effect androgens might have on development is to organize brain circuits as well as peripheral bodily structures. Recently evidence of androgen influence on organization has come from the discovery of anatomical differences between the brains of male and female animals of several species. For example, rats of the two sexes differ in the number of one kind of synapse in the preoptic area. Furthermore, as shown in Figure 9-9, this difference was abolished by administering androgen to newborn females or by castrating newborn males (Raisman and Field, 1973). A nucleus in the medial preoptic area of the rat is eight times as large in male rats as in females (Figure 9-10), and the size of this nucleus can be altered by treating newborns with hormones (Gorski et al., 1977, 1978). This story is still not complete on the behavioral side, since we do not know in detail the behavioral functions of circuits that involve these brain regions, but their importance for sexual behavior will be discussed below.

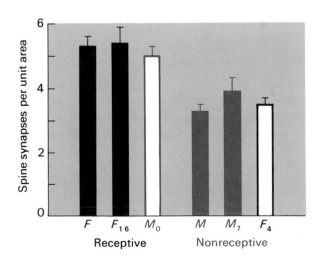

Figure 9-9 Early hormonal status affects the frequency of synapses in the preoptic area of the rat. In adult rats, normal females (F) show significantly more of an identified set of synapses in the preoptic area than do normal males (M). Treatment with androgen at day 16 (F_{16}) does not alter the number, but treatment at day 4 (F_4) results in females whose synapse number is like that of males. Furthermore, the F_4 females do not show estrous cycles. Males castrated on day 7 (M_7) show only a few more of these synapses than normal males, but those castrated within 12 hours of birth (M_0) reach female values. The M_0 animals show behavioral receptivity if primed with estrogen and progesterone, whereas normal males show far less under this hormonal treatment. (Each bar shows the mean of a group of 7–16 animals, ± one standard error.) (Adapted from Raisman and Field, 1973)

Figure 9-10 Sexually dimorphic nucleus of the preoptic area of rat. (a) On a lateral view of the rat brain, the blue line shows the plane of a frontal section through this area. (b) A frontal section at this level. The blue rectangle in (b) shows the region enlarged in the actual brain sections below. (ac, anterior commisure; cc, corpus callosum; oc, optic chiasm; scn, suprachiasmatic nucleus; v, third ventricle.) The enlarged sections show the striking difference in size of the sexually dimorphic nuclei of the proeoptic area (sdn-poa) in normal adult male and female rats. (Sections courtesy of Roger A. Gorski)

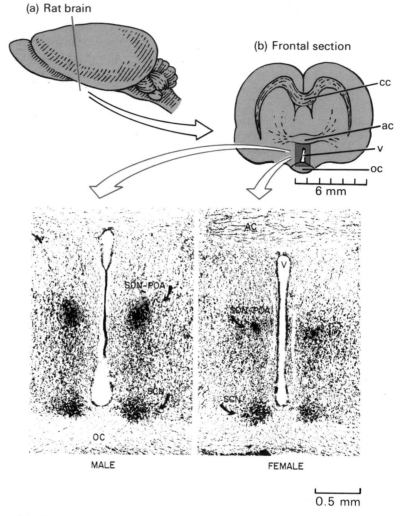

(a) Rat brain

(b) Frontal section

cc

ac

v

oc

6 mm

MALE

FEMALE

0.5 mm

Until recently it appeared that estrogens played no role in the organization of brain circuits. Now some indications are beginning to appear that estrogens may affect, in subtle but measurable ways, both early brain development (e.g., M. C. Diamond, 1980) and behavioral development (e.g., Stewart and Cygan, 1980).

A clear example of the hormonal effects on the brain circuits controlling sexually dimorphic behavior has been found in certain birds. This behavior is the singing that male birds use both to court females and to keep other males out of their territory. The brain circuits that control song behavior have been traced for the canary (Nottebohm, 1980) and the zebra finch (Arnold, 1980). Several of the brain nuclei in these circuits are significantly larger in the male than in the female, and one large nucleus in the male brain cannot be seen at all in the female brain (Figure 9-11). Many of the cells in these nuclei accumulate androgens. In the case of the canary, a female that has already bred and produced eggs can be transformed, by treatment with androgens, to show male behavior, including singing (Nottebohm, 1979). When this treatment is effective, the sizes of the brain nuclei that control song are

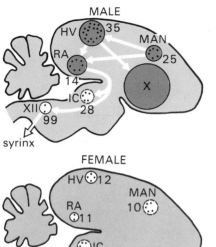

MALE

FEMALE

Figure 9-11   Schematic drawings of the brains of male and female songbirds. The circles represent brain regions involved in song production. The area of each circle is proportional to the volume of the brain region, and these regions have been magnified so that their relative sizes can be seen clearly. Dots mark the regions that pick up testosterone, and the numbers indicate the percentages of cells labeled when radioactive testosterone was injected. (HV, hyperstriatum ventrale; IC, intercollicular nucleus; MAN, magnocellular nucleus of anterior neostriatum; RA, nucleus robustus of the archistriatum; X, area X of the locus parolfactorium; XII, nucleus of the XIIth cranial nerve.) (Adapted from Arnold, 1980)

found to have enlarged toward the sizes seen in males. In the case of the zebra finch, hormonal treatment of the adult female does not cause her to sing, but treatment of a newly hatched female can cause her to acquire song and to show enlarged brain nuclei for song production.

Thus there is rather strong evidence of sex differences in neural organization in at least some species. Surprising as it seems, hormonal stimulation given before birth or around the time of birth can influence behavior years later—long after the effective hormones have disappeared. Investigators are now trying to find out how the sex differences in neural development are related to sex differences in behavior. As Arnold (1980) points out, these animal studies do not tell us whether there are anatomical sex differences in the human brain, but they encourage anatomists to look for such differences. Other kinds of evidence point to sex differences in organization of the human brain, as we will see in the next section.

Does prenatal sexual development influence personality?

Does the normal course of differential sexual development have any influences on personality differences between males and females? Is abnormal exposure to hormones during fetal development reflected in personality? These are difficult questions to answer for several reasons: Personality traits are variable and rather hard to measure; personality development is influenced by many factors, so teasing out one variable is hard to do; the question of sex differences may be difficult to consider dispassionately since it is related to political and social rights of the two sexes. We will note some important findings while remaining aware of the incompleteness of research in this area and, in many cases, its inconclusive nature.

● **Sex differences in personality**   What sex differences in personality are clearly established? Psychologists Eleanor Maccoby and Carol Jacklin (1974) gathered and evaluated thousands of studies that attempted to measure purported differences between boys and girls, men and women. They concluded that many alleged sex differences disappear when attempts are made to measure them objectively, and only four main sex differences were regarded as being fairly well established. In a critical review of the Maccoby and Jacklin book, Jeanne Block (1976) pointed out several methodological difficulties in the attempt to evaluate studies of sex differences. For one thing, most of the studies considered by Maccoby and Jacklin were of children below the age of 5, when some sex differences may not yet have become established. In fact, Block showed that when she classified the studies according to age of the subjects, the older the subjects were (up to young adulthood), the larger was the proportion of studies that showed significant sex differences in personality. Block concluded that there are more sex differences in personality than Maccoby and Jacklin accepted, but let us limit ourselves to these four as a minimum set.

The four main sex differences that Maccoby and Jacklin regarded as established are as follows:

1. Girls have greater verbal ability than boys. The magnitude of the mean difference varies among studies, commonly being about one-quarter of a standard deviation.

2. Boys score higher in visual-spatial ability. The male advantage on spatial tests increases through the high school years and reaches about 0.4 standard deviation.

3. Boys have higher scores in mathematical ability.

4. Boys and men are more aggressive than girls and women.

All four points refer to mean differences, and there is much overlap between members of the two sexes on all of the traits.

To what extent can any of these sex differences be attributed to biological determinants? Maccoby and Jacklin conclude that biological factors are implicated most clearly in measures of aggression and visual-spatial ability. Evidence for a biological component in the greater aggressiveness of males rests on the following bases:

1. It is universal in all cultures that have been studied.

2. A similar sex difference is found among nonhuman primates (Figure 9-12), and the latter do not have a culture that influences sex roles (although they are affected by imitation and social learning).

3. Levels of aggression are increased by androgens and decreased by estrogens; for example, prenatal treatment of female monkeys with androgens significantly increases their aggressiveness and the amount of rough-and-tumble play.

Figure 9-12 Sex differences in aggressive behavior of young rhesus monkeys. Males wrestle frequently, like those in the foreground. Females are more sedate, like those in the background. (Photograph courtesy of H. F. Harlow)

The case for biological determination of visual-spatial ability comes primarily from genetic studies. These indicate the existence of a recessive sex-linked gene that contributes to high scores on tests of spatial ability. About half the men and a quarter of the women show this factor phenotypically. Other genetic factors that also affect spatial ability do not seem to be sex-linked. Of course, training and practice also influence visual-spatial skills, so the sex-linked tendency may be reinforced in some sociocultural circumstances and not in others.

● Fetal endocrine abnormalities and personality   To study effects of unusual prenatal endocrine influences on human personality, investigators depend on spontaneous endocrine abnormalities or on medically prescribed hormonal treatments of pregnant women (Ehrhardt and Meyer-Bahlburg 1981; Rubin, Reinisch, and Haskett, 1981). Prenatal hormonal effects appear in some sexually dimorphic behaviors such as energy expenditure and childhood rehearsal of parental roles, but the effects are rather subtle. Here are a few examples.

In a genetic condition of congenital overgrowth of the adrenal gland (congenital adrenal hyperplasia, or CAH), the adrenal cortex does not secrete cortisol but from fetal life onward secretes an excess of androgens. As a result, if the fetus is female, the external genitalia are masculinized; the appearance of genetic males is not changed because their testes normally produce androgens. Postnatally the condition can be corrected by replacement therapy with corticosteroids that hold adrenal androgen production to a normal level. In girls the external genitalia can be surgically feminized in the first weeks of life. With proper regulation of hormones, pubertal development occurs normally, and sexual functioning and fertility are normal.

Personality studies have shown some differences between such prenatally androgenized children and their siblings or matched normal controls. CAH girls showed a long-term childhood pattern of high energy expenditure (intense outdoor activity, identification as a tomboy) and decreased rehearsal of female parenting (low interest in doll play and baby care). While significant, these trends were not extreme; they fell toward one end of the spectrum of accepted female behavior in our culture. CAH boys differed from controls only in showing higher levels of energy expenditure in play and sports.

A group of 38 genetic males in a rural community in the Dominican Republic was found to have an enzyme deficiency that severely retarded development of masculine external genitalia (Imperato-McGinley et al., 1974, 1979). The internal reproductive structures were male but the external genitalia were ambiguous in form, and 18 of these children were raised as girls. At the age of puberty not only did the genitalia develop masculine form but, despite their upbringing, in 17 of 18 cases gender identity changed, and the boys directed their sexual interest toward females. This report is rather surprising in view of findings noted above that gender identity is usually difficult to change after age 3 or 4. But it should be noted that in most of the cases studied in the United States where sex of rearing was contrary to chromosomal and gonadal sex, further methods were used to reinforce the effects of rearing. These included removal of the gonads and therapy with hormones of the assigned sex. In the case of the subjects in the Dominican Republic, there were social pressures against changing gender identity and gender role, but these were not supplemented by surgical or hormonal treatments. When the presumptive girls did not grow breasts and instead developed a male bodily form at puberty, they changed over to male gender identity. The rather permissive atmosphere of the rural Dominican community did not pose an insurmountable barrier to this change. Thus we see that more research will be needed to define clearly how sociocultural factors and biological factors interact in forming gender identity.

The studies reported in this section suggest that prenatal presence of hormones can have some effects on personality and behavior as well as on bodily structure. Perhaps some subtle differences in personality reflect differences of prenatal exposure that are completely within the normal range of hormone levels, but this result has not been demonstrated.

Evolution of sex

Evolution through natural selection depends on differences in individual animals' reproduction and survival. The success of individuals from an evolutionary point of view means reproduction of their genes. Thus an evolutionary approach to reproductive behavior is particularly appropriate, since it deals with the behavior that makes evolution possible.

Sexual reproduction promotes a richness of genetic combinations, as we mentioned earlier. The result is that offspring of a sexual union can more readily occupy a large range of environments than can offspring of asexual reproduction. "Sex, then, is an adaptation for survival; it is probably the master adaptation" (Adler, 1978, p. 658). Sex means both separateness of male and female and union of sperm and egg. The incredibly varied ways in which this union can occur account for much of the variety of animal form and behavior. In this section we will consider some of the criteria that must be met for successful reproductive behavior and then take up some implications of evolution and of cultural development for human sexuality.

Adaptations for sexual reproduction

Here are some major tests that must be met for successful reproductive behavior in complex animals:

1. Male and female must remain together or come together. This criterion requires mechanisms for attraction, such as those we saw in the ring dove, and for recognition of species, sex, and sexual maturity.

2. Where several potential mates of the right species and reproductive status are available, the individual must select a mate. The selection affects the probability that her or his genes will survive. In many species the female undertakes a larger burden of reproduction than the male in the nutritional and mechanical burdens of pregnancy. So the female may be more careful in selecting a mate, and the male may exhibit elaborate courtship behavior to demonstrate his fitness. In many species both males and females show preferences for particular members of the opposite sex in displaying appetitive behavior. (In this and other points we are not implying that "reproductive strategies" are conscious or intentional. They are bodily and behavioral adaptations that have evolved because they achieve certain consequences, but they do not require any awareness on the part of the actors.)

3. Reproduction is more likely to be successful if it occurs at a favorable time and

place. In many parts of the world food supplies are best only in a short season. Animals that live there may mate at a time that ensures that the young will be born when food supplies are likely to be optimal. Other species may migrate long distances to reproduce in favorable locales.

4. Once the time, place, and partner have been chosen, specific copulatory behavior is required to unite sperm and egg. Copulation involves a complex set of reciprocal behavioral adjustments. Particular neural circuits mediate these behaviors, and in many species these circuits are facilitated by altered levels of hormones. When we described the copulatory patterns of rodents (Table 9-1), we noted that there is much variety among species. Dewsbury (1975) has attempted to relate these differences to the ecologies in which the various species have evolved. Thus whether ejaculation of semen occurs during a single brief insertion of the penis or requires multiple insertions appears to be related to whether the environment is exposed to predators or protected from them. Ejaculation during a single brief intromission occurs in rodent species that live in open habitats and do not burrow. The occurrence of locking (in which the penis remains in the vagina for prolonged periods) requires a safe site for copulation, because a locked pair would be highly susceptible to predation. Locking has been found to occur in rodent species that dig burrows, build large elaborate houses, or live in trees. We don't yet know enough about the behavior of many species of rodents under field conditions to be able to test some hypotheses about the possible significance of their reproductive patterns. Dewsbury has not found any linear pattern in the evolutionary history of reproductive behavior among rodents. Instead certain patterns seem to have evolved repeatedly in response to the particular selection pressures that have acted on particular species.

5. In some species, reproduction requires a postcopulatory physiological response in the female. For example, female cats and rabbits only ovulate after they copulate, a condition called reflex ovulation or coitus-induced ovulation. In such species successful mating is not restricted to a regular ovulatory period of the female's cycle. In species where ovulation spontaneously occurs cyclically, copulation stimulates the secretion of luteinizing hormone and progesterone, which promotes implantation of the fertilized ovum into the wall of the uterus. In some species receptivity is turned off after copulation, which prevents disruption of pregnancy.

6. The behavior of parents can increase the likelihood that their young will survive. A few examples will illustrate the range and variety of this behavior. In some species both parents participate, as in the case of the ring dove. When both parents care for the young, they are usually similar in appearance. In other species only one parent cares for the young. In mammalian species, when only one parent is the care giver, it is always the mother; in other species it may be the father. Among species of birds, if only one parent is the care giver, it usually has the duller, plainer plumage, which probably helps to protect parent and young against predators. Usually this plainer parent is the female, but there are exceptions, such as the phalarope. The female phalarope is larger and more colorful than the male; she displays during courtship, chooses the nesting site, and defends it against other females. Once she lays eggs, the female departs; the male phalarope incubates the eggs and cares for the young.

The class of animals called mammals is characterized by the presence of female mammary glands used to nourish the young. Some theorists have stated that one cannot explain the origin of mammary glands on the basis of selection for fitness of the individual because the glands contribute to the nutrition of another individual. But these glands are clearly important for survival of the mother's genes in her offspring, and it is reproductive survival that is the basis of evolution.

In some vertebrate species neither parent cares for the young. This is true, for example, of turtles, frogs, and some birds. But in these cases the female often helps to favor development of her young by placing the eggs in a location that is likely to foster successful hatching and subsequent growth. The cuckoo often escapes parental duties by laying its eggs in the nest of another species, which then cares for the young cuckoo. (This habit of the cuckoo is the origin of the word "cuckold," applied to the husband of an unfaithful wife.)

● Sexual selection   Trying to understand differences between the sexes has proved to be difficult for everyone, including scientists. Charles Darwin observed the striking anatomical and behavioral differences between males and females of many species, but he was unable to explain these differences by natural selection; so he introduced the concept of **sexual selection** (Darwin, 1871). Darwin conceived of natural selection as depending on the success of both sexes of a species with respect to general conditions such as obtaining food and avoiding being injured or killed. He used sexual selection to explain why certain individuals have a reproductive advantage over others of their sex and species. For example, among elephant seals certain adult males mate with numerous females, while other males are not allowed to mate at all (Figure 9-13). Certain female elephant seals have been

Figure 9-13 Reproductive behavior in elephant seals. (a) Dominant male seal and his harem. The small seals with black pelts are pups. Peripheral adult males are seen beyond the harem. (b) Dominant male prepares to copulate with a member of his harem. Note the large dimorphism of size between male and females. (Photographs by M. R. Rosenzweig)

(a)

(b)

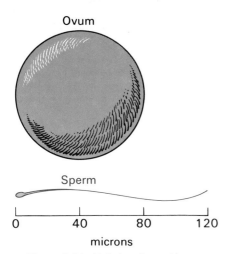

Figure 9-14 Relative sizes of human ovum and sperm; both are magnified about 450 times.

found, season after season, to mate with more vigorous or able males than do other females.

From the start some scientists thought it was incorrect to make a distinction between natural selection and sexual selection, and this is still a matter of debate (Le Boeuf, 1978). The separation is less sharp today than in Darwin's day because geneticists have redefined fitness in terms of the contribution to the gene pool of the next generation rather than in Darwin's general sense of improved chances for survival. Much current research is devoted to the study of the "reproductive strategies" used by males and females in many species to ensure that their genes continue in the next generation. Some of it involves field studies of natural populations whose members are studied over successive generations. As a consequence of these studies sexual selection and reproductive strategies are no longer considered to be limited to the time of mating; they now include all characteristics that facilitate mating and fertilization and those involved in parental care.

The basis of sexual selection is thought to be the unequal investment that the two sexes make in a single offspring. A current formulation of this hypothesis goes along the following lines: Originally the sex cells (gametes) of both sexes were probably of the same size. Organisms simply liberated sex cells into the water where they lived, the way many fish now spawn, and those cells that united formed offspring. These gametes were too large for the organism to produce in great quantities but too small to contain enough food to support extensive development of the embryo. Specialization to produce either tiny gametes or large gametes would yield greater fitness, and both kinds of change occurred (Figure 9-14). Eventually one sex, which we now call males, began to produce smaller sex cells and more of them. Since the small sperm had little food supply, they could not live long and had to make contact with the ova as soon as possible. Mobile sperm therefore evolved. A further development was selection of males that placed sperm closer to females, and this development culminated in internal fertilization. Females specialized in the other direction, producing large gametes with adequate food supplies to permit extensive growth of the embryo. The larger size of the egg relative to that of the sperm meant that the female made a larger investment of energy and metabolism in the individual offspring than did the male. Once she made this greater initial investment, it became advantageous for the female to protect it by additional investments including, in many species, parental care. An indication of the differential investments of female and male ring doves in their offspring is given in Figure 9-15. In many species there is an even greater difference between the investments of the two sexes.

● **Mating systems**   The differential investments by males and females of many species in their offspring have been related to different mating systems among classes and species of animals. There are many possible mating systems; the categories that are most commonly observed are monogamy, polygyny, polyandry, and promiscuity (see Figure 9-16).

In **monogamy** (from the Greek roots "mono," meaning "one," and "gamos," meaning "spouse") one female and one male form a breeding pair. The pair may last for one breeding season or for a lifetime. Lifelong monogamy has been found in many species of birds, such as doves. The constancy of doves has been known for centuries which is why they have been used as a symbol of love. Monogamy is also

Figure 9-15 Hypothetical curves of cumulative investments of a female and a male ring dove in their offspring through the reproductive cycle. (Adapted from Erickson, 1978, and Trivers, 1972)

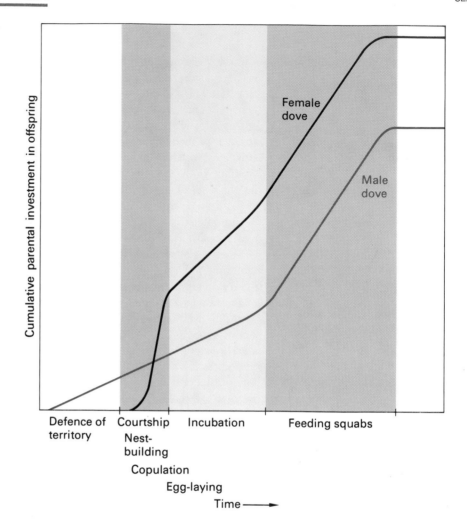

seen in certain species of small antelopes, in some primates (gibbons), and in many human societies. (It does not mean that remating will not occur if the pair are separated or if one member dies.) The term **pair bond** is used to describe this rather durable and exclusive relation between a female and a male. Much current research is studying the conditions under which such relations occur and the mechanisms of pair bonding.

Polygamy (from the Greek roots "poly," meaning "many," and "gamos," meaning "spouse") can take either of two forms. **Polygyny** (from "poly" and "gyny," meaning woman or wife) is the mating of one male with more than one female. Polygyny occurs in some birds (such as the ostrich), in many mammals (such as the elephant seal, deer, and macaque monkeys), and in many human societies. **Polyandry** (from "poly" and "andros," meaning "man") is the mating of one female with more than one male. This system is rather rare. It occurs in a few species of birds (such as the jacana in Figure 9-1) and in a few human societies.

Promiscuity refers to instances where animals mate with several members of the

Figure 9-16 Distributions of mating systems among birds and mammals. The graphs show percentages of species that fall into four main classifications. Estimates for birds (from Lack, 1968) are rather precise, so percentage figures are shown. Estimates for mammals are not very precise, so their graph is shown as a broad band and percentages are not given. (Data for birds from Lack, 1969; estimates for mammals after Daly and Wilson, 1978)

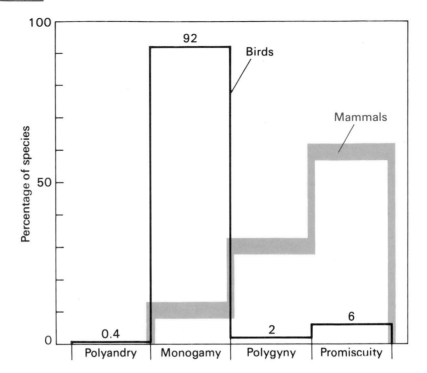

opposite sex and do not establish durable associations with sex partners. In many species of rodents there is intense promiscuous competition of males for females.

Mammals differ from birds in the relative frequencies of these different mating systems, as Figure 9-16 indicates. The distribution for birds is based on estimates by Lack (1968); he estimates that among the approximately 8600 species of birds 92% are monogamous, 2% polygamous, less than 0.5% polyandrous, and 6% show promiscuous male competition for females. Only crude estimates are available for mammals because the mating systems of most of the approximately 4000 species of mammals have not yet been studied. Almost 1700 of the mammalian species are rodents, and in this order polygyny and promiscuous competition of males for females predominate. The same appears to hold true for the other better-known mammalian orders—insectivores (for instance, moles and shrews), pinnipeds (such as seals), ungulates (such as cattle and deer), and primates. Among the carnivores (for example, dogs) monogamy may be more common.

Among both bird and mammalian species the mating system is related to sexual dimorphism in body size. Darwin observed that in birds the two sexes are of closely similar size in monogamous species, whereas in polygynous species the male tends to be larger than the females. The same relation between degree of sexual dimorphism in size and the degree of polygyny (the number of females that mate with a single male) has recently been documented for several orders of mammals (see Figure 9-17). Polygyny for these mammalian species has been quantified from field reports of the sizes of harems. The relationship between polygyny and dimorphism seems to be weaker in primates than in seals or ungulates, but this apparent weakness may be due, in part at least, to the less accurate estimates for the primates under field conditions.

Figure 9-17 Sexual dimorphism in size and degree of polygyny in three orders of mammals: (a) pinnipeds, (b) ungulates, and (c) primates. (Adapted from Alexander, R. D.; Hoogland, J. L.; Howard, R. D.; Noonan, K. M.; and Sherman, P. W.; "Sexual Dimorphisms and Breeding Systems in Pinnipeds, Ungulates, Primates, and Humans," in N. A. Chagnons and W. Irons, eds., *Evolutionary Biology and Human Social Behavior,* © 1979 by Wadsworth, Inc., Belmont, CA., 94002. Reprinted by permission of the publisher, Duxbury Press.)

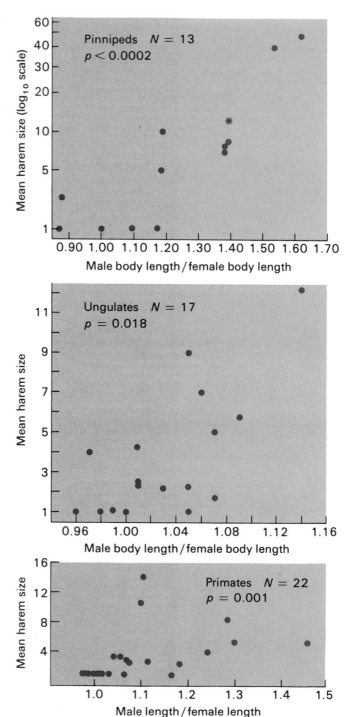

Evolutionary implications for human sexuality

Human beings share the major adaptations of all mammals for reproductive behavior, but they are also molded by the family history of the hominid line and by the cultural developments of our own species, *Homo sapiens.* If we were investigators from another planet and knew that human beings were moderately large mammals with a mild degree of sexual dimorphism of size (the mean ratio of male stature to female stature is 1.08), we might expect to find a slightly polygynous mating system (Alexander et al., 1978). Anthropologists have studied marriage practices in hundreds of human societies (Bourguignon and Greenbaum, 1973) and have found much variety. When the findings are grouped into large categories (Figure 9-18), polygyny is seen to exist in most societies, but in many of them it is practiced by only a small minority. Polyandry exists but is exceedingly rare. Monogamy is the only accepted form in many societies, and it is actually far more prevalent than this statement suggests: Even in societies that accept polygamy, most marriages are monogamous.

Of course, we know much more about our human heritage than just that it is part of the mammalian story. In Chapter 3 we saw that human evolution involved a large increase in brain size and the development of a life style with a division of labor between the sexes. Sex roles became specialized not only with respect to reproductive functions, as in all other mammals, but also in connection with the economy of the group. Women not only bore and cared for their own children but they contributed to the group by gathering plant foods, collecting firewood, and tending fires. Men filled other nonreproductive roles by hunting, protecting the group against attack by animals and other humans, and performing domestic tasks beyond the strength of women. These sex differences in economic roles were not absolute, of course; there was sharing, and different cultures assigned tasks differently. However, all the distinctively human activities required more ability to learn than had simpler ways of life, and as human cultures became steadily more complex, the emphasis on learned behavior increased.

Figure 9-18 Distribution of marriage norms in human societies. The data are based on 854 societies representing all regions of the world and for which rather full information is available in the Human Relations Area Files. Monogamy is the most frequent form of marriage, although in 39% of societies the predominant monagamy is accompanied by occasional polygynous marriages. (Graph based on data from Bourguignon and Greenbaum, 1973)

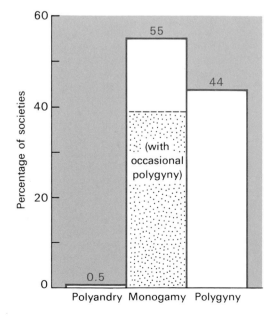

This evolutionary history may help to account both for the wide range of sexual behaviors and sexually differentiated behaviors that exist among groups within our own culture and for the much wider range that has been seen among human cultures. Some anthropologists and psychologists also see in this history a possible basis for those tendencies toward differences in temperament and ability that we have already described. Let us consider briefly this approach to sex differences and then turn to the kaleidoscopic picture of sexuality among human cultures.

From the results of research on human prehistory and studies of anthropology, Beach (1977) has proposed the following explanation of the evolution of behavioral characteristics of human males and females (pp. 18–19):

> It is conceivable that, as human evolution proceeded, natural selection operated to produce or widen genetic differences between males and females, which slowly but progressively improved the capacities of the two sexes to perform their separate roles, and thus increased the effectiveness of the social group as a survival mechanism. Potentially adaptive sex differences could have involved both emotional and intellectual traits, but the most significant variables might well have been sex-related differences in certain motivational characteristics and special types of learning ability.

Beach is not suggesting that evolution provided human males and females with ready-made, instinctively organized behavior patterns for hunting, or child rearing, but that

> as mankind evolved, the male and female genotypes differentiated along lines which provided males with a higher potential for acquiring patterns consonant with the total masculine role, and females with a more marked propensity for developing patterns fitted to the entire feminine role. Sex differences in such "potentials" or "propensities" would be relative rather than absolute. They would be manifest in more rapid and efficient learning of masculine patterns by males and feminine patterns by females. . . . Of course, such sex-related genetic differences, if they existed, could only become manifest in a social environment which stimulated and reinforced their actualization; but this is precisely what every hunting and gathering society did do. The hypothesis is that, over hundreds of millennia, social and genetic forces conspired to encourage the elaboration of primitive mammalian differences in reproductive responsibility into much broader sex differences involving intellectual and emotional traits and capacities quite unrelated to species reproduction.

The power and flexibility of human learning, made possible by the large human brain, have permitted an amazing variety of sexual patterns among human societies and subcultures. It is not that ultimate biological constraints for reproduction can be ignored but rather that human biological capacities can be used with great flexibility and can be incorporated into cultural systems that interpret sexuality in vastly different ways. When Kinsey published his descriptions of sexual behavior in the United States in the 1940s and 1950s, many people were surprised at the differences among American subcultures, which were defined by region, education, and religion. But much more extreme differences have been described by anthropologists (see, for example, Davenport, 1977). Almost opposite attitudes toward sexuality can be found: In some cultures sexuality is evaluated negatively—shunned and even feared—and sexual intercourse is largely restricted to procreation. In other cultures the expression of sexuality is highly valued and encouraged; it is celebrated in art and song, and beauty of all kinds is associated with sex.

Neural and hormonal mechanisms of reproductive behavior

With sexual behaviors showing such variety and complexity, many investigators are seeking to find and understand the bodily mechanisms that mediate them. What are the neural and hormonal mechanisms of female and male reproductive behaviors? If hormones help to organize brain circuits, what are the basic features of these circuits? Are some of the organizational effects of hormones due to their effects on peripheral bodily structures rather than on the nervous system?

Although our understanding of the bodily mechanisms that mediate sex behaviors is still far from complete, many parts of the picture are being filled in by animal experiments and clinical studies with people. We will consider first the attempts to trace the neural pathways and brain regions involved in reproductive behavior, and then we will turn to hormonal modulation of these circuits. Since interactions between the nervous system and the endocrine system are so prominent in reproductive behavior, we cannot present completely separate accounts of them; instead we will go back and forth between neural mechanisms and hormonal influences.

Sexual reflexes

Some motor responses are based on neural circuits within the spinal cord, as we saw in Chapter 8, and this basis has also been found in the case of sexual reflexes. If the spinal cord is transected or severely injured so that no nerve impulses pass between the brain and the part of the spinal cord below the injury, some reflexes can still be elicited in the lower trunk and legs. These reflexes are mediated entirely by spinal circuits. Both erection and ejaculation in males are mediated at the spinal level, in humans as well as other mammals. A paraplegic patient (a person whose spinal cord has been transected or severely injured by an accident or disease) cannot exercise voluntary control over the musculature below the level of the transection, nor is there any sensation from below this level. But by using spinal reflexes, some paraplegic men have been able to impregnate their wives.

● **Sexual reflexes in spinal male animals**   In male dogs, stimulation of different parts of the penis can evoke three different reproductive reflexes (Hart, 1978):

1. Shallow pelvic thrusting with partial erection of the penis. In normal copulation this response precedes achievement of intromission.
2. The intense ejaculatory reaction. Expulsion of seminal fluid is accompanied by strong pelvic movements and alternate stepping of the hind legs. This reflex is the only reproductive reflex with a short duration and an abrupt end. Continued stimulation does not prolong the response.
3. Maintenance of erection and emission of seminal fluid. This response lasts about 10–30 minutes, decreasing in intensity. This reflex probably occurs in the intact male during the copulatory lock.

These reflexes are differentially affected by the hormone testosterone, as we will see below.

Note that these spinal reflex patterns include not only responses mediated by autonomic nerves (such as erection and ejaculation) but also responses mediated by skeletal nerves (for instance, movements of the legs). This is a good example of the coordination of autonomic and skeletal responses.

● **Sexual reflexes in spinal female animals**   Spinal female dogs and cats show several reflexive mating responses to stimulation of the genital region. For example, the hindquarters curve toward the side of stimulation, and the tail is raised or arched to the side. In the intact animal these receptive responses would aid intromission. Elevation of the pelvis (the lordosis response) is not seen in animals whose spinal cord is cut in the midthoracic region, because this reflex requires back muscles above as well as below the level of transection. In animals with spinal transections in the upper thoracic region, elevation of the pelvis can be elicited.

In the rat the lordosis response is so stereotyped that it has been assumed to be a spinal reflex, but so far this assumption has not been proved. This observation has led to the suggestion that the lordosis response is organized in the brain in the rat (Pfaff et al., 1972). But it is hard to believe that a response that is mediated at the spinal cord in the dog and cat requires brain circuits in the rat (Hart, 1978), and study of this issue is continuing.

● **Hormonal influences on spinal reflexes**   Spinal reflexes are not fixed and unchangeable; rather they can be modulated in several ways. Normally nerve impulses from the brain facilitate some spinal circuits and inhibit others. For example, a female cat or dog may be stimulated to assume the full receptive posture just by the presence of the male, without any tactile contact between the two; a sow may show lordosis when stimulated by the mating call of the boar. This stimulation occurs through distance receptors and pattern analysis in the brain. In addition, spinal reflexes show some changes that can be classified as learning—they show habituation, sensitization, and conditioning (such changes will be considered in Chapter 14). Another main source of modulation of spinal reflexes is the action of hormones, which we will take up here.

Studies of nonspinal dogs have shown that surgical removal of the gonads (castration) causes reduced motivation to copulate in some males; even in those dogs that continue to mount and achieve intromission, there is a pronounced decline in duration of the copulatory lock, and the intense ejaculatory response may be less strong than in intact animals. Experiments were therefore undertaken with spinal dogs to see whether testosterone would affect these reflexes.

In the experiments the dogs were castrated, and each animal was given injections of testosterone during one period of testing and no hormone during another period (Hart, 1968). The most obvious effect of lack of testosterone was on the duration of simulated lock response. Dogs that were first tested with testosterone injections had a mean lock duration of 12 min; after hormonal treatment was stopped, the duration declined progressively and fell to 4 min after 60 days. Dogs that were first tested without testosterone treatment showed a lock duration of 2 min; when treatment started, this time increased progressively, reaching 10 min after 60 days. While these autonomic aspects of the responses were clearly affected by presence or absence of testosterone, the skeletal responses of the leg and the back muscles did not reveal any effects of hormonal treatment.

The results just reviewed clearly demonstrate effects of hormone on reflexes that are mediated by spinal circuits, but do they prove that the hormone is acting directly on spinal neurons? Not necessarily. It has been pointed out that both sensory and motor components of the response mechanism are affected by sex hormones. Sensory receptors in the skin of the rat's penis atrophy in the absence of androgens and regenerate when androgens are restored (Beach and Levinson, 1950). Also, the size of the penile muscles that play a role in erection and ejaculation is affected by androgens (Hayes, 1965). Can effects of hormones on such peripheral bodily structures account for all the hormonal influences without any necessary involvement of the nervous system? One way to differentiate between effects of a hormone on the penis and effects on the nervous system is to use a special hormone, dihydro-testosterone (DHT). At low levels (25 micrograms, μg) DHT maintains the size and sensitivity of the penis, but it does not maintain sexual behavior in castrated rats (Feder, 1971; Hart, 1973). Thus these findings go against an exclusively peripheral interpretation. Higher doses of this hormone (200 μg or more) do restore sexual responses, and with these doses the hormone was found to accumulate in ventral horn cells in the spinal cord (Sar and Stumpf, 1977). Thus it appears that at least part of the influence of testosterone must be exerted directly on neurons if sexual behavior is to occur.

Brain regions and reproductive behavior

While many aspects of copulatory reflexes are integrated at the spinal level, sexual attraction and appetitive behavior in vertebrates require the involvement of brain regions. Furthermore, brain regions modulate the activity of the spinal circuits, either facilitating or inhibiting them. The preoptic area has been demonstrated to be important for male reproductive behavior in a wide range of vertebrate classes— mammals, birds, frogs, and fish. For female reproductive behavior the important brain regions lie in the anterior or lateral hypothalamus, posterior to the preoptic area. Let us survey briefly some of the main evidence that has led to these conclusions about preoptic and hypothalamic sites. Figure 9-19 shows these regions in the rat, a species used in much of this research.

● **The preoptic area and male reproductive behavior**   Several experimental techniques provide convergent evidence elucidating involvement of the preoptic area (POA) in male reproductive behavior. Recall that a nucleus in the medial preoptic

(a) Rat brain, showing the locations of the frontal sections illustrated below

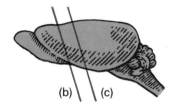

(b) Frontal section through the preoptic area

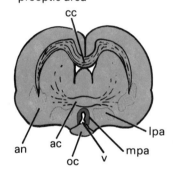

(c) Frontal section through the hypothalamus

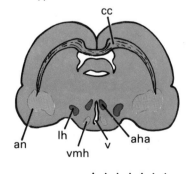

6 mm

Figure 9-19 Areas of the rat brain important to reproductive behavior. The lateral view of the rat brain in (a) shows where the sections in (b) and (c) were made. (ac, anterior commissure; aha, anterior hypothalamic area; an, amygdaloid nuclei; cc, corpus callosum; lh, lateral hypothalamus; lpa, lateral preoptic area; mpa, medial preoptic area; oc, optic chiasm; v, third ventricle; vmh, ventromedial hypothalamus.)

area is much larger in the male rat than in the female, as we saw in Figure 9-10. Bilateral destruction of this area abolishes copulatory behavior in male rats (Larsson and Heimer, 1964), cats (Hart et al., 1973), dogs (Hart, 1974), and monkeys (Sling et al., 1978). Although the spinal circuits are intact in these animals, they lack facilitation from brain circuits, and only occasional mounting without intromission is seen in the brain-lesioned males. In intact rats, facilitating the POA by stimulating it with implanted electrodes increases or even elicits male sex behavior (for example, van Dis and Larsson, 1971; Perachio et al., 1973). Cells in the POA pick up androgens from the blood. Male sex behavior can be restored in castrates by implanting small quantities of testosterone directly into the brain; in the rat, at least, the POA is the most sensitive region for producing this effect (Johnston and Davidson, 1972).

The preoptic area also is involved in the male copulatory behavior shown by female rats. Female rats often mount other females and sometimes show pelvic thrusts. These behaviors were abolished in females after lesions of the POA, but typical female sex behavior was not affected (Singer, 1968). Implants of testosterone in the POA of females facilitated mounting behavior; estradiol also facilitated mounting, but only if implanted posterior to the POA (Dörner et al., 1968a, b).

● **Hypothalamic areas and female reproductive behavior**   The hypothalamic foci where lesions effectively abolish female sex behavior vary somewhat from species to species. In the rat, lesions of the anterior hypothalamus were most effective in abolishing typical female reproductive behavior, whereas in the female hamster, lesions of the ventromedial nucleus were more effective than those in the anterior hypothalamus (Kow et al., 1974). But lesions in some hypothalamic regions posterior to the preoptic area have been found to be effective in several mammalian species. (Studies of nonmammalian species have focused more on male sex behavior than on female sex behavior.) Implants of estradiol into the hypothalamus facilitate female sex behavior in several species of rodents; usually these sites are slightly anterior to the sites of effective lesions. Thus in the rat, hormone implants into the medial preoptic area increase lordosis responses, whereas lesions in the anterior hypothalamus abolish these responses (Singer, 1968). It is chiefly the lesion experiments that differentiate between the neural substrates that underlie male and female sex behavior. Another technique used for this purpose is described in Box 9-1.

Hormonal influences on reproductive behavior

Hormones are involved in at least three different ways in reproductive behavior:

1. As we saw above, a fetal testicular hormone plays an organizational role in forming the reproductive structures and shaping certain brain circuits.

2. Hormones also play an activational role in eliciting or facilitating reproductive behavior that is based on already organized neural circuits and effector structures.

3. Beyond these two generally acknowledged roles, it now appears that hormones play a further **modulatory role** (or maintenance role) in maintaining the sensitivity of neural circuits and other structures to hormonal influences. That is, the presence of hormones over prolonged periods affects the susceptibility of tissues to respond to short-term changes in hormonal level.

BOX 9-1   A Male Head on a Female Body: Genetic Mosaics

Neural control of *Drosophila* mating has been studied by a technique that can transpose heads, although not exactly in the way described in the legend at the start of Chapter 1. Geneticists have found a way to produce *Drosophila* in which the cells of one part of the body have a different chromosomal makeup from the cells in another part; such animals are called **genetic mosaics** (Hotta and Benzer, 1976). In some cases, for example, the head is male and the rest of the body is female. This method can be used to pinpoint the neural structures that control various behaviors.

    Drosophila with male heads but female bodies ap-proach females to commence mating. Originally it appeared that a male head could command a female body to engage in the courting behavior of wing vibration. Further work showed that male tissue must also be present in the thoracic neural ganglion, for this behavior to occur (von Schilcher and Hall, 1979). Apparently a command component is present in the head ganglion, and a motor-pattern generator for wing vibration is located in the thoracic ganglion. These can function to carry out attraction and appetitive behavior without any hormonal stimulation and despite the fact that the animal is not equipped to carry out the third stage, copulatory behavior.

As we hinted earlier, the successive phases of the ring dove's reproductive behavior can be related to the activational and modulatory roles of hormones. In this section we will first look at these hormonal influences on the behavior of the dove. Then we will consider hormonal influences on reproductive behavior in nonhuman mammals, and finally we will examine hormonal influences on human sexual behavior.

● **Hormonal influences on reproductive behavior of the dove**   Investigators are trying to cross-check hypotheses that specific hormones elicit or modulate certain behaviors by performing three kinds of experiments:

1. Remove the hormone or the source of the hormone and see if the behavior disappears or at least declines substantially.
2. Replace the hormone and see if the behavior then reappears.
3. Determine, under normal conditions, whether the concentration of the hormone increases in the system when the behavior appears and decreases when it disappears.

Research with the ring dove illustrates the use of these methods.

    The roles of hormones in the complementary sequences of reproductive behaviors of the female and the male dove have been the subject of intensive research for over thirty years. Although the full story is still not known, this work demonstrates several major relations between hormones and behavior.

    The initiation of courtship behavior by the male dove requires both a normal adult level of testosterone and also the presence of an adult female. An adult male that has been castrated for several weeks will not show much courtship even in the presence of a female. (Circulating testosterone is metabolized by the body in a few hours, but androgens set up effects in the nervous system that last for days or weeks.) Replacement of testosterone by injection then leads to courtship of the female. Even a

Figure 9-20 Hormonal changes in male and female ring doves during the reproductive cycle. Levels of estradiol, progesterone, and testosterone were measured in blood plasma. The weight of the crop gives an index of the level of the hormone prolactin, which cannot yet be measured directly in the dove. Note the rapid rise of estradiol in the female and of testosterone in the male early in courtship (prelaying days). (Adapted from Silver, 1978)

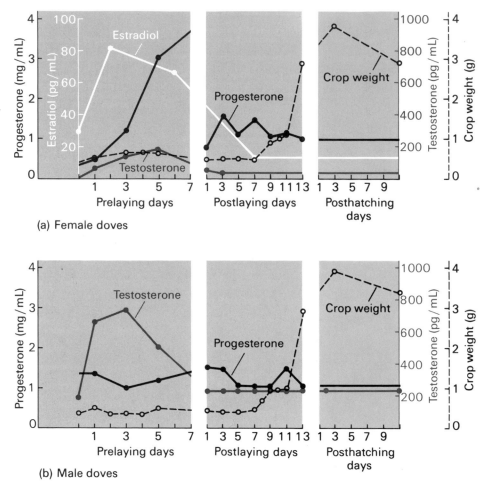

normal adult male will not court unless a female is present, so the stimulus situation is just as important as the hormonal and neural factors. When a male that has been isolated is placed in the presence of a female, the concentration of testosterone begins to rise. An increase can be detected within a few hours, and the level continues to rise during the first few days of courtship (see Figure 9-20). This rise is not necessary for initiation of courtship, however, because it occurs after courtship has begun.

To determine whether the increase in the level of androgen is directly related to the performance of courtship, researchers studied males through two successive breeding cycles with the same mates. In the second period of courtship the male showed far less bow-cooing and charging at the female, but he showed just as great an increase in secretion of androgen (Silver, 1978). Thus, although a normal level of androgen is needed for the male's initiation of reproductive behavior, the increase in concentration does not seem to be correlated with this behavior. The rise probably serves as a safety factor to ensure that performance will not suffer from fluctuations in the rate of secretion.

The behavior of the female dove during courtship shows a clearer relation to levels of sex hormone than does that of the male. The sight of a male directing courting responses toward her causes a rise in the female's level of estrogen; this rise begins a day or two after the pair is caged together and continues until about the start of nest building (Figure 9-20). The different responses of the female during successive stages of courtship correlate closely with the rise in the level of estrogen (Cheng, 1974). Removal of the ovaries abolishes the female's attractive and proceptive responses. Administration of estrogen restores these responses, and they return to the normal order of stages, from wing flipping to proceptive crouching. Estrogen alone does not restore nest-orientated behaviors, however; these require the addition of progesterone. Normally progesterone also rises during courtship, but it lags behind estrogen (Figure 9-20). The combination of these two hormones leads to nest-cooing, nest building, egg laying, and incubation.

Normally birds that have not gone through courtship and nest building will not incubate eggs that are presented to them. But if an isolated female is given estrogen and progesterone injections for a few days before the eggs are offered, then she will incubate. Similarly, an isolated male will incubate if he has been prepared by injections of testosterone and progesterone. Whether progesterone normally plays a role in initiation of incubation in the male is still a subject of debate (Cheng, 1979; Silver, 1978). It may be that under normal circumstances the male follows the lead of the female's behavior in starting to incubate, just as he does in starting nest-building behavior.

The suppression of mating behavior during incubation has been attributed to secretion of prolactin from the anterior pituitary. Here again, although prolactin certainly causes production of crop-milk by both parents, the effect on willingness to mate seems to be exerted chiefly on the female. Tests of willingness to mate have been made by taking birds at various stages of the reproductive cycle and placing them in another cage with a new partner. A female will accept a new partner at certain parts of the cycle but not while prolactin secretion is high. Secretion of prolactin falls off sooner in the female than in the male, and this result corresponds with the fact that the female stops feeding the young a few days earlier than does the male. When prolactin has declined in the female and she has stopped feeding the squabs, the female is ready to breed again. The male, even though his prolactin level remains substantial, is willing to recommence mating with his partner, so prolactin does not inhibit mating in the male.

Thus the progress from one behavioral stage to the next in the reproductive cycle is guided in the female by changing amounts of estrogen, progesterone, and prolactin. The changes in the ovarian hormones, estrogen and progesterone, are elicited by perception of the courtship of the male, and the increase in prolactin is elicited by tactile and visual stimulation from the eggs. The synchrony between the behavior of the two parents that is necessary for successful reproduction is mainly achieved by the male's adjusting his behavior to that of the female; it does not appear to be influenced by changing levels of hormones. Except for the secretion of crop-milk, the only hormonal requirement of the male is a steady supply of testosterone. This hormone, plus stimulation by the behavior of the female, allows him to play his successive roles during the reproductive cycle.

It is worth stressing the bidirectionality of the behavioral interactions. In terms of

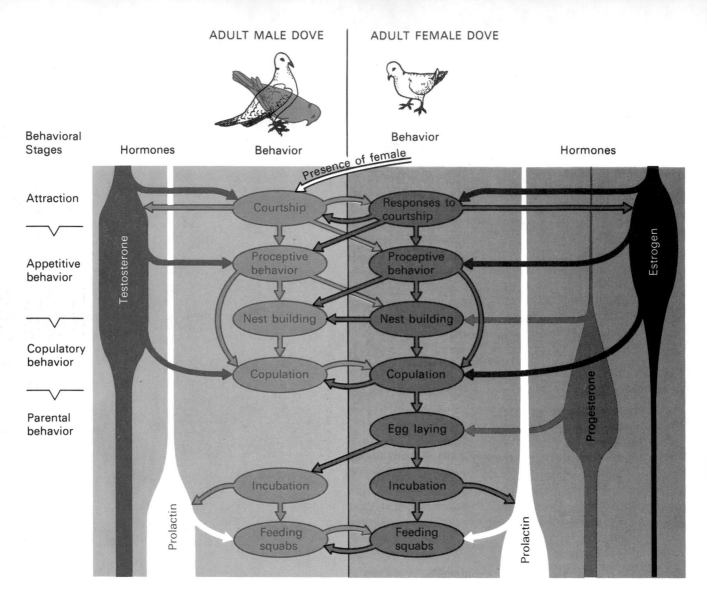

Figure 9-21 Summary of behavioral and hormonal changes during the reproductive cycle of ring doves. The figure shows the reciprocal relations between male and female and between behavioral and somatic variables.

our circle schema, interventions into the hormonal system affect behavior, and behavioral interventions (such as allowing a female to see a courting male) affect levels of hormones. Some of these interventions and effects are summarized in Figure 9-21.

● **Hormonal influences on reproductive behavior in nonhuman mammals**
How do hormones influence the reproductive behaviors of mammals? To what extent is the story similar or different for different species of mammals? To what extent is it the same or different for the two sexes? We will pursue these questions next.

In some species of mammals the nonpregnant adult female goes through a regular cycle of production of estrogen and progesterone. In the rat this cycle lasts 4–5 days, and in women the cycle lasts about 28 days (whence the term "menstrual cycle," from the Latin word "mens," meaning "month"). Reproductive males of these species maintain a rather steady day-to-day average level of androgens (although there are marked short-time fluctuations). The cyclical production of hormones in females is necessary for regular production of ova and associated changes in the reproductive tract. Do these hormonal changes also govern attractive, proceptive, and receptive behavior? In the case of males, do individual differences in levels of androgens account for individual differences in strength and amount of reproductive behavior? We will consider these questions in the following paragraphs.

Hormonal effects in nonprimate females   In rats, and in practically all non-primates, the levels of ovarian hormones are a major determinant of female reproductive behavior. Removing the ovaries results in virtually complete disappearance of sexual receptivity. Over two thousand years ago Aristotle reported a fact already well known to animal husbandmen: "The ovaries of sows are excised with a view to quenching their sexual appetites." Modern knowledge of hormones has enabled investigators to perform replacement experiments in order to find the respective roles of estrogen and progesterone and to determine relations between levels of hormones and various behaviors. In some species estrogen alone will restore receptive behavior (for example, in cats, dogs, rabbits, goats, and monkeys), whereas in others the two hormones appear to be necessary (such as in rats, mice, guinea pigs, and cows). In rats repeated low doses of estrogen restore the lordosis response. Receptivity can be quantified by the "lordosis quotient," the number of times a female shows lordosis divided by the number of times she is mounted by a male. The lordosis quotient was found to be a monotonic function of the dose level of replacement estrogen, as shown in Figure 9-22 (Davidson et al., 1968). Estrogen does not produce its be-

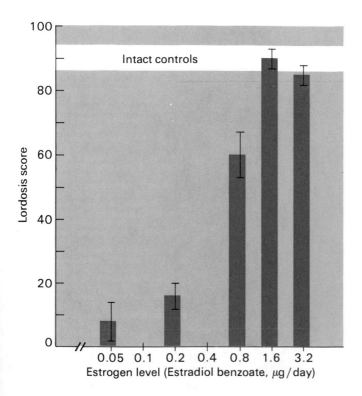

Figure 9-22   Relation between level of estrogen and sexual behavior in female rats. Adult rats with ovaries removed were given daily injections of estradiol benzoate; 5 groups each received a different dosage over a 12-day period. On days 8, 10, and 12 each rat was given about 10 test trials with a sexually active male. The behavioral measure was the lordosis score, that is, the percentage of trials on which a female showed a lordosis response when the male attempted to mount. Scores are means of group performance over the three test days. Vertical bars show ±1 standard error. Note that each point on the scale of dosages indicates twice the preceding value. (From data of Davidson et al., 1968)

havioral effects promptly; it must be present at least one or two days before any behavioral effect is seen. Progesterone then takes a few hours to produce its effects. The complete series of events that intervene between the rise of ovarian hormones in the circulation and the facilitation of neural circuits is still only incompletely known.

Hormonal effects in primate females   Among primates the dependence of female reproductive behavior on hormones is less clear, and there is much individual variability. Some female monkeys remain receptive after removal of the ovaries, although males are less attracted to them. Attempts to correlate female proceptivity with the stage of the menstrual cycle have not produced completely consistent results. Furthermore, testosterone as well as estrogen and progesterone seem to play a role in behavioral changes during the cycle. It is important to note that animal studies show larger interindividual differences in initiative (proceptivity) than in receptivity. In the face of these complexities, we can only sketch some of the better-established findings and some current conclusions.

The attractiveness of female monkeys to males is increased by the surge of estrogen that occurs slightly before the middle of the menstrual cycle (Figure 9-23). The estrogen causes changes in secretions of the vagina and causes swelling of the "sexual skin" on the buttocks (Figure 9-24). Males respond to both the olfactory and the visual stimulation. In an ovariectomized female, replacement therapy with estrogen restores attractiveness, as measured by responses of males. This effect holds whether the estrogen is put into the general circulation or whether it is placed directly into the vagina, so the nervous system need not be involved. Adding progesterone, which normally increases after ovulation (Figure 9-23), decreases attractiveness.

Some investigators think that proceptive behavior—attempts by the female to get the male to copulate—is affected especially by the androgens that are secreted by the female's ovaries and adrenal glands. Note in Figure 9-23 that female monkeys actually have higher blood concentrations of testosterone than of estradiol (the most

Figure 9-23   Fluctuations in hormone levels of female monkeys during the menstrual cycle. (picogram = 10^{-12} gram; nanogram = 10^{-9} gram) (Adapted from Herbert, 1978)

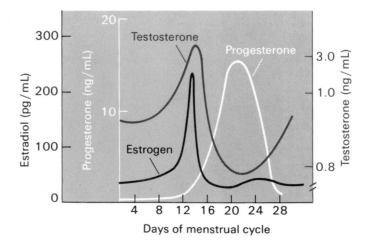

Figure 9-24 Proceptive behavior of female rhesus monkeys. (a) The "presentation" posture in which the female turns her genitalia toward the male, the tail deviated aside. The "sex skin," indicated in blue, is actually pink. (b) The "head duck" in which the female bobs her head up and down and raises her genitalia from the ground. (Herbert, 1978)

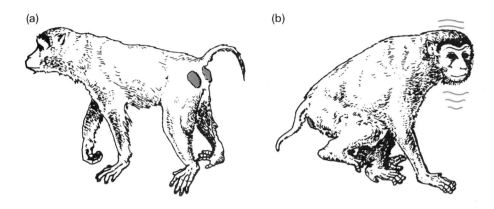

(a)

(b)

common estrogen), but estradiol is a far more potent hormone on a per-weight basis. Note also that the level of testosterone fluctuates more or less in parallel with the level of estrogen during the menstrual cycle. If both the ovaries and the adrenal glands are removed, then no more testosterone is secreted. Replacement therapy with cortisol makes up for basic adrenal functions, and replacement with estrogen restores attractiveness, but the otherwise normal, healthy female makes few attempts to gain access to the male (Everitt and Herbert, 1972). Thus estrogen, which makes female primates attractive and receptive, does not cause proceptive behavior. Injections of testosterone restore proceptive behavior, and so does implantation of a small amount of testosterone into the hypothalamus (Everitt and Herbert, 1975), so this effect is mediated by the nervous system. Whether proceptivity varies with the changes in testosterone levels during the menstrual cycle is not entirely clear. Irregular variations in secretion and in cycle length complicate such research. Using statistical procedures to allow for such variability, Bonsall and collaborators (1978) conclude that there is a statistically significant peak in proceptivity of female rhesus monkeys in midcycle, and seven of nine females showed such an effect. On the other hand, Johnson and Phoenix (1978) were unable to find a significant relation between proceptive behavior and hormonal fluctuations during the menstrual cycles of ten female rhesus monkeys. If there is indeed a cycle of proceptivity in female monkeys, it is largely overshadowed by interindividual and intraindividual variability.

The need for care in interpreting observations in this field is shown by the apparent effects of progesterone on proceptivity. Injection of this hormone increases the attempt of female monkeys to gain access to males. Does this mean that progesterone stimulates brain regions for proceptive behavior, just as testosterone does? Further work showed that very small doses of progesterone placed in the vagina counteracted the local effects of estrogen but did not alter blood levels. In this case, too, the females increased their sexual invitations to males. The experimenters suggest that the progesterone made the females less attractive to males, who were therefore responding sluggishly. So the females had to increase their attempts to invite copulation in order to obtain responses from the males (Baum et al., 1977).

Female primates show some receptivity even though they are ovariectomized and adrenalectomized. Replacement of estrogen causes a major increase in receptivity, and adding androgen brings receptivity to fully normal levels. Progesterone seems to have little or no effect on receptivity. Thus the different aspects of reproductive behavior of female primates are all affected by hormonal levels, and the sex hormones—estrogens, progesterones, and androgens—play clearly different roles in this behavior.

Hormonal effects in male mammals   Male mammals show less prompt effects of gonadal hormones on reproductive behavior than do females. In the rat, for example, some males show the full copulatory pattern for weeks after castration, even though androgens disappear from the body within a few hours; the behavior does decline, but not nearly as rapidly as the levels of androgens (Davidson, 1966b). Among cats, males with mating experience continue to mate for weeks after castration, but few males without prior experience copulate in tests that follow castration (Rosenblatt and Aronson, 1958). Thus neural circuits that have been altered by experience may not require hormonal facilitation.

Differences among males in reproductive behavior seem to depend less on levels of androgens in the circulation than on differences in sensitivity of brain cells to the hormones. The first clue to individual differences in sensitivity came from surprising results on the measurement of reproductive behavior in male guinea pigs before and after castration (Figure 9-25; Grunt and Young, 1953). The animals were divided into three groups—high, medium, and low—according to their preoperative performance on mating tests. Under replacement therapy the groups showed the same ranking (Figure 9-25), and doubling the dose of testosterone did not alter this ranking. In male ring doves individual differences in male courtship behavior are also restored after castration by androgen replacement therapy (Hutchison, 1971). Results such as these have led workers to consider the possibility of individual differences in sensitivity of neurons to hormones.

In our discussion of the development of the reproductive structures, we noted that

Figure 9-25 Hormone level does not completely determine amount of sex behavior. After castration of male guinea pigs reduced their sex activity, the same amount of testosterone was given to each animal, beginning at week 26. The group that had shown high sex activity before castration became high again; the animals that were originally the lowest remained lowest. Doubling the amount of hormone did not increase the ratings. (Adapted from Grunt and Young, 1952)

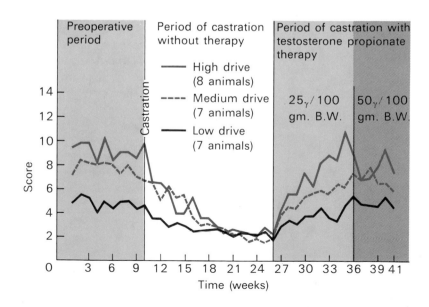

occasional genetic males are insensitive to androgens and therefore develop an external female appearance. Less complete differences in sensitivity are also possible. Sensitivity to hormones can also vary over time. It has often been observed that the longer the number of weeks after castration before replacement therapy has begun, the larger are the doses needed to restore reproductive behavior. The same effect has now been shown for replacement by brain implants of testosterone in the dove (Hutchison, 1976). This result demonstrates that the decline in sensitivity is a cerebral effect and is not caused by peripheral (sensory or muscular) changes. Moreover, brain circuits may normally be more sensitive to androgens than are peripheral structures. Thus to keep rats mating normally requires only half the level of testosterone needed to keep their seminal vesicles at normal weight (Davidson, 1972). Thus variations of androgen levels within or above the normal range do not affect sexual performance. Somewhat higher levels of secretion provide a safety factor, ensuring that performance will not be adversely affected by fluctuations in the rate of secretion (Damassa et al., 1977), but they do not cause superior performance.

● Hormonal influences on the sexual behavior of women   Attempts to relate hormonal levels to sexual behavior in women are based on several sorts of evidence—the variations in hormonal levels that occur normally during the menstrual cycle, departures from the normal cycle because of some deficiency in the neuroendocrine system, and effects of administered hormones, usually for purposes of birth control. Many studies, reviewed by Bancroft (1978), have investigated the relative frequency of sexual intercourse during the menstrual cycle, but the results are not clear-cut. Most studies report a peak following menstruation, although some report a peak before menstruation and some report a peak around midcycle at the time of ovulation. A peak at midcycle would be understandable in that it would increase the possibility of fertilization, but the evidence for such a peak is mixed and inconclusive. Rather the picture is one of individual variability.

The use of oral contraceptives does not seem to have major effects on the timing of intercourse during the cycle. This observation indicates that the exact timing of the ovarian hormones is not of major behavioral importance; neither is the timing of the hypothalamic and pituitary hormones, since they are inhibited by the oral contraceptives. (See Box 9-2.)

Cessation of menstruation in a women before the age of menopause may be traced to any of three levels in the neuroendocrine system. The most common cause is at the hypothalamic level. The surge of luteinizing hormone (LH) that is required for ovulation does not occur, although there is a steady level of secretion of LH and follicle-stimulating hormone (FSH). This surge appears to be the most vulnerable stage in the female reproductive sequence (Federman, 1979). It is inhibited in many conditions, including nutritional deficiency, pathological refusal to eat (anorexia nervosa), and many kinds of psychological distress or anxiety. This condition, often called "hypothalamic amenorrhea" or "psychic amenorrhea," demonstrates the importance of neural control of the ovarian hormones. A rarer cause of amenorrhea is a pituitary defect; in this case the levels of both LH and FSH are low, unlike the condition in hypothalamic amenorrhea. Amenorrhea may also be caused by ovarian failure, but this condition is rare in young women.

BOX 9-2 Hormones in Reproduction and Contraception

Investigation of the female endocrine cycle is making it possible to control reproduction both to aid people in having the children they want and in avoiding having unwanted children. The human menstrual cycle will be discussed here in relation to reproduction. Whether this cycle can be related to changes in behavior is considered in this chapter.

During a 28-day menstrual cycle, follicle-stimulating hormone (FSH) from the anterior pituitary begins to rise a few days before the menses and stimulates development of an ovarian follicle with its egg (Box Figure 9-1). FSH also stimulates the ovary to secrete estrogens, principally estradiol, which act on the uterus to build up its inner lining. The estrogens reach their peak around day 12, which triggers a surge in production of luteinizing hormone (LH) that occurs the next day; ovulation follows within 24 hours. The follicle that released the ovum now becomes a corpus luteum, which secretes the hormone progesterone. Progesterone causes further development of the uterine wall that prepares it for implantation of a fertilized egg. If an egg is fertilized, after undergoing several cell divisions, it secretes a hormone that keeps the corpus luteum producing progesterone. Later the placenta secretes progesterone. If fertilization does not occur, the secretion of progesterone declines after about day 24, which leads to the sloughing off of the lining of the uterine wall in menstruation.

For women in whom ovulation does not occur regularly, the regularity can often be improved by hormonal treatment. Sometimes such treatment causes several eggs to be released at the same time, so that births of quintuplets or sextuplets are more common than they were before the advent of induced ovulation.

Prevention of ovulation can also be accomplished by hormonal treatments, which is the basis of the birth control pills that have been developed since the 1950s. These pills combine a synthetic estrogen with progestin, a progesteronelike compound. These synthetic hormones perform two functions:

1. They suppress the pituitary gonadotropic hormones through negative feedback, so there is no stimulation

of a follicle to develop an ovum. That is, the brain detects the elevated level of steroid hormones in the blood and therefore does not send gonadotropic-releasing factor to the pituitary.

2. They act to stimulate the uterine wall and thus cause a menstrual cycle.

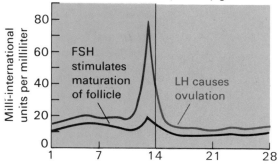

(a) Tropic hormones of anterior pituitary gland

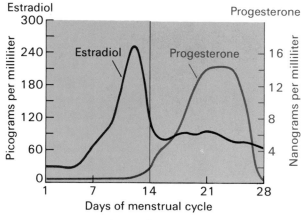

(b) Ovarian hormones

(c) Changes in ovary

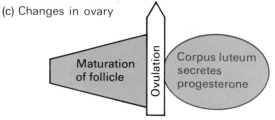

Box Figure 9-1 Cycles of changes during the human menstrual cycle: (a) tropic hormones of the adrenal pituitary gland, (b) ovarian hormones, and (c) the ovary.

At the average age of 48 in the United States, a woman stops producing ripe follicles in the ovaries, and menopause occurs. There is a sharp increase in FSH at this time, showing that the failure is not in the central command but in the ability of the ovaries to respond. Because of the feedback relations in control of the ovarian hormones, a decline in their level causes a rise in FSH (Figure 5-12). The failure of production of ripe ova, of course, makes conception impossible. Lack of development of follicles also prevents the secretion of estrogen and progesterone by the ovaries, although some estrogen may still be secreted by the adrenal cortex. The decline in the level of estrogen may produce a variety of symptoms, but it does not cause cessation of sexual behavior.

Thus while the endocrine system is vital for reproduction, individual differences in hormonal levels have not been shown to influence strongly the frequency or quality of sexual behavior. Bancroft concludes: "There has been a widespread need to find a simple hormonal key to the understanding of human sexual behavior. There is no reason why we should expect to find simple relationships" (1978, p. 514).

● Hormonal influences on the sexual behavior of men   In healthy men from ages 18 to 60, the values of testosterone show a rather wide normal range from about 350 to 1000 nanograms per 100 milliliters of blood. Individual differences within this range appear to have no significance for sexual behavior. Beyond the age of 60 or so the mean value of testosterone tends to fall progressively, although about half the healthy men over 80 still have values that are within the normal range for younger men.

A man who complains of lack of potency or fertility often also shows a testosterone value below 400 and/or a low sperm count. Current methods often permit diagnosis of the level of the neuroendocrine system that is deficient, and appropriate therapies then aid many cases. A disorder may occur at any of three levels:

1. The hypothalamus may not furnish normal amounts of the gonadotropin-releasing hormone (GnRH).

2. The pituitary may not release sufficient amounts of luteinizing hormone (LH) and follicle-stimulating hormone (FSH). The pituitary gonadotropins are not released steadily but in pulses, so more than one sample is required for an adequate test. If the values are low, GnRH can be administered to see whether the pituitary will respond with normal release of LH and FSH.

3. The failure may be in the testes, which, although they are being stimulated by adequate amounts of pituitary gonadotropin, are not producing enough testosterone. In this case the level of LH is found to be above normal, since the hypothalamus and pituitary are not receiving enough negative feedback from testosterone.

Thus in men 60 and over the fall in testosterone is accompanied by a rise in LH, which indicates a primary decline in gonadal function.

For men in whom the level of testosterone is below the threshold level and who complain of lack of sexual responsiveness, administration of testosterone every few weeks has been shown to be helpful in restoring sexual activity. Thus in one double-blind study six hypogonadal men were given either a long-lasting form of testosterone or an inactive control substance once every four weeks, and they kept daily records of their sexual activity and experience. In five of the six subjects stimulatory effects of testosterone on sexual activity were rapid and reliable, and they were not due to a placebo effect (Davidson et al., 1979).

Several studies have asked whether homosexuals differ from heterosexuals in gonadotropins or in gonadal hormones. The results, reviewed by Bancroft (1978), have varied widely. Among studies that appear to have been done carefully, some have found male homosexuals to have lower testosterone levels than heterosexuals, some have reported no significant difference, and some have found higher values for the homosexuals. Relatively little investigation has been made so far of possible endocrine factors in female homosexuality. Bancroft doubts that any simple answer about homosexuality will emerge from endocrine studies, but research in this area continues.

Thus in the adult human male, as in the adult female, most individual differences in sexual behavior cannot be explained by individual differences in hormonal levels. Hormones are certainly important in early development of reproductive structures and in later development of secondary sexual characteristics. They also play an activational role in facilitating the initiation of sexual behaviors and in maintaining them. But wide variations in hormonal levels do not have clear effects on the amount or quality of human sexual activities. Once the neural circuits for these behaviors have been established, other sources of stimulation can suffice even in the absence of endocrine facilitation.

SUMMARY / MAIN POINTS

1. Sex brings variety to life in many ways, including sex differences in appearance and behavior, sex-related changes in appearance and behavior over the life span, and genetic permutations that have made rapid evolution possible.

2. Mating behavior shows four stages: sexual attraction, appetitive or proceptive behavior, copulatory behavior, and postcopulatory behavior. Each stage demands interaction between the female and the male.

3. The XY or XX chromosomal pattern determines whether the gonads of the embryo will develop into testes or ovaries. It also determines the relative responsiveness of the body tissues to different sex hormones.

4. Two systems of primitive ducts exist in each embryo; they allow for the possible development of either masculine or feminine internal reproductive structures. The female system will develop unless a fetal testicular substance is secreted. Similarly, the external genitals assume the femi- nine form unless androgens transform them to the masculine appearance.

5. Sex differentiation of brain structures has been found both in rats and in songbirds. The two sexes differ in the sizes and connections of some brain structures, and these differences can be altered by hormonal treatments.

6. Prenatal sexual development appears to exert some influences on human personality and behavior. Although many alleged sex differences in personality have not been substantiated, there is good evidence that, on the average, girls exceed boys in verbal ability, boys exceed girls in visual-spatial ability and in mathematics, and males of all ages are more aggressive than females.

7. Successful sexual reproduction requires that the sexes come together and select suitable partners, that the time and place for reproduction be suitable, and that specific copu- latory (and sometimes postcopulatory) behavior occurs.

Furthermore, parental care can increase the probability that offspring will survive.

8. Sexual selection has been used to explain the reproductive advantage of certain individuals over others of their sex and species. The basis of sexual selection is the unequal investment that the two sexes make in a single offspring.

9. Evolutionary implications for human sexuality are found both in adaptations shared with other mammals and in the specific history of human evolution. The tripling of brain size in the hominid line has promoted variety and flexibility of human behavior, including reproductive behavior. During human evolution there may also have been selection for somewhat different sex roles.

10. Many of the motor responses involved in copulation are integrated by spinal circuits. Testosterone directly affects these responses in males. These spinal responses are normally modulated by the activity of brain regions.

11. Sexual attraction and appetitive behavior in vertebrates require brain activity. The preoptic area is especially involved in male reproductive behavior; hypothalamic areas posterior to the preoptic area are especially involved in female behaviors.

12. Hormones play an organizational role in developing reproductive organs and neural circuits; later they play an activational role in eliciting or facilitating reproductive behavior. They also help to maintain and modulate the sensitivity of neural circuits to hormones.

13. In the ring dove the complementary sequences of behaviors in female and male are beautifully integrated. The female's transition from one stage to the next is marked by changes in the levels of estrogen, progesterone, and prolactin. The male can ensure his role at most stages with an adequate and steady supply of androgens and a tendency to follow the behavioral lead of the female as she moves from one stage to the next.

14. In mammals, reproductive females of some species go through a regular cycle in which levels of estrogen and progesterone rise and fall. In the rat, proceptivity and receptivity depend on the hormonal cycle. In nonhuman primates the dependence on hormonal changes is less complete.

15. Estrogen is the main determinant of attractiveness of the female primate to the male. Progesterone decreases attractiveness by acting on peripheral structures such as the sexual skin on the buttocks. Proceptive behavior is determined largely by the androgens secreted by the ovaries and adrenal glands. Both estrogens and androgens enhance receptivity, although some receptivity remains even in the absence of either hormone.

16. Male mammals show less clear-cut effects of hormones on reproductive behavior than do females. Males will continue to copulate for weeks after castration or even indefinitely, especially if they were experienced. Differences among males seem to depend less on their levels of androgens than on the sensitivity of brain cells to androgens.

17. In human females and males, hormones are important in early development of reproductive structures, in later development of secondary sexual characteristics, in activating and initiating sexual behaviors, and in maintaining these behaviors. But wide variations in hormonal levels do not seem to affect the quality or quantity of sexual activities.

18. Once neural circuits for reproductive behaviors have been established, other sources of stimulation can suffice in the absence of hormonal facilitation.

RECOMMENDED READING

Adler, N. T. (Ed.). *Neuroendocrinology of reproduction*. New York: Plenum, 1981.

Beach, F. A. (Ed.). *Human sexuality in four perspectives*. Baltimore: Johns Hopkins University Press, 1977.

Daly, M., and Wilson, M. *Sex, evolution and behavior*. North Scituate, Mass.: Duxbury Press, 1978.

Hutchison, J. B. (Ed.). *Biological determinants of sexual behaviour*. New York: Wiley, 1978.

Katchadourian, H. A., and Lunde, D. T. *Fundamentals of human sexuality* (3rd ed.). New York: Holt, Rinehart and Winston, 1980.

McGill, T. E., Dewsbury, D. A., and Sachs, B. D. *Sex and behavior*. New York: Plenum, 1978.

Orientation

Properties of homeostatic mechanisms

Multiple control systems

Regulation of Body Temperature

Types of regulation

External regulation

Internal regulation

Learned temperature regulation

Development of temperature regulation

Evolution of temperature regulation

Thirst

Monitoring the body's supplies of water

Initiation of drinking

Termination of drinking

Taste and drinking

Summary/Main Points

10

Homeostatic Mechanisms I: Heating/Cooling, Drinking

Orientation

Naked inhabitants of central Australia sleep comfortably without shelter through a winter night when the temperature falls to 4°C. An American anthropologist visiting this semi-arid desert region shivers miserably under a light blanket, but after a few weeks the American adapts to the stress of the nighttime cold. Throughout this time the anthropologist and the aborigines have maintained core body temperatures close to 37°C (98.6°F).

Just as responses to cold differ among human groups, dietary habits differ amazingly among the regions and peoples of the world, even though all people share the same basic nutritional needs. Eskimo and Northwest Coast Indians traditionally lived most of the year on diets of meat and fish; they had no agriculture and did little gathering of plant foods. On the plains of India large groups maintain strict vegetarian diets, which exclude even animal products such as eggs. In the dusty grasslands of East Africa the main daily meal of adult Masai men used to be a bowl of blood drawn from a domestic cow. By adapting to local conditions, people have been able to live on almost all the earth's surface, except in regions of extreme cold or extreme altitude (Figure 10-1). Now human beings are even learning how to live for extended periods beneath the seas and in outer space.

Our bodies, and those of other animals, are complex life-support systems that have evolved over millions of years. Within the body the cells are kept within a narrow range of temperatures that ensures optimal functioning, even though the external temperature may be much colder or warmer. The cells are immersed in a fluid me-

(a)

Figure 10-1 Adaptation to extreme climates involves changes in behavior, physiology, and anatomy. Examples are seen in comparing (a) an Eskimo from arctic Alaska with (b) a Nilotic inhabitant of tropical Africa. [(a) © Karl H. Maslowski, 1977/Photo Researchers, Inc. (b) © Lynn McLaren/Photo Researchers, Inc.]

(b)

dium with nearly constant characteristics and are supplied with nutriments. These internal constancies are characteristic of mammals and birds (although we will consider certain exceptions later). As we noted in Chapter 5, Claude Bernard stressed the importance of constancy of the internal environment, and Walter Cannon coined the term **homeostasis** to describe it.

In this chapter we will consider processes that regulate body temperature and thirst (fluid content); Chapter 11 takes up the related topic of hunger (food stocks and metabolism). In many cases the regulation keeps conditions relatively constant, but in some cases there is a controlled change, such as a small drop of body temperature during sleep or a large drop during hibernation. Each of these three systems is vital in itself, and all are interrelated. For instance, maintaining body heat requires metabolic expenditure, which draws on the body's stocks of food; cooling the body involves evaporation of moisture from the lungs or body surface and thus entails loss of water. We will see other interactions among these systems later on.

Properties of homeostatic mechanisms

The homeostatic mechanisms that regulate temperature, body fluids, and metabolism are all **negative-feedback systems.** That is, in each case a desired value or zone is established; this desired value is called the **set point,** or set zone, by analogy with the setting of a thermostat (Figure 10-2). (We first discussed negative-feedback systems in connection with regulation of hormonal secretion in Chapter 5.) When the heating system of a building is controlled by a thermostat, a drop in temperature below the set level will activate the thermostat, which turns on the heating system. When the thermostat registers a small rise in temperature, it turns off the heating system. (Note that there is a small range of temperature between the "turn on" and "turn off" signals, otherwise the heating system would be going on and off very frequently. Thus there is really a "set zone" rather than a "set point.") The setting of the thermostat can be changed; for example, it can be turned down at night to save energy. The building may also have a cooling system that is thermostatically controlled with set temperatures that cause it to go on and off. Thus active systems prevent the internal temperature from getting either unpleasantly hot or uncomfortably cool.

The body temperature for most mammals and birds is usually held within a narrow range, about 36°–38°C (97°–100°F)—though the set zone can be altered depending on overall conditions and current goals of the organism. Temperatures in certain parts of the body are monitored closely by internal receptors, and deviations from the desired value are noted. If the deviation exceeds a threshold amount, then corrective action brings the temperature back within the set zone. Physiological adjustments are carried out automatically and internally whereas other corrective actions require behavioral interaction with the environment, including learned behaviors in some cases. This model appeals to many investigators because it is similar to an un-

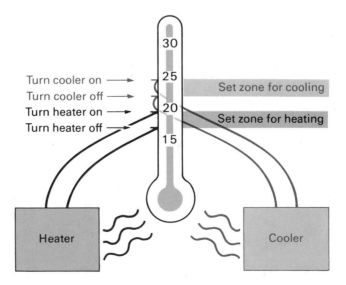

Figure 10-2 Diagram of thermostatically controlled heating and cooling systems.

derstood physical system and can encompass many behavioral observations. Nevertheless, a negative-feedback circuit with a built-in set zone is not the only kind of model being considered, as we will see below.

Multiple control systems

For guaranteed performance of vital mechanical and electrical functions, space capsules are designed with multiple monitoring units and with parallel systems or backup devices. Thus the failure of one unit or system is not lethal, since other systems can guarantee the same objective. Evolution has similarly endowed our bodies with multiple systems. In fact, this endowment has complicated researchers' attempts to find the mechanisms that ensure the constancy of bodily conditions; interfering with one or another mechanism often produces little or no effect, since parallel or alternative mechanisms assume the burden. Nevertheless, we will seek to find the signals that initiate corrective action and the signals that terminate it for each homeostatic bodily system.

Regulation of body temperature

Our cells cannot remain alive outside certain limits of temperature, and much narrower limits mark the boundaries of effective functioning. Above about 45°C (113°F) most proteins become inactivated and begin to lose the precise three-dimensional structure they need for their bodily functions. Below 0°C (32°F) the water inside cells begins to form ice crystals that disturb the internal organization and the membranes of cells, killing them. The enzyme systems of mammals and birds are most efficient only within a narrow range around 37°C; a departure of a few degrees from this value seriously impairs their functioning. Even though cells can survive wider fluctuations, the integrated actions of bodily systems are impaired. Children, for example, may become delirious with a few degrees of fever. Other animals have a wider tolerance for changes of bodily temperature. Isolated nerves and muscles continue to function reasonably well in physiology laboratories even though their temperature is changed over 10°C or more, but the integrated behavior of mammals cannot survive such a change of internal temperature.

Types of regulation

For centuries it has been recognized that mammals and birds differ from other animals in the way they regulate body temperatures. Our ways of characterizing the difference have become more accurate and meaningful over time, but popular terminology still reflects the old division into "warm-blooded" and "cold-blooded" species; "warm-blooded" included mammals and birds, while all other creatures were called "cold-blooded." As more species were studied, it became evident that this classification was inadequate. A fence lizard or a desert iguana—both "cold-blooded"—usually has a body temperature only a degree or two below ours and so is *not* cold. Therefore the next distinction was made between animals that maintain a constant body temperature, called **homeotherms** (from the Greek "homeo," meaning "same," and "therm," meaning "heat"), and those whose body temperature varies with their environment, called **poikilotherms** (from the Greek root "poikilo," meaning "varied"). But this classification also proved inadequate, because among mammals there are many that vary their body temperatures during hibernation. Furthermore, many invertebrates that live in the depths of the ocean never experience a change in the chill of the deep waters, and their body temperatures remain constant.

The current distinction is between animals whose body temperature is regulated chiefly by internal metabolic processes and those whose temperature is regulated by, and who get most of their heat from, the environment. The former are called **endotherms** (from the Greek root "endo," meaning "internal"), and the latter are called **ectotherms** (from the Greek root "ecto," meaning "exterior"). Most ectotherms do regulate their body temperature, and they do so mainly by locomoting to favorable sites or by changing their exposure to external sources of heat. Endotherms (mainly mammals and birds) also regulate their temperature by choosing favorable environments, but primarily they regulate their temperatures by making a variety of internal adjustments.

Regulation by use of external heat sources was the first to evolve and uses rather simple mechanisms, so we will discuss ectothermy before endothermy.

External regulation   The marine iguana of the Galapagos Islands stays underwater for an hour or more eating seaweed in water that is 10° to 15°C cooler than its preferred body temperature. Then it emerges and lies on a warm rock to restore its temperature. While warming up, it lies broadside to the sun to absorb as much heat as possible (Figure 10-3a). When its temperature has reached the desired level, 37°, the iguana turns to face the sun and thus absorb less heat, and it may extend its legs to keep its body away from warm surfaces (Figure 10-3b). Many ectotherms regulate their tempera-

Figure 10-3 Behavioral control of body temperature. (a) A Galapagos marine iguana, upon emerging from the cold sea, raises its body temperature by hugging a warm rock and lying broadside to the sun. (b) Once its temperature is sufficiently high, the iguana reduces its surface contact with the rock and faces the sun to minimize its exposure. These behaviors afford considerable control over body temperature. (Photographs by M. R. Rosenzweig)

(a)   (b)

tures in similar ways. Some snakes, for example, adjust their coils to expose more or less surface to the sun and thus keep their internal temperature relatively constant during the day.

Bees regulate the temperature inside the hive by their behavior. When there are larvae or pupae, the bees keep the temperature in the brood area of the hive at 35–36°C. When the air temperature is low, the bees crowd into the brood area and shiver, thus generating heat. When the air temperature is high, the bees reduce the temperature in the brood area by fanning with their wings and by evaporative cooling (Heinrich, 1981).

Mammals and birds, which are endotherms, also control their exposure to the sun and to hot or cold surfaces in order to avoid making excessive demands on their internal regulatory mechanisms. For example, herring gulls stand oriented toward the sun or broadside to it, depending on the ambient temperature (Lustick, Battersby, and Kelty, 1978). In hot desert regions many small mammals, such as the kangaroo rat, remain in underground burrows during the day and appear aboveground only at night when the environment is relatively cool.

Human populations have devised many cultural practices to adapt to conditions of cold or heat. For example, Eskimos learned to design clothing that insulates well but permits dissipation of heat through vents. Other Eskimo cultural adaptations include the design of efficient shelters, sharing of body heat, choice of diet, and use of seal oil lamps (Moran, 1981).

Whether an animal is an ectotherm or an endotherm, if it is placed in a laboratory situation where there is a gradient of temperature from warm to cold, it will spend most of its time at its preferred environmental temperature. The choices show that the preferred temperature differs from species to species. Even animals as simple as bacteria converge on an optimal temperature zone. A nude sedentary person prefers an air temperature of about 28°C (82°F); a well-clothed sedentary person prefers an air temperature of about 22°C (72°F). If a person or animal is placed in an experimental situation that consists of two compartments, one heated above the subject's preferred temperature and the other cooled below the preferred temperature, then the subject alternates frequently between the two regions and thereby helps to keep its internal temperature within the desired range.

Internal regulation   Our usually accurate regulation of body temperature results from a precise balancing of processes that increase and maintain heat against processes that lose heat. What are some of these processes of heat gain and heat loss? How and where is temperature monitored in the body? How are the processes that gain, conserve, and lose heat controlled? When an animal reduces the burden of regulating temperature by entering a state of torpor (as some species of bats do daily) or by hibernating for months (as ground squirrels do), is the animal's temperature still controlled, or does it simply fall to that of the environment? We will answer these questions in the following paragraphs.

● **Mechanisms of heat gain**   Metabolism—utilization of stored food in the body—releases heat, so all living tissues produce heat. Table 10-1 shows the amounts of heat produced by an adult person engaging in different activities, from sleep to stren-

TABLE 10-1   Influence of Activity on Heat Production of an Adult Person

ACTIVITY	HEAT (KCAL/H)
Resting or sleeping	65
Awake, sitting quietly	100
Light exercise	170
Moderate exercise	290
Strenuous exercise	450
Very strenuous exercise	600

uous exercise. [The unit of heat is a kilocalorie, abbreviated kcal; 1 kcal is enough heat to raise the temperature of 1000 cubic centimeters (cc) of water 1°C.] When the body is at rest, a considerable proportion of the heat is produced by the brain (about 20 out of 65 kcal). As bodily activity increases, the heat production of the brain does not rise much, but that of the muscles can increase nearly tenfold. Muscles, like mechanical devices, produce a good deal of heat while they are accomplishing work. Muscles and gasoline engines have about the same efficiency; each produces about four or five times as much heat as mechanical work. Some of the main ways of gaining and of dissipating heat are shown in Figure 10-4.

Heat production is closely related to the area of body surface, since heat exchanges with the environment occur largely at the surface of the body. A big animal like an elephant has relatively little skin surface compared to the volume of its body; a small animal like a canary or a rat has a large surface-to-volume ratio. The ratio of surface to volume decreases with increasing volume, as shown in Figure 10-5. Surface-to-volume relations are important for generating and dissipating body heat, because heat is produced by body tissue (volume) and dissipated at the body surface.

Table 10-2 shows the body sizes of several species in terms of weight, surface area, and heat production. Smaller animals, because of their larger surface-to-volume ratios, lose heat more rapidly to the environment, so they must produce more heat in relation to body size than do larger animals. For example, from the data of Table 10-2 we see that it takes 20 cats to equal the weight of a person, but the 20 cats produce twice the heat of the person of equal weight. (And that is why we have to buy so much cat food.) Per unit of body weight, small animals produce much more heat than large ones; from canary to elephant the ratio is more than 20 to 1.

TABLE 10-2   Body Size and Heat Production of Some Birds and Mammals

SPECIES	BODY WEIGHT (KG)	BODY SURFACE (M²)	ENERGY OUTPUT PER DAY		
			Total (kcal)	Per Unit of Body Weight (kcal/kg)	Per Unit of Body Surface (kcal/m²)
Canary	0.016	0.006	5	310	760
Rat	0.2	0.03	25	130	830
Pigeon	0.3	0.04	30	100	670
Cat	3.0	0.2	150	50	750
Human	60	1.7	1,500	25	850
Elephant	3,600	24	47,000	13	2,000

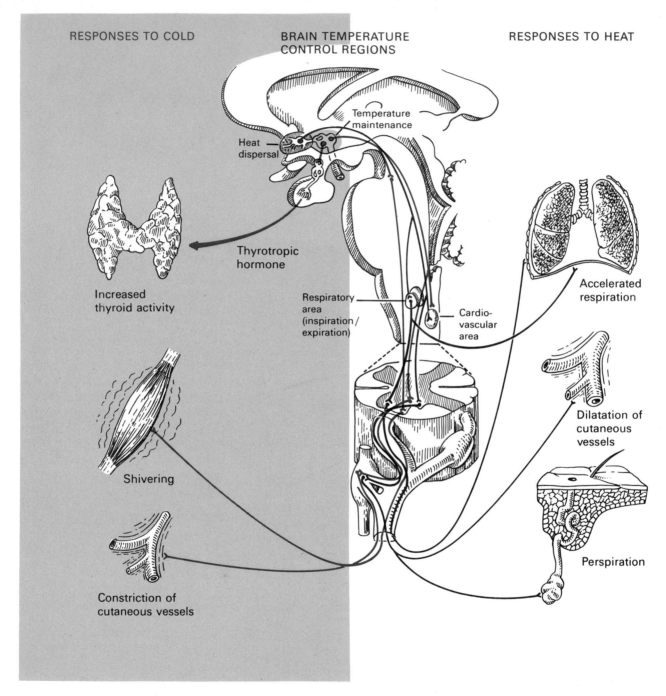

Figure 10-4 Some of the primary ways the human body gains and loses heat and their neural controls.

The rate of heat production can be adjusted to suit conditions, particularly in certain organs. Deposits of brown fat are found especially around vital organs in the trunk and around the cervical and thoracic levels of the spinal cord. Under cold conditions the sympathetic nervous system stimulates increased metabolism of brown fat cells. The most conspicuous means by which heat is generated is muscular

Figure 10-5 The ratio of surface to volume of a solid decreases as the volume increases.

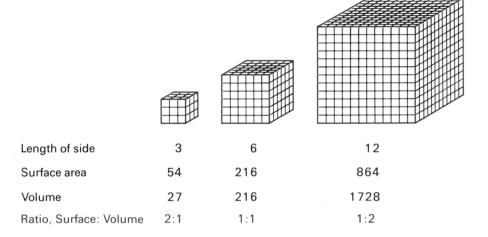

Length of side	3	6	12
Surface area	54	216	864
Volume	27	216	1728
Ratio, Surface: Volume	2:1	1:1	1:2

activity. At low temperatures nerve impulses cause muscle cells to contract out of synchrony, producing shivering rather than movements. Shivering of small amplitude, not visible to casual observation, can be detected by fine intramuscular electrodes.

● **Mechanisms of conserving heat**   In the face of an internal energy crunch, conservation in the body is important. When the environmental temperature is considerably lower than the preferred internal temperature, it requires great metabolic expense to keep body heat at the desired level. If animals did not have effective ways of conserving heat, they would die. With strong selection pressure for heat conservation, many different adaptations have evolved; a few of the principal ones are body size, body shape, and skin adaptations.

Body size is an important means of conserving heat. Since the main need for warmth is at the core of the body, peripheral tissues can insulate the inner organs; the skin and the extremities are usually cooler than the core of the body. Because large animals do not need to make up as much heat loss as do smaller animals, the larger animals have lower metabolic rates, as we saw above. Within a group of closely related mammals or birds, those living at lower temperatures will be larger than those living in warmer environments. And even in the temperate zone a very small mammal like the shrew has to eat almost incessantly to meet its metabolic needs.

Shape also affects heat conservation. The humanoid form in Figure 10-6 has exactly the same volume as the squat figure beside it, but the more slender form has almost twice as much surface area as the compact form. Because of its lower surface-to-volume ratio, the more compact body conserves heat better and therefore is better able to protect its internal temperature in a cold climate. Among human groups there has been a tendency for taller, more slender body forms to evolve in the tropics and for shorter stockier physiques to evolve in the colder regions (Figure 10-1), but migrations and intermixture of human stocks have blurred this tendency. Among many animal groups body appendages are smaller in arctic species than in

Figure 10-6 Two forms with the same volume but different surface areas.

related tropical species. Figure 10-7 illustrates this by showing variations in the size of the external ear in species of foxes from different climatic zones.

Fur of mammals and feathers of birds—these are special adaptations of the skin that serve as insulation from the environment. In cold environments large mammals usually have a thick coat of fur, but small mammals cannot grow thick fur without interfering with their locomotion. If fur or feathers are to serve their function of insulation properly, they must be kept in good condition, which is one reason why many mammals and birds spend a great deal of time grooming and preening. For an animal like the sea otter that spends its life in cold water, insulation is vital. A small area of matted fur that provides a channel for heat loss could be fatal to the otter. Most species of birds have a preen gland or oil gland near the base of the tail; the oil from this gland is used to dress the feathers and waterproof them.

● Mechanisms of heat loss   Getting rid of heat can be important too. Even in a cold climate energetic muscular activity produces heat that must be dissipated rapidly. In a hot climate body temperature must be kept below that of the surrounding environment. Evaporation is an effective way to dissipate heat, and many ways of promoting evaporation have evolved. In people, horses, and cattle, sweating helps to prevent overheating. Many species, such as dogs, cats, and rats, have no sweat glands over most of their body surface, so they pant to evaporate moisture from the mouth, throat, and lungs. Rats have been observed to spread saliva over their fur to increase the area for evaporation. Honeybees have been found to prevent overheating of the head by using evaporation (Heinrich, 1979). At high air temperatures they regurgitate droplets of nectar onto the tongue; evaporation reduces their temperature and at the same time concentrates the nectar.

Sending blood to the surface of the body helps to dissipate heat, as long as the environment is cooler than the body, and many animals lose heat in this way. The large ears of the elephant increase its surface appreciably; they are highly vascular and blood is shunted there to dissipate heat. Rabbits also use their ears as major heat exchange surfaces. In some species the ears account for a quarter of the body

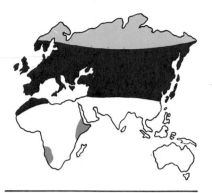

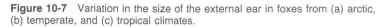

Figure 10-7 Variation in the size of the external ear in foxes from (a) arctic, (b) temperate, and (c) tropical climates.

(a)

(b)

(c)

surface. The amount of blood flow in the ear is controlled by the autonomic nervous system; when blood flow to the ear is constricted, body temperature rises.

Camels adjust to heat in one of two ways, depending on the availability of water. When water is freely available, the camel uses evaporation through panting and respiration to keep its temperature between 36° and 38°C. When water is scarce, the camel lets its temperature drop to 34° in the cool of the night and allows it to rise as high as 41° in the afternoon. This process economizes about 5 liters of water a day. By allowing its temperature to fall below normal during the night, the camel is capable of storing more heat during the day than if it started at 37°C (Schmidt-Nielsen, 1964).

On a hot day a dog can chase a rabbit until the rabbit dies from overheating of the brain. Why is this exertion lethal for the rabbit but not for the dog? Although running raises the body temperature of both animals, the dog's brain has a special cooling system that the rabbit's brain does not (Baker, 1979). This cooling system combines adaptations of the respiratory system for evaporation and of the circulatory system for a heat exchange network (see Figure 10-8). This network of blood vessels is located just below the base of the brain. In it, cooler venous blood coming from the periphery reduces the temperature of arterial blood before it enters the brain. The heat exchange occurs because the veins and arteries both subdivide into many fine vessels that come into close contact with each other. This intricate network of vessels was called the **rete mirabile,** or "wonderful net," by Galen, the great Roman anatomist of the second century. Galen observed this network in the brains of domestic animals and supposed that it must be present in human beings. He thought that it was the site of transformation of the "animal spirit" (or animate fluid) from the arteries into the "psychic spirit" (or fluid) that he believed traveled through the hollow tubes of nerves. Actually there is no rete in human beings nor in other primates, nor is there one in horses, rodents, marsupials, and many other species. Carnivores possess the rete, and so do sheep and cattle.

The venous blood that cools the rete comes mainly from the regions of the nose and mouth, and increased evaporative cooling occurs here during exercise. In the dog the extensive branching of the bones in the nasal passages provides a surface that is larger than all the rest of the body. The combined evaporative and heat exchange system is so effective that during the first 5–10 minutes of exercise, the dog's brain temperature actually falls below the resting level.

● **Monitoring and regulating body temperature**   The nervous system controls and regulates all the processes of heat production and heat loss that we have just reviewed, with assists in some cases from the endocrine system. What parts of the nervous system are active in these processes and what principles operate? Research, which has been conducted on these topics since the last century and at a rapid pace in recent years, has provided some answers.

Figure 10-8 Why exertion overheats some animals but not others. Exercise produces heat, but some species, such as the dog, have a special heat-exchange cooling system. Other species, such as the rabbit, do not possess this special cooling system.

In the 1880s physiologists observed that localized destruction of tissue in the hypothalamus of dogs elevated the body temperature. In classic experiments Barbour (1912) manipulated the temperature of the hypothalamus in dogs by implanting silver wires. When the wires were heated, body temperature fell; when the wires were cooled, body temperature rose. These results suggested that body temperature is monitored in the hypothalamus and that when temperature there departs in either direction from the desired level, compensatory actions are initiated. Later work involving electrical recording from single cells revealed cells that responded specifically to small increases or decreases of brain temperature; these cells are scattered throughout the preoptic area (POA) and the anterior hypothalamus.

Lesion experiments in mammals indicate that there are different sites for two kinds of regulation: (1) regulation by locomotor and other behaviors that mammals share with ectotherms and (2) physiological regulations that are characteristic of endotherms. Lesions in the lateral hypothalamus of rats abolished behavioral regulation of temperature but did not affect the autonomic thermoregulatory responses such as shivering and vasoconstriction (Satinoff and Shan, 1971; Van Zoeren and Stricker, 1977). On the other hand, lesions in the POA of rats impaired the autonomic responses but did not interfere with behaviors such as pressing levers to turn heating lamps or cooling fans on or off (Satinoff and Rutstein, 1970; Van Zoeren and Stricker, 1977). Here is a clear example of parallel circuits for two different ways of regulating the same variable.

Receptors at the surface of the body monitor temperature and provide information used in controlling thermoregulatory processes. If you enter a cold environment without protective clothing, you soon begin to shiver—long before there is a fall in your core temperature. If you enter a hot greenhouse or a sauna bath, you begin to sweat before there is any rise in your hypothalamic temperature. So the skin provides information to central circuits which promptly initiate corrective action. The spinal cord has also been found to be a temperature-monitoring region; heating or cooling the cord in experimental animals causes compensatory responses. Information from different regions—hypothalamus, skin, and spinal cord—converges on the thermoregulatory circuits, a topic we will take up next.

● **Thermoregulatory circuits**   The neural circuits that regulate temperature are known only in part, and debate continues over which of a few possible basic designs is actually employed. Some possibilities that we will consider are these:

1. A feedback circuit with an endogenous (within the body) set point.

2. Multiple feedback systems, each controlling a different thermoregulatory response.

3. Cross-linked reflex circuits for warmth sensors and cold sensors without an endogenous set point.

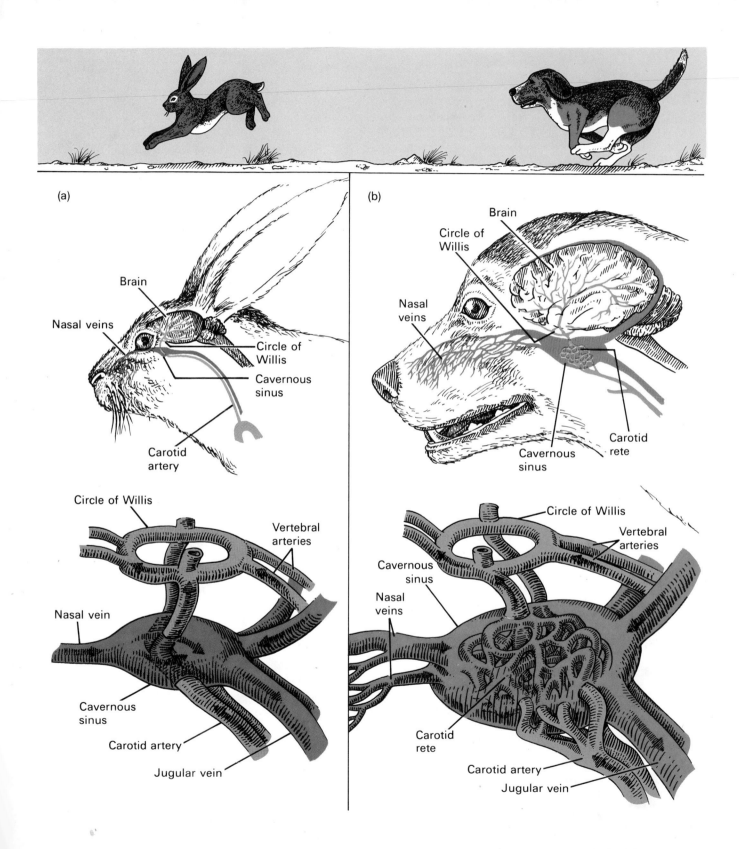

(a)

Brain

Nasal veins

Circle of Willis

Cavernous sinus

Carotid artery

Circle of Willis

Vertebral arteries

Nasal vein

Cavernous sinus

Carotid artery

Jugular vein

(b)

Brain

Circle of Willis

Nasal veins

Cavernous sinus

Carotid rete

Circle of Willis

Vertebral arteries

Cavernous sinus

Nasal veins

Carotid rete

Carotid artery

Jugular vein

(a) Hypothalamus

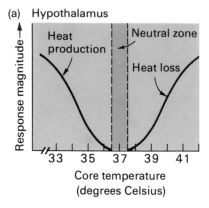

(b) Brain stem

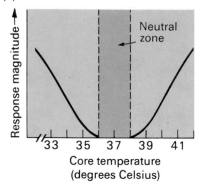

(c) Spinal cord

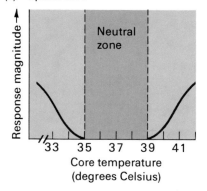

Figure 10-9 Thermal neutral zones of thermoregulatory systems at different levels of the nervous system. The neutral zones are narrower at the higher levels of the nervous system than at the lower levels. (Adapted from Satinoff, 1978)

Many investigators employ the model of a negative-feedback circuit with an endogenous set point; this model is the thermostat model that we mentioned early in this chapter and showed in Figure 10-2. Later in this chapter we will see a feedback model for control of the body's stores of water, and Chapter 11 includes a feedback model for control of food.

A single "thermostat" seems inadequate, however, to account for all the facets of thermoregulation. For one thing, there appear to be different brain sites for behavioral and autonomic regulation of temperature, as we noted above. But even two thermoregulatory circuits are not sufficient, as Satinoff (1978) emphasizes. For example, Roberts and Mooney (1974) warmed small sites in the diencephalon and mesencephalon of rats and measured three responses in the repertoire of heat loss behaviors. As a rat is exposed to increasing heat, it first grooms, then it moves about actively, and finally it lies quietly in a sprawled-out position. Local heating of brain did not produce this sequence; instead each of these behaviors tended to be elicited by heating points in a different region. The sprawled extension posture was elicited by heating points in the preoptic area, whereas grooming was elicited only from points in the posterior hypothalamus and ventral medulla. Locomotion was elicited by heating points that ranged from the septal area through the midbrain to the medulla, and it could occur in combination with sprawling or with grooming. These data indicate multiple independent channels from thermal detectors to motor effectors. There seems, in addition, to be a hierarchy of thermoregulatory circuits, some located at the spinal level, some centered in the midbrain, and others at the diencephalic level. Transections of the nervous system or ablations reveal some capacity for regulation at each of these levels. But spinal or decerebrate animals die in the cold or heat because they do not respond until body temperature deviates by 2° or 3°C from normal values.

Satinoff (1978) interprets these findings in the following way: The thermal neutral zones are broader in lower regions of the nervous system (Figure 10-9). The thermoregulatory systems at the diencephalic level have the narrowest neutral zones, and they normally coordinate and adjust the activity of the other systems. This arrangement can give the impression of a single system, although in reality there are multiple interlinked systems.

While most investigators have conceived of a system with an established (although adjustable) set point, others have claimed that it is unnecessary to postulate a reference signal or set point (Bligh, 1979). These investigators suggest that the facts of temperature regulation can be accounted for in the following way: Stimulation of cold sensors activates heat production, and stimulation of warmth sensors activates heat loss. The apparent set point would then be the crossover point of the sensitivities of the two kinds of receptors (Figure 10-10). As body temperature deviated in either direction from this neutral point, heat production or heat loss would be elicited, thus tending to drive temperature back to the neutral point. In other words, the reciprocal antagonism of the two systems would accomplish homeostatic regulation of temperature. So that only one of the two processes would be active at a time, even though the distributions of sensitivities of the two kinds of receptors might overlap, there could be crossed inhibitory influences between the two pathways; only the more strongly excited of the two would then lead to its response. Figure 10-11 shows the basic layout of such a circuit.

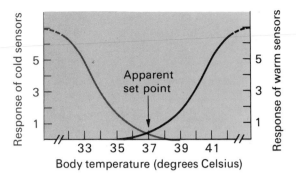

Figure 10-10 Apparent temperature set point at the crossover of response curves of cold sensors and warm sensors.

Could such a circuit without an explicit set point accommodate changes in the neutral or target temperature, such as those that occur with circadian rhythms, torpor, or hibernation? Such changes could be accomplished by modulating the activity of the receptor inputs of the two main circuits. Thermosensitive neurons in the mammalian hypothalamus are active over a range of temperatures, so there is scope for modulation. Although most of these neurons in a nonhibernator (guinea pig) became silent below 30°C, many in a hibernator (golden hamster) remained active to 15°C or below (Heller et al., 1978).

● **Temperature control during hibernation**   Ground squirrels in the Sierra of California hibernate for about eight months of the year. During much of this time they conserve energy by allowing their temperature to fall to within a few degrees of their surroundings; core temperature may fall to 10°C or less. The hibernating ground squirrel curls up into a fur-covered ball, and its respiration and heart rates fall far below the waking values. At intervals during the long period underground

Figure 10-11 A thermoregulatory system involving reciprocally antagonistic components. No set point or internal reference signal is required. (Adapted from Bligh, 1979)

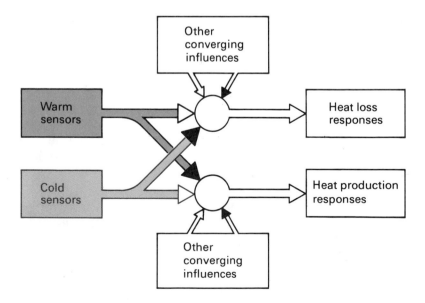

they wake up and warm up for a few hours, and then they hibernate again. Many species of small mammals show similar patterns.

The fall of body temperature as ground squirrels enter hibernation does not mean that they have abandoned endothermic regulation and returned to a more primitive ectothermic level. Unlike ectotherms, hibernators can rouse and return to a normal body temperature of 37° even when the surrounding temperature remains low. Recent laboratory studies have indicated that they lower their set point for temperature in a regular progressive manner. At any given hypothalamic temperature, if an implanted hypothalamic probe is cooled by only a few degrees, the squirrel responds by rewarming. Thus it appears that the animal's thermostat is turned down gradually as it enters into hibernation (Heller, Cranshaw, and Hammel, 1978). If the ambient temperature falls to dangerously low levels, the squirrel rouses; this "fail-safe" mechanism prevents it from freezing.

The alarm signal for rewarming and arousal is not located in the same place for all species. In the ground squirrel it is in the head; if the hypothalamus is slightly warmed while the rest of the body is chilled below the alarm level, the squirrel continues to hibernate. In contrast, the garden dormouse can be aroused by applying a cold stimulus to its feet. The dormouse hibernates on its back with its feet sticking up into the air, whereas the ground squirrel tucks its feet inside its ball-shaped hibernation posture.

It has been suggested that hibernation evolved as an adaptive extension of the decrease in temperature that occurs during the phase of sleep when EEG activity is slow (Heller, 1979). Electrophysiological studies have indicated similarities between hibernation and slow-wave sleep.

Learned temperature regulation

The Australian aborigines mentioned at the beginning of this chapter are able to withstand cold nights by exerting precise and localized vasomotor control over skin temperature. Unlike European or American subjects, they do not increase heat production during cold nights to compensate for loss. Rather they prevent loss by constricting their peripheral blood vessels, starting at temperatures higher than those at which Europeans first begin to show constriction. When the aborigines use fires, their vasomotor control shows precisely localized responses. The arterioles on the side of the body toward the fire are dilated, allowing heat to radiate in, while the arterioles on the other side are closed to prevent loss of heat (Hicks, 1964). This control is exerted through neural regulation of the constriction of blood vessels. A familiar and visible example of this control is seen when a person blushes. Since the nervous system regulates temperatues, people can learn to gain some control over it, as we will see next.

● **Learned control of skin temperature**   Probably all of us are capable of exerting precise localized control over peripheral circulation and skin temperature with suitable training. This notion has been studied not only out of curiosity but also to aid people who suffer from conditions such as Raynaud's disease and migraine headaches. In Raynaud's disease the blood supply to the fingers may shut off upon exposure to the cold and sometimes in response to emotional states. Raynaud's disease can make it hard for a person to work in the cold and may subject its sufferers to frostbite.

Biofeedback training is effective in conferring self-regulation of skin temperature (Taub, 1977; Taub and School, 1978). Here are the basic procedures: The subject is seated comfortably in a dimly illuminated room with temperature-sensing devices attached to various points on one hand. The mean hand temperature is shown to the subject in terms of the intensity of a white feedback light. After a period of stabilization the subject is instructed either to increase hand temperature (and the brightness of the light) or to decrease it. Subjects are told, "You will be able to change hand temperature without moving. In fact, it has been found that tensing the muscles interferes with this. Simply stay relaxed and think of your hand as being warmer [cooler]." Subjects are usually trained for a few successive days.

While many experimenters and laboratories have reported success with biofeedback training for temperature control, some have not, and the size of the effects varies considerably. Taub and School (1978) have reported experimental evidence that the "person factor" is extremely important in thermal biofeedback training—that is, the quality of interaction between the experimenter (or therapist) and the subject (or patient). With one group the experimenter maintained an impersonal attitude, using last names, discouraging extraneous conversation, and avoiding eye contact. With another group the same experimenter adopted a friendly attitude, using first names, making frequent eye contact, and encouraging development of a friendly relationship. Both groups showed significant learning, but at the end of the ten-day training period the impersonally treated group showed a mean effect of only 0.7°C, whereas the group treated in a friendly manner achieved a mean change of 2.3°. This striking difference was the largest effect found for any of the numerous variables tested in these experiments. The investigators conclude: "It is almost impossible to overemphasize the importance of the experimenter-attitude variable for the success of thermal biofeedback training. It seems highly probable that the person factor is equally critical for the success of other types of biofeedback training" (p. 617). It is not yet known how the "person factor" translates into physiological mechanisms. Perhaps it involves no more than setting a level of muscular tension that favors learning.

Patients with Raynaud's disease were found to be as capable as normal subjects of learning to control skin temperature. Several studies have indicated that such training helps these patients to deal with cold and other stresses and to avoid disabling vasoconstriction. Positive results have also been reported for control of migraine headaches by biofeedback training of vascular responses. This subject appears to be a promising one for further research and application.

● **Learned control of core temperature**   Central or core temperature can also be affected by training. This has been studied in experiments in which animals are conditioned to the administration of morphine, which induces a rise in body temperature (hyperthermia). If the drug is given in conjunction with specific stimuli, those stimuli alone eventually elicit the rise in body temperature. Thus if a rat is injected with morphine once a day for several days in a particular experimental room, then just placing the animal in that room will elicit the rise in temperature. But the situation is more complex. The animal responds to the morphine-induced hyperthermia by mobilizing heat-dissipating responses and reducing its temperature. Therefore if a rat is given an injection of morphine at the same time every day for several days and then the drug is withheld, a hypothermic response will occur at about the time that the morphine had been given.

Understandably, reports have been somewhat varied and even contradictory, since both hyperthermia and hypothermia were being conditioned. In experimental conditions to test different hypotheses it has recently been found that hyperthermia and hypothermia become associated with different kinds of stimuli. Hyperthermia becomes associated with environmental stimuli such as visual or auditory stimuli, but it does not become conditioned to the time of day at which the drug is administered. In contrast, hypothermia becomes conditioned to temporal cues but not to environmental cues (Eikelboom and Stewart, 1981). Thus both increases and decreases of body temperature can be learned, depending on the circumstances.

Development of temperature regulation

The young of many species cannot regulate their temperatures well and must be protected by their parents. Most birds must keep their eggs warm. For this purpose the parents of many species develop a specially vascularized area of skin (the brood patch), which transfers heat efficiently to the eggs. Rat pups, which are born without hair, cannot maintain body temperature if they are exposed individually to cold. The rat mother keeps her pups protected in a warm nest, and this response of the mother is related to her own thermoregulation (see Box 10-1). By the time their eyes open and they begin to stray from the nest at about 13 days of age, rat pups have developed physiological thermoregulatory reflexes and have grown a coat of fur. Other rodents, such as guinea pigs, are born in a more mature state. They show endothermic regulation from the start and do not need maternal protection.

Even though young rat pups are not capable of endothermic regulation, they do show ectothermic regulation, which evolved earlier. They accomplish ectothermic regulation by huddling together and varying their positions in the huddle in accordance with changes in temperature (Figure 10-12). Rectal temperatures and oxygen

Figure 10-12 Rat-pups regulate their temperature by huddling together. The arrows show direction of movement within the huddle. [Reprinted from J. Alberts, *Journal of Comparative and Physiological Psychology,* vol. 92 (1978): 241, Figure 6. Copyright 1978 by the American Psychological Association. Reprinted by permission of the publisher and the author.]

BOX 10-1   The Warmth of Maternal Care

The rat mother's nesting with her young is determined largely by her own thermoregulation. That is, the mother receives thermal stimulation from the young, and this stimulation is a major determinant of how long she stays in contact with the young on successive visits to the nest (Leon, Croskerry, and Smith, 1978). The nursing mother has a somewhat elevated body temperature caused by increased levels of prolactin and ACTH. When she returns to the nest, contact with the pups helps to dissipate heat until they become warmed and no longer remove heat from the mother; at this point she leaves the nest. As the pups become larger and produce more heat, the mother progressively shortens her stays in the nest.

The role of maternal temperature in duration of mother-pup contact was tested in experiments in which the temperature of the mother was raised artificially (Woodside, Pelchat, and Leon, 1980). Different sites of warming were used—subcutaneous, body core, or brain. For the first two sites a fine coil of wire was inserted in a surgical operation; the wire was used to raise temperature by about 10° C over the existing level. Such heating reduced mean nest stays to about half the normal duration. In tests of effects of heating the brain, warming electrodes were implanted surgically into the medial preoptic area in some rats and into the caudate-putamen in others. On trials in which heating was used, it began 15 min after a mother had started contact with her litter. On trials where no brain stimulation was delivered, contact lasted about 70 min. When the preoptic area was heated, the mother left the nest in about 3 min, that is, about 50 min earlier than she would have done without the brain stimulation. When the caudate-putamen was heated, the mother terminated contact about 25 min later; this slow response presumably occurred because the spread of heat from the caudate eventually warmed thermosensitive neurons elsewhere in the brain. So the contact in the nest that helps to keep the young rat pups warm is actually regulated, not in terms of the temperature of the pups but in terms of that of the mother.

consumption were measured in pups of different ages placed in a cool chamber (23°–24°C), either singly or in a group of four. In the 5-day-old rats, the temperature of the isolated pups fell below 30° in less than an hour, whereas those in the group maintained their temperatures above 30° for four hours (Alberts, 1978). Huddling also significantly reduced oxygen consumption. The form of the huddle changes according to ambient temperatures; it is loose in warm temperatures but tightly cohesive in the cold. The pups frequently change positions in the clump, sometimes being inside and at other times at the periphery. In effect, they share the costs and benefits of this group activity. Thus early in the rat's development its thermoregulation depends on social interaction, whereas later in its development the rat becomes capable of individual endothermic regulation.

Evolution of temperature regulation

Endotherms pay substantial costs for maintaining a high body temperature and keeping it within narrow limits. Much food must be obtained and metabolized; elaborate regulatory systems are required; and departures of body temperature of a few degrees in either direction impair functioning. What benefits may have led to the evolution of such a complicated and costly system in comparison with that of the ectotherms who get along with somewhat lower mean body temperatures and who have a greater tolerance for changes in temperature?

Increasing the capacity to sustain a high level of muscular activity over prolonged periods may have been the principal gain in the evolution of endothermy (Bennett and Ruben, 1979). Table 10-1 showed that a person's metabolic rate (or heat production) can rise almost tenfold between resting and very strenuous exercise. A five- to tenfold increase above the resting level is the greatest that vertebrates can achieve, whether they are ectotherms or endotherms. It would probably be advantageous to have a higher differential between rest and maximal activity, but apparently about 1:10 is the best that vertebrate metabolic processes can handle. So to be able to engage in a high level of activity for a sustained period of time, an organism must maintain a relatively high basal level of metabolism.

Ectotherms are capable of bursts of high activity for a few minutes; in this case a major contribution is made by anaerobic metabolism. But a high level of anaerobic metabolism can be maintained for only a few minutes, and then the animal must rest and repay the oxygen debt. So reptiles and amphibians can perform as well as mammals and birds for short periods but not for long ones. Ectotherms can escape from and sometimes even pursue endotherms over short distances, but in a long-distance race the endotherm will win. It is likely that the capacity for internal thermoregulation evolved along with increasing capacity to sustain a high level of muscular activity through aerobic metabolism.

The thermoregulatory system, with its several mechanisms and different loci and levels of representation in the nervous system, has been cited by Satinoff (1978) as an illustration of the principle of evolutionary coadaptation. That is, a mechanism that evolved to serve one function turns out to have an adaptive value for a different system and evolves further to improve its value for the second system. The ectotherms already had a basic thermoregulatory system since they sensed internal and external temperatures and used this sensory ability to regulate locomotor behavior, moving into and out of different temperature zones in their environments. Then control of muscular activity, including shivering, was brought into the thermoregulatory system for internal heat production. A higher rate of heat production then made it advantageous to be able to dissipate heat quickly. Since animals at this stage already breathed and for that purpose had a good control of the vascular system, it was possible for thermal monitors to influence the rates of respiration and of peripheral blood flow. Thus different systems that already existed at the spinal and midbrain levels could be adapted to new requirements. There was no need to transfer these circuits to the forebrain. But to the extent that these functions were not handled perfectly well at the lower levels of the nervous system—if, for example, the narrower set zone of the hypothalamus conferred an advantage in natural selection—then an impetus toward a hierarchical organization evolved, with the higher centers tending to control the lower ones in thermoregulation.

Human evolution shows particular adaptations for thermoregulation. There has been much speculation on why human beings have hair on only part of the body surface, whereas other primates have full coats of hair. Perhaps humans evolved into "naked apes" to facilitate rapid dissipation of heat produced during prolonged pursuit of prey in their original tropical homelands. We may never be sure of the answer, but many studies have investigated differences among human groups that appear to be related to thermoregulation. Here are a few examples from a recent review (So, 1980): Human body forms tend to be more linear in the tropics and more compact in arctic regions; these forms favor heat dissipation in the tropics and heat conservation in the arctic. Nostrils tend to be narrower in arctic regions, which aids conservation of heat. One worldwide survey of populations shows a correlation of 0.72 between breadth of the nose and an index that combines temperature and relative humidity (Roberts, 1973). The characteristic eyelid of Chinese people is believed to have evolved in the north to protect against loss of heat by evaporation from the eyes. Eskimos have fewer sweat glands on the limbs and trunk than do Europeans, but they have more sweat glands on the face. This distribution in the Eskimos is adaptive for the following reasons: Eskimos insulate the body from the cold by well-designed clothing, so sweat on the limbs or trunk would be uncomfortable and would defeat the insulation. When Eskimos are active, they need to dissipate heat, and the face is the only uncovered surface, so the face has to be richly supplied with sweat glands. Thus many differences in appearance among human groups appear to reflect adaptations to the thermal characteristics of the climatic zones in which they live.

Thirst

Human beings are watery creatures. Water makes up more than half the weight of most adults. It is the main constituent of most of our tissues; blood, which carries nutrients and oxygen to the tissues, is mainly water; and many ions are bound to molecules of water as they pass through cell membranes. Water is also used to eliminate wastes from the body. Under average conditions in a mild climate, an adult human being turns over about 2500 milliliters (mL) of water per day, as shown in Table 10-3. We do not notice the evaporation of water from the lungs or from the surface of the skin when there is no visible sweating, so this process is called "insensible water loss." Under very high heat, sweating may equal the other types of output, thus doubling the daily loss of water. Unless the output is balanced by input, a person's life is soon menaced. Figure 10-13 illustrates the many parts of the body involved in keeping a water balance.

Problems of regulating the intake and excretion of fluids have grown more complicated during the course of evolution. The first primitive organisms evolved in the ocean, and the composition of their internal fluids was very similar to the composition of the ocean in terms of ion content. But even these primitive organisms had to take in food and eliminate wastes and thus regulate exchanges with the environment. When marine animals invaded fresh water, with its lower osmotic pressure, the problems of fluid balance became more difficult. More elaborate systems of intake and excretion were required, and levels of various ions in the body fluids gradually changed. Then when animals left the water and emerged onto dry land, even more difficult problems had to be faced. The liquid internal environment of the cells had to be maintained in a non-liquid external environment. Internal regulation of

TABLE 10-3   Average Daily Water Balance of an Adult Person (mL)

APPROXIMATE WATER INTAKE		APPROXIMATE WATER OUTPUT	
Fluid water, including beverages	1200	Urine	1400
Water content of food	1000	Insensible water loss	900
Water from oxidation of food	300	Feces	200
	2500		2500

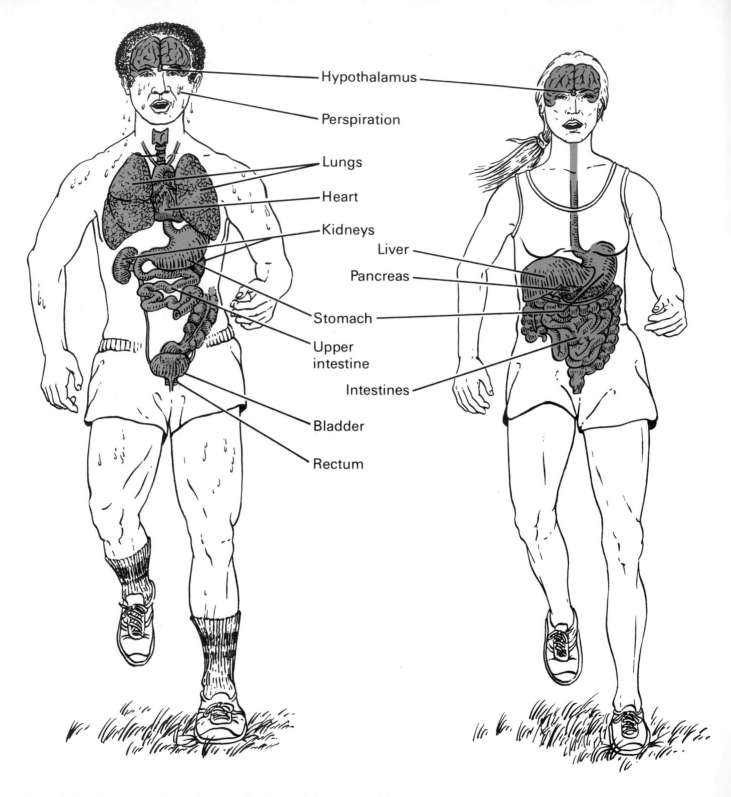

Figure 10-13 Many parts of the body are involved in regulation of the body's water balance (left) and food supplies (right).

different fluid compartments became more elaborate, and behavioral regulation was required to secure adequate amounts of fluid.

Different kinds of animals show very different patterns of fluid regulation, depending on their evolutionary histories and their ecological niches. Even among the mammals there are major differences. Some small desert mammals, such as the kangaroo rat, have no access to water and never drink. They live on seeds and other vegetation and obtain their water from food. On the other side of their fluid balance, they urinate very little and their urine is highly concentrated. Elephant seals get by without taking in fluids or food during the four or five months of each year when they are ashore during the mating season. They derive all the fluid they need by metabolizing stored food, and they excrete very little during this period. Elephant seals do not drink during the rest of the year, either. As mammals that have returned to the ocean, seals are no more able to live on salt water than are human beings, so they must obtain their water from the fish they eat.

Since the need for water is so vital, it is not surprising that animals have evolved effective mechanisms to regulate both the intake and the excretion of fluids. These mechanisms involve both internal physiological processes and behavior with regard to the environment. We will focus on the controls over the behavioral responses, but it is important to keep in mind that this is only one aspect of the regulation of the fluid balance of the body. A simplified version of the basic systems that regulate drinking is shown in Figure 10-14. (A more complete diagram will be shown later in Figure 10-18.)

Among the basic questions that investigators are studying are these: How are fluid supplies in the body monitored? What factors cause a person or animal to start drinking? What factors cause drinking to stop? (In Chapter 11 we will take up similar questions about food supplies and eating, and we will see that eating and drinking are interdependent.) In the following sections we will consider each of these questions in detail.

Figure 10-14 A simplified version of the basic systems that regulate fluid intake.

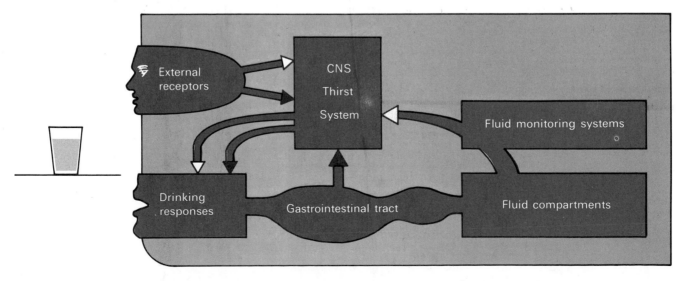

Monitoring the body's
supplies of water

About four-tenths of our body weight consists of water located inside the billions of cells of the body; another two-tenths is located outside the cells, either in the blood plasma or in the spaces between cells. It is usual to state that the water is divided between two compartments: **intracellular fluid** (or, simply, **cellular fluid**) and **extracellular fluid.** Extracellular fluid includes both fluid in the spaces between cells (interstitial fluid) and fluid in the vascular system. The body monitors the intracellular and extracellular compartments separately, as we will see. Usually the supplies of water in the two compartments vary in parallel, and water can move from one compartment to another. However, some disease conditions affect the two compartments separately, and investigators have found out how to manipulate and assess the two compartments separately. Depletion of intracellular fluid is normally more important in causing drinking than is depletion of extracellular fluid. Different mechanisms monitor intracellular and extracellular fluid, and we will consider them in succession.

● Monitoring intracellular fluid   To see how intracellular fluid is monitored, we must first consider how water moves into and out of cells. Cell membranes are permeable to some substances and not to others. For instance, the membranes permit ions of potassium (K^+) to pass easily, as we saw for neurons in Chapter 4, but they are less permeable to sodium ions (Na^+); proteins are retained within cells and do not pass out through their membranes; molecules of water pass readily in and out through the membranes. The interstitial fluid and blood plasma contain about 0.9% salt (NaCl). A solution with a larger concentration of salt than 0.9% is called **hypertonic;** a solution with a lower concentration is **hypotonic.** If a person drinks a hypertonic solution or if salt is placed in a body cavity, the concentration of sodium ions in the blood and interstitial fluid soon increases. Sodium ions do not enter the cells, so there is a greater concentration of particles in the extracellular fluid than in the intracellular fluid. Whenever there is an unequal concentration of particles in the fluids on the two sides of a semipermeable membrane, fluid moves to the side with the greater concentration. This process is called **osmosis,** and the force involved is called **osmotic pressure.** Since the Na^+ ions cannot enter the cells, water leaves the cells in order to equalize the concentrations. As the volume of intracellular fluid decreases, the cells become smaller. If glucose is ingested or placed into the bloodstream, it enters cells easily and therefore does not cause a shift in water, but it does increase the **osmolality** (the number of particles per unit volume of solute) in both compartments.

Exactly what change in body fluids initiates drinking? Three competing hypotheses have been suggested. All are consistent with the observation that administering a hypertonic NaCl solution causes drinking. One hypothesis is that the concentration of sodium ions in the interstitial fluid is the effective stimulus (Andersson, 1978). A second hypothesis is that the concentration of particles of all sorts in the interstitial fluid (that is, the osmolality) is the effective stimulus. The third, and most generally accepted, hypothesis is that cellular dehydration is the effective stimulus (Gilman, 1937), and this hypothesis has been supported by recent experiments.

It had been shown in the 1950s that injecting small amounts of hypertonic NaCl solution into regions of the hypothalamus of experimental animals caused the animals to start drinking. This observation led to the suggestion that some of the cells in the hypothalamus are **osmoreceptors**—that is, they respond to changes in osmotic pressure. More recent experiments have applied other substances to these cells to characterize them better. Investigators tested responses to substances such as glucose (which readily crosses the cell membrane) and sucrose (which does not cross the membrane). Sucrose was found to stimulate the hypothalamic cells that responded to NaCl, but glucose did not. Thus these cells were not responding just to NaCl or to any increase in osmolality; rather they responded to a change in osmotic pressure that caused an outflow of intracellular water. That is, the cells reported their own dehydration and decrease in volume. It might be appropriate to call these cells dehydration receptors, but it has become conventional to refer to them as osmoreceptors. Similarly, the response to a decrease of cellular fluid is often called **osmotic thirst.**

Electrical recording from single cells has shown that osmoreceptors are widely scattered throughout the preoptic area, the anterior hypothalamus, and the supraoptic nucleus. Research is still needed to define the connections of these cells to others and to trace the neural circuits by which drinking is initiated. We will see shortly that electrical stimulation of the preoptic area (POA) can lead to impressive increases in water intake.

● **Monitoring extracellular fluid**   The response to a reduced volume of extracellular fluid is often called **hypovolemic thirst** (from the Greek root "hypo," meaning "low," and the root "volemic," which pertains to volume). The heart cannot function properly unless the amount of fluid in the vascular system is kept within fairly close limits. Loss of blood, as in hemorrhaging, reduces the fluids of the heart; reduced output of the heart lowers blood pressure, further reducing the supply to the heart. To prevent such an impairment of the circulatory system, a fall in blood volume must be reported and counteracted promptly. Neural reflexes accomplish this, and a chemical system may also be involved. Pressure receptors in the heart and in some arteries initiate neural signals in response to the fall of blood pressure; these signals help to elicit compensatory responses. One kind of response is to increase the muscular tension in the walls of the blood vessels. Another response is to release antidiuretic hormone (or vasopressin) from the posterior pituitary gland. This hormone acts to inhibit the removal of water by the kidneys and thus to hold water in the body.

Many investigators are convinced that yet another response to hypovolemia involves the kidneys and special chemicals in the blood. Other investigators are skeptical. Let us examine the hypothesis first and then come to the questions.

Diminished blood flow through the kidneys causes release of a substance called renin from the walls of the arterioles in the kidneys. Renin reacts with a substance in the blood to form angiotensin, which is then converted into **angiotensin II.** (The first demonstrated effect of angiotensin was to increase blood pressure, which is how it got its name: The Greek root "angeio," means "blood vessel" and "tensio" pertains to tension or pressure.) Very low doses of angiotensin II injected into the POA were found to be extremely effective in eliciting drinking, even in animals that were not deprived of water (Epstein et al., 1970). When administered to rats that had been

Figure 10-15 Mid-sagittal section of rat brain showing the circumventricular organs, which mediate between the brain and the cerebrospinal fluid. The circumventricular organs are shown in blue, and the ventricles and channels for cerebrospinal fluid are shown in gray. (OVLT, organum vasculosum of the lamina terminalis)

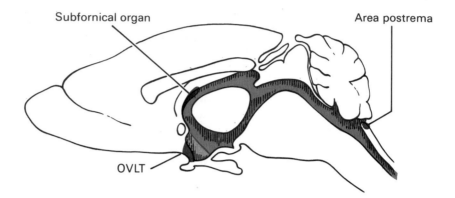

deprived of food but not water, angiotensin II caused them to stop eating and start drinking; thus its effect is highly specific.

Exactly where in the brain angiotensin II has its effect is the subject of much current research. Although the original work on this question found the POA to be the most sensitive site, it was difficult to see how angiotensin II could reach receptors in this region since it does not penetrate the blood-brain barrier. Attention then focused on the **circumventricular organs.** As their name suggests, these organs lie in the walls of the cerebral ventricles (see Figure 10-15). They contain receptor sites that can be affected by substances in the cerebrospinal fluid, and information about stimulation of these sites is carried by axons of the circumventricular cells into other parts of the nervous system.

Some researchers continue to maintain that cells in the POA respond to angiotensin II in experiments where leakage of the injected material into the ventricles could not have occurred. They suggest that angiotensin II may be generated in the brain as well as in the bloodstream. Determination of whether or not there are receptors for angiotensin II in the POA as well as in circumventricular organs and determination of the brain circuits that control the drinking responses stimulated by these receptors are topics of ongoing research.

A further problem related to the angiotensin story is whether the amount formed in the blood by reductions in blood volume is enough to stimulate thirst. Careful recent measurements indicate that not enough angiotensin is normally produced to evoke thirst (Abraham et al., 1975; Stricker, 1977). Therefore some investigators argue that many previous experiments involved responses to angiotensin II administered as a drug—pharmacological effects rather than normal physiological effects. Further research is needed to resolve this issue. Meanwhile there is no doubt that responses of pressure receptors in the heart and arteries cause neural signals of hypovolemia.

Initiation of drinking   Stimulating the preoptic area through implanted electrodes in unanesthetized, freely moving rats causes them to go promptly to a water spout and start to drink. As the POA stimulation continues, some animals may drink as much in 1 hour (h) as they normally drink in 24 h. During a 10-h period of stimulation of the POA in a group of rats, the rats ingested almost their entire body weight in water. (Urination kept pace with intake, so the animals did not become waterlogged.) If instead of stimulating the POA, investigators destroy it, the animals totally refuse to drink, a condition called **adipsia** (from the Greek roots "a," meaning "without," and "dipas," meaning "thirst").

Normally a deprived individual lacks water to about the same degree in both the cellular and extracellular compartments. How can we find the relative importance of osmotic and hypovolemic deficits in initiating drinking? A telling method has been to vary salt concentration separately in either the cerebral circulation or the peripheral circulation of water-deprived dogs. Surgery was performed to bring a loop of the carotid artery to the surface of the skin on each side of the neck, and these loops were used for injections (Figure 10-16). Since the carotid arteries provide the main blood supply to the brain, injections into the loops can alter the concentration of the blood reaching the brain without significantly changing the blood in the rest of the body. The concentrations in the cerebral circulation were measured by withdrawing blood as it left the brain through the jugular vein; the concentrations in the peripheral circulation were measured in samples taken from a leg vein. Bilateral infusion of water into the carotid arteries at a rate that brought the tonicity of cerebral plasma down to the predeprivation level reduced water intake by three-quarters; infusion of isotonic saline had no effect on drinking. These results furnish further support for the conclusion that the body monitors cellular hydration in the brain and not in the rest of the body, since reducing saline in the brain but leaving it high in the body caused a marked reduction of drinking. The dogs drank only a small amount in a few minutes and then stopped, although the cells in the body were still dehydrated and the volume of extracellular fluid was still below normal (Ramsay, Rolls, and Wood, 1977).

The role of extracellular dehydration was tested in the dogs by infusing isotonic saline solution into the jugular vein. Restoring the plasma volume to predeprivation levels reduced drinking of water-deprived dogs by only one-quarter. Thus extracellular depletion is less important than is cellular depletion in controlling drinking. Tests with a small number of monkeys indicate that the same conclusion is true for them (Rolls, Wood, and Rolls, 1980).

Destruction of the lateral hypothalamus in rats causes them to refuse to drink or eat. This lateral hypothalamic syndrome has been investigated chiefly with regard to feeding behavior, so we will discuss it in detail in Chapter 11. Here we note, however, that even if the lesioned animals recover their ability to eat and to regulate their food consumption, they show a peculiar reluctance to initiate drinking. They confine their drinking to mealtimes, especially when dry food is being eaten. It seem as if water is used by these rats to lubricate the passage of food rather than being ingested for its own sake. It is not yet clear how the lateral hypothalamus enters into the system that controls consumption of water. It is probably not primarily concerned with monitoring water supplies. Perhaps it is important in facilitating the motor circuits that accomplish drinking.

Water-deprived animals or animals whose POA is stimulated will drink readily, but only if an appropriate liquid is available. This result shows that sensory input must combine with diencephalic activity in order to initiate drinking. How and

Figure 10-16 Method used to vary salt concentration separately in the cerebral circulation and the peripheral circulation.

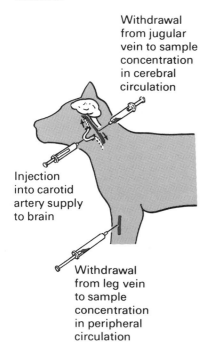

Withdrawal from jugular vein to sample concentration in cerebral circulation

Injection into carotid artery supply to brain

Withdrawal from leg vein to sample concentration in peripheral circulation

where these two kinds of information are combined has apparently not been investigated, but there has been productive research into the comparable question of initiation of feeding, as we will see in Chapter 11.

Termination of drinking

A dog deprived of water for 24 h will drink avidly, consuming almost all it needs in only 2 to 3 min. A rat makes up its deficit more slowly, making up about half the deficit in 5 min and continuing to drink intermittently for about an hour. People fall in between these extremes, making up about two-thirds of their deficit in the first 2.5 min.

What mechanism operates to terminate drinking? One possibility is that the person or animal monitors the amount being ingested and that intake continues until an amount known to be equal to the deficit is reached. Another possibility is that the drinker continues until the deficits that initiated the behavior are completely overcome. But actually an animal's deficit is not in the stomach but in the tissues, and it takes some time for fluid to get from the stomach to the upper intestine and then into the cells. This time delay between drinking and rehydration of tissues makes even more striking the rapid termination of drinking in species like the dog. Clearly there are two phases in the controls for termination: First, there are signals that a sufficient amount of fluids has been ingested. Second, the fluid reaches the bodily compartments and thus eliminates the signals of deficit that helped to initiate drinking.

The factors that affect termination have been investigated by measuring the rate of change in bodily deficits after drinking and by stimulating one or another stage of the processes of ingestion and rehydration. Also, human subjects have made various ratings of their sensation of thirst and other feelings during rehydration. In the dog it is clear that drinking stops while the water is still in the gut and long before rehydration of either compartment has occurred. Although drinking stops in 2 to 3 min, it takes about 10 min before cellular or extracellular dehydration begins to fall. Thereafter they return to predeprivation levels in a period of 40 to 60 min (Rolls, Wood, and Rolls, 1980). Although people make up two-thirds of their deficit in the first 2.5 min, the beginning of dilution of plasma concentrations is first apparent only about 5 min later, and by another 10 to 15 min the changes in the cellular and extracellular compartments may become important in limiting further drinking.

How dogs can make up their water deficits so accurately and rapidly remains a mystery, in spite of much research. For instance, some investigators thought that monitoring intake through the mouth and throat was a possibility. This idea was investigated by attaching a tube surgically to the esophagus so that the water swallowed passed out through the tube and did not reach the stomach. In this case dogs drank far more water than their deficit, so monitoring oral intake by itself does not terminate drinking. The next factor studied was loading the stomach. But placing a balloon in the stomach and inflating it to distend the stomach had little effect on checking drinking. Water ingested reaches the small intestine of the dog in 2 to 3 min, and receptors there may play a role in terminating drinking. This theory has not been studied directly in the dog, but it has in the monkey, as we will see next.

In the monkey, as in the dog and the rat, stimulation of the mouth and throat is not sufficient to terminate drinking. But monitoring by the stomach seems to be more important in the monkey than in the dog, as shown by the following experiment: Monkeys were equipped with a tube to the stomach. They were allowed to drink until they stopped, and then the tube was used to drain the stomach; the monkeys resumed drinking almost immediately. In other monkeys surgically implanted tubes were used to place water directly in the small intestine (duodenum). Infusion of even a small amount of water into the small intestine would stop drinking, at least for a short period. Perhaps placing water directly into the intestine made the monkey uncomfortable, and it refused to drink not because its thirst was slaked but because it was under stress. The experimenters therefore performed two other tests. One was to see whether infusing water into the duodenum stopped eating as well as drinking. But the monkeys continued to eat, indicating both that the treatment did not make the animals uncomfortable and that it was specific to thirst. An even more telling test placed isotonic saline solution rather than plain water in the intestine. The saline did not stop drinking as the water did. This comparison showed that the monkeys responded to the tonicity of the water rather than simply to its bulk (Rolls, Wood, and Rolls, 1980). Thus the duodenum seems to contain osmoreceptors that monitor whether water has been ingested.

Taste and drinking

How pleasant a liquid tastes helps to determine how much is consumed, and the state of hydration or dehydration helps to determine how good a fluid tastes. The influence of taste can easily be measured by seeing how much a person or animal drinks when offered a choice of fluids. When a fluid tastes sweet because sugar or saccharine has been added, people or rats or monkeys increase their intake significantly, but no such effect is seen in cats. Rats also prefer slightly salty water (0.7%) to plain water and will drink much more of the salt solution. Variety of flavors also increases consumption; both humans and rats drink significantly more when offered several palatable flavors in succession rather than having the same flavor repeatedly.

Perhaps less expected is the finding that people change their ratings of the palatability of water depending on their degree of deprivation or satiety (Cabanac, 1971). Subjects tasted a small amount of water and rated its pleasantness on a numerical scale. After being deprived of water overnight, subjects rated the taste of a sample as highly pleasant. Ratings of subsequent small samples taken at 5-min intervals diminished slightly in pleasantness. But if subjects were allowed to drink to satiety, then the ratings of the next sample showed a large drop, to about 0.8 of the initial rating, and over the next few samples the palatability dropped to about 0.6 of the initial value. Some neurons in the hypothalamus of the monkey show similar changes in their firing rates. These neurons respond when the monkey drinks water. The rate of response goes up with deprivation or with intracarotid infusion of hypertonic saline solution but goes down as the monkey continues to drink water (Arnauld et al., 1975). Thus taste can contribute to drinking, and decrease of taste stimulation may play a role in termination of drinking.

The basic systems that regulate drinking are summarized in Figure 10-17. This diagram can help you to review the material on thirst and regulation of body fluids.

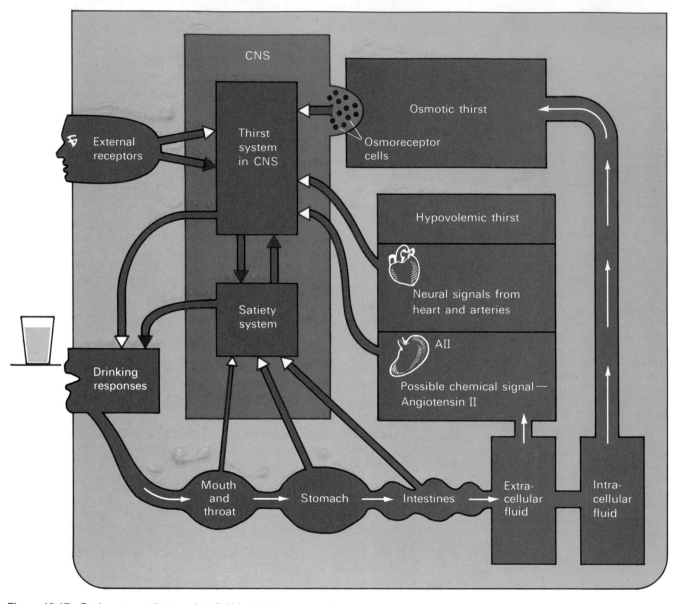

Figure 10-17 Basic systems that regulate fluid intake in a mammal.

SUMMARY / MAIN POINTS

1. Homeostatic mechanisms maintain relative constancy of internal bodily conditions such as temperature, water content, and food supplies. These mechanisms include both behavioral adjustments and internal physiological processes.

2. Ectotherms (such as amphibia and reptiles) regulate their body temperature chiefly by moving to favorable sites or by changing their exposure to external sources of heat. Endotherms (mainly mammals and birds) also use these behavioral methods and in addition make a variety of internal adjustments.

3. The lateral hypothalamus is involved in behavioral regulation of temperature; the preoptic area is involved in physiological regulation.

4. Temperature is monitored not only by regions in the basal forebrain but also by the spinal cord and receptors at the body surface. The higher levels of thermal regulation in the nervous system have narrow set zones and the lower levels have wider ones.

5. Temperature regulation is usually thought to be accomplished by a negative-feedback system with a fixed set point (or set zone), but the data could also be explained by opposed heat gain and heat loss systems, perhaps with reciprocal inhibitory influences.

6. It is possible through training to gain some control over both skin temperature and core temperature.

7. Ectothermy evolved before endothermy, and some species (such as the rat) develop behavioral thermoregulation before they develop physiological thermoregulation. Endothermy may have evolved in order to increase the capacity for aerobic metabolism to sustain a high level of muscular activity over a prolonged period.

8. Water in our bodies is needed for blood circulation, temperature regulation, digestion, and elimination. About two-thirds of the human body is water, most of it within cells.

9. Intracellular fluid is monitored primarily by osmoreceptor neurons in the preoptic area. Extracellular fluid is monitored by pressure receptors in the heart and in certain arteries and possibly by angiotensin II, which may act on receptors in the circumventricular organs and on neurons in the preoptic area.

10. Depletion of intracellular fluid (called osmotic thirst) is a more potent stimulus to drinking than is depletion of extracellular fluid (hypovolemic thirst), but usually both effects work in parallel.

11. Stimulation of receptors in the mouth and throat does not terminate drinking. Rather, monitoring by the stomach and duodenum seems to provide the main signals that water has been ingested. As water moves into the fluid compartments, it eliminates the signals of deficit that initiated drinking.

12. Taste contributes to drinking, and water depletion causes fluids to be more palatable.

RECOMMENDED READING

Bligh, J. The central neurology of mammalian thermoregulation. *Neuroscience,* 1979, *4,* 1213–1236.

Heller, H. C., Cranshaw, L. I., and Hammel, H. T. The thermostat of vertebrate animals. *Scientific American,* 1978, *239* (2), 102–113.

Rolls, B. J., Wood, R. J., and Rolls, E. T. Thirst: The initiation, maintenance, and termination of drinking. In J. M. Sprague and A. N. Epstein (Eds.), *Progress in psychobiology and physiological psychology* (Vol. 9). New York: Academic Press, 1980.

11

Homeostatic Mechanisms II: Eating

Orientation

Control of eating and of the body's food stores is intimately related to control of temperature and water, but it is considerably more complicated. One reason for the complexity is that there are many different kinds of foods and a large number of nutritional requirements. Even for our own species not all nutritional requirements have yet been determined. We do know that to be healthy, human beings must regularly ingest 22 different amino acids, at least a dozen vitamins, and several trace elements. We also need to consume enough calories to supply our current needs for energy. Other mammals have similarly elaborate dietary requirements.

How do we and other animals manage to fulfill all these specific requirements for food intake? Part of the answer is that the plant and animal foods we consume are themselves complex, and many of them can furnish several of our dietary requirements. In addition, each species has evolved in such a way as to be able to obtain, consume, digest, and metabolize adequate foods in its ecological niche, or it would not have survived.

Most individuals can monitor internal food supplies so as to take in enough for current requirements. For some individuals the monitoring systems maintain their present size; for others it allows them to grow along a genetically determined curve. These monitoring systems do not always work perfectly, as shown by cases of obesity or anorexia (lack of appetite), and we will consider these problems in this chapter. Also, special nutritional needs arise in certain conditions such as pregnancy or dietary deficiencies; these needs may be made up by specific hungers or by the ability to learn which foods supply the needed nutriment(s).

In this chapter we will emphasize comparative and neurophysiological approaches to control of eating. We will consider the internal and external signals that regulate the initiation and termination of eating, and how this information is represented in terms of neural and hormonal messages. Finally we will see how some of the research and concepts in this field are being applied to the problem of obesity.

Basic feeding systems

The essentials of feeding systems are illustrated in relatively simple invertebrates such as the fly (Dethier, 1976) or the sea snail *Aplysia* (Kandel, 1976). When such animals are deprived of food, they become more active and start moving, more or less at random, until they encounter a smell or taste that signals food. Recognition of these stimuli is built into the animal's nervous system. The strength of the eating response varies, however, with sensory adaptation and with internal signals of fullness of the digestive tract. The tendency of a fly to consume a sugar solution increases with the strength of the solution up to a certain level, but as the solution becomes even more concentrated, it repels the fly. As the fly continues to taste the solution, its receptors adapt to the stimulus; this adaptation may proceed to the point at which the receptors stop firing, whereupon the fly ceases to consume that food. It will, however, be ready to ingest a food with a different flavor, a feature that promotes consumption of a variety of foods. When the digestive tract becomes full, mechanoreceptors in the gut send signals to the central nervous system and the feeding reflexes are turned off. Feeding stops even if the sensory receptors are still signaling that tasty food is available. If the nerve from the gut to the neural centers is cut, the fly may continue to eat until it literally bursts.

Note that the basic tendency of the fly is to eat; feeding occurs whenever food is available unless the taste receptors are adapted or unless the gut receptors signal fullness. The basic components of the fly's feeding system are diagramed in Figure 11-1. Although the fly has a simple feeding system, it nevertheless competes rather successfully with us for food. Later, in Figure 11-11, we will see a diagram of the more complex feeding system of a mammal.

Figure 11-1 Diagram of the basic system that regulates feeding in the fly.

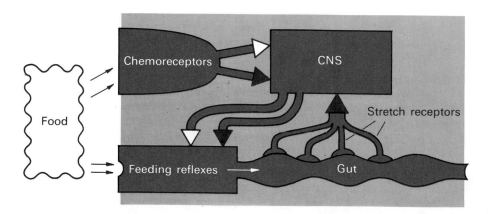

The pattern of intake of the fly is not absolutely constant. For instance, the female fly increases its intake of protein for a day or two every seven days or so, just after it lays eggs; in this way it secures the protein needed for the next clutch of eggs. The temporary increase in preference for protein is an example of a **specific hunger.**

The basic characteristics of the invertebrate feeding systems are also found in the feeding systems of mammals. In this chapter we will see where and how relevant information about the external and internal environments is obtained and processed and how responses to food are coordinated. In the mammal, however, these patterns are built into complex, multilevel nervous systems, and they allow feeding behavior to be integrated with a wide range and variety of behavioral patterns. Monitoring of food supplies is more elaborate than simply detecting the quantity of food in the gut. These complexities have made the task of identifying and describing the feeding systems much more difficult. We will see some of the aspects of mammalian feeding systems that have been well explored and others that are still open to investigation and controversy.

Comparative feeding behavior

Species differ greatly in respect to the way they get their food, the kinds of food they select, and the timing of their feeding. Some examples of these species differences will be noted here; the mechanisms will be discussed later.

Securing food: Structural adaptations

The initial step in dealing with hunger is securing food from the environment. For some marine animals this step is relatively simple; they remain in place and extract food from the water that flows past them. Browsing animals eat plant food and in some cases migrate to follow available plants as the seasons change. Predators hunt other animals for their food. Each of these life styles requires many structural adaptations. Let us consider some that are specifically concerned with ingestion of food.

Devices animals use to obtain and direct food into the mouth exhibit a wide range of structural variations. Dramatic examples are seen among birds, which show extraordinary differences in beak size and shape (Figure 11-2). Major modes for obtaining food among birds include fishing, crushing seeds, catching insects in the air, extracting insects from bark, sipping nectar, and tearing flesh. Giant birds of prey like eagles tear up food and have powerful curved or hooked beaks; nectar feeders have long and slender bills that are effective in probing flowers. Some birds crack seeds and nuts to select particular parts, and these animals, such as finches and parrots, have short and stout beaks. Some birds, such as ducks and spoonbills, have special bills that allow them to strain small particles of food from the water. Of course, beak size and shape are only two of the many attributes related to bird feeding. Overall physical appearance, behavior, and habitat are certainly other significant determinants of feeding strategies and habits.

The food supply of mammals is extremely diverse, including other animals, seeds, grasses, roots, and the bark of trees. The teeth of mammals reflect their diversity of diet (Figure 11-3). Gnawing rodents have large incisors, and carnivorous animals usually have impressive canine teeth. Mammals that eat leaves and grasses

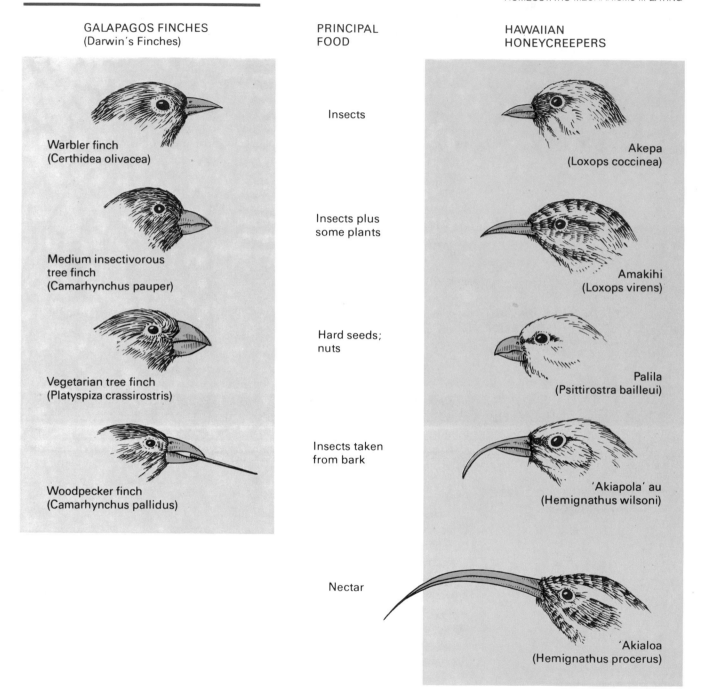

GALAPAGOS FINCHES
(Darwin's Finches)

PRINCIPAL
FOOD

HAWAIIAN
HONEYCREEPERS

Warbler finch
(Certhidea olivacea)

Insects

Akepa
(Loxops coccinea)

Medium insectivorous
tree finch
(Camarhynchus pauper)

Insects plus
some plants

Amakihi
(Loxops virens)

Vegetarian tree finch
(Platyspiza crassirostris)

Hard seeds;
nuts

Palila
(Psittirostra bailleui)

Woodpecker finch
(Camarhynchus pallidus)

Insects taken
from bark

'Akiapola' au
(Hemignathus wilsoni)

Nectar

'Akialoa
(Hemignathus procerus)

Figure 11-2 Beaks of birds have evolved different shapes and sizes to cope with different kinds of food. The varied finches of the Galapagos Islands probably all evolved from one ancestral form. They provided an important clue to Darwin when he was formulating his theory of evolution by natural selection. The Hawaiian honeycreepers show even more divergent evolution over a longer period of time.

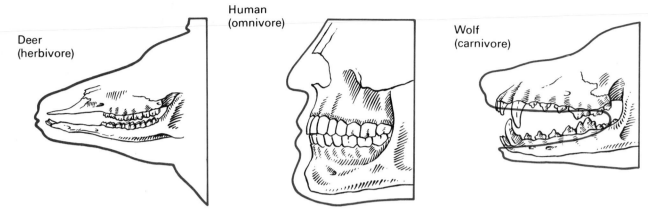

Figure 11-3   The forms of teeth in mammals reflect the diversity of diets of different species.

have large teeth with flat grinding surfaces. An expert can identify a species, including fossil animals, by seeing a single tooth.

Food selection among animals

For all animals survival depends on obtaining and using nutrients. Metabolism of nutrients provides the ingredients that form the structures of cells and the energy that supports body activities. Although many environments offer a range of possible nutrients, most animals select particular diets. In fact, some animals have adapted to such a narrow range of foods that they starve if their food choice becomes unavailable.

Zoologists make broad classifications of animals according to the foods usually eaten. Those that eat other animal material are carnivorous. Those that eat plant material are herbivorous. Insect-eating animals (such as many species of birds) are insectivorous. And nectar-eating animals (such as bees and hummingbirds) are nectivorous.

Temporal patterns of feeding

Some species eat almost continuously, and others eat a few meals restricted to particular times during either the day or the night. Ecological factors such as the availability of food sources are particularly important in determining the frequency and timing of meals. Other determinants include the nutritive characteristics of food, pacing by internal clocks, and social learning, which is especially evident in humans. Some of these determinants will be discussed below in relation to the initiation and termination of feeding.

Many species go for weeks or even months without eating—for example, seals during breeding, whales during migration, penguins during incubation, and bears during hibernation. Apparently these long fasts occur when eating would be incompatible with some other more important activity. The mechanisms of long fasts will be considered later.

Mammalian alimentary tract and digestion

For the cells of the body to receive and use vital nutrients, ingested food must be changed into simpler chemicals. These simpler substances are the products of digestion, a series of mechanical and chemical processes that take place in the digestive tract. A brief review of some of the main processes of digestion will set the stage for our consideration of control of feeding behavior.

The digestive tract begins at the mouth, where mechanical breakdown of food prepares for the chemical processes of digestion. Taste buds of the tongue are vital to the accurate recognition of food. Saliva provides a medium for dissolving food and also contains an enzyme that initiates the chemical breakdown of carbohydrates. Tasting and chewing food produce signals that start the secretion of disgestive enzymes in the stomach.

Food passes to the stomach with the act of swallowing, a complex reflex involving an elaborate set of muscles of the mouth and throat. The esophagus is a tube that connects the mouth and stomach. Waves of movements in this tube propel food toward the stomach. The most intense digestive processes occur in the stomach. Structural characteristics of the stomach vary among animals; especially elaborate morphology is found among grazing animals (herbivores) because of their diet of varied grasses. Within the stomach waves of movements keep food mixed while enzymes break down the substances. One enzyme breaks down protein into simpler constituents, amino acids. Another enzyme changes the proteins characteristically found in milk, while still another aids in the digestion of fats. Since the stomach also acts as a reservoir for food undergoing digestion, the presence and amount of food in the stomach could be expected to influence the timing of eating.

The contents of the stomach are directed in spurts to the small intestine. A muscular valve, the pyloric sphincter, separates the stomach from the small intestine. Within the small intestine, enzymatic action continues. Enzymes from the pancreas act on proteins, carbohydrates, and fat. Secretions from the liver and the small intestine further contribute to the digestive process. Rhythmic movements in the intestine contribute to mixing of the digestive process. Further along the length of the small intestine absorption of the final simplified products of digestion takes place. These substances pass into capillaries and enter the bloodstream leading to the liver. Undigestible substances pass into the large intestine to form feces.

In addition to enzymes, hormones are secreted by cells of the stomach, and these regulate certain aspects of the digestive process. Some hormones regulate enzyme production. Some hormones may also act on brain cells to influence feeding behavior, as we will see later.

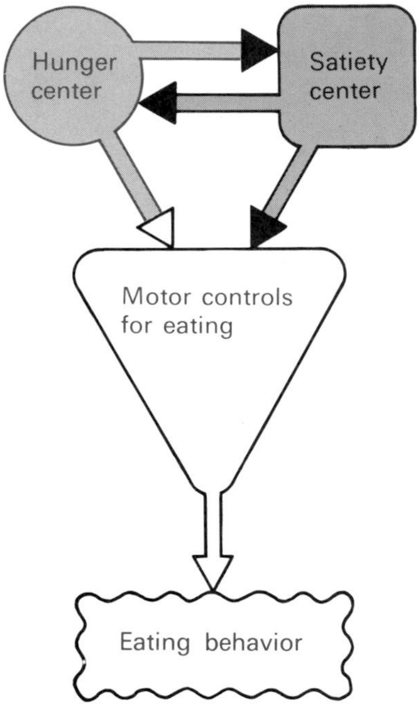

Figure 11-4 Diagram of dual-center theory of control of eating.

Feeding control systems in the brain

Discoveries by the early 1950s had given rise to a "dual-center theory" of control of eating (Figure 11-4). According to this theory the hypothalamus contains the primary control centers for hunger and satiety: A "hunger center" in the **lateral hypothalamus** (LH) facilitates eating, whereas a "satiety center" in the **ventromedial hypothalamus** (VMH) inhibits eating. All the other regions and factors that influence eating were presumed to act through these hypothalamic control centers. Further research aimed at filling in the details of this picture soon resulted in dethroning the hypothalamic regions from their exclusive status, and even the concept of a center or centers was challenged.

*Ventromedial hypothalamus:
The satiety center?*

Occasionally a person develops a pathologically voracious appetite and soon becomes obese. Box 11-1 describes such a case. In the last century physicians began to find that some of these patients had lesions or tumors at the base of the brain. In 1940 Hetherington and Ranson reported that bilateral lesions of the ventromedial hypothalamus (see Figure 11-5) caused rats to become obese. Further research by others showed that VMH lesions produce obesity in all the species that have been tested—monkeys, dogs and cats, several species of rodents, and some species of birds. Most of the studies have been done on rats, so our data will come mainly from them, but we will show the relevance of these data to human behavior.

The VMH was promptly called a "satiety center" because destroying it seemed to prevent animals from ever being satiated with food, but this characterization was soon seen to be inadequate. Destruction of the VMH did not simply cause the rats to become mere feeding machines. Rather the eating habits of VMH-lesioned rats were still controlled by both the palatability of food and body weight, but these controls were no longer exerted in normal ways. If palatable food of high caloric content is available, VMH-lesioned rats typically show two phases of postoperative weight gain. At first they show an amazing increase in consumption, eating two or three times as much as normal; this condition is called **hyperphagia** (from the Greek roots "hyper," meaning "over," and "phagia," meaning "eating"). Body weight shoots up, a stage called the **dynamic phase of weight gain** (see Figure 11-6). But after a few weeks weight stabilizes at an obese level, and food intake is not much above normal; this stage is called the **static phase of obesity.**

Some observations indicate that the obese VMH-lesioned rat regulates its weight at a new target value, considerably above the preoperative norm, but this regulation is not as complete as normal regulation. If an obese rat in the static phase is force-fed, its weight will rise above the plateau level; but when it is again allowed to eat on its own, body weight returns to the plateau level. Similarly, after an obese rat has been deprived of food and has lost weight, when given free access to food, it will regain its plateau level. This regulation is incomplete, however, because the plateau level depends on the availability of a palatable high-fat diet. If VMH-lesioned rats are kept on a diet of laboratory chow pellets, their weight does not rise much above that of control animals. If the food is adulterated with quinine to make it bitter, then body weight of the VMH-lesioned rats may fall below that of controls (Sclafani, Springer, and Kluge, 1976). VMH-lesioned rats tend to be finicky, not only in their exaggerated feeding reactions to the palatability but also in the amount of work they will perform to obtain food. Although they are happy to be freeloaders, the lesioned rats will not work as much as normals to obtain food.

Genes can result in a high target weight, as is seen in rats of the Zucker strain (Zucker and Zucker, 1961). Rats that are homozygous for the recessive fatty gene have fat cells that are more numerous and of larger size than those of their heterozygous littermates. These fat rats maintain their obesity even on diets strongly adulterated with quinine or when they are required to work hard to obtain food (Cruce et al., 1974). The Zucker fat rats provide a better example of the set-point interpreta-

(a) Rat brain,showing the locations of the frontal sections illustrated below

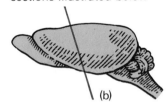

(b) Frontal section through the hypothalamus

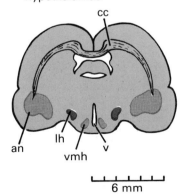

6 mm

Figure 11-5 Areas of the rat brain involved in control of eating. The lateral view of the brain in (a) shows the plane of the frontal section illustrated in (b). (an, amygdaloid nuclei; cc, corpus callosum; lh, lateral hypothalamus; v, third ventricle; and vmh, ventromedial hypothalamus)

BOX 11-1　Effects of a Hypothalamic Tumor on Human Behavior

A case involving a small, sharply localized tumor in a woman's brain demonstrates the multiple functions of the hypothalamus and shows how results of animal experiments can help in the interpretation of a person's motivated behavior (Reeves and Plum, 1969).

The patient was a twenty-year-old bookkeeper. She first came to the hospital about a year after she had developed an abnormal appetite; she ate and drank large amounts and gained weight rapidly. She also had frequent headaches, and her menstrual periods had stopped. She was mentally alert, performed her work well, and showed no emotional abnormalities.

Another year passed, and her family brought her back to the hospital because of changes in her behavior. Now she was often uncooperative and at times attacked people around her. She was confused and sometimes could not remember correctly. She would no longer attempt arithmetic calculations. Tests showed reduced endocrine function involving the gonads, the thyroid gland, and the adrenal cortex. An operation revealed a tumor at the base of the brain, but it could not be removed. The young woman's outbursts of violent behavior became more frequent, especially if she was not fed frequently. Toward the end of her hospitalization she had to be fed almost continuously in order to keep her reasonably tractable, and she was eating about 10,000 calories a day.

When she died, three years after the onset of her illness, the position of the tumor was determined precisely; it is shown in Box Figure 11-1. The tumor had destroyed the ventromedial nucleus of the hypothalamus. In animal studies destruction of the ventromedial nucleus has been found frequently to cause overeating and obesity. In some species, such as the cat, the same operation usually makes the animal display rage behavior more often and more readily than a normal animal does. Hypothalamic areas involved particularly in sexual receptivity and in mating behavior are also found nearby, but in the case of this patient the reduced gonadal function was probably caused by interruption of pathways by which the hypothalamus regulates the pituitary gland. This dysfunction would also explain the observed decreases in thyroid and adrenal cortex function, since these endocrine glands are also regulated by the anterior pituitary gland. The causes of the confusion and the malfunctioning of memory are not clear, although hypothalamic structures have been implicated in learning and memory.

In a similar case described recently by Beal et al. (1981), the patient also showed loss of memory. He slept most of the time but when he was awake he ate almost continuously when food was available. At autopsy a tumor 2 cm in diameter was found in the third ventricle. The tumor had destroyed both the posterior hypothalamic nuclei, which probably caused the somnolence, and the ventromedial nuclei, which probably caused the hyperphagia.

These cases show how a small tumor—about the size of the last joint of the little finger—because of its location in a critical region of the brain, could affect a variety of motivated behaviors: eating, aggression, and sex. The neurologists who reported the first case concluded: "The findings provide a close functional correlation between the human and homologous lower mammalian ventromedial hypothalamic structures" (Reeves and Plum, 1969, p. 622).

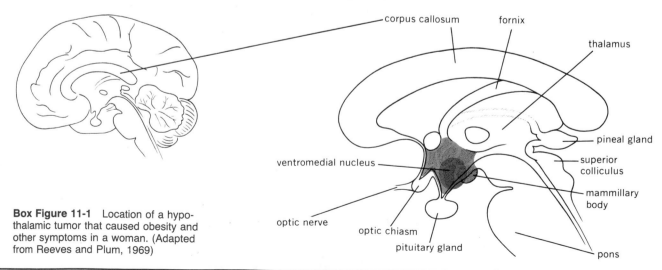

Box Figure 11-1 Location of a hypothalamic tumor that caused obesity and other symptoms in a woman. (Adapted from Reeves and Plum, 1969)

Figure 11-6 Phases of weight gain after lesioning of the ventromedial hypothalamus.

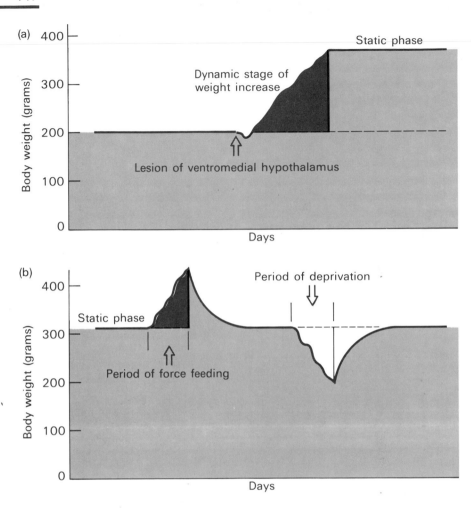

tion of the control of feeding than do VMH-lesioned rats. Rats with lesions of the VMH and those with genetically caused obesity may provide models for two different kinds of human obesity.

Lateral hypothalamus: The hunger center?

The other part of the dual-center hypothesis was the hunger center. In 1951 Anand and Brobeck announced that bilateral destruction of the lateral aspect of the LH caused rats or cats to refuse to eat. This **aphagia** was so severe in some cases that animals died of starvation even in the presence of their usual food. The investigators proposed that the LH contains a "feeding center" and that the VMH normally acts as a brake on feeding by inhibiting the LH. Two important features about the effects of LH damage soon emerged (Teitelbaum and Stellar, 1954). First, the rats refused not only to eat but also to drink; they showed **adipsia** as well as aphagia. If the experimenters placed a bit of food or a drop of water on the lips or in the mouth of the rat, it spat out the food or water as if it were distasteful. Second, the aphagia and adipsia were not necessarily permanent. A few rats began to eat and drink spontaneously after about a week. Even those who did not recover in this way would eventually eat spontaneously if they were kept alive meanwhile by having food and water tubed into the stomach. So just as VMH destruction does not abolish all inhibition of eating, LH destruction does not permanently prevent eating and drinking.

The recovery after an LH lesion shows four main stages (Teitelbaum and Epstein, 1962): In stage 1 the animal is aphagic and adipsic; food or water seem aversive and are avoided, and body weight drops rapidly. In stage 2 the animal remains adipsic but becomes **anorexic** (showing lack of appetite) rather than refusing food. It will accept palatable foods but not water; even with palatable foods available, intake remains so low that tube feeding remains necessary to sustain life. In stage 3 the animal can regulate food intake but continues to refuse water. If water is the only liquid available, the animal does not drink and therefore soon stops eating. However, it can be trained gradually to accept water flavored with saccharine. Some rats with large lesions never recover beyond stage 3, but some get to stage 4, in which they can live on dry food and water. Even after recovery, LH-lesioned rats are deficient in their response to treatments that lower blood glucose, such as injections of insulin. Also, they tend to drink water only while they are eating; that is, they drink to aid ingestion of food rather than to regulate fluid.

While many investigators have verified this sequence of recovery and have used the four stages to describe their results, Teitelbaum and colleagues have recently suggested a rather different interpretation, especially of the first two stages (Wolgin, Cytawa, and Teitelbaum, 1976). They have proposed that stages 1 and 2 represent general behavioral deficits and that only in stages 3 and 4 can specific deficits of eating and drinking be seen. The first two stages show both a general neglect of sensory inputs and also a loss of behavioral activation. If a cat or a rat in stage 2 is aroused by painful stimulation, it will eat; but when the painful stimulation ceases, the animal falls back into lethargy.

The difference between general and specific effects on eating can be illustrated by different effects of the drug amphetamine. Many people use amphetamine or related drugs to suppress appetite and thus to help in weight loss. Others use amphetamine as a stimulant. Curiously, although amphetamine decreases food intake of normal animals, it enhances the eating of cats and rats in stage 2 and early in stage 3. In the early stages of recovery from an LH lesion, the stimulating effect seems to be the more important effect. Thus activation, both internal and through sensory stimulation, provides a necessary support for feeding behavior.

Recovered LH-lesioned rats regulate their body weights with precision at a nearly constant percentage of the weights of control rats. The larger the size of the LH lesion, the lower is the target level of body weight. If food is restricted, the weights of LH-lesioned and control rats fall in parallel, and then the predeprivation level is regained when ad libitum feeding is restored (see Figure 11-7). Similarly, if eggnog is the only food available, both lesioned and control rats gain weight in parallel; and when the usual diet is restored, both groups then fall to their previous level. When food is adulterated with quinine, the LH-lesioned rats again show changes strictly in parallel with normal controls (Keesey and Boyle, 1973), whereas we saw that VMH-lesioned rats displayed an exaggerated reaction to quinine. Thus the LH-lesioned rats are said to defend a lowered weight target or set point (Keesey, 1980).

Figure 11-7 Regulation of body weight by normal rats (black line) and by rats that have recovered from lesioning of the lateral hypothalamus (blue line). The LH-lesioned rats regulate around a lowered target weight but in parallel with normal rats.

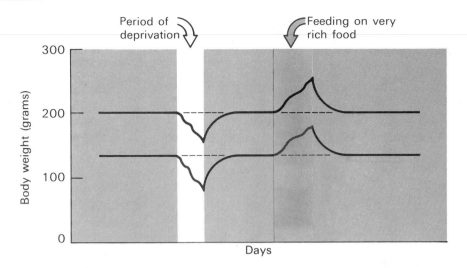

Human beings may become emaciated if they suffer from lesions or tumors in the lateral hypothalamus. Bilateral damage to the LH through accident or disease is, of course, rare, but even unilateral damage to the LH sometimes produces aphagia and adipsia in animals. Cases of LH anorexia in humans are about a quarter as frequent as cases of hypothalamic obesity (White and Hain, 1959).

Reciprocal activities of VMH and LH

Several kinds of evidence indicate that the VMH and the LH reciprocally inhibit each other (Hernandez and Hoebel, 1980). The effect of a partial lesion of one of these regions can be moderated by a partial lesion in the other. Thus a rat with small bilateral lesions in the LH is more likely to accept food if it also sustains damage in the VMH. Recording the electrical activity of single neurons in the VMH and the LH also demonstrates reciprocal innervation. Excitation of some of the cells in the one area causes decreases in the firing rate of certain cells in the other area. This result has been observed with electrical stimulation and also with injections of glucose or insulin, either systemically or to individual cells.

The two regions have opposite influences on both external behavior and internal adjustments. Activity of the LH enhances positive feeding stimuli, facilitates feeding responses, and promotes the mobilization and utilization of the body's food supplies. Activity of the VMH potentiates aversive feeding stimuli, facilitates withdrawal from food, and promotes storage and conservation of internal food supplies.

Dual-center or multifactor system?

The adequacy of the dual-center hypothesis was soon challenged by further observations. For one thing, controversies arose as to whether the lesions were effective because they destroyed integrative centers, as originally believed, or because they interrupted fiber tracts that passed through these regions. For another thing, it was found that many brain regions outside the hypothalamus are involved in regulation of feeding behavior, and they do not contribute solely by their connections to the hypothalamus. Among the regions whose destruction impairs the regulation of feeding are the amygdaloid nuclei, the frontal cortex, and the substantia nigra. In the next two sections we present some examples of research on the question of centers versus tracts and the roles of amygdaloid nuclei.

● Centers or tracts?   When Anand and Brobeck (1951) first reported that LH lesions caused aphagia, they were aware that these lesions invaded the medial forebrain bundle and certain other tracts. Their analysis of the results convinced them, however, that no aphagia occurred in cases where the lesion missed the intended target in the LH and destroyed adjacent tissue, including the nearby tracts. More recently other investigators have studied this question in detail, cutting tracts anterior, posterior, or lateral to the LH. They have found clear effects on feeding behavior even when the LH was not invaded. Similar transection experiments have been conducted with tracts that run close to the VMH in order to determine whether the VMH actually plays a role in regulation of feeding. In complementary experiments investigators have employed techniques to destroy cells in a region without injuring fibers that pass through it.

Selective damage to the **nigrostriatal bundle** (NSB) causess many of the symptoms of LH destruction. The NSB is a dopaminergic tract that originates in the substantia nigra of the midbrain, passes through the LH and then through the globus pallidus, to terminate in the caudate-putamen. Cutting this tract or depleting its dopamine by using the drug 6-hydroxydopamine (6-OHDA) causes aphagia and adipsia (Marshall, Richardson, and Teitelbaum, 1974). Other effects are finickiness to quinine-adulterated food and failure to respond to lowered glucose. Does destruction of the NSB account for all the effects of lesioning LH? Further techniques were then used to answer this question.

Two recently developed techniques have been employed in the attempt to destroy cells of the LH without impairing the fiber tracts that pass through it. The first employed kainic acid, a neurotoxin that overexcites and destroys some cell bodies close to its site of injection but that does not affect fibers that pass through the region. When a small amount of kainic acid was slowly infused into the LH over several minutes, rats became aphagic and adipsic. Histological examinations revealed a marked reduction of neurons in the LH but no signs of damage to axons of passage. Biochemical assays revealed no difference in dopamine levels in the brains of the experimental animals, confirming that NSB fibers were unaffected (Grossman et al., 1978; Stricker et al., 1978). Thus killing cell bodies in the LH, without affecting axons that pass through the region, impairs feeding and drinking behavior.

The second technique involved making lesions in the LH in 10-day-old rats, before fiber tracts had completely grown through this region or had become functionally mature (Almli, 1978; Almli, Fisher, and Hill, 1979). The lesioned pups stopped nursing and had to be fed until they were more than 30 days old, whereas normal rats are weaned by 25 days of age. Eventually the lesioned rats survived on wet mash, but they refused to eat dry food or to drink water; the anorexia and adipsia persisted as long as the rats were kept, up to 375 days in some cases. While these symptoms were severe, the rats lesioned as infants did not show either the sensory neglect or the lack of arousal that characterizes stages 1 and 2 of recovery in rats lesioned as adults. Specific behavioral tests had to be designed to assess the sensory and motor capacities of infant and young rats before this research could be carried out. From their results the investigators suggested that when LH lesions are made in adults, the specific problems of feeding and drinking are caused by damage to the hypothalamic neurons, while the sensory and arousal deficits are caused by interruption of fibers of passage. Although some fibers are damaged in the infant lesions, the immature fiber system seems to be capable of recovering its function. Thus from the experiments in which either the LH neurons or the fiber bundles were impaired separately, we see that the hypothalamic cells play a more specific role in the resulting deficits of eating and drinking than do the fibers of passage, although impairing the fibers can also interfere with eating and drinking.

● **Amygdaloid nuclei and control of feeding**   Lesions of the amygdaloid complex can cause either aphagia or hyperphagia, depending on the parts of the amygdala destroyed (Figure 11-8). Bilateral lesions of the basolateral subdivisions of the amygdala cause hyperphagia, while bilateral lesions of the corticomedial subdivisions cause aphagia. These effects have been reported in cats, dogs, and monkeys, but they are most striking in rats (C. I. Thompson, 1980). With large lesions that

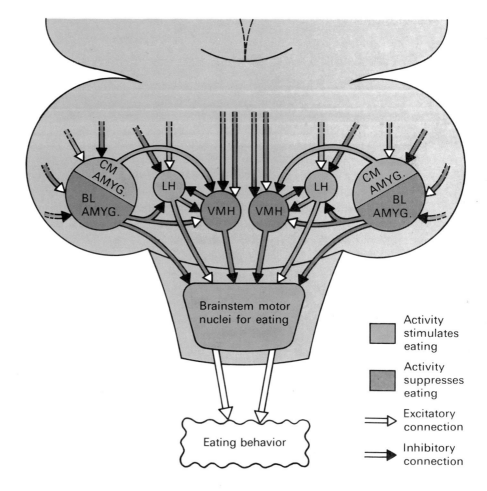

Figure 11-8   Diagram of presumed connections from amygdaloid nuclei and hypothalamic nuclei to brainstem motor nuclei for eating behavior. The amygdaloid nuclei exert effects on the brainstem nuclei both directly and through the ventromedial and lateral nuclei of the hypothalamus. Note that the two main divisions of the amygdala have opposite effects on eating. (BL AMYG., basal lateral amygdala; CM AMYG., cortical medial amygdala) Activity of the basolateral amygdala suppresses eating, so ablation of this region causes hyperphagia.

destroy the amygdala and surrounding tissue, the basolateral effect predominates, and hyperphagia results.

The basolateral divisions send fibers to the LH, where they exert an inhibitory effect; that is, stimulation of the basolateral amygdala leads to inhibition of neurons in the LH. The same stimulation also excites cells in the VMH, probably across a synaptic relay. The corticomedial amygdala inhibits the same VMH cells that are excited by the basolateral amygdala.

But the effects of the amygdala on feeding are not exerted entirely through the LH and the VMH. This result is shown by the finding that the hyperphagia caused by amygdaloid damage still persists after destruction of the VMH and the LH (Morgane and Kosman, 1960). Also, bilateral destruction of the amygdala leads to the peculiar symptom of indiscriminate eating, which is not found with hypothalamic lesions. For example, monkeys with bilateral temporal lobectomy were found to put anything into their mouths, including hardware, live mice, and snakes (which monkeys normally fear); later this symptom was attributed specifically to destruction of the amygdala. A human patient with extensive destruction of the temporal lobe was reported to exhibit an enormous and indiscriminate appetite, ingesting "virtually everything within reach, including the plastic wrapper from bread, cleaning pastes, dog food, and feces" (Marlowe, Mancall, and Thomas, 1975). So the amygdala affects eating both through the hypothalamus and independently of the hypothalamus.

Initiation of feeding

How do the neural systems operate to initiate and terminate eating? In adult human beings the time of starting to eat is largely a matter of custom and habit. Most of us eat on a rather regular schedule that is largely a matter of social convenience. In the United States the usual schedule consists of three meals a day, with the last meal at the end of the afternoon or early evening. In some parts of Europe there are five regular meals—breakfast, second breakfast or coffee break, lunch, teatime, and a late supper. Among some African tribes adults eat only one meal a day. This diversity of human meal patterns shows that learning and habit play major roles in initiation of eating.

Among different species of mammals there is great diversity in spacing and duration of meals. Many animals must spend most of their waking hours eating. This phenomenon is true of most small mammals, because with their large surface-to-volume ratios they lose heat rapidly to the environment. It is also true of herbivores since their food is low in caloric content and large amounts must be ingested in order to meet nutritional needs. Even these animals do not eat all the time, however, and research has studied the factors that initiate and terminate their feeding. Most intriguing is the case of large carnivores.

We are used to seeing large carnivores such as African leopards receive a single daily meal in a zoo. The timing of the meal is scheduled for the convenience of the viewing public, and the amount of food is planned to keep the leopard in good health. The leopard "wolfs" it down. In nature the timing and size of a carnivore's meals are much less regular. On one day the leopard may make several small kills and consume each promptly. On another day the leopard may kill a large antelope that proves too much to eat at a sitting. Rather than abandoning the rest of its prey to scavengers, the leopard may carry it up into a tree and stash it where the foliage hides it from the vultures above and where it is safe from jackels or hyenas. What factors determine when the leopard will stop one meal and when it will start another?

Future needs as well as present needs influence the feeding of many species. For example, animals that hibernate accumulate large stocks of fat, which enable them to survive the long period when they do not eat. Elephant seals also store fat in advance of the mating season, a period when they do not eat. Some species of birds accumulate fat resources before starting long migratory flights. Many species that do not undergo such extreme tests—like the leopard—nevertheless store some reserves so that they are not always on the edge of hunger. Thus the signals that initiate feeding are not the disappearance of bodily stores but rather indications that they are below some target level.

For many centuries it seemed obvious what signal initiates eating: A person eats when he or she feels hungry. Physiologists in the last century and the early part of the present century attributed feelings of hunger to some state of the stomach: Some claimed it was an increase in secretion of gastric juices and others claimed it was a decrease; some claimed that feelings of hunger were induced by activity of the stomach and others claimed that inactivity of the stomach was responsible. Then as investigators became capable of doing research on the brain—stimulating neurons, recording their electrical activity, and making localized brain lesions—interest in the control of feeding shifted from processes in the gut to neural processes. From the 1940s on, brain processes and brain circuits held the center of the stage. Then in the 1970s and 1980s an effort was made to bring peripheral processes back into the picture along with central processes. Now an account of the control of feeding includes taste and shifts in palatability, stomach activity and gastric secretions, monitoring of substances in the blood, and the interaction of excitation and inhibition in brain regions. In this section we will examine research that has supported this modern view. First we will take up studies that explore the effects of localized stimulation of the brain on eating. Then we review some investigations of how internal and external stimuli affect activity of brain sites that are related to eating.

Effects of localized stimulation of the brain

Localized stimulation in different sites in the brain of an experimental animal can evoke different kinds of motivational behaviors—eating, drinking, copulation, aggressive attack, or fearful escape. This result was demonstrated by the Swiss physiologist Walter R. Hess in the 1940s, and his research brought him a Nobel Prize in 1949. Other investigators readily confirmed the occurrence of **stimulation-elicited behavior** (stimulation-induced feeding, stimulation-induced drinking, and the like). Nevertheless, the interpretation of these phenomena has stirred up much controversy and engendered a great deal of further research. One issue has been whether the stimulation really elicits a motivational state or whether it only forces the animal to perform consummatory acts as if it were a puppet whose strings were being pulled. Another issue has been whether stimulation at a particular site really elicits a specific motive; perhaps the brain stimulation only facilitates whatever motive is strongest at the time or most appropriate to the external circumstances (such as presence of food or water or a mate).

Tests have shown that electrical stimulation of the LH does not simply elicit sterotyped feeding movements. Quite different locomotor movements may be evoked on successive trials, depending on where the animal happens to be in relation to the food source when the brain stimulation starts. Also, the feeding responses are appropriate to the nature of the food, whether it is a liquid, a soft mash, or hard pellets. If the animal had previously learned when food-deprived to press a lever to obtain food pellets, then it will readily begin to press the lever when the LH is stimulated. These results suggest that the stimulation produces a feeling not unlike that caused by food deprivation.

The specificity of the motive state induced by brain stimulation is an issue that is not yet completely resolved. Some investigators have reported that a variety of motivational responses might be obtained within a relatively large LH area without any specificity of location (Valenstein et al., 1970). Other investigators have found more specific effects. For example, even if both drinking and eating can be elicited from the same electrodes, water deprivation increases stimulation-induced drinking and preloads of water reduce it, but these treatments do not affect eating. Conversely, analogous treatments with food affect eating but not drinking. The apparent lack of specificity may be due in part to the small size of the rat brain. Use of very fine electrodes was reported to yield greater specificity (Olds, Allan, and Briese, 1971). Also, studies in the larger brains of the dog, cat, and opossum have shown clear separation of sites for different kinds of motivation (Wise, 1974). It appears that localized stimulation of brain sites can help us to understand motivation circuits in the brain.

Signals that initiate feeding   Granted that feeding is initiated by activation of a neural system that includes the LH, what signals cause this activation? These could be either signals that act in an excitatory way on the feeding system (including the LH) or signals that inhibit the satiety system (including the VMH). Inhibiting the satiety system could initiate feeding, because the satiety system normally inhibits the feeding system.

● **Internal monitoring of food stores**   Many investigators have proposed that the body monitors its food stores. An indication that these supplies are falling below a set value could be the trigger that activates the feeding system. Many different indices of food stocks have been suggested. Among the most prominent are the rate of utilization of glucose and the supply of fat, which may be indicated by some by-product, such as free fatty acids.

For a little background before considering the research on these hypotheses, let us note briefly some differences in the fuels used by the brain and the rest of the body and also shifts in these fuels as a function of time after eating (Figure 11-9). Note that the brain utilizes chiefly glucose and, unlike other organs, does not require insulin for this purpose. Under conditions of deficiency the brain can also use ketone bodies, but these cannot completely replace glucose. The rest of the body has more flexible requirements, and when glucose is in short supply, the body shifts to other fuels to spare glucose for the brain.

Since glucose is the primary fuel of the brain, it was logical to suppose that the brain might monitor directly the supplies of glucose. Evidence for this hypothesis

Figure 11-9 Main sources of energy of the brain and the rest of the body, as a function of time since the last meal.

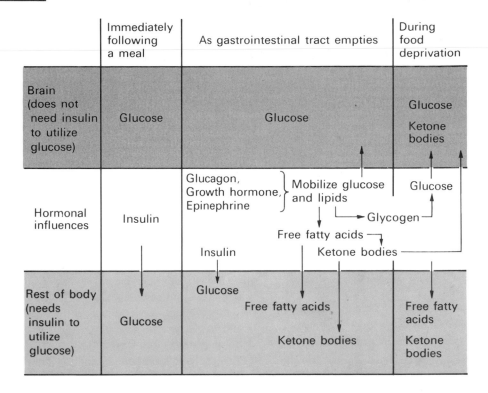

Figure 11-10 Schematic representation of responses of cells of ventromedial hypothalamus (VMH) and lateral hypothalamus (LH) to glucose, insulin, and free fatty acids. Response frequencies are indicated as increases (up) or decreases (down) from the baseline frequency. [Adapted from Y. Oomura; Figure 2, in D. Novin et al. (Eds.), *Hunger: Basic Mechanisms and Clinical Implication* (New York: Raven Press, 1976), p. 149.]

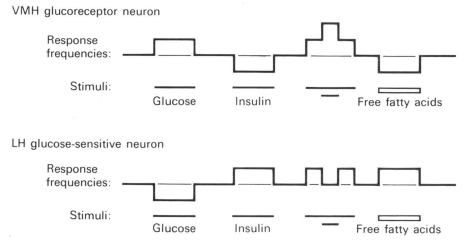

has been accumulating since the 1950s. Some of the most convincing evidence has come from recent recordings of the activity of single neurons in the VMH and the LH (Oomura, 1976). Application of glucose to single neurons was found to stimulate about a third of the VMH neurons and a sixth of the LH neurons, whereas it has an inhibitory effect on about a third of the LH neurons. The generally opposite effects found in the two hypothalamic regions are shown diagrammatically in Figure 11-10. Insulin alone tended to hyperpolarize and inhibit VMH neurons, but it potentiated the response to glucose. The response of most brain cells to glucose is not facilitated by insulin; the fact that the VMH acts like body cells in this regard suggests that the VMH may be capable of monitoring the glucose utilization of tissues that depend on insulin for uptake of glucose. Note that glucose, especially in the presence of insulin, stimulates the VMH (a part of the satiety system) and inhibits the LH (a part of the feeding system). On the other hand, free fatty acids stimulate the LH and inhibit the VMH; their presence in the blood may indicate that lipid stores are being drawn upon. Thus initiation of the disposition to eat could be signaled by lack of glucose or by presence of free fatty acids or both.

Mayer (1953) proposed that it is not the absolute level of glucose but rather the rate of glucose utilization that is monitored by cells in the hypothalamus. Glucose utilization can be estimated by measuring the difference between concentrations of glucose in the arterial and venous blood (the A–V difference). A large A–V difference means that glucose is being taken up by the cells, and this uptake is correlated with satiety in human subjects. A small A–V difference reflects low uptake of glucose, a condition found to be associated with hunger. Diabetics feel hungry with high levels of glucose because without sufficient insulin most body organs cannot take up much glucose, so diabetics have a low A–V difference. Thus a low A–V difference of glucose may be one of the main signals leading to the state of readiness to eat.

Human beings usually report feeling hungry at mealtimes, even if they have eaten only a few hours previously and are in no significant state of depletion. Is this just habit or "imagination," or may there actually be a reduced A–V glucose difference at the usual mealtime? In rats that were put on a schedule of one meal per day at a fixed hour, a conditioned release of insulin and consequent lowering of blood glucose were observed in the few minutes before the expected meal (Wiley and Leveille, 1970; Woods et al., 1977). It seems likely that such conditioning occurs in people, since release of insulin has been measured when they look at food at mealtime (Rodin, 1976) or when they imagine food intake under hypnotic suggestion (Goldfine et al., 1970).

All glucoreceptors need not reside in the brain. Russek (1963) proposed that glucoreceptors in the liver fire more rapidly whenever glucose becomes less available and that these signals, transmitted to the CNS, are important in initiation of eating. Since the liver is so important in storage and conversion of food, the hypothesis had some plausibility. Several experiments have in fact shown that injection of glucose into the hepatic circulation prevents hungry animals from eating, though there have also been failures to confirm this effect. But although this hypothesis has attracted considerable attention, researchers have shown that the liver is not necessary for initiation or termination of feeding: Total denervation of the liver does not affect intake of food (Bellinger, Trietley, and Bernardis, 1976), nor does a liver transplant in animals or in human beings abolish hunger (Calne et al., 1968).

It is an old idea that contractions of the empty stomach cause hunger pangs and that it is these sensations that initiate eating. But hunger sensations and regulation of food intake have been found to persist in human beings in whom removal of vagus nerve connections to the stomach has eliminated stomach contractions. Human patients who have sustained total removal of the stomach report that they continue to experience hunger just as they did before the operation. Thus it is quite clear that it is monitoring in the central nervous system that provides the main signals that make mammals ready to eat.

● **External stimuli and initiation of feeding**   It is obvious that hungry people or animals do not eat unless there are edible objects available, but the importance of sensory information about such objects and other aspects of the environment is often overlooked in discussions of feeding behavior. Part of the initiation of feeding lies in perception of appropriate food objects. There is a two-way interaction: Perception of food objects can heighten the motivation to eat, and increased motivation can enhance the salience and palatability of food.

The importance of sensory stimulation for eating has been demonstrated both in LH-lesioned animals and in intact animals. Part of the difficulty with LH-lesioned animals is that they tend to ignore sensory stimuli. In stage 1 of recovery, sensory neglect and apathy can be counteracted by painful stimulation or by amphetamine. Later the stimuli from food objects can play this role. When cats make the transition from stage 1 (aphagia) to stage 2 (anorexia), visual stimuli are of primary importance (Wolgin, Cytawa, and Teitelbaum, 1976). If opaque occluders are placed over the eyes of cats in this stage, they will not approach food and they will not eat even if food is placed right in front of their mouths. Needless to say, a normal cat that is blindfolded will find food placed anywhere in a room and will accept food presented to it. The transition to stage 3, when animals become able to maintain their weight on palatable food, coincides with the emergence of olfactory control over feeding. At this stage blindfolded cats will accept food and can find it in their cages. Smell also seems to activate the recovering animals both to search for food and to consume it.

Some hypothalamic cells respond specifically to the sight of food objects—but only when the animal is hungry! This result was found in recording the activity of single neurons with implanted electrodes in awake monkeys (Mora, Rolls, and Burton, 1976; Rolls, 1978). In a sample of several hundred neurons examined in the lateral hypothalamus, 13% had activity related to perception of food objects. In most of these neurons the response occurred before the food was placed in the monkey's mouth, while the monkey looked at such objects as a peanut, a banana, or mash. These neurons did not respond to the presentation of nonfood objects, to muscular movements, or to emotional arousal. When the monkeys were fed until they were satiated, the neurons lost their responsiveness to food stimuli. When the monkeys were trained during a recording session to associate a neutral object with food, then the conditioned stimulus elicited responses from the "food" neurons.

The discovery of hypothalamic neurons that respond specifically to food does not, of course, show that such cells are unique to the hypothalmic areas; perhaps such neurons occur in other regions as well. Also, it does not prove that these cells play a role in initiation of feeding; perhaps they merely reflect responses to food objects, either muscular responses or glandular responses such as salivation. Experiments were therefore undertaken to test alternative interpretations. The route of visual information to the LH probably passes through the inferotemporal visual association cortex and the lateral amygdala. Ablation of either of these regions produces a syndrome in which monkeys do not recognize objects and tend to place all sorts of objects in their mouths. Recordings of single neurons in the inferotemporal cortex or the amygdala did not, however, reveal cells with specific responses to food objects.

To test whether the specific LH neurons might be participating in initiation of feeding responses, the investigators trained monkeys to respond in a special situation. The monkey, restrained in a chair for electrophysiological recording, faced a shutter that could open to reveal a stimulus object. When certain objects were shown, the monkey could obtain a small amount of fruit juice by licking a tube positioned just in front of its mouth. But when other objects were presented, a lick yielded aversive hypertonic saline solution. The monkey therefore learned to pay attention and to discriminate the food signals from the negative stimuli. Under these conditions the latency of response of hypothalamic neurons to food stimuli was 150–200 milliseconds (msec); the latency of response of the tongue muscles was about 300 msec; and the latency of contact with the tube was at least 400 msec. Thus the hypothalamic units clearly responded before the motor units. They may well participate in the initiation of feeding responses, but further research will be required to establish this definitively.

The research to date suggests the following conclusion: A disposition to eat, or a central motive state of hunger, is induced by internal signals that indicate either a lack of available food stores in the body or a level of stores that is below the current target value. Feeding behavior is initiated when the disposition to eat is accompanied by perception of appropriate food objects or of stimuli that have been conditioned to food. Feeding behavior can be terminated or weakened by activity of the satiety system, a subject we consider next.

Termination of feeding

Fullness of the stomach has long been thought to be the signal to stop eating. This condition has been demonstrated to be the main signal that terminates feeding in the fly. Does the same simple arrangement work in mammals? Research has shown that the stomach also signals satiety in mammals, but chemoreceptors as well as mechanoreceptors in the stomach may be involved, and the stomach may not be the only part of the gastrointestinal tract involved in satiety.

Monitoring food intake through the mouth and throat does not produce satiation, any more than oral monitoring terminates drinking. This result was found by feeding animals that had been equipped with esophageal fistulas (just as such tubes were used in the study of the control of thirst). But tasting food may play a role in satiation, in combination with other signals.

Controversy rages over whether neural signals from the stomach or a hormonal signal from the duodenum is the major factor that produces satiety. There is good evidence that the stomach not only senses the bulk of food ingested but that it also assesses the caloric value of the food. The arrival of food into the duodenum causes the release of a hormone from the mucosal lining of the duodenum; several lines of evidence suggest that this hormone, **cholecystokinin** (CCK), is involved in satiety. (This hormone was originally found to cause contraction of the gallbladder which aids in digestion; hence its name, from the Greek roots "cholo," meaning "gall" or "bile," "cysto," meaning "bladder," and "kinein," meaning "causing movement or contraction.") Assessing the roles of the gastric and duodenal factors is important both in tracing out the specific processes involved in satiety and in developing therapies for dysfunctions such as obesity.

Evidence that CCK is important in satiety can be summarized briefly (J. Gibbs et al., 1973; Smith and Gibbs, 1976). Increased levels of CCK are measured in the blood within a few minutes after the start of eating; release is also elicited by placing emulsified fats, weak hydrochloric acid, or other materials into the duodenum of anesthetized cats or dogs. Eating can be suppressed in hungry rats, cats, or dogs by giving them intraperitoneal injections of CCK. The suppression of eating appears to be specific, because CCK does not reduce water intake in thirsty animals. If a rat equipped with an esophageal fistula is sham feeding, an intraperitoneal injection of CCK produces the normal sequence of behaviors that rats show when they have eaten their fill—a short period of grooming or exploration, then rest or sleep (Antin et al., 1975). The satiety does not appear to be produced by making the animal feel ill or nauseous. Gibbs and colleagues reached this conclusion because pairing CCK with saccharine does not cause the animal to develop an aversion of saccharine, whereas aversions are easily established by pairing flavors with substances known to produce illness, such as lithium chloride.

Recent research has shown that CCK also exists in neurons of the cerebral cortex. (This is one case among many in which compounds that act as hormones in the digestive tract have also been found recently as probable neurotransmitters in the brain.) Furthermore, genetically obese mice have significantly lower amounts of this substance in their brains than do nonobese littermates (Straus and Yalow, 1979). A ten-peptide chain that is part of the larger CCK molecule has been found to bind selectively to the VMH and to suppress eating. Thus CCK may be a hormone or neurotransmitter at several levels of the feeding-digestive system—the gallbladder, the duodenum, and the cerebral cortex. A deficiency of CCK in the brain may be related to the unrestrained appetites of the obese mice.

Strong challenges to much of the evidence implicating CCK in satiety have come from Deutsch (1978). To study the role of the stomach separately from that of the duodenum and CCK, Deutsch implanted into rats a small inflatable cuff around the passage between the stomach and the duodenum (the pyloric sphincter). When the cuff was inflated from outside the animal, food could not pass from the stomach to the duodenum. An abnormal buildup of pressure in the stomach was prevented by implanting a tube and valve; ingested material would move out when the level of pressure in normal feeding was reached. When the cuff was inflated so that food could reach the stomach but not the duodenum, rats ate meals of normal sizes and then stopped, showing that satiety can be signaled by the stomach. If some of the food is withdrawn from the stomach of normal rats at the end of a meal and then they are allowed to feed again, they compensate by ingesting approximately the amount that had been removed. Deutsch tested this observation with rats with the pyloric cuffs and found that the compensation was as accurate when the cuff was inflated as when it was not; this result provided further evidence that the stomach can measure the amount of food and that the duodenum need not be involved.

Deutsch also found no clear evidence that CCK in physiological amounts causes satiety. Using more sensitive behavioral tests than had Gibbs and co-workers (1973), Deutsch found that pairing CCK with a flavor did produce aversion for that flavor.

Although CCK does not produce as strong an aversion as does lithium chloride, it is aversive in the doses used. Deutsch then assayed CCK to see whether the experimental doses were similar to the amounts released by ingestion of food. He found that the level of CCK secreted during normal satiety is lower than had been supposed and lower than the amounts employed in previous experiments. Thus some investigators may have been making their animals sick and therefore unwilling to eat—rather than satiated.

When small doses of CCK were administered to human volunteers, they decreased their food intake during the experimental session (Sturdevant and Goetz, 1976). But an attempt to use a larger amount produced nausea and abdominal cramps, even though the authors noted that this dose was smaller than that used to demonstrate decreased eating in animals. Species differ markedly in the appropriate doses of hormones and drugs, so the right dose for one species cannot be determined by tests with another.

Other researchers have discounted the criticisms directed against the hypothesized role of CCK in satiety. Thus researchers are continuing to try to determine the site(s) in the body at which CCK acts to produce satiety. Intraperitoneally injected CCK causes satiety even in rats with lesions of the ventromedial hypothalamus (Kulkowsky et al., 1976), so apparently it does not act on brain receptors. But the satiety effect is blocked if the branch of the vagus nerve to the stomach is cut (Smith et al., 1981). Further evidence suggests that the critical fibers in the vagus nerve are afferents from the stomach. Smith and colleagues (1981) therefore hypothesize that CCK administered intraperitoneally causes satiety by activating vagal afferent fibers either through a direct effect on afferent terminals or receptors or through an effect on smooth muscles that stimulate gastric receptors. By inference, this vagal mechanism is also activated by CCK released naturally when food stimulates the small intestine.

It is clear that more research is required in order to determine whether or not CCK is a satiety signal, in addition to the effective gastric signals. We may have here another example of the fact that the same behavioral effect is often achieved by multiple parallel mechanisms. As matters stand, we know of at least one set of neural signals that terminate feeding, and perhaps they are supplemented by a hormonal signal.

Now that we have considered the basic systems that regulate initiation and termination of eating in mammals, we summarize these systems in Figure 11-11.

Specific hungers and learning

Food preferences change, partly because of shifting bodily needs and partly because of learning. People and animals learn (at least part of the time) to eat foods that improve their health and to avoid foods that poison them.

Some bodily needs seem to elicit unlearned specific hungers. We saw earlier that female flies increase their intake of protein in preparation for each clutch of eggs they produce. If the adrenal glands of a rat are removed so that it cannot retain much sodium chloride, it promptly begins to consume salt. A similar craving for salt was reported by Wilkins and Richter (1940) in a classic case. A 3-and-a-half-year-old boy was brought to a hospital for examination because he showed marked development of secondary sexual characteristics. He refused most of the hospital diet and died suddenly one week after admission. Postmortem examination revealed an ab-

Figure 11-11 Basic systems that regulate feeding in a mammal.

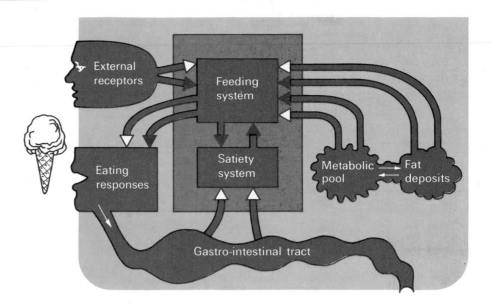

normality of the adrenal glands: The adrenal cells that produce gonadal hormones had overgrown and destroyed the cells that produce salt-regulating hormones. Inquiries then revealed that the boy had previously kept himself alive by eating great quantities of salt. He had refused foods that were not heavily salted, and "salt" was one of the first words he had learned. Many patients with Addison's disease, which involves destruction of the adrenal cortex, report a craving for salt; this craving can aid in early diagnosis of the disease.

Some substances that are important to health are not connected with specific hungers, but animals can learn to prefer foods that contain them. An example is thiamine (vitamin B). Rats made deficient in thiamine do not promptly recognize which of several available foods contains thiamine, but many of them will come, over a number of days, to prefer that food. A flavor that has been associated with recovery from thiamine deficiency comes to be preferred over other flavors (Zahorik, Maier, and Pies, 1974). This effect has been called the "medicine preference" effect.

The opposite effect is called "bait shyness" or taste aversion learning. If an animal eats a bit of a substance and then experiences a toxic effect, it will tend to avoid that substance in the future. Such learned aversions have been demonstrated in simple animals like slugs (Gelperin, 1975) and also in mammals, including people (Garb and Stunkard, 1976). It is not necessary that the ingested substance actually cause the toxic effect; if a harmless flavor is followed by injection of lithium chloride or by exposure to a high level of X-irradiation (both of which cause nausea), then a taste aversion is produced. For birds, visual cues (color or appearance of food) are more important than taste. Learning to avoid foods with negative consequences seems to occur very readily and strongly. It can occur in one trial and even if an interval of hours separates the experience of the flavor and the illness. It is reported to occur even if the toxic treatment is delivered while the animal is anesthetized, whereas other kinds of learning require wakefulness (Bureš and Burešová, 1981). Taste aversion learning in rats is impaired by damage to the gustatory region of the neocortex, the lateral hypothalamus, or the basolateral amygdala.

Obesity   Many people overeat and become obese, and some people abstain from food and become dangerously underweight. These facts test our knowledge of the processes of weight regulation and our capacity to use them effectively. We have seen that ventromedial hypothalamic brain lesions in people can give rise to hyperphagia and that lateral hypothalamic lesions can cause anorexia. So the animal lesion models help us to understand these cases. But we now know that many other lesions or transections in experimental animals can also cause disorders of weight control, and perhaps these have analogs in a variety of disease states in people. Beyond this, many obese or anorexic people do not show evidence of brain impairment, even on postmortem examinations. Perhaps the difficulties are more subtle, and some may require neurochemical rather than neuroanatomical analyses, as indicated by the finding of low CCK in the brains of obese mice. With control systems that are distributed at several levels of the nervous system and that include neurochemical and hormonal links, there are many possibilities for dysfunction.

The discrepancies between modern civilization and the conditions in which humankind evolved certainly contribute to obesity. Instead of scarcity of food and the need for exertion, we now have an abundance of rich, palatable food and very little need to exercise. Obese patients have been characterized as having the behavioral repertoire of a clever, carnivorous tiger and the continual access to food of a lucky, herbivorous cow. Yet even under these conditions many people manage to remain trim and fit. Why do these individual differences occur?

Externality: A basic cause of obesity?   A hypothesis that posits a single factor to account for a wide range of behaviors is always attractive, even though experience shows that most such hypotheses will not live up to their promise. An example of such a hypothesis is Schachter's (1968, 1971) external-internal distinction: Overweight people are hypothesized to be more responsive to external stimuli of all sorts than are their peers of average weight; they are also hypothesized to be less responsive to internal physiological cues that affect eating. This hypothesis became very popular and is said to have appeared in almost every introductory psychology textbook published in the last eight years (Rodin, 1981).

According to Schachter, the heightened susceptibility of obese individuals to external cues is evident in their spontaneous pattern of eating. For example, he reported that obese people, being more responsive to food, eat longer meals, but they also tend to eat fewer meals, presumably because when food is not present, they exert less effort to obtain it. In one often-cited experiment, individual overweight and normal-weight subjects performed a task and could eat cashews while they did so. When the cashews were prominent under a bright light, the overweight ate many more than when the nuts were under a dim light, whereas normal-weight subjects ate slightly less when the cashews were under the bright light. Schachter pointed out similarities between overweight people and rats with VMH lesions; among the similarities were the tendency to eat longer meals but to work less hard to obtain food than normal subjects.

In reviewing further research on this topic, Rodin (1980) concludes that most people, and not just the obese, are strongly influenced by external dietary stimuli and are poor at judging internal cues to nutritional need or satiety. Not all obese people are highly responsive to external cues; the most responsive tend to be the moderately obese. Nisbett (1972) has turned this observation around and suggested that dieting makes people more responsive to food; thus people whose set point for weight is high and who are trying to restrain their intake are the ones who are especially stimulated by the presence of food. Even the original observations have not been confirmed: ". . . a number of well-controlled studies of eating patterns both in the laboratory and in natural settings have documented that there is scant difference in the eating rates or styles of obese persons and those of normal weight adults" (Wilson, 1980, p. 326). Thus the attempt to attribute obesity to the single factor of relative sensitivity to external versus internal stimuli has proved oversimple. What we have learned about the many factors involved in control of food intake should have prepared us for this result.

Reducing the set-point for body weight

Earlier in this chapter we mentioned that many species typically go for weeks or months without eating and lose a great deal of weight. Could the same mechanisms be used by obese people? Do these animals become hungrier and hungrier as they abstain from eating, or do they show a progressive decrease in their set-point for body weight (Mrosovosky and Sherry, 1980)? For example, weight of the golden-mantled ground squirrel shows a regular annual cycle. Even ground squirrels that remain awake with food available during the winter lose weight, although not as much as squirrels that hibernate. When a squirrel emerges from hibernation and starts eating, it reaches the weight appropriate for the season rather than the higher weight at which it started hibernation. For another example, the female red junglefowl loses weight while it incubates its eggs. During this period it leaves the nest for less than 20 minutes per day. But even if food is made available at the nest, the junglefowl eats little and loses weight at the usual rate. If it is completely deprived of food for several days, however, the junglefowl then will eat more when food is restored and will regain the lower weight level that it was maintaining.

The neural mechanisms by which the set-points for body weight are modified are not yet known. An intriguing study has indicated hormonal control of weight regulation in the octopus (Wodinsky, 1977). The female octopus spawns only once in its life, eats less while caring for the eggs, and dies shortly after the eggs hatch. Removal of small endocrine glands in the optic lobes of the brain causes the octopus to stop caring for the eggs and to resume eating, and this operation greatly extends the lifespan. Mrosovosky and Sherry (1980) urge investigators to find natural physiological mechanisms for altering set-points. They hold out the possibility that such research might eventually make it possible for obese people to lose weight effortlessly even in the presence of palatable food.

Defense of body weight

Although adults differ greatly in their body weights, at any stage of life each person tends to keep his or her body weight quite constant. For this reason some investigators state that each person "defends" a set point or target value of body weight. People whose body weight had been reduced an average of 25% through a semi-starvation diet in an experiment, rapidly regained their predeprivation weight when allowed to eat as they pleased (Keys et al., 1950). In another experiment men who

BOX 11-2 Advantages of Obesity?

Is obesity a major American problem? The U.S. Public Health Service has estimated that 25–45% of the American population over 30 is "overweight" (1966). In a sample of Californians, 32% of the men and 46% of the women described themselves as "too heavy." Many medical and psychological disadvantages of being overweight have been asserted. Some investigators who study this topic, however, are urging a more skeptical and balanced view. Thus Fitzgerald (1981), a physician active in this area, has proposed the following iconoclastic views for consideration:

1. "Obesity, as we commonly use the term, may be more an aesthetic and moral problem than one of physical health." There certainly are medical problems associated with obesity, such as the increased mechanical burden of weight. But diagnoses of obesity are often made by eyeball, and Americans are inclined to judge themselves as overweight when people of some other culture would not. "What an American fashion model calls chubby, a Russian grandmother considers pathologically thin." Furthermore, some of the psychological stresses that are said to be associated with obesity may be culturally imposed.
2. "The therapy of obesity may be, in some circumstances, more morbid than fatness." For example, unnecessary dieting in people who are mildly to moderately fat may be life-threatening. Drug addiction has been (and perhaps still is) a major danger in the use of amphetamines to reduce weight. The therapy of obesity is costly and wasteful, since most weight reduction schemes fail.
3. "There may be some advantages, in medical and other senses, to being fat." For example, some studies indicate that fat people are more likely to survive various diseases, including tuberculosis and cancer. Obese people have a lower suicide rate than the nonobese.

For your consideration, here is Fitzgerald's conclusion concerning the possible selective advantages of obesity (1981, p. 228):

A well-adapted animal has the ability to store fat during periods of abundant food supply in preparation for the inevitable intervals of famine. . . . It may be, then, that the prevalence of obesity in the United States is due to the conjunction of millions of years of evolutionary thrust with a remarkable sufficiency of food available at minimal exertion. The fat may be the most highly evolved among us. And should food become scarce through natural disaster, war, or shortages of energy, the fat may be the most likely survivors.

were induced to consume a diet that contained up to 8000 calories per day increased their weights by 15 to 25%; when they were then permitted to eat normally, their weights quickly returned to the preexperimental level (Sims and Horton, 1968). These results are analogous to those we saw earlier in animal experiments (Figure 11-7).

Adjustments in the rate of energy expenditure play a significant role in maintaining the energy balance and in keeping body weight relatively constant (Keesey, 1980). The reductions and increases of food intake mentioned in the last paragraph did not lead to as rapid changes in body weight as might have been supposed. The subjects in the semistarvation experiment showed decreased activity and a drop of almost 30% in basal metabolic rate. Obese patients put on diets also decrease their metabolic rates and lose less weight than their reduced caloric intake would indicate. Overfeeding human subjects leads to increased muscular activity and to an elevated basal metabolic rate. Thus changes in energy expenditure compensate, in part, for changes in diet and help to maintain the person's normal or target body weight. This change in expenditure is probably a major reason why it is difficult to change the weight that a person has maintained for a long period and why changes that are achieved are likely to be short-lived.

Body weight is being defended, in another sense, by some current investigators who suggest that the problem of obesity has been exaggerated; see Box 11-2.

SUMMARY / MAIN POINTS

1. A relatively simple animal like the fly provides a model system for regulation of feeding. The fly is ready to eat whenever acceptable tastes or odors are encountered unless the relevant receptors are adapted or unless receptors in the gut signal fullness.

2. The ventromedial hypothalamus (VMH) used to be called the "satiety center" because its destruction can lead to overeating and obesity. But overeating occurs mainly during the dynamic phase of weight gain, and then weight stabilizes at a plateau. Also, weight gain occurs only if palatable food is available.

3. The lateral hypothalamus (LH) was called the "eating center" because its destruction causes aphagia and adipsia. However, if the animal is nursed through this stage, it may become able to regulate its food intake, although at a lowered target weight.

4. Some of the tracts that pass through the VMH or the LH account for some of the effects found when these regions are lesioned. But in general the functions of the tracts differ somewhat from the functions of the nuclei.

5. Other brain regions, such as the anterior neocortex and the amygdaloid nuclei, also contribute to control of feeding.

6. Stimulation-induced feeding occurs when electrical stimulation of the LH causes an animal promptly to begin eating available food even if it is satiated. The stimulated behavior is appropriate to the situation and is not simply forced motor movements.

7. Different brain sites have been found where stimulation elicits different motive states (hunger, thirst, copulation).

8. The feeding system is activated by signals that the body's food stores are falling below a set value. One such signal may be a low rate of glucose consumption, reflected in a low arterial-venous glucose difference.

9. Sensory information about the availability of food is needed along with internal signals if feeding is to be initiated. Sensory signals may also heighten motivation. Some cells in the hypothalamus respond specifically to the presence of food objects in the environment.

10. Termination of feeding is triggered by neural signals from the stomach and perhaps also by a hormonal signal—the release of the hormone cholecystokinin (CCK) when food reaches the duodenum.

11. Food preferences change, partly because of specific hungers and partly because of learning both to accept beneficial foods and to avoid foods that are accompanied by adverse consequences.

12. A popular hypothesis to explain obesity is that obese people are more sensitive to external stimuli and less responsive to internal physiological cues than are people of average weight. This hypothesis has been found to be oversimple, and some of the observations that appeared to support it have not proved to be repeatable.

13. Adjustments in the rate of energy expenditure play a significant role in maintaining the energy balance and in keeping body weight relatively constant.

RECOMMENDED READING

Novin, D., Wyrwicka, W., and Bray, G. A. (Eds.). *Hunger: Basic mechanisms and clinical implications*. New York: Raven Press, 1976.

Stunkard, A. J. (Ed.). *Obesity*. Philadelphia: Saunders, 1980.

Thompson, C. I. *Controls of eating*. Jamaica, New York: Spectrum, 1980.

12

Sleeping and Waking

Orientation

By the time we reach 60 years of age, most of us have spent 20 of those years asleep! However, some of us were awake for many of those 20 years; these are the few humans who survive without distress on just 2–4 hours of sleep per day. Among animals some sleep considerably more than humans (cats sleep about 12 hours a day), and some sleep much less (horses sleep about 2 hours a day).

Since sleep accounts for so large a slice of our lives and those of many other animals, it is quite surprising that the behavioral and biological features of sleep remained unstudied for so long. However, within the last twenty years sleep has become a major focus of investigation in physiological psychology. Attention has been directed to this issue for several reasons, and perhaps foremost among them is the recognition of the complexity of this state; sleep isn't simply nonwaking but rather the interlocking of elaborate cyclical processes, an alternation of different states. Further, the behavioral correlates of these different sleep states range from the suspension of thought to a galaxy of images and dreams. In this chapter we will discuss the characteristic patterns of sleep in human beings and other animals, the factors that influence sleep patterns, and the physiological events of sleep. We will look at mechanisms that might control the onset, duration, and alternation of sleep states. We will also consider some speculations about the biological role(s) of sleep—that is, why do we sleep? (We hope that not too many hedonists will raise the reverse question!) Hypotheses about the roles of dreaming will also be considered in the light of recent research.

Defining and describing human sleep

Sleep seems to be characterized by the absence of behavior; it is a period of inactivity with raised thresholds to arousal by external stimuli. For some animals we can add to this definition the feature of a distinctive reclining sleep posture, although this posture is less evident in hoofed mammals.

Sleep research gained momentum after the early 1960s, when experimenters found that brain potentials recorded from electrodes on the human scalp (EEG) provide a way to define and describe levels of arousal and states of sleep. What are the EEG criteria or distinctions defining different sleep states? The pattern of gross electrical activity in the fully awake, vigilant person appears as a desynchronized mixture of many frequencies dominated by waves of relatively fast frequencies [greater than 15–20 hertz (Hz)] and low amplitude. With relaxation and closing of the eyes a distinctive rhythm appears, consisting of a regular oscillation at a frequency of 9–12 Hz, known as the **alpha rhythm** (Figure 12-1a). It is particularly prominent in posterior scalp regions. As drowsiness sets in, the amplitude of the alpha rhythm decreases, and at some point it disappears and is replaced by much smaller-amplitude events of irregular frequencies (Figure 12-1b). This stage is called **stage 1 sleep;** during this period there is a slowing of heart rate and a reduction of muscle tension. Many subjects awakened during this stage would not acknowledge that they had been asleep, although they might have failed to respond to instructions or signals demanding action. This period usually lasts for several minutes and gives way to **stage 2 sleep,** which is defined by EEG events called spindles that occur in periodic bursts (Figure 12-1c). These are bursts of regular 14–18-Hz waves that progressively increase and then decrease in amplitude. Now our subject is quite unresponsive to the external environment, and under the closed eyelids the eyes begin to roll about in a slow, uncoordinated manner. In the early part of a night of sleep this stage leads to **stage 3 sleep,** which is defined by the appearance of spindles mixed with quite large-amplitude slow waves (about one per second) (Figure 12-1d). During this period the muscles continue to relax, and heart rate and respiration rate fall lower. **Stage 4 sleep,** which follows, is defined by a continuous train of high-amplitude slow waves (Figure 12-1e). Stages 1 through 4 are all classified as **slow-wave sleep.**

After one hour a person has probably progressed through these stages in the first period of sleep. The human sleeper then returns quite briefly to stage 2, and a transition to something totally different occurs. Quite abruptly, scalp recordings display a pattern of small-amplitude, fast activity similar in many ways to that of the aroused vigilant person, but tension in postural neck muscles has disappeared (Figure 12-1f). (Because of this seeming contradiction—the brain waves look awake but the musculature is deeply relaxed and unresponsive—one name for this state is **paradoxical sleep.**) Breathing and pulse rates become fast and quite irregular. The eyes now show rapid movements under the closed lids, so this stage is also referred to as **REM sleep,** or **rapid-eye-movement sleep.** A host of quite distinctive physiological changes now occur while our subject remains recumbent and, in terms of common behavioral descriptions, is decidedly asleep (see Table 12-1). Thus the EEG portrait shows that sleep consists of a sequence of states instead of just an "inactive" period.

Now let us consider the progression of these states through an ordinary night's sleep in humans, because the pattern changes somewhat during the course of the night.

Figure 12-1 EEG descriptions of sleep stages. Scalp-recorded EEG of a person during relaxed waking, stages 1, 2, 3, and 4 of slow-wave sleep and REM. The arrow in the stage 1 tracing points to a sharp wave called a vertex spike that appears during this period. The arrow in the stage 2 tracing points to a brief period of sleep spindles characteristic of this stage.

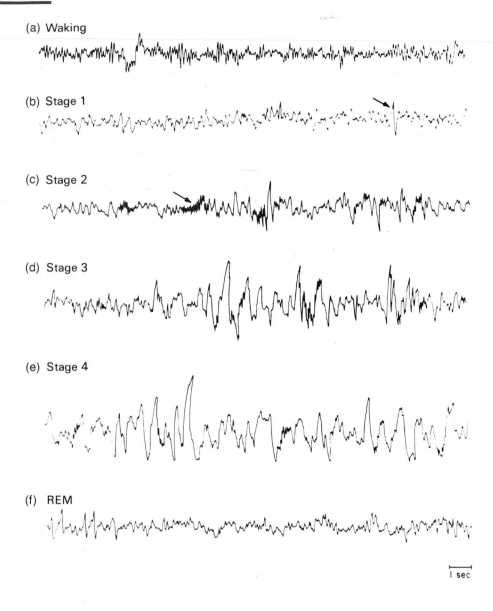

(a) Waking

(b) Stage 1

(c) Stage 2

(d) Stage 3

(e) Stage 4

(f) REM

1 sec

A night's sleep

By now, many subjects all around the world have displayed their sleep life to researchers in sleep laboratories. The bedroom the sleep subject walks into differs little from the usual sleep environment except for the presence of many wires. These lead to an adjacent room where machines record brain waves and experimenters stand by observing. The setting is aptly described by the title of a book by William C. Dement, a leading sleep researcher: *Some Must Sleep While Some Must Watch* (1974).

In this setting the subject goes to sleep in a usual way except that scalp electrodes are pasted in position on the scalp. In some studies cameras take pictures of changing body postures. Electrical recordings and behavior observation offer a portrait of a

TABLE 12-1   Properties of Slow-Wave and REM Sleep

	SLOW-WAVE	REM
Autonomic activities		
Heart rate	Slow decline	Variable with high bursts
Respiration	Slow decline	Variable with high bursts
Thermoregulation	Maintained	Impaired
Brain temperature	Decreased	Increased
Cerebral blood flow	Reduced	High
Skeletal muscular system		
Postural tonus	Progressively reduced	Eliminated
Knee jerk reflex	Normal	Suppressed
Phasic twitches	Reduced	Increased
Eye movements	Infrequent, slow, nonconjugate	Rapid, conjugate
Cognitive state	Vague thoughts	Vivid dreams, well organized
Hormone secretion		
Growth hormone secretion	High	Low
Neural firing rates		
Cerebral cortex	Many cells reduced and more phasic	Increased firing rates; tonic activity
Event-related potentials		
Sensory-evoked	Large	Reduced
Drug effects		
Antidepressants	Increased	Decreased

characteristic human sleep period. Although the onset, pattern, duration, and termination of sleep are affected by many variables, there is a regularity that allows a portrait to be drawn of the typical sleep state of adults.

Many different measures of the pattern of sleep can be obtained by scoring the several volumes of EEG records provided from a single night's observations. Incidentally, computer analysis techniques are permitting the development of automatic scoring and assessment of EEG records, although for the present most studies continue to rely on the human observers' page-by-page assessment of EEG signals. Typical measures of a night's sleep include total sleep time, duration and frequency of different sleep states, and measures of the sequencing of sleep states.

The total sleep time of young adults usually ranges from 7 to 8 h, and analysis of the distribution of sleep states shows that 45–50% of sleep is stage 2 sleep. REM sleep accounts for 25% of total sleep. An overall look at a graph of a typical night of adult human sleep (Figure 12-2) shows that repeating cycles of about 90–110 minutes (min) duration recur four or five times in a typical night. The components of these cycles change in a regular manner through the sleep period. Cycles early in the night are shorter and are characterized by greater amounts of stages 3 and 4 slow-wave sleep. The latter half of a typical night's sleep is usually virtually bereft of stages 3 and 4 slow-wave sleep. In contrast, REM sleep is typically more prominent in the later cycles of sleep. The first REM period is the shortest, some-

Figure 12-2 The course of a typical night's sleep in a young adult. (From Kales and Kales, 1970)

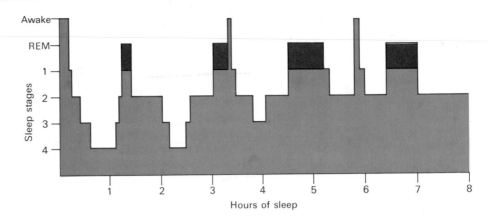

times lasting only 5–10 min, while the last REM period just before awaking can last as long as 40 min in normal adults.

Regularities of sequence are also evident in examining human sleep cycles. REM sleep is invariably preceded by stage 2 slow-wave sleep. Exceptions to this pattern are seen only with infants and with some cases of disturbed nervous system functioning. Brief arousals occasionally occur immediately after a REM period.

The sleep cycle of 90–110 min has been viewed by some researchers as the manifestation of a **basic rest-activity cycle** (Kleitman, 1969), and some have searched for cycles of similar duration during waking periods. For example, cycles of daydreaming during waking have an interval of approximately 100 min (Lavie and Kripke, 1981). Many other psychological and physiological properties show a 90–110 min cycle; these include eating and drinking, play behavior of children, heart rate, and the relative dominance of the cerebral hemispheres (D. B. Cohen, 1979).

Variations in the human pattern of sleep

The portrait of human sleep shows many variations. Some differences can be clearly related to maturational status, functional states like stress, impact of drugs, and many other external and internal states. Changes over the life span will be considered below. We should note that some departures from this "normal" state of human sleep can be quite marked. Newspapers and scientific journals have both made much of the unusual person who hardly sleeps at all. These cases are rare but are more than folktales. Dement (1974) reported that a Stanford University professor slept for only 3–4 h a night for over fifty years and died at age 80. Meddis (1979) verified by EEG recordings the claims of a healthy woman that she slept only an hour a night. It would appear, then, that some marked departures from the modal pattern can be seen in quite benign conditions.

Some differences in sleep characteristics may be related to variations in human personality. Hartmann (1978) has offered some controversial work that compared and contrasted groups of short sleepers and long sleepers. Both groups consisted of normal volunteers who viewed themselves as sleeping for either a shorter or a longer time than most other people. Each subject slept several days in a laboratory and completed personality inventories and detailed interviews. Recording confirmed the subjects' reports of their characteristic duration of sleep and revealed interesting differences among them. The principal difference between short sleepers and long sleepers is in the time spent in REM sleep. Long sleepers spend an average of 121 min per night in this state, compared with 65 min for short sleepers. Slow-wave sleep differences between these groups are less marked, suggesting a fairly constant requirement for this phase. Psychological profile differences reveal that the short sleepers tend to show greater sociability, less nervousness, and can be described as efficient, energetic, sociable, adroit, and optimistic about life. Long sleepers include many more individuals who show greater personal stresses and appear mildly depressed. Generally they seem more indecisive than short sleepers and would be regarded as worriers. Hartmann (1978) suggests that certain life styles, especially those that generate worried concern about the world, may require more sleep and that the long REM periods of this group reflect the importance of this state in psychological recovery processes.

Evolutionary-comparative perspectives: Sleep in different animals

EEG descriptions of sleep states let us make precise comparisons of different sleep stages in a variety of animals. To date this technique has resulted in the description of sleep in a wide assortment of mammals and, to a lesser extent, in reptiles, birds, and amphibians. Since animals differ widely in various measures of sleep (for example, total sleep time per day or average length of REM sleep), it is hoped that such comparisons may enable researchers to determine what factors control the timing and periodic properties of sleep. How does the adaptive niche of an animal influence the properties of sleep? Do predators sleep differently from animals that are commonly preyed upon? What kind of story about the evolution of sleep can we develop from the study of contemporary animals? How is the evolution of sleep behavior related to evolutionary changes in nervous system structure?

The amount of daily life occupied by sleep and the percentage of sleep devoted to paradoxical sleep for a variety of animals are listed in Table 12-2. Several comparative generalizations can be drawn from these and many other observations in the experimental literature. Among mammals, all that have been investigated thus far, with the exception of the echidna (spiny anteater), display both REM and slow-wave sleep. The spiny anteater is an egg-laying mammal that shows prolonged slow-wave sleep but no REM sleep. This creature is believed to have the oldest continuous history among current mammals. Its near rival for ancientness among existing mammals is the opossum, described by some sleep investigators as a "living fossil." The opposum (a marsupial—that is, an animal born at a very early developmental stage and spending a period of its development in a pouch) displays both slow-wave and REM sleep, with EEG characteristics that are not distinguishably different from placental mammals. The comparisons between these two ancient mammals have suggested to some investigators that slow-wave sleep developed first (echidna date to about 130 million years ago). Comparisons of brain anatomy between these mammals or between echidna and all others may provide useful information about the structural developments during evolution that enable REM sleep to occur.

Although some researchers regard REM sleep as a more recent evolutionary development, Meddis (1979) has offered an interesting argument to the contrary. He notes that cycles of two main stages of sleep (REM and slow-wave or, as he

TABLE 12-2   Comparisons of Sleep States in Various Mammals

| | STATES (% TIME/DAY) | | |
ANIMAL	Waking	Slow-Wave Sleep	REM Sleep
Cat	42.3	42.2	15.5
Fox	59.2	30.8	10.0
Dog (pointer)	66.2	30.0	3.0
Seal	55.7	33.5	10.7
Rabbit	50.0	48.0	2.0
Kangaroo rat	55.7	38.5	5.8
Rat	42.9	48.2	8.6
Cow	82.6	15.8	1.6
Opossum	19.2	76.7	4.1
Armadillo	28.0	59.0	13.0
Echidna	64.2	35.8	0
Squirrel monkey	17.0	59.3	22.9
Baboon	18.0	71.3	10.5
Human	60.6	32.8	6.6

SOURCE: From Rojas-Ramirez and Drucker-Colin (1977).

describes them, active sleep and quiet sleep) are seen only in animals that regulate their temperature physiologically, that is, endotherms. Many data show that temperature regulation during REM sleep is poor, and this result leads him to suggest that REM sleep might be derived from ectotherms, animals that could survive with less accurate temperature regulation. It would be disastrous for endotherms to remain in a state in which they could not regulate their temperatures closely. Meddis offers a solution to the danger posed by REM sleep: slow-wave or quiet sleep, during which temperature regulation functions well. Thus slow-wave, quiet sleep may have evolved to rescue endotherms from markedly changing body temperature. According to Meddis, small animals have short periods of REM and short sleep cycles precisely because, given their limited body mass, they are more vulnerable to temperature changes produced by surrounding environmental variations.

Several other generalizations have been derived from comparative studies of sleep. In general, hoofed animals (donkey, cow, horse) sleep much less than other mammals, although the immature hoofed animals may display appreciable amounts of both slow wave and REM sleep. Small animals have quite short epoch durations; an epoch is a period that consists of one episode of slow wave sleep and a following episode of REM sleep. For example, for the laboratory rat one sleep epoch lasts an average of 10–11 min, while for humans it lasts 90–110 min. This observation has contributed to the generalization that epoch duration is inversely related to metabolic rate (small animals tend to have high metabolic rates). But short epochs can also be caused by other demands. For example, dolphins must rise to breathe, so their periods of sleep are very brief. Some birds such as the swift and the sooty tern sleep briefly while gliding. The swift spends almost all its time in the air, except during the nesting season, and the sooty tern spends months flying or gliding above water, never alighting but catching fish at the surface.

Comparing the sleep of primates, we can see wide variations in temporal pattern, although the EEG waves look very similar and can be classified into the same stages of slow-wave and REM sleep. Stages 1 and 2 of slow-wave sleep predominate in the sleep of one primate, the baboon, which sleeps way out on the ends of smaller limbs of trees. Bert (1971) suggests that this location, which protects the baboon from predators, makes the total muscular relaxation of REM sleep more dangerous—the animal can fall out of the tree during REM sleep. Higher amounts of REM sleep are shown by the chimpanzee, which builds temporary nests on large branches.

Most of the studies of sleep have been done with animals confined to the unusual environment of a laboratory, and some critics have suggested that the constraints of such a setting might tend to minimize the distinctive features of sleep for particular species. However, while this criticism might feel right intuitively, attempts to assess this possible limitation of laboratory studies do not offer much support. In a comparison of patterns of primates in the laboratory and in the field, several investigators have failed to note significant differences.

One way of organizing current comparative work has been offered by Meddis (1975). He suggests comparing animal groups according to these main features of sleep:

1. A circadian distribution of rest and activity (see Box 12-1).
2. At least one long period of inactivity per day.
3. Increased arousal thresholds to external inputs during the period(s) of inactivity.
4. Slow waves and associated inactivity.
5. REM sleep epochs.
6. Species-typical sleep niches and a typical body position during sleep.

All vertebrates show a circadian distribution with a prolonged phase of inactivity, raised thresholds to external stimuli, and a characteristic posture during inactivity. In comparisons of various vertebrate classes, REM sleep is found in mammals, birds, and reptiles but not in monotremes, amphibia, or fish. Slow waves and associated sleep are evident only in mammals, birds, and monotremes.

Developmental perspectives: Life span and sleep

In any mammal the characteristics of sleep-waking cycles change during the course of life. These changes are most evident during early development, although the infant EEG in many species cannot be classified in precisely the same manner as that of an adult animal. In fact, the characteristic EEG picture of different stages of slow wave sleep is not evident until age 5–6 in humans. At this age EEG data can be classified into stages just like adult EEG data. Infant behavior related to EEG findings enable researchers to distinguish between quiet sleep (similar to slow-wave sleep) and active sleep (similar to REM sleep). This distinction is drawn by differences in responses, such as muscle twitches, eye movements, respiration, and heart rate. Quiet sleep of infants is characterized by slower EEG, strong sucking, and irregular respiration. Active sleep is defined by the presence of phasic increases in respiration accompanying bursts of eye movements, very low amplitude EEG, facial grimacing, and occasional smiles. Let us look at the changing sleep patterns over the life span.

Sleep: Infancy through adulthood

Infants of virtually all mammalian species show larger amounts of total daily sleep than adults of the same species. They also show large percentages of REM or paradoxical sleep. For example, Figure 12-3 shows that in humans within the first

Figure 12-3 Changes in sleep with age in humans. (From Roffwarg, Muzio, and Dement, 1966)

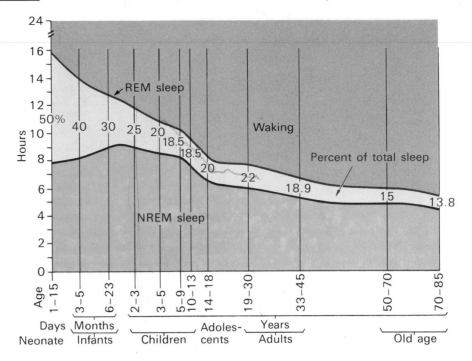

two weeks of life, 50% of sleep is REM. Unlike normal adults, human infants can move directly from an awake state to REM sleep. This feature is also evident in infant cats and rats.

A clear cycle of sleeping and waking takes several weeks to become established in human infants. The establishment of a distinct 24-h rhythm is illustrated for an infant in Figure 12-4. It is generally evident by 16 weeks of age. A further feature distinguishing infant from adult sleep is the number of changes of state and their average duration. Infant sleep is characterized by frequent state changes of shorter average duration than those seen in adulthood.

These features of the sleep of infants are attributable to the relative immaturity of the brain. This assertion can be demonstrated in several ways. First, premature human infants show even greater amounts of total sleep than full-term children. Second, some animals born in an advanced state of development (precocial animals), such as the guinea pig, show much less marked sleep pattern changes with aging.

The sleep patterns of mentally retarded children are different from normal children (Petre-Quadens, 1972). This difference is evident in both the qualitative properties of sleep states (for example, retarded children show fewer eye movements during sleep) and the quantitative properties (for example, many retarded subjects show reduced amounts of REM sleep). Sleep EEG recordings at birth might be useful in identifying some suspected retarded children and facilitate early therapeutic intervention, especially in forms of mental retardation without biochemical or anatomical indicants.

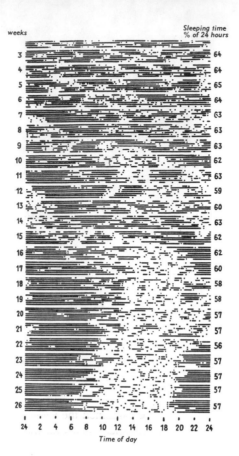

Figure 12-4 Development of circadian rhythm in the sleep-activity patterns during early infancy. On this kind of chart, for each day the dark portions indicate time asleep and the blank portions, time awake. (From Kleitman and Engelmann, 1953)

Sleep in the aged   In older age the parameters of sleep change more slowly than in early development. Table 12-3 lists some differences among adolescence, middle age, and old age. A decline in the total amount of sleep is evident, as is an increase in the number of arousals during a night's sleep. In the very elderly insomnia (which may be partially

TABLE 12-3   Comparisons of Sleep of Adolescence, Middle Age, and Old Age

SLEEP VARIABLE	13–15 YEARS Mean	S.D.	41–46 YEARS Mean	S.D.	60–69 YEARS Mean	S.D.
Total sleep time (min)	489.85	12.02	376.65	35.68	388.36	26.12
No. of sleep stages	46.50	7.98	44.25	10.03	50.98	5.46
No. of awakenings	4.40	2.88	6.50	2.53	9.38	2.94
REM period length (min)	30.26	4.25	21.18	6.84	19.45	5.58
Percent stage 0	1.16	1.00	6.22	5.29	10.20	4.57
Percent stage 1	3.79	1.66	5.95	2.23	12.11	4.46
Percent stage REM	26.97	2.77	21.88	4.28	21.33	4.37
Percent stage 2	43.92	5.22	50.76	11.72	51.49	7.46
Percent stage 3	6.05	2.55	7.19	2.78	3.73	2.93
Percent stage 4	18.10	3.81	7.99	10.49	1.14	2.37
Percent REM in first third of night	8.56	4.46	20.15	8.69	22.50	8.68
Percent REM in last third of night	53.14	8.03	39.01	11.46	39.37	9.40

confounded by daytime naps) is a common complaint (Miles and Dement, 1980). The most dramatic progressive decline is in stages 3 and 4 sleep—their amounts at age 60 are only 55% of what they are at age 20. The decline of amounts of stages 3 and 4 sleep in the aged is partly related to diminished cognitive capabilities at this age. This feature is emphasized by the marked reduction of stages 3 and 4 sleep in aged humans who show senile dementia.

What are the functional implications of these changes in sleep over the life span? The preponderance of REM sleep early in life led some investigators to suggest that this state provides some stimulation that is essential to the maturation of the nervous system. This hypothesis has not been developed in any detail and may confront some difficulties. For example, REM activity would appear to be rather random, and at an intuitive level an argument can be offered that patterned stimulation is an important developmental consideration. Another hypothesis is that REM sleep is important for consolidation of long-term memories. Since infancy is a time when much learning is taking place, this hypothesis may account for the large amount of REM sleep early in life. Other theoretical views suggest that the progressive changes in sleep states reflect comparable changes in the rate of development of information-processing capabilities. However, this assertion fails to establish close links of a causal nature between these parallel developments. The story of development and sleep is an intriguing but unfinished one.

Factors that affect onset and duration of sleep

Many studies have examined the impact of different environmental stimuli, social influences, and biological states on the pattern and temporal properties of sleep. From one viewpoint, sleep is an amazingly stable state. Major changes in the characteristics of waking behavior have only minor impact on subsequent sleep. For example, exercise before sleep seems to produce a shortening of the latency to the onset of the first sleep episode but has no impact on any other sleep parameter. Even social arrangements during sleep seem to have little impact. For example, Leiman and Aldrich in unpublished observations compared a sleeping-alone condition in cats with a condition of sleep with a more dominant or more submissive animal. During waking, dominance was strongly displayed by hissing and striking. However, continuous recording of waking and sleeping states revealed no significant impact on timing or pattern of sleep in either animal.

There are some conditions that can be manipulated by experimenters that do produce major shifts in sleep measures. These conditions are especially interesting because they reveal properties of sleep that give insight to its underlying mechanisms. We will examine some of these conditions in this section.

Sleep deprivation

All of us at one time or another have been willing or not-so-willing participants in informal sleep deprivation experiments. Thus we are all aware of some of the effects of partial or total sleep deprivation. Notably, it makes us sleepy! Why then do researchers examine the consequences of short- or long-term deprivation? A burst of sadism, perhaps? Or is sleep deprivation a way to explore some of the potential regulatory mechanisms of sleeping and waking? In general, the latter sentiment has guided the experimental investigation of deprivation as a factor affecting sleep-waking cycles. The majority of studies in this area have been concerned with the phenomenon of sleep recovery. Does a sleep-deprived organism "keep track" of the

BOX 12-1   Circadian Rhythms

When you walk through a meadow at night, you share this area with many little rodents that leave their burrows with the arrival of darkness. By day these nocturnal animals are replaced by other animals, especially large mammals. There seems to be a basic rhythm of "taking turns," typical of species. More formally this rhythm is described as resource partitioning; diurnal or daytime animals use daytime periods for obtaining food, and nocturnal animals are adapted for satisfying the demands of active life during dark periods.

Most animals show behavioral, biochemical, and physiological variability throughout the course of a typical day. These changes of state are not random fluctuations; they are rhythmic, and some changes have a clocklike regularity. Many fluctuations have a 24-h period, and these are known as **circadian rhythms** (from the Latin roots "circa," meaning "about," and "dies," meaning "day"). There are many regularly occurring changes in bodily and behavioral states that are shorter than 24 h and others, like seasonal rhythms, that are much longer.

Circadian rhythms are valuable because they synchronize behavior and bodily states to changes in the environment. Light and dark fluctuations during the course of a single day have significance for survival. Picture the small nocturnal rodent who can avoid many predators during the day by remaining hidden but moves about hurriedly in the darkened night.

Many examples of circadian rhythm (reviewed by Rusak and Zucker, 1979) can be seen in the behavior of all animals. The sleep-waking cycle is the most prominent example of a circadian process. Temperature fluctuations also closely follow a regular 24-h rhythm, and many endocrine secretions are modulated by this kind of cycle.

What are the origins of the timing for this rhythm? Most researchers argue, with strong evidence, that the timing of circadian rhythms is provided by endogenous events—that there are biological clocks that time a single day. These clocks are probably found at many levels of biological organization, since both isolated cells and intact whole animals show circadian rhythms. They can be described as endogenous timekeeping mechanisms that measure about 24 h. Although the rhythm of such clocks is difficult to change, environmental influences, particularly light, can synchronize a circadian rhythm. Such synchronizers are called "zeitgebers" (German for "time givers").

Light can entrain rhythms to a period of either more or less than 24 h, although there are limits to entrainability. At the low end is a 21-h day and at the high end, a 27-h day (Box Figure 12-1). The pathways involving light entrainment of circadian rhythms diverge from the visual pathways mediating perceptual responses. For example, a retinal-hypothalamic pathway may be a significant part of the visual networks that control light entrainment (Box Figure 12-2).

Where in the nervous system are these circadian rhythms generated? This question is difficult to answer decisively, but studies involving assessments of the effects of brain lesions offer some possibilities. Damage to a small region of the hypothalamus—the suprachiasmatic nucleus—obliterates activity rhythms in hamsters, as illustrated in Box Figure 12-3 (Rusak, 1977; Stephan and Zucker, 1974). Furthermore, lesions of this area also affect sleep rhythms and various circadian neuroendocrine responses. This lesion produces a breakup of the basic circadian rhythm, with some much shorter cycles evident in lesioned animals. Such rhythm splitting might indicate that the suprachiasmatic nucleus is important in coupling together many other shorter rhythms to produce a longer circadian period.

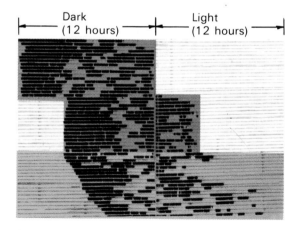

Box Figure 12-1   Light entrainment of activity rhythms (wheel running) in hamster. Dark blue indicates the period of darkness and light blue indicates continuous light. (From Zucker, 1976, based on Rusak, 1975)

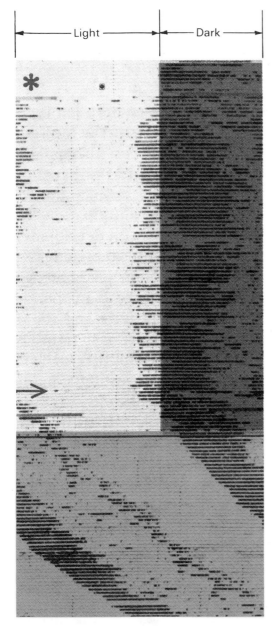

Box Figure 12-2 Effects of destruction of optic tract (indicated by arrow) on activity rhythms. Dark blue indicates the period of darkness and light blue indicates continuous light. (From Zucker, 1976, based on Rusak, 1975)

Box Figure 12-3 Effects of lesions of suprachiasmatic nucleus on activity rhythms in hamster. Dark blue indicates the period of darkness and light blue indicates continuous light. (From Zucker, 1976, based on Rusak, 1975)

amounts and type of lost sleep? And when the organism is given the opportunity to compensate, is recovery partial or complete? Can you pay off sleep debts? How many days of recovery sleep are necessary for any kind of compensation?

● **Disturbances during sleep deprivation**   Another interest in sleep deprivation has drawn the attention of psychiatric researchers: Early reports in the sleep deprivation literature emphasized a similarity between instances of "bizarre" behavior provoked by sleep deprivation and features of psychosis, particularly schizophrenia. Partial or total sleep deprivation has been examined by these investigators in the hopes that it may illuminate some aspects of the genesis of psychotic behavior. A frequent emphasis in this work has been the functional role of dreams as a "guardian of sanity," partially inspired by early reports that REM deprivation can produce unusual emotional consequences that can be enduring. Tests of this hypothesis employing schizophrenic patients do not seem to confirm this view. For example, these patients can show sleep-waking cycles similar to nonpatients, and sleep deprivation does not exacerbate symptoms.

The behavioral effects of prolonged total sleep deprivation vary appreciably and may depend on some general personality factors and age. In several studies employing quite prolonged total deprivation—205 h or 8 to 9 days—some subjects showed occasional episodes of hallucinations. Only rarely is a psychotic state provoked by sleep deprivation in excess of 100 h. The most common behavior changes noted in these experiments are increases in irritability, difficulty in concentrating, and episodes of disorientation. During each deprivation day the effects are more prominent in the morning; by late afternoon and early evening the subjects seem much less affected by the accumulating sleep loss. The subject's ability to perform tasks is best described in a quote from a review by L. C. Johnson (1969, p. 216): "His performance is like a motor that after much use misfires, runs normally for a while, then falters again." Tasks that elicit strong motivation and are brief in duration may show almost no impairment, even with prolonged sleep deprivation.

EEG effects during the course of sleep deprivation are particularly evident in measures of alpha rhythm—there is a progressive decline in the prominence of alpha rhythm. The EEG of these subjects takes on an appearance resembling stage 1 sleep, although the subjects move about. There is abundant evidence that sleep deprivation can provoke EEG and behavioral signs similar to those of people with seizure disorders.

● **Compensation for lost sleep**   Many studies have been concerned with a possible compensation for sleep loss following total or partial sleep deprivation. To illustrate the recovery process in humans, Table 12-4 provides data about 264 h (11 days) of sleep deprivation in a young man. No evidence of a psychotic state was noted, and the incentive for this unusually long act was simply the young man's curiosity. This study was reported in scientific journals in 1966, and the self-appointed subject received considerable publicity at the time. Researchers got into the act only after the subject started his deprivation schedule, which is the reason for the absence of predeprivation sleep data. Nevertheless, these effects are comparable to many other data (although this subject appears to be the record holder for intentional sleep deprivation).

In the first recovery night (column 1 of Table 12-4), stage 4 sleep shows the greatest relative difference from normal. This increase in stage 4 sleep is usually at

TABLE 12-4 Recovery of Sleep After Eleven Days (264 h) of Total Sleep Deprivation

	RECOVERY SLEEP SESSIONS MIN/STAGE/NIGHT OF SLEEP: %/STAGE/NIGHT IN PARENTHESES			POSTRECOVERY SLEEP		
Stages	1	2	3	1 Week	6 Weeks	10 Weeks
Awake	0	0	11	15	33	16
	(0)	(0)	(2.02)	(3.54)	(8.57)	(4.0)
1	1	3	1	6	36	22
	(0.11)	(0.5)	(0.18)	(1.42)	(9.31)	(6.0)
2	397	258	224	255	183	227
	(45.2)	(41.3)	(41.4)	(60.1)	(47.13)	(58.0)
3	133	109	98	57	46	39
	(15.1)	(17.4)	(17.9)	(13.3)	(11.86)	(10.0)
4	113	67	60	18	34	12
	(12.8)	(10.7)	(11.0)	(4.24)	(8.85)	(3.0)
REM	236	188	152	73	56	75
	(26.8)	(30.1)	(27.8)	(17.4)	(13.64)	(19.0)
Total sleep (min)	880	625	543	424	388	391

SOURCE: From Gulevich, Dement, and Johnson (1966).

the expense of stage 2 sleep. However, the rise in stage 4 sleep during recovery does not completely make up for the deficit accumulated over the deprivation period. In fact, it is no more than reported for deprivation periods half as long. REM sleep with prolonged sleep deprivation shows its greatest recovery during the second postdeprivation night. The REM debt comes closer to being paid off, although it probably takes longer (that is, requires more recovery nights).

There have been many experiments with humans and other animals involving the "repayment of sleep debts." The experiments of the early 1970s dealing with this feature primarily involved rather short-term deprivation effects. These studies involved either total deprivation or, more usually, REM deprivation. The latter condition was achieved by forceful awakening of a subject whenever EEG signs of REM sleep appeared. These short-run, early-REM deprivation studies generally showed that in postdeprivation recovery sessions subjects made up for the loss of REM sleep in the form of longer-duration REM episodes. With longer-duration REM deprivation this debt is paid off somewhat differently. In these instances recovery in terms of number of hours of REM sleep is not complete, but other forms of REM recovery become evident. For example, the loss of tension of postural muscles (for example, neck muscles), which is part of the signature of REM sleep, may appear in slow-wave sleep following prolonged deprivation. Thus the usual properties of REM sleep may be reallocated to other stages of sleep. This phenomenon has been observed in both humans and cats.

Recovery sessions may also involve another form of compensation. Several studies have noted that recovery night REM sleep is more "intense" than predeprivation REM episodes. Intensity in these experiments is evidenced by the number of rapid eye movements per period of time. Less consistent results have been obtained by using the arousal thresholds to either a sensory stimulus (such as a tone or buzzer) or direct stimulation of brain regions. Several investigators have noted that thresholds on REM recovery nights are higher than those of predeprivation REM sessions.

These observations show that recovery REM sleep is somewhat dissimilar from usual REM sleep.

There is some evidence that the REM compensation phenomenon is particularly sensitive to the deprivation of the phasic events generally characteristic of this stage (for example, rapid eye movements). The pertinent data were derived from experiments with cats. One group of animals was totally deprived of REM sleep for two days, while another group was awakened for two days when phasic events occurred in either slow-wave sleep or REM sleep. The duration of these events in the slow-wave sleep of cats is rather trivial (1–2 min per sleep epoch). The rebound of REM sleep was greater in cats deprived of phasic events.

Many aspects of compensation following sleep deprivation remain to be explored. In recent years difficulties with experimentation in this area and the confounding effects of stress induced by deprivation have limited research interest, although many important questions have not yet been resolved.

Effects of drugs on sleep processes

Throughout recorded history humans have reached for substances that could enhance the prospects of sleep. Both sleep onset and maintenance have been aided by elixirs, potions, and, more recently, drugs. Early civilizations discovered substances in the plant world that induced sleep (Hartmann, 1978). Ancient Greeks used the juice of the poppy to obtain opium. Greek medicinals also included products of the mandrake tree, which we recognize today as scopolamine and atropine. Elixirs that combined the products of various plants provided sleep for many people until the birth of sleep pharmacology, which started with the synthesis of morphine from opium at the beginning of the nineteenth century. The preparation of barbituric acid in the mid-nineteenth century by the discoverer of aspirin, Adolph von Bayer, provided the basis for the development of an enormous number of substances—barbiturates that continue to be used for sleep dysfunctions.

Many chemicals that are not common sleeping pills can have consequences for sleep. Indeed, there are some suggestions in the clinical and experimental literature that drugs employed to control or ameliorate particular diseases may, through the roundabout route of modifying sleep, compromise their effectiveness. For example, the intense cardiovascular activation characteristic of REM sleep can be dangerous for heart disease patients. If drugs employed in the treatment of such diseases promote the likelihood of REM sleep, the vulnerability of the individual may, quite paradoxically, be increased.

The assessment of drug effects on sleep is beset with methodological difficulties. In the usual experiment some substance is administered to a subject and the sleep pattern is measured. Many studies clearly show that the effects of certain substances generally regarded as sleep inducers depend on both dosage and whether the assessment is made during a single night or over an extended period of time. The mode in which the drug is withdrawn also influences rebound or postdrug effects. As our knowledge of some of the underlying neurochemical events increases, some of the variability of results may become more understandable. One final critical note: Many assessments of the effects of drugs on sleep use normal young subjects who do not have apparent sleep disorders or complaints. Perhaps the use of such subjects limits the range of phenomena that could be examined. To provide an analogy: If you were

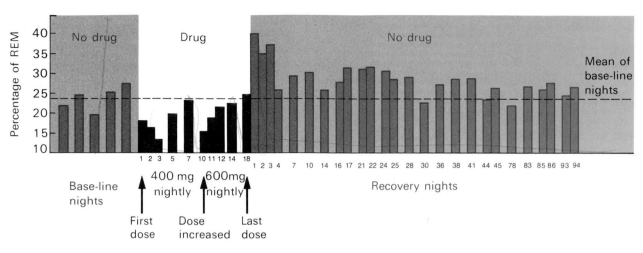

Figure 12-5 Rebound of REM following a period of use of barbiturates to promote sleep. (From Oswald and Priest, 1965)

interested in the antitubercular properties of some drugs, it is highly unlikely that you would assess this substance with subjects who show no signs of tuberculosis. There's simply no possibility of seeing a change in state since the tubercular state was not there in the first place.

One of mankind's oldest and simplest drugs is alcohol. Its effects on sleep seem to be typical of a larger class of "depressant" substances. That is, a relatively moderate dosage (comparable to two shots of whiskey within an hour) depresses REM sleep time. With continued consumption at this level over successive days, REM sleep recovers, and no effect is observable within three to five days. This result has suggested to some investigators that alcohol and similar drugs (such as barbiturates like those commonly used as sleeping pills) activate a REM compensation mechanism. Some data pertinent to this belief have been obtained from alcoholics during a withdrawal period. Following the cessation of alcohol intake, REM is markedly suppressed by the third day (which is also the period of maximum likelihood of delirium tremors in alcoholics). Then REM sleep becomes elevated for several days and again goes through a phase of suppression and recovery. A persistent REM rebound effect after stopping the use of barbiturates is illustrated in Figure 12-5.

Marked suppression of REM sleep occurs with administration of antidepressant drugs (or "pep pills"). Amphetamine addicts may show a virtually complete absence of REM sleep during the period of use of this drug. Following cessation of drug use, rebound REM sleep in some cases may amount to 75% of the night's sleep and may occur as a rapid sleep onset phenomenon, unlike the normal case of a latency of 40 to 90 min. The preponderance of REM in the withdrawal sleep of amphetamine addicts may be related to the terrifying dreams they have during withdrawal from amphetamines. In a later section we note that some other antidepressants inhibit REM sleep, but no subsequent rebound is evident.

A relation is evident between drug dependency and REM sleep. Substances that produce REM suppression and rebound are drugs that also cause dependency. In contrast, drugs that produce suppression without rebound do not lead to dependency.

Some investigators (such as Hartman, 1973) speculate that the physiological activities elicited by this second class of substances might replace the need for REM sleep. This class of drugs includes those used as antidepressants, such as monoamine oxidase inhibitors.

A 1979 report of a presidential commission has examined national reliance on and abuse of sleeping pills. They note that at least three-quarters of all prescriptions are written for sleep problems; very few of us have never taken medication to induce or maintain sleep. Viewed solely as a way to deal with sleep problems, current drugs fall far short of being a suitable remedy for several reasons. First, continual use of sleep medication results in a loss of the sleep-inducing property of these substances. Declining ability to induce sleep frequently leads to increased dosages that are self-prescribed and pose a health hazard. A second major drawback in the use of sleeping pills is that they produce marked changes in the pattern of sleep, both during the period of drug use and for a following period that may last for days. Most commonly during the initial phase of drug use a reduction of REM sleep occurs, especially during the first half of a night's sleep. A gradual adaptation to drug use is evident in the return of REM sleep with continued use of sleeping pills. Sudden withdrawal of many types of sleeping pill results in a period of REM rebound with an intensity that many people experience as unpleasant and may lead to a return to reliance on sleeping pills. A final major problem in the frequent use of sleeping pills is the impact of these drugs on waking behavior. A persistent "sleep drunkardness" coupled with drowsiness, even with intense efforts at maintaining vigilance, impair productive activities during waking hours.

These problems in the use of sleep drugs have led to other biochemical approaches to sleep disorders. Primary among these is the attempt to promote increases in the concentration and release of neurotransmitters that may be involved in some aspect of sleep induction. Hartmann (1978) has emphasized serotonin as an important transmitter in this process. Serotonin levels in the brain can be strongly influenced by the administration of tryptophan, which is a precursor in the synthesis of serotonin. Human studies by Hartmann (1978) show that low doses of the precursor under double-blind conditions reduced sleep latency without changing the basic pattern of sleep. This observation in normal subjects has been confirmed in a population with mild insomnia. Further promise for this substance is shown by the absence of long-term tolerance effects and the absence of daytime effects on vigilance. More extensive clinical trials are urged by Hartmann. Meanwhile, grandmother's suggestion to take a glass of warm milk before sleep isn't too far away from current neurobiological insights, since milk is a good source of tryptophan.

Circadian rhythms and sleep

Most of us are accustomed to a single period of sleep enjoyed over an interval starting late in the day and lasting until morning. The onset and termination of sleep seem synchronized to many external events, including light and dark periods determined by the earth's rotations. What happens to sleep when all the customary synchronizing or entrainment stimuli are removed, including changes of light or temperature? One way to get away from such stimuli is to find deep caves and to spend weeks in this setting. Several experiments on sleep patterns in caves have been performed in which all cues to external time have been removed. Under such

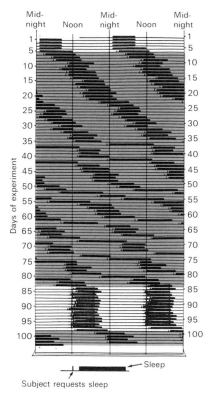

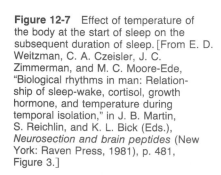

Figure 12-6 Sleep–waking pattern of a subject during periods of isolation from cues about the time of day. During these periods (indicated by blue shading) the subject drifts away from a 24-h day. (From Weitzman et al., 1981)

conditions a circadian rhythm of sleep-waking remains evident, although the biological clock slowly shifts away from 24 to 25 h. Some individuals adopt much longer days, lasting up to 35 h.

A systematic study of sleep rhythms in humans under isolated conditions has recently been offered by Weitzman and collaborators (1981). Their subjects, ten adult men, spent 25–105 days individually in a small apartment totally free of time cues. A subject could go to sleep and awaken any time he desired; however, this sleep interval had to be the regular sleep period since naps were not allowed. Several physiological measurements were recorded, including body temperature and circulating hormone levels. EEGs were also recorded during these sleep periods. Unlike the subjects of cave experiments, these subjects had direct social contact with laboratory workers.

Under these conditions all subjects showed a sleep-waking rhythm that was longer than 24 h (Figure 12-6). Three subjects adopted a "day" that ranged between 24.4 and 26.2 h. However, three subjects had periods greater than 37 h. These subjects demonstrated that some circadian rhythms can become uncoupled from each other, since the subjects continued to show a 24-h temperature rhythm. This latter group of subjects had some sleep periods that were short (less than 10 h) and others that lasted as long as 20 h. Whether these episodes were long or short was related to the 24-h temperature rhythm. Short sleep episodes began when body temperature was at its lowest level, while long sleep episodes began while body temperature was at its peak (Figure 12-7). Some changes in the distribution of sleep states were also seen in the experiment. For example, REM sleep occurred earlier during the sleep period, although its total percentage of sleep time remained the same. REM sleep also showed a specific time relation to body temperature, so the basic REM rhythm is not locked under these conditions to slow-wave sleep. These data show that sleep-waking rhythms are connected to oscillations in the brain that time other biological rhythms.

Figure 12-7 Effect of temperature of the body at the start of sleep on the subsequent duration of sleep. [From E. D. Weitzman, C. A. Czeisler, J. C. Zimmerman, and M. C. Moore-Ede, "Biological rhythms in man: Relationship of sleep-wake, cortisol, growth hormone, and temperature during temporal isolation," in J. B. Martin, S. Reichlin, and K. L. Bick (Eds.), *Neurosection and brain peptides* (New York: Raven Press, 1981), p. 481, Figure 3.]

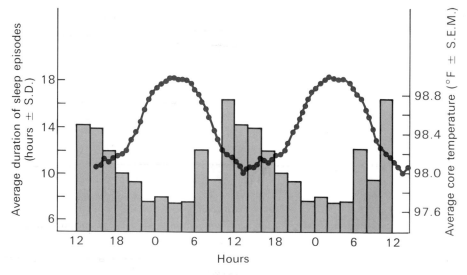

Psychological aspects of sleep states

By this point we can see that sleep is not analogous to switching off a motor. Rather it consists of different stages, and many brain cells continue to be active, although in different modes. Since the brain continues to be active, it is reasonable to inquire about the properties of mental activity during sleep. This work has focused on dreams, learning, and thresholds of arousal to external stimulation, subjects that we will consider next.

Mental experiences during sleep: The world of dreams

One of the most exciting aspects of contemporary work in the psychobiology of sleep has been the active examination of the properties of thinking and imagery during various stages of sleep. In a typical experiment the EEG is recorded and the subject is awakened at particular stages—stages 1, 2, 3, 4, and REM—and questioned about thoughts or percepts immediately prior to awakening.

Until recent years the data strongly indicated that dreams were largely restricted to REM sleep. Studies during the early 1960s commonly showed that subjects reported dreams between 70% and 90% of the times that they were awakened in this stage—in contrast to an incidence of 10% to 15% for non-REM sleep periods. Indeed, at first it was thought that the rapid eye movements characteristic of this period were related to "viewing" dream scenes! In other words, if your dream was one of viewing a ping-pong match, your eyes would reveal that rapid to-and-fro movement of real life observations of such a match. This scanning theory of eye movements during REM dreams now seems unlikely, particularly since there are many differences between the characteristics of eye movements during actual viewing of scenes and those of REM sleep.

Many studies have been concerned with dream reports after subjects were awakened from different states of sleep. Quite consistent across all these studies is a large percentage of dream reports on awakening from REM sleep. However, some investigators have increasingly questioned whether REM is the sole sleep state associated with dreams. Thus current studies have been directed at attempting to distinguish between the qualitative features of slow-wave and REM dreams. These data show that the dream reports of REM sleep are characterized by visual dream imagery, whereas the dream reports of slow-wave sleep are of a more "thinking" type. REM dreams are apt to include a story that involves odd perceptual experiences and the sense that "you are there" experiencing sights, sounds, smells, and acts. During such a dream these events seem real. Slow-wave dreams, on the other hand, are characterized more as thoughts than sights. Subjects awakened from this state report thinking about problems rather than seeing themselves in a stage presentation. Cartwright (1978) has shown that the dreams of these two states are so different that judges can indicate the sleep state in which a dream occurred with 90% accuracy. Furthermore, awakenings from REM sleep result in more frequent reports of dreams than arousals from slow-wave sleep.

Studies of the content of dreams, especially during REM sleep, suggest that dreams during the first half of sleep are oriented toward reality. Details of these dreams show an incorporation of the day's experience, and the sequence of events is ordinary. In contrast, dreams during the second half of sleep become more unusual and less readily connected with the day's events. The sequence of events and the content of dreams become more emotionally intense and bizarre. The emotional quality of REM dreams may also reflect clinical variables, as indicated in sleep studies of depression. Dreams of depressed patients during the depths of this state are emotionally bland, with very reduced activity and mood.

Views about the functional role of dreams venture into a very ancient and persistent riddle which is not likely to be answered by currently available experimental approaches. In the history of humans, dreams have been viewed in many different lights. Van de Castle (1971) provides some interesting illustrations from primitive societies around the world. For example, Cuna Indians off the coast of Panama viewed dreams as predictors of imminent disaster, and their dream "analysts" had a variety of objects to ward off both dreams and their presumed consequences. For instance, a tomahawk-like object was used to treat dreams of thunder and lightning. (These dreams were probably hypnagogic hallucinations—vivid sensory experiences reported by many normal humans that may occur at the start of sleep.) Primitive cultures placed great emphasis on the truthfulness of dreams. Perhaps this view continues in the arguments of some contemporary investigators who believe that dreams are important in resolving problems.

For some, dreams are considered as an innocent by-product of basic bodily restorative processes and have no significance by themselves. From this perspective there is no way to accomplish the biological role of sleep without the "accidental" provocation of dreams, since certain regions of the brainstem produce phasic activity of neurons that affects the visual cortex. This activity may excite visual cortical neurons to produce the perceptual elements of a dream. These random bursts are made more coherent by the cognitive activity of the dreamer. However, dreams per se, although reflecting personal attributes, may have little functional role.

At the other end of the spectrum is the perspective that emphasizes dimensions like "wish fulfillment" and the problem-solving role of these nightly adventures. For many individuals sleep without the ability to recollect these interludes is unsatisfactory sleep. Whether this response reflects acquired tastes for dreams or provides a hint about their functional role(s) is yet another problem for contemporary and future investigators.

Learning and sleep

Every now and then we are confronted with newspaper reports and advertisements that herald some new technique or gadget that will enable us to learn something during sleep and remember it afterward. The appeal of such possibilities is overwhelming to some, including those who begrudgingly accept sleep as a necessary interference with the pursuit of knowledge and those who sport the fantasy that information can be transmitted by a deep embrace of a book. More seriously, sleep is obviously a living state in which many neurons are active; can we learn during this state? Also, do the learning experiences of a day influence the pattern of a night's sleep? Some researchers have suggested a relationship between REM sleep and the establishment of permanent memory. Others have suggested that REM sleep may serve as a kind of filter of the day's experiences.

Some things that happen during the course of a typical day are important for adaptive success, while others are trivial, repetitive events. Metabolic processes involved in establishing memory are "expensive" (as you will see in Chapter 15), and it might be that sleep serves to consolidate some of the day's events. Experiments in this area have examined whether sleep influences the effectiveness of subsequent learning. Further studies have looked at the effects of sleep deprivation—either selective or total—on learning. Additional questions in the study of sleep-learning connections are concerned with the effectiveness of retention when sleep occurs following learning. (Many students participating in the ritual of cramming for exams can provide personal data for this question.) Let us look at some of the experimental evidence.

● **Learning during sleep**   This controversial area has been beset with many conflicting claims. And about the only overall conclusion one can confidently draw from a large range of studies is that if you are relying on information acquisition and retention during sleep, you had best find a backup system. Although several nonhuman experiments indicate that a simple conditioned response can be acquired during various sleep stages, evidence for people learning verbal materials is generally negative. We will consider one experimental example. Two investigators, Tani and Yoshii (1970), asked whether a simple form of verbal associative learning could occur during sleep. Pairs of words were read to subjects of one group during sleep; then the subject was awakened and checked to see if he could provide the associate to a single word of the pair. The task was readily accomplished by a separate control group given the test during an awake state. Some form of learning was evident in the sleep group only when the word pair transiently caused the subject to go from a sleep state to one characterized by alpha rhythms. Those with a persistent EEG pattern of sleep showed no evidence of learning. Under no condition of sleep, ranging from stage 1 to REM, was learning possible if an alpha kind of alertness was not provoked. Thus verbal learning occurred only if the stimulation awakened the subject, at least briefly.

Some forms of learning less complicated than that of the previous example are possible in both humans and other animals, as shown by habituation experiments—experiments in which a stimulus is repeated without consequence over some period of time. For example, if a sudden loud sound is presented during slow-wave sleep, the subject—human or cat—will show EEG signs of arousal. Repetition of the stimulus becomes less likely to produce arousal. In some sense this response is not sleep learning since arousal is produced. However, this phenomenon indicates that the novelty of a stimulus can be detected in the sleeping state.

Another aspect of learning during sleep focuses on internally generated information. Common experience indicates that sleep includes episodes of cognitive and perceptual events that range from the mundane to the quite unusual. This is the stuff of dreams. Laboratory studies of dreams show that the mental life of sleep is quite active. These studies also show that memory for such events is quite fragmentary. No amount of therapy, drugs, cajolery, or whatever unearths much of the information generated by internal processes during sleep.

Formal studies of this phenomenon have involved waking subjects at varying intervals following the end of a REM episode. Many of those awakened within the first few minutes of the end of a REM episode report dreaming experiences. However, those subjects awakened 5 min after the end of a REM period have no recollection for the events of a REM period (Dement, 1974). It appears that no permanent memory traces are established for the cognitive and perceptual events of the REM episodes. An exception occurs if the dreamer awakens briefly just after the dream. (It is not always true, as psychoanalysts have hypothesized, that dreams protect us from awakening.) If waking occurs soon after a dream, then the dream may be recalled the next day.

It is probably beneficial that most dreams are never stored in long-term memory, since it would pose difficulties to store permanent traces of events that may not be accurate descriptions of a person's experience. Perhaps one of the roles of the slow-wave sleep that follows REM episodes is to provide the neural condition that precludes lasting storage of the events of REM periods.

● **Effects of sleep on long-term memory**   In 1924 Jenkins and Dallenbach reported an experiment that continues to provoke research. They trained subjects in a verbal learning task at bedtime and tested them 8 h later on arising; they also trained the subjects early in the day and tested them 8 h later. The results showed better retention when a period of sleep occurred between a learning period and tests of recall.

What accounts for such an effect? Several differing psychological explanations have been offered. One suggests that during the waking period intervening between learning and recall, diverse experiences interfere with accurate recall. Sleep during this interval appreciably reduces the range of interfering stimulation. A second explanation notes that memory tends to decay and that this relentless process simply occurs more slowly during sleep. This is a passive process. A third explanation ties more directly to an emphasis on a positive functional contribution of sleep to learning. This view says that sleep includes processes that consolidate the learning of waking periods. Sleep is then seen as providing the conditions for a firm "printing" of enduring memory traces.

Recent experiments by Ekstrand and collaborators (1977) add complexity to the original Jenkins and Dallenbach observations. In one experiment they compared the magnitude of memory loss in three groups, all of whom learned lists of paired associates. Group 1 learned a list in the evening and was tested for retention after an interval of 8 h of no sleep; group 2 slept for half the night, was then awakened, learned the list, and allowed 4 h of sleep before retention testing; group 3 learned the list of paired associates, slept 4 h, and was then awakened and tested for retention. Group 2 showed the best recall. The experimenters' interpretation is that slow-wave sleep favors retention, but other interpretations are possible.

Other studies of sleep and learning have examined the importance of REM sleep for the consolidation of memory—that is, the transfer of memories from some short-term storage system to a permanent form. Some experiments investigate this idea by depriving an animal of REM sleep after a learning session and determining the resultant price of sleep deprivation on retention or acquisition of some response. For example, the sequence of steps in such an experiment might proceed like this: (1) train animals; (2) deprive them of REM sleep; (3) test retention; (4) allow sleep recovery; (5) test retention again. This experimental paradigm shows consistent memory impairment as a consequence of REM deprivation (McGrath and Cohen, 1978).

Other experiments (Bloch, 1976) have shown that when animals receive training the percentage of REM sleep increases in subsequent periods of sleep. If learning

Figure 12-8 Amounts of REM sleep and learning in rats: Sleep is recorded after learning sessions. (From Bloch, 1976)

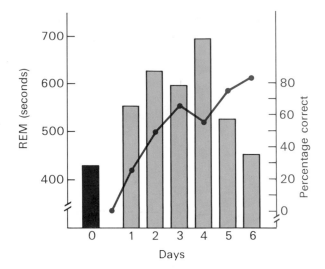

extends over several days, the increase in REM sleep is largest during the steepest part of the learning curve (Figure 12-8). Thus the day's activities affect the night's sleep.

Sleep and arousal thresholds

The ease of waking an individual depends on many factors and especially on the stage of sleep. Variations in arousal thresholds suggest that sleep states differ in depth. A common way to assess this depth is to examine differences in stimulus intensity needed to awaken an individual in different sleep states. For example, stimuli are presented at different points in slow-wave or REM sleep, and the difference in the depth of these sleep states is measured by either the duration or the intensity of the stimulus needed to produce EEG signs of arousal.

Early studies with animal subjects seemed to show that arousal became more difficult during the progression from slow-wave to REM sleep. This result implied that REM periods are those of greatest depth of sleep. Further refinements in these studies (Wright and Leiman, 1971) showed that arousal thresholds during REM sleep are not homogeneous. Arousal thresholds are higher during REM periods of frequent eye movements (Price and Kreinen, 1980).

Arousal from sleep also depends on the relevance of the stimulus. In a classical demonstration Oswald (1962) showed that the threshold of waking is lowest for the oral presentation of one's own name in contrast to other names. This stimulus preference is lost when these names are played backward from a tape recorder, so it is the meaning of the name and not just the acoustical stimulation that is important.

Neurobiological aspects of sleep states

During the course of sleep many nervous and hormonal functions are dramatically modified. Some of these changes have strong implications for hypotheses about the presumed restorative role of sleep. In this section we will discuss some of the major physiological modifications that occur during sleep.

Neural and motor changes during sleep

During sleep physiological changes are evident in many systems. In the autonomic nervous system such functions as heart rate, blood pressure, and respiration show progressive declines during slow-wave sleep but marked increases in REM sleep (Figure 12-9). During REM sleep cerebral blood flow increases in some areas, which provides another example of the increased metabolic demands of REM.

For virtually all animals sleep means the absence of activity of the skeletal musculature. How does the motor system become quiescent? This feature is especially puzzling since at the same time much of the brain is quite active. This contrast implies that motor pathways become reversibly uncoupled from the rest of the brain. Another motor system puzzle is the unusual episodic activity in nonpostural muscles during REM sleep—the rapid eye movements and sudden twitches of fingers, hands, and other muscle groups.

During the course of slow-wave sleep there is a reduction in monosynaptic and polysynaptic spinal reflexes. With REM sleep these reflexes are virtually abolished, resulting in profound loss of muscle tone. Some of this motor decrement depends on descending influences from the brain to the spinal cord, since reflex depression

Figure 12-9 Some comparisons of the physiology of slow-wave and REM sleep. During REM sleep (indicated by blue shading) blood pressure rises and respiration and pulse rate become variable, but there are few body movements. (From Snyder et al., 1964)

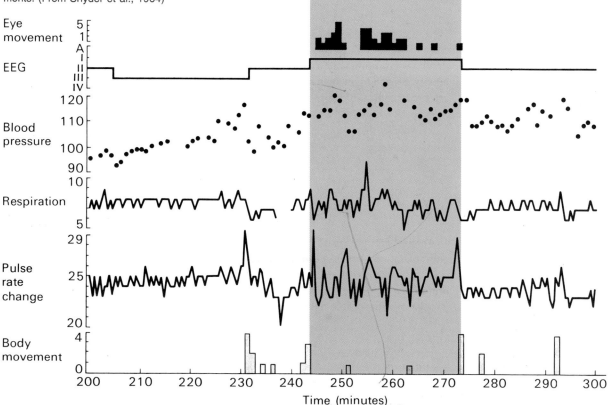

Figure 12-10 PGO spikes recorded
from the lateral geniculate of a sleeping
cat during an REM episode. (A. L. Leiman)

(a) NREM sleep

(b) REM sleep

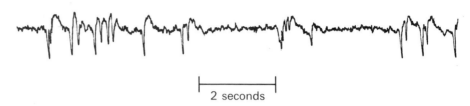

|———————|
2 seconds

during sleep does not occur with spinal transection. Direct production of inhibitory
postsynaptic potentials on spinal motoneurons during sleep has been recorded in
cats. The usual loss of muscle tone during sleep can be abolished by lesions in the
pons, suggesting a role for this region in producing motor uncoupling during sleep,
especially REM sleep.

A brain potential correlated with phasic motor events can be seen during REM
sleep in recordings at the level of the pons, the lateral geniculate nucleus, and the
occipital cortex; these potentials are called "PGO spikes" (pons, geniculate, occipital). Their occurrence during a period of slow-wave and REM sleep is shown in
Figure 12-10. In cats they appear 1–2 min before the onset of REM sleep and continue in bursts throughout the period of REM sleep. Studies of the origins of PGO
spikes by Morrison (1979) reveal that they are controlled by distinct brainstem
regions. He believes that PGO spikes are masked during slow-wave sleep but can
be provoked during waking and REM sleep; he also believes that they represent the
brain's response to novel or alerting stimulation. The role of the PGO spikes during
REM sleep remains unknown, but Morrison suggests that the brain is functioning as
though it were presented with intense barrages of novel stimulation.

Some views of the function of sleep emphasize that this state is important in
providing a period of restoration following the demands of a prolonged waking
period. From this viewpoint we would expect nerve cells of sensory and motor
regions to show reduced firing rates during sleep. Studies of single nerve cells in the
cerebral cortex reveal something different from this expectation, though. Some
nerve cells actually increase their firing rates during sleep. This emphasizes that the
brain does not stop working during sleep.

Hormones and sleep   Hormonal relations to sleep have been explored from two different perspectives.
First, some studies have examined whether the release of particular hormones is
especially prominent during sleep and related to particular sleep states. This work
has mainly involved the pituitary growth hormone. Second, a larger group of
investigations have looked at the effects of hormones on sleep states. This work was
instigated when researchers found differences between males and females in various
measures of sleep processes.

Daily rhythms are apparent in the secretion of hormones, including various pituitary hormones like growth hormone, thyroid-stimulating hormone, and follicle-stimulating hormone. A specific link to sleep processes has been established for the pituitary growth hormone. (Recall Box 5-1 on psychosocial dwarfism.) This hormone, in addition to being involved in growth processes, also participates in mechanisms governing the metabolism of proteins and carbohydrates. Several studies, which involved taking samples of human blood throughout the day, have shown that the highest concentrations of growth hormone in blood are evident at night. Blood plasma levels of growth hormone show a rise after the start of sleep. The direct tie to sleep is shown by observations that if sleep is advanced or delayed, the rise in blood plasma levels of growth hormone follows the onset of sleep, even if this involves a complete inversion of the day's schedule (Figure 12-11). More detailed examinations of the relation to sleep stages have shown that release is related to

Figure 12-11 Growth hormone secretion during a 24-hour period. Increases in the rate of secretion are seen during the early phase of sleep. (From Takahashi, 1979)

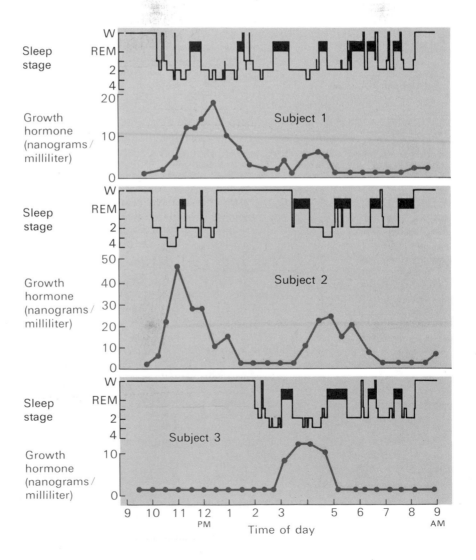

slow-wave sleep and particularly to stages 3 and 4. The exact nature of sleep control or regulation remains to be explored. For instance, is slow-wave sleep the exclusive causal condition for growth hormone release? How these events are synchronized also remains to be determined.

Hormones involved in pituitary-adrenal relations also seem related in a comparable manner to sleep, in this case especially to REM sleep. Recall that the anterior pituitary is controlled by the hypothalamus and releases a hormone, adrenocorticotropin (ACTH), which stimulates the adrenal cortex to release glucocorticoids. The latter substances are referred to as stress hormones, partially because of the conditions for their release and their anti-inflammatory actions. One class of these substances released by the adrenal cortex, 17-hydroxycorticosteroids, reaches a peak level in the blood of humans during a late phase of sleep, 4 to 6 A.M. In one study peak level appeared in spurts, with rises occurring after REM onset. Many other observations point to the sleep dependency of this response, as opposed to a circadian effect; that is, there was evidence of a continued relation to REM sleep when days were made artificially long or short.

Neural mechanisms of sleep

Any complete theory of nervous system mechanisms that control sleep must explain the following basic questions:

1. Why and how does sleep start?
2. What accounts for the periodic properties of this state, including the daily sleep-arousal cycle and the timing of successive episodes of slow-wave and REM.
3. What stops a prolonged period of sleep?

Various hypotheses, guesses, and conjectures have been offered by workers in this field, but there is still no comprehensive theory that successfully deals with these major questions. We will explore a variety of hypotheses. Some of them appear increasingly plausible; others, however tantalizing, still yearn for confirmation. Particular hypotheses treat only limited aspects of the broad phenomena of sleep. Some hypotheses are exclusively anatomical, dealing with neural circuits of sleep, whereas others are neurochemical.

Two alternative conditions that might govern the onset of sleep have been posited:

1. Sleep starts because the mechanisms promoting waking simply run down from a period of use. From this perspective sleep occurs as a passive process.
2. Sleep starts because the mechanisms promoting waking are actively inhibited. From this perspective sleep occurs as a result of the buildup of activity in an inhibitory center (or centers) whose output is directed to waking centers.

This distinction between active and passive processes has deeply influenced thinking in this area, with the passive view being dominant until quite recently. To develop some perspective on current views of active mechanisms, let us review briefly the progression of research and theories since the 1930s.

Sleep as a passive phenomenon

In the late 1930s the Belgian neurophysiologist Frédéric Bremer performed some experiments that became the foundation of passive views of sleep onset and maintenance. In one group of cats he examined cortical electrical activity after the brain-

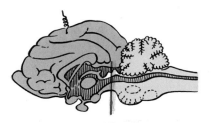

(a) cerveau isolé

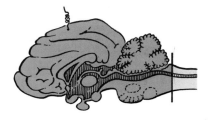

(b) encephale isolé

Figure 12-12 The levels of brain section in encéphale isolé and cerveau isolé preparations.

stem was isolated from the spinal cord by a cut below the medulla. This physiological preparation he called an **encéphale isolé** (isolated brain); see Figure 12-12. These animals showed EEG signs of waking and sleeping. During EEG-defined wakeful periods the pupils were dilated and the eyes followed moving objects. During EEG-defined sleep the pupils were small, as is characteristic of normal sleep. (It should be noted that Bremer did not distinguish between slow-wave and REM sleep; this distinction was not discovered until the 1950s. By sleep Bremer meant slow-wave sleep.)

In another group of animals he examined cortical electrical activity following a cut at the upper level of the midbrain (between the inferior and superior colliculi). This preparation was called the **cerveau isolé** (isolated forebrain). These animals displayed persistent EEG sleep patterns with no instance of wakefulness, either in terms of the EEG or pupil size and eye movements. These data were, at the time, interpreted to mean that sleep starts and is maintained by the loss of sensory input, a state of **deafferentation.** The cerveau isolé animals showed no signs of wakefulness, according to this interpretation, because transecting the upper brainstem reduced the normal flow of afferent input, which, according to this view, is a prerequisite for the waking condition.

Sleep as an inhibition of waking

In the late 1940s Bremer's experiments were reinterpreted on the basis of experiments involving electrical stimulation of an extensive region of the brainstem known as the **reticular formation** (Figure 12-13). The reticular formation consists of a diffuse group of cells whose axons and dendrites course in many directions, extending from the medulla through the thalamus. Moruzzi and Magoun, two scientists prominent in the study of the role of the reticular formation, found that they could awaken sleeping animals by electrical stimulation of the reticular formation; the animals showed rapid arousal. Lesions of these regions produced persistent sleep in the animals, although this phenomenon was not observed if the lesions interrupted only the sensory pathways in the brainstem. This latter observation led to new views about the phenomena displayed in Bremer's experiments. The effects noted by Bremer were now interpreted as arising from interference from a waking or activating system within the brainstem. This mechanism remained intact in the encéphale isolé animal, but its output was precluded from reaching the cortex in the cerveau isolé animal. This "reticular formation" school argued that waking results from activity of brainstem reticular formation systems and that sleep results from the passive decline of activity in this system.

This conclusion started a long series of continuing experiments concerned with factors that control the excitability of the waking mechanisms of the reticular formation. Current views emphasize the importance of midbrain and pontine portions of the reticular formation in the maintenance of arousal, although there may be other processes involving more extensive regions that also mediate the maintenance of arousal.

Many influences seem to exert a dampening effect on the brainstem mechanisms of arousal. These include blood pressure, receptor afferent inputs, deactivation influences from the cerebral cortex, and influences from caudal regions of the brainstem. The existence of a caudal brainstem mechanism that can inhibit rostral activating mechanisms was shown in experiments in which sections were made between these two systems. Animals subjected to this treatment display persistent signs of wakefulness, suggesting that there is a dampening effect on the upper levels of the reticular formation from caudal regions. Stimulation of this caudal brainstem region also inhibits motor systems.

Defining the circuits for the inhibition of arousal mechanisms is complicated by experiments showing that several regions can exert quite similar controls over activating systems. Jouvet (1967) emphasized particularly a system of neurons coursing in the midline of the brainstem, called the **raphe nucleus.** These neurons contain the substance serotonin, which is considered to be a synaptic transmitter. We will consider this region in more detail below when we consider a broad theory by Jouvet. Other regions that have been implicated in the onset and maintenance of sleep, particularly slow-wave sleep, include portions of the medial thalamus, whose stimulation can produce sleep behavior in cats. Similar results have been observed by excitation of a group of forebrain regions, including the anterior hypothalamus. The integration of these various regions, in terms of a more defined circuit that depicts the forms of interaction in these diverse systems, has yet to be accomplished. For the moment it looks as though many regions of the brain are capable of controlling or modulating sleep induction. Perhaps all of them function by deactivating arousal mechanisms, although this assertion is not conclusively proved at this point.

Neurochemical controls of sleep and waking

Some of the apparent complexity of circuitry relevant to sleep-waking control has led, in recent years, to an approach that has emphasized a neurochemical perspective. One inspiration for this approach is derived from classical experiments and their contemporary relatives. Many years ago it was thought that sleep might result from the accumulation in the brain and body of a sleep-producing substance, a "hypnogen." The existence of such a substance was suggested by the experiments of Piéron in 1910. Piéron showed that the injection of cerebrospinal fluid from fatigued dogs into rested animals resulted in sleep in the rested animals. This basic kind of experiment has been done in many ways since that time, including injections of filtered blood derived from animals in which sleep was induced by thalamic stimulation. A "humoral" factor in body fluids has also been implicated in experiments with animals whose circulatory systems have been linked together (parabiotic rats). These experiments show that such linkages produce considerable similarity in the sleep patterns of the two animals only when some blood exchange is possible. The latter point is particularly important, since some critics have pointed out that human "Siamese" twins may not sleep at the same time. That observation may not be significant in the assessment of humoral theories since many forms of Siamese twins in humans do not involve the sharing of vascular systems but rather the joining of bone or connective tissue, which would provide minimal opportunity for exchange of fluids.

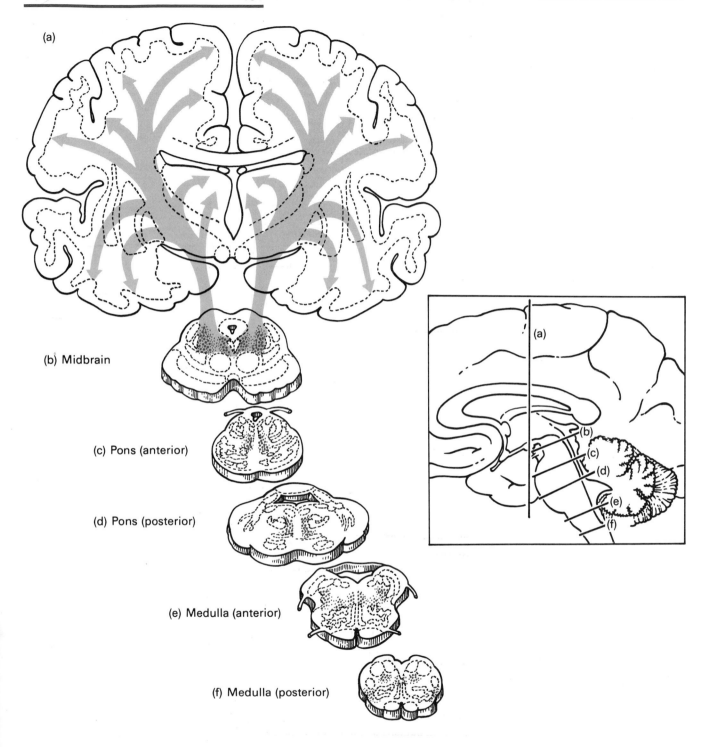

Figure 12-13 Location of the reticular formation in different levels of the brainstem. The diagram to the right shows the levels of the separated sections on the left.

How do such humoral effects arise? One possible answer to this question brings us closer to a consideration of synaptic transmitter systems. This answer suggests that humoral effects might derive from transmitter substances themselves, that is, from metabolites that are delivered in small quantities to the vascular system from the brain regions in which they are released. This conjecture has directed attention to the organization of various transmitter substances within the brainstem. Intensive work in this area during the past five years has resulted in a rather complete portrait of the types of transmitters and their locations in the brainstem. Almost all the serotonin of the brain is made by the cells of the raphe nucleus. A large concentration of norepinephrine is found in the cells of the brainstem region called the **locus coeruleus.** The knowledge thus gained about the neuroanatomy and neurochemistry of these synaptic transmitters has led to a comprehensive theory by Michel Jouvet (1972, 1977), which we will now consider.

Jouvet proposes that slow-wave sleep is initiated by the release of serotonin from the cells of the anterior nucleus of the raphe (Figure 12-14). These neurons inhibit waking systems, particularly those involving two other brainstem regions, the substantia nigra and locus coeruleus. There is considerable neuropharmacological evidence that links serotonin to slow-wave sleep. Injections of a substance called PCPA, which reduces the level of serotonin, can produce insomnia in cats. In these animals raising the level of serotonin by injections of a precursor substance can result in the return of slow-wave sleep. Furthermore, circadian variations in the concentration of serotonin have been reported to be closely related to activity cycles in rats.

How does REM sleep come about in this scheme? Jouvet argues that the serotonin-containing neurons of the caudal raphe nucleus prime REM sleep. These neurons send terminals to the locus coeruleus and initiate the onset of REM sleep as a function of the rate at which the serotonin that promotes slow-wave sleep is released. As the level of serotonin diminishes with slow-wave sleep, the caudal raphe initiates REM sleep at the level of the locus coeruleus. The locus coeruleus controls the phenomena of REM sleep, including tonic inhibition of skeletal muscle activity and production of rapid eye movements. The inhibition of skeletal muscle activity is controlled by caudal regions of the locus coeruleus, and stimulation of extraocular muscles is controlled by its medial portions. The neurons of these regions employ norepinephrine as the synaptic transmitter. Thus the alternation of slow-wave sleep and paradoxical sleep results from the interaction of these two regions. Waking occurs when the norepinephrine-containing neurons of the anterior locus coeruleus tonically inhibit the anterior raphe nucleus.

To summarize this position: Sleep is caused by the tonic inhibition of a norepinephrine and dopamine waking system by the serotonin-containing neurons of the raphe nucleus. Waking is caused by tonic inhibition of the serotonin-containing system by the norepinephrine-containing neurons of the anterior locus coeruleus. The alternation between slow-wave and REM sleep involves interactions between the raphe and the locus coerulcus.

While this formulation encompasses many observations, newer data challenge it. Recent evidence provided by Mouret and Coindet (1980) shows that lesions of the raphe nucleus in rats do not affect daily amounts of REM and slow-wave sleep. Furthermore, in some animals, nearby lesions in other structures change amounts of REM and slow-wave sleep.

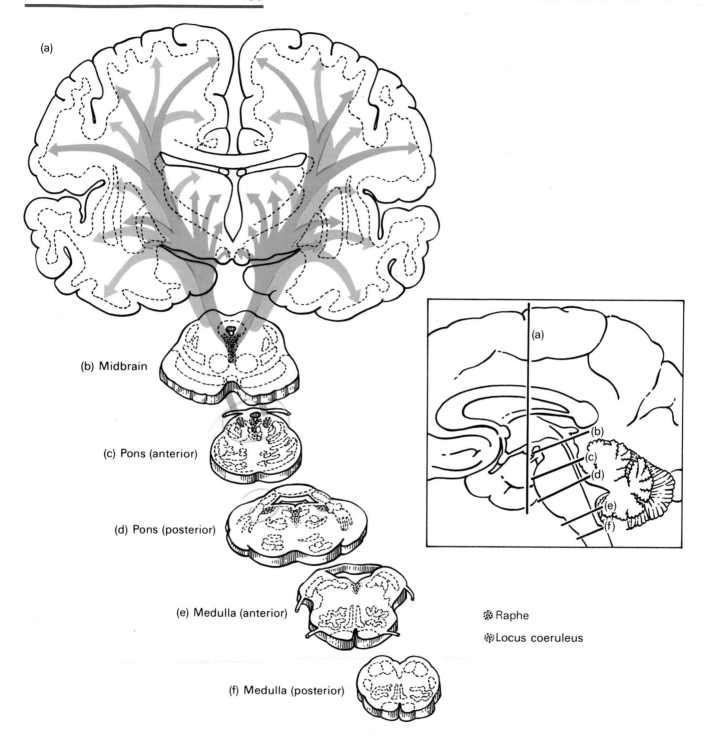

Figure 12-14 The location of the raphe nucleus and locus coeruleus in the brainstem.

Biological functions of sleep

Why do most of us spend one-third of our lifetime asleep? However comforting that figure is to some of us, it magnifies the significance of questions about the biological role of sleep. The mystery is deepened by the existence of two dissimilar states of sleep with distinct physiological attributes.

Inquiries about the functions served by sleep are many, and our discussion emphasizes the major ideas. We should note that these proposed functions or biological roles of sleep are not mutually exclusive. There may be many roles served by sleep, and the list may include virtually all the suggestions offered in this section.

However profound the hypotheses and speculations about the functions of sleep, we must recognize that none is proved as yet. Furthermore, no theory has explained the phenomena of people who get along with little sleep or the occasional rare case of a patient who goes for months without sleep and nevertheless shows apparently normal intellect and personality. (Such a patient is described in Box 12-2.)

Sleep conserves energy

Diminished energy expenditure is a property of an appreciable portion of sleep periods. For example, reduced muscular tension, lowered heart rate, reduced blood pressure, and slower respiration all occur during sleep. Reduced metabolic processes are also related to the characteristic lowered body temperature of sleep. These many indications of diminished metabolic activity during sleep suggest that one role of sleep might be to conserve energy. From this perspective sleep enforces the cessation of ongoing activities and thus ensures rest; it is a state of diminished metabolic requirements.

The importance of this function can be seen by looking at the world from the perspective of small animals. These animals have very high metabolic rates, and activity for them is metabolically expensive. It is very easy for demand to outstrip supply in these animals. And periods of reduced activity can be especially valuable if they occur when food is less likely to be located and secured. Some support for this view can be seen in comparative sleep data, which reveal a high correlation between total amount of sleep per day and waking metabolic rate. Some problems for this view become apparent, however, when we remember that at least part of sleep is characterized by intense metabolic expenditure, such as the phasic events of REM sleep and similar events during a short period of slow-wave sleep.

Sleep aids predator avoidance

The natural world has a large cast of characters who frequently interact in awkward ways. Notably, some kinds of animals eat other kinds. Intense evolutionary pressures have generated a variety of tactics for avoiding predators. Some researchers have suggested that the stratagems of biological adaptation directly involve sleep. Meddis (1975) suggests that the immobility of sleep enhances survival. For some animals this immobility lessens the likelihood of encountering potential predators. In this manner, sleep can provide the device that leads to effective sharing of some ecological niche—survival without becoming a meal.

This possible functional role for sleep is underscored by some speculations about a distinct contribution of REM sleep. Snyder (1969) used the term "sentinel" hypothesis to explain a REM function as a periodic quasi arousal that enabled the animal to assess possible danger. Recurrent REM sleep is then a protective device against

BOX 12-2 Four Months without Sleep

Rare cases have been described in which patients with encephalitis stop sleeping completely. In a recent case the lack of sleep for at least four months was verified by EEG recordings (Fisher-Perroudon, Mouret, and Jouvet, 1974). The patient, Monsieur M., was hospitalized in January 1970 with a syndrome that included a mild temperature, fibrillation (fine trembling) of the muscles, rapid heartbeat, pain in the extremities, and itching. He also reported total lack of sleep and nighttime hallucinations. EEG recordings showed that over several successive nights the mean total sleep time was only 26 min. Nor did the patient sleep during the daytime; telemetry recordings during several successive days showed an average of only 35 min of sleep, and that small amount was stage 1 sleep.

Intellectual performance and personality seemed normal during the ten months of hospitalization. M. was cooperative and showed normal intelligence, attention, and memory. Personality test results were also normal, although M. was somewhat depressive. The lack of impairment of intellectual capacity and of personality is in striking contrast to people who are deprived of sleep for several days in a row. So, too, was M.'s inability to sleep even when lying on a bed in the dark, whereas subjects in sleep deprivation experiments have to stay on their feet and receive constant stimulation in order to stay awake.

About the only behavioral abnormality that M. showed, apart from his insomnia, was a tendency to hallucinations. Brief hallucinations appeared 10–15 times a night. Usually these took the form of conversations with relatives, and they were usually forgotten promptly. Some evenings between 8 and 10 there were hallucinations that lasted 20 to 60 min. Usually these were visual, and a few themes occurred repeatedly—a space trip and moon landing, or hunting pheasants.

Classical sleep-inducing drugs had no effect on M.'s insomnia, but high doses of serotonin increased sleep time and restored deeper phases of sleep and REM sleep (Box Figure 12-4). Tryptophan caused the hallucinations to become worse. After several weeks of treatment with serotonin, the drug became ineffective; the patient showed a general worsening of his physical condition and died eleven months after being hospitalized.

The investigators of this case conclude with a note of bewilderment:

> Without sleeping or dreaming for 3 months, and with only a few minutes of hallucinations per night, a man can read newspapers, make plans for the

future, play and win at cards, recall recent or old memories without trouble, learn a complex maze, and lie all night on a bed in the dark without falling asleep. We conclude that these observations make obsolete almost all theories about the functions of sleep and of REM, but they do not provide us with any new hypothesis.

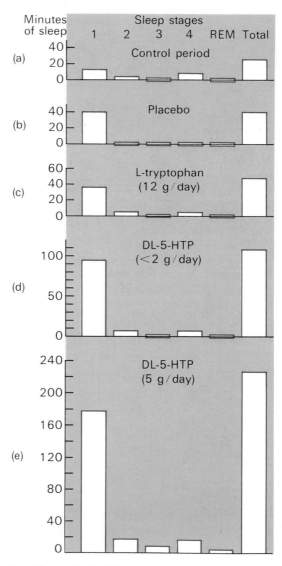

Box Figure 12-4 Effects of drug treatments for a person who could not sleep. High doses of precursor for the synthesis of serotonin produce some sleep periods.

predator dangers that might arise during sleep. From this view REM sleep complements the protection offered by a sleep habitat like a burrow or a tree. Support for this idea is scant, although it is true that small, frequently preyed upon animals have shorter sleep cycles.

Sleep restores weary bodies

Why do we sleep? Obviously, we sleep because we are tired, or so goes the most common refrain. Daily waking activities involve a vast expenditure of energy or body use, and some investigators view sleep as the state of restoration. The function of sleep is simply the rebuilding or restoration of materials used during waking, such as proteins.

Unfortunately, this commonsensical perspective is not supported by research. In fact, what seems so simple at first glance becomes quite paradoxical. For example, a simple way to test this idea would be to look at the effects of changes in presleep activity on the duration or cycle of sleep. Can intense metabolic expenditure during the day influence sleep duration? The answers to this question deepen the mystery. In humans, physical exercise before sleep shortens the latency of sleep onset without affecting overall duration. Some studies show a small lengthening of early slow-wave sleep stages, but many do not provide unequivocal support for the notion of restoration. In addition, the wide variety of sleep patterns in the animal kingdom is not obviously related to differences in restorative needs or processes. If restoration were the main function of sleep, how could horses get along with only 2 h of sleep per day while cats sleep 12 h?

Some researchers have emphasized the special restorative needs of the brain in contrast to the rest of the body. They emphasize the complexity of the neurochemical machinery of the body and indicate that waking activities profoundly affect processes like the state of neurotransmitters. Morruzzi (1972), a famed researcher in this area, particularly argues that use affects the small neurons of the brain and that sleep is especially restorative to these cells. Larger nerve cells, according to this view, have a greater metabolic reserve.

Sleep helps information processing

Many different events occur during the course of a single day, ranging from the casual inspection of a new face to a major reward honoring a distinct accomplishment. Moment by moment these events occur, some to be recalled years later, others to decay into oblivion with considerable ease. Previously we noted several connections between the phenomena of learning and the features of sleep. Many of these studies argue that sleep serves as a kind of information arbiter for the day. Accordingly, sleep is seen as a state that functions to sort and consolidate the memories of the day. Thus persistence of memory appears to be affected in an operation controlled by sleep processes.

Sleep disorders

The peace and comfort of regular, uninterrupted sleep each day may occasionally be disturbed by such occurrences as an inability to fall asleep, prolonged sleep, or unusual awakenings. What is unusual for some individuals may, however, be the customary and unsatisfactory sleep of others. Intensive work during the past decade concerned with unraveling sleep mechanisms in animals now offers some possibilities for understanding and treating human sleep dysfunctions. In turn, the study

TABLE 12-5   A Classification of Sleep Disorders

1. **Disorders of initiating and maintaining sleep (insomnia)**
   Ordinary, uncomplicated insomnia
      Transient
      Persistent
   Drug-related
      Use of stimulants
      Withdrawal of depressants
      Chronic alcoholism
   Associated with psychiatric disorders
   Associated with sleep-induced respiratory impairment
      Sleep apnea

2. **Disorders of excessive somnolence**
   Narcolepsy
   Associated with psychiatric problems
   Associated with psychiatric disorders
   Drug-related
   Associated with sleep-induced respiratory impairment

3. **Disorders of sleep-waking schedule**
   A. Transient
      Time zone change by airplane flight
      Work shift, especially night work
   B. Persistent
      Irregular rhythm

4. **Dysfunctions associated with sleep, sleep stages, or partial arousals**
   Sleepwalking (somnambulism)
   Sleep enuresis (bed-wetting)
   Sleep terror
   Nightmares
   Sleep-related seizures
   Teeth grinding
   Sleep-related activation of cardiac and gastrointestinal symptoms

SOURCE: Adapted from Weitzman (1981).

of sleep disorders is also contributing to our basic knowledge regarding sleep processes. In this section we will examine examples of disordered sleep, ranging from routine, commonplace experiences of many persons to quite unusual states found in a few individuals.

A recent meeting of researchers from sleep disorder clinics has led to a diagnostic classification scheme for disorders of sleep and arousal (Weitzman, 1981). Table 12-5 lists the main diagnostic classes with examples. Our discussion follows that organization.

Insomnias: Disorders of initiating and maintaining sleep

Difficulty in falling asleep (insomnia) is the most common manifestation of disordered sleep. The form of insomnia in humans that has been examined in sleep laboratories is the chronic type—the person who habitually feels tortured by an inability to fall asleep and remain sleeping for the usual period of time. Frequently such studies have found a discrepancy between the subject's reported failure to sleep

Figure 12-15 Example of sleep apnea in an adult human. Breathing stops during the course of slow-wave sleep and this produces arousal from sleep (not shown on this record). (From Mitler et al., 1975. Reprinted from *Psychology Today Magazine.* Copyright © 1975 Ziff-Davis Publishing Company.)

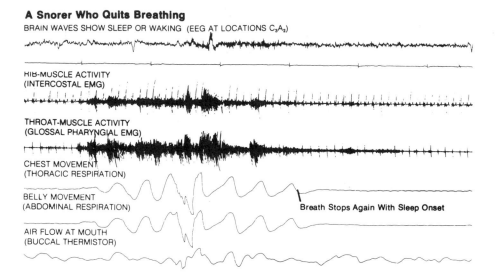

and EEG indicants of sleep. Thus some insomniacs report that they did not sleep when actually they showed EEG signs of sleep and did not respond to stimuli during this EEG sleep state. In many studies, however, insomniacs show less REM sleep and more stage 2 sleep than normal sleepers. No differences are evident in the amounts of stages 3 and 4 sleep.

During sleep, respiration in some people becomes unreliable. In these cases respiration can cease or slow to dangerous levels; blood levels of oxygen show a marked drop. This syndrome, called **sleep apnea** (Figure 12-15), arises from either the progressive relaxation of muscles of the chest, diaphragm, and throat cavity or changes in the pacemaker respiratory neurons of the brainstem. In the former instance, relaxation of the throat obstructs the airway—a kind of self-choking. This feature is common in very obese people who sleep lying on their back. Frequent arousals are seen in these people so they are sleepy in the daytime. Insertion of a removable tube in the throat can restore a normal sleep pattern and eliminates excess daytime sleepiness.

Some investigators of sleep disorders have speculated that crib death (sudden infant death syndrome) arises from sleep apnea that develops from reduction in brainstem neural activity that paces respiration. Continuous monitoring of the sleep of infants at risk for crib death has helped to save the lives of some children.

Disorders of excessive somnolence

There are some people who are sleepy all day long or have sudden bursts of sleep. Excessive daytime sleepiness occurs with the sleep apnea syndrome, as we noted above. The most dramatic syndrome of excessive sleepiness is **narcolepsy,** an unusual disorder that involves frequent, intense attacks of sleep, which last from 5 to 30 min and can occur anytime during the usual waking hours. Narcoleptics frequently have associated problems like a sudden loss of muscle tone that can be provoked by sudden or intense stimuli, including some that are generally considered

Figure 12-16 Sleep of a narcoleptic subject. (From Mitler et al., 1975. Reprinted from *Psychology Today Magazine*. Copyright © 1975 Ziff-Davis Publishing Company.)

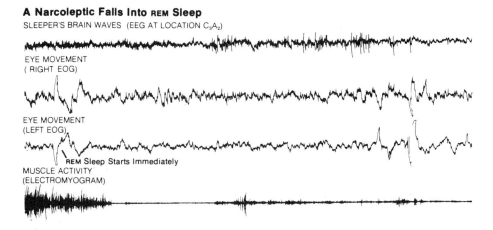

A Narcoleptic Falls Into REM Sleep
SLEEPER'S BRAIN WAVES (EEG AT LOCATION C₃A₂)

EYE MOVEMENT
(RIGHT EOG)

EYE MOVEMENT
(LEFT EOG)

REM Sleep Starts Immediately
MUSCLE ACTIVITY
(ELECTROMYOGRAM)

"nontraumatic," such as a burst of laughter. Individuals with this sleep disorder are distinguished from others by the appearance of REM at the onset of sleep (Figure 12-16). Indeed, the duration of a narcoleptic attack is quite similar to the usual period of a REM episode. Night sleep of narcoleptics is quite similar to normal sleep. Some investigators consider this disorder to involve a brainstem dysfunction that involves the failure of a waking mechanism to suppress the brainstem centers controlling REM sleep.

Many narcoleptics also show catalepsy, which is a sudden episode of muscle weakness leading to collapse of the body without loss of consciousness. These episodes, like narcoleptic attacks, are also triggered by sudden, intense emotional stimuli. In afflicted individuals this disorder continues throughout life and may show genetic transmission. No structural changes in the brain have been connected to this problem.

Recently the study of narcolepsy has been advanced by the discovery of a comparable disorder in dogs. In the sleep laboratories of William Dement several strains of dog have been shown to exhibit several properties of narcolepsy. These animals show sudden motor inhibition (cataplexy) and very short latencies to sleep onset. Many instances of sleep onset REM episodes are evident, just like those seen in human narcoleptics. Strong genetic control of this disorder is apparent in all strains of dog that have shown the phenomenon.

Disorders of the sleep-waking schedule

Airplane travel across several time zones can wreak havoc on circadian sleep-waking cycles. This rapid shifting of time zones is matched by the circadian shifts seen in people who work at night. Irregular patterns characterize the sleep of such people, who also show shortened sleep.

More serious sleep pattern impairments are seen in people who show "delayed sleep phase syndrome" (Weitzman, 1981). These people have an exceptionally long latency to sleep onset and just seem out of synchrony with normal sleep scheduling. Success in resetting the sleep rhythm is reported by Czeisler and collaborators (1981), who delay the time of sleep by 3 h each day until the person is "in phase"

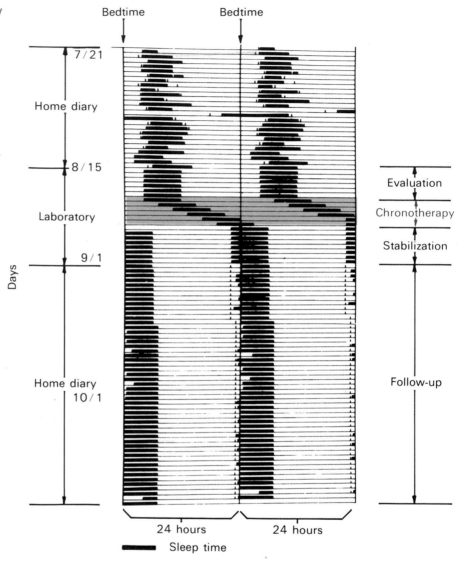

Figure 12-17 Impact of chronotherapy on a form of insomnia. Delay in the start of sleep resets the rhythm of sleep. (From Czeisler, 1981)

again (Figure 12-17). This circadian therapy allows an effective new sleep onset rhythm to be established, sometimes after years of disorder.

Dysfunctions associated with sleep

Some people have sleep periods that are usual in terms of onset and duration of sleep but unusual in terms of events that occur during sleep. These range from the embarassing to the life threatening.

One group of unusual behaviors provoked during sleep occurs most frequently in children. Sleepwalking (somnambulism) can consist of getting out of bed, walking around a room, and appearing awake. Studies in children show that such episodes arise out of slow-wave sleep, particularly stages 3 and 4. Children have no recollection of these periods, and with further maturation sleepwalking disappears for most individuals. Slow-wave sleep is also related to two other common sleep disorders in children, night terrors and bed-wetting. Night terrors occur after about a hour of sleep and are signaled by a sudden intense shriek. The adult equivalent of the nightmare results in awakening and a frequent report of a sense of pressure on the chest. In both children and adults these experiences arise from stage 4 sleep and, in the absence of awakening, there is no recollection of these events. Bed-wetting episodes predominate in the first third of a night's sleep and also seem to be triggered during stages 3 and 4 sleep. Pharmacological approaches to these episodic interferences with sleep emphasize the use of drugs that reduce the amount of stages 3 and 4 sleep (and also decrease REM time) while elevating amounts of stage 2 sleep.

A common view of sleep (emphasized by parents) is its ability to heal and promote well-being. But there's another side to this story. REM sleep can aggravate some health problems, especially the class of "stress diseases." Intense activation of autonomically innervated visceral organs can lead to an increase in the severity of tissue impairments in these systems. Gastric ulcers provide a good example of tissue pathology affected by REM sleep. Many ulcer patients report intense epigastric pain that awakens them from sleep. A ready explanation of this phenomenon is provided in Figure 12-18. Note that although normal subjects show no elevation of gastric acids during REM episodes, gastric ulcer patients secrete three to twenty times more acid at night than do controls. Peaks of acid concentration are reached during REM episodes.

Figure 12-18 Gastric acid secretion during sleep. A marked increase is seen during REM periods. (From Kales and Kales, 1970)

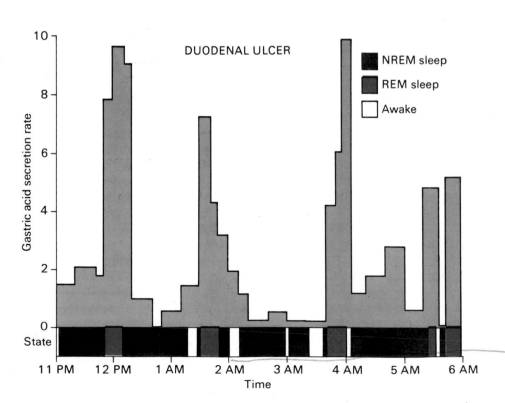

Similar attacks of illness occur among cardiovascular patients. A sad reminder is seen in hospital reports which show that cardiac patients are most likely to die during the hours of 4–6 A.M., the period of most intense and prolonged REM episodes. Further data are provided by the study of the time of occurrence of angina episodes. This chest pain syndrome is related to coronary artery disease. Kales (1971) showed that 32 of 39 such episodes in a hospitalized population occurred during REM episodes.

These examples indicate that REM states may involve significant physiological stresses in diseased persons. Thus appropriate medical care for some patients might well include efforts to reduce the hazards of REM sleep.

SUMMARY / MAIN POINTS

1. During sleep almost all mammals alternate between two main states, slow-wave sleep and rapid-eye-movement (REM) sleep.

2. Slow-wave sleep in humans shows several stages defined by EEG criteria that include bursts of spindles and persistent trains of large, slow waves (1–4 Hz). During slow-wave sleep there is a progressive decline in muscle tension, heart rate, respiratory rate, and temperature.

3. REM sleep is characterized by a rapid EEG of low amplitude, almost like the EEG during active waking behavior, but the postural muscles are profoundly relaxed.

4. In adult humans slow-wave sleep and REM sleep alternate every 90–110 min. Smaller animals have shorter sleep cycles and spend more time asleep per 24 h.

5. The characteristics of sleep-waking cycles change during the course of life. Mature animals sleep less than the young, and REM sleep accounts for a smaller fraction of their sleep.

6. The prominence of REM sleep in infants suggests that REM sleep contributes to development of the brain and to learning.

7. Mental activity does not cease during sleep. Vivid perceptual experiences (active dreams) are frequently reported by subjects awakened from REM sleep; reports of "ideas" or "thinking" are often given by subjects awakened from slow-wave sleep.

8. Verbal learning during sleep is unlikely, although habituation can be shown. Formation of memory is impaired when sleep deprivation—particularly REM sleep deprivation—follows learning sessions, so sleep may aid consolidation of memory.

9. Deprivation of sleep for a few nights in a row leads to impairment in performances that require sustained vigilance. During recovery nights following deprivation, the lost slow-wave sleep and REM sleep are partially restored over several nights.

10. Many drugs used to induce sleep inhibit REM sleep during the first few nights. When the drug is withdrawn, there is a rebound increase of REM sleep on the following nights.

11. Many brain structures are involved in the initiation and maintenance of sleep. Particular emphasis has been placed on brainstem structures, including the reticular formation, the raphe nucleus, and the locus coeruleus. The synaptic transmitters serotonin and norepinephrine are prominent in these structures and are involved in control of sleep.

12. Researchers have suggested several biological roles for sleep including conservation of energy, avoidance of predators, restoration of depleted resources, and consolidation of memory.

13. Sleep disorders fall into three major categories: (1) disorders of initiation and maintenance of sleep (e.g., insomnia); (2) disorders of excessive somnolence (e.g., narcolepsy); and (3) disorders of the sleep-waking schedule.

RECOMMENDED READING

Arkin, A. M., Antrobus, J. S., and Ellman, S. J. (Eds.). *The mind in sleep: Psychology and psychophysiology*. Hillsdale, N.J.: Lawrence Erlbaum, 1978.

Drucker-Colin, R., Shkurovich, M., and Sterman, M. B. (Eds.). *The functions of sleep*. New York: Academic, 1979.

Hartmann, E. L. *The functions of sleep*. New Haven: Yale University, 1973.

Orem, J., and Barnes, C. D. (Eds.). *Physiology in sleep*. New York: Academic, 1980.

Williams, R. L., and Karacan, I. *Sleep disorders: Diagnosis and treatment*. New York: Wiley, 1978.

Orientation

Bodily Responses in Emotion

Theories of emotion

Differentiation of skeletal muscular responses and autonomic responses in emotional states

Individual patterns of autonomic responses

Endocrine correlates of emotion

Control of autonomic responses: Biofeedback

Psychosomatic medicine

Bodily responses to stress

Brain Mechanisms and Emotion

Brain lesions and emotion

Electrical stimulation of the brain and emotion

Psychobiology of Aggression

What is aggression?

Hormones and aggression

Neural mechanisms of aggression

Controversies about the neurology of human violence

Biology of Mental Disorders

Genetic studies of schizophrenia

Physiological and biochemical theories of schizophrenia

Affective disorders

Surgical treatment in psychiatry

Summary/Main Points

13

Emotions and Mental Disorders

Orientation

The sound of unexpected footsteps in the eerie quiet of the night brings fear for many of us. But the sound of music we enjoy or the voice of someone we love can summon feelings of warmth. No story about our behavior is complete without consideration of the many events of a single day that involve feelings of one type or another.

The world of emotions is quite complicated; it includes a wide range of observable behaviors, expressed feelings, and changes in body states. Indeed, the diversity of meanings of the word "emotion" has made the subject hard to study. After all, for many of us these are very personal states, difficult to define, describe, or identify except in the most obvious instances. Even simple emotional states seem much more complicated than states related to other conditions, such as hunger and thirst. Things become even more puzzling when we seek to describe emotions in nonhuman animals. Is the hissing cat frightened, angry, or perhaps enjoying the experience of tormenting another cat or its solicitous but apprehensive owner?

At least two meanings of the word "emotion" are evident in the psychobiological research literature:

1. Emotion as a private subjective feeling. Humans can report an extraordinary range of states, which they say they "feel" or experience. At times such reports are accompanied by quite obvious signs of enjoyment or distress. But quite frequently these reports of subjective experience are without overt indicators.

2. Emotion as an expression or display of distinctive somatic and autonomic responses. This emphasis suggests that emotional states can be defined by particular constellations of bodily responses. Specifically, these responses involve autonomically innervated visceral organs, like heart, stomach, and intestines. Presumably they are provoked by equally distinctive emotional stimuli, although the attributes that make a stimulus "emotional" are not precisely defined. Taking this second meaning, we can examine emotion in nonhuman animals as well as in human beings.

The biological study of emotions moves along many different lines. We will consider two of them: bodily responses during emotional states and brain mechanisms that control the diverse forms of emotional expression. Aggression is emphasized in many studies of both kinds, partly because of its importance in human existence and partly because its lack of subtlety makes it relatively easy to examine experimentally. We will also consider mental disorders in humans, since marked emotional changes are among the most prominent features of these conditions.

Bodily responses in emotion   In many emotional states we can sense our heart beating fast, our hands and face feeling warm, our palms sweating, and a queasy feeling in the stomach. There seems to be an especially close tie between the subjective psychological phenomena we know as emotions and the activity of visceral organs controlled by the autonomic nervous system. Several theories have tried to explain the connections between emotions and visceral activity. These theories have raised the question of whether we can experience emotions without the activity of visceral organs.

Theories of emotion   Among the many theories of emotion, some focus on peripheral bodily events, some on central brain processes, and some seek to integrate both kinds of events. In this section we will discuss three prominent examples of such theories—the James-Lange theory, the Cannon-Bard theory, and Schachter's cognitive theory.

● **James-Lange theory**   Strong emotions and activation of the skeletal muscle and/or autonomic nervous systems are virtually inseparable. Expressions common in many languages capture this association—"trembling with rage," "with all my heart," "hair standing on end," "a sinking feeling in the stomach." William James, the leading figure in American psychology around the turn of the twentieth century, suggested that emotions were the perception of bodily changes provoked by particular stimuli. His idea is sketched in Figure 13-1. From this perspective fear is evident because particular stimuli produce changes in bodily activity, which are then noted as an emotion. Thus our feeling of body changes *is* emotion, as indicated in Figure 13-1.

James's notion (independently offered by a Danish physician, Carl Lange) started research on the relations between visceral responses and feelings or emotions. Questions such as "What are the responses of the heart in love, anger, fear?" continue to form a prominent part of the biological study of emotions. Although the James-Lange theory initiated this research, it has not survived critical assessment.

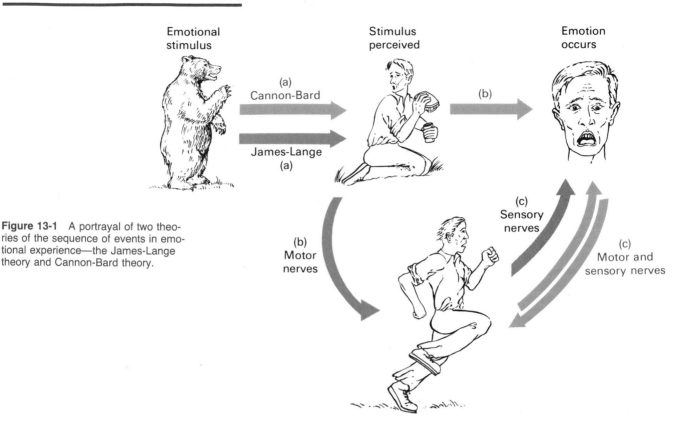

Emotional stimulus   Stimulus perceived   Emotion occurs

(a) Cannon-Bard

(b)

James-Lange (a)

(b) Motor nerves

(c) Sensory nerves

(c) Motor and sensory nerves

Figure 13-1 A portrayal of two theories of the sequence of events in emotional experience—the James-Lange theory and Cannon-Bard theory.

● **Cannon-Bard theory**   If body states are emotions, then different emotions should be characterized by different visceral conditions. Also, provoking changes in the body by various experimental treatments, such as surgical procedures or drugs, should change emotional responses. The simplicity of the James-Lange theory thus presented ready opportunity for experimental assessments.

Physiologist Walter Cannon provided strong criticism of the James-Lange theory. For example, he noted that emotions are not lost in people with high transections of the spinal cord, even though such patients cannot feel visceral changes because the brain is separated from the visceral organs. The force of this criticism has been somewhat blunted by a study of emotional feelings in people with high or low spinal transections (Hohman, 1966). The higher the transection, and therefore the less the information from visceral organs, the less is the reported intensity of emotional feelings, although emotional reports were present in all cases.

Cannon further argued that visceral changes may be similar in different emotions and that some visceral changes may have very different emotional consequences, depending on the context. For example, there is a marked difference between tearfulness produced by sadness-inducing situations and that produced by an irritating stimulus like tear gas.

Cannon's own theory stressed cerebral integration of both emotional experience and emotional response. Noting that emotional states involved considerable energy expenditure, Cannon (1929) emphasized that some emotions are an emergency response of an organism to a sudden threatening condition. This response produced maximal activation of the sympathetic component of the autonomic nervous system, according to Cannon. Activation of the viscera by the sympathetic system, according to his theory, comes about because emotional stimuli excite the cerebral cortex, which in turn releases inhibition of thalamic control mechanisms. Activation of the thalamus then produces cortical excitation, resulting in emotional experiences and autonomic nervous system activity. This theory is sketched in Figure 13-1.

In a subsequent section we will consider theories based on direct study of the brain, especially brain stimulation studies. The James-Lange and Cannon-Bard theories directed attention to physiological patterns of visceral activity during emotional states. Questions such as "Are there distinct patterns of visceral activation that distinguish emotional states?" continue to be fruitful areas of experimental work. Before considering these data, though, we will take up a different theoretical perspective on peripheral events and emotions, a cognitive theory of emotions.

• **Cognitive theory of emotions**   We have noted in our criticism of the James-Lange theory that activation of a physiological system by itself is not sufficient to provoke an emotion. For example, tears produced by a noxious gas do not ordinarily provoke sadness. Stanley Schachter (1975) suggests that individuals interpret visceral activation in terms of the eliciting stimuli, the surrounding situations, and their cognitive states. An emotion is thus not relentlessly driven by physiological activation—especially that controlled by the sympathetic nervous system. Rather bodily states are interpreted in the context of cognitions and are molded by experience. According to Schachter, emotional labels—anger, fear, joy—depend on the interpretations of a situation, interpretations that are controlled by internal cognitive systems.

Schachter has conducted many studies whose results underscore the significance of cognitive evaluation. His observations remain controversial, though; some have been confirmed by others, while some seem idiosyncratic to his laboratory. His basic experiment involved injections of epinephrine to manipulate sympathetic arousal in ways that resemble the activation of the sympathetic nervous system. Cognitive activity of subjects in these experiments was manipulated by "explanations" of drug effects presented to the subjects. For example, one group of "epinephrine-informed" subjects received the following explanation from the experimenter about effects of the drug, which was called by the fictitious name "Suproxin":

> I should . . . tell you . . . our subjects have experienced side effects from Suproxin. These effects are transitory . . . What will probably happen is that your hand will start to shake, your heart will start to pound and your face may get warm and flushed. . . .

An "epinephrine-ignorant" group was told nothing about the "side effects," and an "epinephrine-misinformed" group was told that the side effects would include itching and numbness, responses that are not actually elicited by epinephrine.

After the injections were given, emotional states were manipulated by contrived social situations, usually involving an accomplice of the researcher. This "stooge" in some situations acted silly and in others sought to provoke the subject's anger. Results offered by Schachter (summarized in 1975) show that emotions described by the subject in this situation are not determined by sympathetic activation per se. Rather, emotional responses are a result of the interpretation of physiological effects produced by the drug.

The situation provides the subject with cognitive data that lead to interpretations of physiological arousal. Emotions, as noted by self-report during epinephrine-induced arousal, can be directed toward euphoria or anger by the cognitive manipulations of the researcher. However, if the subject is provided with an accurate interpretation of the induced physiological state, manipulation of reported emotion is not possible. A representation of this theory is presented in Figure 13-2.

A critical reexamination of Schachter's hypothesis has been presented in a comprehensive study by Erdmann and Janke (1978). These investigators noted some limitations in Schachter's experiments, among them poorly controlled social situations and minimal effects in some major comparisons of different groups. In the Erdmann and Janke study the situations manipulated by the experimenter were "anger," "happiness," "anxiety," and "neutral." Two drug conditions were used, a placebo state and a sympathetic arousal produced by ephedrine. Situational manipulations were produced by reports to the subject about performance attained in a presumed intelligence test. Anger situations developed from the subject being informed about how badly he had done on this test. The opposite report was given to

Figure 13-2 A cognitive theory of emotions presented by Schachter.

Individual emotional response is a function of both:

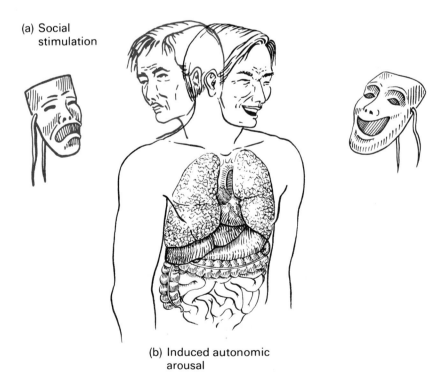

(a) Social stimulation

(b) Induced autonomic arousal

produce happiness. Discussion about electrical shock and a brief experience with this stimulus provided an anxiety manipulation. Measurements of effects included an adjective checklist and heart rate and blood pressure. Mood rating by subjects clearly showed that the happiness and anger conditions influenced the judgments of the effects of drug administration. However, the anxiety condition did not show an impact of ephedrine administration. The failure to find any effect with anxiety shows that impact of cognition on emotional response cannot be generalized to all emotional states.

Differentiation of skeletal muscular responses and autonomic responses in emotional states

Our bodies reveal emotions in overt ways involving the skeletal muscular systems and in ways less apparent to the casual observer. Overt expressions of emotion are evident in posture, gesture, and facial expressions; all these dimensions are well cultivated by the accomplished actor. Visceral responses involve activities of many different internal organs, and their patterning is especially important in studies of emotion. Our discussion starts with examples of skeletal muscle activities seen in facial expressions and then proceeds to some autonomic responses.

● Facial expression and emotion   Expressions of happiness, anger, and sadness are familiar parts of human communication. Since the human face is hard to hide from view, it is a ready source of information for others. This prospect for communication is enhanced by the elaborate and finely controlled musculature of the face, which provides possibilities for an enormous range of facial expression. Diverse examples of facial expressions produced by small muscle changes are shown in Figure 13-3. Motor control of the face is provided by a large set of neural fibers, many of which control small sets of muscles; this system allows for delicate control of expression.

An emphasis on facial expressions and emotion was noted quite early by the work of Charles Darwin, "The Expression of the Emotions in Man and Animals" (1872). In this book Darwin cataloged facial expressions of humans and other animals and emphasized the universal nature of these expressions. He emphasized especially that facial expressions are connected to distinctive emotional states both in humans and in nonhuman primates. Facial expressions were partly viewed as information communicated to other animals.

More recently the work of Paul Ekman (1972, 1979) has provided rich insight into the information properties of facial expression. Across many cultures facial expressions of emotions are similarly recognized or identified. No explicit training is needed to interpret facial expressions in any of these cultures. Cross-cultural similarity is also noted in the production of facial expressions specific to particular emotions. For example, people in a preliterate New Guinea society, when posing particular emotions, show facial expressions like those of advanced societies. Universal facial expression in humans is seen for anger, disgust, happiness, sadness, fear, and surprise. Of course, universal facial expressions do not account for the full complement of human facial expressions (Ekman and Oster, 1979). Cultural differences may emerge in culture-specific display rules, which stipulate social contexts for facial expression. Thus some anthropologists have suggested that cultures that prescribe rules for facial expression and control enforced by culture conditioning

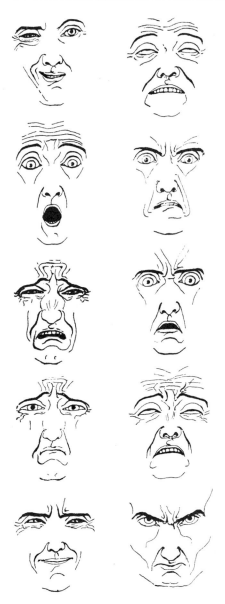

Figure 13-3 Facial expressions as illustrated in a book on mime techniques. These are exaggerated but show the flexibility and range of facial communication of emotions.

might mask the universal property of facial expressions. The stimuli for expression may also differ among cultures.

Facial expressions that resemble particular adult expressions are evident in early infancy. For example, newborn humans show smiles during REM sleep periods. By 3–4 months infants show differential responses to various facial expressions of adults. Much research indicates that by the ages of 4–5 years children have acquired full knowledge about the appearance and meaning of many common facial expressions.

● **Autonomic responses**   Although it is hard to hide the changing expressions of the face, the detection of visceral changes requires the scrutiny of electronic gadgets. When a subject is connected to devices that measure heart rate, blood pressure, stomach motility, dilation or constriction of blood vessels, skin resistance, or sweating of the palms or soles, we see a wealth of changes that are sensitive to emotional states. Devices that measure several of these bodily responses are called polygraphs. These machines are popularly known as "lie detectors."

Does the pattern of bodily response indicate the kind of emotion being experienced? This question, arising from the emphasis of the James-Lange theory, continues to intrigue investigators. Experimental studies in this area explore whether people show patterns of reactions that are specific to particular events or stimuli. For example, if we recorded heart activity, stomach motility, skin temperature, respiration, and blood pressure during states of anger and fear, we would expect to see profiles distinctive for each state. Albert Ax (1953) reported an oft-quoted experiment that shows such specificity in response to anger- and fear-provoking stimuli. In this study subjects had wires connected to them for recordings of several physiological measures. The states of anger and fear were induced by a confederate; he provoked anger by insulting behavior and fear by acting worrisome and incompetent in the presence of sparks deliberately contrived to elicit fear of electrocution. However hesitant one might now be about this kind of subject manipulation, it produced potent emotional states. Several differences in physiological patterns were seen, including greater increases in pulse rate and blood pressure in fear than in anger.

Individual patterns of autonomic responses

Responses of various bodily systems reveal distinct patterns that are characteristic of the individual. This feature of visceral responses has been studied by John and Beatrice Lacey (1970), who refer to this characteristic as **autonomic response specificity.** Their work involved longitudinal studies of people extending over many years, from early childhood to adulthood. The stimulus situations they used to provoke autonomic responses included stress conditions such as immersing the hand in ice-cold water, performing rapidly paced arithmetic calculations, and presenting intense stimuli to the skin. They noted that across these conditions an individual profile of response can be seen, which is evident even in human neonates. For example, some neonates respond vigorously with heart rate changes, others with gastric motility changes, still others with blood pressure responses. Response patterns are remarkably consistent throughout life. This observation may provide the basis for understanding why the same intense stress might cause pathology of different organs in different individuals. It would seem that constitutional factors lead some of us to develop ulcers and others to develop high blood pressure in similar emotion-provoking situations. The concept of autonomic response specificity is therefore of considerable significance in the field of psychosomatic medicine.

Endocrine correlates of emotion

Humoral theories of emotion have a long history and have involved many body organs including liver, spleen, and endocrine glands. This history is reflected in some common words used to express emotion like "bilious" (derived from "bile"), meaning irritable, cranky, or unpleasant, and "phlegmatic" (from "phlegm"), meaning apathetic or sluggish. Current research explores the relations between hormones and emotions in two ways:

1. Observing changes of hormone levels in the blood during experimentally or naturally produced emotional states. The technology of biochemical measurement of hormones has become quite precise and allows measurement of minute changes.

2. Observing changes in emotional states after administering hormones or after noting hormone deficiencies produced by endocrine disease. In the former case a frequent interest has been mood changes produced by hormone treatments in women, generally birth control pills.

We will consider some examples of research in each of these two directions.

Endocrine measurements accompanying emotional experiences have generally emphasized (1) assessment of epinephrine, released by the adrenal medulla and reflecting sympathetic activation of this gland, and (2) measurements of 17-hydroxycorticosteroids in blood or urine, which reflect the activities of the pituitary-adrenal cortical systems. Many studies clearly show that emotional stimuli or situations are accompanied by hormone secretions. Elevated urinary and blood levels of epinephrine or norepinephrine have been seen both prior to and during stressful and energetic activities like professional sport encounters, military maneuvers, and many other anxiety-provoking situations. Studies by Elmadjian and collaborators (1957, 1958) show that norepinephrine levels might be related to the intensity of the emotional encounter. Their data show elevated norepinephrine levels for individuals who deal with an interview situation with intense emotional responses, including aggression, in contrast with those who respond more passively. However, norepinephrine levels may not distinguish the type of emotional display, since Levi (1965) has found similar epinephrine increases in women presented with film material that elicits pleasant and unpleasant responses. Adrenocortical responses also do not seem to differentiate the type of emotion. Brown and Heninger (1975) presented films that were either erotic or suspenseful and noted that both types of stimuli produced elevated cortisol levels in blood.

Figure 13-4 Pattern of hormonal responses to stress in a monkey. These graphs show control hormone levels and those during a three-day period of avoidance training and a six-day post-training period. Note that some stress-induced hormone effects are quite persistent. (From Mason, 1972)

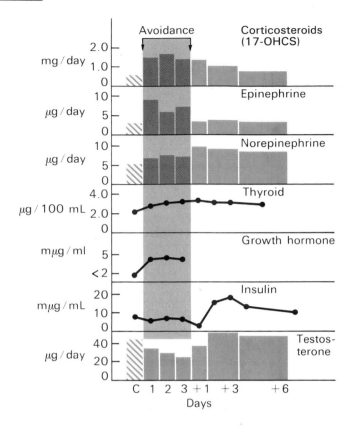

Various measures of fear and avoidance behavior of nonhuman primates and other animals have been investigated in many experiments. Figure 13-4 shows an extensive series of measures obtained in monkeys in the studies of Mason (1972). These animals engaged in an extended period of avoidance behavior in which they performed a lever-pressing response to avoid shock. The only cue controlling this behavior was time; responses had to be presented at some criterion rate (like once per minute) to avoid shock. In this situation hormone measures that show an increase during avoidance periods include epinephrine, 17-hydroxycorticosteroids, thyroid activity, and growth hormone, while decreases are evident in insulin and testosterone.

Diminished hormone output produced by various disease states also influences emotional responses. Decreased thyroid output is frequently associated with depression. Depression is also seen in Addison's disease, an adrenal gland disorder that is accompanied by decreased glucocorticoid secretions.

Control of autonomic responses: Biofeedback

Heart rate, blood pressure, and respiration, among other autonomic responses, are influenced by many internal and external conditions. Yogis and others have dramatically demonstrated ways to control some internal conditions. Stories of their success in reducing heart rate and respiration to death-defying levels are part of the folklore surrounding mystics. Laboratory observations have documented unusual autonomic control in some of these individuals. Efforts of this sort powerfully demonstrate learned modulations of physiological systems that were at one time thought to be controlled by automatic mechanisms that could not be affected by experience.

Biofeedback procedures can increase as well as decrease the level of activity in autonomically controlled systems, a result shown in work on the blood pressure levels of people who have suffered spinal transections (Miller, 1980). Many of us have experienced a quite transient light-headedness that occurs when we rapidly stand up after a night's sleep. This fleeting response occurs because blood pressure transiently falls under the impact of gravitational forces. In the ordinary case vascular reflexes rapidly adjust to normal. But paraplegic humans, especially those with high spinal lesions, may show a marked and maintained drop in blood pressure when moved to an upright posture. The absence of muscle tension over a large part of the body modifies the regulatory mechanisms of the vascular system, partly by changing the mechanical impact on blood vessels. This blood pressure failure forces some spinal-injured humans to maintain a horizontal position.

Miller (1980) has described biofeedback procedures that result in sustained elevation of blood pressure in such patients when they are moved to an upright position. Subjects are instructed to "try to increase" their blood pressure (Figure 13-5). Although they can make only tiny changes at the start, training that involves direct knowledge of results has been successful in many cases. Blood pressure information is continuously provided to the patient, and increases of systolic pressure cause a tone to sound. The patient is told to try to make the sound come on as frequently as possible. With success at one blood pressure level, the criterion is changed so that sound comes on only with yet higher blood pressure responses. Following such a regimen, spinal humans with this problem learn to increase their blood pressure when moved to an upright posture. This has enabled some to be fitted with braces and crutches and thus to become mobile. This learned increase in blood pressure becomes highly specific; that is, eventually it is not accompanied by heart rate changes. Biofeedback training to control skin temperature and thus alleviate such conditions as Reynaud's disease and migraine headaches was described in Chapter 10.

Psychosomatic medicine

The role of psychological factors in disease has been strongly emphasized by many psychiatrists and psychologists during the past fifty years. This field came to be known as "psychosomatic medicine" after an eminent psychoanalyst, Thomas French, suggested that particular diseases arise from distinctive sets of psychological characteristics. From this perspective ulcers were related to frustration of "oral" needs and the development of "oral dependency," hypertension was seen as arising from hostile competitive activities, and migraine headaches represented repressed hostile needs or impulses. Each disease state or illness was thought to be associated with a specific set of psychological characteristics—those that generated some form of unresolved conflict.

Although these ideas were prominent in the early development of psychosomatic medicine, current views make fewer claims for highly particular associations. In-

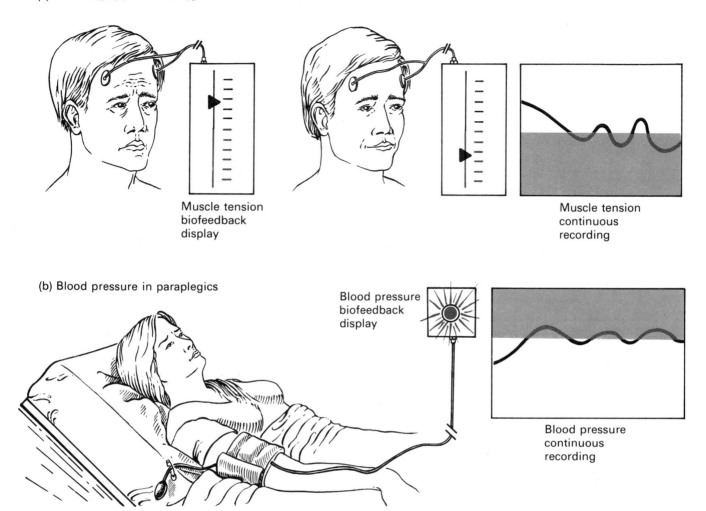

(a) Muscle tension headaches

Muscle tension
biofeedback
display

Muscle tension
continuous
recording

(b) Blood pressure in paraplegics

Blood pressure
biofeedback
display

Blood pressure
continuous
recording

Figure 13-5 Two examples of biofeedback training to modify physiological responses. (a) Biofeedback training to diminish frontal muscle tension that generates headaches. Signals to the subject in a display of muscle tension (electromyograms) show the current level and the optimal level (reduced tension). Muscle recording on the right shows progressive reduction with training. (b) Biofeedback modification of blood pressure in a paraplegic. The display (light) shows when optimal level is reached, and the subject's task is to keep the light on for longer and longer periods as a progressively more upright posture is produced.

stead they emphasize that emotional responsiveness is only one factor among many that determine the onset, maintenance, and treatment of bodily disorders. Emotional stimuli activate a diversity of neural and hormonal changes that influence pathological processes of bodily organs. Studies in psychosomatic medicine have broadened in scope and now range from global evaluations of emotions, stress, and sickness to unraveling particular relations between emotions and bodily responses or conditions. A field called psychological medicine, or behavioral medicine seems to be emerging in the wake of this developing interest (Stone, 1980).

Connections between stress and human disease have been drawn in many different ways. Each new piece of evidence is tantalizing but generally several steps away from being conclusive. Perhaps the ambiguity is determined less by lack of ingenuity of experimenters than by the vast range of individual differences among people with regard to susceptibility to different diseases. Some of us are more constitutionally prone to failure in certain organs than others. Further, research on stress and human disease is bedeviled by the fact that stress is only a contributory condition to most disease states. Health habits, including nutritional variables, and patterns of coping with stress are probably of equal significance. This area is a difficult one to study, although it is of major importance to human life.

One global approach to linking stress and human disease is to study the covariation between precisely defined stressful life events and the incidence of particular diseases over a long period of time. Cancer and heart disease are leading causes of death and misery in human beings. The toll of these diseases in many countries has generated large scale studies of the health habits, quality of life, and personal adjustment of large samples of people, including whole communities (Hurst et al., 1976). Most of these studies have been retrospective; that is, participants have been asked to report and rate experiences and emotional responses prior to the onset of an illness. In some instances relatives of deceased subjects provide this information. Behavior scales have been developed that allow a quantitative assessment of the frequency and number of stressful events that precede an illness. Although many methodological problems are evident in this approach, some consistent relations between stressful events and illness have been found.

Most research in this area seeks to show temporal relations between onset of illness and recent changes in the frequency of stressful events. A study of naval shipboard personnel by Rahb and his collaborators (1972) provides an example. Navy personnel were asked to report major life events associated with stress (such as death of family members or divorce) and a history of illness for a ten-year period. Results showed that subjects who reported few stressful events for a particular period had few episodes of illness in the following years. In contrast, subjects who experienced many stressful events reported a much higher level of illness for the following year. Many other studies seem to support this association between frequency of stressful life events and probability of illness in the future. However, cause and effect are intertwined in this research (Rabkin and Struening, 1976).

Mere frequency of stressful life events may be less related to serious illness than earlier studies emphasized. In a study of stressful events and heart attack, Byrne and White (1980) compared a group of coronary patients with a "control" group of people who were admitted to emergency rooms with suspected heart difficulties but who were rapidly diagnosed as not being heart attack cases. Questionnaires completed by the coronary patients gave researchers an estimate of the frequency and intensity of stressful life events for the year prior to hospitalization. Analysis of these data show that heart attack patients did not have a higher frequency of stressful events during the year prior to illness than did the controls. Nor was the intensity of stress events a factor that distinguished these groups. However, heart attack patients were significantly more distressed by stressful life events and tended to be more anxious. It would seem that the emotional impact of stress has greater significance for future serious illness than does the occurrence of stressful events.

Bodily responses to stress   Studies of stress have examined bodily responses both in laboratory situations and in real-life circumstances. Let us see examples of research in both sorts of settings.

● **Stress and the stomach**   The emphasis on stress, emotions, and human disease evident in psychosomatic medicine has generated many experimental inquiries concerned with autonomic reactivity during stress. A critical set of observations by Harold Wolff in the 1940s involved the case of a patient known as Tom. This patient had swallowed a caustic solution that had seared his esophagus and thus he could not eat normally. To enable Tom to take in food, surgeons made a hole through the body wall into the stomach; a tube through this hole provided a route for nutrient fluids. The tube also let Wolff and his collaborators directly observe the surface lining of the stomach during the course of interviews that provoked emotional responses. During intensely emotionally laden phases of these interviews, Tom showed marked changes in the gastric mucosa, along with a dramatic buildup of stomach acid (Figure 13-6). Subsequent studies of humans with ulcers have shown marked elevation of hydrochloric acid in the stomach.

Figure 13-6 Changes in stomach mucosa and gastric acid secretion in the case of Tom. Portions of this person's stomach mucosa were connected to the skin of the abdomen, creating a hole through which food could be delivered into the stomach. With emotion, the mucosa can be seen to redden and enlarge because it has become engorged with blood. Studies of the stomach contents show a progressive rise in gastric acidity during emotion-arousing interviews. (From Wolf and Wolff, 1943)

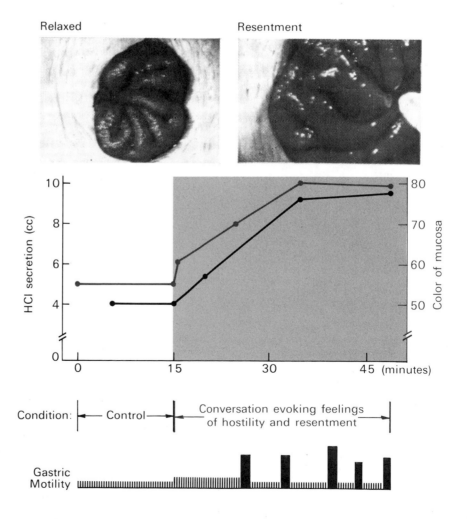

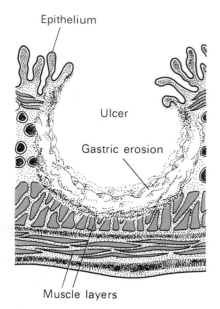

Epithelium

Ulcer

Gastric erosion

Muscle layers

Figure 13-7 Drawing of a gastric ulcer, showing erosion of outer layer of cells.

Laboratory studies of ulcer development in animals (for example, Ader, 1972) have involved stressful stimuli such as electric shock; these conditions can generate ulcers in some animals (Figure 13-7). Because the gastric erosions or ulcers produced in rats exposed to such conditions are believed to partially resemble the gastric ulcers seen in humans, it is of considerable interest to understand the psychobiological factors that lead to ulcer development in rats.

Various experimental conditions can be used to generate ulcers in rats. Preventing these animals from moving by using a body restraint is one of the oldest methods. The effect is especially evident in younger animals, particularly those that have sustained early separation from their mother. Section of the vagus nerve input to the stomach (which lowers stomach acid secretion) reduces the number of gastric lesions. Another determinant of ulcer formation in this experimental context is the level of the digestive substance pepsinogen secreted into the stomach. High levels in the stomach increase the probability of stomach lesions in rats.

Another experimental technique used to induce stomach lesions in experimental rats is the generation of strong emotional responses by employing electric shock. A variable that has been found to be especially important in this kind of experiment is the predictability of shock. Weiss (1977) has claimed that unpredictable electric shocks are more likely to contribute to gastric ulcer formation than predictable shocks.

An experiment involving ulcer formation in monkeys by Brady (1958) came to be known as the "executive monkey" experiment. Pairs of monkeys in primate restraint chairs were placed next to each other. One animal, the "executive monkey," pressed a lever to avoid shock under conditions in which this response had to be repeated every 20 seconds to maintain continued shock avoidance. Whenever this monkey failed to press the lever within this interval, it received a shock. The second monkey received shocks at the same time, but it would not perform any response that could protect it from shocks. Executive monkeys in this experiment developed ulcers, whereas their adjacent partners failed to show gastric lesions. This experiment, in the years after its initial presentation, stimulated many research efforts, and most of them have failed to confirm Brady's finding. Indeed, in some rat experiments the responding animal is *less* likely to get ulcers, especially if shock is preceded by a warning signal. Experiments like these point to some of the psychological factors that contribute to gastric lesions. The links between these conditions and stomach pathology remain topics of continuing research efforts.

● **Stress outside the laboratory**   Laboratory studies of human stress have used painful stimuli like exposure to electric shock or hand immersion in ice-cold water. Researchers of stress have frequently criticized the artificiality of such laboratory studies. Placing a hand in a bucket of ice cubes is certainly pale in comparison with dangerous situations that threaten life or produce psychological trauma. Some researchers have sought to use real-life situations as the arena in which to explore the biology of stress, but, of course, most human stress situations are not predictable in advance, so baseline prestress assessments are not available. A few studies have avoided this difficulty and offered controlled observations of baseline conditions and prolonged observations through the course of a continuing potentially harmful situation. The most commonly used real-life situation is military training, especially aviator training and parachute training, where stress involves fear of bodily harm and fear of failure.

A recent monograph by Ursin, Baade, and Levine (1978) is the most recent example of the study of the psychobiology of stress in a parachute-training condition. The classical work in this area by Grinker and colleagues (1955) provided a comprehensive study of stress in this situation, involving both tower training and airplane jumps. However, this pioneering study took place long before the development of modern chemical assessments of circulating substances like hormones. The latest work by Ursin and his collaborators took advantage of contemporary analytic tools that allow the study of minute changes of hormone levels in blood. A group of young recruits in the Norwegian military were studied by using a variety of psychological and physiological measures before and during the early phase of parachute training. This training period involved a sliding ride along a long sloping wire suspended from a tower 12 meters high. Recruits were dressed in a suit that provided a hook to a guide wire and they slid along its course. This familiar situation in parachute training involves an experience somewhat like that of free-fall. Initial apprehension is high, and at first the sense of danger is acute, although recruits know that they are not likely to lose their life in this part of the training. Physiological measures were obtained during a basal period prior to training and with successive jumps. On jump days two samples of blood were drawn to chart the time course of neuroendocrine events.

A portrayal of autonomic activation in this situation is presented in Figure 13-8. Pituitary activation of the adrenal cortex during stress has been shown in many animal experiments, as noted in an earlier section. Figure 13-9 (a) shows an elevation in cortisol in blood with initial exposure to the practice jump. Success in this task produces a rapid fall in the pituitary-adrenal response. Plasma testosterone levels fall below control levels on the first jump (Figure 13-9b), a finding that is also seen in rats and primates with exposure to noxious stimuli. In the parachute-training study the effect is due to fear and disappeared after initial exposure to the situation. Since this effect coincided with cortisol changes the experimenters suggested that it might be mediated through the pituitary.

Urinary levels of epinephrine show a somewhat different pattern (Figure 13-9c). The initial jump day involved a marked elevation of urinary epinephrine, with a slow return to baseline with further parachute jumps. The pattern of norepinephrine secretion is somewhat different (Figure 13-9d), a finding evident in other studies, which emphasize that elevated epinephrine might be related to active coping responses whereas norepinephrine might be related to less direct coping.

Clear-cut endocrine responses were also seen in changes of blood level of growth hormone (Figure 13-9d). In this experiment an evident elevation of growth hormone was seen during the day of the first jump.

Less dramatic real-life situations also evoke clear endocrine responses, as shown by research of Frankenhaueser and her associates (1979). For example, riding in a commuter train was found to provoke release of epinephrine; the longer the ride and the more crowded the train, the greater was the hormonal response (Figure 13-10a). Factory work also led to release of epinephrine; the shorter the work cycle—that is, the more frequently the person had to repeat the same operations—the higher were the levels of epinephrine. The stress of a Ph.D oral exam led to a dramatic increase in both epinephrine and norepinephrine (Figure 13-10b, c).

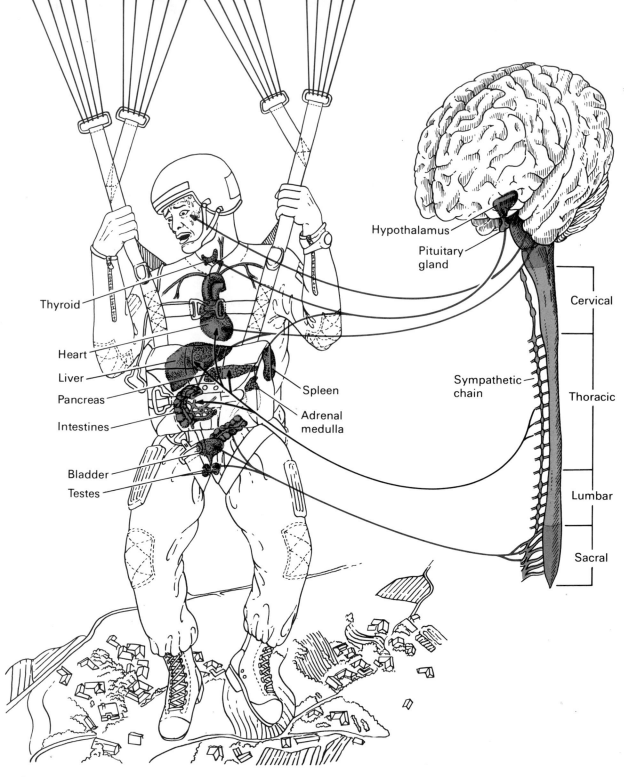

Figure 13-8 Autonomic activation during a stress situation—parachute training.

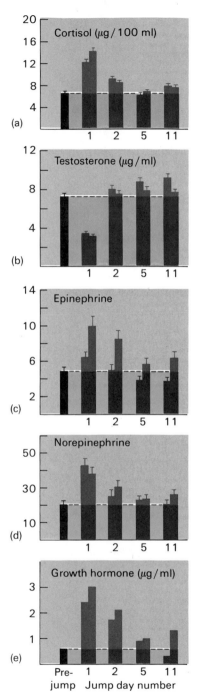

(a)

(b)

(c)

(d)

(e)

Figure 13-9 Hormone changes during parachute training in military trainees. (From Ursin, Baade, and Levine, 1978)

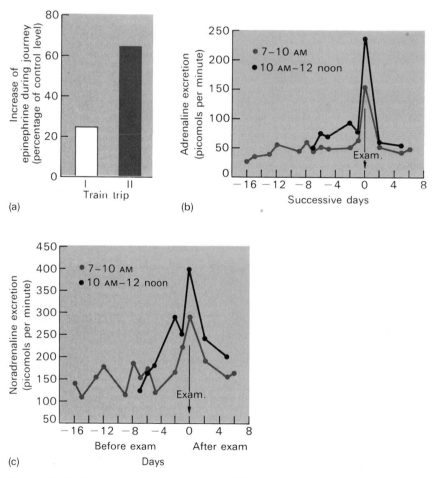

Figure 13-10 Hormone changes in humans arising from common social stresses. (a) Effects of small changes in crowding on a morning commuter train ride. Level I indicates percent increment of adrenaline secretion during a usual ride while II shows percent increment with a 10% increase in the number of passengers during a period of gasoline rationing. Levels of adrenaline (b) and noradrenaline (c) in a graduate student during a two-week period before thesis exams, during the exam, and following. (Adapted from "Psychoneuroendocrine Endocrine Approaches to the Study of Emotion as Related to Stress and Coping" by M. Frankenhauser, *Nebraska Symposium on Motivation,* 1979, by permission of University of Nebraska Press.)

Brain mechanisms and emotion

Are there particular neural circuits for emotions localized in particular regions of the brain? This question has been explored in studies involving either localized brain lesions or electrical stimulation. Neuropharmacological studies have tried to determine the role of specific transmitters in particular emotions. Brain lesion studies involving clinical observations in humans or experimenter-produced lesions in non-human animals have focused on some dramatic syndromes of emotional change, such as the taming of monkeys following temporal lobe lesions. Brain stimulation studies have generated brain maps for various emotional responses, especially those involving aggression. In this section we will look at both types of studies and their results.

Brain lesions and emotion

Many studies have explored brain mechanisms of emotion by investigating effects of destruction of brain regions on behavior. These studies include both clinical investigations and surgical experiments with animal subjects.

- **Decorticate rage**   Ablation of the neocortex provided the oldest experimental demonstration of brain mechanisms and emotion. Early in this century, decorticate dogs were shown to respond to routine handling with sudden intense rage—sometimes referred to as "sham rage" because it lacked well-directed attack. Snarling, barking, and growling were provoked by ordinary handling, and this behavior also included strong visceral responses. Clearly, emotional behaviors of this type are organized at a subcortical level, and these observations suggested that the cerebral cortex provides inhibitory control of emotional responsiveness.

- **Klüver-Bucy syndrome**   Studies of brain mechanisms and emotion were advanced by the work of Klüver and Bucy (1938), who described a most unusual syndrome in primates following temporal lobe surgery. In the course of studies concerned with cortical mechanisms in perception, they removed large portions of the temporal lobe of monkeys. A dramatic portrait of behavior change was evident in these animals postoperatively. The syndrome was highlighted by an extraordinary taming effect. Animals who were wild and fearful of humans prior to surgery became tame and docile and showed neither fear nor aggression. In addition, they seemed to lose a sense of the meaning of many objects, as indicated by their ingestion of inedible objects. Frequent mounting behavior was seen and was described as hypersexuality. Lesions restricted to the cerebral neocortex did not produce these results, which implicated deeper-lying regions of the temporal lobe, including sites within the **limbic system.** These observations formed a cornerstone in the subsequent attempts to understand the role of subcortical structures in emotion.

- **Papez circuit of emotion**   Knowledge about brain anatomy and emotion has been derived from both experimental and clinical sources. In 1937, James W. Papez, a neuropathologist, proposed a neural circuit of emotions. Papez (pronounced Papes) derived his proposal from brain autopsies of humans with emotional disorders, including psychiatric patients. He also studied the brains of animal subjects, such as rabid dogs. He noted the sites of brain destruction in these cases and concluded that

Figure 13-11 Papez circuit
of emotion.

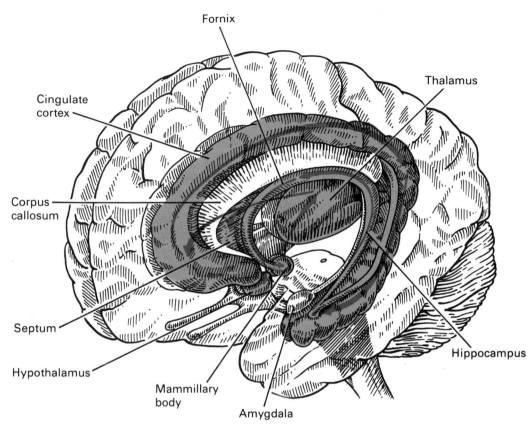

the necessary and sufficient destruction associated with impairment of emotional
feelings involved a set of interconnected pathways in the limbic system. According
to his circuit model, emotional expressions involved hypothalamic control of visceral organs, and feeling arose from connections to a circuit that includes the
hypothalamus, the mammillary bodies, the anterior thalamus, and the cingulate
cortex. The progression of activity in this circuit, as hypothesized by Papez, is
shown by the arrows in Figure 13-11.

Papez's proposed circuit has been the source of much experimental work in the
past 40 years. Each region in this circuit has been lesioned or electrically stimulated
to determine the relation to emotional processing. Aggression in particular has been
a focus of many studies of the Papez circuit because of its importance in human
affairs and the ease with which it can be observed in nonhumans. These studies have
expanded the complexity of the circuitry, especially by adding roles for other
structures in the limbic system, including the amygdala and the septal area.

● **The triune brain**   A broad, speculative neural model of emotion has been
presented by Paul MacLean (1970). His model arises from a diverse array of
observations, including the study of limbic system seizures in humans, maps of
behavior elicited by brain stimulation in monkeys, and an interpretation of the
research literature on the evolution of the mammalian brain.

According to MacLean, the human brain can be viewed as a three-layered system, with each layer marking a significant evolutionary development. The oldest and deepest layer represents our reptilian brain heritage and is seen in the current organization of the brainstem. It serves to mediate highly stereotyped acts that are part of a limited repertoire, including acts that creatures have to perform to survive, like breathing and eating. Routine maintenance is one way of describing these functions. In time, another layer wrapped around the reptilian core; this two-layered system is seen in some lower mammals. This additional layer, MacLean argues, deals with species and individual preservation and includes the neural apparatus mediating emotions, feeding, pain escape and avoidance, fighting, and pleasure seeking. The set of relevant structures in this layer is the limbic system. With a further progression of evolution, a final, third layer developed; it consisted of the dramatic elaboration of the cerebral cortex and provided the substrate for rational thought, according to this speculative model.

MacLean has viewed his model as providing an understanding of the common features of emotional responses among many animals and an understanding of changes evident with progressively higher animals. From the standpoint of understanding the advantage of the development of the limbic system, he sees the elaboration of these structures as offering the reptilian brain freedom from stereotyped behavior and a flexibility that is driven by emotions. Many aspects of his speculation suggest interesting thoughts about neural aspects of emotions, although assessments of the broad scope of his model are not yet available.

Electrical stimulation of the brain and emotion

Another productive approach to the neuroanatomy of emotion is to stimulate electrically sites in the brains of awake, freely moving animals and to note the effects on behavior. Such stimulation may produce either rewarding or aversive effects or may elicit sequences of emotional behavior.

● **Stimulation of the brain and positive reinforcement**   In 1954 psychologists James Olds and Peter Milner reported a remarkable experimental finding. They found that rats could learn to press a lever when the reward or reinforcement was a brief burst of electrical stimulation of the septal area within the limbic system. Another way to describe this phenomenon is brain "self-stimulation." Patients receiving electrical stimulation in this region are reported by Heath (1972) to feel a sense of pleasure or warmth, and in some instances stimulation in this region provoked sexual excitation.

The report of Olds and Milner (1954) is one of those rare scientific discoveries that starts a new field. Many investigators have employed brain self-stimulation techniques over the past 25 years. Some work has been concerned with mapping the distribution of brain sites that yield self-stimulation responses. Such studies can provide a portrait of the circuits of positive reinforcement. Other studies have analyzed the similarities and differences between positive responses elicited by brain stimulation and those elicited by other rewarding situations, such as presentation of food to a hungry animal or water to a thirsty animal. Perhaps electrical stimulation taps in on the circuits mediating these more customary rewards. Quite recently the direction of research in this area has moved in a neurochemical direction with many efforts being made to identify the relevant transmitters in brain pathways that mediate self-stimulation behavior. Work in this area can be of particular importance in understanding the impact of many drugs on emotional responses of humans.

Self-stimulation is not a peculiar property of rat brains. It can be shown in diverse mammals including cats, dogs, monkeys, and humans. Nevertheless, it has been most extensively studied in rats. In these animals self-stimulation by lever pressing can go on for hours; response rates vary with both electrical current values and brain site (Figure 13-12a). Early studies comparing self-stimulation with conditions that involve natural rewards—like food and water—seemed to reveal significant differences in reinforcement properties. For example, sudden extinction was seen with

Figure 13-12 Distribution of self stimulation regions in (a) rats and (b) humans. In (a) the rectangular boxes show where brain self-stimulation has been obtained in lever-pressing tasks. In (b) reward systems in the human brain are indicated by arrows. (Adapted from A. Routtenberg, "The reward system of the brain." Copyright © 1978 by Scientific American, Inc. All rights reserved.)

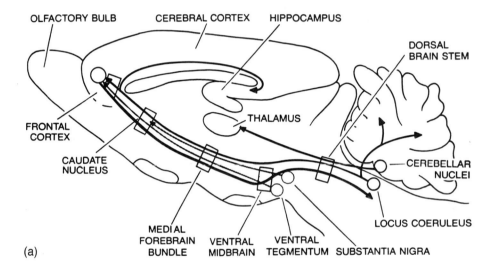

(a)

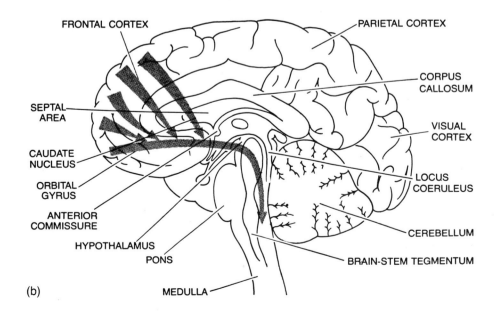

(b)

behavior reinforced by direct brain stimulation of self-stimulation regions; as soon as the electrical stimulation was interrupted, lever pressing ceased. However, more recent studies directly comparing responses for food, water, and electrical stimulation of the brain show similar features no matter which reinforcing condition is employed (reviewed in M.E. Olds and Fobes, 1981).

Self-stimulation is found with electrical stimulation of many different subcortical sites; however, cortical stimulation does not have positive reinforcement properties. Concentration of positive brain sites is seen in the hypothalamus, although these sites also extend into the brainstem. A large tract that ascends from the midbrain to the hypothalamus—the medial forebrain bundle—contains many sites that yield strong self-stimulation behavior. This bundle of axons is characterized by widespread origins and an extensive set of brain regions where terminals of these axons can be found. The anatomical arrangements of self-stimulation sites seem similar in different animals, although positive sites are spread more extensively throughout the rat brain than in the cat brain. More recently the maps of self-stimulation sites have been matched to those of various neurotransmitters. A very controversial idea that developed from observation of these maps is that dopamine is the transmitter for reward circuits. This notion is currently in doubt but has some supporters.

● Maps of elicited emotional responses   Electrical stimulation of the brains of alert, awake cats and monkeys implanted with electrodes has provided maps of the distribution of emotional responses. This work has especially emphasized limbic system sites and has focused particularly on aggression (described below). An example of the integration of behavioral and autonomic responses provoked by hypothalamic stimulation is shown in Figure 13-13, taken from the work of Kaada (1967). These maps show that very discrete components of both autonomic and behavioral responses are represented at selected loci in the limbic system and the hypothalamic regions. No instance of emotional response has been elicited by stimulation of the cerebral cortex.

Psychobiology of aggression

Violence, assaults, and homicide exact a high toll in many human societies; for example, homicide is the most prominent cause of death in young adults in the United States. Many different approaches to understanding aggression have investigated its psychological, anthropological, and biological dimensions. These concerted efforts have clarified many aspects of aggression along with its biological bases in hormonal and neurophysiological mechanisms. We will examine the results of these studies in this section.

What is aggression?

Surely we all know aggression! Alas, a more sustained consideration suggests that this all-too-familiar term is laden with many different meanings. In its ordinary, common usage, aggression defines an emotional state that many humans describe as consisting of feelings of hate and a desire to inflict harm. This perspective emphasizes aggression as a powerful inner feeling. However, when we view aggression as

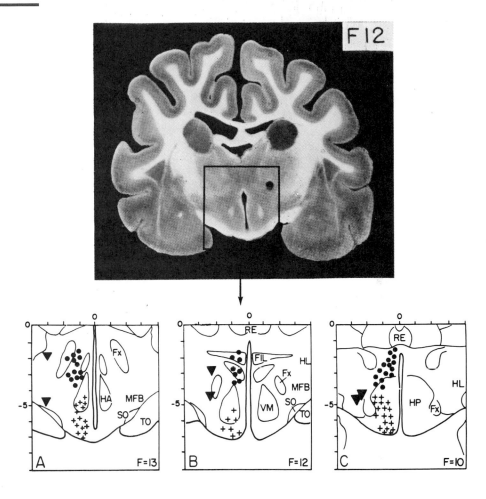

Figure 13-13 Distribution of sites in the hypothalamus from which electrical stimulation elicited defensive responses, flight, and attack and/or killing of prey. (+, defense; •, flight; ▼, prey-killing) Three different cross sections of the hypothalamus are shown. A is the most anterior. (FIL, nucleus filiformis; Fx, fornix; HA, anterior hypothalamus; HL, lateral hypothalamus; MFB, median forebrain bundle; SO, supraoptic nucleus; TO, optic tract; VM, ventro-medial nucleus) (Adapted from Kaada, 1967)

an overt response—overt behavior that involves actual or intended destruction of another organism—we see several different forms.

Attack behavior of an animal directed to a natural prey is seen by some as predatory aggression. However, Glickman (1977) has argued that this behavior is more appropriately designated as feeding behavior. Intermale aggression within the same species is found in virtually all vertebrates. Perhaps the relevance to humans is seen in the fact that the ratio of males to females arrested on charges of murder in the United States is 5:1, with a dominance in the age group 14–24. Further, aggressive behavior between boys, in contrast to that between girls, is seen quite early in the form of vigorous and destructive play behavior. (See Chapter 9.) Maternal aggression is seen in some animals and reaches an extreme form in the cannibalism of young by rodent mothers. Fear-induced aggression is seen in animals who are cornered and unable to escape. Some forms of aggression are seen as a component of sexual behavior. And, lastly, one form of aggression is referred to as irritable aggression; it can emerge from frustration or pain and frequently has the quality described as uncontrollable rage.

Hormones and aggression

Male sex hormones play a major role in some forms of aggressive behavior, especially that seen in intermale social encounters. This association has been found in several types of experiments. One set of data relates levels of circulating androgens to different measures of aggressive behavior. Variation in hormones among a group of animals can arise from processes of development or seasonal circadian changes. With the advent of sexual maturity intermale aggression markedly increases in many species. McKinney and Desjardins (1972) have shown aggressiveness changes in mice that start at puberty. Immature mice treated with androgen display increased aggression. Seasonal changes in testosterone are seen in many species, and increases in testicular size seem related to increased aggression in animals as diverse as birds and primates.

An additional line of evidence for the relation between hormones and aggression comes from observations of the behavioral effects of castration. Reductions in the level of circulating androgen produced in this manner are commonly associated with profound reduction in intermale aggressive behavior. Restoring testosterone by injection in castrated animals increases fighting behavior in mice in a dose-related manner (Figure 13-14).

Figure 13-14 Effects of androgen on aggressive behavior of mice. During each session, the number of biting attacks on an inanimate object is counted. (a) Male behavior before and after castration. (b) Female behavior before and after the removal of the ovaries. (c) The effects of hormone replacement on the attack behavior of castrated males. Testosterone reinstates aggressive behavior in castrated males. (From Wagner, Beauving, and Hutchinson, 1980)

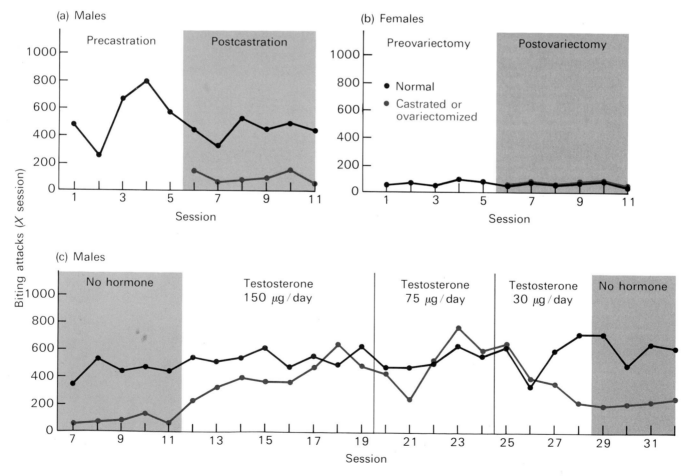

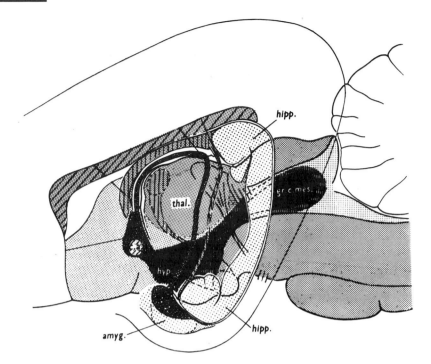

Figure 13-15 Distribution of brain sites in the cat that, during electrical stimulation, yield emotional responses. Stimulation of the inner zone of the hypothalamus (black) and the central gray elicits hissing. Stimulation of the outer zone (hatched) produces flight. (hipp., hippocampus; gr. c. mes., central gray; amyg., amygdala; hyp., hypothalamus; thal., thalamus) (From de Molina and Hunsperger, 1959)

The idea of a relationship between hormones—especially androgens—and human aggression is laden with controversy. For example, some males in jail for violent acts have sought castration in order to obtain parole. Arguments summoned in related legal briefs frequently cite the results of the literature on nonhuman animals. Some human studies have shown a positive correlation between testosterone levels and magnitude of hostility, as measured by behavior rating scales. But one study of prisoners (Kreuz and Rose, 1972) shows no relation between testosterone levels and several measures of aggressiveness; another study (Ehrenkrantz, Bliss, and Sheard, 1974) shows positive relations. Thus it is not clear that levels of androgens in intact men is related to aggressiveness.

Neural mechanisms of aggression

For many years researchers have electrically stimulated various brain regions in awake, behaving animals and thus sought to provide maps of the anatomy of aggressive acts. This work started with the pioneering experiments of Hess in the 1920s. The dramatic character of various components of feline aggressive behavior has made cats a favorite experimental animal. Figure 13-15 provides an example of the mapping of various aggressive displays in cats. Most of the sites that elicit aggressive behavior are found within the limbic system and connected brainstem regions. Regions differ in the patterning of elicited behavior and the emphasis on particular components. For example, brainstem stimulation in the central grey area produces piloerection, hissing, claw retraction, and especially prominent, loud, characteristic vocalizations.

Controversies about the neurology of human violence

Some forms of human violence exhibited by individuals are characterized by sudden intense physical assaults. In a very controversial book, "Violence and the Brain," Mark and Ervin (1970) have suggested that some forms of intense human violence are derived from temporal lobe seizure disorders. They offer horrifying examples from newspaper accounts as preliminary evidence. For example, in 1966, Charles Whitman climbed a tower at the University of Texas and murdered by wanton shooting a number of passing individuals. Earlier he had killed family members, and letters he left behind revealed a portrait of a bewildered young man possessed by an intense need to commit violence. Postmortem analysis of his brain suggested the presence of a tumor deep in the temporal lobe. Other, more formal data cited by Mark and Ervin include the common occurrence of aggression in temporal lobe seizure patients and the long-controversial claim that a large percentage of habitually aggressive criminals display abnormal EEGs that indicate likely temporal lobe disease. They argue that temporal lobe disorders may underlie many forms of human violence and produce a disorder they label "dyscontrol syndrome."

Mark and Erwin presented several detailed clinical reports of humans with possible temporal lobe seizure disorders. These patients had depth electrodes implanted within the temporal lobe. Electrical stimulation of various sites along the electrode tracts resulted in seizures typical of the patient. Characteristic data are shown in Figure 13-16. Intense assaultive behavior directly related to elicitation of temporal lobe seizure was seen. In some patients neurosurgical intervention—removal of some temporal lobe regions, especially the region of the amygdala—produced profound reduction in both seizure activity and reports of assaultive behavior.

Much of the controversy surrounding this monograph deals with the claim that a large proportion of human violence has this neuropathological origin (Valenstein, 1973). Vigorous controversy is also promoted by the implicit argument that neu-

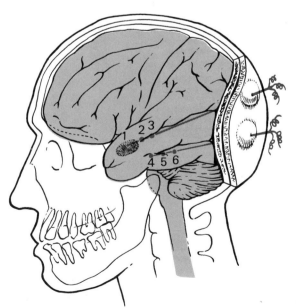

Figure 13-16 Human aggression and temporal lobe stimulation. Responses of this patient to stimulation at different sites within the temporal lobe are shown. The amygdala is the oval body penetrated by the tip of the upper electrode. (Adapted from Mark and Ervin, 1970)

1. Pleasant; hopeful; relaxed; confident; complete opposite of seizure; creative; elated; floating; warm; peaceful; calm
2. Unpleasant; "radio waves" in chest
3. Feeling of "looking on" scene
4. Power gone; weak; weird
5. Odd; warm; floating; blurred vision
6. Breathless; difficult to communicate thoughts

rosurgery can alleviate forms of violent behavior that many others feel are more readily understood as products of social distress and developmental impairment.

Discussions about the biology of human violence have also given considerable emphasis to certain abnormalities of human sex chromosomes. This interest was partially fostered by the observation that a murderer who had killed a group of nurses in their home had the rare XYY chromosome pattern. Some investigators noting the link to male hormones seen in infrahuman studies of hormones and aggression suggested a connection between an extra Y chromosome and violence. This chromosome disorder is a very rare occurrence, so testing of this relation proved difficult. A group of investigators who were aware of the very thorough birth and life history data in Denmark pursued a thorough analysis of the relation between human aggression and the XYY chromosome type (Mednick and Christiansen, 1977). To the surprise of some, they found that although XYY chromosome males were more likely to be in jail than normals the crime that resulted in jailing was less likely to have been violent in nature. In fact, the cause for jailing was usually petty theft and similar offenses; diminished social intelligence of many of these men seemed to preclude the ability to hide their crimes.

Biology of mental disorders

Around the turn of the twentieth century one widely prevalent psychosis accounted for 20–25% of the patient populations in mental hospitals. Descriptions of the patients emphasized these attributes: profound delusions, grandiosity and euphoria, poor judgment, impulsive and capricious behavior, and profound changes in thought structure.

This disorder was known in virtually all societies of the world and had been known for centuries. Many people regarded it as a functional psychosis derived from the stresses and strains of personal and social interactions. Then in 1911 the microbiologist Hideyo Noguchi discovered the cause of this profound psychosis. Examining the brains of patients during autopsy, he established that extensive brain changes were wrought by *treponema pallidum,* a bacterium of the class spirochete. This psychosis was produced by syphilis, a venereal infection that has journeyed through history with humans. Noguchi's discovery ushered in an era of biological psychiatry, which many believe is now reaching its golden age. Since one kind of psychosis was demonstrated to be caused by physical changes produced in brain cells, investigators sought to find neurological causes for other psychotic conditions (see Box 13-1).

Genetic studies of schizophrenia

In many cultures heredity has been emphasized as a causal factor in the development of mental disorders. Vigorous debate stirs meetings of psychiatrists whenever the issue of genetics and mental disorder is raised. Some of this controversy stems from the limitations of human genetics data in so complicated an area as mental illness. Argument also stems from misunderstanding about the implications of genetic contributions to mental illness. Some view such prospects with a sense of fatalism and see genetic influence as inevitable. But as we will see shortly, even where a genetic factor has been demonstrated for a disorder, one twin in a pair of identical twins may develop the disorder while the other does not. The role of genetic research in psychiatry is to contribute to an understanding of the causal chain of predisposing, precipitating, and maintaining factors that are involved in mental illness. Knowledge

BOX 13-1   Changes in the Brain Anatomy of Schizophrenics

Since in many patients the symptoms of schizophrenia are so marked and persistent, is there a measurable structural change in their brains? Postmortem investigations of the brains of schizophrenics during the past hundred years have yielded occasional exciting findings that have been rapidly challenged by better-controlled studies. Studies in this field usually involved aged patients or those who had been hospitalized for long periods. Recent developments in radiology, notably tomography, have made it possible to study brain anatomy in living patients at all stages of their illness. Data obtained from such cases have begun to show a consistent finding of changes in the size of the lateral ventricles in schizophrenic patients. Brain changes do occur in schizophrenia!

Weinberger and colleagues (1979) performed computer tomogram scans on psychiatric patients and com-

pared them with tomograms from a large control group of healthy individuals. Ventricular size was measured, and the results revealed a significant difference: The ventricles of chronic schizophrenics were larger than those of normals. Ventricular enlargement was not related to length of illness or to duration of hospitalization. In a follow-up study Weinberger (1980) has indicated that the degree of ventricular enlargement predicts the patient's response to antipsychotic drugs. Patients with the more enlarged ventricles show poorer response to these drugs in terms of reducing the psychotic symptoms. The ventricular enlargement found in schizophrenics implies atrophy of adjacent neural tissue. These studies may provide clues to the loci of changes in neural tissue that may account for the symptoms of schizophrenia.

of the role of genetic mechanisms may foster a clearer understanding of those aspects of mental disorders that originate from inheritable mechanisms, in contrast with those that are more directly connected with the experiences of patients.

The world population of schizophrenics is estimated at about 10 million. The size of this health problem is also reflected in the large percentage of mental hospital patients diagnosed as schizophrenic; estimates have ranged as high as 50% of all mental hospital patients in the United States. Because of the large number of patients, scientists have been able to conduct a variety of genetic studies (Schulsinger, 1980). These include family or pedigree studies, twin studies, and adoption studies. We will take up each of these in turn.

● Family studies   Family studies involve determinations of the number of relatives of schizophrenics—parents, siblings, and more distant relatives—who are also schizophrenic. The proportion of schizophrenics among a patient's relatives is called his or her "morbidity risk." Such data are compared with the risk rate of the general population. In general, parents and siblings of patients have a higher risk of being or becoming schizophrenic than do individuals in the general population. The risk is greater the closer the biological relatedness.

It is easy to find fault with family studies. For one thing, they involve a thorough confusion of hereditary and experiential factors, since members of a family share both of these. In addition, the data usually depend on the recollections of relatives whose memories are likely to be clouded by zealous efforts to attribute "blame" in consideration of the origins of the disorder. Funny aunts and uncles now departed are easily designated as the responsible agents in the etiology of mental disorder. But better family studies restrict data to professionally diagnosed cases.

TABLE 13-1
Concordance Rates of
Schizophrenia for Monozygotic
and Dizygotic Twins

	CONCORDANCE RATES (%)	
Study	*Monozygotic*	*Dizygotic*
A	61	10
B	82	15
C	75	14
D	42	9
E	38	10

● **Twin studies**   In providing twins, nature gives researchers what would seem on casual glance to be the conditions for a perfect genetic experiment. Human twins can arise either from the same egg (identical twins) or from two different eggs (fraternal twins). Additionally, many twins have other siblings as well. Twin studies of schizophrenia are concerned with determining the occurrence of schizophrenia in twins, especially the difference in rate of occurrence between identical and fraternal twins. When both individuals of a twin pair are schizophrenic, they are described as being concordant for this trait. If only one member of the pair is schizophrenic, the pair is described as discordant. Table 13-1 compares concordance rates in identical and fraternal twins. Concordance rates in these studies are much higher in identical twins. This fact is clear.

But can we accept such data as reflecting the inheritability of schizophrenia? Twin studies of schizophrenia have been criticized on several grounds. Some data indicate that twins are unusual from a developmental perspective in that they usually show lighter birth weights and different developmental progress than nontwins. In addition, parental treatment of identical twins differs considerably from their interaction with fraternal twins, thus generating a compounding environmental variable.

Despite these weaknesses, twin studies do indicate the importance of genetic mechanisms in the development of psychotic disorders, particularly schizophrenia. They regularly show higher concordance rates for schizophrenia in identical twins than those observed in fraternal twins or ordinary siblings. However, it is important to note that even with identical twins concordance for schizophrenia is less than 100%. Although the genetic constitution is identical for both identical twins, one member of the identical twin pair may be schizophrenic and the other normal.

Studies of identical twins discordant for schizophrenia can provide useful information about the possible factors that lead to schizophrenia and those that protect against the emergence of it. An excellent review of this problem by Wahl (1976) highlights some of the major findings. Many studies emphasize the finding that the twin that developed schizophrenia tended to be the one who was more abnormal throughout life. The symptomatic twin frequently weighed less at birth and had an early developmental history that included more instances of physiological distress. This developmental history is also connected with the parents' view of the symptomatic twin as more vulnerable. During development this twin was more submissive, fearful, and sensitive than the identical sibling. More controversial findings include observations of elevated urinary 17-OH steroid levels in the symptomatic twin; but this result may reflect the ongoing stresses of the schizophrenic disorder rather than indicating a physiological state related to pathogenesis. This type of study is in its infancy and may yet provide indications about how to protect against schizophrenia. We mention this aspect of genetic studies to show that genetic studies of schizophrenia are not "fatalistic" in design but rather can provide a positive view of prevention.

● **Adoption studies**   Criticisms of twin techniques led to adoption studies, which have produced substantial support for the significance of genetic factors in many psychiatric disorders. Most of the relevant data have come from Scandinavian countries, where quite complete data are available for follow-up studies of adoptees. In studies reported by Kety and his collaborators (1975) the biological and adopting parents of all children given up for adoption early in life in a particular time period were identified, and a determination was made of those who had been hospitalized for psychiatric difficulties. Psychiatric disorder was found to a higher degree among the offspring of schizophrenic parents than in a control group of children of non-schizophrenic parents who gave their children up for adoption. Further, if we change the point of reference and look at comparisons of the biological and foster parents of schizophrenic adoptees, striking evidence is displayed. The biological parents of schizophrenic adoptees are far more likely to have been schizophrenic than are the adopting parents. It should be emphasized that the rearing of these patients was almost entirely by adopting parents and therefore social influences from a schizophrenic parent were virtually nil. Although the group of parents giving children up for adoption early in life is in general more likely to involve psychiatric problems than the general population, the differences between control and patient comparisons remain striking. The findings provide conclusive evidence for genetic factors that predispose to schizophrenia.

Although the evidence for genetic transmission of predisposition to schizophrenia is clear, there is still controversy about alternative genetic models. Neither single gene models nor multifactor models fit all the data. This poses a problem as to what advice to give in genetic counselling. More research is needed to clarify the mechanism of genetic transmission in schizophrenia. A promising new experimental design called "family of twins" includes adult identical twins, their spouses, and their children. This design allows testing assumptions over several degrees of relationship within a single study (Henderson, 1982).

Physiological and biochemical theories of schizophrenia

Throughout history explanations of mental disorder have emphasized biological origins. Bodily factors claimed to be related to schizophrenia have included injury, infection, diet, and brain disease. As knowledge about the neurochemistry of the brain has grown, hypotheses about the basis of schizophrenia have become more precise. Several major views backed by large amounts of experimental data and clinical observation characterize contemporary orientations to the biological origins of schizophrenia. One view holds that schizophrenia arises from faulty metabolic processes in the brain that lead to excesses or insufficiencies of neurochemicals that are ordinarily found in the brain. In most cases these substances are neurotransmitters. An example is provided by the most influential view in current work in schizophrenia, which focuses on the role of dopamine (described below). A second general perspective proposes that schizophrenia develops from faulty metabolic processes in the brain that produce abnormal substances that generate psychotic behavior. Such hypothetical substances, called **psychotogens** or **schizotoxins,** might be similar in some of their properties to hallucinogenic agents. The "transmethylation" hypothesis (also described below) is an example of this orientation.

Although exciting ideas and data are apparent in the research, several problems continue to frustrate major progress. First, it is very hard to separate biological events that are primary causes of psychiatric disorder from those that are secondary effects. Secondary effects are those that arise from the profound impairments of social behavior and may range from dietary limitations to prolonged stress. Treatment variables also can mask or distort the search for primary causes, since they frequently produce marked changes in brain and body physiology and biochemistry. A second major problem in schizophrenia research is the definition of the term "schizophrenia." Is it a single disorder or many disorders with very different origins and outcomes? Psychiatrists have wrestled with this problem for a long time, and many have suggested that "schizophrenia" is not a uniform label, since two major types of schizophrenia can be distinguished. One type, called process schizophrenia, shows an early history of social reclusiveness, and these patients become psychotic in later adolescence; very often they show a chronic lifelong course of intermittent or continuing psychotic episodes. No apparent situational factors appear to provoke the psychotic breakdown. The other type, called reactive schizophrenia, by contrast shows a more obvious connection to situational stress factors. These patients have a more acute psychotic period and have greater chances of making a satisfactory adjustment.

● **Dopamine hypothesis**   Many clinical and basic research findings have argued that abnormal levels of dopamine form the basis of schizophrenia. Dopamine (as we saw in Chapter 4) is a synaptic transmitter in the brain. Findings suggesting this basis have converged from several sources, including amphetamine psychosis, effects of tranquilizing agents, and Parkinson's disease.

Part of the dopamine story starts with the search for experimental models of schizophrenia. Basic scientific advances in the understanding of human disease frequently depend on the development of a controllable model of a disorder, usually an animal replica that can be turned on and off by experimenters. Some scientists involved in psychiatric research have suggested the effects of certain hallucinogenic agents as models of schizophrenia. There is no question that many drugs, such as LSD and mescaline, produce profound perceptual, cognitive, and emotional changes. And many aspects of psychoses are reproduced by these agents. However, several features of the behavioral effects of these drugs are quite dissimilar from those of schizophrenia. Most drug-induced psychoses are characterized by confusion, disorientation, and frank delirium; these are not typical symptoms of schizophrenia. Hallucinations produced by these drugs are usually visual, in contrast to the predominantly auditory hallucinations of schizophrenia. Schizophrenic patients given LSD report that the experience produced by the drug is very different from the experiences of their disorder, and psychiatrists can readily distinguish taped conversations of schizophrenics from those of subjects given hallucinogenic agents. One drug state, however, has come close to replicating the schizophrenic state—amphetamine psychosis.

Amphetamine abuse causes an unusual psychosis. Some individuals use amphetamine on an everyday basis as a stimulant. But if the same level of euphoria is to be maintained, the self-administered dose must be progressively increased and may reach as much as 3000 milligrams per day (mg/day). Contrast this level with the usual 5 mg taken to control appetite or prolong wakefulness. Many of these individuals develop paranoid symptoms, often involving delusions of persecution with auditory hallucinations. Suspiciousness and bizarre postures also are included in the portrait of this state. The similarity of amphetamine psychosis to schizophrenia is also suggested by the finding that amphetamine exacerbates symptoms in

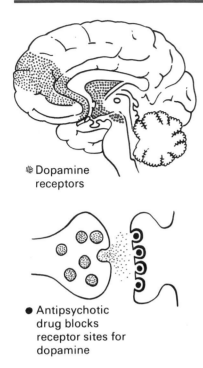

● Dopamine
receptors

● Antipsychotic
drug blocks
receptor sites for
dopamine

Figure 13-17 Distribution of dopamine
receptors in the brain.

schizophrenia. The neurochemical effects of amphetamine are to promote release of catecholamines, particularly dopamine, and to prolong the action of the released transmitter by blocking reuptake. Rapid relief of the amphetamine psychosis is provided by an injection of chlorpromazine—a substance that brings us to the second part of the story leading to the dopamine hypothesis.

In the early 1950s the population of psychiatric hospitals in the United States was about half a million. This hospital population has dramatically decreased in size in the years since then. Several factors contributed to this reduction, the most significant being the introduction of a remarkable drug in the treatment of schizophrenia. In the search for a substance to produce muscle relaxation for surgery, French surgeon Henri Laborit discovered a compound that also reduced worry and preoperative tension. An insightful investigator, Laborit then collaborated with psychiatrists in using this substance on psychiatric patients; they found remarkable antipsychotic effects. This drug, **chlorpromazine,** was then introduced on a large scale in the psychiatric hospitals around the world and produced a profound impact on psychiatry. By now, a massive number of well-controlled studies point to the fact that this substance and many related to it (called phenothiazines) have a specific antipsychotic effect. Neurochemical studies show that this substance acts in the brain by blocking postsynaptic receptor sites for dopamine (Figure 13-17). In fact, the clinical effectiveness of antipsychotic agents (also called tranquilizers) is directly related to the magnitude of postsynaptic receptor blockage of dopamine sites. This result suggests that schizophrenia may be produced either by abnormal levels of available and released dopamine or by excessive postsynaptic sensitivity to released dopamine, which might involve an excessively large population of postsynaptic dopamine receptor sites.

Another trail leading to the dopamine hypothesis of schizophrenia involves Parkinson's disease (discussed in Chapter 8). As we have noted, this disorder is caused by degeneration of nerve cells located in the brainstem (in a region called the substantia nigra). These cells contain dopamine, and some relief is produced by the administration of the substance L-dopa, which is a precursor for the synthesis of dopamine. L-dopa increases the amount of released dopamine. Two connections to schizophrenia and the dopamine hypothesis are apparent in the study of parkinsonian patients. First, some patients given L-dopa to relieve the symptoms of Parkinson's disease become psychotic. Second, some schizophrenic patients receiving chlorpromazine develop parkinsonian symptoms. In fact, movement disorders as a consequence of tranquilizer treatment may be permanent (see Box 13-2 on tardive dyskinesia).

Recently criticisms of a dopamine model of schizophrenia have been presented (Alpert and Friedhoff, 1980). Emphasized in these assessments is the fact that direct evidence of the level of functioning of dopamine receptors in patients is lacking or confusing. Although schizophrenic brains show an increase in dopamine receptors (Lee and Seeman, 1980), this result could develop from reduced dopamine turnover. Critics note that an increase in dopamine receptors is significant only in the presence of normal levels of dopamine. A further difficulty for this hypothesis is the lack of correspondence between the time at which drugs produce dopamine blockade (quite rapidly) and the behavior changes that signal the clinical effectiveness of the drug (usually on the order of weeks). Thus the relation of dopamine to schizophrenia

BOX 13-2 Tardive Dyskinesia and Supersensitivity Psychosis: Dilemmas in Drug Treatment of Schizophrenia

Few would dispute the view that drugs like chlorpromazine have had a revolutionary impact in the treatment of schizophrenia. Many people who might otherwise have been in mental hospitals for the remainder of their lives can take care of themselves in nonhospital settings. Drugs of this class can justly be regarded as antipsychotic.

However, these drugs often have other effects that raise questions in psychiatry and pose novel research problems for the neurosciences. Soon after the introduction of these drugs, users were seen to develop various maladaptive motor symptoms **(dyskinesia).** Many of these symptoms were transient and were eliminated with a reduction in dose levels. But some drug-induced motor changes only emerge after prolonged drug treatment—after months and, in some cases, years—hence the term **tardive,** or late. Included in this set of motor effects are an array of involuntary movements, especially those involving the face, mouth, lips, and tongue. Elaborate uncontrollable movements of the tongue are particularly prominent, including incessant rolling movements and sucking or smacking movements of the lips. Twisting and sudden jerking movements of the arms or legs are seen occasionally in some patients. These effects of anti-psychotic substances are seen in a large percentage of patients; estimates range as high as a third of all drug-treated patients. Female patients are usually more severely affected than males (Smith et al., 1979). The alarming aspect of this motor impairment is that it frequently continues as a permanent disability even when drug treatment is halted.

Another unusual effect of long-term drug treatment occurs in the nonmotor realm. Prolonged blockage of dopamine receptors with these drugs seems to increase the number of dopamine receptors and lead to receptor supersensitivity. In some patients discontinuation of the drugs or a lowering of dosage results in a sudden, marked increase in "positive" symptoms of schizophrenia, such as delusions or hallucinations. The effect is often reversible by increasing the dose level of dopamine-receptor blocking agents. However, there are some data suggesting that this "supersensitivity psychosis" might be enduring.

Both tardive dyskinesia and supersensitivity psychosis are pressing problems for future research, since they may limit the effectiveness of these substances in the treatment of schizophrenia.

may be more complex than that envisioned in the simple model of hyperactive dopamine synapses.

In this section we have seen several lines of evidence pointing to the involvement of dopamine in the schizophrenic psychosis. Several other transmitters have been linked to schizophrenia; these are described and discussed in Box 13-3.

● **Schizotoxin theories**   Organic chemists have noticed a similarity in the chemical structure of manufactured hallucinogens and some substances found as normal ingredients in the brain. This structural similarity of natural and artificial substances raised the prospect that the brain might accidentally produce a psychotogen—a chemical substance that produces psychotic behavior. Metabolic faults in particular pathways might allow particular reactions to go on in the brain and convert an innocuous molecule into a behaviorally maladaptive substance capable of producing schizophrenic symptoms. A major hypothesis generated by this view suggests a particular chemical mechanism. According to this view, the addition of a methyl group (CH_3) to some naturally occurring brain compounds can convert some substances to known hallucinogenic agents. This hypothesis is known as the **transmethylation hypothesis;** it was initiated by the work of Osmond and Smythies in

BOX 13-3 Endorphins and Schizophrenia

Excitement in neuroscience circles is running high about the roles of endorphins in the brain. Their significance in the control of transmission in pain pathways of the spinal cord and brain was explored in Chapter 7. As new substances are discovered in the brain, scientists examine their roles in many different kinds of behavior, especially in the realms of major human disorders. And possible connections between schizophrenia and endorphins have been drawn by several experimental observations.

Using the behavior of endorphin-injected rats as a clue, Bloom and his collaborators (1978) suggested that levels of endorphins are related to schizophrenia. They based this suggestion on the appearance of a "catatonic"-like state in injected animals. More decisive (although controversial) data have come from one study showing high endorphin levels in the cerebrospinal fluid of schizophrenics. This observation led Barchas and collaborators (1979) to examine the effects of naloxone on schizophrenic behavior. Naloxone is a specific antagonist to morphine and related substances like endorphins. If excess levels of endorphins are related to some aspects of psychotic states, it would then follow that blocking the effects of endorphins might attenuate the symptoms of schizophrenia. Although still fraught with controversy, the data presented by Barchas's group (1979) indicate that naloxone can produce a dramatic transient reduction in hallucinations and other signs of psychotic distress. This dramatic finding was not confirmed by another group, although differences of dose level may account for the discrepancy.

Further studies in this area may yield a connection to dopamine pathways, which appear to be involved in the action of many antipsychotic drugs like phenothiazines. As we noted in Chapter 7, a growing research literature suggests that endorphins have many roles in integrating and mediating behaviors rather than in simply controlling pain.

---

the 1950s, which showed hallucinogenic properties for a substance called adrenochrome. This substance was viewed as a possible metabolic product of norepinephrine—now known to be a neurotransmitter in the brain as well as in the peripheral autonomic nervous system.

More recently many experiments have tested the idea that transmethylation could produce a compound that might act as a substance that produces schizophrenia—a schizotoxin. One way to test this idea is to administer substances (methyl donors) that provide a good supply of methyl groups. When administered to patients, some of these substances produce an exacerbation of symptoms, although the effect is not general to all such substances. This inconsistency, coupled with problems in understanding how this mechanism could account for the effects of tranquilizers, limits the current credibility of this proposal.

Can the body produce amphetaminelike substances by metabolizing norepinephrine? Amphetamine psychosis resembles paranoid schizophrenia, and production of an amphetaminelike substance would be an extremely interesting finding. Recently several investigators have argued that phenylethylamine is produced in small quantities by the metabolism of norepinephrine. This substance has amphetaminelike properties. Current work seeks to assess levels of this metabolite in the bodies of schizophrenics.

Lastly, some (for example, see Stein and Wise, 1971) have suggested a metabolic fault in schizophrenic brains that results in the production of a neurotoxin that destroys particular synaptic terminals. Destruction of dopaminergic and noradrenergic terminals by a substance called 6-hydroxy-dopamine is well known, and

Stein and Wise suggest that this unusual substance might be produced in the brains of schizophrenics by the incomplete conversion of dopamine to norepinephrine. They suggest that a reduction in the level of the enzyme dopamine beta hydroxylase might result in this consequence. Preliminary studies using brain samples of deceased patients initially showed a reduction in the level of this substance. Controversy surrounds this result, and further research is needed.

Affective disorders

Many of us go through periods of unhappiness that we commonly describe as **depression.** However, in some persons a depressive state is more than a passing malaise and occurs over and over with a cyclical regularity. These people are usually over 40 years old, and women are two to three times as likely to suffer from depression as men. For such individuals this state is characterized by an unhappy mood, loss of interests, energy, and appetite, difficulty in concentration, and restless agitation. Pessimism seems to seep into every act. Periods of such **unipolar depressions** (that is, depressions that alternate with normal emotional states) can occur with no readily apparent stress. Without treatment the depression lasts for several months.

Some individuals have depressed periods that alternate with periods of excessively expansive moods that include sustained overactivity, talkativeness, increased energy, and strange grandiosity. This condition is called **bipolar illness** (also known as **manic-depressive psychosis**). Men and women are equally affected, and the age of onset is usually much younger than that in unipolar depression.

Genetic studies of unipolar and bipolar disorders reveal strong hereditary contributions. Concordance is much higher for monozygotic as opposed to dizygotic twins. In monozygotic twins concordance rates are similar for twins reared apart and those reared together. Adoption studies show high rates of affective illness in the biological parents in comparison to foster parents.

Work on the psychobiology of affective illness has been very much influenced over the past 20 years by a theory offered by Joseph Schildkraut and Seymour Kety (1967) called the **monoamine hypothesis of depression.** According to this view, depressive illness is associated with a decrease in synaptic activity of connections that employ the synaptic transmitters norepinephrine and serotonin. This decrease is especially characteristic of hypothalamic and associated limbic system circuitry. Evidence offered for this hypothesis emphasizes the clinical effectiveness of two forms of treatment (Figure 13-18). Some antidepressant drugs inhibit monoamine oxidase and thus raise the level of available norepinephrine. Electroconvulsive treatment is especially valuable in many depressed patients, and these seizures have a strong impact on biogenic amines. In contrast, the drug reserpine, which depletes the norepinephrine and serotonin of the brain (by releasing intraneuronal monoamine oxidase, thereby breaking down these transmitters), results in a profound depression. This hypothesis continues to be summoned as a biological explanation of affective illness, although the clinical effectiveness of many drugs is not easily related to the monoamine system. An alternative hypothesis is that antidepressant drugs work by blocking neural receptors for histamine (Kanof and Greengard, 1978).

The treatment of manic episodes has advanced greatly in recent years with the use of lithium, a simple metallic ion. In the nervous system lithium has an action similar to sodium: It can replace sodium in determining the resting and action potentials of

Comparative Effectiveness of EST and Chemotherapy

Diagnosis	EST	Chemotherapy			
		Tricyclics	Antipsychotics	MAO Inhibitors	Lithium
Depression					
Psychotic	●—	○	●	○	●
Neurotic	○	●	○	●	○
Endogenous	●—	●—	●	○	●
Involutional	●—	◐	●	?	?
Schizophrenic	●	○	◐	○	?
Manic-Depressive Disease					
Manic phase	◐	?	◐	?	●—
Depressive phase	●—		●	?	●
Catatonia	●—	?	◐	?	?
Schizophrenia					
Acute	●	○	◐	○	?
Childhood	○	○	●	○	?
Anorexia nervosa	?	○	○	●	?
Drug psychosis	○	○	●	○	?
Personality disorder	○	○	○	?	?

●— Highly effective   ◐ Moderately effective   ● Possibly effective   ○ Ineffective   ? Efficacy uncertain

Figure 13-18 Efficacy of different clinical treatments for depression and other disorders. EST refers to electroshock therapy. (From Fink, 1978)

nerves. It has diverse effects on various transmitters including decreased responses to norepinephrine. It is particularly potent in preventing manic excitement periods, and some infrahuman studies show that lithium reduces aggressive behaviors in rats and cats.

Surgical treatment in psychiatry

Down through the ages the mentally disabled have been treated by methods limited only by the human imagination. Some of the methods have been gruesome and were inspired by views that the mentally disordered were controlled by demonical forces. While twentieth-century psychiatry has been purged of such moralistic views, until recently treatment was on a trial-and-error basis, and inspiration for new efforts came from diverse sources. In the 1930s experiments on frontal lobe lesions in chimpanzees inspired Egas Moniz to attempt similar operations in patients. He was intrigued by the report of a calming influence in nonhuman primates, and at the time he tried frontal surgery little else was available. His observations led to the beginning of **psychosurgery,** defined as the use of surgically produced brain lesions to modify severe psychiatric disorders. Throughout its use there has been vigorous debate, which continues to the present (Valenstein, 1980).

During the 1940s frontal lobe surgery was forcefully advocated by several neurosurgeons and psychiatrists. A recent presidential commission on psychosurgery estimates that during this period 10,000–50,000 patients underwent this surgery. During the most intense period of enthusiasm, patients of all diagnostic types were operated on, and varieties of surgery were employed (Figure 13-19).

Interest in psychosurgery arose from the saddening sight of so many people in mental hospitals living empty, disturbed lives without hope of change. No drug to that point aided chronic schizophrenics, and the population of permanently hospitalized continued to mount. Since psychiatric hospitals were becoming very crowded, many unusual remedies were tried. Today frontal surgery is limited to

(a)

(b)

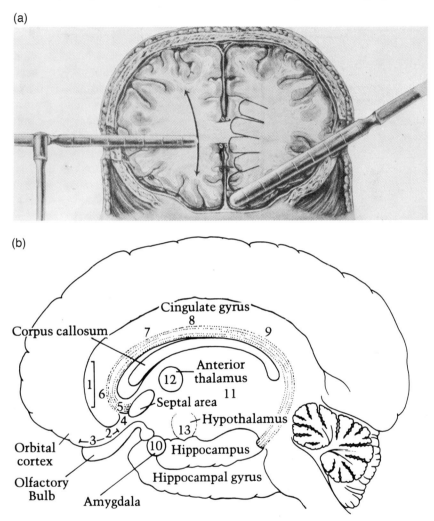

Figure 13-19 Forms of psychosurgery used in the treatment of mental illness. (a) An early lobotomy procedure employed by Freeman and Watts in the frontal lobes. A cutting device was placed in the frontal lobes and rotated, severing connections between the frontal lobe and the thalamus. (b) More recent psychosurgical procedures. Numbers indicate sites of intended tissue destruction. These procedures are more localized than that noted in (a). 1. Leucotomy severing some frontal lobe connections. 2. Lesion in subcortical white matter. 3. Partial cutting of orbital frontal cortex. 4. Section of some tissue below the caudate nucleus. 5. Destruction of fibers of the internal capsule. 6. Lesions near the knee of the corpus callosum. 7, 8, and 9 include sections at different points in the cingulate cortex. 10. Amygdalectomy. 11 and 12. Lesions of thalamic nuclei. 13. Hypothalamic surgery. [(a) From Freeman and Watts, *Psychosurgery in the treatment of mental disorders, second edition,* 1950. Courtesy of Charles C. Thomas, Publisher, Springfield, Illinois. (b) From Valenstein, 1980]

controlling emotional arousal accompanying intense pain. Its use in psychiatry has practically ended, although the commission on psychosurgery has urged further consideration of the role of surgery in psychiatry. (In an earlier section in this chapter we noted the related use of temporal lobe surgery for relief from violent behavior attributed to seizure activity.)

Assessments of the value of frontal lobe surgery on psychiatric treatment are steeped in controversy. Some researchers showed clinical improvements, and even recently William Sweet (1973) argued that more localized brain lesions might provide significant aid in particular psychiatric disorders. However, the use of drugs has overshadowed psychosurgery, especially since surgical results seem much less reversible than brain lesions produced by neurosurgery.

The development of techniques for accurate placement of depth electrodes in humans has led some surgeons to use subcortical lesions in psychiatric disorders. Newer surgical targets include the amygdala, the cingulate, and the hypothalamus. Some of these new surgical targets were chosen on the basis of research results with nonhumans. For example, in Germany several surgeons have used hypothalamic lesions to "cure" sexual deviations (Roeder, Orthner, and Muller, 1972). But the ethical implications of such interventions are complex (Valenstein, 1980). This kind of work is partly inspired by lesion experiments in rats, but Beach (1979) has warned that this may reflect an inappropriate use of animal models.

SUMMARY / MAIN POINTS

1. The term "emotion" includes both private subjective feelings and expressions or displays of particular somatic and autonomic responses.

2. The James-Lange theory considered emotions as the perception of stimulus-induced bodily changes, whereas the Cannon-Bard theory emphasized brain integration of emotional experiences and responses. A cognitive theory of emotion argues that activity in a physiological system is not enough to provoke an emotion. Rather the key feature in emotion is the interpretation of visceral activities.

3. Facial expressions of particular emotions are similarly presented and recognized in many quite different human societies.

4. Biofeedback experiments involving visceral activity have shown learned modifications of heart rate and blood pressure that can be very specific.

5. The impact of emotions on human health can be seen in measures of illness following stress. Reports of illness tend to be higher in groups that sustain prolonged stress, although constitutional factors are also important.

6. The pathological toll of stress can be seen in experiments on ulcer formation in rats, especially when the animal performs any adaptive response to the stressful stimulus.

7. Assessment of physiological effects of stress in real-life situations, in contrast to artificial laboratory situations, shows that stress produces elevations in several hormones, such as cortisol, growth hormone, and epinephrine. Successful completion of a stressful task reduces the level of hormone response on subsequent exposure to the same situation.

8. Brain regions involved in emotion include an array of interconnected sites within the limbic system.

9. Electrical stimulation of many sites within the limbic system is rewarding, as seen in self-stimulation experiments. Electrical stimulation of the cerebral cortex does not result in positive reinforcement.

10. Aggression has several hormonal relations, the most prominent being the association with the level of circulating androgens. In humans, however, the relation between the level of testosterone and criminal behavior is controversial. Argument also abounds about the role of temporal lobe epilepsy and the human "dyscontrol syndrome."

11. There is strong evidence for a genetic factor in the etiology of schizophrenia. Consistent evidence comes from the study of the incidence of schizophrenia in families, twins, and foster-reared people.

12. Biological theories of schizophrenia include two general classes of ideas: (a) the view that schizophrenia comes about because of a failure at some level in the operation of neurotransmitters at synapses, and (b) the view that schizophrenia develops from a metabolic fault that results in the production of a toxic substance, a psychotogen with properties similar to known hallucinogenic agents.

13. The dopamine hypothesis attributes schizophrenia to excess release or sensitivity to dopamine. Supporting evidence comes from studies on the effects of antipsychotic drugs, amphetamine psychosis, and Parkinson's disease.

14. Biological studies of affective disorders like unipolar depression reveal a strong genetic factor and also note the importance of levels of neurotransmitters.

RECOMMENDED READING

Grings, W. W., and Davison, M. E. *Emotions and bodily responses: A psychophysiological approach*. New York: Academic Press, 1978.

Maser, J. D., and Seligman, M. E. P. (Eds.). *Psychopathology: Experimental models*. San Francisco: Freeman, 1977.

Plutchik, R., and Kellerman, H. (Eds.). *Emotion: Theory, research, and experience*. Vol. 1: *Theories of emotion*. New York: Academic Press, 1980.

Snyder, S. H. *Biological aspects of mental disorder*. New York: Oxford University Press, 1980.

Stern, R. M., Ray, W. J., and Davis, C. M. *Psychophysiological recording*. New York: Oxford University Press, 1980.

Valenstein, E. S. *The psychosurgery debate: Scientific, legal, and ethical perspectives*. San Francisco: Freeman, 1980.

Valzelli, L. *Psychobiology of aggression and violence*. New York: Raven Press, 1980.

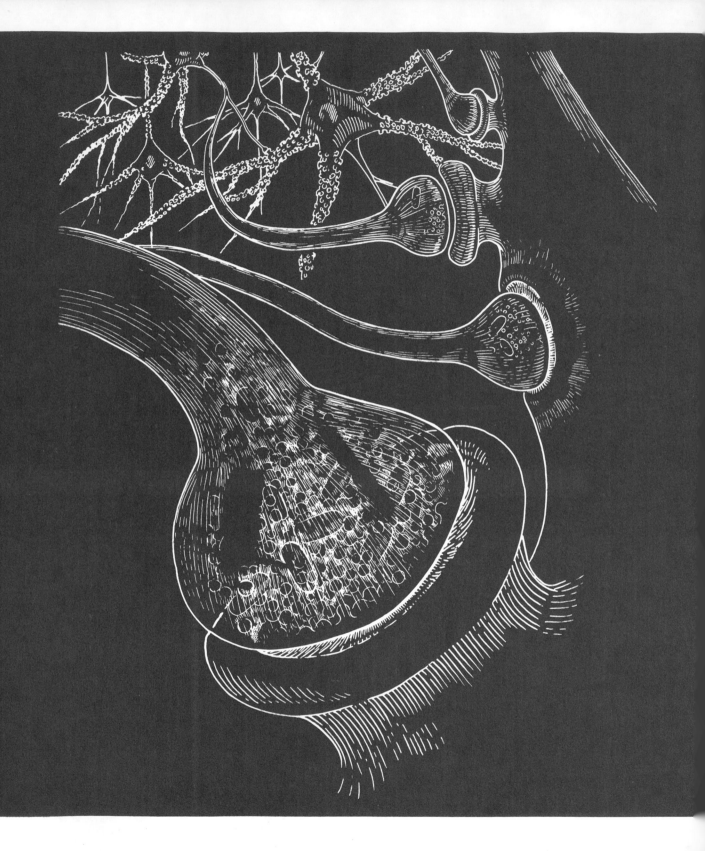

Part Four

LEARNING, MEMORY, AND COGNITION

THERE IS HARDLY A LIVING CREATURE THAT cannot change its behavior as a result of experience. The capacity to learn and remember makes it possible to deal with a complex and changing world and thus increases adaptive success. The language we speak, our skills in writing, driving, skiing, dressing, manipulating eating utensils—these and many more human behaviors depend upon our learning and memory. Storing the lessons of experience implies that the properties of the nervous system can be enduringly changed. How this feat is accomplished is the major mystery of the biological sciences. By now, investigators have developed many ideas and experimental strategies to try to find out how nervous systems accomplish the exploits of learning and memory. In this section we will consider many aspects of research in the biology of learning. Further, we will discuss the most elaborate products of brain function—the biology of language and cognitive states that are so distinctively human.

Orientation

Forms of Learning and Memory

Associative learning

Nonassociative learning

Types of memory

Pathology of Memory

Interventive approaches to the study of memory

Amnesic syndromes and neuropathology

Research inspired by "hippocampal amnesia"

Failures of encoding and of retention

Developmental Approaches to Learning and Memory

Comparative and Evolutionary Approaches to Learning

Distribution of learning abilities among classes of animals

Comparisons of learning ability among species

Evolution of learning and intelligence

Relations Between Brain Size and Intelligence

Interspecies comparisons of brain size and intelligence

Within-species relations between brain size and intelligence

Alterations of brain size and intelligence

Costs and benefits of larger brains

Generality of Learning in the Central Nervous System

Summary/Main Points

14

Learning and Memory: Biological Perspectives

Orientation

Since evolution through natural selection produces animals whose structures and behaviors are adapted to their environments, what further advantages do learning and memory confer? In other words, why did learning and memory evolve?

Adaptation of animals to their environments occurs slowly over successive generations through natural selection, but learning allows individuals to alter their responses rapidly to fit particular circumstances. Thus bees have evolved to fly and to forage for nectar in flowers, but on any particular day a bee must learn where nectar is available so that it can make repeated trips back to those flowers and not waste time on plants that do not provide reward.

A newly hatched chick requires no learning to begin pecking at small objects on the ground around it. But there are many kinds of objects in the chick's environment—grains of corn, pebbles, and chicken excreta—and the chick has to learn which to peck and which to ignore. Corn tastes good, pebbles are hard, and excrement tastes bad (the chick shakes its head and wipes its beak on the ground after tasting it). In only a few trials the chick learns to associate the sight of each of these objects with the consequence of pecking it, and thereafter it confines its pecking mainly to edible objects.

Since the abilities to learn and to remember are advantageous to many ecological niches, the capacities for these behaviors have evolved. Thus there has been evolution to yield more rapid adaptation than evolution itself affords!

To understand human behavior, we must also understand learning and memory. This chapter takes up behavioral and neurobehavioral perspectives on learning and memory, focusing on the following questions: What are the main kinds of learning and memory, and how are these distributed through the animal kingdom? How can damage to the human brain affect learning and memory, and what has study of such cases told us about brain mechanisms? How do the abilities to learn and to remember vary over the life span? Does a larger brain mean greater learning ability? Are special parts of the brain or special kinds of neural circuits required for learning and memory?

Forms of learning and memory

Psychologists have attempted to categorize some of the main kinds of learning and memory as a step toward understanding these behaviors and their biological mechanisms. Let us note first some examples of learning in natural environments that will come up again in experimental settings and then see some of the useful categories that investigators have established.

A mouse hesitates briefly before going through a hole into the area beyond; but the coast seems clear, so out it goes. No sooner has it emerged than a dark shape descends rapidly on the mouse, who darts back into the hole, nursing a scratch inflicted by the cat's paw. When the mouse comes back to that hole, whether it is later the same day or a week later, it may not go through it at all—at the least it will peer very carefully all around and hesitate much more than it would have if it had not had the frightening experience. Learning and memory lead the mouse not to make a response that it would have made otherwise; in scientific terminology it now shows a **passive avoidance response.** More generally, this is an example of **associative learning** because the mouse has learned to associate going through the hole with a particular consequence.

Now consider a crayfish walking at the bottom of a shallow bay. If a predator—a racoon or a fisherman—starts to grasp the crayfish, pressure on the sides evokes a powerful tail flip that may whisk the crayfish out of danger. This response is a valuable one, but it cannot be given all the time—to each wave in the bay, for example—or the crayfish would waste energy and be unable to feed. Instead the crayfish becomes unresponsive to repeated stimuli—it is said to **habituate** to them. But if an unusually strong or painful stimulus occurs, then the crayfish becomes more responsive to most stimuli—it is said to be **sensitized.** Every kind of animal, including human beings, shows both habituation and sensitization. Note that unlike the mouse above, the crayfish has made no association here; the magnitude or likelihood of the response is a function of the strength of the stimulus and of the temporal course of its presentation over the past. This is an example of **nonassociative learning.**

In the rest of this section we will review briefly the concepts of associative learning (classical conditioning, instrumental conditioning, imprinting), nonassociative learning (habituation, sensitization), and memories of different duration (iconic, short-term, intermediate-term, long-term).

Associative learning

Two kinds of learning often studied in the laboratory are **classical conditioning** (also called **Pavlovian conditioning**) and **instrumental conditioning** (also called **operant conditioning**). Both are kinds of **associative learning;** that is, an association is formed between two particular stimuli or between a particular stimulus and a particular response. We will define both classical and instrumental conditioning in the following paragraphs. Meanwhile we should note that some kinds of learning occur only early in life and are irreversible, such as a duckling or a lamb learning to follow

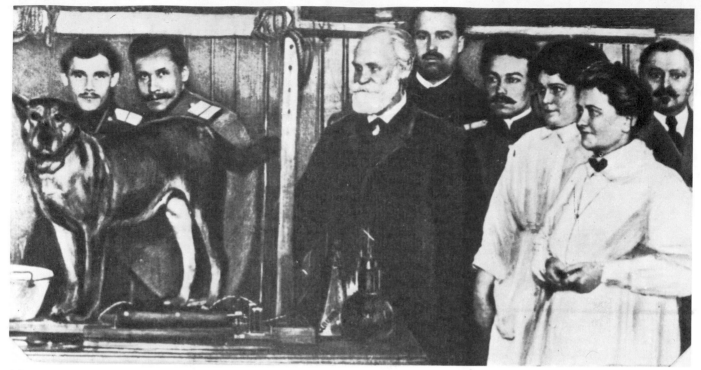

(a)

Figure 14-1 Classical conditioning. (a) The photograph shows Pavlov demonstrating his research at the Russian Military Medical Academy. (Culver Pictures) (b) The drawing of the dog in the conditioning setup is from the first major English-language account of Pavlov's experiments in conditioning.

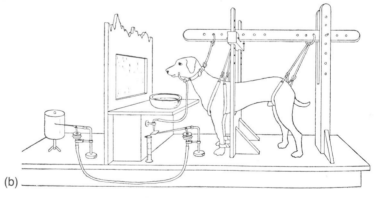

(b)

the first relatively large moving object it sees—usually its mother. This kind of learning is called **imprinting.**

● Classical conditioning In classical conditioning an originally neutral stimulus, through repeated pairing with a stimulus that elicits a particular response, acquires the power of eliciting that response. Thus, for example, sounding a tone normally has no effect on the response of the salivary gland. But if the tone regularly precedes delivery of a drop of mild acid into the mouth, it will come to evoke salivation. Similarly, if the tone regularly precedes a puff of air to the eye, it will come to elicit blinking. In more formal terms, the originally neutral **conditioned stimulus** (the tone), through repeated pairing with the **unconditioned stimulus** (the acid or the puff of air), is able to elicit the response. What is learned in classical conditioning is the relationship between the conditioned stimulus (CS) and the unconditioned stimulus (US). The Russian physiologist Ivan P. Pavlov studied classical conditioning intensively from the beginning of the present century (see Figure 14-1).

Classical conditioning also formed an important part of the program of American behaviorism.

As the pairing of the conditioned and unconditioned stimuli is repeated several times, the response to the conditioned stimulus is acquired; that is, it gains in reliability of occurrence and in magnitude. When the response has been established, if the CS is then presented several times unaccompanied by the US, **extinction** may occur; that is, the response to the CS may drop out (become extinguished). Then if no testing is done for a period of time, **spontaneous recovery** may occur; that is, the extinguished response may appear again. Another feature of conditioning is **generalization.** Once a conditioned response has been established, not only can the CS elicit it, but so can a variety of other stimuli. The more similar these other stimuli are to the conditioned stimulus, the more likely they are to elicit the conditioned response.

Conditioning occurs only if the US occurs simultaneously with the CS or follows it, and in most cases the time interval between the two stimuli cannot exceed 1 second. No conditioning occurs if the order is reversed (US, then CS), or if the stimuli are given in random fashion without a strict temporal relation. These facts are often used in control experiments to discriminate between conditioning and sensitization.

● Instrumental conditioning   In instrumental conditioning, the likelihood that an act will be performed depends upon the consequences that follow it. Thus, for example, the likelihood that a laboratory rat will press on a lever in its cage is increased if, shortly after each press, a small pellet of food drops into the cage. The lever press is called an **instrumental response** because it is a means of obtaining a reward. Presenting a **reinforcing stimulus** (such as the food pellet) in a regular relationship with the instrumental response establishes a contingency, and the tendency to perform the instrumental response is strengthened. If punishment (negative reinforcement) follows a response, its likelihood of occurrence decreases. What is learned in instrumental conditioning is the relationship between the response and the reinforcer.

● Acquiring sets of associations   The acquisition of single associations such as those described above is very useful for research purposes, because the behavior is relatively simple and investigators can study the changes in amplitude and frequency of a single response in relation to the timing of presentations of the stimuli. But investigators often want to study more complex behavior involving sets of associations. For example, they may wish to test the capacity of a subject more fully than the use of a single response allows. Or they may wish to study behaviors that are natural to a species and that are more complex than the acquisition of single associations. Thus from early in the present century many investigators have studied the abilities of animals of many species (including human beings) to find their ways in mazes of varying complexity. This technique continues to be useful, although it is used less often today than it was earlier in the century. Also, studies of verbal learning usually deal with situations more complex than that of learning single paired associates; often short-term memory is tested by the digit span—that is, the number of successive digits that the subject can repeat accurately. More complex sets of verbal associates are usually used to test long-term memory.

● Imprinting   A striking kind of learning, imprinting, occurs only early in the life of animals of many species. The young animal learns to follow the first relatively large moving object that it sees. Thus the duckling becomes imprinted on the duck and stays close to it; the lamb learns to remain close to the ewe. If the first moving object the duckling sees is a mechanical apparatus in the laboratory, the duckling imprints on it; if it is an experimenter, the duckling imprints on him or her. Imprinting occurs quickly and usually lasts a lifetime. If a duckling of one species imprints on a duck of another species, when it becomes adult it will prefer to mate with the other species rather than with its own.

Nonassociative learning   The example of crayfish behavior that we considered above showed **habituation**. Animals of every sort show such declines in response to the familiar—a kind of acquired insensitivity to stimulation. This form of decreased responsiveness should be distinguished from a decline that reflects either receptor adaptation or muscle fatigue. Habituation is a form of **nonassociative learning** because it occurs with mere repetition of a single kind of stimulus; no relation to any other stimulus is required.

Behavioral studies of habituation show that it follows several rules, including the following:

1. Repeated stimulation leads to a progressive decrease in the amplitude of the response. An example is given in Figure 14-2, which shows electrical responses of human abdominal muscles to mechanical or electrical stimuli applied to the abdomen (Hagbarth and Kugelberg, 1958). As successive stimuli of the same strength are delivered, the responses are seen to decline progressively.

2. The weaker the stimulus, the more rapidly the response declines in amplitude. Strong stimuli may not lead to habituation and may even increase response strength.

3. The more often the stimulus is presented in a given period of time, the more rapid and pronounced is the decrease in amplitude of the response.

4. If the stimulus is no longer presented for a sufficiently long period of time, the response will recover spontaneously.

5. Habituation to one stimulus may cause at least partial habituation to a similar stimulus, but this result is not always found. In Figure 14-2 habituation did not generalize; the stimulus at point (b) still shows its full response even though the response at nearby point (a) has been habituated by 29 successive trials.

When a response has become habituated, a strong stimulus (either of the same sort or even in another sensory modality) will often cause the response to succeeding presentations of the habituated stimulus to increase sharply in amplitude; it may become even larger than the original response before habituation (Figure 14-3). This increase in response amplitude has often been called "dishabituation," the idea being that the habituation has been removed. Further investigation has shown, however, that **sensitization** is a more accurate description of this phenomenon, for several reasons. For one thing, even a response that has not been habituated may increase in amplitude after a strong stimulus. For another thing, a response that has been habituated may not simply regain its prehabituation amplitude after the strong stimulus but may reach a greater amplitude than before.

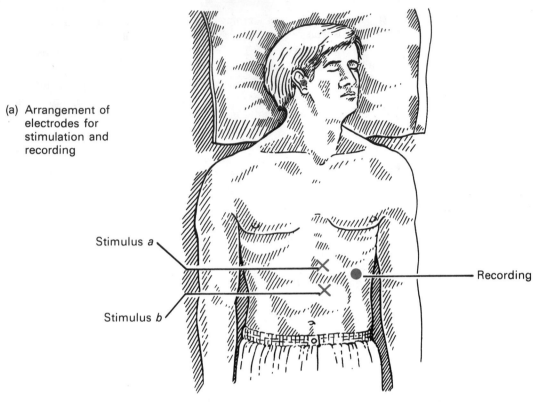

(a) Arrangement of
    electrodes for
    stimulation and
    recording

Stimulus *a*

Stimulus *b*

Recording

(b) Electrical responses of abdominal muscles

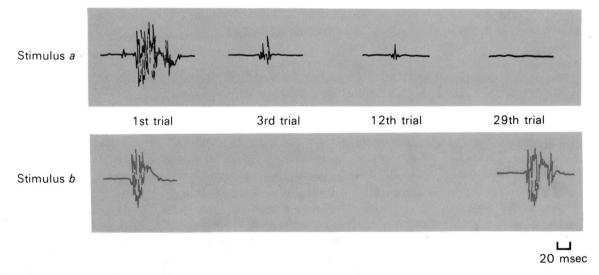

Stimulus *a*

1st trial   3rd trial   12th trial   29th trial

Stimulus *b*

20 msec

Figure 14-2   Habituation of the human abdominal reflex. While the subject reclines with eyes closed and wearing ear plugs, electrical stimulation of the skin elicits reflex responses of the abdominal muscles. When stimuli were applied at site *a* every 5–10 sec, the amplitude of the muscular response diminished progressively, showing habituation. A single initial stimulus at site *b* elicited a large response. Then *b* was left unstimulated while site *a* received 29 successive stimuli and habituated. A single stimulus then applied again to *b* evoked a large response, so the habituation at *a* had not generalized to *b*. (Adapted from Hagbarth and Kugelberg, 1958)

Figure 14-3 Sensitization of the human abdominal reflex. (b) The reflex response of the abdominal muscles was first habituated to weak mechanical taps to the skin. A series of strong blows to the skin then sensitized the reflex. After a series of 3 sensitization stimuli, responses were elicited by the next 17 weak taps; after 10 sensitization stimuli, weak taps elicited responses for over 100 trials. (c) Sensitization by strong stimulation. After the habituation response in 1, a single electrical shock to the skin sensitized the response to the following tap, as shown in 2. (d) Sensitization by verbal stimuli. A weak electrical stimulus to the skin elicited no muscular response. The same weak stimulus became effective after the subject was told that the next shock would be painful. (Adapted from Hagbarth and Kugelberg, 1958)

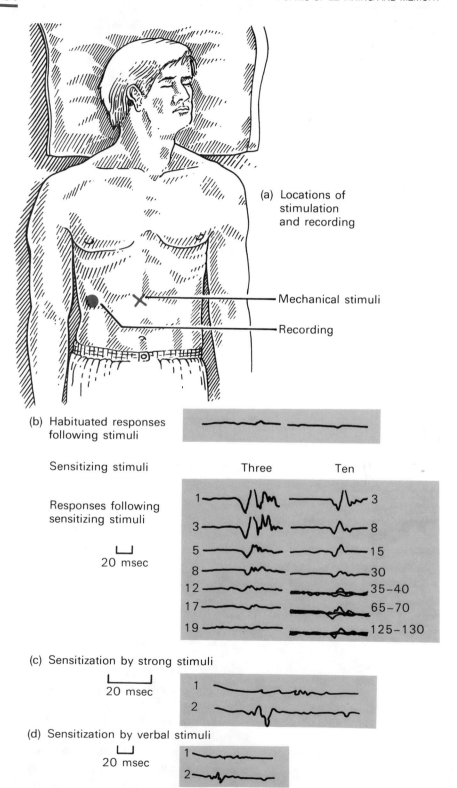

(a) Locations of stimulation and recording

Mechanical stimuli

Recording

(b) Habituated responses following stimuli

Sensitizing stimuli   Three   Ten

Responses following sensitizing stimuli

20 msec

(c) Sensitization by strong stimuli

20 msec

(d) Sensitization by verbal stimuli

20 msec

Figure 14-4 Diagram of a multiple-trace hypothesis of memory storage. (Adapted from McGaugh, 1968)

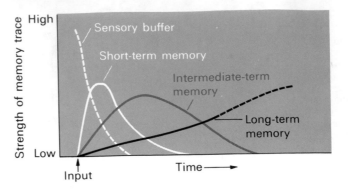

It appears that sensitization is a separate phenomenon, superimposed on the existing level of responsiveness, rather than simply a removal of habituation. Two special characteristics of sensitization are the following:

1. The stronger the stimulus, the more apt it is to produce sensitization.
2. With repeated presentations of the same sensitizing stimulus, it tends to lose its effect; that is, there is habituation of sensitization.

Types of memory   The terms "learning" and "memory" are so often paired that it sometimes seems as if one of them necessarily implies the other. We cannot be sure that learning has occurred unless a memory can be elicited at some later time. But even if we can show that learning did occur, this observation does not guarantee that memory for the learned material can be retrieved again in the future. Even though short-term memory occurred, a long-lasting memory may never have been formed, or it may decay in time or be impaired by injuries to the brain, or the subject may be temporarily in a particular state in which a given memory cannot be retrieved.

The briefest memories are called **iconic** (from the Greek word for "image"). An example would be your impressions of a scene that is illuminated for only a moment. You may be able to grasp one part of the display, but the rest vanishes in seconds. (A very brief auditory memory is called "echoic," as if you could still hear it ringing in your ears.) More generally, these brief memories are attributed to sensory buffers. (See Figure 14-4.)

Somewhat longer than iconic memories are **short-term memories.** For example, suppose that you want to call a person on the telephone, using a number that you have never used before. You look up the number and, if nothing distracts or interrupts you, you dial the number successfully. You have used a short-term memory of the telephone number. If the line is busy, however, and you want to call back a minute or so later, you may have to look the number up again, unless you have been repeating it to yourself in the meantime. If you rehearse or use the number, then it can remain in short-term memory until you turn to some other activity. Unfortunately there is no consistency in the use of the label "short-term memory" among investigators from different fields. Physiological psychologists and other biologists often use it to cover memories that are not permanent but that fade out over minutes or hours; some investigators have even used short-term memory to mean memories that last a few days. But researchers who study human verbal behavior usually restrict the term short-term memory to memories that last for seconds up to a minute or so, if rehearsal is not permitted.

As an example of memory that lasts somewhat beyond the short-term, suppose that you drive to school or work and park your car in a different place each day. If things go well, you remember each afternoon where you parked your car that morning, but you may very well not recall where you parked your car yesterday or a week ago. This is an example of what is sometimes called **intermediate-term memory,** that is, a memory that outlasts short-term memory but that is far from being permanent.

Beyond the memories that last for hours are memories that last for weeks, months, and years; these are called **long-term memories.** Many memories that do last for days or weeks nevertheless become weaker and may even fade out completely over time, so some investigators also use the term **permanent memory** to designate memories that appear to continue without decline for the rest of the life of an organism, or at least as long as the organism remains in good health.

The fact that some memories last only for seconds and others for months is not proof that short-term memories are based on different biological mechanisms than are long-term memories. It is the scientist's task to find out whether these memories are based on the same processes or on different processes. And as we will see, there are good reasons—both clinical and experimental—to conclude that different biological processes underlie short-term and long-term memory storage.

Memory processes   Psychologists who study learning and memory suggest that several successive processes seem to be necessary to guarantee recall of a past event; these are **encoding, consolidation,** and **retrieval** (see Figure 14-5). The original information

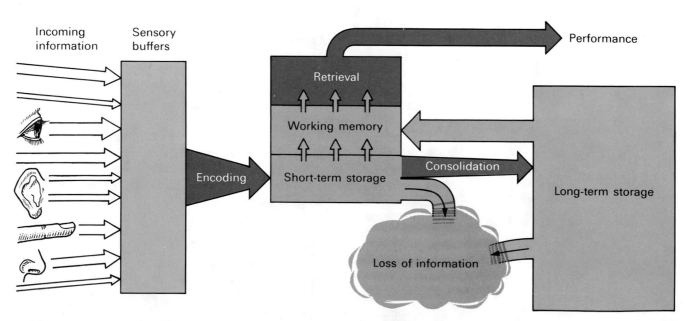

Figure 14-5 A schema of memory processes that includes encoding, consolidation, and retrieval.

must enter sensory channels and then be encoded rapidly into a form that passes into short-term memory. Some of this information is then consolidated in long-term storage. Some cognitive psychologists hold that there is no essential difference between short-term and long-term storages; they claim that more deeply processed information is stored longer. Others claim that storage is accomplished by different neural processes in the short-term and long-term stores. Finally there are the processes of retrieval. With these stages in mind, investigators have tried to find out whether particular examples of failure of recall in normal subjects involve failure of encoding or of consolidation or of retrieval, and whether pathological impairments of memory involve selectively one or another of these main processes.

Pathology of memory

Enormous capacities to learn and remember are salient characteristics of humankind. We all know the meanings of thousands of words, and even vaster vocabularies are readily acquired by many people who live in border regions of the world or who have other reasons to master several languages. Most of us recognize hundreds or thousands of faces and countless visual scenes and objects, hundreds of voices and many other familiar sounds, and hundreds of different odors. In addition, depending on our interests and experiences, we may be able to recognize and sing or play a large number of tunes and identify and supply information about a great many athletes, musical performers, actors, or historical characters. Impairments of learning and memory occur through disease or accidents, and the types of impairment have long been scrutinized both to find clues to the mechanisms of memory and to find ways of treating its malfunctions.

How can we investigate the neural bases of the enormous and essential human abilities to learn and remember? Although we naturally want to learn about brain mechanisms of learning and memory in human beings, ethical reasons preclude the use of many kinds of somatic intervention that are employed in experiments with animal subjects. Much has been discovered and is being discovered, however, by studying "experiments of nature"—cases of damage to the brain that come about through diseases or accidents. In this way neurologists and brain scientists have made considerable progress in relating sites of brain damage to kinds of behavioral impairments. Also, they have studied learning and memory in isolated parts of the nervous system, such as one hemisphere of the brain separated from the other when the corpus callosum has been transected for medical reasons. Many of the clues that have been obtained by study of clinical cases have then been followed up and extended by research with animal subjects, where the intervention can be controlled and specified more accurately and results obtained more rapidly. Let us consider the interventive approaches a bit further; then we will take up some examples of research that employ them.

Somatic intervention and the study of memory

One type of intervention involves the destruction of particular regions of the brain and study of the resultant effects on learning and memory. Another type does not damage the brain but alters its functioning by the use of various treatments such as electrical stimulation or drugs.

● **Correlating sites of brain damage with impairment of memory**   Impairment of memory may occur because of a disease or an accident that destroys brain tissue. For over a century neurologists have tried to correlate the location of such damage with behavioral impairment. Until recently this study could be done only at post-mortem examinations, but now the site of damage can be ascertained in living patients by means of computerized X-ray tomography or positron emission tomography. Also, since brain surgery is now common, sites of damage can be seen directly in some patients during surgical interventions.

For many suggested relations between locus of damage and behavioral impairment, neuroscientists try to cross-check their hypotheses by conducting research on animal subjects. Animal research permits precise control of the area(s) destroyed and allows relatively rapid accumulation of information. We have seen this technique applied to the study of perception, control of movement, and motivation, and it is prominent in the study of mechanisms of learning and memory.

● **Altering brain activity**   Many agents or conditions that alter the activity of the brain—including concussions, shock therapy, drugs, and sleep states—have been found to affect the formation of memories. Much of the research in this area is related to the **perseveration-consolidation hypothesis** first put forth in 1900 by Müller and Pilzecker to account for aspects of human verbal learning. These German psychologists proposed that the neural processes that are responsible for memory "perseverate" for a time after the learning experience, but that this process accounts for only a **labile memory,** that is, one that is easily disrupted. In some cases the memory becomes fixed or "consolidated" in a stable form, and it then can last for long periods. The psychologist William McDougall was quick to point out that this perseveration-consolidation hypothesis could be used to explain the **retroactive amnesia** that is often observed after head injuries. That is, a person who suffers a concussion in an accident may find, upon regaining consciousness, that he has no memory for the events just before the accident; in severe cases amnesia may extend to days or weeks before the concussion. According to the consolidation hypothesis, the accident did not blot out memories retroactively but rather it interrupted the neural activity necessary to put memories into a stable long-term form.

When electroconvulsive shock was introduced as a treatment for mental illness in the late 1930s, it was soon found to produce retroactive amnesia. The technique was then taken into the psychological laboratory for precise experimentation with animal subjects. The closer in time the shock followed the learning, the more effective it was found to be in weakening or preventing the formation of long-term memory. Electroconvulsive shock is still used therapeutically, often to counteract depression, and it continues to be used in experiments on formation of memory, occasionally with human patients and more frequently with animal subjects.

Certain therapeutic drugs have also been found to affect memory formation. One example is the anticholinergic agent scopolamine. This drug has been used, in combination with other agents, during childbirth. Scopolamine relaxed the mother, and it also prevented formation of memory; thus the awake, relaxed woman could cooperate with the obstetrician, but she formed no long-lasting memories. (The use of drugs to prevent or to modulate many aspects of neural activity during the minutes and hours following learning is prominent in current research, as we will see in Chapter 15.)

Now let us examine representative research that uses the approaches described above. Chapter 15 will deal mainly with research that attempts to track mechanisms of learning and memory to the cellular level.

Amnesic syndromes and
neuropathology

In the 1880s a Russian neurologist published a paper about a syndrome of impaired memory that became a classic and caused the condition to be named after him— **Korsakoff's syndrome.** People suffering from this syndrome fail to recall many items or events of the past; if such an item is presented again or if it happens to be recalled, the patient does not show a feeling of familiarity with it. Korsakoff patients frequently deny that anything is wrong with them. They often show disorientation for time and place, and they may "confabulate," that is, fill a gap in memory with a falsification that they accept as correct.

The main cause of Korsakoff's syndrome is lack of the vitamin thiamine; this lack occurs in alcoholics who obtain most of their calories from alcohol and neglect their diet. Treating such a person with thiamine can prevent further deterioration; if the treatment is started before the person has become a full-blown Korsakoff case, the condition can be ameliorated. Over the years neurologists have examined brains of many patients who suffered from Korsakoff's syndrome in an attempt to locate the site(s) of damage. Unfortunately, as pointed out by Mair and colleagues (1979), very few patients have had both careful determination of their capacities and also detailed postmortem examination of the brain, so that one cannot have full confidence in the findings reported to date. Some of the cases may not actually have shown the specific memory deficits of Korsakoff's syndrome, since they were described as showing "mental confusion" or "clouding of consciousness" rather than being characterized in terms of performance on appropriate tests of memory. Also, some of the autopsy reports were sketchy and limited as to the brain regions considered. In these studies both the mammillary bodies and the dorsomedial nucleus of the thalamus have frequently, but not invariably, been found to be severely damaged (Figure 14-6).

In a recent, thorough study Mair and colleagues (1979) examined two patients over several years with a battery of behavioral tests; the brains of both were later examined in detail. Both brains showed shrunken, diseased mammillary bodies, and there was some damage in the dorsomedial thalamus. Temporal lobe structures, including the hippocampus and the temporal stem, were normal. Thus these cases confirm the less precise, earlier studies. Mair and co-workers characterize the mammillary bodies as "a narrow funnel through which connections from the midbrain as well as the temporal lobe neocortex and limbic system gain access to the frontal lobes" (p. 778).

In another kind of patient, impairment of the hippocampus seemed to produce a striking deficit of memory formation, and this report has engendered both research and controversy ever since it first appeared (Scoville and Milner, 1957). One of these patients became famous through a series of studies made of his case because he showed unusual symptoms after a brain operation in 1953; he is known by his initials, H. M. This man had suffered from epilepsy since childhood. His condition became progressively worse and was uncontrollable by medication; he had to stop

Figure 14-6 Regions of the human brain that have been implicated in the formulation of long-term memories. (a) A lateral view of the brain shows the levels of the transverse sections shown in (b).

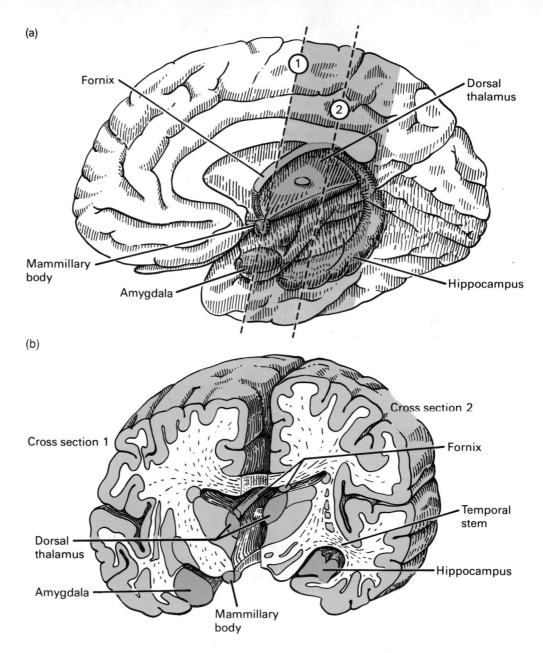

(a)

Fornix

Dorsal thalamus

Mammillary body

Amygdala

Hippocampus

(b)

Cross section 1

Cross section 2

Fornix

Dorsal thalamus

Temporal stem

Amygdala

Hippocampus

Mammillary body

work at the age of 27. The symptoms indicated that the neurological origins of the seizures were in the medial basal regions of both temporal lobes, so the neurologist removed such tissue bilaterally, including much of the hippocampus (see Figure 14-7). Similar operations had been performed before without harmful effects, although less tissue had been removed than in this case. Upon recovery from the operation H. M. was unable to retain new material for more than brief periods. Most of his old memories were intact, although there was amnesia for most events during the three years before the operation. Here is one example of his inability to learn new

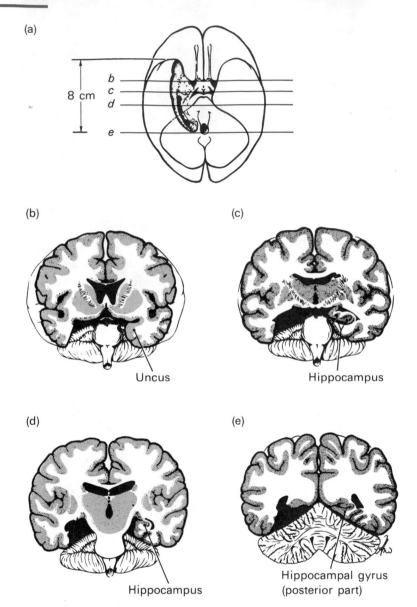

(a)

8 cm

b
c
d
e

(b)

Uncus

(c)

Hippocampus

(d)

Hippocampus

(e)

Hippocampal gyrus
(posterior part)

Figure 14-7 Brain tissue removed in the operation on patient H. M. The operation was performed bilaterally, but the diagram shows only unilateral removal so that the forms of the structures can be seen. (a) The base of the brain, showing the extent of the operation and the levels of the transverse sections (b–e). (From Scoville and Milner, 1957)

information: Six months after the operation H. M.'s family moved to another house on the same street; when H. M. went out, he could not remember the new address and kept returning to the old house. Also, H. M. could no longer learn the names of people he met, although he recognized the people he knew before the operation. He still retains a new fact only briefly; as soon as a distraction occurs, the newly acquired information vanishes. But H. M. does converse easily, and his IQ remains above average—118 when tested in 1962 and in 1977 but declining to 104 in 1981 (Corkin et al., 1981). Short-term memory is normal, but very few long-term memories are formed.

H. M. recognizes that something is wrong with him because he has no memories of the past several years or even of what he did earlier in the same day. His description of this strange state of isolation from his own past is poignant (Milner, 1970, p. 37):

> Every day is alone in itself, whatever enjoyment I've had, and whatever sorrow I've had. . . . Right now, I'm wondering, have I done or said anything amiss? You see, at this moment everything looks clear to me, but what happened just before? That's what worries me. It's like waking from a dream. I just don't remember.

After publication of the case of H. M., similar cases were reported that resulted not from brain surgery but from disease. Occasionally herpes simplex virus attacks the brain and destroys tissue in the medial temporal lobe, and this destruction can produce a severe failure to form new long-term memories although acquisition of short-term memories is normal (for example, see Rose and Simonds, 1960; Starr and Phillips, 1970). The temporal lobe patients, unlike patients with Korsakoff's syndrome, are not disoriented, and they do not confabulate, although they too are cut off from their recent past.

Research inspired by "hippocampal amnesia"

H. M.'s memory deficit was ascribed to bilateral destruction of much of the hippocampus. This conclusion was reached because earlier surgical cases that had not shown memory impairment had involved less damage to the hippocampus, although they shared with H. M. damage to more anterior structures, including the amygdala. Soon after description of this case, investigators began to remove the hippocampus in experimental animals in order to try to reproduce the deficit and then study the mechanisms of formation of long-term memories. But after years of research brain scientists had to confess failure: Neither in rats nor in monkeys did it appear possible to demonstrate failure of memory consolidation after bilateral destruction of the hippocampus (Douglas, 1967; Kimble, 1968; Isaacson, 1972). Different investigators have attempted to account for this puzzling discrepancy in different ways, and the widening research on this problem has led to considerable gains in knowledge—about the amnesic syndrome in people, about functions of the hippocampus, and about brain mechanisms of memory.

Four alternative hypotheses are these:

1. The human impairment involves chiefly verbal material, and animals could not be tested for such deficits.

2. The tests of amnesia in patients may not have been adequate. If properly tested, their memories may be better than supposed.

3. When adequate tests are employed with animal subjects, they do show serious impairment of memory formation after the hippocampus is destroyed.

4. The impairment in H. M. and other patients with damage to the medial temporal lobe should not have been ascribed to destruction of the hippocampus. Either another nearby structure is responsible for the amnesia or another structure must be damaged in addition to the hippocampus in order to produce the impairments of memory formation.

Another possibility, which most investigators are reluctant to accept, is that the formation of memory involves different brain structures in human beings and in other animals.

Now let's examine some of the main findings of research conducted to test the four hypotheses.

● **Does temporal lobe amnesia involve chiefly verbal memory?**   An interesting finding with H. M. suggested that his difficulty might be chiefly with verbal learning and not with motor performance. Milner (1965) presented a mirror-tracing test to H. M. In this test (see Figure 14-8) the subject looks at both a printed star and his hand in a mirror and tries to stay inside the double boundaries while tracing the contour with a pencil. H. M. showed considerable improvement over several trials. The next day the test was presented again. When asked if he remembered it,

Figure 14-8 Mirror-tracing test, and learning by H. M. (a) The subject attempts to trace the outline of a form, keeping his pencil within the double boundary, while observing the form and his hand through a mirror. A barrier prevents direct observation of hand and form. (b) Performance of H. M. over three successive days. The record shows improvement within days (short-term memory) and retention from one day to another (long-term memory). (Data from Milner, 1965)

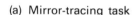

(a) Mirror-tracing task

(b) Performance of H. M. on mirror-tracing task

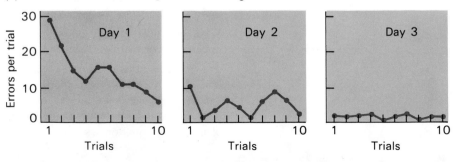

H. M. said no, but his performance was better than at the start of the first day (Figure 14-8). Over three successive days H. M. never reported recognizing the problem, but his tracings showed memory. If an animal subject showed similar proof of memory, we would have no doubts, because we don't ask our animal subjects whether they recognize the test. Korsakoff patients have also been tested with mirror tracing, and they too retain improvements of performance while failing to show recognition of the task.

Two kinds of findings indicate that the memory problems of H. M. and other patients cannot be attributed solely to difficulties with verbal materials as such. First, such patients also have difficulty in reproducing or recognizing pictures and spatial designs that are not recalled in verbal terms. Second, although the patients have difficulty with the specific content of verbal material, they can learn procedural or rule-based information about verbal material (N. J. Cohen and Squire, 1980). A brief look at this research will make the distinction clear.

Subjects were asked to read successive sets of three moderately long words printed mirror-reversed, like this:

bɘlggɒɿbɘd   zuoioiɿqɒɔ   ɘzoibnɒɿg

The task is difficult, but subjects improve markedly with practice. No motor skill is involved but rather the ability to deal with abstract rules or procedures. If some words are used repeatedly, normal subjects come to recognize them and to read them easily. Brain-lesioned patient N. A., Korsakoff subjects, and patients who received electroconvulsive shock learned the skill of mirror reading but not the specific words, nor did they recognize the task on successive occasions. Thus the important distinction is probably not between motor and verbal performances but between procedural or rule-based information, on the one hand, and specific item content or data-based information, on the other hand. As Cohen puts it, the patients learned *how* but they didn't learn *what*. So it is probably not animals' inability to speak that accounts for their immunity to effects of hippocampal lesions on storing memories.

● **Memory formation in people with hippocampal damage**   Indications that patients with "hippocampal amnesia" may suffer more from difficulties of retrieval of memories than from inability to form memories were found by Warrington and Weiskrantz (1968). These investigators observed that the patients seemed to be unable to learn even simple lists of words after several repetitions. But as the patients were given one list after another, the experimenters began to recognize as familiar many of the wrong responses that their patients produced. Analysis showed that many of the wrong responses were actually words from earlier lists in the experiment. Thus the words were being stored by the patients but were emerging at the wrong time. Further experiments showed that providing cues at the time of recall could substantially improve the performance of amnesic patients (Weiskrantz and Warrington, 1975). This result was taken as evidence that the defect was more in the retrieval than in the storage of memories. This finding may be of value in helping patients with partial destruction of medial temporal structures whose deficits are less severe than those of H. M. Amnesic patients and others who suffer from problems of memory can be aided both by using strategies of encoding and by cuing at retrieval (Signoret and Lhermitte, 1976; Poon, 1980).

But the technique of prompting does not completely overcome the memory deficits of amnesic patients; in fact, prompting helps normal subjects more than it helps patients (Squire and Slater, 1978). Thus the results indicate that both amnesics and normals possess more information than they can produce by free recall but that the amnesics have stored less information than normals. Therefore we cannot agree with Weiskrantz (1977, p. 438) when he concludes that there no longer need be "any embarrassment over being unable to find a blockade of input into long-term memory in the animal, because there is no such blockade in man either" as a consequence of hippocampal destruction.

Although the retrieval impairment hypothesis can account for a number of observations and suggests useful techniques for recovering memories, Rozin (1976b) has pointed out that it does not account for certain salient phenomena. If the deficit is one of retrieval, how is it that memories acquired before brain damage can be retrieved readily, whereas only those acquired later are difficult to retrieve without special cuing? Also, amnesic patients show a striking lack of familiarity for post-lesion memories even if they are retrieved, and this result is not explained by the retrieval impairment hypothesis.

● **Impairment of memory in animals with hippocampal lesions**   Some investigators have attempted to narrow the gap between human and animal results by finding evidence of impairment of memory storage in animals with hippocampal lesions. Experiments with hippocampectomized animals revealed that they had greater difficulty than normals in abandoning earlier learning or strategies; they showed greater interference of earlier learning on later tasks (for example, see Douglas, 1967; Kimble, 1968). The persistence of response in the animal subjects agreed with the observation of Warrington and Weiskrantz (1968) concerning persistence of responses from earlier lists of words. The animal subjects also showed difficulty in remembering spatial problems, but this result probably reflects difficulty with spatial discrimination of the operated animals rather than impairment of memory as such. Tests of memory for nonspatial materials (such as visual patterns or sounds) do not show important impairment as a result of hippocampal lesions. It seems clear that complete bilateral destruction of the hippocampus in animals does not produce the massive impairments of memory seen in such patients as H. M. (Focus of attention on the hippocampus has led to the discovery of important kinds of plasticity in this structure, however, and we will take up electrophysiological studies of hippocampal plasticity in Chapter 15.)

● **Study of other sites in the medial temporal lobe**   A very different approach followed recently by Horel (1978) has been to reexamine critically whether the site of the lesion responsible for the memory deficits is in fact the hippocampus or some other structure in the ventromedial part of the temporal lobe. After scrutinizing published reports, Horel concluded that the critical site is probably not the hippocampus but rather the temporal stem (see Figure 14-6). This structure, also called the albal stalk, carries the afferent and efferent connections of the temporal cortex and the amygdala but does not carry connections of the hippocampus. The position of the temporal stem makes it vulnerable to the surgical approach that was used in the human medial temporal lobectomies. Furthermore, when the stem was sectioned in monkeys, without damaging the hippocampus, severe deficits were produced in

Figure 14-9 Coronal section of the brain of a patient who became unable to form long-term memories after an episode of anoxia. The hippocampus is seen to be shrunken (compare with the hippocampus in Figures 14-6 and 14-7). (Courtesy of R. Escourolle and J.-L. Signoret, Laboratory of Neuropathology Charles Foix, Hôpital de la Salpetrière, Paris, France)

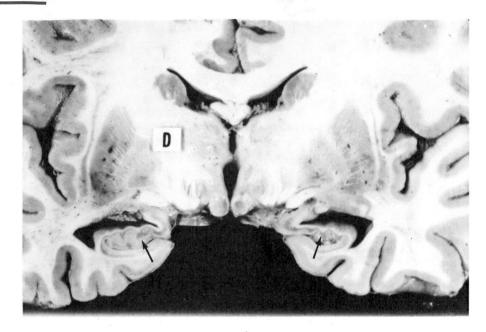

visual discrimination learning and retention (Horel and Misantone, 1974, 1976). Among the connections of the temporal lobe whose damage might be responsible for the memory defect, Horel emphasized those to the medial magnocellular part of the medial dorsal nucleus of the thalamus. Pathology in this nucleus has been strongly implicated in the memory defects that occur in Korsakoff's syndrome (Victor, Adams, and Collins, 1971) and in patient N. A.

The critical evaluation of Horel has had the beneficial effect of arousing renewed interest in this problem and stimulating investigators to publish further case reports. Some of these reports have challenged Horel's reevaluation and have reaffirmed the importance of the hippocampus for memory formation. For example, Figure 14-9 shows a section through the brain of a patient who became unable to form long-term memories after an episode of anoxia. The hippocampus is seen to have been largely destroyed, whereas the temporal stalk was not impaired. The publication of full behavioral and neuroanatomical reports on more amnesic patients should permit us to resolve this problem in the near future.

In focusing on the medial dorsal nucleus of the thalamus, Horel was attempting to account for the amnesia of Korsakoff patients as well as that of patients with temporal lobe involvement. It is not clear, however, that the memory defects of the two groups of patients are identical. Some workers have concluded that the temporal lobe patients are similar in many essential respects to the Korsakoff amnesic state in their memory impairments (Weiskrantz and Warrington, 1975). But other investigators have emphasized that rather simple tasks of memory and problem solving differentiate the two kinds of patients reliably (Lhermitte and Signoret, 1976; Cohen and Squire, 1980). Therefore one should be cautious about amalgamating the two groups, and it is possible that the brain regions impaired in Korsakoff and temporal lobe patients will also differ, at least in part.

BOX 14-1   How Do You Live When You Can't Form New Memories?

What is life like for a person who suddenly loses the ability to form memories? Such a disaster has befallen some people as a consequence of disease, brain operations, or injury to the brain. A few of these cases have been investigated carefully, and they have furnished valuable information about memory and its mechanisms. Now the daily life of one of these people has been studied (Kaushall, Zetin, and Squire, 1981), and the description is illuminating.

N. A. had done well in school, both scholastically and athletically, and he graduated in 1958. After a year of junior college, he joined the Air Force. One day in 1960 while N. A. was assembling a model airplane, a roommate took a miniature fencing foil from the wall, tapped N. A. from behind, and thrust forward as N. A. turned around. The blade entered the right nostril and penetrated the left hemisphere of N. A.'s brain. N. A. reports memories of the accident and of the minute or two afterwards until he lost consciousness. During hospitalization, several not uncommon neurological symptoms were noted, and they cleared up. But there was one unusual symptom and it persisted: N. A. was practically unable to form new long-term memories, especially for verbal material.

After several months, N. A. was returned to the care of his parents. During the several years after the accident, psychologist H. L. Teuber and colleagues followed this case (Teuber, Milner, and Vaughan, 1968). Since 1975 a psychological-medical team has tested N. A. frequently and has also visited his home often (Kaushall et al., 1981).

Upon first meeting N. A., visitors are impressed with his normality. He has a relaxed and amiable manner and is polite and hospitable. He invites you to inspect his collection of guns and model airplanes and hundreds of souvenirs that he has acquired on trips with his parents. He describes the objects lucidly and intelligently, although he is sometimes unsure where he obtained a particular object. He does not exhibit confusion, and during a visit he does not show the same object twice.

But when you return for repeated visits, N. A. apologizes each time for not remembering your name and asks each time whether he has shown you his collections. By the third or fourth visit, these repetitions and other aspects of N. A.'s behavior " . . . come to reveal a devastated life and an isolated mental world" (Kaushall et al., 1981, p. 384).

Although N. A. has an IQ of 124 he can neither hold a job nor form close personal relationships. N. A. has attended an outpatient treatment center for many years and is popular among staff and patients, but he cannot remember their names or their histories. He is alert, and enjoys humor, but his socializing is limited by his inability to keep a topic of conversation in mind, especially if there are interruptions. Also, his failure to acquire knowledge about current events or people prevent him from contributing much to conversations. Although N. A. was sexually active before his accident, he has had virtually no sexual contact since. He once made a date with a young woman he met at a picnic, but he failed to remember the appointment until two weeks later, and did not pursue the acquaintanceship further. His relationship with his mother is the dominant feature of his emotional life. He has said that he would have had a wife and family if he had not been injured but now believes that he will not be able to do so.

The only routines that N. A. can perform reliably are ones that he has learned through years of practice. Cooking or other activities that require correct sequencing of steps are very difficult for him. Even watching television is a problem because a commercial interruption may cause him to forget the subject. He spends much of his time tidying around the house, doing small woodworking projects, and assembling models. He constantly arranges objects and shows obsessive concern that everything be in its right place; he is irritated if he finds that anything has been moved. N. A.'s mother insists that his obsessiveness and irritability developed since the accident. Probably he strives for a rigorously stable environment to compensate for his deficient memory.

Despite his handicap, N. A. maintains a generally optimistic view of his life. In part this may reflect the fact that he remembers mainly experiences prior to 1960 when he was successful socially, athletically, and scholastically. Although he has had many frustrating experiences since his accident, these are not remembered in detail and apparently they do not lead to depression. N. A.'s inability to form memories is as severe as that of patients with Korsakoff's syndrome, but he does not show the apathy, blandness, and loss of initiative that characterize them.

N. A. has formed some verbal memories after the accident, but they are spotty. Thus he knows that "Watergate" signifies some political scandal that took place in "Washington or Florida" but he cannot give any details or tell who was involved. Only occasionally does he write notes or instructions to himself as memory aids, and he tends to lose track of such notes. At one recent session when N. A.'s memory was being tested, he repeatedly tried to recall a question that he wanted to ask the investigator. Finally he searched his pockets and found a note that he had written to himself: "Ask Dr. Squire if my memory is getting better."

(a) Tomogram showing horizontal section of the brain

Anterior

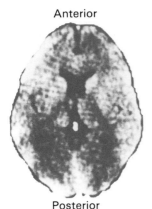

Posterior

(b) Diagram of the tomogram above

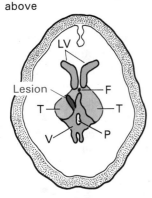

Figure 14-10 Brain damage in patient N. A. (a) Computerized axial tomogram. (b) Line drawing of the tomogram. (Adapted from L. R. Squire and R. Y. Moore, "Dorsal thalamic lesion in a noted case of human memory dysfunction," *Annals of Neurology*, vol. 6 (1979): 504.)

An independent indication that damage to the dorsomedial thalamus can impair memory formation comes from the case of the patient N. A. (Teuber, Milner, and Vaughan, 1968; Squire and Moore, 1979). N. A. became amnesic as a result of an accident in which a miniature fencing foil entered his brain through the nostril. N. A. is markedly amnesic, primarily for verbal material, and he can give little information about events since his accident in 1960, but he shows almost normal recall for events of the 1940s and 1950s. Computerized tomography scans were made of N. A. in 1978, and the only indication of damage was in the left dorsal thalamus (Figure 14-10). There may be subtle damage elsewhere, but damage in the dorsomedial thalamus alone may be sufficient to impair gravely the formation of long-term memories. (The effects of this deficit on N. A.'s daily life are shown in Box 14-1.)

Like Horel, Mishkin (1978) also asked whether temporal lobe damage that impairs memory might involve a structure other than the hippocampus, but he reached a conclusion different from Horel's. Mishkin tested the effects of destroying either the hippocampus or the amygdala or both (Figure 14-11). The subjects were monkeys and the task was to discriminate a novel object from any of a series of objects that had been shown in familiarization presentations; in each test trial one previously seen object was paired with a novel object. The results showed that neither the hippocampus nor the amygdala is essential for acquisition of this task (see Table 14-1). But monkeys deprived of both structures required far more trials to reacquire this task postoperatively than they had needed to learn it originally. In addition to this failure of recognition memory, animals with the combined ablation were unable to recall on the basis of a single trial whether or not an object had been rewarded. The amygdala and hippocampus share many input and output connections, so it is not surprising that they may be able to serve as alternative pathways between cortical association areas and subcortical targets. This is not to state that the amygdala and the hippocampus are identical in function but only that the functions of the two structures may overlap in an important way in regard to formation of memory.

In a further study to test the hypotheses of Horel and of Mishkin, two kinds of intervention were employed: The temporal stem was transected bilaterally in some monkeys whereas both the amygdala and the hippocampus were ablated bilaterally in others (Zola-Morgan, Squire, and Mishkin, 1981). The animals were tested both on a visual discrimination task and on formation of memory for familiar versus novel objects. The results demonstrated that transection of the temporal stem impaired

(a)

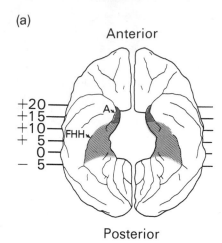

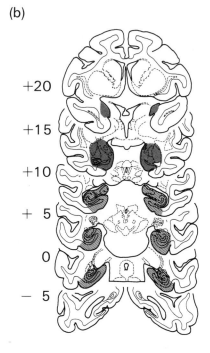

0 10 20 mm

Figure 14-11 Sites of experimental lesions of the amygdala and hippocampus in rhesus monkey brain. (a) The lesions are projected on a ventral view of the brain. The amygdalar lesion (A) is shown in dark blue and the hippocampal lesion (FHH) in light blue. The levels indicated at the left of diagram (a) show where the series of transverse sections in (b) were taken. (Courtesy of Dr. Mortimer Mishkin, Laboratory of Neuropsychology, National Institute of Mental Health)

TABLE 14-1
Effects of Removal of the Amygdala and the Hippocampus on Memory in Monkeys

	PREOPERATIVE		POSTOPERATIVE	
	Trials	*Errors*	*Trials*	*Errors*
Normal controls	73	24	0	0
Amygdala removed	100	33	140	39
Hippocampus removed	93	25	73	19
Combined removal of amygdala and hippocampus	130	32	987	270

Note: Data are numbers of trials and errors to criterion of 90% correct.
SOURCE: From Mishkin (1978).

visual discrimination but did not affect ability on the memory task. On the contrary, ablation of the amygdala and hippocampus left visual discrimination intact but severely impaired formation of memory. The histological verification of the lesions in this experiment is not yet complete, and one would like to see the experiment replicated in another laboratory. As results stand to date, they favor the hypothesis that destruction of either the amygdala or the hippocampus does not have serious effects on ability to form memories, but that combined lesions of these structures is devastating for memory.

Horel and Mishkin both remind us that the temporal lobe includes several important structures and that investigators have shown tunnel vision in concentrating almost exclusively on the hippocampus for 20 years in attempting to explain the temporal lobe amnesic syndrome. Now we should be cautious about concluding that the amygdala and/or hippocampus are involved in all kinds of learning. In fact, a recent study by Pigareva (1982) reports that in learning to switch the significance of conditioned stimuli, intact rats do more poorly than rats in which both the amygdala and the hippocampus have been largely destroyed! Much research will be needed to determine the roles that different brain structures play in different kinds of learning and in memory formation.

Failures of encoding and of retention

Do patients with different kinds of brain damage differ in the basic learning-memory processes in which they are deficient? Some recent evidence suggests that this is the case. Patients with Korsakoff's syndrome are commonly supposed to have trouble encoding information, and their ability to retrieve has also been implicated in their poor performance. In tests of these possible sources of difficulty, Huppert and Piercy (1978) found that Korsakoff subjects had to be given longer exposure to stimuli in order for their recognition of the stimuli to equal that of normals. Thus they showed a deficiency of encoding. Then measures of recall were taken after varying periods of time, and forgetting was found to occur at the same rate in Korsakoff and normal subjects. Thus a main difficulty in the Korsakoff syndrome appears to be in encoding information.

In some patients whose brain damage is different from that of Korsakoff subjects, the rate of forgetting is faster than normal. H. M., for example, has no trouble in encoding, as shown by good short-term memory, but he definitely forgets more rapidly than normal subjects (Huppert and Piercy, 1979). Also, patients who have recently received a series of therapeutic electroconvulsive shocks show more rapid forgetting than they do four months later (Squire, 1981). More rapid forgetting means poorer consolidation of long-term memories. Thus the ability to form long-term memories distinguishes some classes of subjects; it may also vary—although less dramatically—among normal subjects.

Developmental approaches to learning and memory

Changes in the abilities to learn and to remember over the life span are important not only to understanding behavior at different ages but also to providing clues about the neural mechanisms of learning and memory. We are all familiar with the increasing ability of children to learn more complex material and to solve more difficult problems as they grow older. Some theorists have speculated about the importance of education, informal as well as formal, in developing learning ability; others have emphasized the importance of language in directing learning and aiding problem solving. But neither of these proposed explanations can account for the following finding about the maturation of problem-solving ability (Harlow, 1959): Monkeys a few months old can solve simple problems but they do poorly on more complex problems; monkeys that have been kept in a simple laboratory environment with no training or testing until the age of 3 years can solve complex problems with relative ease. The increase in ability without training continues through the age of 4 or 5. These results suggest the importance of maturation of neural circuits for complex learning.

The ability to form long-term memories also requires maturation. If you have tried to recall your earliest memories, you probably have not been able to get back beyond the age of 2 or 3, and you probably have few memories from before your fifth year. This "amnesia of early childhood" is curious, because children are obviously learning a great deal and undergoing interesting experiences in their first few years. Why should these experiences not be remembered in later years? Here again theorists have varying interpretations. Some have suggested that memories for these years are repressed; others, that the memories were not coded effectively into linguistic terms. Here, too, research with animal subjects has suggested a more satisfying explanation: Research with rodents has shown that in species like rats and mice the ability to form long-term memories matures more slowly than does learning ability (Campbell and Coulter, 1976). Human babies and rat pups are alike in being born at a relatively early stage of their development; such species are called **altricial.** Altricial infants tend to remember only what they have learned over and over again. Thus children remember words and faces that they have relearned repeatedly over a long period, but memories for particular incidents (so-called episodic memories) are not retained from early life. On the other hand, some species are born at a rather advanced stage of development; they are called **precocial.** The guinea pig is precocial, and infant guinea pigs can remember as well as can adults. Thus the ability to form long-term memories appears to depend upon the relative maturity of the nervous system.

A further test of this maturational hypothesis was performed by accelerating or retarding the maturation of the nervous system in mice (Nagy, 1979). Treatment with thyroid hormone, which accelerates brain development, led to the ability to remember for 24 hours (h) at 10 days of age rather than at 12 days for controls. On the other hand, underfeeding retarded neural maturation, and 24-h memory appeared only at 14 days of age in these mice. These results added fresh support to the hypothesis that the ability to form long-term memories is related to maturation of the central nervous system. Further research is being conducted to try to find what aspects of nervous system maturation are required for efficient formation of long-term memories.

Comparative and evolutionary approaches to learning

There has been a good deal of speculation about the evolution of abilities to learn and remember; but it is not possible to do direct research on this subject, since we cannot measure the behavior of animals now extinct. We can, of course, compare the learning and memory capacities of existing species, some of which are more primitive than others in the sense that they resemble their ancient ancestors more closely, but this is not a direct route to the past. As we survey attempts at comparing learning ability among existing species in the paragraphs below, we will see that this is not a simple matter; just as it is difficult and perhaps impossible to devise a "culture-free" intelligence test for human beings, so it has been difficult to devise tests for animals that do not favor the sensory and/or motor capacities of some species and work against others. Nevertheless, we will see ingenious efforts to devise appropriate comparative tests of intelligence, and the suggestive results that they have yielded. Findings from the comparative approach will be helpful when we then consider the evolution of learning and intelligence.

Distribution of learning abilities among classes of animals

Nonassociative learning appears to be very widely distributed throughout the animal kingdom. Rather simple animals with small nervous systems readily habituate to repeated stimuli, and the courses of habituation and of sensitization are similar whether studied in an earthworm, a mollusc, or a mammal. Some investigators have reported learning even in paramecia, one-celled animals that, of course, do not have a nervous system. It appears that there are not any animals that do not show some kind of learning and memory.

Associative learning probably has a somewhat more restricted distribution than nonassociative learning, although it too is found in a great variety of animals. For example, insects can learn to associate a location or a particular stimulus with food. Bees, as we saw earlier, identify sources of food in nature and return to them; in experimental conditions they readily learn to associate the color of a dish with nectar. The octopus learns easily that one particular geometrical form signals food whereas another stands for punishment; it learns to approach the first and to avoid the second. Some animals may show associative learning only under special conditions, and unless and until these have been discovered the animal is classed as incapable of associative learning. Thus a marine snail, *Pleurobranchea,* that had been used for studies of neural processes in habituation has recently been conditioned to avoid one of its usual foods—if the food is paired with electrical shock. But trials cannot be given more frequently than once an hour if success is to be obtained. So this snail is a "slow learner" even if it does not require many trials. The sea hare, *Aplysia,* is used extensively to study neural processes in habituation, but only in 1980 was it first reported to be capable of associative learning.

Part of the problem of assessing the capacity of a species to learn and remember is that these capacities may be highly specific. In recent years it has become evident that certain species can learn particular associations well even though they are very poor at other tasks that do not seem more difficult to us. Therefore testing learning and memory in one or two situations may not furnish a valid indication of the capacities of a species. In particular, it is important to consider the specific circumstances of the animal's natural habitat—the kinds of occasions that call for it to learn and remember.

Now that species-specific aspects of learning are being studied actively, it may be hard to believe that eminent investigators ignored or even denied them, but that is the case. Thus Pavlov (1927, p. 7) stated that in studying conditioning one could choose any response that a particular animal is capable of and find how it can become linked to any sensory signal that the animal can receive. Skinner also held to a general approach. Two of his students used his techniques of operant conditioning to train thousands of animals for zoo shows and television programs and commercials (Breland and Breland, 1961, 1966). Generally they were quite successful, but there were failures, and they finally perceived a pattern in their unsuccessful cases. Many failures occurred when the desired behavior competed with a species-specific response that the animal performs in the wild. This feature of species-specific characteristics is in keeping with the evolutionary approach to the study of behavior.

A recent review calls it a "revolution" that has brought evolutionary concepts back into the study of learning (D'Amato, 1974). The revolution occurred when investigators could no longer ignore evidence of four kinds:

1. **The nonequivalence of stimuli.** All stimuli are not alike, even in a general sense, for the purposes of learning. Even among the stimuli to which a given species can respond, some are much more compelling in evoking learning than are others.

2. **The nonequivalence of responses.** The rapidity of learning a given instrumental behavior varies enormously among species.

3. **The nonequivalence of associations.** There is a great variety of possibilities for forming associations, especially those that bridge long time intervals. Some associations are learned only if the consequence follows the response very promptly, a result generally true of Pavlovian conditioning, as when a sound is followed by presentation of food. Other associations can be formed over a long time interval; for example, if a gastric disturbance occurs hours after eating a new food, many animals learn to avoid that food. (This result accounts for bait shyness.)

4. **The selectivity of reinforcement.** It now seems doubtful that reinforcement automatically strengthens all neural links that have been employed recently.

These **constraints on learning,** as they are often called, have the following consequences: An animal's inability to learn one thing doesn't mean that it can't learn another that might seem to us to be equally difficult. For example, a rat that becomes ill after eating a food will not learn to avoid food of similar color or texture or food in the same dish, but it will avoid food of the same taste. Quails—highly visual animals—learn to avoid the color as well as the taste. Bees can learn to come for a particular food on a 24-h schedule but not on any other schedule; if you tried to train them to come on a 12-h schedule, you would conclude that they can't learn to time their feeding. *Drosophila* (fruit flies) have been so thoroughly studied in terms of their genetics that many investigators have sought to study their learning processes. But it was only in 1974 that investigators announced successful training of *Drosophila;* they are now beginning to find how differences in learning and memory are related to genetic differences among lines of *Drosophila* (Dudai and Quinn, 1980).

Research on the comparative distribution of learning abilities is being pursued actively, both by observing animals in their natural settings and by studying behavior in the laboratory. What kinds of ecological niches favor the development of ability for rapid and powerful learning? Are there ecological niches that make learning a dispensable luxury and neural plasticity unnecessary? These are basic questions that remain for future research to answer.

Comparisons of learning ability among species

Since the beginning of this century many American psychologists have attempted to compare the learning abilities of different species. Thorndike's puzzle boxes were the first attempt at a "general intelligence test" that would be appropriate for work with many species (Figure 14-12). With each species Thorndike recorded the trials and errors needed to solve problems, and he noted the rate at which errors decreased on successive trials.

Figure 14-12 Puzzle box devised by Edward L. Thorndike in 1898 to study animal learning.

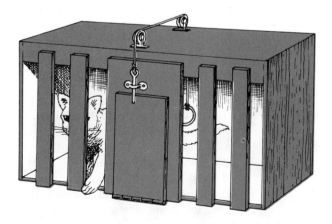

Figure 14-13 Delayed response test devised by Walter S. Hunter in 1913. The animal is retained in a transparent start box while one of the three lights is illuminated briefly. After a delay interval, the animal is released. If it chooses the correct path, it can reach the food reward. If not, it is returned to the start compartment for another trial.

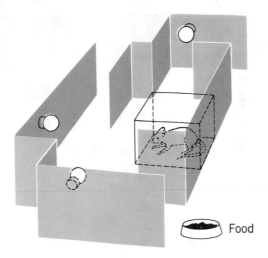

Food

In 1913 W. S. Hunter published a report concerning the ability of several species in the delayed response test. In this test the animal is shown which of a few choices is correct, but a time delay is imposed between the signal and the opportunity to respond (Figure 14-13). At first it seemed that higher mammals could tolerate longer delays than rodents, but later work indicated that under appropriate circumstances a rat could perform at as long a delay as a chimpanzee. Moreover, the ethologist Tinbergen (1961) pointed out that if delayed response was used as the measure of intellectual ability, the digger wasp would be considered among the most intelligent of animals. It can "remember" exactly how much food to bring to each of its many larva nests (of varying population) even if delayed by as much as 24 h; this delay is longer than most mammals can tolerate in Hunter's test. Although this criticism is telling, it is not completely fair. The digger wasp can delay only in a very specific task, one on which the survival of its species depends. Animals that can delay in a variety of situations may be demonstrating a capacity for flexibility—which is certainly part of intellectual ability—that far exceeds that of the wasp. Still, the attempt to scale animal intelligence by means of the delayed response test came to a not undeserved end.

The study of formation of **learning sets** (Harlow, 1949) provided another trial-and-error explanation of complex behavior, and it was also an attempt to find a general-purpose intelligence test for animals. Essentially, learning sets are formed when an animal—a monkey, for example—is given as many as 300 problems, one after the other, all based on the same principle. For example, the animal may be trained to choose one of a pair of objects (circle versus triangle) that the experimenter has arbitrarily designated as correct (Figure 14-14). This problem is called the object discrimination problem. On each trial that the monkey chooses the correct object, it is given a bit of food. After a number of trials the monkey masters that problem, and then it is given another pair of objects and again has to learn which is correct. After hundreds of successive problems of this type, each with a different pair of objects, the monkey can solve a new problem very quickly. If its choice on the first

Figure 14-14 Monkey making an object discrimination during an experiment on formation of learning sets. (Courtesy of H. F. Harlow)

trial is rewarded, it stays with that choice and makes no errors at all; if not rewarded, it switches to the other object and thereafter never errs. If one were to observe these monkeys after 300 prior problems, one might see their brilliant performance as insight, but we know that would be a mistake.

The degree to which different species improve in their performance from the 1st to the 10th, to the 50th, to the 100th problem, and so on, has been used to scale the "intelligence" of species (Hodos, 1970). Results of this learning set measure (see Figure 14-15) conform rather well to our intuitive ideas about the relative intel-

Figure 14-15 Comparison of species according to their rates of improvement in formation of learning sets. (Hodos, 1970)

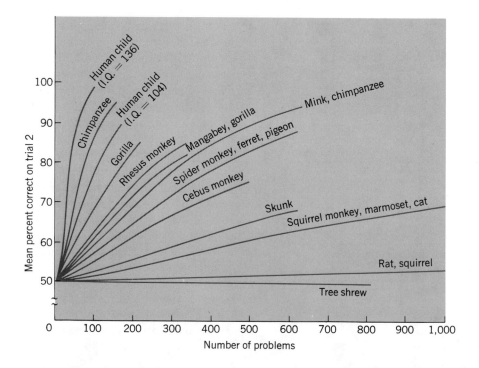

ligence of species. This measure is not free of the difficulties of the other measures that have been tried, but at least it involves an ability—discrimination learning—that is common and useful in a wide variety of species.

Many psychologists have concluded that it is not possible to scale the general learning ability or intelligence of different species; they view the intelligence of each species as the sum of specialized abilities or as composed of special-purpose systems (see Lockard, 1971). That is, members of a given species may be very good at solving a particular sort of problem for which they are adapted by evolution but poor at others, so it is difficult or impossible to make an overall classification. On the other hand, some psychologists continue to design methods to determine general intelligence, or at least general factors of intelligence. Thus Riddell (1980) has designed tests of animals' abilities to inhibit a recently learned response (such as a visual choice—the light rather than the dark alternative) and go back to a previously learned response (such as a spatial choice—right or left). The absolute numbers of errors in the problems may be related to specific factors, but the relative numbers can be used as a measure of general ability. Among mammals this index appears to separate species in a reasonable way; we will see later that the behavioral index correlates rather well with a measure of relative brain size. The problem of comparing intelligence of different species remains unsettled, however, and work on it continues. The fact that some of the interspecies behavioral scores correlate highly with the interspecies brain measures supports the value of both measures.

Evolution of learning and intelligence

From our survey of comparative aspects of learning and intelligence we can draw some tentative conclusions about how these capacities evolved, and we will supplement these conclusions with some proposals of Rozin (1976a). We have seen that "lower" or simpler animals tend to have specific sensory and motor abilities that are adapted to particular environmental niches. Sometimes these abilities are quite keen and precise, such as the abilities of bees to distinguish colors and patterns of blossoms and to learn to come to a particular location for food on a 24-h schedule. But these abilities are highly specific and constrained; they do not make it possible to learn other tasks that would seem similar to us, such as learning to come to food on an 8-h or 12-h schedule. Of course, those shorter schedules don't occur in the bees' world.

It seems likely that the powerful and flexible brain systems for learning and memory in humans and other complex animals have been built on prior specific adaptations in simpler animals. In the course of time the specific circuits of the simpler animals probably came to be used in more general and more plastic ways in higher animals. A complex system cannot be built from the ground up without building stable subsystems on the way. Simon (1962) has pointed to the need for a hierarchical structure of subsystems as a basis for complex systems, since errors or mistakes in evolution or development could otherwise bring down the whole system. Building a system out of self-contained subsystems ensures that a failure in one part of the mechanism results, at worst, only in loss of that particular subsystem.

Much of the evolution of learning and intelligence probably consisted first of the development of precise and elaborate systems to handle specific situations and then of the liberation of these systems from their restricted context. In other words, particular circuitry that evolved to handle particular problems (such as size constancy in perception or memory for food location) was initially accessible only to those input and output systems that it was designed to serve. With evolution some of these systems became connected to other systems; thus they became components in a hierarchy and hence could be used more widely. Also, circuits that were successful in a particular context probably served as models for circuits in related systems. Thus we see the modular structure of the cerebral cortex, where similar basic circuits are replicated many times to fit into different networks. This manifold replication of basic units in complex brains is one of the causes of the increase in brain size with evolution, a topic we considered in Chapter 3.

Relations between brain size and intelligence

Does brain size predict intelligence? Ever since the brain was recognized as the seat of intellect and the organ that coordinates behavior, its size and complex shape have intrigued thinkers. Many attempts have been made to relate the size of the brain to intelligence, and work on this correlational approach continues actively. We will consider three basic questions:

1. Can interspecies differences in brain size be related to interspecies differences in intelligence?
2. Among members of a given species, are those with larger brains more intelligent?
3. If brain size is altered experimentally, is there a subsequent change in intelligence?

Interspecies comparisons of brain size and intelligence

We saw in Chapter 3 that there is a general rule that relates brain size to body size among all the vertebrates: Brain weight is proportional to the two-thirds power of body weight. We also saw that this general rule is modified by a constant k, which tends to be greater for more recently evolved species within each line of evolutionary radiation. Several investigators have tried to determine whether k (or similar measures) can be related to the relative intelligence of different species. The most promising attempts have used the rate of formation of learning sets as the index of intelligence.

Recall that when animals of different species formed learning sets, some improved their performance much faster than others (Figure 14-15). Given enough problems, most species performed rather well, but the initial slopes of their learning curves differed greatly. Riddell and Corl (1977) calculated the brain index, Nc ("extra" cortical neurons, related to k), for mammalian species and plotted it against the initial linear slope of the learning curve (Figure 14-16). The rank-order correlation between the behavioral measure and the cerebral index was 0.98, an extremely high value. So the rate of formation of learning sets seems to be closely related to relative brain size, at least among species of mammals.

Riddell (1979) also tested six species of mammals on his own test of ability to inhibit a recently learned response and to return to a previously learned one. This ability was quantified by an index labeled K. Figure 14-17 shows the results when K was plotted against Nc. Here the rank-order correlation was 0.94, again extremely high. Encouraged by this success, Riddell attempted to extend the range of obser-

Figure 14-16 Plot of rate of acquisition of learning sets versus a measure related to relative brain weights for subjects of 11 mammalian species. The learning set measure for each species is the slope of the initial linear section of its curve in Figure 14-15. The brain measure is the index of "extra" cortical neurons (Nc), which is related to the encephalization index. (Adapted from Riddell and Corl, 1977)

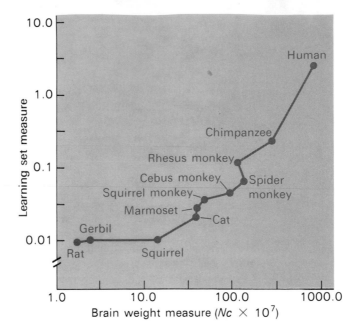

Figure 14-17 Plot of Riddell's index of behavioral flexibility versus a brain index for subjects of five mammalian species. The lower the index K, the greater the behavioral flexibility. (Adapted from Riddell, 1979)

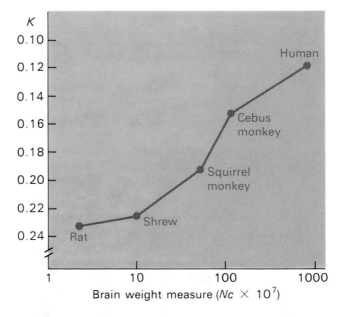

vations by including fish, the class of vertebrates with the smallest relative brain size. The index Nc could not be used, since fish do not have a cerebral cortex, so Riddell used an index of relative size of brain, the encephalization quotient (EQ) that we discussed in Chapter 3. When the data were plotted, it was found that fish of the species tested (chub) performed better than expected—in fact, about as well as a squirrel monkey (Figure 14-18). Riddell noted that the pattern of responses of the

Figure 14-18 Plot of Riddell's index of behavioral flexibility versus a brain index, for a species of fish (chub) and five mammalian species. (Adapted from Riddell, 1979)

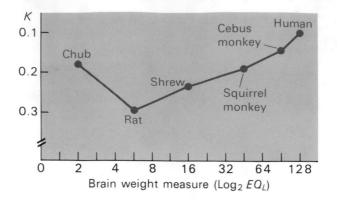

fish were very different from those of mammals; this qualitative difference indicates that a true comparison was not being made. So the problem of devising a test suitable for use across classes of animals reappeared, although the two tests did function well within the class of mammals. We do not yet know whether the rule that holds within the mammals—that brain index predicts learning ability—will also hold within other classes of animals, or whether *any* relation will hold among all classes of animals.

Within-species relations between brain size and intelligence

There is an age-old belief that a high forehead is a sign of intelligence. This notion has even been extended to animals, giving the owl and the elephant their reputations for sagacity.

When measurements of intelligence began to be made in the twentieth century, they revealed only low relations between cranial size and intelligence, yet the old belief died hard. Thus Karl Pearson reported that at the turn of the century the well-known psychologist and statistician Sir Francis Galton "was very unhappy about the low correlations I found between intelligence and size of head . . . it was one of the few instances I noticed when impressions seemed to have more weight than measurements" (Pearson, 1924, p. 24, note 2). G. A. Miller claims that "to the day he died [Galton] was unwilling to admit that the size of a man's skull had no value as a measure of his intelligence" (1962, p. 137). But we should note that Pearson's evidence of intelligence came from teachers' ratings, not from formal testing, and Galton's "impressions" may have been of equal value.

A recent review by Van Valen (1974) shows only a few studies that have correlated head size with intelligence test scores. The observed correlations ranged from 0.08 to 0.22, but Van Valen argued that when allowance is made for errors inherent in the methods used in these tests, the true correlation between intelligence and brain size may be as high as 0.3. That is, skull size is not a very good measure of brain size, and test scores are not perfect measures of intelligence, so the true correlation between brain size and intelligence may be higher than the observed correlation between skull circumferences and test scores.

Variation in the volume of the cerebral ventricles also tends to lower the observed correlations between head size and intelligence. The ventricles vary considerably even among normal individuals. In some cases they are greatly enlarged, a condition called hydrocephaly ("water in the head"). In a mild case that begins in infancy, the skull enlarges to accommodate the increased volume of cerebrospinal fluid; the circumference of the head is large, and intelligence is unaffected. In more extreme cases the brain tissue is crushed by the fluid; the individual has a large, rather globe-shaped head and low intelligence. Clearly such cases of pathologically en- larged skulls accompanied by low intelligence diminish the correlation between head size (or brain size, as it is usually measured) and intelligence. A few cases have recently been reported in which head size is normal but where over half the cranial cavity is occupied by cerebrospinal fluid, yet intelligence is normal (Lewin, 1980). Brain size in some of these cases has been estimated from tomograms, but this technique leaves a wide margin of uncertainty. Study of such cases has led one investigator, John Lorber of Sheffield, England, to ask half-seriously, "Is the brain necessary for intelligence?" But his doubt is clearly a minority view.

Age also introduces variation in brain size without clearly affecting intelligence. The effects of age on brain weight were shown in Figure 3-1. As the brain becomes smaller, past the age of 40 or so, skull size does not diminish; here is another way in which head size does not accurately measure brain size. Because of the effects of age on brain size, it would be best to conduct correlational studies within subjects of the same age or to allow explicitly for age, but neither of these precautions has been taken in most studies.

A recent unpublished analysis based on data for U.S. children (Jerison) yielded a small but significant correlation (0.3) between head circumferences and intel- ligence; but after the influence of height was separated out, the correlation fell to 0.1. A recent study in England was based on data for 415 men and women, ranging in age from 18 to 75 (Passingham, 1979). Cranial capacity was estimated from head measures, and IQ was measured on the Wechsler Adult Intelligence Scale. A small but significant correlation of 0.15 was found, but this fell to 0.03 (nonsignificant) when the influence of height was factored out. If there is a correlation of 0.1–0.2 between brain size and intelligence, this correlation is not enough to help you predict the intelligence of individuals, but it is large enough to be a factor in natural selection over many generations and thus to lead to increasing size of brain and head.

● **Brain size and ability in animals**   Some of the difficulties of research with hu- man subjects can be overcome when laboratory rodents are used as subjects, because the experimenter can measure brain weights at the conclusion of behavioral testing rather than having to rely on skull size. Also extensive behavioral measures can be taken. A study of this sort was performed recently with male and female mice from each of three heterogeneous stocks (C. Jensen and Fuller, 1978; Jensen, 1979). Table 14-2 shows correlations between brain weights and scores of performance on four different learning tasks; for the first two tasks, two different scores were obtained. Three of the six correlations were statistically significant, indicating that larger brains do predict better performance, at least in this species.

● **Size of specific brain regions and learning ability**   It may be possible to relate some kinds of learning to particular parts of the brain or to specific nuclei. Thus problem-solving scores among rats of several strains were found to correlate signifi- cantly with the weight of the cerebral cortex (Rosenzweig, Bennett, and Diamond,

TABLE 14-2 Correlations Between Brain Weights and Learning Performance in Mice

ACTIVE AVOIDANCE		WATER MAZE		OPERANT DISCRIMINATION	PASSIVE AVOIDANCE
Training	_Extinction_	_Trials to First Criterion_	_Total Criterion_		
−0.17	0.37*	−0.24	0.40†	0.42†	0.07

SOURCE: From C. Jensen and J. L. Fuller, "Learning performance varies with brain weight in heterogeneous mouse lines," _Journal of Comparative and Physiological Psychology, 92,_ 5(1978): 830–836. Copyright 1978 by the American Psychological Association. Reprinted by permission of the publisher and author.
*$p < 0.05$
$^\dagger p < 0.02$

1967). In songbirds particular brain nuclei control singing, and the size of these nuclei has been reported to correlate with ability to acquire songs. Among male canaries the size of a bird's repertoire of songs correlates significantly with the volumes of two brain nuclei (HVC and RA: see Figure 9-11) (Nottebohm et al., in press). This finding in laboratory canaries has been replicated in wild marsh wrens, a species in which males show marked differences in the size of their repertoires (Canady, Kroodama, and Nottebohm, 1981). While birds with small song nuclei tend to have small repertoires, those with large nuclei show considerable variation in size of repertoire. Nottebohm suggests that these observations follow the "library principle":: If you want to house a lot of books, you have to have a large library building, but having a large building doesn't guarantee that you have a lot of books.

Alterations of brain size and intelligence

If larger brain size is correlated with superior learning, then can better learning be produced by increasing brain size? Several kinds of animal experiments have produced conflicting answers to this question. One kind of experiment has been to breed selectively to obtain a high-brain-weight line and a low-brain-weight line from the same foundation stock. Several generations of selective breeding produced a clear separation of brain weights, and members of the high and low lines could then be tested. Overall, the test results have given only weak, inconsistent support for the hypothesis that learning ability increases with a genetic increase in brain weight (Jensen, 1977, 1980). One explanation for these results is that selection may have led to fixation of other traits that have affected intellectual ability in a variety of ways.

Another kind of experiment increased the brain size of rodents by raising them in a relatively complex environment (Rosenzweig and Bennett, 1978). It is chiefly the cerebral cortex that is increased by this treatment, as we will see in Chapter 15. In this case learning ability also increased with complex experience, but the behavioral and cerebral effects may be separate and independent. The increase in the cortex, it should be noted, is not in the form of "extra neurons" but rather in greater dendritic branching and increased numbers of synaptic contacts.

A third kind of experiment yielded larger rat brains with greater numbers of neurons by allowing only a single fetus to develop instead of the six or more in a normal litter (van Marthens et al., 1974). Preliminary behavioral measures indicate that these larger-brained singletons are better learners than normal rats from multiple litters.

While the results of these animal experiments provide some support for the hypothesis that altering brain size causes a corresponding alteration of learning ability, the support is far from conclusive.

Costs and benefits of larger brains

What can we conclude about relations between brain size and intelligence, both among and within species? Also, what are the costs as well as the benefits of larger brains?

Evidence from the evolution of brain size, considered in Chapter 3, as well as three lines of evidence just reviewed all indicate a positive relation between brain size and intelligence, while leaving considerable room for other determinants. We saw in Chapter 3 evidence for the following conclusions:

1. Within each line of vertebrate evolution the more recently evolved species tend to have larger brains than the older, more conservative forms.
2. Within several families of mammals, larger brain sizes have been found in those species whose food is distributed less densely and less uniformly.
3. A study of cranial endocasts of North American fossil ungulates and carnivores suggested that predator-prey interaction favored selection of larger brains over a period of more than 60 million years.
4. The increase of brain size among hominids, along with increasing ability to make complex tools, is consistent with the selective value of brain size.

In this chapter we have seen reports of high correlations between relative brain size and behavioral scores among species. It must be recognized, however, that the adequacy of interspecies comparisons of intelligence remains a matter of controversy. Within a species, where at least the same test or tests can be used with all individuals, correlations between brain size and intelligence have tended to be low. Almost all these within-species studies have been done with human subjects, where the measures of brain size have been indirect and subject to considerable error. The recent animal study of Jensen (1979) showed moderately strong correlations. Overall these varied kinds of evidence suggest to us that greater brain size promotes greater intelligence.

Much of the research on brain size and intelligence has focused only on the possible benefits of larger brains. It is important, however, to consider possible costs as well as benefits of increased brain size. One cost is metabolic. As we have noted, the weight of the human brain is only about 2% of the weight of the body, but as you sit reading, your brain consumes about 20% of your energy expenditure. Clearly a brain that was larger than necessary would be wasteful of energy. A large brain also poses mechanical problems. First is the problem of getting the head through the birth canal. Although the human pelvis evolved along with increasing head size, birth is not an easy experience for human babies (or their mothers). Then there is the problem of carrying a large head poised at the top of the spine, where its mass predisposes it to injuries such as "whiplash" of the cranial part of the spinal cord.

Brain size of any given species has been determined during evolution through a balance of costs and benefits for life in a particular ecological niche. Thus plasticity of brain size may provide an aspect of flexibility. That is, in several species brain size has been found to increase slightly when greater functional demands are placed on individuals, as we will see in Chapter 15. Plasticity in brain size may make it possible to hold down brain size when functional demand is low but to increase brain size and functional capacity when demand increases. Such an adaptive response may be one reason for evolution of anatomical plasticity of the brain (Rosenzweig, 1979).

Generality of learning in the central nervous system

Are special parts of the brain and particular kinds of neural circuits devoted to learning and memory? We have seen that certain tracts and brain nuclei are specialized for sensory-perceptual functions and that others are involved in motor functions. Is there a similar assignment of brain regions for learning and memory? Pavlov maintained that the "higher functions" of learning and memory require the cerebral cortex, but most current investigators believe that much of the central nervous system is capable of learning.

In 1912 an investigator in Pavlov's laboratory tried to condition a dog from which most of the cerebral cortex had been removed; the experimenter reported failure to find conditioning. From this and other results Pavlov concluded that conditioning involves the formation of what he called "temporary links" in the cortex. These links were supposed to bridge the sensory and motor areas of the cortex, forming new reflex circuits. Later research showed that although decorticate dogs are somewhat unstable subjects, they can be conditioned (for example, Poltyrev and Zeliony, 1930; Culler and Metter, 1934). We saw earlier that species that possess little or no cerebral cortex are capable of learning, and this observation demonstrated in another way that the cortex is not required for learning. Further work showed that conditioning can be produced in the spinal cord after its connections with the brain have been severed. Such spinal conditioning has been found in several species including dogs (Shurrager and Culler, 1938) and cats (Patterson, 1975). Research with invertebrates has shown that habituation can occur in the simplest of neural circuits—a two-neuron reflex arc in which a sensory neuron makes synaptic contact with a motor neuron (Kandel, 1979); we will take this work up in more detail in Chapter 15. It may be, then, that many synapses in many parts of the nervous system are capable of modifying their properties in ways that produce learning. Also, as we will see in Chapter 15, new synapses can be formed in many parts of the nervous system in response to functional demand, and this feature may offer another widely distributed mechanism of learning.

Storage of memory also seems to be widely distributed in the nervous system. Certainly the many investigators who have made experimental lesions to study the mechanisms of learning and memory have never discovered a specific memory bank. That is, removing any particular brain region has not been found to destroy particular memories. In at least some cases the memory of a particular behavior appears to reside in the same neural circuit that mediates that behavior.

The fact that the mechanisms of learning and memory are widely distributed in the brain does not necessarily mean that particular brain regions may not have special functions in learning or memory. For example, experimental results reported above suggest that the hippocampus and amygdala may facilitate the formation and storage of memories by other brain regions. Destroying the hippocampus or the amygdala or both does not impair existing memories, though, so these are not storage regions. Instead they may modulate learning or memory storage by other brain regions. (In Chapter 15 we will see further suggestions of specific roles for certain brain regions.)

SUMMARY / MAIN POINTS

1. The abilities to learn and remember affect all behaviors that are characteristically human, and they are used extensively by animals. Whereas evolution by natural selection brings about adaptation over successive generations, learning permits adaptation within the lifetime of the individual.

2. Learning includes both nonassociative forms such as habituation and sensitization and associative forms such as classical conditioning, instrumental learning, and imprinting. Memories are often classified by how long they last; these classifications are iconic, short-term, intermediate-term, and long-term.

3. The pathological impairment of memory called Korsakoff's disease results from prolonged alcoholism. Korsakoff patients show gaps in memory, which they may attempt to fill by confabulation, and deficits in problem solving; they are also impaired in encoding new information. Korsakoff patients usually show severe bilateral damage to the mammillary bodies and the dorsomedial nucleus of the thalamus.

4. Some patients with damage in the temporal lobe show particular impairment in consolidation of long-term memories. The critical site of damage was thought to be the hippocampus, but animals with hippocampal lesions do not show a similar impairment of memory, so alternative hypotheses are being explored.

5. The ability to form long-term memories develops more slowly than the ability to learn. The "amnesia of early childhood" is a phenomenon that humans share with other species that are born in a relatively immature state.

6. Nonassociative learning is widely distributed throughout the animal kingdom. Associative learning seems to have a more restricted distribution among species, and for a given species it may occur only with regard to particular stimuli and/or responses; that is, it shows "constraints of learning."

7. The evolution of powerful and flexible brain mechanisms of learning and memory may have resulted first from development of precise and elaborate systems to handle specific sensorimotor adjustments and then from the liberation of these systems for more general use.

8. Relative brain size among mammalian species correlates highly with the rate of formation of learning sets.

9. Within-species correlations of brain size and intelligence are low for human beings, where the measures of brain size are indirect and subject to major sources of variability. A study conducted with mice showed significant correlations between direct measures of brain weight and various measures of learning.

10. Although larger brains appear to confer benefits in terms of learning and memory, at least across species, they also exact costs in terms of metabolic and mechanical requirements. Brain size of any given species has been determined through evolution by a balance of costs and benefits for life in a particular ecological niche.

11. Mechanisms for learning and memory appear to be widely distributed in the central nervous system rather than being restricted to a single region or formation, such as the cerebral cortex.

RECOMMENDED READING

Butters, N., and Cermak, L. S. *Alcoholic Korsakoff's syndrome: An information-processing approach to amnesia.* New York: Academic Press, 1980.

Rosenzweig, M. R., and Bennett, E. L. (Eds.). *Neural mechanisms of learning and memory.* Cambridge, Mass.: MIT Press, 1976.

Sinz, R. and Rosenzweig, M. R. *Psychophysiology 1980: Memory, Motivation, and Event-Related Potentials in Mental Operations.* (Symposia and papers from the XXIInd International Congress of Psychology, Leipzig). Amsterdam: North-Holland Press, 1982.

Thompson, R. F., Hicks, L. H., and Shvyrok, V. B. (Eds.). *Neural mechanisms of goal-directed behavior and learning.* New York: Academic Press, 1980

Orientation

Possible mechanisms of memory storage

Behavioral and somatic interventions

Neuroanatomical Effects of Experience

Effects of experience on gross anatomy of the brain

Effects of experience on synapses

Mechanisms producing neuroanatomical effects

Neurochemical Effects of Experience

Effects of enriched or impoverished experience on brain chemistry

Effects of formal training on brain chemistry

Possible roles of protein synthesis in memory storage

Electrophysiological Correlates of Learning

Habituation and sensitization in simple systems

Associative learning in simple systems

Conditioning in vertebrates

Consolidation Hypothesis of Memory Formation

Testing the consolidation hypothesis with electroconvulsive shock

Varying the locus and kind of treatment

Improving memory with posttrial treatments

Sequential Neurochemical Processes in Memory Formation

Time courses of effects of different agents

Protein synthesis and memory

Modulation of Formation of Memory

Cholinergic modulation

Catecholamine modulation

Mechanisms of modulation

Applications to Problems of Human Memory

Improving memory with pharmacological agents

Application to mental retardation and dementia

Summary/Main Points

15

Neural Mechanisms of Learning and Memory

Orientation

An experience that lasts only a few seconds may result in a memory that lasts a lifetime. If memories are to be maintained, enduring changes must be brought about in the nervous system. Such memory-holding processes, sometimes called **memory traces,** have proved to be elusive, but recent research is yielding evidence of functional and structural changes that may store memories. In previous chapters we have seen how perception, motor coordination, and motivated behavior are based on processing of neural impulses that travel over defined circuits. Now we will see indications of how neural circuits can change so that responses are modified as a result of experience.

Since the 1940s research has been narrowing in on the neural mechanisms of learning and memory, going beyond correlational techniques to behavioral and somatic interventions. By the 1960s the level of analysis had reached the synapse, and we now have evidence that experience produces anatomical, biochemical, and electrophysiological changes in synapses. Some examples of research will illustrate the main themes and accomplishments of modern investigators.

How are neural circuits modified during learning? What kinds of modifications persist to provide the basis for memories? From the time that synaptic junctions were discovered toward the end of the last century, many investigators have suggested that synaptic changes could be the mechanisms of memory storage. As knowledge of synaptic anatomy and chemistry has increased, hypotheses have become more numerous and more precise. Both changes in existing synapses and changes in numbers of synapses have been proposed; Figure 15-1 presents some of these hypotheses. Each will be considered in the following discussions.

● **Physiological changes at synapses**   Many physiological changes during learning could alter the postsynaptic response to a presynaptic impulse at existing synapses. The charge could be either presynaptic or postsynaptic, or possibly both. One possibility is that the number of transmitter molecules released per nerve impulse could increase, thus altering the response of the postsynaptic cell; this idea is depicted at (a) in Figure 15-1. A change in release of transmitter could be caused by chemical changes within the end bouton. It could also be caused by the influence of terminals on the end boutons, as shown in (b) of Figure 15-1; they could alter the polarization of the boutons. The responsiveness or sensitivity of the postsynaptic endings could also change, so that the same amount of transmitter release would initiate a larger effect; this situation is indicated in (c) of Figure 15-1.

● **Structural changes**   Structural changes at existing synapses could also provide memory mechanisms. In many parts of the body, exercise causes structural changes; these changes are well known in the cases of muscles and bone. In somewhat the same way the synaptic contact area could increase or decrease as a function of training [see (d) in Figure 15-1].

We do not have to limit ourselves to existing synapses in hypothesizing changes induced by experience. Training could lead to an increase in the number of terminals for the pathway being used, as shown in Figure 15-1 (e), or it could cause a more used pathway to take over endings formerly occupied by a less active competitor (f).

● **Limitations and qualifications to synaptic models of memory**   Our treatment of synaptic models up to this point should be tempered by three considerations.

First, single synapses are tiny subunits of neural systems. Most behaviors of vertebrates depend on the cooperative action of thousands or millions of neurons (each with tens of thousands of synaptic inputs) and not on a decision by one "pontifical cell."

Second, for some functions, at least, it may not be possible to find behavioral correlates by examining responses of cellular units; only sets or ensembles of neurons may yield correlates of some behaviors (John, 1978). In Chapter 2 we used the analogy of card displays in a cheering section at a football game, where looking at one or a few cards cannot reveal the pattern made by hundreds of cards. The same conclusion can be drawn for many sensory fields. This possibility should also be kept in mind as we consider many of the attempts to trace learning and memory to synaptic mechanisms. Certainly the behavior of ensembles depends on unit activity, but it is not entirely reducible to activity of units.

Third, we have mentioned only increases in synaptic effects with training. Actually changes in the opposite direction could just as well mediate learning and

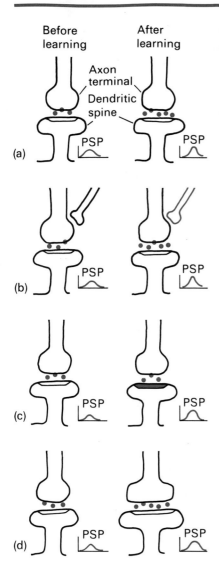

(a)

(b)

(c)

(d)

Before learning | After learning

Axon terminal

Dendritic spine

PSP

Figure 15-1 Diagrammatic portrayal of synaptic changes that could provide bases for storage of memory. (a) After training, each nerve impulse in the relevant neural circuit causes increased release of transmitter molecules (symbolized by blue dots). The size of the postsynaptic potential (PSP), indicated in the small graph, therefore increases. (b) An interneuron (shown in blue) modulates the polarization of the axon terminal and causes release of more transmitter molecules per nerve impulse. (c) Modification of the postsynaptic receptor membrane (shown in blue) causes a larger response to the same amount of transmitter release. (d) The size of the synaptic contact area increases with training. (e) A neural circuit being used more often (the one shown in blue) increases the number of synaptic contacts. (f) A more frequently used neural pathway (shown in blue) takes over synaptic sites formerly occupied by a less active competitor.

memory, since both making and breaking contacts alter circuits. You can't build a circuit by subtracting contacts, but you can modify an existing one. So listing ways of increasing synaptic activity or numbers should be considered only as shorthand notation for "increasing or decreasing."

● **Memory formation within single neurons?** The idea that changes at synaptic junctions between neurons provide the basis of memory is widely accepted. But E. N. Sokolov and his collaborators at the University of Moscow (Sinz, Grechenko, and Sokolov, 1982) have made the unorthodox suggestion that changes *within* neurons may account for at least part of the memory capacity of the nervous system. These investigators have worked with isolated nerve cells taken from snails. In an appropriate fluid environment these cells can maintain their excitability and spontaneous activity. They can be stimulated either by chemical substances applied to

Before learning | After learning

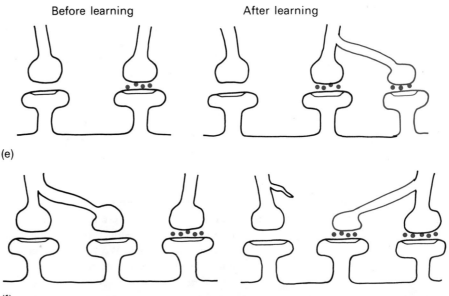

(e)

(f)

various sites on the cell body or by electrical pulses. It has been reported that if a subthreshold amount of acetylcholine (ACh) is regularly followed by a supra-threshold intracellular electrical pulse, then the chemical stimulus becomes capable of evoking an action potential. This change shows the basic features of classical conditioning. It occurs only if the unconditioned stimulus (the electrical pulse) follows the conditioned stimulus (ACh) within 120 milliseconds and does not occur if the CS and US are presented in reversed order, noncontiguously, or separately. Thus habituation and sensitization cannot account for the results, and associative learning seems to have occurred. The conditioning extinguishes after several minutes, and extinction can be hastened by eliciting trials that are not reinforced by the US. Following extinction the response can be reconditioned more rapidly than in the original series.

The investigators suggest that the conditioning produces a greater number of active sites on the membrane, but it may be that the change is in the sensitivity of existing sites. The discovery of conditioning within single neurons demonstrates, according to these investigators, that the synaptic model of the memory trace is not the only possible one. This may be so, but fuller reports from the Moscow laboratory and attempts at confirmation from other laboratories will be necessary for evaluation of the novel hypothesis that the information-processing capacities of the neurons include the formation of memories.

Behavioral and somatic interventions

We now know that the anatomy and chemistry of the nervous system are far more changeable by experience than was realized 10 or 15 years ago. This new view has come about because of experiments in which investigators have altered stimulation and/or experience of animal subjects and then looked for resultant changes in the nervous system. The kinds of manipulations of experience include a wide range: (1) repeated presentations of a single stimulus in habituation experiments; (2) classical conditioning of the eyeblink reflex; (3) training animals to solve mazes; and (4) differential experience of animals that live in enriched or impoverished environments. The dependent variables in these experiments include anatomical measures, such as dendritic branching, numbers of dendritic spines, and sizes of synaptic contacts; neurochemical measures, such as levels of RNA; and electrophysiological responses of nerve cells. Many species of animals have been used as subjects in this research. Indeed, recent innovations include use of isolated parts of the nervous system.

In the next three sections we will take up, in turn, changes in brain anatomy, chemistry, and electrophysiology that are produced by experience. Then we will consider the sequence of processes that occur during the formation of memories.

Neuroanatomical effects of experience

In a well-known series of studies informal experience in differential environments and formal training were found to alter the brain anatomy and chemistry of laboratory rodents. The results provide evidence for some of the possible synaptic changes that we have listed. We will consider first the effects of experience on the gross anatomy of the brain and then the effects on the detailed anatomy of synapses and dendrites.

Effects of experience on the gross anatomy of the brain

A study of relations between individual differences in problem-solving ability and brain measures in laboratory rats has shown significant correlations. The brain measure chosen for this work was activity of the enzyme acetylcholinesterase (AChE), taken as an index of the flux of cholinergic nerve impulses. The better an animal's score on a test, the greater the activity of AChE tended to be in the cerebral cortex. But an unexpected finding emerged from this study: The different groups of rats differed in mean levels of AChE activity; the more difficult the test to which they had been subjected, the higher the level of AChE tended to be (Rosenzweig, Krech, and Bennett, 1961). This finding was a surprise to the investigators who had supposed that the level of enzyme would be a fixed characteristic of each animal; instead, behavioral testing itself had altered the brain characteristic that was being measured! Since the possibility of measuring a change in the brain due to experience seemed even more interesting than the correlational work, the study was soon redirected into an investigation of brain responses to differential experience.

Instead of giving differential experience by running rats through problem-solving tests, which is a time-consuming and expensive procedure, the investigators decided to house the animals in different environments that would provide differential opportunities for informal learning (Figure 15-2). Littermate animals of the same sex were assigned by a random procedure to various laboratory environments, the three most commonly used being the following:

1. The standard colony (SC) situation with three animals in a small but adequate cage provided with food and water. This condition is the one in which laboratory rodents are typically kept in behavioral and biological laboratories.

2. A relatively large cage containing groups of 10 to 12 animals and a variety of stimulus objects, which were changed daily. This condition was called the **enriched condition** (EC) because it provided greater opportunities for informal learning than did the SC condition.

Figure 15-2 Laboratory environments that provide differential opportunities for informal learning. (a) Standard colony environment with 3 rats per cage. (b) Impoverished environment with an isolated rat. (c) Enriched laboratory environment with 10–12 rats per cage and a variety of stimulus objects. (From M. R. Rosenzweig, E. L. Bennett, and M. C. Diamond, "Brain changes in response to experience." Copyright © 1972 by Scientific American, Inc. All rights reserved.)

(a)

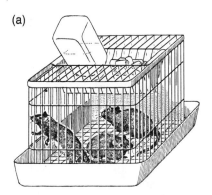

(b)

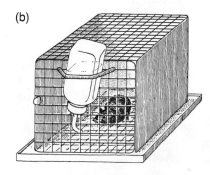

(c)

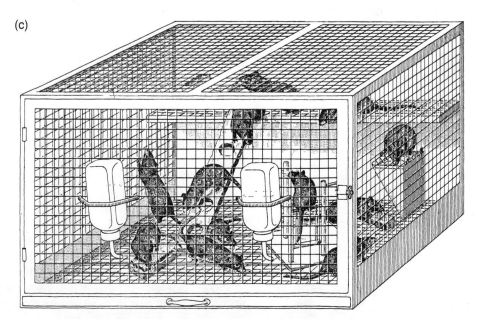

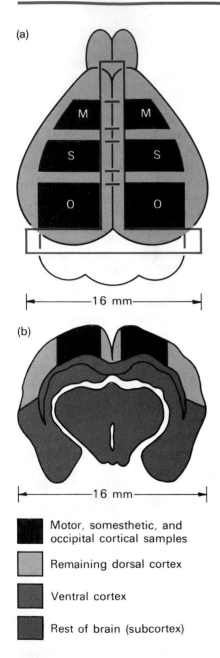

(a)

M   M

S   S

O   O

|—— 16 mm ——|

(b)

|—— 16 mm ——|

■ Motor, somesthetic, and occipital cortical samples

▨ Remaining dorsal cortex

▨ Ventral cortex

▨ Rest of brain (subcortex)

Figure 15-3 Dissection of rat brain into standard samples for measurement of effects of experience. (a) Dorsal view of brain with calibrated plastic T square used to delimit samples of specific cortical regions. (b) Transverse section of brain.

3. SC-size cages housing single animals; this condition was called the **impover-ished condition** or isolated condition (IC).

In the initial experiments of this series, rats were assigned to the differential conditions at weaning (about 25 days after birth), and they were kept in the conditions for 80 days. In later experiments both the age at assignment and the duration of the period of differential experience were varied.

At the end of the period of differential experience, each brain was dissected into standard samples for chemical analysis (Figure 15-3). In the initial experiments animals in the enriched condition (EC) developed greater cortical AChE than did their littermates in IC. Moreover, control experiments showed that this effect could not be attributed to either greater handling of the EC animals or greater locomotor activity in the EC situation (Rosenzweig, Krech, and Bennett, 1961). Enzymatic activity was measured by dividing total activity by the weight of the tissue sample— AChE/weight. Scrutiny of the data then revealed that the experimental groups differed not only in total enzymatic activity but also in weight of the cortical samples: The EC animals developed a greater weight of the cerebral cortex than did their littermates in IC (Rosenzweig et al., 1962). This result was a real surprise, because since the beginning of the century it had been accepted that brain weight is a very stable characteristic of the organism.

Further experiments showed the brain weight differences to be extremely reliable, although small in percentage terms. Moreover, these differences were not uniformly distributed throughout the cerebral cortex. They were almost invariably largest in occipital cortex and smallest in the adjacent somesthetic cortex. The rest of the brain outside the cerebral cortex tended to show very little effect (Figure 15-4).

The differences in cortical weights among groups were then related to differences in cortical thickness; that is, animals exposed to the EC environment developed slightly thicker cerebral cortices than did their littermates in other conditions (Diamond, Krech, and Rosenzweig, 1964; Diamond, 1976). More refined neuroanatomical measures were then undertaken; these included counts of dendritic spines, measures of dendritic branching, and measurement of size of synaptic contacts. All three measures were taken on pyramidal cells in the occipital cortex. Each of these measures showed significant effects of differential experience, as we will see in the next sections of this chapter.

Effects of experience on synapses

The idea that learning and memory might be mediated by the formation of new synaptic contacts has had its ups and downs. It was proposed in the 1890s and was supported by eminent investigators such as Cajal (1894) and Sherrington (1897). But then the hypothesis waned, since no concrete evidence was produced to back it up. In 1965 Eccles (the neurophysiologist who shared the Nobel Prize in 1963) remained firm in his belief that learning and memory storage involve "growth just of bigger

Figure 15-4 Effects of differential experience on weights of brain regions. Percentage differences are shown between means of enriched condition (EC) and impoverished condition (IC) rats, and between means of EC and standard colony condition (SC) rats. Eighty-seven animals were put into each condition at 25 days of age, and they remained there for 30 days. (From data of Rosenzweig and Bennett, 1978)

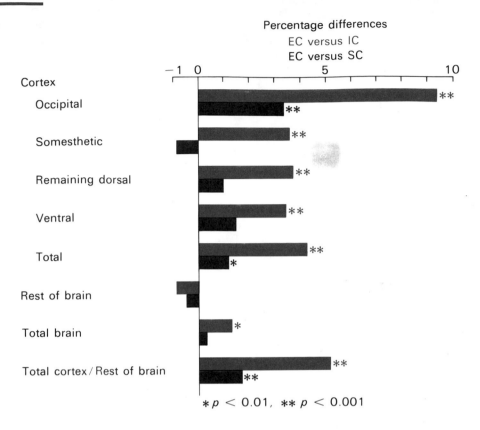

and better synapses that are already there, not growth of new connections." It was only in the 1970s that experiments with laboratory rats assigned to enriched or impoverished environments produced evidence to test this hypothesis.

Dendritic spines were shown in Chapters 2 and 3 to be a late aspect of the differentiation of neurons and to be affected by experience. When dendritic spines were counted in EC–IC experiments, numbers of spines per unit of length of dendrite were found to be significantly greater in EC than in IC animals (Globus et al., 1973). This effect was not obtained uniformly over the dendritic tree; rather it was most pronounced for basal dendrites, as shown in Table 15-1. Different aspects of the dendritic tree receive inputs from different sources, and the basal dendrites of these cells have been shown to receive input especially from adjacent neurons in the same region. Thus it appears that enriched experience leads to development of increased numbers of synaptic contacts; such a change, you remember, was one of the possible mechanisms of memory storage mentioned above [see (e) in Figure 15-1].

Following the lead of these experiments, William Greenough also placed laboratory rats in SC, EC, and IC environments and looked for anatomical effects. Greenough quantified **dendritic branching** by methods shown in Figure 15-5. EC animals were shown to develop significantly greater dendritic branching than IC animals (Greenough and Volkmar, 1973; Volkmar and Greenough, 1972). The SC values fell in between and tended to be closer to the IC than to the EC values. With

TABLE 15-1

Effects of Experience on Numbers of Dendritic Spines

Apical dendrites	0.2
Terminal dendrites	3.1*
Oblique dendrites	3.6*
Basal dendrites	9.7[†]

SOURCE: From M. R. Rosenzweig, E. L. Bennett, and M. C. Diamond, "Effects of differential experience on dendritic spine counts in rat cerebral cortex," *Journal of Comparative and Physiological Psychology,* 1973, *82*(2):175–181. Copyright 1973 by the American Psychological Association. Reprinted by permission of the publisher and the authors.

(a)

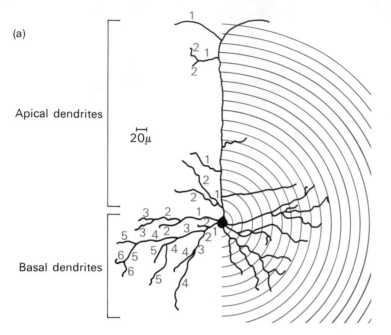

Apical dendrites

20μ

Basal dendrites

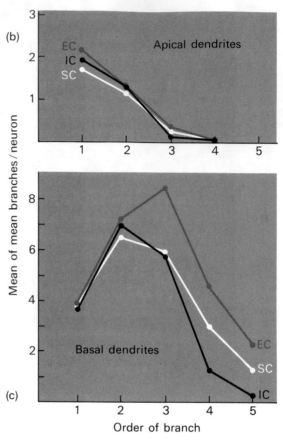

(b)

(c)

Figure 15-5 Measurement of dendritic branching. Using an enlarged photograph of a neuron, branching is quantified either by counting the number of branches of different orders, as shown in the left in (a), or by counting the numbers of intersections with concentric rings, as shown to the right in (a). The results of (b) and (c) were obtained by the first of these methods. They show significant differences in branching between rats kept for 30 days in enriched, standard colony, or impoverished environments. (From Greenough, 1976)

enriched experience each cell did not send its dendrites out further but instead tended to fill its allotted volume more densely with branches. These results together with those of the dendritic spine counts indicate that the enriched-experience animals become equipped with more elaborate information-processing circuits. More generally, the results provide strong support for Cajal's and Sherrington's hypothesis that learning and long-term memory involve the formation of new synaptic contacts.

The size of synaptic contacts has also been shown to change as a result of differential experience. The mean length of the postsynaptic thickening (see Figure 15-6) has been found to be significantly greater in EC rats than in their IC littermates (West and Greenough, 1972; Diamond et al., 1975). These results demonstrate the reality of another of the possible mechanisms mentioned earlier [see (d) in Figure 15-1].

We now see some reasons for the increased weight and thickness of the cerebral cortex reported earlier. The greater number of dendritic branches is probably the main factor, since in cortical pyramidal cells the dendrites account for about 95% of the bulk of the cell. Both the cell body and the nucleus of these neurons are significantly greater in the EC animals (Diamond et al., 1975); the larger cell body

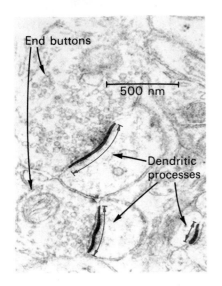

Figure 15-6 Measurement of the size of synaptic contacts. Contacts can be measured on electron micrographs in terms of the length of the thickened region (shown in blue) of the postsynaptic membrane. Note that the end buttons contain many small synaptic vesicles and occasional large mitochondria.

and nucleus are probably needed to sustain the larger dendritic tree and its more active metabolism. There also appears to be an increase in the number of glial cells in the EC animals, perhaps to provide metabolic support to the more active neurons (Diamond et al., 1966; Szeligo and Leblond, 1977).

Mechanisms producing neuroanatomical effects

What mechanisms could account for these unexpected effects of experience on brain structures? It is true that the experiments with differential environments were undertaken to vary opportunities for informal learning and thus to study effects of experience on brain measures. Nevertheless, once results were obtained, it was important to test whether the observed effects might be attributed to causes other than learning and memory storage. Let us look at these tests.

● **Testing alternatives to learning**   Could the cerebral differences between rats in the enriched (EC) and impoverished (IC) conditions be caused by obvious differences in stimulation or life styles? For example, could the facts that rats in the EC were handled more often and that they showed more locomotor activity than their IC littermates account for the effects? Or could they be caused by the lesser activity of the IC rats and their greater gain in body weight? Tests indicate that the answer is no. Control groups were used to test the variables of handling, differential locomotor activity, and food intake, and none of them contributed to the cerebral differences (Rosenzweig et al., 1961). In some brain measures young EC animals seemed more like adults than did ICs, so could the effects of enriched experience be attributed to speeded maturation? Again the answer is no, because typical, although somewhat smaller, effects are obtained even if the animals remain under standard colony conditions until adulthood and then are assigned to the differential environments. Could the results be attributed to increased stress in one or another of the experimental groups? Again no, since the animals in these conditions do not show physiological signs of stress, nor does imposition of direct stress bring about brain changes similar to those produced in the differential environments.

It has been suggested that the effects of experience in differential environments can be assimilated to the effects of sensory inputs on development of the nervous system. (Recall that sensory deprivation and distortion were shown in Chapter 3 to alter development of the visual system.) Three lines of evidence suggest a distinction between effects of differential experience, on the one hand, and effects of sensory deprivation or distortion, on the other. First, effects of sensory deprivation or distortion on development of receptive fields in cats or monkeys can be induced only during a critical period early in the life of the animal (Blakemore and Cooper, 1970; Hubel and Wiesel, 1962), whereas many cerebral effects of experience can be caused throughout the life span of rats. Second, the changes in cortical receptive fields have been induced by simply restricting stimulation or by distorting it. No requirement for active participation by the animal has been stated, and it has even been reported that receptive fields can be altered by presenting restricted stimuli to animals that have been immobilized by pharmacological agents (Pettigrew and Garey, 1972). In contrast, the effects of differential experience on brain measures require active participation of the subjects, and passive exposure to the complex environment is ineffective (Ferchmin, Bennett, and Rosenzweig, 1975). Third, the amount of visual stimulation in the impoverished condition, which is not sufficient for full development of the rodent brain, is perfectly adequate for development of normal visual receptive fields in cats and monkeys. Thus the visual effects that are described by such investigators as Hubel and Wiesel, Blakemore, and others appear to be more specifically sensory and to require much more severe restriction of stimulation than do the effects of differential experience that we have been describing.

Might social stimulation be the important factor, since the EC and IC experiments differ in the amount of social interaction they provide? Systematic variation of this factor has demonstrated that differences in social experience are not required to produce the cerebral effects:

1. Rats placed individually in large cages with varied stimulus objects developed cerebral effects similar to those shown by rats placed in groups in the complex experiment (Rosenzweig and Bennett, 1972).

2. Although social experience causes some brain changes, it cannot account for the full cerebral effects seen in the EC environment. Groups of 12 rats were placed in environments that ranged from a laboratory cage without stimulus objects to an outdoor cage that measured 30 × 30 feet. The more complex the environment in which the group was placed, the greater were the cerebral differences from SC or IC littermates (Rosenzweig et al., 1978).

● **Testing the learning hypothesis**   Let us return to the original hypothesis with which these experiments began. Can it be proved that learning as such, rather than some stimulus factor, is responsible for the cerebral effects? Positive evidence has been reported recently from two laboratories. In one series of experiments individually housed rats ran self-paced maze trials (shown in Figure 15-7). This experiment produced significant cerebral effects similar to, but not as large as, those caused by exposure of grouped rats to the EC (Bennett et al., 1979). Rats that traversed a similar field but without maze barriers did not develop the cerebral effects, although they were housed in the same room as the learners, were handled as often, made about as many trials per day, and were surrounded by the same ambient stimulation. Thus learning seems to be the only factor that accounts for the anatomical and chemical changes found in the brains of the rats who learned.

Chang and Greenough (1978) have also produced rather strong evidence that learning produces the neuroanatomical effects they measure. They did experiments with split-brain rats that learned a series of maze patterns, a different pattern each day for 30 days. While in the maze situation some of the rats wore an opaque contact lens over one eye, so that information about the maze reached only one cerebral hemisphere in these animals. (In the rat each eye projects its axons almost entirely to the contralateral hemisphere and sends very few axons to the ipsilateral hemisphere.) At the conclusion of the 30-day learning period, samples of tissue were taken from the visual cortex of the two hemispheres, and branching of dendrites was measured. The cortex that received information during the maze-running experience showed significantly greater branching of dendrites than did the other hemisphere. In the other cortex the dendritic measures were similar those of control animals that

Figure 15-7 Rats run self-paced maze trials between food and water stations in this situation.

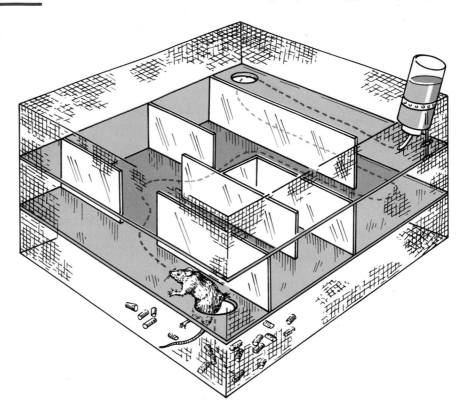

had not been exposed to the maze situation at all. In these maze-trained animals one hemisphere could be used as a control for the other, since the background conditions were very similar for both hemispheres.

As the evidence stands now, it supports the conclusion that learning can bring about measurable and significant changes in anatomical characteristics of the brain. A recent review presents evidence that synapses throughout the nervous system are turned over continuously and suggests that the synaptic changes in learning are related to this ongoing plasticity (Cotman and Nieto-Sampedro, 1982).

Neurochemical effects of experience

Along with the changes in neuroanatomy changes in brain chemistry as a result of both informal and formal experience have been reported by many investigators. How can we tell whether any of these changes are actually related to learning and are not just side effects of the experimental conditions? Several criteria for genuine correlates of learning have been proposed; here are a few criteria (from Entingh et al., 1975) that we can refer to as we consider experiments and results in this section:

1. The neurochemical change should be related to learning and not just to stimulation or muscular activity.

2. If the strength of the memory can be quantified, then the magnitude of the chemical change should show a positive relation to the strength of the memory. (A linear relation cannot be expected, of course, because memory is not translated directly into performance.)

3. The first stages of the chemical processes should occur at the beginning of memory storage processes, and the chemical (or anatomical) correlates of long-term memory should be present as long as the memory lasts.

4. The distribution of neurochemical changes should be consistent with locations of memory-related events, as determined anatomically and electrophysiologically. (This criterion would be more useful if we had a clearer map of memory formation than we have.)

5. Preventing the neurochemical change should prevent the formation of memory. (This criterion has been very useful. We will see some use of this test in this section and much more use of it when we look at effects of biochemical or pharmacological treatments.)

In this section we will first take up effects of enriched or impoverished experience on brain chemistry and then we will see effects of formal training on brain chemistry.

Effects of enriched or impoverished experience on brain chemistry

Results of experiments employing differential experience meet some of the criteria just listed. Let us note some of these results, criterion by criterion.

1. The requirement for learning was shown by the finding that chemical effects occurred in rats that interacted directly with the enriched environment but not in those that only observed it. Also, these effects were found in rats that ran self-paced maze trials but not in those for whom no barriers were present.

2. The size of the chemical effects was found to increase with duration of exposure to the differential environments, from a few days up to 30 days. Also, the more complex the environment, the greater was the size of the cerebral effect.

3. Changes in RNA were significant after only 4 days of differential experience. In a test of the duration of the effects of differential experience, rats were returned to the IC after either 30 or 80 days in the EC. The magnitude of differences in cortical weights and AChE declined somewhat over time, but there were still significant differences at the longest interval tested, 45 days. Moreover, the decline was slower and smaller for the rats that had been in the EC for 80 days than for those that had only 30 days of EC experience (Bennett et al., 1974).

Effects of formal training on brain chemistry

Almost as soon as the genetic code was cracked (see Box 3-1), investigators began to try to determine whether learning involved synthesis of RNA and of proteins. Some hypotheses in this area were soon discarded. They included the suggestion that just as "genetic memory" is stored in the structure of DNA molecules, so acquired memories might be stored in the structure of the newly synthesized molecules of RNA; it was even suggested that these latter molecules might be considered "tape recorder" molecules of RNA. There were reports that memories could be transferred from trained to naive animals by making an extract of brain RNA from the former and injecting it into the latter, but such results could not be replicated consistently. While these hypotheses were entertained for only short periods, it was seen that changes in the nervous system produced by learning would probably involve synthesis of RNA and then of protein, and research along these lines has been productive. In this section we will examine some of the research.

● Varied training procedures alter brain chemistry   One of the first investigators to contribute to this field was Holger Hydén in Sweden, and his work on the chemistry of learning continues to the present. Some of his studies involved changing the paw preferences of rats. The rats were first tested to see which paw they preferred to use when reaching into a tube to obtain small pellets of food. About equal numbers of rats were found to have right-paw preference and left-paw preference. Then for each animal the tube was set up next to a partition so that food was accessible only to the nonpreferred paw. Rats were trained for four days with two 25-minute (min) sessions each day. Upon completion of training the animals were sacrificed, and samples of tissue were taken from the motor cortex (paw region) and hippocampus in both hemispheres. Training was reported to bring about a difference between the two hemispheres in RNA content in both the cortex and the hippocampus (Hydén and Egyhazi, 1964).

Even single training sessions have been reported to alter brain chemistry. The effects of active avoidance training on the incorporation of radioactively labeled uridine into RNA were studied by Glassman and his colleagues at the University of North Carolina (Glassman, 1974). Individual mice were placed in a small box and trained to jump to a platform in order to avoid foot shock delivered through floor grids. Yoked control animals received the conditioned stimuli (the light and buzzer that preceded and accompanied the shock) and the unconditioned stimulus (foot shock) but they were trained in a box with no platform, so the shock could not be avoided. The brains of the experimental and control animals were removed for analysis 15 min after the end of the training session. The results indicated that the avoidance training increased the incorporation of uridine into RNA, particularly in the hippocampus and the diencephalon. In other words, more RNA was synthesized during avoidance training than during the control procedure. It should be noted that control animals were also learning something: Their active responses to the onset of light and buzzer showed that they had learned to anticipate the shock. Thus this experiment was really a comparison between two kinds of learning rather than learning versus no learning. To test whether learning was really involved, and not just sensory stimulation or activity in the situation, the experimenters analyzed the brains of mice that had been trained previously in the jump box. The mice did not show increased synthesis of RNA after their second session in the apparatus, strengthening the interpretation that the changes measured in naive mice were due to learning and not to performance.

A sequence of neurochemical effects during and following training has been found by Matthies and associates (1979) in East Germany. They trained rats to escape foot shock by running to the lighted side on each trial in an apparatus with three alleys (Figure 15-8). The experimental design included both "passive controls" (animals that remained in their home cages throughout) and "active controls" (animals that ran to escape foot shock but that were not given a light-dark discrimination to learn). Brains were taken for analysis at various times during or following the training session. Trained rats were found to differ from both active and passive controls by showing increased incorporation of radioactive uridine into RNA in the hippocampus, the visual cortex, and the cingulate cortex. Other brain regions examined did not show any change; these included other cortical regions as well as thalamic and hypothalamic structures.

Analysis of sequential changes in the hippocampus was then made. The earliest changes were related to synaptic activity. Increased concentration of acetylcholine was observed, even during the training session. At first the increase of ACh was seen in the cytoplasm and then during the hour after training an increase was found in the synaptic vesicles. The number of synapses observable in the hippocampus increased during training and continued to increase for about an hour thereafter, reaching a peak of about 30% above normal. The number was still about 20% above control values 24 hours (h) later but had fallen to normal by 2 weeks after training. About 8 h after training there was a peak of protein synthesis. Matthies has speculated that this wave may reflect the formation of specific proteins and glycoproteins necessary for construction of the postsynaptic structures involved in memory. These promising experiments should be extended to other brain regions.

● **Effects of imprinting on brain chemistry**   Imprinting has been used by some experimenters to try to produce rather large and meaningful changes in the brain. In these studies chicks are maintained in darkness for 18–24 h after hatching and then

Figure 15-8 Automatic discrimination apparatus used to study effects of training on brain chemistry. (Adapted from Matthies et al., 1979)

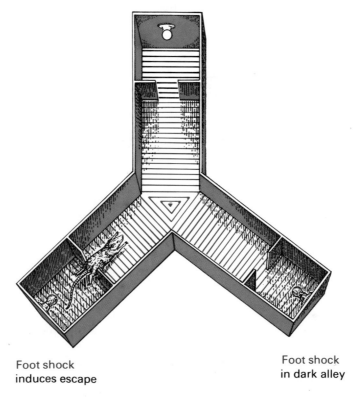

Foot shock
induces escape

Foot shock
in dark alley

they are put in the presence of a flashing light for 60 min. This training procedure produces a strong and sustained approach response when the animal is later tested— thus it has imprinted on the flashing light. The training procedure also produces increased incorporation of radioactively labeled precursors into RNA and into protein in parts of the brain used in vision (Horn et al., 1973; Rose et al., 1976).

Interpretation of these effects is complicated by the possibility that such factors as stress and differential motor activity may have caused differences between the imprinting and control chicks. In tests to see if these alternatives could be ruled out, one hemisphere of the chick was used as control for the other. Split-brain chicks were produced by transecting the supraoptic commissure. The chicks were then exposed to the flashing light while one eye was covered with an opaque patch; thus only one side of the brain received the visual imprinting information but both sides of the brain were influenced by such other factors as arousal and stress. When the chicks' brains were then analyzed for incorporation of the radioactive precursors, the incorporation was found to be greater in the hemisphere of the brain that had received the visual input than in the other hemisphere.

The experiments reported in this section and many others offer presumptive evidence that training leads to an increased synthesis of RNA and of proteins in the brain. But both the behavioral and the biochemical findings are still open to alternative interpretations, since, for one thing, setting up adequate control groups is difficult, as we have seen above. In some cases the comparison involves two different kinds of training without an untrained control group. In other cases trained animals are compared with nontrained animals. Here there must be differences in arousal and attention as well as learning itself; therefore the cerebral differences may be due to motivational factors rather than to learning. On the biochemical side there are difficult problems of interpretation that we will not go into here; for discussion of these biochemical problems see the recent reviews (for example, Agranoff, 1980; Dunn, 1980).

Possible roles of protein synthesis in memory storage

It is likely that synthesis of protein plays several different roles in establishing and maintaining storage of memories:

1. Since structural proteins form an important component of the cell membrane, the increased branching of dendrites and the increased numbers of dendritic spines observed as consequences of training and enriched experience require increased synthesis of structural proteins.

2. The increase in numbers and in size of synaptic junctions requires more receptor proteins in the postsynaptic membranes.

3. Increased amounts of enzymes (which are proteins) are needed to direct the building of dendrites, spines, and receptor areas.

4. Some proteins may serve as reinforcing or confirming signals to establish certain memories.

More work will be needed to test these various roles of protein synthesis and to find the time courses over which each occurs and the locations of each.

Electrophysiological correlates of learning

Since the basic transactions of the nervous system involve electrical signals, many investigators are studying the mechanisms of learning and memory by recording the electrical activity of neurons during various kinds of training. Their aims are two-fold: (1) to identify the sites at which crucial changes occur and (2) to ascertain the processes involved. The subjects of such experiments range from isolated parts of the nervous system of molluscs to intact mammals, and the kinds of learning vary from habituation and sensitization to classical conditioning. We will start with mechanisms of simple kinds of learning in a simple nervous system and then take up more complex kinds of learning in more complex nervous systems.

Habituation and sensitization in simple systems

Habituation, you will recall, is a decrease in the response to a repeated stimulus. As we said in Chapter 14, habituation occurs in all animals, from the simplest to the most complex, and is a way of becoming insensitive to stimuli that have no special relevance or consequence for current behavior. The mechanisms of habituation have been studied in intact mammals, in spinal preparations of mammals, and in simpler invertebrate systems. Invertebrate preparations are now being used extensively because they offer several advantages:

1. The number of nerve cells in a ganglion is relatively small compared to that in a mammal, although the number in the invertebrate ganglion is still of the order of 1000.

2. In the anatomy of the invertebrate ganglion the cell bodies form the outside and the dendritic processes are on the inside. This arrangement is the reverse of that

Figure 15-9 Identified nerve cells in a ganglion of an invertebrate, the sea hare *Aplysia*. (a) Dorsal view of *Aplysia* with the positions of the ganglia indicated in blue. (For lateral views of *Aplysia*, see Figure 15-11). (b) Dorsal view of the abdominal ganglion with several identified neurons labeled. Neurons included in the circuit for habituation (Figure 15-10) are labeled in blue. (c) Ventral view of abdominal ganglion with several identified neurons labeled. [(a) Adapted from *Cellular basis of behavior: An introduction to behavioral neurobiology* by Eric R. Kandel. W. H. Freeman and Company. Copyright © 1976. (b) and (c) from Frazier et al., 1967, and Koester and Kandel, unpublished.]

(a) Dorsal view of *Aplysia*

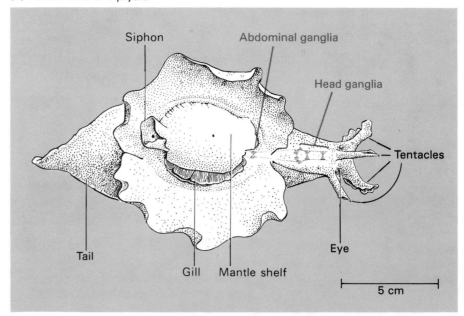

in the mammal, and it makes it easy to identify and record from cells of invertebrates.

3. Many individual cells in invertebrate ganglia can be recognized both because of their shapes and sizes and because the cellular structure of the ganglion is uniform from individual to individual of the species (Figure 15-9). Thus it is possible to identify certain cells and to trace out their sensory and motor connections. Hence when one isolates a ganglion in a particular invertebrate, one already knows the basic connections of many of the larger cell bodies.

When the complete circuit of a response has been traced out, it is possible to investigate the site or sites where habituation occurs. Figure 15-10 diagrams an invertebrate neural circuit in which habituation has been studied in the large sea snail *Aplysia*. This circuit includes neurons in the abdominal ganglion, shown in Figure 15-10.

Eric Kandel and his collaborators have conducted a major program of experimentation on synaptic processes of habituation and sensitization in *Aplysia* (Kandel, 1976, 1979). Figure 15-11 shows some of *Aplysia*'s characteristic behaviors as it moves across the bottom of shallow bodies of seawater. The animal's gill is usually spread out on the back, protected only by a light mantle shelf, and the siphon is extended in order to draw in water and circulate it over the gill. If anything touches the mantle shelf or the siphon, the animal retracts its gill so that it is much smaller and less vulnerable. This gill-withdrawal reflex is controlled by the abdominal ganglion illustrated in Figure 15-9. For experimental purposes a preparation that is often made consists of the siphon, mantle shelf, gill, and the sensory and motor

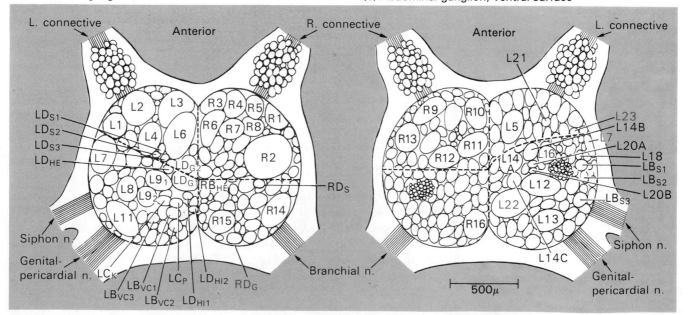

(b) Abdominal ganglion, dorsal surface   (c) Abdominal ganglion, ventral surface

Figure 15-10 Diagram of the basic neural circuits involved in the gill-withdrawal reflex of *Aplysia* and its habituation. A monosynaptic circuit is shown in dark blue; it starts at sensory neurons with endings in the siphon and mantle shelf, synapses on neuron L7, and runs to motor endings in the gill. Other monosynaptic circuits run through cells LD$_{G1}$, LD$_{G2}$, and so forth. Polysynaptic links occur through excitatory interneurons L22 and L23 and inhibitory interneuron L16. (Adapted from Kupferman, Carew, and Kandel, 1974)

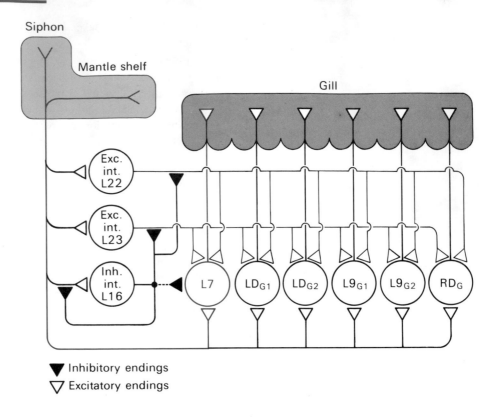

nerves connecting these structures to the abdominal ganglion. With these structures fixed in position, the experimenters can stimulate the siphon or mantle with precisely calibrated jets of water at precisely determined times, and they can accurately record the size of the gill-withdrawal reflex.

The gill-withdrawal reflex habituates readily upon repeated stimulation; moreover, this habituation has all the characteristics that have been found for habituation in human beings and other animals. *Aplysia* shows sensitization as well as habituation; when the animal is presented with a painful stimulus to the head, the gill-withdrawal reflex is greatly enhanced. The close correspondence between the characteristics of habituation and sensitization in *Aplysia* and these behaviors in mammals justifies our looking further into the neural mechanisms of these behaviors in *Aplysia*, even if we are not particularly interested in this sea snail in itself.

● **Site and mechanism of habituation** Pinpointing the site of habituation for the gill-withdrawal response of *Aplysia* has been accomplished, and the goal of spelling out the neurochemical mechanisms of the habituation is well advanced. To accomplish this goal Kandel and his collaborators tested several possible loci of altered activity; these loci are indicated in Figure 15-12. As had been found for the mammal, habituation was not caused by receptor adaptation (locus 1 in Figure 15-12) or by either fatigue of the muscles (locus 3) or depression of the junctions between motor neurons and muscles (locus 2).

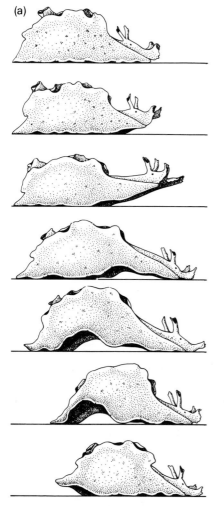

(a)

Turning then to the ganglion, the experimenters found that intracellular recordings from the motor neurons did show decreases in firing rates during the course of habituation. Several mechanisms could be hypothesized as causes of this effect. For example, Pavlov had hypothesized that habituation is caused by a buildup of inhibition (locus 4); but recording did not reveal a buildup of hyperpolarization as habituation was induced, so this possibility was excluded. Inhibition of excitatory interneurons (locus 5) was ruled out by the observation that the rate of arrival of impulses at the motor neuron did not decrease during habituation. The decreased firing rate of the motor neuron could reflect either an increase of the input resistance (decreased sensitivity) of the motor neuron (locus 6 in Figure 15-12) or a change in synaptic input to the motor neuron (locus 7 or 8). The threshold of the motor neuron for initiating a spike was found to remain constant during habituation, so the change in habituation could not be attributed to altered resistance of the postsynaptic membrane (locus 6).

The excitatory postsynaptic potentials (EPSPs) to synaptic input were found to decrease progressively during repeated sensory stimulation, and this decrease could account for the decreased firing rate of the motor neuron during habituation. With a period of rest and no stimulation, the amplitude of the EPSPs recovers. Depression of the EPSPs caused by repeated stimulation of one part of the receptive field (such as the siphon) did not cause a decrease of the EPSPs to stimulation of another part of the sensory field (for instance, the mantle), so the depression is strictly localized. The contribution of the interneurons to the EPSPs of the motor cells was small relative to the monosynaptic pathway, so the effect must be localized chiefly at the monosynaptic sensorimotor junctions (locus 8 in Figure 15-12). The depression of the EPSPs was found to be caused by a decrease in the number of quanta of synaptic transmitter released by each sensory impulse; the size of the individual quanta remained constant. This feature was determined by studying the variability in the EPSPs, which are graded in quantal units, that is, units of fixed size. The change

Figure 15-11 Some behaviors of *Aplysia*. (a) Locomotion. (b) Usual posture with the siphon extended and the gill spread out on the back. Ordinarily only the tip of the siphon would be visible in a lateral view, but here the rest of the siphon and the gill are shown as if the animal were transparent. (c) Retraction of the siphon and of the gill in response to a light touch. (d) Retraction of the head and release of ink in response to a strong stimulus. (From *Cellular basis of behavior: An introduction to behavioral neurobiology* by Eric R. Kandel. W. H. Freeman and Company. Copyright © 1976.)

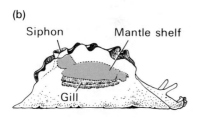

(b)
Siphon   Mantle shelf

Gill

(c)

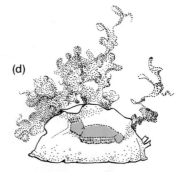

(d)

Figure 15-12 Possible loci of habituation in the circuits that control the gill-withdrawal reflex of *Aplysia*. Each possible locus is indicated by a blue number. The neurons are labeled as in Figure 15-10. (Adapted from Kandel, 1976)

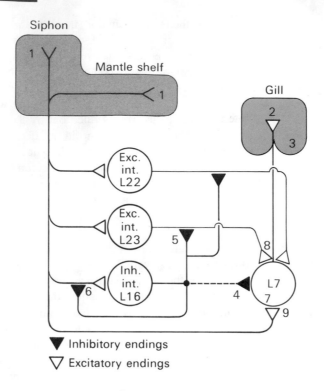

in the amount of transmitter released upon arrival of a nerve impulse is, you will recall, one of the hypothesized mechanisms of memory [(a) in Figure 15-1].

Within this neural circuit, then, the alteration due to habituation was precisely localized, and it occurs mainly at one site—the presynaptic terminals on the motor nerve. Thus although the anatomy of the circuit is determined and fixed, the gain of the sensorimotor synapses can be modified.

Studies with several other species of invertebrates have shown that these results with *Aplysia* have some generality. For example, investigators have been able to trace the circuits of several responses, especially escape or defensive responses. When there are several levels or branches in the circuit, not all are plastic (Krasne, 1976). As an example, consider the circuit of the escape response of the crayfish

Figure 15-13 Modifiability in the circuit of the escape response of the crayfish. The modifiable junctions are shown in blue. In this circuit some of the neuromuscular junctions are modifiable as well as synapses on interneurons. (Adapted from Krasne, 1976)

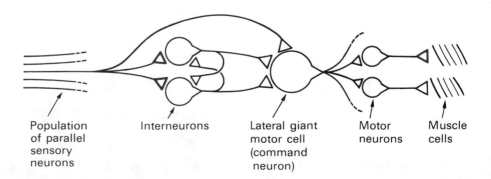

(Figure 15-13). Here the main modifiability is found at synapses of sensory neurons or interneurons, and some of the neuromuscular junctions also exhibit plasticity. But the other synapses in the circuit do not alter their response characteristics during habituation.

● **Site and mechanism of sensitization**   The same responses that habituate can also be sensitized. The circuit involved in sensitization of the gill-withdrawal reflex of *Aplysia* is shown diagrammatically in Figure 15-14. Painful stimulation of the head was found to activate sensory neurons that, among other connections, excite facilitating interneurons. These interneurons end on the synaptic terminals of the sensory neurons from the siphon or mantle. The transmitter agent of the facilitating interneurons, thought to be serotonin, apparently modulates the release of sensory neuron transmitter to the motor neuron. The sensitization effect appears to act through a second messenger in the terminals of the sensory cells.

Strong stimulation of the pathway from the head that mediates sensitization in *Aplysia* gave rise to an increase in cyclic adenosine monophosphate (cyclic AMP) in cells throughout the abdominal ganglion. (The mechanism of cyclic AMP as a second messenger in neural and hormonal communication was considered in Chapter 4.) Cyclic AMP increases the influx of calcium ions into the terminal bouton, perhaps by making more calcium channels available in the membrane. The internal calcium then causes a greater binding of synaptic vesicles to release sites, increasing the probability that the neuron will release the transmitter into the synaptic cleft.

Figure 15-15 illustrates this hypothesized mechanism of sensitization as well as a related possibility for habituation. In the case of habituation it is hypothesized that repeated impulses over the terminals could decrease the number of open calcium channels, thus depressing the level of calcium within the terminal and decreasing the number of active release sites and so inactivating the synapse.

Figure 15-14   Circuit for sensitization of the gill-withdrawal response of *Aplysia*. Strong stimulation of the head leads to sensitization of this reflex. The sensitization circuit involves interneurons [L22 and L23 (see also Figure 15-10)] and includes presynaptic endings on the plastic terminal from the sensory neuron to the motor neuron (L7). (Adapted from Kandel, 1976)

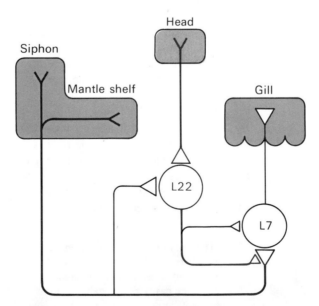

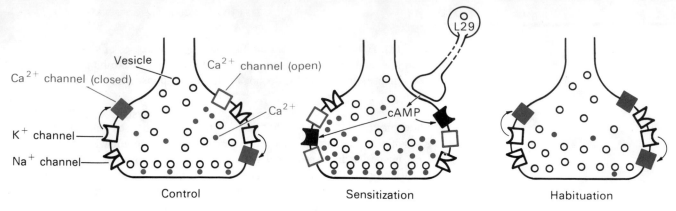

Ca²⁺ channel (closed)

Vesicle

Ca²⁺ channel (open)

Ca²⁺

L29

cAMP

K⁺ channel

Na⁺ channel

Control

Sensitization

Habituation

Figure 15-15 Hypothesized presynaptic mechanisms of sensitization and habituation. Axon terminals are represented in control, sensitized, and habituated conditions. Their membranes are studded with a variety of specialized channels. In the control condition, most of the K⁺ channels are open, and this tends to inhibit the Ca²⁺ channels. (Closed channels are indicated by solid symbols.) Ca²⁺ is required for vesicles to bind to release sites and thus liberate the transmitter into the synaptic cleft. In sensitization, the activity of a modulatory neuron causes release of the second messenger cAMP inside the axon terminal; this closes K⁺ channels and allows Ca²⁺ channels to open. More release sites then become available. In habituation, repeated impulses decrease the number of open Ca²⁺ channels and therefore there is little binding of vesicles and release of transmitter. (Adapted from Klein and Kandel, 1980)

Associative learning in simple systems

With so much information about mechanisms of nonassociative learning coming from the analysis of the gill-withdrawal reflex of *Aplysia,* investigators have been eagerly trying to condition this response and to find other examples of associative learning in relatively simple invertebrate preparations. Years of attempts to condition the gill-withdrawal reflex were unsuccessful until an effective method was announced in 1981 (Carew, Walters, and Kandel, 1981). A light touch to the mantle soon habituates, but if the touch is promptly followed by a strong shock to the tail, after a few trials the touch alone elicits a strong withdrawal response. The touch (CS) and shock (US) must be paired and the interval between them kept brief for this conditioning to occur; tests demonstrate that this is conditioning and not sensitization. Now it should be possible to compare the mechanisms of conditioning and of nonassociative learning in the same relatively simple preparation.

Other invertebrate preparations are also being used in the study of mechanisms of learning and memory. These include the nudibranch mollusc *Hermissenda* (e.g., Farley and Alkon, 1981) and the marine gastropod mollusc *Pleurobranchea* (e.g., Mpitsos et al., 1980).

As we mentioned in Chapter 3, so much is known about the genetics of the fruit fly *Drosophila* that the discovery of associative learning in this insect has opened up many possibilities (Benzer, Quinn, and Gould, 1979). Mutant strains of *Drosophila* have been found that are poor in learning or whose memory is abnormally brief, and attempts are being made to identify neural correlates of these behavioral deficiencies. Again, though, the small size of the neurons is an impediment. So the ideal subject has not yet been found, prompting William Quinn to prescribe the following specifications:

The organism should have no more than three genes, a generation time of twelve hours, be able to play the cello or at least recite classical Greek, and learn these tasks with a nervous system containing only ten large, differently colored, and therefore easily recognizable neurons.

Conditioning in vertebrates   While some investigators have been making progress in understanding the cellular mechanisms of learning in relatively simple neural circuits, others have been attempting to study the basic mechanism of learning in the much more complex nervous systems of vertebrates. Among the strategies used to find electrophysiological correlates of learning in vertebrate nervous systems are these:

1. Exploring many sites and looking for indications of learning at each.
2. Focusing on events at a particular site that other kinds of research had already implicated in learning.
3. Patiently tracing the entire neural circuit involved in an example of learning and determining at what site(s) in the circuit evidence of learning occurs.

Each of these strategies has produced interesting results.

Electrophysiological recording from the intact brain has been used to study conditioning since the 1940s. The first electrophysiological observations of conditioning were made by accident on a human subject, in the following way: The French physiologists Durup and Fessard (1943) were studying how the alpha rhythm of the EEG is blocked when the subject's visual field is illuminated. After switching on the light several times one day and seeing the subject's alpha rhythm disappear each time, the experimenter again threw the light switch. But the bulb failed and so the room remained dark—nevertheless the alpha rhythm again disappeared! Instead of ignoring this puzzling occurrence, the experimenters realized that the subject might have become conditioned so that the sound of the switch became a conditioned stimulus to appearance of light. Tests with other subjects soon demonstrated that the sound did not block the alpha rhythm in naive subjects but did do so after pairings of sound and light.

In the late 1940s and 1950s many studies of EEG conditioning were carried out. Some of these tried to localize the signs of conditioning over various parts of the brain. Precise localization is difficult, however, because of the overlying skull and tissue. Besides, the critical events might not be occurring in the cortex but in deeper brain structures. So the focus of research shifted. Instead of recording from the human skull, investigators began to record from the animal brain, often with indwelling electrodes.

How can investigators tell whether a site from which they record is critically related to learning? Even if the electrical activity varies in parallel with the progress of learning, the site of recording might simply be reflecting events determined elsewhere in the nervous system. Experimental designs that try to answer this question include these:

1. Attempting to find the sites with the earliest (shortest-latency) responses related to learning.
2. Testing to see whether the inputs to a site already show relations to learning.

● **Finding specific learning sites in the brain**   James Olds and his associates (1972) sought to identify sites critical to the learning process by finding locations that gave the shortest-latency conditioned responses. They trained rats to orient to a pellet dispenser when a given tone (CS+) sounded; another tone (CS−) did not

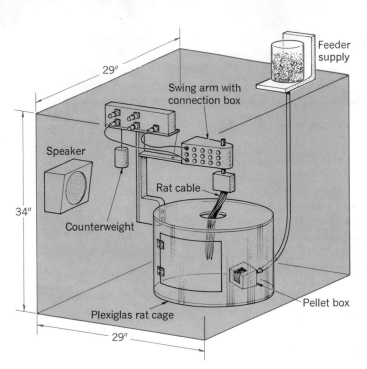

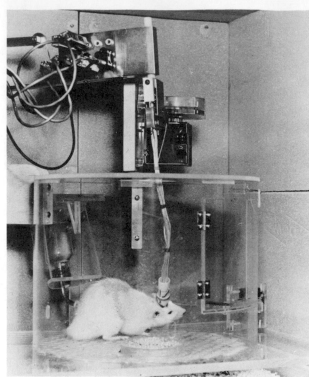

Figure 15-16 Recording the activity of single neurons in the search for localized changes in the brain during training. (From Olds et al., 1973. Photograph courtesy of James Olds.)

signal the presentation of a food pellet. Responses of single neurons in various locations were recorded from the active animals with indwelling electrodes; the experimental setup is shown in Figure 15-16. Some brain areas were found in which, as conditioning occurred, responses to CS+ appeared with latencies of less than 20 msec. Some of these regions were classified as "nonspecific" because the responses generalized readily when the frequency of CS+ was varied, and the cells also gave similar responses to novel stimuli. It was hypothesized that such cells play a role in arousal of the nervous system during learning. Other sites were called "specific" because cells there did not generalize readily and were not activated by novel stimuli. Such cells appeared to be related specifically to learning and not to the arousal that accompanies learning. Specific learning activity was found in the frontal and sensorimotor regions of the cortex and in a part of the hippocampus called the CA3 region. It would be valuable to test these findings by using other methods. For example, would learning these tasks become impossible if the "critical sites," as defined by Olds, were destroyed by circumscribed lesions?

● Studies of conditioning in the hippocampus   Richard Thompson (1976, 1980) and co-workers have looked for electrophysiological signs of conditioning especially in the hippocampus and related structures. The choice of site was made because of previous experimental and clinical studies that suggested a special role for the hippocampus in learning and memory. Thompson used a preparation that had already yielded a great deal of behavioral information about the formation of a classically conditioned response, the conditioning of the nictitating membrane (NM) in the rabbit, as developed by Gormezano (1972). The nictitating membrane is the so-called third eyelid that many species of mammals possess. During conditioning the awake rabbit is held in position and a puff of air to the eye is the US that elicits movement of the NM across the cornea; the timing, extent, and shape of the NM response can be recorded accurately by attaching a thread to the NM. A tone is used as the CS.

This system has several characteristics that are valuable for study of the neural mechanisms of conditioning. The conditioned response is acquired over a single training session but it requires a substantial number of trials, so the progress of conditioning can be followed in detail. The CS (tone) does not produce an NM response before training, and repeated unpaired presentations of the CS or the US do not cause sensitization. The behavioral response is reliable and is rarely given spontaneously, and the exact time course and the amplitude of the response are readily measurable. The animal preparation is normal and intact, does not require any use of drugs, and remains essentially motionless, except for the NM response, during the training session. Responses of hippocampal units are recorded with electrodes implanted in the hippocampus prior to the start of the conditioning sessions.

When paired stimuli are delivered to the animal (CS tone and US air puff), the activity of hippocampal neurons soon begins to change. First there is an increase in the magnitude of response to the US. Then this response to the US moves forward in time, occurring as a response to the tone (CS), prior to delivery of the air puff. These neuronal changes occur early in conditioning, even before a reliable response of the NM to the CS occurs. When the conditioned motor response does occur, it lags behind the hippocampal response by a brief and relatively constant interval of 25–35 msec. Not only does the neural response regularly precede the NM response, but the neural response has a waveform over time that is very similar to the waveform of the NM response (Figure 15-17). Thus the hippocampal neurons seem to set the pattern of muscular movements of the NM response. On the other hand, it is clear that the hippocampal neurons are not simply part of the motor pathway for the NM. No hippocampal activity accompanied NM responses before the conditioning, and even after conditioning is established, hippocampal activity does not accompany spontaneous blinks of the NM.

Because the hippocampal unit activity developed so rapidly during the first block of conditioning trials, a trial-by-trial analysis was made for the first eight stimulus pairings for several animals. An example is shown in Figure 15-18a. During the first four trials, even though a clear and large NM response occurred to each presentation of the air puff, no response of hippocampal units was seen. Hippocampal responses first occurred on the fifth or sixth trial, and thereafter appeared regularly. Figure 15-18b shows the further development of the response. The NM response following the US grew rapidly in size, while the increase in the response during the CS–US interval grew more slowly but regularly. The white lines in these graphs show that if the stimuli were presented unpaired, then there was no increase in magnitude of the hippocampal response. Thus the hippocampal neurons of the rabbit do not respond to either type of stimulation by itself, but they appear to detect very rapidly the existence of contingencies between stimuli. The regular pairing of the CS and the US brings about a response that is not given to either stimulus alone or to the two presented without temporal relation to each other. Furthermore, during training the form of the response of the hippocampus resembles more and more the form of the response of the nictitating membrane. This resemblance was quantified by calculating correlation coefficients of the amplitude versus time courses of responses in 21 animals over two days of training (Figure 15-19).

For tests of species generality of these observations, similar experiments were conducted with cats as subjects (Patterson, Berger, and Thompson, 1979). In the cat, unlike the rabbit, the hippocampus was responsive from the start to both tone and air puff stimulation. However, paired presentation of the CS and the US rapidly

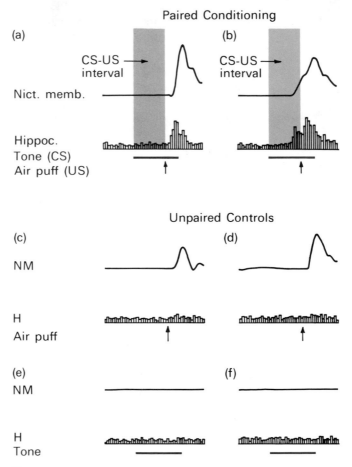

Figure 15-17 Conditioning of the response of the nictitating membrane (Nict. memb. or NM) and associated responses of neurons in the hippocampus (Hippoc. or H). The responses of hippocampal neurons are shown as histograms in 15-msec intervals. Each trace is 750 msec in duration. The tone (CS) lasted 350 msec and overlapped with the air puff (US). When tone and air puff were paired, a hippocampal response appeared during the first 8 paired trials (a). By the last 13 blocks of 8 trials on Day 1 (b), both the nictitating membrane response and the hippocampal response preceded the air puff, so conditioning had occurred. When only air puffs were given and no tones were delivered, each air puff elicited a blink of the nictitating membrane, but the hippocampus showed only spontaneous activity; this was true from the first block of trials on Day 1 (c) through the last block on Day 2 (d). Presentation of tone pulses alone did not yield responses of either the nictitating membrane or the hippocampus, from the first block of trials on Day 1 (e) through the last block on Day 2 (f). The control responses (c–f) show that the conditioning in (b) cannot be attributed to sensitization. (Adapted from Berger and Thompson, 1978)

(a) Single-trial analysis of the first block of conditioning trials

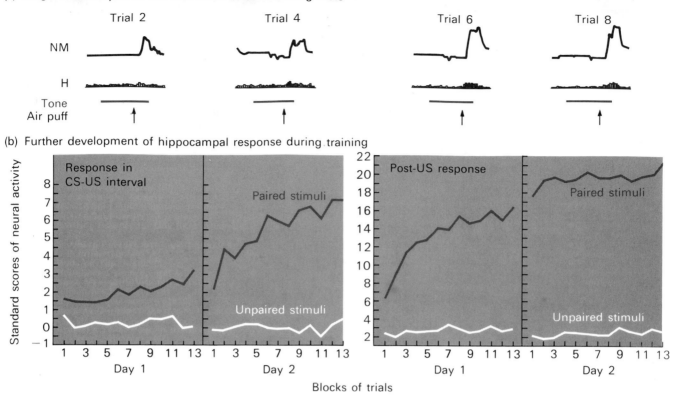

(b) Further development of hippocampal response during training

Figure 15-18 Appearance and growth of the hippocampal response during conditioning of the nictitating membrane. (a) Analysis of single trials during the first block of 8 paired presentations of CS and US. Although the air puff elicits a blink of the nictitating membrane (NM) from the first trials, no response occurs in the hippocampus (H) until trial 6. (b) Further growth of the hippocampal response over 2 days of training. Amplitude grows steadily, but more slowly in the CS–US interval than post-US. For animals that receive the unpaired presentation of the tone and the air puff, no response develops in the hippocampus, as shown by the white curves. Note the difference of scale on the y axes of the two graphs in (b). (From Berger and Thompson, 1978)

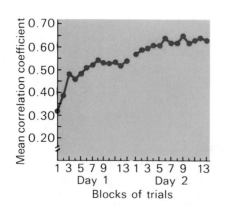

led to increased amplitude of hippocampal responses, and this increase did not occur with unpaired presentations. The experimenters concluded that the basic characteristics of hippocampal neural plasticity during classical conditioning were highly similar in cat and rabbit.

The responses of other structures in the limbic system were also studied in order to see whether the hippocampus might simply be reflecting changes in response that developed at some prior site. The medial septum is a source of input to the hippocampus, and the lateral septum receives output from the hippocampus. Recordings

Figure 15-19 Graph of correlation coefficients between amplitude–time courses of the responses of the nictitating membrane and the responses of hippocampal units. Responses were recorded from 21 animals during 2 days of training. The hippocampal response precedes the membrane response by about 40 msec and predicts its pattern well. When the time difference is taken into account by shifting the hippocampal and membrane patterns so that they coincide in time, the correlation reaches a value of 0.82 by the end of training. (From Berger, Laham, and Thompson, 1980)

were made from both sites during conditioning of the rabbit, and recordings were also made from the mammillary bodies that have been implicated in learning. Units in the medial septum were found to respond to both the CS and the US from the outset, but these responses did not change as a function of pairing of the stimuli. Thus there was no evidence of conditioning in responses of a main input to the hippocampus. Units in the lateral septum reflected the development of responses to paired stimuli seen in the hippocampus; thus the conditioned responses were maintained in an output target of the hippocampus. Units in the mammillary nuclei showed only small, diffuse excitation that exhibited no consistent changes over training and that was not related to activity seen in either the hippocampal or septal regions. Thus there are clear differences in responsiveness of these parts of the limbic system during conditioning. The hippocampus seems to play a primary role in detecting contingencies of environmental stimulation and responding to them.

Even though hippocampal activity parallels so closely the course of conditioning and does so more clearly than does activity of the other limbic structures, this result does not prove that the hippocampus is required for conditioning to occur. In fact, destruction of either the hippocampus or the septum has little effect on acquisition or retention of the conditioned NM response in rabbits (Lockhart and Moore, 1975). Therefore the hippocampus is not indispensable for conditioning, although a further experiment indicates that if the hippocampus is present, it does take part in conditioning. In this experiment lesions made in the medial septum significantly altered spontaneous electrical activity of the hippocampus and slowed the acquisition of the conditioned NM response (Berry and Thompson, 1979). The investigators interpret this result as showing that abnormal hippocampal activity disrupts the acquisition of conditioning; in other words, the animal is better able to learn without any hippocampus at all than with an impaired hippocampus. In Chapter 14 we mentioned that destruction of both the amygdala and hippocampus in monkeys severely impaired acquisition, whereas there was little impairment with destruction of one or the other of these structures (Mishkin, 1978). Perhaps in the rabbit when the hippocampus is destroyed, it is the amygdala that is able to mediate classical conditioning, but this possibility has not yet been subjected to experimental tests.

One further experimental result should be noted: A small change in the training situation makes it impossible for the rabbit to acquire the conditioned response after destruction of the hippocampus (Weisz, Solomon, and Thompson, 1980). In the original experiments the tone continued until the air puff was delivered; this situation is called "delayed conditioning." In what is called "trace conditioning," the CS is terminated shortly before the US is presented. Investigators from Pavlov on down have reported that trace conditioning is harder to acquire than delayed conditioning. Now it is reported that whereas intact rabbits learn well in the trace-conditioning situation, hippocampectomized rabbits cannot be conditioned in this situation. Perhaps, then, the hippocampus is indispensable for the more complex contingency of trace conditioning.

● Tracing the circuit of a conditioned response   David H. Cohen (1974, 1982) and his collaborators have been engaged in a long-term project of tracing the complete circuit of a conditioned response in the brain of a vertebrate and identifying sites where electrophysiological signs of plasticity occur. Their experimental animal is the pigeon. In the training situation an increase in light intensity precedes an electric shock delivered to the pigeon's feet; the response recorded is an increase in heart rate. After several paired presentations of light and shock, heart rate increases promptly upon presentation of the light before the foot shock occurs; that is, the pigeon shows conditioned cardiac acceleration to the light (CS). Cohen and his collaborators have traced the sensory pathways from the eyes into the brain and the motor pathways back from the heart into the brain, trying to map the complete circuit that mediates the conditioned response.

Although a mapping of the entire circuit is not yet complete, it is well advanced, as shown in Figure 15-20. Furthermore, the investigators have already found indications of plastic sites in this circuit. The visual circuits include three parallel pathways, and any one of them can mediate the conditioning if the other two are interrupted surgically. Electrophysiological recording during conditioning showed that no changes occurred in the retina but that neurons in the visual thalamus do show training-induced increases in their responses to the CS. On the other hand, presentation of light alone or unpaired presentations of light and foot shock diminished the response. This aspect of the research is still preliminary, but it indicates that the modifications in a known circuit may be found in vertebrates. Development of this work will allow critical comparisons between findings in vertebrates and invertebrates as to whether their mechanisms of plasticity are the same or different. And research with vertebrates may be more suitable for the study of mechanisms of associative learning, once the relevant circuits have been adequately defined.

Figure 15-20 Circuit involved in conditioning of cardiac response to light flash in pigeon. (The ascending branches through the cortex are adapted from D. H. Cohen, 1974; the descending branches are adapted from D. H. Cohen, 1982.)

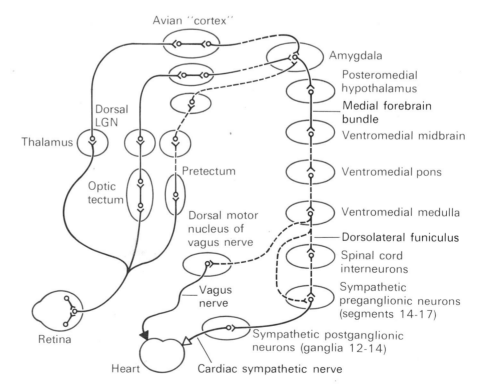

Consolidation hypothesis of memory formation

A person who suffers a severe blow to the head is likely to have a gap in his memory for the events just preceding the accident. At the beginning of this century an explanation was offered for such puzzling gaps in memory: The blow did not wipe out memories; rather it interfered with ongoing processes needed to translate short-term into long-term memories. This interpretation was based on the influential **perseveration-consolidation hypothesis** formulated in 1900 by Müller and Pilzecker on the basis of their experiments on human verbal learning. Müller and Pilzecker hypothesized that studying material tends to set up continuing activity, and these perseverating short-term processes help to consolidate stable long-term memory.

In 1949 Hebb formulated the dual-trace hypothesis of memory, which was essentially a neurophysiological restatement of the perseveration-consolidation hypothesis. According to Hebb, a memory trace first takes the form of circulating neural impulses, and these impulses help to establish a long-term structural trace in the form of altered synaptic connections. The basic insight of these theorists now usually goes by the simplified designation of **consolidation hypothesis.** Experiments guided by this hypothesis used, first, electroconvulsive shock and then a variety of pharmacological agents to alter the formation of memory. In this section we will examine some of these experiments and their results.

Testing the consolidation hypothesis with electroconvulsive shock

Forty years after the consolidation hypothesis was formulated, investigators finally found a way to test it. When cerebral electroshock was introduced in 1938 as a psychiatric treatment, several investigators noticed that it caused retrograde amnesia. The patients showed impaired memory, especially for a period of seconds to minutes that preceded the shock. The observation was then confirmed and extended in research with animal subjects beginning in the late 1940s.

A typical experiment used a form of the mouse hole situation. A mouse (or rat) is placed in the start chamber of a small two-compartment apparatus (see Figure 15-21). Within a few seconds the mouse usually steps from the start box into the second compartment. Once its feet are on the floor bars of the second compartment, the bars are energized electrically, and the mouse hops back to the start chamber, where there is no shock. The shock is not strong enough to be harmful, but the mouse tends to remember it. The stronger the shock, the better the mouse tends to remember it. If a mouse is put back into the apparatus a week or a month later, it will probably refuse to go through the hole or at least it will hesitate for a few hundred seconds before going through.

This result is true if nothing is done to interfere with formation of memory. Suppose, however, that a short time after the mouse has had the learning experience, it is given an electroconvulsive shock (ECS), that is, an electrical current is passed through the head. If the time interval between the training trial and the ECS is relatively brief, then the mouse may not form a long-term memory of the experience. If it is put into the apparatus a day or a week later, it will probably step into the second compartment within a few seconds, just as if it had never received foot shock. The longer the interval between the training experience and the ECS, the more likely the mouse is to remember.

The increase in the percentage of mice that remember as a function of increasing time between training and ECS was thought by early workers on this topic to show

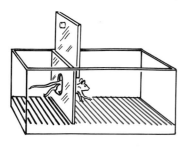

(a) Step through

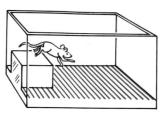

(b) Step down

(c) Pole jump

(d) T-maze

Figure 15-21 Behavioral tests used to determine the effects on memory of interventions in brain chemistry. The first three are tests of passive avoidance, and the last involves active avoidance. The blue grids indicate where shock can be delivered. (a) Step-through test. When the door is opened, the animal steps through and receives foot shock. (b) Step-down test. (c) Pole-jump test. (d) T-maze. When the door is opened, the animal must leave the start area and go to the correct side or it will receive foot shock.

a temporal gradient of consolidation of memory. If one could accurately measure the time necessary to establish memory traces, this result would furnish important information to indicate the neural and biochemical processes involved in memory storage. Biochemists hoped to use such findings to eliminate certain biochemical processes as possible bases of memory storage. Unfortunately, experiments soon showed a widespread diversity in temporal gradients (see Figure 15-22). In certain experiments the treatment was effective in eliminating memory only if the delay between the trial and the subsequent electroconvulsive shock did not exceed 30 sec; in other experiments there were still strong effects after a delay of several minutes; in still other experiments effects of cerebral electroshock could be found even if 10 h intervened between training and electroshock. Several factors were found to influence the apparent duration of consolidation: the behavioral criterion employed, the intensity of the amnestic (amnesia-producing) treatment, the difficulty of the learning task, the site of the shock to the brain, and the strain or species of subject studied. Thus the situation is far from being as simple as was originally supposed.

Varying the locus and kind of treatment

Giving an electroconvulsive shock across the head is not a very precise method. To obtain more specific information, a few investigators have placed electrodes either on different areas of the cortex or in different brain centers, and these experiments have yielded unexpected results. In experiments where electroshock is given across the head or directly to the cortex, most investigators have found that amnesia occurs

Figure 15-22 Diversity of temporal gradients of memory consolidation. Each of these curves comes from a different published experiment in which rodents were given single-trial passive avoidance training and then, after a fixed interval of time, were given electroconvulsive shock (ECS). Within each experiment, a different group of animals was used for each training–ECS interval. In each experiment memory at a subsequent test was better the longer the training–ECS interval, but the alleged "temporal gradients of consolidation" differ so widely in slope as to raise questions about the concept of consolidation.

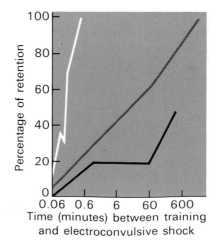

only if the animal shows a convulsion. But if the electrodes are implanted in certain subcortical sites, amnesia can be obtained with quite weak currents that do not cause convulsions. One such site is the amygdaloid nuclei, where a weak current of 50 microamperes given on only one side of the brain is enough to produce amnesia, even if the interval after the trial is as long as an hour (Gold, Macri, and McGaugh, 1973). At the cortex currents of a few milliamperes—that is, currents 100 times stronger—are needed to produce amnesia.

Do these results indicate that the amygdaloid nuclei are essential to formation of memory? Apparently not, since rats in which experimenters have destroyed these centers in both hemispheres learn the tasks easily and recall them as well as control animals. As we saw in Chapter 14, the amygdaloid nuclei and the hippocampus may work in parallel in certain kinds of learning, with either region being able to carry the burden alone. The amygdaloid nuclei are therefore not necessary for learning or for memory, but disrupting the activity of these nuclei can impair formation of long-term memory.

Many other kinds of posttraining treatments have been found to affect formation of memory. For example, reduction of available oxygen, changes in body temperature, spreading depression of cortical activity, anesthesia, inhibition of protein synthesis in the brain, and deprivation of REM sleep all affect formation of memory. Some of these treatments are almost as easy to use as electroshock. For example, anesthetic agents that work by inhalation start their activity rapidly, the duration can easily be regulated, and the intensity of the effect varies with the concentration. Drugs that inhibit protein synthesis in the brain have been very helpful in discovering a route that is necessary for forming long-term memory, as we will see later.

Improving memory with posttrial treatments

It is possible to improve as well as inhibit the formation of memory. Lashley showed in 1917 that rats given low dosages of strychnine before daily trials in a maze learned more rapidly than control animals. McGaugh and Petrinovich (1959) confirmed these results and went even further. With pretrial administration the drug might have affected either the encoding of the information or the subsequent consolidation of memory. The experimenters therefore gave the drug to some groups at various periods after their daily maze trials and to other groups at various periods before the trials (Figure 15-23). The results showed that strychnine has as much effect if it is given after the trials as it has if it is given before the daily trials. Even if strychnine is given as long as 60 min before or 60 min after the trials, a large reduction in errors occurs. But if the drug is given 120 min before or 240 min after the trials, there is no effect on the number of errors. So the drug has to act in temporal proximity to the trials if it is to affect memory. The results obtained with injections made after the learning trial support the hypothesis of consolidation of memory. Furthermore they extend that hypothesis by showing that during the period in which memory is forming, it can be either impaired or reinforced.

Weak electrical stimulation given, after trials, to the activating reticular formation in the brainstem can improve consolidation (Bloch, Deweer, and Hennevin, 1970). These results support the hypothesis that the efficiency of consolidation processes can be affected by the level of alertness. It has long been known in a general way that the level of attention influences learning and memory.

Figure 15-23 Strychnine in low doses improves the consolidation of memory in rodents if given shortly before or shortly after training. A different group of animals was used for each time condition. Animals received injections at the same time before or after each daily training trial on a visual discrimination table. Better performance is shown by fewer errors to criterion. Control groups received injections of physiological saline solution, which has no effect on memory. (From McGaugh and Krivanek, 1970)

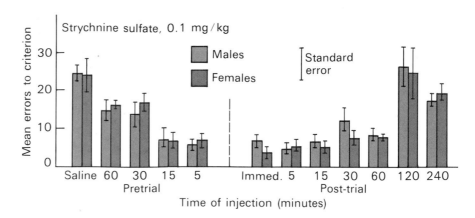

Sequential neurochemical processes in memory formation

The use of biochemical and pharmacological agents in the study of memory formation, which began in the 1950s, has led to many interesting discoveries and to new concepts. Chemical treatments have many advantages for this research, since many of them are reversible, unlike brain lesions or other permanent interventions. The chemical treatments can be used for relatively brief, accurately timed effects, and subjects can be tested in their normal state both before and after treatment. Chemical agents can be given systemically or locally. Systemic administration permits the study of a whole system of widely separated neurons, such as neurons that employ a particular synaptic transmitter. Local injection into a specific brain site can be used to investigate localized processes.

The different courses of effects found with various agents suggest that different neurochemical processes may mediate memory storage over different time periods— short-term, intermediate-term, and long-term memories. This result has given rise to the concept of sequential neurochemical processes in memory formation, which we will discuss in this section. The same chemical or pharmacological agent may aid memory formation under certain conditions but impair it under other conditions. This result has given rise to the concept of modulation of memory formation, a topic we will discuss in a later section.

Time courses of effects of different agents

A set of experiments that suggest three biochemical stages in memory formation has been reported by Gibbs and Ng (1977). The existence of these stages is indicated by the finding that all the many effects of chemical or pharmacological agents on memory can be grouped into just three time periods. These are shown in Figure 15-24, and some of the agents are listed in Table 15-2. Figure 15-24 shows first a brief stage that is not specified in chemical terms but that can be abolished by electroconvulsive shock; here memory may be held momentarily by some residual activity that briefly survives the initial electrical responses. The first chemical stage appears to be related to hyperpolarization of neurons caused by a change in K^+ conductance. This so-called short-term stage holds memory for about 10–15 min and can be abolished or enhanced by agents that alter K^+ conductance. The second

TABLE 15-2   Stages of Memory in the Chick and Agents That Affect Their Formation

STAGE	MAXIMUM DURATION	PROCESSES HYPOTHESIZED TO MEDIATE	AGENTS THAT FACILITATE	AGENTS THAT INHIBIT
Short-term	30 min	Hyperpolarization involving K^+ conductance change	Calcium chloride	Lithium chloride, potassium chloride
Intermediate-term	90 min	Hyperpolarization involving Na^+-K^+ pump activity	Diphenyl-hydantoin, pargyline	Ouabain, ethacrynic acid
Long-term	Days	Protein synthesis	Pargyline, amphetamine	Anisomycin, cycloheximide, aminoisobutyrate

chemical stage holds memory for about 30 min; Gibbs and Ng called it "labile memory," although "intermediate-term" is a more suitable designation since the earlier stage is also labile. This stage appears to be related to hyperpolarization caused by changes in activity of the sodium-potassium pump. The third stage is characterized by protein synthesis, which is necessary to establish long-term memory. It is probable that these stages are sequentially dependent; that is, abolishing any stage eliminates the next one.

Identification of these stages and of the underlying processes came from experiments with day-old chicks. Most of the training involved a one-trial, passive-avoidance task carried out in the following way: A small shiny bead that had been dipped in water was presented at the end of a wire, and the chick pecked at it. If the bead had been dipped in a bitter solution, after pecking it, the chick would shake its

Figure 15-24 Stages of memory formation and processes that may underlie each stage. Note that the stages in this schema of Gibbs and Ng (1977) are similar to those of McGaugh (1968) presented in Figure 14-4. For each stage, a treatment is indicated that can impair the underlying process of memory formation. (Adapted from Gibbs and Ng, 1977)

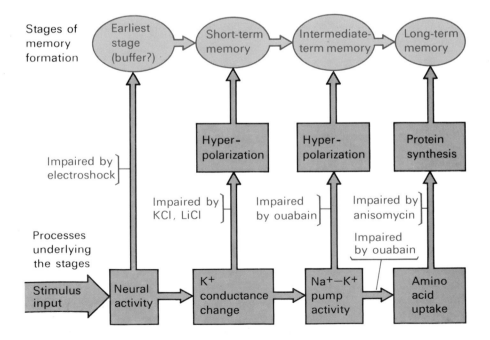

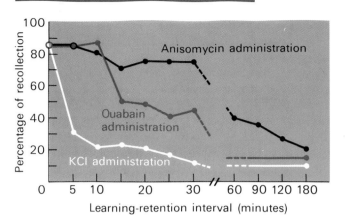

Figure 15-25 *Percentages of chicks showing learned avoidance response on retention test. The percentage of recollection varied with both the substance injected into the brain and the interval of time between learning and retention. Each point is based on data from a separate group of chicks. Administration of anisomycin (black curve) prevented formation of long-term memory, but intermediate-term memory (30 min) and short-term memory (5–10 min) were intact. Administration of ouabain (blue curve) prevented formation of intermediate-term memory, but short-term memory (5–10 min) was intact. Administration of KCl prevented formation of even short-term memory. (Adapted from Gibbs and Ng, 1977)*

head and wipe its beak vigorously on the floor of the cage. Without any further treatment a chick would remember such an experience and refuse to peck the bead again, whether the test trial occurred 3 h or 24 h later. The specificity of this learning was tested by presenting the bitter substance on a colored bead (red for some chicks and blue for others). At subsequent testing chicks did not peck the bead of the color that had been coupled with the bitter taste, yet they readily pecked the other bead. But if certain chemicals are injected into the animal, shortly before or shortly after training, it forgets the bitter taste and pecks at the test bead on a recall trial.

In a study of the temporal gradients of drug effects, a drug was given at one of various times before or after the avoidance training trial, and the retention trial was given at one of various time intervals after training. A different group of chicks was used for each combination of injection time and test time, and each animal was tested only once. Thus thousands of chicks were used in this study, which is why an inexpensive test animal and a rapid, reliable procedure were indispensible. Results for different classes of agents are shown in Figure 15-25. Depending on the class of drug used, memory was abolished after different durations. Other agents can enhance memory at each of these stages, which lends further support to this three-stage model of memory formation. Investigators have begun to look for these stages in mammals; results so far are positive, although the exact time courses may differ somewhat among species.

If these stages also hold for human beings, we may find it strange that our short-term and long-term memories for an event are apparently mediated by different mechanisms. We do not notice any change in our memories when they are switched from one method of storage to another. But this phenomenon is just one more example of the fact that we are not aware of our bodily mechanisms but only of the behavioral results that they achieve. (In Chapter 7 we remarked that our localization of high and low tones depends on different mechanisms, though we are not aware of this feature either.)

Protein synthesis and memory   Of all the proposed processes of memory storage, the best-studied and most soundly established is the synthesis of protein, which appears to be necessary for forming long-term memory. This field of work provides a good example of the rigorous testing and elimination of alternatives that characterize an advancing area of research. The proposed alternatives are also worth examining because they reveal some of the complexities in both the behavior and the biological processes involved in learning and memory.

The behavioral criteria of learning and memory are, of course, crucial to our study, because they provide our only way of knowing whether or not learning has occurred and memory has been formed and retained. Yet the behavioral tests do not always provide clear and unambiguous answers. If a subject fails to make a learned response when tested for retention, is this result a clear sign of forgetting? Not necessarily. The response may be stored but may not be retrievable at the moment, like a name that you are sure you know but just can't bring out. An easier test— recognition rather than recall—may yield the response and thus demonstrate that the memory was present all along. Some investigators tend to ignore the fact that memories are graded in strength. Memories are not simply present or absent, rather they may range all the way from very weak to very strong. Strong memories are easy to retrieve, but weak memories can be retrieved only under favorable circumstances. Also, a response may be available but the subject is not motivated to produce it, so psychologists stress the performance aspects of tests. Investigators have to be keenly aware of behavioral aspects of their experiments and must cross-check one test with another to be sure of the accuracy of their interpretations.

Research to test the effects of inhibitors of protein synthesis on formation of long-term memory began in the 1960s and has continued to the present. Most of this work has been done with rodents, especially mice. Why have investigators still not been able to decide conclusively whether or not synthesis of protein is required for formation of long-term memories? The answer to the question includes several parts:

1. The pharmacological agents used in the experiments have more than one effect, and it is not a simple task to test and rule out all the side effects. For example, drugs that inhibit protein synthesis also decrease the synthesis of adrenal steroids and of catecholamine neurotransmitters; one of these effects, rather than inhibition of protein synthesis, may be the reason that the drugs impair memory.

2. Many behavioral findings lend themselves to diverse interpretations. For example, some investigators have hypothesized that protein synthesis inhibitors impair retrieval of memory rather than impairing formation of the memory. Such alternative interpretations then require separate tests.

3. Research on the basic question has given rise to related questions, such as the conditions necessary for inhibitors to take their effect, interaction with other drugs, and so on.

Let us note some of the main steps in research in this area and some of the main findings.

● Use of varied antibiotic drugs   Several antibiotic drugs have been tested for possible amnestic qualities. Many new antibiotics are created each year, and some have been found to inhibit the formation of memory. Puromycin was the antibiotic used in initial research to test the hypothesis that protein synthesis is required for formation of long-term memory (Flexner et al., 1962). Injection of puromycin bilaterally into the temporal cortex blocked retention of Y maze training in mice,

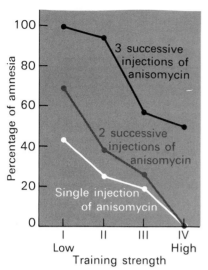

Figure 15-26 Percentage of mice showing amnesia after having had one of four levels of training in passive avoidance and subcutaneous injections of anisomycin, an inhibitor of protein synthesis. Some groups received a single injection 15 min before training (white curve). Some also received a second injection 2 h after the first (blue curve), and some received a third injection 2 h after the second (black curve). The level of amnesia was greater the weaker the training and the longer the duration of inhibition of protein synthesis. (From Flood et al., 1973)

whereas similar injection of saline solution or of various compounds related to puromycin did not interfere with recall. A few years later it was found that puromycin produces abnormal electrical activity in the hippocampus (Cohen et al., 1966), so administering puromycin was similar to delivering electrical shocks to the brain, and this similarity might explain its amnestic action. Puromycin blocks protein synthesis by being taken into a growing peptide chain as if it were a combination of transfer RNA and a molecule of the amino acid phenylalanine. The abnormal compounds that result appear to be toxic to the cell; this toxicity may provide another explanation for the amnestic effect of puromycin. So puromycin was largely abandoned in this work and other agents were taken up.

The protein synthesis inhibitor cycloheximide has been widely used since the middle 1960s. It is an effective amnestic agent if it is administered shortly before training in a dose that inhibits protein synthesis in the brain by about 90% (Barondes and Cohen, 1967). A single dose inhibits protein synthesis for a few hours. It may seem surprising that the body can get along with protein synthesis almost completely blocked for hours, but cells contain large supplies of proteins; existing enzymes, for example, can continue directing the cell's metabolism. Memory research with this inhibitor suffered, however, from two major flaws. First, the level of inhibition necessary to produce amnesia required toxic doses of the drug; the animals showed signs of illness and some died during an experiment or on the following days. Second, even strong inhibition seemed to overcome only weak training. If mice were trained to a criterion of 3 correct responses in 4 successive T maze trials, cycloheximide could wipe out memory for the habit, but training to a criterion of 9 out of 10 overrode effects of the drug. Investigators therefore wondered whether inhibition of protein synthesis affected only weak memories.

Then Bennett introduced to this field an inhibitor that overcame previous problems, anisomycin (Flood et al., 1973). This inhibitor is an effective amnestic agent at low doses; 25 times the effective amnestic dose is nonlethal. Because anisomycin is safe, it can be given in repeated doses; administering it every 2 h keeps inhibition of cerebral protein synthesis at about 90%. With such repeated administration Flood and co-workers demonstrated that even relatively strong training could be overcome by inhibition of protein synthesis; the stronger the training, the longer the inhibition had to be maintained to cause amnesia.

Figure 15-26 shows results of an experiment in which mice were trained in one-trial passive avoidance and received either one, two or three successive subcutaneous injections of anisomycin; the first injection was given 15 min before the training trial, and the subsequent injections were given at 2-h intervals. With the foot shock strength used in this experiment, two successive injections—4 h of inhibition of protein synthesis—were not enough to cause amnesia. Averaging across all four levels of training strength, 70% of the mice showed recall at the retention test two weeks after training. But three injections of anisomycin—6 h of inhibition—did cause amnesia; only 20% of the mice recalled at the retention test. Note that the injection that made the difference was given $3\frac{3}{4}$ h after training, so the synthesis of protein(s) necessary for long-term memory may take place hours after training if inhibition of synthesis has been prevented up to this time. With stronger training an even longer period of inhibition of protein synthesis may be necessary to cause amnesia. Thus, in principle at least, even strong training can be overcome by a sufficiently long period of inhibition of protein synthesis.

TABLE 15-3 Percentage of Animals Showing Amnesia at Test As a Function of Strength of Training and Duration of Inhibition of Protein Synthesis

STRENGTH OF TRAINING (NUMBER OF TRAINING TRIALS)	LENGTH OF INHIBITION (HOURS)					
	0	*2*	*8*	*10*	*12*	*14*
6	0	10	77	73	70	90
8	0	10	44	50	71	77
10	0	0	36	38	60	62

SOURCE: Flood, Bennett, Orme, and Rosenzweig 1975).

Normally the synthesis of protein related to memory storage occurs during the minutes that follow the training trial; if, in mice, the first injection of inhibitor is given only 15 min after training, there is no amnesia even if thereafter a long series of injections is administered. But the necessary synthesis, which without the drug occurs rapidly, can be delayed by inhibiting synthesis for a few hours. In that case it can take place even 4–6 h after training. This result is shown by the experiments we have just considered. The capacity to form proteins related to memory may therefore persist for a few hours, at least under the effects of inhibitors of synthesis.

To test further the generality of the findings with passive avoidance and to study the effects of even longer periods of inhibition of protein synthesis, Flood and co-workers (1975, 1977) did experiments with active-avoidance training and extended the duration of inhibition up to 14 h. Active avoidance in a T maze requires several trials to learn and is, of course, more complex than single-trial passive avoidance; it was used to determine whether the same principles applied. Different groups of mice were given 6, 8, or 10 trials in a T maze, motivated by foot shock. For different subgroups inhibition of protein synthesis lasted for 2, 8, 10, 12, or 14 h. Retention tests run one week after training demonstrated that even in well-trained mice (10 training trials), 14 h of inhibition produced a significant percentage of amnesia (see Table 15-3). The longer the duration of inhibition, the higher was the percentage of amnesia. Also, the weaker the training, the higher was the percentage of amnesia. Thus the same principles that had been demonstrated for passive avoidance also apply to the more complex and more variable behavior of active avoidance. The results of this program of experimentation have brought new and integrated support to the hypothesis that synthesis of protein is necessary for the formation of long-term memory.

Modulation of formation of memory

Many other kinds of agents alter memory storage besides those that affect the basic or direct memory processes. Some of these agents include stimulants (such as amphetamine and caffeine), depressants (such as chloral hydrate and phenobarbital), neuropeptides, the catecholamine neurotransmitters (dopamine, serotonin, and norepinephrine), and drugs that affect the catecholamines or the acetylcholine transmitter system. Experiments with such agents have led to the concept of **modulation of formation of memory** or **modulation of memory storage processes.**

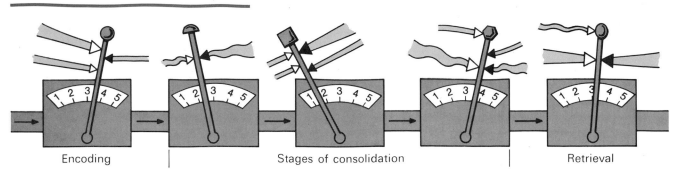

Encoding | Stages of consolidation | Retrieval

Figure 15-27 Schematic presentation of direct and modulatory processes in memory. Each direct process, or stage of memory (shown in gray), can have its rate or level facilitated or inhibited by various modulatory processes (symbolized by arrows with blue shafts). Facilitation is indicated by white arrowheads and inhibition by black arrowheads.

Two things are implied by the use of the term "modulation." One is that memory formation can be either impaired or enhanced by the same agent, depending on the time of administration or other conditions. The other implication is controversial: namely that we know the fundamental biological processes involved in the formation of memories and that other treatments are secondary ones, superimposed on the basic processes. Figure 15-27 indicates this view of basic and modulatory processes in the formation of memory. It may be overoptimistic to think that we can really distinguish what is modulatory from what is a basic storage process. But many modulatory effects are large and important, so it is worth investigating them, especially since some of them may yet turn out to be basic. In this section we will survey results obtained with two kinds of chemical modulators, and then we will consider mechanisms of modulation.

Cholinergic modulation

Agents that affect the cholinergic system can alter both the storage and the retrieval of memories, as shown by studies with both human and animal subjects. Acetylcholine (ACh) is the transmitter at many synapses in the neocortex and the hippocampus, as well as elsewhere in the brain. Scopolamine (which blocks muscarinic ACh receptors) has been used during childbirth because it prevents formation of long-term memories; under the influence of the drug the mother can aid in the delivery of the child but will not subsequently recall the delivery. Experimental studies with human subjects have confirmed that scopolamine does not affect short-term memory but significantly impairs long-term memory (D. A. Drachman, 1978). Moreover, the pattern of impairment over a battery of tests was quite similar to the pattern shown by elderly subjects. Agents that enhance cholinergic action have been found to improve formation of long-term memory in normal human subjects (K. L. Davis et al., 1978; Sitaram et al., 1978). Because of the foregoing findings, work is being done to try to improve the memory of aged and demented patients by giving them drugs that prolong the action of ACh at synapses and also by giving ACh precursors (that is, compounds used by the body to manufacture ACh).

Retrieval can also be affected by modulating the cholinergic system, as shown by Deutsch (1971) in studies with rats. In the case of rather strong, recent memories, the drug DFP impairs recall, whereas with rather weak, older memories, DFP aids recall. How can the same drug have opposite modulatory effects on memories of different strengths? DFP is an inhibitor of cholinesterase, the enzyme that breaks up

ACh and terminates its action at synapses. Administering DFP, then, allows prolonged activity of the molecules of ACh released at a synapse. According to Deutsch, when memories are strong, the activity of ACh is optimal for synaptic transmission. Greater ACh activity would block the junction in a depolarized state, while weaker ACh activity would result in insufficient depolarization. Thus in the case of strong memories DFP drives the level of ACh activity away from optimal; in the case of weak memories DFP drives the level toward optimal.

Catecholamine modulation

Modifying activity of the catecholamine transmitters can affect memory formation, as we noted briefly above. These transmitters normally are active for moderately long periods when released or injected. Posttrial injections of catecholamines into the cerebral ventricles of mice aids memory formation (Haycock et al., 1977). Conversely, posttrial injection of a drug (DDC) that lowers the levels of catecholamines impairs subsequent memory (Stein, Belluzzi, and Wise, 1975; Jensen et al., 1977). To test whether the impairment might be due to some side effect of the drug, other than lowering catecholamine levels, the investigators administered posttrial injections of norepinephrine, and these injections reduced the impairment caused by DDC (Stein, Belluzzi, and Wise, 1975). Thus memory formation can be modulated up or down by altering levels of brain catecholamines.

The best opportunity for finding modulatory effects occurs when the strength of memory is neither too strong nor too weak; the middle range allows sensitive tests and is not stuck at "ceiling" or "floor" levels. The experimenter can control training conditions and also use a drug such as anisomycin in order to put memory strength near a sensitive "balance point," that is, near the behavioral dividing line that classifies an animal as having either "memory" or "amnesia" (Figure 15-28). The

Figure 15-28 Varied strengths of memories as a function of training strength and time after training. The white curve represents memory strength after weak training; it does not reach the criterion of recall. The blue curve indicates memory strength after training of intermediate strength; the memory is suprathreshold for a time but then falls below the criterion. The black curve represents memory strength after strong training. Different tests for memory can shift the level of criterion up or down.

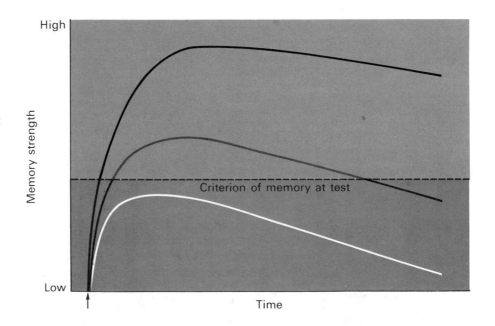

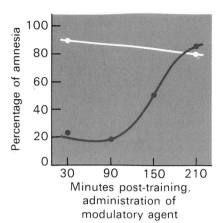

Figure 15-29 Effects of amphetamine administered at various times post-training to animals made amnesic by anisomycin. Giving amphetamine (blue curve) at 30 or 90 min post-training was effective in combatting the amnesic effects of anisomycin, but injections at later times had lesser or no effect. Giving saline (white curve) had no effect on the level of amnesia; this served as a control for the injection procedures. Twenty mice were used per point. (Adapted from Bennett, Rosenzweig, and Flood, 1979)

general procedure is to administer anisomycin 15 min prior to training, train the mouse, and at a suitable interval after training administer the drug under investigation. A week or so later the animals are tested. This procedure permits the administration of the drug at an extended time after training—30 min to 1 h—and thus serves to eliminate possible effects of the drug on the training itself. Results of an experiment using d-amphetamine (which causes release of norepinephrine) are shown in Figure 15-29. d-Amphetamine administered either 30 or 90 min after training attenuated the amnesic effect of two successive doses of anisomycin. But if d-amphetamine administration was delayed until 150 min after training, little attenuating effect was seen.

Developmental changes in catecholamine levels may help to explain why some kinds of learning or plastic effects show critical periods—that is, occur only during relatively brief parts of the life span. Examples of effects that can be induced only during a critical period are imprinting and the changes in ocular dominance that occur when one eye is occluded for several weeks. The susceptibility to shifts of ocular dominance can be modulated by norepinephrine, according to recent reports (Kasamatsu and Pettigrew, 1979). If norepinephrine levels are artificially reduced in the visual cortex of kittens, a shift in ocular dominance cannot be induced, as it can be in normal kittens. Conversely, in adult cats in which a shift in dominance cannot normally be brought about, prolonged perfusion of the visual cortex with norepinephrine produces a shift in dominance. If these results can be verified and extended to other brain regions and behaviors, many therapeutic uses of such a technique can be imagined. For example, pharmacological treatments might be used to overcome some kinds of mental retardation or to aid recovery of function after brain lesions.

Mechanisms of modulation   It is clear that there are modulatory effects, but how do they occur? There are many possible ways in which modulators might work, and different classes of modulators may have different mechanisms of action. Let us review some of these possibilities.

Stimulant and depressant drugs that modulate memory might actually alter the rates of protein synthesis. That is, perhaps these drugs alter protein synthesis directly, or perhaps they do so in interaction with anisomycin. Direct tests ruled out these possibilities: The stimulant and depressant drugs had only slight effects on protein synthesis, either by themselves or used in conjuction with anisomycin (Flood et al., 1977).

Another hypothesis—and a more plausible one—is that the level of arousal following acquisition plays an important role in determining the length of time and the rate of the biosynthetic phase of memory formation. This hypothesis is consistent with the finding that treatments, other than drugs, that affect the level of arousal can alter formation of long-term memory. For example, the use of foot shock in training increases arousal as well as furnishing information about behavioral contingencies, and foot shock usually leads to strong memory formation. Electrical stimulation of the reticular formation following learning trials can also foster the production of long-term memories.

According to another hypothesis, modulating agents could alter motivational feedback that may be important for formulation of long-term memories. That is, among all the information that an individual takes in and stores briefly, only a small fraction is selected for long-term storage. If certain stimuli or behaviors turn out to have important motivational consequences, they are more apt to be put into long-term memory. Kety (1976) has pointed out that the catecholamines, and especially norepinephrine, are often involved in such motivational feedback, and he has hypothesized that these neurotransmitters thus play a special modulating role in memory storage. This role could include both central and peripheral feedback.

Applications to problems of human memory

If we understood the biological mechanisms of acquisition, memory storage, and retrieval, this knowledge could be used to prevent or alleviate many human problems. Even our present fragmentary knowledge has yielded some useful applications—chiefly in the form of drug therapies—and prospects for further application. In this section we will consider a few of these applications.

Improving memory with pharmacological agents

Some drugs that have been shown to modulate memory formation and/or to affect memory retrieval in laboratory animals have now been found to be effective in human beings. For example, arecholine, a cholinergic agonist, and choline, a precursor of acetylcholine, improve serial verbal learning in normal human subjects; scopolamine, a cholinergic antagonist, impairs it. Those subjects who were more affected by both drugs were the ones who showed the poorer learning scores under control conditions. In other words, these drugs may be useful in bringing individuals toward an optimal level of cholinergic activity but may not be able to improve those who are already at that level (Sitaram, Weingartner, and Gillin, 1978). Physostigmine improved both storage and retrieval of verbal material in normal human subjects; this drug inhibits the enzyme AChE and thus prolongs activity of ACh (Davis et al., 1978).

Both the Sitaram and the Davis reports noted that in Alzheimer's disease and other presenile dementias the cortex shows a decrease in the enzyme that synthesizes ACh, and both groups suggested that research should be done to see whether cholinergic agents might aid such patients. A subsequent pilot study with Alzheimer's disease patients has reported that while physostigmine alone did not cause improvement, memory was facilitated when physostigmine was coupled with lecithin, a precursor of ACh (Peters and Levin, 1979). Perhaps these agents could also aid some kinds of retarded individuals.

BOX 15-1   Do Multiple Memory Systems Exist?

Many and varied changes occur in the nervous system as consequences of learning or of differential experience. These include anatomical changes at existing synapses, changes in the number of synapses, numerous alterations in neurochemistry, and changes in electrophysiological responses. Such changes probably contribute to alterations of functional neural circuits.

Many investigators have sought *the* neural change that underlies learning and memory—that is, a single key that could unlock these mysteries. In keeping with this unitary focus, some claim that the same fundamental memory process must be involved in all animal species, and this claim has been coupled with statements about the overall conservatism of nature. On the other hand, some investigators have stressed the variety and diversity of processes involved in memory. Consider, for example, this statement of psychobiologist Seymour Kety (1976, pp. 321–322):

> I have always been impressed with the prolific diversity of nature, and the unity of memory processes . . . seems to be something of an oversimplification.

So profound and powerful an adaptation as learning or memory is not apt to rest upon a single modality. Rather, I suspect that advantage is taken of every opportunity provided by evolution. There were forms of memory before organisms developed nervous systems, and after that remarkable leap forward it is likely that every new pathway and neural complexity, every new neurotransmitter, hormone, or metabolic process that played upon the nervous system and subserved a learning process was preserved and incorporated.

A program for future research will be to find under what circumstances each of these mechanisms is employed—that is, in what combinations of tasks, species, and brain regions. Only then will we have fulfilled the objective of being able to describe in orderly progression the processes that must occur from the initial acquisition of information until later retrieval that demonstrates that long-term storage was achieved.

Vasopressin (antidiuretic hormone) has recently been shown to occur in the brain, where it may be a synaptic transmitter. Administering vasopressin to rodents has been shown to aid memory formation (for example, see de Wied et al., 1976). Following up on this lead, a pilot study with four cases of amnesia (three caused by concussions and one by alcoholism) found that administering vasopressin over a few days brought recovery of memory in each case (Oliveros et al., 1978). Further research on this topic is being carried out in several laboratories.

We noted earlier that Korsakoff's syndrome develops in alcoholics because of thiamine deficiency. Therapeutic use of thiamine has substantially reduced the proportion of alcoholics who develop Korsakoff's syndrome. But abuse of alcohol impairs the nervous system, even if intake of thiamine is adequate, and measurable impairments of memory and problem-solving abilities are found even in heavy social drinkers. In fact, there is a regular progression of impairment of memory from light social drinkers to heavy social drinkers to alcoholics to Korsakoff's patients (Butters and Ryan, 1979). Confirming these results and making them widely known might help to combat a common cause of memory impairment.

Since many stages and processes are involved in the formation of memory, it is likely that cases of deficient memory often involve more than a single process. For this reason combinations of pharmacological agents may often be much more effective in improving memory than any dose of a single agent (Flood and Cherkin, 1981).

Application to mental retardation and dementia

Many kinds of human suffering and waste of human potential could be alleviated if we could prevent or ameliorate deficiencies of learning and memory that are caused by abnormal neural conditions. Among these conditions are mental retardation and senile decline, two topics we will discuss here.

● Mental retardation   Mental retardation is caused by many known factors, but the etiology of most cases is not known. In Chapter 3 we noted that lack of a specific enzyme has been established as the cause of one kind of retardation, phenylketonuria. This condition is now diagnosed by a simple test, and infants who have the condition can develop normally if they are given a diet that does not contain the amino acid phenylalanine, which they cannot metabolize. In other cases, such as Tay-Sachs disease, no treatment has yet been discovered. It is possible that "genetic engineering" will remedy such cases by restoring to the DNA of affected infants the genetic instructions that they lack. The more that becomes known about brain mechanisms of learning and memory, the better will investigators be able to direct their search toward discerning faulty or lacking brain structures or genetic sequences. The President's Commission on Mental Retardation (1976, p. 44) has predicted that by the end of the present century it should be possible to reduce the incidence of biologically caused mental retardation in the United States by one-half.

Many cases of mental retardation are considered to arise from sociocultural causes—that is, because of lack of adequate stimulation and training. Earlier in this chapter we saw that adequate experience is necessary to achieve full anatomical and neurochemical development of the brain. Supplementary educational programs have been organized in many communities, especially in an attempt to ensure full intellectual development among poor and minority children. The President's Commission on Mental Retardation (1976, p. 45) predicted that retardation caused by socioeconomic factors can reasonably be expected to drop by a third by the end of the present century.

● Dementia   The decline of mental abilities in many elderly people is saddening, and even more pathetic is the similar decline that overtakes many people as early as their forties or fifties. The "presenile decline" was given its own name—Alzheimer's disease—to distinguish it from the similar condition in the elderly. Now, however, most investigators believe that dementia is the same disease whether it strikes early or late; in either case the behavioral symptoms and brain pathology are similar.

The first clear symptom of dementia is loss of memory. It can progress so rapidly that within a year or two patients may become unable to care for themselves. With the steady increase of the over-65 population, nearly 4 million people in the United States may be afflicted by this disorder by the year 2020 unless ways are found to prevent it. Dementia could be the worst public health problem of the next century.

As we saw in Chapter 3, clues about the neural bases of dementia are the presence of neurofibrillary tangles and plaques (Figure 3-23); these occur most frequently in the cerebral cortex and the hippocampus. There appears to be a genetic predisposition to Alzheimer's disease, since it is more frequent in near relatives of patients, although no clear-cut pattern of inheritance is evident. It is also more common in families where a member has Down's syndrome, and sufferers from Down's syndrome are especially apt to develop Alzheimer's disease. Trauma due to head injury may predispose a person to the disease, and so may long-term exposure to certain metals.

While the search for the biological causes of dementia goes on, behavioral and pharmacological treatments are being used to aid the sufferers as much as possible. Research with cholinergic agents was mentioned above. Encouraging patients to be as active as possible may help to slow the course of the disease. Showing patients how to organize their activities and encouraging them to write down reminders help them remain active and care for themselves. Prevention and cure of this disorder are high on the agenda of neurological research.

SUMMARY / MAIN POINTS

1. Memory storage has long been hypothesized to involve changes in neural circuits. Research since the 1960s has demonstrated functional and structural changes at synapses related to learning.

2. Anatomical changes at synapses caused by differential experience and training include modifications in the size of synaptic contact areas, the numbers of dendritic spines, and the branching of dendrites. Several possible causes for these effects other than learning appear to have been ruled out experimentally.

3. Training also causes changes in brain chemistry, including increased synthesis of RNA, changes in ACh levels, and synthesis of proteins.

4. Habituation and sensitization have been studied in identified neural circuits in invertebrates. In the monosynaptic circuits for the gill-withdrawal response of *Aplysia*, habituation involves a decrease in the number of quanta of neurotransmitter released from the presynaptic sensory neuron. In sensitization of this response an interneuron modulates increased release of transmitter from the sensory neuron.

5. Electrophysiological techniques have been used to find sites and processes of conditioning in the vertebrate brain. Several specific sites have been identified. The hippocampus appears to detect contingencies between stimuli and to model the process of conditioning, but it is not essential to the occurrence of conditioning.

6. Formation of memory can be impaired or facilitated by interventions made shortly after learning. Effective treatments include electrical stimulation of the brain and administration of a variety of pharmacological agents. Some of these treatments affect the consolidation of memory.

7. Formation of memory appears to involve a sequence of at least three different biochemical stages, which hold memory for different lengths of time. Formation of long-term memory requires the synthesis of protein.

8. Treatments not only affect directly the basic processes involved in formation of memory but also modulate these processes. The same modulatory treatment may either impair or enhance memory, depending on the time of administration and other conditions. For example, an anticholinesterase agent can impair strong memories but facilitate weak ones.

9. Cholinergic drugs have been shown to improve memory both in normal humans and in some people who suffer from dementia.

10. Substantial reduction in the incidence of mental retardation is predicted by the end of this century both through increasing knowledge of biological causes and through efforts to overcome sociocultural causes.

RECOMMENDED READING

Rosenzweig, M. R., and Bennett, E. L. (Eds.). *Neural mechanisms of learning and memory*. Cambridge, Mass.: MIT Press, 1976.

Teyler, T. (Ed.). *Brain and learning*. Stamford, Conn.: Greylock Publishers, 1978.

Thompson, R. F., Hicks, L. H., and Shvyrok, V. B. (Eds.). *Neural mechanisms of goal-directed behavior and learning*. New York: Academic Press, 1980.

Orientation

Evolutionary and Comparative Perspectives on Speech and Language

Vocal behavior of nonhumans

Fossils and language

Language learning by nonhuman primates

Brain Impairments and Language Disorders

Types of aphasia correlated with location of brain injury

Aphasia in users of sign language

Aphasia in bilinguals

Dyslexia

Electrical stimulation and language impairments

Recovery from aphasia

Hemispheric Specialization and Lateralization

Split-brain patients

Information-processing differences between the hemispheres of normal humans

The left-handed

Anatomical and physiological relations to hemispheric differences

Origins of hemispheric specialization

Theories of cognitive differences between human cerebral hemispheres

Language Development and the Brain

Frontal Lobes and Behavior

Analysis of frontal lobe injury

Prefrontal lesions in nonhumans

Parietal Cortex Syndromes in Humans

Perceptual deficits

Unilateral neglect

Recovery of Function Following Brain Injury

Recovery from general physiological abnormalities

Anatomical regrowth in the brain following injury

Education and rehabilitation

Substitution by remaining brain structures

Age and recovery of function

Lesion momentum and deficits

Summary / Main Points

16

Language and Cognition

Orientation

Inspection of this week's best-seller list readily confirms the impression that only humans write books, though chimps may dabble in paint and rats may occasionally eat books. By this and many other measures human mental life is distinctive in the animal world. But, as yet, the biological foundations of our complex cognitive abilities, especially language, are barely known. Clues to the workings of the brain related to human cognition come from studies of individuals with brain disorders, especially those arising from strokes, and also from differences in hemispheric function of normal individuals. Specific brain regions have been shown to be related to particular classes of cognitive disorder. This is especially evident with injuries that interfere with language.

In the late nineteenth century the neurologist Paul Broca discovered that lesions in the left hemisphere impair speech and language. Now, one hundred years later, studies of normal humans at all ages have provided interesting ideas about brain organization and cognition. Starting with simple observations of handedness, asymmetry of brain mechanisms can be readily noted. Only 5 to 10% of humans are left-handed. Does this fact imply a different functional relation between the cerebral hemispheres in these individuals than that characteristic of the majority? Moving on to more complex functions in normal humans, many investigators have offered data that point to a large range of hemispheric differences in cognitive functions. From

TABLE 16-1
Proposed Cognitive Modes of
the Two Cerebral
Hemispheres

LEFT HEMISPHERE	RIGHT HEMISPHERE
Phonetic	Nonlinguistic
Sequential	Holistic
Analytic	Synthetic
Propositional	Gestalt
Discrete temporal analysis	Form perception
	Spatial
Language	

this collection of experimental facts an edifice of speculation has been built. Proposed differences between the cerebral hemispheres even include the notion that they differ in fundamental modes of thought (Table 16-1). Popular concern has been aroused by these ideas because some speculative writers have suggested that current educational practices fail to consider intrinsic differences between the cerebral hemispheres. There is a threat that specialists in providing separate educational counsel to each hemisphere may emerge. More extreme arguments have even suggested that within a single brain there are two forms of consciousness that may vie with each other for behavioral fulfillment.

In this chapter we will seek clues about brain processes and structures involved in human mental life. Guesses, hunches, and data will be viewed from the realms of both the brain-injured and the hemispheric specialization in normals. Obviously many simpler questions about the brain and behavior have yet to be successfully answered. So it is difficult to offer more than a beginning to an understanding of those distinctive aspects of human life—the ability to generate complex language and thought.

Although brain injury in humans can produce profound losses, there are many observations that offer hope. In many cases following stroke or trauma, behavior recovers. In the most dramatic instances seen in children, almost complete restitution of behavior occurs, even though a large part of the brain may be damaged or missing. In the last section of this chapter we will present some ideas about the ways in which function might be recovered in brain-damaged individuals.

Evolutionary and comparative perspectives on speech and language

There are five to ten thousand languages in the world and countless local dialects. All these languages have similar basic elements, and each is composed of a set of sounds and symbols that have distinct meanings. These elements are arranged in distinct orders according to rules characteristic of that language. Anyone who knows the sounds, symbols, and rules of a particular language can generate sentences that convey information to others with similar knowledge. Looking at language acquisition, we see a remarkable regularity to the development of language across virtually all human languages. The abilities fundamental to production of language seem to be inherent in the biological structure of human brains.

Over the centuries scholars have offered many speculations about the origins of language, but data in this area are scarce. The oldest written records available to modern researchers are only about 6000 years old. The absence of older records has promoted a sense of mystery and elaborate tales about the beginnings of language. At one point over a hundred years ago, the French Academy banned speculations about the origin of languages as being merely fruitless speculation, incapable of being verified. Nevertheless, some old ideas have a vitality that leads to their continued restatement. A common notion of the past, which has recently been given new life, states that speech and language originally developed from gestures, especially involving facial movements. Even today, hand movements are a common accompaniment during speech. Gordon Hewes (1973), an anthropologist, has suggested that gestures came under volitional control quite early in human history and became an easy mode of communication before the emergence of speech. Perhaps tongue and mouth movements slowly came to replace grosser body movements. In time, sounds connected to these tongue and mouth movements may have provided the substrate of speech. Other speculations note that primitive humans were surrounded by sounds produced in the natural world, sounds that they might have attempted to imitate. Sounds caused by the wind, like the rustling of leaves, or vocalizations by other animals are always part of our surroundings. Imitations of these sounds by humans might have formed the beginning of vocal communication, which, in time, came to be shaped into speech.

Vocal behavior of nonhumans   Chirps, barks, meows, songs and other sounds are among the many produced by nonhuman animals. Many mammals, especially primates, have a large repertoire of species-typical vocalizations that seem to be related to distinct situations significant in promoting adaptive behavior. Many of these sounds are related to reproductive behavior, especially calls that serve to separate species or signal readiness to mate. Other vocalizations alert the group to the prospect of danger. Is it possible that the vocal behavior of nonhuman animals is related to the biological history of human speech and language? Are there any attributes of nonhuman vocal behavior that are akin to human speech? We will explore these questions by focusing on the songs of birds and the sounds of nonhuman primates.

● Birdsong   Many sounds of birds are pleasant tunes, and these sounds offer some intriguing analogies to human speech. Birdsongs vary in complexity; some repeat a simple basic unit, while others are more elaborate (Figure 16-1). The intricate

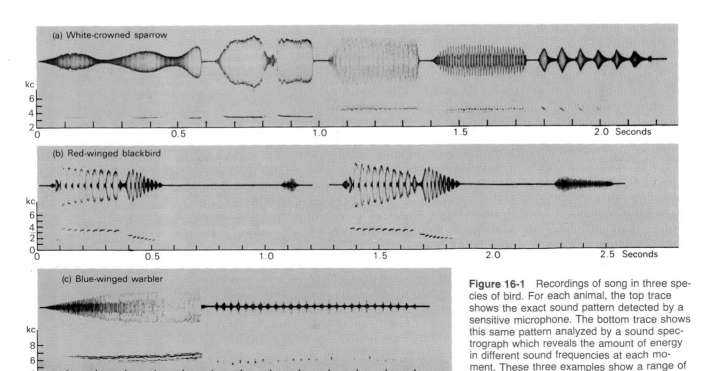

Figure 16-1 Recordings of song in three species of bird. For each animal, the top trace shows the exact sound pattern detected by a sensitive microphone. The bottom trace shows this same pattern analyzed by a sound spectrograph which reveals the amount of energy in different sound frequencies at each moment. These three examples show a range of birdsong complexity. (From Greenewalt, 1968)

Figure 16-2 The effects of early sound isolation and deafening on the characteristics of the typical song of two species of sparrow. The top row shows the typical adult pattern, the middle row shows songs produced by males reared in isolation from songs of other birds, and the bottom row shows the songs of birds deafened in infancy. (From Marler, 1981)

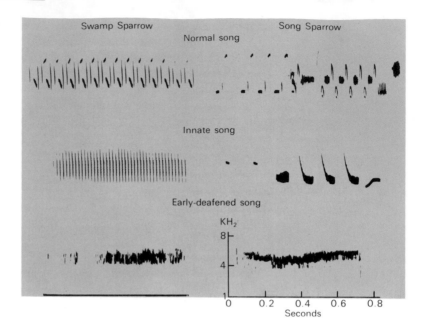

patterning of some songs promotes the idea that there is a connection to human speech. Parallels to human speech and language are examined in terms of importance of early experience and similarities of neural mechanisms controlling sound production in birds and humans. Note that no investigator believes that birdsong is an evolutionary precursor to human speech. Rather, the hope is that birdsong can give an interesting analogy that could be useful as an experimental tool.

The vocal behavior of some birds is not affected by early deafening or rearing in isolation. For example, neither early deafening nor rearing by another species changes the vocalizations of ring doves (Nottebohm, 1977). Deafened canaries can develop song although a few unusual sounds appear.

On the other hand, some birds, much like humans, require exposure to birdsong in order to develop the characteristic patterns of their species. These birds, such as white-crowned sparrows, chaffinches, and cardinals, show quite abnormal song if they are deafened before the maturation stage when song customarily appears (Figure 16-2). Another example of the strong role of acoustic experience in bird vocalization is seen in birds that mimic humans (and other animals). The mynah bird, for example, mimics human speech with astonishing fidelity even though its vocal tract is very different from that of humans. Like the development of human speech, song acquisition in some birds depends on an early, critical period of song exposure.

Some birds show a striking similarity to humans in the neurology of vocal control. The sound production machinery of birds consists of a voice organ, the syrinx, from which sound originates. Changes in membranes of this organ are produced by adjacent muscles innervated by the right and left hypoglossal nerves—cranial nerves that control the musculature of the neck. When these nerves are cut, the effects on song differ markedly between the right and left hypoglossal nerves. Section of the right hypoglossal nerve produces barely any change in song. Section of the left

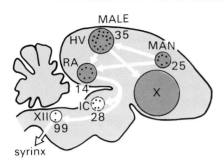

Figure 16-3 Vocal control centers of the male songbird brain. (HV, hyperstriatum ventrale; IC, intercollicular nucleus; MAN, magnocellular nucleus of anterior neostriatum; RA, nucleus robustus of the archistriatum; X, area X of the locus parolfactorium; XII, nucleus of the XIIth cranial nerve.) (From Arnold, 1980)

hypoglossal nerve produces a virtually silent bird; such birds "look like actors in silent cinema film" (Nottebohm, 1977). All the correct body movements are made, but no sound comes out. This observation indicates left dominance of vocal-control mechanisms in these birds.

Peripheral dominance is matched by differences in brain hemispheres. Investigators have mapped the vocal-control centers of the canary brain (Figure 16-3). Nottebohm (1980) has shown that lesions of the left-hemisphere vocal-control regions markedly impair production of the usual song; singing becomes unstable and monotonous. Minimal changes were seen following lesions in comparable right-hemisphere structures. An interesting parallel to human language impairment following brain injury is seen: In left-hemisphere-damaged animals some song elements are recovered seven months after lesions, as the right hemisphere takes over this function.

● **Vocal behavior of nonhuman primates**   The calls of nonhuman primates have been intensively examined in both field and laboratory studies. Ploog and his collaborators in Munich (Ploog, 1981) have studied the vocal behavior of squirrel monkeys, cataloging the calls they produce and the communication properties of those sounds in a social context. Their calls include shrieking, quacking, chirping, growling, and yapping sounds. Many of these calls can penetrate a forest for some distance, communicating alarm, territoriality, and other emotional statements. Direct electrical stimulation of some regions of a squirrel monkey's brain can elicit some calls, but stimulation of the cerebral cortex generally fails to elicit vocal behavior. Brain regions that elicit vocalizations also seem to be involved in defense, attack, feeding, and sex behavior. These regions include sites in the limbic lobe and related structures. Other investigators have shown that removing parts of the cerebral cortex of nonhuman primates has little effect on vocalization, whereas in humans it can dramatically affect language. Thus human speech requires the cortex, whereas animal cries do not.

Nonhuman primate vocalizations differ from human speech in several ways. In most cases these vocalizations seem elicited by emotional stimuli and are bound to particular situations. Further, even in the most talkative nonhuman primate, the number of distinct sounds is small.

Fossils and language   Sound production ability forms a special focus for evolutionary studies of language. The use of sound for communication often has advantages over the use of other sensory channels. For example, sound enables animals to communicate at night or in other situations in which they cannot see each other. The development of spoken communication clearly has survival value. Of course, sounds do not fossilize. However, parts of the skull concerned with speech sounds do form fossils and may provide clues about the origins of language.

On the basis of his studies of the probable shape and length of the vocal tract of various ancient human specimens, Lieberman (1979) has suggested that the capability for speech production of *Homo sapiens* may be only 50,000 years old. At about that time the human vocal tract developed a size and shape that could generate adequate signals for complex communication. The increase in the size and shape of the vocal tract, according to Lieberman, enables the production of certain key vowel sounds like "i" and "u." The ability to produce these sounds evolved along with the development of perceptual detectors that were especially sensitive to these sounds. Lieberman further argues that the vocal tracts in human infants and in nonhuman primates (monkeys) are shaped so that they cannot produce all the sounds that speech requires. These are interesting speculations, but there are strong criticisms of these ideas (for example, Dingwall, 1979). Some concern the reconstruction of the vocal tract; others challenge the sound limitations that this model suggests.

Language learning by nonhuman primates

Throughout history people have tried to teach animals to talk. But in most cases if any communication occurred, it was because the person learned to meow, grunt, or bark, rather than because the animal learned to produce sounds of human speech. Many such efforts lead to the conclusion that in order to speak like a human, an animal must have a vocal apparatus like that of a human.

Since both the vocal tracts and the basic vocal repertoires of modern nonhuman primates are different from those of humans, scientists have given up attempting to train animals to produce human speech. Instead they have asked whether nonhuman primates can be taught other forms of communication that have features similar to human language, including the ability to represent objects with symbols and to manipulate these symbols. An especially important objective of these studies is to determine whether animals other than humans can generate novel strings of symbols, such as a new sentence.

A switch in tactics came with the work of Allen and Beatrice Gardner (1969). They have been successful in training chimpanzees to acquire a gesture type of language called American Sign Language—the sign language used by the deaf in the United States. These animals have learned many signs and appear to be able to use them spontaneously and to generate new sequences of these signs.

David Premack (1972) has used another approach. He teaches chimpanzees a system based on an assortment of colored chips (symbols) that can adhere to a magnetic board. After extensive training the chimpanzees can manipulate these chips in ways that may reflect an acquired ability to form short sentences and to note various logical classifications.

At the Yerkes Primate Center, Project Lana has involved teaching "Yerkish" to a chimpanzee (Rumbaugh, 1977). Yerkish is a computer-based language, with different keys on a console acting as words. Apes are quite facile in acquiring many words in this language and appear to string together novel, meaningful chains.

Thus while nonhuman primates (at least those as intelligent as the chimpanzee) do not have a vocal system that permits speech, they appear to have a capacity for learning at least some components of language. Neurological studies of such animals may provide an experimental approach to understanding brain mechanisms related to human language.

Debate about chimpanzee language learning has always been vigorous and has recently intensified. Challenges to studies of language learning in nonhuman primates, including both methodological and theoretical issues, have come from several quarters. One of the main critics is Herbert Terrace (1979), who raised a young chimp and taught it many signs. Terrace tested carefully to see whether his chimp or others really could construct sentences. According to linguists, grammar is the essence of language, so investigators in this area look for the ability of sign-using chimps to generate meaningful and novel sequences of signs. As we noted above, the Gardners' studies suggested that sign-using chimps make distinctive series of signs, just as though they were using words in a sentence. However, Terrace argues that strings of signs have been explicitly presented to the chimps and that these animals merely imitate rather than generate new combinations. He suggests that this imitation happens in a quite subtle manner and may involve cuing practices of which the experimenter is unaware.

A broader debate emphasizing the nature of language has been opened by Rumbaugh, Rumbaugh, and Boysen (1980). True symbolization, they argue, involves something more than representing objects or action. It involves an intention to communicate an internal representational process akin to thoughts. This process may not be a component in chimpanzee language learning, although, of course, interrogation of the animals about this feature of language use is quite difficult. This debate is far from being settled, but the accomplishments of the trained chimpanzees have at least forced investigators to sharpen their criteria of language. Whether nonhuman primates are really capable of language is not yet clear.

Brain impairments and language disorders

Most of our understanding of the relationship of brain mechanisms and language is derived from observation of language impairments following brain injury due to accidents, diseases, or strokes. Unfortunately, it is hard to ascertain how localized the damage is. Nevertheless, some common syndromes of language impairment appear to be related to distinct brain regions. Specifically, in approximately 90–95% of the cases of language disorders due to brain injury—called **aphasia** —the damage is to the left cerebral hemisphere. Damage to the right hemisphere is responsible for the remaining 5–10% of the cases of aphasia.

Types of aphasia correlated with location of brain injury

The particular form of language disorder depends on the region of injury. Figure 16-4 shows two areas in the left cerebral cortex where damage affects language ability. Damage to **Broca's area** results in marked speech impairments. In this disorder, called **Broca's aphasia,** the patient has difficulty producing words even with considerable prompting and other forms of assistance. Nouns are used more often than verbs, and frequent errors in grammar occur. Speech production is severely impaired; it is quite slow and very labored, if present at all. These patients can often write words correctly and can readily understand written and spoken language. The impairment of speech may be related to the fact that this cortical area is close to motor cortical zones, especially those controlling the lips and face. Patients with Broca's aphasia also show right-side weakness or paralysis since the effects of stroke, at least in the early phases, involve extensive cortical areas. In studies of the effects of electrical stimulation of this area, Wilder Penfield and Lamar Roberts (1959) showed that excitation of this region can arrest ongoing speech (Figure 16-6 discussed below). Injury to Broca's area seems to affect an executive control for speech, and output from this region probably goes to motor cortical areas directly involved in activating relevant musculature in the face and throat.

Figure 16-4 Cortical speech and language areas in the human cerebral cortex (left hemisphere). Lesions in the anterior frontal region called Broca's area interfere with speech production; injury to an area of temporal-parietal cortex called Wernicke's area interferes with language comprehension.

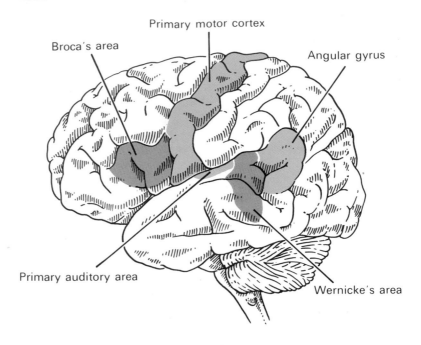

In contrast to Broca's aphasia, injury to a more posterior region of the left cortex, **Wernicke's area** (Figure 16-4), produces a marked, enduring deficit in language comprehension. In this form of aphasia, called **Wernicke's aphasia,** speech appears effortless and fluent and has its characteristic rhythm. The trouble is that it doesn't make any sense; frequently it is composed of gibberish and many unusual forms of language usage. These patients show little comprehension of language, and both speech and writing are equally affected.

A model of language mechanisms of the left hemisphere presented by Norman Geschwind (1972) notes that Wernicke's area borders on auditory cortical areas. He argues that output of the auditory cortex is transmitted to Wernicke's regions, where some forms of language analysis occur. In turn, pathways from Wernicke's area to Broca's area (Figure 16-4) control the elicitation of appropriate forms of speech. Language analysis of visually presented stimuli, like reading material, according to Geschwind, involves the angular gyrus, a region adjacent to Wernicke's area. The role of this region is to convert visual inputs to a form appropriate for language analysis.

A third form of aphasia reveals the role of the pathways connecting Wernicke's area to Broca's area. This impairment, called **conduction aphasia,** occurs when these pathways are damaged but without injury to either Wernicke's or Broca's areas. It is characterized by intact comprehension but poor repetition of spoken language; speech includes incorrect sounds. This patient also cannot read aloud.

It is important to note that the study of language impairments following brain injury has never shown deficits for specific linguistic or grammatical categories. For

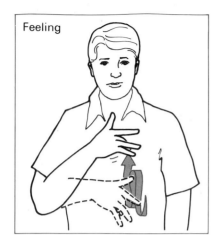

Feeling

Quiet

Secret

Figure 16-5 Examples from a language based on gestures—American sign language of the deaf. (From Klima and Bellugi, 1980)

example, specific linguistic units like prepositions or particular phonemes are not lost. Rather, as Lenneberg (1967) has emphasized, injury to the brain changes modes of language functioning, especially as they relate to general rules of language usage.

Aphasia in users of sign language

Human hands and arms are remarkable in the ability to move in many different and elaborate ways. Some gestures of the hand convey meanings that seem almost universal; some have been used for centuries. Formal hand and arm gestures with specific rules of arrangement form the basis of nonvocal languages such as American Sign Language of the deaf. This language involves an elaborate code and grammar; some examples are displayed in Figure 16-5. An exhaustive analysis of American Sign Language by two linguists (Klima and Bellugi, 1979) clearly establishes this gesture-based set of symbols as a language as elaborate as its vocal counterparts. In fact, even features as subtle as dialect are seen in sign languages. For this reason investigators have been interested in finding out whether sign language is similar to spoken language in its neural organization. Is there hemisphere specialization for a language system based on hand signals most of which are formed by the right hand although some involve both hands?

Several recent case histories provide interesting data about aphasia in users of sign language. Meckler, Mack, and Bennett (1979) described a young man who was raised by deaf-mute parents and who became aphasic after an accident. Previously he had used both spoken and sign language for communication. Afterward impairments in his spoken language, sign language, and writing were equally severe. He could copy complicated hand and finger movements when he was provided with the model of the experimenter's gestures, but he could not offer gestures in a spontaneous manner. A comprehensive analysis of sign language deficits in an older deaf-mute has been offered by Chiarello and Knight (1981). This person was deafened in childhood prior to the onset of speech and could not communicate vocally. She had well-developed sign language skills. Following a stroke sustained at age 59, she showed a total inability to generate hand signals with either hand. Computer tomograph scans indicated extensive damage in the left temporal cortex. Months later testing showed some return of sign language, although it was restricted to simple phrases. Errors in these signals bore a striking resemblance to language mistakes seen in the speech and writing of people with comparable lesions who had used spoken language. These case histories indicate that the neural mechanisms of spoken and sign languages are identical. Cerebral injury in these cases affects a mechanism that controls rules for the ordering of symbolic information whether conveyed by speech or by hand.

Aphasia in bilinguals   People who can speak and write in more than one language have always been fascinating to researchers in aphasia. Do cerebral cortical injuries produce similar impairments in both languages? Do very different languages share common neural systems? The understanding of this issue is partly obscured by definitions of bilingualism. A possible critical factor in these studies is the age at which a second language is acquired, even extending into adulthood. Very few bilinguals acquire two languages simultaneously in early childhood. Furthermore, most studies have concerned a small group of Indo-European languages that have many similar characteristics. Few reports of aphasia in bilinguals involve Asian languages, most of which are very different from English, German, French, and Spanish.

Most of the data on aphasia in bilinguals has been presented in a clinical format of individual case histories, which makes it difficult to see the common or most characteristic findings. Searching for the general themes, Paradis (1977) reviewed all published case histories and has characterized the classes of symptoms and recovery of aphasia in bilinguals. There are many different patterns of recovery, but the most common form, shown by almost half of all cases in the research literature, is that in which both languages are similarly impaired and there is equal recovery in both. This observation suggests that each language is similarly organized in the brain. In a smaller number of instances recovery is successive, although there is no consistent rule as to which language is first to recover; it is not as simple as "last in, first out." In rarer cases recovery is antagonistic; as one language recovers, it inhibits recovery of the other language.

After reviewing many of the facts and theories of bilingual aphasia, Paradis concludes that multiple factors account for the pattern of loss and restitution, and these include psychological considerations and differential fluency. Clearly there is no evidence for loss in one language without some impairment in others.

Dyslexia   Some children do not readily acquire the ability to read although intellectual prowess in other areas can be demonstrated. This inability to read is called **dyslexia** (from the Greek roots for faulty reading). Some dyslexic children show very high IQ performance. Dyslexia is more common in boys and left-handed persons.

There is considerable controversy about this syndrome, and its characteristics may be broader than a reading disorder. Denckla (1979) sees this inability to read as a symptom of a broader developmental language disorder that encompasses other aspects of language functioning. Dyslexia is a fuzzy clinical category, but recently it has been connected to some interesting anatomical findings.

In a single-case presentation Galaburda and Kemper (1978) described structural abnormalities in the brain of a person with major developmental language problems. Early in life this person showed delayed speech acquisition and major reading difficulties, despite normal intelligence test levels. Repeated testing from age 13 to 19 showed continued major reading difficulties. (Both his father and brother also showed reading impairments.)

After this dyslexic man died suddenly in an accident at age 20, anatomical studies of his brain revealed malformations in the left temporal lobe, which consisted of abnormal gyri that were numerous and small. The location of the disorder was posterior to the auditory region. This region is part of Wernicke's language region.

In other cortical regions there seemed to be abnormal cell layering, with accumulations of cells in clumps in unusual positions. The right cerebral cortex was regarded as normal in all respects. These findings suggest that focal left-hemisphere structural abnormalities produce reading disabilities. Of course, there may be other routes to developmental failures in reading attainment, and further research may clarify this issue.

Electrical stimulation and language impairments

Electrical stimulation of the brain is one of the tools used to explore language functions of the human cerebral cortex. Subjects in these studies are patients undergoing temporal lobe surgery for the relief of seizures. Electrical stimulation helps the neurosurgeon locate—and thus avoid—language-related cortical regions. These regions are found by observing language interference produced by the stimuli. Patients are given only local anesthesia so that they can communicate verbally.

Pioneering work by Penfield and Roberts (1959) provided a map of language-related zones of the left hemisphere (Figure 16-6). A pooling of data from many patients showed a large anterior zone, stimulation of which produced speech arrest. Speech simply stopped during the period of applied stimulation. Other forms of language interference, like misnaming or repetition of words, was evident from stimulation of both this region and more posterior temporal-parietal cortex regions (Figure 16-7).

In the years since this study new techniques in the analysis of language and electrical stimulation have been introduced and observations have been expanded. Using tasks that assessed movements of the mouth and lips, sound identification, naming, and memory, Ojemann and Mateer (1979) present more detailed cortical maps (Figure 16-8). Maps of sites that affected language functions revealed several

Figure 16-6 Interference with speech production by electrical stimulation at the points indicated. This is a summary of data obtained from many patients. [From Wilder Penfield and Lamar Roberts, *Speech and brain-mechanisms* (copyright © 1959 by Princeton University Press): Figure VIII-3, p. 122. Reprinted by permission of Princeton University Press.]

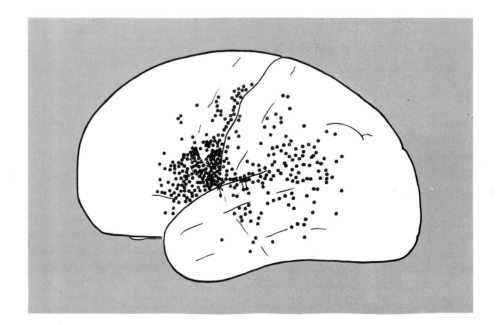

Figure 16-7 Aphasic type of responses produced by electrical stimulation at the points marked "A." These responses include confusion when counting, inability to name, and distortions of words. [From Wilder Penfield and Lamar Roberts, *Speech and brain mechanisms* (copyright © 1959 by Princeton University Press): Figure VIII-11, p. 130. Reprinted by permission of Princeton University Press.]

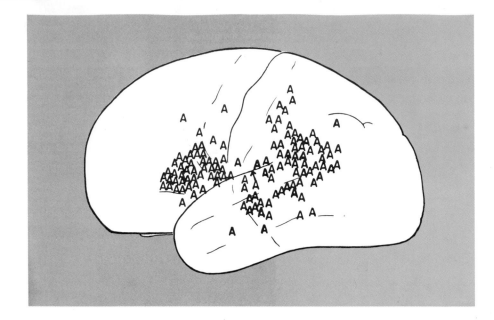

Figure 16-8 Detailed analysis of changes in language functions produced by electrical stimulation of the cerebral cortex: a summary of the cognitive effects of cortical electrical stimulation in four human subjects. Performance in naming (N), repeating movements (R), short-term memory (S), and language (L) was assessed during and after stimulation of the left hemisphere. A memory system (blue region) is posterior to systems for language production and understanding. The final motor pathway for speech is shown by the dark gray region. (Adapted from Ojemann and Mateer, 1979)

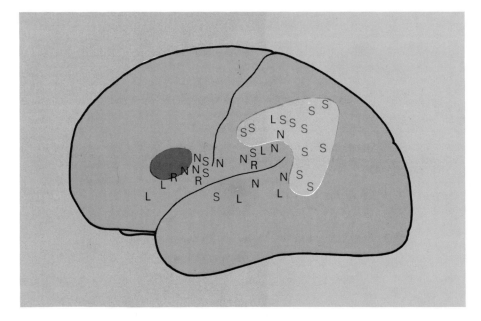

different systems. Stimulation of one system arrested speech and impaired all facial movements. This system was regarded as the cortical, final motor pathway for speech; it is located in the inferior premotor frontal cortex. Stimulation of a second system altered sequential facial movements and impaired phoneme identification. This system included sites in the inferior frontal, temporal, and parietal cortex. A third system was defined by stimulation-induced memory errors; it surrounds the sites of the systems that impair phoneme identification. Reading errors were evident from stimulation of other cortical positions.

Recovery from aphasia Many persons who survive the brain disorders that produce aphasia recover some language abilities. For some people language recovery depends on specific forms of speech therapy. The exact forms of speech therapy are mainly improvisations supported by some degree of clinical success rather than generated by theories.

The course of recovery from aphasia can be predicted from several factors. For example, recovery is better in survivors of brain damage due to trauma, like a blow to the head, than in those whose brain damage is caused by stroke. Patients with more severe language loss recover less. Left-handed persons show better recovery than right-handers. In fact, right-handed individuals with near relatives who are left-handed recover from aphasia better than right-handers without a family history of left-handedness.

Studies by Kertesz (1979) illustrate the typical course of recovery (Figure 16-9). The largest amount of recovery occurs during the initial three months following brain damage. In many instances little further improvement is noted after the lapse of one year, although this result may reflect impoverished therapeutic tools rather than a property of neural plasticity. Kertesz suggests that there is a sequence of stages of recovery that are distinguished by linguistic properties and that patients show a transformation of type of aphasia. According to Kertesz, a common end-point, no matter what the initial diagnosis, is **anomic aphasia,** a difficulty in "finding" words, although comprehension and ability to repeat words are normal. Anomic aphasia frequently stands as the residual symptom. In a later section we describe the remarkable and virtually complete recovery from aphasia characteristic of children.

Figure 16-9 The course of recovery following brain damage that produces (a) Broca's aphasia and (b) Wernicke's aphasia. Data in these graphs show the Aphasia Quotient (AQ), a score derived from a clinical test battery. (From Kertesz, 1979)

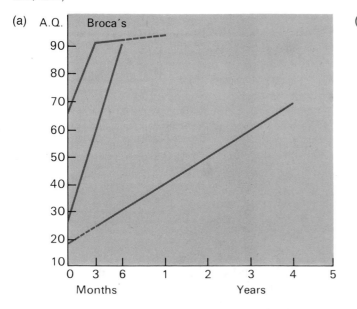

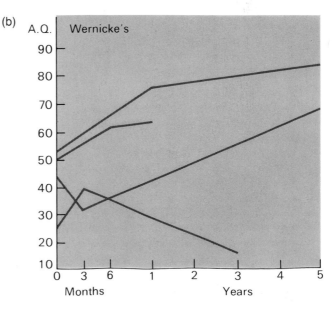

BOX 16-1   Anesthetizing One Hemisphere at a Time: The Sodium Amytal Test

In the process of making clinical assessments and decisions, neurologists must know which hemisphere is specialized for language processing. Although clinical observations of brain-injured humans indicate that 95% of us show left-hemisphere specialization for verbal activities, typical psychological tests would have led us to expect a smaller group. A technique that comes close to producing effects like that of brain injury without inflicting damage to the brain would be very valuable for neurosurgeons who seek to minimize language impairments from brain operations.

Wada and Rasmussen (1960) provided a tool that is much like a reversible lesion. The effect is accomplished by injection of a short-acting anesthetic—sodium amytal—into a single carotid artery, first on one side and then, several minutes later, on the other. From our discussion in Chapter 2 you will recall that the circulation of the anterior two-thirds of the cerebral hemisphere comes from branches of the carotid artery. Most of the anesthetic in the first pass through the vascular system remains on the side of the brain where it was injected. The patient shows arrest of speech for a brief period when injected on the side of hemispheric specialization for language processing. After a few minutes the effects wear off, so the injection is much like a reversible brain lesion. The sodium amytal test (sometimes named the Wada test after its discoverer) shows that about 95% of humans are left-hemisphere-specialized for language.

Improvement in language abilities following stroke might involve a shift to right-hemisphere language control. Evidence for such hemispheric shifts in children is presented later in this chapter. A recent case presentation by Cummings, Benson, Walsh and Levine (1979) lends some support to the hypothesis of left-to-right-hemisphere change in language control of an adult following left-hemisphere injury. The case they described followed a massive stroke. Computerized tomograms showed total destruction of Wernicke's and Broca's areas in the left hemisphere. Immediately after the stroke language was limited to small groups of words virtually bereft of meaning. Further, verbal comprehension was severely impaired. Three years later the patient was able to produce comprehensible short phrases and correctly identify objects. Since his left-hemisphere language areas were totally destroyed, the investigators concluded that the elements of recovered language are mediated by right-hemisphere mechanisms.

It is important to note that a concern for remediation following brain injury is relatively recent. For many years researchers regarded the nervous system as a rigidly organized organ without prospects of structural or functional plasticity. We are now in the midst of a major change toward views that seem more optimistic about the prospects of a rational basis for rehabilitation following brain injury (Bach-y-Rita, 1980). Recovery of language is a top priority of these renewed efforts.

Various forms of therapy are a significant factor in the long-term recovery pattern of aphasia. As mentioned earlier, strategies employed by therapists tend to be improvised rather than based on knowledge of the brain mechanisms of speech. An emphasis on auditory stimulation and repetition characterizes many approaches. An unusual innovation called "melodic intonation therapy" draws attention to the differences between song and speech. Aphasics can frequently sing words and phrases even though they show major handicaps with spoken words. This technique tries to enhance communication by instructing patients to sing sentences they would ordinarily attempt to deliver in conversational form. Therapists have had some success in slowly transferring subjects from a song mode to a nonmelodic speech pattern. The rapid pace of developments in computerized devices, including machines that speak, may provide new dimensions in rehabilitation of language disorders.

Hemispheric specialization and lateralization

By the early twentieth century it was firmly established that the cerebral hemispheres were not equivalent in mediating language functions. The left hemisphere seemed to be the controller for this function and was commonly described as the dominant hemisphere. However, the right hemisphere does not just sit within the skull awaiting the call to duty when the left side of the brain is injured. In fact, many researchers slowly drifted from notions of cerebral dominance to ideas of hemispheric specialization, or lateralization. This newer emphasis implies that some functional systems are connected more to one side of the brain than the other, that functions become lateralized, and that each hemisphere is specialized for particular ways of working.

Lateralization of function is not a surprising idea; a broad look at the distribution of body organs shows considerable asymmetry between the right and left sides—for example, the heart on the left and the liver on the right. Virtually every species, even very simple ones, shows such lateral differences. Nevertheless, at the level of brain processing in normal individuals, the interconnections of the hemispheres ordinarily mask ready evidence of hemisphere specialization. But by studying patients whose interhemispheric pathways have been disconnected—**split-brain** patients— researchers have been able to see cerebral hemispheric specialization in cognitive, perceptual, emotional, and motor activities. Study of split-brain individuals has also provided the impetus for many research studies using normals. In this section we will consider some of the many forms of evidence that lead us to further understanding of the similarities and differences of functions of the two cerebral hemispheres.

Split-brain patients

The differential properties of the cerebral hemispheres are best illustrated in a recent series of studies by Roger Sperry and his collaborators at the California Institute of Technology (1974). These experiments involved a small group of human patients who underwent a surgical procedure designed to provide relief from frequent, disabling epileptic seizures. In these patients epileptic activity initiated in one hemisphere spread to the other hemisphere via the corpus callosum, the large bundle of fibers that connect the two hemispheres. Surgically cutting the corpus callosum appreciably reduces the frequency and severity of the patient's seizures.

Studies by other investigators in the 1930s had shown that this remedy for seizures was not accompanied by any apparent changes in brain function, as assessed by general behavior testing methods such as IQ tests. But the human corpus callosum is a huge bundle of over a million axons, and it seemed strange that the principal connection between the cerebral hemispheres could be cut without producing detectable changes in behavior. Lashley, with his characteristic sardonic humor, suggested that perhaps the only function of the corpus callosum was to keep the two hemispheres from floating apart in the cerebrospinal fluid. Subsequent animal research showed, however, that with careful testing one could demonstrate deficits in behavior as consequences of hemispheric disconnection.

Results of hemisphere disconnection were first studied extensively in animals in the 1950s. For example, in one study cats had both the corpus callosum and the optic chiasm sectioned so that each eye was connected only to the hemisphere on its own side. Such cats learned with their left eye that a particular symbol stood for reward but that the inverted symbol did not, while with the right eye they learned the opposite—that the inverted symbol was rewarded rather than the upright symbol. Thus each hemisphere was ignorant of what the other had learned (Sperry, Stamm, and Miner, 1956).

In 1960 Joseph Bogen proposed, after a careful review of the earlier studies, that splitting the brain could control interhemispheric spread of epilepsy. His operations on patients proved his belief to be correct, and several of his split-brain patients were studied extensively both pre- and postoperatively through a series of psychological tests devised by Sperry and his co-workers. Stimuli can be directed to either hemisphere by presenting them to different places on the surface of the body. For example, objects the patient feels with the left hand result in activity in nerve cells of the sensory regions in the right hemisphere. Since the corpus callosum is cut in these patients, most of the information sent to one half of the brain cannot travel to the other half. By controlling stimuli in this fashion, the experimenter can present stimuli selectively to one hemisphere or the other and thus test the capabilities of each hemisphere.

In some of Sperry's studies words were projected to either the left or the right hemisphere. Visual stimuli were presented in either the right or the left side of the visual field. Words projected to the left hemisphere of split-brain people can be read easily and communicated verbally. No such linguistic capabilities were evident when the information was directed to the right hemisphere (Figure 16-10). More recently Zaidel (1976), a colleague of Sperry's, has shown that the right hemisphere has a small amount of linguistic ability. For example, it can recognize simple words. In general, the vocabulary and grammatical capabilities of the right hemisphere are far less developed than they are in the left hemisphere. On the other hand, the right hemisphere is superior on tasks involving spatial relations.

Sperry's findings not only confirmed the earlier animal research but were more dramatic, since they showed that only the processes taking place in the left hemisphere could be described verbally by the patients. Thus it is the left hemisphere that possesses language and speech mechanisms in most people. For our present concern the important result is that each hemisphere by itself can process and store information without any participation by the other hemisphere. The ability of the "mute" right hemisphere could be tested by nonverbal means. For example, in a test a picture of a key might be projected to the left of the fixation point and so reach only the right visual cortex. The subject would then be asked to touch a number of objects that she could not see and hold up the correct one to the experimenter. Such a task could be performed correctly with the left hand (controlled by the right hemisphere) but not by the right hand (controlled by the left hemisphere). In such a patient it is literally true that the left hemisphere does not know what the left hand is doing.

This research also indicated that while the left hemisphere controlled speech, the right hemisphere seemed to be somewhat better for processing spatial information, especially if the response was a manual one rather than simply a recognition of a correct or appropriate visual pattern. The apparent differences in functioning of the

Figure 16-10 Testing of a split-brain patient (right) compared with a normal subject (left). Words projected to the left visual field activate the right visual cortex (1). In normals, right-visual-cortex activation excites corpus callosum fibers, which transmit verbal information to the left hemisphere (2) where analysis and production of language takes place (3). In split-brain patients, the absence of callosal connections prevents language production in response to left-visual-field stimuli.

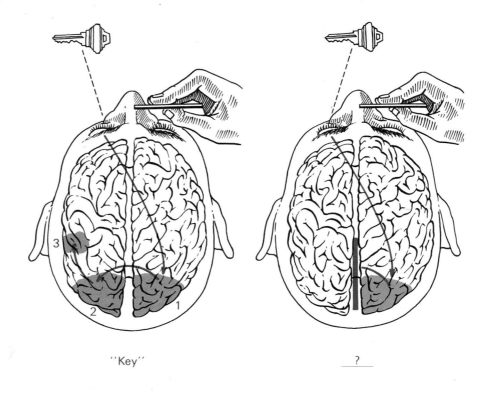

left and right hemispheres then became exaggerated. Two researchers in this field have put it in the following way (Gazzaniga and Le Doux, 1978, p. 6):

> There arose a barrage of popular and overdramatized accounts of the uniqueness of mind left and mind right. These representations of the implications of the split-brain observations gave rise to cult-like following and were largely written by people who had never seen a patient, but they were fed, in part, by new studies carried out by those directly involved in the experimental enterprise. We believe that these "pop" versions of hemisphere function are in error. . . .

These two investigators wrote a book called *The Integrated Mind* (1978), from which the previous sentences were taken; the purpose of their book was to present a sober framework for considering studies on cerebral commissurotomy and to show the necessity of the integrated functioning of the two hemispheres for normal behavior.

Research with split-brain humans has sometimes been criticized because these patients have suffered from seizures for many years before surgery. Since prolonged seizure activity produces many changes in the brain, critics have argued that the apparent consequences of cutting the corpus callosum might have arisen from changes in epileptic brains. This argument has been weakened by the publication of observations of the effects of a partial callosal section in nonepileptics. For example, a posterior callosal section in a 16-year-old boy was reported by Damascio, Chui, Corbett, and Kassel (1980). The patient had a tumor just below the posterior part of the corpus callosum, and removing it required partial cutting of the corpus callosum.

Following surgery the boy showed some of the classic signs of failure of inter-hemispheric transfer seen in epileptic split-brain patients. These signs included right visual field superiority in reading three-letter words and greater accuracy in naming objects presented in the right half of the visual field. Since the surgery severed most of the interhemispheric visual fibers, impairment of interhemispheric integration with visual input was predictable. On the other hand, since callosal fibers connecting somatosensory cortical regions remained intact, it was therefore understandable that the subject was able to name objects placed in either hand. The impairment of visual function and the integrity of somatosensory function in this patient provide strong evidence of the necessity of callosal fibers for interhemispheric communication.

Information-processing differences between the hemispheres of normal humans

● Auditory specialization: Dichotic listening   With earphones it is possible to present different sounds to each ear at the same time; this process is called the **dichotic-listening technique.** The subject hears a particular speech sound in one ear and, at the same time, a different vowel, consonant, or word in the other ear. The task for the subject is to identify or recall these sounds. Are speech sounds presented to each ear recalled equally well?

Although this technique may seem to be a program designed to produce confusion, it yields consistent observations linked to cerebral specialization. In general, data from dichotic-listening experiments indicate that right-handed persons identify verbal stimuli delivered to the right ear more accurately than simultaneously presented stimuli presented to the left ear. This result is described as a right-ear "advantage" for verbal information. In contrast, about 50% of left-handers reveal a reverse pattern, showing a left-ear advantage—more accurate performance for verbal stimuli delivered to the left ear. Some data also show that the pattern of ear advantage in right-handers changes when the stimuli are nonverbal, such as identification of musical sounds.

Figure 16-11   A representation of Kimura's model of the dichotic listening experiment (Kimura, 1973). (a) A word delivered to the left ear results in stronger stimulation of the right auditory cortex. (b) A word to the right ear results in stronger input to the left hemisphere. (c) When words are delivered to both ears simultaneously, the one to the right ear is usually perceived because it has more direct connections to the left hemisphere.

(a)

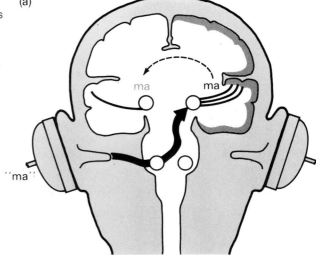

An explanation for these findings by Kimura (1973) argues that auditory information exerts stronger contralateral than ipsilateral neural effects (Figure 16-11). Accordingly, auditory stimuli presented to the right ear produce stronger left-auditory-cortex effects than right-auditory-cortex effects, and vice versa. Thus sounds presented to the right ear exert stronger control over left-hemispheric language mechanisms, whereas speech sounds presented to the left ear are less potent in activating left-cerebral-hemisphere language-processing regions.

Several recent studies have shown that right-handers' right-ear advantage for speech sounds is restricted to particular kinds of speech sounds (Tallal and Schwartz, 1980). The right-ear advantage is evident with simultaneously presented consonants like "b," "d," "t," and "k" but not with vowel sounds. Some investigators suggest that the right-ear advantage reflects a special feature of sound processing per se rather than verbal features. Tallal and Schwartz have suggested that the right-ear–left-hemisphere advantage for processing speech sounds reflects a left-hemisphere specialization for processing *any* sounds with rapidly changing acoustic properties. Of course, rapid change characterizes some speech sounds but not all. When the same speech sounds are artificially changed by extending them in time, the right-ear advantage for speech sounds is diminished. Hence in the dichotic-listening experiment, the right-ear advantage reflects a specialization for processing rapidly changing sounds, not a verbal specialization. Some speech sounds are included in this acoustic criterion for left-hemisphere processing; others are not.

● **Visual hemispheric specialization**   Hemispheric specialization in normal humans can be studied by using brief exposures to stimuli presented to visual half-fields (Figure 16-12). If the stimulus exposure is kept to less than 100–150 milliseconds, then input can be restricted to one hemisphere, since this time is not sufficient for the eyes to shift their direction. Of course, in intact humans further processing may involve information transmitted through the corpus callosum to the other hemisphere.

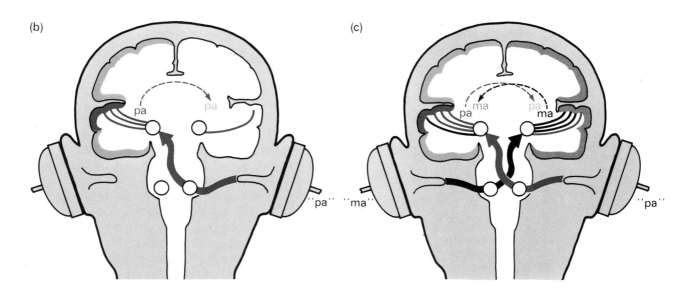

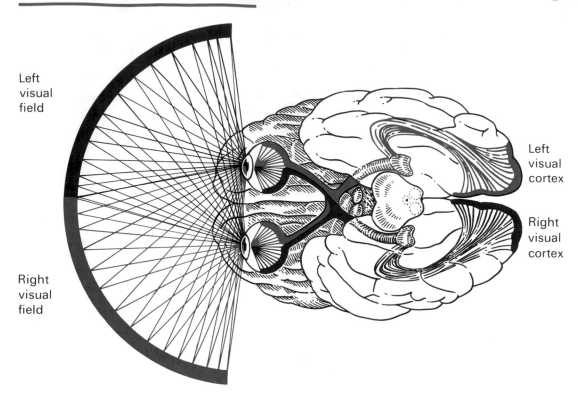

Figure 16-12 Representation of the visual fields on the retina and cerebral hemispheres. The right visual field projects to the left cerebral hemisphere and the left visual field projects to the right cerebral hemisphere.

Left visual field

Right visual field

Left visual cortex

Right visual cortex

Most studies with visual half-field presentations show that verbal stimuli (words and letters) presented to the right visual field (going to the left hemisphere) are better recognized than the same input presented in the left visual field (going to the right hemisphere). On the other hand, nonverbal visual stimuli (like faces) presented to the left visual field are better recognized than the same stimuli presented to the right visual field. Simpler visual processing such as detection of light, hue, or simple patterns is equivalent in the two hemispheres. But for more complex materials, in vision as well as audition, certain verbal stimuli are better processed in the left hemisphere of most individuals.

The left-handed Anthropologists speculate that right-handedness goes back a long time into prehistory. People portrayed in cave paintings held things in their right hand, and Stone Age tools seem to be shaped to a right hand. Some of the evidence comes from studying skull fractures of animals preyed upon by ancient humans. Since the fractures are on the animal's left side, anthropologists conclude that the attacker held an implement in the right hand. So right-hand preference and use goes back a long way. Throughout history many unusual attributes have been ascribed to the left-handed person—from the possession of an evil personality to a diffuse form of cerebral cortex organization. Indeed, the term "sinistral" ("left-handed") comes from the same Latin root as the word "sinister"!

Left-handed people comprise a small percentage of human populations. A figure of around 10% is commonly reported, although this percentage may be lower in parts of the world where teachers actively discourage left-handedness. For example, a higher percentage of left-handed Chinese-Americans is seen in more tolerant U.S. schools than among Chinese in China.

Many studies have sought to show cognitive and emotional differences between left- and right-handed humans, the implication being that these groups differ in cerebral cortex organization. Some studies (using relatively small samples of subjects) linked left-handedness to cognitive deficits. Such data tend to be contradictory, perhaps because some studies classify handedness with a single criterion (such as writing), whereas others employ many behaviors. Further, some individuals are ambidextrous—at least with regard to some tasks—or alternate their hand preference from task to task.

Hardyck, Petrinovich, and Goldman (1976) undertook a large-scale study of handedness and cognitive performance. They examined over 7000 children in grades one through six for school achievement, intellectual ability, motivation, socioeconomic level, and the like. In a detailed analysis of the resultant data they clearly showed that left-handed children did not differ from right-handed children on any measure of cognitive performance.

However, the idea that the left-handed are "damaged" humans has been common in the past and has even found occasional support. Silva and Satz (1979) note that several studies show a higher incidence of left-handedness in clinical populations than in the general population. They examined handedness in over 1400 patients in a school for the mentally retarded and showed an incidence of 17.8% left-handers, about double the level in the general population. In this population more left-handers than right-handers had abnormal EEGs. To explain the high rate of left-handedness in this retarded population, investigators have suggested that the rate is the result of injuries to the brain. Early brain injury, these investigators argue, can cause a shift in handedness. Since most people are right-handed, early one-sided brain injury is more likely to effect a change from right-handedness to left-handedness than the reverse.

Some left-handed persons write by using an inverted hand posture in which the hand is held curved, resting above the written line. This posture contrasts with that of other left-handers, which appears as a mirror image of the writing posture of most right-handers. The awkwardness of the inverted left-handed posture has been viewed as a product of either an attempt to model the characteristic slant of right-handers or a way to gain a better view of the written line. However, a different perspective is offered by the work of Levy and Reid (1976), who argue that these hand postures can be used to predict which hemisphere controls language functions. In their study they compared inverted and noninverted left-handers on visual field tasks. A similarity was noted between right-handers and inverted left-handers in that both showed superiority of right-visual-field verbal tasks, implying left-hemisphere language control. In contrast, noninverted left-handers showed left-visual-field superiority for verbal tasks. A similar right-hemisphere language control was shown by one right-hander with an inverted writing posture—an extreme rarity. This work is controversial; although the relationship to visual field tasks continues to be seen, writing posture of left-handers is not related to other measures of hemispheric specialization, like dichotic-listening tasks (Springer and Deutsch, 1981).

Anatomical and physiological relations to hemispheric differences

The search for the biological bases of hemispheric differences has included both anatomical and neurophysiological studies. Recent research suggests that the two hemispheres have a slightly different form. Comparing the structures of the left and right sides of the body, we note that they are not mirror halves. Marked asymmetry is evident for the heart and liver. Look in the mirror and smile—or if you are not up to that, grimace. Careful examination of facial folding and the edges of the lips shows decided asymmetry. The functional role of these facial asymmetries is unknown (although it has been claimed that expressions on the left side of the face are judged as more emotional). Investigators have not yet explored whether a viewer's interpretation of another person's face is similarly asymmetrical.

In a study of adult temporal lobes Geschwind and Levitsky (1968) at the Harvard Medical School found that in 65% of the brains examined, a region of the cerebral cortex known as the planum temporale was larger in the left hemisphere than in the right hemisphere (Figure 16-13). In 11% the right side was larger. In some studies the magnitude of this left-right difference is almost 2 to 1. The region examined, the upper surface of the temporal lobe, includes part of Wernicke's speech area. Presumably the difference in the size of the area reflects the specialization (dominance) of one cerebral hemisphere for language. The larger left area implies more elaborate development of that side, which might include more nerve cells or greater elaboration of dendrites. This difference in cortical size is even more evident at birth. It appeared in 86% of the infant brains examined. This evidence suggests an intrinsic basis for cerebral dominance in language, since the asymmetry appears before any environmental reinforcement of dominance can occur.

Direct anatomical observations and functional measures like handedness and verbal abilities are not yet available from the same subjects. However, some indirect measures of temporal cortex size can be obtained from arteriograms that reveal the size and course of the middle cerebral artery (LeMay and Culebras, 1972; Hochberg and LeMay, 1975). Of a group of 44 right-handed patients, 86% showed a blood vessel pattern that implied greater left temporal-parietal size, whereas this pattern was seen in only 17% of left-handers. The bulk of left-handers showed no right-left differences.

Figure 16-13 Structural asymmetry of the human temporal lobe. The planum temporale (darker blue area) is larger in the left hemisphere in 65–75% of humans. (Adapted from Geschwind and Levitsky, 1968, copyright 1968 by the American Association for the Advancement of Science.)

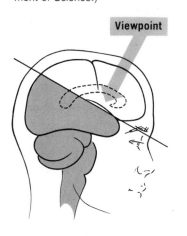

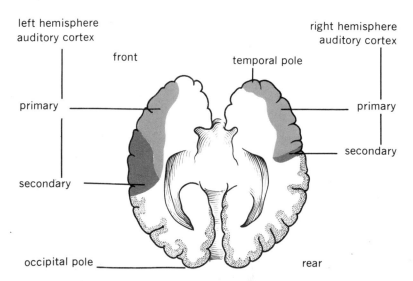

Computer tomograms reveal size differences in some large brain regions, and these differences can be related to overlying skull shape. Using this technique, LeMay (1977) has shown that a majority of right-handers (61%) have wider frontal regions on the right, whereas this pattern was seen in only 40% of left-handers. In contrast, more left-handers had greater left frontal regions. The differences were more pronounced when only familial left-handers were compared with right-handers.

Right-left asymmetry is also seen in both vascular structures of the cerebral hemispheres and measures of cerebral blood flow responses to verbal and nonverbal stimuli. Blood flow to any organ changes with tissue activity. This change is produced by varying the caliber of the blood vessel—producing dilation or constriction. Greater left-hemisphere blood flow has been observed in response to verbal stimuli. Positron emission tomography has recently revealed some startling examples of metabolic differences between the hemispheres with verbal and spatial stimuli.

Origins of hemispheric specialization

To understand some of the workings of the brain it is useful to reflect on the advantages of certain biological states. Of course, the complete story of the rationale of some biological advantages is lost in the history of evolution. The failure of behavior to fossilize might even generate more elaborate speculations. Such is the case in the scrutiny of the biological advantage and presumed evolutionary origins of hemispheric specialization. Let us examine some of these speculations.

Some see the origins of hemispheric specialization in the differential use of the limbs displayed in many routine tasks. Picture an early version of humans hunting. One hand holds the weapon and provides power, while the other is used in more delicate guidance or body balance. Archeological studies of human skulls imply differential use of the limbs in attacking other humans. Proof offered in support of this idea is the more common observations of left skull fracture in fossilized specimens of ancient people. In time the evolutionary successes offered by handedness might have been used in the emergence of language and speech.

Several different theories about the emergence of speech and language have been suggested. Some focus on the motor aspects of speech and others on the cognitive properties of language. The speech motor apparatus involves many delicate muscle systems situated in the midline of the body, like the tip of the tongue. Sensitivity and precision of stimulus analysis on the body surface are reduced in the exact midline. Perhaps this result reflects the mutual antagonism of right and left axon terminals in the skin. For speech this peculiarity of the midline would be catastrophic for precise control. Symmetry of motor control of speech production might then offer better unchallenged control of relevant parts of the speech apparatus. Such sidedness in motor sound production is even seen in the vocal control of singing in birds as we discussed above (Figure 16-3).

Other connections to language and evolutionary advantages of cerebral specialization are seen in arguments that propose a fundamental difference in cognitive style between the hemispheres. According to this view, the left hemisphere provides processing that is analytic, and the right hemisphere offers a more holistic or general analysis of information. Hemisphere specialization allows for separate cognitive modes, which, it is argued, are mutually incompatible. Any linguistic or cognitive response involves acting on elements differently, and hemisphere specialization, it is argued, is a good solution to this need.

We noted earlier that the French Academy had once banned speculations on the origin of language, but no similar movement is afoot with respect to the topic of cerebral specialization. We have discussed only a small sample of current speculations. Further discussion might offer support for the wisdom of the French Academy in the late eighteenth century.

Theories of cognitive differences between human cerebral hemispheres

In the wake of research work on human split-brain patients, considerable speculation developed about cognitive and emotional differences between the hemispheres. This speculation has been further fueled by experimentation with normal humans. Educators concerned about declining accomplishments in primary and secondary schools now speak of educating "both halves of the brain." Bogen (1977), one of the surgeons involved in split-brain operations, urges equal time for each hemisphere in schools. Increasing popularization of the themes of research in this area seems to lead to speculative leaps unbridled by facts.

Actually, distinctions between "left brain" and "right brain" have been drawn even since the dichotomy of verbal versus nonverbal grew from clinical observations of language disorders following left temporal and frontal injuries. Table 16-1 presented a list of differences in cognitive processing proposed by various researchers. Leading this list is the distinction between verbal and nonverbal born from studies of aphasia. However, several experimental observations lead us to question this dichotomy. We have already noted that several studies using split-brain patients show language processing in the right hemisphere. This result becomes increasingly apparent as researchers move away from using speech as the sole measure of linguistic abilities. For example, patients can point to objects whose name is flashed to the left visual fields.

Although some experiments do show task differences between the cerebral hemispheres, the leap to the notion that we harbor two cognitive selves is quite beyond even inspired speculation. We must remember that many differences between the cerebral hemispheres are small and do not indicate that one side is more involved in accomplishment of a particular function. It is very difficult in usual circumstances to direct information exclusively to one hemisphere. Simultaneous processing by the two is the more likely story, and mutual interaction between the cerebral hemispheres is the modal state. Studying hemispheric specialization provides clues about information processing, and these clues indicate that mental unity is the customary human experience. Separate education of each hemisphere is not justified, at least from the vantage point of scientific inquiry to date.

Language development and the brain

Both extrinsic and intrinsic processes determine the acquisition of language. On one hand, there is considerable regularity across all human languages in the timing of stages of language development. During the first year of life, the babbling of all children, no matter in what culture they are reared, sounds similar. On the other hand, the highly specialized attributes of specific languages require the processes of learning during early development. Rare cases of profound isolation in children during early development point to the importance of experience during critical periods early in development.

One focus of developmental studies is the acquisition of lateralization in children as seen in structures of the brain and functions like dichotic listening. Previously we noted that hemispheric asymmetry appears in human infants at birth. Newborn babies turn their heads far more often to the right than to the left (Turkewitz, 1977). Electrophysiological asymmetry of the infant cerebral hemispheres is evident in response to speech sounds. Thus from quite early on structural and functional lateralization exist in the human brain.

Maturation of language development takes time, a result that is reflected in several features of recovery from language impairment following brain injury. This idea is discussed in the last section of this chapter. The essence of these observations is that the brain slowly loses the ability to compensate for injury.

Frontal lobes and behavior

Because the complexity of human beings far exceeds that of other animals, researchers have sought characteristics of the brain that might account for human preeminence. Among the most striking differences is the comparative size of the human prefrontal cortex. In part because of its size, the frontal region has been regarded as the seat of intelligence and abstract thinking. Adding to the mystery of frontal lobe function is the unusual assortment of behavior changes that follow surgical or accidental lesions of this region. The complexity of change following prefrontal damage remains best epitomized by the last sentence of a report written by a physician describing the behavior changes seen in the classical case of Phineas Gage after accidental brain damage. Recall from Chapter 1 that in 1848 Mr. Gage exploded gunpowder which sent an iron rod through his skull, producing a massive lesion of the prefrontal cortex. The last sentence of the physician's report reads, ". . . his mind was radically changed, so decidedly that his friends and acquaintances said that he was 'no longer Gage.' " Now, over 130 years later, research provides some clues to the bases of Phineas Gage's transformation. As we will see in this section, some of the mystery of frontal lobe function has begun to yield to intense experimental analysis.

Analysis of frontal lobe injury

In humans approximately half of the volume of the cerebral cortex consists of frontal cortex. In other animals the frontal cortex, especially prefrontal regions, is a smaller portion of the cerebral cortex (Figure 16-14). The clinical portrait of humans with frontal lesions reveals an unusual collection of emotional, motor, and cognitive changes. Observations of the emotional reactivity of these patients shows a persistent strange apathy, broken by bouts of euphoria with an exalted sense of well-being. Ordinary social conventions seem readily cast aside by impulsive activity. Concern for the past or the future is rarely evident.

Frontal patients show quite shallow emotions, even including reduced responsiveness to pain. Frequently, though, there are episodes in which this apathy is replaced by boastfulness and silliness and, sometimes, unbridled sexual activities.

Cognitive changes in human frontal patients are very complicated and difficult to pinpoint, although one senses that something very different characterizes the frontal patient. Standard IQ test performance shows only slight pre-to-postsurgery changes. Forgetfulness is shown in many tasks requiring sustained attention. In fact, some investigators have commented that these patients even forget their own warnings "to remember."

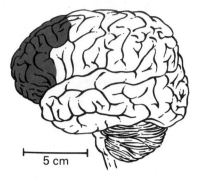

Figure 16-14 Comparisons of the size of prefrontal cortex in various mammals. The relative percentage of prefrontal cortex is greatest in humans and decreases successively in other primates, carnivores, and rodents.

5 cm

(a) Human

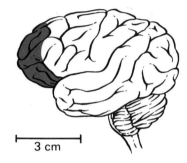

3 cm

(b) Spider monkey

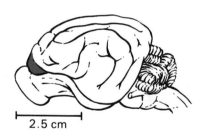

2.5 cm

(c) Cat

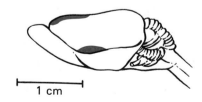

1 cm

(d) Rat

Clinical examination of frontal patients also reveals an array of strange impairments in motor activities, especially in the realm of "plans" for action. The patients seem to perseverate in any activity. For example, if the patient is asked to open and then close the fist, once this activity has begun—and it is difficult to initiate acts like this in frontal patients—the patient continues an unending sequence of fist opening and closing. Overall level of motor activity is quite diminished in frontal patients, especially in the realm of ordinary, spontaneous movements. For example, facial expression becomes quite blank, and there is a marked reduction in head and eye movements. Some reflexes evident only very early in life reappear in frontal cases, such as the infantile grasp reflex of the hand. Many clinical assessments of these patients have emphasized an impairment in goal-directed behavior, especially an inability to plan acts and use foresight. Daily activities of these patients seem disorganized and without a clear program for successive activities.

Prefrontal lesions in nonhumans

The study of prefrontal cortical function in animals starts with the work of Carlyle Jacobsen in the 1930s. In his experiments with chimpanzees he employed delayed-response learning. In this procedure (which has several variants) an animal is presented with two empty food wells within reach of its cage. While the animal views these cups, a morsel of food—a grape, a raisin, or a peanut—is placed in one of the wells. The cups are then covered and an opaque screen is lowered in front of the animal, preventing maintained observation of the wells. After a delay of time, ranging from seconds to minutes, the animal is allowed access to the wells and can retrieve the bit of food. A correct response consists of reaching toward the cup with the food as the initial response. This basic task can be made more difficult by the addition of more cups, and particular cues can be added to alter the information available to the animal in the solution of the problem. Typically normal primates can retrieve the food from the baited cup after an interval of minutes.

This simple test situation revealed a remarkable impairment in chimpanzees with prefrontal lesions. These animals did very poorly in this task, in contrast with animals that sustained lesions in other brain regions. The interpretation of this phenomenon offered by Jacobsen emphasized the memory function of the frontal cortex.

Experimental and clinical observations of humans and other animals with frontal lesions have generated some hypotheses about the functions of the frontal lobes. A large variety of symptoms becomes evident—almost an overabundance—and there are no immediately available generalizations that could account for all these deficits. Some ideas fit more data than others and have thus become a strong focus for work in this area. These hypotheses include memory functions, planning controls, inhibitory control of behavior, and feedback control of behavior. Current evidence offers support for many of these theories.

Parietal cortex syndromes in humans

Injury to the parietal lobe produces impairments such as these: Objects placed in the hand cannot be recognized by touch alone. One side of the body may be completed neglected even to the point of being rejected as one's own. Faces cannot be recognized from photographs. Spatial orientation can become severely disturbed. Diversity of behavior changes following injury to this region is partly related to its large expanse and its critical position adjacent to occipital, temporal, and frontal regions.

The anterior end of the parietal region includes the postcentral gyrus, which is the primary cortical receiving area for somatic sensation. Brain injury in this area does not produce numbness; rather it produces contralateral sensory deficits that seem to involve complex sensory processing. For example, objects placed in the hand contralateral to the injured somatosensory area cannot be identified by touch and active manipulation. This deficit is called **astereognosis,** (from the Greek roots "a," meaning "not" or "lacking," "stereo," meaning "solid," and "gnosis," meaning "knowledge"). It occurs even though primary somatosensory capabilities are relatively intact—that is, the subject feels something in his hand although he cannot identify it. In some cases the deficit occurs on the same side as the brain injury (Corkin, Milner, and Rasmussen, 1970). More extensive injuries in the parietal cortex, not restricted to the somatosensory cortex, affect interactions between or among sensory modalities, such as visual-tactual matching tasks, which require the subject to identify visually an object that was touched, or the reverse.

Perceptual deficits

Through the course of life people acquire a large memory store of familiar faces, ranging from family members to prominent figures appearing on television programs. Recognition of these faces involves both integration of visual inputs and connections with memories of these faces. The process of facial recognition is so commonplace that it is startling to come across instances in which the ability to recognize faces is abolished following brain injury. Over the years a small number of patients have been described who lose the ability to recognize a familiar face on the basis of visual information, although these patients are able to perceive a face as a face. Here is an example of this disability in a man following a stroke (Cohn,

Neumann, and Woods, 1977): He became unable to recognize his wife when she stood among a group of people in front of him until she spoke; he also had difficulty recognizing his own face from photographs. This deficit is never seen in isolation from other difficulties, which include visual field defects, memory loss, and spatial disorientation (Benton, 1979).

Although some investigators have attributed this syndrome to right-hemisphere parietal-occipital lesions, most data point to a bilateral origin. The patient of Cohn, Neumann, and Woods (1977) showed bilateral obstruction of the posterior cerebral artery, which affected large regions of the visual cortex and the hippocampal gyrus. The lateral geniculate bodies in this patient showed extensive cell loss, which suggests that decreased transmission of visual information may be an ingredient in this syndrome, although these patients are far from being blind.

In other reported cases it was not faces but some other category for which individuals lost the ability to recognize specific items with which they had been familiar. For example, after her stroke a woman who loved flowers could no longer recognize individual species. She could see and describe a flower that was presented to her, but she could no longer recognize what kind of flower it was. Her loss was rather specific, because she could identify correctly other plants such as vegetables. In another case a man who knew all the makes of automobiles could no longer recognize them, although he could correctly classify vehicles into categories such as fire engine, truck, and automobile.

Deficits of spatial orientation following parietal lesions can be revealed in many simple ways. For example, a patient might be quite familiar with the geography of an area, but when asked to produce a broad-scale map of an area, would mislocate places. This deficit even extends to tasks like drawing a route from home to work—a path the patient might have followed for years. Defective performance in simple tasks like mazes is also evident, especially with right-hemisphere parietal damage.

Unilateral neglect

Brain damage involving the right inferior parietal cortex produces a very unusual set of behavior changes. The key feature is the neglect of the left side of both the body and space. For example, when a patient is asked to draw the face of a clock all the hour positions are crowded onto the right side (Figure 16-15). Patients may fail to dress the left side of their body and may even disclaim "ownership" of their left arm or leg. In some instances familiar people presented on the left side of the patient are completely neglected, although there may be no apparent visual field defect. The

(a)

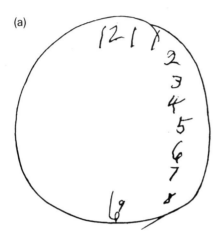

(b)

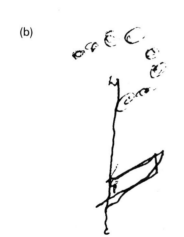

Figure 16-15 The neglect syndrome following right parietal cortex damage. (a) If such a patient is asked to draw a typical clock face, the left side is ignored and all hours are placed on the right. (b) When asked to copy a drawing of a daisy, the patient draws petals only on the right (Heilman, 1979). When asked to bisect a line, the patient places a mark well to the right of the midpoint, showing that he largely ignores the left.

(c)

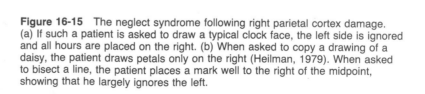

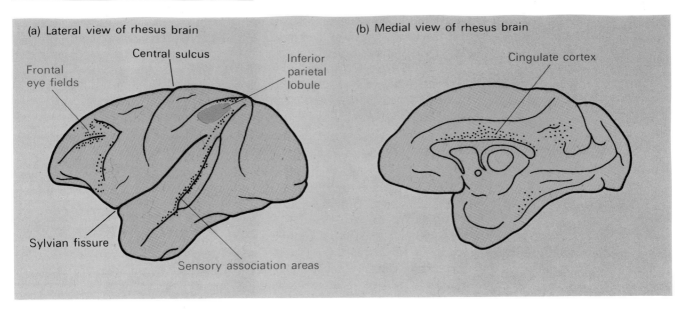

Figure 16-16 Regions of the cortex that are implicated in different aspects of unilateral neglect, shown on lateral (a) and medial (b) views of the monkey brain. (Adapted from Mesulam et al., 1977)

phenomenon of hemispatial neglect can also be seen in simple test situations. A common test requires the patient to bisect a horizontal line presented on a piece of paper. Estimates of the center are markedly shifted to the right, and this effect is particularly marked when lines are presented to the left of the center of the body (Schenkerberg, Bradford, and Ajax, 1980).

Associated with this dramatic change is a feature called "extinction of simultaneous double stimulation." Most people can readily report the presence of two stimuli when stimulated simultaneously on both sides of the body. Patients with right inferior parietal lesions are completely unable to note the double nature of the stimulation and usually report only the stimulus presented to the right side. Although many patients with injury to this region show recovery from the symptom of unilateral neglect, the feature of extinction is quite persistent.

Yet another dramatic feature of this syndrome is the frequent failure to recognize illness, referred to as "denial of illness." Such patients may adamantly maintain that they are quite capable of engaging in their customary activities and do not recognize the impressive signs of unilateral neglect.

Many hypotheses have been offered to account for these symptoms. Some have regarded the disorder as the consequence of the loss of spatial pattern analysis; this hypothesis is consistent with the fact that unilateral neglect occurs with lesions of the right hemisphere but not with lesions of the left hemisphere. Others regard it as an attentional deficit.

A recent theory of the neurologist Mesulam (1981) offers an explanation of some properties of the neglect syndrome. Mesulam notes that single-cell recordings from posterior parietal cortex in monkeys show firing patterns that are sensitive to manipulations of attention. For example, some nerve cells in this area increase their discharge rates when the animal's eyes follow or track a meaningful object, frequently one that has been associated with reward. Anatomical studies of the sources of inputs to the posterior parietal region show origins in several distinct cortical sectors (Figure 16-16) including polymodal cortical sensory areas, cingulate cortex, and frontal cortex especially frontal eye fields. In turn, posterior parietal cortex has outputs that go back to these regions. Mesulam has proposed that each of these regions has some distinctive role in a network governing attention. The posterior parietal component involves processes that yield an internal sensory map, while frontal cortex governs relevant searching movements, and cingulate cortex processing provides motivational values.

Recovery of function following brain injury

The course of behavior following brain injury often reveals striking changes. Aphasia following a stroke that involves regions of the left hemisphere may not have disappeared a year later. Yet striking examples of language recovery following removal of an entire hemisphere have been shown in children. For example, data cited by Woods and Teuber (1979) show complete language recovery for several children who were aphasic from a brain injury sustained before the age of 8. Strokes in adults also reveal striking examples of restoration of many behaviors lost after immobilizing brain injury. For many injuries in adults, deficits seen in acute or early stages show decisive changes in time—a clear recovery of function.

Many theories are currently being offered to describe the mechanisms mediating recovery of function after lesions. Of course, recovery of function is characteristic of lesions involving many different organs. The surprise and puzzle of such effects following brain injury comes from the knowledge that, unlike other organs, the nervous system does not add neurons to any significant extent following birth. In addition, views that were quite common until the last few years emphasized structural and functional fixedness of the brain—rigidity that seemed to provide little opportunity to compensate for a loss of elements. Within the last ten years, research in recovery of brain functions has provided an exciting array of ideas and data that reveal several forms of brain plasticity. Studies in this area offer prospects for rehabilitation that are quite striking. We will consider some of the findings and notions of recovery mechanisms in this active area of research. Perhaps many different mechanisms together contribute to the patterns of recovery, so no single explanation can be offered as the sole basis.

Recovery from general physiological abnormalities

Any brain injury destroys particular collections of nerve cells and produces more generalized disturbances that transiently affect the responsiveness of other nerve cells. For example, in the region of a brain injury there is frequently a change in the properties of the blood-brain barrier. Some researchers have suggested that the time course of functional deficits following structural damage to nerve cells might reflect the inhibitory impact of blood-borne substances, which are ordinarily prevented from reaching the environment of nerve cells (Seil, Leiman, and Kelly, 1976). In time the changes in the blood vessels around a site of injury reestablish the blood-brain barrier and also increase blood flow to transiently distressed but intact tissue. Many years ago the term **diaschisis** was coined by the anatomist von Monakow (1914) to describe the distant inhibitory effects of brain lesions that seemed to be reversible. Over time the usage of the term diaschisis has expanded to include a host of potentially reversible, nonspecific effects that make the immediate consequences of a brain lesion more intense than persistent deficits.

Anatomical regrowth in the brain following injury

Anatomical dogma for many years declared that anatomical changes in the adult central nervous system are solely destructive. The intricate structure and connections of nerve cells were considered to be structurally fixed once adulthood was reached. Injury, it was thought, could only lead to the shrinkage or death of nerve cells. Many impressive contemporary demonstrations to the contrary have now led us to emphasize structural plasticity of nerve cells and their connections (see Chapter 15). Of course, regeneration of the axons of the peripheral nervous system has always been accepted. Now comparable structural regrowth has been seen in the brain and spinal cord (Veraa and Grafstein, 1981). For example, injury to catecholamine-containing fibers in the medial forebrain bundle leads to degeneration of terminal portions of the axon and regrowth of axonal portions connected to nerve cells. Dendritic regrowth following injury may also occur in the brain.

Another form of structural change is seen in the spinal cord and brain—collateral sprouting. This change has been described in the peripheral nervous system, and the story goes like this: If a peripheral sensory or motor fiber is injured, there follows degeneration of the terminal portions and an immediate loss of sensory or motor function in the affected region. Nerve fibers adjacent to the injured fibers recognize this injury (perhaps by a chemical signal delivered from the injured site), and they respond by developing sprouts or branches from intact axons. In time, usually weeks, these sprouts connect to denervated skin or muscle and acquire functional control of these regions on the periphery of the body (J. Diamond et al., 1976). This mechanism seems to result in functional compensation for a loss of neuronal connections. Incidentally, it should be noted that the injured nerve fiber (axon) slowly regrows, and, as it approaches the skin or muscles it had been connected to, there is a retraction of the sprouts. Again, chemical signals from the regrowing original fiber probably produce this change. Mark (1980) has suggested that a stage prior to the actual physical withdrawal of the fiber includes the cessation of synaptic effectiveness of the sprout-borne connections—a phenomenon he labeled "synaptic repression." This result implies that synapses can be turned off even though the structural connection is still present. This switching of effectiveness of synapses is probably a significant feature of neural plasticity.

Demonstrations of collateral sprouting in the brain and spinal cord, which at one time were never observed, are now reported with regularity. Some investigators (such as Raisman, 1978) suggest that collateral sprouting in the brain offers hope for functional repair following injury.

Observations of this sort indicate that brain connections are not as rigid anatomically as was once emphasized. The brain's response to injury does include structural modifications. However, are these anatomical changes relevant to the processes of functional repair? Around this question, controversy swirls. Although structural repair in the brain in the form of collateral sprouting is now generally accepted, there is no evidence that links this change with functional recovery following injury to the brain or spinal cord. In fact, some investigators (Wall, 1980) suggest that collateral sprouting might generate behavioral abnormalities, since nerve cells come under the control of unusual inputs. This form of regeneration in the spinal cord has been linked to spasticity in reflexes elicited below the level of a spinal injury (Liu and Chambers, 1958). Intensive research currently in progress is aimed at evaluating the functional value of such brain regrowth as collateral sprouting.

Education and rehabilitation

For years hospitals and physicians have devoted considerable attention to providing rehabilitation for injuries that impair movement, especially if these defects developed from injury or disease of muscle or bone. For instance, teaching amputees to use prosthetic devices like artificial limbs has been a common effort. But until recently work with cognitive or perceptual handicaps that develop from brain impairments had received less intensive clinical and research interest. Several factors have provided the stimulus for a change of emphasis.

Some recent studies have demonstrated that postinjury experience can affect recovery. It is important at this point to distinguish between the role of experience in compensating for brain injury and its role in restoring behavior lost after injury. It is well known that experiences significantly reduce the impact of brain injury by fostering the elaboration of compensatory behavior. For example, vigorous eye movements can make up for large scotomas that result from injury to the visual pathways. Behavior strategies can change after a brain injury to allow for successful performance on a variety of tests. The role of experience following a lesion in possible reorganization of pathways is also evident in several studies.

Recently, Teodoru and Berman (1980) described a striking phenomenon of recovery that involves a change in feedback signals governing behavior. In experiments with monkeys they showed that unilateral section of the dorsal roots as they enter the spinal cord results in animals that do not show spontaneous use of the affected limb. It is placed at the side as though paralyzed. To facilitate use of this limb, these investigators placed a hollow ball over the intact hand. This technique allowed free movement of the hand within the ball, but movements of the normal arm could not be used in securing food or other adaptive acts. With such maximal demands placed on the affected limb, it began to move more frequently. After four months the monkey showed coordinated activity of the denervated limb, including finger movement and reaching behavior. Performance of the denervated limb continued when the intact limb was removed from the ball. However, if the duration of this recovery experience was less than four months, coordinated movements of the two limbs did not persist and the denervated limb resumed its paralyzed posture.

The importance of training and experience in promoting recovery has been suggested by clinical observations and has been studied in animal experiments. A well-known case of aphasia and slow but excellent recovery is that of the actress Patricia Neal. Before she had a stroke at the age of 39, Patricia Neal had won an Academy Award. She was the mother of three children, and at the time of her stroke she was pregnant. A series of strokes crippled one leg and left her aphasic, unable to speak, read, or write. Speech therapy was begun as soon as possible. Then her husband organized friends to come in on schedule to talk with Pat and encourage her to speak and be active. Her baby was born normally. At this point Pat was still rather apathetic and was reluctant to continue to strive for further small gains: "I got fed up with working so hard. I felt certain that I was as good as I'd ever be. I was about eighty percent recovered. Still plenty of problems. But I was really ready to take a breather. And that's exactly what I would have done if Roald [her husband] hadn't made me go on. I had reached the danger point. The point where so many people stop work and just cruise along" (Griffith, 1970, p. 89). Her husband then hired a gifted nurse, Valerie Eaton Griffith, who devised a program of motivation and training that helped Pat to make further gains. Four years after her stroke Patricia

Neal was able to star in another movie. Recovery is probably never absolutely complete after a major brain lesion, but it can be full enough to permit an active life and even a resumption of professional activities, as this example shows.

Animal experiments have shown that both formal training and informal enriched experience can promote recovery of function. Several studies performed with brain-lesioned rats have demonstrated that postlesion experience in a complex environment can improve subsequent problem-solving behavior (Will et al., 1977). Animals were placed in impoverished or enriched environments of the same kinds that had been shown to lead to changes in brain measures (Chapter 15). Although the brain-injured animals still made more errors than intact rats, those from the enriched environments made significantly fewer errors than those from the impoverished environments. Simply placing a group of animals together in a large cage had a measurable beneficial effect, but giving the animals access to varied stimuli was still more helpful (Rosenzweig, 1980). Thus even an injured brain can profit from experience. In the case of human patients, some experts in rehabilitation have questioned the wisdom of placing certain patients in virtual sensory isolation (coma patients, or patients kept in fixed positions in isolated rooms for intravenous therapy). Quite possibly such patients, even if they cannot respond, might be aided by visitors, music, and changing visual stimuli.

Substitution by remaining brain structures

Recovery following brain injury demonstrates that remaining neural tissue can mediate required behaviors. One perspective suggests that there is appreciable "redundancy" of neural systems and that recovery involves the use of redundant pathways. However, what appears to be redundancy may arise from the complexity of the neural substrates of behavior and the simple ways in which recovery is assessed. Thus if the neural substrate for some behavior is broadly represented in the brain, behavior may be reinstated because of the extensiveness of neural controls rather than because of redundant or repeated systems.

Another kind of unusual substitution has been described by Wall (1980). He studied the receptive field properties of dorsal column and thalamic cells following peripheral denervation. Wall noted that sizes of receptive fields of cells in this system change with denervation, especially in the direction of increasing size. Cells may also become responsive to bilateral inputs. Thus change occurs rapidly, and Wall suggests that denervation unmasks weakly excitable paths that come to control some neurons. He refers to this effect as a "homeostatic adjustment" of nerve cell excitability. Switching of nerve cell responsiveness in sensory paths is also evident in the vestibular system. Section of the vestibular nerve or unilateral removal of the labyrinth on one side results in head tilting or deviation and other signs of postural asymmetry. In time these effects abate, illustrating a phenomenon known as "vestibular compensation." Some of this recovery depends on inputs from the spinal cord (Jensen, 1979). Another independent aspect of recovery is a change in the activity of brainstem vestibular neurons.

Age and recovery of function

Many clinical observations have led to the general proposition that brain lesions earlier in life have less disastrous consequences than similar injuries sustained later in life. The explanation offered for this phenomenon is that the younger brain

BOX 16-3   Childhood Loss of One Hemisphere

During early development the brain is a vulnerable organ, a phenomenon especially apparent when looking at the effect of a prolonged, difficult birth involving a period of oxygen loss. Some children with this early physiological deficit show lateralized brain injury involving a single cerebral hemisphere. Early on, such a child may show paralysis on one side of the body and frequent seizures. These seizures can be quite difficult to control with medication, and they may occur so often that they endanger life. Major brain damage on one side is shown in radiological data; the injured hemisphere can be quite shrunken.

Surgical removal of the malfunctioning hemisphere reduces seizures. Although at first some severe effects of the surgery are evident, over a long period of time the restoration of behavior is practically complete. This result is strikingly illustrated in a case presentation of Smith and

Sugar (1975). As an infant, the boy showed a right-side paralysis and by $5\frac{1}{2}$ years of age he was experiencing 10 to 12 seizures a day. Although the boy's verbal comprehension was normal, his speech was hard to understand. All the cerebral cortex of the left hemisphere was therefore removed. Long-term follow-up studies extended to age $26\frac{1}{2}$, when he had almost completed college. Tests revealed an above-normal IQ and superior language abilities; thus the early loss of the left hemisphere did not preclude language development. This patient also has remarkable development of nonverbal functions, including visuospatial tasks and manual tasks. Note that adult hemispherectomy of the left side usually results in drastic impairment of language affecting both speech and writing. This case thus provides an example of extensive functional recovery after childhood loss.

possesses greater plasticity, although it is also acknowledged that especially the infant brain is more vulnerable to some destructive agents like viruses. A recent study of human language impairments and age provides an example of the relations between maturational state and recovery of function.

In a survey of childhood aphasia Woods and Teuber (1978) examined records of a large group of children who lost language abilities following brain damage. The age of 8 looms as a critical point in recovery from brain trauma. All children who became aphasic before the age of 8 regained speech no matter how great the impairment observed immediately following brain injury. (An example is given in Box 16-3.) The time for recovery of language ranged from one month to two years. Many children who became aphasic after age 8 showed less complete recovery.

Differences in nerve cell regrowth processes have been related to age in several studies. Kalil and Rey (1979) noted that section of the pyramidal tract at the level of the medulla in infant hamsters is followed by massive regrowth. They also note that, in contrast to adult hamsters, these infant hamsters develop normal motor functions of the forepaw. Regenerative capabilities seem to change in senescent states, according to Scheff, Bernardo, and Cotman (1978). Reactive regrowth is very sparse in the aged rat brain. The researchers argue that this result implies a reduction in the ability to remodel circuitry with aging.

Studies in nonhumans that explore the factor of age in recovery yield both similarities with and differences from humans. Patricia Goldman (1976) has contributed studies of the relations between maturation of the brain in monkeys and development of their behavior and has reviewed research of others in this field. One of her studies employed the technique of implanting devices in the brains of monkeys by means of which a local area of the cortex could be cooled and thus inactivated for a period of time in an awake monkey. This technique produces, in effect, a reversible brain lesion. Bilateral cooling of the prefrontal cortex in adult monkeys (3 years old or older) was found to impair their performance on a delayed-response task. However, it did not affect their general level of activity or motor coordination. But in juvenile monkeys (18 months old or younger), the cooling had no effect on the test performance. This result is in line with other evidence that the frontal dorsolateral cortex in the monkey does not achieve its adult function until after the monkey is 2 years old.

Lesion momentum and deficits

The impairment caused by a brain lesion is greater the faster the lesion develops. For this reason some investigators speak of the lesion's momentum, or mass × velocity (Finger, 1978). It is curious but true that the same amount of tissue destruction may have much less effect if it occurs gradually than if it occurs swiftly. Investigators have studied this phenomenon by removing a given amount of tissue all at once in some experimental animals and in stages separated by a few weeks in other animals. A lesion in the brainstem that incapacitates animals if the removal is made all at one time may have only slight effect if it is done in two successive stages. Perhaps the partial lesion stimulates regrowth or relearning or both, so that some compensation has already been achieved by the time the rest of the tissue is removed. Some experimenters have reported that sensory stimulation or retraining during the interval between successive lesions is necessary for the reduced impairment observed with staged destruction, but not all studies agree.

Recent experimental findings suggest a mechanism for the staged-lesion effect: When a lesion causes loss of synaptic connections, this may result in the release of chemical signals that facilitate sprouting of terminals. When a small lesion precedes a larger lesion by 4 days to 2 weeks, the response to the second lesion is significantly faster and more extensive than if the earlier lesion had not occurred. Thus the earlier lesion primes the system to respond to the subsequent lesion (Scheff, Bernardo, and Cotman, 1978).

Clinical cases also reveal effects of lesion momentum. For example, an adult patient with a brain tumor encroaching on the speech areas of his left hemisphere had several operations, spaced many months apart (Geschwind, 1976). Each time the tumor regrew, it was necessary to remove more of the cortical speech areas, and each time the patient recovered his speech. Finally he was speaking even though only a fragment of the speech areas remained. The effects of aging on the brain can also be thought of as a slowly developing condition, which probably helps to mitigate them.

The phenomenon of lesion momentum is one of the reasons it is difficult to relate the effects of a disease-caused brain lesion to its size. This phenomenon can help us understand some cases that seem to contradict localization of function. That is, brain lesions in two patients may appear to be the same in size and location, yet one patient will show severe behavioral impairment while the second will not. Perhaps the lesion in the second patient developed slowly, allowing time both for growth in adjacent tissue and also for elaboration of compensatory behavioral strategies. Thus the phenomenon of lesion momentum shows that the brain cannot be regarded as a fixed piece of machinery but must be seen as a plastic structure that adapts to imposed conditions.

In this section we have noted several examples and mechanisms related to functional recovery following brain lesions. These various mechanisms are not mutually exclusive—all may contribute to the pattern of reinstating behavior, for regrowth might provide an opportunity for some forms of recovery but require the sustaining impact of experience. Therefore synaptic regrowth alone may not provide the substrate of recovery. Regrowth in conjunction with appropriately timed experience may be the formula for plasticity.

As the field of neurological rehabilitation develops and efforts to aid the brain-injured become more extensive, we will gain more accurate knowledge of both the possibilities and the limits of recovery.

SUMMARY / MAIN POINTS

1. Humans are distinct in the animal kingdom for their language and associated cognitive abilities. Possible evolutionary origins of human speech may be seen in aspects of gestures.

2. Studies of nonhumans provide analogies to human speech. For example, controls of birdsong are lateralized in the brains of some species of singing birds. Further, in some of these species early experience is essential for proper song development.

3. Limitations of the vocal tract in nonhumans is proposed as one reason they do not have speech. But nonhuman primates like the chimpanzee can learn to use signs of the American Sign Language. However, controversy surrounds claims that these animals can arrange signs in novel orders, such as in the process of creating a new sentence.

4. Left-hemisphere injuries produce language impairments in 95% of people. Left anterior lesions produce an impairment in speech production called Broca's aphasia. More posterior lesions involving the temporal-parietal cortex affect speech comprehension, as seen in Wernicke's aphasia.

5. Left-hemisphere lesions in users of sign language produce impairments in the use of sign language that are similar to impairments in spoken language shown by nondeaf aphasics.

6. Split-brain patients show striking examples of hemispheric specialization. Most words projected to the right hemisphere cannot be read, while the same stimuli directed to the left hemisphere can be read. Verbal abilities of the right hemisphere are also reduced; however, spatial-relation tasks are performed better by the right hemisphere than by the left.

7. Normal humans also show many forms of cognitive specialization of the cerebral hemispheres, although they are not as striking as those shown by split-brain patients. For example, most normal humans show a right-ear advantage and greater right visual field accuracy for verbal stimuli.

8. Anatomical asymmetry of the hemispheres is seen in some structures in the human brain. Especially striking is the large size difference in the planum temporale (which is larger in the left hemisphere of most right-handers).

9. Broad theoretical statements about different cognitive modes of the two hemispheres exceed confirmations from current experimental and clinical data. In most cases mental activity depends on interactions between the cerebral hemispheres.

10. The frontal lobes of humans are quite large in comparison with those of other animals. Injury in this region produces an unusual syndrome of profound emotional changes, including reduced responsiveness to many stimuli. Tasks that require sustained attention show drastic impairment after frontal lesions.

11. In most patients parietal cortex injuries on the right side produce many perceptual changes. A dramatic example is the inability to recognize familiar objects and the faces of familiar people. Some patients with right parietal injury neglect or ignore the left side of both the body and space.

12. Many functional losses following brain injury show

at least partial recovery. In aphasia the bulk of recovery occurs in the year following stroke, with fewer changes evident after that.

13. Mechanisms of functional recovery may involve structural regrowth of cell extensions—dendrites and axons—and the formation of new synapses.

14. Retraining is a significant part of function recovery and may involve both compensation, by establishing new solutions to adaptive demands, and reorganization of surviving networks.

15. Greater recovery is evident in younger individuals. Less impairment occurs when lesions are produced over a period of time.

RECOMMENDED READING

Bach-y-Rita, P. (Ed.). *Recovery of function following brain injury: Theoretical considerations*. Bern: Hans Huber, 1980.

Finger, F. *Recovery from brain damage: Research and theory*. New York: Plenum, 1978.

Heilman, K., and Valenstein, E. (Eds.). *Clinical neuropsychology*. New York: Oxford University Press, 1979.

Herron, J. (Ed.). *Neuropsychology of left-handedness*. New York: Academic Press, 1980.

Springer, S. P., and Deutsch, G. *Left brain, right brain*. San Francisco: Freeman, 1981.

Glossary

absolute refractory phase A period of complete unresponsiveness. The absolute refractory phase of the neuron is shown in Figure 4–5. The absolute refractory phase of the male sexual response cycle is indicated in Figure 9–6(a).

acetylcholine (ACh) One of the best known synaptic transmitters. Acetylcholine acts as an excitatory transmitter at synapses between motor nerves and skeletal muscles but as an inhibitory transmitter between vagus nerve and heart muscle.

acetylcholinesterase (AChE) An enzyme that inactivates the transmitter *acetylcholine** both at synaptic sites and elsewhere in the nervous system, thus halting its effects.

ACh See *acetylcholine.*

AChE See *acetylcholinesterase.*

ACTH See *adrenocorticotropic hormone.*

action potential See *nerve impulse.*

acupuncture The insertion and rotation of needles in various parts of the body for relief of pain.

adaptation A progressive loss of receptor sensitivity as stimulation is maintained. See Figure 6–15.

adenohypophysis See *anterior pituitary.*

adequate stimulus The type of stimulus for which a given sense organ is particularly adapted, e.g., light energy for photoreceptors.

ADH See *antidiuretic hormone.*

adipsia A condition in which an individual refuses to drink.

adrenal cortex The outer bark of the adrenal gland. The three cellular layers of the adrenal cortex each produce different hormones.

adrenal gland An endocrine gland adjacent to each kidney; see Figure 5–1.

adrenal medulla The inner core of the adrenal gland.

adrenocorticotropic hormone (ACTH) A tropic hormone secreted by the anterior pituitary gland which controls the production and release of hormones of the *adrenal cortex.* See Figure 5–6.

afferent fibers Axons carrying nerve impulses from sense organs to the central nervous system; opposite of *efferent.*

after potentials Positive and negative changes of membrane potential that may follow a nerve impulse.

aldosterone A *mineralocorticoid* hormone that helps maintain homeostasis in the concentrations of ions in blood and extracellular fluid.

all-or-none Refers to the fact that the amplitude of the nerve impulse is independent of stimulus magnitude. Stimuli above a certain threshold produce nerve impulses of identical magnitude (although they may vary in frequency); stimuli below this threshold do not produce nerve impulses. See Figure 4–3.

alpha motoneurons Motoneurons that control the main contractile fibers (extrafusal fibers) of a muscle. See Figure 8–9.

alpha rhythm A brain potential that occurs during relaxed wakefulness, especially at the back of the head; frequency 8–12 Hz. See Figure 4–24.

altricial Refers to animals born in a relatively developed state who are able to survive without maternal care; opposite of *precocial.*

Alzheimer's disease Dementia which occurs in middle age (45–60).

amblyopia Reduced visual acuity not caused by optical or retinal impairments.

ampulla An enlarged region of each *semicircular canal* that contains the receptor cells (hair cells) of the vestibular system. See Figure 6–9.

amygdala A group of nuclei in the medial anterior part of the temporal lobe. See Figures 11–8, 13–16, and 14–6.

angiogram A technique for examining brain structure in intact humans by taking X-rays after special dyes are injected into cerebral blood vessels. Inferences about adjacent tissue can be made by examining the outline of the principal blood vessels. See Figure 2–16.

angiotensin II A substance produced in the blood by the action of renin and which may be involved in control of thirst.

anions Negatively charged ions, such as protein and chloride ions.

anorexic Lacking in appetite for food.

anterior pituitary The front lobe of the pituitary gland which secretes tropic hormones; also called *adenohypophysis.* See Figure 5–5.

anterograde degeneration Loss of the distal portion of the axon resulting from injury to the axon; also called *Wallerian degeneration.* See Box Figure 3–4.

antidiuretic hormone (ADH) A hormone from the posterior pituitary that controls the removal of water from blood by the kidneys. Also called *vasopressin.*

aphagia Refusal to eat, often related to damage to the lateral hypothalamus.

aphasia Impairments in language understanding and/or production due to brain injury.

appetitive behavior The second stage of mating behavior that

*Italicised words are defined in the Glossary.

i

helps establish or maintain sexual interaction. See Figure 9–2.

apraxia An impairment in the ability to begin and execute skilled voluntary movements although there is no muscle paralysis.

associative learning A form of learning in which an association is formed between two stimuli or between a stimulus and a response; includes both classical and instrumental conditioning. Contrast with *nonassociative learning*.

astrocyte A star-shaped glial cell with numerous processes or extensions that run in all directions. Their extensions provide structural support for the brain and may isolate receptive surfaces. See Figure 2–27.

ataxia Impairment in the direction, extent, and rate of muscular movement; often due to cerebellar pathology.

auditory cortex A region of the temporal lobe that receives input from the *medial geniculate nucleus*. See Figures 6–19, 7–17.

autonomic nervous system Part of the peripheral nervous system that supplies neural connections to glands and to smooth muscles of internal organs. Composed of two divisions (sympathetic and parasympathetic) that act in opposite fashion. See Figure 2–15.

autonomic response specificity Patterns of bodily response governed by the autonomic nervous system, that are characteristic of an individual.

autoradiography A histological technique that shows the distribution of radioactive chemicals.

autoreceptors Receptors for synaptic transmitters located in the presynaptic membrane. These receptors inform the axon terminal of the amount of transmitter released. See 6 in Figure 4–19.

autosomes Pairs of chromosomes that are identical; that is, all chromosomes except the sex chromosomes.

axon A single extension from the cell body which carries nerve impulses from the cell body to other neurons. See Figure 2–21.

axon hillock A cone-shaped area from which the axon originates out of the cell body. Depolarization must reach a critical threshold here for the neuron to transmit a nerve impulse. See Figure 2–21.

axoplasmic streaming The process that transports materials synthesized in the cell body to distant regions in the dendrites and axons.

basal ganglia A group of forebrain nuclei found deep within the cerebral hemispheres. See Figure 8–19.

bases Components of a DNA or RNA molecule. DNA contains four bases (adenine, thyamine, cytosine, and guanine), a pair of which forms each rung of the molecule. The order of these bases determines the genetic information of a DNA molecule. See Box Figure 3–1.

basic neuroglial compartment A level of brain organization which includes a single nerve cell with all its synaptic endings, associated glial cells surrounding extracellular space, and vascular elements. See Figure 2–17.

basic rest-activity cycle Repeating cycles of rest and activity that occur both in waking hours and during sleep.

basilar artery An artery formed by the fusion of the vertebral arteries; its branches supply blood to the brainstem and to posterior portions of the cerebral hemispheres. See Figure 2–10.

basilar membrane A membrane in the cochlea containing the principal structures involved in auditory transduction. See Figure 6–7.

ballism Uncontrollable violent tossing of the limbs due to basal ganglia dysfunction.

ballistic Classes of rapid muscular movements thought to be organized or programmed by the cerebellum. Contrast with *ramp*.

behavioral intervention An approach to finding relations between bodily variables and behavioral variables that involves intervening in the behavior of an organism and looking for resultant changes in bodily structure or function. See Figure 1–7.

behavioral teratology Impairments in behavior produced by early exposure to toxic substances.

binocular disparity The slight difference between the views from the two eyes, important in depth perception. See Figure 7–8.

biofeedback A technique that allows a person to monitor some bodily variable such as skin temperature or the gross electrical activity of the brain. This information allows the person to gain some control over the bodily variable and may be used in the treatment of various disorders. See Figure 13–5.

bipolar depression Depression that alternates with mania. Contrast with *unipolar depression*.

bipolar neurons Nerve cells with a single dendrite at one end of the nerve cell and a single axon at the other end. Found in some vertebrate sensory systems. See Figure 2–20.

blind spot A place through which blood vessels enter the retina. Because there are no receptors in this region, light striking it cannot be seen. See Figure 7–6.

blood-brain barrier The mechanisms that make the movement of substances from capillaries into brain cells more difficult than exchanges in other body organs, thus affording the brain a greater protection from exposure to some substances found in the blood. See Figure 2–11.

brainstem reticular formation Part of the brainstem involved in arousal. See Figure 12–13.

brightness One of the basic dimensions of light perception. This varies from dark to light. See Figure 7–2.

Broca's aphasia Impairment in speech production, related to damage in Broca's area.

Broca's area An area in the frontal region of the left hemisphere involved in the production of speech. See Figure 16–4.

calcitonin A hormone released by the thyroid gland.

cAMP See *cyclic adenosine monophosphate*.

cations Positively charged ions, such as potassium and sodium.

caudal An anatomical term meaning toward the tail end. Opposed to *rostral*.

caudate nucleus One of the basal ganglia with a long extension or tail.

CCK See *cholecystokinin*.

cell body The region of a neuron which is defined by the presence of the nucleus. See Figure 2–19.

cell death The final developmental process in shaping the nervous system during which "surplus" nerve cells die.

cell differentiation The prenatal stage in which neuroblasts acquire the distinctive appearance of cells characteristic of a region of the nervous system. See Figure 3–7.

cell proliferation The production of nerve cells. See Figure 3–5.

cellular fluid See *intracellular fluid*.

central deafness Hearing impairments related to lesions in auditory pathways or centers, including sites in the brainstem, thalamus, or cortex.

central nervous system (CNS) The portion of the nervous system that includes the brain and the spinal cord. See Figure 2–8.

cephalic An anatomical term referring to the head end. Also called *rostral*.

cerebellar cortex The outer surface of the cerebellum. See Figure 2–29.

cerebellum A structure located at the back of the brain, dorsal to the pons; it is involved in the central regulation of movement. See Figure 2–29.

cerebral cortex The outer bark or cortex of the cerebral hemispheres which consists largely of nerve cell bodies and their branches. See Figure 2–30.

cerebral hemispheres The right and left halves of the forebrain. See Figure 2–1.

cerebrospinal fluid The fluid filling the cerebral *ventricles*. See Figure 2–9.

cerveau isolé An animal with the nervous system transected at the upper level of the midbrain (between the inferior and superior colliculus). Contrast with the *encéphale isolé*. See Figure 12–12.

cervical Pertaining to the neck region.

chemical transmitter See *synaptic transmitter*.

chlorpromazine An antipsychotic drug, one of the class of phenothiazines.

cholecystokinin (CCK) A hormone released from the lining of the duodenum which may be involved in the satiation of hunger.

cholinergic Refers to cells that use *acetylcholine* as their synaptic transmitter.

chorda tympani A portion of the facial nerve that serves taste receptors in the anterior two-thirds of the tongue.

choreic movements Uncontrollable, brief, and forceful muscular movements related to basal ganglia dysfunction.

chromosomes Structures in the nucleus of the cell which contain a *DNA* molecule and associated protein molecules.

cingulum A region of medial cerebral cortex lying dorsal to the *corpus callosum*. Also called *cingulate cortex*. See Figure 13–11.

circadian rhythms Behavioral, biochemical, and physiological fluctations that have a 24-hour period.

circle of Willis A structure at the base of the brain formed by the joining of the carotid and basilar arteries. See Figure 2–10.

circuit A level of brain organization which includes an arrangement of neurons and their interconnections. These assemblages often perform a particular limited function. A local circuit is a circuit wholly contained within a particular region.

circumventricular organs Organs lying in the walls of the cerebral ventricles. These organs contain receptor sites that can be affected by substances in the *cerebrospinal fluid*. See Figure 10–15.

classical conditioning A form of associative learning in which an originally neutral stimulus [a *conditioned stimulus (CS)*], through pairing with a stimulus that elicits a particular response [an unconditioned stimulus *(US)*], acquires the power of eliciting that response. Also called *Pavlovian conditioning*.

cloaca The sex organ in many birds through which sperm are discharged (in the male) and eggs are laid (in the female). This is the same passage through which wastes are eliminated.

clones Asexually produced organisms that are genetically identical.

closed-loop mechanism A form of control mechanism that

provides a flow of information from whatever is being controlled to the device that controls it. See Figure 8–6.

CNS See *central nervous system.*

CNV See *contingent negative variation.*

coactivation A central nervous system control program that activates or inhibits the skeletal motoneurons at the same time as it alters the sensitivity of the *muscle spindles.*

cochlea A snail-shaped structure in the inner ear which contains the primary receptors for hearing. See Figure 6–6.

cochlear duct One of three principal canals running along the length of the cochlea. See Figure 6–7.

cochlear microphonic potential An electrical potential produced by hair cells that accurately copies the acoustic waveform of the stimulus. See Figure 6–8.

cochlear nuclei Brainstem nuclei that receive input from auditory hair cells and send output to the superior olivary complex. See Figure 7–17.

codon A sequence of three bases on a DNA molecule. See Box Figure 3–3.

colliculus One of two pairs of structures on the dorsal midbrain. See *inferior colliculus, superior colliculus.*

common carotid arteries Arteries that ascend the left and right sides of the neck. The branch that enters the brain is called the *internal carotid artery.*

complex cortical cells Cells in the visual cortex that respond best to a bar of a particular width and direction anywhere within a particular area of the visual field. See Figure 7–9.

computer axial tomogram A technique for examining brain structure in intact humans through a computer analysis of X-ray absorption at several positions around the head. This technique affords a virtual direct view of the brain. See Figure 2–16(c).

concordant Any trait that is seen in both individuals of an identical twin pair.

conditioned stimulus (CS) See *classical conditioning.*

conduction aphasia A language disorder, involving intact comprehension but poor repetition of spoken language, related to damage of the pathways connecting *Wernicke's area* and *Broca's area.*

conductive deafness Hearing impairments associated with pathology of the external or middle ear cavities.

cones Receptor cells in the retina that are responsible for color vision. The three types of cones have somewhat different sensitivities to light of different wavelengths. See Figures 6–4 and 7–3.

consolidation A stage of memory formation in which information in short-term or intermediate-term memory is transferred to long-term memory. See Figure 14–5.

consolidation hypothesis See *perseveration-consolidation hypothesis.*

constraints on learning Factors that restrict the ease of different kinds of learning in different species.

contingent negative variation (CNV) A slow event-related potential recorded from the scalp. It arises in the interval between a warning signal and a signal that directs action. See Figure 4–25.

contrast sensitivity function (CSF) A psychophysical function determined by finding the contrast necessary for perceiving different spacings of dark and light bars. Used to measure spatial acuity of the visual system. See Figure 7–13.

copulatory behavior The third stage of mating behavior during which the male mounts the female, inserts the erect penis, and ejaculates.

coronal (plane) The plane dividing the body or brain into front and back parts. Also called frontal or transverse. See Box Figure 2–1.

corpus callosum The band of axons that connects the two cerebral hemispheres. See Figure 2–1.

correlational approach An approach to finding relations between bodily variables and behavioral variables that involves finding the extent to which some bodily measure co-varies with some behavioral measure. See Figure 1–7.

corticotropin-releasing hormone (CRH) A releasing hormone from the hypothalamus that controls the daily rhythm of ACTH release.

cortisol A glucocorticoid hormone of the adrenal cortex.

cranial nerves One of the three main subdivisions of the peripheral nervous system, composed of a set of pathways mainly concerned with sensory and motor systems associated with the head. See Figure 2–12.

cretinism Reduced stature and mental retardation caused by thyroid deficiency.

CRH See *corticotropin-releasing hormone.*

CS Conditioned stimulus. See *classical conditioning.*

CSF See *contrast sensitivity function.*

cyclic adenosine monophosphate (cyclic AMP or cAMP) A *second messenger* involved in the synaptic activities of dopamine, norepinephrine, and serotonin.

cyclic AMP See *cyclic adenosine monophosphate.*

cytoarchitectonics The study of anatomical divisions of the brain based on the kinds and spacing of cells and distribution of axons.

DA See *dopamine.*

dB See *decibel.*

decibel (dB) A logarithmic expression of sound intensity.

dendrites Extensions of the cell body which are the receptive surfaces of the neuron. See Figure 2–20.

dendritic branching The pattern and quantity of branching of dendrites. See Figure 15–5.

dendritic spines Outgrowths along the dendrites of neurons. See Figure 2–25.

dendritic tree The full arrangement of a single cell's dendrites.

deoxyribonucleic acid (DNA) A nucleic acid present in the chromosomes of cells; it codes hereditary information. See Box Figures 3–1 and 3–2.

depolarization A reduction in membrane potential (the inner membrane surface becomes less negative in relation to the outer surface); this is caused by excitatory neural messages. See Figure 4–3.

derepression The mechanism through which regions of the DNA molecule that are repressed from transcription become unblocked. This process allows for the selection of genetic information that will be utilized by a particular cell.

dermatome A strip of skin innervated by a particular spinal root. See Figure 7–25.

diaschisis A temporary period of generalized impairment following brain injury.

dichotic listening technique A technique involving presentation of different sounds to each ear at the same time. Used to determine hemispheric differences in processing auditory information. See Figure 16–11.

diencephalon The posterior part of the forebrain; it includes the thalamus and hypothalamus. See Figures 2–7 and 2–8.

discordant Any trait that is seen in only one individual of an identical twin pair.

distal An anatomical term meaning toward the periphery or toward the end of a limb. See Box Figure 2–1.

divergence A system of neural connections that allows one cell to send signals to many other cells. See Figure 4–12.

DNA See *deoxyribonucleic acid.*

dopamine (DA) A neurotransmitter produced mainly in the basal forebrain and diencephalon that is active in the basal ganglia, the olfactory system, and limited parts of the cerebral cortex. For location of dopaminergic fibers, see Figure 4–23.

dopaminergic Refers to cells that use dopamine as their synaptic transmitter.

dorsal An anatomical term meaning toward the back of the body or the top of the brain; opposite of *ventral*. See Box Figure 2–1.

dorsal root Root at the back of the spinal cord. See Figure 2–13.

Down's syndrome A form of mental retardation associated with an extra chromosome.

duplex theory A theory of pitch perception combining the *place theory* and *volley theory*. Volley theory operates for sounds from about 20 to 1000 Hz, and place theory operates for sounds above 1000 Hz.

duplication of DNA A process through which a cell duplicates (or replicates) its genetic information during mitosis. See Box Figure 3–3.

dynamic phase of weight gain The initial period following destruction of the ventromedial hypothalamus during which the animal's body weight shoots up. See Figure 11–6.

dyskinesia See *tardive dyskinesia.*

dyslexia A reading disorder attributed to brain impairment.

EC See *Enriched condition.*

ectoderm The outer cellular layer of the developing fetus; this layer gives rise to the skin and to the nervous system.

ectotherms Animals whose body temperature is regulated by, and who get most of their heat from, the environment. Contrast with *endotherms.*

edema The swelling of tissue, especially in the brain, in response to brain injury.

EEG See *electroencephalography.*

efferent fibers Axons carrying information from the nervous system to the periphery; opposite of *afferent.*

ejaculation The forceful expulsion of semen from the penis.

electrical synapse Junctional region where the presynaptic and postsynaptic membranes approach so closely that the nerve impulse can jump to the postsynaptic membrane without being translated into a chemical message. See Figure 4–8.

electroencephalography (EEG) The recording and study of gross electrical activity of the brain recorded from large electrodes placed on the scalp. See EEG recordings made during sleep; Figure 12–1.

embryo The earliest stage in a developing animal; in the human, up to 8 to 10 weeks after conception.

encéphale isolé An animal in which the brainstem is separated from the spinal cord by a cut below the medulla. Contrast with *cerveau isolé*. See Figure 12–12.

encoding A process of memory formation in which the information entering sensory channels is passed into short-term memory. See Figure 14–5.

endocast A cast of the cranial cavity of a skull. Used to determine brain shape and size of extinct animals.

endocrine Refers to glands that secrete products into the bloodstream to act on distant targets; opposite of *exocrine*. See Figure 5–1.

endorphins Neurotransmitters that have been called the body's own narcotics.

endothelial cells The tightly fitting cells that make up the walls of the capillaries in the brain. See Figure 2–11.

endotherms Animals, such as mammals and birds, whose body temperature is regulated chiefly by internal metabolic processes; contrast with *ectotherms*.

enkephalin A type of *endorphin*.

enriched condition (EC) An experimental condition with a complex environment. See Figure 15–2.

ependymal layer See *ventricular layer*.

epilepsy A brain disorder marked by major sudden changes in the electrophysiological state of the brain referred to as seizures. See Figures 4–28 and 4–29.

epinephrine A compound that acts both as a hormone (secreted by the adrenal medulla) and as a neurotransmitter; also called *adrenalin*. For location of adrenergic neurons, see Figure 4–21.

EPSP See *excitatory postsynaptic potential*.

equilibrium potential The state in which the tendency of ions to flow from regions of high concentration is exactly balanced by the opposing potential difference across the membrane.

estrogen A hormone produced by female gonads. See Figure 5–12.

estrus The period during which female animals are sexually receptive.

event-related potentials Gross electrical potential changes in the brain that are elicited by discrete sensory or motor events. See Figure 4–25.

evoked potential See *event-related potentials*.

evolution through natural selection The Darwinian theory that evolution proceeds by differential success in reproduction.

excitatory postsynaptic potentials (EPSPs) Depolarizing potentials in the postsynaptic neuron caused by excitatory presynaptic impulses. These potentials may summate to trigger a nerve impulse in the postsynaptic cell. See Figure 4–7.

exocrine Refers to glands that secrete their products through ducts to the site of action; opposite of *endocrine*.

extinction A feature of conditioning in which the learned response wanes when reinforcement is not presented.

extracellular space The space between cells.

extraocular muscles Muscles attached to the eyeball that control its position and movements. See Figure 8–22.

extrapyramidal system A motor system that includes the basal ganglia and some closely related brainstem structures. See Figure 8–19.

5HT See *serotonin*.

facial nerve A cranial nerve that innervates facial musculature and some sensory receptors. See Figure 2–12.

feature detector model A model of visual pattern analysis in terms of linear and angular components of the stimulus array. Contrast with *spatial frequency filter model*.

fixed action patterns Complex preprogrammed species-specific behaviors triggered by particular stimuli and carried out without sensory feedback. See also *modal action pattern*.

flexion reflex Abrupt withdrawal of a limb in response to intense stimulation of the foot.

folia Folds or convolutions of the cerebellar cortex.

follicle-stimulating hormone (FSH) A tropic hormone released by the anterior pituitary that controls the production of estrogen and progesterone. See Figure 5–12.

forebrain The frontal division of the neural tube that contains the *cerebral hemispheres*, the *thalamus*, and the *hypothalamus*. Also called the *prosencephalon*. See Figure 2–7.

fornix A fiber tract that runs from the hippocampus to the mammillary body. See Figures 2–3 and 13–11.

Fourier analysis The analysis of a complex pattern into the sum of sine waves. See Box Figure 6–3.

fovea A small depression in the center of the retina with a dense concentration of cones and maximal visual acuity. See Figure 7–6.

frequency The number of cycles per second in a sound wave, measured in hertz (Hz). See Box Figure 6–2.

frontal See *coronal*.

FSH See *follicle-stimulating hormone*.

gametes The sex cells which, unlike autosomes, contain only unpaired chromosomes therefore having only half the number of autosomal chromosomes. One gamete from a female and one from a male organism join during sexual reproduction.

gamma efferents Motors neurons by means of which the central nervous system controls *muscle spindle*, sensitivity. See Figure 8–9.

ganglion A collection of nerve cell bodies. Also called a *nucleus*.

ganglion cells Cells in the retina whose axons form the optic nerve. See Figure 6–4.

gender identity The way one identifies one's self, and is identified by others, as a male or a female.

generalization A feature of conditioning in which stimuli similar to the conditioned stimulus can elicit a conditioned response.

generalized seizures Epileptic seizures that arise from pathology at brain sites that project to widespread regions of the brain. These seizures involve loss of consciousness and symmetrical involvement of body musculature. See Figures 4–28 and 4–29.

generator potential Local changes in the resting potential of receptor cells that mediate between the impact of stimuli and the initiation of nerve impulse. See Figure 6-3.

genetic mosaics Animals in which the cells of one part of the body have a different chromosomal makeup from the cells in another part. For example, the head of a male fruit fly can be put on the body of a female fruit fly. Study of genetic mosaics helps determine which neural structures control various behaviors.

giant axons Large diameter axons found in some invertebrates. The size of these axons facilitates research on the properties of neural membrane structure and function. See Figure 4-2.

glia See *glial cells*.

glial cells Nonneural brain cells that provide structural, nutritional, and other supports to the brain. Also called *glia* or *neuroglia*. See Figure 2-27.

gliomas Brain tumors resulting from the aberrant production of glial cells.

glossopharyngeal nerve A cranial nerve that serves taste receptors in the tongue. See Figure 2-12.

glucagon A hormone released by alpha cells in the islets of Langerhans that increases blood glucose. See Figure 5-9.

glucocorticoids Hormones released by the adrenal cortex that affect carbohydrate metabolism.

GnRH See *gonadotropin-releasing hormone*.

Golgi tendon organs Receptors located in tendons that send impulses to the central nervous system when a muscle contracts. See Figure 8-9.

Golgi type 1 A type of large nerve cell.

gonadotropin-releasing hormone (GnRH) A hypothalamic hormone that controls the release of luteinizing hormone (or interstitial-cell-stimulating hormone). Also called *luteinizing-hormone-releasing hormone*. See Figure 5-12.

graded potentials Potentials that can vary continuously in size; also called local potentials; contrast with *all-or-none potentials*. See Figure 4-7.

grand mal seizures A type of generalized epileptic seizure that involves nerve cells firing in high frequency bursts. These seizures cause loss of consciousness and sudden muscle contraction. See Figure 4-28.

grandmother cell An extrapolation of the feature detector model suggesting that if there were enough levels of analysis, a unit could be constructed that would enable a person to recognize his or her grandmother.

granule (cell) A type of small nerve cell.

growth hormone A tropic hormone secreted by the anterior pituitary that influences the growth of cells and tissues. Also called *somatotropic hormone* (STH). See Figure 5-6.

gyri The ridged or raised portions of a convoluted brain surface. Contrast with *sulci*. See Figure 2-1.

habituation A form of nonassociative learning characterized by a reduction in response strength following repeated presentations of a stimulus. See Figure 14-2.

hair cells The receptor cells for hearing in the cochlea. Displacement of these cells by sound waves generates nerve impulses that travel to the brain. See Figure 6-7.

hindbrain The rear division of the brain; it contains the *cerebellum, pons,* and *medulla* in the mature vertebrate. Also called the *rhombencephalon*. See Figure 2-7.

hippocampus A portion of the cerebral hemispheres found curled in the basal medial part of the temporal lobe. See Figures 2-3 and 14-6.

homeostasis The tendency for the internal environment to remain constant.

homeotherms Animals, such as birds and mammals, that maintain a relatively constant body temperature. Contrast with *poikilotherms*.

hominids Primates of the family *Hominidae*, of which humans are the only living species.

horizontal cells A specialized type of retinal cell. See Figure 6-4.

horizontal plane The plane dividing the body or brain into upper and lower parts. See Box Figure 2-1.

hormone A chemical secreted by an endocrine gland that is conveyed by the bloodstream and regulates target organs or tissues. Table 5-2 lists main hormones.

hue One of the basic dimensions of light perception. It varies around the color circle though blue, green, yellow, orange, and red. See Figure 7-2.

Huntington's chorea A progressive genetic disorder characterized by *choreic movements* and profound changes in mental functioning.

hypercomplex 1 Cells in the visual cortex that respond best to visual stimulation by bars of a given orientation and of limited length.

hypercomplex 2 Cells of the visual cortex that respond best to visual stimulation by two line segments meeting at a particular angle.

hyperphagia A condition involving increasing food intake, often related to damage to the ventromedial hypothalamus.

hyperpolarization Increases in membrane potential (the inner surface of the membrane becomes more negative in relation to the outer surface); caused by inhibitory neural messages. See Figure 4-3.

hypertonic A solution with a larger concentration of salt than that found in interstitial fluid and blood plasma (above about 0.9% salt); opposite of *hypotonic*.

hypothalamus Part of the diencephalon, lying ventral to the thalamus. See Figures 2-8 and 2-34.

hypotonic A solution with a lesser concentration of salt than that found in interstitial fluid and blood plasma (below about 0.9% salt); opposite of *hypertonic*.

hypovolemic thirst The response to a reduced volume of extracellular fluid. Contrast with *osmotic thirst*.

IC See *Impoverished condition*.

iconic memory A very brief type of memory that stores the sensory impression of a scene.

ICSH See interstitial-cell-stimulating hormone or luteinizing hormone.

impoverished condition (IC) An experimental condition with a drastically simplified environment. See Figure 15–2.

imprinting A form of learning in which young animals learn to follow the first relatively large moving object they see.

inferior colliculus The auditory center in the midbrain; it receives input from the brainstem auditory nuclei and sends output to the medial geniculate nucleus. See Figure 7–17.

infundibulum The stalk of the pituitary gland. See Figure 5–5.

inhibitory postsynaptic potentials (IPSPs) Hyperpolarizing potentials in the postsynaptic neuron caused by inhibitory connections. These potentials decrease the probability that the postsynaptic neuron will fire a nerve impulse. See Figure 4–7.

inner hair cells Receptor cells for hearing in the cochlea. See Figure 6–7.

innervation ratio The ratio expressing the number of muscle fibers innervated by a single motor axon. The fewer muscle fibers an axon innervates (the lower the ratio) the finer the control of movements.

instrumental conditioning A form of associative learning in which the likelihood that an act will be performed depends upon the consequences (reinforcing stimuli) that follow it.

instrumental response See *instrumental conditioning*.

insulin A hormone released by beta cells in the islets of Langerhans that lowers blood glucose. See Figure 5–9.

intention tremor A tremor that occurs only during voluntary movement, e.g., when the person reaches out to grasp an object.

intermediate-term memory A form of memory lasting longer than short-term, and requiring no rehearsal, but not lasting as long as long-term memory.

internal carotid artery See *common carotid artery*. See Figure 2–10.

interstitial-cell-stimulating hormone (ICSH) See *luteinizing hormone*.

intracellular fluid Water within cells. Also called *cellular fluid*.

intromission Insertion of the erect penis into the vagina during copulatory behavior.

ion channels Pores in the cell membrane which permit the passage of certain ions through the membrane when the channels are open. See Figure 4–13.

IPSP See *inhibitory postsynaptic potential*.

islets of Langerhans Clusters of cells in the pancreas which release two hormones (insulin and glucagon) with opposite effects on glucose utilization. See Figure 5–9.

Korsakoff's syndrome A memory disorder, related to a thiamine deficiency, generally associated with chronic alcoholism.

kuru A slow virus of the brain which produces trembling and eventually paralysis of the limbs.

labeled lines A view of stimulus coding stating that particular nerve cells are intrinsically labeled for particular sensory experiences such as cold, touch, pain, and so forth. See Figure 6–14.

labile memory An early stage of memory formation during which formation of a memory can be easily disrupted by conditions that influence brain activity.

laminar (form of organization) The horizontal layering of cells found in some brain regions. See Figure 2–30 for laminar organization of the cerebral cortex.

lateral An anatomical term meaning toward the side; opposite of *medial*. See Box Figure 2–1.

lateral geniculate nucleus Part of the thalamus which receives information from the optic tract and sends it to visual areas in the occipital cortex. See Figure 7–1.

lateral hypothalamus (LH) A hypothalamic region involved in facilitating eating. See Figure 11–5.

lateral inhibition A phenomenon produced by interconnected neurons that inhibit their neighbors, producing contrast at the edges of the stimulus. See Figure 4–12.

lateral-line system A sensory system found in many kinds of fish and some amphibians that informs the animal of water motion in relation to the body surface.

learning set The ability to solve a particular type of problem efficiently after prolonged experience with that type of problem.

LH See *lateral hypothalamus*.

LH See *luteinizing hormone*.

local circuit See *circuit*.

local circuit neurons Small neurons that make contact only with neurons that are within the same functional unit.

localization of function The concept that specific brain regions are responsible for various types of experience, behavior, and psychological processes.

long-term memory An enduring form of memory lasting for weeks, months, or years.

lordosis A female receptive posture in quadrupeds in which the hindquarters are raised and the tail is turned to one side, facilitating intromission by the male. See Figure 9–4.

lumbar Referring to the lower part of the spinal cord or back.

luteinizing hormone (LH) A tropic hormone released by the anterior pituitary that influences the hormonal activities of the gonads. In males this hormone is called *interstitial-cell-stimulating hormone* (ICSH). See Figure 5–12.

luteinizing hormone-releasing hormone See *gonadotropin-releasing hormone*.

malleus A middle ear bone, connected to the tympanic membrane; one of the chain of three ossicles that transmit sound across the middle ear.

mammillary bodies Paired nuclei at the base of the brain slightly posterior to the pituitary stalk. See Figure 2–3 and 14–6.

manic depressive psychosis See *bipolar depression*.

medial An anatomical term meaning toward the middle; opposite of *lateral*. See Box Figure 2–1.

medial geniculate nucleus A nucleus in the thalamus that receives input from the *inferior colliculus* and sends output to the *auditory cortex*. See Figure 7–17.

medulla The lowest part of the brain, also called *myelencephalon*. See Figure 2–8.

meiosis The process of forming gametes in which each new cell receives half the chromosomes, therefore not requiring duplication of DNA.

membrane potential See *resting potential*.

memory traces Persistent changes in the brain that reflect the storage of memory.

mesencephalon The midbrain. See Figure 2–8.

messenger RNA (mRNA) A strand of RNA that carries the code of a section of a strand of DNA to the cytoplasm. See Box Figure 3–2.

metencephalon A subdivision of the hindbrain that includes the cerebellum and the pons. See Figure 2–8.

microglia Extremely small glial cells that remove cellular debris from injured or dead cells.

microtubules Hollow cylindrical structures in axons that are involved in axoplasmic streaming. See Figure 2–24.

midbrain The middle division of the brain. Also called *mesencephalon*. See Figures 2–7 and 2–8.

middle ear The cavity between the eardrum and the cochlea. See Figure 6–6.

mineralocorticoids Hormones released by the adrenal cortex that affect ion concentrations in body tissues.

mitosis The process of division of somatic cells that involves duplication of DNA.

modal action pattern A modification of the concept of a *fixed action pattern* which allows for some variability of the response between different individuals and within the same individual at different times.

modulation of formation of memory Facilitation or inhibition of memory formation by factors other than those directly involved in memory formation. Also called *modulation of memory storage processes*.

modulation of memory storage processes See *modulation of formation of memory*.

monogamy A mating system in which a female and a male form a breeding pair that may last for one breeding period or for a lifetime. A rather durable and exclusive relation between a male and a female is called a *pair bond*.

monopolar neurons Nerve cells with a single branch leaving the cell body which then extends in two directions—one end is the receptive pole, the other end the output zone. See Figure 2–20.

motoneurons Nerve cells in the spinal cord that transmit motor messages from the spinal cord to muscles.

motor cortex A region of cerebral cortex that sends impulses to motoneurons. See Figure 8–16.

motor unit A single motor axon and all the muscle fibers it innervates.

mRNA See *messenger RNA*.

Müllerian duct system A primitive duct system in each embryo that will develop into female reproductive structures—the oviducts, uterus, and upper vagina—if testes are not present in the embryo. Contrast with *Wolffian duct system*. See Figure 9–7.

multipolar neurons Nerve cells with many dendrites and a single axon. See Figure 2–20.

muscarinic A cholinergic receptor (one responsive to *acetylcholine*) that mediates chiefly the inhibitory activities of acetylcholine.

muscle fibers Contractile fibers of a muscle; also called *extrafusal fibers*. See Box Figure 8–1.

muscle spindle A muscle receptor that lies parallel to the muscle and sends impulses to the central nervous system when a muscle is stretched. See Figure 8–10.

muscular dystrophy Diseases that lead to degeneration and functional changes in muscles.

myasthenia gravis A neurological disease characterized by easy fatiguability and weakness of muscles. See Box 4–5.

myelencephalon A subdivision of the hindbrain; the medulla. See Figures 2–7 and 2–8.

myelin The fatty insulation around an axon, formed by accessory cells; this improves the speed of conduction of nerve impulses. See Figure 2–22 and 2–23.

myelinization The process of formation of myelin. See Figure 2–22.

narcolepsy A disorder involving frequent, intense episodes of sleep, which last from 5 to 30 minutes and can occur anytime during the usual waking hours.

NE See *norepinephrine*.

negative feedback system A regulatory system in which output is used to reduce the effect of input signals. See Figure 5–2.

neocortex The relatively recently evolved portions of the cerebral cortex.

Nernst equation An equation used to calculate the equilibrium potential.

nerve growth factor A substance that controls the growth of neurons of the spinal ganglia and the ganglia of the sympathetic nervous system. See Figure 3–15.

nerve impulses The propagated electrical messages of a neuron which travel down the axon to adjacent neurons. Also called *action potentials*. See Figure 4–4.

neural folds Ridges of ectoderm which form around the neural groove and which come together to form the neural tube in the embryo. See Figure 3–3.

neural groove The groove between the neural folds which becomes the neural tube when these folds come together in the embryo. See Figure 3–3.

neural tube A prenatal structure with subdivisions which correspond to the future forebrain, midbrain, and hindbrain. The cavity of this tube will include the cerebral ventricles and the passages that connect them. See Figure 3–3.

neuroblasts Early forms of cells during the stage of cell migration. See Figures 3–5 and 3–6.

neurofibrillary tangles Abnormal whorls of neurofilaments within nerve cells that are especially apparent in people suffering from dementia. See Figure 3–23.

neurofilaments Small rod-like structures in axons that are involved in transport of materials. See Figure 2–24.

neuroglia See *glial cells*.

neurohypophysis See *posterior pituitary*.

neuromodulators Substances that influence the activity of synaptic transmitters.

neuron The basic unit of the nervous system, composed of a cell body, receptive extension(s), and a transmitting extension (axon). See Figure 2–20.

neuron doctrine A hypothesis which states that the brain is composed of separate cells that are distinct structurally, metabolically, and functionally.

neuropathies Peripheral nerve destruction.

neurosecretory cells Neurons that manufacture and secrete hormones.

neurospecificity A theory of nervous system development which states that each axon grows to a particular site. See Figure 3–13.

neurotransmitter See *synaptic transmitter*.

nicotinic A cholinergic receptor that mediates chiefly the excitatory activities of acetylcholine.

nigrostriatal bundle (NSB) A dopaminergic tract that runs from the substantia nigra of the midbrain to the lateral hypothalamus, the globus pallidus, and the caudate-patamen.

nociceptors Receptors that respond to stimuli that produce tissue damage or pose the threat of damage.

node of Ranvier A gap between successive segments of the myelin sheath where the axon membrane is exposed. See Figure 2–21.

nonassociative learning A form of learning in which presentation of a particular stimulus leads to altered strength or probability of a response according to the strength and temporal spacing of that stimulus. Includes habituation and sensitization. Contrast with *associative learning*.

nonequivalence of associations A constraint of learning stating that a given association is learned with differential ease by different species.

nonequivalence of response A constraint on learning stating that the rapidity of learning a given instrumental behavior varies between species.

nonequivalence of stimuli A constraint on learning stating that the same stimulus has a differential ability to be learned by different species.

norepinephrine (NE) A neurotransmitter produced mainly in brainstem nuclei, also called *noradrenalin*. See Figure 4–21.

NSB See *nigrostriatal bundle*.

nucleotide A portion of a DNA molecule composed of a single base and the adjoining sugar-phosphate unit of the strand.

nucleus An anatomical collection of neurons, e.g., caudate nucleus.

nystagmus Abnormal to and fro movements of the eye during attempts to fixate.

occipital cortex The cortex of the occipital (posterior) lobe of the brain. See Figure 7–1.

ocular-dominance histogram A graph that shows the strength of a neuron's response to stimuli presented to either the left or right eye. Used to determine the effects of depriving one eye of visual experience. See Figure 3–20.

operant conditioning See *instrumental conditioning*.

optic radiation Axons of the *lateral geniculate nucleus* that terminate in the primary visual areas of the occipital cortex. See Figure 7–1.

optic tract The axons of the retinal ganglion cells after they have passed the optic chiasm; most terminate in the lateral geniculate nucleus. See Figure 7–1.

optokinetic system A closed loop system controlling eye movement and keeping the gaze on target.

organ of Corti A structure in the inner ear that lies on the basilar membrane of the cochlea. It contains the hair cells and the terminations of the auditory nerve. See Figure 6–7.

organizational role The role that hormones play in the development and differentiation of body structure.

orgasm The climax of sexual experience, marked by extremely pleasureable sensations.

osmolality The number of particles per unit volume of a solute.

osmoreceptors Cells in the hypothalamus that were thought to respond to changes in osmotic pressure.

osmosis When there are unequal concentrations of particles in the fluids on two sides of a semipermeable membrane, fluid moves to the side with the greater concentration.

osmotic pressure The force involved in osmosis.

osmotic thirst The response to increased osmotic pressure in brain cells. Contrast with *hypovolemic thirst*.

ossicles Small bones that transmit sound across the middle ear, from the tympanic membrane to the oval window.

outer hair cells Receptor cells of the cochlea. See Figure 6–7.

oval window The opening from the middle ear to the inner ear.

oxytocin A hormone released by the posterior pituitary which triggers milk let-down in the nursing female. See Figure 5–7.

Pacinian corpuscle A kind of receptor found especially in tissue overlying the abdominal cavity. See Figure 6–3.

pair bond A form of monogamy.

paleocortex Evolutionary old cortex, e.g., the hippocampus.

pancreas An endocrine gland located near the posterior wall of the abdominal cavity; it secretes insulin and glucagon. See Figure 5–9.

paradoxical sleep See *rapid-eye-movement sleep (REM)*.

parallel processing Using several different circuits at the same time to process the same stimuli.

parasympathetic division One of the two systems that compose the *autonomic nervous system*. The parasympathetic division arises from both the cranial and sacral parts of the spinal cord. See Figure 2–15.

paraventricular nucleus A nucleus of the hypothalamus. See Figure 5–5(b).

Parkinson's disease A degenerative neurological disorder involving dopaminergic neurons of the substantia nigra.

partial seizures Epileptic seizures arising from pathological foci that do not have widespread distribution. These include focal repetitive motor spasms and do not involve loss of consciousness.

passive avoidance response A response that an organism has learned not to make, i.e., learning not to enter a compartment where it has been given a shock.

Pavlovian conditioning See *classical conditioning*.

peripheral nervous system The portion of the nervous system that includes all the nerves outside the brain and spinal cord.

permanent memory A type of memory that lasts without decline for the life of an organism.

perseveration-consolidation hypothesis A hypothesis stating that information passes through two stages in memory formation. During the first stage the memory is held by perseveration of neural activity and is easily disrupted. During the second stage the memory becomes fixed, or consolidated, and is no longer easily disrupted.

petit mal seizures A type of generalized epileptic seizure characterized by a spike-and-wave electrical pattern (Figure 4–29). During these seizures the person is unaware of the environment and later cannot recall what happened.

phantom limb The experience of sensory messages attributed to an amputated limb.

phasic receptors Receptors that show a rapid fall in nerve impulse discharge as stimulation is maintained.

phenylketonuria (PKU) An inherited disorder of protein metabolism in which the absence of an enzyme leads to a toxic build up of a certain compound, causing mental retardation.

phosphenes Perceived flashes of light provoked by electrical or mechanical stimulation of the eyeball.

photon A quantum of light energy.

photopic system A system in the retina that operates at high levels of light, shows sensitivity to color, and involves the cones; contrast with *scotopic system*.

phrenology The belief that bumps on the skull reflect enlargements of brain regions responsible for certain behavioral faculties. See Figure 2–5.

pitch A dimension of auditory experience in which sounds vary from low to high.

pituitary gland A small complex endocrine gland located in a socket at the base of the skull. The anterior pituitary and posterior pituitary are separate in function. See Figure 5–5.

PKU See *phenylketonuria*.

place theory A theory of frequency discrimination according to which pitch perception depends on the place of maximal displacement of the basilar membrane produced by a sound. Contrast with *volley theory*.

placebo effect A reponse to an inert substance which mimics the effects of an actual drug, i.e., the relief pain sufferers frequently get from sugar tablets presented as medicine.

planum temporale A region of superior temporal cortex adjacent to the primary auditory area. See Figure 16–13.

pneumoencephalogram A technique for examining brain structure in intact humans by taking X rays after a gas is injected into the ventricles. See Figure 2–16(b).

poikilotherms Animals whose body temperature varies with the environment, such as reptiles. Contrast with *homeotherms*.

polyandry A mating system in which one female mates with several males.

polygamy A mating system in which an individual mates with more than one other animal. *Polygyny* is the mating of one male with.more than one female. *Polyandry* is the mating of one female with more than one male.

polygyny See *polygamy*.

pons A portion of the metencephalon. See Figures 2–3 and 2–8.

positron emission tomography A technique for examining brain structure and function in intact humans by combining tomography with injections of radioactive substances used by the brain. An analysis of metabolism of these substances reflects regional differences in brain activity. See the cover of this book and Figure 2–16(d) and (e).

postcopulatory behavior The final stage in mating behavior. These species-specific behaviors include rolling (in the cat) and grooming (in the rat).

posterior pituitary The rear division of the pituitary gland. Also called *neurohypophysis*. See Figure 5–5.

postsynaptic potentials See *graded potentials*.

postural tremor A tremor that occurs when a person attempts to maintain a posture such as holding an arm or leg extended, resulting from pathology of the basal ganglia or cerebellum.

potassium equilibrium potential See *equilibrium potential*.

precocial Refers to animals born in an undeveloped state that depend on maternal care, such as a human infant; opposite of *altricial*.

proceptive behavior Pertaining to female appetitive sexual behavior.

progestogen A class of hormone produced by female gonads, e.g., progesterone. See Figure 5–12.

projection neuron Large neurons that transmit messages to widely separated parts of the brain.

promiscuity A mating system in which animals mate with several members of the opposite sex and do not establish durable associations with sex partners.

prosencephalon See *forebrain*.

prosthetic devices Artificial replacements of body parts lost by accident or disease, such as an artificial limb.

proximal An anatomical directional term meaning near the trunk or center; opposite of *distal*.

psychosocial dwarfism Reduced stature caused by stress early in life which inhibits deep sleep. See Box 5–1.

psychosurgery Surgically produced brain lesions to modify severe psychiatric disorders.

psychotogens Subtances that generate psychotic behavior.

pure tone A tone with a single frequency of vibration. See Box Figure 6–2.

Purkinje cell A type of large nerve cell in the cerebellar cortex. See Figures 2–29 and 3–7.

pyramidal cell A type of large nerve cell in the cerebral cortex. See Figure 2–18.

pyramidal system A motor system including neurons within the cerebral cortex and their axons which form the pyramidal tract. See Figure 8–16.

quantum A unit of radiant energy.

ramp movements Slow, sustained motions thought to be generated in the basal ganglia. Also called *smooth movements*. Contrast with *ballistic*.

range fractionation A hypothesis of stimulus intensity perception stating that a wide range of intensity values can be encoded by a group of cells each of which is a specialist for a particular range of an intensity scale. See Figure 6–13.

raphe nucleus A group of neurons in the midline of the brainstem which contains serotonin, involved in sleep mechanisms. See Figure 12–14.

rapid-eye-movement sleep (REM) A stage of sleep characterized by small-amplitude, fast EEG waves, no postural tension, and rapid eye movements. Also called *paradoxical sleep*. See Figure 12–1.

Raynaud's disease A circulatory disorder which may shut off blood supply to the fingers upon exposure to the cold and sometimes in response to emotional states.

readiness potential An electrical potential which occurs over widespread posterior regions of the scalp prior to the onset of a voluntary movement. See Figure 8–22.

receptive field The stimulus region and features that cause the maximal response of a cell in a sensory system. See Figures 6–18 and 7–9.

receptivity The state of readiness to show the female responses that are necessary for the male to achieve intravaginal ejaculation, e.g., assuming the posture that facilitates intromission during copulatory behavior.

receptor proteins Substances at synaptic receptor sites

whose reaction to certain transmitters causes a change in the postsynaptic membrane potential.

receptors The initial elements in sensory systems, responsible for stimulus transduction, e.g., hair cells in the cochlea or rods and cones in the retina. See Figure 6–2.

receptor sites Regions of specialized membrane containing receptor proteins located on the postsynaptic surface of a synapse; these sites receive and react with the chemical transmitter.

reflex A simple, highly stereotyped, and unlearned response to a particular stimulus (i.e., an eyeblink in response to a puff of air). See Figure 8–14.

reflex ovulation Ovulation that is induced by copulation, thus not restricting successful mating to a regular ovulatory period of the female's cycle.

refractory A period during and after a nerve impulse in which the axon membrane's responsiveness is reduced. A brief period of complete insensitivity to stimuli (absolute refractory phase) is followed by a longer period of reduced sensitivity (relative refractory phase) during which only strong stimulation produces a nerve impulse. See Figure 4–5.

reinforcing stimulus See *instrumental conditioning*.

relative refractory phase See *refractory*.

REM See *rapid-eye-movement sleep*.

resting potential Potential differences across the membrane of nerve cells during an inactive period. Also called *membrane potential*. See Figure 4–1.

rete mirabile A network of fine blood vessels located at the base of the brain in which blood coming from the periphery reduces the temperature of arterial blood before it enters the brain. See Figure 10–8.

reticular formation A region of the brainstem (extending from the medulla through the thalamus) which is involved in arousal. See Figure 12–13.

retina The receptive surface inside the eye which contains the rods and cones. See Figure 6–4.

retrieval A process in memory during which a stored memory is utilized by an organism.

retroactive amnesia A type of memory loss in which events just before a head injury are not recalled.

retrograde degeneration Destruction of the nerve cell body following injury. See Box Figure 3–4.

re-uptake A mechanism by which a synaptic transmitter released at a synapse is taken back into the presynaptic terminal, thus stopping synaptic activity.

rhodopsin The photopigment in *rods* that responds to light.

rhombencephalon See *hindbrain*.

ribonucleic acid A nucleic acid present in the cell body. Two forms of RNA are *transfer RNA* and *messenger RNA*.

ribosomes Structures in the cell body where translation of genetic information takes place. See Box Figure 3–2.

RNA See *ribonucleic acid*. See Box Figure 3–2.

rods Light sensitive receptor cells in the retina which are most active at low levels of light. See Figure 6–5.

roots The two distinct branches of a spinal nerve, each of which serves a separate function. The *dorsal root* carries sensory information from the peripheral nervous system to the spinal cord. The *ventral root* carries motor messages from the spinal cord to the peripheral nervous system. See Figure 2–13.

rostral An anatomical term meaning toward the head end; opposite of *caudal*.

round window A membrane separating the cochlear duct from the middle ear cavity.

saccades Rapid movements of the eyes which occur regularly during normal viewing.

saccadic suppression The suppression of vision during saccades, which provides the viewer with perception free of these abrupt movements. See Figure 8–11.

saccule A small fluid-filled sac under the utricle that responds to static positions of the head. See Figure 6–9.

sacral Refers to the lower part of the back or spinal cord.

sagittal plane The plane that bisects the body or brain into right and left halves. See Box Figure 2–1.

saltatory conduction The form of conduction seen in myelinated axons in which the nerve impulse jumps from one node of Ranvier to the next.

saturation One of the basic dimensions of light perception. This varies from rich to pale, i.e., from red to pink to gray in the color solid of Figure 7–2.

Schwann cell The kind of accessory cell that forms myelin in the peripheral nervous system. See Figure 2–27.

scotoma A region of blindness caused by injury to the visual pathway.

scotopic system A system in the retina which responds to low levels of light intensity and involves the rods. Contrast with *photopic system*.

second messenger A relatively slow acting substance in the postsynaptic cell which amplifies the effects of nerve impulses and can initiate processes that lead to changes in electrical potentials at the membrane.

secretin A hormone that is released during digestion.

selectivity of reinforcement A constraint on learning: across species, different reinforcements are differentially effective in strengthening associations.

semicircular canals Three fluid-filled tubes in the inner ear that are part of the *vestibular system*. Each of the tubes, which are at right angles to each other, detects angular acceleration. See Figure 6–9.

senile dementia A neurological disorder of the aged involving progressive behavioral deterioration including personality change and profound intellectual decline.

senile plaques Neuroanatomical changes correlated with senile dementia. These plaques are small areas of the brain containing abnormal cellular and chemical patterns. See Figure 3–23.

sensitization A form of nonassociative learning in which an organism becomes more responsive to most stimuli after being exposed to unusually strong or painful stimulation.

sensorineural deafness A hearing impairment originating from cochlear or auditory nerve lesions.

serotonergic Refers to neurons that use serotonin as their synaptic transmitter.

serotonin (5HT) A neurotransmitter produced in the raphe nuclei and active in structures throughout the cerebral hemispheres. Figure 4–13 shows the distribution of serotoninergic cells in the brain.

set-point The point of reference in a feedback system like a setting of a thermostat.

sex chromosomes Pairs of chromosomes which are identical in females (XX) but which are different in males (XY). Contrast with *autosomes*.

sexual attractiveness The first step in the mating behavior of many animals in which animals emit stimuli that attract members of the opposite sex.

sexual selection A theory concerning the evolution of anatomical and behavioral differences between males and females.

short-term memory Memory that usually lasts only for seconds or as long as rehearsal continues.

simple cortical cells Cells in the visual cortex that respond best to an edge or a bar of a particular width and with a particular direction and location in the visual field. See Figure 7–9.

sinistral Left-handed.

sleep apnea A sleep disorder that involves slowing or cessation of respiration during sleep, which wakens the patient. Excessive daytime somnolence results from frequent nocturnal awakening.

slow-wave sleep Stages of sleep including stages 1 through 4, defined by presence of slow EEG activity. See Figure 12–1.

smooth movements See *ramp movements*.

sodium equilibrium potential See *equilibrium potential*.

somatic intervention An approach to finding relations between bodily variables and behavioral variables that involves manipulating bodily structure or function and looking for resultant changes in behavior. See Figure 1–7.

somatotropic hormone See *growth hormone*.

spatial frequency filter model A model of pattern analysis emphasizing Fourier analysis of visual stimuli. Contrast with *feature detector model*.

spatial summation The summation at the axon hillock of postsynaptic potentials from across the cell body. If this summation reaches threshold a nerve impulse will be triggered. See Figure 4–10.

specific hunger The temporary unlearned increase in preference for a particular food, related to a specific need.

spectrally opponent cell A visual receptor cell with opposite firing responses to different regions of the spectrum. See Figure 7–4.

spinal animals Animals whose spinal cord has been surgically disconnected from the brain. Used to study behaviors that do not require brain control.

spinal nerves The 31 pairs of nerves that emerge from the spinal cord. See Figure 2–13.

spinal shock A period of decreased synaptic excitability in the neurons of the spinal cord after it is isolated surgically from the brain.

spindle cell A kind of small nerve cell.

split-brain Individuals who have had the corpus callosum severed, halting communication between the right and left hemispheres.

spontaneous recovery A feature of classical conditioning in which, if no testing is done after extinction occurs, the conditioned stimulus may again elicit a response.

stage 1 sleep The initial stage of slow-wave sleep involving small-amplitude EEG waves of irregular frequency, slow heart rate, and a reduction of muscle tension. See Figure 12–1(b).

stage 2 sleep A stage of slow-wave sleep defined by bursts of regular 14–18-Hz EEG waves that progressively increase and then decrease in amplitude (called spindles). See Figure 12–1(c).

stage 3 sleep A stage of slow-wave sleep defined by the spindles seen in stage 2 sleep mixed with larger amplitude slow waves. See Figure 12–1(d).

stage 4 sleep A stage of slow-wave sleep defined by the presence of high amplitude slow waves of 1–4 Hz. See Figures 12–1(d) and (e).

stapes A middle ear bone, connected to the oval window. One of the three ossicles that conducts sounds across the middle ear.

static phase of weight gain A later period following destruction of the ventromedial hypothalamus during which the animal's weight stabilizes at an obese level and food intake is not much above normal.

stellate cell A kind of small nerve cell with many branches.

stereocilia The hairs that protrude from the upper end of each hair cell.

stereopsis The ability to perceive depth, utilizing the slight difference in visual information from the two eyes. See Figure 7–8.

STH See *growth hormone*.

stimulation-elicited behavior Motivational behaviors such as eating, drinking, or fearful escape elicited by electrical stimulation of sites in the brain.

stretch reflex Contraction of a muscle resulting from stretch of that muscle. See Figure 8–13.

striate cortex A portion of the visual cortex with input from the lateral geniculate nucleus. Area V-1 in Figure 6–20.

subventricular zones Regions around the brain ventricle which continue to manufacture the precursors of nerve cells after birth.

sulci The furrows of convoluted brain surface. Contrast with *gyri*.

summating potential An electrical potential produced by a hair cell. See Figure 6–8.

superior colliculus A structure in the midbrain that receives information from the optic tract. See Figure 7–1.

superior olivary complex A brainstem structure that receives input from both right and left cochlear nuclei, providing the first binaural analysis of auditory information.

supraoptic nucleus A nucleus of the hypothalamus. See Figure 5–5(b).

sympathetic chains One of two systems that compose the autonomic nervous system. See Figure 2–15.

synapse An area composed of the presynaptic (axonal) terminal, the postsynaptic (usually dendritic) membrane, and the space (or cleft) between them. This is the site at which neural messages travel from one neuron to another. Also called the *synaptic region*. See Figures 4–15 and 4–19.

synaptic assembly A level of brain organization which includes the total collection of all synapses on a single cell. See Figure 2–17.

synaptic bouton The presynaptic swelling of the axon terminal from which neural messages travel across the synaptic cleft to other neurons. See Figure 2–25.

synaptic cleft The space between the presynaptic and postsynaptic membranes. See Figures 4–8 and 4–15.

synaptic region See *synapse*.

synaptic transmitter The chemical in the presynaptic bouton that serves as the basis of neural-neural communication. It travels across the synaptic cleft and reacts with the postsynaptic membrane when triggered by a nerve impulse. Also called *neurotransmitter*.

synaptic vesicles The small, spherically shaped structures which contain molecules of synaptic transmitter. See Figure 4–16.

system A higher level of brain organization that includes specialized circuits, e.g., the visual system. Contrast with *circuit*.

tardive dyskinesia Involuntary movements—especially those involving the face, mouth, lips, and tongue—related to prolonged use of antipsychotic drugs, such as chlorpromazine. See Box 13–2.

taste buds Taste receptor cells on the surface of the tongue.

tectorial membrane A structure in the cochlear duct. See Figure 6–7.

telencephalon The frontal subdivision of the forebrain which includes the cerebral hemispheres when fully developed. See Figures 2–7 and 2–8.

temporal summation The summation of postsynaptic potentials which reach the axon hillock at different times. The closer together they are, the more complete the summation.

testosterone A hormone produced by male gonads which controls a variety of bodily changes that become visible at puberty. See Figure 5–11.

thalamus The brain regions that surround the third ventricle. See Figures 2–2 and 6–19.

thoracic Refers to the level of the chest.

threshold The stimulus intensity just adequate to trigger a nerve impulse at the axon hillock.

thyroid gland An endocrine gland located below the vocal apparatus in the throat which regulates metabolic processes, especially carbohydrate utilization and body growth. See Figure 5–6.

thyroid-stimulating hormone (TSH) A tropic hormone released by the anterior pituitary gland which increases the release of thyroxine and the uptake of iodide by the thyroid gland. See Figure 5–6.

thyrotropin-releasing hormone (TRH) A hypothalamic hormone that regulates the release of thyroid-stimulating hormone. See Figure 5–6.

thyroxine A hormone released by the thyroid gland.

tomogram See *computer axial tomogram*.

tonic receptors Receptors in which the frequency of nerve impulse discharge declines slowly or not at all as stimulation is maintained.

transcription The process during which mRNA forms bases complementary to a strand of DNA. This message is then used to translate the DNA code into protein molecules.

transducers Devices that convert energy from one form to another, e.g., sensory receptor cells.

transduction The process of converting one form of energy to another.

transfer RNA (tRNA) Small molecules of RNA that convey amino acids to ribosomes for translation. See Box Figure 3–2.

translation The process by which amino acids are linked together (directed by an mRNA molecule) to form protein molecules. See Box Figure 3–2.

transmethylation hypothesis A hypothesized explanation of schizophrenia suggesting that the addition of a methyl group to some naturally occuring brain compounds can convert some substances to hallucinogenic agents, or psychotogens.

transverse See *coronal*.

tremors Rhythmic repetitive movements caused by brain pathology.

tremor-at-rest A tremor that occurs when the affected region, such as a limb, is fully supported.

TRH See *thyrotropin-releasing hormone*.

trichromatic hypothesis A theory of color perception which states that there are three different types of cones, each excited by a different region of the spectrum and each having a separate pathway to the brain.

trigger features Particular stimulus characteristics that are most effective in evoking responses from a particular cell.

triplet code A code for an amino acid specified by three successive bases of a DNA molecule.

tRNA See *transfer RNA*.

tropic hormones Anterior pituitary hormones that affect the secretion of other endocrine glands. See Figures 5–4 and 5–6.

TSH See *thyroid-stimulating hormone*.

tympanic canal One of three principal canals running along the length of the cochlea. See Figure 6–7.

tympanic membrane The partition between the external and middle ear. Also called *eardrum*. See Figure 6–6.

unconditioned stimulus (US) See *classical conditioning*.

unipolar depression Emotional depression that alternates with normal emotional states. Contrast with *bipolar depression*.

unmyelinated Refers to fine diameter axons that lack a *myelin* sheath.

US Unconditioned stimulus. See *classical conditioning*.

utricle A small fluid-filled sac in the *vestibular system* that responds to static positions of the head. See Figure 6–9.

vagus nerve One of the cranial nerves. See Figure 2–12.

vasopressin See *antidiuretic hormone*.

ventral An anatomical term meaning toward the belly or front of the body or the bottom of the brain; opposite of *dorsal*.

ventral root See *roots*.

ventricles Cavities in the brain which contain cerebrospinal fluid. See Figure 2–9.

ventricular layer A layer of homogeneous cells in the neural tube of the developing organism which is the source of all neural and glial cells in the mature organism. Also called the *ependymal layer*. See Figure 3–12.

ventromedial hypothalamus (VMH) A hypothalamic region involved in inhibiting eating, among other functions. See Figure 11–5.

vertebral arteries Arteries which ascend the vertebrae, enter the base of the skull, and join together to form the basilar artery. See Figure 2–10.

vestibular canal One of three principal canals running along the length of the cochlea. See Figure 6–7.

vestibular system A receptor system in the inner ear that responds to mechanical forces, such as gravity and acceleration. See Figure 6–9.

vestibuloocular reflex A rapid response that adjusts the eye to a change in head position.

VMH See *ventromedial hypothalamus*.

volley theory A theory of frequency discrimination which emphasizes the relation between sound frequency and the firing pattern of nerve cells (i.e., a 500-Hz tone would produce 500 neural discharges per second by a nerve cell or group of nerve cells). Contrast with *place theory*. See Figure 7–20.

vomeronasal system A collection of olfactory receptor cells on the floor of the nose found in some animals in addition to the olfactory epithelium.

Wallerian degeneration See *anterograde degeneration*.

Wernicke's aphasia A language impairment—involving fluent, meaningless speech and little language comprehension—related to damage to *Wernicke's area*.

Wernicke's area A region of the left hemisphere involved in language comprehension. See Figure 16–4.

white matter A shiny layer underneath the cortex consisting largely of axons with white, myelin sheaths.

Wolffian duct system A primitive duct system in each embryo which will develop into male structures—the epidymides, the vas deferens, and the seminal vesicles—if testes are present in the embryo. Contrast with *Müllerian duct system*. See Figure 9–7.

X cells Retinal ganglion cells that continue to respond to maintained visual stimuli.

Y cells Retinal ganglion cells that respond strongly initially, but rapidly decrease frequency of response as the visual stimuli is maintained.

References

Abraham, S. F., Denton, D. A., and Weisinger, B. S. "Effect of an angiotensin antagonist, Sar-Ala-Angiotensin II on physiological thirst." *Pharmacology, Biochemistry and Behavior*, 1976, *4*, 243–247.

Ader, R. "Experimentally induced gastric lesions: Results and implications of studies in animals." *Advances in Psychosomatic Medicine*, 1971, *6*, 1–39.

Adler, N. T. (Ed.), *Neuroendocrinology of reproduction*. New York: Plenum, 1981.

Adler, N. T. "On the mechanisms of sexual behaviour and their evolutionary constraints." In J. B. Hutchison (Ed.), *Biological determinants of sexual behaviour*. New York: Wiley, 1978. 657–695.

Aghajanian, G. K., and Bloom, F. E. "The formation of synaptic junctions in developing rat brain: A quantitative electron microscopic study." *Brain Research*, 1967, *6*, 716–727.

Agranoff, B. W. "Biochemical events mediating the formation of short-term and long-term memory." In Y. Tsukada and B. W. Agranoff (Eds.), *Neurobiological basis of learning and Memory*. New York: Wiley, 1980.

Alberts, J. R. "Huddling by rat pups: Multisensory control of contact behavior." *Journal of Comparative and Physiological Psychology*, 1978, *92*(2), 220–230.

Albrecht, D. G. "Analysis of visual form." Ph.D. thesis. University of California, Berkeley, 1978.

Alexander, R. D., Hoogland, J. L., Howard, R. D., Noonan, K. M., and Sherman, P. W. "Sexual dimorphisms and breeding systems in pinnipeds, ungulates, primates, and humans." In N. A. Chagnon and W. Irons (Eds.), *Evolutionary biology and human social behavior*. North Scituate, Mass.: Duxbury, 1979. 402–435.

Allman, J. M., and Kaas, J. H., "Representation of the visual field in the medial wall of occipital-parietal cortex in the owl monkey." *Science*, 1976, *191*, 572–575.

Almli, C. R. "The ontogeny of feeding and drinking behaviors: effects of early brain damage." *Neuroscience and Biobehavioral Reviews*, 1978, *2*, 281–300.

Almli, C. R., Fisher, R. S., and Hill, D. L. "Lateral hypothalamus destruction in infant rats produces consummatory deficits without sensory neglect or attenuated arousal." *Experimental Neurology*, 1979, *66*, 146–157.

Alpert, M., and Friedhoff, A. J. "An un-dopamine hypothesis of schizophrenia." *Schizophrenia Bulletin*, 1980, *6*, 387–390.

Altman, J. "Experimental reorganization of the cerebellar cortex. VII. Effects of late x-irradiation." *Journal of Comparative Neurology*, 1976, *165*, 65–76.

Altman, J. "Postnatal growth and differentiation of the mammalian brain with implications for a morphological theory of memory." In G. C. Quarton, T. Melnechuk, and F. O. Schmitt (Eds.), *The Neurosciences*. New York: Rockefellar University, 1967.

Amaral, D. G. "A Golgi study of cell types in the hilar region of the hippocampus in the rat." *Journal of Comparative Neurology*, 1978, *182*, 851–914.

Anand, B. K., and Brobeck, J. R. "Localization of a 'feeding center' in the hypothalamus of the rat." *Proceedings of the Society for Experimental Biology and Medicine*, 1951, *77*, 323–324.

Andersson, B. "Regulation of water intake." *Physiological Reviews*, 1978, *58*, 582–603.

Antin, J., Gibbs, J., Holt, J., Young, R. C., and Smith, G. P. "Cholecystokinin elicits the complete behavioral sequence of satiety in rats." *Journal of Comparative and Physiological Psychology*, 1975, *89*, 784–790.

Apgar, V. "A proposal for a new method of evaluation of the newborn infant." *Current Research in Anesthesia and Analgesia*, 1973, *32*, 260.

Arkin, A. M., Antrobus, J. S., and Ellman, S. J. (Eds.), *The mind in sleep: Psychology and psychophysiology*. Hillsdale, N. J.: Lawrence Erlbaum, 1978.

Arnauld, E., Dufy, B., and Vincent, J. D. "Hypothalamic supraoptic neurones: Rates and patterns of action potential firing during water deprivation in the unanesthetized monkey." *Brain Research*, 1975, *100*, 315–325.

Arnold, A. P. "Sexual differences in the brain." *American Scientist*, 1980, *68*, 165–173.

Autrum, H., Jung, R., Loewenstein, W. R., MacKay, D. M., and Teuber, H. L. (Eds.), *Handbook of Sensory Physiology* (9 vols.), Berlin and New York: Springer-Verlag, 1971–1981.

Ax, A. F. "The physiological differentiation between fear and anger in humans." *Psychosomatic Medicine*, 1953, *15*, 433–442.

Bach-y-Rita, P. "Brain plasticity as a basis for therapeutic procedures." In P. Bach-y-Rita (Ed.), *Recovery of function: Theoretical considerations for brain injury rehabilitation*. Bern: Hans Huber, 1980.

Bach-y-Rita, P. (Ed.), *Recovery of function following brain injury: Theoretical considerations*. Bern: Hans Huber, 1980.

Baird, I. L. "Anatomical features of the inner ear in submammalian vertebrates." In W. D. Keidel and W. D. Neff (Eds.), *Handbook of Sensory Physiology* Vol. V/1, *Auditory System Anatomy Physiology (Ear)*. New York: Springer-Verlag, 1974, 159–212.

Baker, M. A. "A brain-cooling system in mammals." *Scientific American*, 1979, *240*(5), 130–139.

Bancroft, J. "The relationship between hormones and sexual behaviour in humans." In J. B. Hutchison (Ed.), *Biological determinants of sexual behaviour*. New York: Wiley, 1978, 493–519.

Barbour, H. G. "Die Wirkung unmittelbarer Erwärmung und Abkühlung der Wärmenzentren auf die Körpertemperatur." *Archiv für experimentalle Pathologie und Pharmakologie*, 1912, *70*, 1–26.

Barchas, J. D., Akil, H., Elliott, G. R., Holman, R. B., and Watson, S. J. "Behavioral neurochemistry: Neuroregulators and behavioral states." *Science*, 1978, *200*, 964–973.

Barlow, G. "Modal action patterns." In T. A. Sebeok (Ed.), *How animals communicate*. Bloomington: Indiana University, 1977.

Barlow, H. B., Blakemore, C., and Pettigrew, J. D. "The neural mechanism of binocular depth discrimination." *Journal of Physiology* (London), 1967, *193*, 327–342.

Barnett, S. A. *The rat: A study in behavior*. Revised edition. Chicago: University of Chicago, 1975.

Barondes, S. H., and Cohen, H. D. "Comparative effects of cycloheximide and puromycin on cerebral protein synthesis and consolidation of memory in mice." *Brain Research*, 1967, *4*, 44–51.

Bartoshuk, L. "Taste." In R. B. Masterton, *Handbook of Neurobiology* V. 1 New York: Plenum, 1978.

Baum, M. J., Keverne, E. B., Everitt, B. J., Herbert, J., and de Vrees, P. "Reduction of sexual interaction in rhesus monkeys by a vaginal action of progesterone." *Nature*, 1976, *263*, 606–608.

Beach, F. A. "Behavioral endocrinology: An emerging discipline." *American Scientist*, 1975, *63*, 178–187.

Beach, F. A. "Human sexuality in four perspectives." In F. A. Beach (Ed.), *Human sexuality in four perspectives*. Baltimore: Johns Hopkins University, 1977, 1–21.

Beach, F. A., and Levinson, G. "Effects of androgen on the glans penis and mating behavior of castrated male rats." *Journal of Experimental Zoology*, 1950, *144*, 159–171.

Beal, M. F., Kleinman, G. M., Ojemann, R. C., and Hockberg, F. H. "Gangliocytoma of third ventricle: Hyperphagia, somnolence and dementia." *Neurology*, 1981, *31*, 1224–1227.

Beamish, P., and Kiloh, L. G. "Psychoses due to amphetamine consumption." *Journal of Mental Science*, 1960, *106*, 337–343.

Bellinger, L. L., Trietley, G. J., and Bernardis, L. L. "Failure of portal glucose and adrenaline infusions or liver denervation to affect food intake in dogs." *Physiology and Behavior*, 1976, *16*, 299–304.

Bennett, E. L., Rosenzweig, M. R., Diamond, M. C., Morimoto, H., and Hebert, M. "Effects of successive environments on brain measures." *Physiology and Behavior*, 1974, *12*, 621–631.

Bennett, E. L., Rosenzweig, M. R., and Flood, J. F. "Role of neurotransmitters and protein synthesis in short- and long-term memory." In J. Obiols, C. Ballus, E. Gonzales Monclus, and J. Pujol (Eds.), *Biological Psychiatry Today*. Amsterdam: Elsevier/North-Holland Biomedical Press, 1979.

Bennett, E. L., Rosenzweig, M. R., Morimoto, H., and Hebert, M. "Maze training alters brain weights and cortical RNA/DNA." *Behavioral and Neural Biology*, 1979, *26*, 1–22.

Bennett, M. V. L. "Function of electronic junctions in embryonic and adult tissues." *Federation Proceedings*, 1973, *32*, 65–75.

Bentley, D. "Genetic analysis of the nervous system." In J. C. Fentress (Ed.), *Simpler networks and behavior*. Sunderland, Mass.: Sinauer Associates, 1976.

Benton, A. "Visuoperceptive, visuospatial, and visuocoustinctive disorders." In K. M. Heilman and E. Valenstein (Eds.), *Clinical Neuropsychology*, New York: Oxford, 1979.

Benzer, S. "Genetic dissection of behavior." *Scientific American*, 1973, *229*(12), 24–37.

Berger, T. W., Laham, R. I., and Thompson, R. F. "Hippocampal unit-behavior correlations during classical conditioning." *Brain Research*, 1980, *193*, 229–248.

Berger, T. W., and Thompson, R. F. "Neuronal plasticity in the limbic system during classical conditioning of the rabbit nictitating membrane response, I. The hippocampus." *Brain Research*, 1978, *145*, 323–346.

Bernstein, N. *The co-ordination and regulation of movements*. New York: Pergamon, 1967.

Berry, M., Rogers, A. W., and Eayrs, J. T. "Pattern of cell migration during cortical histogenesis." *Nature*, 1964, *203*, 591–593.

Berry, S. D., and Thompson, R. F. "Medial septal lesions retard classical conditioning of the nictitating membrane response in rabbits." *Science*, 1979, *205*, 209–211.

Bert, J. "Sleep in primates: A review of various results." *Medical Primatology*. Basel: Karger, 1971, 308–315.

Bierce, A. *The devil's dictionary*. New York: Boni, 1935 (Original printing, 1911).

Bilger, R. C., and Hopkinson, N. T. "Hearing performance with the auditory prosthesis." *Annals of Otology, Rhinology and Laryngology*, 1977, Supplement 38.

Bindra, D. (Ed.), *The brain's mind: A neuroscience perspective on the mind-body problem*. New York: Gardner, 1980.

Blakemore, C. "The conditions required for the maintenance of binocularity in the kitten's visual cortex." *Journal of Physiology* (London), 1976, *261*, 423–444.

Blakemore, C. "Developmental factors in the formation of feature extracting neurons." In F. G. Worden and F. O. Schmitt (Eds.), *The Neurosciences, Third Study Program*. Cambridge: MIT, 1974.

Blakemore, C., and Campbell, F. W. "On the existence of neurones in the human visual system selectively sensitive to the orientation and size of retinal images." *Journal of Physiology* (London), 1969, *203*, 237–260.

Blakemore, C., and Cooper, G. F. "Development of the brain depends on the visual environment." *Nature*, 1970, *228*, 477–478.

Bligh, J. "The central neurology of mammalian thermoregulation." *Neuroscience*, 1979, *4*, 1213–1236.

Bloch, V. "Brain activation and memory consolidation." In M. R. Rosenzweig and E. L. Bennett (Eds.), *Neural mechanisms of learning and memory*. Cambridge: MIT, 1976.

Bloch, V., Deweer, B., and Hennevin, E. "Suppression de l'amnésie rétrograde et consolidation d'un apprentissage à essai unique par stimulation réticulaire." *Physiology and Behavior*, 1970, *5*, 1235–1241.

Block, J. H. "Issues, problems, and pitfalls in assessing sex differences: A critical review of *The Psychology of Sex Differences*." *Merrill-Palmer Quarterly*, 1976, *22*, 283–308.

Bodis-Wollner, I. "Visual acuity and contrast sensitivity in patients with cerebral lesions." *Science*, 1972, *178*, 769–771.

Bogen, J. E. "Educational implications of recent research on the human brain." In Wittrock, M. C. (Ed.), *The human brain*. Englewood Cliffs, N. J.: Prentice-Hall, 1977.

Bolles, R. C., and Faneslow, M. S. "Endorphins and behavior." *Annual Review of Psychology*, 1982, *33*, 87–101.

Bonica, J. J. (Ed.) "Pain." Vol. 58 in *Research publication: Associ-*

ation for research in nervous and mental disease. New York: Raven, 1980.

Bonsall, R. W., Zumpe, D., and Michael, R. P. "Menstrual cycle influences on operant behavior of female rhesus monkeys." *Journal of Comparative and Physiological Psychology*, 1978, *92*, 846–855.

Bourguignon, E., and Greenbaum, L. S. *Diversity and homogeneity in world societies.* New Haven: HRAF, 1973.

Brady, J. V. "Ulcers in 'executive' monkeys." *Scientific American*, 1958, *10*, 95–100.

Brasel, J. A., and Blizzard, R. M. "The influence of the endocrine glands upon growth and development." In R. H. Williams (Ed.), *Textbook of endocrinology.* Philadelphia: Saunders, 1974.

Brazier, M. A. B. "The historical development of neurophysiology." In *Handbook of Physiology. Section I. Neurophysiology. Vol. 1*, Washington, D. C.: American Physiological Society, 1959.

Bredberg, G. "Cellular pattern and nerve supply of the human organ of Corti." *Acta Otolaryngologica*, 1968, Supplement 236.

Breland, K., and Breland, M. *Animal Behavior.* New York: Macmillan, 1966.

Breland, K., and Breland, M. "The Misbehavior of Organisms." *The American Psychologist*, 1961, *16*, 681–684.

Brown, W. A., and Heninger, G. "Cortisol, growth hormone, free fatty acids and experimentally evoked affective arousal." *American Journal of Psychiatry*, 1975, *132*, 1172–1176.

Brudny, J., Korein, J., Grynbaum, B. B., Friedmann, L. W., Weinstein, S., Sachs-Frankel, G., and Belandres, P. V. "EMG feedback therapy: Review of treatment of 114 patients." *Archives of Physical Medicine and Rehabilitation*, 1976, *57*, 55–61.

Bullock, T. H., Orkand, R., and Grinell, A. *Introduction to nervous systems.* San Francisco: Freeman, 1977.

Bureš, J., and Burešová, O. "Elementary learning phenomena in food selection." *Proceedings of the International Union of Physiological Sciences*, 1980, *14*, 13–14.

Bushnell, M. C., Robinson, D. L., and Goldberg, M. "Dissociation of movement and attention: Neuronal correlates in posterior parietal cortex." *Society for Neuroscience Abstracts*, 1978, *4*, 621.

Butters, N., and Cermak, L. S. *Alcoholic Korsakoff's syndrome: An information-processing approach to amnesia.* New York: Academic, 1980.

Butters, N., and Ryan, C. "Memory deficits of detoxified alcoholics: evidence for the premature aging and continuity hypotheses." *International Neuropsychological Society Bulletin*, 1979, *12*.

Byrne, D. G., and Whyte, H. M. "Life events and myocardial infarction revisited." *Psychosomatic Medicine*, 1980, *42*, 1–10.

Cabanac, M. "Physiological role of pleasure." *Science*, 1971, *173*, 1103–1107.

Callaway, E. *Brain electrical potentials and individual psychological differences.* New York: Grune & Stratton, 1975.

Calne, R., Williams, R., Dawson, J., Ansell, I., Evans, D., Flute, P., Herbertson, B., Joysey, V., Keates, G., Knill-Jones, R., Mason, S., Millard, P., Pena, J., Pentlow, B., Salaman, J., Sells, R., and Cullum, P. "Liver transplantation in Man-II, a report of two orthotopic liver transplants in adult recipients." *British Medical Journal*, 1968, *4*, 541–546.

Campbell, F. W. "The transmission of spatial information through the visual system." In F. O. Schmitt and F. G. Warden (Eds.), *The neurosciences: Third study program.* Cambridge: MIT, 1974.

Campbell, F. W., and Robson, J. G. "Application of Fourier analysis to the visibility of gratings." *Journal of Physiology* (London), 1968, *197*, 551–566.

Canady, R., Kroodama, D., and Nottebohm, F. "Significant differences in volume of song control nuclei is associated with variance in song repertoire in a free ranging song bird." *Society for Neuroscience Abstracts*, 1981, *7*, 845.

Cannon, W. B. *Bodily changes in pain, hunger, fear and rage.* New York: Appleton, 1929.

Carew, T. J., Walters, E. T., and Kandel, E. R. "Associative learning in a simple reflex of *Aplysia*." *Society for Neuroscience Abstracts*, 1981, *7*, 353.

Carew, T. J., Walters, E. T., and Kandel, E. R. "Classical conditioning in a simple withdrawal reflex in *Aplysia Californica*." *The Journal of Neuroscience*, 1981, *1*, 1426–1437.

Cartwright, R. D. *Night life.* Englewood Cliffs, N. J.: Prentice-Hall.

Caviness, V. S., Jr. "The developmental consequences of abnormal cell position in the reeler mouse." *Trends in Neurosciences*, 1980, *3*, 31–33.

Chang, E.-L., and Greenough, W. T. "Lateralized effects of monocular training on dendritic branching in adult split-brain rats." *Brain Research*, 1982, *232*, 283–292.

Cheng, M.-F. "Ovarian development in the female ring dove in response to stimulation by intact and castrated male ring doves." *Journal of Endocrinology*, 1974, *63*, 43–53.

Cheng, M.-F. "Egg fertility and prolactin as determinants of reproductive recycling in doves." *Hormones and Behavior*, 1977, *9*, 85–98.

Cheng, M.-F. "Progress and prospects in ring dove research: A personal view." *Advances in the Study of Behavior*, 1979, *9*, 97–129.

Chiarello, C., Knight, R., and Mundel, M. "Aphasia in a prelingually deaf woman." *Brain*, 1982, *105*, 29–52.

Cohen, D. B. *Sleep and dreaming: Origin, nature and functions.* Oxford: Pergamon, 1979.

Cohen, D. H. "The neural pathways and informational flow mediating a conditioned autonomic response." In L. V. Di Cara (Ed.), *Limbic and autonomic system research.* New York: Plenum, 1974.

Cohen, D. H. "Cardiovascular neurobiology: the substrate for biobehavioral approaches to hypertension." In Ruth Johnsson Hegyeli (Ed.), *1981 joint USA-USSR symposium on biobehavioral and epidemiological aspects of hypertension.* Washington, D.C.: National Institute of Health, 1982.

Cohen, H. D., Ervin, F., and Barondes, S. H. "Puromycin and cycloheximide: different effects on hippocampal electrical activity." *Science*, 1966, *154*, 1552–1558.

Cohen, N. J., and Squire, L. R. "Preserved learning and retention of pattern-analyzing skill in amnesia: dissociation of knowing how and knowing what." *Science*, 1980, *210*, 207–210.

Cohen, N. J., and Squire, L. R. "Retrograde amnesia and remote memory impairment." *Neuropsychologia*, 1981, *19*, 337–356.

Cohn, R., Neumann, M. A., and Wood, D. H. "Prosopagnosia: A clinicopathological study." *Annals of Neurology* 1977, *1*, 177–182.

Cole, K. S., and Curtis, H. J. "Electric impedance of the squid giant axon during activity." *Journal of General Physiology*, 1939, *22*, 649–670.

Cooper, J. R., Bloom, F. E., and Roth, R. H. *The biochemical basis of neuropharmacology*. New York: Oxford, 1978.

Cooper, I. S., Riklan, M., Amin, I., Waltz, J. M., and Cullinan, T. "Chronic cerebellar stimulation in cerebral palsy." *Neurology*, 1976, *26*, 744–753.

Corkin, S., Milner, B., and Rasmussen, T. "Somatosensory thresholds: Contrasting effects of postcentral-gyrus and posterior parietal-lobe excisions." *Archives of Neurology*, 1970, *23*, 41–58.

Corkin, S., Sullivan, E. V., Twitchell, T. E., and Grove, E. "The amnesic patient H. M.: clinical observations and test performance 28 years after operation." *Society for Neuroscience Abstracts*, 1981, *7*, 235.

Cotman, C., and Nieto-Sampedro, M. "Brain function, synapse renewal, and plasticity." *Annual Review of Psychology*, 1982, *33*, 371–402.

Cowan, W. M. "The development of the brain." *Scientific American*, 1979, *241*(3), 112–133.

Cowey, A. "Perimetric study of field defects after cortical and retinal ablations." *Quarterly Journal of Experimental Psychology*, 1967, *19*, 232–245.

Cragg, B. G. "Changes in visual cortex on first exposure of rats to light: Effect on synaptic dimensions." *Nature*, 1967, *215*, 251–253.

Cragg, B. G. "The development of synapses in the visual system of the cat." *Journal of Comparative Neurology*, 1975, *160*, 147–166.

Crile, G., and Quiring, D. P. "A record of the body weight and certain organ and gland weights of 3690 animals." *Ohio Journal of Science*, 1940, *40*, 219–259.

Cruce, J. A. F., Greenwood, M. R. C., Johnson, P. R., and Quartermain, D. "Genetic versus hypothalamic obesity: Studies of intake and dietary manipulation in rats. *Journal of Comparative and Physiological Psychology*, 1974, *87*, 295–301.

Culler, E., and Mettler, F. A. "Conditioned behavior in a decorticate dog." *Journal of Comparative Psychology*, 1934, *18*, 291–303.

Cummings, J. L., Benson, D. F., Walsh, M. J., and Levine, H. L. "Left-to-right transfer of language dominance: A case study." *Neurology*, 1979, *29*, 1547–1550.

Curtis, S. Genie. "A psycholinguistic study of a modern day 'wild child'." *Perspectives in neurolinguistics and psycholinguistics series*. New York: Academic, 1977.

Cutting, J. E. "Generation of synthetic male and female walkers through manipulation of a biomechanical invariant." *Perception*, 1978, *7*, 393–405.

Czeisler, C. A., Richardson, G. S., Coleman, R. M., Zimmerman, J. C., Moore-Ede, M. C., Dement, W. C., and Weitzman, E. D. "Chronotherapy: Resetting the circadian clocks of patients with delayed sleep phase insomnia." *Sleep*, 1981, *4*, 1–21.

Dallos, P. *The auditory periphery. Biophysics and physiology*. New York: Academic, 1973.

Daly, M., and Wilson, M. *Sex, evolution and behavior*. Belmont, Cal.: Duxbury, 1978.

Damascio, A. R., Chui, H. C., Corbett, J., and Kassel, N. "Posterior callosal section in a non-epileptic patient." *Journal of Neurology, Neurosurgery, and Psychiatry*, 1980, *43*, 351–356.

Damassa, D. A., Smith, E. R., Tennent, B., and Davidson, J. M. "The relationship between circulating testosterone levels and male sexual behavior in rats." *Hormones and Behavior*, 1977, *8*, 275–286.

D'Amato, M. R. "Derived motives." In M. R. Rosenzweig and L. W. Porter (Eds.), *Annual review of psychology* (Vol. 25). Palo Alto: Annual Reviews, 1974.

Darian-Smith, I. "Touch in primates." *Annual Review of Psychology*, 1982, *33*, 155–194.

Darian-Smith, I., Davidson, I., and Johnson, K. O. "Peripheral neural representations of the two spatial dimensions of a textured surface moving over the monkey's finger pad." *Journal of Physiology*, 1980, *309*, 135–146.

Darwin, C. *The descent of man and selection in relation to sex*. London: John Murray, 1871.

Davenport, J. W. "Environmental therapy in hypothyroid and other disadvantaged animal populations." In R. N. Walsh and W. T. Greenough (Eds.), *Environments as therapy for brain dysfunction*. New York: Plenum, 1976.

Davenport, W. H. "Sex in cross-cultural perspective." In F. A. Beach (Ed.), *Human sexuality in four perspectives*. Baltimore: Johns Hopkins University, 1977, 115–163.

Davidson, J. "Hormones and reproductive behavior." In H. Balin and S. Glasser (Eds.), *Reproductive Biology*. Amsterdam: Exerpta Medica, 1972.

Davidson, J. M. "Activation of the male rat's sexual behavior by intracerebral implantation of androgen." *Endocrinology*, 1966, *79*, 783–794.

Davidson, J. M. "Characteristics of sex behaviour in male rats following castration." *Animal Behaviour*, 1966, *14*, 266–272.

Davidson, J. M., Camargo, C. A., and Smith, E. R. "Effects of androgen on sexual behavior in hypogonadal men." *Journal of Clinical Endocrinology and Metabolism*, 1979, *48*, 955–958.

Davidson, J. M., Smith, E. R., Rodgers, C. H., and Bloch, F. J. "Relative thresholds of behavioral and somatic responses to estrogen." *Physiology and Behavior*, 1968, *3*, 227–229.

Davis, K. L., Mohs, R. C., Tinklenberg, J. R., Pfefferbau, A., Hollister, L. E., and Kopell, B. S. "Physostigmine: improvement of long-term memory processes in normal humans." *Science*, 1978, *201*, 272–274.

DeArmond, S. J., Fusco, M. M., and Dewey, M. M. *Structure of the human brain*. New York: Oxford, 1976.

Dekaban, A. S., and Sadowsky, D. "Changes in brain weights during the span of human life: Relation of brain weights to body heights and body weights." *Annals of Neurology*, 1978, *4*, 345–356.

DeLong, M. R. "Motor functions of the basal ganglion: Single-unit activity during movement." In F. O. Schmitt and F. G. Worden

(Eds.), *The neurosciences: Third study program*. Cambridge: MIT, 1974.

Denckla, M. B. "Childhood learning disabilities." In K. M. Heilman and E. Valenstein. (Eds.), *Clinical neuropsychology*. New York: Oxford, 1979.

Desaki, J., and Uehara, Y. "The overall morphology of neuromuscular junction as revealed by scanning electron microscopy." *Journal of Neurocytology*, 1981, *10*, 101–110.

Desmedt, J. E. (Ed.), *Progress in clinical neurophysiology. (Vol. 4): Cerebral motor control in man: Long loop mechanisms*. Basel: Karger, 1978.

Dethier, V. G. *The hungry fly: A physiological study of behavior associated with feeding*. Cambridge: Harvard, 1976.

Deutsch, J. A. "The cholinergic synapse and the site of memory." *Science*, 1971, *174*, 788–794.

Deutsch, J. A. "The stomach in food satiation and the regulation of appetite." *Progress in Neurobiology*, 1978, *10*, 135–153.

De Valois, R. L., and De Valois, K. K. "Neural coding of color." In *Handbook of perception: Seeing* (Vol. 5). New York: Academic, 1975.

De Valois, R. L., and De Valois, K. K. "Spatial vision." *Annual Review of Psychology*, 1980, *31*, 309–341.

De Valois, R. L., Morgan, H., and Snodderly, M. "Psychophysical studies of monkey vision—III. Spatial luminance contrast sensitivity tests of macaque and human observers." *Vision Research*, 1974, *14*, 75–81.

De Valois, R. L., Albrecht, D. G., and Thorell, L. G. "Spatial tuning of LGN and cortical cells in monkey visual system." In H. Spekreijse and L. H. van der Tweel (Eds.), *Spatial Contrast*. Amsterdam: North Holland, 1977.

Dewsbury, D. A. "Diversity and adaptation in rodent copulatory behavior." *Science*, 1975, *190*, 947–954.

Dewson, J. H. "Efferent olivocochlear bundle: Some relationships to stimulus discrimination in noise." *Journal of Neurophysiology*, 1968, *31*, 122–130.

Diamond, I. T. "The functional significance of architectonic subdivisions of the cortex: Lashley's criticism of the traditional view." In J. Orbach (Ed.), *Neuropsychology after Lashley*. New York: Plenum, 1982, 101–135.

Diamond, J., Cooper, E., Turner, C., and Macintyre, L. "Trophic regulation of nerve sprouting." *Science*, 1976, *193*, 371–377.

Diamond, M. C. "Anatomical brain changes induced by environment." In L. Petrinovich and J. L. McGaugh (Eds.), *Knowing, Thinking, and Believing*. New York: Plenum, 1976, 215–241.

Diamond, M. C. "New data supporting cortical asymmetry differences in males and females." *The Behavioral and Brain Sciences*, 1980, *3*, 233–234.

Diamond, M. C., Krech, D., and Rosenzweig, M. R. "The effects of an enriched environment on the histology of the rat cerebral cortex." *Journal of Comparative Neurology*, 1964, *123*, 111–119.

Diamond, M. C., Law, F., Rhodes, H., Lindner, B., Rosenzweig, M. R., Krech, D., and Bennett, E. L. "Increases in cortical depth and glia numbers in rats subjected to enriched environment." *Journal of Comparative Neurology*, 1966, *128*, 117–125.

Diamond, M. C., Lindner, B., Johnson, R., Bennett, E. L., and

Rosenzweig, M. R. "Differences in occipital cortical synapses from environmentally enriched, impoverished, and standard colony rats." *Journal of Neuroscience Research*, 1975, *1*, 109–119.

Dobelle, W. H., and Mladejovsky, M. G. "Phosphenes produced by electrical stimulation of human occipital cortex and their application to the development of a prosthesis for the blind." *Journal of Physiology* (London), 1974, *243*, 553–577.

Dörner, G., Döcke, F., and Moustafa, S. "Differential localization of a male and a female hypothalamic mating centre." *Journal of Reproduction and Fertility*, 1968b, *17*, 583–586.

Dörner, G., Döcke, F., and Moustafa, S. "Homosexuality in female rats following testosterone implantation in the anterior hypothalamus." *Journal of Reproduction and Fertility*, 1968a, *17*, 173–175.

Douglas, R. J. "The hippocampus and behavior." *Psychological Bulletin*, 1967, *67*, 416–422.

Drachman, D. B. "The biology of myasthenia gravis." *Annual Review of Neurosciences*, 1981, *4*, 195–225.

Drachman, D. A. "Central cholinergic system and memory." In M. A. Lipton, A. DiMascio, and K. F. Killam (Eds.), *Psychopharmacology: a generation of progress*. New York: Raven, 1978.

Drucker-Colin, R., Shkurovich, M., and Sterman, M. B. (Eds.), *The functions of sleep*. New Haven: Yale, 1973.

Dudai, Y. and Quinn, W. G. "Genes and learning in *Drosophila*." *Trends in Neurosciences*, 1980, *3*(2), 28–30.

Dunn, A. J. "Neurochemistry of learning and memory: An evaluation of recent data." *Annual Review of Psychology*, 1980, *31*, 343–390.

Durup, G., and Fessard, A. "L'électroencéphalogramme de l'homme." *L'Année Psychologique*, 1935, *36*, 1–32.

Eccles, J. C. "Possible ways in which synaptic mechanisms participate in learning, remembering and forgetting." In D. P. Kimble (Ed.), *The anatomy of memory*. Palo Alto: Science and Behavior Books, Inc., 1965, 12–87.

Eccles, J. C. "The synapse: From electrical to chemical transmission." *Annual Review of Neuroscience*, 1982, *5*, 325–339.

Eccles, J. C. *The understanding of the brain*. New York: McGraw-Hill, 1973.

Ehrenkranz, J., Bliss, E., and Sheard, M. H. "Plasma testosterone: correlation with aggressive behavior and social dominance in men." *Psychosomatic Medicine*, 1974, *36*, 469–475.

Ehrhardt, A. A., and Meyer-Bahlburg, H.F.L. "Effects of prenatal sex hormones on gender-related behavior." *Science*, 1981, *211*, 1312–1318.

Ehrhardt, A. A., and Meyer Bahlburg, H.F.L. "Prenatal sex hormones and the developing brain: Effects on psychosexual differentiation and cognitive function." *Annual Review of Medicine*, 1979, *30*, 417–430.

Eikelboom, R., and Stewart, J. "Temporal and environmental cues in conditioned hypothermia and hyperthermia associated with morphine." *Psychopharmacology*, 1981, *72*, 147–153.

Eisenberg, J. F. and Wilson, D. E. "Relative brain size and feeding strategies in the Chiroptera." *Evolution*, 1978, *32*, 740–751.

Ekman, P. "Universals and cultural differences in facial expressions of emotion." *Nebraska Symposium on Motivation*, 1972, 207–283.

Ekman, P., and Oster, H. "Facial expressions of emotion." *Annual Review of Psychology*, 1979, *30*, 527–554.

Ekstrand, B. R., Barrett, T. R., West, J. M., and Maier, W. G. "The effect on human long-term memory." In R. R. Drucker-Colin and J. L. McGaugh (Eds.), *Neurobiology of sleep and memory*. New York: Academic, 1977.

Eliasson, S. G., Prensky, A. L., and Hardin, W. B. *Neurological pathophysiology*. New York: Oxford, 1974.

Elmadjian, F., Hope, J. M., and Lamson, E. T. "Excretion of epinephrine and norepinephrine in various emotional states." *Journal of Clinical Endocrinology*, 1957, *17*, 608–620.

Elmadjian, F., Hope, J. M., and Lamson, E. T. "Excretion of epinephrine and norepinephrine under stress." *Recent Progress in Hormone Research*, 1958, *14*, 513.

Entingh, D., Dunn, A., Wilson, J. E., Glassman, E., and Hogan, E. "Biochemical approaches to the biological basis of memory." In M. S. Gazzaniga and C. Blakemore (Eds.), *Handbook of Psychobiology*. New York: Academic, 1975.

Epstein, A. N., Fitzsimons, J. T., and Rolls, B. J. "Drinking induced by injection of angiotensin into the brain of the rat." *Journal of Physiology*, (London), 1970, *210*, 457–474.

Erdmann, G., and Janke, W. "Interaction between physiological and cognitive determinants of emotions: Experimental studies on Schachter's theory of emotions." *Biological Psychology*, 1978, *6*, 61–74.

Erickson, C. J. "Sexual affiliation in animals: Pair bonds and reproductive strategies." In J. B. Hutchison (Ed.), *Biological determinants of sexual behaviour*. New York: Wiley, 1978, 697–725.

Evarts, E. V. "Contrasts between activity of precentral and postcentral neurons of cerebral cortex during movement in the monkey." *Brain Research*, 1972, *40*, 25–31.

Evarts, E. V. "Feedback and corollary discharge: A merging of the concepts." *Neurosciences Research Program Bulletin*, 1971, *9*, 86–112.

Evarts, E. V. "Relation of pyramidal tract activity to force exerted during voluntary movement." *Journal of Neurophysiology*, 1968, *31*, 14–28.

Everitt, B. J. "A neuroanatomical approach to the study of monoamines and sexual behaviour." In J. B. Hutchison (Ed.), *Biological determinants of sexual behaviour*. New York: Wiley, 1978, 555–574.

Everitt, B. J., and Herbert, J. "The effects of dexamethasone and androgens on sexual receptivity of female rhesus monkeys." *Journal of Endocrinology*, 1971, *51*, 575–588.

Everitt, B. J., and Herbert, J. "The effects of implanting testosterone propionate into the central nervous system on the sexual behavior of adrenalectomized female rhesus monkeys." *Brain Research*, 1975, *86*, 109–120.

Farley, J., and Alkon, D. L. "Associative neural and behavioral change in *Hermissenda*: consequences of nervous system orientation for light- and pairing-specificity." *Society for Neuroscience Abstracts*, 1981, *7*, 352.

Feder, H. H. "The comparative actions of testosterone propionate and 5α-androstran-17βol-3-one propionate on the reproductive behaviour, physiology, and morphology of male rats." *Journal of Endocrinology*, 1971, *51*, 241–252.

Federman, D. D. "Endocrinology." Chapter 3, *Scientific American Medicine*. New York: Scientific American, 1979.

Ferchmin, P. A., Bennett, E. L., and Rosenzweig, M. R. "Direct contact with enriched environments is required to alter cerebral weights in rats." *Journal of Comparative and Physiological Psychology*, 1975, *88*, 360–367.

Fields, H. "Pain II. New approaches to pain management." *Annals of Neurology*, 1981, *9*, 100–106.

Finger, S. (Ed.), *Recovery from brain damage: Research and theory*. New York: Plenum, 1978.

Fink, M. "Electroshock therapy." *Hospital Practice*, 1978, *13*, 77.

Fisher-Perroudon, C., Mouret, J., and Jouvet, M. "Sur un cas d'agrypnie (4 mois sans sommeil) au cours d'une maladies de Morvan. Effet favorable du 5-hydroxytryptophane." *Electroencephalography and Clinical Neurophysiology*, 1974, *36*, 1–18.

Fitzgerald, F. T. "The problem of obesity." *Annual Review of Medicine*, 1981, *32*, 221–231.

Flexner, J. B., Flexner, L. B., Stellar, E., de la Haba, G., and Roberts, R. B. "Inhibition of protein synthesis in brain and learning following puromycin." *Journal of Neurochemistry*, 1962, *9*, 595–605.

Flood, J. F., Bennett, E. L., Orme, A. E., and Rosenzweig, M. R. "Relation of memory formation to controlled amounts of brain protein synthesis." *Physiology and Behavior*, 1975, *15*, 97–102.

Flood, J. F., Bennett, E. L., Rosenzweig, M. R., and Orme, A. E. "The influence of duration of protein synthesis inhibition on memory." *Physiology and Behavior*, 1973, *10*, 555–562.

Flood, J. F., and Cherkin, A. "Cholinergic drug interactions: enhancement and impairment of memory retention." *Society for Neuroscience Abstracts*, 1981, *7*, 359.

Flood, J. F., Jarvik, M. E., Bennett, E. L., Orme, A. E., and Rosenzweig, M. R. "The effect of stimulants, depressants and protein synthesis inhibition on retention." *Behavioral Biology*, 1977, *20*, 168–183.

Foster, F. M. *Reflex epilepsy, behavioral therapy and conditional reflexes*. Springfield, Ill.: Charles C. Thomas, 1977.

Foster, F. M., and Sherrington, C. S. *A textbook of physiology. Part 3. The central nervous system*. New York: Macmillan, 1897.

Fox, M. W. "Reflex development and behavioral organization." In W. A. Himwich (Ed.), *Developmental neurobiology*. Springfield, Ill.: Charles C. Thomas, 1970.

Franhaeuser, M. "Psychoneuroendocrine approaches to the study of emotion as related to stress and coping." *Current theory and research in motivation*, 1979, *26*, 123–162.

Frazier, W. T., Kandel, E. R., Kupfermann, I., Waziri, R., and Coggeshall, R. E. "Morphological and functional properties of identified neurons in the abdominal ganglion of *Aplysia californica*." *Journal of Neurophysiology*, 1967, *30*, 1288–1351.

Freeman, W. J. *Mass action in the nervous system*. New York: Academic, 1975.

Freeman, W. J., and Watts, J. W. *Psychosurgery in the treatment of mental disorders and intractable pain*. Springfield, Ill.: Charles C. Thomas, 1950.

Friedman, M. B. "Interactions between visual and vocal courtship stimuli in the neuroendocrine response of female doves." *Journal of Comparative and Physiological Psychology*, 1977, *91*, 1408–1416.

Furshpan, E. J., and Potter, D. D. "Mechanism of nerve impulse transmission at a crayfish synapse." *Nature*, 1957, *180*, 342–343.

Gadjusek, D. C. "Unconventional viruses and the origin and distribution of Kuru." *Science*, 1977, *197*, 943–960.

Galaburda, A. M., and Kemper, T. L. Cytoarchitectonic abnormalities in developmental dyslexia: A case study." *Annals of Neurology*, 1978, *6*, 94–100.

Garb, J. L., and Stunkard, A. J. "Taste aversions in man." *American Journal of Psychiatry*, 1974, *131*, 1204–1207.

Gardner, L. I. "Deprivation dwarfism." *Scientific American*, 1972, *227*(1), 76–82.

Gardner, R. A., and Gardner, B. J. "Teaching sign language to a chimpanzee." *Science*, 1969, *165*, 664–672.

Gazzaniga, M. S., and Le Doux, J. E. *The integrated mind*. New York: Plenum, 1978.

Gelperin, A. "Rapid food-aversion learning by a terrestrial mollusk." *Science*, 1975, *189*, 567–570.

Geschwind, N. "Language and cerebral dominance." In T. N. Chase (Ed.), *Nervous system* Vol. 2 *The clinical neurosciences*, New York: Raven, 1976, 433–439.

Geschwind, N. "Language and the brain." *Scientific American*, 1972, *226*(4), 76–83.

Geschwind, N., and Levitsky, W. "Human brain: Left-right asymmetries in temporal speech region." *Science*, 1968, *161*, 186–187.

Gibbs, J., Young, R. C., and Smith, G. P. "Cholecystokinin decreases food intake in rats." *Journal of Comparative and Physiological Psychology*, 1973, *84*, 488–495.

Gibbs, M. E., and Ng, K. T. "Psychobiology of memory formation." *Biobehavioral Reviews*, 1977, *1*, 113–136.

Gilman, A. "The relation between blood osmotic pressure, fluid distribution and voluntary water intake." *American Journal of Physiology*, 1937, *120*, 323–328.

Ginsburg, A. P. "Psychological correlates of a model of the human visual system." Masters thesis. Wright-Patterson AFB, Ohio, Air Force Institute of Technology, 1971.

Ginsburg, A. P., and Campbell, F. W. "Optical transforms and the 'pincushion grid' illusion?" *Science*, 1977, *198*, 961–962.

Glassman, E., Machlus, B., and Wilson, J. E. "The effect of short experiences on the incorporation of radioactive phosphate into acid-soluble nuclear proteins of rat brain." In J. L. McGaugh (Ed.), *The chemistry of mood, motivation and memory*. New York: Plenum, 1972.

Glickman, S. E. "Comparative psychology." In P. Mussen and M. R. Rosenzweig (Eds.), *Psychology: An introduction, second edition*. Lexington, Mass.: D. C. Heath, 1977.

Globus, A., Rosenzweig, M. R., Bennett, E. L., and Diamond, M. C. "Effects of differential experience on dendritic spine counts in rat cerebral cortex." *Journal of Comparative and Physiological Psychology*, 1973, *82*, 175–181.

Gluhbegovic, N., and Williams, T. H. *The human brain*. New York: Harper & Row, 1980.

Gold, P. E., Macri, J., and McGaugh, J. L. "Retrograde amnesia produced by subseizure amygdala stimulation." *Behavioral Biology*. 1973, *9*, 671–680.

Goldfine, I. D., Abraira, C., Gruenwald, D., and Goldstein, M. S. "Plasma insulin levels during imaginary food ingestion under hypnosis." *Proceedings of the Society for Experimental Biology and Medicine*, 1970, *133*, 274–276.

Goldman, P. S. "Maturation of the mammalian nervous system and the ontogeny of behavior." In J. S. Rosenblatt, *Advances in the study of behavior*, 1976, *7*, 1–90.

Goodman, C. "Isogenic grasshoppers: Genetic variability and development of identified neurons." In X. O. Breakefield (Ed.), *Neurogenetics*. New York: Elsevier, 1979.

Gormezano, I. "Investigations of defense and reward conditioning in the rabbit." A. H. Black and W. F. Prokasy (Eds.), *Classical Conditioning II: Current Research and Theory*. New York: Appleton-Century-Crofts, 1972, 151–181.

Gorski, R. A., Gordon, J. H., Shryne, J. E., and Southam, A. M. "Evidence for a morphological sex difference within the medial preoptic area of the rat brain." *Brain Research*, 1978, *148*, 333–346.

Gottlieb, G. "The roles of experience in the development of behavior and the nervous system." In G. Gottlieb (Ed.), *Studies on the development of behavior and the nervous system*, (Vol. 3), *Neural and behavioral specificity*. New York: Academic, 1976.

Granit, R. *The purposive brain*. Cambridge: MIT, 1977.

Graziadei, P. P. C., Levine, R. R., and Graziadei, G. A. M. "Plasticity of connections of the olfactory sensory neuron: regeneration into the forebrain following bulbectomy in the neonatal mouse." *Neuroscience*, 1979, *4*, 713–728.

Graziadei, P. P. C., and Monti Graziadei, G. A. "Continuous nerve cell renewal in the olfactory system." In M. Jacobson (Ed.), *Handbook of sensory physiology: Development of sensory systems* (Vol. 9). Berlin: Springer, 1978.

Greenewalt, C. H. *Bird song: Acoustics and physiology*. Washington, D. C.: Smithsonian, 1968.

Greenough, W. T. "Enduring brain effects of differential experience and training." In M. R. Rosenzweig and E. L. Bennett (Eds.), *Neural mechanisms of learning and memory*. Cambridge: MIT, 1976.

Greenough, W. T., and Volkmar, F. R. "Pattern of dendritic branching in occipital cortex of rats reared in complex environments." *Experimental Neurology*, 1973, *40*, 491–504.

Griffith, V. E. *A Stroke in the Family: A Manual of Home Therapy*. New York: Delacorte, 1970.

Grillner, S., and Zangger, P. "On the central generation of locomotion in the low spinal cat." *Experimental Brain Research*, 1979, *34*, 241–261.

Grings, W. W., and Davison, M. E. *Emotions and bodily responses: A psychophysiological approach*. New York: Academic, 1978.

Grossman, S. P., Dacey, D., Halaris, A. E., Collier, T., and Routtenberg, A. "Aphagia and adipsia after preferential destruction of nerve cell bodies in hypothalamus." *Science*, 1978, *202*, 537–539.

Groves, P. M., and Rebec, G. V. "Biochemistry and behavior: Some central actions of amphetamine and antipsychotic drugs." *Annual Review of Psychology*, 1976, *27*, 97–128.

Grunt, J. A., and Young, W. C. "Consistency of sexual behavior patterns in individual male guinea pigs following castration and androgen therapy." *Journal of Comparative Physiology and Psychology*, 1953, *46*, 138–144.

Hagbarth, K. E., and Kugelberg, E. "Plasticity of the human abdominal skin reflex." *Brain*, 1958, *81*, 305–318.

Hall, J. C., and Greenspan, R. J. "Genetic analysis of Drosophila neurobiology." *Annual Review of Genetics*, 1979, *13*, 127–195.

Hallett, P. E., and Lightstone, A. D. "Saccadic eye movements towards stimuli triggered by prior saccades." *Vision Research*, 1976, *16*, 99–106.

Hampson, J. L. "Determinants of psychosexual orientation." In F. A. Beach (Ed.), *Sex and behavior*. New York: Wiley, 1965.

Hardy, J. B. "Fetal consequences of maternal viral infections in pregnancy." *Archives of Otolaryngology*, 1973, *98*, 218–227.

Hardyck, C., Petrinovich, L., and Goldman, R. "Left-handedness and cognitive deficit." *Cortex*, 1976, *12*, 266–279.

Harlow, H. F. "The development of learning in the rhesus monkey." *American Scientist*, 1959, *47*, 459–479.

Harlow, H. F. "The formation of learning sets." *Psychological Review*, 1949, *56*, 51–65.

Hart, B. L. "Effects of testosterone propionate and dihydrotestosterone on penile morphology and sexual reflexes of spinal male rats." *Hormones and Behavior*, 1973, *4*, 239–246.

Hart, B. L. "Gonadal androgen and sociosexual behavior of male mammals: A comparative analysis." *Psychological Bulletin*, 1974, *81*, 383–400.

Hart, B. L. "Hormones, spinal reflexes, and sexual behaviour." In. J. B. Hutchison (Ed.), *Biological determinants of sexual behaviour*. New York: Wiley, 1978, 319–347.

Hartmann, E. L. *The functions of sleep*. New Haven: Yale, 1973.

Hartmann, E. L. *The sleeping pill*. New Haven: Yale, 1978.

Haycock, J. W., van Buskirk, R., and McGaugh, J. L. "Effects of catecholaminergic drugs upon memory storage processes in mice." *Behavioral Biology*, 1977, *20*, 281–310.

Heath, R. G. "Pleasure and brain activity in man." *Journal of Nervous and Mental Diseases*, 1972, *154*, 3–18.

Hebb, D. O. *Essay on mind*. Hillsdale, N.J.: Lawrence Erlbaum, 1980.

Hebb, D. O. *The organization of behavior*. New York: Wiley, 1949.

Heilman, K., and Valenstein, E. (Eds.), *Clinical neuropsychology*. New York: Oxford, 1979.

Heinrich, B. "Keeping a cool head: Honeybee thermoregulation." *Science*, 1979, *205*, 1269–1271.

Heinrich, B. "The regulation of temperature in the honeybee swarm." *Scientific American*, 1981, *244*(6), 146–160.

Held, R., and Hein, A. "Movement-produced stimulation in the development of visually guided behavior." *Journal of Comparative and Physiological Psychology*, 1963, *56*, 872–876.

Heller, H. C., Cranshaw, L. I., and Hammel, H. T. "The thermostat of vertebrate animals." *Scientific American*, 1978, *239*(2), 102–113.

Henderson, N. "Human behavior genetics." *Annual Review of Psychology*, 1982, *33*, 403–440.

Herbert, J. "Neuro-hormonal integration of sexual behaviours in female primates." In J. B. Hutchison (Ed.), *Biological determinants of sexual behaviour*. New York: Wiley, 1978, 467–491.

Hernandez, L., and Hoebel, B. G. "Basic mechanisms of feeding and weight regulation." In A. J. Stunkard (Ed.), *Obesity*. Philadelphia: Saunders, 1980.

Herron, J. (Ed.), *Neuropsychology of left-handedness*. New York: Academic, 1980.

Hetherington, A. W., and Ranson, S. W. "Hypothalamic lesions and adiposity in the rat." *Anatomical record*, 1940, *78*, 149–172.

Hewes, G. "Primate communication and the gestural origin of language." *Current Anthropology*, 1973, *14*, 5–24.

Hicks, C. S. "Terrestrial animals in cold: Exploratory studies of primitive man." In D. B. Dill (Ed.), *Handbook of Physiology* (Sec. 4, Vol 1), Washington, D. C.: American Physiological Society, 1964.

Hille, B. "The receptor for tetrodotoxin and saxitoxin: A structural hypothesis." *Biophysical Journal*, 1975, *15*, 615–619.

Hirsch, H. V. B., and Spinelli, D. N. "Modification of the distribution of receptive field orientation in cats by selective visual exposure during development." *Experimental Brain Research*, 1971, *12*, 509–527.

Hlinak, Z., and Madlafousek, J. "The dependence of sexual behaviour of inexperienced males on the precopulatory behaviour of female albino rats." *Physiologia bohemoslovenica*, 1972, *21*, 83–84.

Hochberg, F. H., and Le May, M. "Arteriographic correlates of handedness. *Neurology*, 1975, *25*, 218–222.

Hodgkin, A. L., and Huxley, A. F. "A quantitative description of membrane current and its application to conduction and excitation in nerve." *Journal of Physiology* (London), 1952, *117*, 500–544.

Hodgkin, A. L., and Katz, B. "The effect of sodium ions on the electrical activity of the giant axon of the squid." *Journal of Physiology* (London), 1949, *108*, 37–77.

Hodos, W. "Evolutionary interpretation of neural and behavioral studies of living vertebrates." In F. O. Schmitt (Ed.), *The neurosciences: Second study program*. New York: Rockefeller University, 1970.

Hoffman, K.-P., Stone, J. "Conduction velocity of afferents to cat visual cortex: A correlation with cortical receptive field properties." *Brain Research*, 1971, *32*, 460–466.

Hopkins, C. D. "Electric communication in fish." *American Scientist*, 1974, *62*, 426–437.

Horel, J. A. "The neuroanatomy of amnesia: A critique of the hippocampal memory hypothesis." *Brain*, 1978, *101*, 403–445.

Horel, J. A., and Misantone, L. G. "The Klüver-Bucy syndrome produced by partial isolation of the temporal lobe." *Experimental Neurology*, 1974, *42*, 101–112.

Horel, J. A., and Misantone, L. G. "Visual discrimination impaired by cutting temporal lobe connections." *Science*, 1976, *193*. 336–338.

Horn, G., Rose, S. P. R., and Bateson, P. P. G. "Experience and plasticity in the central nervous system. Is the nervous system modified by experience? Are such modifications involved in learning?" *Science*, 1973, *181*, 506–514.

Hosobuchi, Y., Adams, J. E., and Linchitz, R. "Pain relief by electrical stimulation of the central gray matter in humans and its reversal by naloxone." *Science*, 1977, *197*, 183–186.

Hosobuchi, Y., Rossier, J., Bloom, F. E., and Guillemin, R. "Stimulation of human periaqueductal gray for pain relief increases immunoreactive β-Endorphin in ventricular fluid." *Science*, 1979, *203*, 279–281.

Hohman, G. W. "Some effects of spinal cord lesions on experienced emotional feelings." *Psychophysiology*, 1966, *3*, 143–156.

Hotta, Y., and Benzer, S. "Courtship in *Drosophila* mosaics: Sex-specific foci of sequential action patterns." *Proceedings of the National Academy of Sciences*, U.S.A., 1976, *73*, 4154–4158.

Hoyle, G. "How is muscle turned on?" *Scientific American*, 1970, *222*(4), 84–93.

Hubel, D. H., and Wiesel, T. N. "Binocular interaction in striate cortex kittens reared with artificial squint." *Journal of Neurophysiology*, 1965, *28*, 1041–1059.

Hubel, D. H., and Wiesel, T. N. "Brain mechanisms of vision." *Scientific American*, 1979, *241*(3), 150–168.

Hubel, D. H., and Wiesel, T. N. "The period of susceptibility to the physiological effects of unilateral eye closure in kittens." *Journal of Physiology* (London), 1970, *206*, 419–436.

Hubel, D. H., and Wiesel, T. N. "Receptive fields, binocular interaction, and functional architecture in the cat's visual cortex." *Journal of Physiology*, 1962, *160*, 106–154.

Hughes, J., Smith, T. W., Kosterlitz, H. W., Fothergill, L. A., Morgan, B. A., and Morris, H. R. "Identification of two related pentapeptides from the brain with potent opiate agonist activity." *Nature*, 1975, *258*, 577–579.

Humphrey, N. K. "What the frog's eye tells the monkey's brain." *Brain, behavior and evolution*, 1970, *3*, 324–337.

Humphrey, T. "Some correlations between the appearance of human fetal reflexes and the development of the nervous system." *Progress in Brain Research*, 1964, *4*, 93–135.

Hunter, W. S. "The delayed reaction in animals and children." *Behavior Monographs*, 1913, *2*.

Huppert, F. A., and Piercy, M. "Dissociation between learning and remembering in organic amnesia." *Nature*, 1978, *275*, 317–318.

Huppert, F. A., and Piercy, M. "Normal and abnormal forgetting in organic amnesia: Effect of locus of lesion." *Cortex*, 1979, *15*, 385–390.

Hurst, M. W., Jenkins, D., and Rose, R. M. "The relation of psychological stress to onset of medical illness." *Annual Review of Medicine*, 1976, 301–312.

Hutchison, J. B. (Ed.), *Biological determinants of sexual behaviour*. New York: Wiley, 1978.

Hutchison, J. B. "Effects of hypothalamic implants of gonadal steroids on courtship behaviour in Barbary doves (*Streptopelia risoria*)." *Journal of Endocrinology*, 1971, *50*, 97–113.

Hutchison, J. B. "Hypothalamic mechanisms of sexual behaviour, with special reference to birds." In J. S. Rosenblatt, R. A. Hinde, E. Shaw, and C. Beer (Eds.), *Advances in the study of behaviour* (Vol. 6). New York: Academic, 1976.

Hutchison, J. B. "Hypothalamic regulation of male sexual responsiveness to androgen." In J. B. Hutchison (Ed.), *Biological determinants of sexual behaviour*. New York: Wiley, 1978, 277–317.

Hydén, H., and Egyházi, E. "Changes in RNA content and base composition in cortical neurons of rats in a learning experiment involving transfer of handedness." *Proceedings of the National Academy of Sciences*, U.S.A., 1964, *52*, 1030–1035.

Imperato-McGinley, J., Guerrero, L., Gautier, T., and Peterson, R. E. "Steroid 5 α-reductase deficiency in man: an inherited form of male pseudohermaphroditism." *Science*, 1974, *186*, 1213–1215.

Imperato-McGinley, J., Peterson, R. E., Gautier, T., and Sturla, E. "Androgens and the evolution of male-gender identity among male pseudohermaphrodites with 5α reductase deficiency." *New England Journal of Medicine*, 1979, *300*, 1233–1237.

Ingvar, D. H., and Lassen, N. A. "Activity distribution in the cerebral cortex in organic dementia as revealed by measurements of regional cerebral blood flow." *Bayer Symposium VII, Brain Function in Old Age*, 1979, 268–277.

Isaacson, R. L. "Hippocampal destruction in man and other animals." *Neuropsychologia*, 1972, *10*, 47–64.

Iversen, L. L., and Bloom, F. E. "Studies of the uptake of ^{3}H-GABA and (^{3}H) glycine in slices and homogenates of rat brain and spinal cord by electric microscopic autoradiography." *Brain Research*, 1972, *41*, 131–143.

Iwamura, Y., and Tanaka, M. "Postcentral neurons in hand region of area 2: Their possible role in the form discrimination of tactile objects." *Brain Research*, 1978, *150*, 662–666.

Jacobs, B. L., and Trulson, M. E. "Mechanisms of action of LSD." *American Scientist*, 1979, *67*, 397–404.

Jacobson, M. *Developmental neurobiology*. New York: Plenum, 1978.

Jacobson, M. "A plentitude of neurons." In G. Gottlieb (Ed.), *Studies of the development of behavior and the nervous system*, (Vol. 2), *Aspects of neurogenesis*. New York: Academic, 1974.

Jenkins, J., and Dallenbach, K. "Oblivescence during sleep and waking." *American Journal of Psychology*, 1924, *35*, 605–612.

Jenkinson, D. H., and Nicholls, J. G. "Contractures and permeability changes produced by acetylcholine in depolarized denervated muscle." *Journal of Physiology* (London), 1961, *159*, 111–127.

Jensen, C. "Generality of learning differences in brain-weight-selected mice." *Journal of Comparative and Physiological Psychology*, 1977, *91*, 629–641.

Jensen, C. "Learning performance in mice genetically selected for brain weight: Problems of generality." In M. E. Hahn, C. Jensen, and B. C. Dudek (Eds.), *Development and evolution of brain size*. New York: Academic, 1979.

Jensen, C., and Fuller, J. L. "Learning performance varies with brain weight in heterogeneous mouse lines." *Journal of Comparative and Physiological Psychology*, 1978, *92*, 830–836.

Jensen, D. W. "Vestibular compensation: tonic spinal influence upon spontaneous descending vestibular nuclear activity." *Neuroscience*, 1979, *4*, 1075–1084.

Jensen, R. A., Martinez, J. L., Messing, R. B., Spiehler, V. R., Vasquez, B. J., Soumireu-Mourat, B., Liang, K. C., and McGaugh, J. L. "Morphine and naloxone alter memory in rats." *Society for Neuroscience Abstracts*, 1978, *4*, 260.

Jerison, H. J. *Evolution of the brain and intelligence*. New York: Academic, 1973.

John, E. R. *Functional neuroscience Vol. 2 Neurometrics: Clinical applications of quantitative electrophysiology*. Hillsdale, N.J.: Erlbaum, 1977.

John, E. R., and Schwartz, E. L. "The neurophysiology of information processing and cognition." *Annual Review of Psychology*, 1978, *29*, 1–29.

Johnson, D. F., and Phoenix, C. H. "Sexual behavior and hormone levels during the menstrual cycles of rhesus monkeys." *Hormones and Behavior*, 1978, *11*, 160–174.

Johnson, L. C. "Psychological and physiological changes following total sleep deprivation." In Kales, A. (Ed.), *Sleep: Physiology and pathology*. Philadelphia: Lippincott, 1969.

Johnston, P., and Davidson, J. M. "Intracerebral androgens and sexual behavior in the male rat. *Hormones and Behavior*, 1973, *3*, 345–357.

Jouvet, M. "Neurophysiology of the states of sleep." In G. C. Quarton, T. Melnechuk, and F. O. Schmitt (Eds.), *The Neurosciences*. New York: Rockefeller University, 1967, 529–544.

Jouvet, M. "The role of monoamines and acetylcholine containing neurons in the regulation of the sleep waking cycle." *Ergebnisse der Physcologie* (Reviews of Physiology), 1972, *64*, 166–307.

Julesz, B. *Foundations of cyclopean perception*. Chicago: University of Chicago, 1971.

Julesz, B., and Spivack, G. J. "Stereopsis based on vernier acuity cues alone." *Science*, 1967, *157*, 563–565.

Kaada, B. "Brain mechanisms related to aggressive behavior. In C. D. Clemente and D. B. Lindsley (Eds.), *Aggression and defense*. Berkeley: University of California, 1967.

Kales, A., and Kales, J. "Evaluation, diagnosis and treatment of clinical conditions related to sleep." *Journal of the American Medical Association*, 1970, *213*, 2229–2235.

Kalil, K. and Reh, T. "Regrowth of severed axons in the neonatal central nervous system: establishment of normal connections." *Science*, 1979, *205*, 1158–1161.

Kandel, E. R. *Cellular basis of behavior*. San Francisco: W. H. Freeman, 1976.

Kandel, E. R. "Small systems of neurons." *Scientific American*, 1979, *241*(3), 66–76.

Kandel, E. R., and Schwartz, J. H. *Principles of neural science*. New York: Elsevier/North-Holland, 1981.

Kanof, P., and Greengard, P. "Brain histamine receptors as targets for antidepressant drugs." *Nature*, 1978, *272*, 329–333.

Kaplan, H. S. *The New Sex Therapy*. New York: Brunner/Mazel, 1974.

Karp, L. E. *Genetic engineering: Threat or promise*. Chicago: Nelson-Hall, 1976.

Kasamatsu, T., and Pettigrew, J. D. "Preservation of binocularity after monocular deprivation in the striate cortex of kittens treated with 6-hydroxydopamine." *Journal of Comparative Neurology*, 1979, *185*, 139–162.

Katchadourian, H. A., and Lunde, D. T. *Fundamentals of human sexuality (3rd ed.)*. New York: Holt, Rinehart & Winston, 1980.

Kaushall, P. I., Zetin, M., and Squire, L. R. "A psychosocial study of chronic, circumscribed amnesia." *The Journal of Nervous and Mental Disease*, 1981, *169*(6), 383–389.

Keele, S. W., and Summers, J. J. "The structure of motor programs." In Stelmach, G. E. (Ed.), *Motor control: Issues and trends*. New York: Academic, 1976.

Keesey, R. E. "A set-point analysis of the regulation of body weight." In A. J. Stunkard (Ed.), *Obesity*. Philadelphia: Saunders, 1980.

Keesey, R. E., and Boyle, P. C. "Effects of quinine adulteration upon body weight of LH-lesioned and intact male rats." *Journal of comparative and physiological psychology*, 1973, *84*, 38–46.

Kelley, D. B., and Pfaff, D. W. "Generalizations from comparative studies on neuroanatomical and endocrine mechanisms of sexual behaviour." In J. B. Hutchison (Ed.), *Biological determinants of sexual behaviour*. New York: Wiley, 1978, 225–254.

Kelly, R. B., Deutsch, J. W., Carlson, S. S., and Wanger, J. A. "Biochemistry of neurotransmitter release." *Annual Review of Neuroscience*, 1979, *2*, 399–397.

Kertesz, A. "Recovery and treatment." In K. M. Heilman and E. Valenstein (Eds.), *Clinical neuropsychology*. New York: Oxford, 1979.

Kety, S. S. "Biological concomitants of affective states and their possible role in memory processes." In M. R. Rosenzweig and E. L. Bennett (Eds.), *Neural mechanisms of learning and memory*. Cambridge: MIT, 1976.

Kety, S. S., Rosenthal, D., Wender, P. H., Schulsinger, F., and Jacobsen, B. "Mental illness in the biological and adoptive families of adopted individuals who have become schizophrenic. A preliminary report based on psychiatric interviews." In R. R. Fieve, D. Rosenthal, and H. Brill (Eds.), *Genetic research in psychiatry*. Baltimore: Johns Hopkins University, 1975.

Keys, A., Brozek, J., Henschel, A., Mickelsen, O., and Taylor, H. L. *The biology of human starvation*. Minneapolis: University of Minnesota, 1950.

Khanna, S. M., and Leonard, D. G. B. "Basilar membrane tuning in cat cochlea." *Science*, 1982, *215*, 305–306.

Kimble, D. P. "Hippocampus and internal inhibition." *Psychological Bulletin*, 1968, *70*, 285–295.

Kimura, D. "The asymmetry of the human brain." *Scientific American*, 1973, 360–368.

Kinsey, A. C., Pomeroy, W. B., and Martin, C. E. *Sexual behavior in the human male*. Philadelphia: Saunders, 1948.

Kinsey, A. C., Pomeroy, W. B., Martin, C. E., and Gebhard, P. H. *Sexual behavior in the human female*. Philadelphia: Saunders, 1953.

Klein, M., and Kandel, E. R. "Mechanism of calcium modulation underlying presynaptic facilitation and behavioral sensitization in Aplysia." *Proceedings of the National Academy of Science*, 1980, *77*(11), 6912.

Kleitman, N. "Basic rest-activity cycle in relation to sleep and wakefulness." In A. Kales (Ed.), *Sleep: Physiology and pathology*. Philadelphia: Lippincott, 1969.

Klima, E. S., and Bellugi, U. *The sign's of language*. Cambridge: Harvard, 1979.

Kluckhohn, C. *Mirror for man*. New York: Whittlesey House, 1949.

Klüver, H., and Bucy, P. C. "An analysis of certain effects of bilateral temporal lobectomy in rhesus monkey with special reference to 'psychic blindness'." *Journal of Psychology*, 1938, *5*, 33–54.

Knibestol, M., and Valbo, A. B. "Single unit analysis of

mechanoreceptor activity from the human glabrous skin." *Acta Physiologica Scandinavica*, 1970, *80*, 178–195.

Knudsen, E. I. "Auditory and visual maps of space in the optic tectum of the owl." *Journal of Neuroscience*, 1982, *2* (in press).

Knudsen, E. I., and Konishi, M. "Mechanisms of sound localization in the barn owl (Tyto alba)." *Journal of Comparative Physiology*, 1979, *133*, 13–21.

Koester, J., and Kandel, E. R. "Further identification of neurons in the abdomincal ganglion of *Aplysia* using behavioral criteria." (Unpublished)

Kolata, G. B. "Clues to the cause of senile dementia." *Science*, 1981, *211*, 1032–1033.

Kornetsky, C. and Eliasson, M. "Reticular stimulation and chlorpromazine: An animal model for schizophrenic overarousal." *Science*, 1969, *165*, 1273–1274.

Kornhuber, H. "Cerebral cortex, cerebellum, and basal ganglia: An introduction to their motor functions." In F. O. Schmitt and F. G. Worden (Eds.), *The neurosciences: Third study program*. Cambridge: MIT, 1974.

Korsakoff, S. S. "Etude médico-psychologique sur une forme des maladies de la mémoire." *Revue philosophique*, 1889, *5*, 501–530.

Kow, L.-M., Malsbury, C., and Pfaff, D. "Effects of medial hypothalamic lesions on the lordosis response in female hamsters." *Society for Neuroscience, Abstracts*, 1974, *4*, 291.

Krasne, F. B. "Invertebrate systems as a means of gaining insight into the nature of learning and memory." In M. R. Rosenzweig and E. L. Bennett (Eds.), *Neural mechanisms of learning and memory*. Cambridge: MIT, 1976, 401–429.

Kreuz, L. E., and Rose, R. M. "Assessment of aggressive behavior and plasma testosterone in a young criminal population." *Psychosomatic Medicine*, 1972, *34*, 321–332.

Krieger, D. T., and Liotta, A. S. "Pituitary hormones in brain: Where, how, and why?" *Science*, 1979, *205*, 366–372.

Kuffler, S. W., and Nicholls, J. G. *From neuron to brain*. Sunderland, Mass.: Sinauer Associates, 1976.

Kulkosky, P. J., Breckenridge, C., Krinsky, R., and Woods, S. C. "Satiety elicited by the C-terminal octapeptide of cholecystokinin-pancreozymin in normal and VMH-lesioned rats." *Behavioral Biology*, 1976, *18*, 227–234.

Kupferman, I. T., Carew, T. J., and Kandel, E. R. "Local, reflex, and central commands controlling gill and siphon movements in *Aplysia*." *Journal of Neurophysiology*, 1974, *37*, 996–1019.

Lacey, J. I., and Lacey, B. C. "Some autonomic-central nervous system interrelationships." In P. Black (Ed.), *Physiological correlates of emotion*. New York: Academic, 1970.

Lack, D. *Ecological adaptations for breeding in birds*. London: Methuen, 1968.

Larroche, J. C. "The development of the central nervous system during intrauterine life." In F. Falkner (Ed.), *Human development*. Philadelphia: Saunders, 1966.

Larsson, K., and Heimer, L. "Mating behavior of male rats after lesions in the preoptic area." *Nature*, 1964, *202*, 413–414.

Lashley, K. S., and Clark, G. The cytoarchitecture of the cerebral cortex of Ateles: A critical examination of architectonic studies." *Journal of Comparative Neurology*, 1946, *85*, 223–306.

Latour, P. L. "Visual thresholds during eye movements." *Vision Research*, 1962, *2*, 261–262.

Lavie, P., and Kripke, D. F. "Ultradian circa 1½ hour rhythms: A multioscillatory system." *Life Sciences*, 1981, *29*, 2445–2450.

Lavine, R. A. "Phase-locking in response of single neurons in cochlear nucleus complex of the cat to low-frequency tonal stimuli." *Journal of Neurophysiology* 1971, *34*, 467–483.

Le Boeuf, B. J. "Sex and evolution." In McGill, T. E., Dewsbury, D. A. and Sachs, B. D. (Eds.), *Sex and Behavior*. New York: Plenum, 1978.

Lee, T., and Seeman, P. "Elevation of brain neuroleptic dopamine receptors in schizophrenia." *American Journal of Psychiatry*, 1980, *137*, 191–197.

Lehrman, D. S. "Interaction between internal and external environments in the regulation of the reproductive cycle in the ring dove." In F. A. Beach (Ed.), *Sex and Behavior*. New York: Wiley, 1965.

Lehrman, D. S. "The reproductive behavior of ring doves." *Scientific American*, 1964.

Leiman, A. L., and Hafter, E. R. "Responses of inferior colliculus neurons to free field stimuli." *Experimental Neurology*, 1972, *35*, 431–450.

LeMay, M. "Asymmetries of the skull and handedness." *Journal of the Neurological Sciences*, 1977, *32*, 243–253.

LeMay, M., and Culebras, A. "Human brain morphological differences in the hemispheres demonstrable by carotid arteriography." *The New England Journal of Medicine*, 1972, *287*, 168–170.

Lenneberg, E. H. *Biological foundations of language*. New York: Wiley, 1967.

Leon, M., Croskerry, P. G., and Smith, G. K. "Thermal control of mother-young contact in rats." *Physiology & Behavior*, 1978, *21*(5), 793–811.

Leshner, A. *An introduction to behavioral endocrinology*. New York: Oxford, 1978.

Levi, L. "The urinary output of adrenalin and noradrenalin during pleasant and unpleasant emotional states." *Psychosomatic Medicine*, 1965, *27*, 80.

Levi-Montalcini, R. "Developmental neurobiology and the natural history of nerve growth factor." *Annual Review of Neuroscience*, 1982, *5*, 341–362.

Levi-Montalcini, R. "Growth and differentiation in the nervous system." In J. Allen (Ed.), *The nature of biological diversity*. New York: McGraw-Hill, 1963.

Levi-Montalcini, R., and Calissano, P. "The nerve growth factor." *Scientific American*, 1979, *240*, 68–77.

Levine, J. D., Gordon, N. C., Bornstein, J. C., and Fields, H. L. "Role of pain in placebo analgesia." *Proceedings of the National Academy of Sciences*, 1979, *76*, 3528–3531.

Levy, J., and Reid, M. "Variations in writing posture and cerebral organization." *Science*, 1976, *194*, 337–339.

Lewin, R. "Is your brain really necessary?" *Science*, 1980, *210*, 1232–1234.

Lewis, J. W., Cannon, J. T., and Liebeskind, J. C. "Opioid and nonopioid mechanisms of stress analgesia." *Science*, 1980, *208*, 623–625.

Lhermitte, F., and Signoret, J.-L. "The amnesic syndromes and the hippocampal-mammillary system." In M. R. Rosenzweig and E. L. Bennett (Eds.), *Neural Mechanisms of Learning and Memory*, Cambridge, Mass., and London, England: MIT Press, 1976, 49–56.

Lieberman, P. "Hominid evolution, supralaryngeal vocal-tract physiology and the fossil evidence for reconstructions." *Brain and Language*, 1979, 7, 101–126.

Liu, C. N., and Chambers, W. W. "Intraspinal sprouting of dorsal root axons." *Archives of Neurology and Psychiatry*, 1958, 79, 46–61.

Lockhart, M., and Moore, J. W. "Classical differential and operant conditioning in rabbits (*Orycytolagus cuniculus*) with septal lesions." *Journal of Comparative and Physiological Psychology*, 1975, 88, 147–154.

Loewenstein, W. R. "Biological transducers." *Scientific American*, 1960, 203(2), 98–108.

Loewenstein, W. R. "Mechano-electric transduction in the Pacinian corpuscle. Initiation of sensory impulses in mechanoreception." *Handbook of Sensory Physiology*, Vol. 1, 269–290. Berlin: Springer-Verlag, 1971.

Ludel, J. *Introduction to sensory processes*. San Francisco: Freeman, 1978.

Lund, R. D. *Development and plasticity of the brain*. New York: Oxford, 1978.

Lund, R. D., and Hanschka, S. D. "Transplanted neural tissue develops connections with host rat brain." *Science*, 1976, 193, 582–584.

Lustick, S., Battersby, B., and Kelty, M. "Behavioral thermoregulation: Orientation toward the sun in Herring Gulls." *Science*, 1978, 200, 81–82.

Maccoby, E. E., and Jacklin, C. M. *The psychology of sex differences*. Stanford: Stanford University, 1974.

Mace, G. M., Harvey, P. H., and Clutton-Brock, T. H. "Is brain size an ecological variable?" *Trends in Neuroscience*, 1980, 3, 193–196.

MacLean, P. D. "The triune brain, emotion, and scientific bias." In F. O. Schmitt (Ed.), *The neurosciences*. New York: Rockefeller University, 1970, 336–348.

Maffei, L., and Fiorentini, A. "The visual cortex as a spatial frequency analyser." *Vision Research*, 1973, 13, 1255–1267.

Mair, W.G.P., Warrington, E. K., and Wieskrantz, L. "Memory disorder in Korsakoff's psychosis." *Brain*, 1979, 102, 749–783.

Manfredi, M., Bini, G., Cruccu, G., Accornero, N., Berardelli, A., and Medolago, L. "Congential absence of pain." *Archives of Neurology*, 1981, 38, 507–511.

Mann, T. *The transposed heads: A legend of India*. New York: Knopf, 1941.

Manning, A. "Drosophila and the evolution of behaviour." In J. D. Carthy and C. L. Duddington (Eds.), *Viewpoints in biology*. London: Butterworth, 1965, 125–169.

Marchisio, P. C., Circillo, D., Naldini, L., and Calissano, P. "Distribution of nerve growth factor in chick embryo sympathetic neurons in vitro." *Journal of Neurocytology*, 1981, 10, 45–55.

Mark, R. F. "Synaptic repression at neuromuscular junctions." *Physiological Reviews*, 1980, 60, 355–395.

Mark, V. H., and Ervin, F. R. *Violence and the brain*. New York: Harper & Row, 1970.

Marlowe, W. B., Mancall, E. L., and Thomas, J. J. "Complete Klüver-Bucy syndrome in man." *Cortex*, 1975, 11, 53–59.

Marshall, J. F., and Berrios, N. "Movement disorders of aged rats: reversal by dopamine receptor stimulation." *Science*, 1979, 206, 477–479.

Marshall, J. F., Richardson, J. S., and Teitelbaum, P. "Nigrostriatal bundle damage and the lateral hypothalamic syndrome." *Journal of comparative and physiological psychology*, 1974, 87, 800–830.

Marten, P. "Birdsong: The acquisition of a learned motor skill." *Trends in Neurosciences*, 1981, 4, 88–94.

Martin, A. R., and Pilar, G. "Dual mode of synaptic transmission in the avian ciliary ganglion." *Journal of Physiology* (London), 1963, 443–463.

Mason, J. W. "Organization of psychoendocrine mechanisms: A review and reconsideration of research." In N. S. Greenfield, and R. A. Sternbach (Eds.), *Handbook of Psychophysiology*. New York: Holt, Rhinehart, & Winston, 1972.

Masters, W. H., and Johnson, V. E. "The sexual response cycles of the human male and female: Comparative anatomy and physiology." In F. A. Beach (Ed.), *Sex and behavior*. New York: Wiley, 1965.

Masters, W. H., and Johnson, V. E. *Human sexual response*. Boston: Little, Brown, 1966.

Masters, W. H., and Johnson, V. E. *Human sexual inadequacy*. Boston: Little, Brown, 1970.

Maser, J. D., and Seligman, M. E. P. (Eds.), *Psychopathology: Experimental models*. San Francisco: Freeman, 1977.

Masterton, R. B. (Ed.), *Handbook of behavioral neurobiology. (Vol. 1): Sensory Integration*. New York: Plenum, 1978.

Masterton, R. B., and Berkley, M. A. "Brain function: Changing ideas on the role of sensory, motor, and association cortex in behavior." *Annual Review of Psychology*, 1974, 25, 277–312.

Matthies, H. "Biochemical, electrophysiological, and morphological correlates of brightness discrimination in rats." In M. A. B. Brazier (Ed.), *Brain mechanisms in memory and learning: From the single neuron to man*. New York: Raven, 1979.

Mayer, J. "Glucostatic mechanisms of regulation of food intake." *New England Journal of Medicine*, 1953, 249, 13–16.

Mayer, D. J., and Liebskind, J. C. "Pain reduction by focal electrical stimulation of the brain: an anatomical and behavioral analysis." *Brain Research*, 1974, 68, 73–93.

McGaugh, J. L. "A multi-trace view of memory storage processes." In D. Bovet (Ed.), *Attuali orientamenti della ricerca sull'apprendimento e la memoria*. Academia Nazionale dei Lincei, Quaderno N. 109, 1968.

McGaugh, J. L., and Krivanek, J. A. "Strychnine effects on discrimination learning in mice: effects of dose and time of administration." *Physiology and Behavior*, 1970, 5, 1437–1442.

McGaugh, J. L., and Petrinovich, L. F. "The effect of strychnine sulphate on maze learning." *American Journal of Psychology*, 1959, 72, 99–102.

McGeer, E. G., and McGeer, P. L. "Neurotransmitter metabolism in the aging brain." In R. D. Terry and S. Gershon (Eds.), *Neurobiology of aging*. Vol. 3. New York: Raven, 1976.

McGill, T. E., Dewsbury, D. A., and Sachs, B. D. *Sex and behavior*. New York: Plenum, 1978.

McKinney, T. D., and Desjardins, C. "Postnatal development of the testis, fighting behavior and fertility in house mice." *Biology of Reproduction*, 1973, *9*, 279–294.

Meckler, R. J., Mack, J. L., and Bennett, R. "Sign language aphasia in a non-deaf mute." *Neurology*, 1979, *29*, 1037–1040.

Meddis, R. "The evolution and function of sleep." In D. A. Oakley and H. C. Plotkin (Eds.), *Brain, behavior and evolution*. London: Methuen, 1979.

Meddis, R. "On the function of sleep." *Animal Behavior*, 1975, *23*, 676–691.

Mednick, S. A., and Christiansen, K. D. (Eds.), "Biosocial bases of criminal behavior." New York: Gardner, 1977.

Meisami, E. "Influence of early anosmia on the developing olfactory bulb." *Progress in Brain Research*, 1978, *48*, 211–230.

Melzack, R. *The puzzle of pain*. New York: Basic Books, 1973.

Melzack, R. "Psychological aspects of pain." In J. J. Bonica (Ed.), *Pain* (Association for Research in Nervous and Mental Disease, Vol. 58). New York: Raven, 1980.

Melzack, R., and Casey, K. L. "Sensory, motivational, and central control determinants of pain." In D. R. Kenshals (Ed.), *The skin senses*. Springfield, Ill.: Charles C. Thomas, 1968.

Melzack, R., and Watt, P. D. "On the nature of cutaneous sensory mechanisms." *Brain*, 1962, *85*, 331–356.

Merzenich, M. M., and Kaas, J. H. "Principles of organization of sensory-perceptual systems in mammals." In J. M. Sprague and Alan N. Epstein (Eds.), *Progress in psychobiology and physiological psychology* (Vol. 9). New York: Academic, 1980.

Mesulam, M. M. "A cortical network for directed attention and unilateral neglect." *Annals of Neurology*, 1981, *10*, 309–325.

Mesulam, M. M., Van Hoesen, G. W., Pandya, D. N., and Geschwind, N., "Limbic and sensory connections of the inferior parietal lobule (area PG) in the rhesus monkey: a study with a new method for horseradish peroxidase histochemistry." *Brain Research*, 1977, *136*, 393–414.

Michelson, R. P. "Multichannel cochlear implants." *Otolaryngological Clinics of North America*, 1978, *11*, 209–216.

Middlebrooks, J. C., and Pettigrew, J. D. "Functional classes of neurons in primary auditory cortex of the cat distinguished by sensitivity to sound location." *Journal of Neuroscience*, 1981, *1*, 107–120.

Mihailoff, G. A., McArdle, C. G., and Adams, C. E. "The cytoarchitecture cytology, and synaptic organization of the basilar pontine nuclei in the rat. 1. Nissl and Golgi studies." *Journal of Comparative Neurology*, 1981, *195*, 181–201.

Miller, G. A. *Psychology: The science of mental life*. New York: Harper & Row, 1962.

Miller, N. E. "Biofeedback and visceral learning." *Annual Review of Psychology*, 1978, *29*, 373–404.

Milner, B. "Memory and the medial temporal regions of the brain." In D. H. Pribram and D. E. Broadbent (Eds.), *Biology of Memory*. New York: Academic, 1970.

Milner, B. "Memory disturbance after bilateral hippocampal lesions." In P. M. Milner and S. E. Glickman (Eds.), *Cognitive processes and the brain*. Princeton: Van Nostrand, 1965.

Milner, B., Corkin, S., and Teuber, H.-L. "Further analysis of the hippocampal amnesic syndrome: 14-year follow-up study of H. M." *Neuropsychologia*, 1968, *6*, 215–234.

Mishkin, M. "Memory in monkeys severely impaired by combined but not by separate removal of amygdala and hippocampus." *Nature*, 1978, *273*, 297–298.

Mohler, C. W., and Wurtz, R. H. "Role of striate cortex and superior colliculus is visual guidance of saccadic eye movements in monkeys." *Journal of Neurophysiology*, 1977, *40*, 74–94.

Mollon, J. D. "Color vision." *Annual Review of Psychology*, 1982, *33*, 41–85.

Money, J. "Human hermaphroditism." In F. A. Beach (Ed.), *Human sexuality in four perspectives*. Baltimore: Johns Hopkins University, 1976, 62–86.

Money, J., and Ehrhardt, A. A. *Man and woman, boy and girl*. Baltimore: Johns Hopkins University, 1972.

Moore, R. Y., and Bloom, F. E. "Central catecholamine neuron systems: Anatomy and physiology of the dopamine systems." *Annual Review of Neurosciences*, 1978, *1*, 129–169.

Moore, R. Y., and Bloom, F. E. "Central catecholamine neuron systems: Anatomy and physiology of the norepinephrine and epinephrine systems." *Annual Review of Neurosciences*, 1979, *2*, 113–168.

Mora, F., Rolls, E. T., and Burton, M. J. "Modulation during learning of the responses of neurones in the lateral hypothalamus to the sight of food." *Experimental Neurology*, 1976, *53*, 508–519.

Moran, E. F. "Human adaptation to arctic zones." *Annual Review of Anthropology*, 1981, *10*, 1–25.

Morgane, P. J., and Kosman, A. J. "Relationship of the middle hypothalamus to amygdalar hyperphagia." *American Journal of Physiology*, 1960, *198*, 1315–1318.

Morrison, A. "Brain-stem regulation of behavior during sleep and wakefulness." *Progress in Psychobiology and Physiological Psychology*, 1979, *8*, 91–131.

Moruzzi, G. "The sleep-waking cycle." *Ergebnisse der Physiologie* (Reviews of Physiology), 1972, *64*, 1–165.

Moulton, D. G. "Spatial patterning of response to odors in the peripheral olfactory system." *Physiological Reviews*, 1976, *56*, 578–593.

Mountcastle, V. B. "An organizing principle for cerebral function: the unit module and the distributed system." In F. O. Schmitt and F. G. Worden (Eds.), *The neurosciences: fourth study program*, Cambridge: MIT, 1979.

Mountcastle, V. B. "The problem of sensing and the neural coding of sensory events." In G. C. Quarton, T. Melnechuk, and F. O. Schmitt (Eds.), *The Neurosciences*. New York: Rockefeller University, 1967, 393–408.

Mountcastle, V. B., Andersen, R. A., and Motter, B. C. "The influence of attentive fixation upon the excitability of the light-sensitive neurons of the posterior parietal cortex." *Journal of Neuroscience*, 1981, *1*, 1218–1235.

Mouret, J., and Coindet, J. "Polygraphic evidence against a critical role of the raphe nuclei in sleep in the rat." *Brain Research*, 1980, *186*, 273–287.

Movshon, J. A., and van Sluyters, R. C. "Visual neural development." *Annual Review of Psychology*, 1981, *32*, 477–522.

Mpitsos, G. J., Collins, S. D., and McClellan, A. D. "Learning: a model system for physiological studies." *Science*, 1978, *199*, 497–506.

Mrosovsky, N., and Sherry, D. F. "Animal anorexias." *Science*, 1980, *207*, 837–842.

Müller, G. E., and Pilzecker, A. "Experimentale Beiträge zur Lehre vom Gedächtnis." *Zeitschrift für Psychologie*, 1900, Suppl., 1–288.

Nagy, Z. M. "Development of learning and memory processes in infant mice." In N. E. Spear and B. A. Campbell (Eds.), *Ontogeny of learning and memory*. Hillsdale, N.J.: Lawrence Erlbaum, 1979.

Nakamura, R. K., and Mishkin, M. "Chronic blindness following nonvisual cortical lesions in monkeys." *Society for Neuroscience Abstracts*, 1979, *5*, 800.

Netter, F. *Nervous system*. Vol. 1 in the Ciba Collection of Medical Illustrations, 1957.

Newman, E. A., and Hartline, P. H. "Integration of visual and infrared information in bimodal neurons of the rattlesnake optic tectum." *Science*, 1981, *213*, 789–791.

Newsome, W. T., Baker, J. F., Meizen, F. M. Myerson, J., Petersen, S. E., and Allman, J. M. "Functional localization of neuronal response properties in extrastriate visual cortex of the owl monkey." *ARVO Abstracts*, 1978 *1*, 174.

Nguyen, My Lien, Meyer, K. K., and Winick, M. "Early malnutrition and 'late' adoption: A study of their effects on the development of Korean orphans adopted into American families." *American Journal of Clinical Nutrition*, 1977, *30*, 1734–39.

Nisbett, R. E. "Hunger, obesity, and the ventromedial hypothalamus." *Psychological Review*, 1972, *79*, 433–453.

Norback, C. R. *The human nervous system*. New York: McGraw-Hill, 1981.

Norback, C. R., and Montagna, W. *The Primate Brain*. New York: Appleton-Century-Crofts, 1970.

Northcutt, R. G. "Evolution of the telencephalon in nonmammals." *Annual Review of Neuroscience*, 1981, *4*, 301–350.

Nottebohm, F. "Asymmetries in neural control of vocalization in the canary." In S. Harnad, R. W. Dory, L. Goldstein, J. Jaynes, and G. Krauthamer (Eds.), *Lateralization in the nervous system*. New York: Academic, 1979.

Nottebohm, F. "Brain pathways for vocal learning in birds: A review of the first 10 years." In J. M. Sprague and Alan N. Epstein (Eds.), *Progress in psychobiology and physiological psychology* (Vol. 9). New York: Academic, 1980.

Novin, D. Wyrwicka, W., and Bray, G. A. (Eds.), *Hunger: Basic mechanisms and clinical implications*. New York: Raven, 1976.

Ojemann, G., and Mateer, C. "Human language cortex: Localization of memory, syntax, and sequential motor-phoneme identification systems." *Science*, 1979, *205*, 1401–1403.

Olds, J., Allan, W. S., and Briese, E. "Differentiation of hypothalamic drive and reward centers. *American Journal of Physiology*, 1971, *221*, 672–674.

Olds, J., Disterhoft, J. F., Segal, M., Kornblith, C. L., and Hirsh, R. "Learning centers of rat brain mapped by measuring latencies of conditioned unit responses." *Journal of Neurophysiology*, 1972, *35*, 202–219.

Olds, J., and Milner, P. "Positive reinforcement produced by electrical stimulation of septal area and other regions of the rat brain." *Journal of Comparative and Physiological Psychology*, 1954, *47*, 419–427.

Olds, M. E., and Fobes, J. L. "The central basis of motivation: Intracranial self-stimulation studies." *Annual Review of Psychology*, 1981, *32*, 523–574.

O'Leary, J. L., and Goldring, S. *Science and epilepsy: Neuroscience gains in epilepsy research*. New York: Raven, 1976.

Oliveros, J. C., Jondali, M. K., Timsit-Berthier, M., Remy, R., Benghezal, A., Audibert, A., and Moeglen, J. M. "Vasopressin in amnesia." *Lancet*, 1978, 42.

Olson, E. C. *Vertebrate paleozoology*. New York: Wiley, 1971.

Oomura, Y. "Significance of glucose, insulin, and free fatty acid on the hypothalamic feeding and satiety neurons." In D. Novin, W. Wywricka, and G. A. Bray (Eds.), *Hunger: Basic mechanisms and clinical implications*. New York: Raven, 1976.

Orbach, J. and Chow, K. L. "Differential effects of resections of somatic areas I and II in monkeys." *Journal of Neurophysiology*, 1959, *22*, 195–203.

Orem, J., and Barnes, C. D. (Eds.), *Physiology in sleep*. New York: Academic, 1980.

Østerberg, G. "Topography of the rods and cones in the human retina." *Acta ophthalmologica*, 1935 (Supplement 6).

Oswald, I. *Sleeping and waking*. Amsterdam: Elsevier, 1962.

Oswald, I., and Priest, R. G. "Five weeks to escape the sleeping pill habit." *British Medical Journal*, 1965, *2*, 1093–1095.

Palay, S. L., and Chan-Palay, V. *Cerebellar cortex: cytology and organization*. New York: Springer-Verlag, 1974.

Papez, J. W. "A proposed mechanism of emotion." *Archives of Neurology and Psychiatry*, 1937, *38*, 725–745.

Pappas, G. D., and Purpura, D. P. *Structure and function of synapses*. New York: Raven, 1972.

Pappas, G. D., and Waxman, S. G. "Synaptic fine structure—morphological correlates of chemical and electrotonic transmission." In G. D. Pappas and D. P. Purpura (Eds.), *Structure and function of synapses*. New York: Raven, 1972.

Paradis, M. "Bilingualism and aphasia." In H. Whitaker and H. Whitaker (Eds.), *Studies in neurolinguistics* (Vol. 3). New York: Academic, 1977.

Patterson, M. M. "Effects of forward and backward classical conditioning procedures on a spinal cat hind-limb flexor nerve response." *Physiological Psychology*, 1975, *3*, 86–91.

Patterson, M. M., Berger, T. W., and Thompson, R. F. "Neuronal plasticity recorded from cat hippocampus during classical conditioning." *Brain Research*, 1979, *163*, 339–343.

Pavlov, I. P. *Conditioned Reflexes*. London: Oxford, 1927.

Pearson, K. *The life, letters and labours of Francis Galton* (Vol. 2). Cambridge, England: Cambridge University, 1924.

Pellegrino, L. J., and Altman, J. "Effects of differential interference with postnatal cerebellar neurogenesis on motor performance activity level and maze learning of rats: A developmental study." *Journal of Comparative and Physiological Psychology*, 1979, *93*, 1–33.

Perachio, A. A., Alexander, M., and Marr, L. D. "Hormonal and social factors affecting evoked sexual behavior in rhesus monkeys." *American Journal of Physical Anthropology*, 1973, *38*, 227–232.

Peters, A., Palay, S. L., and Webster, H. de F. *The fine structure of the nervous system*. Philadelphia: Saunders, 1976.

Peters, B. H., and Levin, H. S. "Effects of physostigmine and lecithin on memory in Alzheimer disease." *Annals of Neurology*, 1979, *6*, 219–222.

Petre-Quadens, O. "Sleep in mental retardation." In C. D. Clemente, D. R. Purpura, and F. E. Mayer (Eds.), *Sleep and the maturing nervous system*. New York: Academic, 1972.

Pettigrew, J. D., and Freeman, R. D. "Visual experience without lines: Effect on developing cortical neurons." *Science*, 1973, *182*, 599–601.

Pettigrew, J. D., and Garey, L. J. Selective modification of single neuron properties in the visual cortex of kittens. *Brain Research*, 1974, *66*, 160–164.

Pettigrew, J. D., Nikara, T., and Bishop, P. O. "Binocular interaction on single units in cat striate cortex: Simultaneous stimulation by single moving slit with receptive fields in correspondence." *Experimental Brain Research*, 1968, *6*, 391–410.

Pieron, H. "Le problème physiologique du sommeil." Thèse. Paris: Masson & Cie, 1912.

Pigareva, M. L. "Limbic lesions and switching-over of the conditioned reflex in rats." In R. Sinz and M. R. Rosenzweig (Eds.), *Psychophysiology 1980*. Amsterdam: North-Holland Press, 1982.

Ploog, D. "Neurobiology of primate audio-vocal behavior." *Brain Research Reviews*, 1981, *3*, 35–62.

Poggio, G. F., and Fischer, B. "Binocular interaction and depth sensitivity of striate and prestriate cortical neurons of behaving rhesus monkeys." *Journal of Neurophysiology*, 1977, *40*, 1392–1405.

Plutchik, R., and Kellerman, H. (Eds.), *Emotion: Theory, research, and experience. Vol. 1: Theories of emotion*. New York: Academic, 1980.

Poltyrev, S. S., and Zeliony, G. P. "Grosshirnrinde und Assoziationsfunktion." *Zeitschrift für Biologie*, 1930, *90*, 157–160.

Poon, L. W. "A systems approach for the assessment and treatment of memory problems." In J. W. Ferguson and C. B. Taylor (Eds.), *The comprehensive handbook of behavioral medicine. Vol. 1. Systems intervention*. New York: SP Medican and Scientific Books, 1980, 191–212.

Poritsky, R. "Reconstruction from serial electron micrographs of a motoneuron." *Journal of Comparative Neurology*, 1969, *135*, 423–452.

Premack, A. J., and Premack, D. "Teaching language to an ape." *Scientific American*, 1972, *227*(4), 92–99.

Price, L. J., and Kreinen, I. "Variations in behavioral response threshold within the REM period of human sleep." *Psychophysiology*, 1980, *17*, 133–141.

Prohovnik, I., and Risbert, J. "Anatomical distribution and physiological correlates of cognitive function as revealed by blood flow studies during mental activity." In R. Sinz and M. R. Rosenzweig (Eds.), *Psychophysiology 1980*. Amsterdam: North-Holland, 1982.

Purpura, D. P. "Pathobiology of cortical neurons in metabolic and unclassified amentias." *Association for research in nervous and mental diseases* (Vol. 52). New York: Raven, 1978.

Rabkin, J. G., and Struening, E. L. "Life events, stress, and illness." *Science*, 1976, *194*, 1013–1020.

Rahe, R. H. "Subjects recent life changes and their near-future illness reports." *Annals of Clinical Research*, 1972, *4*, 250–265.

Raisman, G. "What hope for repair of the brain?" *Annals of Neurology*, 1978, *3*, 101–106.

Raisman, G., and Field, P. M. "Sexual dimorphism in the neuropil of the preoptic area of the rat and its dependence on neonatal androgen." *Brain Research*, 1973, *54*, 1–29.

Rakic, P. "Genetic and epigenetic determinants of local neuronal circuits in the mammalian central nervous system." In F. O. Schmitt and F. G. Worden (Eds.), *The Neurosciences: Fourth Study Program*. Cambridge: MIT, 1979.

Ramsay, D. J., Rolls, B. J., and Wood, R. J. "Thirst following water deprivation in dogs." *American Journal of Physiology*, 1977, *232*, R93–R100.

Reeves, A. G., and Plum, F. "Hyperphagia, rage, and dementia accompanying a ventromedial hypothalamic neoplasm." *Archives of Neurology*, 1969, *20*, 616–624.

Retzius, G. *Das Gehörorgan der Wirbelthiere*. Vol. I, 1881, vol. II, 1884. Stockholm: Samson and Wallin.

Richards, W. "Selective stereoblindness." 1977. See De Valois *et al.* 1977, 109–111.

Richards, W. "Stereopsis and stereoblindness." *Experimental Brain Research*, 1970, *10*, 380–388.

Riddell, W. I. "Cerebral indices and behavioral differences." In M. E. Hahn, C. Jensen, and B. C. Dudek (Eds.), *Development and evolution of brain size*. New York: Academic, 1979.

Riddell, W. I., and Corl, K. G. "Comparative investigation of the relationship between cerebral indices and learning abilities." *Brain, behavior and evolution*, 1977, *14*, 385–398.

Ritchie, J. M. "A pharmacological approach to the structure of sodium channels in myelinated axons." *Annual Review of Neuroscience*, 1979, *2*, 341–362.

Roberts, D. F. *Climate and human variability*. Addison-Wesley Module Anthropology, No. 34. Reading, Mass.: Addison-Wesley, 1973.

Rockel, A. J., Hiorns, R. W., and T. P. S. Powell "Numbers of neurons through full depth of neocortex." *Proceedings of the Anatomical Society of Great Britain and Ireland*, 1974, *118*, 371.

Rodin, J. "Current status of the internal-external hypothesis for obesity." *American Psychologist*, 1981, *36*, 361–372.

Rodin, J. "The role of perception of internal and external signals on regulation of feeding in overweight and nonobese individuals. In T. Silverstone (Ed.) *Appetite and food intake*. Braunschweig: Pergamon, 1976.

Roeder, F., Orthner, H., and Müller, D. "The stereotaxic treatment of pedophilic homosexuality and other sexual deviations." In E. Hitchcock, L. Laitinen, and K. Vaernet (Eds.), *Psychosurgery*. Springfield, Ill.: Charles C. Thomas, 1972, 87–111.

Rojas-Ramirez, J. A., and Drucker-Colin, R. R. "Phylogenetic correlations between sleep and memory." In R. R. Drucker-Colin and J. L. McGaugh (Eds.), *Neurobiology of sleep and memory*. New York: Academic, 1977.

Roland, E., and Larson, B. "Focal increase of cerebral blood flow during stereognostic testing in man." *Archives of Neurology*, 1976, *33*, 551–558.

Rolls, B. J., Wood, R. J., and Rolls, E. T. "Thirst: The initiation, maintenance, and termination of drinking." In J. M. Sprague and Alan N. Epstein (Eds.), *Progress in psychobiology and physiological psychology* (Vol. 9). New York: Academic, 1980.

Rolls, E. T. "Neurophysiology of feeding." *Trends in Neurosciences*, 1978, *1*, 1–3.

Rose, F. C., and Symonds, C. P. "Persistent memory defect following encephalitis." *Brain*, 1971, *94*, 661–668.

Rose, S.P.R., Hambley, J., and Haywood, J. "Neurochemical approaches to developmental plasticity and learning." In M. R. Rosenzweig and E. L. Bennett (Eds.), *Neural Mechanisms of Learning and Memory*, Cambridge, Mass.: MIT, 1976.

Rosen, S., Olin, P., and Rosen, H. V. "Dietary prevention of hearing loss." *Acta Otolaryngologica*, 1970, *70*, 242–247.

Rosenblatt, J. S., and Aronson, L. R. "The decline of sexual behavior in male cats after castration with special reference to the role of prior sexual experience." *Behaviour*, 1958, *12*, 285–338.

Rosenzweig, M. R. "Animal models for effects of brain lesions and for rehabilitation." In P. Bach-y-Rita (Ed.), *Recovery of function: Theoretical considerations for brain injury rehabilitation*. Bern: Hans Huber, 1980.

Rosenzweig, M. R. "Electrophysiological correlates of auditory localization." Doctoral thesis, Harvard, 1949.

Rosenzweig, M. R. "Representations of the two ears at the auditory cortex." *The American Journal of Physiology*, 1951, *167*, 147–158.

Rosenzweig, M. R. "Responsiveness of brain size to individual experience: Behavioral and evolutionary implications." In M. E. Hahn, C. Jensen, and B. C. Dudek (Eds.), *Development and evolution of brain size*. New York: Academic, 1979.

Rosenzweig, M. R., and Bennett, E. L. "Cerebral changes in rats exposed individually to an enriched environment." *Journal of Comparative and Physiological Psychology*, 1972, *80*, 304–313.

Rosenzweig, M. R., and Bennett, E. L. "Effects of environmental enrichment or impoverishment on learning and on brain values in rodents." In A. Oliverio (Ed.), *Genetics, environment, and intelligence*. Amsterdam: Elsevier/North-Holland, 1977.

Rosenzweig, M. R., and Bennett, E. L. "Experimental influences on brain anatomy and brain chemistry in rodents." In G. Gottlieb (Ed.), *Studies on the development of behavior and the nervous system*. Vol. 4. Early influences. New York: Academic, 1978, 289–327.

Rosenzweig, M. R., and Bennett, E. L. (Eds.), *Neural mechanisms of learning and memory*. Cambridge: MIT, 1976.

Rosenzweig, M. R., Bennett, E. L., and Diamond, M. C. "Brain changes in response to experience." *Scientific American*, 1972, *226*(2), 22–29.

Rosenzweig, M. R., Bennett, E. L., and Diamond, M. C. "Effects of differential environments on brain anatomy and brain chemistry." In J. Zubin and G. Jervis (Eds.), *Psychopathology of mental development*. New York: Grune & Stratton, 1967, 45–56.

Rosenzweig, M. R., Bennett, E. L., Hebert, M., and Morimoto, H.

"Social grouping cannot account for cerebral effects of enriched environments." *Brain Research*, 1978, *153*, 563–576.

Rosenzweig, M. R., Krech, D., and Bennett, E. L. "Heredity, environment, brain biochemistry, and learning." *In Current trends in psychological theory*. Pittsburgh: University of Pittsburgh, 1961.

Rosenzweig, M., Krech, D., Bennett, E. L., and Diamond, M. "Effects of environmental complexity and training on brain chemistry and anatomy: A replication and extension." *Journal of Comparative and Physiological Psychology*, 1962, *55*, 429–437.

Roufogalis, B. D. "Calmodulin: Its role in synaptic transmission. *Trends in Neurosciences*, 1980, *3*, 238–241.

Routtenberg, A. "The reward system of the brain." *Scientific American* 1978, *239*(5), 154–164.

Rozin, P. "The evolution of intelligence and access to the cognitive unconscious." In J. M. Sprague and A. N. Epstein (Eds.), *Progress in Psychobiology and Physiological Psychology* (VI). New York: Academic, 1976a.

Rozin, P. "The psychobiological approach to human memory." In M. R. Rosenzweig and E. L. Bennett (Eds.), *Neural mechanisms of learning and memory*. Cambridge: MIT, 1976b.

Rubin, R. T., Reinisch, J. M., and Haskett, R. F. "Postnatal gonadal steroid effects on human behavior." *Science*, 1981, *211*, 1318–1324.

Rumbaugh, D. M. (Ed.), *Language learning by a chimpanzee: The LANA project*. New York: Academic, 1977.

Rusak, B. "The role of the suprachiasmatic nuclei in the generation of circadian rhythms in the golden hamster Mesocricetus auratus." *Journal of Comparative Physiology*, 1977, *118*, 145–164.

Rusak, B., and Zucker, I. "Neural regulation of circadian rhythms." *Physiological Reviews*, 1979, *59*, 449–526.

Russek, M. "Hepatic receptors and the neurophysiological mechanisms controlling feeding behavior." In S. Ehrenpreis (Ed.), *Neurosciences Research, 4*. New York: Academic, 1971.

Sanders, M. D., Warrington, E. K., Marshall, J., and Weiskrantz, L. "Blindsight": Vision in a field defect. *Lancet*, 1974, 707–708.

Sar, M., and Stumpf, W. E. "Androgen concentration in motor neurons of cranial nerves and spinal cord." *Science*, 1977, *197*, 77–79.

Sarich, V. "A molecular approach to the question of human origins." In P. Dolhinow and V. Sarich (Eds.), *Background for Man*. Boston: Little, Brown, 1971.

Sarnat, H. B., and Netsky, M. G. *Evolution of the nervous system*, 2nd Ed., New York: Oxford, 1981.

Satinoff, E. "Neural organization and evolution of thermal regulation in mammals." *Science*, 1978, *201*, 16–22.

Satinoff, E., and Rutstein, J. "Behavioral thermoregulation in rats with anterior hypothalamic lesions." *Journal of Comparative and Physiological Psychology*, 1970, *71*, 77–82.

Satinoff, E., and Shan, S. Y. "Loss of behavioral thermoregulation after lateral hypothalamic lesions in rats." *Journal of Comparative and Physiological Psychology*, 1971, *77*, 302–312.

Savage-Rumbaugh, E. S., Rumbaugh, D. M., and Boysen, S. "Do apes use language?" *American Scientist*, 1980, *68*, 49–61.

Schachter, S. *Emotion, obesity, and crime*. New York: Academic, 1971.

Schacter, S. "Cognition and peripheralist-centralist controversies in motivation and emotion." In M. S. Gazzaniga and C. Blakemore, (Eds.), *Handbook of Psychobiology*, New York: Academic, 1975.

Schachter, S. "Obesity and eating." *Science*, 1968, *161*, 751–756.

Scheff, S. W., Bernardo, L. S., and Cotman, C. W. "Decrease in adrenergic axon sprouting in the senescent rat." *Science*, 1978, *202*, 775–778.

Scheff, S. W., Bernardo, L. S., and Cotman, C. W. "Effect of serial lesions on sprouting in the dentate gyrus: Onset and decline of the catalytic effect." *Brain Research*, 1978, *150*, 45–53.

Scheibel, M. E., Tomiyasu, U., and Scheibel, A. B. "The aging human Betz cells." *Experimental Neurology*, 1977, *56*, 598–609.

Schenkenberg, T., Bradford, D. C., and Ajax, E. T. "Line bisection and unilateral visual neglect in patients with neurologic impairment." *Neurology*, 1980, *30*, 509–518.

Schildkraut, J. J., and Kety, S. S. "Biogenic amines and emotion." *Science*, 1967, *156*, 21–30.

Schmidt, R. F. *Fundamentals of sensory physiology*. New York: Springer-Verlag, 1978.

Schmidt, R. S. "Neural mechanisms of releasing (unclasping) in American toad." *Behaviour*, 1974, *48*, 315–326.

Schmidt-Nielsen, K. *Desert animals: Physiological problems of heat and water*. New York: Oxford, 1964.

Schneider, G. E. "Two visual systems." *Science*, 1969, *163*, 895–902.

Schoppmann, A., Nelson, R. J., Stryker, M. P., Cynader, M., Zook, J., and Merzenich, M. M. "Reorganization of hand representation within area 3b following digit amputation in owl monkey." *Society for Neuroscience Abstracts*, 1981, *7*, 842.

Schulsinger, F. "Biological psychopathology." *Annual Review of Psychology*, 1980, *31*, 583–606.

Schutz, F. "Sexuelle Prägung bei Anatiden." *Zeitschrift für Tierpsychologie*, 1965, *22*, 50–103.

Schwartz, J. H. "Axonal transport: Components, mechanisms, and specificity." In W. M. Cowan, Z. W. Hall, and E. R. Kandel (Eds.), *Annual Review of Neuroscience*, Vol. 2. Palo Alto: Annual Reviews, 1979, 467–504.

Sclafani, A., Springer, D., and Kluge, L. "Effects of quinine adulteration on the food intake and body weight of obese and nonobese hypothalamic hyperphagic rats." *Physiology and behavior*, 1976, *16*, 631–640.

Scoville, W. B., and Milner, B. "Loss of recent memory after bilateral hippocampal lesions." *Journal of Neurology, Neurosurgery and Psychiatry*, 1957, *20*, 11–21.

Seeman, P., and Lee, T. "Antipsychotic drugs: Direct correlation between clinical potency and presynaptic action on dopamine neurons." *Science*, 1975, *188*, 1217–1219.

Seil, F. J., Leiman, A. L., and Kelly, J. "Neuroelectric blocking factors in multiple sclerosis and normal human sera." *Archives of Neurology*, 1976, *33*, 418–422.

Sholl, D. A. *The organization of the cerebral cortex*. London: Methuen, 1956.

Shurrager, P. S., and Culler, E. A. "Phenomena allied to conditioning in the spinal dog." *American Journal of Physiology*, 1938, *123*, 186–187.

Sidman, R. L., Green, M. C., and Appel, S. H. *Catalog of the neurological mutants of the mouse*. Cambridge: Harvard, 1965.

Signoret, J.-L., and Lhermitte, F. "The amnesic syndromes and the encoding process." In M. R. Rosenzweig and E. L. Bennett (Eds.), *Neural mechanisms of learning and memory*. Cambridge: MIT, 1976, 67–75.

Silva, D. A., and Satz, P. "Pathological left-handedness. Evaluation of a model." *Brain and language*, 1979, *7*, 8–16.

Silver, R. "The parental behavior of ring doves." *American Scientist*, 1978, *66*, 209–215.

Simon, H. A. "The architecture of complexity." *Proceedings of the American Philosophical Society*, 1962, *106*, 467–482.

Simantov, R., and Snyder, S. H. "Isolation and structure identification of a morphine-like peptide enkephalin in bovine brain." *Life Sciences*, 1976, *18*, 781–788.

Simpson, G. G. *The meaning of evolution*. New Haven: Yale, Second Edition, 1967.

Sims, E. A. H., and Horton, E. S. "Endocrine and metabolic adaptation to obesity and starvation." *American Journal of Clinical Nutrition*, 1968, *21*, 1455–1470.

Singer, J. J. "Hypothalamic control of male and female sexual behavior in female rats." *Journal of Comparative and Physiological Psychology*, 1968, *66*, 738–742.

Sinz, R., Grechenko, T. N., and Sokolov, Y. N. "The memory neuron concept: A psychophysiological approach." In R. Sinz and M. R. Rosenzweig (Eds.), *Psychophysiology 1980*. Amsterdam: North-Holland, 1982, 227–254.

Sinz, R., and Rosenzweig, M. R. *Psychophysiology 1980: Memory, Motivation, and Event-Related Potentials in Mental Operations*. (Symposia and papers from the XXIInd International Congress of Psychology, Leipzig). Amsterdam: North-Holland, 1982.

Sitaram, N., Weingartner, H., and Gillin, J. C. "Human serial learning: Enhancement with arecholine and choline and impairment with scopolamine." *Science*, 1978, *201*, 274–276.

Skavenski, A. A., and Hansen, R. M. "Role of eye position information in visual space perception." In J. Senders, D. Fisher, and R. Monty (Eds.), *Eye movements and the higher psychological functions*. New York: Erlbaum, 1978.

Slimp, J. C., Hart, B. L., and Goy, R. W. "Heterosexual, autosexual and social behavior of adult male rhesus monkeys with medial preoptic-anterior hypothalamic lesions." *Brain Research*, 1978, *142*, 105–122.

Smith, A., and Sugar, O. "Development of above normal language and intelligence 21 years after hemispherectomy." *Neurology*, 1975, *25*, 813–818.

Smith, G. P., and Gibbs, J. "Cholecystokinin and satiety: Theoretic and therapeutic implications." In D. Novin, W. Wyrwicka, and G. Bray (Eds.), *Hunger: Basic Mechanisms and Clinical Implications*. New York: Raven, 1976.

Smith, G. P., Jerome, C., Cuslien, B. J., Eterno, R., and Simansky, K. J. "Abdominal vagotomy blocks the satiety effect of cholecystokinin in the rat." *Science*, 1981, *213*, 1036–1037.

Smith, J. M., Kucharski, L., Oswald, W. T., and Waterman, L. J. "A systematic investigation of tardive dyskinesia in inpatients." *American Journal of Psychiatry*, 1979, *136*, 918–922.

Snyder, F., "Sleep and REM as biological enigmas." In A. Kales (Ed.), *Sleep: Physiology and pathology*. Philadelphia: Lippincott, 1969, 266–280.

Snyder, F. and Scott, J. "The psychophysiology of sleep." In N. S. Greenfield and R. A. Sternbach (Eds.), *Handbook of Psychophysiology*. New York: Holt, Rhinehart and Winston, 1972, 645–708.

Snyder, S. H. *Biological aspects of mental disorder*. New York: Oxford, 1980.

Snyder, S. H., and Bennett, J. P. "Neurotransmitter receptors in the brain: biochemical identification." *Annual Review of Physiology*, 1976, *38*, 153–175.

Snyder, S. H., and Childers, W. R. "Opiate receptors and opioid peptides." In W. M. Cowan, Z. W. Hall, and E. R. Kandel (Eds.), *Annual Review of Neuroscience*, Vol. 2. Palo Alto: Annual Reviews, 1979, 35–64.

So, J. K. "Human biological adaptation to arctic and subarctic zones." In B. Siegel, A. Beals, and S. Tyler (Eds.), *Annual Review of Anthropology*, 1980, *9*, 63–82.

Sotaniemi, K. A. "Brain damage and neurological outcome after open-heart surgery." *Journal of Neurology, Neurosurgery and Psychiatry*, 1980, *43*, 127–135.

Sotelo, C. "Mutant mice and the formation of cerebellar circuity." *Trends in Neurosciences*, 1980, *3*, 33–36.

Spearing, D. L., and Poppen, R. "Use of feedback in reduction of foot dragging in a cerebral-palsied client." *Journal of Nervous and Mental Diseases*, 1974, *159*, 148–151.

Sperry, R. W., "Lateral specialization in the surgically separated hemispheres." In F. O. Schmitt and F. G. Worden (Eds.), *Neurosciences: Third study program*. Cambridge: MIT, 1974.

Sperry, R. W. "Mechanisms of neural maturation." In S. S. Stevens (Ed.), *Handbook of Experimental Psychology*. New York: Wiley, 1951.

Sperry, R. W., Stamm, J., and Miner, N. "Relearning tests for interocular transfer following division of optic chiasma and corpus callosum in cats." *Journal of Comparative and Physiological Psychology*, 1956, *49*, 529–533.

Spinelli, D. N., Hirsch, H. V. B., Phelps, R. W., and Metzler, J. "Visual experience as a determinant of the response characteristics of cortical receptive fields in cats." *Experimental Brain Research*, 1972, *15*, 289–304.

Springer, S. P., and Deutsch, G. *Left brain, right brain*. San Francisco: Freeman, 1981.

Squire, L. R. "A stable impairment in remote memory following electroconvulsive therapy. *Neuropsychologia*, 1975, *13*, 51–58.

Squire, L. R. "Two forms of human amnesia: an analysis of forgetting." *Journal of Neuroscience*, 1981, *1*, 635–640.

Squire, L. R., and Moore, R. Y. "Dorsal thalamic lesion in a noted case of chronic memory dysfunction." *Annals of Neurology*, 1979, *6*, 503–506.

Squire, L. R., and Slater, P. C. "Anterograde and retrograde memory impairment in chronic amnesia." *Neuropsychologia*, 1978, *16*, 313–322.

Starr, A. "Sensory evoked potentials in clinical disorders of the nervous system." *Annual Review of Neurosciences*, 1978, *1*, 103–129.

Starr, A., and Phillips, L. "Verbal and motor memory in the amnestic syndrome." *Neuropsychologia*, 1970, *8*, 75–88.

Stein, L., Belluzzi, J. D., and Wise, C. D. "Memory enhancement by central administration of norepinephrine." *Brain Research*, 1975, *84*, 329–335.

Stein, L., and Wise, C. D. "Possible etiology of schizophrenia: progressive damage to the noradrenergic reward system by 6-hydroxydopamine." *Science*, 1971, *171*, 1032–1036.

Stelmach, G. E. (Ed.), *Information processing in motor control and learning*. New York: Academic, 1978.

Stent, G. S., Kristan, W. B. Jr., Friesen, W. O., Ort, C. A., Poon, M., and Calabrese, R. L. "Neuronal generation of the leech swimming movement." *Science*, 1978, *200*, 1348–1357.

Stephan, F. K., and Zucker, I. "Circadian rhythms in drinking behavior and locomotor activity of rats are eliminated by hypothalamic lesions." *Proceedings of the National Academy of Sciences* (WSA), 1972, *69*, 1583–1586.

Stern, R. M., Ray, W. J., and Davis, C. M. *Psychophysiological Recording*. New York: Oxford, 1980.

Stewart, J., and Cygan, D. "Ovarian hormones act early in development to feminize adult open-field behavior in the rat." *Hormones and Behavior*, 1980, *14*, 20–32.

Stone, G. S. (Ed.), *Health Psychology*. San Francisco: Jossey-Bass, 1980.

Straus, E., and Yalow, R. S. "Cholecystokinin in the brains of obese and nonobese mice." *Science*, 1979, *203*, 68–69.

Stricker, E. M., Swerdloff, A. F., and Zigmond, M. J. "Intrahypothalamic injections of kainic acid produce deficits in feeding and drinking during acute homeostatic imbalances." *Society for Neuroscience Abstracts*, 1978, *4*, 181.

Stunkard, A. J., (Ed.) *Obesity*, Philadelphia: Saunders, 1980.

Sturdevant, R. A. L., and Goetz, H. "Cholecystokinin both stimulates and inhibits human food intake." *Nature*, 1976, *261*, 713–715.

Swazey, J. P. *Chlorpromazine in psychiatry*. Cambridge: MIT, 1974.

Sweet, W. H. "Treatment of medically intractable mental disease by limited frontal leucotomy—Justifiable?" *New England Journal of Medicine*, 1973, *289*, 1117–1125.

Szeligo, F., and Leblond, C. P. "Response of the three main types of glial cells of cortex and corpus callosum in rats handled during suckling or exposed to enriched, control and impoverished environments following weaning." *Journal of Comparative Neurology*, 1977, *172*, 247–264.

Takahashi, Y. "Growth hormone secretion related to the sleep and waking rhythm." In R. Drucker-Colin, M. Shkurovich, and M. B. Sterman (Eds.), *The Functions of Sleep*. New York: Academic, 1979.

Talbot, R. E., and Humphrey, D. R. (Eds.), *Posture and movement*. New York: Raven, 1979.

Tallal, P., and Schwartz, J. "Temporal processing, speech perception and hemispheric asymmetry." *Trends in Neurosciences*, 1980, *3*, 309–311.

Tani, K., and Yoshii, N. "Efficiency of verbal learning during sleep as related to EEG pattern." *Brain Research*, 1970, *17*, 277–283.

Taub, E. "Self-regulation of human tissue temperature." In G. E.

Schwartz and J. Beatty (Eds.), *Biofeedback: Theory and Research*. New York: Academic, 1977.

Taub, E., and Berman, A. J. "Movement and learning in the absence of sensory feedback." In S. J. Freedman (Ed.), *The Neuropsychology of Spatially Oriented Behavior*. Homewood, Ill.: Dorsey, 1968.

Taub, E., and School, P. J. "Some methodological considerations in thermal biofeedback training." *Behavior Research Methods and Instrumentation*, 1978, *10*(5), 617–622.

Teitelbaum, P., and Epstein, A. N. "The lateral hypothalamic syndrome: Recovery of feeding and drinking after lateral hypothalamic lesions." *Psychological Review*, 1962, *69*, 74–94.

Teitelbaum, P., and Stellar, E. "Recovery from failure to eat produced by hypothalamic lesions." *Science*, 1954, *120*, 894–895.

Teodoru, D. E., and Berman, A. J. "The role of attempted movements in recovery from lateral dorsal rhizotomy." *Society for Neuroscience Abstracts*, 1980, *G*, 25.

Terrace, H. *Nim*. New York: Knopf, 1979.

Teuber, H.-L. "Alterations of perception after brain injury." In Eccles, J. C. (Ed.), *Brain and conscious experience*. New York: Springer-Verlag, 1966.

Teuber, H.-L., Milner B., and Vaughan, H. G. "Persistent anterograde amnesia after stab wound of the basal brain." *Neuropsychologia*, 1968, *6*, 267–282.

Teyler, T. (Ed.), *Brain and Learning*, Stamford, Conn.: Greylock, 1978.

Thompson, C. I. *Controls of eating*. Jamaica, New York: Spectrum, 1980.

Thompson, R. F., Berger, T. W., Cegavske, C. F., Patterson, M. M., Roemer, R. A., Teyler, T. J., and Young, R. A. "The search for the engram." *American Psychologist*, 1976, *31*, 209–227.

Thompson, R. F., Hicks, L. H., and Shvyrok, V. B. (Eds.), *Neural mechanisms of goal-directed behavior and learning*. New York: Academic, 1980.

Thorndike, E. L. "Animal intelligence: An experimental study of the associative processes in animals." *Psychological Review Monograph Supplement*, 1898, *2*.

Tinbergen, N. *The Study of Instinct*. Oxford: Clarendon, 1951.

Tizard, J. "Early malnutrition, growth and mental development." *British Medical Bulletin*, 1974, *30*, 169–174.

Tobias, P. V. "L'évolution du cerveau humain." *La Recherche*, 1980, *11*, 282–292.

Tomlinson, B. E., and Henderson, G. "Some quantitative cerebral findings in normal and demented old people." In R. D. Terry and S. Gershon (Eds.), *Neurobiology of Aging*. New York: Raven, 1976.

Towe, A. "Relative numbers of pyramidal tract neurons in mammals of different sizes." *Brain, Behavior and Evolution*, 1973, *7*, 1–17.

Towe, A., and Luschei, E. (Eds.), *Handbook of behavioral neurobiology, Vol. 5, Motor coordination*. New York: Plenum, 1981.

Trivers, R. L. "Parental investment and sexual selection." In B. Campbell (Ed.), *Sexual selection and the descent of man, 1871–1971*. Chicago: Aldine, 1972, 136–230.

Turkewitz, G. "The development of lateral differences in the human infant." In S. Harnad, R. W., Doty, L., Goldstein, J. Jaynes, and G. Krauthamer (Eds.), *Lateralization in the nervous system*. New York: Academic, 1977.

Turner, C. D., and Bagnara, J. T. *General endocrinology, 6th ed.* Philadelphia: Saunders, 1976.

Ungerstedt, U. "Sterotaxic mapping of the monoamine pathways in the rat brain." *Acta Physiologica Scandinavica*, Supplementum, 1971, *367*, 1–48.

Ursin, H., Baade, E., and Levine, S. *Psychobiology of stress: A study of coping men*. New York: Academic, 1978.

U. S. President's Committee on Mental Retardation. *Mental retardation: Century of decision*. (DHEW Publication No. (OHD) 76–21013). Washington, D. C., 1976.

Uttal, W. R. *The psychobiology of sensory coding*. New York: Harper & Row, 1973.

Valbo, A. B. "Muscle spindle responses at the onset of isometric voluntary contractions in man. Time difference between fusimotor and skeletomotor effects." *Journal of Physiology* (London), 1971, *218*, 405–431.

Valenstein, E. S. *Brain control*. New York: Wiley-Interscience, 1973.

Valenstein, E. S. *The psychosurgery debate: Scientific, legal, and ethical perspectives*. San Francisco: Freeman, 1980.

Valenstein, E. S., Cox, V. C., and Kakolewski, J. W. "Reexamination of the role of the hypothalamus in motivation." *Psychological Review*, 1970, *77*, 16–31.

Valzelli, L. *Psychobiology of aggression and violence*. New York: Raven, 1980.

van Bergeijk, W. A. "The evolution of vertebrate hearing." In W. D. Neff (Ed.), *Contributions to sensory physiology*, Vol. 3. New York: Academic, 1967.

van de Castle, R. L. *The psychology of dreaming*. New York: General Learning, 1971.

van Dis, H., and Larsson, K. "Induction of sexual arousal in the castrated male rat by intracranial stimulation." *Physiology and Behavior*, 1971, *6*, 85–86.

van Marthens, E., Grauel, L., and Zamenhof, S. "Enhancement of prenatal development in the rat by operative restriction of litter size." *Biology of the Neonate*, 1974, *25*, 53–56.

van Valen, L. "Brain size and intelligence in man." *American Journal of Physical Anthropology*, 1974, *40*, 417–424.

van Zoeren, J. G., and Stricker, E. M. "Effects of preoptic, lateral hypothalamic, or dopamine-depleting lesions on behavioral thermoregulation in rats exposed to the cold." *Journal of Comparative and Physiological Psychology*, 1977, *91*, 989–999.

Veraa, R. P., and Graftein, B. "Cellular mechanisms for recovery from nervous system injury: A conference report." *Experimental Neurology*, 1981, *71*, 6–75.

Victor, M., Adams, R. D., and Collins, G. H. *The Wernicke-Korsakoff Syndrome*. Philadelphia: F. A. Davis, 1971.

Volkmann, F. C., Riggs, L. A., and Moore, R. K. "Eyeblinks and visual suppression." *Science*, 1980, *207*, 900–902.

Volkmann, F. C., Schick, A. M., and Riggs, L. A. "Time course of visual inhibition during voluntary saccades." *Journal of the Optical Society of America*, 1969, *58*, 562–569.

Volkmar, F. R., and Greenough, W. T. "Rearing complexity affects branching of dendrites in the visual cortex of the rat." *Science*, 1972, *176*, 1445–1447.

vom Saal, F. S., and Bronson, F. H. "*In utero* proximity of female mouse fetuses to males: Effect on reproductive performance occurring in later life." *Biology of Reproduction*, 1978, *19*, 842–853.

von der Heydt, R., Adorjani, Cs., Hanny, P., and Baumgartner, G. "Disparity sensitivity and receptive field incongruity of units in the cat striate cortex." *Experimental Brain Research*, 1978, *31*, 523–545.

von Holst, E. "Relations between the central nervous system and the peripheral organs." *British Journal of Animal Behaviour*, 1954, *2*, 89–94.

von Schilcher, F., and Hall, J. C. "Neural topography of courtship song in sex mosaics of *Drosophila melanogaster*." *Journal of Comparative Physiology*, 1979, *129*, 85–95.

Wada, J. A., and Rasmussen, T. "Intracarotid injection of sodium amytal for the lateralization of cerebral speech dominance: Experimental and clinical observations." *Journal of Neurosurgery*, 1960, *17*, 266–282.

Wagner, G. C., Beuving, L. J., and Hutchinson, R. R. "The effects of gonadal hormone manipulations on aggressive target-biting in mice." *Aggressive Behavior*, 1980, *6*, 1–7.

Wahl, O. F. "Monzygotic twins discordant for schizophrenia: A review." *Psychological Bulletin*, 1976, *83*, 91–106.

Wald, G. "The receptors of human color vision." *Science*, 1964, *145*, 1007–1016.

Walk, R. D., Shepherd, J. D., and Miller, D. R. "Attention as an alternative to self-induced motion for perceptual behavior of kittens." *Society for Neuroscience Abstracts*, 1978, *4*, 129.

Wall, P. D. "Mechanisms of plasticity of connection following damage of adult mammalian nervous systems." In P. Bach-y-Rita (Ed.), *Recovery of function: Theoretical considerations for brain injury rehabilitation*. Bern: Hans Huber, 1980.

Walls, G. L. *The vertebrate eye*, Vol. 1. Bloomfield Hills, Mich.: Crankbrook Institute of Science, 1942.

Warrington, E. K., and Weiskrantz, L. "A study of learning and retention in amnesic patients." *Neuropsychologia*, 1968, *6*, 283–291.

Weddell, A.G.M. "Activity pattern hypothesis for sensation of pain." In R. G. Grenell (Ed.), *Neural physiopathology*. New York: Harper & Row, 1962.

Weinberger, D. R., Bigelow, L. B., Kleinman, J. E., Klein, S. T., Rosenblatt, J. E., and Wyatt, R. J. "Cerebral ventricular enlargement in chronic schizophrenia." *Archives of General Psychiatry*, 1980, *37*, 11–13.

Weinberger, D. R., Torrey, E. F., Neophytides, A. N., and Wyatt, R. J. "Lateral cerebral ventricular enlargement in chronic schizophrenia." *Archives of General Psychiatry*, 1979, *36*, 735–739.

Weiskrantz, L. "Trying to bridge some neuropsychological gaps between monkey and man." *British Journal of Psychology*, 1977, *68*, 431–445.

Weiskrantz, L., and Warrington, E. K. "The problem of the amnesic syndrome in man and animals." In R. L. Isaacson and K. H. Pribram (Eds.), *The Hippocampus* (Vol. 2) New York: Plenum, 1975, 411–428.

Weiskrantz, L., Warrington, E. K., Sanders, M. D., and Marshall, J. "Visual capacity in the hemianopic field following a restricted occipital ablation." *Brain*, 1974, *97*, 709–728.

Weiss, J. M. "Psychological and behavioral influences on gastrointestinal lesions in animal models." In J. D. Maser and M. E. P. Seligman (Eds.), *Psychopathology: Experimental methods*. San Francisco: W. H. Freeman, 1977.

Weisz, D. J., Solomon, P. R., and Thompson, R. F. "The hippocampus appears necessary for trace conditioning." *Bulletin of the Psychonomic Society*, 1980, *16*, 164.

Weitzman, E. D. "Sleep and its disorders." *Annual Review of Neurosciences*, 1981, *4*, 381–417.

Weitzman, E. D., Czeisler, C. A., Coleman, R. M., Spielman, A. J., Zimmerman, J. C., and Dement, W. "Delayed sleep phase syndrome." *Archives of General Psychiatry*, 1981, *38*, 737–746.

Weitzman, E. D., Czeisler, C. A., Zimmerman, J. C., and Moore-Ede, M. C. "Biological rhythms in man: Relationship of sleep-wake, cortisol, growth hormone, and temperature during temporal isolation." In J. B. Martin, S. Reichlin, and K. L. Bick (Eds.), *Neurosecretion and brain peptides*. New York: Raven, 1981.

West, J. R., Hodges, C. A., and Black, A. C. "Prenatal exposure to ethanol alters the organization of hippocampal mossy fibers in rats." *Science*, 1981, *211*, 957–959.

West, R. W., and Greenough, W. T. "Effect of environmental complexity on cortical synapses of rats: Preliminary results." *Behavioral Biology*, 1972, *7*, 279–284.

Westby, G.W.M. "Communication and jamming avoidance in electric fish." *Trends in Neurosciences*, 1981, *4*, 205–210.

Wever, E. G. "The evolution of vertebrate hearing." In *Handbook of sensory physiology*. Vol. 1, *Audition*. New York: Springer-Verlag, 1974.

White, L. E., and Hain, R. F. "Anorexia in association with a destructive lesion of the hypothalamus." *Archives of Pathology*, 1959, *68*, 275–281.

Wiesel, T. N., and Hubel, D. H. "Extent of recovery from the effects of visual deprivation in kittens." *Journal of Neurophysiology*, 1965, *28*, 1060–1072.

Wiley, J. H., and Leveille, G. A. "Significance of insulin in the metabolic adaptation of rats to meal ingestion." *Journal of Nutrition*. 1970, *100*, 1073–1080.

Wilkins, L., and Richter, C. P. "A great craving for salt by a child with cortico-adrenal insufficiency." *Journal of the American Medical Association*, 1940, *114*, 866–868.

Will, B. E., Rosenzweig, M. R., Bennett, E. L., Hebert, M., and Morimoto, H. "Relatively brief environmental enrichment aids recovery of learning capacity and alters brain measures after post-weaning brain lesions in rats." *Journal of Comparative and Physiological Psychology*, 1977, *91*, 33–50.

Williams, R. H. (Ed.), *Textbook of endocrinology*. Philadelphia: Saunders, 1974.

Williams, R. L., and Karacan, I. *Sleep disorders: Diagnosis and treatment*. New York: Wiley, 1978.

Wilson, D. M. "The origin of the flight-motor command in grasshoppers." In R. F. Reis (Ed.), *Neural theory and modeling*. Standford, Cal.: Stanford University, 1964, 331–345.

Wilson, G. T. "Behavior modification and the treatment of obesity." In A. J. Stunkard (Ed.), *Obesity*. Philadelphia: Saunders, 1980, 325–344.

Wilson, J. R., and Sherman, S. M. "Receptive-field characteristics of neurons in cat striate cortex: Changes with visual field eccentricity." *Journal of Neurophysiology*, 1976, *39*, 512–533.

Windle, W. "Brain damage by asphyxia at birth." *Scientific American*, 1969, *221*(4), 76–84.

Winick, M. *Malnutrition and brain development*. New York: Oxford, 1976.

Winick, M., Meyer, N. K., and Harris, R. C. "Malnutrition and environmental enrichment by early adoption." *Science*, 1975, *190*, 1173–1175.

Wise, R. A. "Lateral hypothalamic electrical stimulation: Does it make animals 'hungry'?" *Brain research*, 1974, *67*, 187–209.

Wodinsky, J. "Hormonal inhibition of feeding and death in *Octopus:* control by optic gland secretion." *Science*, 1977, *198*, 948–951.

Wolf, S., and Wolff, H. G. *Human gastric function: An experimental study of a man and his stomach*. New York: Oxford, 1947.

Wolgin, D. L., Cytawa, J., and Teitelbaum, P. "The role of activation in the regulation of food intake. In D. Novin, W. Wyrwicka, and G. Bray (Eds.), *Hunger: Basic mechanisms and clinical implications*. New York: Raven, 1976.

Woods, B. T., and Teuber, H.-L. "Changing patterns of childhood aphasia." *Annals of Neurology*, 1978, *3*, 273–280.

Woods, S. C., Vasselli, J. R., Kaestner, E., Szakmary, G. A., Milburn, P., and Vitiello, M. V. "Conditioned insulin secretion and meal feeding in rats." *Journal of Comparative and Physiological Psychology*, 1977, *91*, 128–133.

Woodside, B., Pelchat, R., and Leon, M. "Acute elevation of the heat load of mother rats curtails maternal nest bouts." *Journal of Comparative and Physiological Psychology*, 1980, *94*, 61–68.

Woolsey, C. N. *Cortical sensory organization: Multiple auditory areas*. Crescent Manor, N.J.: Humana, 1981.

Woolsey, C. N. *Cortical sensory organization: Multiple somatic areas*. Crescent Manor, N.J.: Humana, 1981.

Woolsey, C. N. *Cortical sensory organization: Multiple visual areas*. Crescent Manor, N.J.: Humana, 1981.

Woolsey, T. A., Durhann, D., Harris, R. M., Simous, D. T., and

Valentino, K. "Somatosensory development." In R. S. Aslin, J. R. Alberts, and M. R. Peterson (Eds.), *Sensory and perceptual development: Influences of genetic and experiential factors*. New York: Academic, 1981.

Woolsey, T. A., and Wann, J. R. "Areal changes in mouse cortical barrels following vibrissal damage at different postnatal ages." *Journal of Comparative Neurology*, 1976, *170*, 53–66.

Wurtman, R. J. "Food for thought." *The Sciences* (New York Academy of Sciences), 1978 (April), 6–9.

Yamada, M. "A search for odour encoding in the olfactory lobe." *Journal of Physiology* (London), 1971, *214*, 127–143.

Yoon, M. "Specificity and plasticity of retinotectal connections." *Neuroscience Research Program Bulletin*, 1979, *17*, 255–359.

Zahorik, D. M., Maier, S. F., and Pies, R. W. "Preferences for tastes paired with recovery from thiamine deficiency in rats: Appetitive conditioning or learned safety?" *Journal of Comparative and Physiological Psychology*, 1974, *87*, 1083–1091.

Zaidel, E. "Auditory vocabulary of the right hemisphere following brain bisection or hemidecortication." *Cortex*, 1976, *12*, 191–211.

Zecevic, N., and Rakic, P. "Differentiation of Purkinje cells and their relationship to other components of developing cerebellar cortex in man." *Journal of Comparative Neurology*, 1976, *167*, Fig. 6, 27–48.

Zeki, S. M. "Color coding in the superior temporal sulcus of rhesus monkey visual cortex." *Proceedings of the Royal Society of London*, 1977, *197*, 195–223.

Zeki, S. M. "Functional specialization in the visual cortex of the rhesus monkey." *Nature*, 1978, *274*, 423–428.

Zihl, J., and von Cramon, D. "Restitution of visual function in patients with cerebral blindness." *Journal of Neurology, Neurosurgery and Psychiatry*, 1979, *42*, 312–322.

Zucker, I. "Light, behavior, and biologic rhythms." *Hospital Practice*, 1976 (October), 83–91.

Zucker, L. M., and Zucker, T. F. "Fatty, a new mutation in the rat." *Journal of Heredity*, 1961, *52*, 275–278.

Zola-Morgan, S., Squire, L. R., and Mishkin, M. "The anatomy of amnesia: amygdala-hippocampus vs. temporal stem." *Society for Neuroscience Abstracts*, 1981, *7*, 236.

Name Index

Subject Index

*Boldface numbers indicate figure numbers.
†Boldface numbers preceded by **T** indicate table numbers.